lonely planet

KT-420-100

Costa Rica

Mara Vorhees
Matthew Firestone

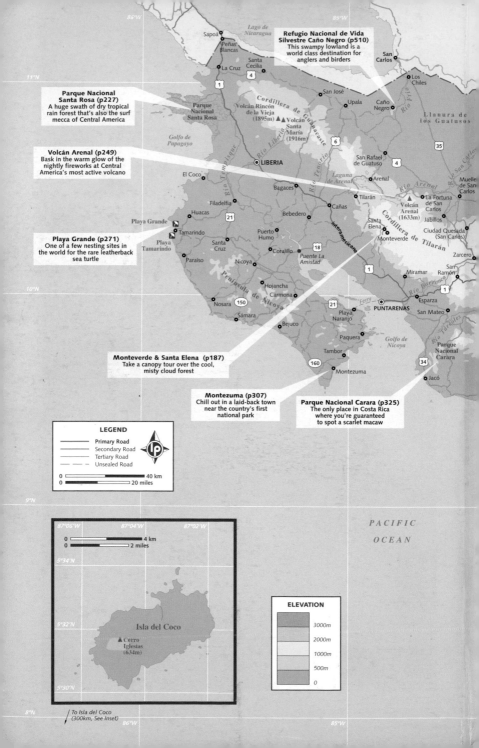

Parque Nacional Santa Rosa (p227)
A huge swath of dry tropical rain forest that's also the surf mecca of Central America

Refugio Nacional de Vida Silvestre Caño Negro (p510)
This swampy lowland is a world class destination for anglers and birders

Volcán Arenal (p249)
Bask in the warm glow of the nightly fireworks at Central America's most active volcano

Playa Grande (p271)
One of a few nesting sites in the world for the rare leatherback sea turtle

Monteverde & Santa Elena (p187)
Take a canopy tour over the cool, misty cloud forest

Montezuma (p307)
Chill out in a laid-back town near the country's first national park

Parque Nacional Carara (p325)
The only place in Costa Rica where you're guaranteed to spot a scarlet macaw

LEGEND

Primary Road
Secondary Road
Tertiary Road
Unsealed Road

0 —————— 40 km
0 —————— 20 miles

ELEVATION

3000m
2000m
1000m
500m
0

PACIFIC OCEAN

Isla del Coco
▲ Cerro Iglestas (634m)

0 ———— 4 km
0 ———— 2 miles

To Isla del Coco (300km, See inset)

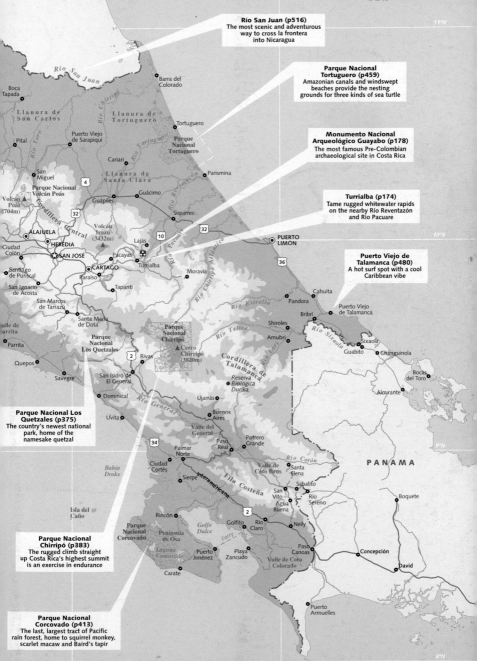

Río San Juan (p516)
The most scenic and adventurous way to cross la frontera into Nicaragua

Parque Nacional Tortuguero (p459)
Amazonian canals and windswept beaches provide the nesting grounds for three kinds of sea turtle

Monumento Nacional Arqueológico Guayabo (p178)
The most famous Pre-Colombian archaeological site in Costa Rica

Turrialba (p174)
Tame rugged whitewater rapids on the nearby Río Reventazón and Río Pacuare

Puerto Viejo de Talamanca (p480)
A hot surf spot with a cool Caribbean vibe

Parque Nacional Los Quetzales (p375)
The country's newest national park, home of the namesake quetzal

Parque Nacional Chirripó (p383)
The rugged climb straight up Costa Rica's highest summit is an exercise in endurance

Parque Nacional Corcovado (p413)
The last, largest tract of Pacific rain forest, home to squirrel monkey, scarlet macaw and Baird's tapir

Destination Costa Rica

The bellowing of the howler monkeys echoes across the treetops and you wonder if it was wise to venture into the jungle at the crack of dawn. You spot the creatures in a nearby fig tree, feasting on fruit. Out on the deserted beach magnificent frigate birds are circling high overhead. Less-than-sonorous squawking gives away a pair of scarlet macaws, alighting from an almond tree. Morning has broken in the coastal rain forest.

Similar scenes are unfolding across Costa Rica: from the dry tropical forest along the Pacific coast to the misty cloud forest at higher altitudes, this wildlife wonderland is coming alive. More than 27% of the country's area is protected, creating a haven for countless species of flora and fauna.

The value of this natural resource is unquantifiable: annually Costa Rica attracts more than one million visitors eager to catch a wave, bathe under a waterfall, spot a sloth or otherwise partake of paradise. Tourism is the country's top source of employment and investment.

It's not easy to maintain the delicate balance between preserving natural resources and cashing in on economic opportunity. But most Ticos are proud of their natural heritage, and they recognize that the goals of environmental conservation and economic prosperity are not mutually exclusive. This is the enlightened approach that has earned Costa Rica its reputation as the paradigm of ecotourism.

It's no wonder that the Ticos extend such a warm welcome to travelers. This peace-loving people is eager to share – the staggering scenery, the bountiful biodiversity and the complete contentment that comes with *pura vida*, the 'pure life' of Costa Rica.

OPPOSITE: ERIC L WHEATER   DANITA DELIMONT / ALAMY

Explore Natural Wonders

ALFREDO MAIQUEZ

Get up close and personal with the smouldering giant, Volcán Arenal (p249)

OTHER HIGHLIGHTS

- Get all hot and sweaty exploring the rugged Bahía Drake (p405).
- Catch a glimpse of the nocturnal river rhino, the Baird's tapir (p415), at Serena station.

RALPH LEE HOPKIN

Visit during the rainy season for the spectacular eruption of wild flowers (p66)

Be as lazy as you want on the stunning white sand at Playa Nancite (p227) in Parque Nacional Santa Rosa

KEVIN SCHAFER / ALAMY

CHRIS FREDRIKSSON / ALAMY

Live life on the edge of Volcán Irazú's (p168) active crater

Explore the forest floor of Parque
Nacional Corcovado (p413)

RALPH LEE HOPKINS

LUKE HUNTER

Immerse yourself in the Parque Nacional Palo Verde (p216),
a wetland sanctuary in Costa Rica's driest province

It's a Wild, Wild World

MARK NEWMAN

Catch a glimpse of the basilisk lizard (p58), which looks like a small dinosaur

TOM BOYDEN

View the morpho butterfly (p58) with its distinctive electric blue upper wings

See Central America's most culturally important bird, the quetzal (p60)

TOM BOYDEN

OTHER HIGHLIGHTS

- Get to know the fascinating habits of the beautiful and endangered turtles (p62) of Costa Rica.
- Check out the brightly colored toucan (p61) with its huge bill and flamboyant plumage.

LUKE HUNTER

Take a look at the many species of heron (p461) seen at the Parque Nacional Tortuguero

Laugh at the cheeky spider monkey (p63), which glides through the forest canopy

RALPH LEE HOPKINS

Track down the nocturnal Hoffman's two-toed sloth (p62)

JOHN HAY

The Life Aquatic

AARON McCOY

Soak up the inviting cool water of La Catarata de la Fortuna (p239)

OTHER HIGHLIGHTS

- Challenge yourself and take on the rapids for some seriously good white-water rafting (p75).
- Explore some the more-remote areas of Costa Rica's 1228km of coastline by sea kayak (p76).

DAVID SOUTH / ALAMY

Take a dip in the patrolled waters off the party town of Dominical (p362)

Facing page:
Catch a wave or two at Playa Tamarindo (p274)
MACDUFF EVERTON

La Vida Activa

MARTIN SIEPMANN / IMAGEBROKER / ALAMY

Horse ride your way around Volcán Rincón de la Vieja (p224)

Sweat it out on the gruelling climb up Cerro Chirripó (p384)

LUKE HUNTER

OTHER HIGHLIGHTS

- Do something different and try waterfall rappelling (p79) – rock climbing for those who like to get wet.
- Get beneath the surface of the blissfully warm water with a spot of diving (p75).

MARK NEWMAN

Ride the rapids through a series of spectacular canyons on the foaming Río Pacuare (p177)

Get down and dirty by mountain biking in the Bosque del Río Tigre (p422)

MACDUFF EVERTON

Pura Vida

Solve the mystery of La Negrita (p167) at the Basílica de Nuestra Señora de los Ángeles in Cartago

M.TIMOTHY O'KEEFE / ALAMY

Watch the magic unveil as day turns to night (p24)

CHRIS BARTON

OTHER HIGHLIGHTS

- Indulge in the drink of choice for most Costa Ricans – coffee (p82), served strong with hot milk to taste.

- Join in an impromtu *fútbol* (p47) game, played anytime, anywhere among enthusiastic youngsters aspiring to make the national team.

DAVID SANGER PHOTOGRAPHY / ALAMY

Enjoy a slice of traditional life

Browse the bustling stalls at San José's Mercado Central (p96)

IMAGESYNC LTD / ALAMY

Relax with the kids in the family environment of Costa Rica

AARON McCOY

Up in the Clouds

JAN CSERNOCH / ALAMY

Admire the stunning blue waterfall on the Río Celeste near Volcán Tenorio (p214)

Gaze at the greenery in the Reserva Biológica Bosque Nuboso Monteverde (p207)

DAVID M WATSON

OTHER HIGHLIGHTS

- Check out some of the 230 species of birds at Ecolodge San Luis & Research Station (p211).
- Marvel at the 2028m high Volcán Miravalles (p215).
- Enjoy the peace and solitude at Costa Rica's newest national park, Parque Nacional Los Quetzales (p375).

Contents

Regional Map Contents

The Authors

MARA VORHEES
Coordinating Author, Southern Costa Rica, Península de Osa & Golfo Dulce, Caribbean Coast

The first time Mara strayed from the jungle trail was in 1996, in Corcovado, where she spotted her first toucan. The second was in Parque Nacional Cahuita, where she found herself sipping *jugos* at a café. Her most recent fiasco was in La Amistad, where she found – or rather, was found by – a park ranger named Henry. She has learned from Costa Rica that getting lost in the jungle leads to brilliant discoveries. In the meantime, Mara spent four years working on a sustainable development research program at Harvard University. But she prefers to witness sustainable development first-hand.

My Favorite Trip

I traveled this route across the Península de Osa with my husband, which made it all the more enjoyable (he carried the heavy pack across Corcovado). We flew into Sierpe (p402) and took a boat through the mangroves of the Humedal Nacional Térraba-Sierpe (p404). Off the shores of dazzling Bahía Drake (p405), we swam, snorkeled and spied on scarlet macaws. From here, we did the trek across Parque Nacional Corcovado (p413), spending time at Sirena station (p414) for unmatched wildlife-watching. We recovered amidst luxury at Ojo del Mar (p427), near Cabo Matapalo. At Köbö Farm (p421) we saw cocoa cultivation and sampled homemade chocolate. On our last night in Puerto Jiménez (p422) we dined on fresh seafood at Jade Luna (426).

MATTHEW D FIRESTONE
San José, Central Valley & Highlands, Northwestern Costa Rica, Península de Nicoya, Central Pacific Coast, Northern Lowlands

Matt is a biological anthropologist and epidemiologist interested in the health and nutrition of indigenous populations. His first visit to Costa Rica took him into the rain forests of Parque Nacional Chirripó, where he did a field study on the modern diet of the Cabécar. Unfortunately, Matt's career was postponed due to a case of wanderlust, though he has traveled to over 50 different countries in search of a cure. Matt is hoping that this book will ease the pain of others bitten by the travel bug, though he fears that there is a growing epidemic.

CONTRIBUTING AUTHORS

David Goldberg MD wrote the Health chapter (p555). He completed his training in internal medicine and infectious diseases at Columbia-Presbyterian Medical Center in New York City, where he has also served as voluntary faculty. At present he is an infectious diseases specialist in Scarsdale, New York, and the editor-in-chief of the website MDTravelHealth.com.

David Lukas wrote the Environment chapter (p53) and Wildlife Guide (p57). He is an avid student of natural history who has traveled widely to study tropical ecosystems, including Borneo and the Amazon. He has also spent several years leading natural history tours to all corners of Costa Rica, Belize and Guatemala.

Getting Started

Costa Rica has something for everyone. If you are an impulsive adventurer seeking an adrenaline rush, you will definitely find it in Costa Rica. If you prefer to spend some quality time with a good book on a sun swept beach, we've got a few of those too.

For budget types, transport around the country is plentiful: local buses can carry you to just about every nook and cranny; boats will pick up where buses leave off. For the more discriminating or time-pressed, minivans with air-con, domestic flights and charters can reach even the most remote corners. Accommodations also range from bargain-basement cabins, campsites and hammock hotels, all the way up to first-class resorts loaded with luxury.

See the Directory for more information on climate (p532) and festivals (p535).

Lodging is abundant and it's usually easy to find someplace to stay when you arrive in town. The exceptions to this rule are the weeks between Christmas and New Year's Day and before and during Semana Santa (the week preceding Easter Sunday). It is also a good idea to book accommodations ahead of time during the school vacation in January and February.

Note that because Costa Rica has a high standard of living, prices here tend to be a good deal higher than those of other Central and Latin American nations.

WHEN TO GO

Generally, the best time to visit Costa Rica is the dry season from December through April, which locals refer to as *verano* (summer). Dry season does not mean it does not rain; it just rains less (so perhaps should be called the 'drier season'). Costa Rican schools are closed from December to February, when beach towns are busy, especially on weekends. Lodgings during Semana Santa are usually booked months ahead.

In May begins the rainy season, or *invierno* (winter) as it's known locally. The tourism ministry has come up with the more attractive

---

DON'T LEAVE HOME WITHOUT...

- Checking the latest visa situation (p541) and government travel advisories (p532)
- Insect repellent containing DEET; and if you're planning large-scale jungle adventures (or staying in budget lodging), a mosquito net
- Pepto-Bismol or an antidiarrheal, in case you get a bad dose of the trots
- Sunblock and a hat, so you don't get cooked by the tropical sun
- Clothes that you don't mind getting absolutely filthy or wet
- Swimsuit and beach towel
- A pair of river sandals or reef-walkers and sturdy jungle boots
- A waterproof, windproof jacket and warm layers for highland hiking
- A flashlight (torch)
- Binoculars and a field guide
- Miscellaneous necessities: umbrella, padlock, matches, pocketknife
- Your sense of adventure

denomination of 'green season'. The early months of the rainy season are actually a wonderful time to travel to Costa Rica: you can avoid the tourist bustle and lodging is slightly cheaper. During this time, however, rivers start to swell and dirt roads get muddy, making travel more challenging. Some more remote roads may not be accessible to public transportation, so always ask locally before setting out. Bring your umbrella and a little patience.

Because of the number of North American and European tourists, some Costa Rican towns experience a mini-high season in June and July, during the northern summer holidays. Expect to pay high-season prices in some towns at this time.

For surfers the travel seasons vary slightly. For the most part, the Pacific coast sees increased swells and bigger, faster waves during the rainy season, starting in late June and peaking in the worst rainy months of September and October. The Caribbean side, however, has better waves from November through May. Some breaks are consistent year-round.

Wildlife enthusiasts may wish to plan their trip around the seasons of the critters. Turtle season on the Caribbean coast is from late-February to October, with the peak season for leatherbacks in April and May and for green turtles in August and September. On the Caribbean coast, the season for leatherbacks is from October to March.

Birders will be overwhelmed by feathered friends any time of year, but the best season to spot the resplendent quetzal is between November and April. Spring (March through May) and autumn (September through November) are good times to watch the migratory flocks.

Fishing, also, is good year-round, but you might choose your season if you have your heart set on a specific fish. Anglers head to the Caribbean coast between January and May in search of tarpon, while the autumn (September through November) is the season for snook. On the Pacific coast and in the Golfo Dulce, the best time to snag that sailfish is between November and May.

COSTS & MONEY

Travel costs are significantly higher here than in most Central American countries, but cheaper than in the USA or Europe. And if you're arriving from inexpensive Central American nations such as Nicaragua, get ready to bust that wallet wide open.

Prices in Costa Rica are frequently listed in US dollars, especially at upmarket hotels and restaurants, where you can expect to pay international prices. Most types of tours are charged in US dollars. In fact, US dollars are widely accepted, but the standard unit of currency is still the colon.

Shoestring travelers can survive on US$20 to US$30 a day, covering just the basics of food, lodging and public transportation. The cheapest hotels start at about US$5 per person for a bed, four walls and shared bathrooms. Better rooms with private bathrooms start at roughly US$10 per person, depending on the area. It is possible to eat cheaply at the many *sodas* (lunch counters), where you can fill up on tasty casados (set meals) for about US$2 to US$3.

Midrange budgeters can travel comfortably for anywhere from US$50 to US$100 per day. Hotels in this category offer very good value, and double rooms come with comfortable beds, private bathrooms, hot water (most of the time) and even breakfast, for US$20 to US$50 per night. Many hotels in this price range also have shared or private kitchenettes, which allows travelers the opportunity to cook. (This is a great option

HOW MUCH?

SkyTrek zip-line adventure in Monteverde US$40

Admission to Parque Nacional Manuel Antonio US$7

A bus from San José to Puerto Viejo de Talamanca US$7.75

Taxi from the international airport into central San José US$12-15

Two hours of surfing lessons in Tamarindo US$30

TOP TENS

Idyllic Sunset Sites

Abundant nature + peaceful surroundings + great views = No more worries

- The mountaintop hostel on Cerro Chirripó (p385)
- From the lookout above El Mirador Lodge in Bahía Drake (p408)
- The view of Volcán Arenal from Cabina La Fortuna (p237)
- A sunset sail from Tamarindo (p276)
- At La Taberna in Tortuguero (p466) sipping a *cerveza*
- Sunset from Ronny's Place in Manuel Antonio (p353)
- Reggae-listening at the Sunset Bar in Puerto Viejo de Talamanca (p490)
- Twilight hike in the Children's Eternal Forest (p193) in Monteverde
- On the dock of the bay at the Banana Bay Marina (p431) in Golfito
- The hills of San José from the Plaza de la Democracia (p100)

Worst Roads

It is a badge of honor for travelers to boast about the disastrous roads they've survived in Costa Rica. A list of the most bragworthy:

- Oldie, but goodie – the road from Tilarán to Monteverde
- The punisher – Puerto Jiménez to Carate
- Dude, where's the transmission? – bumping and grinding to the waves at Playa Naranjo
- A river runs through it – crossing the Río Ora between Playa Carrillo and Islita
- You call this a road? – Golfito to Pavones
- Bone-cruncher – Buenos Aires to Reserva Biológica Dúrika reserve
- Car-nivore – the stretch between Tamarindo and Avellana gobbles up vehicles like candy
- Road less traveled – the steep climb up to Altamira and La Amistad
- Keep on truckin' – swerving with the big rigs on the Interamericana between Cañas and Liberia
- Lake defect – dodging huge potholes on the road around Laguna Arenal

Best Beaches

This is what we came for…

- Manzanillo (p494) – surfing and snorkeling along the Caribbean's most scenic stretch
- Playas Coyote & San Miguel (p301) – abandoned beach, backed by rugged wilderness
- Playa Conchal (p271) – crushed shells and turquoise water
- Playa Grande (p271) – sweeping blonde sand backed by mangroves, great surf
- Playa Matapalo (p360) – surfing the waves, hiking to waterfalls
- Playa Montezuma (p308) – empty white sands and rocky coves, killer sunrises
- Playa Mal País (p313) – huge, crashing surf for kilometers in every direction
- Playa Negra (p471) – people of color, beaches of color
- Playa San Josecito (p411) – scarlet macaws roosting in the almond trees overhead
- Playa Sámara (p295) – destination of sophisticated beach goers
- Playa Zancudo (p437) – gentle, luminescent waters and vast, empty sands

for families.) A variety of restaurants cater to midrange travelers, offering starters (often as filling as a main meal) that range in price from US$5 to US$10.

Top-end visitors can find a good selection of restaurants and hotels in the touristy towns and within some of the major resorts. Luxurious beach-side lodges and boutique hotels can cost anywhere from US$80 – and all the way up – and offer meals that begin at US$20.

Lodging prices are generally higher in the dry season (December to April), and highest during holiday periods (between Christmas and New Year and during Semana Santa). During slower seasons, most hotels are eager for your business, so you can try to negotiate a lower rate. Some of the more popular tourist areas (Monteverde, Jacó, Manuel Antonio and many of the beaches on the Península de Nicoya) are also more expensive than the rest of the country.

TRAVEL LITERATURE

There are surprisingly few travelogues specifically about Costa Rica. Dr Alexander Skutch – who lived for years near San Isidro de El General – wrote *A Naturalist in Costa Rica,* which is part natural history, part memoir. An icon among birders, Dr Skutch weaves his philosophies into his beautiful descriptions of flora and fauna.

Green Phoenix, by science journalist William Allen, is an absorbing and inspiring account of his efforts, alongside American and Costa Rican scientists and activists, to conserve and restore the rainforest in Guanacaste.

In *Walk These Stones,* by Leslie Hawthorne Klingler, this Mennonite service worker writes about her experiences living, working, praying and sharing in the small village of Cuatro Cruces. Her account of village life is poignant, but if you are not into spiritual questions it is not for you.

Many more books are accounts of journeys through Central America by various means. *Ninety-Nine Days to Panama,* by John and Harriet Halkyard, is a retired couple's detailed and entertaining account of driving an RV (complete with pet dog Brindle) from Texas to Panama. Peter Ford's *Around the Edge* is the story of the author's travels along the Caribbean coast from Belize to Panama, on foot and by boat. *The Old Patagonian Express: By Train Through the Americas,* by Paul Theroux, details the author's journey by train from a suburb of Boston all the way to Patagonia. Sadly, many of the train routes he took are no longer in operation, but it's still a great book.

In Lonely Planet's *Green Dreams: Travels in Central America* by Stephen Benz, the author astutely analyzes and questions the impact visitors are having on a region and its people. *Traveler's Tales Central America,* edited by Larry Habegger and Natanya Pearlman, is a collection of striking travel essays on the region from renowned writers such as Paul Theroux and Tim Cahill.

So Far from God: A Journey to Central America, by Patrick Marnham, was the winner of the 1985 Thomas Cook Travel Book Award. It's an insightful and often amusing account of a leisurely meander from Texas down to Mexico City and on into Central America.

Though not specifically about Costa Rica, bird-watchers will enjoy *Birders: Birds of Tribe* by Mark Cocker, a true celebration of the bird enthusiast's determination to endure hours of boredom and terrible weather – all to catch a glimpse of some rare and spectacular avian species.

INTERNET RESOURCES

Costa Rica Guide (www.costa-rica-guide.com) Nicely organized website with detailed maps and travel information on each region.

Costa Rica Link (www.1costaricalink.com) An online directory that provides a great deal of information on transport, hotels, activities and more.

Guías Costa Rica (www.guiascostarica.com) Links that connect you with everything you'd ever need to know – from entertainment to health to government websites.

Lanic (http://lanic.utexas.edu/la/ca/cr) An exceptional collection of links to sites of many Costa Rican organizations (mostly in Spanish), from the University of Texas.

Lonely Planet (www.lonelyplanet.com) Provides summaries on traveling to most places on earth, including the all-important Thorn Tree bulletin board, where you can ask questions of travelers who've been to Costa Rica recently; the site can link you to useful travel resources elsewhere on the Web.

Tico Times (www.ticotimes.net) The online edition of Costa Rica's excellent English-language weekly newspaper.

Itineraries

CLASSIC ROUTES

SURF & TURF
One Week / San José to Playas Avellana & Negra

This popular route takes travelers by bubbling volcanoes, steamy hot springs and tranquil cloud forest before hitting the beach.

From San José head north to **La Fortuna** (p237) on the eastern folds of Cordillera de Tilarán, where you hike through thick forest on the flanks of **Volcán Arenal** (p249), followed by a good soak in the hot springs. Then hop on the jeep-boat-jeep service across Laguna de Arenal to **Monteverde** (p187) and search for the elusive quetzal at **Reserva Biológica Bosque Nuboso Monteverde** (p207). End your stay with a zip-line canopy tour.

Then, make a beeline to the pretty surf of **Playa Tamarindo** (p274), where travelers can loll by the beach, or pursue water- and land-based frolics. Nature buffs will not want to miss the nesting leatherback turtles at **Playa Grande** (p271).

From here, continue south along a dismal dirt road for more sun and surf at **Playas Avellana & Negra** (p281). Now, sufficiently suntanned and surf-weary, you can head back to San José.

This 605km loop could take more than three weeks if you study Spanish or volunteer in Monteverde, make a stop for world-class windsurfing in Laguna de Arenal, celebrate Guanacaste Day in Santa Cruz, or explore the beaches south of Tamarindo.

COAST TO COAST
Two Weeks / Jacó to Uvita & Cahuita to Manzanillo

Surfers, sun-worshippers and party-goers may want to catch some waves and some rays on both coasts. First head to **Jacó** (p329), the quintessential beach-party town on the Pacific coast. Take the jet boat to lovely, laid-back **Montezuma** (p307) for a different vibe. Surfers will want to head to the other side of the Nicoya Peninsula to check out the swells at **Mal País** and **Santa Teresa** (p313).

Backtrack to Jacó, and then continue on to **Manuel Antonio** (p354) for a chance to see the endangered squirrel monkey at the world famous **Parque Nacional Manuel Antonio** (p356). If you haven't yet had enough of the post-card-perfect Pacific coast, continue further south to **Dominical** (p362) to catch some more waves, or to **Uvita** (p366) to escape the tourist crowds.

Now it's time to explore the Caribbean side, but first you have to make it back to **San José** (p88). Hop on the first eastbound bus out of the capital and get off at **Cahuita** (p470), capital of Afro-Caribbean culture and gateway to **Parque Nacional Cahuita** (p478). Stick around and get your fill of this mellow little village, before moving on to **Puerto Viejo de Talamanca** (p480), the Caribbean's center for nightlife, cuisine and positive vibes. Rent a bike and ride to **Manzanillo** (p494), from where you can snorkel, kayak and hike in the **Refugio Nacional de Vida Silvestre Gandoca-Manzanillo** (p496).

You'll cover 575km on the Pacific side (plus the boat ride to Montezuma) and 580km on the Caribbean side, making this the ultimate road trip. One week on each coast is the bare minimum.

PEAK TO BEACH

Two Weeks / San José to Jacó

From the highest summit down to tropical beaches, this itinerary takes you high and low and through everything in between.

Start by heading south on the Interamericana out of San José, into the Zona de Los Santos. Visit the coffee plantations in the valley near **Santa María de Dota** (p371) or go bird-watching in the highlands of the **Parque Nacional Los Quetzales** (p375). Continue past the looming **Cerro de la Muerte** (p376) and straight down the mountain to the pleasant agricultural city of **San Isidro de El General** (p377). From here, ride the winding dirt road northeast to **San Gerardo de Rivas** (p381) and prepare for the two-day climb up Costa Rica's highest peak, **Cerro Chirripó** (p384). Linger around the summit for incredible day hikes before making your way back down.

Return through San Isidro to **Dominical** (p362) and enjoy a laid-back vibe and powerful surf. If you're addicted to Pacific sunsets, stay in **Escaleras** (p364) for staggering views. Continue on north to **Hacienda Barú** (p361), where you can clamber on a canopy platform and sloth-spot in the trees. Head further up the coast to the port of **Quepos** (p343), before dipping south and landing in the country's most popular national park, **Parque Nacional Manuel Antonio** (p356). Wind down your trip with some fun and sun in the resort town of **Jacó** (p329), an adequate reintroduction to gringo-life before flying out of San José.

A 675km loop leads from San José inland to San Isidro and then on to the Pacific coast at Dominical and up the coast, so there's no need to backtrack. Add another week if you decide to use Dominical as a base for exploring the wonders of the southern coast.

ROADS LESS TRAVELED

OSA ADVENTURE   One Week / Puerto Jiménez to Puerto Jiménez

You only have a week but you still want to see the most distant corner of Costa Rica?

Fly into **Puerto Jiménez** (p422), where you can spend a few days kayaking around the mangroves, panning for gold and otherwise soaking up the charm of this tiny town. Head north to **La Palma** (p419), from where you can visit the **Reserva Indígena Guaymí de Osa** (p422) and observe firsthand the lifestyle of one of Costa Rica's indigenous groups. Next, head to **Los Patos ranger station** (p414), which will be the starting point for a trek across the **Parque Nacional Corcovado** (p413). The first day of the trek lands you at **Sirena station** (p414), one of the country's best wildlife-watching spots, especially for squirrel monkeys and Baird's tapirs. It's worth spending an extra day exploring the trails around this area without a pack on your back. Finally, the last day of the hike brings you to La Leona ranger station. In the nearby village of **Carate** (p428), catch the *taxi collectivo* to the **Cabo Matapalo** (p427), where you can chill out for the rest of the week, enjoying some of the country's most beautiful beaches. From here, it's a quick taxi ride back to Puerto Jiménez, for your return flight to San José.

This 120km round-trip fits perfectly into a one-week vacation. But if you have time to spare, you can undertake the more strenuous hike to San Pedrillo station and spend some time in Agujitas on beautiful Bahía Drake.

RIDING THE RÍO SAN JUAN   10 Days / La Virgen to Tortuguero

Travel exclusively by boat in some of Costa Rica's (and Nicaragua's) most remote regions near the sparsely populated northern Caribbean coast.

From San José, head to the tiny town of **La Virgen** (p515), a rafting and kayaking mecca where you can take a ride on the Río Sarapiquí and spend the night at the luxurious lodge **Centro Neotrópico Sarapiquís** (p518). Then head up the river to **Puerto Viejo de Sarapiquí** (p520): take a day to wander through banana plantations, spot wildlife and mingle with busy scientists at the **Estación Biológica La Selva** (p522). Leave terra firma and grab the morning boat up the Río Sarapiquí to **Trinidad Lodge** (p521), on the south bank of the Río San Juan. Stay on a working ranch, ride horses and go birding before setting out, again by boat, along the Río San Juan, with your eye to the Caribbean coast.

This river (Nicaraguan territory) offers an incredible ride, which will take you through a combination of ranches, forest, wildlife and old war zones (from when Contras inhabited the area), and through the remote **Refugio Nacional de Vida Silvestre Barra del Colorado** (p467), to the village of **Barra del Colorado** (p467) and its loose assortment of lodges, where travelers can go sportfishing, bird-watching and looking for crocs. Afterwards, continue to the more touristed village of **Tortuguero** (p461), to watch green sea and leatherback turtles and to canoe through the infinite canals of **Parque Nacional Tortuguero** (p459), Costa Rica's mini-Amazon. Then head to San José via water taxi and bus through **Cariari** (p448) and **Guápiles** (p445).

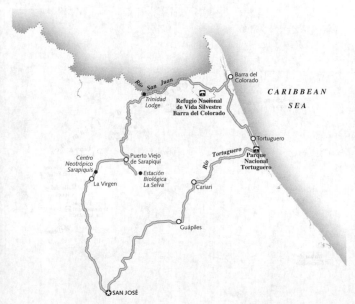

This trip is only 200km, and could be done in a week if the tides, weather and the various independent boatmen you'll need all work out. But if you're going to the trouble (and expense), get your captain to take it slowly and you'll see more wildlife and incredible scenery than you ever imagined.

EXPLORING THE TALAMANCAS

Two Weeks / San Isidro to Parque Internacional La Amistad

Delve into the mountainous area that remains Costa Rica's most unexplored. You can do either of the following hikes separately (for a shorter trip) or bundle them into one if you've got plenty of time.

Gear up in **San Isidro de El General** (p377) before heading southeast through pineapple plantations to the small agricultural town of **Buenos Aires** (p386). Arrangements can be made here for transport via dirt road to the wonderfully remote **Reserva Biológica Dúrika** (p387), a self-sustaining community nestled in the Cordillera de Talamanca. From this point, undertake the six-day, round-trip hike-and-climb of **Cerro Dúrika** (3280m), situated inside the Parque Internacional La Amistad. Visits to the neighboring indigenous community of **Ujarrás** (p387) are also available.

If you haven't had your fill of nature yet, then continue on south from Buenos Aires to Altamira, where you'll find the headquarters for **Parque Internacional La Amistad** (p398). From here you can make the 20km guided trek through **Valle del Silencio** (p399), one of the most isolated and remote areas in all of Costa Rica, ending up at a small refuge at the base of the Cerro Kamuk. From here, make the return trip through Altamira and back to the rowdy roads near the Interamericana.

It's 210km straight up and down mountains in the isolated Cordillera de Talamanca, one of the most remote areas in the country and home to various indigenous communities, unspoiled wildlife and incredible vistas. Stay and work as a volunteer in the Dúrika reserve if you wish.

TAILORED TRIPS

SURFING COSTA RICA

Costa Rican shores have been attracting surfers since *Endless Summer II* profiled some of the country's most appealing breaks.

Playa Tamarindo (p274) serves as a good base for several tasty surfing sites. Start with a boat trip to the granddaddies of all surf breaks, Witch's Rock and Ollie's Point in the **Parque Nacional Santa Rosa** (p227). Then hit the isolated beaches at **Playas Avellana** and **Negra** (p281), whose famous waves were featured in the movie. Down the coast **Playa Guiones** (p291) is cooking all year long, and from there it's just a hop, skip and long jump to the oh-so-trendy **Mal País** (p313).

The next big stop is **Jacó** (p329) and **Playa Hermosa** (p339) on the central Pacific coast, offering consistent waves, but keep moving south for good reef breaks at **Matapalo** (p360) and **Dominical** (p362). Afterwards, hightail it way south to **Cabo Matapalo** (p427) on the Península de Osa, before skipping back to the mainland for one of the continent's longest left-hand breaks at **Pavones** (p440).

And don't forget the Caribbean. Catch a boat to the uninhabited **Isla Uvita** (p456) off the coast of Puerto Limón or frolic in the waves on the endless Playa Negra north of **Cahuita** (p470). Further south the famous Salsa Brava at **Puerto Viejo de Talamanca** (p480) is for experts only, while Playa Cocles has consistent waves that service surfers of all skill levels.

RAFTING SAFARI

Experience the country's world-class rivers while soaking in the sight of pristine rain forests and wildlife on a 10-day safari.

From San José head east to the **Río Pacuare** (p177) for two days of enchanted Class IV white water. Move on to the nearby Pascua section of the **Río Reventazón** (p177) for 24km of heart-pumping Class IV+. Travel west to the central Pacific coast and spend a day of gentler rafting, taking in the beach-fringed rain forest of **Parque Nacional Manuel Antonio** (p356), home to more than 350 species of birds. After, suit-up for a quick half-day down the challenging **Río Naranjo** (p348), close by. Cap it all off with two days on the largely unexplored **Río Savegre** (p348), putting in on the remote, Class IV+ upper **Río División** (p378), the main tributary of the Savegre. The next day will have you continuing downstream to the bridge take-out on the Costanera, the Pacific coastal highway leading north to San José.

Snapshot

In the February 2006 presidential election, former president and Nobel Peace Prize Laureate Oscar Arias narrowly beat Citizens' Action Party (CAP) candidate Otton Solís. After weeks of investigating potential irregularities and re-counting votes – reminiscent of another presidential election you might remember – Solís conceded. Arias earned just 18,169 votes more than his opponent, winning the popular election by a 1.2% margin.

Solís' showing was significant, as his CAP was a newcomer on the political scene, founded only in 2000. Attempting to break into Costa Rica's two-party system, CAP's platform promotes citizen participation and condemns corruption – issues made relevant by the previous administration.

The topic that dominated this election, however, was the Central American Free Trade Agreement (Cafta), the regional treaty that is currently hung up in the Legislative Assembly. Costa Rica is the only one of the six signatories that has not ratified the agreement.

Proponents of Cafta – including Arias – tout its economic benefits, including increased access to US markets and thousands of new jobs. Critics argue that the accord does not protect Costa Rica's small farmers and domestic industries, which will struggle to compete with the anticipated flood of cheap US products. As Solís explained, 'The law of the jungle benefits the big beast. We are a very small beast.' Opponents have vowed to strike, demonstrate and do anything to keep the agreement from proceeding.

Critics are also concerned about Cafta's effects on the environment – always a hot issue (literally and figuratively). They fear that the international trade agreement will take precedent over local conservation laws, forcing Costa Rica to allow off-shore oil drilling and open-pit mining, among other detrimental activities.

While these questions are pertinent – and activists are right to ask them – there are more pressing threats to the environment in Costa Rica. Soaring tourist numbers and increased infrastructure create stress on ecological habitats – ironic, as that is what people come to enjoy. The proliferation of small hotels is difficult to regulate, while big-business developers pose an ongoing threat. Sustainable tourism – that fine line between economic profits and environmental conservation – is proving difficult to execute (see p66). Communities experience other side effects of the tourist boom, like child prostitution and drug addiction.

Fortunately, local communities are active and aware. Conservationist, educational and cultural organizations have helped protect the environment, preserve local culture and enhance education. For travelers, these organizations offer a great opportunity to get involved – see p542.

Meanwhile, Costa Rica is becoming more diverse, more cosmopolitan. North Americans and Europeans continue to arrive in droves, in search of their own piece of tropical paradise. They bring much-needed investment, but also drive up property prices and displace cash-strapped Ticos.

Nicaraguans are coming south in search of employment, education and other opportunities lacking in their poorer homeland. Rightly or wrongly, immigrants are often blamed for increases in crime, fueling ongoing animosity between Nicas and Ticos (see p235).

Despite these tensions, typical of a multicultural society, Ticos are not blind to the value of increasing globalization – even in their own communities. In a country that boasts about its biodiversity, they are wise to welcome a little 'human diversity' too.

FAST FACTS

Population: four million

Life expectancy at birth: 78 years (USA: 78 years)

Adult literacy: 96% (USA: 97%)

Population living below the poverty line: 18% (USA: 12%)

Percentage of population using the Internet: 29% (USA: 56%)

Annual carbon dioxide emissions per person (metric tons): 1.2 (USA: 19.9)

Annual coffee consumption per person: 4.1kg (USA: 4kg)

Passenger cars per 1000 people: 82.2 (USA: 477.8)

Percentage of protected land: 27% (USA: 16%)

Number of species of birds: 850 (USA: 508)

History

Costa Rica is unique. While sharing with its neighbors the experiences of colonial exploitation and commodity-export dependency, Costa Rica managed to rise above. Instead of recurring cycles of dictatorship and poverty, Costa Rica boasts an enduring democracy and the highest standards of living in Central America. What's more, Costa Rica is unique among all nations for its 'unarmed' political democracy and 'green' economic revolution.

LOST CIVILIZATION

Humans have inhabited the rain forests of Costa Rica for 10,000 years. The region long served as an intersection for America's native cultures. About 500 years ago, on the eve of European discovery, it is guesstimated that as many as 400,000 people lived in today's Costa Rica.

Knowledge about these pre-Columbian cultures is scant. The remains of lost civilizations were washed away by torrential rains, and Spanish conquerors were more intent on destroying rather than describing native lifestyles. Until recently, Costa Ricans showed little interest in their ancient past.

The region hosted roughly 20 small tribes, organized into chiefdoms, indicating a permanent leader, or cacique, who sat atop a hierarchical society that included shaman, warriors, toilers and slaves. The language of the Central Valley Huetar Indians was known throughout all regions. The Central Valley contains the only major archaeological site uncovered in Costa Rica at Guayabo (p178). Thought to be an ancient ceremonial center, it featured paved streets, an aqueduct and decorative gold.

To the east, the Carib Indians, naked and fierce, dominated the Atlantic coastal lowlands. Adept at seafaring, the Carib tribes were a conduit of trade with the South American mainland. The Indians in the northwest were connected to the great Meso-American cultures. Aztec religious practices and Mayan jade and craftsmanship are in evidence in the Península de Nicoya, while Costa Rican quetzal feathers and golden trinkets have turned up in Mexico. These more concentrated tribes tended corn fields. The three chiefdoms found in the southwest showed the influence of Andean Indian cultures, including coca leaves, yucca and sweet potatoes.

Still a puzzle are the hundreds of hand-sculpted, monolithic stone spheres that dot the landscape of the southwest's Diquis Valley (p389), as well as the Isla del Caño (p413). Weighing up to 16 tons and ranging in size from a baseball to a Volkswagen, the spheres have inspired many theories: an ancient calendar, extraterrestrial meddling, or a game of bocce gone terribly awry.

> The origin of earth – according to Bribrí and Cabécar creation myth – is the subject of the beautifully illustrated story *When Woman Became Sea* by Susan Strauss.

> Visit World Mysteries at www.world-mysteries .com/sar_12.htm for an investigation of the mysterious stone spheres.

HEIRS OF COLUMBUS

On his fourth and final voyage to the New World, in 1502, Christopher Columbus was forced to drop anchor near today's Puerto Limón after a hurricane damaged his ship. Waiting for repairs, Columbus ventured

TIMELINE	1000 BC	AD 800
	Construction and habitation of Guayabo begins	Production of granite spheres in Diquis region begins

into the verdant terrain and exchanged gifts with the friendly natives. He returned from this encounter, claiming to have seen 'more gold in two days than in four years in Española.' Columbus dubbed the stretch of shoreline from Honduras to Panama as Veragua, but it was his excited descriptions of 'la costa rica' that gave the region its lasting name.

Anxious to claim its bounty, Columbus petitioned the Spanish Crown to have himself appointed governor. But by the time he returned to Seville, his royal patron Queen Isabella was on her deathbed, and King Ferdinand awarded the prize to a rival. Columbus never returned to the 'Rich Coast'. Worn down by ill health and court politics, he died in 1506, a very wealthy man.

To the disappointment of his conquistador heirs, the region was not abundant with gold and the locals were not so affable. The king commissioned Diego de Nicuesa to settle the newly claimed land. But this first colony was abruptly abandoned when tropical disease and tenacious natives decimated its ranks. Successive expeditions launched from the Caribbean coast also failed. The pestilent swamps, oppressive jungles and volcano-topped mountains made Columbus's paradise seem more like hell.

In 1513 Balboa made it across Panama and gazed at the Pacific. The conquistadors now had a western beachhead from which to assault Costa Rica. They targeted the indigenous groups living near the Golfo de Nicoya. To the glory of God and king, aristocratic adventurers plundered villages, executed resisters and enslaved survivors. None of these bloodstained campaigns led to a permanent presence, however. Intercontinental germ warfare caused outbreaks of feverish death on both sides. Scarce in mineral wealth and indigenous laborers, the Spanish eventually came to regard the region as the 'poorest and most miserable in all the Americas.'

It was not until the 1560s that a Spanish colony was established. In the interior, at Cartago, a small community eventually settled to cultivate the rich volcanic soil of the Central Valley. Costa Rica's first church (see p166) was built here on the banks of the Río Reventazón. The fledgling colony survived under the leadership of its first governor, Juan Vasquez de Coronado. He used diplomacy instead of firearms to counter the Indian threat, surveyed the lands south to Panama and west to the Pacific, and secured deed and title over the colony. Though Vasquez was lost at sea in a shipwreck, his legacy endured: Costa Rica was an officially recognized province of New Spain.

In Cartago, you can visit Las Ruinas de la Parroquia (p167) on the site of the original 1575 Iglesia del Convento.

CENTRAL VALLEY SUNDAY

Central America was a loosely administered colony. Its political-military headquarters was in Guatemala and the closest bishop was in Nicaragua. Lacking strategic significance or exploitable riches, Costa Rica became a minor provincial outpost.

Costa Rica's colonial path diverged from the typical Spanish pattern in that a powerful landholding elite and slave-based economy never gained prominence. Instead of large estates, mining operations and coastal cities, modest-sized villages of small-holders developed in the interior Central Valley. They toiled six days a week, while Central Valley Sundays were for

Thirty-three out of 44 presidents prior to 1970 were descended from just three original colonizing families.

1502	1563
Christopher Columbus docks his boat at Puerto Limón during his fourth and final voyagex	First permanent colonial settlement established in Cartago by Juan Vásquez de Coronado

prayer and rest. In national lore, the stoic, self-sufficient farmer provided the backbone for 'rural democracy.' Recent historical research shows that colonial society was more complex than this view suggests; still, the Central Valley was a relatively egalitarian corner of the Spanish empire.

Colonial life centered on agriculture. Costa Ricans grew corn, beans and plantains for subsistence, and produced sugar, cacao and tobacco for sale. Despite ample rainfall and rich soil, the Central Valley struggled to prosper. Indian raids and pirate attacks kept villagers on nervous guard. Much of Cartago was leveled in 1723 by Volcán Irazú (p168). New settlements eventually sprouted in Heredia (1706), San José (1737) and Alajuela (1782). As the 18th century closed, the population topped 50,000.

The colony exhibited social hierarchy and ethnic diversity. It is not that Costa Rica lacked an upper class, rather its elite was neither extravagantly affluent nor exclusive. There were several well-connected families, whose lineage went back to the founding of the colony; but anyone could acquire wealth by agricultural processing or trade.

Below the elite, villages included small-holders, tenant laborers and domestic servants. Social mobility existed, but was crimped by economic dearth and cultural conservatism. Patriarchy prevailed at home, an arrangement reinforced by the Church, which was empowered to mediate in family affairs.

The Central Valley population also included free blacks, mulattos and mestizos. With labor in short supply, nonwhites eked out a living on the edge of the colonial economy, but they were denied legal status. The scarcity of European women meant that over time the Central Valley's white population turned browner.

As Spanish settlement expanded, the indigenous population plummeted. From 400,000 at the time Columbus first sailed, the number was reduced to 20,000 a century later, and to 8000 a century after that. While disease was the main source of death, the Spanish were relentless in their effort to exploit the natives as an economic resource. Central Valley indigenous groups were the first to fall. Outside the valley, several tribes managed to survive a bit longer under forest cover, staging occasional raids. Repeated military campaigns eventually forced them into submission and slavery as well.

In 1676, the governor of Cartago granted official recognition to a group of mixed-race individuals who had helped to save the town from pirates.

NOBLE HOMELAND

In 1821 the Americas wriggled free of Spain's imperial grip. Mexico declared independence for itself as well as Central America. The Central American colonies declared independence from Mexico. These events hardly disturbed Costa Rica, which learned of its liberation a month after the fact. With an empire up for grabs, the region descended into conflict.

Independence set off a struggle between Conservatives, Spanish-bred elites who previously dominated colonial administration, and Liberals, New World elites who were denied the status and power that they believed they deserved. Conservatives promoted an orderly continuation of tradition, monarchy and the Church; Liberals favored enlightened progress, a constitutional republic, and secular reform. In the Central Valley, this clash led to a short civil war between Conservatives of Cartago

1737	1821
San José founded	Costa Rica gains independence from Spain

GARABITO

The area encompassed by Parque Nacional Carara (p325) was once home to a legendary indigenous hero, a local cacique named Garabito. Commanding a vast area from the Golfo de Nicoya to the Central Valley, he led a fierce struggle against the Spanish.

A favorite tactic of the Spanish to weaken native resistance was to decapitate tribal leadership – literally. In 1560, the Guatemalan high command dispatched a military force to arrest Garabito. The wily chieftain used the forest to elude capture, but the Spanish managed to seize his wife, Biriteka, as a hostage. Garabito countered by having one of his followers dress up as the chieftain and allow himself to be captured. While the camp celebrated its prize catch, Garabito escaped with his wife.

Garabito's ploy, however, was the exception. The more common fate of captured caciques was to star in an imperial morality play. In Act One, the shackled chief sat through a trial at which his numerous transgressions against God and king were expounded. The chief responded to the charges, then was sentenced to death. In Act Two, a public execution was staged, whereby the guilty chief had his eyes and tongue cut out, was shot with a crossbow, was beheaded with an axe, had his severed head displayed on a pike, and finally had his body burned to ashes. The End.

---

and Liberals of San José. The upstart Liberals prevailed and, as a spoil of war, the victors moved the capital to San José in 1823.

The newly liberated colonies pondered their fate: stay together in a United States of Central America or go their separate national ways. At first, they came up with something in between – the Central American Federation (CAF). But it could neither field an army nor collect taxes. Accustomed to being at the center of things, Guatemala attempted to dominate the CAF, alienating smaller colonies and hastening its demise. Costa Rica formally withdrew in 1938. Future attempts to unite the region would likewise fail.

Meanwhile, an independent Costa Rica was taking shape under Juan Mora Fernandez, first head of state (1824–33). Mora tended to nation-building. He organized new towns, built roads, published a newspaper and coined a currency. His wife designed a new flag. Life returned to normal, unlike the rest of the region where post-independence civil wars raged on. In 1824 the Nicoya-Guanacaste province seceded from Nicaragua and joined its more easygoing southern neighbor, defining the territorial borders. In 1852 Costa Rica received its first diplomatic emissaries from the United States and Great Britain.

Legend has it that the president ordered a popular local musician – under threat of arrest – to compose the national anthem, a hymn entitled *Our Noble Homeland*.

As one empire receded, another arose. In the 19th century, the US was in an expansive mood and Spanish America looked vulnerable. In 1856 the soldier of fortune William Walker landed in Nicaragua intending to conquer Central America, establish slavery, and construct an interoceanic canal. Walker was soon marching on Costa Rica. A volunteer army of 9000 civilians was hastily mobilized. The Yankee mercenaries were stopped at Santa Rosa, and chased back into Nicaragua. During the fight, a drummer boy from Alajuela, Juan Santamaría, was killed while daringly setting fire to Walker's defenses. The battle became a national legend and Santamaría a national hero (and inspiration for an airport). Walker's messianic ambitions were soon quenched by a Honduran firing squad. You can see a memorial to this battle in Parque Nacional in San José (p100).

1823	1824
The capital moves to San José after skirmishes with the residents of Cartago	The Nicoya-Guanacaste region secedes from Nicaragua and becomes a part of Costa Rica

COFFEE RICA

In the 19th century, the riches that Costa Rica had long promised were uncovered, when it was realized that the soil and climate of the Central Valley highlands were ideal for coffee cultivation. Costa Rica led Central America in introducing the caffeinated red bean, which remade the impoverished country into the wealthiest in the region.

When an export market was discovered, the government actively promoted coffee to farmers by providing free saplings. At first, Costa Rican producers exported their crop to nearby South Americans, who processed the beans and re-exported the product to Europe. By the 1840s, local merchants had wised up. They built up domestic capacity and scoped out their own overseas markets. They persuaded the captain of the HMS *Monarch* to transport several hundred sacks of Costa Rican coffee to London, percolating the beginning of a beautiful friendship.

The Costa Rican coffee boom was on. The drink's quick fix made it popular among working-class consumers in the industrializing north. The aroma of riches lured a wave of enterprising German immigrants to Costa Rica, enhancing the technical and financial skills of the business sector. By century's end, more than one-third of the Central Valley was dedicated to coffee cultivation, and coffee accounted for more than 90% of all exports and 80% of foreign-currency earnings.

The coffee industry in Costa Rica developed differently than in the rest of Central America. As elsewhere, there arose a group of coffee barons, elites that reaped the rewards for the export bonanza. Costa Rican coffee barons, however, lacked the land and labor to cultivate the crop. Coffee production is labor intensive, with a long painstaking harvest season. The small farmers became the principal planters. The coffee barons, instead, monopolized processing, marketing and financing. The coffee economy in Costa Rica created a wide network of high-end traders and small-scale growers; in the rest of Central America, a narrow elite controlled large estates, worked by tenant laborers.

Coffee wealth became a power resource in politics. Costa Rica's traditional aristocratic families were at the forefront of the enterprise. At midcentury, three-quarters of the coffee barons were descended from just two colonial families. The country's leading coffee exporter at this time was President Juan Rafael Mora (1849–59), whose lineage went back to the colony's founder Juan Vasquez. In 1860 Mora was overthrown by his brother-in-law, after the president proposed to form a national bank independent of the coffee barons. The economic interests of the coffee elite would thereafter become a priority in Costa Rican politics.

BANANA EMPIRE

The coffee trade unintentionally gave rise to Costa Rica's next export boom – bananas. Getting coffee out to world markets necessitated a rail link from the central highlands to the coast and Limón's deep harbor made it an ideal port. Inland was dense jungle and infested swamps. The government contracted the task to Minor Keith, nephew of an American railroad tycoon.

The project was a disaster. Malaria and accidents forced a constant replenishing of workers. Tico recruits gave way to US convicts and Chinese

---

The land in Santa Rosa where William Walker was defeated in 1856 would later be owned by Nicaraguan dictator Anastasio Somoza in the 1950s. These were expropriated in 1978 when the Costa Rican government severed diplomatic relations with Nicaragua.

In the 1940s children learned to read with a text that stated, 'Coffee is good for me. I drink coffee every morning.'

Today in Costa Rica there are an estimated 130,000 coffee farms.

1856	1889
Costa Rica defeats American filibuster William Walker in the battle of Santa Rosa	First democratic elections held (blacks and women not allowed to vote)

For details on the role of Minor Keith and United Fruit in lobbying for a CIA-led coup in Guatemala, pick up a copy of the highly readable *Bitter Fruit* by Stephen Schlesinger and Stephen Kinzer.

indentured servants, who were replaced by freed Jamaican slaves. Keith's two brothers died during the arduous first decade that laid 100km of track. The government defaulted on funding and construction costs soared over budget. To entice Keith to continue, the government turned over 800,000 acres of land along the route and a 99-year lease to run the railroad. In 1890, the line was finally completed, and running at a loss.

Keith had begun to grow banana plants along the tracks as a cheap food source for the workers. Desperate to recoup his investment, he shipped some bananas to New Orleans in the hope of starting a side venture. Keith struck gold, or rather yellow. Consumers went crazy for the elongated finger fruit. Banana fincas (plantations) replaced lowland forests. By the early 20th century, bananas surpassed coffee as Costa Rica's most lucrative export. Costa Rica was the world's leading banana exporter. Unlike the coffee industry, however, the profits were exported along with the bananas.

Costa Rica was transformed by the rise of Keith's banana empire. He joined with another American importer to found the infamous United Fruit Company, soon the largest employer in Central America. To the locals, it was known as *el pulpo*, the octopus. Its tentacles stretched across the region, becoming entangled with the local economy and politics. United Fruit owned huge swathes of lush lowlands, much of the transportation and communication infrastructure, and bunches of bureaucrats. United Fruit promoted a wave of migrant laborers from Jamaica, changing the country's ethnic complexion and provoking racial tensions (see the boxed text The Great Banana Strike, opposite).

In 1913 a banana blight known as 'Panama disease' shut down many Caribbean plantations and the industry relocated to the Pacific. Eventually United Fruit lost its banana monopoly in Costa Rica.

UNARMED DEMOCRACY

The modern-day successor to the United Fruit Company is Chiquita.

Early Costa Rican politics followed the Central American pattern of violence and dictatorship. In the 19th century, a few favored aristocrats competed to control patronage in the new state. The military, the Church and, most of all, the coffee barons were the main sources of influence. Presidents were more often removed at gunpoint, than by the ballot box.

In 1842 Francisco Morazan, the last head of the CAF, returned to Costa Rica and became president via a coup. Morazan set the precedent for using arms to come to power, but he also confirmed that power was fleeting without elite support. He was executed shortly thereafter.

After this inauspicious start, political life slowly became more civil. A number of democratically inspired constitutions were enacted, and just as quickly discarded when elite fears were aroused. By the late 19th century, the eligible electorate expanded from 2% to 10% of the adult population. Military strongman, Tomas Guardia, forced higher taxes on the coffee barons to finance social reform. By the early 20th century, Costa Rica had free public education, a guaranteed minimum wage and child protection laws. Denied the right to participate, disenfranchised groups resorted to protest politics. In 1918 women school teachers and students staged effective strikes against the despotic displays of President Frederico Tinoco, who soon resigned.

1890	1900
Construction of the railroad between San José and Puerto Limón is completed	The population of Costa Rica reaches 50,000

THE GREAT BANANA STRIKE

In the mid-19th century, liberated West Indian slaves became a workforce for hire. United Fruit actively recruited English-speaking Jamaican blacks to be banana workers. Tens of thousands migrated to Costa Rica, creating an Afro-Caribbean enclave around Limón, 30,000 strong. Their presence provoked conflict with Costa Rican Hispanics in competition for banana jobs, which intensified when the industry moved to the Pacific coast. United Fruit exploited racial antagonisms to keep labor divided and weak.

Former banana employees turned to radical politics, organizing a series of often bloody strikes against the company. The movement culminated in Puerto Limón in August 1934 with the largest protest in Costa Rica's history. Thousands staged a general strike: the docks shut down, federal troops were called in, shots were fired and negotiations held. In a victory duplicated nowhere else in Central America, United Fruit capitulated, forgiving debts to the company store and promising to improve living conditions.

But the outcome of the banana strike proved devastating to Costa Rica's Afro-Caribbean community. Although Hispanics were the main participants in the strike, black workers were punished. The Costa Rican government now became actively involved in segregating and discriminating against the blacks. Further immigration was banned out of fear of an 'Africanization' of the country. Moreover, blacks were forbidden from moving to the Pacific coast to follow the banana jobs. Stranded in the least-developed part of the country, many turned to subsistence farming, fishing or cocoa plantations. Younger blacks left the country to find jobs elsewhere. The Afro-Caribbean community in Limón declined by nearly half by the mid-20th century.

Beginning in 1940, events would lead Costa Rica onto a more democratic path. At this time, President Rafael Calderon defied elite expectations, by championing the rights of the working class and the poor. Calderon orchestrated a powerful alliance between workers and the Church. The inevitable conservative reaction was unleashed in full force in the 1948 presidential election. Costa Rica briefly descended into civil war. The business community staged its own strike threatening an economic crisis, armed workers battled military forces, and Nicaraguan and US forces joined in the fray. Peace was restored in less than two months, but with 2000 deaths.

Out of the chaos came a coffee grower and utopian democrat, José Figueres Ferrer. As head of a temporary junta government, Figueres enacted nearly 1000 decrees. He taxed the wealthy, nationalized the banks, and built a modern welfare state. His 1949 constitution granted full citizenship and voting rights to women, blacks, indigenous groups and Chinese minorities. Most extraordinarily, he abolished the military, calling it a threat to democracy. Figueres proved to be a transformative figure in Costa Rican politics. His revolutionary regime became the foundation for Costa Rica's unique and unarmed democracy (see the boxed text The Struggle Without End, p42).

The old army headquarters in San José now house the Museo Nacional de Costa Rica (p100). You can still see where the walls were riddled by bullets in the 1948 civil war.

OLIVER'S ARMY

The sovereignty of the small nations of Central America was limited by their northern neighbor, the USA. Big sticks, gun boats and dollar diplomacy were instruments of Yankee hegemony. The USA was actively hostile toward leftist politics. In the 1970s, radical socialists forced the

1940	1948
Rafael Angel Calderón Guardia elected president; minimum-wage laws and eight-hour day introduced	Six-week civil war leaves 2000 dead

THE STRUGGLE WITHOUT END

José Figueres Ferrer was a self-described farmer-philosopher and the father of Costa Rica's un-armed democracy. He was born in Alajuela in 1906, the son of Catalan immigrant coffee planters. Figueres excelled in school and went abroad to MIT to study engineering. Instead, he spent this time at the Boston Public Library studying political philosophy. Figueres returned to Costa Rica and set up his own coffee plantation in 1928. Inspired by his readings, he organized the hundreds of laborers on his farm into a utopian socialist community, and appropriately named the property *La Luz Sin Fin,* or 'The Struggle without End.'

In the 1940s, Figueres became involved in national politics as an outspoken critic of President Calderon. In the midst of a radio interview in which he badmouthed the president, police broke into the studio and arrested Figueres. He was accused of having fascist sympathies and banished to Mexico. While in exile he formed the Caribbean League, a collection of students and demo-cratic agitators from all over Central America, who pledged to bring down the region's military dictators. When he returned to Costa Rica, the Caribbean League, now 700-men strong, went with him and helped stir up protest against the powers that be.

When government troops descended on the farm with the intention of arresting Figueres and disarming the Caribbean League, it touched off a civil war. The moment had arrived: the diminu-tive farmer-philosopher now played the man on horseback. Figueres emerged victorious from the brief conflict and seized the opportunity to put into place his vision of Costa Rican social democracy. When he dissolved the military, Figueres quoted HG Wells, who said, 'the future of mankind cannot include the armed forces.'

military oligarchies of Guatemala, El Salvador and Nicaragua onto the de-fensive. In 1979 the rebellious Sandinistas toppled the American-backed Somoza dictatorship in Nicaragua. Alarmed by the Sandinistas' Soviet and Cuban ties, fervently anticommunist President Ronald Reagan de-cided it was time to intervene. The Cold War arrived in the hot tropics.

Costa Rica did not experience the same upsurge in radical politics as its northern neighbor. Its more inclusive social democracy effectively moderated the extremist tendencies visible elsewhere in the region. The political left in Costa Rica was reformist, not revolutionary.

The surf destination known as Ollie's Point is named after US Colonel Oliver North. Situated near the break is an old airstrip that was used by US airplanes to smuggle goods to the Nicaraguan Contras in the 1980s.

The organizational details of the counter-revolution were delegated to Oliver North, an eager-to-please junior officer working out of the White House basement. North's can-do creativity helped to prop up a collection of *caudillo* wannabes – the Contra rebels – to incite civil war in Nicara-gua. While both sides invoked the rhetoric of freedom and democracy, the war was really a turf battle between left-wing and right-wing thugs.

Under intense US pressure, Costa Rica was reluctantly dragged in. The Contras set up camp in northern Costa Rica, from where they staged gue-rilla raids. Not-so-clandestine CIA operatives and US military advisors were dispatched to assist the effort. Costa Rican authorities were bribed to keep quiet. A secret jungle airstrip was built near the border to fly in weapons and supplies. To raise cash for the rebels, North neatly used his covert supply network to traffic illegal narcotics through the region. Diplomatic relations between Costa Rica and Nicaragua grew nastier; border clashes between the two became bloodier.

The war polarized Costa Rica. From conservative quarters came a loud call to re-establish the military and join the anticommunist crusade.

1949	1963
The new constitution abolishes the army, desegregates the country and grants women and blacks the right to vote	Cabo Blanco becomes Costa Rica's first federally protected conservation area

The Pentagon agreed to underwrite this proposal. On the opposing side, in May 1984, over 20,000 demonstrators marched through San José to give peace a chance. The debate came to climax in the 1986 presidential election. The victor was 44-year-old Oscar Arias. Born to coffee wealth, Arias was an intellectual reformer in the mold of Figueres, his political patron.

Once in office, Arias affirmed his commitment to a negotiated resolution and reasserted Costa Rican national independence. He vowed to uphold his country's pledge of neutrality and to vanquish the Contras from the territory. His stance prompted the US ambassador to suddenly quit his post. In a public ceremony, Costa Rican school children planted trees on top of the CIA's secret airfield. Most notably, Arias became the driving force in uniting Central America around a peace plan, which ended the Nicaraguan war. In 1987 he was awarded the Nobel Peace Prize.

When not in the office of the president, Oscar Arias founded the Arias Foundation for Peace and Human Progress; on the web at www.arias.or.cr.

PARADISE FOUND
As Spanish conquistadors hacked their way into Costa Rica, the dense rain forest was an obstacle to the quest for treasure. Five hundred years later, the hidden wealth was discovered to be the rain forest itself. Today Costa Rica is a glittering gem of the world environmental movement.

The 18th-century Spanish naturalist Fernandez de Oveido was awestruck by the rich stock of flora and fauna. His plea to Costa Ricans to take care of the forests went unheeded. Only quirky foreign scientists seemed to show an aesthetic interest. Well into the 20th century, clearing the jungle was considered the best way to improve the land.

In the 1970s, world coffee prices rapidly dropped due to oversupply. The unpredictability of commodity markets brought together an unusual alliance of economic developers and environmental conservationists. If wealth could not be sustained through exports, then what about imports – of tourists? Costa Rica embarked on a green revolution.

In 1963, the Reserva Natural Absoluta Cabo Blanco became the first federally protected conservation area (p315). By 1995 there were more than 125 government protected sites, including national parks, forest preserves and wildlife reserves. Success encouraged private landholders to build reserves as well. Almost one-third of the entire country is now under some form of environmental protection.

The ecotourism boom was on: the rain forest was essentially paying for itself. In 1975 the Monteverde reserve recorded only 500 tourists; by 1995 the number surpassed 50,000. Tourism contributed $100 million to the economy in 1985, and more than $750 million a decade later. It passed coffee and bananas as the main source of foreign currency earnings. In 1999 more than one million tourists visited Costa Rica.

For the most part, tourism profits stay in the country and have contributed to rising living standards.

Costa Rica is a pioneer in sustainable development, providing a model in which economic and environmental interests are complementary. But it is not without some contention. Conservation and ecotourism are administered by two powerful bureaucracies – the Ministry for Environment & Energy (Minae) and the Costa Rica Tourism Board (ICT) – which frequently clash. The San José-based eco-elite often seem removed

Costa Rica's parks didn't just happen. Pick up The Quetzal and the Macaw: The Story of Costa Rica's National Parks, by David Rains Wallace, for the full contentious history that pitted the government against communities against environmental activists.

The jaguar's share of ecotourists comes from the USA – 43% of visitors to Costa Rica are americanos.

1987	2000
Oscar Arias Sánchez wins the Nobel Prize for his work on the Central American peace accords	The population of Costa Rica reaches 3.8 million

from the concerns of local residents, who still use the land to survive. The lure of paradise has attracted foreign capital, which inflates property values and displaces the local populace.

Furthermore, the success of the green revolution creates a new concern – sustainable tourism. The increasing number of visitors to Costa Rica leads to more hotels, more transportation and more infrastructure upgrades. This tourist-driven encroachment into the rain forest inevitably places stress on its fragile ecosystem.

TICOS TODAY

Costa Rica is sometimes referred to as the Switzerland of Central America for its natural beauty, comfortable lifestyle and peaceful democracy. But is this merely the depiction on a postcard or does it have relevance for today's Tico?

Early in the 20th century, this view could rightly be called an optimistic caricature. At best, Costa Rica was an occasional democracy with widespread poverty. In the second half of the century, however, the postcard was truer to life. Sustained economic growth created a viable middle class and more generous social welfare that benefited the majority.

By most indicators, Costa Rica ranks well above its poorer neighbors. In 1950, one out of two Ticos lived below the poverty line; today the number is one out of five. In 1950, average life expectancy was less than 50 years; today it is over 75 years. In 1980, zero Ticos had visited a shopping mall; today more than one million have visited within the past month. Older Ticos especially have witnessed significant change: a *supermercado* replacing the *pulpería*, urban sprawl replacing family farms, and satellite TV replacing the state radio.

With economic change comes social change. More women have entered the workforce though opportunities in the tourist and service sectors. Divorce rates have increased and family size has shrunk. More Ticos are entering higher education, and they are doing so in Costa Rica. Migrant laborers from Nicaragua work the coffee plantations, while Tico tenants seek better jobs in the city. Rice and beans is still a staple at most tables, but fast-food burgers increasingly substitute.

Costa Rican democracy is still dominated by the old family elites, although politics is now peppered with popular protest. Economic growth produced a larger public sector, which stays busy regulating and redistributing. Patronage and corruption remain accepted currencies in politics. Protectionist politics has caused resistance to outside pressures for more privatization as well as to the Central American Free Trade Agreement (Cafta), the proposed regional free trade zone (see p34).

Ticos are sometimes criticized for being self-content and passive about politics. But underneath the easygoing veneer is discernable pride and support for their unarmed democracy. As stated by recently re-elected President Oscar Arias in his Nobel Peace Prize acceptance speech, 'we seek peace and democracy together, indivisible, an end to the shedding of human blood, which is inseparable from an end to the suppression of human rights.' A unique point of view – not only in Central America, but in the world.

The excellent *Costa Rica Reader*, by Steven Palmer and Iván Molina, is a collection of vignettes about ordinary Costa Ricans – past and present – from all walks of life.

The Last Country the Gods Made, by Adrian Colesberry, is an unexpected collection of essays and photographs, providing an overview of Costa Rican history, geography and society.

2005	2006
A fire at San José's Calderon Guardia hospital kills 17 patients and two nurses	Oscar Arias is elected president for the second time

The Culture

THE NATIONAL PSYCHE

Costa Ricans take pride in defining themselves by what they are not. In comparison with their Central American neighbors, they aren't poor, they aren't illiterate and they aren't beleaguered by political tumult. It's a curious line-up of negatives that somehow adds up to one big positive.

Ticos (Costa Ricans) are very proud of their country, from its ecological jewels, high standard of living and education levels to, above all, the fact that it has flourished without an army for the past 50-plus years. They view their country as an oasis of calm in a land that has been continuously degraded by warfare. The Nobel Prize that Oscar Arias received for his work on the Central American peace accords is a point of pride and confirms the general feeling that they are somehow different from a grosser, more violent world. Peace is priceless.

And to maintain it, Ticos will avoid conflict at all costs, no matter how trifling the topic. People will say 'yes' even if they mean 'no', and 'maybe' often replaces 'I don't know.' This is a habit that can flummox foreigners, who try to figure out if anyone really means what they say. Tough negotiating is not a strong suit.

Ticos are well-mannered to a fault and will do everything they can to *quedar bien* (leave a good impression). Conversations start with a cordial *buenos días* or *buenas tardes* and friendly inquiries about your well-being before delving into business. Bullying and yelling will get you nowhere, but a smile and a friendly greeting goes a long way.

Ticos are cautious and rarely get passionately involved in a debate or fight. Disputes tend to be settled amicably through careful negotiation and compromise. And while the stereotype of Costa Rican friendliness is largely true, it's also just as true that they wouldn't tell you if they didn't like you because, well, it'd be rude.

LIFESTYLE

A lack of war, strong exports and stronger tourism have meant that Costa Rica enjoys the highest standard of living in Central America. Even though 18% of the populace lives below the poverty line, beggars are few and you won't see the packs of ragged street kids that seem to roam around other Latin American capitals.

In the poorer lowland areas, *campesinos* (peasants) and *indígenas* (indigenous people) often live in windowless houses made of *caña brava*, a local cane. Urban areas have hastily constructed shanty towns where many of the urban poor dwell, but certainly not on the scale of some other Latin American countries.

For the most part, Costa Ricans live fairly comfortably. The home of an average Tico is a one-story construction made of concrete blocks, wood or a combination of both. According to Unicef, 92% of households have adequate sanitation systems, while 97% have access to potable water.

The Caribbean coast has long suffered from a lack of attention by the federal government. Here, poverty levels are higher and standards of living are lower than in the rest of the country. Even in this deprived region, however, most people have adequate facilities and improved drinking water.

Life expectancy exceeds that of the USA. Most Costa Ricans are more likely to die of heart disease or cancer, as opposed to the childhood diseases

The most comprehensive and complete book on Costa Rican history and culture is *The Ticos: Culture and Social Change in Costa Rica* by Mavis, Richard and Karen Biesanz. A must-read for anyone interested in the country.

If you are operating on *hora tica*, or Tico time, you should feel no need to end a conversation to be on time to a prearranged appointment.

The expression *matando la culebra* (meaning 'to be idle', literally 'killing the snake') originates with peons from banana plantations. When foremen would ask what they'd been doing, the response was, '¡Matando la culebra!'

that tend to claim lives in many developing nations. A nationwide health-care system (if overburdened) and proper sanitation systems account for these positive statistics.

Family remains the nucleus of social and cultural life in Costa Rica. Families socialize together, and groups of the same clan will often live near each other in clusters. Similar to the industrialized world, families have an average of 2.2 children. For the most part, Costa Rican youths spend ample time on middle-class worries such as dating, music, belly-baring fashions and *fútbol* (soccer). Primary education is free and compulsory, contributing to the 97% literacy rate.

Modernization is continually affecting family ways. Society is increasingly geographically mobile and the Tico that was born in Puntarenas might end up managing a lodge on the Península de Osa. And, with the advent of better paved roads, cell (mobile) phones, electrification and the presence of 50,000 North American ex-pats, change will continue to come at a steady pace for the Tico family unit.

POPULATION

Costa Ricans call themselves Ticos (men and groups of men and women) or Ticas (females). Two-thirds of the nation's almost four million people live in the Meseta Central (Central Valley), and almost one-third is under the age of 15.

In the 1940s, Costa Rica was an overwhelmingly agricultural society, with the vast majority of the population employed by coffee and banana plantations. By the end of the century, the economy had shifted quite dramatically, and only one-fifth of the labor force was employed by agriculture. These days, industry (especially agro-industry) employs another one-fifth, while the service sector employs more than half of the labor force. Banking and commerce are prominent, but tourism alone employs more than 10% of the labor force and produces an equal portion of the GDP.

Most inhabitants are mestizo, a mix of Spanish with Indian and/or black roots (though most Ticos consider themselves white). Indigenous Costa Ricans make up only 1% of the population; groups include the Bribrí and Cabécar (see p498), Brunka (p388), Guaymí (p442) and Maleku (p508). A growing interest in indigenous cultures – mostly on the part of foreign tourists – is beginning to draw a bit of attention to these long-ignored groups. The indigenous groups are responding with varying degrees of receptivity, but many recognize the economic potential of encouraging tourism. See the boxed text Endangered Cultures, p49, for more information.

Less than 3% of the population is black, much of it concentrated on the Caribbean coast. Tracing its ancestry to Jamaican immigrants who were brought to build railroads in the 19th century, this population speaks Mecatelio, a patois of English, Spanish and Jamaican English. This population identifies strongly with its counterparts in other Caribbean countries; coconut spiced cuisine and calypso music are only a few elements that travelers can enjoy. In Limón, still common are the rituals of *obeah*, or sorcery, passed down from African ancestors (see the boxed text Local Lore, p454).

Chinese immigrants (1%) arrived in Costa Rica through similar routes, though there have been regular, more voluntary waves of immigration since then. In recent years North American and European immigration has greatly increased and it is estimated that roughly 50,000 North American ex-pats live in the country.

The Space Propulsion Lab at NASA is run by a Tico. Renowned astronaut Franklin Chang-Díaz is designing an engine that will someday get humans to Mars. He is revered in Costa Rica and even has a beetle named after him: *Phanaeus changdiazi*.

A winning oral history of the black communities on the Caribbean coast is covered in Paula Palmer's *What Happen*. It can be difficult to find because it's out of print, but used copies pop up on www .amazon.com and www .half.com.

SPORTS

The national sport is, you guessed it, *fútbol*. Every town has a soccer field (which usually serves as the most conspicuous landmark), where neighborhood aficionados play in heated matches.

The *selección nacional* (national selection) team is known affectionately as La Sele. Legions of rabid Tico fans still recall La Sele's most memorable moments, including an unlikely showing in the quarter-finals at the 1990 World Cup in Italy and a solid (if not long-lasting) performance in the 2002 World Cup. Most recently, Tico fans were celebrating La Sele's qualification to participate in the 2006 World Cup in Germany, although the team failed to progress beyond the first round. Costa Rica has also played several times in the Copa America, twice making it to the quarter-finals. Women's soccer is not followed with as much devotion, but there is a female national team. The regular season is from August to May.

Surfing is growing in popularity among Ticos. Costa Rica annually hosts numerous national and international competitions that are widely covered by local media. Bullfighting is also popular, particularly in the Guanacaste region. (The bull isn't killed in the Costa Rican version of the sport, which is really a ceremonial opportunity to watch a drunk cowboy run around with a bull.) The popular Latin American sport of cockfighting is illegal.

Get player statistics, game schedules and find out everything you ever needed to know about La Sele, the Costa Rican national soccer team, at www.fedefutbol.com (in Spanish).

MULTICULTURALISM

The mix of mainstream mestizo society with blacks, Asians, Indians and North Americans provides the country with an interesting fusion of culture and cuisine. And while the image of the welcoming Tico is largely true, tensions always exist.

For the black population, racism has been a reality for more than a century. About 75% of the country's black population resides on the Caribbean coast, and this area has been historically marginalized and deprived of services by a succession of governments (black Costa Ricans were not allowed in the Central Valley until after 1948). Nonetheless, good manners prevail and black visitors can feel comfortable traveling

Costa Rica hosts an annual tennis tournament known as La Copa del Café, or the Coffee Cup.

NORTH AMERICAN IMMIGRATION

Costa Rica is currently grappling with identity issues raised by the influx of North American (and some European) settlers. Many Ticos are starting to feel that they are being discriminated against in their own country. It is not hard to see why. About 80% of all coastal property is owned by foreigners. Signs are in English, prices are in dollars and many top-end resorts are managed exclusively by foreigners, with locals serving primarily as maids and gardeners.

Some foreign hotel owners make a point of keeping their business in exclusively foreign hands. 'No Ticos,' one hotel manager on the Pacific coast said proudly. Yet another confided, 'These Latin Americans don't like to work.' This is certainly not the attitude of the majority of North American immigrants, but nobody can deny that discrimination exists.

In contrast, some travelers have complained that Costa Rica is somehow a 'less authentic' destination because of the large numbers of North Americans. The country is certainly in a state of cultural evolution. But it is worth recognizing the contributions immigrants have made. Many European and North American immigrants have been responsible for organizing, supporting and financing the nation's major conservation and environmental efforts. It was two immigrants from Scandinavia who helped found the country's first national park, the Reserva Natural Absoluta Cabo Blanco (p315).

Immigration is part of history and part of society. We only hope the immigrants will give as much as they get.

around the entire country. Asian Ticos and the small Jewish population have frequently been the subject of immature jokes, though Jewish and Asian travelers alike can expect to be treated well.

It is Nicaraguans who are currently the butt of some of society's worst prejudice. During the 1980s, the civil war provoked a wave of immigration from Nicaragua. While the violence in this neighboring country has ended, most immigrants prefer to stay in Costa Rica for its economic opportunities. Many nationals like to blame Nicas for an increase in violent crime, though no proof of this claim exists (see the boxed text Nica vs Tico, p235).

Indigenous populations remain largely invisible to many in Costa Rican society. While many indigenous people lead Westernized, inherently Tico, lives, others inhabit the country's reserves and maintain a more traditional lifestyle (see the boxed text Endangered Cultures, opposite). Note that one translation of Indian is *indio*, which is an insulting term; *indígena* is the preferred term, meaning 'indigenous.'

<aside>For Costa Rica news in English, check out the weekly *Tico Times* at www.ticotimes.net or the tabloid *Inside Costa Rica* at www.insidecostarica.com.</aside>

MEDIA

The law guaranteeing freedom of the press in Costa Rica is the oldest in Central America, dating from 1835. While Costa Rica certainly enjoys more press freedom than most Latin American countries, do not expect a great deal of probity from its media. The outlets are limited and coverage tends to be cautious, largely due to conservative media laws.

At the time of research the country still had a *desacato* – insult law – on its books. This is common in most Latin American countries and allows public figures to sue journalists if their honor has been 'damaged' by the media. A 'right of response' law allows individuals who have been criticized in the media equal attention (time or space) to reply to the charges. These laws are considered to limit the freedom of the press and provide officials with a shield from public scrutiny. Indeed, in a 2003 survey, 41% of reporters polled indicated that they had left out some information due to legal concerns, while 79% said they felt some pressure to forego investigation of certain issues.

The 2001 assassination of radio journalist Parmenio Medina gave reporters another reason not to dig deep. Medina was the host of a popular investigative program called *La Patada* (The Kick). Shortly before broadcasting a series on financial irregularities at a now-defunct Catholic radio station, he was shot to death outside his home in Heredia. Nine men, including a priest, were brought to trial in connection with the murder at the end of 2005.

Other laws prevent journalists from doing an effective job. Libel and slander laws put the burden of proof on reporters and they are frequently required to reveal their sources in court. In July 2004, the Inter-American Court of Human Rights struck down a defamation decision against Mauricio Herrera Ulloa of *La Nación*. The Costa Rican government has promised to abide by the ruling, which called for a revision of the criminal libel laws. At the time of writing, however, no changes had been made.

RELIGION

More than 75% of Ticos are Catholic (at least in principle). And while many show a healthy reverence for the Virgin Mary, they rarely profess blind faith to the dictates coming from Rome – apparently 'pure life' doesn't require being excessively penitent. Most people tend to go to church for the sacraments (baptism, first communion, confirmation, marriage and death) and the holidays.

Religious processions on holy days are generally less fervent and colorful than those found in Latin American countries such as Guatemala or Peru. (Though the procession for the patron virgin, La Virgen de los Ángeles, held annually on August 2 does draw penitents who walk from all over Central America to Cartago to show devotion. For details, see the boxed text Local Lore, p168.) Semana Santa (the week before Easter) is a national holiday: everything (even buses) stops operating at lunchtime on Maundy Thursday and doesn't start up again until the afternoon of Holy Saturday.

Follow current events in Costa Rica at the website of the top daily, *La Nación*, at www.nacion.com.

Roughly 14% of Costa Ricans are evangelical Christians; increased interest in evangelical religions is attributed to a greater sense of community spirit within the churches. The black community on the Caribbean is largely Protestant and there are small Jewish populations in San José and Jacó. There are sprinklings of Middle Easterners and Asians who practice Islam and Buddhism, respectively.

ENDANGERED CULTURES

The Europeans that made the long journey across the Atlantic did not come to admire the native culture. Spanish conquistadors valued the indigenous populations as an economic resource: they ruthlessly leveled tribal society, plundered its meager wealth, and hunted down and enslaved the survivors. Catholic missionaries followed closely behind, charged with eradicating heathen beliefs and instilling a more civilized lifestyle. All and all, they were quite successful as native culture in Costa Rica came close to extinction.

The remnants of a traditional native lifestyle survived at the outer margins, kept alive by isolated families beyond the reach of law and popular culture. The indigenous groups were not even encouraged to assimilate, but instead were actively excluded from Spanish-dominated society. Well into the 20th century, they were forbidden from entering populated regions and were denied fundamental political and legal rights. Indigenous peoples were not granted citizenship until the 1949 constitution, though in practice their status did not change much as a result.

In 1977, the government created the reservation system, which allowed indigenous groups to organize themselves into self-governing communities. The government, however, retained title to the land. With this change, it was now permitted to engage in traditional languages and customs – for those descendants who could still remember their roots. Ironically, this more tolerant government policy also meant access to public education and job opportunities, which accelerated native language loss and Tico acculturation.

Presently, there are 22 reservations in Costa Rica but indigenous cultures remain highly endangered. The language of the once-robust Central Valley Huetar is already extinct. In Guanacaste, the cultural inheritance of the Chorotega tribe, descendants of the rich Meso-American tradition, is now all but depleted. In remote pockets of the south, the Guaymí still speak the native tongue, wear traditional garments, and hunt and gather to subsist (see the boxed text Guaymí, p442). Many of the Bribrí Indians who remained in the Caribbean lowlands shed their native ways after finding employment on the banana plantations (see the boxed text Bribrí & Cabécar, p498).

The Brunka, also called Boruca, is what remains of three great chiefdoms that once inhabited the Península de Osa and much of the south; now they are restricted to a reservation in the valley of the Río Grande de Térraba. While their annual Fiesta de los Diablitos attracts much outside attention, their language is nearly extinct and their land is threatened by a proposal for a huge hydroelectric project (see p388).

The rise of ecotourism has had more success preserving indigenous fauna than indigenous cultures. Nonetheless, traditional native culture has at last found some source of sustenance as a result of tourism. A consumer market now exists for indigenous arts and crafts. Some villages will accommodate visitors who are curious for a glimpse of a traditional lifestyle or seek to learn the healing powers of medicinal forest plants. Costa Rican universities have taken up the task to study Indian cultures and languages. After suffering disparagement and neglect for so long, a better understanding and appreciation of the native cultures would be welcomed.

WOMEN IN COSTA RICA

Women are traditionally respected in Costa Rica (Mother's Day is a national holiday), and since 1974 the Costa Rican family code has stipulated that husband and wife have equal duties and rights. In addition, women can draw up contracts, assume loans and inherit property; sexual harassment and sex discrimination are against the law. In 1996, Costa Rica passed a landmark law against domestic violence, one of the most progressive in Latin America.

In conjunction with two indigenous women, Paula Palmer wrote Taking Care of Sibö's Gifts, an inspiring account of the intersection between the spiritual and environmental values of the Bribrí.

But only recently have women made gains in the workplace, with growing roles in political, legal, scientific and medical fields. In 1993 Margarita Penon (Oscar Arias Sánchez's wife) ran as a presidential candidate and in 1998 both vice presidents (Costa Rica has two) were women: Astrid Fischel and Elizabeth Odio.

Despite some advances, machismo is not a thing of the past. Antidiscrimination laws are rarely enforced and women are generally lower paid and are less likely to be considered for high-level jobs. They also have more difficulty getting loans, even though their repayment record is better than that of men. In the countryside many women maintain traditional roles: raising children, cooking and running the home.

ARTS

When New Flowers Bloomed: Short Stories by Women Writers from Costa Rica & Panama edited by Enrique Jaramillo Levi is a worthwhile read.

Costa Rica is famous more for its natural beauty and tropical ecology than for its culture. There is little indigenous cultural influence in the nation's arts, and cultural activities of any kind tend to be centered on Western-style entertainment.

San José is not only the political capital, but the artistic one as well, and it is here that you will find the lion's share of the nation's museums, in addition to a lively theater, gallery and music scene.

Literature

Few writers or novelists are available in translation and, unfortunately, much of what is written about Costa Rica and available in English (fiction or otherwise) is written by foreigners.

Costa Rica: A Traveler's Literary Companion, edited by Barbara Ras, is a fine collection of 26 short stories by modern Costa Rican writers, offering a valuable glimpse of society from Ticos themselves.

Carmen Naranjo (1930–) is one of the few contemporary Costa Rican writers who has risen to international acclaim. She is a novelist, poet and short-story writer who also served as ambassador to India in the 1970s and, a few years later, as Minister of Culture. In 1996 she was awarded the prestigious Gabriela Mistral medal from the Chilean government. Her collection of short stories *There Never Was a Once Upon a Time* is widely available in English. Two of her stories can also be found in *Costa Rica: A Traveler's Literary Companion*.

Tatiana Lobo (1939–) was actually born in Chile but has lived since 1967 in Costa Rica, where her many books are set. She received the noteworthy Premio Sor Juana Inés de la Cruz for Latin American women novelists for her novel *Asalto al Paraíso* (Assault on Paradise).

José León Sánchez (1930–) is an internationally renowned memoirist. A Huetar Indian from the border of Costa Rica with Nicaragua, he was convicted for stealing from the famous Basílica de Nuestra Señora de los Ángeles (p166) in Cartago and sentenced to serve his term at Isla San Lucas, one of Latin America's most notorious jails. Illiterate when he was incarcerated, Sánchez taught himself how to read and write, and clandestinely authored one of the continent's most poignant memoirs: *La Isla de los Hombres Solos* (called *God Was Looking the Other Way* in the translated version). He served 20 years of his 45-year sentence and went on to produce 14 other novels and serve in several high-level public appointments.

Theater

San José is the center of a thriving acting community. Plays are produced mainly in Spanish, but the Little Theater Group (p121) stages English-language performances.

The most famous theater in the country is the Teatro Nacional (p121) in San José. The story goes that a noted European opera company was on a Latin American tour but declined to perform in Costa Rica for lack of a suitable hall. Immediately, the coffee elite put a special cultural tax on coffee exports for the construction of a world-class theater. The Teatro Nacional is now the premier venue for plays, opera, performances by the national symphony orchestra, ballet, poetry readings and other cultural events. It also is an architectural work in its own right and a landmark in any city tour of San José.

Visual Arts

The visual arts in Costa Rica first took on a national character in the 1920s, when Teodórico Quirós, Fausto Pacheco and their contemporaries began painting landscapes that varied from traditional European styles, depicting the rolling hills and lush forest of Costa Rican countryside, often sprinkled with characteristic adobe houses.

The contemporary scene is more varied, and it is difficult to define a unique Tico style. Several individual artists have garnered acclaim for their art work, including the magical realism of Isidro Con Wong; the surreal paintings and primitive engravings of Francisco Amighetti; and the mystical female figures painted by Rafa Fernández. Other artists incorporate an infinite variety of themes in various media, from painting and sculpture to video and site-specific installations. The Museo de Arte y Diseño Contemporáneo (p96) is the top place to see this type of work and its permanent collection is a great primer.

Many art galleries are geared toward tourists and specialize in 'tropical art' (for lack of an official description): brightly colored, whimsical folk paintings depicting flora and fauna are evocative of the work of French artist Henri Rousseau. To get a firsthand account of artists at work, spend a day on the Costa Rica art tour (see p105), which visits artists' studios around San José.

Folk art and handicrafts are not as widely produced or readily available as in other Central American countries. But the dedicated souvenir hunter will have no problem finding the colorful Sarchí oxcarts (p152) that have become a symbol of Costa Rica. Escazú (p139) is known for its woodwork. Indigenous craftsmanship includes intricately carved and painted masks and hand-woven bags and linens. These items are available for purchase in Guaitil (p286), in Boruca (p388) or at the Galería Namu (p123) in San José.

See a stunning and comprehensive visual database on Central American contemporary art at the website for the Museo de Arte y Diseño Contemporáneo at www.madc.ac.cr/.

Music & Dance

The mix of cultures in Costa Rica has resulted in a lively music scene, incorporating elements from North and South America and the Caribbean islands. San José features a regular line-up of domestic and international rock, folk and hip-hop artists, but you'll find that the regional sounds are equally vibrant, featuring their own special rhythms, instruments and styles. The Monteverde Music Festival (p197) focuses on Latin, jazz and folk music, while another festival in Barva (p162) is primarily for classical music.

Popular dance music includes Latin dances such as salsa, merengue, bolero and cumbia. These invigorating rhythms are oft heard (and danced) in clubs across the country (although they are not traditionally Costa Rican). One Tico salsa group that has made a significant name for itself at a regional level is Los Brillanticos, which once shared the stage with Cuban legend Celia Cruz during a tour stop she made in San José. Timbaleo is a salsa orchestra founded by Ramsés Araya, who became famous as the drummer for Panamanian salsa superstar Ruben Blades. Taboga Band is another long-standing Costa Rican group that plays jazz-influenced salsa and merengue music.

Orquesta Maribel is a popular group that makes dance music by combining marimbas with traditional orchestral music.

The Península de Nicoya has a rich musical history, most of it made with marimbas. A marimba is akin to a xylophone, with wooden bars usually made of rosewood. Traditional music in Guanacaste is usually played with guitars, maracas and marimbas. Romantic ballads often recount the life of a *campesino* or praise the beauty of a homeland.

Guanacaste is also the birthplace of many traditional dances, most of which depict courtship rituals between country folk. The most famous – sometimes considered the national dance – is the *punto guanacasteco* (see the boxed text La Fiestas de Guanacaste, p220). What keeps it lively is the *bomba*, a funny (and usually racy) rhymed verse, shouted out by the male dancers during the musical interlude.

The Riverside Orchestra is a longtime calypso favorite from the 1930s, while El Charro Limonense is a contemporary singer who preserves the calypso tradition.

The traditional sound on the Caribbean coast is calypso, which has roots in the Afro-Carib slave culture. Slaves were not allowed to talk to each other, so they communicated in song. Calypso music is still mostly vocal, with plenty of percussion for emphasis; satirical ballads often touch on political and social issues. Music on the Caribbean coast is also infused with reggae flavor. The South Caribbean Music & Arts Festival (p484) in Puerto Viejo de Talamanca is an excellent opportunity to sample some of the region's musical talents.

Environment David Lukas

THE LAND

Despite its tiny size, Costa Rica is an extremely varied country. At 51,100 sq km, it is slightly smaller than the state of West Virginia in the USA and slightly larger than Switzerland, yet it encompasses one of the world's most diverse natural landscapes. Divided neatly by a series of volcanic mountain chains that run the length of the country from Nicaragua to Panama, Costa Rica hosts markedly different climates on its Pacific and Caribbean sides. These in turn support entirely separate assemblages of plants and animals.

With a length of 1016km, the Pacific coastline is infinitely varied as it twists and turns around gulfs, peninsulas, and many small coves. Rugged, rocky headlands alternating with classic white- and black-sand beaches and palm trees make this a tropical paradise along some stretches. Strong tidal action creates an excellent habitat for waterbirds as well as visually dramatic crashing surf (an excellent habitat for surfers). Inland, the landscapes of the Pacific lowlands are equally dynamic, ranging from dry deciduous forests and open cattle country in the north to lush and magnificent tropical rain forests in the south.

Monotonous in comparison, the Caribbean coastline runs a straight 212km along a low, flat plain that is strongly inundated with brackish lagoons and waterlogged forests. A lack of strong tides allows plants to grow right over the water's edge along inland sloughs, creating a wall of green vegetation. Broad, humid plains that scarcely rise above sea level and murky waters characterize much of this coastal region, though agriculture is now widespread on all upland areas.

Running down the center of the country, the mountainous spine of Costa Rica is a land of active volcanoes, clear tumbling streams and chilled peaks clad in impenetrable cloud forests. These mountain ranges generally follow a northwest to southeast line, with the highest and most dramatic peaks near the Panamanian border (culminating at the 3820m-high Cerro Chirripó). The difficulties of traveling through and farming

Les D Beletsky's Costa Rica: The EcoTraveller's Wildlife Guide provides a handy overview of the country's flora and fauna.

Costa Rica's national tree is the guanacaste, commonly found in the lowlands of the Pacific slope.

TOP FIVE WAYS TO SAVE THE RAIN FOREST

Ask not what the rain forest can do for you, but what *you* can do for the rain forest.

- Reforest a former banana plantation: plant a tree at the Selva Bananito Lodge (p471).

- Drink organic, shade-grown coffee. Organic means avoiding the use of chemical pesticides and fertilizers to minimize the impact on the other flora and fauna. Shade-grown means the survival of old-growth forests and shade plants that produce nitrogen and improve the quality of both the soil and the coffee crop.

- Work on a community education program with the Fundación Corcovado (p414).

- Say no to beef. The number-one cause of forest clearing in Central America is to make way for cattle pasture – mostly to feed the export market. If you can't bypass that burger, make sure you know where your cow came from. Consider indulging in grass-fed beef, which is better for your health and better for the environment.

- Make a donation to the **Monteverde Conservation League** (☎ 645 5003; www.monteverdeinfo .com/monteverde_conservation_league.htm) in support of the Bosque Eterno de los Niños (p193). Yes, we know, that's the cloud forest. But why should the rain forest get all the goods?

LOOK BUT DON'T JUMP IN

As of 2006, it is illegal in Costa Rica to swim with dolphins and whales, just as it is illegal to attempt to capture or harass them. Dolphin- and whale-watching tours have become increasingly popular in recent years, leading to an explosion in the number of operators. Unfortunately, too many operators are out for a quick buck.

In a survey conducted by the Cetacean Society International, 17 of the operators refused to cooperate by answering survey questions, and all of the tour companies investigated made mistakes ranging from harassing animals, to not carrying lifejackets and having motor problems. Only one company had knowledgeable guides that could provide 'reasonable natural-history information.' Lacking experience and knowledge, many operators have been conducting their tours without due attention to the integrity of the star players – the animals themselves.

In short, too much attention from tourists has been causing the dolphins and whales to stress out. Research indicated that in some heavily touristed areas, dolphins were actually leaving their natural habitat in search of calmer seas. Some scientists believed that the close proximity of human beings in the water was disrupting feeding, nursing and other behavior. There was growing concern about the long-term impact on the health of entire populations of these marine mammals. The legislation banning swimming with marine mammals was enacted with their best interest in mind.

When your boat comes across these amazing creatures of the sea, do not jump in the water. From the comfort of the boat, you can have an equally awe-inspiring and longer-lasting experience (the dolphins and whales usually swim away quickly when humans are in the water, but they might stay and swim around a boat indefinitely). And more importantly, you can do so without disturbing the peace of these gentle giants.

on these steep slopes have, until recently, saved much of this area from development and made it a haven for wildlife.

In the midst of the highlands is Meseta Central – or Central Valley – which is surrounded by mountains (the Cordillera Central to the north and east and the Cordillera de Talamanca to the south). It is this fertile central plain, between about 1000m and 1500m above sea level, that contains four of Costa Rica's five largest cities and more than half of the country's population.

Like most of Central America, Costa Rica's geological history can be traced to the impact of the Cocos Plate moving northeast and crashing into the Caribbean Plate at a rate of about 10cm every year – quite fast by geological standards. The point of impact is called a 'subduction zone,' and this is where the Cocos Plate forces the edge of the Caribbean Plate to break up and become uplifted. It is not a smooth process, and hence Central America is an area prone to earthquakes and volcanic activity (see p532).

This process began when most of Costa Rica was under water and has been going on for about five million years. Costa Rica itself is about three million years old, with the exception of the Península de Nicoya, which is many millions of years older. Most of the mountain ranges in Costa Rica are volcanic; the exception is the massive Cordillera de Talamanca in the south, the largest range in Costa Rica. This is a granite batholith of intruded igneous rock that formed under great pressure below the surface of the earth and was uplifted.

Adrian Forsyth has written several colorful children's books about the rain forest, including Journey through a Tropical Jungle *and* How Monkeys make Chocolate.

WILDLIFE

Nowhere else in the world are so many types of habitats squeezed into such a tiny area. The range of habitats in Costa Rica, a consequence of its unique geography, creates an incredibly rich diversity of flora and fauna – in fact no other country on the planet has such variety. Measured in terms of number of species per 10,000 sq km Costa Rica tops the list of countries at 615 species, compared to a wildlife-rich country such as Rwanda that has 596, or to the comparatively impoverished USA with its 104 species. This simple fact alone (not to mention the ease of travel and friendly residents!) makes Costa Rica the premier destination for nature lovers from all over the world.

Along with its diverse geography, the large number of species in Costa Rica is also due to the relatively recent appearance of the country.

If wildlife is your thing bring along Lonely Planet's Watching Wildlife in Central America *by Luke Hunter and David Andrew.*

DREAM OF THE BOUNTIFUL TURTLES

There are seven kinds of sea turtles, four of which frequent Costa Rica's beaches: olive ridley, leatherback, green and hawksbill. All four species are classified as endangered or critically endangered, meaning they face an imminent threat of extinction. While populations of some species are increasing, thanks to various protection programs along the Caribbean coast, the risk for these tortugas is still very real.

Destruction of habitat is a huge problem. With the exception of the leatherbacks, all of these species return to their natal beach to nest. That means that the ecological state of the beach directly affects that turtle's ability to reproduce. All of the species prefer dark, undisturbed beaches, and any sort of development or artificial lighting will inhibit nesting (even flashlights!).

A devastating number of turtles are killed every year when they get caught in loglines or gill nets, which are sometimes used by commercial fisheries. The Leatherback Trust estimates that 63% of all Pacific leatherbacks get hooked by loglines, resulting in a 15% to 18% death rate.

Hunting and harvesting eggs are also major causes of declining populations. Green turtles are actually hunted for their meat. Leatherbacks and olive ridleys are not killed for meat, but their eggs are considered a delicacy – an aphrodisiac no less. The hawksbill turtles are hunted for their unusual shells, which are sometimes used to make jewelry and hair ornaments. Of course any trade in tortoise-shell products and turtle eggs and meat is illegal, but a significant black market exists for these products.

Enforcement of hunting and harvesting bans requires lots of nighttime beach patrols during turtle-nesting season. There are many opportunities for volunteers to assist with beach patrols and education programs (see p463):

Olive Ridley Endangered (world population of nesting females est 800,000). Olive ridleys are unique in that thousands of turtles descend on one beach to nest *en masse*. This happens in Parque Nacional Santa Rosa (p227) and Refugio Nacional de Fauna Silvestre Ostional (p294) between July and November. They are also unique in that it is legal to harvest a limited number of eggs from the first laying – usually for sale in San José. The idea is to give locals a stake in protecting the nests from illegal poachers from the outside. Unfortunately, it also has the effect of encouraging illegal harvesting in other areas, as the sale is not regulated.

Leatherback Critically endangered (world population of nesting females est 35,000). Leatherbacks nest on the northern Caribbean coast – around Parque Nacional Tortuguero (p459) and the beaches of Parismina (p457) – from March to June. Pacific leatherbacks have laid eggs on Playa Grande in the Parque Nacional Marino Las Baulas de Guanacaste (p272) for thousands of years, but the number of nesting turtles has declined dramatically in recent years. In the 2005–06 season, Playa Grande attracted only 51 turtles, which is nonetheless an improvement from the previous year.

Green Endangered (world population of nesting females est 88,520). Green turtles nest in Parque Nacional Tortuguero (p459) and surrounding beaches from mid-June to mid-September. They represent the rare success story. Thanks to information collected by the Caribbean Conservation Corporation (see p462), scientists realized in the 1980s that fewer than 3000 female green turtles were nesting in Tortuguero annually, compared to tens of thousands in earlier decades. The alarming data helped them convince a coalition of public and private groups to initiate long-term conservation efforts geared toward bringing the turtles back. Today, more than 20,000 of the lovely ladies show up on these shores to breed during the year, and the number continues to climb.

Hawksbill Critically endangered (world population of nesting females est 22,900). These beauties only make rare appearances on beaches around Tortuguero between February and September, while they are more common at Parque Nacional Marino Ballena (p368) from May to November.

Roughly three million years ago Costa Rica rose from the ocean and formed a land bridge between North and South America, and as species from these two vast biological provinces started to mingle and mix, the number of species was essentially 'doubled.'

Animals

Though tropical in nature – with a substantial number of tropical animals such as poison-arrow frogs and spider monkeys – Costa Rica is also the winter home for more than 200 species of migrating birds that arrive from as far away as Alaska and Australia. So don't be surprised to see one of your familiar backyard birds here feeding alongside trogons and toucans. For more details on individual animals and insects, see the Wildlife Guide.

With over 850 species recorded in Costa Rica, it's understandable that birds are one of the primary attractions for naturalists. You could stay for months and you'll still have scratched the surface in terms of seeing all these species. Birds in Costa Rica come in every color, from strawberry-red scarlet macaws to the iridescent jewels called violet sabrewings (a type of hummingbird). Because many birds in Costa Rica have restricted ranges, you are guaranteed to find different species everywhere you travel.

Though visitors will almost certainly see one of Costa Rica's four monkey or two sloth species, there are an additional 260 animal species awaiting the patient observer. More exotic sightings might include amazing species such as the four-eyed opossum and silky anteater while a lucky few might spot the elusive tapir, or have a jaguarundi cross their path.

The extensive network of national parks, wildlife refuges and other protected areas are prime places to spot wildlife. But remember that these creatures do not know park boundaries, so keep your eyes peeled in the forested areas and buffer zones that often surround these sanctuaries. Early morning is the best time to see animals, as many species stay still during the hotter part of the day. Nocturnal species – such as Baird's tapir, the silky anteater and the kinkajou – require going out at night, preferably with a guide.

If you are serious about spotting birds and animals, the value of a knowledgeable guide cannot be underestimated. Their keen eyes are trained to recognize the slightest movement in the leaves, and they can recognize the many exotic calls of the wild. Most professional bird guides are proficient in many dialects of bird, which enhances your ability to hear and see them. Furthermore, a good local guide will often have an idea where certain species tend to congregate – whether because they like the fruit of a certain tree (as the quetzal in the avocado tree), or because they like to catch the fish at the mouth of the river (as the American crocodile). Knowing the habits of your prey vastly improves your chances of finding them.

No season is a bad season for exploring Costa Rica's natural environment, though most visitors arrive during the peak dry season when trails are less muddy and more accessible. An added bonus of visiting between December and February is that many of the wintering migrant birds are still hanging around. A trip after the peak season may mean fewer birds, but it is a stupendous time to see dried forests transform into vibrant greens and it's the time when resident birds begin their nesting season.

ENDANGERED SPECIES

As expected in a country that has both unique habitats and widespread cutting of its forests, there are numerous species whose populations are declining or in danger of extinction. The number-one

Dr Alexander Skutch is famous for the Guide to the Birds of Costa Rica, *but he also wrote several other contemplative books about his feathered friends, including* A Naturalist in Costa Rica *and* The Minds of Birds.

Two-toed sloths descend from the trees once every two weeks to defecate.

(Continued on page 65)

Wildlife Guide David Lukas

Costa Rica has some of the most diverse wildlife in the world, and it's the reason many people travel here. From stunning, colorful birds to fleeting glimpses of rare mammals, it is a land of surprises and enchantment. Included in this guide are a tiny fraction of the common or 'target' species that you could see in Costa Rica. Wildlife enthusiasts are encouraged to bring along one of the many excellent wildlife guides (listed throughout the Environment chapter) for suggestions.

Scarlet macaw pairs mate for life (as is generally true for all parrots).
PHOTO BY LUKE HUNTER

The morpho butterfly has a wingspan of 15cm.
PHOTO BY TOM BOYDEN

INSECTS

More than 35,000 species of insects have been recorded in Costa Rica, but thousands remain undiscovered. Butterflies and moths are so abundant that Costa Rica claims 10% of the world's butterfly species. In excess of 3000 species have been recorded in Parque Nacional Santa Rosa (p227) alone.

The distinctive morpho butterfly, with its electric-blue upper wings, lazily flaps and glides along tropical rivers and through openings in the forests across Costa Rica. When it lands, though, the wings close and only the mottled brown underwings become visible, an instantaneous change from outrageous display to modest camouflage.

The red-black poison arrow frog is also known as the strawberry poison dart frog.
PHOTO BY MARK NEWMAN

AMPHIBIANS

The 160 species of amphibians include the tiny and colorful poison-dart frogs, in the family of Dendrobatidae. Some are bright red with black legs, others are red with blue legs, and still others are bright green with black markings. Several species have skin glands exuding toxins that can cause paralysis and death in many animals, including humans. Dendrobatids, which are widespread in tropical areas, have been used by forest Indians for a poison to dip the tips of their hunting arrows.

The green iguana can be seen in the Refugio Nacional de Vida Silvestre Caño Negro.
PHOTO BY LUKE HUNTER

REPTILES

Over half of the 220-plus species of reptiles in Costa Rica are snakes. Though much talked about, snakes are rarely seen. But keep an eye out for the fer-de-lance and the bushmaster, two deadly poisonous snakes. Both have broadly triangular heads and are widespread at lower elevations. The fer-de-lance, which can be anything from olive to brown or black in color, has a pattern of X's and triangles on its back, while the bushmaster is usually tan-colored with dark diamond-shaped blotches.

Of the country's lizards, the most frequently seen are the abundant ameiva lizards, which have a white stripe running down their backs. Also common are bright-green basilisk lizards, noted for the huge crests running the length of their heads, bodies and tails, which gives them the appearance of small dinosaurs almost 1m in length. They are common along watercourses in lowland areas. Also seen in the same areas is the stocky green iguana, which is regularly encountered draping its 2m-long body across a branch over water.

BIRDS

The wealth of Costa Rica's world-famous avifauna is one of the top reasons visitors choose to travel here. The country hosts more bird species (approximately 850) than huge areas such as Europe, North America or Australia. The sheer numbers and variety is somewhat baffling and overwhelming and, in patches of healthy rain forest, the din of countless birds all calling at once will leave a lasting impression on even the most hardened travelers.

In addition to diverse forest birds, Costa Rica also hosts a spectacular assortment of seabirds, including the magnificent frigatebird. This distinctive black bird, with an inflatable red throat pouch, is large, elegant and streamlined. It makes an acrobatic living by aerial piracy, often harassing smaller birds into dropping or regurgitating their catch and then swooping to catch their stolen meal in midair. Frigatebirds are found along both coasts but are more common along the Pacific.

The brown pelican is unmistakable with its large size and huge pouched bill. Pelicans are often seen in squadron-like formation, flapping and gliding in unison. They are found on both coasts but are more common on the Pacific. A pelican feeds by shallow plunge-diving and scooping up fish and water in its distensible pouch, then draining the water through the bill.

Larger species of herons include the boat-billed heron, a stocky, mostly gray bird with a black cap and crest and distinctively large and wide bill. The yellow-crowned night-heron is quite common in coastal areas and has an unmistakable black-and-white head with a yellow crown. Despite its name, it's mainly active by day.

The descriptively named roseate spoonbill is most often seen in the Palo Verde (p216) and Caño Negro (p510) areas. It has a white head and a distinctive spoon-shaped bill. Unlike most birds, which feed by sight, spoonbills, ibises and many storks feed by touch. The spoonbill swings its open bill back and forth, submerged underwater, while stirring up the bottom with its feet, until it feels a small fish, frog or crustacean and then snaps the bill shut.

Vultures are often seen hovering ominously in the sky, searching for carrion. The largest vulture in Costa Rica is the king vulture, which is easily identified by its off-white body and legs, black primary wing feathers and tail, and a wattled head colored black with various shades of orange-yellow. It's most frequently seen in Corcovado (p413), though it lives almost countrywide in small numbers.

A favorite waterbird for many visitors is the northern jacana, which has extremely long, thin toes that enable it to walk on top of aquatic plants,

The roseate spoonbill has a white head and a distinctive spoon-shaped bill.

PHOTO BY DAVID M WATSON

The northern jacana has long, thin toes that enable it to walk on top of aquatic plants.
PHOTO BY TOM BOYDEN

earning it the nickname 'lily-trotter.' It is common on many lowland lakes and waterways. At first glance its brown body, black head, yellow bill and frontal shield seem rather nondescript, but when disturbed the bird stretches its wings to reveal startling yellow flight feathers.

Of the 16 species of parrots recorded in Costa Rica, none is as spectacular as the scarlet macaw – unmistakable for its size (84cm long), bright red body, blue-and-yellow wings, long red tail and white face. Macaws are often seen flying overhead, in pairs or small flocks, calling raucously to one another. Recorded as common in 1900, they have suffered devastating reductions in numbers due to deforestation and poaching for the pet trade. Now it is rare to see these birds outside of Carara (p325) and Corcovado (p413).

The violet sabrewing hummingbird has a striking violet head and body, with dark green wings.
PHOTO BY MICHAEL FOGDEN / BRUCE COLEMAN INC. / ALAMY

More than 50 species of hummingbirds have been recorded and their delicate beauty is matched only by their extravagant names. Largest is the violet sabrewing, which has a striking violet head and body, with dark green wings. It is found in mid-elevations. Upwards of 20 species have been seen at local feeders, including such jewels as the purple-throated mountain-gem and crowned woodnymph.

The most famous of Costa Rica's 10 species of trogons is undoubtedly the resplendent quetzal (ket-sal), easily the most dazzling and culturally important bird of Central America. It had great ceremonial significance to the Aztecs and the Mayas and is now the national bird and symbol of Guatemala. It is extremely difficult to keep in captivity, where it usually dies quickly, which is perhaps why it became a symbol of liberty to Central Americans during the colonial period. The male lives up to its name with glittering green plumage set off by a crimson belly, and white tail feathers contrasting with bright-green tail coverts that stream over 60cm beyond the bird's body. The head feathers stick out in a spiky green helmet through which the yellow bill peeks coyly. A glimpse of this bird is the highlight of many a birder's trip. The quetzal is fairly common from 1300m to 3000m in forested or partially forested areas. Locals usually know where to find one; good places to look are in Reserva Biológica Bosque Nuboso Monteverde (p207) and the namesake Parque Nacional Los Quetzales (p375). The best time to see the birds depends on the altitude: they hang around slightly lower altitudes like Monteverde for nesting season (March to June); but are easily spotted at higher altitudes between November and April. At other times they are less active and quite wary, as are all the trogons.

Toucans are classic rain forest birds and six species are found in lowland forests throughout Costa Rica. Huge bills and flamboyant plumage make species such as the chestnut-mandibled toucan and keel-billed toucan hard to miss. The chestnut-mandibled toucan is mainly black with a yellow face and chest and red under the tail, and has a bicolored bill – yellow above and chestnut below. The keel-billed toucan is similarly plumaged but the bill is multicolored. But with toucans, even smaller species such as the collared aracari (top right) are notable.

About half of Costa Rica's birds are passerines, a sprawling category that includes warblers, sparrows, finches and many other types of birds. Nearly limited to the tropics, however, are tanagers and cotingas. One of the country's most common birds is the blue-gray tanager, a resident of open, humid areas up to 2300m. The male scarlet-rumped tanager is jet black with a bright-scarlet rump and lower back, a flashy and unmistakable combination.

The male red-headed barbet is striking with its bright-red head and chest, yellow bill, green back, and yellow belly. It forages in trees at mid-elevations. The white-fronted nunbird is an upright-perching black bird of the Caribbean lowlands. It's immediately identified by its red bill with white feathers at the base.

Cotingas are even more dramatic and include two species that are pure white and two that are a sparkling blue color. One of the strangest cotingas is the three-wattled bellbird, a highlight for visitors to Monteverde reserve (p207) because of its penetrating metallic *bonk!* and eerie whistling calls (not to mention the male's odd appearance).

The chestnut-mandibled toucan is mainly black with a yellow face and chest with red under the tail.

PHOTO BY TOM BOYDEN

MARINE ANIMALS

Long famous are the giant sea turtles of Costa Rica, impetus for the establishment of Tortuguero and several other coastal national parks. With a shell up to 1.6m long, the massive 360kg leatherback turtle is a stunning creature. The smaller olive ridleys are legendary for their remarkable synchronized nesting, when tens of thousands of females emerge from the sea on the same night. All sea turtles are highly endangered and the conservation efforts on their behalf are some of the most important projects in Costa Rica.

In a few of the rivers, estuaries and coastal areas (especially around Tortuguero, p459) you may glimpse the endangered West Indian manatee, a large marine mammal (up to 4m long and weighing 600kg, though usually smaller), which feeds on aquatic vegetation. There are no seals or sea lions in Costa Rica, so a manatee is easy to recognize.

Because Costa Rica has one of the most biologically diverse marine ecosystems in the world, there is an astounding variety of marine mammals found here. Migrating whales arrive from both the northern and southern hemispheres. The deepwater upwellings that make these waters so productive are constant year-round, creating ideal viewing conditions at any season. Humpback whales may be seen almost every month – perhaps the only place in the world where this is possible – while common, bottle-nosed and spotted dolphins are year-round residents. Seeing more than a dozen other species of dolphins and whales is possible, including orca, blue and sperm whales, and several species of poorly known beaked whales. All of these animals are best seen on guided boat tours along both coasts.

The giant sea turtle lays its eggs on secluded beaches.
PHOTO BY TRAVELPIX / ALAMY

LAND MAMMALS

Five species of sloths are found in the neotropics, and the two species widespread in Costa Rica are the brown-throated three-toed sloth and Hoffman's two-toed sloth. The diurnal three-toed sloth is often sighted, whereas the nocturnal two-toed sloth is less often seen. Both are 50cm to 75cm in length with stumpy tails. Sloths hang motionless from branches or slowly progress upside down along a branch toward leaves, which are their primary food.

Anteaters lack teeth and use a long, sticky tongue to slurp up ants and termites. There are three species of anteaters in Costa Rica including the giant anteater, which reaches almost 2m in length and has an amazing tongue that protrudes an astonishing 60cm up to 150 times a minute!

Two species of armadillo inhabit Costa Rica. The best known is the nine-banded armadillo. Despite its name, there can be from seven to 10 bands. These armadillos grow up to 1m long, of which about one-third is tail. Mainly nocturnal, they have a diet of mainly insects, and some fruit, fungi and carrion.

The white-faced capuchin monkey is inquisitive and is easily seen in the wild.
PHOTO BY ALFREDO MAIQUEZ

Costa Rica has four monkey species, all members of the family Cebidae. These are the tropical mammals most likely to be seen and enjoyed by travelers, and in some places you can see all four at the same location. The Central American spider monkey is named for its long and thin legs, arms and tail, which enables it to pursue an arboreal existence in forests throughout Costa Rica. Spider monkeys swing from arm to arm through the canopy and can hang supported just by their prehensile tail while using their long limbs to pick fruit. They rarely descend to the ground, and require large tracts of unbroken forest. Logging, hunting (their flesh is eaten) and other disturbances have made them endangered.

The loud vocalizations of a male mantled howler monkey can carry for more than 1km even in dense rain forest. Variously described as grunting, roaring or howling, this crescendo of noise is one of the most characteristic and memorable of all rain-forest sounds. Inhabiting wet lowland forests, howlers live in small groups. These stocky blackish monkeys with coiled prehensile tails reside high in the canopy so they can be hard to spot.

The small and inquisitive white-faced capuchin is the easiest to observe in the wild. Unlike the squirrel monkey, it has a prehensile tail that is typically carried with the tip coiled. Capuchins occasionally descend to the ground where foods such as corn and even oysters are part of their diet. Their meticulous foraging and prying into leaves, litter and bark makes them enjoyable to watch.

The diminutive Central American squirrel monkey persists only in isolated areas of the south Pacific coastal rain forests, including Manuel Antonio (p356) and Corcovado (p413) national parks, where it travels in small to medium-size groups during the day, squealing or chirping noisily and leaping and crashing through vegetation in search of insects and fruit in the middle and lower levels of lowland forests.

The white-nosed coati is the most frequently seen member of the raccoon family. It is brownish and longer, but slimmer and lighter, than a raccoon. Its most distinctive features are a long, mobile, upturned whitish snout with which it snuffles around on the forest floor looking for insects, fruit and small animals; and a long, faintly ringed tail held straight up in the air when foraging. Coatis are found countrywide in all types of forest up to 3000m.

The squirrel monkey persists only in isolated areas of the south Pacific coastal rain forests.
PHOTO BY RALPH LEE HOPKINS

Lacking the facial markings and ringed tail of its cousins, the cuddly kinkajou is a raccoon relative found in lowland forests. It is an attractive

The cuddly kinkajou jumps from tree to tree in search of fruit.
PHOTO BY TOM BOYDEN

reddish-brown color and is hunted both for food and the pet trade. Nocturnal and mainly arboreal, it jumps from tree to tree searching for fruits (especially figs), which comprise most of its diet.

The southern river otter lives in and by fast-moving lowland rivers, but is infrequently seen. It is a rich brown color with whitish undersides and has the streamlined shape of an aquatic weasel. The similarly shaped tayra is more easily spotted; it is blackish brown, with a tan head, and is territorial and arboreal. It is over 1m long (the tail is about 40cm) and is found in forests up to 2000m.

Distinctive for its color is the large weasel called the grison. Its body, tail and the crown of its head are light gray and the legs, chest and lower face are black. A white band across the forehead, ears and sides of the neck gives the head a black/white/gray tricolor. The tail is shorter than that of most weasels. It is found in the lowland rain forests but is uncommon.

It is every wildlife-watcher's dream to see a jaguar in the wild. However, these big cats are extremely rare and well camouflaged, so the chance of seeing one is remote. Jaguars have large territories and you may see their prints or droppings in large lowland parks with extensive forest such as Corcovado (p413). Occasionally you may hear them roaring – a sound more like a series of deep coughs. There's no mistaking this 2m-long yellow cat with black spots in rosettes and a whitish belly. Good luck seeing one.

Other Costa Rican felids include the spotted ocelot, a little more than 1m in length with a short tail. Though it is the most common of the Costa Rican cats, it is shy and rarely seen. It adapts well to a variety of terrain, wet and dry, forested and open, and has been recorded in most of the larger national parks.

Known as javelinas in the USA, the widespread collared peccary lives in a wide variety of habitats. An adult is about 80cm long, weighs around 20kg, and has coarse gray hair with a light collar. The larger white-lipped peccary is darker and lacks the collar but has a whitish area on the lower chin. Peccaries are noisy and rather aggressive with audible tooth gnashing and clicking – rather frightening if you hear 300 animals at once!

The jaguar is the largest Central American carnivore.
PHOTO BY CHRIS FREDRIKSSON / ALAMY

Some large rodents are among the most commonly seen rain-forest mammals, including the Central American agouti and the paca. The agouti is diurnal and terrestrial and found in forests up to 2000m. It looks like an oversize cross between a rabbit and a squirrel, with a very small tail and short ears. The closely related paca looks similar, except it has white stripy marks on its sides and is twice the size of an agouti. It is common but nocturnal.

(Continued from page 56)

threat to most of Costa Rica's endangered species is habitat destruction, followed closely by hunting and trapping.

The legendary resplendent quetzal – the bird at the top of every naturalist's must-see list – teeters precariously as its home forests are felled at an alarming rate. Sightings of the large, squawky scarlet macaw are a highlight of birding in Costa Rica. But trapping for the pet trade has extirpated these magnificent birds from much of their former range. Although populations are thriving in the Península de Osa, the scarlet macaw is now extinct over most of Central America, including the entire Caribbean coast.

Sea turtles get a lot of attention in Costa Rica, with a wide variety of programs supporting population growth. See the boxed text The Dream of the Bountiful Turtles, p55.

Central America's largest land mammal, Baird's tapir, is a sought-after source of protein, making it a target for hunters. The tapirs' habit of commuting between feeding patches and waterholes on distinctive 'tapir trails' makes them extremely vulnerable to hunting. Tapirs are now restricted to the least accessible wilderness areas. Similarly, the gigantic West Indian manatee is an easy victim for hunters, especially since they are extremely placid and have no defenses. Manatees still populate the canals of Parque Nacional Tortuguero, though they are elusive.

Costa Rica's sexiest endangered species is undoubtedly the sleek, speedy jaguar. Jaguars require a large area to support enough prey to survive. Annually, an individual jaguar needs the equivalent of 53 white-tailed deer, 18 peccaries, 40 coatis, 25 armadillos and 55 ctenosaurs. That is for one jaguar! Owing to clearing for cattle ranches and overhunting of jaguar prey, suitable habitat for viable populations of jaguars now occurs in only a handful of protected areas, such as Parque Nacional Corcovado (p413) and Parque Internacional La Amistad (p398).

Plants

Floral biodiversity is also high – well over 10,000 species of vascular plants have been described in Costa Rica, and more are being added to the list every year. Orchids alone account for about 1300 species.

Experiencing a tropical forest for the first time can be a bit of a surprise for visitors from North America or Europe, where temperate forests tend to have little variety. Such regions are either dominated by conifers, or have endless tracts of oaks, beech and birch. Tropical forests, on the other hand, have a staggering number of species – in Costa Rica, for example, almost 2000 tree species have been recorded. If you stand in one spot and look around, you'll see scores of different plants, and if you walk several hundred meters you're likely to find even more.

The diversity of habitats created as these many species mix is a wonder to behold – one day you may find yourself canoeing in a muggy mangrove swamp, and the next day squinting through bone-chilling fog to see orchids in a montane cloud forest. If at all possible, it is worth planning your trip with the goal of seeing some of Costa Rica's most distinctive plant communities, including a few of the following examples.

Classic rain-forest habitats are well represented in parks of the southwest corner of Costa Rica or in mid-elevation portions of the central mountains. Here you will find towering trees that block out the sky, long looping vines and many overlapping layers of vegetation. Many large trees may show buttresses, a feature of tropical trees whereby they grow wing-like ribs extending out from the base of their trunks for added structural support.

While the female scarlet macaw sits on her nest, the male regurgitates food for her to eat, and later does the same for their chicks.

The tale of the green turtle's rebound in Tortuguero are told in two popular books by Archie Carr: *The Windward Road: Adventures of a Naturalist on Remote Caribbean Shores* and *The Sea Turtle: So Excellent a Fishe.*

The seven species of poison-dart frog in Costa Rica are beautiful to look at but have exceedingly toxic skin secretions that cause paralysis and death.

THE PRICE OF ECOTOURISM

Costa Rica has so much to offer the wildlife enthusiast that it is no small wonder that ecotourism is growing in the country. More than 70% of foreign travelers visit one or more nature destinations, and half of these visitors come specifically to see Costa Rica's wildlife.

Such has been its popularity that, from the late 1980s to the mid-1990s, the annual number of visitors has doubled, and now 1.4 million foreign tourists visit every year. Tourism revenues recently surpassed those of the banana and coffee industries, and prices for the traveler have risen in tandem. At first, the growth in tourism took the nation by surprise – there was no overall development plan and growth was poorly controlled. Some people wanted to cash in over the short term with little thought for the future. Unfortunately, this attitude has changed little even as pressure has grown to regulate the industry more closely.

Traditionally, tourism in Costa Rica has been on a small and intimate scale. The great majority of the country's hotels are small (fewer than 50 rooms), staffed with friendly local people who work closely with tourists, to the benefit of both. This intimacy and friendliness has been a hallmark of a visit to Costa Rica.

But this is changing. The financial bonanza generated by the tourism boom means that new operations are starting up all the time – many are good, some are not. The big word in Costa Rica is 'ecotourism' and everyone wants to jump on the green bandwagon. There are 'ecological' car-rental agencies and 'ecological' menus in restaurants. People want tourists, they want the money that tourists carry, but unfortunately there's little infrastructure to take care that these very tourists don't wreck the environment or have a role in despoiling any more wilderness.

Taking advantage of Costa Rica's 'green' image, some developers are promoting mass tourism by building large hotels with accompanying environmental problems (for more see the boxed text

Along brackish stretches of both coasts, mangrove swamps are a world unto themselves. Growing stiltlike out of muddy tidal flats, five species of trees crowd together so densely that no boat and few animals can penetrate. Striking in their adaptations for dealing with salt, mangrove trees thrive where no other land plant dares tread. Though often thought of as a mosquito-filled nuisance, mangrove swamps play some extremely important roles. Not only do they buffer coastlines from the erosive power of waves, they also have very high levels of productivity because they trap so much nutrient-rich sediment, and serve as spawning and nursery areas for many species of fish and invertebrates.

Most famous of all, and a highlight for many visitors, are the fabulous cloud forests of Monteverde reserve (p207), with fog-drenched trees so thickly coated in mosses, ferns, bromeliads, and orchids that you can hardly discern their true shapes. Cloud forests, however, are widespread at high elevations throughout Costa Rica (such as the Cerro de la Muerte area, p376) and any of them would be worth visiting. Be forewarned, however, that in these habitats the term 'rainy season' has little meaning because it's always dripping wet from the fog.

For a complete change of pace try exploring the unique drier forests along the northwest coast. During the dry season many trees drop their leaves, creating carpets of crackling, sun-drenched leaves and a sense of openness that is largely absent in other Costa Rican habitats. The large trees here, such as Costa Rica's national tree, the guanacaste, have broad, umbrellalike canopies, while spiny shrubs and vines or cacti dominate the understory. At times, large numbers of trees erupt into spectacular displays of flowers, and at the beginning of the rainy season everything is transformed with a wonderful flush of new green foliage.

Michael Crichton's book *Jurassic Park* is set on Isla del Coco. In it, he refers to Ticos as 'Ticans.'

Costa Rica's national bird is the clay-colored robin.

Clamor in Tambor, p309, and discussion of the Papagayo Project, p266). Apart from the immediate impacts, such as cutting down vegetation, diverting or damming rivers and driving away wildlife, there are secondary impacts such as erosion, lack of adequate waste-treatment facilities for huge hotels in areas away from sewage lines, and the building of socially, environmentally and economically inadequate 'shanty towns' to house the maids, waiters, cooks, janitors etc.

Another problem is that many developers are foreigners – they say that they are giving the local people jobs, but locals don't want to spend their lives being waiters and maids while watching the big money go out of the country. We recommend staying in smaller hotels that have a positive attitude about the environment and are more beneficial to the locals, rather than the large, foreign-owned, mass-tourism destinations.

Amid all this, the government tourist board (ICT; Instituto Costarricense de Turismo) has launched mass-marketing campaigns all over the world, touting 'Costa Rica: No Artificial Ingredients,' yet hasn't followed up with the kind of infrastructure necessary to preserve those ingredients (nor does it lobby for them). Many people feel a certain degree of frustration with the ICT for selling Costa Rica as a green paradise but doing little to help preserve it.

The big question is whether future tourism developments should continue to focus on the traditional small-hotel, ecotourism approach, or turn to mass tourism, with planeloads of visitors accommodated in 'megaresorts' such as the ones in Cancún, Mexico. From the top levels of government down, the debate has been fierce. Local and international tour operators and travel agents, journalists, developers, airline operators, hotel owners, writers, environmentalists and politicians have all been vocal in their support of either ecotourism or mass tourism. Many believe that the country is too small to handle both forms of tourism properly. It remains to be seen which faction will win out – or if both can co-exist peacefully together.

NATIONAL PARKS

The national-park system began in the 1960s, and at the time of research, there were 35 national parks, comprising 11% of the country. In addition, there are scores of other protected zones, wetlands and mangroves, as well as a slew of privately owned and operated reserves. Therefore, the Costa Rican authorities enjoy their claim that more than 25% of the country has been set aside for conservation. In addition, there are various buffer zones, such as indigenous reservations, that boost the total area of 'protected' land to about 27%. These buffer zones still allow farming, logging and other exploitation, however, so the environment within them is not totally protected.

The tallest tree in the rain forest is usually the silk cotton tree, or the ceiba. The most famous example is a 70m elder in Corcovado.

What this means for the traveler is that, in addition to the national-park system, there are hundreds of small, privately owned lodges, reserves and haciendas that have been set up to protect the land, and many of these are well worth visiting.

Although the national-park system appears wonderful on paper, a report from the national conservation body (Sinac; Sistema Nacional de Areas de Conservación) amplifies the fact that much of the protected area is, in fact, at risk. The government doesn't exactly own all of this land – almost half of the areas are in private ownership – and there isn't a budget to buy it. Technically, the private lands are protected from development, but many landowners are finding loopholes in the restrictions and selling or developing their properties.

The National Biodiversity Institute is a clearing-house of information on both biodiversity and efforts to conserve it. It's at www.inbio.ac.cr.

Sinac (☎ 1283 8004; www.sinac.go.cr in Spanish) is a branch of the oddly paired environmental and energy ministry (Minae; Ministerio del Ambiente y Energía). The agency has developed a project to link geographically close groups of national parks and reserves, private reserves and national forests into 11 conservation areas that cover the country. The system has two major effects. First, larger areas of wildlife habitats are protected in

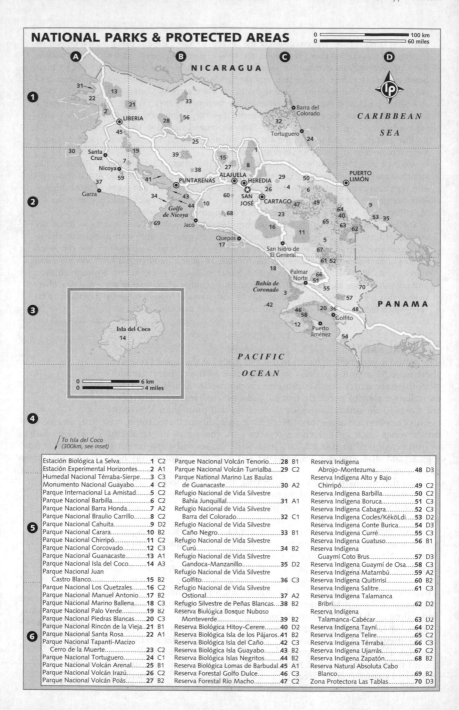

NATIONAL PARKS & PROTECTED AREAS

WORLD HERITAGE SITES IN COSTA RICA

Out of Costa Rica's many outstanding natural sites, two have been highlighted for special protection as Unesco World Heritage sites. Parque Nacional Isla del Coco (p420), located 550km off the Pacific coast of Costa Rica, is important as the only island in the eastern Pacific with a tropical rain forest, and it is famous as one of the best places in the world to view large pelagic species such as sharks, rays, tuna and dolphins. Area de Conservación Guanacaste (encompassing four national parks and reserves in the northwest corner of the country) is recognized as the best remaining example of dry forest habitat left in Central America and Mexico, but even more importantly this area protects a complete transect from marine ecosystem to high altitude cloud forest – a biological corridor – where animals can migrate with the seasons. Efforts to earn recognition of the Parque Nacional Corcovado (p413) as a Unesco World Heritage site are ongoing. Sadly, recent reports of uncontrolled hunting highlighted the government's inability to protect and preserve this valuable site, and the nomination has been temporarily withdrawn.

blocks (so-called megaparks), allowing greater numbers of species and individual plants and animals to exist. Second, the administration of the national parks is delegated to regional offices, allowing a more individualized management approach for each area. Each conservation area has regional and subregional offices delegated to provide effective education, enforcement, research and management, although some regional offices play what appear to be only obscure bureaucratic roles.

Most of the national parks have been created in order to protect the different habitats and wildlife of Costa Rica. A few parks are designed to preserve other valued areas, such as the country's best pre-Columbian ruins at Monumento Nacional Arqueológico Guayabo (p178); an important cave system at Parque Nacional Barra Honda (p287); and a series of geologically active and inactive volcanoes in several parks and reserves.

For maps and descriptions of the national parks, go to www.costarica national parks.com.

Most national parks can be entered without permits, though a few limit the number they admit on a daily basis and others require advance reservations for accommodations within the park's boundaries (Chirripó, Corcovado and La Amistad). The entrance fee to most parks is US$6 to US$8 per day for foreigners, plus an additional US$2 to US$5 for overnight camping where it is permitted. Some of the more isolated parks may charge higher rates.

Many national parks are in remote areas and are rarely visited – they also suffer from a lack of rangers and protection. Others are extremely – and deservedly – popular for their world-class scenic and natural beauty, as well as their wildlife. In the idyllic Parque Nacional Manuel Antonio (p356), a tiny park on the Pacific coast, the number of visitors reached 1000 per day in the high season as annual visits rocketed from about 36,000 visitors in 1982 to more than 150,000 by 1991. This number of visitors threatened to ruin the diminutive area by driving away the wildlife, polluting the beaches, and replacing wilderness with hotel development. In response, park visitors have since been limited to 600 per day, and the park is closed on Mondays to allow it a brief respite from the onslaught.

The fabulous limestone caves of Parque Nacional Barra Honda were formed in the remains of ancient coral reefs that were subsequently uplifted out of the ocean.

Costa Rica has a world-famous reputation for the excellence and far-sightedness of its national-park system – but lack of funds, concentrated visitor use and sometimes fuzzy leadership have shown that there are problems in paradise. A further complication is that the Costa Rican government changes every four years, and this can mean a lack of cohesive, standard-operation plans.

With Costa Rican parks contributing significantly to both national and local economies through the huge influx of tourist monies, there is little

POPULAR PROTECTED AREAS

Popular Protected Areas	Features	Activities	Best Time to Visit	Page
Parque Nacional Cahuita	easily accessible hiking trail, coral reef, beaches, howler monkeysp478	beach walking, snorkeling	year-round	p479
Parque Nacional Chirripó	Costa Rica's highest summit, cloud forest, beautiful mountain views, diverse animal and plant life at varying altitudes	strenuous two-day hike to summit	dry season (Jan-Mar), closed in May	p383
Parque Nacional Corcovado	vast remote rain forest: giant trees, jaguar, scarlet macaw, tapir	exploring off-the-beaten path, wildlife-watching	anytime, though trails bad in rainy season (May-Nov)p413	p413
Parque Nacional Manuel Antonio	beautiful accessible beaches, mangrove swamp, diverse marine life, eroded rocks	beach walking, exploring	avoid peak season if possible (Jan-Mar)	p356
Parque Nacional Santa Rosa	unique dry forest: guanacaste (Costa Rica's national tree), monkey, peccary, coati	wildlife-watching, hiking	dry season (Jan-Mar) for spectacular flowering trees	p227
Parque Nacional Tortuguero	wild Caribbean coast: sea turtle, sloth, manatee, crocodile, river otter	beach walking, canoeing, turtle-watching	best during turtle egg-laying season, check with park for details	p459
Reserva Biológica Bosque Nuboso Monteverde	world-famous cloud forest: resplendent quetzal, epiphytes, orchid, three-wattled bellbird	bird-watching, wildlife-viewing	avoid peak season if possible	p207
Reserva Natural Absoluta Cabo Blanco	scenic remote beaches, seabirds, marine life, three species of monkey	beach walking, bird-watching	anytime	p315

question that the country's healthy ecosystems are important to most citizens. In general, national support for land preservation remains high because it provides income and jobs to so many people. An added benefit is that the parks offer important opportunities for scientific investigation. Most adversely affected are agricultural enterprises that rely on the regular clearing of rain forest to open up new plots.

More than 30% of Costa Rica's forests have been cut to raise low-grade beef that goes into American fast-food hamburgers, TV dinners and pet food.

ENVIRONMENTAL ISSUES

Despite Costa Rica's national-park system, the major problem facing the nation's environment is deforestation. Costa Rica's natural vegetation was originally almost all forest, but most of this has been cleared, mainly for pasture or agriculture. Illegal logging also contributes to this problem. It is estimated that only 5% of the lands outside of parks and reserves remains forested, while only 1% of the dry forests of northwestern Costa Rica are left.

The World Resources Institute recently calculated that Costa Rican forests were still being cleared at the rate of almost 4% a year, making it one of the world's most rapidly disappearing forests. Tree plantations are being developed, however, and the availability of commercially grown timber (hopefully) means there may be less pressure to log the natural forests.

Nevertheless, deforestation continues at a high rate and, even within national parks, some of the more remote areas have been logged illegally because there is not enough money to hire guards to enforce the law.

Apart from the direct loss of tropical forests and the plants and animals that depend on them, deforestation has led directly or indirectly to other severe environmental problems. The first and greatest issue is soil erosion. Forests protect the soil beneath them from the ravages of tropical rainstorms; after deforestation much of the topsoil is washed away, lowering the productivity of the land and silting up watersheds. Some deforested lands are planted with Costa Rica's main agricultural product, bananas, the production of which entails the use of pesticides and blue plastic bags to protect the fruit. Both the pesticides and the plastic bags end up polluting the environment (see the boxed text Tallying the True Cost of Bananas, p449, for information on how this has affected humans as well).

Green Phoenix, by science journalist William Allen, is an absorbing account of his efforts, alongside scientists and activists, to conserve and restore the rain forest in Guanacaste.

Deforestation and related logging activities also create inroads into formerly inaccessible regions, leading to an influx of humans. One consequence, especially in national parks where wildlife is concentrated, is unrestrained poaching. This problem has become so serious in Parque Nacional Corcovado that there's been recent discussion about temporarily closing the park so that guards can take a stand against the poachers.

The other great environmental issue facing Costa Rica comes from the country being loved to death, directly through the passage of one million foreign tourists every year, and indirectly through the development of extensive infrastructure to support this influx (see the boxed text The

RESPONSIBLE TRAVEL: DOS & DON'TS

The impact you have on other people's as well as your own experiences while traveling are both functions of being responsible and having respect for another country's environment. Common sense and awareness are your best guides.

- Do shop responsibly. Don't purchase animal products, no matter how cute. Despite the assurances of the salesperson, there is virtually no way to guarantee that they were collected in an ecologically sensible or legal manner. This includes turtle shells, feathers, skins, skulls, coral, shells, and almost anything made of wood.

- Don't litter. Do patronize hotels that have recycling programs. Do carry out all of your trash from trails and parks, because most facilities are too underfunded and understaffed to collect trash regularly.

- Do stay on trails: they lessen the erosion caused by human transit. Don't disturb animals or damage plants. Do observe wildlife from a distance with binoculars.

- Don't feed the animals! Feeding the animals interferes with their natural diets. They can be susceptible to bacteria transferred by humans or pesticides contained within fruit, which may cause illness or death. Not only do they become more vulnerable to hunting and trapping, but they may stop seeking out their own natural food sources and become dependent on this human source.

- Do follow the instructions of trained naturalist guides. Don't request that guides disturb animals so you can have a better look.

- Don't visit the conservation areas that are saturated by travelers. Do support tourism companies and environmental groups that promote conservation initiatives and long-term management plans.

- Do learn about wildlife and local conservation, environmental and cultural issues before your trip and during your visit. Do ask questions and listen to what locals have to say.

Price of Ecotourism, p66). Every year, more resort hotels and lodges pop up, most notably on formerly pristine beaches or in the middle of intact rain forest. These necessitate additional support systems, including roads and countless vehicle trips, and much of this activity appears to be unregulated and largely unmonitored. For instance, there is growing concern that many hotels and lodges are simply dumping wastewater into the ocean or nearby creeks rather than following expensive procedures for treating it. With an official estimate that only 4% of the country's wastewater is treated and with thousands of unregulated hotels in operation there's a good bet that even some of the fanciest 'ecolodges' aren't taking care of their wastes.

Other times, lodges keep wild animals under the guise that they are running a rescue center. This serves as a draw for tourists who are enchanted with many a hotel operator's claim that they are 'saving' these animals from grave dangers. Unfortunately, this has created a black market for supplying wildlife that is already under threat. Permits from Minae are required to keep wild animals, and visitors can ask hotel operators to see this paperwork (many will claim to have it but will likely be unable to actually produce it).

It is worth noting, however, that many private lodges and reserves are also doing some of the best conservation work in the country, and it's incredibly inspiring to run across homespun efforts to protect Costa Rica's environment spearheaded by hardworking families or small organizations tucked away in some forgotten corner of the country. These include projects to boost rural economies by raising butterflies or native flowers, efforts by villagers to document their local biodiversity, or amazingly resourceful campaigns to raise funds to purchase endangered lands. The Refugio Nacional de Vida Silvestre Curú (p305), Tiskita Lodge in Pavones (p443), La Amistad Lodge (p400) and Rara Avis (p524) near Puerto Viejo de Sarapiquí are but a few examples. Costa Rica is full of wonderful tales about folks who are extremely passionate and generous in their efforts to protect the planet's resources.

Few organizations are as involved in building sustainable rain forest–based economies as the Rainforest Alliance. See the website for special initiatives in Costa Rica: www.rainforest -alliance.org.

The world-famous Organization for Tropical Studies runs three field stations and offers numerous classes for students seriously interested in tropical ecology. See www .ots.ac.cr.

Adventure Travel

If you want it, Costa Rica's got it. The extraordinary array of national parks and reserves provides an incredible stage for the adventure traveler in search of everything from mountain-biking excursions to multiday jungle treks to some of the best white water in Central America. Seafaring types will appreciate the good surfing and diving opportunities that abound on both of Costa Rica's coasts.

While Costa Rica is the place for a good adrenaline rush, travelers should be aware that there is a small but ever-present risk of injury or death in any adventure-tourism activity. Numerous tourism-related deaths early this century led the government to pass sweeping laws in an attempt to regulate the industry. In 2003 Costa Rica became the first country in Latin America to pass a universal set of safety standards to which all adventure-tour operators need comply. Unfortunately, compliance is dependent on enforcement, which in Costa Rica always tends to be weak. The goodwill is there, but the money for checking up isn't.

By and large, most of these activities are safe, but be careful and choose adventure-tour operators who are recommended and have a good safety track record. Do your homework and then enjoy!

The Big Book of Adventure Travel, by James C Simmons, is a worthwhile investment for anyone interested in the subject; it covers the entire planet, but numerous itineraries in Costa Rica are featured.

HIKING & TREKKING

There is no shortage of hiking opportunities around Costa Rica, from day hikes in the countless private reserves to more-extended trips in some of the national parks.

Especially notable for day hikes are the fumaroles and tropical dry forest in Parque Nacional Rincón de la Vieja (p225), the pretty beaches of Parque Nacional Cahuita (p478) and the cloud forest reserves of Santa Elena (p211) and Monteverde (p208).

For those who want multiday adventures, the (minimum) two-day hike through Parque Nacional Corcovado (p415) is nothing less than incredible. This last remaining strand of coastal Pacific rain forest is packed with macaws, monkeys, tapirs and peccaries, and offers totally rugged adventure.

Historic Parque Nacional Santa Rosa (p230) offers opportunities to hike and camp in tropical dry forest. Easily accessible from the Interamericana, travelers here may spot peccaries, coatis and tapirs concentrated at watering holes during the dry season. Longer trips can be made through the park and to the pristine beaches of Nancite and Naranjo.

Trail Source (www.trailsource.com) provides information on hiking in Costa Rica. It also has info on horse riding and mountain biking. A monthly fee applies.

PUTTING DOWN THE GUIDE

No, we're not talking about insulting the local guy who is leading you through the rain forest. We're talking about closing this book that you have in your hands and leaving it behind. We're talking about following your own trail, catching your own wave and paddling up your own stream. It is bound to be an adventure more memorable than the one you'll find along the Gringo Trail.

We at Lonely Planet are dedicated to providing comprehensive coverage of every country and region that we cover, but we recognize the sometimes detrimental effect of places being 'discovered'. Even more than that, we are dedicated to creating a sustainable global traveler culture, and we recognize the universal benefit of 'discovery.'

So put your guidebook down for a day or – even better – a week. Explore the places that are not covered in the pages of this guidebook. And discover your own lonely planet.

In recent years, more than 6000 people climbed Cerro Chirripó each year. In 2005 Minae started limiting this number to 5100 to minimize tourist impact.

Mountaineers will enjoy the steep and arduous hike through the *páramo* (highland shrub forests and grasslands) up Cerro Chirripó (p385) – the highest mountain in Costa Rica. And for the trekker that appreciates complete solitude in absolute wilderness, there's Parque Internacional La Amistad (p399). This heavily forested and rarely traversed park offers some of the most breathtaking scenery in the country.

Many local companies offer guided hikes in different parts of Costa Rica (p528).

Safety on the Trail

Costa Rica is hot and humid: hiking in these tropical conditions can really take it out of you. Overheating and dehydration are the main sources of misery on the trails, so be sure to bring plenty of water and don't be afraid to stop and rest. Make sure you have sturdy, comfortable footwear (see below) and a lightweight rain jacket.

You can take a 50km ride *down* the Cerro de la Muerte to Manuel Antonio.

Unfortunately, some readers have told horror stories of getting robbed while on some of the more remote hiking trails. This is not a common occurrence. Nonetheless, it is always advisable to hike in a group for added safety. Hiring a local guide is another excellent way to enhance your experience, avoid getting lost and learn an enormous amount about the flora and fauna in your midst.

Some of the local park offices have maps, but this is the exception rather than the rule. If you are planning to do independent hiking on long-distance trails, be sure to purchase your maps in San José in advance (see p537).

MOUNTAIN BIKING

Some cyclists claim that the steep, narrow, winding and potholed roads and aggressive Costa Rican drivers add up to a poor cycling experience. This may be true of the main roads, but there are numerous less-trafficked roads that offer plenty of adventure – from winding and scenic mountain paths with sweeping views to rugged trails that take riders through streams and by volcanoes. For information on tour operators, see p529.

THESE BOOTS WERE MADE FOR WALKING

With its ample supply of mud, streams and army ants, hiking through Costa Rica's parks can be quite an adventure – particularly for your shoes. Footwear is a personal issue, but here are some options for keeping your feet happy in the jungle.

- Do as the locals and invest in galoshes (rubber boots), especially for the rainy season. (If you're larger than a size 44 – men's 10 in the USA – consider buying them abroad.) Rubber boots are indestructible, protect you from snakes and ticks, provide excellent traction and can be easily hosed off at the end of the day. The downside of the rubber boots is that they are not very comfortable. Plus, river crossings guarantee that the boots will fill up with water at some point, and then your feet are wet for the rest of the day. Price US$6.

- High-end sport sandals (like Chacos or Tevas) are used by climbers to scramble up boulders to the starting points for climbing routes. These are great for crossing rivers, as the water runs right off them (and your feet). However, be aware that there are lots of creepy crawlies living in the rain forest, some of which might like to make lunch out of your toes, and sandals offer little protection. Price US$50 to US$100.

- There is something to be said for good, solid, waterproof hiking boots. You don't have to pay an arm and a leg for sturdy boots that offer strong support and keep your feet marginally dry. If you can't stand the idea of walking around with wet feet, consider tossing a pair of sandals into your pack too, and change your shoes for the river crossings. Price US$80 to US$200.

DIVING

There's good news and there's bad news. The good news is that Costa Rica offers body-temperature water with few humans and abundant marine life. The bad news is that the visibility is low because of silt and plankton. If you are looking for turquoise waters and plenty of hard coral, head for Belize. However, if you're looking for fine opportunities to see massive schools of fish as well as larger marine animals such as turtles, sharks, dolphins and whales, then you have arrived.

Some of the best areas for diving are off the northern part of the Península de Nicoya at Playas del Coco (p259), Ocotal (p267) and Hermosa (p265), where you can expect to see manta rays, sharks and dozens of species of fish, all in large numbers. See also the boxed text Divers Do It Deeper, p262. Dive shops in the area provide gear and guides, as well as offer courses.

Another top dive center is Bahía Drake (p406). Several of the hotels organize excursions to Isla del Caño (p413) and other sites, offering the opportunity to put yourself in the path of giant schools of barracuda, grouper, manta ray, Moorish idol and puffer fish.

The Caribbean coast offers fewer opportunities for diving, although Puerto Viejo de Talamanca (p483) and nearby Manzanillo (p497) are emerging dive centers. Visibility is generally better than on the Pacific coast (especially if you go when it's not raining and the swells are down), but the diving is a completely different experience, offering small reefs and colorful fish. Most dives are fairly easy and nontechnical, making this a good place for beginners.

The mack daddy of dive sites is Isla del Coco (p420), 500km to the southwest of the Costa Rican mainland. There you can expect to find 18 species of coral reef, 57 types of crustacean, three species of dolphin and innumerable other types of marine life. It's a 36-hour ocean journey to get there and it's for intermediate and advanced divers only. In addition, the island does not allow camping and does not provide accommodations, so you'll be spending a lot of quality time on your boat.

For practical information about diving see p527.

RIVER RAFTING

Rivers tumbling from the central mountains down to the coast afford fantastic white-water rafting opportunities. The wildest months are from June through October though rafting can be done year-round.

Since the mid-1980s, white-water rafting and kayaking have been major contributors to the country's ecotourism-based economy. From Class II to Class V, Costa Rica's rivers offer magical white-water experiences for both first-time runners and seasoned enthusiasts.

Thousands of travelers go river running in Costa Rica each year, and the vast majority enjoy a memorable, safe trip. However, wild rivers are powerful and uncontrollable by nature, and white-water river running is a risky and potentially dangerous undertaking. River-running companies are not bound by safety regulations in Costa Rica, so be sure to choose an outfitter with bilingual guides certified in swift-water rescue and emergency medical training.

The country's most popular rivers are the Pacuare and Reventazón, both located in the Northern Lowlands town of Turrialba (p177). Home to toucans, herons, monkeys and sloths, the Río Pacuare is often flooded during the rainy season (June to October) due to erosion from rampant deforestation upstream, and is best run during the dry season (November to early April). Considered one of the world's top 10 white-water runs, the

As of 2006, it is illegal to swim with dolphins and whales in Costa Rica.

The waters off of Isla del Coco are home to schooling scalloped hammerheads, countless white-tip reef sharks and even whale sharks.

The Rivers of Costa Rica, a kayaking and rafting guide by Michael W Mayfield, is just the ticket for river runners.

Pacuare is currently threatened by a hydroelectric project (see the boxed text Damming the Rivers?, p179). If constructed, the dam would greatly diminish ecotourism in the area and impact lands vital to the Cabécar and Awari indigenous groups. The white water and fragile wilderness desperately need protection from future hydroelectric projects. Contact **Fundación Ríos Tropicales** (www.riostropicales.com) for more information.

In the late 1990s the Río Reventazón Class V Peralta section was destroyed by a hydroelectric dam built for energy to export to neighboring countries.

North of Turrialba, the little-known town of La Virgen (p516) is famous in white-water circles as a base for rafting and kayaking on the Río Sarapiquí. You can run the Sarapiquí year-round, but July through December are considered peak months. This river offers a wide range of rafting options for all skill levels, from the Class I-II Chilamate put-in, all the way up to the Class IV-V rapids of the Upper Sarapiquí. Most people choose to put in near La Virgen and ride the Lower Sarapiquí, an adventurous Class III-IV river run that does not require rafting experience.

Several rivers near the thriving tourist mecca of Manuel Antonio (p348) on the central Pacific coast offer great white water and wildlife viewing year-round. The Río Naranjo boasts an experts-only Class V upper section known as the Labyrinth (which is best run from December to early March, depending on flows), with the more forgiving Class III-IV Villa Nueva section downstream. The neighboring Class III-IV+ Río Savegre, plunging from its source near 3820m Cerro Chirripó in the Cordillera de Talamanca, offers continuous, world-class white water, and is touted as one of the cleanest rivers in Central America. A family favorite, the nearby Class II+ Río Parrita has excellent bird-watching and frequent wildlife sightings in a luscious, tropical-wilderness setting.

In the Shadow of a Sphere, by Tom Youngholm, is an imaginative – almost supernatural – novel about a young musician's adventures on Costa Rica's white water.

Details on river trips and outfitters are given in the regional chapters of this book, or see p529.

KAYAKING

With 1228km of coastline, two gulfs and plentiful mangrove estuaries, Costa Rica is an ideal destination for sea kayaking. Several outfitters offer guided coastal or estuary tours with trained bilingual naturalists, as well as renting out equipment for self-guided excursions. Sea kayaking is a great way for beginning or expert paddlers to comfortably access remote areas and catch rare glimpses of birds and wildlife.

On the Pacific side, the Península de Nicoya's Refugio de Vida Silvestre Curú (p305) offers stunning paddling along palm-lined beaches, rock arch formations and estuaries teeming with birds and colorful crabs.

Sometimes you can see salt crystals on the edge of the leaves of the Pacific black mangrove, which absorbs salinated water through its roots, then secretes the salt through its leaves.

On the central Pacific coast, Isla Damas (p341) and the nearby Parque Nacional Manuel Antonio (p356) are equally as riveting. The delicate mangrove ecosystem of Isla Damas is home to a wealth of wildlife including boa constrictors, white-faced monkeys, crocodiles and shore birds best described by the naturalist guides of Amigo Tico Complete Adventure Tours (p344). Following the tide out to the Pacific Ocean, it's not far to Parque Nacional Manuel Antonio and the nearby tiny Islas Gemelas and Olinga, where nesting shore birds may be spotted.

On the Península de Osa, the Río Agujitas in Bahía Drake (p407) and the mangroves around Puerto Jiménez (p422) are optimal for exploration by kayak.

Heading over to the Caribbean side, Parque Nacional Tortuguero (p460), a 192-sq-km coastal park, is well known for its amazing network of lagoons and canals. Paddling provides unlimited opportunities for solitude and wildlife sightings (monkeys, sloths, anteaters, kinkajous, peccaries, tapirs and manatees).

SURFING

Point and beach breaks, lefts and rights, reefs and river mouths, warm water and year-round waves make Costa Rica a favorite surfing destination. Some beaches may be difficult to get to, but the trade-off is that they are usually less crowded. Even the more accessible spots tend to be much more sparsely populated than the beaches of California or Sydney. See the surfer's map on p78 for an idea of what's around.

Waves are big (though not Hawaii-big) and the many reef breaks offer hollow and fast rides. For the most part, the Pacific coast has bigger swells and better waves during the latter part of the rainy season, but the Caribbean cooks from November to May. Basically there is a wave, somewhere, waiting to be surfed at any time of the year.

Surfers should pick up a copy of Mike Parise's *Surfer's Guide to Costa Rica* for detailed information about Costa Rica's surf breaks.

If you are in the market for a good, cheap board, good places to start your search include Jacó (p331), Mal País & Santa Teresa (p313) and Tamarindo (p276). It's usually possible to buy a cheap long board for about US$250 to US$300, and a cheap short board for about US$150 to US$200. Most surf shops will buy back your board for about 50% of the price you paid.

Short boards are preferred in Costa Rica, mainly because they are easier to travel with (both Nature Air and Sansa have restrictions on surf-board sizes). That said, long boards are recommended for beginners, as they are easier to vault up on.

For the uninitiated, lessons are available at almost all of the major surfing destinations. On the Pacific, Jacó and Tamarindo are good (though crowded) places to learn, as is Pavones (p441) on the Golfo Dulce. One veteran surfer recommends that even for newbies, it is worth trying some of the more aggressive waves (just not when they are at their peaks).

See the boxed text Top Five Breaks, below, for Costa Rica's best surfing spots, but these are only the white caps in a sea of magnificent waves.

Península de Nicoya & Northwestern Costa Rica

Playa Tamarindo (p276) is Surf City, USA. Tamarindo has been a major surfing mecca ever since Patrick and Wingnut stopped here in the film classic *Endless Summer II*. These days, it is filled with surf shops, surf schools and surfer dudes. The smaller beaches in town may be good places to learn, but more-experienced surfers will appreciate the bigger, faster (and less-crowded) waves at Playas Negra and Avellana (p281) as well as Playa Junquillal (p283), to the south. These are also possible jumping-off points for excursions to the infamous beach breaks at Ollie's Point and Witches Rock in Parque Nacional Santa Rosa (p230). The most consistent waves are north of Tamarindo on the deserted beaches of Playa Grande (p271).

Mal País and Santa Teresa (p313) are in the second generation as surf destinations, and have a groovy scene to match the powerful waves.

TOP FIVE BREAKS

Greg Gordon of *Costa Rica Surf Report* ranks Costa Rica's top breaks.

- Pavones (p441) – The legendary longest left in the country.
- Playa Hermosa (p339) – The country's most consistent waves.
- Playa Grande (p271) – Great waves and a gorgeous beach, in the midst of the national park.
- Salsa Brava (p481) – The rough reef has earned this break its nasty reputation.
- Witches Rock/Ollie's Point (p230) – Way out-of-the-way (but worth the trip) waves in the Parque Nacional Santa Rosa.

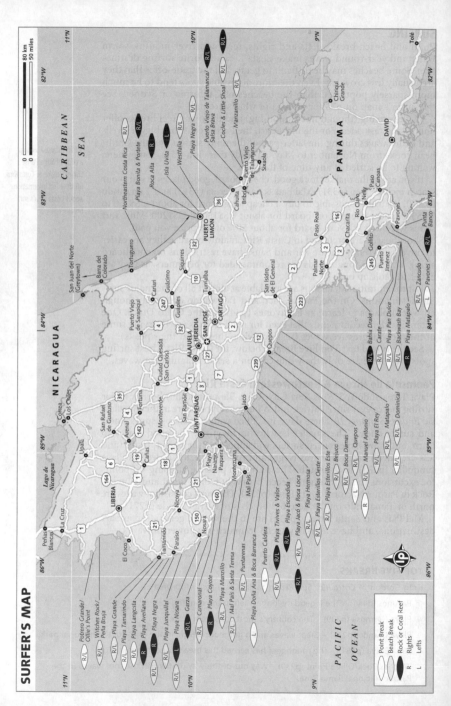

SURFER'S MAP

Central Pacific Coast

Surfing is generally better during the rainy season on the Pacific coast. But Jacó (p331) is perhaps the exception that proves the rule, offering consistent surf year-round. Jacó is another place that is overrun with surf shops and surf schools; it is an excellent place for beginners to surf by day and party by night. If you can't stand the crowds, head south to Playa Hermosa (p339), where bigger, faster curls attract a more determined (and experienced) crew of wave-chasers.

Further south on the Pacific coast, Dominical (p362) is a laidback surfing destination with some wicked waves. It is less developed than the other Pacific-coast destinations, but still has something of a scene (including one surf camp and a few places to rent boards). Nearby, Matapalo (p360) also offers amazing surf, though it is relatively unknown (meaning more waves for you).

Península de Osa & Golfo Dulce

On the Península de Osa, you'll find good, steady surf at the beaches of Cabo Matapalo (p427). There are plenty of waves for locals and tourists alike at this still-undiscovered spot. Three different beaches provide opportunities for both long and short boards, beginners and experts (but no surf schools). The limited degree of development in these parts means there are not a lot of facilities: bring your own board.

Across the sweet waters of the Golfo Dulce lies the legendary long left at Pavones (p441). During the rainy season, die-hard surfers make the grueling four-hour journey over rocky roads to reach this mecca; in the off season, the waves are usually somewhat better at the nearby Punta Banco.

Caribbean Coast

The southern Caribbean coast is basically one long surf paradise, from Puerto Limón south to the Panamanian border. Puerto Viejo de Talamanca (p481) is infamous for the reef break at Salsa Brava, but it is for experts only. The slightly less intimidating beach break at Playa Cocles is also popular and excellent for learners. You'll find boards for rent and surf lessons advertised all over this little village.

If you are not into the surf scene, but still appreciate a good wave, Playa Negra in Cahuita (p471) is less competitive and less crowded (but the waves are still consistent). And you can still rent a decent board, take a lesson and end your evening watching surfing videos in the local surfer bar.

Off the coast of Puerto Limón, Isla Uvita (p456) is a destination for adventurous surfers, as it is uninhabited and has no facilities. Another off-the-beaten-track destination is Manzanillo (p494), but bring your board from Puerto Viejo.

WATERFALL RAPPELLING

With its many pretty waterfalls, it just had to be a matter of time before someone in Costa Rica decided it'd be a good idea to rappel down one of them. (Great fun for rock-climbing types who like to get wet.)

The main destination for waterfall rappelling is the area around Puerto Jiménez and Cabo Matapalo (p427) on the Península de Osa. Everyday Adventures (p427) specializes in the sport, but most of the lodges in the Jiménez area can book you on tours. In the Monteverde area, Desafío Adventure Company (p195) also offers these types of adventures. In the Central Valley, try Exploranatura (p175) in Turrialba.

Log on to the *Costa Rica Surf Report* (www.crsurf.com) and check out Costa Rica's surf scene.

Allen Weisbecker recounts his adventures trying to track down his long-lost pal and a few good waves in *In Search of Captain Zero*. Don't be surprised if you run into Captain Zero in Puerto Viejo.

SPORTFISHING

Fishing enthusiasts flock to both of Costa Rica's coasts for the thrill of reeling in mammoth marlins and supersized sailfish. Many lodges are willing to cook and serve your fish, if you bring it back from the boat. However, a good day of fishing often produces more fish than the clients can eat. Most sportfishing companies encourage 'catch and release' practices so as not to deplete fish populations.

Despite this conscientious effort, sportfishing is often the target of local criticism, mainly for the big-spending, free-wheeling reputation of the clientele, who are closely associated with the increase in prostitution in some areas (see the boxed text Sportfishing, p300).

On the Pacific coast, both Tamarindo (p276) and Quepos (p344) offer plenty of opportunities for offshore fishing. The main attraction is the Pacific sailfish, which swims in these waters between December and April.

The Golfo Dulce is probably Costa Rica's top spot for fishing, especially for dorado, marlin, sailfish and tuna. Fishing operators work out of Puerto Jiménez (p424), Golfito (p431) and Zancudo (p438). The latter is also excellent for snook, which inhabit the surrounding mangrove swamps, especially from May to September.

Nearby, Bahía Drake (p407) claims more than 40 fishing records, including sailfish, three kinds of marlin, yellow fin tuna, wahoo, cubera snapper, Spanish and sierra mackerel and roosterfish. Fishing is excellent year-round, although the catch may vary according to the season.

There is also fishing up and down the Caribbean coast, especially in the remote northern outposts of Barra del Colorado (p467) and Parismina (p458). High-end fishing lodges attract world-class anglers in search of snook (September through November) and tarpon (January through May). These luxury lodges go to great lengths to provide their clients with all the creature comforts, even in the furthest corners of Costa Rica. In Cahuita (p471) you'll find more barebones operations catering to simple folk who wish to drop a line.

Food & Drink

From sushi to *sangría*, this little country can sate your appetite. Typical hearty local cooking – *cocina típica* – is available far and wide and at every price range. Thatched country kitchens can be found all over, with local women ladling out basic home-cooked specials. But you can get your Tico (Costa Rican) fare upscale and with a nouveau twist in trendier, more touristed areas.

In the most popular tourist destinations, the high level of immigration from the USA assures a wide selection of just about anything you might want to munch on: Italian, Spanish, Chinese, Japanese, French, Mexican, American and even Greek.

STAPLES & SPECIALTIES

Costa Rican food, for the most part, is very basic. Some might even call it bland. The complex and varied dishes concocted in Mexico and Guatemala just didn't make it over the border to here. The diet consists largely of rice and beans – and beans and rice – and any combination thereof.

Breakfast is usually *gallo pinto*, a stir-fry of rice and beans served with eggs, cheese or *natilla* (sour cream). This is generally cheap (US$2) and filling and sometimes can be downright tasty. If you'll be spending the whole day surfing or hiking you'll have energy to spare! Many hotels will provide what they refer to as a 'tropical breakfast' – usually bread along with a selection of fresh fruits. American-style breakfasts are available in many eateries.

Most restaurants offer a set meal at lunch and dinner called a *casado*, or a 'married man's' lunch. This meal is always cheap and filling. It usually includes meat, beans, rice, cabbage salad and fried plantains.

Breakfast and lunch is often served with bread or toast, though some places will offer fresh tortillas (most popular in Guanacaste), made from a thickly ground corn.

Food is not heavily spiced, unless you're having traditional Caribbean-style cuisine. The vast majority of Ticos have a distinct aversion to hot sauce, though most local restaurants will lay out a spicy *curtido* (a pickle of hot peppers and vegetables) or little bottles of Tabasco-style sauce for the diehards. Another popular condiment is *salsa lizano*, the Tico version of Worcestershire sauce.

When Ticos share a meal they wish each other *'Buen provecho!'* or 'Bon appetit!'

Entradas: Journeys in Latin American Cuisine, by Joan Chatfield-Taylor, has some of Costa Rica's most popular recipes – and many others.

TRAVEL YOUR TASTE BUDS

Perhaps the tastiest local cuisine is found on the Caribbean coast. Spicy coconut-milk stews (*rondón*), garlic potatoes, well-seasoned fish and chicken dishes are all lip-smacking good. Also, don't miss the savory 'rice and beans' (in English), red beans and rice cooked in coconut milk.

In the Guanacaste region, keep your eye out for *chan*, the black seeds of the chan plant, soaked and served in *agua dulce* (sugar-cane water) or with tamarind juice. It's space-age looking and rather slimy, but the locals swear that nothing will refresh you more. In rural areas, especially at festivals and local celebrations, you might sample *chicha*, fermented corn and sugar liquor.

In palm-producing regions, expect to find *palmitos* (hearts of palm) in just about everything: salad dishes, stews and even lasagna. In Guanacaste, the locals produce a palm wine (only available in the dry season) called *vino coyol*. You think *guaro* (local firewater made from sugar cane) is intense? Try this stuff. It's not usually available in bars, so keep your eyes peeled for signs offering it outside private homes and *pulperías* (corner grocery stores).

Concinando con Tia
Florita is a popular Tico
cooking show. Check out
the recipes and meet Tia
Florita herself at www
.concinancdocontia
florita.com.

Considering the extent of the coastline, it is no surprise that seafood is plentiful and fish dishes are usually fresh and delicious. Fish is often fried, but may also be grilled or blackened. While not traditional Tico fare, *ceviche* is on most menus. Raw fish is marinated in lime juice with chilies, tomatoes and herbs. Served chilled, it is a delectable way to enjoy fresh seafood. Emphasis is on 'fresh' here. This is raw fish, so if you have reason to believe it is not fresh, don't risk eating it.

At Christmas, and other times, some restaurants will serve *tamales*, banana leaves packed with a cornmeal and meat filling and then steamed.

The most popular foreign foods in Costa Rica are Chinese and Italian. Nearly every town has a Chinese place, and even if it doesn't, menus will likely include *arroz cantonés* (fried rice). Pizza parlors and Italian restaurants of varying quality abound, though the locally produced pizza can sometimes be heavily loaded (read: cheese bomb).

If an establishment doesn't exactly impress you with its cleanliness, then it might be advisable not to eat fruits, vegetables or salads there. If they are improperly washed, you could be sending your stomach a little bacteria surprise. See more on this in the Health chapter (p559).

DRINKS

Order gourmet coffee and
other treats at www
.cafébritt.com.

Coffee is probably the most popular beverage in the country and wherever you go, someone is likely to offer you a *cafécito*. Traditionally, it is served strong and mixed with hot milk to taste, also known as *café con leche*. Most drinkers get *café negro*, and for those who want a little milk, you can ask for *leche al lado* (milk on the side). Many trendier places serve cappuccinos and espressos. The milk is pasteurized and safe to drink.

For a refresher, nothing beats *batidos* – fresh fruit drinks (like smoothies) made either *al agua* (with water) or *con leche* (with milk). The array can be mind-boggling, and includes mango, papaya, *piña* (pineapple), *sandía* (watermelon), *melón* (cantaloupe), *mora* (blackberry), *zanahoria* (carrot), *cebada* (barley) or *tamarindo* (made from the fruit of the tamarind tree). If you are wary about the condition of the drinking water, ask that your *batido* be made with *agua enbotellada* (bottled water) and *sin hielo* (without ice.)

GALLO PINTO

How to start your day the Tico way: put on a pot of delicious organic coffee and whip up your morning rice and beans.

2 cups cooked rice
2 cups cooked black beans
½ cup stock from cooking beans
½ onion, chopped
1 bell pepper, chopped
2 cloves garlic
2 tablespoons fresh coriander
2 tablespoons vegetable oil
Heavy cream

Fry the onion and bell pepper in the vegetable oil, then add garlic. Pour in beans and bean stock; bring to a simmer, taking care that the mixture doesn't dry up. Add in the rice and stir thoroughly but gently – you don't want to mash the beans! Season to taste with salt and pepper. Just before serving, stir in the fresh coriander and top with a little heavy cream.

Recipe courtesy of Food Cards, foodcards@hotmail.com

A bottled, though far less-tasty alternative, is a local fruit beverage called 'Tropical'. It's sold in many stores and restaurants and the most common flavors are *mora, piña, cas* (a tart local fruit) and *frutas mixtas.* Just shake vigorously before drinking or the powder-like substance at the bottom will remain intact.

Pipas are green coconuts that have a hole macheted into the top of them and a straw for drinking the 'milk' – a very refreshing and filling drink.

Agua dulce is sugar-cane water, or in many cases boiled water mixed with brown sugar. *Horchata*, found mostly in the countryside, is a sweet drink made from cornmeal and flavored with cinnamon.

The usual brands of soft drinks are available, including some favorites you thought were long-gone, like Crush and Squirt. In rural areas, and especially on buses, don't be surprised if your soda (or your juice) is served in a plastic bag. Plastic bags are undoubtedly cheaper than plastic bottles or other containers. So locals fill plastic bags with a variety of beverages and sell them from coolers at the side of the road. If you are lucky, they will also have straws, which makes it a lot easier to enjoy your drink.

The most popular alcoholic drink is beer and there are several local brands. Imperial is perhaps the most popular – either for its smooth flavor or for the ubiquitous T-shirts emblazoned with their eagle-crest logo. Pilsen, with a higher alcohol content, is also known for its saucy calendars featuring *las chicas Pilsen* (the Pilsen girls). Both are tasty pilsners. Bavaria produces a lager and Bavaria Negro, a delicious, full-bodied dark beer. This brand is popular among the young and well-educated, but it's not so easy to find outside of the trendiest spots.

Most of these beers contain 4% or 4.5% alcohol. Rock Ice, with 4.7% alcohol content, has a slightly more bitter taste. Domestic beer costs about US$0.75 in the cheapest places, but will generally run about US$1.50 per bottle or US$3 in fancier tourist lodges. Other beers are imported and expensive.

After beer, the poison of choice is *guaro*, which is a colorless alcohol distilled from sugar cane and usually consumed by the shot, though you can order it as a sour. It goes down mighty easily, but leaves one hell of a hangover.

Local vodka, gin and whisky is not recommended. One locally made liqueur is Café Rica, which, predictably, is based on coffee and tastes like the better-known Mexican Kahlua. Mix *guaro* with Café Rica to make a uniquely Tico Black Russian.

Also inexpensive and worthwhile is local rum, usually drunk as a *cuba libre* (rum and cola). Premixed cans of *cuba libre* are available in stores but it'd be a lie to say the contents didn't taste weirdly like aluminum. The best rum available is Ron Centenario, which is definitely worth the price (US$12 a bottle at a liquor store; US$9 at airport duty-free).

Most Costa Rican wines are cheap, taste cheap, and will be unkindly remembered the next morning. Imported wines are available but expensive (and difficult to store at proper temperatures). Chilean brands are your best bet for a palatable wine at an affordable price.

WHERE TO EAT & DRINK

Lunch is usually the main meal of the day and is typically served at around noon. Dinner tends to be a lighter version of lunch and is eaten around 7pm.

By far the most popular eating establishment in Costa Rica is the *soda*. These are small and informal lunch counters dishing up a few daily casados (US$2 to US$3). These are the best places to eat if you are on

Coffee was thought to energize workers, so in 1840 the government decreed that all laborers building roads should be provided with one cup of coffee every day.

No alcohol is served on Election Day or in the three days prior to Easter Sunday.

Are you worried that you'll head back home and dearly miss *salsa lizano* or Tropical drinks? Thankfully www.lapulpe .com sells Costa Rican products and will ship the goods to just about anywhere in the world.

TOP FIVE EATS

- Asian fusion at Restaurante Tin Jo (p115) in San José.
- Spicy, delicious fish tacos from El Loco Natural (p489) in Puerto Viejo de Talamanca.
- Ronny's Place (p353) in Manuel Antonio.
- Homemade coconut ice cream from Jade Luna (p426) in Puerto Jiménez.
- Anything off the menu at Pachanga (p280) in Tamarindo.

a budget and they are easily found in any neighborhood as well as the *mercado central* (central market) of any town. The cheapest *sodas* are usually inside the *mercado*. Look for the places that are packed: they're always the best and serve the freshest food. Many *sodas* are only open for breakfast and lunch. Other popular cheapies include the omnipresent fried- and rotisserie-chicken stands.

A regular *restaurante* is usually higher on the price scale and has slightly more atmosphere. There will often be a more formal menu *(carta)* and just about everything – from *comida típica* to American and foreign specialties – will be served. Many *restaurantes* serve casados, while the fancier places refer to the set lunch as the *almuerzo ejecutivo*.

In San José and in touristy areas, eg Tamarindo, Manuel Antonio and Jacó, specialty and ethnic restaurants are widely available. Prices at *restaurantes* can range from US$3 for a casado to US$40 for lobster in Manuel Antonio. Pizza parlors and Chinese restaurants are usually the cheapest ethnic eats. Pizzas are usually personal size and generally start at US$3. Prices at Chinese restaurants start at US$2 for fried rice; a plate of cashew chicken can run to about US$6, depending on the establishment. Upmarket restaurants add a 13% tax plus 10% service to the bill, so check the menu to see if the tax is included in the list prices.

Pastelerías and *panaderías* sell pastries and bread, respectively, and sometimes a combination of the two. Some also sell sandwiches.

Many bars serve snacks called *bocas*. In the countryside, these were frequently provided free of charge, but this practice is getting harder to find. Most times, *bocas* are snack-sized portions of main meals, including *ceviche* (marinated fish cocktail), *arroz con pollo* (chicken and rice) or *patacones* (thick wedges of fried plantain bananas with bean dip). Order a few *bocas* and you'll have a delicious (and varied) dinner on your hands.

> You can pick up the necessary skills to make a good *casado* at the Costa Rican Language Academy in San José (p104).

> Many Tico men believe that eating turtle eggs will give them increased sexual prowess. Hopefully Viagra will alleviate the illegal traffic in these eggs.

Quick Eats

There is not a vast selection of street snacks to choose from in Costa Rica. For the most part, street vendors sell fresh fruit (sometimes pre-chopped and ready to go), cookies, chips (crisps) and fried plantains. Many *sodas* have little windows that face the street, and from there dispense *empanadas* (a meat or chicken turnover), tacos (usually a tortilla with meat) or *enchilados* (pastry with spicy meat). Many of these places also offer fried chicken, which has to be one of the most consistently popular foods in all of Costa Rica.

VEGETARIANS & VEGANS

If you don't mind rice and beans, Costa Rica is a relatively comfortable place for vegetarians to travel. Most restaurants will make veggie casados on request and many are now including them on the menu. They usually include rice and beans, cabbage salad and one or two selections of variously prepared vegetables or legumes.

With the high influx of tourism, there are also many specialty vegetarian restaurants or restaurants with a veggie menu in San José and tourist-centric towns. The Vishnu chain in San José (p117) enjoys a popular local following and has an outlet in Heredia (p161). The many yoga and holistic retreat centers also offer veggie cooking. Also check out Luna Lodge (p429) in Carate, Pura Vida Retreat & Spa (p148) near Alajuela, Samasati Retreat Center (p488) near Puerto Viejo de Talamanca or Yoga Farm (p443) near Pavones.

Lodges in remote areas that offer all-inclusive meal plans can all accommodate vegetarian diets with advance notice. Be sure to note your preference at the time you make your reservation.

Vegans, macrobiotic and raw-foods-only travelers will have a tougher time as there are fewer outlets accommodating those diets. A couple of places include Restaurant Shakti (p118) in San José, Pura Vida Retreat & Spa (p148) near Alajuela and Veronica's Place (p488) in Puerto Viejo de Talamanca. If you intend to keep to your diet, it's best to choose a lodging where you can prepare foods yourself. Many towns have health-food stores (macrobióticas), but selection varies. Fresh vegetables can be hard to come by in isolated areas and will often be quite expensive.

> *Costa Rican Typical Foods*, by Carmen de Musmani and Lupita de Weiler, is out of print, but it is perhaps the only Tico-specific cookbook.

EATING WITH KIDS

If you're traveling with the tots, you'll find that 'kids' meals' (small portions at small prices) are not normally offered in restaurants, though some fancy lodges do them. However, most local eateries will accommodate two children splitting a meal or can produce child-size portions on request. You can ask for restaurant staff to bring you simple food, rice with chicken or steak cooked on the grill (a la plancha).

If you are traveling with an infant, stock up on formula and baby food before heading to remote areas. Avocados are safe, easy to eat and nutritious and they can be served to children as young as six months old. Young children should avoid water and ice in drinks as they are more susceptible to stomach illnesses.

Always carry snacks for long drives in remote areas – sometimes there are no places to stop for a bite.

For other tips on traveling with the tykes, see p531.

> The best ice-cream treat is, by far, the 'Mmmio': vanilla ice cream topped with caramel and nuts and bathed in chocolate – it's mmm-good and available just about everywhere.

EAT YOUR WORDS

The thrill of eating; the agony of ordering in a foreign language. This handy guide is set up to help you eat – and order – well. For further guidance with Spanish pronunciation, see p562.

DOS & DON'TS

- When you sit down to eat, it is polite to say *buenos días* or *buenas tardes* to the waitstaff or any people you might be sharing a table with.
- If you're eating with a group of locals, it's polite to say *buen provecho (bon appetit)* at the start of the meal.
- Tipping is not customary at low-end *sodas*, though leaving spare change is always appreciated.
- Midrange and top-end restaurants frequently include a service charge in the bill.

Useful Phrases

Do you have a menu (in English)?
¿Hay una carta (en Inglés)?   ai oo-na kar-ta (en een-gles)?
What is there for breakfast/lunch/dinner?
¿Qué hay para el desayuno/   ke ai pa-ra el de-sa-yoo-no/
el almuerzo/la cena?   el al-mwer-so/la se-na?
Is this water purified?
¿Ésta agua es purificada?   es-ta a-gwa es poo-ree-fee-ka-da?
I'm a vegetarian.
Soy vegetariano/a.   soy ve-khe-te-rya-no/a
I don't eat meat, chicken, fish or eggs.
No como carne, pollo, pescado o huevos.   no ko-mo kar-ne po-yo pes-ka-do o we-vos
I'd like the set lunch.
Quisiera un casado.   kee-sye-ra oon ka-sa-do
The bill, please.
La cuenta, por favor.   la kwen-ta por fa-vor

Menu Decoder
Food Glossary

a la parrilla/plancha	a la pa-ree-lya/plan-cha)	grilled over charcoal/in a pan
agua (enbotellada)	a-gwa (en-bot-el-a-da)	(bottled) water
almuerzo	al-mwer-so	lunch
almuerzo ejecutivo	al-mwer-so e-khe-koo-tee-vo	inexpensive set lunch; special of the day (literally 'business lunch')
arreglados	a-re-gla-dos	puff pastries stuffed with beef, chicken or cheese
arroz	a-ros	rice
arroz con pollo	a-ros kon po-lyo	a basic dish of rice and chicken
azúcar	a-soo-kar	sugar
batido	ba-tee-do	fresh fruit shake made with water or milk
bebida	be-bee-da	drink, soda
bistek	bis-tek	steak
bocas	bo-kas	small savory dishes served in bars
cajeta	ka-khe-ta	a thick caramel fudge
caldo	kal-do	broth, often meat-based
camarones	ka-ma-ro-nes	shrimp
carne	kar-ne	meat; though frequently refers to beef
casado	ka-sa-do	a set meal, normally rice, black beans, a small salad, a cooked vegetable and either chicken, fish, meat or cheese
cerveza	ser-ve-sa	beer
ceviche	se-vee-che	seafood marinated with lemon, onion, sweet red peppers and cilantro; can be made with fish, shrimp or conch
chicharrón	chee-cha-ron	pork crackling
chorreada	cho-re-a-da	pan-fried cornmeal cake served with sour cream
churrasco	choo-ras-ko	grilled steak; frequently a skirt steak
coco	ko-ko	coconut
comida/ cocina típica	ko-mee-da/ ko-see-na tee-pee-ka	typical Costa Rican fare
cuba libre	koo-ba lee-bre	rum and cola
dorado	do-ra-do	mahi mahi fish
dulce de leche	dool-se de le-che	milk and sugar boiled to make a thick caramel paste often used in pastries
elote	e-lo-te	corn on the cob served boiled (elote cocinado) or roasted (elote asado)

empanadas	em-pa-*na*-das	turnovers stuffed with chicken, beef or cheese
enchilados	en-chee-*la*-dos	pastries stuffed with potatoes and cheese and sometimes meat
ensalada	en-sa-*la*-da	salad
filete de pescado	fee-*le*-te de pes-*ka*-do	fish fillet
flan	flan	cold caramel custard
frijoles	free-*kho*-les	black beans
frutas	*froo*-tas	fruit
gallo pinto	ga-lyo peen-to	stir-fry of rice and beans, served with eggs, cheese or sour cream
gallos	ga-lyos	tortilla sandwiches with meat, beans or cheese
guaro	gwa-ro	local firewater made from sugar cane
hamburguesa	am-boor-*gwe*-sa	hamburger
helado	e-*la*-do	ice cream
huevos fritos/revueltos	we-vos free-tos/re-*vwel*-tos	fried/scrambled eggs
jugo	hoo-go	juice
leche	*le*-che	milk
limón	lee-mon	lime or lemon
maíz	mai-*ees*	dried corn or corn meal
mantequilla	man-te-*kee*-ya	butter
manzana	man-*za*-na	apple
mariscos	ma-*rees*-kos	seafood
mazamorra	ma-sa-*mo*-ra	a pudding made from cornstarch
mora	mo-*ra*	blackberry
naranja	na-*ran*-kha	orange
natilla	na-*tee*-lya	sour cream
olla de carne	o-lya de *kar*-ne	a hearty soup containing beef, potatoes, corn, squash, plantains and yuca, a type of tuber
pan	pan	bread
papa/papas fritas	pa-pa/pa-pas free-tas	potato/French fries
pargo rojo	par-go ro-ho	red snapper
pastel	pas-*tel*	pastry or cake
patacones	pa-ta-*ko*-nes	slices of plantain deep-fried like french-fried potatoes; usually served with bean dip
pejibaye	pe-khee-*ba*-ye	starchy tasting palm fruit also eaten as a salad
pescado al ajo	pes-*ka*-do al a-kho)	fish in garlic sauce (frequently butter)
pescado	pes-*ka*-do	fish
pimienta	pee-*myen*-ta	pepper (black)
piña	pee-nya	pineapple
plátano	pla-ta-no	fried sweet plantain
pollo	po-lyo	chicken
postre	pos-tre	dessert
puerco	pwer-ko	pork
queso	ke-so	cheese
rice and beans (in English)		rice and red beans cooked in coconut milk, served on the Caribbean side
rondón	ron-*don*	thick seafood-based soup blended with coconut milk, found on the Caribbean
sal sal	salt	
taco	ta-ko	a snack or hors d'oeuvres
tamales	ta-*ma*-les	boiled cornmeal pies usually wrapped in a banana leaf (you don't eat the leaf) and stuffed with chicken or pork
verduras	ver-*doo*-ras	vegetables
zanahoria	sa-na-o-rya	carrot

SAN JOSÉ

San José

For much of the 20th century, San José was predominantly an agricultural city. However, following the post-war baby boom, increasing urban migration completely transformed the capital in a few decades. Between the 1950s and 1980s, the city's population increased exponentially, and explosive growth, abysmal architectural preservation and unregulated development transformed the elegant capital into a sprawling and unsightly metropolis.

Today, Chepe, as it's called by Ticos, is the most cosmopolitan capital in Central America. The city is packed with office towers, shopping malls and fast-food restaurants, though booming capitalism has left a large portion of the city's residents disenfranchised. With each passing year, the outlying *tugurios* (slums) become more desperate and increasingly more violent, and the city is struggling to manage the growing crime rate that is atypical of the *pura vida* spirit.

For most travelers, a stopover in San José is regarded as a necessary evil before heading to the 'real' Costa Rica. However, to josefinos, as inhabitants of San José are called, San José might not be a thing of beauty, but it is the center of it all.

A few days in San José can offer a perspective on the true face of the nation and indeed there is truth to the concept of 'beauty on your doorstep.' The markets are vibrant and the nightlife is as sophisticated (or debaucherous) as you want it to be. San José is home numerous museums and there are a few neighborhoods where colonial stylings still radiate. More importantly however, San José is home to over one-third of all Ticos, and the assault on the sense that is Chepe is perhaps your best opportunity for understanding modern-day Costa Rica.

HIGHLIGHTS

- Enjoying the museum scene – from **contemporary art** (p96) to priceless **jade** (p96)

- Strolling through the historic **Barrio Amón** (p96) or the extensive greens of **La Sabana** (p97)

- Dancing all night long in **Centro Comercial El Pueblo** (p119) or on **Calle de la Amargura** (p132)

- Munching on a hot **churro** (doughnut tube; p117) while strolling amid the crowds on Avenida Central

- Sipping cocktails in **Escazú** (p139), a well-to-do San José 'burb

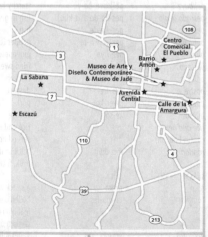

- POPULATION: CITY 350,000, GREATER METRO AREA OVER 1.5 MILLION   - ELEVATION: 1150M

HISTORY

The future capital of Costa Rica was established in 1737 as Villanueva de la Boca del Monte del Valle de Abra (New Village of the Mountain's Mouth in the Open Valley), though the name was later changed to a more manageable San José in honor of Joseph, the town's patron saint. Interestingly enough, the founding of San José was the result of an edict from the Catholic Church, which decreed that the populace must settle near a place of worship (attendance was down, times were bad, and churches were cheap to build).

For much of the colonial period, San José played second fiddle to the bigger and relatively more established Cartago. Following the surprise announcement in 1821 that Spain had abandoned its colonial holdings in Central America, Cartago and San José signed a series of empty-worded accords while secretly preparing for battle. On April 5, 1823, San José defeated Cartago at the Battle of Ochomongo, and subsequently declared itself capital. (Much to the chagrin of modern-day residents of Cartago, this rivalry still remains one-sided on the football field.)

Although San José generously offered to rotate capital status, bitterness ensued, and on September 26, 1835, Cartago, Heredia and Alajuela joined forces in an attempt to sack the city. In a siege that become known as La Guerra de la Liga (the War of the Leagues), San José defeated its attackers and retained its status as the capital. (Much to the chagrin also of modern-day residents of Heredia, this rivalry still remains one-sided on the football field, though Alajuela manages to hold its own.)

Recent years have been marked by a massive urban migration as Ticos (and increasingly Nicaraguans, see the boxed text Nica vs Tico, p235) move to the capital in search of increased economic opportunities. Unfortunately, this has resulted in the creation of shantytowns on the outskirts of the capital, and crime is increasingly becoming a way of life for many poverty-stricken inhabitants. Ticos are quick to point fingers at the Nicaraguans (as well as the Panamanians and Colombians) for causing to the degradation of their capital, and although these groups are certainly part of the problem, the total picture is much more complex.

ORIENTATION

The city is in the heart of a wide and fertile valley called the Meseta Central (Central Valley). San José's center is arranged in a grid with Avenidas running east to west and Calles running north to south. Avenida Central is the nucleus of the city center and is a pedestrian mall between Calles 6 and 9. It becomes Paseo Colón to the west of Calle 14.

Street addresses are given by the nearest street intersection. Thus the address of the tourist office is Calle 5 between Avenidas Central and 2. Note that the map used in this book shows the streets and avenues However, most locals do not use street addresses and instead use landmarks to guide themselves. Learn how to decipher Tico directions by turning to the boxed text What's That Address?, p539.

The center has several districts, or *barrios,* which are all loosely defined. The central area is home to innumerable businesses, shops, bus stops and cultural sights. Perhaps the most interesting district to visitors is Barrio Amón, northeast of Avenida 5 and Calle 1, with its concentration of landmark mansions, largely converted into hotels and fine-dining establishments. Just west of the city center is La Sabana, named after the park, and just north of it is the elegant suburb of Rohrmoser. Further west again is the affluent outer suburb of Escazú. Southeast of the downtown area are the lively student areas of Los Yoses and San Pedro.

Look for maps at either Lehmann's (p91), Librería Universal (p91), or the tourist center (p92).

INFORMATION

Bookstores

English-language magazines, newspapers and books are also available in the gift shops of the international airport and several of the top-end hotels. The following bookstores are among the most noteworthy.

7th Street Books (Map p98; ☎ 256 8251; Calle 7 btwn Avs Central & 1; ⏰ 9am-6pm) An attractive shop with new and used books in English and other languages as well as magazines and newspapers.

Mora Books (Map p98; ☎ 255 4136, 383 8385; Omni Center, Av 1 btwn Calles 3 & 5) Highly recommended secondhand bookstore has books mainly in English; guidebooks and comic books are a specialty.

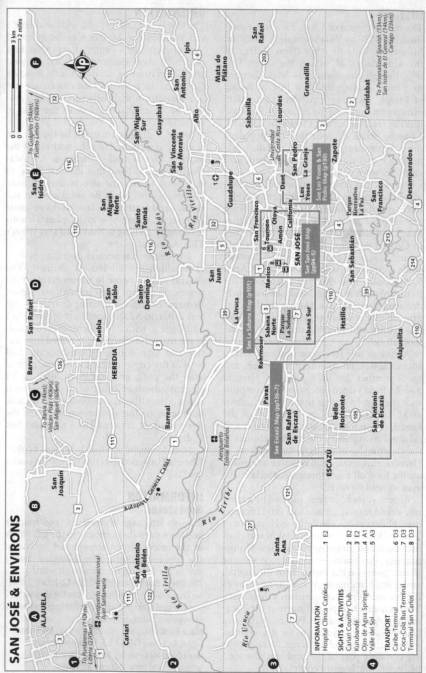

SAN JOSÉ & ENVIRONS

GETTING INTO TOWN

Taxis to downtown San José from Juan Santamaría airport will cost between US$12 and US$15 depending on traffic. When leaving the airport terminal, look for the official **Taxi Aeropuerto stand** (☎ 221 6865; www.taxiaeropuerto.com) as you exit the baggage-claim area, and pay the flat rate of US$12 in advance. The official airport taxis are orange. The ride generally lasts about 20 minutes, but may take over an hour during rush hour.

The cheapest option however is the red **Tuasa bus** (US$0.60, up to 45 minutes), which runs between Alajuela and San José, and passes the airport every few minutes from 5am to 11pm. The stop is on the far side of the parking lot outside the terminal (it's a short walk, even with luggage). Some taxi drivers will tell you there are no buses; don't believe them. The **Interbus** (☎ 283 5573; www.interbusonline.com) is a good deal and it runs an airport shuttle service that costs US$5 per person. Reservations can be made online.

International and domestic buses all arrive at one of the many bus terminals sprinkled around the west and south of downtown San José. The downtown area is perfectly walkable provided you aren't hauling a lot of luggage. If arriving at night, take a taxi to your hotel as most bus terminals are in seedy areas; a cab to any part of downtown costs US$1 to US$2.

Be aware that many taxi drivers in San José (and other parts of Costa Rica) are commissioned by hotels to bring them customers. In the capital, the hotel scene is so competitive that drivers will say just about anything to steer you to the places they represent. They'll tell you the establishment you've chosen is a notorious drug den, it's closed down, or that, sadly, it's overbooked. (Many owners will tell you wild stories about the horrible condition of the rooms at the competition down the street.) Do not believe everything you hear. Tell drivers firmly where it is you would like to go, and if you're still being met with resistance, get out of the cab and try another.

Lehmann's (Map p98; ☎ 223 1212; Av Central btwn Calles 1 & 3) It has some books, magazines and newspapers in English, and a selection of topographical and other Costa Rican maps in the upstairs map department.

Librería Francesa (Map p98; ☎ 223 7979; Av 1 btwn Calles 5 & 7) Spanish books and magazines, as well as a selection of French, German and English titles, are sold here.

Librería Universal (Map p98; ☎ 222 2222; Av Central btwn Calles Central & 1) Situated on the 2nd floor of the Universal department store, the shop has road and topographical maps, a few books in English and a small bookstore café.

Libro Azul (Map p98; Av 10 btwn Calles Central & 1; ☿ 8:30am-12:30pm & 1:30-5:30pm Mon-Fri, 9am-noon Sat) A tiny, well-known shop offering secondhand books, mostly in Spanish and some in English.

Emergency
Emergencies (☎ 911) Ambulance, fire, police.
Fire (☎ 118)
Police (☎ 117)
Red Cross (☎ 128)
Traffic Police (☎ 222 9330)

Internet Access
Checking email is easy in San José, where cybercafés are more plentiful than fruit peddlers. Rates are generally US$1 to US$2 per hour, though these days most hotels

(even budget hostels) provide free Internet to guests.

1@10 Café Internet (Map p98; ☎ 258 4561; www .1en10.com; per hr US$1; Calle 3 btwn Avs 5 & 7) Also serves as the gay and lesbian information center.

CyberCafé searchcostarica.com (Map p98; ☎ 233 3310; Las Arcadas, Av 2 btwn Calles 1 & 3; per hr US$0.75; ☿ 7am-11pm) Also houses a book exchange and a pizza and fresh-juice bar.

Laundry
Plan on dragging your dirty socks around town since a do-it-yourself laundry service is hard to find in San José. Most lavanderías offer only dry-cleaning services. Many hotels and hostels offer laundry service, but beware of top-end places that charge by the piece – this gets pricey.

Medical Services
For details of a hospital in Escazú, see p133. Note that both the Bíblica and Católica have pharmacies.

Clínica Bíblica (Map pp94-5; ☎ 257 5252; www.clinica biblica.com; Av 14 btwn Calles Central & 1) The top private clinic in the downtown area; doctors speak English, French and German; an emergency room is open 24 hours. Be prepared to pay for medical attention, though costs are generally much cheaper than in the USA or Europe.

Hospital San Juan de Dios (Map pp94-5; ☎ 257 6282; cnr Paseo Colón & Calle 14) The free public hospital is centrally located, but waits are long.

Hospital Clínica Católica (Map p90; ☎ 246 3000; www .clinicacatolica.com; Guadalupe) A private clinic located north of downtown.

Money

Any bank will change foreign currency into colones, but US dollars are by far the most accepted currency for exchange, with euros following a distant second. Upmarket hotels have exchange windows for their guests, but commissions can be steep, so check before changing large sums.

Credit cards are widely accepted in San José, though Visa tends to be preferred over MasterCard and American Express. (For more information on money issues in Costa Rica, see p538).

Banco de Costa Rica (Map p98; ☎ 221 8143; www .bancobcr.com; Av 1 btwn Calles 7 & 9; ☺ 8:30am-6pm Mon-Fri)

Banco de San José (Map p98; ☎ 295 9595; www .bancosanjose.fi.cr; Av 2 btwn Calles Central & 1; ☺ 8am-7pm Mon-Fri, 9am-1pm Sat) Has ATMs on the Plus and Cirrus systems.

Banco Nacional de Costa Rica Exchange House (Map p98; cnr Av Central & Calle 4; ☺ 10:30am-6pm) A good find in the event of a Sunday cash-exchange emergency since it's open seven days; expect long lines.

Compañía Financiera de Londres (Map p98; ☎ 222 8155; cnr Calle Central & Av Central, 3rd fl; ☺ 8:15am-4pm Mon-Fri) No commission on cash transactions and accepts US and Canadian dollars, euros and yen. Will also change traveler's checks.

Credomatic (Map p98; ☎ 295 9000; inside Banco de San José; Calle Central btwn Avs 3 & 5) Gives cash advances on Visa and MasterCard.

Scotiabank (Map p98; ☎ 287 8700; www.scotiabank .com; Av 1 btwn Calles 2 & 4; ☺ 8:15am-5pm Mon-Fri) Good service and ATMs on the Cirrus system dispense US dollars too.

Post

Correo Central (Central Post Office; Map p98; ☎ 223 9766; www.correos.go.cr; Calle 2 btwn Avs 1 & 3; ☺ 8am-5pm Mon-Fri, 7:30am-noon Sat) The most efficient place to send and receive mail in Costa Rica. It also offers express and overnight services to various parts of the world. A small stamp museum is upstairs on the 2nd floor, and there's also a pleasant café.

Telephone

Local and international calls can be made from most public phones, which are found all over town – several dozen are on the west side of Parque Central and around Plaza de la Cultura. Many hotels also have public phones in their lobbies. Chip and Colibrí cards are sold at souvenir shops, newsstands and Más X Menos supermarkets. Telephone directories are usually available in hotels. For general information on phone services, see p540.

Tourist Information

Canatur (☎ 234 6222; www.costarica.tourism.co.cr; Juan Santamaría international airport; ☺ 8am-10pm) The Costa Rican National Chamber of Tourism provides information on member services from a small stand next to the international baggage claim.

Instituto Costarricense de Turismo (ICT) (www.visit costarica.com; ☎ 223 1733, ext 277; ☺ 9am-5pm with flexible lunch Mon-Fri); Correo Central (Map p98; post office, Calle 2 btwn Avs 1 & 3); Plaza de la Cultura (Map p98; Calle 5 btwn Av Central & 2) The government tourism office is good for a copy of the master bus schedule and handy free maps of San José and Costa Rica.

Travel Agencies

The following are long-standing and reputable agencies. For a list of tour companies, see p105.

OTEC (Map p98; ☎ 256 0633; www.turismojoven.com; Calle 3 btwn Avs 1 & 3) Specializes in youth travel; can also issue student discount cards.

TAM Travel Corporation (Map p98 ☎ 256 0203; www .tamtravel.com; Calle 1 btwn Avs Central & 1) Airline ticketing, local travel and more.

DANGERS & ANNOYANCES

Street crime is on the rise in San José, and it's the principle concern of most travelers in the city. Fortunately, violent crime is still low compared to American cities, though pickpocketing is extremely common. Always carry your money and your passport in an inside pocket or a money belt and never ever leave money, passports and important documents in the outer pocket of your backpack or you will most likely regret it later. Also, it's a good idea to keep daypacks in front of you rather than on your back where they can be unzipped and pilfered.

Be advised that a common scam is getting something spilled on you and then being pickpocketed by the person who steps in to help 'clean up'.

Unfortunately, muggings are on the rise in San José. Between January 2004 and

April 2005 in Costa Rica, there were 599 reported tourist assaults, the vast majority of which occurred in San José. If any point you're held at knife or gunpoint, do not resist or fight back. Take your wallet out of your pocket slowly and calmly, and either hand it to your assailant or place it on the ground and step back. Do not try to be a hero!

Be advised that a common crime trend consists of groups of people in cars that mug pedestrians and then speed off.

The best way to prevent problems is to first find out from your hotel or other travelers about the area you are going to and if possible, to go with a friend. As a general rule, it's best to avoid wearing jewelry or watches in the city, and always walk confidently – do not stop on the street to read a map in broad sight! If you are lost, it's safer to first step into a store or restaurant and then discreetly check the map. After dark, you should always travel by taxi as they're cheap, and they'll save you plenty of aggravation. If you are bar-hopping at night, never go alone and again, always travel by taxi.

If you have been the victim of a crime, it is advised that you file a report in person at the **Organismo de Investigacíon Judicial** (Map pp94-5; ☾ 9am-5pm Mon-Fri) in the Supreme Court of Justice building.

The neighborhoods reviewed in this book are generally safe during the day, though you should be especially careful around the Coca-Cola bus terminal and the red-light district south of Parque Central, particularly at night. The following neighborhoods are reportedly dodgy during the day and unsafe at night: Leon XIII, 15 de Septiembre, Cuba, Cristo Rey, Sagrada Familia, México, Bajo Piuses, Los Cuadros, Torremolinos, Desamparados and Pavas. Be advised that like most major cities, adjacent neighborhoods can vary greatly in terms of safety. If you are going to spend time in an area of the city that you are not familiar with, always inquire locally before setting out.

It is not recommended that you drive in San José, and there is very little reason to as most car-rental agencies are located near the airport. However, if you have business in the city, never leave your car parked on the street – use guarded lots. And don't leave anything inside your car – even in a guarded lot. Most importantly, take care not to be swallowed up by the pit-sized gutters and potholes.

Women traveling alone should take extra precautions. In the past, some women have complained of being harassed by cab drivers at night – avoid taking unlicensed taxis. Also, it is not safe to walk around alone at night, and women should be advised that men in bars and clubs can get aggressive. (Further information for women travelers is available on p541.)

Men should beware of friendly prostitutes as they are known for their abilities to take more than their customers bargained for – namely their wallets. Also, AIDS is on the rise in Central America, and although the Costa Rican government is tolerant of prostitution, it's certainly not regulated (this isn't Holland) – be smart and wrap it.

Finally, noise and smog are unavoidable components of the San José experience, and most central hotels are victim to a considerable amount of street noise, no matter how nice they are.

SIGHTS

The downtown area is fairly small and is best visited on foot as the streets are congested with heavy traffic and parking is difficult. Pedestrian walkways are located on Avenida Central between Plaza de la Cultura and Calle 8, and on Blvd Ricardo Jimenez south of the Parque Nacional.

The sights here are listed in counter-clockwise fashion around the city, beginning with the contemporary art museum just east of Parque España.

LOOKING TO SCORE SOME?

Although it's a good idea to be wary of drug dealers throughout Costa Rica, it's especially important to play it smart (and safe) in San José. Buying drugs in the capital can be extremely dangerous, and generally quality is lower than you'll find in more touristy areas. However, remember that drugs are 100% illegal in Costa Rica, and you can (and most likely will) be prosecuted if caught. For more information, see the boxed text Got Drugs, Will Travel, p333.

SAN JOSÉ

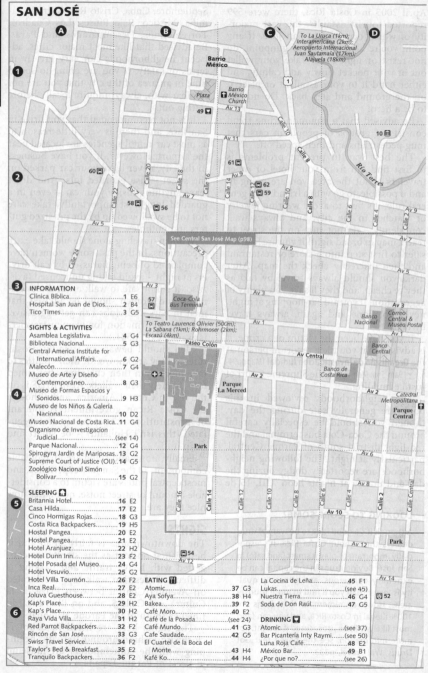

Barrio
México

Plaza

Barrio
México
Church

Av 13

49

Av 11

Calle 10

Calle 8

Río Torres

10

61

60

58

56

62

59

Calle 22

Calle 20

Calle 18

Calle 16

Calle 14

Calle 12

Calle 10

Calle 8

Calle 6

Calle 4

Calle 2

Av 7

Av 9

Av 7

Av 5

Av 5

Av 2

Av 9

See Central San José Map (p98)

Av 5

Av 3

Av 3

Av 3

Av 3

Av 1

Av 1

Av 1

57

Coca-Cola
Bus Terminal

To Teatro Laurence Olivier (500m);
La Sabana (1km); Rohrmoser (2km);
Escazú (4km)

Paseo Colón

Banco
Nacional

Correo
Central &
Museo Postal

Banco
Central

Av Central

Banco de
Costa Rica

Parque
La Merced

Av 2

Av 2

Catedral
Metropolitana

Parque
Central

Av 4

Park

Av 4

Av 6

Av 8

Av 10

Calle 16

Calle 14

Calle 12

Calle 10

Calle 8

Calle 6

Calle 4

Calle 2

Calle Central

54

Av 12

Av 12

Park

Av 14

52

To La Uruca (1km);
Interamericana (2km);
Aeropuerto Internacional
Juan Santamaría (17km);
Alajuela (18km)

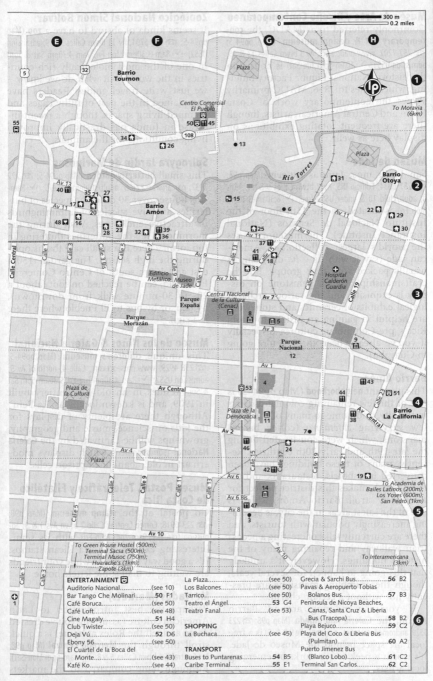

Museo de Arte y Diseño Contemporáneo

Commonly referred to as MADC, the **contemporary art & design museum** (Map pp94–5; ☎ 257 7202; www.madc.ac.cr; Av 3 btwn Calles 13 & 15; admission US$1; ⌚ 10am-5pm Tue-Sat) is housed in the historic National Liquor Factory building, which dates to 1856. MADC primarily shows the contemporary work of Costa Rican and Central American artists, though there are frequent rotating exhibitions on display here as well.

Museo de Jade

San José's most famous **museum** (Map p98; ☎ 287 6034; Edificio INS, Av 7 btwn Calles 9 & 11, 11th fl; adult/child 10 & under US$2/free; ⌚ 8:30am-3:30pm Mon-Fri) is located on the 11th floor of the Instituto Nacional de Seguros (National Insurance Institute). The museum houses the world's largest collection of American jade (say it with us – ha-day), and is usually packed with tour groups. But the craftsmanship of each gemstone on display is exquisite, and the various archaeological exhibits of ceramics and stonework are helpful in gaining an insight to Costa Rica's pre-Columbian cultures (especially if you've already been to or you're going to Guayabo).

Barrio Amón

This pleasant **neighborhood** (Map pp94–5) is one of the few remaining colonial districts in the city, and home to many of the city's few surviving cafétalero (coffee baron) mansions, which were constructed during the late-19th and early-20th centuries. Recently, many of these buildings have been converted into hotels, restaurants and offices, which makes this district perfect for a leisurely stroll. Barrio Amón, which is one of the safest areas in the city, is becoming increasingly popular with tourists, and there are currently talks of creating a pedestrian walkway and repairing many of the historic buildings. However, it's unlikely that this going to happen for several years, though the crumbling mansions are presently not without a certain charm.

If you're wandering around Barrio Amón, the **Galería Andrómeda** (Map p98; ☎ 223 3529; andromeda@amnet.co.cr; cnr Calle 9 & Av 9) is a free local art space behind the Museo de Jade. It's worth a peek to see works by emerging local artists.

Zoológico Nacional Simón Bolívar

It seems kinda of absurd to have a **zoo** (Map pp94–5; ☎ 233 6701; Av 11 btwn Calles 7 & 9; admission US$2; ⌚ 8am-3:30pm Mon-Fri, 9am-4:30pm Sat & Sun) in one of the most biologically rich countries in the world, but what do we know – we just write travel guides. Readers have complained in the past of filthy cages and cramped living spaces, though a recent increase in funds has drastically improved living conditions for the animals.

Spirogyra Jardín de Mariposas

This small **butterfly garden** (Map pp94–5; ☎ 222 2937; parcar@racsa.co.cr; adult/student US$6/5; ⌚ 8am-4pm) houses over 30 different species of butterflies and five species of hummingbirds in attractive enclosures. Visit during the morning to see the butterflies fluttering in top form. There is a small café that is open during the high season. The garden, 150m east and 150m south of Centro Comercial El Pueblo, can be reached on foot (about a 20- to 30-minute walk from downtown), by taxi, or by bus to El Pueblo where there is a sign.

Museo de los Niños & Galería Nacional

This unique **children's museum** (Map pp94–5; ☎ 258 4929; www.museocr.com; Calle 4, north of Av 9; admission US$2; ⌚ 8am-4:30pm Tue-Fri, 9:30am-5pm Sat & Sun) resides in an old penitentiary built in 1909, and is known locally as 'La Peni'. Although there are plenty of displays for the kids on science, music and geography, grown-ups will be captivated by the **Galería Nacional** (admission free), which displays modern art in old, abandoned prison cells.

Museo Postal, Telegráfico y Filatélico de Costa Rica

Go postal at the **stamp museum** (Map p98; ☎ 223 6918; Correo Central; Calle 2 btwn Avs 1 & 3; admission free; ⌚ 9am-2pm Mon-Fri) with its semi-interesting exhibit of Costa Rican stamps. It's a good way to kill time while your friends are waiting to mail some letters home.

Mercados (Markets)

Perhaps the best introduction to Latin American culture (assuming you've dressed down and left the Rolex at home) is a quick stroll through the **Mercado Central** (Map p98; Avs Central & 1 btwn Calles 6 & 8; ⌚ 6am-6pm Mon-Sat). Although tame compared to the markets of countries like Perú or Guatemala (you can't find pig's heart by the kilo here – we looked), the market is nevertheless crowded and bustling, and you can buy anything from produce and fresh sausage to organic coffee beans and the obligatory *pura vida* souvenir T-shirt. In addition, some of the cheapest fresh meals in town are served here. One block away is the similar **Mercado Borbón** (Map p98; cnr Av 3 & Calle 8), which is also jam-packed with vendors and pickpockets.

Parque Metropolitano La Sabana

This spacious **park** (Map p101) at the west end of the Paseo Colón was once the site of the country's main airport. After an impressive landscape project, it's now the most popular retreat from the grit and the grime of the city. La Sabana is also home to two museums (following), a lagoon, a fountain and a variety of sports facilities including the Estadio Nacional (National Stadium), where international and Division-1 soccer matches are played. During the daytime, it's a great place for a daytime stroll, a quiet picnic or a relaxed jog. During the night-time, it's a great place for getting mugged.

At the west end of Paseo Colón (or the eastern entrance to the park) is the **Museo de Arte Costarricense** (Map p101; ☎ 222 7155; www .musarco.go.cr; Parque La Sabana; admission US$1, Sun free; ✆ 10am-4pm Tue-Sun), which houses a permanent collection of Costa Rican art from the 19th and 20th centuries. The museum itself is an attractive Spanish colonial-style building that served as San José's airport until 1955, and is situated next to an impressive open-air sculpture garden. Regular rotating exhibits feature works by Tico artists past and present.

Near the southwest corner of the park is the **Museo de Ciencias Naturales La Salle** (Map p101; ☎ 232 1306; admission US$2; ✆ 7:30am-4pm), which has an extensive collection of dusty and dated stuffed animals and butterflies. The exhibit has definitely seen better days, and although some of the animals look like they're about to fall apart, you'd be hard pressed to find a more bizarre display of taxidermy. There are also a number of exhibits on paleontology and Pre-Columbian archaeology. It's in the old Colegio La Salle (high school).

Parque Central

The city's central **park** (Map p98; Avs 2 & 4 btwn Calles Central & 2) is home to a strange installation art, which was donated to the city by former Nicaraguan dictator Anastasio Somoza. It's a bit of a controversial piece actually, though josefinos voted several years ago to keep it because, well, what else were they going to do with it?

To the east of the square is the modern though classically inspired **Catedral Metropolitana** (Map p98; Avs 2 & 4 btwn Calles Central & 1), which is among the more popular cathedrals in the city for Sunday mass.

On the north side of the park is **Teatro Melico Salazar** (Map p98; Av 2 btwn Calle Central & 2), which was built with the intention of serving as the poor man's alternative to the Teatro Nacional (following). However, it was the sight of the 2002 presidential inauguration, and regularly hosts a variety of fine arts engagements and musical performances (p121).

Plaza de la Cultura

Though it's not particularly striking, virtually every Tico refers to the **Culture Plaza** (Map p98; Avs Central & 2 btwn Calles 3 & 5) as the geographic heart of Costa Rica. Coincidentally, it's also the safest place in the city as the entire plaza is the ceiling of the **Museo de Oro Precolombino**, and is considered private property (this gives security guards the right to shoo out away 'unsavory' characters). It's also home to the Teatro Nacional, and there is great birding here – feral pigeons are commonly sighted.

The plaza is also home to the only *real* **tourist information center** in the city, p89.

MUSEO DE ORO PRECOLOMBINO Y NUMISMÁTICA

Beneath the Plaza de la Cultura is this three-in-one **museum** (Map p98; ☎ 243 4202; www.museos delbancocentral.org; basement, Plaza de la Cultura; admission US$5; ✆ 10am-4:30pm Tue-Sun), owned by the Banco Central and its architecture brings to mind all the warmth and comfort of a bank vault. The museum is a favorite of tourists as the glittering collection of pre-Columbian gold is well presented, though smaller than similar collections in Mexico and Peru. A small exhibit details the history of Costa Rican currency and another room houses a temporary display space for local art.

SAN JOSÉ

CENTRAL SAN JOSÉ

TEATRO NACIONAL

The **national theater** (Map p98; ☎ 221 1329; Calles 3 & 5 btw Avs Central & 2; admission US$3; ⏰ 9am-5pm Mon-Fri, 9am-12:30pm & 1:30-5:30pm Sat) is considered San José's most impressive public building. Built in 1897, the building features a columned neoclassical facade and is flanked by statues of Beethoven and Calderón de la Barca, a 17th-century Spanish dramatist. The lavish lobby and auditorium are lined with paintings depicting various facets of 19th-century life. The most famous is *Alegoría al café y el banano*, an idyllic canvas showing coffee and banana harvests. The painting was produced in Italy and shipped to Costa Rica for installation in the theater and the image was reproduced on the five-colón note (now out of circulation), which you can find in some souvenir shops. However, it is clear that the painter never witnessed a banana harvest because of the way he portrayed a central man awkwardly grasping a bunch. In case you're wondering, actual banana workers hoist the stem onto their shoulders.

For information on viewing a performance, see p121.

There is also an excellent café (p118) here.

Belonging to the national theatre is the very worthwhile **Galería García Monge** (Map p98;

cnr Av 2 & Calle 5; admission free), which is located across the street and has rotating exhibits by contemporary artists.

Museo Para la Paz

The **Peace Museum** (Map pp94-5; ☎ 223 4664; cnr Av 2 & Calle 13; admission free; ☒ 8am-noon & 1:30pm-4:30pm Mon-Fri) is operated by the Arias Foundation, and catalogs Nobel Peace Prize laureate and President Oscar Arias's past efforts to bring peace to Central America. It also exhibits the work of other laureates including the Dalai Lama, Jimmy Carter and Lech Walesa. At the time of writing the Peace Museum had just opened and was still in the process of defining individual exhibits, though there were ambitious plans on display that detailed future expansion.

Museo Nacional de Costa Rica

The **National Museum** is located inside the Bellavista (Good View) Fortress (Map pp94-5; ☎ 257 1433; Calle 17 btwn Avs Central & 2; adult/student US$4/2; ☒ 8:30am-4:30pm Tue-Sun), which served as the old army headquarters and saw fierce fighting (hence the pockmarks) in both the 1931 army mutiny and the 1948 civil war. Ironically, Bellavista was also the site where Costa Rican President José Figueres announced in 1949 that he was abolishing the country's military.

The museum itself is ideal for getting a quick survey of Costa Rican history. You'll find a wide range of pre-Columbian artifacts from ongoing digs at archeological sites such as Guayabo, as well as numerous colonial objects and plenty of religious art. There is also a natural-history wing that has flora and fauna specimens, minerals and fossils.

Museo de Formas, Espacios y Sonidos

This **interactive museum** (Map pp94-5; ☎ 222 9462; Av 3 btwn Calles 17 & 23; admission US$1; ☒ 9:30am-3pm Mon-Fri) is geared to small kids or people who like to act like them. Housed in the old San José Atlantic train station, you can clamber on an antique locomotive and traipse through old rail cars. There are also several small exhibits dedicated to the senses of sound, touch and sight.

A curious sight is the bust outside the museum of Tomás Guardia, who has the curious distinction of constructing the first railroad, and of being one of the only dictators in Costa Rican history.

Eastern Parks & Plazas

Numerous other green areas dot downtown San José, providing a small respite from the steel and concrete of the capital. Note that these parks are not safe after dark, and most of them become centers of prostitution during the twilight hours.

One of the nicest parks in San José is the shady, cobblestone-lined **Parque Nacional** (Map pp94-5; Avs 1 & 3 btwn Calles 15 & 19). In the center of the park is the dramatic **Monumento Nacional**, which depicts the Central American nations (with Costa Rica in the lead of course) driving out the American filibuster William Walker.

Important buildings surrounding the park include the **Biblioteca Nacional** (National Library) to the north, the Cenac complex, which houses the modern art museum (p96) to the northwest and the **Asamblea Legislativa** (Legislative Assembly) to the south. In the Assembly's gardens is a statue of national hero Juan Santamaría, who's best know for kicking out a certain pesky gringo out of Costa Rica.

South of the Asamblea Legislativa is the stark **Plaza de la Democracia** (Map p98; Avs Central & 2 btwn Calles 13 & 15), which was constructed by President Oscar Arias in 1989 to commemorate 100 years of Costa Rican democracy. The plaza itself is architecturally unremarkable, though it does provide decent views of the mountains surrounding San José (especially at sunset). On its western flank, you'll find an open-air crafts market that has a good selection of gifts (see p122).

Parque España (Map p98; Avs 3 & 7 btwn Calles 9 & 11) is surrounded by heavy traffic, but manages to become a riot of birdsong every day at sunset when the local avians come here to roost. The park is bordered by the black-glass INS building to the north, which serves as the home of the Museo de Jade (p96). A block to the west is the **edificio metálico** (Map p98; cnr Av 7 & Calle 9) an interesting two-story yellow-and-blue metal building that was designed in France and prefabricated in Belgium. During the 1890s, the entire structure was shipped piece by piece to the city of San José. Today, it functions as an elite school.

To the northeast of Parque España is the **Casa Amarilla** (Map p98; Av 7 btwn Calles 11 & 13), an elegant colonial house that is home to the ministry of foreign affairs (and is closed to the public). The glorious ceiba tree in front of the building was planted by John F Kennedy during his 1963 visit to Costa Rica.

To the southwest, you'll come across the slightly rundown **Parque Morazán** (Map p98; Avs 3 & 5 btwn Calles 5 & 9), which happens to be the most notorious prostitution center in the country. Tragically (or perhaps fittingly), the concrete gazebo in the center of park is commonly referred to as the **Templo de Música** (Music Temple), and is regarded by many as the symbol of San José. The park is named after General Francisco Morazán, who failed to unite the newly independent Central American countries under one flag in the 1830s.

ACTIVITIES

Parque Metropolitano La Sabana (Map p101) has a variety of sporting facilities including tennis courts, volleyball, basketball and baseball areas, jogging paths and soccer pitches – pick-up soccer games can be had on most days, though you'd better be good (Ticos can already sink a drop shot by age seven).

There is also an Olympic-sized **swimming pool** (admission US$3; ☉ noon-2pm), though most Ticos prefer the excursion to the Ojo de Agua springs (in San Antonio de Belén, see p143), where swimming is available all day.

Tennis, gym facilities and a swimming pool are also available at the **Costa Rica Tennis Club** (☎ 232 1266) on the south side of La Sabana for US$10 per person per day. There

LA SABANA

0 — 500 m
0 — 0.3 miles

INFORMATION	
Banco de Costa Rica	1 C3
Spanish Embassy	2 C3

SIGHTS & ACTIVITIES	
Centro Linguistico Conversa	3 C3
Museo de Arte Costarricense	4 C3
Museo de Ciencias Naturales La Salle	5 A3

SLEEPING	
Galileo Hostel	6 C3
Gaudy's	7 C2
Hostel La Mariposa Azul	8 C3
Hotel Cacts	9 D2
Hotel Grano de Oro	10 D3
Hotel Occidental Torremolinos	11 C2

Hotel Petite Victoria	12 D3
JC & Friends	13 C3
Meliá Tryp Corobici	14 C2
Mi Casa Hostel	15 B2
Ritmo del Caribe	16 C3
Rosa del Paseo	17 D3

EATING	
Arirang	(see 1)
El Chicote	18 A2
Fuji	(see 14)
La Piazzetta	19 C3
Lubnán	20 D3
Machu Picchu	21 C3
Marisquería Sabor a Oceano	22 C3
Restaurant Grano de Oro	(see 10)

Restaurant y Galeria La Bastille	23 D3
Restaurante Pacifico	24 C3
Soda Tapia	25 C3

ENTERTAINMENT	
Estadio Nacional	26 A3
Sala Garbo	27 D3

TRANSPORT	
Alitalia	28 D3
American Airlines	29 C2
Buses to San Isidro de El General	30 D3
Delta Airlines	31 C3
Iberia Airlines	32 C3
Japan Airlines	33 C3
SAM/Avianca	(see 32)

To Interamericana (2km);
Aeropuerto Internacional Juan
Santamaria (15km);
Alajuela (16km)

Autopista
General Canas

To Kalexma
Inn (1.6km)

Americas

Rincon
de Cubillos

To Colours Oasis
Resort (200m)

ICE
Building

Ave 7

Ave Las Américas

Parque Metropolitano
La Sabana

Centro
Colón

Ave 5

Ave 3

Monumento
Leon Cortes

Ave 1

Paseo Colón

To Central
San José
(1km)

Pool

Ave 2

Ave 4

Ave 6

Ave 10

Ave 8

Las Vegas

San Martin

Perpetuo
Socorro

Ave Campos

Sabana Sur

Bolivar

are 11 indoor and outdoor courts, three pools, a sauna and gym facilities.

You can sign up with a local gym for about US$20 to US$40 a month. Look under 'Gimnasios' in the yellow pages telephone directory. Or go a couple rounds with the locals at the **Thaiboxing Center** (Map p130; ☎ 225 7386) or **Atemi Ryu Martial Arts Center** (Map p130; ☎ 524 0781) in San Pedro.

Golfers can lose their golf balls (and their patience) at either the **Cariari Country Club** (Map p90; ☎ 293 3211; cariari@racsa.co.cr), the **Costa Rica Country Club** (Map pp136-7; ☎ 228 9333, 208 5000) or **Valle del Sol** (Map p90; ☎ 282 9222, ext 218/219).

Adrenaline junkies can sign up for the daily bungee jumps at the nearby Río Colorado Bridge in Grecia with **Tropical Bungee** (☎ 248 2212, 383 9724; www.bungee.co.cr; 1st/2nd jump US$60/30). Transportation from San José included.

WALKING TOUR

OK, so now that you've taken off the jewelry, studied the map, buried a bit of extra cash in your sock and called your mom to tell her you love her, are you ready to see what the big, bad city is all about? San José may not have colonial promenades

Start	Plaza de la Cultura
Finish	Mercado Central
Distance	2km
Duration	30 minutes

and towering skyscrapers, but it sure oozes character (in a slightly seedy, film-noir sort of way). The following walking tour is recommended for anyone who wants to learn about all the things that the tourist information center *won't* tell you.

Starting in the **Plaza de la Cultura** (**1**; p97), cross the street and head north for two blocks until you reach the **Parque Morazón** (**2**; p101). Sure, it's attractive enough during the day, but if you came here at night (which you shouldn't), you'd soon realize that the park also serves as an office for San José's sex workers (p112). Sure, they're beautiful, but moral deviance aside, keep in mind that some of these women are under 18, and some of these women aren't, well, women.

Before leaving the park, look towards the towering steel and glass building to the northeast. Most tourists know this building as the **Museo de Jade** (**3**; p96), but the 10 stories underneath the museum are home to the Instituto Nacional Seguros (National Insurance Institute), which is the government-owned insurance monopoly. Why should I care, you ask? Well, in case you were wondering why car rental is so expensive in Costa Rica, look no further. Curse silently under your breath. Now turn around.

The reasonably attractive pink building you're now staring at is the **Key Largo** (**4**), which is mentioned here solely because some regard a visit to this club as a part of the country's wildlife experience. Ageing anglers and their slinky young Latina

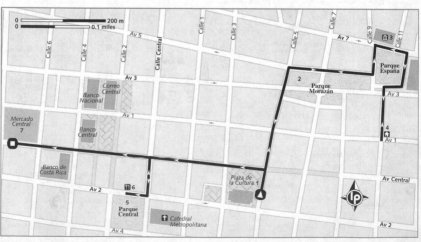

escorts are the most commonly sighted species. Attached to this fine establishment is the **Hotel Del Rey**, a top-end hotel that's popular with ageing anglers and their suspiciously absent wives.

Are you having fun yet? If so, let's backtrack to the Plaza de la Cultura and then walk west along the pedestrian boulevard for three blocks. When you get to the intersection, turn left and walk south for two blocks where you'll find the **Parque Central** (5; p97). Aside from the unlikely tribute to General Samoza, the famous Nicaraguan humanitarian whose charitable work was supported by the US government, take a moment to look at the **Food Mall (6)** on the north side of the plaza. Although this shrine of fast-food consumerism is packed on weekends with Tico families, it was once the Palace Theater, a famous art house and performance space – if you can find a more perfect symbol of globalization, let us know!

Backtrack one more time to the boulevard, and continue to head west for three more blocks where you'll see the **Mercado Central** (7; p96), the number-one place in San José for getting robbed. Every day, doe-eyed tourists armed with Nikon cameras and heavily armored wallets are vanquished by mere 'snatch-and-run' guerilla warfare. But you were smart enough to leave all your valuables at home, so jump headfirst into the consumer chaos and see if you get a good bargain on a Costa Rica snowglobe. Happy shopping!

COURSES
Dancing
If you want to improve your moves on the dancefloor, then check out one of the many classes offered in the San José area. These are geared at Ticos, not tourists, but travelers who speak Spanish are welcome. You can learn all types of Latin dancing – salsa, cha-cha, merengue, bolero, tango. Classes cost around US$20 for two hours of group lessons per week. Travelers can also find dance classes by inquiring at many language schools.

Academia de Bailes Latinos (Map pp94-5; ☎ 233 8938; Av Central btwn Calles 25 & 27) Next to Pizza Hut in Barrio Escalante.
Malecón (Map pp94-5; ☎ 222 3214; Av 2 btwn Calles 17 & 19)
Merecumbé (Map p130; ☎ 228 6253; Escazú)
Kurubandé (Map p90; ☎ 234 0682; Guadalupe)

SAN JOSÉ FOR CHILDREN
Most children will probably want to get out of San José as fast as possible – if you think the city is a little rough around the edges, imagine how they feel. But if you're spending a day – or two or three – in San José there are a number of activities to keep the tykes busy and/or exhausted.

The **Museo de los Niños** (p96) and the **Museo de Formas, Espacios y Sonidos** (p100) are a hit with young children who just can't keep their hands off the exhibits. Interactive is what they're all about.

Both **Teatro Eugene O'Neill** (p122) and **Teatro Fanal** (p121) have children's theater groups. If your child is learning Spanish, this experience might make a vivid lesson.

Young nature lovers will enjoy getting up close and personal with butterflies at the **Spirogyra Jardín de Mariposas** (p96) or checking out all of the exotic animals over at the **Zoológico Nacional Simón Bolívar** (p96).

Teens might dig checking each other out at the **Plaza de la Cultura** (p97), which has a number of nearby fast-food outlets and ice-cream shops. In the suburbs, **Mall San Pedro** (p132) and **Escazú Multiplaza** (p139) are good for young consumers craving mall action.

To wear them out with a day of outdoor activities, there are always the swimming pools at the **Costa Rica Tennis Club** (p101), which are open to the public. For more extensive water-based activities, head northwest of San José for **Ojo de Agua** (p143).

If you're planning on spending more than a week in the city with your lovable offspring, most Spanish schools (p104) offer special custom-tailored lessons for young *chicos y chicas* (boys and girls).

QUIRKY SAN JOSÉ
Every Sunday, the **Tico Train** (adult/child US$2/1) picks up riders from the eastern side of the Plaza de la Cultura (p97) and takes them on a 45-minute joyride through the city. The train itself looks like it was stolen from a county carnival somewhere in Iowa, though the *cumbia* music (traditional provincial ballads) emanating from the train is about as Costa Rican as it gets. The Tico Train was started by the city council in an effort to inject more life and personality into the city center, and is intended to recall the days when josefinos traveled through their capital on trains. Even if you're not nostalgic for

TALK LIKE A TICO

There are fine Spanish-language schools in the San José area. The schools listed have been operating since at least 1998 and/or they have received reader recommendations. Most of the reviewed language schools also organize volunteer placements, which is a great way to learn Spanish while giving back to those who need it most.

Unless otherwise noted, prices are given for five four-hour days of instruction, with/without a week's homestay with a local family. All prices include breakfast and dinner. Note that program fees are usually less if you study for an extended period of time.

Academia Latinoamericana de Español (☎ 224 9917; www.alespanish.com; Av 8 btwn Calles 31 & 33, San Pedro; courses with/without homestay US$290/135) This highly professional institute caters to groups of less than six students, and is staffed with linguists and philologists.

Amerispan Unlimited (☎ in the USA & Canada 800-879 6640; www.amerispan.com; courses with/without homestay US$570/430) Offers a variety of educational travel programs including language programs, volunteer/Internship placements, academic study abroad and specialized programs such as Salud, a medical Spanish program.

Central America Institute for International Affairs (ICAI; ☎ 233 8571; www.educaturs.com; courses with/without homestay US$450/300) This institute has been teaching the Spanish language for over 20 years, and offers substantially cheaper rates for longer courses of study. Find it 100m west, 25m north then 25m west from the emergency room entrance of Hospital Calderón Guardia.

Centro Lingüístico Conversa (Map p101; ☎ 221 7649, in the USA 800-367 7726, in the Caribbean 880-354 5036; www.conversa.net; Centro Colón, cnr Calle 38 & Paseo Colón; courses US$500) Students have the option of living on the school's private campus for US$125 to US$220 per week, depending on occupancy.

Costa Rican Language Academy (Map p130; ☎ 280 1685, in the USA 866-230 6361; www.learn-spanish .com; courses with/without homestay US$411/286) This organization also offers cooking classes, Latin dance lessons and can provide you with enrollment information for a variety of volunteer programs. From the Subaru dealership, go 300m north and 50m west.

Forester Instituto Internacional (Map p130; ☎ 225 3155, 225 1649, 225 0135; www.fores.com; Los Yoses; courses with/without homestay US$650/520) This professional institute in suburban Lose Yoses also arranges cultural excursions and offers free Latin dance classes. It's 75m south of the Automercado.

Institute for Central American Development Studies (Icads; ☎ 225 0508; www.icadscr.com) This school offers month long programs (with/without homestay US$2100/1700) that are combined with lectures and activities focused on environmental and regional sociopolitical issues. It can also help place you in a variety of local volunteer positions depending on your interests. It's off the main road to Curridabat about 1km from the center of town.

Instituto Británico (Map p130; ☎ 225 0256; www.institutobritanico.co.cr; Los Yoses; courses with/without homestay US$305/180) This institute offers a high level of Spanish-language education that's also suited for teacher training and corporate instruction. Find it 75m south of the Subaru dealership.

Instituto Latinoamericano de Idiomas (ILDI; Map p130; ☎ 280 0700, in the USA 800-454 7248; www .ilisa.com; with homestay US$570-1230) Though pricey, this San Pedro school is customized for professional businesspeople and includes curricula such as 'Spanish for CEOs' and less exclusive management titles. Cultural outings and cooking classes are part of the deal. Go 100m east, 400m south, 50m east from the San Pedro church.

Instituto Universal de Idiomas (Map p98; ☎ 223 9662; www.universal-edu.com; Av 2 btwn Calles 7 & 9, 2nd fl; courses with/without homestay US$318/178) This institute offers a wide range of programs ranging from 'survivial Spanish courses' to business and medical Spanish courses.

Intensa (☎ 281 1818, in the USA & Canada 866-277 1352; www.intensa.com; Calle 33 btwn Avs 1 & 3, San Pedro; courses with/without homestay US$428/303) This language school blends intensive courses with a variety of cultural distractions including field trips to national parks and beaches.

Personalized Spanish (Map p90; ☎ 278 3254; www.personalizedspanish.com; Tres Rios; courses with/without homestay US$383/488) This institute comes highly recommended by readers, and is located in a beautiful suburb of the capital.

Universidad Veritas (☎ 283 4747; www.uveritas.ac.cr; Edificio ITAN, Carretera a Zapote, 1-month courses with/without homestay US$1145/620) This Costa Rican university is dedicated to art, architecture and design, though they host have some exceptional study-abroad programs. Go 1km west of Casa Presidencial.

the good old days, the train ride itself is a total riot, especially when the driver overtakes cars while ringing an oversized bell.

TOURS

The city is easily navigable by the independent traveler and walking tours aren't necessary if you have a little time on your hands. If you have just a few hours and don't want to miss the key sights, Swiss Travel Service offers a recommended three-hour tour that covers the San José basics.

Calypso Tours (☎ 256 2727; www.calypsotours.com) Does tours to the islands near Bahía Gigante by bus and 70ft motorized catamaran.

Costa Rica Art Tour (☎ 288 0896, 359 5571; www .costaricaarttour.com; tours US$95) If you're an art-lover, this reader-recommended day tour goes to five different studios in the city, some of which are located in the houses of the artists. Routes through the city change daily, so no two tours are ever the same. The tour emphasizes painting, sculpting, printmaking, ceramics, jewelry-making and mixed media, and there are plenty of opportunities to purchase original art direct from the artist. Lunch and hotel pick-up is included in the price. Group, senior and student discounts are available.

Lava Tours (☎ 281 2458; www.lava-tours.com) Organizes a number of tours including reader-recommended mountain-biking tours around the Central Valley.

Swiss Travel Service (Map pp94–5; ☎ 221 0944) Longtime, reputable travel agency for tours all over Costa Rica. Find it 250m west of Centro Comercial El Pueblo; there is a branch office at the Radisson Europa.

Tiquicia Travel (☎ 256 9682; www.tiquiciatravel.com; Condominios Pie Montel, La Uruca) A small agency focusing on tours to gay and gay-friendly locales around Costa Rica.

FESTIVALS & EVENTS

Festival de Arte Every even year, San José becomes host to the biennial citywide arts showcase featuring theater, music, dance and film. It is held for two weeks in March. Keep an eye out for information in the daily newspapers.

Día de San José On March 19, San José marks the day for its patron saint with masses in some churches. The day used to be a holiday, but modernization has quickly done away with that.

Festival de las Carretas (Ox-cart Festival) Takes place every November, and is a celebration of the country's agricultural heritage. The highlight is a parade of ox-carts down Paseo Colón.

Festival de Luz (Festival of Light) A month later on Paseo Colón is the a Christmas parade, marked by an absurd amount of plastic 'snow.'

Las Fiestas de Zapote, If you're in the San José area between Christmas and New Year's Eve, you absolutely have to visit this weeklong holiday celebration of all things Costa Rican (namely rodeos, cowboys, carnival rides, fried food and a whole lot of drinking). The celebration, which annually draws in tens of thousands of Ticos, takes place in the suburb of Zapote, just southeast of the city.

SLEEPING

Accommodations in San José run the gamut from grim little boxes to sumptuous world-class luxury. The cheapest hotels in the city are located near the Coca-Cola bus terminal. However, this neighborhood is growing increasingly dangerous for travelers, and unless you're a diehard fan of grunge, bustle and crime, it's recommended that you stay elsewhere.

If you want to spend the night in San José proper, the two nicest areas to stay are in Barrio Amón and La Sabana. Midrange and top-end accommodations tend to cluster in these well-to-do neighborhoods, though they are also home to the city's top budget hostels. There are also a number of good choices in central San José.

If you're looking for a quieter, more relaxed stay, consider spending the night in the city's wealthiest suburbs, namely Los Yoses and San Pedro and Escazú. Both neighborhoods are located a few kilometers outside the city center, and can be easily reached by public bus or taxi.

If you're either flying into or out of Costa Rica, it's actually more convenient to stay in Alajuela as the city (contrary to what cab drivers will tell you) is actually closer than San José to the airport.

There are also several options for lodging in the suburb of Cariari, which is easy for getting to the airport (though a bit hard on the wallet).

Reservations are recommended during the high season (December through April) and the two weeks around Christmas and Semana Santa (the week before Easter Sunday). For more general information on hotels in Costa Rica, see p525. High-season prices are listed throughout.

Before reserving with a credit card, see p527 for advice.

Barrio Amón & Around

BUDGET

Red Parrot Backpackers (Map pp94–5; ☎ 256 1215; www.redparrotbackpackers.com; Calle 7 btwn Avs 9 & 11; dm/d US$7/16; 🖳) The owners of this sterile and boring hostel are definitely shrewd businessmen – open up a hostel across the street from one of the most popular places in the city (see below), charge a dollar less and people will show up. Rooms with shared bathrooms are OK, though the fluorescent-light ambience leaves a lot to be desired.

Tranquilo Backpackers (Map pp94-5; ☎ 223 3189, 222 2493, 355 5103; www.tranquilobackpackers.com; Calle 7 btwn Avs 9 & 11; dm US$8, s/d small room US$11/13, s/d large room US$19/22, all incl breakfast; ☑) Located in an old mansion in Barrio Amón, Tranquilo is one of the top reader-recommended hostels in the city, and radiates mellow vibes and relaxing times. Big common rooms are decorated with hanging Japanese lanterns, bright murals, ample hammocks and enough mounted guitars to satisfy all your

impromptu needs. There are also whimsically decorated mosaic-tile shared showers and a communal kitchens, as well as free luggage storage, Internet access and the famous (and universally loved) pancake breakfast. Airport transfer can be arranged.

Costa Rica Backpackers (Map pp94-5; ☎ 221 6191; www.costaricabackpackers.com; Av 6 btwn Calles 21 & 23; dm US$9, d US$22; ⓟ ☑ ☎) Located near the Supreme Court Building, this perennial reader favorite is located in a sprawling complex that's centered on a beautiful freeform pool surrounded by hammock-strung gardens. Chill-out music completes the laid-back ambience, though you can always take things up a notch in the attached bar-restaurant, which also doubles certain evenings as a movie theater. Rooms

---

THE AUTHOR'S CHOICE

Budget

Hostel Pangea (Map p98; ☎ 221 1992; www.hostelpangea.com; cnr Av 13 & Calle 3 bis, Av 11 btwn Calles 3 & 3 bis, Av 7 btwn Calles 3 & 3 bis; dm US$10, r per person with/without bathroom US$14/12; ⓟ ☒ ☑ ☎) Run by a pair of animated Tico twin brothers, this backpackers paradise is located in three nearby buildings in Barrio Amón, each of which is covered in vibrant murals, and features dormitory and private rooms with hot showers and orthopedic mattresses. The two smaller buildings are perfect if you want a chilled-out atmosphere, though revelers and partiers go ga-ga over the newest building, which has a solar-heated freeform pool with swim-up bar, a rooftop bar-restaurant that has some of the best views in the city, and (are you ready for this one?) a mechanical bull. Seriously. Other perks include free Internet (and wi-fi), free phone calls to North America, free luggage storage, free lockers, airport pick-up (US$14) and a fully bilingual staff.

Midrange

Kap's Place (Map pp94-5; ☎ 221 1169; www.kapsplace.com; Calle 19 btwn Avs 11 & 13, Av 11 btwn Calle 19 & 21; s US$22-38, d US$24-48, tr US$36-58, 2-/3-/4-/5-person apt US$90/100/110/120; ⓟ ☑) 'Knowledge, Accommodation and Personalized Service' are on offer at owner Karla Arias' meticulously maintained and delightfully original guesthouse, which offers rooms of varying prices and sizes in two nearby sprawling buildings. Every inch of this hotel has been adorned with an artist's touch, from the incredible mosaic mural floors to the kaleidoscope of colors that washes across the walls and ceilings. There are even Indian sarongs on all the beds, fish lights in the bathrooms and a gurgling, cactus-laden fountain in the center of the house. Guests share a kitchen with free tea (15 choices!) and coffee, and there's free Internet. Spanish, English and French spoken.

Top End

Hotel Grano de Oro (Map p101; ☎ 255 3322; www.hotelgranodeoro.com; Calle 30 btwn Avs 2 & 4; s US$94, d standard/superior/deluxe US$95/115/130, ste US$150-260; ⓟ ☒) This early-20th-century mansion is located on a quiet sidestreet from Paseo Colón, and belongs to the group of 'Small Distinctive Hotels of Costa Rica.' The design scheme here is 'Tropical Victorian,' which blends traditional stylistic elements such as dark colors and wrought-iron fixtures with locally crafted furniture and original artwork from prominent Costa Rican painters. Private bathrooms sparkle with blue and white Italian tiles adorned with gleaming base fixtures. No two rooms are alike. There is also a top-notch restaurant here that's highly recommended (p117). Credit cards accepted.

and shared bathrooms are well decorated with tropical-themed murals, and there's two communal kitchens and a TV lounge, as well as free luggage storage and Internet access. Airport transfer can be arranged.

Casa Ridgway (Map p98; ☎ 233 6168; www.ami gosparalapaz.org; casaridgway@yahoo.es; cnr Calle 15 & Av 6 bis; dm US$10, s/d US$12/24; ✗) This welcoming guesthouse, on a quiet side street near the Supreme Court building, is run by the adjacent Friends' Peace Center, which promotes peace, social justice and collaboration between peoples. Rooms are immaculate, the shared showers are hot, the communal kitchen is spotless and the atmosphere is, well, peaceful. A lending library offers an extensive collection of books on Central American politics and society. This isn't the place for party people – there's no smoking, alcohol or drugs allowed and quiet hours are from 10pm to 6am.

Casa Hilda (Map pp94-5; ☎ 221 0037; c1hilda@ racsa.co.cr; Av 11 btwn Calles 3 & 3 bis; s/d incl breakfast US$26/36) The Quesadas will make you feel like you're returning home at this peaceful, peach-colored inn in Barrio Amón. Rooms with private hot-water bathrooms are very simple, but the entire property is glows with domestic warmth – this is an excellent choice if you want to spend some time with a real Costa Rican family. Check out the natural spring in the center of the house that has been bubbling potable water for 90 years (even during the dry season).

Hotel Aranjuez (Map pp94-5; ☎ 256 1825; www .hotelaranjuez.com; Calle 19 btwn Avs 11 & 13; s with/without bathroom US$28/22, d with/without bathroom US$38/25, all incl breakfast; P 🖳) This rambling wooden hotel consists of several nicely maintained vintage homes strung together with connecting gardens and a lush backyard containing a mango tree. Spotless rooms vary in size and price and the hosts serve a sumptuous daily breakfast buffet in the garden courtyard.

MIDRANGE
All of the hotels listed have private hot-water showers and cable TV unless otherwise stated, and can arrange tours throughout the country.

Cinco Hormigas Rojas (Map pp94-5; ☎ 257 8581, 255 3412; www.cincohormigasrojas.com; Calle 15 btwn Av 9 & 11; r US$30-58; ✗) This highly recommended traveler's refuge and artistic retreat is run

by the multilingual and insanely talented Mayra, a Tica artist and naturalist who's nurtured the grounds of her small guesthouse for over 10 years. Today, 'Five Red Ants' is a micro-ecosystem that's teeming with tropical birds, and indeed it's easy to forget that you're staying in San José. The guesthouse itself has three rooms of varying sizes and amenities (if you need TV in your life, this is not the place for you), each of which is uniquely themed and displays her incredible artwork. Mayra's specialty is covering household objects in *papier-mâché*, and then sculpting and painting them into intricate designs – their originality and beauty is impossible to describe. Art is available for purchase, and every traveler leaves after breakfast with a small gift in hand.

Joluva Guesthouse (Map pp94-5; ☎ 223 7961; www.joluva.com; Calle 3 bis btwn Avs 9 & 11; s/d US$36/50; 🖳) This quaint gay-operated guesthouse in Barrio Amón has seven small but well-appointed rooms (check out the massage heads on the showers) that are scattered around a number of cozy public areas. The management speaks English and can provide information on the Costa Rican gay scene.

Inca Real (Map pp94-5; ☎ 222 5318; www.gruporeal internacional.com/hotelincareal; Av 11 btwn Calles 3 & 5; s/d standard US$39/49; P ✗ 🖳) This Ecuadorian-run hotel has modern rooms with air-con that feature a heavy dose of Incan-inspired artwork – you may find yourself planning your next trip before you even finish the one you're on.

Hotel Vesuvio (Map pp94-5; ☎ 221 8325, 256 1616; www.hotelvesuvio.com; Av 11 btwn Calles 13 & 15; s/d/tr US$40/50/60, deluxe US$70, all incl breakfast; P 🖳) This family-owned hotel is on a quiet street in Barrio Otoya, and has 20 carpeted rooms (deluxe rooms have a bathtub) arranged along a corridor. Rooms are fairly standard, though the owners are welcoming and very accommodating. An onsite restaurant (dishes US$4 to US$7) prepares tasty Italian fare.

Taylor's Bed & Breakfast (☎ 257 4333; taylorsinn@ catours.co.cr; Av 13 btwn Calles 3 & 3 bis; s/d incl breakfast US$40/58; P ✗ 🖳) This attractive brick mansion in Barrio Amón has elegant rooms with lofty ceilings and attractive wood accents. Hot breakfasts are served in the interior courtyard, which has a bubbling goldfish pond that's backed with a vine-laden stone wall.

Rincón de San José (Map pp94-5; ☎ 221 9702; www.hotelrincondesanjose.com; Av 9 btwn Calle 13 & 15; s/d/tr incl breakfast US$44/55/66; 💻) This charming little hotel in a landmark colonial house in Barrio Amón is beautifully maintained and furnished with period pieces. Large rooms with polished-wood or ceramic-tile floors surround an attractive courtyard. Breakfast is served in an attractive garden courtyard and a small bar is open until 10pm. Credit cards accepted.

Hotel Posada del Museo (Map pp94-5; ☎ 258 1027; www.hotelposadadelmuseo.com; s/d standard US$45/ 50, superior US$55/60, ste US$65/75) This *posada* (country-style inn) is diagonal from the Museo Nacional, located on a pedestrian street in a beautiful district of the capital. The building dates from 1928, and has a dramatic entrance complete with a Juliet balcony overlooking the foyer. French doors line the entrances to each of the rooms, which are named after Costa Rican birds and flowers, and are furnished with period pieces. The Argentinean managers are multilingual (English, Spanish, French and Italian), and are committed to offering guests personalized surface. The attached café is a perfect location for people-watching or for simply enjoying the ambience of this tranquil neighborhood.

Casa Morazan (Map p98; ☎ 257 4187; www .casamorazan.com; cnr Calle 7 & Av 9; s/d incl breakfast) US$45/55 This art-deco mansion in Barrio Amón was built in the 1930s as the residence of John Keith, the cousin of Minor Keith, the famous banana baron who helped construct the Atlantic railroad. The house is fully furnished in period antiques, and rooms are well appointed with bathtubs, bidets and regal beds.

Hotel Dunn Inn (Map pp94-5; ☎ 223 3232, 222 3426; www.hoteldunninn.com; cnr Calle 5 & Av 11; d standard/ deluxe US$47/57, ste US$80; 🅿 💻) This pale yellow, rambling brick-and-wood mansion was constructed in 1929, and features fully restored rooms with modern fixtures that are named after different words in Costa's Rica's indigenous languages (plaques in the rooms explain the derivations and usage of the words). There is also a restaurant and a small bar, which stays open late. Visa is accepted.

Hotel Kekoldi (Map p98; ☎ 248 0804; www.ke koldi.com; Av 9 btwn Calles 5 & 7; s/d US$49/59, d master queen US$72, all incl breakfast) The Kekoldi is in a fabulously light and airy art-deco building in Barrio Amón that features spotless, freshly painted pastel rooms with sky blue tiled bathrooms. There are fresh flowers in virtually every corner of the hotel, and tranquil murals of beach landscapes adorn the common areas. This hotel is gay-friendly and popular with younger travelers. It has a sister hotel in Manuel Antonio (p349). Credit cards are accepted. English, German and Italian are spoken.

Hotel Don Carlos (Map p98; ☎ 221 6707; www .doncarlos.co.cr; Calle 9 btwn Avs 7 & 9; s/d standard US$60/ 70, superior US$70/80, all incl tropical breakfast; 🅿 💻) This converted mansion in Bario Amón features 33 unique rooms with colonial design schemes and huge, tiled bathrooms. The entire property is decked with various artwork, ranging from Sarchí-style ox-carts to oil paintings of dead white conquistadores. There is a also a Pre-Columbian-themed sculpture garden, bar and restaurant as well as a sundeck with tables, a small Jacuzzi and an excellent gift shop. Rates include a welcome cocktail.

Fleur de Lys Hotel (Map p98; ☎ 257 2621; www .hotelfleurdelys.com; Calle 13 btwn Avs 2 & 6; s/d US$79-89, ste US$104-135, all incl breakfast; 🅿 ❌) Housed in a beautifully restored 1926 pink Victorian mansion, this sophisticated hotel features 31 individually decorated rooms and suites (three with a Jacuzzi), each named after a native flower of Costa Rica. Both public areas and private rooms feature Costa Rican art, attractive furnishings and beautifully polished woodwork. You can eat at the attached restaurant anytime of day.

TOP END

All of the following hotels accept credit cards.

Hotel Santo Tomás (Map p98; ☎ 255 0448; www .hotelsantotomas.com; Av 7 btwn Calles 3 & 5; d standard/superior/deluxe incl breakfast US$70/80/105, extra person US$15; 💻 🐾) This early-20th-century French-colonial mansion is a Barrio Amón landmark, and once belonged to the Salazar family of *cafétaleros*. Twenty elegant rooms of varying sizes have polished wood floors, 4m-high ceilings and antique furnishings. There is a garden courtyard with a solar-heated swimming pool, a Jacuzzi and a small gym. Also there is a small, recommended restaurant, the El Oasis (see p322). English and Spanish are spoken.

Britannia Hotel (Map pp94–5; ☎ 223 6667; in the USA 800-263 2618, 888-535 8832; www.hotelbritan niacostarica.com; cnr Calle 3 & Av 11; s/d US$79/89, deluxe US$93/105, ste US$106/117, child under 10 free; 🔀 💻) The Britannia is a small but elegant hotel that is located in the heart of Barrio Amón. The building was constructed in 1910, and features heavy walls of bent brick, elevated ceilings and Victorian-style windows. The well-appointed rooms conserve this design scheme, and are decorated with English-style wallpaper, carpeting, mosaics and colonial furniture. There is a good bar-restaurant that's popular with well-to-do josefinos.

Raya Vida Villa (Map pp94–5; ☎ 223 4168; www .rayavida.com; off Av 11; s/d US$80/95 incl breakfast; P) This secluded hilltop villa is an absolute treasure of a B&B. The bedrooms, dining and sitting areas reflect the owner's interest in art and antiques, and visitors can expect to spot original works by Dalí and Toulouse-Lautrec (seriously, we're not kidding!). Rooms have been decorated with the highest possible level of luxury, straight down to the orthopedic mattresses, imported European linens and flawless bathrooms (one of which has a whirlpool tub). The house itself is an elegant colonial mansion featuring stained-glass windows, hardwood floors, a patio with fountain, a fireplace and a small garden. Owner Michael Long can help with reservations at other B&Bs, and can arrange for airport pick-up if you call in advance. For the cab driver: the hotel is 100m north

---

HOMESTAYS

Bell's Home Hospitality (☎ 225 4752; www .homestay.thebells.org; s/d/tr incl breakfast US$30/45/50) This recommended agency is run by Vernon Bell, a Kansan who has lived in Costa Rica for more than 30 years, and his Tica wife, Marcela. The couple can arrange homestays in over 70 local homes, each of which has been personally inspected to maintain high standards of cleanliness and wholesomeness. All are close to public transportation and readers have sent only positive comments about these places. Note that there is a US$5 surcharge for one-night-only stays and for private bathrooms. The Bells can also arrange airport transfers (US$15), car rental and tours.

---

of Hospital Calderón Guardia on Calle 17, then 50m west on Avenida 11, then another 50m north.

Hotel Villa Tournón (Map pp94–5; ☎ 233 6622; www.hotel-costa-rica.com; d standard/superior US$80/97; 100m east of the República newspaper office; 🔀 💻) This well-run modern hotel primarily caters to business travelers, who take advantage of the Internet ports in the room and the onsite conference center (as well as the kidney-shaped pool and Jacuzzi in the gardens). The hotel has a decent restaurant, the Rincón Azul (open 6:30am to 11pm), which serves a mix of Tico and Western standards, as well as a popular bar called ¿Por que no?.

La Sabana & Around

This section covers hotels in the neighborhoods of La Sabana, La Uruca, La Pitahaya and Rohrmoser.

BUDGET

Gaudy's (Map p101; ☎ 258 2937; www.backpacker.co.cr; Av 5 btwn Calles 36 & 38; dm US$7, d with bathroom US$20-25; 💻) Located in a residential area east of Parque La Sabana is this homey hostel, which has been popular among shoestring travelers for years. The Columbian owners operate one of the cheapest hostels in the city, and although the design scheme is fairly basic, the service is professional and the house is well maintained. There's a communal kitchen, hot showers, a TV lounge, a hammock-strung outdoor patio and free Internet. Find it 200m north and 150m east of the Banco de Costa Rica.

Galileo Hostel (Map p101; ☎ 221 8831, 248 2094; www.galileohostel.com; dm/d US$7/16; 💻) Also located east of Parque La Sabana (and also popular with shoestringers), this hostel is lacking a bit in personality, though the dormitories and private rooms are adequate, and there are plenty of communal areas for kicking back with other travelers. There is also a communal kitchen, shared hot-water bathrooms and free Internet. It's 100m south of the Banco de Costa Rica

Mi Casa Hostel (Map p101; ☎ 231 4700; www.mi casahostel.com; dm US$8-10, r US$25-30, all incl breakfast; P 💻) This beautiful old mansion with polished-wooden floors and antique furnishings has a variety of dormitories and private rooms to choose from – the nicer ones have tiled hot-water bathrooms and balconies overlooking the attractive neighborhood of La Sabana. Communal areas are well furnished, and the kitchen and hot showers are clean and comfortable. There's free Internet. It's 50m west and 150m north of the ICE Building.

Hostel La Mariposa Azul (Map p101; ☎ 258 7878; www.lamariposaazul.com; dm US$8, s/d US$20/22; 🖳) This isn't a bad option as rooms are clean enough, and the 'Blue Butterfly' has all the services you'd expect from a hostel, though the atmosphere is completely neutral (bordering on sterile). Find it 200m south and 150m east of the Subway.

JC & Friends (Map p101; ☎ 374 8246; www.jcfriends hostel.com; cnr Calle 34 & Av 3; dm US$9, r per person US$12, camping US$7, all incl breakfast; 🖳) This recommended hostel is owned and managed by Juan Carlos (he's JC, and you're the friends), a Costa Rican–born, Spanish-raised and American-educated all-round great guy, whose personal attention makes this intimate place a winner. At time of writing, JC was just starting things up, though he's already installed a pool table, bar, TV room and outdoor hammock lounge (complete with artificial 'sand'). If you're just arriving in Costa Rica, JC is a great source of info on the country, and he swears that he has the cheapest tours and car rentals in town. There's also a communal kitchen, hot water, free Internet access (and wi-fi) and volcano views from the 2nd floor. And here's the best part – the Tuasa airport bus conveniently stops directly in front of the hostel.

Kalexma Inn (Map p101; ☎ 232 0115, 290 2624; www.kalexma.com; s with/without bathroom US$25/18, d with/without bathroom US$35/25; 🖳) Located in the quiet neighborhood of La Uruca, this is a good choice if you want to avoid the hustle and bustle of the city. The Tica owner is very welcoming of guests, speaks English and can arrange area homestays as well as Spanish-language classes. Rooms with private hot-water bathrooms and cable TV are simple, though you'll enjoy the warm, familial ambience of the inn. It's 50m west, 25m south of John Paul II traffic circle.

MIDRANGE
All hotels have private hot showers unless otherwise stated.

Hotel Petite Victoria (Map p101; ☎ 225 8488; victoria@amnet.com; cnr Calle 28 & Av 2; s/d incl breakfast US$25/30) This English Victorian–style house

is decorated with period chandeliers and furnishings, and still retains its original colonial tiling. Unfortunately, rooms and bathrooms are a little worn, though it's still a comfortable place to spend the night.

Hotel Cacts (Map p101; ☎ 233 0486, 221 6546, 221 2928; www.hotelcacts.com; Av 3 bis btwn Calles 28 & 30; s/d/tr US$40/45/55, s/d without bathroom US$25/35; 🖳 🕿) Located north of Paseo Colón in the residential neighborhood of La Pitahaya, this hotel has a good range of amenities including a pool, Jacuzzi, TV lounge, rooftop terrace and onsite travel agency. Whitewashed, tiled rooms are spacious and bright, and a Tico breakfast is included in the price. English, German and French are spoken. Directions for taxis: 100m north and 50m west from Pizza Hut on Paseo Colón. Credit cards are accepted.

Ritmo del Caribe (Map p101; ☎ 256 1636; www.ritmo -del-caribe.com; Paseo Colón btwn Calles 32 & 34; s/d/tr incl breakfast US$28/35/45; 🅿 🖳) This German-Tica run inn has comfortable rooms with thick mattresses and colorful bedding, though the real attraction is the pleasant outdoor breakfast nook (and the accompanying all-you-can-eat breakfast buffet). The owners also run an on-site travel agency, and are helpful in arranging tours and car (or motor cycle) rentals (p127).

Rosa del Paseo (Map p101; ☎ 257 3258; www.rosa delpaseo.com; Paseo Colón btwn Calles 28 & 30; s/d US$65/70, d ste US$90-120; 🅿 🖳) This 'Caribbean Victorian–style' mansion was built in 1897 by the Montealegre family, who were one of the first coffee exporters in Costa Rica. Today, the mansion has been converted into a highly recommended guesthouse, though much of the original ambience is intact. The original tiled floors and polished-wooden ceilings are preserved, and period pieces including oil paintings and sculptures are scattered throughout the hotel. There is also a stunning garden of heliconias and bougainvilleas, where a tropical breakfast is served each morning. Although it's hard to find the San José of yesteryear, this is one place where it's easy to imagine yourself in another epoch.

TOP END
All of the following hotels accept credit cards.

Colours Oasis Resort (☎ 296 1880, in the USA 877-932 6652; www.colours.net; Blvd Rohrmoser, northwest cnr of 'El Triangulo'; d US$79-109, ste US$139-189; 🕿) This self-proclaimed 'full-service gay resort' is located in the quiet and elegant Rohrmoser district, and is affiliated with 'Colours Destinations International,' a collection of gay-friendly hotels throughout the world. Rooms in this sprawling Spanish-colonial complex have romantic paddle fans, modern furnishings and impeccable bathrooms. Facilities at the resort include a TV lounge, bar-restaurant, pool, sundeck and Jacuzzi. Call ahead for directions.

Hotel Occidental Torremolinos (Map p101; ☎ 222 5266, 222 9129; www.occidental-hoteles.com; Calle 40 btwn Av 5 & 7; d US$80, ste US$110, all incl breakfast; P ⌘ 🖳 🖳) The San José branch of this Iberian hotel chain caters primarily to international business travelers. Standard-issue luxury rooms with cable TV and air-con are a little on the smallish side, though the larger suites have plenty of breathing room, and the balconies have good views of the capital lights. There is also a restaurant, bar, conference center, garden-lined pool, Jacuzzi and several meetings rooms. Credit cards accepted.

Meliá Tryp Corobicí (Map p101; ☎ 232 8122; www.solmelia.com; Calle 42, d standard/executive US$125/140, ste US$160; P ⌘ 🖳 🖳) The architecture is all *Battlestar Galactica* (seriously, what were the architects thinking?), but otherwise this hotel is pretty swanky (in a chain hotel sort of way). The 213 fully equipped modern rooms have access to the casino, spa, sauna, pool, massage service and gym. The restaurants, although expensive (see Fuji, p116), serve excellent food and a coffee shop provides 24-hour room service. Check the website for inexpensive, last-minute bookings. It's 200m north of Parque La Sabana.

Central San José

Noise is a drawback at some of the following places, though you are in the center of everything (for better or worse).

BUDGET

All showers are hot unless otherwise stated.

Hotel Compostela (Map p98; ☎ 257 1514; Calle 6 btwn Avs 3 & 5; r per person without bathroom US$8) Despite the sketchy neighborhood, the owners of this hotel are proud of the fact that there is no funny business going on at this hotel. Rooms are bare but very cheap – ask for the ones in the back to avoid listening to the street noise.

Green House Hostel (☎ 258 0102; www.greenhouse hostel.altervista.org; Calle 11 btwn Ave 16 & 18; dm US$13, s/d/tr US$20/30/40) This is a very attractive hostel that's brimming with personality – the entire building is adorned with hanging plants, historic photographs and an interesting variety of antiques. The rooms themselves are a bit more modest, though the huge perk here is that they all have en suite bathrooms (even the dorms). Unfortunately, it's a bit pricey compared with other hostels in the city, and it's inconveniently located in Plaza Víquez, which isn't exactly the nicest of neighborhoods.

Pensión de la Cuesta (Map p98; ☎ 256 7946; www.suntoursandfun.com/lacuesta; Av 1 btwn Calles 11 & 15; s/d/tr incl breakfast US$14/28/39, child under 12 free) Situated on a little hill behind the Asamblea Legislativa is this 1920s wooden house, which looks like it was designed and decorated by Barbie and Ken. Nine small but appealing rooms with private bathrooms share a homey TV lounge that's perfect for relaxing with the owners and guests.

Gran Hotel Centroamericano (Map p98; ☎ 221 3362; Av 2 btwn Calles 6 & 8; s/d/tr/q/5-person/6-person US$20/25/30/35/40/45) One of the most popular hotels in the city for Tico travelers is a hive of activity. The main attraction is the central location – and that fact that you can stuff five of your best friends into some of the rooms. Credit cards are accepted and there is a 10% discount for students with a valid ISIC card.

Hotel Los Recuerdos (Map p98; ☎ 222 7320; Av 8, cnr Calle 6; d weekday/weekend US$20/26; ⌘) This Spanish-style terra-cotta building is surprisingly nice for a neighborhood that isn't – clean, well-lit hallways lead to tiled rooms with private hot-water bathrooms.

MIDRANGE & TOP END

Hotel Colonial (Map p98; ☎ 223 0109; www.hotelcol onialcr.com; cnr Calle 11 btwn Avs 2 & 6; s/d US$40/50, ste US$80; 🖳) This 60-year-old Spanish-colonial mansion with distinct Moorish influences is highlighted with latticed iron work, expansive wood working and an arched, poolside promenade. Classically accented rooms have modern furnishings, and some (the ones on the higher floors) have sweeping views of the city and outlying mountains.

Hotel La Gran Vía (Map p98; ☎ 222 7737, 222 7706; Av Central btwn Calles 1 & 3; s/d incl breakfast US$45/60) This hotel, which is popular with Tico

THE SEX TRADE

Although the majority of travelers to Central America are searching for sandy beaches, tropical breezes and a Latin vibe, an increasing number of 'sex tourists' are unfortunately finding their way to Costa Rica.

According to organizations such as Unicef and Human Rights Watch, the sexual exploitation of men and women in Costa Rica, despite the fact that the country retains a cute and cuddly PR image.

Although it's difficult to explain the dynamics of the sex trade with complete certainty, experts have suggested two likely reasons for this phenomenon. First, traditional sex tourism destinations such as Thailand and the Philippines have in recent years enacted stricter laws and strong public awareness campaigns, which has greatly blunted the sex industry in both countries. Second, the growth of tourism in Costa Rica has attracted a greater number of European and North American sex tourists, especially considering that prostitution is completely legal. Furthermore, despite the lack of statistics proving rises in sexual exploitation, anecdotal evidence, independent surveys and high-profile arrests of foreign pedophiles gives credibility to this assertion.

In Costa Rica, the sex trade is centered in San José, and it's certainly frustrating to see the growing number of luxury hotels that cater to sex tourists (particularly wealthy Americans). Although it's favorably reviewed in most other guidebooks, one need only visit some of the several well-known bars to see evidence of the problem. Again, Costa Rican law allows women over the age of 18 to work as prostitutes, so it's commonly argued that sex tourists are not committing any crimes. However, it's estimated that over 40 million children in Central America are working in the sex trade. And it's not surprising that the former executive president of Costa Rica's National Child Trust acknowledged in 2004 that there had been an accelerated increase in child prostitution in the country.

There are several reasons why the sexual exploitation of children is on the rise. Regarding the perpetrators, experts believe that the increased demand for child prostitutes is partly due to the mistaken belief that younger men and women are less likely to have HIV or AIDS. Also, the advent of the Internet has made it easier for sex tourists to learn about the availability of underage sex in various destinations. Regarding children, minors are often pushed into prostitution when poor families lose the ability to support themselves. Studies also show that many child prostitutes are often victims of sexual abuse at home, and are driven to prostitution as a means of survival. Finally, it has also been shown that drug abuse is correlated with child prostitution, and that minors often use sex as a means of feeding their addiction.

Fortunately, there are signs that the Costa Rican government is starting to crack down on offenders. First of all, there are stiff penalties for anyone convicted of buying sex from a minor including hefty fines and lengthy prison sentences. In addition, the Costa Rica Tourism Bureau (ICT) recently began a highly visible campaign to discourage tourists from engaging in the sex trade. At present, there are signs and leaflets in both of Costa Rica's international airports that alert arriving travelers to the penalties for having sex with a minor. Similar billboards can also be seen on major highways and at tourist sites throughout the country. In addition, the tourism industry in Costa Rica recently adopted a code of conduct to help discourage domestic workers from helping foreigners find prostitutes. For example, taxi drivers, waiters and hotel staff are often eager to help guests find prostitutes since they can usually earn a hefty commission. In an effort to combat this practice, some businesses are investing in 're-education' classes for their staff, though unfortunately, it's easy to remain skeptical of the effectiveness of this program.

Throughout this book, we've done our best to ensure that the businesses we list do not support or encourage the practice of prostitution. We understand that many of our readers are traveling with their families, and it is appalling that supposedly reputable hotels in San José tolerate prostitution (and worse yet encourage the act). If however you observe suspicious practices at any of the hotels we list, please let us know, and we will investigate the matter to the best of our ability.

business travelers, has 32 modern, carpeted rooms with hot-water bathrooms, cable TV and balconies facing down to the pedestrian walkway below. There is a decent bar-restaurant that serves typical Tico fare.

Gran Hotel Doña Inés (Map p98; ☎ 222 7443, 222 7553; www.donaines.com; Calle 11 btwn Avs 2 & 6; s/d/tr incl breakfast US$40/50/60) This Italian-owned hotel is located in an old colonial home, which has a handful of quaint rooms decorated with period furniture. Rooms are set back from the street so they're fairly quiet, and they surround a small but pleasant courtyard. The staff speaks English, Spanish and Italian and can help with travel arrangements. Credit cards are accepted.

Gran Hotel Costa Rica (Map p98; ☎ 221 4000; www.grandhotelcostarica.com; Calle 3 btwn Avs Central & 2; d standard/superior US$72/78, ste US$110-165, all incl breakfast) The city's first prominent hotel was constructed in 1930, and is today recognized as a national landmark. Frequent renovations have kept the rooms modern and comfortable, though there are still subtle architectural reminders of the hotel's history including exposed beams, molded ceilings and the dramatic entrance hall. The 24-hour alfresco Café Parisienne (p119) is one of the most popular tourist cafés in the city. There are also two restaurants, a bar and a 24-hour casino. Credit cards accepted.

Aurola Holiday Inn (Map p98; ☎ 222 2424, in the USA 800-465 4329; www.aurola-holidayinn.com; cnr Calle 5 & Av 5; d standard US$125, ste US$150-650, child under 12 free; P X R) You'll find this luxurious hotel conveniently situated downtown, right off Parque Morazán. Its 18-story luxury tower serves as one of San José's most visible landmarks, and it has all the four-star amenities you'd expect. Rooms are modern and typical of Holiday Inns throughout the world (though the views are pretty spectacular). On most nights, however, occupancy looks to be less than 10%, and indeed it's usually possible to get cheap rooms here if you book in advance on the web. Credit cards accepted.

Coca-Cola Bus Terminal Area

It is not recommended that you stay in this area – crime is on the increase, and travelers are easy targets, particularly at night. However, if you're just looking to crash near the station for a night, the following hotels are better than most.

BUDGET

Gran Hotel Imperial (Map p98; ☎ 222 8463; gran himp@racsa.co.cr, Calle 8 btwn Avs Central & 1; s/d without bathroom US$5/10, d with bathroom US$14; 🖵) Despite its unwelcoming 1950s office-building facade, this hotel is quite popular with shoestringers and is the best choice in the area. Security is tight and the desk manager doesn't take any funny business from anyone. Rooms consist of dimly lit wooden stalls with fairly clean hard beds. Internet access is available and a restaurant serves cheap breakfasts.

Hotel Musoc (Map p98; ☎ 222 9437; Calle 16 btwn Avs 1 & 3; s/d US$9/15, s/d/tr with bathroom US$12/16/18) This large building close to the Coca-Cola is nicer inside than it would appear on the outside. The linoleum-tiled rooms are simple and clean and showers are hot, but noise can be a problem with all the buses passing below. The staff speaks some English and credit cards are accepted.

Hotel Nuevo Johnson (Map p98; ☎ 223 7633; www.hotelnuevojohnson.com; Calle 8 btwn Avs Central & 2; r per person US$10) The dark hallways aren't exactly welcoming, but the decent-sized rooms with hot showers are clean and the management is competent. There is also a games room with a pool table, in case you're too scared to go out at night.

By the Airport

The residential district of Cariari is located in the nether region between San José and Alajuela. It's a convenient base if you're either coming from or going to the international airport (assuming you have some dough to spare). There's no shortage of expensive hotels in this section of the city, though the following spots are particularly recommended. All of the listed hotels are easily reached by cab. Note that these hotels are not mapped.

MIDRANGE & TOP END

Cariari Bed & Breakfast (☎ 239 2585; www.cariaribb .com; d incl breakfast US$65-85; Av de la Marina; P 🖵) This charming B&B is run by a friendly North American named Laurie, and comes as a welcome respite from the area's absurdly priced hotels. Three suites of varying sizes and amenities (one room shares a bathroom, one has a private shower and the other a bathtub) are available for guests, though there are plenty of common areas in this stunning Spanish-colonial home including a tropical garden, a TV lounge and a roof-deck. To reach the B&B, go straight on the access road past the Herradura and Meliá Cariari Hotels, and then turn when you see the AM/PM convenience store. Follow this road for 200m – the B&B will be on your left-hand side before the bridge (house number 12).

Meliá Cariari Hotel (☎ 239 0022; www.solmelia .com; d superior/deluxe US$150/165, ste US$250-500; P X Q R) This luxurious hotel has a presidential suite that isn't presidential in name only: numerous foreign leaders from around the world frequently stay here during their trips to Costa Rica. If you're not a visiting dignitary, however, there are 221 spacious, carpeted rooms and suites to choose from, all of which have air-con, cable TV and a private balcony. Amenities include a large pool, sauna, children's play area, convention facilities, casino, shopping mall, restaurants (24-hour room service) and bars. In addition, guests receive privileges at the neighboring Cariari Country Club. Check the website for inexpensive, last-minute bookings.

Hotel Herradura (☎ 293 0033; www.hotelherra dura.com; s/d US$150/165, ste US$250-1000; P X R) This golf resort and conference center also has privileges at the neighboring country club as well as ample convention facilities. Modern rooms have plush carpets and all the trimmings, though it's the amenities that you're paying for – we're talking three pools, including one with waterfalls and a swim-up bar, five Jacuzzis, a casino, a sauna, a concierge service, three restaurants and two bars. One of the restaurants, Sakura (☎ 293 0033, meals from US$10, open 11:30am to 3pm and 6pm to 11pm Tuesday to Sunday), is one of the top locally recommended Japanese places in the San José area. The menu has traditional dishes, including sushi, sashimi and teppanyaki, as well as an impressive selection of sake.

EATING

Costa Ricans are fond of the following proverb: *'Pansa llena, corazón contento,'* or 'When the stomach is full, the heart is happy.' Not surprisingly, food is the glue that holds together Costa Rican families together, and josefinos are no different. Cosmopolitan San José has an impressive number and variety restaurants, and it's easy to find something to satisfy most tastes and budgets.

Although Ticos have an increasing love of American fast food, keep in mind that these restaurants are comparatively expensive. Tico families save all week so they can bring the kids to McDonald's or Pizza Hut, which are usually formal sit-down affairs, and the pumping air-con is a reason to linger.

Note that approximate prices for meals are given as a guide throughout the book, though generally anything with shrimp, lobster or crab will be more expensive. Many of the better restaurants in San José get very busy (especially on evenings and weekends), so it's best to make a reservation.

Eateries in the suburbs of Escazú and Los Yoses and San Pedro are listed later in this chapter.

Supermarkets are spread throughout the city, and several are marked on each neighborhood map.

Bario Amón & Surrounds
BUDGET

Soda de don Raúl (Map pp94-5; Calle 15 btwn Avs 6 bis & 8; dishes US$1.50-3) This basic soda (small and informal lunch counter) has hearty gallo pinto (stir-fry of rice and beans) and abundant lunch specials (US$2.50) that attract a steady stream of suited Ticos from the nearby courts.

El Cuartel de la Boca del Monte (Map pp94-5; Av 1 btwn Calles 21 & 23; dishes US$3-6; ☽ 11:30am-2pm & 6-10pm) This popular nightclub doubles as greasy-spoon during the day. Sure, the exposed-brick walls and worn-wooden floors aren't exactly the most pleasant of surroundings, but the typical fare here is cheap, filling and perfect for filling the gut before a long night of drinking.

MIDRANGE

Cafe de la Posada (Map pp94-5; ☎ 258 1027; Calle 17 btwn Avs 2 & 4; dishes US$3-6; ☽ 11am-7pm Mon-Fri, to 5pm Sat & Sun) This Argentinean-run café, which fronts a pedestrian walkway in a quiet and scenic district of the city, is one of the few spots in San José where you can dine alfresco. The specialties here are superbly brewed coffees and authentic Argentinean-style empanadas, though the US$5 'plate of the day' is always a good choice. The café also displays rotating exhibitions of local and international art.

THE AUTHOR'S CHOICE

Budget
Nuestra Tierra (Map pp94-5; cnr Av 2 & Calle 15; casados US$3-5; ⏰ 24hr) This country-style restaurant is nestled underneath a traditional thatched patio strung with bunches of onions and plantain bananas, and serves typical food that is anything but typical. The menu features tasty casados and traditional favorites such as *chorreadas* (pan-grilled corn cake served with cheese or sour cream) and tamales. The ingredients are fresh, the sauces are thick, the service is friendly and the prices are right.

Midrange
Atomic (Map pp94-5; ☎ 222 2868; cnr Av 11 & Calle 15; dishes US$5-8; ⏰ noon-3:30pm & 5:30pm-midnight Mon-Fri, 11am-5pm Sat) There really are certain places that defy description – take Atomic, for example. The interior is a 1950s diner complete with white-and-black checkered tiles and red leather couches. The cuisine is 'complete food,' which is anything and everything from burgers and pizzas to burritos and sushi. The ambience is hip and artsy, and focuses on a bizarre collection of pop culture memorabilia combined with rotating photography and art exhibits. The music changes nightly depending on the crowd, which is just as eclectic as everything else.

Top End
Restaurante Tin-Jo (Map p98; ☎ 222 2868; cnr Av 11 & Calle 15; appetizers US$3-5, mains US$6-12; ⏰ 11:30am-3pm & 5:30-10pm Mon-Thu, 11:30am-3pm & 5:30-11pm Fri & Sat, 11:30am-10pm Sun) There are few restaurants in San José with a more dramatic interior than Tin-Jo. Each dining room at this long-standing San José establishment is decorated with artwork and traditional crafts from a different Asian country. However, the decoration isn't nearly as varied as the menu, which incorporates elements of Szechuan, Thai, Indian, Cantonese, Indonesian and Japanese cuisine. Reservations are highly recommended – this place gets packed.

Cafe Saudade (Map pp94-5; ☎ 233 2534; Calle 17 btwn Avs 2 & 4; US$4-12; ⏰ 10am-6:30pm Mon-Thu, 11am-5pm Fri & Sat) This hidden gem of a place has an eclectic menu of tempting international foods including sushi, humus, crepes and salads as well as your standard café offerings. It also serves as an exhibition hall for local artists and photographers (the tables are actually display cases). Dance and yoga classes are occasionally held in the upstairs room.

La Cocina de Leña (Map pp94-5; ☎ 223 3704, 255 1360; Centro Comercial El Pueblo; dishes US$5-9; ⏰ 11am-11pm Sun-Thu, to midnight Fri & Sat) One of the best-known restaurants in town, 'the Wood Stove' has the endearing tradition of printing its menu on brown paper bags. Typical dishes include corn soup with pork, black-bean soup, tamales, *gallo pinto* with meat and eggs, stuffed peppers and oxtail served with yucca and fried plantain. It also serves local desserts and alcoholic concoctions, including *guaro*, which is the highly recommended local firewater. There's live marimba music on some nights.

Aya Sofya (Map pp94-5; cnr Av Central & Calle 21; dishes US$5-8; ⏰ 11:30am-3pm & 6-11pm Mon-Fri, 11:30am-midnight Sat) Named after the most famous mosque in Istanbul, this Turkish restaurant is a great choice, especially if you've eaten your fill of rice and beans. The menu features traditional kebabs, stews and syrupy pastries, and twice a month the restaurant hosts a belly-dancing party.

Café Mundo (Map pp94-5; ☎ 222 6190; cnr Av 9 & Calle 15; dishes US$5-10; ⏰ 11am-11pm Mon-Fri, 5pm-12:30am Sat) This reader-recommended restaurant is housed in a beautiful old mansion, and has a relaxing outdoor terrace that overlooks a lush garden and a bubbling fountain. This is the perfect spot for an afternoon *cafécito* (cup of coffee), though its diverse menu of pastas, meats and gourmet salads is reason enough linger on until dinner.

Kafé Ko (Map pp94-5; ☎ 258 7453; cnr Av Central & Calle 21; dishes US$5-10; ⏰ 11am-midnight Mon-Fri, 5pm-1am Sat) This hip, candlelit 'kafé' serves simple but gourmet Western-style sandwiches, quiches and salads, though during the evening it evolves into a popular nightspot.

There's occasional live music during the week, though things really get going on weekends in the evening when live DJs come here to spin.

Lukas (Map pp94-5; ☎ 233 2309, 233 8145; Centro Comercial El Pueblo; dishes US$7-12; ☒ 11-2am) If you have a long night of drinking ahead of you in El Pueblo (p119), consider carbo-loading at this popular local spot. Lukas has a good midpriced selection of standard meat and seafood meals, as well as Italian dishes and sandwiches.

Obelisko (Map p98; ☎ 223 1206; Calle 13 btwn Av 2 & 6; dishes US$8-12; ☒ 6:30am-9:30pm) The restaurant at Hotel Fleur de Lys has a good reputation for its 'new Costa Rican cuisine,' which blends local recipes with traditional Continental stylings. There is live music on Friday nights and a popular happy hour on Tuesday and Friday from 5pm to 7pm.

TOP END

Bakea (Map pp94-5; ☎ 248 0303; cnr Av 11 & Calle 7; appetizers US$3-7, dishes US$7-16; ☒ noon-midnight Tue-Fri, 7pm-midnight Sat) The trendiest restaurant in the capital resides in a beautiful converted vintage home, which features numerous intimate dining rooms, a softly lit patio and a small art gallery. The menu consists of nouveau international dishes – from risotto to steak frites to seafood – all of it world class. Don't miss the delectable *desgustación* dessert sampler. Credit cards accepted.

El Oasis (Map p98; ☎ 255 0448; Av 7 btwn Calles 3 & 5; mains US$9-15; ☒ 4-11pm Tue-Sat, 3-11pm Sun) Situated in the Hotel Santo Tomá, this well-reviewed restaurant has a very simple French colonial–inspired ambience, which focuses your attention on the quality of the cuisine. The international menu at the Oasis has traditional Western specialties and a rich seafood menu, as well as some modern Latin American dishes.

Café Moro (Map pp94-5; ☎ 223 3116; cnr Calle 3 & Av 13; mains US$9-15; ☒ 11:30am-9:30pm Mon-Fri, to 10:30pm Sat) This Middle Eastern–inspired restaurant is located on the ground floor of a 75-year-old Moorish-style mansion, and elaborately decorated with Arabic murals and darkly painted walls. The menu features traditional regional dishes such as kabobs, falafel, couscous, and dolmades as well as a variety of pastas, meats and fishes. The coffee here is strong and potent, blending well with the honey-drenched pastries.

La Sabana & Surrounds

BUDGET

Marisquería Sabor a Océano (Map p101; ☎ 255 0994; cnr Av 3 & Calle 34; casados US$2-6; ☒ 11am-10pm) The 'Taste of the Ocean' has a great variety of seafood dishes including *ceviche* (local dish of uncooked but well-marinated seafood), octopus, squid, fish fillets and fish fries, none of which will break your budget.

Soda Tapia (Map p101; cnr Av 2 & Calle 42; casados US$3-4; ☒ 6am-midnight) This unpretentious spot is a local favorite – you can't go wrong with any of its featured casados, though it's worth saving some room for the sinful sundaes.

MIDRANGE

Restaurante Pacifico (Map p101; ☎ 257 9523; Calle 24 btwn Paseo Colón & Av 2; casados US$4-7; ☒ 11am-10pm) This no-frills eatery serves up spicy Korean and Chinese-style stir-fries as well as a various sushi assortments.

Arirang (Map p101; ☎ 223 2838; Edificio Centro Colón, Paseo Colón btwn Calles 38 & 40, 2nd fl; dishes US$5-9; ☒ 11:30am-3pm & 5:30-10pm Mon-Fri, 11:30am-10pm Sat) If you're looking for slightly fancier surrounds, Arirang is the place for Korean barbecues, which are cooked right at your table.

Lubnán (Map p101; ☎ 257 6071, Paseo Colón btwn Calles 22 & 24; dishes US$5-9; ☒ 11am-3pm & 6-11pm Tue-Sat, 11am-4pm Sun) The beauty of San José is being able to find diverse places such as Lubnán, an excellent Lebanese eatery that serves Middle Eastern specialties including shish kabobs, falafel and lamb stews.

Machu Picchu (Map p101; ☎ 222 7384; Calle 32 btwn Av 1 & 3; mains US$6-11; ☒ 11am-3pm & 6-10pm Mon-Sat) This highly recommended Peruvian outpost is one of the most popular restaurants in the city – and with good reason. The menu includes a variety of *ceviches*, tremendous seafood stews and traditionally prepared meats and fishes. If you've never been to Peru, this is a great place to try the country's famous national cocktail, the pisco sour.

TOP END

El Chicote (Map p101; ☎ 232 0936; appetizers US$4-8, mains US$8-13; ☒ 11am-3pm & 6-11pm Mon-Fri, 11am-11pm Sat & Sun) Protein fiends can go wild at this venerable steakhouse, which grills beefy sirloins in the middle of the restaurant and then serves them up with black beans and fried banana slices, along with a baked potato. A small pavement patio has seating and the large interior is filled with flowers. El Chicote is located near the northwestern corner of the park.

La Piazzetta (Map p101; ☎ 222 7896; cnr F Colón & Calle 40; dishes US$8-18; ☯ noon-2:30pm & 6:30-11pm Mon-Fri, 6-11pm Sat) Some of the best Italian fare in the city is served to guests on a silver platter (literally). The house specialties include homemade pastas, creamy risottos and tender cuts of veal and beef. There is an extensive list of imported wines, and several luscious desserts to choose from.

Fuji (Map p101; ☎ 232 8122, ext 191; Calle 42, mains US$10-30; ☯ noon-3pm & 6:30-11pm Mon-Sat, noon-10pm Sun) Arguably the top Japanese restaurant in town is located in the Hotel Meliá Tryp Corobicí, 200m north of Parque La Sabana. The restaurant serves skillfully prepared sushi and traditional Japanese dishes including teppanyaki and bento. Credit cards accepted.

Restaurant y Galería La Bastille (Map p101; ☎ 255 4994; cnr Paseo Colón & Calle 22; dishes US$12-16; ☯ 11:30am-2pm & 6:30pm-midnight Mon-Fri, 6pm-midnight Sat) This cheerfully elegant bistro is one of San José's longest-standing French restaurants. Dishes emphasizing local meats and thick sauces are simply impeccable. The restaurant also serves as a colorful art gallery, and displays rotating exhibits that highlight local artists.

Restaurant Grano de Oro (Map p101; ☎ 255 3322; Calle 30 btwn Avs 2 & 4; dinner mains US$20; ☯ 6am-10pm) Foremost among small hotel-restaurants in San José is Grano de Oro, which is applauded for its historic dining area and superb international cuisine. Dishes include inventive items such as chicken basted in coconut milk with grilled pineapple or Chilean sea bass in orange herb sauce with macadamia nuts. The restaurant is popular, so reservations are highly recommended – even for weeknights. Guests can have their meals delivered to their rooms at no additional charge. Credit cards accepted.

Central San José & Coca-Cola Bus Terminal Area
BUDGET

Pastelería Merayo (Map p98; Calle 16 btwn Paseo Colón & Av 1; pastries US$1-2) This busy pastry shop has a wide variety of cavity-inducing goodies. The coffee is strong and it's a sweet way to pass the time if you're waiting for a bus at the Coca-Cola.

Soda Castro (Map p98; Av 10 btwn Calles 2 & 4; dishes US$2-4) The area outside is frightful, but inside it's so delightful. So it's not in the best neighborhood, but if you happen to be coming through here, Castro is a good place to feed a sweet tooth. The vast hall is an old-fashioned Tico family spot (there's a sign prohibiting public displays of affection) where you can get heaping ice-cream sundaes and banana splits.

Mariscar (Map p98; Av Central btwn Calles 7 & 9; dishes US$2-4) This popular Chinese/Costa Rican restaurant is locally famous for its heaping and fresh food. The chicken soup can halt any flu in its tracks and the fried rice is a meal in itself. In the evenings, the open-air bar at the back gets cranking with loud music and plenty of young Ticos engaged in rapt conversation.

Restaurante El Pollo Campesino (Map p98; Calle 7, btwn Avs 2 & 4; meals US$2-4; ☯ 10am-11pm) The chicken from a wood-burning spit will satisfy any post-beer need for munchies at this pleasant place with booth seating and homey atmosphere (though plan on smelling like dead poultry when you leave).

Huarache's (Av 22 btwn Calles 5 & 7; dishes US$2-5; ☯ 11am-11pm) This bustling Mexican restaurant makes up for all the bland meals you've had in Costa Rica. Here you'll find fresh honest-to-goodness tacos, quesadillas, guacamole, tortilla soup and hot sauces that'll make you think you've died and gone to Mexico.

Vishnu (Map p98; dishes US$3-5) Av 1 (Av 1 btwn Calles 1 & 3); Calle Central (Calle Central btwn Calles 6 & 8) Vegheads go nuts at this famous San José chain, which is known for its bounteous fare and affordable prices. A US$3 lunch special buys you soup, brown rice, veggies, a fruit drink and dessert. But it's worth coming back for dinner as well – their veggie burger and fruit-drink combo is so good it'll make your carnivorous friends jealous.

Churrería Manolo's (Map p98; churros US$0.50, meals US$3-5; ☯ 24hr) Downtown West (Av Central btwn Calles Central & 2); Branch 2 (Av Central btwn Calles 9 & 11) This San José institution is famous for its cream-filled *churros* (doughnut tubes), which draws in crowds of hungry josefinos in search of a quick sugar rush day or night. Here's a tip – the churros are the freshest around 5pm when hungry office workers beeline here straight from the office. If you're looking for something a little more filling, the Downtown West location serves killer casados, and the 2nd-floor balcony is great for spying on passers-by on the pedestrian mall below.

Chelle's (Map p98; cnr Av Central & Calle 9; dishes US$3-6; ⏲ 24hr) This unpretentious spot is centrally located and serves local dishes – none of which are very exciting. Regardless, some Ticos say you haven't really experienced San José until you've had a wee-hours breakfast here after a night of drinking. (And there's even a bar in case you want to keep on going.)

Restaurant Shakti (Map p98; ☎ 222 4475; cnr Av 8 & Calle 13; dishes US$4-6; ⏲ 7am-7pm) This recommended vegetarian restaurant is a more sophisticated version of Vishnu. The highlights of the menu are the fresh baked breads, veggie burgers, macrobiotic produce and local root vegetables. And in case your travel companions retch at the thought of eating wholesome food, the friendly staff will even cook up a chicken for your unenlightened friends.

Restaurante y Cafetería La Criollita (Map p98; Av 7 btwn Calle 7 & 9; meals US$4-6; ⏲ 7am-8pm Mon-Sat) This recommended eatery serves full American or Tico breakfasts, with coffee and juice included for only US$4 – there are even free refills on coffee and the service is fast and friendly. Lunch or dinner is also a good time to come for huge casados that attract crowds of in-the-know office workers. There's even a nice bar and garden terrace, which is a fine place for a drink.

Restaurante Don Wang (Map p98; Calle 11 btwn Avs 6 & 8; dishes US$4-8; ⏲ 8am-3pm & 6-11pm Mon, 8am-11pm Tue-Sat, 8am-10pm Sun) If you travel for long enough in Costa Rica, you'll be surprised to learn what passes for Chinese food in this country. At the Don Wang, you're getting

the real deal, especially if you come in the morning for its recommended Cantonese dim sum.

One of the cheapest places for a good lunch is at the **Mercado Central** (Map p98; Av Central btwn Calles 6 & 8), where you'll find a variety of restaurants and *sodas* serving casados, tamales, seafood and everything in between. If you happen to be here, stop for dessert at **Las Delicias** (Map p98; ice cream US$0.75), a San José institution that has been whipping up ice cream for more than a century. Get the tasty homemade cinnamon-spiced vanilla and do as the locals and order *barquillos* (cylindrical sugar cookies) to go with it.

MIDRANGE & TOP END

Tin-Jo (see the boxed text The Author's Choice, p115) is the author's choice for this price range.

Café de Correo (Map p98; Calle 2 near Av 3; ⏲ 9am-7pm Mon-Fri, to 5pm Sat; dishes US$5-6) Located in the Correo Central, this is an excellent place to sip a hot (or iced) espresso while writing postcards – the drop box is literally right around the corner. There is also as a small selection of pasta dishes for the hungry.

Café del Teatro Nacional (Map p98; Plaza de la Cultura; dishes US$5-6; ⏲ 9am-5pm Mon-Fri, to 12:30pm & 1:30-5:30pm Sat) The most beautiful café in the city is not surprisingly located in the most beautiful building in the city. The coffees and small sandwiches are good enough, though the real reason you're here is to soak up the ambience of the building's stunning frescoes.

Dos Gringos (Map p98; cnr Av 1 & Calle 7; dishes US$5-11; ⏲ 11-2am) This bar and restaurant is run by two gringos, namely a Bostonian and a Floridian, and has a good mix of American dishes. During the evening, this is a popular

---

EATING VEGGIE IN SAN JOSÉ

Of all the cities in Costa Rica, San José is the best equipped to cater to vegetarians. Beyond the obvious veggie havens of **Vishnu** (p117) and **Shakti** (above), the city's numerous Chinese restaurants offer plenty of vegetable stir-fries, while in many Italian places you can carbo-load on simple dishes of pasta with tomato or cheese sauces. And of course, there is always the ubiquitous rice and beans. For the most part, restaurants are very conscientious about the needs of vegetarians, so if you specify that you want a meat-free dish, most kitchens will be happy to oblige.

While they're not exclusively vegetarian, other good places to eat at are **Tin-Jo** (p115), **Don Wang** (above) and **Restaurante y Cafetería La Criollita** (above), all of which have regular vegetarian items featured on their menus. See also **Comida Para Sentir** (p131).

For more tips on veggie eating in Costa Rica, see the Food & Drink chapter (p81).

spot for middle-aged tourists, who dance to classic rock while sipping a cocktail or two.

Café Parisienne (Map p98; Plaza de la Cultura; dishes US$6-10; 24hr) Part of the Gran Hotel Costa Rica, this European-style café is the perfect place for people-watching, and you can't beat the views of the Teatro Nacional. The meals are definitely overpriced and fairly ordinary, though the waitstaff will leave you alone if you order a coffee.

News Café (Map p98; cnr Av Central & Calle 7; dishes US$6-10; 6am-10pm) On the ground floor of Hotel Presidente is the most popular café in the city for gringo ex-pats. The main draw is the daily selection of foreign newspapers and well as the free wireless Internet. The attached restaurant serves a variety of American-style sandwiches, salads and recommended steaks.

Balcón de Europa (Map p98; ☎ 221 4841, Calle 9 btwn Avs Central & 1; dishes US$6-12; 11:30am-10pm Sun-Fri) One of San José's most popular eateries, this restaurant was established in 1909, and claims to be one of the oldest in Costa Rica. The menu is heavily influenced by European culinary traditions, and features a good selection of pastas, antipasto and salads, though there are plenty of authentic Tico specialties including *palmitos* (hearts of palms).

DRINKING

Whatever your poison may be (ours is a double shot of *guaro* garnished with lime), San José has plenty of options to keep you well lubricated. And there's something for everyone – from hole-in-the-wall dives to trendy lounges to gringolandia.

For listings of nightclubs and gay bars, see p120.

For bars that also have live music, whether regular or occasional, see p121.

For more drinking options, see Los Yoses & San Pedro (p131) and Escazú (p139).

Be advised that San José is not exactly the safest city to go bar-hopping – be smart, and travel by cab at night.

Barrio Amón & Surrounds

Centro Comercial El Pueblo (Map pp94-5; Ⓟ) The recommended 'El Pueblo' is a shopping mall–type complex that's jam-packed with hip bars and clubs, including four that have live music. There is even a 24-hour ATH (A

Toda Hora) ATM on the Cirrus network by the parking lot. The complex usually gets going at about 9pm and shuts down by 3am. Stringent security keeps trouble outside, so this is definitely one place in Chepe where you can kick back a few and let loose (just be careful when you leave as things do get rough outside). Bring your ID. The Peruvian-style Bar Picantería Inty Raymy has potent pisco sours, which always help start the night out right.

¿Por que no? (☎ 233 6622; from 5:30pm) Across the street and about 100m west of Centro Comercial El Pueblo, this is connected to Hotel Villa Tournón. Although the hotel primarily caters to business travelers, its bar is a local favorite, especially on Friday nights when there's live music.

Luna Roja Café (Map pp94-5; ☎ 223 2432; Calle 3 btwn Avs 9 & 11) A bastion of young, hip and trendy josefinos (leave the khakis at home and wear something black). It has a ladies night every Monday and even features the occasional Goth night. It charges a cover (US$2.50) most nights, though Wednesday is free.

Yet another reason to visit the bizarrely hip Atomic (p115) is to drink a cool cocktail while socializing with trendy josefinos.

Central San José

Nashville South Bar (Map p98; Calle 5 btwn Avs 1 & 3) A honky-tonk style bar serves burgers, chili dogs and other fixin's to a bar full of tired-looking gringos. Still, it's a good place if you're looking to meet other gringo travelers, or if you need some time to ease into this whole 'being in a foreign country' thing. Another popular nightspot for the linguistically challenged is nearby Dos Gringos (opposite).

Chelle's (Map p98; ☎ 221 1369; cnr Av Central & Calle 9; 24hr) If you're boozing the night away with Ticos, sooner or later they'll bring you to this 24/7 downtown landmark. In case you're feeling a little woozy, it also serves meals as well.

México Bar (Map pp94-5; cnr Av 13 & Calle 16) An interesting and somewhat upscale (for the neighborhood) bar with good *bocas* and mariachi music some nights. It's next to the Barrio México church. This is definitely a good local hangout, devoid of tourists or ex-pats, but the neighborhood leading to it is a poor one, so take a cab.

SAN JOSÉ

Bar Chavelona (Map p98; Av 10 btwn Calles 10 & 12; ⊙ 24hr) This historic, 77-year-old bar is located in a somewhat deserted neighborhood south of the town center (in other words, take a taxi). The service is good, the atmosphere pleasant and the locale is frequented by radio and theater workers, giving the place an old-world bohemian feel.

ENTERTAINMENT

Pick up *La Nación* on Thursday for a listing (in Spanish) of the coming week's nightlife and cultural events. The *Tico Times* 'Weekend' section (in English) has a calendar of theater, music, museums and events. A handy publication is the *Guía de Ciudad*, published by *El Financiero*, a free city guide featuring the latest events. It is usually available at the tourist office and at better hotels. Visit www.entretenimiento.co.cr for more up-to-date movies, bar and club listings over the San José area.

Nightclubs

Josefinos love to drink almost as much as they love to dance. Whether it's salsa, meringue, hip-hop or reggaeton, Chepe's clubs are always a hot place to be.

Clubs with live music and full-on dance floors will usually charge a cover of US$2 to US$5 depending on the night and the caliber of artist. Don't forget to bring your ID.

See also Los Yoses & San Pedro (p128) for more options in the university district.

In case you missed our first warning, here it is again – be smart, and travel by cab at night.

BARRIO AMÓN & SURROUNDS

Centro Comercial El Pueblo (Map pp94-5; Ⓟ) The top nightspot in San José is a thick density of human activity on weekends. Smaller clubs come and go, so it's best to follow the crowds to see what's in, though there are a few established standards:

Club Twister (☎ 222 5746) Serious dancers (and partiers) should beeline to Twister where there's plenty of room for drinking, dancing and general hell-raising. The DJs play a steady mix of contemporary Latin and international music.

Ebony 56 This sprawling disco has no shortage of dance space, so if you don't like what's playing, move to the next room.

La Plaza (☎ 233 5516) This is one of the classier clubs in El Pueblo, so dress to impress, bust out the Spanish and chat up a few josefinos.

Next door to the Luna Roja, you'll find **Café Loft** (Map pp94-5; ☎ 221 2302; ⊙ 7pm-2am) which has DJs spinning house, ambient and other types of soft electronica on a nightly basis. There's a dress code, so be spiffy or you're not getting in. Nearby Kafé Ko (p115) is also a hot spot for live modern music.

CENTRAL SAN JOSÉ

Ticos describe the downtown scene as being downscale (even dodgy), though there are two recommended places if you're looking for some local flavor.

El Túnel de Tiempo Disco (Map pp94-5; Av Central btwn Calles 7 & 9) Starts pumping the techno late at night and keeps it going 'til the break of dawn.

Complejo Salsa 54 y Zadidas (Map p98; Calle 3 btwn Avs 1 & 3) Another good place to shake it is a vast 2nd-story club that is all Latin, all the time. Be prepared to cut some serious rug here – the local dancers here are expert *salseros*.

Cinemas

Many cinemas show recent Hollywood films with Spanish subtitles and the English soundtrack. Occasionally, films are dubbed over in Spanish *(hablado en español)* rather than subtitled; ask before buying a ticket. Movie tickets cost about US$3, and generally Wednesdays are two-for-one. Check the latest listings in *La Nación*, the *Tico Times* or on www.entretenimiento.co.cr.

Larger and more modern multiplexes are located in the suburbs of San Pedro and Escazú. But in town, try the following:

Cine Magaly (Map pp94-5; ☎ 223 0085; Calle 23 btwn Avs Central & 1)

Omni (Map p98; ☎ 221 7903; Calle 3 btwn Avs Central & 1)

Sala Garbo (Map p101; ☎ 222 1034; cnr Av 2 & Calle 28)

Gay & Lesbian Venues

As a cosmopolitan city, San José is home to a thriving gay and lesbian scene, though it's best to remember that there is still bigotry and intolerance here towards homosexuals. For more additional information, see p535.

Covers are charged on weekends and special nights with prices fluctuating between US$2 and US$5. Clubs may close on some nights and may have women- or men-only nights. To get the latest, log on to **Gay Costa Rica** (www.gaycostarica.com) for up-to-the-minute club info in English and Spanish or drop by the **1@10 Café Internet** (Map pp94-5; ☎ 258 4561; www.1en10.com; Calle 3 btwn Avs 5 & 7), which serves as the gay and lesbian information center.

CENTRAL SAN JOSÉ

The gay scene tends towards the periphery, so expect to find the best clubs in some of the worst areas. As always, travel by cab at night, and if possible, bring a friend.

Bochinche (Map p98; ☎ 221 0500; Calle 11 btwn Avs 10 & 12) This upscale gay bar is popular among young professionals out for a night of drinking and flirting.

Deja Vú (Map pp94-5; ☎ 223 3758; Calle 2 btwn Avs 14 & 16) This massive dance club is one of the most popular spots in the city. The club hosts a men's open-bar night on Wednesday and features go-go boys on Saturday.

La Avispa (Map p98; ☎ 223 5343; Calle 1 btwn Avs 8 & 10) This long-standing gay establishment has been in operation for over 25 years. La Avispa features a bar, pool tables and a boisterous dancefloor that's been recommended by readers. It is most popular with gay men, though it does host a lesbian night once a month.

Los Cucharones (Map p98; ☎ 233 5797; Av 6 btwn Calles Central & 1) This raucous place is frequented by young, working-class men for its over-the-top (and recommended) drag shows.

Live Music

Los Balcones (Map pp94-5; ☎ 223 3704; Centro Comercial El Pueblo; Ⓟ) A small bar specializing in live socially conscious Latin American folk music known as *nueva trova*. There are regular acoustic musicians and no cover charge.

Bar Tango Che Molinari (Map pp94-5; ☎ 226 6904; Centro Comercial El Pueblo; Ⓟ) An intimate Argentinean bar featuring live tango for a small cover charge.

Café Boruca (Map pp94-5; Centro Comercial El Pueblo; Ⓟ) A nice, mellow spot where you can hear folk and acoustic music.

El Cuartel de la Boca del Monte (Map pp94-5; ☎ 221 0327; Av 1 btwn Calles 21 & 23) A restaurant by day, this roomy bar is a major outpost for San José nightlife. The music is sometimes live, but it's always loud. In the back of the club is a small (read as crowded) dancefloor, while the bar toward the front is slightly less frenzied.

Tarrico (Map pp94-5; ☎ 222 1003 Centro Comercial El Pueblo; Ⓟ) This is a popular watering hole where hard-drinking josefinos crowd the big bar and *foosball* table. There is frequent live music.

Theater

There are a wide variety of theatrical options in San José, provided you speak Spanish – though there are a few options in English. Local newspapers, including the *Tico Times*, list current shows. The Teatro Nacional is the city's most important theater. Most other theaters are not very large, performances are popular and ticket prices are quite reasonable. This adds up to sold-out performances, so get tickets as early as possible. Theaters rarely have performances on Monday.

Auditorio Nacional (Map pp94-5; ☎ 249 1208; www .museocr.com; in Museo de los Niños) A grand stage for concerts, dance theater and plays – and even the site of the Miss Costa Rica pageant.

Little Theater Group (LTG; ☎ 289 3910) This English-language theater group has been around since the 1950s and presents several plays a year; call to find out when and where the works will be shown.

Teatro Carpa (☎ 234 2866; Av 1 btwn Calles 29 & 33) Known for alternative and outdoor theater, as well as performances by the Little Theater Group.

Teatro de la Aduana (☎ 225 4563; Calle 25 btwn Avs 3 & 5) The National Theater Company performs here.

Teatro el Ángel (Map pp94-5; ☎ 222 8258, Av Central btwn Calles 13 & 15) A comedy venue.

Teatro Fanal (Map pp94-5; ☎ 257 5524; in the Cenac Complex; Av 3 btwn Calles 11 & 15) Adjacent to the contemporary art museum, it puts on a variety of works, including children's theater – all in Spanish.

Teatro La Máscara (Map p98; ☎ 222 4574; Calle 13 btwn Avs 2 & 6) Dance performances as well as alternative theater.

Teatro Laurence Olivier (☎ 223 1960; cnr Calle 28 & Av 2) LTG also performs at this place, a small theater, coffee shop and gallery.

Teatro Melico Salazar (Map p98; ☎ 233 5434; Av 2 btwn Calles Central & 2) The restored 1920s theater named after one of Costa Rica's most notable coffee barons has a variety of performances, including music and dance, as well as drama.

Teatro Nacional (Map p98; ☎ 221 5341; Av 2 btwn Calles 3 & 5) Stages plays, dance, opera, symphony, Latin American music and other major cultural events. The season runs from March to November, although less frequent performances occur during other months. Tickets start as low as US$4. The National Symphony Orchestra (Orquesta Sinfónica Nacional) plays here.

SAN JOSÉ

Teatro Sala Vargas Calvo (Map p98; ☎ 222 1875; Av 2 btwn Calles 3 & 5) Known for theater-in-the-round performances.

Other important theaters:
Teatro Eugene O'Neill (Map p130; Los Yoses) See p122.
Teatro Lucho Barahona (Map p98; ☎ 223 5972; Calle 11 btwn Avs 6 & 8)
Teatro Moliére (Map p98; ☎ 223 5420; cnr Calle 13 & Av 6)

Casinos

Gamblers will find casinos in several of the larger and more expensive hotels. Most casinos are fairly casual, but in the nicer hotels it is advisable to clean up as there may be a dress code. Be advised that casinos are often frequented by high-end prostitutes, so be suspicious if suddenly you're the most desirable person in the room.
Aurola Holiday Inn (Map p98; ☎ 222 2424; 17th fl, cnr Calle 5 & Av 5)
Casino Club Colonial (Map p98; ☎ 258 2807; Av 1 btwn Calles 9 & 11; ◷ 24hr)
Gran Hotel Costa Rica (Map p98; ☎ 221 4000; Calle 3 btwn Avs Central & 2)
Meliá Tryp Corobicí (Map p101; ☎ 232 8122; Calle 42; ◷ 6pm-2am) It's 200m north of Parque La Sabana.

Sports

International and national football (soccer) games are played in **Estadio Nacional** (☎ 257 6844) in Parque La Sabana. Call ahead for game schedules. For more information on this national passion, turn to p47.

For information on opportunities for sport around the city, see p101.

SHOPPING

Whether you're looking for indigenous handicrafts or a plastic howler monkey, San José has no shortage of shops than run the gamut from artsy boutiques to shameless tourist traps. For the most part however, the capital offers a good selection of handicraft shopping, and stores are generally cheaper here than in tourist towns. With the exception of markets, haggling is not tolerated in stores and shops – this isn't Thailand. For general information on shopping in Costa Rica, turn to p539.

Mercado Central (Map p98; Avs Central & 1 btwn Calles 6 & 8) Assuming you've dressed down and stuck a wad of extra cash in your sock, the Central Market is the best place in city for,

well, pretty much anything you'd want. If you want to do the whole tourist thing, this is the cheapest place to buy a hammock (Hecho en Nicaragua) or a *'Pura Vida'* T-Shirt (Made in China). For something decidedly more Costa Rican, export-quality coffee beans (we like whole-bean organic shade-grown dark roast) can be had at a fraction of the price you'll pay in tourist shops.

Mercado Artesanal (Artensal Market; Map p98; Plaza de la Democracia; Avs Central & 2 btwn Calles 13 & 15) One of the best shopping experiences in the city is here, where you can browse close to a hundred open-air stalls that sell everything from handcrafted jewelry and elaborate woodwork to Cuban cigars and Guatemalan sarongs.

La Casona (Map p98; Calle Central btwn Avs Central & 1; ◷ Mon-Sat) Welcome to the number-one tourist trap in Chepe! Sure, shopping in this multilevel complex is the cultural equivalent of buying art at Wal-Mart, but it's cheap, and the selection is surprisingly good. This is the best place to buy all your tacky souvenirs, be they banana-leaf paper journals or tree-frog stickers, though shop around as there are some quality crafts to be had here.

La Buchaca (Map pp94-5; ☎ 223 6773, 253 8790; Centro Comercial El Pueblo; ◷ 4-8pm Mon-Sat) A tiny oasis in El Pueblo that carries well-made jewelry, ceramics and sculptures – all of Costa Rican origin. Of particular interest are the beautifully executed modern paintings featuring Pre-Columbian motifs from around Central America.

Suraksa (Map p98; ☎ 222 0129; cnr Calle 5 & Av 3; ◷ 9am-6pm Mon-Sat) This artsy boutique has a small selection of high-quality gold work in the pre-Columbian style as well as tropical wood products and fine ceramic ware. The ambience is relaxed, sophisticated and professional, so you won't be hurried if you want some time to shop around.

Annemarie's Boutique (Map p98; ☎ 221 6707; www.doncarloshotel.com; Hotel Don Carlos, cnr Calle 9 & Av 9) This is an exceptional hotel gift shop that is open to the public, and carries an extensive selection of items from all over Costa Rica. The ambience is definitely 'hotel giftshopesque,' though this is off-set by the quality of items for sale.

Sol Maya (Map p98; ☎ 221 0864; Calle 16 btwn Av Central 1; ◷ Sun-Fri) If you're looking to kill some time before getting on the bus, it's worth visiting this small shop near the

---

INDIGENOUS ART

Galería Namu (Map p98; ☎ 256 3412; www.galerianamu.com; Av 7 btwn Calles 5 & 7; ⏱ 9:30am-6:30pm Mon-Sat, 9:30am-1:30pm Sun), which was selected as an official site for the annual Costa Rican Arts Festival in San José, has done an admirable job of bringing together artwork and crafts from Costa Rica's small but diverse population of indigenous tribes. If you want a quick education about indigenous culture in the country, this is a good place to start.

Owner Aisling French regularly visits artists in remote villages around the country and can provide background information on the various traditions represented. Boruca ceremonial masks, Guaymí dolls and dresses, Bribrí dugout canoes, Chorotega ceramics, Huetar carvings and mats and Guatuso blankets are all among the works that can be found at the gallery.

There is also some work by contemporary urban artists, including art produced by Central American street children through a nonprofit program.

English is spoken. In the rainy season it is closed on Sunday, and shop hours may vary.

Coca-Cola bus terminal. This simple but quaint store carries an impressive selection of Guatemalan textiles, and the prices are about as cheap as you'll find anywhere.

If you're in San José it is absolutely worth the trip to go visit Biesanz Woodworks in Escazú (p139). And if you have the time and the inclination, you can also find wide selections of well-priced items in the suburb of Moravia, about 8km northeast of downtown, or by taking a day trip to the village of Sarchí, where Costa Rica's colorful oxcarts and finest woodwork are produced.

GETTING THERE & AWAY

San José is the country's transportation hub, and it's likely that you'll pass through the capital a number of times throughout your travels (whether you'd like to or not). Unfortunately, the transport system is rather bewildering to the first-time visitor, especially considering that most people get around the country by bus, yet there is no central bus terminal. Instead, there are dozens of bus stops, terminals and even an old Coca-Cola bottling plant that are scattered around the city, all serving different destinations. Efforts have been made to consolidate bus services and the use of the Coca-Cola, San Carlo, Caribe and Musoc terminals have definitely helped the situation.

Air

There are two airports serving San José. For information on getting to them, turn to p126. If you're leaving the country, be advised that there is a departure tax of US$26.

Aeropuerto Internacional Juan Santamaría (Map p90; ☎ 437 2626; near Alajuela) handles interna-

tional traffic from its sparkling new terminal and Sansa domestic flights from the diminutive blue building to the right of the main terminal. **Sansa** (☎ 221 9414; www.flysansa.com; cnr Av 5 & Calle 42, La Sabana) also has an office in town.

Aeropuerto Tobías Bolaños (Map p90; ☎ 232 2820; Pavas) is for domestic flights on **Sansa** (☎ 221 9414; www.flysansa.com) and **NatureAir** (☎ 220 3054; www.natureair.com). Any travel agent can book and confirm flights on both Sansa and NatureAir, although you can also make a reservation online. At the time of writing, both airlines were just beginning to expand their services to other destinations in Central America.

INTERNATIONAL AIRLINES

International carriers that have offices in San José are listed here. Airlines serving Costa Rica directly are marked with an asterisk; they also have desks at the airport.

Air France (☎ 280 0069; Curridabat) Go 100m east and 10m north from Pops.

Alitalia (Map p101; ☎ 295 6820; cnr Calle 24 & Paseo Colón)

American Airlines* (Map p101; ☎ 257 1266; Av 5 bis btwn Calles 40 & 42, La Sabana)

British Airways (☎ 257 6912; Barrio Otoya)

Continental* (☎ 296 4911; La Uruca) Next to Hotel Barceló.

COPA* (Map p98; ☎ 222 6640; cnr Calle 1 & Av 5)

Cubana de Aviación* (Map p98; ☎ 221 7625, 221 5881; 5th fl, Edificio Lux, cnr Av Central & Calle 1)

Delta* (Map p101; ☎ 256 7909, press 5 for reservations; Paseo Colón) Office is 100m east & 50m south of Toyota.

Grupo TACA* (☎ 296 0909; cnr Calle 42 & Av 5) Across from Datsun dealership.

Iberia* (Map p101; ☎ 257 8266; 2nd fl, Centro Colón)

Japan Airlines (Map p101; ☎ 257 4646, 257 4023; Calle 42 btwn Avs 2 & 4)

KLM* (☎ 220 4111; Sabana Sur)

LTU (☎ 234 9292; Barrio Dent)

Mexicana* (☎ 295 6969; 3rd fl, Torre Mercedes Benz on Paseo Colón)

SAM/Avianca* (Map p101; ☎ 233 3066; Centro Colón)

United Airlines* (☎ 220 4844; Sabana Sur)

Varig (☎ 290 5222) Find it 150m south of Channel 7, west of Parque La Sabana.

CHARTER AIRCRAFT

Sansa and NatureAir both offer charter flights out of San José as do a number of aerotaxi companies. Most charters are small (three- to five-passenger) aircraft and can fly to any of the many airstrips around Costa Rica. Each listing below includes the San José airport that the company operates out of.

Aero Bell (☎ 290 0000; aerobell@racsa.co.cr; Tobías Bolaños)

Aviones Taxi Aéreo SA (☎ 441 1626; Juan Santamaría)

Helicópteros Turísticos Tropical (☎ 220 3940; Tobías Bolaños)

Pitts Aviation (☎ 296 3600; Tobías Bolaños)

Viajes Especial Aéreos SA (Veasa; ☎ 232 1010, 232 8043; Tobías Bolaños)

Bus

The **Coca-Cola terminal** (Map p98; Coca-Cola; Av 1 btwn Calles 16 & 18) is a well-known landmark in San José and an infinite number of buses leave from a four-block radius around it. Several other terminals serve specific regions. Just northeast of the Coca-Cola, the **Terminal San Carlos** (Map pp94–5; cnr Av 9 & Calle 12) serves northern destinations such as Monteverde, La Fortuna and Sarapiquí. The **Gran Terminal del Caribe** (Caribe Terminal; Map pp94–5; Calle Central, north of Av 13) serves the Caribbean coast. On the south end of town, **Terminal Musoc** (Av 22 btwn Calles Central & 1) caters for San Isidro.

Many of the bus companies, though, have no more than a bus stop (in this case pay the driver directly); some have a tiny office with a window on the street; some operate out of a terminal.

Be aware that bus schedules change regularly. Pick up the useful but not always correct master bus schedule at the ICT office (p92) or look for the helpful *Hop on the Bus*, an up-to-date brochure published by Exintur – the brochure has locations of bus terminals and covers major destinations.

At the time of writing, fuel prices were fluctuating throughout the Americas, and it's likely that the bus prices in this book will change slightly after publication.

Buses are crowded on Friday evening and Saturday morning, even more so during Christmas and Easter.

Thefts are common around the Coca-Cola terminal, so stay alert – especially at night. Theft is an increasing problem on inter-city buses so keep all valuables in your carry-on bag, and don't let it out of your sight.

An excellent way of avoiding the hassle of public buses is to book your onward travel through **A Safe Passage** (☎ 441 7837, 365 9678; www.costaricabustickets.com), which can purchase tickets in advance for a small fee. It also arranges airport transfers, and indeed it's possible to land in San José, and then be shuttled right to your departing intercity bus.

INTERNATIONAL BUSES FROM SAN JOSÉ

Take a copy of your passport when buying tickets to international destinations. For more on border crossings, see the boxed text Border Crossings, on p546.

Changuinola/Bocas del Toro, Panama (Map p98; Panaline; cnr Calle 16 & Av 3) US$15, eight hours, departs at 10am.

David, Panama (Map p98; Tracopa; Calle 14 btwn Avs 3 & 5) US$14, nine hours, departs 7:30am.

Guatemala City (Map p98; Tica Bus, cnr Calle 9 & Av 4) US$39, 60 hours, departs 6am and 7:30am.

Managua, Nicaragua US$12, nine hours; Nica Bus (Map p98; Caribe Terminal) departs at 5:30am and 9am; Transportes Deldu/Sirca Express (Map p98; Calle 16 btwn Avs 3 & 5) departs 4:30am; Tica Bus (Map p98; cnr Calle 9 & Av 4) departs 6am & 7:30am; Trans Nica (Calle 22 btwn Avs 3 & 5) departs 4:30am, 5:30am and 9am.

Panama City US$25/42 for Tica/Panaline, 15 hours; Tica Bus (Map p98; cnr Calle 9 & Av 4) departs 10pm; Panaline (Map p98; cnr Calle 16 & Av 3) departs 1pm.

San Salvador, El Salvador (Map p98; Tica Bus; cnr Calle 9 & Av 4) US$42, 48 hours, departs 6am and 7:30am.

Tegucigalpa, Honduras (Map p98; Tica Bus; cnr Calle 9 & Av 4) US$32, 48 hours, departs 6am and 7:30am.

DOMESTIC BUSES FROM SAN JOSÉ

For destinations within Costa Rica, consult the following.

To the Central Valley

Alajuela (Map pp94–5; Tuasa; Av 2 btwn Calles 12 & 14) US$0.60, 40 minutes, departs every 15 minutes from 4:45am to 11pm.

Cartago US$0.50, 40 minutes, Sacsa (Calle 5 btwn Avs 18 & 20) departs every five minutes, Transtusa (Map p98; Calle 13 btwn Avs 6 & 8) departs hourly from 8am to 8pm.

Grecia, for connection to Sarchí (Map pp94-5; Av 5 btwn Calles 18 & 20) US$0.50, one hour, departs every 30 minutes from 5:30am to 10pm.

Heredia (Map pp94-5; Av 2 btwn Calles 10 & 12) US$0.50, 20 minutes, departs every 20 to 30 minutes from 4:40am to 11pm.

Sarchí (Map pp94-5; Av 5 btwn Calles 18 & 20) US$2, 1½ hours, departs every hour from 5am to 10pm.

Turrialba (Map p98; Calle 13 btwn Avs 6 & 8) US$2, 1¾ hours, departs hourly 8am to 8pm.

Volcán Irazú (Map p98; Av 2 btwn Calles 1 & 3) US$4.50, departs 8am on weekends only.

Volcán Poás (Map pp94-5; Tuasa; Av 2 between Calles 12 and 14) US$4, five hours, departs 8:30am.

To Northwestern Costa Rica

Cañas US$3, 3¼ hours, Tralapa (Map pp94-5; Av 7 btwn Calles 20 & 22) departs hourly; Transportes Cañas (Map pp94-5; Calle 16 btwn Av 1 & 3) departs 8:30am, 9:50am, 11:50am, 1:40pm, 3pm and 4:45pm.

Ciudad Quesada (San Carlos) (Map pp94-5; Autotransportes San Carlos; San Carlos terminal) US$2.50, 2½ hours; departs hourly 5am to 7pm.

La Fortuna (Map pp94-5; San Carlos terminal) US$3, 4½ hours, departs 6:15am, 8:40am and 11:30am.

Liberia US$5, four hours; Pullmitan (Map pp94-5; Calle 24 btwn Avs 5 & 7) departs hourly from 6am to 7pm; Tralapa (Map pp94-5; Av 7 btwn Calles 20 & 22) departs at 3:25pm.

Monteverde/Santa Elena (Map pp94-5; Trans Monteverde; San Carlos terminal) US$4.50, 4½ hours, departs 6:30am & 2:30pm. (This bus fills up very quickly – book ahead.)

Peñas Blancas, the Nicaragua Border Crossing (Map pp94-5; Transportes Deldú; Calle 16 btwn Avs 3 & 5) US$5.50, 4½ hours, departs 4am, 5am, 7am, 7:30am, 10:30am, 1:20pm and 4pm weekdays, every 15 minutes from 3am to 4pm weekends.

Tilarán (Map pp94-5; Autotransportes Tilarán; San Carlos terminal) US$3.50, four hours, departs 7:30am, 9:30am, 12:45pm, 3:45pm and 6:30pm.

To Península de Nicoya

Nicoya (Map pp94-5; Empresas Alfaro; Av 5 btwn Calle 14 &16) US$5.25 to US$6, five hours, departs 6am, 6:30am, 8am, 10am, 10:30am, 12:30am, 1:30pm, 2pm, 3pm, 4pm, 5pm and 6:30pm.

Playa Bejuco (Map pp94-5; Empresas Arza; Calle 12 btwn Avs 7 & 9) US$5.75, 5½ hours, 6am and 3:30pm.

Playa del Coco (Map pp94-5; Pullmitan; Calle 24 btwn Avs 5 & 7) US$5.25, five hours, departs 8am, 2pm and 4pm.

Playa Flamingo, via Brasilito (Map pp94-5; Tralapa; Av 7 btwn Calles 20 & 22) US$6.50, six hours, departs 8am, 10:30am and 3pm.

Playa Junquillal (Map pp94-5; Tralapa; Av 7 btwn Calles 20 & 22) US$8, six hours, departs 2pm.

Playa Nosara (Map pp94-5; Empresas Alfaro; Calle 16 btwn Avs 3 & 5) US$5, seven hours, departs 6am.

Playa Sámara (Map pp94-5; Empresas Alfaro; Calle 16 btwn Avs 3 & 5) US$5, five hours, departs 12:30am.

Playa Panamá & Playa Hermosa (Map pp94-5; Tralapa; Av 7 btwn Calles 20 & 22) US$5, five hours, departs 3:25pm.

Playa Tamarindo (Map pp94-5; Empresas Alfaro; Calle 16 btwn Avs 3 & 5) US$5, five hours, departs 11am and 3:30pm.

Santa Cruz, via Tempisque bridge US$5.25, 4¼ hours; Tralapa (Map pp94-5; Av 7 btwn Calles 20 & 22) departs 7am, 10am, 10:30am, noon, 1pm and 4pm; Empresas Alfaro (Map pp94-5; Calle 16 btwn Avs 3 & 5) departs 6:30am, 8am, 10am, 1:30pm, 3pm and 5pm.

To the Central Pacific Coast

Dominical (Map pp94-5; Transportes Morales; Coca-Cola) US$4.50, 6½ hours, departs 7am, 8am, 1:30pm and 4pm.

Jacó (Map pp94-5; Transportes Jacó; Coca-Cola) US$2.50, three hours, at 7:30am, 10:30am, 1pm, 3:30pm and 6:30pm.

Puntarenas (Map pp94-5; Empresarios Unidos; cnr Av 12 & Calle 16) US$2.50, 2¼ hours, many buses from 6am to 7pm.

Quepos/Manuel Antonio (Map pp94-5; Transportes Morales; Coca-Cola) US$4, four hours, at 6am, 7am, 10am, noon, 2pm, 4pm and 6pm.

Uvita, via Dominical (Map pp94-5; Transportes Morales; Coca-Cola) US$5, seven hours, departs 6am and 3pm.

To Southern Costa Rica & Península de Osa

Ciudad Neily (Map pp94-5; Tracopa; Calle 14 btwn Avs 3 & 5) US$8.25, seven hours, departs 5am, 7:30am, 11am, 1pm, 4:30pm and 6pm.

Golfito (Map pp94-5; Tracopa; Calle 14 btwn Avs 3 & 5) US$8.25, eight hours, departs 7am and 3pm.

Palmar Norte (Map pp94-5; Tracopa; Calle 14 btwn Avs 3 & 5) US$5, five hours, departs 5am, 7am, 8:30am, 10am, 1pm, 2:30pm and 6pm.

Paso Canoas, the Panama Border Crossing (Map pp94-5; Tracopa; Calle 14 btwn Avs 3 & 5) US$9, 7¼ hours, departs 5am, 7:30am, 11am, 1pm, 4:30pm and 6pm.

Puerto Jiménez (Map pp94-5; Blanco Lobo; Calle 12 btwn Avs 9 & 11) US$6.50, eight hours, departs 6:30am & 3:30pm.

San Isidro de El General (Map p101; Transportes Musoc; cnr Calle Central & Av 22) US$3.25, three hours, departs hourly from 5:30am to 6:30pm; (Map p98;Tracopa; Av 4 btwn Calle 14 & 16) US$3.75, three hours, departs hourly from 5am to 6pm.

Santa María de Dota (Map pp94–5; Transportes Los Santos; Av 16 btwn Calles 19 & 21) US$2, 2½ hours, departs 7:15am, 9am, 11:30am, 12:30pm, 3pm, 5pm and 7:30pm.

San Vito (Map pp94–5; Empresa Alfaro; Calle 16 btwn Av 3 & 5) US$7.50, seven hours, departs 5:45am, 8:15am, 11:30am and 2:45pm.

To the Caribbean Coast

All of the following buses depart from the Caribe terminal (Map pp94–5):

Cahuita (Autotransportes Mepe) US$6.50, 3¾ hours, departs 6am, 10am, 1:30pm and 3:30pm.

Cariari, for transfer to Tortuguero (Empresarios Guapileños) US$2.50, 2¼ hours, departs 6:30am, 9am, 10:30am, 1pm, 3pm, 4:30pm, 6pm and 7pm.

Guápiles (Empresarios Guapileños) US$1.75, 1¼ hours, departs hourly from 6:30am to 7pm.

Puerto Limón (Autotransportes Caribeños) US$3.50, three hours, departs every 30 minutes from 5:30am to 7pm.

Puerto Viejo de Talamanca (Autotransportes Mepe) US$7.75, 4¼ hours, departs 6am, 10am, 1:30pm and 3:30pm.

Siquirres (Líneas Nuevo Atlántico) US$2, 1¾ hours, departs 6:30am to 7pm.

Sixaola, the Panama Border Crossing (Autotransportes Mepe) US$9.50, five hours, departs 6am, 10am, 1:30pm and 3:30pm.

To the Northern Lowlands

Ciudad Quesada (San Carlos) See p125.

Los Chiles, the Nicaragua Border Crossing (Map pp94–5; San Carlos terminal) US$3.75, five hours, departs 5:30am and 3:30pm.

Puerto Viejo de Sarapiquí (Map pp94–5; Autotransportes Sarapiquí; Caribe Terminal) US$2.50, 1½ hours, departs 7:30am, 10am, 11:30am, 1:30pm, 2:30pm, 3:30pm, 4:30pm, 5:30pm and 6pm.

Rara Avis (Map pp94–5; San Carlos terminal) US$4.50, four hours, departs 6:30am.

Upala (Map pp94–5; Transportes de Upala; San Carlos terminal) US$6, five hours, departs 6:15am.

TOURIST BUSES

Grayline's Fantasy Bus (☎ 220 2126; www.gray linecostarica.com) and **Interbus** (☎ 283 5573; www .interbusonline.com) shuttle passengers from all over the San José area to a rather long and growing list of popular tourist destinations around Costa Rica. They are more expensive than the standard bus service, but they will get you there faster. Turn to p550 for more information.

GETTING AROUND

Downtown San José is extremely congested – narrow streets, heavy traffic and a complicated one-way system often mean that it is quicker to walk than to take the bus. The same applies to driving: if you rent a car, don't drive downtown – it's a nightmare! If you're in a hurry to get somewhere that is more than 1km away, take a taxi.

To/From the Airports

TO AEROPUERTO INTERNACIONAL JUAN SANTAMARÍA

You can reserve a pick-up with **Taxi Aeropuerto** (☎ 221 6865; www.taxiaeropuerto.com), which charges a flat rate of US$12 from most parts of San José. You can also take a street taxi, but the rates may vary wildly. It should cost roughly US$12 to US$15, but this will depend largely on traffic. A cheaper option is the red **Tuasa bus** (Map p98; cnr Calle 10 & Av 2; fare US$0.60) bound for Alajuela. Be sure to tell the driver that you are getting off at the airport when you board (*Voy al aeropuerto, por favor*). **Interbus** (☎ 283 5573; www.interbuson line.com) runs an airport shuttle service that will pick you up at your hotel for US$5 – good value.

TO AEROPUERTO TOBÍAS BOLAÑOS

Buses to Tobías Bolaños depart every 30 minutes from Avenida 1, 150m west of the Coca-Cola terminal. A taxi to the airport from downtown costs about US$3.

Bus

Local buses are useful to get you into the suburbs and surrounding villages, or to the airport. They leave regularly from particular bus stops downtown – though all of them will pick up passengers on the way. Most buses run between 5am and 10pm and cost US$0.25 to US$0.50.

Buses from Parque La Sabana head into town on Paseo Colón, then go over to Avenida 2 at the San Juan de Dios hospital. They then go three different ways through town before eventually heading back to La Sabana. Buses are marked Sabana–Estadio, Sabana–Cementario, or Cementario–Estadio. These buses are a good bet for a cheap city tour. Buses going east to Los Yoses and San Pedro go back and forth along Avenida 2 and then switch over to Avenida Central at Calle 29. (These buses are easily identifiable because many of them have a big sign that says 'Mall San Pedro' on the front window.) These buses start at the corner of Avenida 2 and Calle 7, near Restaurante El Pollo Campesino.

Buses to the following outlying suburbs and towns begin from bus stops at the indicated blocks. Some places have more than one stop – only the main ones are listed here. If you need buses to other suburbs, inquire at the tourist office (p92).

Escazú Calle 16 (Map p98; Calle 16 btwn Avs 1 & 3);
Avenida 6 (Map p98; Av 6 btwn Calles 12 & 14)
Guadalupe (Map p98; Av 3 btwn Calles Central & 1)
Moravia (Map p98; Av 3 btwn Calles 3 & 5)
Pavas (Map pp94-5; cnr Av 1 & Calle 18)
Santa Ana (Map pp94-5; Calle 16 btwn Avs 1 & 3)
Santo Domingo (Map p98; Av 5 btw Calles Central & 2)

Car

It is not advisable to rent a car just to drive around San José. The traffic is heavy, the streets narrow and the meter-deep curb-side gutters make parking a nerve-wracking experience. In addition, car break-ins are frequent and leaving a car – even in a guarded lot – might result in a smashed window and stolen belongings. (Never ever leave anything in a rental car.) If you are remaining in San José hire the plentiful taxis – available at all hours – instead.

If you are renting a car to travel throughout Costa Rica, you will not be short of choices: there are more than 50 car-rental agencies in and around San José and the travel desks at travel agencies and upmarket hotels can all arrange rentals of various types of vehicles. *Naturally Costa Rica*, a magazine published by the ICT and Canatur (available at many hotels and the ICT office) has an extensive list of car-rental companies in the area. You can also check the local yellow pages (under Alquiler de Automóviles) for a complete listing. See p550 for general information on rental agencies.

Note that there is a surcharge of about US$25 for renting cars from rental agencies at Juan Santamaría airport. Save yourself the expense by renting in town.

Motorcycle

Given the narrow roads, deep gutters and homicidal bus drivers, riding a motorcycle in San José is recommended only for those who are not in complete need of their appendages. But for the foolhardy – and careful – road warrior, renting a bike is an option. Rental bikes are usually small (185cc to 350cc) and rates start at about US$50 per day for a 350cc motorcycle and skyrocket from there. (Plan on paying over US$200 a day for a Harley.) These are a couple of agencies worth trying in San José.

At **Wild Rider** (☎ 258 4604; www.wild-rider.com; in Hotel Ritmo del Caribe, cnr Paseo Colón & Calle 32) Prices start at US$350 per week for a Yamaha TT-R 250 or a Suzuki DR-350 (rates include insurance, taxes, maps and helmets). It will do on- and off-road guided tours as well. Wild Rider also has a handful of used 4WD cars that can be rented at significantly cheaper weekly rates than the big agencies.

Harley Davidson Rentals (see p133) in Escazú rents Harleys.

Taxi

Red taxis can be hailed on the street day or night or you can have your hotel call one for you. You can also hire taxis at any of the taxi stands at the Parque Nacional, Parque Central and near the Teatro Nacional. The most difficult time to flag down a taxi is when it's raining.

Marías (meters) are supposedly used, but some drivers will pretend they are broken and try to charge you more – especially if you're a tourist who doesn't speak Spanish. (Not using a meter is illegal.) Make sure the *maría* is operating when you get in or negotiate the fare up front. Within San José fares are US$0.60 for the first kilometer and US$0.30 for each additional one. Short rides downtown cost about US$1. A cab to Escazú from downtown will cost about US$4, while a ride to Los Yoses or San Pedro will cost less than US$2. There's a 20% surcharge after 10pm that may not appear on the *maría*.

You can hire a taxi and driver for half a day or longer if you want to do some touring around the area, but rates vary wildly depending on the destination and the condition of the roads. For a short trip on reasonably good roads, plan on spending at least US$7.50 an hour for a sedan and significantly more for a 4WD sport utility vehicle or minivan. You can also negotiate a flat fee.

AROUND SAN JOSÉ

Like most sprawling metropolitan areas, San José is home to a number of suburbs, though boundary lines have blurred in recent years due to rapid development. Although a good number of suburbs are strictly off-limits, particularly on the outskirts of the capital where shantytowns are spreading, there are a few areas that offer an appealing alternative to staying in the city proper. About 2km east of downtown are Los Yoses and San Pedro, home to a number of embassies as well as the most prestigious university in the country, namely la Universidad de Costa Rica (UCR). About 7km west of downtown is Escazú, which is the most elite residential area in capital, and the epicenter of a recent wave of Americanization.

Until the mid-20th century, these two suburbs were separate from San José, and were predominantly occupied by the privileged elite. Today Los Yoses, San Pedro and Escazú are contiguous with the city, though they still retain much of their historical airs. For the traveler, spending the night in these well-to-do destinations is recommended if you're looking for a safe and relaxing alternative to the urban grind.

LOS YOSES & SAN PEDRO

College kids are the same the world over, so it shouldn't come as a surprise that this university district is brimming with the highest percentage of bars and clubs in the city. In the evenings, the under-30 crowd takes to the streets in force, and if you spend enough time partying on Calle La Amargura, you may find yourself lingering in the capital for longer than you planned. If you're not the drinking type, this area is also home to some of the nicest malls and movie theaters in the capital (perfect if you're in need of a quick Western culture-fix). And you'd be hard-pressed to find a neighborhood boasting better restaurants than San Pedro and Los Yoses.

These suburbs are centered on a roundabout where Avenida Central meets the road to Zapote. To the west lies Los Yoses, with the Fuente de la Hispanidad (a large fountain) and the Mall San Pedro, both serving as area landmarks. To the east lies San Pedro, anchored by a small plaza and the Iglesia de San Pedro (San Pedro church). A few blocks north of Avenida Central is the tree-lined campus of the national university.

Orientation & Information

Most streets in Los Yoses and San Pedro are unnamed and locals rely almost entirely on the landmark method to orient themselves. (See the boxed text What's That Address?, p539 for more on this.) Three major area landmarks are the old ICE building (el antiguo ICE) and the Spoon in Los Yoses, and the old Banco Popular building (el antiguo Banco Popular) in San Pedro.

The neighborhood abounds with Internet cafés, so there's no problem logging on. Pick up a copy of the student weekly, *Semana Universitaria*, for a comprehensive source of local events.

Internet Café Costa Rica (Map p130; ☎ 224 7295; per hr US$0.60; ⊗ 24hr) As good a place to log on as any, 75m west of the old Banco Popular.

Librería Internacional (Map p130; ☎ 253 9553; Barrio Dent; ⊗ 9:30am-7:30pm Mon-Sat, 1-5pm Sun) This has new books mostly in Spanish (but some in English) as well as travel and wildlife guides. It's 300m west of Taco Bell, behind Mall San Pedro.

Scotiabank (Map p130; ☎ 280 0604; Av Central btwn Calles 5 & 7, San Pedro) Changes cash and has a 24-hour ATM on the Cirrus network.

Sights & Activities

The **Museo de Insectos** (Map p130; ☎ 207 5318, 207 5647; admission US$1; ⊗ 1-5pm Mon-Fri), also known

---

DAY-TRIPPER

Looking for something to do? Here are a few suggestions:

■ Shopping for hardwood handicrafts and mini-oxcarts in **Sarchí** (p153)

■ Shopping for fine leather goods in the colonial town of **Moravia** (p166)

■ Learning everything you've ever wanted to know about coffee at the **Café Britt Finca** (p162)

■ Buying rare orchids for all your friends and family at the **Lankester Gardens** (p170)

■ Gazing into active craters (and fighting off the tourist hordes) at **Volcán Poás** (p156)

as the Museo de Entomología, has a fine collection of insects curated by the Facultad de Agronomía at the Universidad de Costa Rica and housed (incongruously) in the basement of the music building (Facultad de Artes Musicales) on campus. It is claimed that this is the only insect museum of its size in Central America. The collection is certainly extensive and provides a good opportunity to view a vast assortment of exotic – and downright alarming – creepy crawlies. The museum is signposted from San Pedro church, or you can ask for directions. Ring the bell to gain admission if the door isn't open.

If you're interested in knocking down some pins, one block south of the North American–Costa Rican Cultural Center you'll find **Boliche Dent** (Map p130; ☎ 234 2777, cnr Av Central & Calle 23, Los Yoses; bowling per hr US$5) where you can. Just east of the rotunda in San Pedro, you can strap on the roller skates and hang out with what seems like every last teenager in San José at **Salón Los Patines** (Map p130; ☎ 224 6821), the local roller rink.

If you're looking to pick a fight or two, check out the **Thaiboxing Center** (Map p130; ☎ 225 7386) or **Atemi Ryu Martial Arts Center** (Map p130; ☎ 524 0781).

Sleeping

Hostel Bekuo (Map p130; ☎ 234 5486; www.hostel bekuo.com; dm US$9, s/d/tr US$18/26/33; P ▣) This is easily one of the most beautiful hostels in the country – not surprisingly, one of the two Tica owners studied interior design (halfway). Together, Aurora and Michelle run Bekuo, which is a Bribrí word meaning constellation. The common areas of the hostel are heavily influenced by Japanese minimalist design, and feature low tables, beanbag chairs and hanging lanterns. The rooms themselves are naturalist themed, and adorned with stunning mounted photography. Shared facilities include a communal kitchen, hot-water bathrooms, a recreation room with pool table and a TV lounge. Guests have free Internet access (including wireless). It's 325m west of the Spoon.

Casa Yoses (Map p130; ☎ 234 5486; www.casayoses .com; dm US$9, s/d/tr US$18/25/33, all incl breakfast; P ▣) This new addition to the San José hostel scene is a winner. Dorms and private rooms with shared hot-water bathrooms are located in a 19th-century mansion, though the real appeal is the beautiful, fenced-in

garden with hammocks, sun chairs and tropical plants. Guests can also rest in the comfy TV lounge, play a few pick-up games of foosball or cook a meal in the kitchen (or with the outdoor barbecue). There's also free Internet (including wireless). The three Tico owners speak English and French (and Tico), and are all-around cool guys. It's 250m west of the Spoon.

Hostal Toruma (Map p130; ☎ 234 8186; www.hicr .org; Av Central btwn Calles 29 & 31; dm HI member/ nonmember US$10/12; r HI member/nonmember US$20/ 22; P ▣) The longest-standing hostel in San José is affiliated with Hostelling International, and located in a spacious and brightly painted Spanish-colonial mansion. Accommodations at Toruma consist of sex-segregated dorms with bunk beds as well more expensive private rooms, all of which share hot-water bathrooms. There is also a TV lounge, free Internet, a small garden and a communal kitchen, all of which are extremely well kept. Like all HI hostels, there is a strict no alcohol and drugs policy, and quiet hours are enforced after 10pm. This hostel is an excellent choice, but it's definitely not for everyone.

Casa Agua Buena (☎ 234 2411; www.aguabuena .org/casabuena/index.html; Barrio Lourdes, east of San Pedro; r per week US$60-80, month US$160-180) This group house, which caters to long-term renters, is very popular among international students. Two simple peach-colored homes with rooms of various sizes sit side-by-side on a quiet dead-end street. Houses are equipped with a common kitchen, washing machine (use of the machine is included in the rates), a lounge with cable TV and phone. Some rooms share bathrooms, while others have private ones – all with hot water. The house also runs the Agua Buena Human Rights Association, which is working to increase medical access for people living with HIV-AIDS. The Casa is gay-friendly.

Hotel Milvia (☎ 225 4543; www.hotelmilvia.com; s/d/tr incl breakfast US$59/69/75; ▣) This stunning Caribbean-style plantation once served as the home of Ricardo Fernández Peralta, an artillery colonel who fought in Costa Rica's 1948 civil war. It was restored to its original grandeur by his grandson, and now operates as a small and personal hotel. Each spacious room with private hot-water bathroom combines just the right touch of modern and antique. An upstairs terrace provides

LOS YOSES & SAN PEDRO

INFORMATION		
Internet Café Costa Rica	1	D2
Librería Internacional	2	B1
Post Office	3	C2
Scotiabank	4	D2

SIGHTS & ACTIVITIES		
Atemi Ryu Martial Arts Center	5	D2
Boliche Dent	6	A2
Costa Rican Language Academy	7	B1
Forester Instituto Internacional	8	A2
Instituto Británico	9	A2
Instituto Latinoamericano de Idiomas	10	C2
Merecumbé	11	B2
Museo de Insectos	12	D1
Palacio Municipal (City Hall)	13	C2
Salón Los Patines	14	C2
Thaiboxing Center	15	D1

SLEEPING		
Casa Yoses	16	B2
Hostal Toruma	17	A2

Hostel Bekuo	18	A2
Hotel Don Fadrique	19	A2
Hotel Le Bergerac	20	A2

EATING		
Al Muluk	21	D2
Antojitos Cancún	22	B2
Automercado	23	A2
Bagelmen's	24	A2
Comida Para Sentir	25	C1
Il Pont Vecchio	26	C2
La Galería	27	B2
La Masía de Triquell	28	C2
Le Chandelier	29	B2
Más X Menos	30	D2
Restaurant L'Ile de France	(see 20)	
Spoon	31	B2

DRINKING		
Caccio's	32	D2
Centro Comercial Cocorí	33	B2
Fuzion Bar	(see 41)	
La Villa	34	C2

Mosakos	(see 36)	
Mutis	(see 33)	
Reggae Bar Raíces	(see 33)	
Río Bar	35	B2
Rock Bar Sand	(see 33)	
Taos Bar	(see 33)	
Tavarúa	(see 34)	
Terra U	36	D2
Touch Bar	(see 41)	

ENTERTAINMENT		
Cine El Semáforo	37	D2
Costa Rican-North American Cultural Center	(see 43)	
El Retro-visor	38	C1
Jazz Café	39	D2
Multicines San Pedro	40	B1
Planet Mall	41	B2
Teatro Bellas Artes	42	D1
Teatro Eugene O'Neill	43	A1

SHOPPING		
Outlet Mall	44	C2

incredible views of the surrounding residential neighborhood. Credit cards accepted. For cab drivers: it's 100m north and 200m east of Mercado San Pedro Muñoz y Nanne.

Hotel Don Fadrique (Map p130; ☎ 225 8166, 224 7583; www.hoteldonfadrique.com; cnr Calle 37 & Av 8; s/d/tr incl breakfast US$60/70/82; (P)) This family-run hotel is decorated with a private collection of contemporary Central American and Costa Rican art, including the permanent collection of painter Florencia Urbina. Its artsy and sophisticated ambience blends well with the fresh plants and flowers scattered throughout the hotel. Continental breakfast is served on the tropical, plant-filled patio. Credit cards accepted. Take the second entrance to Los Yoses.

Hotel Le Bergerac (Map p130; ☎ 234 7850; www.bergerac.co.cr; Calle 35, Los Yoses; s/d standard US$65/75, s/d superior US$80/90, deluxe US$100/110, d grande US$120, all incl breakfast; (P)(💻)) This boutique luxury hotel, 50m south of Avenida Central, is regarded as one of the most sophisticated places to stay in the capital. The French-colonial building is warm and inviting, though readers predominantly rave about the exceptional professionalism of the staff. Rooms of varying size are furnished with antiques, and highlighted by attractive wooden accents and immaculate bathrooms. The hotel restaurant, Restaurant L'Ile de France (☎ 283 5812; open 6pm to 10pm Monday to Saturday, mains US$8 to US$15), is one of the top spots in the city for French cuisine, and reservations are necessary, even if you're a hotel guest. Credit cards accepted.

Eating

San Pedro and Los Yoses are home to some of the best restaurants in all of Costa Rica (and possibly Central America). There's no shortage of cheap, student spots, though this is one area where it's worth splurging.

Bagelmen's (Map p130; Av Central & Calle 33, Los Yoses) This outpost of the popular bagel chain is just up the street from Hostal Toruma, and serves a decent bagel (US$0.50) considering you're in Central America. Heartier sandwiches (US$3 to US$5) are a good bet, especially when they're packed full of fresh veggies and cream cheese. It's usually very crowded, though it has a drive-thru. This is a wireless hot spot.

Spoon (Map p130; ☎ 253 1331; Cnr Calle 43 & Av 10; dishes US$2-8; ☷ 8am-7pm Mon-Fri, 9am-5pm Sat & Sun) The Los Yoses branch of this universally adored restaurant is so famous that directions are given in relation to it! The menu is extensive, though the big breakfasts are the local favorite (especially after a long night of clubbing).

Al Muluk (Map p130; Calle 3, north of Av Central; dishes US$3-7) Although it has a great selection of traditional Lebanese and Middle Eastern dishes, you're here for the falafel, which is fresh, cheap and damn good.

Antojitos Cancún (Map p130; ☎ 225 9525; Los Yoses; dishes US$3-10; ☷ 11:30-12:30am) Though not terribly authentic (the staff call it 'Mexi-tico'), the local branch of this chain eatery is always packed with hungry students. Choices range from a couple of tacos to a full-blown plate of beef *fajitas*, though the margaritas and nachos are the most popular items on the menu. It's 50m west of the Fuente de Hispanidad.

Comida Para Sentir (Map p130; dishes US$4-8) Vegetarians of the world unite – this jam-packed student haunt 150m north of the church serves up cruelty-free wholegrain sandwiches with all the veggie-riffic fixings you can imagine.

Il Pont Vecchio (Map p130; ☎ 283 1810; mains US$6-15; ☷ noon-2:30pm & 6-10:30pm Mon-Sat) This elegant Italian place vies for the 'best of' in the greater San José area and has been recognized as one of the top restaurants in Central America. Chef Antonio D'Alaimo, who once worked in New York City, makes all of his own fresh pastas and imports many of his ingredients directly from Italy. Credit cards accepted. It's 150m east of Fuente de Hispanidad and 10m north.

La Galería (Map p130; ☎ 234 0850; Los Yoses; dishes US$7-12; ☷ noon-2:30pm & 6:30-10:30pm Mon-Fri, 6:30-10:30pm Sat) This long-standing German-inspired eatery, 125m west of the old ICE Building,. is perennially listed by critics as one of the best restaurants in Central America. Its house specialties are the *schpaetzel* and strudel, and they're good enough to make any homesick German cry. Credit cards accepted.

La Masía de Triquell (Map p130; ☎ 296 3528; Edificio Casa España, Sabana Norte; mains US$10-20; ☷ 11:30am-2pm & 6:45-10:30pm Mon-Sat) The service is excellent and the surroundings unmatched at this refined and long-standing Spanish establishment. The chef specializes in Catalan cuisine, though the lengthy selection of paellas is extremely popular among diners. Credit cards accepted. It's 100m east and 180m north of the old ICE.

Le Chandelier (Map p130; ☎ 225 3980; Los Yoses; meals US$10-25; ☷ 11:30am-2pm & 6:30-11pm Mon-Fri, 6:30-11pm Sat) This is the most famous French restaurant in San José (it even has its own line of sauces that are sold in some of the more upscale supermarkets). The food here is predictably top-notch, and whether you're sitting next to the cozy fireplace or outside on the patio, it's hard to find a more romantic spot. Go 100m west and 100m south of the old ICE Building.

The **Automercado** (Map p130; Av Central btwn Calles 39 & 41, Los Yoses) and the **Más X Menos** (Av Central, San Pedro) are large, modern supermarkets that offer plenty of options for self-caterers.

Drinking

Río Bar (Map p130; cnr Av Central & Calle 39, Los Yoses) Just west of the fountain, this popular bar has live bands on some nights and a pyrotechnic house drink called the *la cucaracha* (the cockroach). There are two-for-one drink specials on Monday night.

Centro Comercial Cocorí (Map p130; south of Av Central, Los Yoses) The nightlife hub, further east and just south of Los Antojitos Cancún. Most of the places here get started after 9pm and run late ('til the last customer leaves). Rock Bar Sand is the regular watering hole for local rockers, as is Mutis out front. Around the back, Reggae Bar Raíces draws in the Rasta crowd, while Taos Bar, next door, is slightly mellower, but still gets packed.

Calle La Amargura (Street of Sorrow; Map p130; San Pedro) This is what Calle 3 is known as, to the north of Avenida Central. However, it should be called Calle de la Cruda (Street of Hangovers) because it has perhaps the highest concentration of bars of any single street in town, many of which are packed with customers even during daylight hours. Terra U, Mosakos, Caccio's and Tavarúa are raucous, beer-soaked places packed with a steady stream of rowdy young customers. A more relaxed (and slightly grown-up) place is La Villa, located in a distinctive wood house with a candlelit back patio. There is live music some weekends.

Mall San Pedro (Map p130; ☎ 283 7516), northwest of Fuente de la Hispanidad, has two popular bars, especially among mall rats who aren't quite ready to go home when the sun goes down. Fuzion Bar alternates between hip hop and reggae, while Touch Bar, as its name implies, is a flirtatious lounge that's great for meeting 'new friends.'

Entertainment

Cinemas are plentiful in the neighborhood. **Multicines San Pedro** (Map p130; ☎ 283 5715/6; top level, Mall San Pedro; admission US$4) has 10 screens showing the latest Hollywood flicks. Better yet, head to **Cine El Semáforo** (Map p130; ☎ 253 9126; www.cineselsemaforo.com; admission US$3; ⏰ 11am-8pm), a hip little theater showing Spanish and Latin American movie classics every day. (It's Spanish only, so it's great if you want to come to practice.) It's beside the train tracks, east of Calle 3.

If live theater is your bag, there are a couple of choices in the area. **Teatro Eugene O'Neill** (Map p130; ☎ 207 7554; www.cccncr.com; cnr Av Central & Calle 37, Los Yoses) has performances sponsored by the Centro Cultural Costarricense Norteamericano (Costa Rican–North American Cultural Center). On the east side of the Universidad de Costa Rica campus is the **Teatro Bellas Artes** (☎ 207 4327) which offers a wide variety of programming, including works produced by the fine-arts department at the university.

Jazz Café (Map p130; ☎ 253 8933; ⏰ 6pm-2am) The destination in San Pedro for live music, with a different band every night. Cover charges vary, depending on the prominence of the musical act featured, but usually fluctuate between US$4 and US$6 for local groups. Find it 50m west of old Banco Popular.

For a full-blown dance party, hit **Planet Mall** (Map p130; ☎ 280 4693; ⏰ 8pm-2:30am Thu-Sat), one of San José's most expensive nightclubs. The enormous, warehouse-sized disco has a couple of levels, several bars and is situated on the 4th and 5th stories of Mall San Pedro where you can admire the twinkling lights of San José from its oversized windows. Covers here can fluctuate depending on who is spinning or performing, but can easily creep up to US$10 on any given night.

One of the hippest spots in the area is the recommended **El Retro-visor** (Map p130; Arte Plaza San Pedro; ⏰ 6pm-2am), an Argentinean-owned retro café that's adorned with 1980s pop culture memorabilia, and very popular among trendy UCR students.

Shopping

Both **Mall San Pedro** (Map p130; ☎ 283 7516; northwest of Fuente de la Hispanidad) and the **Outlet Mall** (Map p130; Av Central) offer ample opportunities for mall rats looking to shop 'til they drop. Look for it east of the road to Zapote.

Getting There & Away

From the Plaza de la Cultura in San José, take any bus marked 'Mall San Pedro.' A taxi ride from downtown will cost US$1.50 to US$2.

ESCAZÚ

Packed with gringo ex-pats and moneyed Tico aristocrats, the affluent suburb of Escazú is spread out on a hillside overlooking San José and Heredia. The area is really comprised of the three adjoining neighborhoods of San Rafael de Escazú, Escazú Centro and San Antonio de Escazú, each of which has its own unique character and flare.

San Rafael, which is one part Costa Rica, two parts USA, is dotted with strip malls, car dealerships, nice homes, nicer cars and chain restaurants that print their menus largely in English. (The US Ambassador lives in this area in a very secure-looking white walled compound.) Escazú Centro thankfully retains a more unhurried Tico ambience, with its narrow streets and numerous shops and *sodas*. And the area around San Antonio remains almost entirely residential. though it does house a handful of hotels that offer spectacular views of the valley.

For the traveler, staying in Escazú is an excellent choice as it's well connected to the city center by public buses, brimming with some of the best restaurants in the city and there are some truly top-notch accommodations to choose from.

Information

Banco Nacional de Costa Rica (Map pp136-7; cnr Calle 2 & Av 2, Escazú Centro; ⊗ 8:30am-3:45pm) On the main plaza, can change money and traveler's checks and it even has a drive-thru window.

Banex (Map pp136-7; Centro Comercial Guachipelín, Carretera JF Kennedy, San Rafael) On the northwestern end you'll find a 24-hour ATM.

Escazú Internet (Map pp136-7; ground fl, Centro Comercial Plaza Escazú, Escazú Centro; per hr US$0.50; ⊗ 8:30am-10pm Mon-Sat, 9am-9pm Sun) Email access.

Hospital CIMA (Map pp136-7; ☎ 208 1000; www.hospitalsanjose.net) Medical care – emergency or otherwise. This is 500m west of the Próspero Fernández toll booth in the area of Guachipelín, on the west side of Escazú, and is one of the most modern hospitals in the greater San José metropolitan area. It is affiliated with Baylor University Medical Center in the USA and is recommended.

Libreria Internacional (Map pp136-7; ☎ 201 8320; Multiplaza Escazú; ⊗ 10am-8pm Mon-Sat, to 7pm Sun) A branch of the bookshop.

Scotiabank (Map pp136-7; Carretera JF Kennedy, San Rafael) With a Cirrus ATM.

Activities

You can arrange motorcycle tours or rent bikes at **Harley Davidson Rentals** (Map pp136-7; ☎ 289 5552; www.mariaalexandra.com), which has an office inside the Apartotel María Alexandra. Riders have to be more than 25 years of age and have a valid motorcycle driving license. Rates start at US$80 per bike per day and include helmet, goggles and unlimited mileage (insurance and tax not included). The agency can deliver bikes to other destinations at an extra charge.

Reputable **Swiss Travel Service** (Map pp136-7; ☎ 282 4898; www.swisstravelcr.com; Autopista Próspero Fernández, 300m west of Cruce de Piedeades de Santa Ana) offers tours all over Costa Rica.

Those who want to practice their golf swing can head to the **Costa Rica Country Club** (Map pp136-7; ☎ 228 9333, 208 5000; www.costaricacountryclub.com), which has a nine-hole course. There are also tennis courts and a pool. In Santa Ana, west of Escazú, is **Valle del Sol** (Map pp136-7; ☎ 282 9222, ext 218/219; www.vallesol.com; greens fees US$7, golf carts US$20), inside a community of the same name, which has a new 18-hole (7000yd, par 72) public course.

Festivals & Events

On the second Sunday of March Escazú celebrates **Día del Boyero**, which is a celebration in honor of ox-cart drivers. Dozens of *boyeros* from all over the country decorate the traditional, brightly painted carts and form a colorful (if slow) parade.

Sleeping

Escazú has a variety of accommodations – all in the midrange to top-end categories. Street addresses aren't given here – refer to the map or call the hotel for directions (which are invariably unwieldy and complicated). All of the listed accommodations can arrange for airport transportation.

Escazú is dotted with a fine selection of B&Bs that all offer a homey alternative to chain hotels. They are listed first.

MIDRANGE

Park Place B&B (Map pp136-7; ☎ 228 9200; Interlink 358, PO Box 025635, Miami, FL 33102; s/d incl breakfast US$45/50; P) Retired dentist Barry Needman runs this small and friendly place, situated in an attractive whitewashed alpine-style house. (There's no sign out the front, so look for the high eaves.) Four immaculate guest bedrooms share two bathrooms, kitchen privileges and a roomy lounge with cable TV. Every morning, Barry cooks a heaping, American-style breakfast for all his guests. Weekly and monthly rates are available.

Costa Verde Inn (Map pp136-7; ☎ 228 4080; www.costaverdeinn.com; s/d/tr US$45/55/65, apt US$70, all incl breakfast; P ☺) The sister lodge of the famous Manuel Antonio hotel is an attractive, country-style home complete with some fairly impressive amenities including a hot tub, lighted tennis court, pool, sundeck, barbecue area and fireplace. The rooms themselves are well decorated with modern furnishings and have a king-size bed, cable TV and private hot shower. Larger loft apartments feature high ceilings, a balcony and a fully equipped kitchen. A Tico breakfast is served on an outdoor terrace. Weekly rates are available, and credit cards are accepted.

Villa Escazú (Map pp136-7; ☎ 289 7971; www.hotels.co.cr/vescazu.html; s/d/tr incl breakfast US$45/65/80; P) A Swiss chalet–type building complete with a wraparound veranda is surrounded

---

LOCAL LORE

Superstition and lore have always been associated with Escazú, so it should come as no surprise that the city's football club is named *Las Brujas* (the witches). Even today, local residents still tread carefully under the cover of night in fear of being attacked by a resident witch, especially La Zegua.

According to legend, Zegua was a beautiful Tica who fell in love with a Spanish officer in Cartago during the colonial era. Unfortunately, after having her heart broken, Zegua changed herself into a witch, and started haunting lonely travelers. La Zegua is said to occasionally appear on the side of the road as a beautiful woman with long black hair and a porcelain face. After luring lonely men to her side, she quickly transforms into a revolting monster that is described as having a horse skull, flaming red eyes and razor-sharp teeth, and enacts revenge for her broken heart.

Another famous Escazú legend is about Mico Malo, an evil monkey with demon eyes and a long arrow-tipped tail that is said to appear in the trees every time a husband and wife quarrel. Mico Malo is extremely wicked, and it's believed that unless a couple settle their differences, the monkey will torment them for the rest of their lives.

---

by terraced gardens and fruit trees and is patrolled by a very friendly pooch named Felíz. Accommodation is in six quaint wood-paneled rooms that feature local artwork as well as comfy couches, and shared hot-water bathrooms. There is also a studio apartment with a small kitchen, cable TV and good-size tiled bathroom (US$250 per week) – an excellent deal. English is spoken.

Posada del Bosque (Map pp136-7; ☎ 228 1164; posada@amerisol.com; d incl breakfast US$70; P ⊠ ⬚) This Tico-run posada is surrounded by tropical gardens, which are home to a swimming pool, barbecue pit, a tennis court and horse-riding trails. The eight-room inn has rustic-style rooms with private hot-water bathrooms as well as plenty of communal areas for chatting with the friendly owners and other guests. There is also a cozy fireplace for those cool, San José nights.

Casa de las Tías (Map pp136-7; ☎ 289 5517; www .hotels.co.cr/casatias.html; Calle León; s/d/tr incl breakfast US$59/79/89; P ⊠) Located in a quiet area of San Rafael, rooms in this brightly painted yellow and turquoise Cape Cod–style house complete with picket fence are decorated crafts from all over Latin America. However, this place is special because of the welcoming owners, Xavier and Pilar, who provide personalized service to all of their guests. Breakfast is served in the lovely backyard, which even has a manmade stream.

Posada El Quijote (Map pp136-7; ☎ 289 8401; www .quijote.co.cr; s/d standard US$75/85, superior US$85/95, deluxe US$95/105, all incl breakfast; P ⊠ ⬚) This hillside *posada* rates as one of the top B&Bs in the San José area. Standard rooms are simple yet homey, with wooden floors, throw rugs, plush bedding, cable TV and private hot-water bathrooms, while larger rooms have either a small patio or a private terrace. However, all guests are free to take a nip at the honor bar, and then relax on the outdoor patio while soaking up the sweeping views of the Central Valley.

Hotel Tapezco Inn (Map pp136-7; ☎ 228 1084; info@ tapezco-inn.co.cr; Calle Central btwn Avs 2 & 4; s/d incl breakfast US$36/45; P ⬚) Located near the Escazú church and on the town plaza, this is the best budget option in the entire area. The brightly painted yellow-and-blue hotel is managed by a friendly Tico family, and has clean and simple rooms with private hot showers and cable TV. The hotel is also conveniently situated – it's less than 100m from the San José bus stop and a short walk from the area's restaurants and cafés.

Hotel Mirador Pico Blanco (Map pp136-7; ☎ 228 1908, 289 6197; pblanco@costarica.net; s/d US$45/65, cottage per month US$400; P) This countryside hotel is located high in the hills about 3km southeast of central Escazú, and has staggering views of the Central Valley from its balconied rooms. The 15 spacious units feature painted rock walls, queen-size beds, cable TV and hot showers. There are also three cottages (which lack views) that sleep up to six and are rented on a monthly basis. There is a small restaurant (US$4 to US$8) that is a good spot for slowing down and appreciating the views. Credit cards accepted.

Apartotel María Alexandra (Map pp136-7; ☎ 228 1507; www.mariaalexandra.com; cnr Calle 3 & Av 23; d

US$80; (P) (X) (R)) This clean, quiet and centrally located apartotel in San Rafael de Escazú is a good option of you're looking for a fully furnished accommodation. Though clean and well maintained, the apartments are completely ordinary, but the bedrooms are totally separate from the kitchen and living areas. Facilities include a sauna, private parking, VCR rental and a washer and dryer. Maid service is included and there are weekly and monthly rates available. Book well ahead in high season. The apartotel is home to Harley Davidson motorbike tours and rentals (see p133).

TOP END

Casa María (Map pp136-7; ☎ 228 0190; www.costarica .org; d US$50-80, tr US$80-100, apt per night/month US$105/1111, all incl breakfast; (P) (R)) Casa María is a seven-room hotel situated in a '70s-style ranch house that's perfect if you're feeling nostalgic for your misspent youth. The common areas are covered in trippy murals adorned with 'period pieces.' Still, rooms are of ample size (the more expensive ones have a private hot-water bathroom), and the banana tree–filled backyard complete with swimming pool is a nice touch.

Hotel San Gildar (☎ 289 8843; www.hotelsangildar .com; Carretera JF Kennedy; d/tr US$98/113; (P) (X) (R)) Just northwest of the Costa Rica Country Club is this trendy hotel that's situated in a Spanish hacienda–style building. The hotel aims to rejuvenate and relax its guests with comfortable, soothing rooms and a picturesque garden-fringed pool. Its chic bar-restaurant (open 6am to 10pm, mains US$7 to US$12) serves Continental cuisine and is locally popular.

Alta Hotel (Map pp136-7; ☎ 282 4160; www.thealta hotel.com; d US$165, ste US$195-820, extra person US$12; (P) (X) (R)) Situated on the road between Escazú and Santa Ana is one of the country's premier boutique hotels, the Alta, which is highly recommended for its professional service, stunning location and top-notch rooms and amenities. The hotel itself is an immaculately sculpted Spanish Mediterranean-style villa, though it's difficult to compete with the grandeur of Mother Nature – on a clear day, there are views from the hotel as far as the Pacific. Fully appointed rooms are highlighted by their spacious patios, regal bathrooms, swish upholstery and

natural wood accents. The on-site restaurant La Luz (🕑 6am to 10pm, mains US$8 to US$18) specializes in nouvelle cuisine that blends Continental, Tico and Californian culinary elements.

Hotel Real InterContinental (Map pp136-7; ☎ 289 7000; www.interconti.com; r US$250, ste US$400-1000; (P) (X) (💻) (R)) About 2km northwest of Escazú is this branch of the well-respected InterContinental hotel chain. The five-story building has 260 deluxe air-con rooms with all the usual upscale business hotel amenities, and an impressive list of facilities including a pool, spa, gym, three restaurants, two bars, a convention and business center, concierge service and a small gift shop. The country's largest shopping mall, the Multiplaza, is located across the street. Check the Web for occasional discounts.

Eating

There are a few inexpensive local *sodas* in Escazú Centro, though for the most part, Escazú is home to expensive, cosmopolitan eateries. If you just can't bear the thought of being separated from all of your favorite American chain eateries, there's everything from a Tony Roma's to a TGI Friday's in San Rafael.

BUDGET

La Casona de Laly (Map pp136-7; cnr Av 3 & Calle Central; US$1-5; 🕑 11am-12:30am) In the heart of Escazú Centro is this much-loved *soda*, which specializes in traditional country-style Tico fare. In the evenings, locals pack the joint for their cheap *bocas* and ice-cold beers.

Perro Loco (Map pp136-7; Centro Comercial El Cruce, cnr Calle L Cortés & Carretera JF Kennedy; dishes US$2-3; 🕑 noon-8pm Mon-Tue, to 4am Wed-Sat, 4-10pm Sun) If you've been boozing it up a little too much, this greasy spoon is just what you need. The menu at the 'Crazy Dog' consists of 10 internationally themed hot dogs, all of which are served with plentiful toppings (our favorite is the Chihuahua dog, which comes loaded with fresh guacamole).

La Paila de la Bruja (dishes US$2-5; 🕑 4pm-midnight Mon-Thu, noon-midnight Fri-Sun) This rustic *soda* in San Antonio de Escazú is a famous institution that prepares traditional Tico specialties using outdoor brick ovens. The terrace is bustling in the evenings, and the dramatic views of the Central Valley make this a memorable spot.

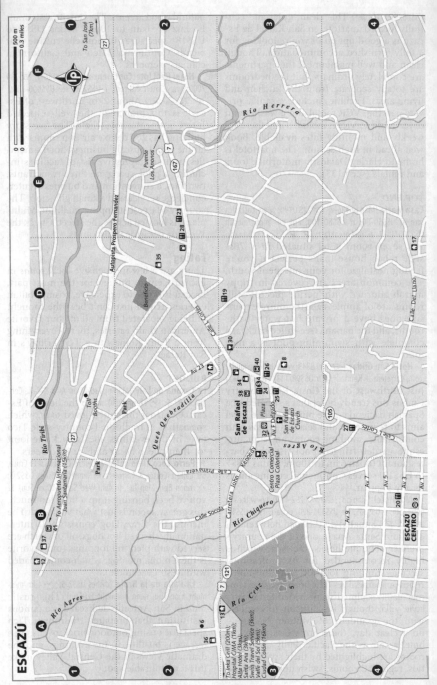

ESCAZÚ

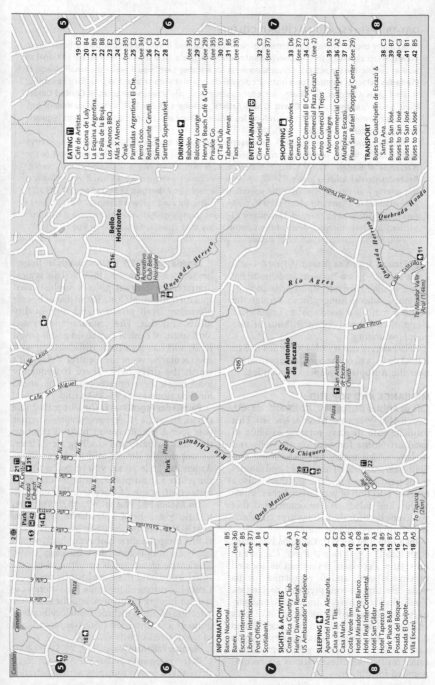

EATING 🍴
Café de Artistas	**19** D3
La Casona de Laly	**20** B4
La Esquina Argentina	**21** B5
La Paila de la Bruja	**22** B8
Los Anonos BBQ	**23** E2
Más X Menos	**24** C3
Órale	(see 35)
Parrilladas Argentinas El Che	**25** C3
Perro Loco	(see 34)
Restaurante Cerutti	**26** C4
Samurai	**27** C4
Saretto Supermarket	**28** E2

DRINKING 🍷
Baboleo	(see 35)
Balcony Lounge	**29** C3
Henry's Beach Café & Grill	(see 35)
Praukie Co	**30** D3
Q'Tal Club	**31** B5
Taberna Arenas	(see 35)
Taos	(see 35)

ENTERTAINMENT 🎭
| Cine Colonial | **32** C3 |
| Cinemark | (see 37) |

SHOPPING 🛍
Biesanz Woodworks	**33** D6
Cemaco	(see 37)
Centro Comercial El Cruce	**34** C3
Centro Comercial Plaza Escazú	(see 2)
Centro Comercial Trejos	
Montealegre	**35** D2
Centro Comercial Guachipelín	**36** A2
Multiplaza Escazú	**37** B1
Plaza San Rafael Shopping Center	(see 29)

TRANSPORT
Buses to Guachipelín de Escazú &	
Santa Ana	**38** C3
Buses to San José	**39** B7
Buses to San José	**40** C3
Buses to San José	**41** B1
Buses to San José	**42** B5

INFORMATION
Banco Nacional	**1** B5
Banex	**2** B5
Escazú Internet	(see 37)
Librería Internacional	**3** B4
Post Office	**4** C3
Scotiabank	**5** A3

SIGHTS & ACTIVITIES
Costa Rica Country Club	(see 7)
Harley Davidson Rentals	**6** A2
US Ambassador's Residence	

SLEEPING 🛏
Aparthotel María Alexandra	**7** C2
Casa de las Tías	**8** C3
Casa María	**9** D5
Costa Verde Inn	**10** A5
Hotel Mirador Pico Blanco	**11** D8
Hotel Real InterContinental	**12** B1
Hotel San Gildar	**13** A3
Hotel Tapezco Inn	**14** B5
Park Place B&B	**15** B7
Posada del Bosque	**16** D5
Posada El Quijote	**17** D4
Villa Escazú	**18** A5

DAY-TRIPPER: ESCAZÚ TO CIUDAD COLÓN

Need a city break? There's an interesting day trip to be had if you have your own wheels. From Escazú, head 3km west to the town of **Santa Ana**, which is a local artisan center for traditional as well as contemporary pottery. Continuing west for another 5km, you'll reach the small village of **Piedades**, which is centered on a historic colonial church that's worth checking out for its beautiful stained-glass windows. Continuing west for another 8km, you'll reach the town of **Ciudad Colón**. Here, you'll find the **Julia & David White Artists' Colony** (☎ 249 1414; www.forjuliaanddavid.org), which was established in 1998 as a refuge for writers, visual artists and composers, and regularly offers a number of workshops and classes.

5km southwest of Ciudad Colón is the **Reserva Forestal el Rodeo**, a 350-hectare private reserve that protects the last stretch of primary forest in the Central Valley. The reserve is a part of the **Hacienda el Rodeo** (☎ 249 1013; ☼ 10am-6pm Sat & Sun), which has a small restaurant, namely **Restaurante del Abuelo** (meals US$4-8), which serves country fare on weekends. If you're looking to prolong your city escape, consider spending the night at **Albergue El Marañon** (☎ 249 1271; www.cultourica.com/frameseteng.html; s/d/tr US$35/49/77; P), located a few kilometers west of Santa Ana in the village of La Trinidad. This quaint 11-room country guesthouse is surrounded by a fruit orchard and has stunning views of the Central Valley that span as far as Volcán Poás.

La Esquina Argentina (Map pp136-7; cnr Av Central & Calle L Cortés; ☼ 7am-2pm weekdays; dishes US$2-6) This popular roadside stand sells piping-hot empanadas to hungry locals, though the outdoor patio is a good spot to linger over a cup of coffee and spend an hour or two people-watching.

Self-caterers can try Más X Menos in San Rafael de Escazú or the Saretto Supermarket near the Autopista Próspero Fernández.

MIDRANGE AND TOP END

Café de Artistas (Map pp136-7; ☎ 228 6045, 288 5082; dishes US$4-8; ☼ 8am-6pm Tue-Sat, to 4pm Sun) This intimate café displays rotating exhibits of local art (some for sale) on its walls and shelves, which makes for a charming and light-hearted meal. The coffees and home-made pastries are excellent, and there's also a heartier selection of vegetarian dishes, sandwiches and salads. It's recommended that you come here for the Sunday brunch, which is accompanied by live music.

Inka Grill (☎ 289 5117; Multicentro Paco Escazú; dishes US$5-13; ☼ 11:30am-11:30pm) The area's most top Peruvian restaurant is located in Guachipelín, and is renowned for its wide selection of well-prepared specialties. You'll find it all here, from *chupe de camarones* (shrimp soup) to *aji de gallina* (spicy chicken). The spice level has been toned down for the milder Tico palate, but you can ask for their scalding homemade hot sauce on the side. Reservations are recommended for dinner.

Tiquicia (☎ 289 5839; ☼ 5pm-midnight Tue-Fri, 1pm-2am Sat, 11am-6pm Sun; mains US$6-10) This typical upmarket restaurant gives a sophisticated spin on traditional Costa Rican dishes by emphasizing fresh produce and high-quality meats and fish. The restaurant is located 5km south of central Escazú on a well-paved road, and has a relaxed, rustic setting with spectacular views of the Central Valley – it's worth the drive here. There is frequently local music here on weekends. Call ahead for directions as it's tricky to find.

Parrilladas Argentinas El Che (Map pp136-7; Calle L Cortés; mains US$6-10; ☼ noon-midnight) Whether you spend the afternoon hours sitting on the outdoor patio and cradling a cold beer, or stop by for dinner and feast on a huge Argentine-style steak, you're going to like the relaxed atmosphere at this popular local restaurant, south of Carretera JF Kennedy.

Los Anonos BBQ (Map pp136-7; ☎ 228 0180; dishes US$7-12; ☼ noon-3pm & 6-10pm Tue-Sat, 11:30am-9pm Sun) On the road between San José and Escazú is this long-standing barbecue shack, which has been in operation since the early 1960s. The entire restaurant is constructed of polished wood, and there are historic photos of Costa Rica along all the walls. Los Anonos caters for hungry carnivores, and the extensive selection of meats includes both locally raised animals and imported USDA-approved cuts of meat. Credit cards accepted.

Mirador Valle Azul (Map pp136-7; ☎ 254 6281; dishes US$8-12; ☼ 4pm-midnight Mon-Sat) A tough steep drive takes you to the aptly named Mirador

Valle Azul (Blue Valley Lookout), from where the views of the San José valley are breathtaking – get there before sunset. The cuisine is European inspired, and features a wide selection of pastas, meats and seafood as well a few Costa Rican standards. On Saturday and Sunday evenings, there's a good chance there will be live music here. It's 700m south and 700m west from Hotel Mirador Pico Blanco.

Samurai (Map pp136-7; ☎ 228 4124; Calle L Cortés; dishes US$9-25; ☉ noon-3pm & 6:30-10pm) Sushi is all the rage these days in Escazú, though this upscale Japanese eatery complete with tableside hibachis also offers authentic teppanyaki, as well as mixed fish and seafood grills. If you're a traditionalist, the sushi here is about as good as it gets, and though it's pricey, the quality is undeniable.

Restaurante Cerutti (Map pp136-7; ☎ 228 4511, 228 9954; Calle L Cortés; dishes US$10-20; ☉ noon-2:30pm & 6-11pm Wed-Mon) This recommended restaurant, south of Carretera JF Kennedy in San Rafael de Escazú, is regarded as one of the best Italian restaurants in the capital. The food here is predictably top-notch, and features hand-selected seafood and delectable homemade pastas. The ravioli with ricotta and mushrooms (US$15) is a local favorite, though you can't go wrong with their big list of risottos. Credit cards accepted.

Drinking

The hottest nightspot in the most exclusive district of San José is the Centro Comercial Trejos Montealegre, a more upscale version of El Pueblo (p119). This complex is packed on weekends with the trendiest scenesters in the capital, and there's no shortage of dance spots to show off all the new threads that daddy's money bought you. The most established clubs are Baboleo, Taos and Praukie Go, though like all things fashionable, this is likely to change. At the time of writing the hottest beats were the Puerto Rican–inspired reggaeton, though again, like all things fashionable, this is likely to change. A recommended spot in Trejos Montealegre is Órale, which serves Tex-Mex fare that's popular among pre-partiers, though things really get hopping on Friday nights when there's cheap drink specials.

Taberna Arenas (Map pp136-7; Escazú Centro; ☉ from 4pm) This delightful, old-fashioned Tico bar, diagonal from the Shell station,

with exceptional *bocas* (US$1) and a good selection of domestic and imported beers is an Escazú institution. Owner Don Israel is a true charmer, and has his photos with various heads of state on the walls, among the agricultural implements that are de rigueur in any decent country bar.

Two hearty drinking options reside in the Plaza San Rafael shopping center a few hundred meters east of the soccer field. **Balcony Lounge** (Map pp136-7; Carretera JF Kennedy; ☉ noon-1am) is an upscale bar and gringo hangout that specializes in well-crafted martinis, while the more laid-back (but equally gringo) **Henry's Beach Café & Grill** (Map pp136-7; Carretera JF Kennedy; ☉ 11-2:30am) is your best spot for partying it up on the dance floor.

On the road into town from San José, you'll find the **Q'tal Club** (Map pp136-7; Calle L Cortés; ☉ 6pm-2am), which is a sophisticated lounge complete with its own house band. There are frequent live jazz performances here, though there is a US$5 cover charge.

Entertainment

For first-run Hollywood movies, check out the **Cine Colonial 1 & 2** (Map pp136-7; ☎ 289 9000; ground fl, Plaza Colonial Escazú, San Rafael; admission US$3) or the **Cinemark** (Map pp136-7; ☎ 288 1111; Multiplaza Escazú; admission US$3).

Shopping

Biesanz Woodworks (Map pp136-7; ☎ 289 4337; www .biesanz.com; ☉ 8am-5pm Mon-Fri, Sat & Sun by appointment) You will find delicate and high-quality wood craftsmanship in the traditional Pre-Columbian style at this showroom in Bello Horizonte. A variety of bowls and other decorative containers are all beautifully produced, the majority using a traditional crafting method in which the natural lines and forms of the wood determine the shape and size of the bowl. This makes every piece unique. The products are expensive (starting at US$50 for a palm-sized bowl), but they are well worth it. Interested shoppers can take a tour of the workshop and learn about how the craftsman selects, ages and prepares the wood for years before he even begins to cut it. A lake, botanical garden and native hardwood nursery are on the property. Call well ahead to make weekend appointments.

Multiplaza Escazú (Map pp136-7; ☎ 289 8984; www .multiplazamall.com; ☉ 10am-8pm Mon-Sat, to 7pm Sun) A full-scale suburban-style mall that has just about everything you need (or don't) – from clothes to eyeglasses to shoes. There is also a good food court. Of particular interest to travelers is the **Cemaco** (☎ 289 7474), a sort of Wal-Mart-style department store that sells basic fishing and camping supplies, including propane gas for your portable stove. If you're coming from San José the mall can be reached by taking any bus that is marked with 'Escazú Multiplaza.' (See p126 for more information on these buses.)

Getting There & Away

Frequent buses between San José and Escazú cost US$0.25 and take 25 minutes. All depart San José from east of the Coca-Cola bus terminal and take several routes: buses labeled 'San Antonio de Escazú' go up the hill to the south of Escazú and end near San Antonio de Escazú church; others labeled 'Escazú' end in Escazú's main plaza; and others, called 'Guachipelín' go west on the Carretera John F Kennedy and pass the Costa Rica Country Club. All go through San Rafael.

Central Valley & Highlands

Although the Central Valley is one of the world's principal coffee-growing centers, the cultural and political environment of the region has matured greatly in recent years. With the booming capital of San José at its core, and the bustling cities of Alajuela, Heredia and Cartago on its perimeter, the Central Valley serves as the main population center of the country as well as embodying the modern-day persona of Costa Rica. The region boasts one of the largest microchip production centers in the world, and the country's young workforce is educated, computer-savvy and increasingly bilingual. With vast cityscapes, a modern infrastructure and dizzying traffic, Costa Rica is clearly much more than 'pretty beaches and rain forest.'

In recent years, hotels have started springing up throughout the Central Valley, particularly near the airport in Alajuela. Although travelers are discovering that the city is a safer and more convenient alternative to staying in San José, tourism remains low-key throughout the region. However, it's worth taking a few days to explore the country's heartland where you can experience Costa Rica from a unique, 'nongringofied' prospective.

As an added bonus, regional roads are generally excellent and public transportation is inexpensive, frequent and comfortable – a bus ride of no more than two hours will bring you to towering waterfalls, active volcanoes, steaming hot springs, enormous coffee fincas (farms or plantations) and some of the best white-water rafting in the world. And, if you have a rental car, there's nothing quite like the thrill of shifting gears on a windy, mountain road.

This chapter is arranged in a roughly west-to-east sequence of the four major population centers, namely Alajuela, Heredia, Cartago and Turrialba.

HIGHLIGHTS

- Whipping down white-water chutes on the **Río Reventazón** and **Río Pacuare** (p177)
- Gazing into the active craters of **Volcánes Irazú** (p168), **Poás** (p156) and **Turrialba** (p180)
- Breathing in the coffee-scented air in the **Valle de Orosi** (p169)
- Traipsing alongside pre-Columbian ruins at **Monumento Nacional Arqueológico Guayabo** (p178)
- Waking up with a hangover after living it up at the country's biggest fiesta in **Palmares** (p153)

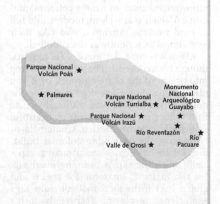

ALAJUELA & THE NORTH OF THE VALLEY

Cradled by the gentle undulations of coffee fincas and tamed jungle parks, the provincial capital of Alajuela lies about 18km northwest of San José. Originally known as Villa Hermosa, it's still a very 'pretty city,' not to mention the country's second largest, with a population of more than 185,000. And, contrary to what most cab drivers will tell you, Alajuela is only 3km from Juan Santamaría international airport, and is rapidly becoming the preferred base for travelers leaving and entering the country.

From coffee barons to conglomerate banks, the pulse and ebb of Alajuela has always been fast-paced and modern, though a short drive into the north of the valley will change your perspective on the area. The colonial heyday of coffee exportation has left its mark on the terraced hillsides, and the lives of many *campesinos* (farmers) still revolve around the cycle of the harvest.

ALAJUELA

Alajuela is known as Costa Rica's second city, though this diminutive status is perhaps unwarranted. In addition to having a rich colonial history, Alajuela is an attractive place resonating with a warm and welcoming vibe that is virtually absent from the capital. Its mango-tree-lined center is as relaxed as any you'll find in the provinces, and the soaring whitewashed cathedral is a testament to the city's past as a colonial administrative center for nearby coffee plantations. Alajuela is also clean, modern and full of hard-working urbanites, who take their jobs almost as seriously as their football.

Alajuela is not a 'destination' for tourists, though it's a convenient base if you're flying into or out of the nearby airport, or if you plan on spending a few days exploring the north of the valley. And although Costa Rican cities are nowhere near as beautiful as historic cities in Mexico, Guatemala or Nicaragua, the crumbling colonial buildings in the city center are attractive, especially when the sun is beaming overhead. So, take a stroll, eat some ice cream and grab a beer if the local football team Liga Alajuelense is playing (especially if it's against its arch-rival Saprissa!).

Orientation & Information

Central Alajuela is a pedestrian-friendly grid of calles (streets) and avenidas (avenues). Although street signs are never a guarantee in Costa Rica (p539), Alajuela is fairly well signed and easy to navigate. The city center is at the intersection of Calle Central and Av 1.

BYTE (☎ 441 1142; cnr Calle 3 & Av 1, 2nd fl; per hr US$0.75; ☒ Mon-Sat) Internet access.

Clínica Norza (☎ 441 3572; Av 4 btwn Calles 2 & 4) Open 24 hours with basic medical services.

Goodlight Books (☎ 430 4083; Av 3 btwn Calles 1 & 3) If you've got a long trip (or flight) ahead of you, stop by and visit the friendly and always helpful owner, Larry. In addition to selling used and new books, Larry also runs a small café and provides Internet access and useful tourist information.

Hospital San Rafael (☎ 441 5011; Av 9 btwn Calles Central & 1)

Instituto Costarricense de Turismo (ICT; ☎ 442 1820) There's no tourist office, but ICT has a desk at the airport.

Scotiabank (☎ 443 2168; cnr Av 3 & Calle 2; ☒ 8am-5pm Mon-Fri, 8am-4pm Sat) There are probably a dozen banks where you can change money, including Scotiabank, which has an ATM on the Cirrus network.

Sights

The shady **Parque Central** is a pleasant place to relax beneath the mango trees. It is surrounded by several 19th-century buildings, including the **cathedral**, which suffered severe damage in an earthquake in 1991. The hemispherical cupola is unusually constructed of sheets of red corrugated metal. The interior is spacious and elegant rather than ornate; two presidents are buried here.

A more baroque-looking church (though it was built in 1941) is the **Iglesia La Agonía**, six blocks east of Parque Central.

Two blocks south of the park is the rather bare **Parque Juan Santamaría**, where there is a statue of the hero (see below) in action, flanked by cannons.

Three kilometers southeast in Río Segundo de Alajuela is **Flor de Mayo** (☎ 441 2658), a very successful green and scarlet macaw breeding program. Visitation is by appointment only, and it's best to get detailed directions as it's difficult to find.

MUSEO JUAN SANTAMARÍA

Alajuela's main claim to fame is as the birthplace of national hero Juan Santamaría, for

TAXI RIDING 101

If you've just arrived at the airport in Costa Rica, here's your quick introduction to how the taxis work. Basically, certain hotels pay cab drivers a small commission for every bleary-eyed tourist they round up. And it's important to realize that the cab fare to San José is nearly five times the fare to Alajuela. So you can expect a song and dance the moment you tell a cabbie your destination, especially if you don't speak Spanish.

It's easy to give in and let your cabbie take you where he wants, though you can almost always expect to pay a higher price for lodging. Besides, you're a discriminating customer (you bought this book, didn't you?), so put some spine into it and speak up. Whether you're told that a hotel listed in this book is 'full' or even worse 'full of prostitutes,' don't believe them, even if they phone the 'receptionist' of the hotel to speak with you. If you're still having problems, simply get out of the cab and try again. *Buena suerte.*

whom the nearby international airport was named and to whom this small **museum** (☎ 441 4775; cnr Av 3 & Calle 2; admission free; ⊙ 10am-6pm Tue-Sun) is devoted.

Santamaría was the drummer boy who volunteered to torch the building that was being defended by North American filibuster William Walker in the war of 1856. Santamaría died after succeeding with his quest. The museum was once the town jail, and it now contains maps, paintings and historical artifacts that are related to the war with Walker, as well as a rotating art exhibition. There is a small auditorium where performances are occasionally staged.

OJO DE AGUA

About 6km south of Alajuela are the **Ojo de Agua** (☎ 441 2808; admission US$2; ⊙ 8am-5pm) springs, a picturesque working-class resort that's packed on weekends with folks from San José and Alajuela. Approximately 20,000L of water gush out from the spring each minute, filling swimming pools and an artificial boating lake before being piped down to Puntarenas, for which the springs are a major supply of water. There are also snack stands, game courts and a small gymnasium From San José, drivers can take the San Antonio de Belén exit off the Interamericana; Ojo de Agua is just past San Antonio.

Courses

The Fundación Castillo language school is in town. See the boxed text Spanish Schools in the Central Valley, p147, as well as the boxed text A Natural Education, p165, for more details.

Festivals & Events

The anniversary of the **Battle of Rivas**, April 11, is particularly celebrated in Alajuela, the hometown of the battle's young hero, Juan Santamaría. After William Walker and the Filibusters were ousted from Santa Rosa on March 20, 1856, the Costa Rican militia chased them into Nicaragua. On April 11 the Battle of Rivas climaxed when Santamaría was shot and killed after torching Walker's stronghold. The event is commemorated with a parade, civic events and a whole lot of firecrackers.

Sleeping

Since Alajuela is so close to the airport, most budget options can arrange transfers for a small fee.

BUDGET

There are some great budget hotels and hostels in Alajuela. All hotels have hot water.

Hostel Trotamundos (☎ 430 5832; www.hosteltrotamundos.com; Av 5 btwn Calles 2 & 4; dm US$10, d US$25-30; **P** 🖳) This reader-recommended hostel is a winner – we're talking cheap dorms, a communal kitchen, TV lounge, free Internet and plenty of communal space for hanging out with other travelers.

Casa Paz B&B (☎ 431 2691; casa-paz@mail.com; Calle 2 btwn Avs 2 & 4; d US$15-45; **P** 🖳) As the name implies (House of Peace), this place is totally mellowed-out with pastel paints and friendly management. There is a variety of different room sizes, depending on your budget, but you'll probably agree that the biggest room (complete with a huge balcony overlooking Parque Juan Santamaría) is worth the splurge – go on, treat yourself!

CENTRAL VALLEY & HIGHLANDS

CENTRAL VALLEY & HIGHLANDS

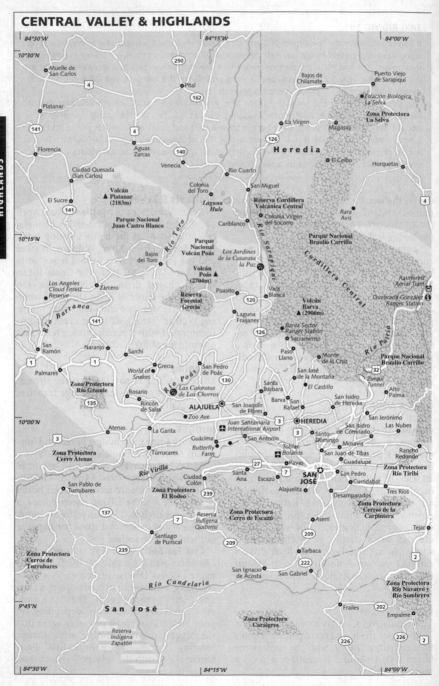

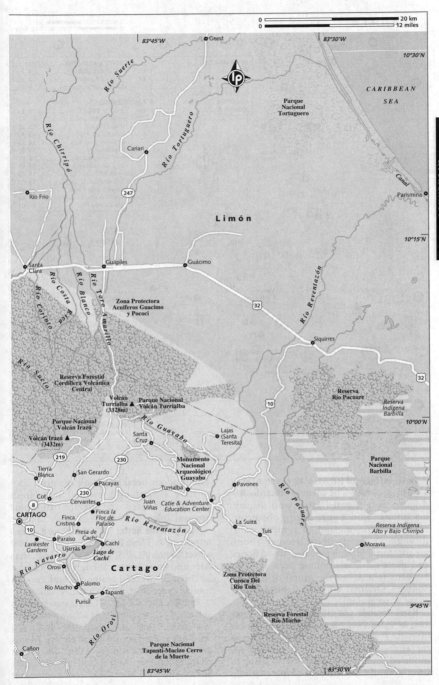

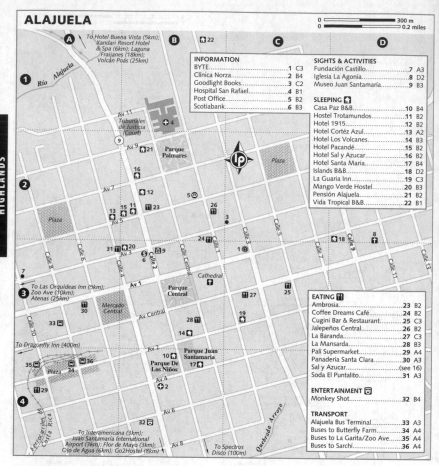

ALAJUELA

INFORMATION
BYTE..................................1 C3
Clínica Norza........................2 B4
Goodlight Books.....................3 C2
Hospital San Rafael.................4 B1
Post Office..........................5 B2
Scotiabank...........................6 B3

SIGHTS & ACTIVITIES
Fundación Castillo...................7 A3
Iglesia La Agonía...................8 D2
Museo Juan Santamaría...............9 B3

SLEEPING
Casa Paz B&B........................10 B4
Hostel Trotamundos.................11 B2
Hotel 1915..........................12 B2
Hotel Cortéz Azul...................13 A2
Hotel Los Volcanes..................14 B2
Hotel Pacandé.......................15 B2
Hotel Sal y Azucar..................16 B2
Hotel Santa Maria...................17 B4
Islands B&B.........................18 D2
La Guaria Inn.......................19 C3
Mango Verde Hostel..................20 B3
Pensión Alajuela....................21 A4
Vida Tropical B&B...................22 B1

EATING
Ambrosia............................23 B2
Coffee Dreams Café..................24 B2
Cugini Bar & Restaurant.............25 C3
Jalepeños Central...................26 B2
La Baranda..........................27 C3
La Mansarda.........................28 B3
Palí Supermarket....................29 A4
Panadería Santa Clara...............30 A3
Sal y Azucar.....................(see 16)
Soda El Puntalito...................31 A3

ENTERTAINMENT
Monkey Shot.........................32 B4

TRANSPORT
Alajuela Bus Terminal...............33 A3
Buses to Butterfly Farm.............34 A4
Buses to La Garita/Zoo Ave..........35 A4
Buses to Sarchí.....................36 A4

Hotel Cortéz Azul (☎ 443 6145; Av 5 btwn Calles 2 & 4; d US$20-30; P) The owner, Eduardo Rodríguez, is a talented artist who displays his 'unique' work (we're talking about surreal vases growing out of cement walls) throughout the property. Homey rooms are comfortable, with polished-wood floors, and there's a fine common area and two kitchens (check out the mural of the Last Supper). Original art is available for purchase at reception.

Hotel Pacandé (☎ 443 8481; www.hotelpacande .com; Av 5 btwn Calles 2 & 4; s US$20, d incl breakfast US$25-45; P 🖳) This is a popular option as the entire property has been recently remodeled, and the owners are welcoming to travelers and a great source of information.

The outdoor breakfast nook is a great spot to have a morning brew and some fresh pineapple. Shared and private bathrooms are available.

Mango Verde Hostel (☎ 441 6330; mirafloresbb@ hotmail.com; Av 3 btwn Calles 2 & 4; r per person with/ without bathroom US$20/15) This popular hostel has bare and basic rooms, though there's a nice kitchen, plenty of hammocks and enough lounge space to strike up a conversation.

Pensión Alajuela (☎ 441 6251; www.pensionala juela.com; Av 9 btwn Calles Central & 2; s/d without bathroom US$25/30, with bathroom US$35/40; P 🖂 🖳) Another great option, as attractive rooms are centered on a 'jungle-lounge' where you chat up other travelers and give (or get) advice on your trip. There's a communal

SPANISH SCHOOLS IN THE CENTRAL VALLEY

Unless otherwise noted, prices are given for five four-hour days of instruction, with/without a week's homestay with a local family. All prices include breakfast and dinner.

Adventure Education Center (☎ 556 4609, 556 4614; www.adventurespanishschool.com; US$415/315) Folks who want to combine Spanish classes and, say, white-water rafting, should head to Turrialba, where this cool school also offers courses tailored for medical professionals.

Centro Panamericano de Idiomas (☎ 265 6306; www.cpi-edu.com; US$395/275) In the Heredia suburb of San Joaquín de Flores, this school also has locations in Monteverde and Flamingo Beach in Guanacaste, with the opportunity to transfer from campus to campus.

Finca la Flor de Paraíso (☎ 534 8003; www.la-flor-de-paraiso.org; with homestay US$370) On an organic farm (see the boxed text A Natural Education (Part II), p171) not far from Cartago, vegetarian meals are the specialty and your cultural experiences could include seeing traditional Costa Rican farming techniques.

Fundación Castillo (☎ 440 8771; US$310/200) A few blocks from central Alajuela, this school also offers courses in business Spanish for a bit extra. There are activities and field trips around town every afternoon, and students get a discount at a local Latin dance school.

Instituto Profesional de Educación Daza (☎ 238 3608; www.learnspanishcostarica.com; US$320/225) Classes emphasizing conversational Spanish are held in central Heredia, and the school organizes student trips throughout the country where you can conjugate verbs while climbing volcanoes or canoeing the Río Sarapiquí.

Intercultura (☎ 260 8480, in the USA 800-552 2051; www.spanish-intercultura.com; US$370/260) This Heredia school also arranges volunteer positions throughout the country, and your new language comes with cooking and dance classes included.

Montaña Linda (☎ 533 3640; www.montanalinda.com; with homestay US$155) All classes are one-on-one at this Orosi outpost, also a fine hostel (see p171). The rate given is for homestays, though you can save money by sleeping in the hostel or camping. Classes are only three hours a day, instead of the customary four.

kitchen, optional air-con (US$10) and wireless Internet.

Hotel Sal y Azucar (☎ 430 7997; salyazucar@hotmail.com; Calle 2 btwn Avs 7 & 9; d US$35; **P**) Three attractive rooms with hip, minimalist decor are available for rent upstairs from a hip café-restaurant (p149). If you stay for more than one night, the friendly owner will take US$5 off the price of the room.

Hotel Santa Maria (☎ 440 6590; www.hotelsanta mariacr.com; Av 4 btwn Calles Central & 2; d incl breakfast US$36; **P**) This parkside inn has antique-cluttered rooms complete with private bathrooms and cable TV. The breakfast nook in the back of the hotel is a cozy spot for relaxing over a cup of coffee and the morning paper.

La Guaria Inn (☎ 440 2948; laguariahotel@netscape .net; Av 2 btwn Calles Central & 1; s/d US$36/38; **P**) Frilly rooms at this bright yellow-and-green B&B have all the trimmings, including private hot showers, cable TV and a big breakfast cooked to order.

Go2Hostel (☎ 265 6563; www.go2hostel.com; dm/d US$14/35; **P**) This solid backpacker option is about 5km east of the airport on the road to San Joaquín. The American-Tico owners spent years managing the famous Toruma

Hostel in San José, and now they've finally got a place of their own. The colonial town of San Joaquín is a pleasant alternative to Alajuela, and the hostel itself is newly constructed and full of like-minded travelers. Rates include breakfast and airport transfer (if there are two people or more).

MIDRANGE

For a few dollars more, there are some lovely B&Bs to choose from.

Vida Tropical B&B (☎ 443 9576; www.vidatropical .com; s/d incl breakfast US$30/40; **P**) In a quiet residential neighborhood just north of the city center is this Colombian-American–run B&B (the owners also own the recommended Jalapeños Central restaurant, see p149). The entire house is awash in bright murals and the backyard garden is perfect for getting some sun. There's also plenty of hammocks, comfy couches and the warm company of the owners.

Hotel Los Volcanes (☎ 441 0525; www.montezuma expeditions.com/hotel.htm; Av 2 btwn Calles Central & 2; d US$45; **P**) This 1920s refurbished home, which has been converted into an intimate six-room B&B, definitely aims to please. Rooms are furnished with period pieces and hardwood accents, and have a combination of private and shared bathrooms. The attentive and professional staff will pick you up at the airport for free, and while you're staying at the hotel they'll help organize any of your future travel plans.

Islands B&B (☎ 442 0573; islandsbb@hotmail.com; Av 1 btwn Calles 7 & 9; d/tr incl continental breakfast US$45/50; P) This unpretentious property has 10 simply furnished rooms with private showers, and a comfortable living room with cable TV that'll suit all your couch-potato needs. The friendly staff will pick you up for free at the airport.

Dragonfly Inn (☎ 443 4152; www.dragonflyinncr .com; s/d incl breakfast US$35/50; P 🖳) About 1km west of the city center, in a quiet residential neighborhood northwest of Parque La Trinidad, this charming inn is run by a North American couple named Dawn and Michael. Bright and airy rooms in this two-story, white colonial home share two immaculate bathrooms (one of which has a Jacuzzi), and the upstairs balcony and 'business center' is perfect for relaxing (or checking your email).

Hotel 1915 (☎ 441 0495; Calle 2 btwn Avs 5 & 7; s/d without air-con US$40/50, s/d/tr with air-con US$50/65/75; P 🖾) This highly recommended hotel is housed in one of the most beautiful buildings in Alajuela. Although it looks closed from the outside (and, indeed, cab drivers will tell you the same), the interior of this 101-year-old Spanish-colonial-style hotel is breathtaking, and it's easy to feel as if you've been transported to a different era. Rooms are impeccable, and everything from the period-piece furnishings to the luxurious bedspreads is a class act.

TOP END

There are few top-end options in the city, so why not exchange the big-city bustle for a little tranquil luxury?

Hotel Buena Vista (☎ 442 8595; www.hotelbuena vistacr.com; d US$70-120; P 🖾 🖾 🖳 🖳) About 5km north of Alajuela on the road to Poás, this whitewashed Mediterranean-style hotel is perched on a mountaintop, and has panoramic views of the nearby volcanoes, particularly from the balconies of the more expensive rooms. Rooms are fully equipped and come in a variety of shapes and sizes, though everyone can walk around the expansive grounds and soak up the dizzying views.

Las Orquídeas Inn (☎ 433 9346; www.orquideas inn.com; d US$69-99, ste US$99-150, apt US$130; P 🖾 🖾 🖳) About 5km west of Alajuela on the road to San Pedro de Poás is this stately Spanish-colonial mansion. Standard rooms are decked out with Guatemalan spreads and are just steps from the pool, while the varied suites are lavish (our favorites are the geodesic domes). The restaurant and bar are both well known: the first for its gourmet cuisine, and the second for its full-on Marilyn Monroe paraphernalia.

Xandari Resort Hotel & Spa (☎ 443 2020; www .xandari.com; d villa US$185-270; P 🖾 🖾 🖳) Set in a coffee plantation overlooking the Central Valley, about 6km north of Alajuela, this relaxed resort seems like it would make for an even better chick trip than a romantic holiday. Rooms are predictably plush and views are postcard perfect, with 3km of private trails and various waterfalls running through them. But the Xandari also offers visitors fitness classes and full spa packages, from facials and pedicures to exotic massages, plus two swimming pools, a Jacuzzi and, the real clincher, a gourmet restaurant that specializes in low-fat and vegetarian meals. It's the perfect place to spend your divorce settlement on the best friend who got you through it all.

Pura Vida Retreat & Spa (☎ 392 8099, in the USA 888-767 7375; www.puravidaspa.com; d tentalows/ ste US$165/185, 7-day package per person US$1200; P 🖾 🖾) Rates include two daily yoga classes, which is your first clue that this is a very different resort. A renowned yoga and alternative-health center that's a destination in itself, the retreat puts guests up in plush but zen 'tentalows' or more comfortable indoor suites, and offers classes and organized outings that usually include a spiritual or alternative-healing angle. Therapies, including lots of different massages and holistic therapies, are also included in the package deal, as are all meals at the on-site restaurant, which specializes in vegetarian and macrobiotic cuisine. It's about 7km north of Alajuela on the road to Carizal, signed from the Estadio.

Eating

Soda El Puntalito (cnr Calle 4 & Av 3; snacks US$1-3) Do as the locals do and grab a bar stool at this dirt-cheap, unassuming roadside stand.

Panadería Santa Clara (Av 1 btwn Calles 6 & 8; items US$1-3) Follow your nose to this outstanding bakery, which is stocked with all types of homemade breads as well as eye-popping pastries and cakes.

Coffee Dreams Café (Calle 1 btwn Avs 1 & 3; dishes US$2-4) This adorable café is a great place to sample the local blend, though it's worth bringing your appetite along too as the tamales here are hot and heavenly.

Jalepeños Central (☎ 430 4027; Calle 1 btwn Avs 3 & 5; dishes US$3-6; ☷ 11:20am-9pm Mon-Sat) Don't leave Alajuela without eating here! Run by an animated Colombian-American from Queens, this Tex-Mex spot provides the much needed spice in your life.

La Baranda (Av Central btwn Calles 1 & 3; dishes US$3-6) Though this *soda* definitely caters to tourists, it's still packed with locals in search of hearty casados and fresh *ceviche*.

Ambrosia (Av 5 btwn Calles Central & 2; meals US$3-6; ☷ 11am-11pm) This open-air Costa Rican diner has everything from Italian pastas to German pastries. It's reasonably priced, always bustling and if you've been traveling for too long, a welcome reprieve from rice and beans.

La Mansarda (☎ 441 4390; Calle Central btwn Avs Central & 2, 2nd fl; meals US$3-7; ☷ 11am-11pm) The top place in town for Costa Rican fare is this wonderfully casual balcony restaurant overlooking the street milieu, where fresh seafood dishes and grilled meats can be complemented by something special from the wine list.

Sal y Azucar (☎ 430 7997; Calle 2 btwn Avs 7 & 9; US$3-7; ☷ 8am-7pm Tue-Fri) This hip café has a good assortment of fresh breads and pastries, though the real draw is the rotating plate of the day, which emphasizes fresh meats and produce.

Cugini Bar & Restaurant (☎ 440 6893; cnr Av Central & Calle 5; meals US$4-10; ☷ noon-midnight Mon-Sat) This Italian-Irish-Tico-American restaurant does excellent American-style pizza plus pastas and other Italian specialties in a sports-bar atmosphere, which true to form serves beer and cocktails until late.

Head to the enclosed **Mercado Central** (Calles 4 & 6 btwn Avs 1 & Central; ☷ 7am-6pm Mon-Sat) for lots of *sodas* (inexpensive eateries), produce stands and much, much more. If you're having a little bit of culture shock, all of your favorite fast-food chains are conveniently located in the town center. Self-caterers can stock up on groceries at the **Palí supermarket** (cnr Av 2 & Calle 10; ☷ 8am-8pm).

Entertainment

The perennial Costa Rican soccer champions, Alajuela's own La Liga, play at the Estadio Morera Soto at the northeast end of town on Sundays during soccer season. If you can't get seats, stop by Cugini Bar & Restaurant (left) and you can catch the game over a brew or two.

There's no shortage of dive bars in Alajuela, and there's a good chance that karaoke will be on offer after 10pm (there's nothing like a bunch of drunken Ticos mumbling *Let It Be*). If this is your first night in Costa Rica, we recommend the Guaro Cacique. Bottoms up!

If you're looking to experience the melodic monotony that is reggaeton, check out **Monkey Shot** (Calle 4), a huge indoor-outdoor bar that sometimes has male and female strippers. Or head to **Spectros Disco** (Calle 2 btwn Avs 10 & 12), which boasts the biggest dance floor in the city.

Getting There & Away

For details of flights to Aeropuerto Internacional Juan Santamaría, see p123 and p548. You can take a taxi (US$3) to the airport from Parque Central.

There are several bus stops in Alajuela, the largest being the **Alajuela bus terminal** (Calle 8 btwn Avs Central & 1) for buses to San José, the international airport, Volcán Poás and other destinations.

Atenas US$0.50, 30 minutes, depart from the corner of Calle 6 and Avenida Central every 30 minutes from 6am to 9pm.

Butterfly Farm US$0.50, 30 minutes, depart from the corner of Calle 8 and Avenida 2 at 6:20am, 9am, 11am and 1pm.

Heredia US$0.50, 30 minutes, depart from Alajuela terminal every 15 minutes from 5am to 11pm.

La Garita/Zoo Ave US$0.50, 30 minutes, depart from the corner of Calle 10 and Avenida 2 every 30 minutes from 6am to 9pm.

Laguna de Fraijanes US$0.50, 30 minutes, depart from Alajuela terminal at 9am, 1pm, 4:15pm and 6:15pm.

San José (Tuasa) US$0.75, 45 minutes, depart from Alajuela terminal every 15 minutes from 5am to 11pm.

Sarchí US$0.50, 30 minutes, depart from Calle 8 between Avenidas Central and 2 every 30 minutes from 5am to 10pm.

BUTTERFLY FARM

Built in 1983, back when tourism was just a small sector of the country's economy, the **Butterfly Farm** (☎ 438 0400; www.butterflyfarm.co.cr; adult/child 5-12 yrs/student US$15/7/10; ☷ 8:30am-5pm) originally opened as the first commercial butterfly farm in Latin America. In the wild it's estimated that less than 2% of caterpillars survive to adulthood, while breeders at the farm boast an astounding 90% survival rate. This ensures a steady supply of pupae for gardens, schools, museums and private collections around the world. If you visit on a Monday or a Thursday from March to August, you can watch thousands of pupae being packed for export.

The butterflies are busiest when it's sunny, particularly in the morning, so try to get there early. Your entrance fee includes a guided two-hour tour, where you can learn about the stages of the complex butterfly life cycle, and the importance of butterflies in nature. Tours in English, German, Spanish or French run three times daily, more often when it's busy.

The complex also has other attractions, primarily gardens devoted to bees, orchids and other tropical species, although you could take a traditional oxcart ride with the obligatory glossy photo: a colorful reward for kids who toughed it out through all those educational videos.

The Butterfly Farm also offers several one-day package tours (adult/child/student US$63/48/53) that include transportation from any San José hotel, lunch and a tour of the farm, plus a Coffee Tour at the Café Britt Finca (see p162) and any number of other side trips.

Drivers can reach the Butterfly Farm by heading 12km south of Alajuela to the village of La Guácima; it's almost in front of the well-signed El Club Campestre Los Reyes. The farm provides a round-trip shuttle service from San José hotels for US$10 per person, or you can take a direct bus from Alajuela (see p149).

WEST TO ATENAS

The road west from Alajuela to Atenas (25km) is a pleasant day trip for anyone who's even remotely interested in corn, though the perfect climate and rural atmosphere are reason enough to linger.

La Garita

This pilgrimage-worthy destination for folks who really appreciate corn is 11km west of Alajuela. At La Garita you can stop for a quick bite at a number of 'corny' restaurants (sorry, we couldn't resist!), as well

as visiting the largest collection of birds in Central America.

Zoo Ave (☎ 433 8989; www.zooave.org; adult/child US$9/1; ⏰ 8:30am-5pm), 10km west of Alajuela, just before La Garita, has more than 80 Costa Rican species of birds on colorful, squawking display in a relaxing parklike setting – this is a great stop for families. All four Costa Rican species of monkey as well as other critters are on view, though the 'zoo' is actually a breeding center that aims to reintroduce native species into the wild. There are volunteer opportunities here as well, especially if you have experience handling animals.

SLEEPING & EATING

Martino Resort & Spa (☎ 433 8382; www.hotelmartino .com; d standard/deluxe US$160/210; P ✖ ✖ ☐ ☑) Couples who can't decide between Las Vegas and Central America can compromise here amid over-the-top, Roman-style luxury, complete with 'Costa Rica's most elegant casino.' Gourmet organic Italian meals, a bird sanctuary, an outrageous spa, huge pools, sauna and full gym are also on offer. It's 2km north of the Alajuela exit from the Interamericana, about 15 minutes from the airport.

Scientists from around the world come to Costa Rica's corn breadbasket to study maize. Everyone else comes to dine at one of a number of unusual restaurants to do their own tasty investigation.

La Fiesta del Maíz (☎ 487 7057; mains US$1-5; ⏰ 6am-9:30pm) This understated spot is famed for its wide variety of corn concoctions, as well as fried pork skins.

Delicias del Maíz (☎ 433 7206; mains US$3-9; ⏰ 8am-9:30pm) Delicias is decidedly more upmarket, with its rustic dining room and grill, and also adapts just about every possible recipe to include corn. Iowa, eat your heart out.

La Casa del Viñedo (☎ 487 6086; mains US$4-15; ⏰ 11am-11pm) Dare we say it – if corn is not your thing, visit this vineyard on the edge of La Garita, which produces small batches of seven different wines. You can sample them alongside the recommended steaks, Argentine or American style.

GETTING THERE & AWAY

Buses (US$0.50, 30 minutes) run between Alajuela and La Garita, via Zoo Ave, every half-hour. If you're driving, take the Atenas exit off the Interamericana, then go 3km east to Zoo Ave.

Atenas

This small village is on the historic *camino de carretas* (oxcart trail) that once carried coffee beans as far as Puntarenas, though it's best known as having the most pleasant climate in the world, at least according to a 1994 issue of *National Geographic*. It's not too heavy on sights, though springtime is always in the air.

Follow the signs to **El Cafetal Inn B&B** (☎ 446 7361; www.cafetal.com; s/d standard US$80/90, d luxury US$100-130; **P**), a sweeping coffee plantation 5km north of Atenas, where you can stay the night or simply stop by to sample the local specialty – that'd be coffee. There's a large garden (with two easy trails to waterfalls), a pool and several attractive rooms that vary in size and amenities, but all with lots of light and great country views. The on-site café **Mirador del Cafetal** (dishes US$1-5; ☽ 7am-5pm) sells its own brand of coffee, La Negrita, as beans or in an outstanding selection of beverages, drunk hot or cold while gazing across the entire Central Valley.

The **Rancho Típico La Trilla** (☎ 446 5637; mains US$3-8), 75m west of the gas station, is a popular tourist stop serving rustic-style casados where you can opt for the caffeine theme at the 'coffee mill.'

Frequent buses connect Atenas to San José and Alajuela.

NORTHWEST TO SARCHÍ

Scattered across the carefully cultivated hills to the northwest of Alajuela are the small towns of Grecia (22km), Sarchí (29km), Naranjo (35km) and Zarcero (52km), which are popular romantic getaways for josefinos in search of flowering trees and fresh country air. In addition to its charming atmosphere, the region also boasts excellent coffee and a subdued collection of eccentric attractions, including the country's most famous topiary bushes as well as its arts-and-crafts capital.

Grecia

Centered on the incongruous, bright-red metal **Catedral de la Mercedes**, which was boxed up in Belgium and shipped to Costa Rica in 1897, Grecia is a modern town spiced up with a fair dash of Costa Rican folklore. The small **Casa de Cultura** (☎ 444 6767) has the official version, with Spanish-colonial artifacts plus articles about Grecia's 'Cleanest Little Town in Latin America' award and an impressive insect collection.

INFORMATION

Theoretically, **Minae** (Ministry of Environment & Energy; ☎ 494 0065; ☽ 8am-4pm Mon-Fri) has information about the surrounding parks. The town has several simple *sodas* and bars plus banks with 24-hour ATMs and a post office.

SIGHTS

Check out the **18th-century rock bridge** south of town connecting the hamlets of Puente de Piedra and Rincón de Salas. Grecians say that the only other rock bridge like this is in China, and some tales tell it was built by the devil. In 1994 it was declared a National Site of Historical Interest.

The premier attraction, however, is **World of Snakes** (☎ 494 3700; adult/child US$12/7; ☽ 8am-4pm), 1.5km southeast of the town center, a well-run attraction with an endangered-snake breeding program. More than 150 snakes (40 species in all) are displayed in comfortable-looking cages as 'Snakes of the World' or 'Snakes of Costa Rica.' Informative tours in English, German or Spanish may include the chance to handle certain snakes if there's time. Any bus to Grecia from Alajuela can drop you at the entrance.

Mariposario Spirogyra (adult/child US$5/3; ☽ 8am-5pm), 150m from the church, is a small but pretty butterfly garden with a few informative plaques. Guided tours are included with the price.

About 5km south of Grecia, toward Santa Gertrudis, are **Las Cataratas de Los Chorros** (admission US$4; ☽ 8am-5pm), two gorgeous waterfalls and a swimming hole surrounded by picnic tables, which is a popular spot for weekending couples.

ACTIVITIES

Is Costa Rica's safe and peaceful image just not doing it for you? Live dangerously at **Tropical Bungee** (☎ 290 5629; www.bungee.co.cr; 1st/2nd jump US$60/30), where you can hurl yourself off the 75m bridge that spans the Río Colorado. Your impending doom is 2km west of the turnoff for Grecia.

SLEEPING & EATING

Healthy Day Country Inn Resort (☎ 444 5903; healthyday@racsa.co.cr; d incl breakfast US$45; ℗ ☒ ☒ 🖳 🖳) Although the crumbling, jungle facade adorning the entrance looks like it's seen better days, this Tico resort is a great city break, especially if you're looking to slim down. Rooms with shared bathrooms are great value considering guests have access to the on-site tennis court, gym and Jacuzzi as well as less taxing weight-loss opportunities including homeopathic therapies, massages and macrobiotic meals. It's 800m northeast of the church on the main road.

Vista del Valle Plantation Inn (☎ 450 0800; www .vistadelvalle.com; s/d US$100/120, ste incl breakfast US$155-200; ℗ ☒ 🖳) In the village of Rosario, about 7km southwest of Grecia as the parrot flies, this choice property with a regular airport shuttle may well be one of the swankiest jungle lodges in Costa Rica. Elegant garden cottages scattered throughout the luxuriously landscaped botanical garden have balconies that overlook the Río Grande, various volcanoes and even San José city lights. Trails lead past a 90m-high waterfall into the adjoining Zona Protectora Río Grande, a cloud forest reserve at about 800m. Horseback tours and massage therapy are available, and there is also a pool and Jacuzzi for soaking off the hike.

There are a few well-stocked markets, bakeries and basic *sodas* in town.

GETTING THERE & AWAY

The bus terminal is about 400m south of the church, behind the *mercado*.

San José US$0.50, one hour, depart every 30 minutes from 5:30am to 10pm.

Sarchí, connecting to Naranjo US$0.25, one hour, depart every 25 minutes from 4:45am to 10pm.

Sarchí

There's just one problem with vacationing in Costa Rica: lousy souvenir shopping. Blame the whole ecotourism thing – it just seems wrong to buy a plastic bauble commemorating your visit to some of the last untouched rain forests in the world. But here it is, the end of your trip, and you've got to face jealous friends and family who won't care that you spotted a rare three-wattled bellbird while trekking through waist-deep mud. Nope, they want presents.

Welcome to Sarchí, Costa Rica's most famous crafts center, where artists showcase the country's deeply ingrained woodworking tradition. Unfortunately, a 45-minute stop in town (especially if you're on a tour bus) is likely to give you the impression that you've landed in a tourist trap, albeit one with free coffee. But keep in mind that there are more than 200 workshops scattered around the nearby countryside, and if you exert a little independence it's often possible to meet different artists, and even custom order your own creation or arrange a lesson or two.

ORIENTATION & INFORMATION

Sarchí is divided by the Río Trojas into Sarchí Norte and Sarchí Sur, and is rather spread out, straggling for several kilometers along the main road from Grecia to Naranjo. In Sarchí Norte you'll find the main plaza with the typical twin-towered church, a hotel and some restaurants. There is a **Banco Nacional** (☎ 454 4262; 🕙 8:30am-3pm Mon-Fri) for changing money.

SLEEPING & EATING

Cabinas Mandy (☎ 454 2397; s/d US$10/15; ℗) Close to the fire station in Sarchí Norte is the best budget option in town. Small but well-kept rooms have cable TV and private hot showers.

Hotel Daniel Zamora (☎ 454 4596; d US$35; ℗) On a quiet street east of the soccer field, this is a slightly more upmarket choice. Rooms have cable TV and private hot showers, and are large and nicely furnished.

A great farmers market is held on Fridays behind Taller Lalo Alfaro, with homemade snacks, palmetto cheese and lots of produce.

Las Carretas (☎ 454 1636; mains US$5-10; 🕙 11am-9pm) The most popular restaurant in town for tour buses and locals alike serves up Tico classics in an elegant dining room adorned with local woodwork.

GETTING THERE & AROUND

Driving, you can take the unpaved road northeast from Sarchí to Bajos del Toro and on through Colonia del Toro to the northern lowlands at Río Cuarto. The main attraction of this route is the beautiful waterfall north of Bajos del Toro. Look for local signs for the 'Catarata.'

A SHOPPERS GUIDE TO SARCHÍ

Elegantly polished or brightly painted, Sarchí work is unmistakable. Although the range of crafts available for purchase is extensive, most travelers are interested in *carretas,* the elaborately painted oxcarts that are the unofficial souvenir of Costa Rica (and official symbol of the Costa Rican worker).

Painting the elaborate mandala designs requires a steady hand and active imagination, and is a process well worth watching. Though pricier models are ready for the road (oxen sold separately), most are scaled-down versions designed for display in gardens and homes, while others have been customized to function as indoor tables, sideboards and minibars. Smaller models are, of course, suitable for every budget and backpack.

In addition to *carretas,* shoppers in the know come to Sarchí for leather-and-wood furniture, specifically rocking chairs that collapse Ikea-style for shipping. Other items you won't find elsewhere include gleaming wooden bowls and other tableware, some carved from rare hardwoods (which you should think twice about buying unless you want to contribute to further deforestation). Most of the hardwoods sculpted in Sarchí are grown locally on plantations, though it's best to inquire about a piece if you're feeling unsure.

What makes Sarchí so much more than another stop on the tourist circuit is that the top artisans are part of renowned woodworking families, many of whom are very welcoming to inquisitive travelers. If you're interested in commissioning a custom piece, artisans will be happy to listen to your ideas as well as to offer suggestions, and prices are generally fair and reasonable. There are also plenty of opportunities in Sarchí for taking woodworking classes or organizing an apprenticeship – talk to different artisans, ask for a few prices and work out a deal that makes everyone happy.

Workshops are usually open from 8am to 4pm daily, and they accept credit cards and US dollars. Below is a listed of recommended spots, though with over 200 places to choose from it pays to shop around and enjoy the experience.

Fábrica de Carretas Joaquín Chaverri (☎ 454 4411) The oldest and best-known factory in Sarchí Sur. This is a good spot for watching artisans from the old school of transportation aesthetic emblazon those incredible patterns on oxcarts by hand.

Los Rodríguez (☎ 454 4097), **La Sarchiseño** (☎ 454 3430) and **El Artesano** (☎ 454 4304) All are located along the main road, and specialize in rocking chairs and other furniture.

Pidesa Souvenirs (☎ 454 4540) By the main plaza, this spot specializes in hand-painting local souvenirs Sarchí style, including full-size milk cans.

Plaza de la Artesanía (☎ 454 3430) In Sarchí Sur, this is the top choice for connoisseurs of kitsch. It's a shopping mall with more than 30 souvenir stores selling everything from truly beautiful furniture to mass-produced key chains.

Taller Lalo Alfaro Two blocks north of the church, is Sarchí's oldest workshop, where they still make working oxcarts using machinery powered by a waterwheel.

Alajuela (Tuasa) US$0.45, 30 minutes, depart every 30 minutes from 6am to 11pm.

Grecia US$0.25, 20 minutes, depart every 30 minutes from 6am to 11pm.

San José US$2, 1½ hours, depart at 6am, 1pm and 4:05pm.

PALMARES

Palmares' claim to fame is the annual **Las Fiestas de Palmares**, a 10-day beer-soaked extravaganza that takes place in mid-January and features carnival rides, parades, a *tope* (horse parade), fireworks, discotheques, big-name bands, small-name bands, exotic dancers, fried food, Guaro Cacique tents and the highest proportion of drunken Ticos you've ever seen. Not surprisingly, it's one of the biggest events in the country, and is widely covered on national TV.

Palmares is a tiny village for 355 days of the year, crowds for the festival can reach upwards of 10,000 people. Over the 10-day period, the fiesta continues unabated virtually day and night, and you won't believe how hard Ticos can party until you've seen it for yourself. If you're traveling in Costa Rica in January, look for posters advertising the festival, which will detail what events are taking place on which days.

CENTRAL VALLEY & HIGHLANDS

Give up any plans you have of staying in Palmares unless you know someone with a house in the area. Buses run continuously from San José to Palmares throughout the festival, though it's common for groups of Ticos to rent private shuttles. If you're driving, the road from Sarchí continues west to Naranjo, where it divides – head south for 13km to reach Palmares.

SAN RAMÓN

The colonial town of San Ramón is no wallflower in the pageant of Costa Rican history. The 'City of Presidents and Poets' has sent five men to the country's highest office, including ex-president Rodrigo Carazo, who built a tourist lodge a few kilometers to the north at the entrance to the Los Angeles Cloud Forest (see right).

Stories of the former presidents, plus poets and more, can be found on plaques around town or at the **Museo de San Ramón** (☎ 437 9851; admission free; ☿ 8:30-11am Wed-Sat & 1-5pm Mon-Fri), on the north side of the park. It's worth working around the museum's schedule to see life-size dioramas depicting colonial Costa Rica and well-done exhibits on the area's impressive history.

At the center of San Ramón are the twin spires of the ash-grey **Iglesia de San Ramón**, which soar high above the town and give it a dignified air. In front of the church is **Parque Central**, which is surrounded by a few colonial buildings and has a bizarre collection of lime-green *torii*, the traditional Japanese gates found at the entrance to a Shinto shrine.

Sleeping & Eating

There are a few inexpensive places to stay in town, as well as two upscale lodges in the nearby reserve (see right).

Hotel Gran (☎ 445 6363; s/d US$10/15; Ⓟ) Three blocks west of the park is this decent budget option, which has completely standard rooms that surround a courtyard and come with private warm-water bathrooms and cable TV.

Hotel la Posada (☎ 445 7359; www.posadahotel .com; s/d incl breakfast US$30/40) Spend the extra money and upgrade to this executive-worthy hotel, which has seriously plush rooms complete with beautiful wooden furniture and huge TVs. Private bathrooms have steaming-hot showers that will make you realize what you've been missing!

Il Giardino (dishes US$4-8) On the southwestern corner of the central park, Il Giardino specializes in wood oven-fired pizzas and thick, juicy steaks.

The Saturday farmers market is a big one, with smaller markets on Wednesday and Sunday.

Getting There & Away

There are hourly buses to San José as well as frequent buses to Ciudad Quesada via Zarcero. Buses depart from Calle 16 between Avenidas 1 and 3.

LOS ANGELES CLOUD FOREST RESERVE

This **private reserve** (☎ 661 1600; per person US$15), about 20km north of San Ramón, is centered on a lodge and dairy ranch that was once owned by ex-president Rodrigo Carazo. Some 800 hectares of primary forest have a short boardwalk and longer horse and foot trails that lead to towering waterfalls and misty cloud forest vistas. The appeal of this cloud forest (which is actually adjacent to the reserve at Monteverde, see p207) is that it is comparatively untouristed, which means you will have a good chance of observing wildlife (jaguars and ocelots are occasionally spotted), and the birding here is simply fantastic. Although quetzals do not roost in the reserve, other trogons are commonly sighted.

Bilingual naturalist guides are available to lead hikes (per person US$25) and you can also rent horses (per hour US$20) or take to the zip lines on a canopy tour (per person US$40). Tours of the reserve are arranged through Villablanca Hotel & Spa (below), though guests of the hotel can enter for free. A taxi to the reserve and hotel costs US$10 from San Ramón, and the turnoff is well signed from the highway.

Sleeping

Villablanca Cloud Forest Hotel & Spa (☎ 228 4603; www.villablanca-costarica.com; d US$135-175) The large main lodge, restaurant and about 30 whitewashed, red-tiled, rustic adobe *casetas* here are surrounded by the Los Angeles Cloud Forest Reserve. Comfortable cabins have refrigerators, bathtubs and fireplaces, and there's a fine on-site restaurant and spa. The big perk here, however, is free and easy access to the adjacent reserve.

POETIC LICENSE

One of the most famous of San Ramón's poets was Lisímaco Chavarría Palma, who was born into a family of farmers in 1878. Although he was forced to drop out of school at an early age, Lisímaco balanced his farming duties with rigorous self-education. During his youth, he became a student of the famous artist Lico Rodríguez Cross, and spent his formative years laboring in a variety of artistic disciplines. In 1901 Lisímaco returned to San Ramón in order to direct a school, and began writing poetry about the customs of the farm.

The modesty of Lisímaco's life and the strength of his words touched Costa Rican society, and he quickly became one of the most famous poets of the day. In 1911 Lisímaco's was offered a position as the curator of the National Library in Guatemala, though he declined in favor of the simple, rural life. On August 27, 1913, Lisímaco tragically died of tuberculosis, though just prior to his death he wrote the following verse:

> …y que manos cariñosas
> me lleven a la huesa muchas rosas
> cortadas con amor…

> …and that caring hands
> take many roses to my tomb
> cut with love.

This short verse spawned a tradition that continues today whereby every August 27, all of the students in the city carry freshly cut roses to the poet's tomb.

Valle Escondido Lodge (☎ 231 0906; www.hotel valleescondido.net; s/d US$70/94) The lodge's collection of luxurious cabinas are adjacent to another private reserve featuring 20km of cloud forest trails and a working ornamental-plant and citrus-fruit farm. Nonguests can pay US$8 just for day use of the trails. There is also a pool, Jacuzzi and a locally popular restaurant with Italian specialties. It's about halfway between Hotel Villablanca and the village of La Tigra.

ZARCERO

North of Naranjo, the road winds for 20km until it reaches Zarcero's 1736m perch at the western end of the Cordillera Central. The mountains are gorgeous and the climate is famously fresh, but the reason you've come is evident as soon as you pull into town.

Parque Francisco Alvarado, in front of the already off-kilter pink and blue 1895 Iglesia de San Rafael, was just a normal plaza until the 1960s (of course), when gardener Evangelisto Blanco suddenly became inspired to shave the ordinary, mild-mannered bushes into bizarre abstract shapes and, over the years, everything from elephants to bull fights (the latest creation is a double tunnel of surreal, melting arches).

Today the trippy topiary is certainly the town's top sight, but space-age trees aren't the only thing growing in Zarcero – this is a center for Costa Rica's organic-farming movement (p281). You can find unusual varieties of pesticide-free goodies all over town, and the surrounding mountains are just perfect for an afternoon picnic.

Activities

The roads around Zarcero are lined with small stores selling picnic supplies – be on the lookout for *queso palmito*, a locally made cheese that has a delicate taste and goes well with fresh tomatoes and basil. Once you've packed your picnic basket, explore the surrounding countryside and find your own grassy spot beneath the shade of a Guanacaste tree.

If you brought your swimsuit, stop into **Piscinas Apamar** (☎ 463 3674; per person US$2; ☼ 7am-4pm Mon-Sat), 500m west of the park on the road to Guadalupe, where there's not only a huge swimming pool but also three hot tubs and a Jacuzzi.

Sleeping

Hotel Don Beto (☎ 463 3137; www.hoteldonbeto .com; d with/without bathroom US$30/25, tr US$35; [P])

Just north of the town church is this recommended hotel, which has homey rooms with either shag rugs or hardwood floors and private balconies. The Tico owners treat everyone has if they were visiting family, and they're a great resource for organizing trips throughout the area, especially to nearby Los Angeles Cloud Forest Reserve and Parque Nacional Juan Castro Blanco.

Getting There & Away

Hourly buses traveling between San José and Ciudad Quesada stop at Zarcero, though some buses may be full by the time they reach Zarcero, particularly on weekends. There are also buses from Alajuela and San Ramón.

PARQUE NACIONAL JUAN CASTRO BLANCO

This 143-sq-km **national park** (admission US$6, camping US$2) was created in 1992 to protect the slopes of Volcán Platanar (2183m) and Volcán Porvenir (2267m) from logging. The headwaters for five major rivers originate here as well, making this one of the most important watersheds in the entire country.

The park is in limbo, federally protected but still privately owned by various plantation families – only those parts that have already been purchased by the government are technically open to the traveler. As yet, there is almost no infrastructure for visitors, though there is a **Minae office** (☎ 460 7600) in El Sucre, next to the only official entrance, where you can pay fees for camping or day use. However, the office is usually closed, and fees are rarely collected.

The park is popular among anglers as each of the five rivers is brimming with trout, and the difficult access means that the park is nearly always abandoned. Also, the lack of infrastructure and tourist traffic means that your chances of spotting rare wildlife are very high. However, since there are no facilities and few marked trails in the park, it's recommended that you hire a guide, which can be arranged at any of the hotels in the area.

PARQUE NACIONAL VOLCÁN POÁS

Just 37km north of Alajuela by a winding and scenic road is the most heavily trafficked **national park** (admission US$7; ☼ 8am-

3:30pm) in Costa Rica. However, there are few places in the world where you can peer into an active volcano – without the hardship of actually hiking up one. The centerpiece of the park is, of course, Volcán Poás (2704m), which had its last blowout in 1953. This event formed the eerie and enormous crater, which is 1.3km across and 300m deep. There are also two other craters, one of which contains a lake, that serve as evidence of the volcano's violent past.

Poás continues to be active to varying extents with different levels of danger. The park was briefly closed in May 1989 after a minor eruption sent volcanic ash spouting more than a kilometer into the air, and lesser activity closed the park intermittently in 1995. In recent years, however, Poás has posed no imminent threat, though scientists are still worried – the water level of the lake has dropped dramatically in the past decade, which is a major warning sign of an impending eruption (see the boxed text Feelin' Hot, Hot, Hot!, p249).

In the meantime, the most common hazard for visitors is the veil of clouds that the mountain gathers around itself almost daily (even in the dry season), starting at around 10am. Even if the day looks clear, get to the park as early as possible or you won't see much. But, crowds and clouds aside, the sight of the bubbling and steaming cauldron is truly astonishing, especially when it belches sulfurous mud and steaming water hundred of meters into the air.

Information

Some 250,000 people visit the park annually, making Poás the most packed national park in the country – visiting on weekends in particular is best avoided. The visitor center has a coffee shop, souvenirs and informative videos hourly from 9am to 3pm. A small museum offers explanations in both Spanish and English. There's no camping at the park.

The best time to visit is during the dry season, especially early in the morning before the clouds roll in and obscure the view. Even if the summit is clouded in, don't despair! Take a hike to the other craters and then return to the cauldron later – winds change rapidly on the summit, and sometimes thick cloud cover is quickly blown away.

Be advised that overnight temperatures can drop below freezing, and it may be windy and cold during the day, particularly in the morning. Also, Poás receives almost 4000mm of rainfall each year. Dress accordingly.

Hiking

From the visitor center, there is a wheelchair-accessible paved road that leads directly to the crater lookout. Because of the toxic sulfuric-acid fumes that are emitted from the cauldron, visitors are prohibited from descending into the crater.

From the crater, there are two trails that branch out – to the right is **Sendero Botos**, to the left **Sendero Escalonia**. Sendero Botos is a short, 30-minute round-trip hike that takes you through dwarf cloud forest, which is the product of acidic air and freezing temperatures. Here you can wander about looking at bromeliads, lichens and mosses clinging to the curiously shaped and twisted trees growing in the volcanic soil. Birds abound, especially the magnificent fiery-throated hummingbird, a high-altitude specialty of Costa Rica. The trail ends at **Laguna Botos**, a peculiar cold-water lake that has filled in one of the extinct craters.

Sendero Escalonia is a slightly longer trail through taller forest, though it gets significantly less traffic than the other parts of the park. While hiking on the trail, look for other highland specialties including the sooty robin, black guans, screech owls and even the odd quetzal (especially from February to April). Although mammals are infrequently sighted in the park, coyotes and the endemic montane squirrel are present.

Tours

Although numerous companies offer daily tours to the volcano, readers frequently complain that they're an overpriced affair. Typically, they cost US$40 to US$100, and the kicker is that you usually arrive at the volcano around 10am – right when the clouds start rolling in. Also, readers complain that they're often rushed off the crater, though there always seems to be time for stopping at a few souvenir stores on the way back.

As always, it's important to shop around and ask questions. Generally, the cheaper tours are large group affairs providing only transportation, park entrance and limited time at the crater. The more expensive tours feature smaller group sizes, bilingual naturalist guides and lunch. However, just remember that it's possible to visit the volcano quite easily using public transportation from San José, and it's definitely cheaper for two people to rent a car for the day and drive themselves.

Sleeping

ON THE ROAD TO POÁS

Lo Que Tu Quieres Lodge (☎ 482 2092; s/d/tr cabins US$19/25/30; P) About 5km before the park entrance, the name of this place translates to 'Whatever You Want Lodge.' This is a good budget option as cabinas are all equipped with heaters and hot water, and the owners will usually let you camp for a few dollars. There is a small restaurant (dishes US$3 to US$8) on the grounds that serves simple, typical food.

Lagunillas Lodge (☎ 448 5506; d/tr US$25/30, cabinas US$30-40; P) The closest accommodation to the volcano is recommended for its stellar views and the warm welcome you'll get on arrival. Rooms and larger cabinas, which can accommodate up to six people, have hot-water showers and heaters, and all are surrounded by good hiking trails. There's also a fish pond out back where you can catch dinner, and the restaurant (mains US$4 to US$10) will prepare it – with side dishes. To get here, a signed turnoff about 2km before the park entrance sends you along a steep 1km dirt road that may require a 4WD – call ahead.

AROUND POÁS

Poás Volcano Lodge (☎ 482 2194; www.poasvolcano lodge.com; s/d US$45/55, s/d with bathroom US$55/75, ste US$90-115; P ▢) About 16km east of the volcano near Vara Blanca, this high-altitude dairy farm frames the attractive stone building, which blends architectural influences from Wales, England and Costa Rica (the original owners were English farmers). Trails radiate from the eclectically decorated rooms, and common areas include a billiard room ('pool' doesn't do it justice). There's a sitting area with a sunken fireplace, and books and board games to while away a stormy night.

Bosque de Paz Rain/Cloud Forest Lodge & Biological Reserve (☎ 234 6676; www.bosquedepaz.com; s/d/tr incl 3 meals US$121/196/279; P) Tastefully decorated in rustic luxury, this 1000-hectare biological reserve offers access to what forms a wild corridor between Parque Nacional Volcán Poás and Parque Nacional Juan Castro Blanco: not your average lodge grounds. There are 22km of trails, sometimes used by researchers from all over the world, and the owners can arrange guided hikes. If driving north from the Interamericana through Zarcero, take a right immediately after the church and head north about 15km. The reserve will be on your right, just before the last bridge to Bajos del Toro.

Eating

On sunny days the road to Poás is lined with stands selling fruit, cheese and snacks – it's worth picking up picnic supplies because the coffee shop has a limited menu. Bring your own bottled water, as proximity to primordial seepage has rendered the tap water undrinkable.

Colbert Restaurant (dishes US$5-10) About 2km east of the Poás Volcano Lodge (p157), on a ridge overlooking the volcano, this reader-recommended rustic French restaurant highlights local Tico-produced cheeses in traditional, continental dishes.

Getting There & Away

You can take a taxi to the park for around US$80 from San José, US$40 from Alajuela. If you're driving, the road from Alajuela to the volcano is well signed. Most visitors using public buses come from San José. Get to the terminal early.

From San José (US$4, three hours) Tuasa buses depart 8:30am daily from Avenida 2 between Calles 12 and 14, stopping in Alajuela at 9:30am, and returning at 2:30pm.

LOS JARDINES DE LA CATARATA LA PAZ

La Paz waterfall gardens (☎ 265 0643; www.waterfallgardens.com; adult/child & student US$21/10; ☉ 8:30am-5:30pm) are built around an almost impossibly scenic series of waterfalls formed as Río La Paz drops 1400m in less than 8km down the flanks of Volcán Poás. The lowest, whose name means 'Peace Waterfall,' is one of the most loved (and photographed) sights in Costa Rica.

Visitors, many on tours from San José, follow 3.5km of well-maintained trails that wind past a butterfly conservatory (the largest in the world), a hummingbird garden and a rare orchids display before plunging down alongside five cascading waterfalls. Small children, city slickers and active seniors won't have any problems with this adventure, especially since there is a shuttle bus at the bottom of the falls that brings hikers back up to the visitor center.

The gardens are administered by the **Peace Lodge** (☎ 482 2720; www.waterfallgardens.com; d regular/deluxe US$185/215), one of six 'Small Distinctive Hotels of Costa Rica.' Take a long, hard look at your travel companion – if you love him or her in the slightest way (and money isn't an option), you'll change your plans and spend the night here. Standard rooms are a work of art with waterfall showers that gush at the slightest turn of a knob, manicured-stone fireplaces for those cool, crisp nights, and exotic design schemes that will bring all of your rainforest fantasies to life. Deluxe rooms are all this and more (we're talking two Jacuzzis for all your indoor and outdoor soaking pleasures).

Even if you're not staying in the hotel, you can still visit the lodge's buffet (adult/child US$10/5), where you can dine alongside a huge fireplace that provides welcome respite from the weather on a rainy day.

HEREDIA AREA

Despite outward appearances and a convenient location, Heredia (population 33,000) isn't just a suburb of San José. Since the late 1990s the city has come into its own as the high-tech capital of Costa Rica – microchips produced here have suddenly become the country's most important export. Career opportunities make Heredia a magnet for this highly educated nation's tech heads, and considering that the historic coffee center also produces some of the world's strongest brew, programmers have little excuse to stop coding. Ever.

But there's much more to this province than its well-to-do capital. The Heredia area retains its heritage as a coffee-production center, and indeed it's possible to visit the headquarters of the most famous roaster in the country, Café Britt Finca (p162). The area is also home to one of Costa Rica's largest swaths of rain forest, namely Parque Nacional Braulio Carrillo (p163).

HEREDIA

During its colonial heyday, la Ciudad de las Flores (the City of the Flowers) was home to the Spanish aristocracy, who made their fortunes by exporting Costa Rica's premium blend. Over the years, the Spanish built an attractive colonial city on an orderly grid, and although Heredia grew in both size and prominence, it managed to retain its charming elegance and small-city feel. Following the independence of Costa Rica, Heredia was even considered for the seat of federal government.

Although it is only 11km from San José, Heredia is a world away from the grit and grime of the capital. The cosmopolitan bustle comes courtesy of the multinational high-tech corporations that have their Central American headquarters here, while more bohemian stylings radiate from the National University. Heredia's historic center is one of the most attractive in the country, and the city serves as a convenient base for exploring the diverse attractions of the province.

Information

Though there's no tourist office, most other services are readily available. The university district is full of copy places, Internet cafés, cell-phone shops, and music and video stores.

Hospital San Vicente de Paul (☎ 261 0001; Av 8 btwn Calles 14 & 16)

Internet Cafe (Av Central btwn Calles 7 & 9; per hr US$0.75) For 24-hour access to the web.

Scotiabank (☎ 262 5303; Av 4 btwn Calles Central & 2; ☼ 8am-5pm Mon-Fri, 8am-4pm Sat) Just one place that changes money, and has a 24-hour ATM that dispenses US dollars.

Sights

Heredia was founded in 1706, and in true Spanish-colonial style it has several interesting old landmarks arranged around **Parque Central**. To the east is **Iglesia de la Inmaculada Concepción**, built in 1797 and still in use. Opposite the church steps you can take a break and watch old men playing checkers at the park tables while weddings and funerals come and go. The church's thick-walled, squat construction is attractive in a Volkswagen Beetle sort of way. The solid shape has withstood the earthquakes that have damaged or destroyed almost all

the other buildings in Costa Rica that date from this time.

To the north of the park is an 1867 guard tower called simply **El Fortín**, which is the last remaining turret of a Spanish fortress and the official symbol of Heredia. This area is a national historic site, but passageways are closed to the public.

At the park's northeast corner, **Casa de la Cultura** (☎ 262 2505; cnr Calle Central & Av Central; www .heredianet.co.cr/casacult.htm in Spanish; admission free; ☼ vary), formerly the residence of President Alfredo González Flores (1913–17), now houses permanent historical exhibits as well as rotating art shows and other events.

The campus of **Universidad Nacional**, six blocks east of Parque Central, is a great place for doing a little guerrilla learning – strap on your backpack (the small one) and follow the student crowds. While you're on campus, keep an eye out for posters advertising cultural offerings and special events happening around the city. Also, check out the marine biology department's **Museo Zoomarino** (☎ 277 3240; admission free; ☼ 8am-4pm Mon-Fri), where more than 2000 displayed specimens give an overview of Costa Rica's marine diversity.

Courses

There are three Spanish-language schools in town: Centro Panamericano de Idiomas, Intercultura and Instituto Profesional de Educación Daza. See the boxed text Spanish Schools in the Central Valley on p147 for more details.

Sleeping

Most travelers prefer to stay in nearby San José, though there are plenty of budget hotels in town that cater to students – if you like paper-thin walls, there are plenty of cheap monthly rates.

Hotel El Verano (☎ 237 1616; Calle 4 btwn Avs 6 & 8; d US$8; **P**) It's in the seedy, noisy area by the bus terminal, but it's cheap and reasonably clean with shared cold showers. Cheaper hourly rates are available (if you catch our drift).

Hotel Las Flores (☎ 261 1477; Av 12 btwn Calles 12 & 14; s/d US$14/20; **P**) Though it's a bit of a walk from the city center, this hotel is recommended for its warm, welcoming management and bright, sunny rooms complete with steamy showers and thick mattresses.

CENTRAL VALLEY & HIGHLANDS

Hotel Heredia (☎ 238 0880; Calle 6 btwn Avs 3 & 5; s/d/tr US$15/20/30; P) This adorable white-and-blue house was recently renovated from the ground up, and now features sparkling rooms with private solar-heated showers and cable TV, not to mention plenty of green space for lounging about.

Hotel Ceos (☎ 262 2628; cnr Calle 4 & Av 1; s/d/tr US$17/27/37; P) This is another good option as newly furnished rooms have private solar-heated showers, cable TV and a large communal balcony – perfect for those Imperial-swigging nights. Check out the old photos that adorn the walls of the ground floor.

Hotel América (☎ 260 9292; Calle Central btwn Avs 2 & 4; s/d incl breakfast US$40/50; P ▣) Spacious rooms are well equipped with private solar-heated showers and cable TV, but they're definitely overpriced (just remember – you're paying for the name). As a consola-tion though, there is a 24-hour restaurant and bar.

Hotel Valladolid (☎ 260 2905; valladol@racsa.co.cr; cnr Calle 7 & Av 7; s/d incl continental breakfast US$62/83; P ✖) Fully equipped rooms at the most established hotel in town caters primarily to discerning business travelers, though it's a good choice if you're looking for a few added comforts, namely a sauna, Jacuzzi and top-floor solarium.

Eating

In the grand tradition of university towns worldwide, Heredia offers plenty of spots for pizza slices and cheap vegetarian grub, not to mention one branch of every fast-food outlet imaginable.

Azzura Heladería y Cafetería Italiana (cnr Calle 2 & Av 2; dishes US$1-4; ✆ 7am-10pm) After a hard morning of designing software, techies flock here for the high-octane coffee and

---

MICROCHIP REPUBLIC

When industry leaders in Heredia heard that Intel, the world's largest microchip manufacturer, was shopping around for a Latin American base of operations, they decided to invite execs down for a quick *cafecito*.

Costa Rica hadn't even made the list, which included Mexico, Brazil and Chile: it was considered too small, too laid-back and too expensive (per capita earnings are among the hemisphere's highest) for the job. But this little country, famed for its exotic wildlife and erupting volcanoes, was conveniently right on the way south. Besides, who wouldn't want to take a 'business trip' here?

The pitch was a pleasant surprise: half a century of investment in schools rather than soldiers had resulted in a highly educated and relatively computer-literate workforce. Costa Rica's track record as a peaceful democracy sat well with the insurance people, and learning that a large percentage of locals already spoke English got human resources' vote. Perhaps most importantly, Intel reps noticed that almost everyone they met was already online, a convenience quite rare in other countries being considered. The tech giant was charmed.

Eager for this massive influx of foreign investment, Heredia officials emailed Intel an offer that included a lovely former finca and some very generous tax breaks. Increased access to computers (subsidized by Intel) and English classes in public schools were also part of the deal.

On some things, however, Heredia would not budge. Microchip production is both water-intensive and ferociously toxic, and Costa Ricans are famously protective of their landscape. Intel finally agreed to ship all waste products out of the country for disposal; moreover, the most environmentally damaging processes continue to take place in the USA, with the final product assembled here.

Pentium processors began rolling out in March 1998, and within three years microchip exports were worth three times as much as bananas and coffee combined. Today Intel products account for almost 10% of Costa Rica's total GDP and over 40% of all exports. The Heredia facility, where local talent is now also responsible for cutting-edge product development and software design, brings in more than US$1 billion annually.

Many other high-tech companies, including Oracle and Microsoft, have since opened up shop in the region hoping to repeat Intel's success, transforming the area into Central America's very own Silicon Valley – but without Starbucks. Its coffee just couldn't compete around here.

sugar-iffic gelato. Healthier souls can indulge in salads, quiche or sandwiches.

El Testy (dishes US$1-5) Here it is folks, your one-stop shopping for burritos, ravioli, hamburgers, tacos, chicken and fries. Feeling indecisive? It also sells ice cream, candy, cookies and snacks!

Mr B (Av 2 btwn Calles 2 & 4) Hungry students line up at this local institution for the US$2 burger and milkshake combo – perfect if you're feeling nostalgic for American grub.

Vishnu Mango Verde (Calle 7 btwn Avs Central & 1; dishes US$3-5; 9am-6pm Mon-Sat) This branch of the famous San José chain is the top spot in town for cheap and healthy vegetarian fare – your stomach (and your karma) will thank you.

Restaurant Fresas (cnr Av 1 & Calle 7; mains US$3-8; 8am-midnight) This popular university hang-out specializes in fresh fruit shakes and salads, though casados and other typical meals complete the menu. The people-watching here is tops.

You can fill up for a few hundred colones at the **Mercado Municipal** (Calle 2 btwn Avs 6 & 8; 6am-6pm), with *sodas* to spare and plenty of very fresh groceries. **Más X Menos** (Av 6 btwn Calles 4 & 6; 8:30am-9pm) has everything else.

Drinking & Entertainment

With a thriving student body, there's no shortage of live music, cultural events and the odd happening. For info on what's going

on, look for fliers near the campus or ask a student to fill you in on the scene.

The university district is hopping most nights of the week (Tico students live it up like you wouldn't believe). **La Choza** (Av Central btwn Calles 7 & 9), **El Bulevar** (cnr Calle 7 & Av Central) and **El Rancho de Fofo** (Av Central btwn Calles 5 & 7) are three popular student spots.

After a few rounds of beers and *bocas* (savory bar snacks), the party really kicks off at the **Miraflores Discotechque** (Av 2 btwn Calles Central & 2), on the southern edge of the Parque Central. Stay aware, however, as Heredia can get dodgy at nighttime, though there is an established police presence.

Getting There & Away

There is no central bus terminal, and buses leave from bus stops near Parque Central and market areas. Buses for Barva leave from near **Cruz Roja** (Red Cross; Calle Central btwn Avs 1 & 3). Buses to San José de la Montaña and Sacramento, with connections to Volcán Barva in Parque Nacional Braulio Carrillo, leave from Avenida 8 between Calles 2 and 4. Ask around the market for information on other destinations.

Alajuela US$0.50, 20 minutes, depart from the corner of Avenida Central and Calle 9 every 15 minutes from 6am to 10pm.

Barva US$0.25, 20 minutes, depart from Calle Central between Avenidas 1 and 3 every 30 minutes from 5:15am to 11:30pm.

Puerto Viejo de Sarapiquí US$2, 3½ hours, depart from the corner of Avenida Central and Calle 9 at 11am, 1:30pm and 3pm.

San José US$0.50, 20 minutes, depart from Avenida 4 between Calles Central and 1 every 20 to 30 minutes from 4:40am to 11pm.

Santa Bárbara US$0.25, 20 minutes, depart from Avenida 6 between Calles 6 and 8 every 10 to 30 minutes from 5:15am to 11:30pm.

Taxis are plentiful and can take you to San José (US$5) or the airport (US$8).

BARVA

Just 2.5km north of Heredia is the historic town of Barva, which dates from 1561 and has been declared a national monument. The town center is packed with 17th- and 18th-century buildings, and is centered on the towering **Iglesia San Bartolomé**. With its scenic mountainside location and colonial ambience, the town is a popular residence among the Costa Rican elite – Cleto González Víquez, twice president of Costa Rica, used to live here. The town is perfect for a lazy afternoon stroll, and although Barva proper doesn't have any lodgings there are some truly spectacular luxury hotels just outside of town.

Festivals & Events

Each July and August, the Hotel Chalet Tirol (opposite) is the site of the **International Music Festival**, which, true to the hotel's Austrian motif, is heavy on the classical music.

Sights

The most famous coffee roaster in Costa Rica, **Café Britt Finca** (☎ 277 1600; www.coffeetour .com, www.cafébritt.com; adult with/without lunch US$30/20, student US$27/18; ☼ tours 11am year-round, 9am & 3pm in high season) is headquartered just 1km south of Barva. Although the tour is a bit pricey, it comes highly recommended by readers. For 90 minutes, bilingual guides will walk you through the plantation and the processing center where you can learn the difference between regular and organic coffee-growing processes, as well as the history of coffee production in Costa Rica. And don't worry – there are plenty of free samples. For an extra US$5, you can combine your tour with a one-hour trip to the *benefico* (processing plant), where you can learn about the wonders of coffee-bean harvesting. Café Britt operates a daily shuttle that will pick you up from San José – call for a reservation. If you drive or take the bus, you can't miss the signs between Heredia and Barva.

Located in Santa Lucía de Barva, about 1.5km southeast of Barva, the **Museo de Cultura Popular** (☎ 260 1619; admission US$2; ☼ 9am-4pm) re-creates colonial Costa Rica in a century-old farmhouse, restored with period pieces and ingenious tools. If you're lucky, docents in period costumes may use the beehive-shaped ovens to make typical Tico foods, which you can purchase anytime at the **garden café** (dishes US$2-5; ☼ 11am-2pm).

INBio (☎ 507 8107; www.inbio.ac.cr/en/default2.html; adult/child/student US$15/8/12; ☼ 7:30am-4pm), the El Instituto Nacional de Bioversidad (the National Biodiversity Institute), is a private research center that was formed in 1989 to catalog the biological diversity of Costa Rica and promote its sustainable use. Visitors to the center spend their time at

INBioparque, a high-quality collection of attractions including biodiversity exhibition halls, wildlife-viewing stations, a butterfly garden, an aquarium, a working farm, medicinal plant garden and sugar mill. However, the center functions primarily as a biodiversity management center, and if you have an appropriate background there are great volunteer opportunities here to work with the highly professional staff.

Sleeping

More affordable accommodations can be found in nearby Heredia (p159), though each of the following luxury hotels comes highly recommended.

Hotel Chalet Tirol (☎ 267 6222; www.costarica bureau.com/hotels/tirol.htm; d chalet US$80; P ☒) Between Monte de la Cruz and Club Campestre El Castillo, you'll find this quaint country hotel, formerly the residence of Costa Rican president Alfredo González Flores. The cloud-forest enclave is rustic-chic, with comfy Austrian-style chalets arranged around open-air common spaces, including a pizza parlor where you can relax and watch the mist drift by. The hotel plays host to an international music festival in the summertime.

Hotel Bougainvillea (☎ 244 1414; www.bougain villea.co.cr; s/d/tr/ste US$75/85/95/105; P ☐ ☒) In the town of Santo Domingo de Heredia, on the road between Heredia and San José, this luxury property is situated among stately coffee fincas, old-growth trees and stunning flowers. Wood-accented rooms and suites have dramatic balconies that overlook either the nearby mountains or the flickering lights of San José. Several private trails wind through the jungle and fruit orchards, passing the swimming pool, restaurant and tennis courts en route to the hills. Best of all, this rural wonderland comes with free hourly shuttles to downtown San José.

Finca Rosa Blanca (☎ 269 9392; www.fincarosa blanca.com; d US$200-300; P ☐ ☒) Just outside Santa Bárbara, this honeymoon-ready confection of gorgeous garden villas and architecturally outstanding suites, cloaked in fruit trees that shade trails and cascading rivers, ranks as one of the most exclusive hotels in Costa Rica. Rooms with balconies overlooking the rain forest are individually and lavishly appointed; one tops a tower with a 360-degree view, reached by a winding staircase made from a single tree trunk. Shower in an artificial waterfall, take a moonlight dip in the sculpted garden pool and hot tub, or have a recommended romantic dinner. Leftovers will be dutifully recycled, and owners happily offer tours of their many other conservation systems, perfect for newlyweds with social consciences.

Getting There & Around

Half-hourly buses travel between Heredia and Barva (US$0.25, 20 minutes), and pick up in front of the church.

PARQUE NACIONAL BRAULIO CARRILLO

Thick virgin forest, countless waterfalls, swift rivers and deep canyons – it will be difficult to believe that you are only 30 minutes north of San José when you're walking around this underexplored national park. Braulio Carrillo has an extraordinary biodiversity attributable to the steep range of altitudes, from the misty 2906m cloud-forest camp sites atop massive Volcán Barva to the lush, humid 50m lowlands stretching toward the Caribbean Sea.

The creation of the park was the result of a unique compromise between conservationists and developers. For more than a century, San José's only link to Puerto Limón was limited to the crumbling railway and a slow rural road. In the 1970s, however, government and industry agreed that a sleek modern highway was required to link the nation's capital to its most important port. But the only feasible route was through a low pass between Volcán Barva and Volcán Irazú, which was still virgin rain forest – conservationists were not happy campers.

The compromise was simple – Parque Nacional Braulio Carrillo (named after Costa Rica's third president, who conceived the cultivation of coffee) was established in 1978, off-limits to development beyond a single major highway to bisect it. Conservationists rejoiced in the creation of a nearly 48,000-hectare national park (we're talking the size of Rhode Island!) that was comprised of 85% primary forest, and protected the watershed for San José. Government and industry rejoiced in the creation of the San José–Guápiles highway, which was completed in 1987, effectively cutting the park into two smaller preserved areas (though it's still administered as a single unit).

Driving through the park will give you an idea of what Costa Rica looked like prior to the 1950s – rolling hills cloaked in mountain rain forest. About 75% of Costa Rica was rain forest in the 1940s, while today less than a quarter of the country retains its natural vegetative cover.

Orientation & Information

The two most popular hiking areas can be accessed from the San José–Guápiles highway. At the southern end of the park is the **Zurquí ranger station** (☎ 257 0992; admission US$6; ⏲ 7am-4pm), 19km northeast of San José, while **Quebrada González ranger station** (☎ 233 4533; admission US$6; ⏲ 7am-4pm) is at the northeast corner, 22km past the Zurquí tunnel. There is a guarded parking lot, toilets and well-marked trails.

People who want to climb Volcán Barva on a day trip or camp overnight can stop by the **Barva Sector ranger station** (☎ 261 2619; ⏲ 7am-4pm), in the southwest of the park, 3km north of Sacramento.

There are also two remote outposts in the extreme northwest corner of the park, namely **El Ceibo** and **Magasay**.

Temperatures can fluctuate drastically in the park, and annual rainfall can be as high as 8000mm. The best time to go is the supposedly 'dry' season (from December to April), but it is liable to rain then, too. Bring warm clothing, appropriate wet-weather gear and good hiking boots.

Wildlife-Watching

Birding in the park is excellent, and commonly sighted species include parrots, toucans, hummingbirds and even quetzals at higher elevations. Other rare but sighted birds include eagles and umbrella birds.

Mammals are difficult to see due to the lushness of the vegetation, though deer, pacas, monkeys and tepezcuintle (the park's mascot) are frequently seen. Pumas, jaguar and ocelots are present but rare.

Hiking

From Zurquí, there is a short but steep 1km trail that leads to a viewpoint. You can also follow the **Sendero Histórico**, which follows the crystal-clear Río Hondura to its meeting point with the Río Sucio (Dirty

River), whose yellow waters carry volcanic minerals.

From Quebrada González, you can follow the 2.8km **Sendero La Botella** past a series of waterfalls into Patria Canyon. There are several other unmarked trails that lead through this area, including several places where you are permitted to camp, although there are no facilities.

Keep an eye out for the distinctive hugeleafed Gunnera plants, which quickly colonize steep and newly exposed parts of the montane rain forest. The large leaves can protect a person from a sudden tropical downpour – hence the plant's nickname *sombrilla del pobre* (poor folks' umbrella).

Climbing Volcán Barva

Climbing Volcán Barva is a good four- to five-hour, round-trip adventure along a well-maintained trail. Because of its relative inaccessibility, there is a good chance you can commune with the volcano solo. Begin on the western side of the park at the Sacramento entrance, north of Heredia. From there the signed track climbs to the summit at a leisurely pace. Trails are often muddy and you should be prepared for rain anytime of the year.

The track leads to three lagoons – Lagos Danta, Barva and Copey – at the volcano's summit, and several spur trails lead to

---

WARNING

Unfortunately, there have been many reports of thefts from cars parked at entrances to some trails in Parque Nacional Braulio Carrillo, as well as armed robbers accosting tourists hiking on the trails or walking along the highway. Readers have reported hearing shots fired on the trails, and hitchhikers have reported being told it is a dangerous area. Stay alert. Don't leave your car parked anywhere along the main highway. As a general rule, you should always register at a station before setting out on a hike. When possible, it's also advised that you either hike with a park ranger or arrange for a guide through any of the stations. You can also visit the park as part of a tour, which is usually arranged in San José.

waterfalls and other scenic spots along the way. If you wish to continue from Barva north into the lowlands, you will find that the trails are not marked and not as obvious. It is possible, regardless, to follow northbound 'trails' (overgrown and unmaintained) all the way through the park to La Selva (p522) and La Virgen (p515). A Tico who has done it reported that it took him four days and it is a bushwhacking adventure only for those used to roughing it and able to use a topographical map and compass.

If you're visiting on a day trip, get there as early as possible as the mornings tend to be clear and the afternoons cloudy. The nighttime temperatures can drop to several degrees below freezing. Camping is allowed at the basic **campsites** (per person US$2) near the chilly but impossibly scenic summit, though you will need to bring your own drinking water.

Getting There & Away

Both Zurqui and Quebrada González stations are on Hwy 32 between San José and Guápiles. Buses between San José and either Guápiles or Puerto Viejo can drop you off 2km from the entrance, but pickup on the major freeway will be dangerous and difficult.

Barva station can be reached by following the decent paved road north from Heredia through Barva and San José de la Montaña to Sacramento, where a signed, 3km-long, 4WD-only trail leads north to the entrance.

El Ceibo and Magasay can be accessed via rough roads from La Virgen (p515).

RAINFOREST AERIAL TRAM

The brainchild of biologist Don Perry, a pioneer of rain-forest canopy research, the **Rainforest Aerial Tram** (☎ 257 5961; www.rainforest tram.com; adult/student & child US$50/27.50) is a highly recommended splurge to the heights of the cloud forest in an airborne gondola.

The pricey entrance fee is worthwhile, as it includes a trained guide who can point out all the small and important things you'll otherwise miss, and who also leads the optional hike through the 400-hectare reserve, contiguous with Parque Nacional Braulio Carrillo. Although the area is rich with wildlife, the sheer density of the vegetation makes observing animals difficult.

The 2.6km aerial-tram ride takes 40 minutes each way, affording a unique view of the rain forest and unusual plant-spotting and birding opportunities. Amazingly, the whole project was constructed with almost no impact on the rain forest (canopy-tour operators could learn a thing or two; see the boxed text Canopy Fighting, p196). A narrow footpath follows the tram and all 250,000kg of construction material was carried in on foot or by a cable system to avoid erosion, with the exception of the 12 towers supporting the tram that were brought in by helicopter by the Nicaraguan Air Force (needless to say, pacifist Costa Rica is decidedly lacking in air support).

From the parking lot a truck takes you about 3km to the tram-loading point, where there is a small exhibit area, restaurant and gift shop. Here you can see an orientation video, and there are short hiking trails that you can use for as long as you want. Tram riders should be prepared for

---

A NATURAL EDUCATION

The **Cerro Dantas Wildlife Refuge** is a research center and education facility that works with scientists, teachers and students to promote environmental conservation. In addition to protecting rare fauna, including jaguars, tapirs and quetzal, Cerro Dantas runs a variety of educational programs aimed at students, teachers and researchers, and day and long-term visitors are welcome.

Programs are varied, though the emphasis is on various facets of the ecosystem including endangered-species preservation, environmental protection, rain-forest ecology and global warming. Basic rates are quoted on individual bases, with or without meals, while special rates are available for students, teachers and researchers. It is advised that you make reservations 30 days in advance as space is often limited.

Cerro Dantas is headquartered in Monte de la Cruz, and is a part of the large Parque Nacional Braulio Carrillo. For more information on the programs offered, visit the website at www.cerro dantas.co.cr or contact the refuge at pavoreal@racsa.co.cr.

rain – although the cars have tarpaulin roofs, the sides are open to the elements.

Driving from San José, the well-signed turnoff to the tram is just past the national-park entrance, on your right. To get here by public transport from San José, take the bus for Guápiles from Terminal Caribe (US$1.50, 1¼ hours), departing hourly from 6:30am to 7pm, and ask the driver to let you out at the *teleferico*. Tram staff will help you flag down a return bus.

MORAVIA

Just 6km northeast of San José, Moravia was an important center for Costa Rica's coffee fincas. Workers hauled sacks of ruby-red fruit down hillsides and into the town, where the beans were packed on ox-carts and transported to nearby *beneficos* (processing plants). After being milled and dried, the beans were then shipped to cafés throughout Europe and North America.

The coffee industry has sadly moved on, though Moravia remains in the spotlight as a famous production center for handi-crafts including leather, ceramics, jewelry and wood. A visit here is a popular day trip from San José, and perfect for filling up on souvenirs prior to heading home.

Around and nearby the spacious Parque Central are several stores. Some started as saddle shops but now sell a variety of leather and other goods. Look for **Artesanía Bribrí**, which sells work made by the Bri-brí people of the Caribbean slope, and the pleasant **Mercado de Artesanías Las Garzas**, a festive complex with arts and crafts stores, a few *sodas* and clean toilets. It's 100m south and 75m east of the *municipio* (town hall).

Local buses to San Vincente de Moravia depart San José from Avenida 3 btwn Calles 3 and 5.

CARTAGO AREA

The stunning riverbank setting of the city of Cartago was handpicked by Spanish Gover-nor Juan Vásquez de Coronado, who said that he had 'never seen a more beautiful valley.' Cartago was founded as Costa Rica's first capital in 1563, and Coronado's suc-cessors endowed the city with the country's finest Spanish colonial architecture. How-ever, as things tend to happen in Costa Rica,

Cartago was destroyed during the 1723 eruption of Volcán Irazú, with remaining landmarks taken care of by earthquakes in 1841 and 1910.

Although the city was relegated to back-water status when the seat of government was moved to San José in 1823, the sur-rounding area, particularly the Orosi Valley, flourished during the days of the coffee trade. Today this tradition continues to leave its mark on the landscape, and although Car-tago is merely a provincial capital, it is an important commercial hub and continues to retain the most important religious site in the country.

CARTAGO

After the rubble was cleared, nobody bothered to rebuild Cartago (population 127,000) to its former quaint specifications – though it is an attractive modern city, in a heavily reinforced sort of way. One excep-tion is the Basílica de Nuestra Señora de los Ángeles, considered to be the holiest shrine in Costa Rica and has been religiously re-built after each of the city's trials and tribulations.

The city is thrown briefly into the spot-light each year on August 2 when pilgrims from every corner of the country descend on the basilica to say their most serious prayers. The remainder of the year, Cartago exists mainly as a bustling commercial and residential center, though the beauty of the surrounding mountains helps to take the edge off modern life.

Information

There is no tourist office in Cartago.

Banco Nacional (cnr Av 4 & Calle 5) Several banks in the town center change money, including Banco Nacional.

Hospital Max Peralta (☎ 550 1999; Av 5 btwn Calles 1 & 3) Offers emergency health care.

Internet Alta Velocidad (Calle 1 btwn Avs 1 & 3; per hr US$1; ☺ 9am-9pm). Check your email here, 50m east of Las Ruinas.

Sights

The most important site in Cartago is the **Basílica de Nuestra Señora de los Ángeles** (cnr Av 2 & Calle 16), which currently boasts a rather formal Byzantine grace and airy spacious-ness with fine stained-glass windows and a polished-wood interior. This latest version is the result of a 1926 makeover that followed its near-total destruction in the 1910 earthquake. Though the outer walls have crumbled numerous times since 1635, La Negrita (see the boxed text Local Lore, p168) has miraculously remained intact, and she continues to sit on a golden altar beset with precious stones. The basilica is absolutely jammed during pilgrimages and holy days, though it's the perfect atmosphere for experiencing the aura of La Negrita.

Las Ruinas de la Parroquia (cnr Av 2 & Calle 2), or Iglesia del Convento, was built in 1575 as a shrine to St James the Apostle, though it was destroyed by the 1841 earthquake, rebuilt a few years later and then destroyed again in the 1910 earthquake. Today only the outer walls of the church remain, though 'the Ruins' are a popular spot for picnicking and people-watching.

For an insight into Costa Rica's pre-Columbian cultures, there are two local museums worth visiting. The **Elias Leiva Museum of Ethnography** (☎ 551 0895; Calle 3 btwn Avs 3 & 5; ☼ 7am-2pm Mon-Fri) has a few displays of historical artifacts while the **Kirieti Indian History Museum** (☎ 573-7113; ☼ 10am-4pm Mon-Fri), 6km

southwest of Cartago in Tobosi, emphasizes history through documentation.

Sleeping & Eating

Lodging options are limited.

Hotel Dinastía (☎ 551 7057; cnr Calle 3; s/d US$7/14) The cheap price and private warm-water bathrooms balance out the thin walls and aging rooms.

San Francisco Lodge (☎ 574 2359; Calle 3; s/d/tr US$18/25/34) Don't let the adult video store downstairs fool you – there isn't any funny business going on at this well-managed hotel. Spacious and comfortable rooms with hot-water showers and cable TV are spotless (and smut free).

Los Ángeles Lodge (☎ 551 0957, 591 4169; Av 4 btwn Calles 14 & 16; s/d incl full breakfast US$25/40; P ☒) With its balconies overlooking the Plaza de la Basílica, this comfy B&B stands out with spacious and comfortable rooms, hot showers and a big breakfast made to order by the cheerful owners.

Your best bet for food is to stroll along Avenidas 2 and 4 downtown, where *sodas* and bakeries congregate.

CARTAGO

0 —————— 300 m
0 —————— 0.2 miles

INFORMATION
Banco Nacional...............................1 A2
Hospital Max Peralta.......................2 A3
Internet Alta Velocidad...................3 A3

SIGHTS & ACTIVITIES
Basílica de Nuestra Señora de los
Ángeles.......................................4 D2
Elias Leiva Museum of Ethnography..5 A3
Las Ruinas de la Parroquia...............6 B2
Padres Capuchinos Church..............7 B3
Tribunales de Justicia......................8 B3

SLEEPING 🏠
Hotel Dinastía.................................9 A2
Los Ángeles Lodge.........................10 D2
San Francisco Lodge......................11 A2

EATING
La Puerta del Sol.......................(see 10)

TRANSPORT
Buses to Finca Flor de Paraíso......12 B3
Buses to Lankester Gardens &
Paraíso.....................................13 B3
Buses to Orosí..........................(see 13)
Buses to San José.........................14 B2
Buses to Turrialba.........................15 B3
Buses to Volcán Irazú................(see 12)
Taxi Stand....................................16 A2

LOCAL LORE

La Negrita or 'The Black Virgin' is a small statuette of an indigenous representation of the Virgin Mary, which was reportedly found by a mulatto woman named Juana Pereira in Cartago on August 2, 1635. According to lore, Juana twice tried to bring the statuette home with her, though on each occasion it reappeared in the same spot where she had found it. Astounded by the miracle that transpired, the townspeople built the Basílica de Nuestra Señora de los Ángeles on the original spot where it was found. In 1824, the year after the capital was moved, the statuette was declared Costa Rica's patron saint.

On two separate occasions, La Negrita was stolen from the basilica, though each time it later reappeared on its altar (once was by the future novelist José León Sánchez, who was sentenced to Isla San Lucas for 20 years; see p303). These strange occurrences have led people to believe that the statuette has curative properties, and it's common for petitioners to offer milagrosos (metal charms) representing the body parts they hope to have healed. Even the spring that flows near the basilica is said to have curative properties, and the statuette has been credited with everything from healing toe fungus to ensuring football victories.

Each August 2, on the anniversary of the statuette's discovery, devotees walk a grueling 22km in the summer heat from San José to Cartago – on their knees. It's an incredible sight to behold, and you're more than welcome (sans kneepads) to participate.

La Puerta del Sol (Av 4 btwn Calles 14 & 16; mains US$3-6; ☺ 8am-midnight) This *soda* opposite the basilica is a good choice for its attractive dining room and good variety of cooked-to-order dishes.

Getting There & Away

While Cartago may not be a hotbed of excitement, the surrounding areas provide plenty to do – from botanical gardens, serene mountain towns and organic farms to an active volcano – all easy to reach via local buses and never more than an hour or two away. Most buses arrive along Avenida 2 and go as far as the basilica before returning to the main terminal on Avenida 4. The following buses serve area destinations.

Finca la Flor de Paraíso US$1. Take a La Flor/Birrisito/El Yas bus from in front of Padres Capuchinos church, 150m southeast of Las Ruinas. Get off at the pink church in La Flor; the entrance to the finca is 100m to the south.

Paraíso & Lankester Gardens US$0.50, depart from the corner of Calle 4 and Avenida 1 hourly from 7am to 10pm. For the gardens, ask the driver to drop you off at the turnoff – from there, walk 750m to the entrance.

Orosi US$0.75, 40 minutes, depart hourly from the corner of Calle 4 and Avenida 1 from 8am to 10pm Monday to Saturday. The bus will stop in front of the Orosi Mirador.

San José US$0.50, 45 minutes, depart every 15 minutes from Avenida 4 between Calles 2 and 4, north of Parque Central.

Turrialba US$1, 1½ hours, depart from Avenida 3 between Calles 8 and 10 (in front of Tribunales de Justicia) every 45 minutes from 6am to 10pm weekdays, 8:30am, 11:30am, 1:30pm, 3pm and 5:45pm weekends.

Volcán Irazú US$4, one hour, depart only on weekends from Padres Capuchinos church, 150m southeast of Las Ruinas. The bus originates in San José at 8am, stops in Cartago at about 8:30am and returns from Irazú at 12:30pm.

PARQUE NACIONAL VOLCÁN IRAZÚ

Looming quietly (though not too quietly) 19km northeast of Cartago, Irazú, which derives its name from the indigenous word *ara-tzu* (thunderpoint), is the largest and highest (3432m) active volcano in Costa Rica. In 1723 the Spanish governor of Costa Rica, Diego de la Haya Fernández, watched helplessly as the volcano unleashed its destruction on the city of Cartago. Since then 15 major eruptions have been recorded, and although Diego de la Haya never restored Cartago to its former grandeur, his name was bestowed upon one of Irazú's craters.

The volcano's most recent major eruption on March 19, 1963, welcomed the visiting US president John F Kennedy with a rain of hot volcanic ash that blanketed most of the Central Valley (it piled up to a depth of more than 0.5m). During the two-year eruption, agricultural lands northeast of the volcano were devastated while clogged waterways flooded the region intermittently. In 1994 Irazú unexpectedly belched a cloud of sulfurous gas, though it quickly quietened down. At the time of writing, Irazú was slumbering peacefully aside from a few hissing fumaroles, though it's likely that farmers will be reminded again why the soil in the Central Valley is so rich. For more information on predicting a volcanic eruption, see the boxed text Feelin' Hot, Hot, Hot!, p249.

The national park was established in 1955 to protect 2309 hectares around the base of the volcano. The summit is a bare landscape of volcanic-ash craters. The principal crater is 1050m in diameter and 300m deep; the Diego de la Haya Crater is 690m in diameter, 100m deep and contains a small lake; and the smallest, Playa Hermosa Crater, is slowly being colonized by sparse vegetation. There is also a pyroclastic cone, which consists of rocks that were fragmented by volcanic activity.

Information

There's a small **information center** (☎ 551 9398; admission to park & center US$7; ☼ 8am-3:30pm) and basic café, but no accommodations or camping facilities. Note that cloud cover starts thickening, even under the best conditions, by about 10am, about the same time that the weekend bus rolls in. If you're on one of those buses, do yourself a favor and don't dally – head straight for the crater. Folks with cars will be glad that they made the extra effort to arrive early.

From the summit it is possible to see both the Pacific and the Caribbean, but it is rarely clear enough. The best chance for a clear view is in the very early morning during the dry season (January to April). It tends to be cold, windy and cloudy on the summit, and there's an annual rainfall of 2160mm – come prepared with warm and rainproof clothes.

Although not nearly as crowded as Volcán Poás (p156), Irazú is still one of the most popular destinations in the Central Valley.

Hiking

From the information center, a 1km trail leads to a viewpoint over the craters; a longer, steeper trail leaves from behind the toilets and gets you closer to the craters (note that this trail is intermittently closed). While hiking, be on the look-out for high-altitude bird species such as the volcano junco.

Tours

Tours are arranged by a variety of San José operators and cost US$30 to US$60 for a half-day tour, and up to US$100 for a full day combined with lunch and visits to the Lankester Gardens and the Orosi Valley (see below).

Tours from hotels in Orosi (US$25 to US$40) can also be arranged – these may include lunch and visits to the basilica in Cartago or sites around the Orosi Valley.

Eating

Restaurant 1910 (☎ 536 6063; mains US$4-9) It's worth stopping here for lunch or dinner to see its collection of old photographs documenting the 1910 earthquake that completed the destruction of colonial Cartago. Cuisine is standard Tico fare, though there are a few European-style dishes available. It's about 500m north of the Pacayas turnoff.

Getting There & Away

Barring a 20km hike, there are three ways to get here on weekdays: an organized tour; a US$30 to US$40 taxi from Tierra Blanca, which includes the driver waiting for you at the park for a few hours; or by car. Drivers can take Hwy 8 from Cartago, which begins at the northeast corner of the plaza and continues 19km to the summit.

Frustratingly, the only public transport to Irazú departs from San José (US$4.50, 1½ hours) on Saturday and Sunday. It stops in Cartago (US$4, one hour), departing at about 8:30am. The bus departs from Irazú at 12:30pm.

VALLE DE OROSI

This river valley and renowned road trip southeast of Cartago is famous for its mountain vistas, colonial churches (one in ruins), hot springs, orchid garden, lake formed by a hydroelectric facility, its truly wild national park, and coffee – lots and lots of coffee. A 60km scenic loop of the valley winds through a landscape of rolling hills terraced with shade-grown coffee plantations and expansive valleys dotted with pastoral villages. If you're lucky enough to have a rental car (or a good bicycle), you're in for a treat, though it's still possible to navigate most of the loop via public buses.

The loop road starts 8km southeast of Cartago in Paraíso, and then heads south to Orosi (p170). At this point you can either continue south to Parque Nacional Tapantí-Macizo Cerro de la Muerte (p172) or loop back to Paraíso via Ujarrás (p173).

CENTRAL VALLEY & HIGHLANDS

Paraíso

The town of Paraíso has been absorbed into the urban sprawl of the provincial capital, only 8km away, and fails to capture the attention of travelers. Although the concrete block houses lining the road into town are hardly picturesque, the Orosi Valley emerges just outside of Paraíso. A few kilometers further along the road to Orosi is the **Mirador Orosi**, which is the official scenic overlook complete with toilets, a parking lot and plenty of great photo opportunities. However, there are two noteworthy sights near Paraíso that are definitely worth visiting before heading into the valley.

The University of Costa Rica now runs the exceptional **Lankester Gardens** (☎ 552 3247; jbl@cariari.ucr.ac.cr; admission US$3.50; ☺ 8:30am-4:30pm), which was started by British orchid enthusiast Charles Lankester in 1917. Orchids are the big draw, with 800 at their showiest from February to April. In addition, lush areas of bromeliads, palms, secondary tropical forest, heliconias and other tropical plants are seen from the paved trails winding through the gardens.

With many plant species labeled and informative plaques throughout the unbelievable grounds, this is a shady introduction to Costa Rica's wealth of flora before you hit the wilder (and unlabeled) national parks. This is also one of the very few places where foreigners can legally purchase orchids to take home. Guided walks through the gardens are offered on the half-hour from 8:30am to about 2:30pm daily. The entrance to the gardens is well signed, 5km west of Paraíso on the road to Cartago.

Two kilometers east of Paraíso on the road to Turrialba is **Finca Cristina** (☎ 574 6426; www .cafecristina.com; US$10), a working organic coffee farm that is open to visitors by appointment only (call ahead for a reservation). Linda and Ernie have been farming in Costa Rica since 1977, and a 90-minute tour of their *microbeneficio* (mini–processing plant) is a fantastic introduction to the processes of organic-coffee growing, harvesting and roasting. Finca Cristina also sells its product to guests at wholesale prices.

About 2km south of Paraíso, **Sanchirí Mirador** (☎ 574 5454; www.sanchiri.com; s/d/tr incl breakfast US$47/60/70 (P 🖳)) is a delightful, family-run hotel that offers as good a reason as any to break up your trip. Older wooden cabins and newer concrete rooms are fairly basic, though it's wonderful to be able to linger amid the beauty of the natural surroundings. Even if you're not staying here, stop by the open-air restaurant (dishes US$4 to US$7), which faces out toward the valley and is a good consolation prize if you're pressing on. The complex is also home to a **butterfly garden** (adult/child US$5/3), a picnic area and a system of trails that can be explored either on foot or horseback.

Orosi

This town was named for a Huetar chief who lived here at the time of the conquest. Spanish colonists quickly became enamored of the town's wealth of water, from lazy hot springs to bracing waterfalls, perfect climate and rich soil. So, in the typical fashion of the day, they decided to take property off of Orosi's hands.

Orosi is one of the few colonial towns to survive Costa Rica's frequent earthquakes, which have left the whitewashed 1743 **Iglesia de San José Orosi** the oldest church still in use in Costa Rica. The roof of the church is a combination of thatched cane and ceramic tiling, while the altar is carved entirely out of wood and adorned with religious paintings of Mexican origin. Adjacent to the church is a small **museum** (☎ 533 3051; admission US$0.50; ☺ 9am-noon & 2-5pm Tue-Fri, 9am-5pm Sat & Sun) with some interesting examples of Spanish-colonial religious art and artifacts.

And while the attractive town has thus far managed to avoid the more rattling aspects of living in a volcanic region, it's got two big perks, namely the hot springs at **Los Balnearios** (☎ 533 2156; admission US$2; ☺ 7:30am-4pm), on the southwest side of town next to the Orosi Lodge, and **Los Patios** (☎ 533 3009; admission US$2; ☺ 8am-4pm Tue-Sun), 1.5km south of town. Los Balnearios is more convenient as it's in town, though Los Patios is a larger complex with a few more springs. Both, however, are modest affairs with simple pools of warm water that are popular with locals and a few foreigners in the know.

INFORMATION

Orosi Tourist Information & Arts Café (Otiac; ☎ 533 3640; ☺ 9am-4pm Mon-Sat), two blocks south of the park, is run by the multilingual Toine and Sara, two long-term residents who have collected a wealth of information on the

---

A NATURAL EDUCATION (PART II)

Finca la Flor de Paraíso is a nonprofit organic farm operated by Asodecah, the Association for the Development of Environmental and Human Consciousness. The farm operates an 'Alternative Spanish Institute,' which combines formal Spanish-language education with themes of environmental conservation and community development.

The farm also operates a volunteer-work program that emphasizes organic agriculture, reforestation, animal husbandry, medicinal-herb cultivation, construction, arts and crafts, community outreach and childhood education. Volunteers can rotate between projects, and are housed in on-site guesthouses and dormitories.

Prices for one week at the Alternative Spanish Institute including 20 hours of classes, a local homestay and three daily vegetarian meals is US$370. Prices for the volunteer-work programs, including full room and board, are US$15 daily for the first two weeks and US$12 after the first two weeks. Prices for visitors on vacation, including private accommodation and guided hikes, are US$22 for a day visit, US$35 for two days and US$210 for six days. All profits are invested directly into a number of community-development initiatives.

Finca la Flor de Paraíso is 7km northeast of Paraíso on the road to El Yas, and can be reached via buses from Cartago. For more information on the programs offered, visit the website at www .la-flor-de-paraiso.org or contact Asodecah at asodecah@racsa.co.cr.

---

valley. They organize a variety of outings to surrounding volcanoes and hot springs for the traveler on a budget, as well as guided walks (US$10), camping and overnight stays at the private **Monte Sky Reserve** (per person incl meals US$25).

In addition to providing the usual tourist services, Otiac functions as a cultural hall, town center and café. It's also a great place for interacting with both travelers and locals. If you're looking for information on volunteering, teaching English or becoming involved in environmental conservation or community development, Otiac is an invaluable resource.

PC Orosi (☎ 533 3302; per hr US$1; ✆ 8am-7pm) has reasonably fast Internet connection.

COURSES

Toine and Sara also run **Montaña Linda** (☎ 533 3640; www.montanalinda.com), one of the most affordable Spanish schools in the country. For more information, see the boxed text Spanish Schools in the Central Valley, p147.

SLEEPING

Montaña Linda (☎ 533 3640; www.montanalinda.com; camping per person US$3.50, dm US$6.50, s/d with shared bathrooms US$10.50/17, d with private bathroom US$25; P ▣) Two blocks south and three blocks west of the bus stop is this great budget option, which has a festive hostel environment, hot showers and kitchen privileges (US$1) or excellent cheap home-cooked meals (US$1

to US$3). Accommodations are in dorms, but there are a few doubles for couples.

Las Torrejas B&B (☎ 533 3534; dm/d US$12/30; P) Near the entrance to town on the left-hand side is this homey option, which is managed by a warm Alabaman family. In addition to renting out comfortable rooms, it also has a small restaurant (dishes US$4 to US$8) that features the owners' home-made tofu and tempeh.

Hotel Reventazón (☎ 533 3838; r US$40; P) Clean, modern rooms sleeping three are two blocks west of Otiac, and come with a nice collection of creature comforts: cable TV, hot-water showers and fridges. The on-site restaurant (dishes US$4 to US$8) is definitely touristy, but it does whip up a good casado.

Orosi Lodge (☎ 533 3578; www.orosilodge.com; d US$52; P) This recommended hotel is run by a friendly German couple named Andreas and Cornelia, and has simple and intimate rooms with excellent views of the valley. Rooms include a private hot shower, a wet bar with minifridge and a shared balcony or patio – the perfect combination for a sundowner. A small garden separates the rooms from the reception area in the highly recommended Cafetería Orosi (mains US$4 to US$8, open from 7am to 7pm), which serves the dreamy coffee you keep smelling in the air as well as a mix of homemade pastries, salads and sandwiches. Los Balnearios hot springs is just a few steps away.

GETTING THERE & AWAY

All buses stop about three blocks west of the football (soccer) field; ask locally about specific destinations. Buses from Cartago (US$0.50, 40 minutes) depart hourly from Calle 6, between Avenidas 1 and 3, close to the church.

Cachí Dam & Ruinas US$0.50, 20 minutes, depart every 30 minutes from 6am to 9pm.

Cartago US$0.75, 40 minutes, depart every 45 minutes from 5am to 9pm.

South of Orosi

If you're continuing south toward Parque Nacional Tapantí-Macizo Cerro de la Muerte rather than looping back via Ujarrás to Paraíso, you'll follow a rough road that slices through coffee plantations while passing the rural villages of Río Macho, Palomo and Purisil (13km). From Purisil, a dirt road leads a few more kilometers to **Parque Purisil** (☎ 228 6630; ☉ 8am-5pm), where nature lovers can take a guided three-hour hike (US$10) into the nearby cloud forests, while anglers can catch dinner at the well-stocked trout pond (price per kilo US$3). The on-site restaurant prepares your catch to order.

Note that buses from Cartago to Orosi occasionally continue as far south as Purisil, though you need to check with the driver to make sure.

Parque Nacional Tapantí-Macizo Cerro de la Muerte

Despite its unwieldy name, this **park** (admission US$7; ☉ 6am-4pm) protects the rain-forested northern slopes of the Cordillera de Talamanca, and boasts a rainy claim to fame – this is the wettest park in the entire country. In 2000 the park was expanded to 583 hectares, and now includes the infamous Cerro de la Muerte (p376). The 'Mountain of Death' marks the highest point on the Interamericana as well as the northernmost extent of the *páramo,* a highland shrub and tussock grass habitat that's commonly found throughout the Andes and is home to a variety of rare bird species.

On the other hand, Tapantí (as it's locally known) protects wild and mossy country that's fed by literally hundreds of rivers. Waterfalls abound, vegetation is thick and the wildlife is prolific, though not easy to see since the terrain is rugged and the trails are few. Nevertheless, Tapantí is a popular destination for dedicated bird-watchers, and opens at 6am to accommodate their avian-searching needs.

INFORMATION

There is an **information center** (☉ 6am-4pm) near the park entrance and a couple of trails leading to various attractions, including a picnic area, a swimming hole and a lookout with great views of a waterfall. Rainfall is about 2700mm in the lower sections but reaches more than 7000mm in some of the highest parts of the park – pack an umbrella. Fishing is allowed in season (from April to October; permit required), but the 'dry' season (from January to April) is generally considered the best time to visit.

WILDLIFE-WATCHING

Quetzals are said to nest on the western slopes of the valley, where the park information center is located. More than 300 other bird species have also been recorded in the park, including hummingbirds, parrots, toucans, trogons and eagles.

Though rarely sighted due to the thick vegetation, monkeys, coatis, pacas, tayras and even pumas, ocelots and oncillas are present.

HIKING

There are three signed trails leading from the information center, the longest a steep 4km round trip, while a well-graded dirt road that is popular with mountain bikers runs through the northern section of the park. Unfortunately, the Tapantí is not open to backcountry hiking, and some visitors walk away feeling as if they only caught a glimpse of the park. However, the birding here is legendary, and most people are satisfied simply being able to spot a large variety of birds in such a small area.

SLEEPING & EATING

There is a basic but adequate **guesthouse** (dm US$5) with a shared kitchen and bathrooms at the ranger station. Cooked meals (US$1 to US$3) are available with prior notice.

Kiri Lodge (☎ 592 0638; s/d incl breakfast US$25/35) This lodge on the road between Purisil and Tapantí has six rustic cabins with private hot showers resting on 50 mossy hectares. There are also expansive trails leading into the Río Macho Forest Preserve, which is

HIGHER GROUNDS

In 1779 Spanish colonists discovered that the cool climate and rich volcanic soil of the Central Valley were perfectly suited for the cultivation of coffee, and began to terrace the hillsides with massive plantations. Since dried beans are relatively nonperishable and thus easy to ship, coffee quickly surpassed cacao, tobacco and sugar in importance, and became the major source of revenue for the colony as early as 1829. By the late 19th century (thanks to a strong push by the young independent government), Costa Rican coffee was being served in cafés throughout Europe, and became famous for its high caffeine content and acidic, multidimensional flavor.

In the past 20 years, however, the Costa Rican coffee market has suffered greatly. Following a collapse in the world quota cartel system, the world coffee price plummeted nearly 40% in just a few years. Although the market eventually stabilized in 1994, this was the same year that Vietnam entered the world market following the lifting of the US trade embargo. Since the market rewarded the efficiency of Vietnamese coffee suppliers, many coffee-exporting nations (Costa Rica included) lost a large percentage of their traditional market share.

Today, Costa Rican coffee continues to be grown in the provinces of Alajuela, Heredia and Cartago. Harvesting occurs primarily in the dry season, and is dependent on cheap, seasonal labor (predominantly Nicaraguan migrant workers). Once picked, the ripened berries are transported to *beneficos* (processing plants) where they are separated from the fruit and dried in the sun. Green coffee beans are then vacuum sealed to retain their characteristic acidity, and shipped to roasters throughout the world.

In recent years, it's ironic that the price of green coffee beans has plummeted at the same time that the price of a cup of coffee has skyrocketed. While coffee suppliers like Starbucks continue to run lucrative enterprises, coffee farmers (not to mention migrant workers) are receiving an absurdly small percentage of the profits. This phenomenon initiated a push for free trade, which is an economic (and increasingly political) term referring to the unhindered flow of goods and services between countries. When a coffee advertises itself as free trade, it is usually sold at a higher price to ensure that profits are more evenly distributed.

With Cafta on the horizon, trade barriers are about to be redefined throughout the Americas. However, since Costa Rica is a comparatively small player in Latin America, it is difficult to say whether this legislation will be enough to secure a market niche in light of the growing production capabilities of countries like Brazil.

---

adjacent to Tapantí and inhabited by much of the same wildlife. The restaurant (mains US$3 to US$6, open from 7am to 9pm) specializes in trout, which can be caught in the well-stocked pond and then served up anyway you like it.

GETTING THERE & AWAY

If you have your own car, you can take a good gravel road passable to all vehicles from Purisil to the park entrance.

Buses are a bit trickier. From Cartago, take an Orosi-bound bus (though make sure it's going to Purisil). From there, it's a 5km walk to the entrance. Or, you can take a **cab** (☎ 771 5116, 551 2797) from Orosi to the park for about US$12 one way.

Orosi to Paraíso

From Orosi, the loop road heads north and parallels the Río Orosi before swinging around the artificial **Lago de Cachi**. The Lake was created following the construction of the **Cachí Dam** (the largest in the country), which supplies San José and the majority of the Central Valley with electricity. Buses run from Orosi to the dam and nearby ruins, though this stretch is best explored by car or bicycle.

About 2km south of the Cachí Dam is the **Casa del Soñador** (Dreamer's House; ☎ 577 1186; admission free; ☒ 8am-6pm), a whimsical house designed and built by the renowned Tico carver Macedonio Quesada. Every detail of the construction, built largely of coffee branches and bamboo, is elaborately chiseled to divine effect. Quesada's sons, who have managed the workshop since Macedonio's death in 1995, continue the family woodworking tradition, and carvings of local *campesinos*, religious figures and other characters, some life-size, are on display. Some of them are available for you to purchase.

Past the dam, you'll find the small village of **Ujarrás** at the bottom of a long, steep hill – a couple of stores with the word 'Ujarrás' tell you that you've arrived. Turn right at a sign for Restaurant La Pipiola to head toward the old village (about 1km), which was damaged by a flood in 1833 and abandoned.

The waters have since receded, revealing the ruins of the 1693 **Iglesia de Nuestra Señora de la Limpia Concepción**, once home to a miraculous painting of the Virgin discovered by a local fisherman. Using similar tactics as La Negrita (see the boxed text Local Lore, p168), the relic refused to move, forcing area clerics to build the church here. In return, the Virgin helped locals defeat a group of marauding British pirates in 1666. After the floods and a few earthquakes, however, the painting conceded to move to Paraíso, leaving the ruins to deteriorate photogenically in an overgrown park. Every year, usually on the Sunday closest to April 14, there is a procession from Paraíso to the ruins where Mass, food and music help celebrate the day of La Virgen de Ujarrás. The church's grassy grounds are a popular picnicking spot on Sunday afternoons.

After Ujarrás, the road continues for a few more kilometers before returning to Paraíso.

SLEEPING & EATING

Cabañas de Montaña Piedras Albas (☎ 577 1462; www .cabinas.co.cr/costa_rica1.htm; s/d US$40/56; **P**) If you're looking to slow down and enjoy the scenery, stay at these well-equipped cabins. You can pretend you're roughing it on the private trails, then relax in front of the cable TV, take a hot shower, fix some dinner in the kitchen and perhaps arrange a tour at the desk. The cabinas are on a signed turnoff just past La Casona.

La Casona del Cafetal Restaurant (☎ 533 3280; mains US$5-15; ⏰ 11am-6pm) This restaurant is about 3km southeast of the dam, where you can enjoy a really fresh cup of coffee (or a recommended meal) while watching the next batch of beans being picked (November to March). It's popular on Sunday, when families with kids go for short horseback or horse-drawn cart rides, also available here.

TURRIALBA AREA

At an elevation of 650m above sea level, the Río Turrialba flows into the Río Reventazón, and gouges a mountain pass through the Cordillera Central. In the 1880s this hydrogeological quirk allowed the 'Jungle Train' between San José and Puerto Limón to roll through, and the mountain village of Turrialba grew prosperous from the coffee trade. Later, the first highway linking the capital to the coast exploited this same quirk. Turrialba thrived.

However, things changed in 1991 when an earthquake shut down the nation's rail system, and the smooth and straight (read as boring) Hwy 32 was completed. Suddenly, Turrialba (population 70,000) found itself off the beaten path, though no one cared to move away – it's too gorgeous here.

Today Turrialba is a low-key agricultural town that's renowned for its mountain air, strong coffee and Central America's best white water. It's also situated in the wake of the undertouristed Volcán Turrialba and close to the country's most important cultural site, Guayabo (p178).

TURRIALBA

The residents of Turrialba are a proud people, and following the relegation of their city to backwater status in 1991, folks here humbly returned to their coffee-cultivating roots. Railways and highways come and go, but life must always go on.

By this time, rafters the world over were already whispering about Turrialba, a modest mountain town with access to some of the best white water on the planet. Tourism was suddenly on the rise, and residents were happy to share their town's charms with curious travelers. However, when the ICE (the national power company) began making good on plans to dam the scenic waterways, the town united with conservation groups and put up a fierce fight (see the boxed text Damming the Rivers?, p179). Fair enough – Turrialba has sacrificed enough to the bulldozers of progress. So far, it seems as if the residents are winning the battle, though it's always a very fine line between conservation and capitalism in Costa Rica.

Information

There's no official tourist office, but better hotels and most white-water rafting outfits can organize tours, accommodations and transportation throughout the region.

Banco Popular (9am-5pm Mon-Fri) Has a 24-hour ATM.

Dimension Internet (per hr US$0.75; 9am-9pm) Check your email here, on the northeast corner of Parque Central.

Sights

About 4km east of Turrialba, and known throughout Costa Rica by its acronym of Catie (which is just as well), **Centro Agronómico Tropical de Investigación y Enseñanza** (Catie; Center for Tropical Agronomy Research & Education; ☎ 556 6431; www.catie.ac.cr; admission free; 7am-4pm) is comprised of about 1000 hectares dedicated to tropical agricultural research and education. Agronomists from all over the world recognize this as one of the most important agricultural stations in the tropics. You need to make reservations for a guided tour of the various agricultural projects, including one of the most extensive libraries of tropical-agriculture literature anywhere in the world, laboratories, greenhouses, a dairy, herbarium, seed bank and experimental plots. Or you can pick up a map and take a self-guided tour through the gardens to the central pond, where waterbirds such as the purple gallinule are a specialty. Another good birding area is the short but steep trail descending from behind the administration building to the Río Reventazón. You can walk to Catie or get a taxi (US$2) from Turrialba.

About 10km east of Turrialba, in the village of Pavones (500m east of the cemetery), **Parque Viborana** (☎ 538 1510; admission US$3; 9am-4pm Mon-Fri) is known for its serpentarium. Here you can see a variety of Costa Rican snakes, including some unusual albino specimens and several boas, one of which weighs as much as a good-sized person. The serpentarium has a rustic visitors area with educational exhibits.

Tours

The following operators all offer either kayaking or rafting, and most can arrange tours throughout the area.

Aventuras de Turrialba (☎ 363 4539; kayakers@latinmail.com) Specializes in kayaking, though it can arrange put-ins and pick-ups.

Costa Rica Ríos (☎ in the USA 888-434 0776; www .costaricarios.com) Offers week-long rafting trips that must be booked in advance. It's 25m north of Parque Central.

Exploranatura (☎ 556 4932; www.costaricacanyoning .com) Also runs a reader-recommended canyoning course.

Loco's (☎ 556 6035; riolocos@racsa.co.cr) A local company that works with small groups.

RainForest World (☎ 556 0014; www.rforestw.com/wel come2.cfm) Offers an overnight in the Cabécar Indigenous Reserve while running the river.

Tico's River Adventures (☎ 556 1231; www.ticoriver .com) A local company that also offers a trip down the Class IV Río Chirripó from June through November.

Sleeping

IN TURRIALBA

Hotel La Roche (☎ 556 7915; Calle 4 btwn Avs 2 & Central; s/d with shared bathroom US$6/8; P) Though a little worn (what do you expect at this price!), bright rooms surrounding a private courtyard are quite cheerful, and those upstairs have nice balconies.

Whittingham's Hotel (☎ 550 8927; Calle 4 btwn Avs 2 & Central; s/d US$6/8) Seasoned budget travelers won't mind the cool, clean (just like the showers) and cavernous rooms with private bathrooms.

Hotel Turrialba (☎ 556 6654; Av 2 btwn Calles 2 & 4; d with/without air-con US$19/15; P) This is great value as small and standard rooms with attractive wood accents are well equipped with air-con, cable TV and private hot showers. The on-site restaurant (dishes US$3 to US$5) whips up a tasty casado.

Hotel Interamericano (☎ 556 0142; www.hotel interamericano.com; Av 1; r per person with/without bathroom US$21/11; P) On the south side of the old train tracks is this recommended hotel, which is regarded by kayakers and rafters as *the* meeting place in Turrialba. Rooms with big windows and shared hot-water bathrooms are well maintained. However, the real reason to stay here is to meet up with like-minded white-water enthusiasts, and to take advantage of the hotel's (white-water)

QUIRKY TURRIALBA

Did you know that Turrialba is home to the oddball industry of baseball-bat manufacturing? San Francisco Giants fans should know that the instrument of Barry Bonds' 73rd home run was fashioned right here in the highlands of Costa Rica.

CENTRAL VALLEY & HIGHLANDS

shuttle services. There is also a bar, restaurant and very professional staff.

Hotel Wagelia (☎ 556 1566; www.hotelwagelia .com; Av 4 btwn Calles 2 & 4; s/d incl breakfast US$46/58; P ⊗) The most established hotel in town is a good choice if you're looking for a bit more comfort in your life. Standard though well-furnished rooms have air-con, private (steaming) hot showers, a huge cable TV and a sitting area for, well, all your sitting needs.

AROUND TURRIALBA

There are some stellar hotels around the Turrialba area. All hotels have private hot-water bathrooms, and can arrange tours and rafting trips.

Hotel Turrialtico (☎ 538 1111; www.turrialtico.com; s/d US$52/62) On the old highway to Siquirres and Limón, 8km from town, this Tico-run lodge has been owned and managed by the García family since 1968. There are 14 wood-paneled rooms in an old farmhouse that feature locally sewn bedspreads and paintings from area artists. The restaurant (dishes US$4 to US$10) shows off the family's wood-

working prowess, though it's hard to beat the dramatic views (and the fresh fish).

Casa Turire Hotel (☎ 531 1111; www.hotelcasatu rire.com; d US$130, ste US$150-230; P ⊗ ⊒ ⊛) This elegant three-story mansion belongs to the group of 'Small, Distinctive Hotels of Costa Rica,' and recalls the colonial heyday of gracious plantation living. The hotel has 12 deluxe rooms and four suites featuring lofty ceilings and private verandas, from where you can gaze wistfully at the sweeping fields of sugar cane, coffee beans and macadamia nuts. Lunch and dinner are taken in the master dining room while evening cocktails are served around the wood-toned bar. And, lest you forget what era you're living in, there's also a luxurious pool and full-service spa.

Rancho Naturalista (☎ 297 4134; www.costarica gateway.com/lodges/index1.php; r per person with 3 meals US$150, 7-day package per person with 3 meals US$1040; P ⊒) Located 20km southeast of Turrialba near the village of Tuis (4WD needed), this Spanish-style, five-bedroom lodge with accompanying cabins is legendary among birders. The North American owners are avid birders who have recorded over 400

TURRIALBA

0 _____ 200 m
0 _____ 0.1 miles

INFORMATION		
Banco Popular	1	C2
Dimension Internet	2	B2
Hospital	3	B3
Police	4	B1
Post Office	5	B1

SIGHTS & ACTIVITIES		
Aventuras de Turrialba	6	C3
Costa Rica Ríos	7	B1
Evangelical Church	8	B2
Exploranatura	9	B2
Palacio Municipal	10	B2

| RainForest World | 11 | C3 |
| Tico's River Adventures | 12 | D3 |

SLEEPING ⌂		
Hotel Interamericano	13	C2
Hotel La Roche	14	B3
Hotel Turrialba	15	B2
Hotel Wagelia	16	B2
Whittingham's Hotel	17	B3

EATING 🍴		
Bar/Restaurant La Garza	18	B2
Café Azul	19	B3
Café Gourmet	20	B2
La Feria	21	B2
Mamma Mias	(see 2)	

TRANSPORT		
Bus Terminal	22	A2
Buses to San José & Siquirres	23	B2
Terminal Turrialba	24	B2

To Restaurant Don Porfi (4km); MN Guayabo (20km); Pacayas (24km); San José (62km)

Río Turrialba

To Parque Viborana (500m)

Plaza

Parque Central

Río Colorado

Quebrada Barahona

Río Colorado

Rail (not in operation)

To Rancho Naturalista (20km); Paraíso (45km); San José (72km)

To Loco's (500m); Catie & Adventure Education Center (4km); Hotel Turrialtico (8km); Casa Turire Hotel (9km); Siquirres (44km)

WHITE-WATER RAFTING (AND KAYAKING) 101

Let's start at the beginning. There are two major rivers in the Turrialba area that most rafters are interested in – the Río Reventazón and the Río Pacuare. The following is a quick guide to the ins, outs, ups and downs of each river, as well as tips on how to organize a trip and estimated costs.

Río Reventazón

The Cachí Dam across the Río Reventazón created the artificial lake, Lago de Cachí, from which the river now tumbles, starting at 1000m above sea level and running down the eastern slopes of the mountains to the Caribbean lowlands. The river is a favorite and is one of the most difficult runs in the country. With more than 65km of rapids, you can get as hardcore as you like.

Tour operators divide the river into four sections between the dam and take-out in Siquirres. **Las Máquinas** (Power House) is a Class II–III float that's perfect for families, while **Florida**, the final and most popular segment, is a scenic Class III with a little more white water to keep things interesting. The **Pascua** section, with 15 Class IV rapids featuring names like 'The Abyss,' is considered to be the classic run. The Class V **Peralta** segment is the most challenging white water in the country, and tour operators will not always run this section due to safety concerns.

Water levels stay fairly constant year-round because of releases from the dam. Note that there are no water releases from the dam on Sunday and, although the river is runnable, this is considered the worst day.

Río Pacuare

The Río Pacuare is the next major river valley east of the Reventazón, and offers arguably the most scenic rafting in Costa Rica, if not Central America. The river plunges down the Caribbean slope through a series of spectacular canyons clothed in virgin rain forest, through runs named for their fury and separated by calm stretches that enable you to stare at the near-vertical green walls towering hundreds of meters above – a magnificent and unique river trip.

The Class III–IV **Lower Pacuare** is the more famous and more accessible run: 28km through rocky gorges and isolated canyons, past an indigenous village, untamed jungle and lots of wildlife curious as to what the screaming is all about. The **Upper Pacuare** is also classified as Class III–IV, but there are a few sections that can go to Class V depending on conditions. It's about a two-hour drive to the put-in, though it's worth it – you'll have the prettiest jungle cruise on earth all to yourself.

The Pacuare can be run year-round, though June to October are considered the best months. The highest water is from October to December, when the river runs fast with huge waves. In March and April the river is at its lowest, and though waves aren't as big, the river is still challenging.

Organizing Trips

Agencies in Turrialba (p175) can organize trips. Children must be at least nine years old for most trips, older for tougher runs.

Day trips usually raft the Class III–IV Lower Pacuare or Class III segments of Río Reventazón, both boasting easy-access put-ins that reduce your travel time. There are other runs, however, including the less accessible (and less crowded) Upper Pacuare and Pascua segment of Reventazón, which folks willing to spend more time in a van will find rewarding. These should be arranged in advance. Most operators also offer rafting on other rivers, including Río Sarapiquí (p516), the Class IV Río Chirripó, white-water-free Río Pejibaye (perfect for families).

Two-day trips are offered by almost every operator, usually including a very comfortable camp site or a fairly plush lodge, guided hikes and borderline gourmet meals.

Prices

For day trips, you can expect to pay anywhere from US$80 to US$120 depending on transportation and accessibility. Generally, the cheapest trips leave from Turrialba, and put-in on the Lower Pacuare or Class III segments of the Reventazón. For two-dray trips, prices vary widely depending on amenities, but expect to pay around US$175 to US$300 per person.

species in the area – over 200 species have been recorded from their balcony alone. Hundreds of species of butterflies can be found on the grounds as well, and there is an expansive trail system leading through the nearby rain forest. Prices include three home-cooked meals a day, and a variety of tours that range from guided birding trips and horseback riding on the low end to plush overnight adventures in Parque Nacional Tortuguero.

Eating

There are several *sodas*, Chinese restaurants, bakeries and grocery stores in town.

Café Gourmet (cnr Calle 4 & Av 4; snacks US$1-3; ☺ 7am-7pm Mon-Sat) This cute little café sells Turrialba's best coffee done up as dozens of different beverages, plus light meals and excellent pastries.

Café Azul (Av Central btwn Calles 2 & 4; snacks US$1-3; ☺ 7am-7pm Mon-Sat) With such great coffee growing on the hillsides, you need plenty of good cafés. Here, the ambience is relaxed, the pastries are fresh and the coffee is strong.

Mamma Mias (pizzas US$2-4; ☺ 11am-11pm) Sometimes you need a slice of greasy pizza, especially when you've just spent the day cascading down raging white water in an inflatable dingy.

Bar/Restaurant La Garza (Cnr Av 6 & Calle Central; mains US$3-6; ☺ 10am-10pm) This Turrialba institution has been serving good seafood, chicken and beef to happy customers, tourists and locals alike for as long as anyone can remember.

La Feria (☎ 556 0386; dishes US$3-8; ☺ 10am-10pm) Whether you're looking for fast food, filling casados or inventive meat and fish dishes, La Feria is a solid choice.

Restaurant Don Porfi (☎ 556 9797; mains US$4-8; ☺ 10am-10pm) Four kilometers north of town on the road to San José is this reader-recommended spot, which is regarded by locals as one of the top eats in the Turrialba area. Portions of European-influenced dishes are sizable, delicious and best when accompanied by a glass of wine. The delightful owner, Sergio, will even arrange transportation for you if you don't have a car.

Getting There & Away

The brand-spanking-new bus terminal is on the western edge of town off Hwy 10. In addition to the services listed below, there are also frequent local buses to the villages of La Suiza, Tuis and Santa Cruz.

Monumento Nacional Guayabo US$0.75, one hour, depart at 11:15am, 3:10pm and 5:20pm.

San José US$2, 1¾ hours, depart hourly from 5am to 9pm.

Siquirres, for transfer to Puerto Limón US$1.50, 1¾ hours, depart almost hourly.

MONUMENTO NACIONAL ARQUEOLÓGICO GUAYABO

The largest and most important archaeological site in the country is 19km northeast of Turrialba. Although Guayabo is not nearly as breathtaking as Maya and Aztec archaeological sites (don't expect pyramids), excavations have unearthed sophisticated infrastructure and mysterious petroglyphs. Polychromatic pottery and gold artifacts found here are exhibited at the Museo Nacional (see p100) in San José.

The most impressive find at Guayabo is the aqueduct system, which may have served more than 20,000 people in AD 800, the height of the city's prominence. It uses enormous stones hauled in from far-off Río Reventazón along an 8km road that's still in pretty good shape, by Costa Rican standards. The extra effort was worth it – the cisterns still work, and (theoretically) potable water remains available on-site, which you can enjoy among various unearthed structures and unexcavated but suspicious-looking mounds.

The site, which may have been occupied as early as 1000 BC, was mysteriously abandoned by AD 1400 – the Spanish conquistadors, explorers and settlers left no record of having found the ruins. Though underfunded archaeologists continue to hypothesize about Guayabo's significance, most believe it was an important cultural, religious and political center. However, it's unfortunate that no written records have been recovered from Guayabo, and it's difficult to credit a particular group with having built the site.

In 1968 Carlos Aguilar Piedra, an archaeologist with the University of Costa Rica, began the first systematic excavations of Guayabo. As its importance became evident, the site was declared a national monument in 1973, with further protection decreed in 1980. Although the site only occupies 232 hectares, most of the ruins are waiting to be uncovered, and there are hopes that future excavations will reveal more about the origins of Guayabo.

Information

There's an information and **exhibit center** (☎ 559 1220; admission US$4; ☽ 8am-3:30pm), though many of the best pieces are on display at the Museo Nacional in San José. Excavations are ongoing during the week, and some sections may be closed to visitors at certain times. Guided tours are not currently available, but it's worth asking around in Turrialba or at the ranger station about independent local guides.

Camping (per person US$2) is permitted, and services include latrines and running water. Keep in mind that the average annual rainfall is about 3500mm; the best time to go is during the January to April dry season, though it might still rain.

Wildlife-Watching

The site currently protects the last remaining premontane forest in the province of Cartago, and although mammals are limited to squirrels, armadillos and coatis, there are good birding opportunities here. Particularly noteworthy among the avifauna are the oropendolas, which colonize the monument by building sacklike nests in the trees. Other birds include toucans and brown jays – the latter are unique among

---

DAMMING THE RIVERS?

Considered one of the most beautiful white-water rafting trips in the world, in 1985 the wild Río Pacuare became the first federally protected river in Central America. Two years later, Instituto Costarricense de Electricidad (ICE), Costa Rica's national energy and communications provider, unveiled plans to build a 200m gravity dam at the conveniently narrow and screamingly scenic ravine of Dos Montañas.

This dam would be the cornerstone of the massive Siquirres Hydroelectric Project, proposed to include four dams in total, linked by a 10km-long tunnel that would divert water from the Río Reventazón to the Río Pacuare. If built, rising waters on the Pacuare would not only flood 12km of rapids, up to the Tres Equis put-in, but also parts of the Awari Indigenous Reserve and a huge swath of primary rain forest where some 800 animal species have been recorded.

When the project was first proposed, ICE was in debt and struggling to keep up with rapidly increasing power demands (tourists, after all, must have their air-conditioning). Costa Rica uses fossil fuels only for vehicles; all other power is generated using renewable resources, including geothermal, solar and wind energy, with a whopping 81% of its power produced by a dozen hydroelectric dams. Technically, this is a renewable resource; in practice, dams not only interrupt rivers and wash away ecosystems, they have long-term impacts that are not completely understood.

As the project moved from speculation toward construction, a loose coalition of local landowners, indigenous leaders, conservation groups and, yep, white-water rafting outfits were already organizing a resistance movement. They filed for the first Environmental Impact Assessment (EIA) in history, an independent audit of such projects that the Central American Commission for Environment and Development first proposed in 1989. The paper-shuffling didn't come to much legally, but it stalled the dam's construction and earned international attention for the Río Pacuare's plight.

Today Costa Rica is a net exporter of electricity (not including oil), primarily to Panama and Nicaragua. Because of new geothermal plants built since the dam was proposed, as well as coordinated national efforts to reduce electricity usage, the dam is not currently needed. For now.

Plans for the project have not been abandoned, not by a long shot. Siquirres would be relatively easy to build, and could generate a tremendous amount of income and electricity in a country modernizing more rapidly than most. However, pressure from international conservation groups is holding ICE at bay, while growth in white-water rafting has helped the Pacuare prove its worth on a spreadsheet somewhere in San José, protecting it for another day.

The neighboring Río Reventazón, however, has not been so lucky: the (in)famous Peralta section has already lost a third of its Class V rapids due to the first phase of the Siquirres Project. Don't put your white-water rafting trip off until the next time you make it down to Costa Rica.

jays in that they have a small, inflatable sac in their chest, which causes the popping sound that is heard at the beginning of their loud and raucous calls.

Getting There & Away

The last 3km of the drive to the monument may be passable to normal cars, if it's dry and you're careful, though your life will be made much easier with a 4WD. Buses from Turrialba (US$0.75, one hour) depart at 11:15am, 3:10pm and 5:20pm, and return at 12:45pm and 4pm. Buses and most taxis (about US$10 one way from Turrialba) drop you at the turnoff to the park, from where it's a 4km hike.

PARQUE NACIONAL VOLCÁN TURRIALBA

This rarely visited active volcano (3328m) was named Torre Alba (White Tower) by early Spanish settlers, who observed plumes of smoke pouring from its summit. Since 1866, however, Turrialba has slumbered quietly, and today the summit is considered safe enough to explore. For more information on predicting a volcanic eruption, see the boxed text Feelin' Hot, Hot, Hot!, p249.

Turrialba was declared a national park in 1955, and protects a 2km radius around the volcano. Below the summit, the park consists of montane rain and cloud forest, dripping with moisture and mosses, full of ferns, bromeliads and even stands of bamboo. Although small, these protected habitats shelter 84 species of birds and 11 species of mammals.

In 2001 the volcano showed its first signs of activity in 135 years, though so far it's been limited to fumaroles and microtremors. While hiking the summit, you can peer into the **Central Crater**, which has minor fumarole activity consisting of bubbling sulfurous mud. The **Main Crater**, which last erupted in 1866, is starting to spew jets of sulfur and steam again, and is thus closed to the public. The smaller **Eastern Crater** lacks fumarole activity, though moisture is present in the crater during the rainy season.

Although the craters are not nearly as dramatic as Poás or Irazú, the lack of infrastructure (and tourists) gives the summit a wild and natural feeling that is absent from more-touristed volcanoes.

Information

At the time of writing, there was neither a ranger station nor admission fee, though there are frequently rangers at the top of the summit. The average temperature up here is only about 15°C, so dress accordingly.

Volcán Turrialba Lodge arranges a variety of guided hikes and horseback rides through the park.

Hiking

From the end of the road, there are trails heading to the Eastern Crater and the Central Crater, though they are unmarked (rangers can usually show you in which direction to head). Be advised that the summit is not developed for tourism, so you need to keep your distance from the craters and be especially careful around their edges – they are very brittle, and can easily break.

From the rim there are views of Irazú, Poás and Barva volcanoes – weather permitting. Although your hiking options are limited, you can explore the edges of the summit without having to navigate the tourist crowds. The hike up the volcano from Santa Cruz is likely to be a solitary slog through montane forest.

Sleeping

Volcán Turrialba Lodge (☎ 273 4335; www.volcan turrialbalodge.com; per person with 3 meals US$45; Ⓟ)) About 14km northwest of Santa Cruz (accessible by 4WD only), this mountain lodge and working cattle ranch is perched between the Turrialba and Irazú volcanoes, and recommended for travelers looking for some highland adventure. Cozy rooms with electric heaters, great views and some with wood stoves are augmented by interesting, well-guided hikes and horseback rides to Volcán Turrialba. The rustic hotel has a blazing wood stove in the bar-restaurant and sitting room, with TV and board games. The bar-restaurant serves excellent buffet-style food, tending toward Tico with an international flair. Quetzals nest on the property from February to April. There are several package deals available.

Getting There & Away

The volcano is only about 15km northwest of Turrialba as the crow flies, but more than twice as far by car than foot. From the village of Santa Cruz (which is 13km from

Turrialba and connected via public buses), an 18km road climbs to the summit. The road is paved for the first 10km, and then becomes increasingly rough – a 4WD is necessary to reach the summit. You can also get a 4WD taxi from Santa Cruz for about US$20 each way (you can arrange for the taxi to wait or pick you up later). There are signs along the way, and this is the official route into the national park.

Another approach is to take a bus from Cartago to the village of San Gerardo on the southern slopes of Volcán Irazú. From here a rough road continues to Volcán Turrialba – it's further than from Santa Cruz, but San Gerardo, at 2400m, is a higher starting point than Santa Cruz is at 1500m. The rough road goes about 25km, then there are a few kilometers of walking, but this route is unsigned.

Northwestern Costa Rica

Awash in hot springs and waterfalls – with an unrivaled collection of national parks and wilderness areas, cloud forests of quetzals, and endless savannah exploding into raucous color come rainfall – there is no end to this region's gifts.

In a few days, your journey can take you from the slopes of active volcanoes to a landscape of bubbling fumaroles. Begin with the organic farms and pristine cloud forest of the Monteverde-Santa Elena ecoplex, and finish in the rare dry tropical forests of Parque Nacional Santa Rosa. Northwestern Costa Rica may be heavily touristed, but the variety of attractions and number of remote spots means that it can be as small (or as big) as you want it to be.

A large portion of this region is the open, dry cattle country of Guanacaste, Costa Rica's equivalent of the American West. While you're traveling in Northwestern Costa Rica, keep an eye out for *sabaneros* (cowboys). They're easily recognized by their straight-backed posture, casual hand on the reins, holster-slung machetes, and the high-stepping gait of their horses.

Guanacastecos take pride in their unique origin and culture and it's not uncommon to see flags proclaiming an independent Guanacaste. Following the independence of Central America from Spain, the newly independent provinces formed the Central American Federation. Then, Guanacaste was part of Nicaragua, though border disputes resulted in skirmishes with Costa Rica. But, on July 25, 1824, Guanacastecos voted to separate and join Costa Rica.

Although most visitors make a beeline towards Arenal and Monteverde, it's worth exploring the far-flung corners of the region – you'll be rewarded with cheaper accommodation, fewer crowds and a more authentic experience.

HIGHLIGHTS

- Watching the nightly fireworks of **Volcán Arenal** (p249) from **La Fortuna** (p237) or the quiet town of **El Castillo** (p251)

- Braving the mud and mists (and crowds) of **Monteverde** (p207) and **Santa Elena** (p210) reserves in search of the elusive quetzal

- Riding wicked waves at Witch's Rock and Ollie's Point at unequaled **Parque Nacional Santa Rosa** (p227)

- Watching wildlife at Costa Rica's largest wetland sanctuary, **Palo Verde** (p216)

- Admiring the thick and creamy blue waterfall and river at the undertouristed **Parque Nacional Volcán Tenorio** (p214)

★ Parque Nacional Santa Rosa

Parque Nacional ★ Volcán Tenorio

Volcán Arenal ★★

Parque Nacional Palo Verde ★ El Castillo ★ La Fortuna

Santa Elena ★ ★ Monteverde

INTERAMERICANA NORTE

Views from the Interamericana don't offer everyone's ideas of the tropics, not during the dry season anyway. Vistas across vast expanses of grassy savannah, which seem more suited to Africa or the American southwest, are broken only by windblown trees, some of which shed their leaves during the hot, dry summer. But complex communications between these seemingly dormant giants will suddenly inspire an entire species to erupt into fountains of pink, yellow or orange blossoms, welling up from the dry grasses in astounding syncopation. This is also where you'll see the signature gait of the *sabanero* as he rounds up a herd of cattle with grace and precision.

The Interamericana Norte is the principal highway connecting San José and Managua, Nicaragua, so you can expect to see big rigs on the road slaloming between potholes with a surprising degree of skill. For travelers, this is the main route for accessing Monteverde, Liberia, the northern volcanoes, Parque Nacional Santa Rosa and the extreme northwest. The Arenal route (p235) connects with the Interamericana Norte in Cañas.

HISTORY

The first occupants of the region are believed to be the Chorotega, who occupied large tracts of land throughout Costa Rica, Honduras and Nicaragua in the 8th century BC. Unfortunately, our knowledge about the group is incomplete due to the lack of extensive ruins typical of populations in other parts of Central America. However, it is known that they were contemporaries of the Maya, and were part of a cultural link extending from Mexico to the Andes. For more information on the Chorotega, see the boxed text A Brief History of the Chorotega, p288.

Although their civilization prospered for over 2000 years, the Chorotega were wiped out by warfare and disease during the Spanish colonial period. During this era, the Spanish systematically clear-cut large tracts of dry tropical rain forest since the table-flat landscape was perfect for growing crops and raising cattle.

Following independence, this region maintained its agrarian roots, though the surrounding rain forest has been severely depleted (see the boxed text A Whopper of a Problem, p229). Today the Interamericana is big-sky country, and you can spot rivers from some kilometers off, snaking through a landscape of fincas and ranches. Fortunately, there are a few large preserves of humid rain forest still left in the Cordillera de Tilarán, and the extreme northwest remains one of the few remaining tracts of dry rain forest in the world.

REFUGIO NACIONAL DE FAUNA SILVESTRE PEÑAS BLANCAS & AROUND

Not to be confused with the Nicaraguan border crossing of the same name, this 2400-hectare **refuge** (admission US$7) is located along the steep southern arm of the Cordillera de Tilarán. Elevations in the small area range from less than 600m to over 1400m above sea level, variations that result in different types of forest, such as tropical dry forest in the lower southwestern sections, semi-deciduous dry and moist forests in middle elevations, and premontane forest in the higher northern sections. The terrain is very rugged, and while there are some hiking trails, they are unmaintained and difficult to follow.

The name Peñas Blancas (White Cliffs) refers to the diatomaceous deposits, similar to a good-quality chalk, found in the reserve. The whitish deposits, remnants of unicellular algae once common here when Central America was underwater, are found in the steep walls of some of the river canyons in the refuge.

The refuge was created to protect the plant species in the varied habitats as well as an important watershed, and until the Ministry of Environment & Energy (Minae) gets the money to develop some tourist infrastructure, the region is inaccessible from all but the most diligent visitors. There are no facilities at the refuge. Camping (per person US$2) is allowed, but you must be self-sufficient and in good shape to handle the very demanding terrain. The dry season (from January to early April) is the best time to go – it's not likely that you'll see anyone else there.

The closest town to the refuge is **Miramar**, a historic gold-mining town that is located

NORTHWESTERN COSTA RICA

NORTHWESTERN COSTA RICA

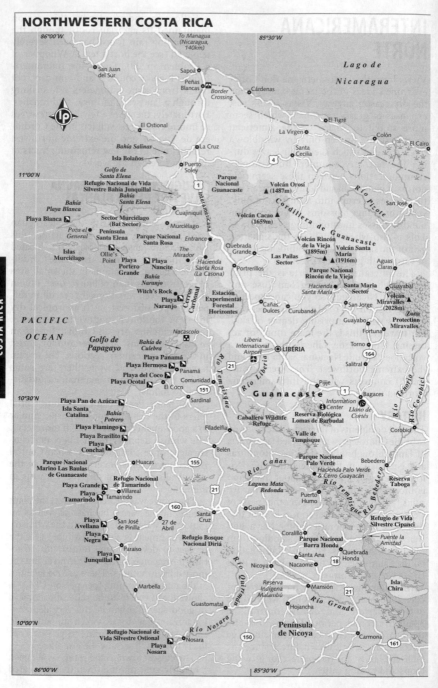

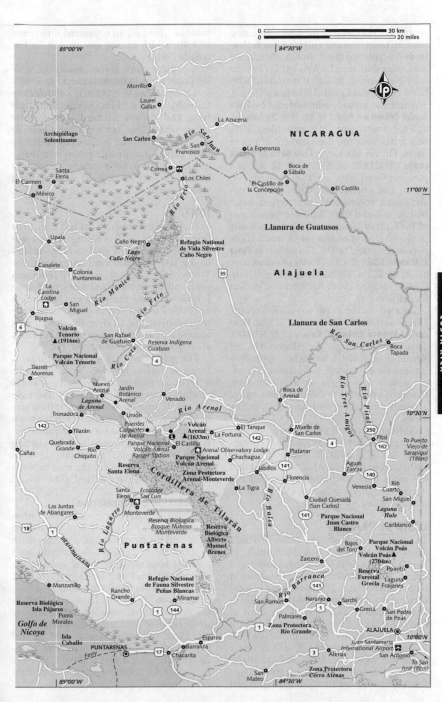

about 8km northeast of the Interamericana. Here, in town, you can visit **Las Minas de Montes de Oro** (guided tour US$45), an old, abandoned gold mine that dates back to 1815. The tour is a bit expensive, though it is coupled with horse riding and a guided hike to a waterfall. The mine is actually administered by **Finca Daniel Adventure Park** (☎ 639 9900; 2hr horse riding US$29, waterfall canopy US$79, guided hiking US$29), which has your usual assortment of pricey tours. The on-site lodge, **Vista Golfo de Nicoya Lodge** (☎ 639 8303; s/d US$55/58; P ▣ ☑), is a pleasant hotel with a tranquil, mountain setting that's perfect for getting a little fresh air. Rustic rooms have private hot-water bathrooms, and some have sweeping views of the Gulf of Nicoya. There's also a shady pool and a good restaurant. A much more personal option is the German-run **Finca El Mirador B&B** (☎ 639 8774; www.finca-mirador.com; d US$45 P ▣), which has three adorable bungalows equipped with full kitchens, perfect for self-caterers.

Located in the small town of Zapotal, 18km northeast of Miramar, is the **Mancuerna Private Ecological Reserve** (☎ 661 8241). This reserve protects the Alberto Manuel Brenes cloud forest, which is famous among birders for its quetzal population. Travelers usually arrive here on a private tour, though it's possible to show up and arrange a number of hiking and horseback-riding tours.

Although there are infrequent buses connecting Miramar to San José and Puntarenas, this is a difficult area to travel in without your own car. Also, be advised that the roads here are frequently washed out during the rainy season, so a 4WD is highly recommended.

COSTA DE PÁJAROS

The 40km stretch of road between Punta Morales in the south and Manzanillo in the north is famous for its mangrove-lined shores, which attracts countless varieties of birds (and birders). The most famous sight in the area is **Isla Pájaros** (Bird Island), which lies less than a kilometer off the coast at Punta Morales. There are no facilities on the 3.8-hectare islet, which protects a rare colony of brown pelicans. It also acts as a refuge for various seabirds, and the island is a virtual forest of wild guava trees. Aside from becoming an ornithologist, you can visit the island on an organized tour (from US$30), which can be arranged at La Enseñada Lodge.

A popular place to stay among the birding population, **La Enseñada Lodge** (☎ 289 6655; www.laensenada.com; s/d US$40/50) is a 380-hectare finca that's also a working cattle ranch, salt farm and papaya orchard. Comfortable villas, which face out onto the Golfo de Nicoya, have private bathrooms heated by solar panels and private patios with hammocks – perfect for watching sunsets (or birds). There is also a pool, restaurant and tennis courts.

JUNTAS

Las Juntas de Abangares (its full name) is a small town on the Río Abangares that was once the center of the gold-mining industry in the late 19th and early 20th centuries. Today, it's simply a pleasant mountain town full of ranchers and farmers, though Juntas was once the premiere destination in Costa Rica for fortune seekers and entrepreneurs from all over the world, who wanted a part of mine-owner Minor Keith's other golden opportunity.

The gold boom is over, though Juntas is trying to reel in travelers by flaunting its attractions, namely an ecomuseum and a recently constructed hot-springs resort. So far, people aren't shaving time off their stay in Monteverde to visit Juntas. But the town does make for a pleasant stop if you've got your own wheels, especially if it's starting to get late. Trust us. The muddy slip-and-slide commonly known as the road to Monteverde is best tackled in daylight.

Orientation & Information

The town of Juntas is centered on the Catholic church, which has some very nice stained glass, and the small but bustling downtown is about 300m north of the church, with a Banco Nacional and several *sodas* (inexpensive eateries) and small markets. The Ecomuseo is 3km from the main road.

Mina Tours (☎ 662 0753), behind the church, is a family-run tour outfit that can arrange transportation and accommodations reservations, and offers several gold-themed tours, including the Ecomuseo and abandoned mines, beginning at about US$30 per person for day trips and more for overnight excursions.

Sights

OK, so the words 'eco' and 'mining' go together about as well as 'China' and 'free speech,' but it's still worth visiting the small **Ecomuseo de las Minas de Abangares** (☎ 662 0129; admission US$2; ✆ 7am-3pm Tue-Fri, to 5pm Sat & Sun), which has a few photographs and models depicting the old mining practices of the area. On the grounds outside the museum are a picnic area and children's play area, and there's a good system of trails that pass by old mining artifacts such as bits of railway. There's also good **birding** (and iguana-ing) along the trails, and monkeys are occasionally sighted.

From the Interamericana, take the paved road 100m past the Parque Central, turn left, cross a bridge, then turn right at the 'Ecomuseo 4km' sign. A couple of kilometers past Juntas, the road forks – a sign indicates a road going left to Monteverde (30km) and to the right to the Ecomuseo (3km).

Sleeping & Eating

Cabinas Las Juntas (☎ 662 0153; 200m south of gas station; s/d US$6/10; ️ P ️ 🕸) The cheapest bed in town is perfectly acceptable if you're just looking to get a bit of shut-eye before heading to Monteverde. Basic but clean, small, tiled rooms with a cold private shower and cable TV. América, the proprietor, will fix breakfast for US$2 extra.

Centro Turistico Cayuco (☎ 662 0868; d with/without air-con US$15/10; ️ P ️ 🕸 ️ 🍴) This is a popular option with vacationing Ticos as there's an on-site pool, hot spring, restaurant and bar, all 200m north of the mining statue. Unfortunately, the pool barely looks swimmable, and the hot spring is a concrete dish that's fed by a pipe bearing 'springwater' of dubious origins. The rooms, however, are decent, and have cable TV and private bathrooms with cold water.

Pueblo Antiguo (☎ 662 0549; www.puebloantiguo .com; d US$56/90; ️ P ️ 🕸 ️ 🍴) This rustic mountain getaway next to the Ecomuseum caters to tourists looking for a rejuvenating escape. OK, so we all know Juntas is not exactly the most exciting of towns, but with on-site hot springs, a swimming pool, Jacuzzi, sauna, nature trails and restaurant, you'll be sufficiently entertained (and relaxed). Ten rooms in wooden cabins have private bathrooms and scenic mountain views, and there's a good chance wildlife will appear

on your front doorstep. The friendly staff members also arrange tours to the nearby ecomuseum and gold mines.

Restaurante Los Mangos (☎ 662 0410; mains US$3-6; ✆ 11-2am Tue-Sun) The nicest restaurant in town (we know it's rundown, but there aren't exactly a lot of options here) is located on the main road, and does your standard mix of casados (set meals), *ceviche* (local dish of uncooked but well-marinated seafood) and fried chicken, and it'll get you liquored up at night.

Pizzeria Reposteria LA (☎ 662 1212; slice US$1.50) Across the street from Restaurante Los Mangos, this is a cheap if somewhat greasy option.

Getting There & Away

Buses from Cañas (US$0.50, 45 minutes) depart at 9:30am and 2:15pm. There are no buses to the Ecomuseo, but a taxi will cost you about US$4, one way.

Drivers can take the turnoff from the Interamericana, 27km south of Cañas at **Irma's Restaurant** (☎ 662 0348; mains US$2-5; ✆ 7am-9pm) a locally popular eatery where you can flag down buses between Liberia and San José. Monteverde is 30km from Las Juntas on a rough dirt road, though it's passable to normal cars in the dry season.

MONTEVERDE & SANTA ELENA

Strung between two lovingly preserved cloud forests is this slim corridor of civilization, which consists of the Tico village of Santa Elena and the Quaker settlement of Monteverde. The history of these settlements dates back to the 1930s when a few Tico families left the gold-mining settlement of Juntas (opposite), and headed up the mountain to try to make a living through logging and farming.

In a completely unrelated turn of events, four Quakers (a pacifist religious group also known as the 'Friends') were jailed in Alabama in 1949 for their refusal to be drafted into the Korean War. Since Quakers are obligated by their religion to be pacifists (p194), the four men were eventually released from prison. However, in response to the incarceration, 44 Quakers from 11 families left the United States and headed for greener pastures – namely Monteverde.

The Quakers chose Monteverde (or Green Mountain) for two reasons – a few years prior, the Costa Rican government had abolished its military and the cool, mountain climate was ideal for grazing cattle. So, the Quakers found their isolated refuge from the ills of the world, and adopted a simple, trouble-free life of dairy farming and cheese production amid a new-found world of religious freedom.

But the story doesn't end there. In an effort to protect the watershed above its 1500-hectare plot in Monteverde, the Quaker community agreed to preserve the mountaintop rain forests. When ecologists arrived in the area years later to investigate the preserve, they discovered that the cloud forests were actually two different ecosystems that straddled both sides of the Continental Divide. In the Monteverde Reserve (p207), the warm, moisture-laden trade winds from the Caribbean sweep up the slopes of the divide where they then cool and condense to form clouds. These clouds also pass over the Reserva Santa Elena (p210), though the absence of the trade winds means that the forests here are a few degrees warmer than in Monteverde. As a result of this temperature differential, each ecosystem boasts several distinct species, most of which you probably won't be able to see.

A 1983 feature article in *National Geographic* described this unique landscape, and subsequently billed the area as *the* place to view one of Central America's most famous birds – the resplendent quetzal. Suddenly, hordes of tourists armed with tripods and telephoto lenses started braving Monteverde's notoriously awful access roads, which of course came as a huge shock to the then-established Quaker community. In an effort to stem the tourist flow, local communities lobbied to stop developers from paving the roads. And it worked. Today, the dirt roads leading to Monteverde and Santa Elena have effectively created a moat around this precious experiment in sustainable ecotourism.

The cloud forests near Monteverde and Santa Elena are Costa Rica's premier destination, and everyone from budget backpackers to well-heeled retirees has it on their to-do list. On a good day, Monteverde is a place where you can be inspired about the possibility of a world where organic farming and alternative energy sources help to salvage the fine mess we've made of the planet. On a bad day, Monteverde is place where you can marvel at the latest in eco-adventure fashion including khaki socks, zipper-pants and multipocketed safari vests. Clearly, the balance here between ecopark and Eco-Disney remains fragile, though the local community continues to fight against the threat of overdevelopment.

Orientation

Driving from either of the Interamericana's first two turnoffs to the region, you'll first arrive in Santa Elena, a bustling little community with lots of budget hotels, restaurants and attractions. A road beginning at the northern point of the triangle leads to Juntas and Tilarán, with a turnoff to Reserva Santa Elena. From the westernmost point of the triangle (to the right as you enter town) you can access a scenic and heavily rutted 6km road to the Monteverde reserve.

This road forms the backbone of this spread-out community, and is lined with hotels and restaurants displaying varying degrees of adorableness. About 2km from Santa Elena, the neighborhood of Cerro Plano has another neat nucleus of cute businesses centered on Casem and the Monteverde Cheese Factory. Almost 5km from town, a turnoff leads three steep kilometers to San Luis Biological Station and Waterfall. Roads are generally paralleled by pedestrian trails.

Information
BOOKSTORES
Chunches Coffeeshop (☎ 645 5147; Santa Elena; ✆ 8am-6pm Mon-Sat) A bookstore and coffee shop with a fine selection of books (many in English), including travel and natural history guides and some US newspapers. There's laundry service (US$5 to wash and dry) and its bulletin board is a good source of information. Also see Bromelia's Books (p205).

EMERGENCY
Police (☎ 645 5127; Santa Elena)

INTERNET ACCESS
Internet access is widely available.
Complejo Atmosphera (☎ 645 6555; Santa Elena; ✆ 8am-9pm; per hr US$2) Surf the web, drink an espresso, have a massage, get a hair treatment, buy art and find inner peace.
Internet Taberna Valverde (☎ 645 5825; Hotel Finca Valverde, Monteverde; ✆ 9am-8pm; per hr US$2)

WHO HAS SEEN THE GOLDEN TOAD?

One animal you used to be able to see so often that it almost became a Monteverde mascot was the golden toad (Bufo periglenes). Monteverde was the only place in the world where this exotic little toad appeared. The gold-colored amphibian used to be frequently seen scrambling along the muddy trails of the cloud forest, adding a bright splash to the surroundings. Unfortunately, the golden toad is believed to be extinct as no one has seen one since 1989, though what happened to it is a mystery.

During an international conference of herpetologists (scientists who study reptiles and amphibians), it was noted that the same puzzling story was occurring with other frog and toad species all over the world. Amphibians once common are now severely depleted or simply not found at all. The scientists were unable to agree upon a reason for the sudden demise of so many amphibian species in so many different habitats.

One of several theories holds that degenerating air quality is the culprit – amphibians breathe both with primitive lungs and through their perpetually moist skin, and they're more susceptible to airborne toxins because of the gas exchange through their skin. Another theory is that deforestation and global warming pushed the frogs ever higher, until there was no higher altitude for them to go. Yet another theory is that their skin gives little protection against UV light, and increasing UV light levels in recent years have proven deadly to amphibians. Perhaps they are like the canaries that miners used in the old days to warn them of toxic air in the mines. When the canary keeled over, it was time for the miners to get out!

Are our dying frogs and toads a symptom of a planet that is already too polluted?

MEDICAL SERVICES
Red Cross (☎ 645 6128; ◷ 24hr) Just north of Santa Elena.

MONEY
Euros, US dollars and traveler's checks can be exchanged at Hotel Camino Verde (p197), although you can expect to pay a fairly hefty commission.
Banco Nacional (☎ 645 5027; Santa Elena; ◷ 8:30am-3:45pm Mon-Fri)

TOURIST INFORMATION
Camara de Empresarios Turisticos y Afines (☎ 645 6565; turismomv@racsa.co.cr; Santa Elena) Here's today's lesson – just because something has a fancy name and looks official doesn't mean you should trust it. Case in point – this company deals only with hotels and tour companies that pay it a regular fee, so don't go here if you're looking for unbiased information.
Monteverde Info (www.monteverdeinfo.com) A great source of information.
Pensión Santa Elena (p199; ☎ 645 6240; www.pension santaelena.com) A better option than the tourist office, even if you're not staying here, is to talk to the friendly folks here, or check out the comprehensive website.

Sights
Ecotourism is big business in Monteverde and Santa Elena, so it's not surprising that there are a number of eco-riffic attractions scattered around both towns. And if there's a certain critter you're itching to see, there are plenty of places where your view won't be obscured by all those pesky trees.

As places possessed of such sublime beauty and loads of service-industry jobs are apt to do, the Santa Elena–Monteverde ecocorridor is attracting an impressive art scene, and there are a growing number of classy galleries scattered throughout the cloud forest. The specialty here is woodwork, but not at all like the Sarchí scene – sculpture, figurative and fluid, is a local art movement worth checking out. Artists from all over the country also display their work in town.

EL JARDÍN DE LAS MARIPOSAS
One of the most interesting activities is visiting the **Butterfly Garden** (☎ 645 5512; adult/student US$8/6; ◷ 9:30am-4pm). Admission entitles you to a guided, naturalist-led tour (in Spanish, English, or German) that begins with an enlightening discussion of butterfly life cycles and the butterfly's importance in nature. A variety of eggs, caterpillars, pupae and adults are examined. Then visitors are taken into the greenhouses, where the butterflies are raised, and on into the screened garden, where hundreds of butterflies of many species are seen. The tour lasts about

MONTEVERDE & SANTA ELENA

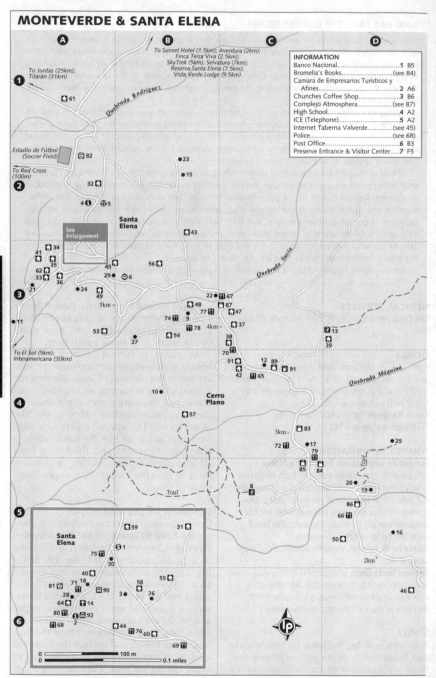

To Sunset Hotel (1.5km); Aventura (2km);
Finca Terra Viva (2.5km);
SkyTrek (5km); Selvatura (7km);
Reserva Santa Elena (7.5km);
Vista Verde Lodge (9.5km)

To Juntas (25km);
Tilarán (31km)

Quebrada Rodríguez

Estadio de Fútbol
(Soccer Field)
To Red Cross
(100m)

Santa
Elena

See
Enlargement

Quebrada Sucia

5km

To El Sol (5km);
Interamericana (30km)

4km

Quebrada Máquina

Cerro
Plano

3km

Trail

Trail

2km

Santa
Elena

0   100 m
0   0.1 miles

NORTHWESTERN COSTA RICA

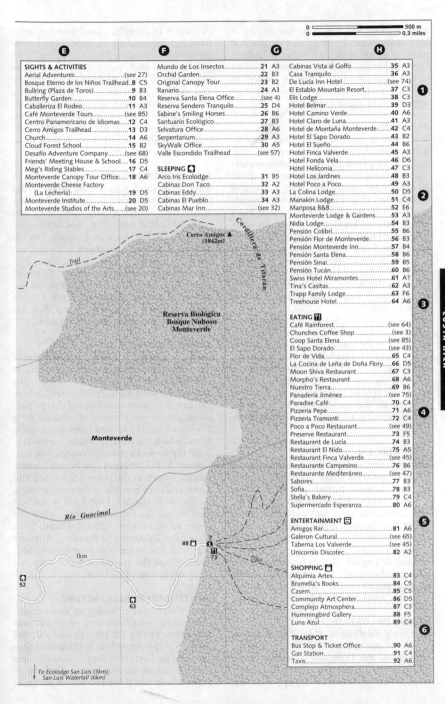

0 500 m
0 0.3 miles

SIGHTS & ACTIVITIES
Aerial Adventures............................(see 27)
Bosque Eterno de los Niños Trailhead..**8** C5
Bullring (Plaza de Toros).................**9** B3
Butterfly Garden...........................**10** B4
Caballeriza El Rodeo......................**11** A3
Café Monteverde Tours..................(see 85)
Centro Panamericano de Idiomas.....**12** C4
Cerro Amigos Trailhead..................**13** D3
Church..**14** A6
Cloud Forest School.......................**15** B2
Desafío Adventure Company..........(see 68)
Friends' Meeting House & School....**16** D5
Meg's Riding Stables......................**17** C4
Monteverde Canopy Tour Office.....**18** A6
Monteverde Cheese Factory
 (La Lechería)...............................**19** D5
Monteverde Institute......................**20** D5
Monteverde Studios of the Arts......(see 20)

Mundo de Los Insectos.................**21** A3
Orchid Garden..............................**22** B3
Original Canopy Tour.....................**23** B2
Ranario.......................................**24** A3
Reserva Santa Elena Office..............(see 4)
Reserva Sendero Tranquilo.............**25** D4
Sabine's Smiling Horses.................**26** B6
Santuario Ecológico......................**27** B3
Selvatura Office............................**28** A6
Serpentarium...............................**29** A3
SkyWalk Office.............................**30** A5
Valle Escondido Trailhead.............(see 57)

SLEEPING
Arco Iris Ecolodge........................**31** B5
Cabinas Don Taco.........................**32** A2
Cabinas Eddy...............................**33** A3
Cabinas El Pueblo.........................**34** A3
Cabinas Mar Inn...........................(see 32)

Cabinas Vista al Golfo....................**35** A3
Casa Tranquilo.............................**36** A3
De Lucía Inn Hotel........................(see 74)
El Establo Mountain Resort............**37** C3
Elis Lodge...................................**38** C3
Hotel Belmar...............................**39** D3
Hotel Camino Verde......................**40** A6
Hotel Claro de Luna......................**41** A3
Hotel de Montaña Monteverde.......**42** C4
Hotel El Sapo Dorado.....................**43** B2
Hotel El Sueño.............................**44** B6
Hotel Finca Valverde.....................**45** A3
Hotel Fonda Vela.........................**46** D6
Hotel Heliconia............................**47** C3
Hotel Los Jardines........................**48** B3
Hotel Poco a Poco........................**49** A3
La Colina Lodge...........................**50** D5
Manakin Lodge.............................**51** C4
Mariposa B&B..............................**52** E6
Monteverde Lodge & Gardens........**53** A3
Nidia Lodge.................................**54** B3
Pensión Colibrí............................**55** B6
Pensión Flor de Monteverde...........**56** B3
Pensión Monteverde Inn.................**57** B4
Pensión Santa Elena......................**58** B6
Pensión Sinaí...............................**59** B5
Pensión Tucán.............................**60** B6
Swiss Hotel Miramontes.................**61** A1
Tina's Casitas...............................**62** A3
Trapp Family Lodge.......................**63** F6
Treehouse Hotel...........................**64** A6

EATING
Café Rainforest.............................(see 64)
Chunches Coffee Shop....................(see 3)
Coop Santa Elena.........................(see 85)
El Sapo Dorado............................(see 43)
Flor de Vida................................**65** C4
La Cocina de Leña de Doña Flory....**66** D5
Moon Shiva Restaurant..................**67** C3
Morpho's Restaurant.....................**68** A6
Nuestro Tierra.............................**69** B6
Panadería Jiménez........................(see 75)
Paradise Café..............................**70** C4
Pizzería Pepe...............................**71** A6
Pizzería Tramonti.........................**72** C4
Poco a Poco Restaurant.................(see 49)
Preserve Restaurant......................**73** F5
Restaurant de Lucía......................**74** B3
Restaurant El Nido........................**75** A5
Restaurant Finca Valverde.............(see 45)
Restaurante Campesino.................**76** B6
Restaurante Mediterráneo.............(see 47)
Sabores.....................................**77** B3
Sofía...**78** B3
Stella's Bakery.............................**79** C4
Supermercado Esperanza...............**80** A6

ENTERTAINMENT
Amigos Bar.................................**81** A6
Galeron Cultural..........................(see 65)
Taberna Los Valverde....................(see 45)
Unicornio Discotec........................**82** A2

SHOPPING
Alquimia Artes.............................**83** C4
Bromelia's Books..........................**84** C5
Casem..**85** C5
Community Art Center...................**86** D5
Complejo Atmosphera....................**87** C3
Hummingbird Gallery.....................**88** F5
Luna Azul...................................**89** C4

TRANSPORT
Bus Stop & Ticket Office................**90** A6
Gas Station.................................**91** C4
Taxis...**92** A6

Cordillera de Tilarán

Cerro Amigos ▲
(1842m)

Trail

Reserva Biológica
Bosque Nuboso
Monteverde

Monteverde

Río Guacimal

1km

52

63

88

7

73

Trail

To Ecolodge San Luis (3km);
San Luis Waterfall (6km)

NORTHWESTERN COSTA RICA

an hour, after which you are free to stay as long as you wish. There's also a theatre that presents an informational video in English, Spanish, French, Dutch or German. It's best to visit in the morning when the butterflies are most active. There are good volunteer opportunities available here.

RANARIUM

With all this mist, it's no wonder that so many amphibians call Monteverde home, and the **Frog Pond** (☎ 645 6320; ranariomv@racsa .co.cr; adult/student US$9/7; ⊙ 9am-8:30pm) has about 30 species on display, including newts and salamanders in addition to the wide assortment of frogs and toads. Guides lead tours in English or Spanish through the well-maintained terraria, and point out the often-poisonous frogs with flashlights. One you won't find, no matter how hard you look, however, is the golden toad (see the boxed text Who Has Seen the Golden Toad?, p189), though there's a spot waiting should it ever again be found.

If you're lucky (tips are always appreciated) your guide may also imitate frog calls, or give you the lowdown on local folklore. Many resident amphibians are more active by night, so it's best to visit during the evening, though your ticket allows you to return for free in the evening. At the time of research, the owners were in the midst of constructing a number of new, outdoor *ranario*.

SERPENTARIUM

Biologist Fernando Valverde has collected about 40 species of snake, plus a fair number of frogs, lizards, turtles and other cold-blooded cuties at his **serpentarium** (☎ 645 6002; www.snaketour.com; adult/student/child US$7/5/3; ⊙ 9am-8pm). Sometimes it's tough to find the slithering stars of the show in their comfy, foliage-filled cages, but guides are available in Spanish or English for free tours; signage is similarly bilingual. The venomous snake displays are awesome, and you'll get to see your first (and hopefully last) fer-de-lance.

MUNDO DE LOS INSECTOS

Sure, the **World of Insects** (☎ 645 6859; klatindancer@ hotmail.com; adult/student US$7/5; ⊙ 8am-9pm) has butterflies, but there are probably more *mariposarios* in this country than canopy tours. What makes this place special is the collection of creepier cloud-forest critters, from hermaphroditic walking sticks to notoriously venomous banana spiders. The yuk factor is high, particularly when viewing hordes of water cockroaches, scorpions and various arachnids – all part of the fun. Fact-filled tours are available in Spanish and English. There's an excellent view from the roof by day, but the insects are more active at night. Luckily, your ticket can be used for two same-day visits.

JARDÍN DE LA ORQUÍDEA

This sweet-smelling roadside **orchid garden** (☎ 645 5510, adult/child US$5/3; ⊙ 8am-5pm) has shady trails winding past more than 400 types of orchid organized into taxonomic groups. Guided tours in Spanish, English and French can be arranged if it's not too busy, where you'll see such rarities as *Plztystele jungermannioides,* the world's smallest orchid, and several others marked for conservation by the Monteverde Orchid Investigation Project, the group that administrates this quiet oasis of flowers.

CAFÉ MONTEVERDE

Coffee-lovers will be excited to find some of the finest coffee in the world right here at **Café Monteverde** (☎ 645 7090; www.cafémonteverde .com; tours per person US$15; ⊙ 7:30am-6pm), where you can sample six roasts free of charge. Better yet, make reservations in advance for a 2½-hour tour (at 8am and 1pm) of the coffee fincas, which use entirely organic methods to build the perfect brew. Afterwards, you'll be brought to the *beneficio* (coffee mill), where you can watch as the beans are washed and dried, and then brought to the roaster where they're, well, roasted. Late April is the best time to see the fields in bloom, while the coffee harvest (done entirely by hand) takes place from December to February. Anytime is a good time to see how your favorite beverage makes the transition from ruby red berry to smooth black brew.

MONTEVERDE CHEESE FACTORY

Until the recent upswing in ecotourism, Monteverde's number-one employer was this **cheese factory** (☎ 645 5522; tours adult/child US$8/5; ⊙ 7:30am-4pm Mon-Sat, to 12:30pm Sun), also called La Lechería (the Dairy). Reservations are required for the two-hour tour of operations, where you'll see old-school methods used to produce everything from a creamy Gouda to a very nice sharp, white cheddar, sold all over the country, as well as other dairy products such as yogurt and, most importantly, ice cream. If you've got a hankering for something sweet, our favorite treat is the coffee milk shake.

Stop by for a cone of soft-serve scrumptiousness here or at a few other select locations around town, including Sabores (p203). The small attached shop also sells deli meats, homemade granola and other picnic goodies, and you can watch cheese being made through the big window Monday through Friday.

SELVATURA

The makers of ecofun really went all out at **Selvatura** (☎ 645 5929; www.selvatura.com; admission gardens each US$10, hanging bridges US$25, exhibition US$10; ☹ 7:30am-4pm), a huge ecocomplex 150m from Reserva Santa Elena complete with butterfly and hummingbird gardens, a canopy tour (p197) and a series of hanging bridges, though the star attraction is the slightly overwhelming **Jewels of the Rainforest Exhibition**. This exhibition houses the majority of the Whitten Entomological Collection, a mind-boggling collection of the strangest and most stunning insects you've ever seen. The entire exhibition is the life's work of Richard Whitten (with a little help from his wife Margaret), and is masterfully presented using a combination of art, video and music. If you only have time to see one sight while you're in Monteverde, this is the one.

Activities

Don't forget your hiking boots, bug spray and the floppiest safari hat you own – there's plenty to do outdoors around here, including lots of action either on horseback or in the jungle canopy.

HIKING

The best hikes are at the two cloud-forest reserves bookending the main road, Reserva Biológica Bosque Nuboso Monteverde (p207) and Reserva Santa Elena (p210), both covered later in the chapter.

If you've ever gotten cynical about schoolchildren asking for money to save the rain forest, then you really must stop by **Bosque Eterno de los Niños** (Children's Eternal Forest; ☎ 645 5003; adult/student day-use US$7/4, guided night hike

US$15/10; ☹ 7:30am-5:30pm) and see what they purchased with all that spare change. Keep in mind, however, that this enormous 22,000-hectare reserve, which dwarfs both the Monteverde and Santa Elena reserves, is largely inaccessible. The international army of children who paid the bills decided that it was more important to provide a home for local wildlife among the primary and secondary forest (and to allow former agricultural land to be slowly reclaimed by the jungle), than to develop a lucrative tourist infrastructure. Kids today, what can you do?

The effort has allowed for one fabulous trail that hooks into a system of unimproved trails that are primarily for researchers, the 3.5km **Sendero Bajo del Tigre** (Jaguar Canyon Trail), which offers more open vistas than do those in the cloud forest, so spotting birds tends to be easier. The reason for this is that a good portion of the surrounding area was clear-cut during the mid-20th century, though there has been significant regrowth since being granted protected status. The resulting landscape is known as premontane forest, which is unique in Costa Rica as most things that are cut down stay cut down. Visitors also report that wildlife-watching tends to be better here than in the reserves at Monteverde or Santa Elena since the tourist volume is considerably lower.

Make reservations in advance for the popular night hikes, which set off at 5:30pm for a two-hour trek by flashlight through a sea of glowing red eyes. The San Gerardo Biological Station at the end of the trail has dorm beds for researchers and students, but you may be able to stay overnight with prior arrangements. If you're looking for a good volunteer program, the administration of the Children's Eternal Forest is always looking for help. For more information, send an email to acmcr@acmcr.org or visit www.acmcr.org.

Santuario Ecológico (Ecological Sanctuary; ☎ 645 5869; adult/student US$7/5; ☹ 7am-5pm) has four loop trails (the longest takes about 2½ hours at a slow pace) offering hikes of varying lengths through private property comprising premontane and secondary forest, coffee and banana plantations, and past a couple of waterfalls and lookout points. Coatis, agoutis and sloths are seen on most days, and monkeys, porcupines, and other animals

NORTHWESTERN
COSTA RICA

HISTORY OF THE QUAKERS

Quakerism (or more correctly the Society of Friends) was started in the 1650s as a breakaway movement from the Anglican Church of England. Although there is some historical uncertainty regarding the original leaders, Quakers attribute the founding of their religion to a man named George Fox, who left home at the age of 19 in 1644 to embark on a religious search that would ultimately last for three years. When his search concluded, Fox reported to have heard the voice of Christ, and claimed that direct experience with God was possible without having to go through the sacraments. Today, this belief is commonly described by Quakers as the 'God in everyone' or the 'inward Christ.'

In 1648 Fox began to preach publicly, in particular about the need to reject the paid priesthood and the governmentally sanctioned church buildings. Fox believed that everyone had within them the capacity to be a minister, and that any worshipful gathering of true Christians was an acceptable means of worship. Even today, Quaker prayer meetings are not conducted by any one individual, and people are encouraged to speak only when they feel moved to by the Spirit. Another tenant of Fox's preaching was the importance of universal pacifism, which was quickly adopted as a religious fundamental.

Starting in 1652, Fox aligned himself with the Seeker movement, which also believed that there was no true church in existence, and that humans were waiting for God to reestablish his kingdom. Fox and his fellow seekers became vocal dissenters against the Church of England, and were subsequently imprisoned on several occasions. In fact, the term 'Quaker' was coined by a judge in the 17th century to describe how defendants quaked in fear of prosecution.

In response to the growing culture of dissent, Parliament passed legislation in the mid-1650s in an attempt to curb the rising number of antichurch movements. Fearful that they would face increased persecution, the Quakers migrated to the Massachusetts Bay Colony in 1656. Although the Massachusetts Puritans were largely intolerant of Quaker beliefs, the Society of Friends later found refuge in New Jersey, Pennsylvania, Delaware and Maryland. In fact, the state of Pennsylvania was specifically founded by William Penn as a safe haven for Quakers.

In 1691, George Fox died, though the movement continued to grow in strength over the next few centuries. Today, the Quaker population in the US is small and confined to several communities, though the Society of Friends is well established in countries throughout the world.

If you're interested in learning more about the Quakers, prayer meetings at the **Friends Meeting House** in Monteverde are held on Sunday at 10:30am and Wednesday at 9am. Also, the Quakers are extremely active in the local community, and if you're willing to give at least a six-week commitment, there are numerous volunteer opportunities available. For more information, contact the **Monteverde Friends School** (www.mfschool.org).

are also common. Birding is also good. Guided tours (excluding admission US$15, three hours) are available throughout the day, and you'll see even more animals on the guided night tours (5:30pm to 7:30pm, adult/student US$14/9).

Sendero Tranquilo Reserve (Tranquil Path Reserve; ☎ 645 5010; admission US$20; ☼ tours at 7:30am & 1pm) is an 81-hectare private reserve located between the Reserva Biológica Bosque Nuboso Monteverde and the Río Guacimal. Trails here are narrow to allow for minimal environmental impact, and the group size is capped at six people, which means you won't have to worry about chattering tourists scaring away all the animals. The trails pass through four distinct types of forest

including a previously destroyed area that's starting to bud again.

Valle Escondido (Hidden Valley Trail; ☎ 645 5156; day-use US$5, night tours adult/child US$15/10; ☼ 7:30am-5:30pm) begins behind the Pensión Monteverde Inn and slowly winds its way through a deep canyon into an 11-hectare reserve. In comparison with the more popular reserves, Valle Escondido is quiet during the day and relatively undertouristed, so it's a good trail for wildlife-watching. However, the reserve's two-hour guided night tour is very popular, so it's best to make reservations for this in advance.

Take a free hike up **Cerro Amigos** (1842m) for good views of the surrounding rain forest and, on a clear day, of Volcán Arenal,

20km away to the northeast. Near the top of the mountain, you'll pass by the TV towers for channels 7 and 13. The trail leaves Monteverde from behind Hotel Belmar and ascends roughly 300m in 3km. From the hotel, take the dirt road going downhill, then the next left. Note that this trail does not connect to the trails in the Monteverde Reserve, so you'll have to double back.

Another popular (but strenuous) hike is to visit the **San Luis Waterfall**, a gorgeous ribbon of water streaming from the cloud forests into a series of swimming holes just screaming for a picnic. The distance from the parking area to the falls is only a few kilometers, but it's steeply graded downhill, and the rocky, mud-filled terrain can get very slick. Readers report that their entire families have been OK on the trail, but it's important to go slow and turn back if it becomes too difficult. However, your efforts will be worth it as the waterfall is simply breathtaking.

Drivers will need 4WD to ford the little river and climb the muddy road out. You can park (US$6 per car) at a private farm, which is located next to the trailhead. Several horseback-riding companies offer excursions to the falls (US$50 per person), but note that much of the road is now paved and this is hard on the horses' knees. ATVs (see Monteverde Off-Roader, below) also make the trek. A taxi from town to the falls will run you about U$12.

ATV RIDING

Hop on an ATV from **Monteverde Off-Roader** (☎ 645 5023; quadadventures@ad.com; tours per ATV US$35-100), because nothing says 'I love nature' better than a trail of sulfurous exhaust.

CANOPY TOURS

Wondering where the whole 'canopy tour' euphemism was coined? Santa Elena is the site of Costa Rica's first zip lines, today eclipsed in adrenaline by the nearly 100 imitators who have followed, some of which are right here in town. Sure, the only way you're going to see a quetzal on one of these things is if you run smack-dab into the poor bird, and the US$35-to-$45 price tag is absolutely ridiculous, but what the heck – they're really fun.

Before you tighten your harness and clip into the ride of your life, you're going to have

to choose which canopy tour will get your hard-earned cash – this is surprisingly harder than you'd think. Much like the rest of Costa Rica, Monteverde works on a commission-based system, so be skeptical of the advice that you're given, and insist on choosing the canopy tour that you want. We can give you the basic info on the four major players in town (p197), though it's good to talk to the friendly, unbiased staff at the Pensión Santa Elena if you want the full scoop (p199).

HORSE RIDING

Until recently, this region was most easily traveled on horseback, and considering the roads around here, that's probably still true. Several operators offer you the chance to test this theory, with guided horse rides ranging from two-hour tours to five-day adventures. Shorter trips generally run about US$15 per hour, while an overnight trek including meals and accommodations runs between US$150 and US$200.

Some outfitters also make the trip to La Fortuna, an intriguing transportation option with several caveats (US$60 to US$100; see the boxed text To Ride Or Not To Ride?, p206). Though a few operators will charge less, remember you (or more likely, the horse) get what you pay for.

Caballeriza El Rodeo (☎ 645 5764; elrodeo@racsa .co.cr) does local tours on private trails, as well as trips to San Luis Waterfall and a sunset tour to a spot overlooking the Golfo de Nicoya.

Desafío Adventure Company (☎ 645 5874; www .monteverdetours.com) does local treks for groups and individuals around town, day trips to San Luis Waterfall (six hours, per person US$50) and several multiday rides. This established outfitter will arrange rides to La Fortuna for US$65, though not on the Castillo Trail. The company also arranges white-water rafting trips on the Ríos Toro, Sarapiquí and others, and can help with transport and hotel reservations.

Meg's Riding Stables (☎ 645 5560; www.guanacaste .com/sites/stellas/stables.htm) takes folks on private trails nearby plus treks to San Luis Waterfall. Kid-sized saddles are also available. The horses are well looked after, and this is the longest-established operation in Monteverde.

Sabine's Smiling Horses (☎ 645 6894; www.horse back-riding-tour.com), run by Sabine, who speaks

English, French, Spanish and German, offers a variety of treks, from US$15-per-hour day trips to specialty tours including a Full Moon Ride (per person US$50, five hours). Several multiday treks are also on offer, and Sabine may also take experienced riders on the Castillo Trail, weather permitting. This outfitter has been highly recommended by readers year after year.

A locally recommended guide who will take experienced riders on the Castillo Trail is **Leonel Quesada** (☎ 645 5354, 200 5174), though the trip is only possible during the dry season and during perfect weather conditions.

TRAMS & HANGING BRIDGES

OK, so you're too scared to zip through the canopy on a steel cable, but fear not as the makers of ecofun have something special for you – trams and hanging bridges, the safe and slightly less expensive way to explore the treetops.

Aerial Adventures & Natural Wonders Tram (☎ 645 5960; naturalwonders@racsa.co.cr; tram adult/child US$15/8, hike US$7, tram & hike US$20) is essentially a ski lift, offering a 1.5km journey in electrically propelled gondola chairs on rails attached to towers; heights reach 12m. The ride lasts an hour, and you have the option of pausing your car briefly to look around. You can also rent golf carts (US$30) that hold up to three people for cruising around the trails afterward, a great choice for folks with limited mobility who want to get out in the woods on their own.

Selvatura, SkyWalk (owned by SkyTrek) and Aventura have systems of hanging bridges that you can traipse across and live out your Indiana Jones fantasies. There are subtle differences between all of them (some are fat, some are thin, some are bouncy, some are saggy), though you're going to enjoy the views of the canopy regardless of which one you pick. They're all priced around US$20 for adults and US$15 for students.

CANOPY FIGHTING   *Carolina A Miranda*

All is not well in the world of zip-line operators. As competition has come to a boil between the nearly 100 canopy-tour operators around the country, the founder of the Original Canopy Tour decided to patent his concept and the words 'canopy tour' with Costa Rica's National Registry. After receiving the title, Darren Hreniuk, the Canadian behind the tour, has claimed that all other operators are running 'pirate tours' and has demanded that they pay him licensing fees or shut down.

The title has been largely ignored by other operators, who insist that the idea of crossing trees on a cable-and-pulley system is hardly a new one. (There is a painting dating back to 1858 in the Museo Nacional that shows people transporting themselves on ropes tied between trees.) Hreniuk insists otherwise. 'I am the inventor of the canopy tour,' he told the *Tico Times* in August of 2003. 'If people like that or not, it is irrelevant.'

The National Registry supported his claim and provided Hreniuk with a cease-and-desist order that demanded that all other tours close up shop. Armed with this, Hreniuk visited more than a dozen tour sites in April and December of 2003 and attempted to shut them down. However, the cease-and-desist order was soon frozen by the government, which claimed that it needed more time to study the matter further.

Locally, Hreniuk's legal moves were poorly regarded. Many Ticos viewed his patent and subsequent enforcement of it as an attempt to create a foreign monopoly on an activity that more than a quarter of all tourists who go to Costa Rica participate in. This is the kind of legal wrangling that can take all the fun out of traveling, in our opinion, and we can only hope that the person who 'invented' rafting doesn't try to do the same.

As an aside, another criticism of Hreniuk's 'invention' is that the environmental impact of canopy tours may be greater then previously believed. Specifically, canopy tours can contribute to ground erosion, the disruption of vegetation and damage to tree trunks. And an increase in the number of screaming gringos flying across the rain-forest canopy can't be good for nearby birders and wildlife-watchers. Regardless, it's likely that at some point during your travels in Costa Rica, you'll probably give in to the temptation and sign up for a quick adrenaline fix. The point is simply to inquire about the environmental impact of a particular canopy tour before you fork over your cash, and to be happy that Costa Rica has a good system of patent law in place.

Tours

Aventura (☎ 645 6901; www.aventuramonteverde.com; adult/student US$35/28; ⏰ 7am-2:30pm) The newest company in town, and has 16 platforms that are spiced up with a Tarzan swing and a 15m rappel. It's located about 3km north of Santa Elena on the road to the reserve, and transportation from your hotel is included in the price.

Original Canopy Tour (☎ 291 4465; www.canopytour .com; adult/student/child US$45/35/25; ⏰ 7:30am-2:30pm) On the grounds of Cloud Forest Lodge, this has the fabled zip lines that started an ecotourism movement of questionable ecological value. These lines aren't as elaborate as the others, but with 14 platforms, a rappel through the center of an old fig tree and 5km of private trails worth a wander afterward, you can enjoy a piece of history that's far more entertaining than most museums.

Selvatura (☎ 645 5929; www.selvatura.com; adult/child US$40/30; ⏰ 7:30am-4pm) Claims to be the longest canopy tour in the country, though by the time you finished measuring them, six more would have opened. In case you're the kind of person who finds numbers sexy, it's got 3km of cables, 18 platforms and one Tarzan swing. It's also the only canopy tour located in primary forest. The office is located across the street from the church in Santa Elena.

SkyTrek (☎ 645 5796; www.skywalk.co.cr; adult/student US$40/32; ⏰ 7:30am-5pm) If you're not buying the whole 'eco' element of canopy tours, then this is definitely for you. This seriously fast canopy tour consists of 11 platforms attached to steel towers that are spread out along a road. We're talking about some serious speed here, which is probably why SkyTrek is the only canopy tour that has a real brake system.

Courses

Centro Panamericano de Idiomas (☎ 265 6306; www.cpi-edu.com; classes with/without homestay US$380/255) Specializes in Spanish language education. Also has locations in Heredia and Playa Flamingo, with the opportunity to transfer from campus to campus.

Monteverde Institute (☎ 645 5053; www.mvinstitute .org) A nonprofit educational institute, founded in 1986, that offers interdisciplinary courses in tropical biology, conservation, sustainable development and Spanish, among other topics. These courses are occasionally open to the general public – check the website. There is also a volunteer-placement program for people who wish to teach in local schools or work in reforestation programs.

The institute's short courses (US$800 to US$1800, two weeks) teach both high-school and college students about conservation and land use in the Monteverde area. Long courses (US$4000, 10 weeks) are university-accredited programs for undergraduates and they emphasize tropical community ecology.

Monteverde Studios of the Arts Administered by Monteverde Institute, this offers a variety of classes and workshops, sometimes open to visitors, covering everything from woodworking to papermaking, with a special emphasis on pottery.

Festivals & Events

Monteverde Music Festival is held annually on variable dates from late January to early April. It's gained a well-deserved reputation as one of the top music festivals in Central America. Music is mainly classical, jazz, and Latin, with an occasional experimental group to spice things up. Concerts are held on Thursday, Friday and Saturday, at different venues all over town. Some performances are free, but most events ask US$5 to US$15 – proceeds go toward teaching music and the arts in local schools.

Monteverde is a magnet for artists, travelers and dreamers alike, so you can usually count on the odd cultural offering or two. A good place to inquire about special events is Moon Shiva (p203), an Israeli-run restaurant that's the vanguard of all things hip.

Sleeping

During Christmas and Easter, many hotels are booked up weeks in advance. During the January-to-April busy season and also in July, reservations are a good idea, though you can almost always find somewhere to stay. Note that Monteverde can get very cool at night, so don't be surprised if your room doesn't have a fan (but do if it doesn't have a warm blanket!).

The rates given are high-season rates, but low-season rates could be as much as 30% to 40% lower.

BUDGET

Competition has kept costs low and budget spots usually offer warm(ish) showers.

Hotel Camino Verde (☎ 645 5204; www.monteverde infocenter.com/caminoverde; r per person with/without bathroom US$7/5) This budget hotel has clean, basic rooms with hot showers, a central location and one of the cheapest prices in town. The hotel also has a comprehensive tour-booking service, and can exchange money and traveler's checks. Camino Verde operates the only public transportation to the Reserva Santa Elena.

Pensión Sinai (☎ 645 5343; lucreciajc@yahoo.com; r per person with/without bathroom US$10/5) Brand new tiled rooms in this homey family-owned pension are pristine, and readers rave about the friendly staff and the warm communal feel. Showers have warm water, and there is a small kitchen available.

Pensión Tucán (☎ 645 5017; r per person with/without bathroom US$10/5) Small wooden rooms are clean and comfortable enough, but it's next to a 'major' Santa Elena intersection that can get noisy, even at night. It's a popular option that's perfectly acceptable, but you can probably do better. Breakfast (US$3) is available, and there's a tour office downstairs.

Pensión Colibrí (☎ 645 5682; r per person with/without bathroom US$11/6; P) Another popular budget option, this small, family-run pension is located on a quiet lane and feels like it's perched among the trees. The larger rooms with private bathrooms are worth the money as they have balconies overlooking the woods, which are perfect for breathing in the cool, mountain air. There's also a small communal kitchen that everyone can use.

Tina's Casitas (☎ 645 5641; www.tinascasitas.de; tinas casitas@hotmail.com; s/d/tr US$8/12/15; P ▯) Located west of the La Esperanza supermarket, this terrific German-run spot is a great value, and consistently packed with backpackers from all around the world. The rooms are spotlessly maintained and feature handcarved furniture of Tina's own design, firm beds and private bathrooms. There's also a shared kitchenette and Internet access, and you're bound to meet some great travelers here.

Cabinas Mar Inn (☎ 645 5279; cabmarin@racsa.co.cr; d incl breakfast with/without bathroom US$12/10; P) On a hill about 50m north of the high school, this is a great option as the managers are welcoming, and the breakfasts are filling. Wood-paneled rooms are rustic and airy, and the quiet location means you'll get a restful night's sleep. There's a nice outdoor patio overlooking the town.

Cabinas Eddy (☎ 645 6635; d US$12; P ▯) One of the newest places in town comes reader recommended due to its delightful staff and cheap, cheap price (all rooms have a private hot shower). The English-speaking staff members are extremely helpful, and you've got to hear the marimba-playing prowess of Eddy, the owner and manager.

Pensión Flor de Monteverde (☎ 645 5236; d incl breakfast with/without bathroom US$15/12, incl all meals extra US$15; P) Though it's definitely further out than other hotels, you'll be glad you came to this sheltered hideaway. Owner Eduardo Venegas Castro is a fountain of information. In the past, he worked at both the Monteverde and Santa Elena reserves, and was director of the latter. Rooms are basic, though comfortable. Tours and transportation can be arranged.

Casa Tranquilo (☎ 645 6782; www.casatranquilo.net; tranquilo@racsa.co.cr; s/d/tr incl breakfast US$15/20/30; P ▯) Also west of the supermarket is this reader-recommended hotel, owned and managed by a delightful couple, David and Elena. Wood-paneled rooms with skylights have views of the Gulf, and the private showers are as hot as they come. Check out the great outdoor patio, perfect for a few late-night ballads on the guitar. There's also a communal kitchen, free Internet, free coffee and tea, CD burning and printing, and a buffet breakfast with granola, bread and eggs.

Cabinas El Pueblo (☎ 645 6192; www.cabinaselpueblo.com; s with/without bathroom US$15/10; d with/without bathroom US$20/15; P) These pleasant cabinas are run by an attentive Tico couple who will do everything possible to make your stay memorable. Well-furnished rooms have firm mattresses and hot private showers, and there's a fully equipped kitchen.

Hotel El Sueño (☎ 645 6695; d incl breakfast US$20; ▯) This Tico-run hotel has huge, recently renovated wooden rooms with private hot showers. Upstairs rooms are airier, though the best ones are in the new addition toward the back of the property. There's also a great balcony with sweeping views of the area.

Pensión Monteverde Inn (☎ 645 5156; s/d US$15/25; P) Located in a tranquil corner of Cerro Plano is this small inn, which is conveniently located next to the trailhead for the Hidden Valley Trail (p194). Spartan rooms have private hot showers, though the remote location is primarily why you're here. The owners can pick you up at the bus stop if you have a reservation.

Cabinas Vista al Golfo (☎ 645 6321; vistaalgolfo@racsa.co.cr; d US$30; P) This is a very comfortable, homey locale run by a congenial Costa Rican family. Rooms are well kept, the showers are hot and the owners will make you feel right at home. The upstairs balcony has great views of the rain forest and, on a clear day, the Gulf of Nicoya. There's also a small, communal kitchen.

Elis Lodge (☎ 645 5586; elislodge@yahoo.com; d with/without bathroom US$30/20; P) This cozy family home in Cerro Plano has lots of cutesy personal touches along with clean, bright rooms with a private hot-water bathroom. There's also a comfortable common area with a cable TV and fireplace.

MIDRANGE

Hotel Los Jardines (☎ 645 6038; www.hoteljardines demonteverde.com; s US$18-38, d US$36-56) This delightful hotel is recommended for its variety of rooms, which come in all different shapes and sizes. Don't worry though – you really can't choose wrong as every one is

wood-paneled and lovingly decorated by Grace, the delightful Tica owner. The hotel also has a great balcony lined with hammocks, which will suit all your swinging needs.

Mariposa B&B (☎ 645 5013; umfamilia@costarri cense.cr; s/d incl breakfast US$25/40; **P**) Just 1.5km from the reserve, this friendly family-run place has simple but very nice rooms with private hot showers. In addition to breakfast (and we're talking a real breakfast of fruits, pancakes, eggs and tortillas), there is a huge, shared kitchen that's perfect for

---

THE AUTHOR'S CHOICE

Budget

Pensión Santa Elena (☎ 645 6240; www.pensionsantaelena.com; camping per person US$3.50, dm US$6, s with/without bathroom US$15/10, d with/without bathroom US$20/12-14, tr with/without bathroom US$25/21, cabinas s/d/tr/q US$20/25/30/40; **P** 🖳) This full-service shoestringer's hostel is *the* place to stay in the area, and easily one of the top hostels in all of Costa Rica. OK, so the old, rambling house is definitely not going to win any beauty contests, but Ran and Shannon, the brother-sister duo from Austin, Texas, are committed to offering budget travelers top-notch, five-star service. They operate the only nonbiased tourist information office in town, and they'll take the time to sit down with travelers and explain all their options. They're also environmentalists at heart, and they're working with the local community on projects such as the reduction of gray water by installing septic tanks. And, if this isn't enough to help you sleep at night, all beds have firm, orthopedic mattresses. Other amenities include hot, tank showers, a message board, shared kitchen, cozy, communal atmosphere, free Internet (wireless too) and coffee all day. The Costa Rican staff is also fully bilingual, extremely professional and altogether charming.

Midrange

Arco Iris Ecolodge (☎ 645 5067; www.arcoirislodge.com; d US$45-85; **P**) This clutch of pretty cabins is on a little hill overlooking Santa Elena and the surrounding forests, and has the privacy and intimacy of a mountain retreat. The lodge features a system of private trails that wind throughout the property, including one that leads to a lookout point where you can see the Pacific on a clear day. There are a variety of different room sizes and styles to choose from, so you can either go rustic or live it up. If you're traveling in a group, the four-to-five-person split-level cabin (US$100 to US$140) is highly recommended – it's adorned with rich tapestries and features volcanic rock–laden showers. The multilingual German-owners are delightful, and they make excellent meals that sometimes feature organic vegetables grown on the grounds.

Top End

Hotel Fonda Vela (☎ 645 5125; www.fondavela.com; s/d US$86/94, junior ste US$94/112, additional person US$9; **P** 🗙 🖳) With a convenient location near the Monteverde reserve, unique architectural styling, 14 hectares of trail-laden grounds and a private stable, this classy retreat is a sophisticated home base for enjoying the pleasures of the area. Standard rooms are spacious and light, with wood accents and large windows, though the suites here are among the nicest rooms in town, and feature bathtubs, balconies and sitting rooms with huge TVs. Many rooms are wheelchair-accessible. The restaurant (mains US$8 to US$16, open 6:15am to 9am, noon to 2pm and 6:30pm to 8:30pm) is open to the public, and recommended for its excellent food that emphasizes fresh, local ingredients. The hotel is owned by the two sons of Paul Smith, who first arrived in Monteverde in the 1950s and is a well-known local artist whose work graces the walls.

self-caterers. There's also a little balcony out back for observing wildlife, because nothing is cuter than a passel of *pizotes*.

Treehouse Hotel (☎ 645 7475; s/d incl breakfast US$30/40; ℗ 🖳) This hotel, which is located at the top of a complex of restaurants and cafés, is built around the canopy of a 45-year-old fig tree that was planted by the grandfather of the owner. The rooms themselves have all been recently renovated, and have private hot-water bathrooms, cable TV and balconies overlooking the town of Santa Elena. If you're traveling in a group, inquire about the seven-person penthouse.

Finca Terra Viva (☎ 645 5454; www.terravivacr.com; d per 1/2 or more nights US$40/30, extra person US$5, incl 3 meals extra US$15; ℗ 🖳) About 2.5km out on the road toward Reserva Santa Elena, this 135-hectare finca is being gradually returned to the forest; about 60% is already there. In the meantime, cattle, pigs, goats, horses and chickens offer guests a typically Costa Rican rural experience – kids love this place. Each of the four rustic, wooden rooms sleeps up to four and has a private hot shower; for an extra US$5 per person there's access to a full kitchen. Or it'll whip up three Costa Rican meals per day for an additional US$15 per person. Owner Federico is a well-known naturalist and guide who has long envisioned living in a finca that combines education, conservation and farming – this is the result. Horse riding can be arranged, and you can try your hand at milking cows and making cheese.

Sunset Hotel (☎ 645 5228; s/d/tr US$30/40/50; ℗) About 1.5km out of Santa Elena toward Reserva Santa Elena, this intimate guesthouse is in a secluded location with great views of the Golfo de Nicoya and ample opportunities for bird-watching on private trails. Clean, standard rooms with porches have two little luxuries: real hot showers (not suicide machines), and toilets with enough pressure to flush paper. German and English are spoken.

Nidia Lodge (☎ 645 6082; s/d US$35/40; ℗) The proprietor of Pensión Flor de Monteverde, Eduardo Venegas Castro, has a beautiful new inn named for his wife. The area is peaceful and just steps away from the Santuario Ecológico, so there's a good chance that wildlife will grace your front doorstep. The accommodations are first-rate, with hot water and private balconies upstairs,

plus there's a nice restaurant. Eduardo, an expert naturalist, clearly revels in offering guided walks of area forests.

Manakín Lodge (☎ 645 5835; www.manakinlodge .com; d standard/superior US$40/60; ℗ 🖳) This simple Tico family-run lodge in Cerro Plano is surrounded by shady gardens and has a friendly, laid-back feel. All rooms have homey furnishings and private hot-water showers, though the 2nd-floor superior rooms have better views and small, private balconies.

Swiss Hotel Miramontes (☎ 645 5152; www.swiss hotelmiramontes.com; s/d US$40/50, d chalet US$70; ℗) Just outside Santa Elena on the road to Juntas is this delightful European-inspired retreat, well situated in a grove of pine trees and tropical flowers. Eight rooms of varying size come with fabulous private hot-water bathrooms, while the two chalets have a little more breathing space, and a private porch where you can kick off your shoes. Kids love the expansive landscaped grounds, with trails through the well-stocked orchid garden (US$5 for nonguests) and everyone enjoys the huge, pretty chalets. The restaurant (mains US$4 to US$10, open 1pm to 10pm) specializes in Swiss treats such as *ge-schnetzeltes* (Zürich-style cut of meat) with *rösti* (grated potatoes), made with locally grown manioc instead of potatoes, and *café fertig*, coffee with real Swiss schnapps.

La Colina Lodge (☎ 645 5009; www.lacolinalodge .com; per person camping US$5, d with/without bathroom US$49/42, tr with/without bathroom US$61/54) This is the former 'Flor Mar' opened in 1977 by Marvin Rockwell, one of the area's original Quakers, who was jailed for refusing to sign up for the draft in 1949 and then spent three months driving down from Alabama. The property was recently purchased by North Americans Kevin and Nancy, who were in the process of renovating it at the time of writing. Expect good things to come as Nancy is a talented painter, who's giving everything she sees the artist's touch, and Kevin's working on his own project – namely a bar and Jacuzzi.

Cabinas Don Taco (☎ 645 5263; www.cabinasdon taco.com; d standard/cabina incl breakfast US$45/50; ℗) Sure, the name is a tad ridiculous, but with big porches, great murals and an outdoor dining–chill-out area, this spot is fabulous. Cabinas come with TV, refrigerator and a balcony overlooking the Golfo de Nicoya.

Street life, San José (p88)

Teatro Nacional (p99), San José

Local poses with motorcycle

Catedral Metropolitana (p97), San José

Traditional handicraft (p539)

It's located just north of Santa Elena proper, so you can rest easy at night.

Hotel Poco a Poco (☎ 645 6000; www.hotelpoco apoco.com; s/d/tr US$50/65/70; P ☒) A short walk from the village of Santa Elena will bring you to this funky property, which is adorned with ceramic mushrooms, tree frogs and other Costa Rican critters. Yellow-stuccoed rooms sleep three, and they have some great perks – full bathtubs, big cable TVs and a DVD library (rental US$3) to dip into during those rainy nights. The best perk, however, is the excellent restaurant (mains US$6 to US$11, open 6:30am to 9am and noon to 9:30pm), also open to the public, which specializes in reader-recommended barbecue.

Hotel Claro de Luna (☎ 645 5269; www.hotelclaro deluna.com; d incl breakfast standard/deluxe US$55/72; P) This mountain chalet just southwest of Santa Elena is the perfect get-away for lovers. If you squint your eyes just a bit while staring at the hotel's Swiss-inspired architecture, you'll think you're summering high up in the Alps. All nine rooms have hardwood floors and ceilings and feature luxurious, hot-water bathrooms with regal tiles.

El Sol (☎ 645 5838; www.elsolnuestro.com; d small/ large cabin US$60/80; P) Located 5km outside of Santa Elena near Guacimal is this 'sunny' spot (El Sol translates to 'the Sun'). This small farm with two guest cabins is located at a lower elevation than Santa Elena – the climate is drier and the sun is warmer. The owners of this highly recommended accommodation are Elisabeth and Ignacio, a German-Spanish couple who will pamper you with strong massages and delicious home cooking. Their young son, Javier, is an absolute delight, and he's a great guide around the private trails on foot or on horseback.

Hotel Finca Valverde (☎ 645 5157; www.monte verde.co.cr; d cabin/ste US$65/70, extra person US$12; P) Just outside Santa Elena, this working coffee farm is a great choice if you're looking for something a bit different. Cabins each have two bare units with private hot-water showers, an upstairs loft and a balcony, though the real reason you're here is to soak up the rural atmosphere. Junior suites are only slightly more expensive, though they have full baths and cable TV. A simple but pleasant restaurant (mains US$4 to US$11, open 6am to 9:30pm) serves good fish and

meat dishes as well as vegetables from the backyard garden. The attached bar is locally popular.

Hotel Belmar (☎ 645 5201; www.hotelbelmar.net; s/d US$65/70, chalet s/d US$75/85; P ☐ ☎) Despite being a 'real' ecoresort, the Hotel Belmar admirably doesn't flaunt it in its name. Rooms here are definitely upscale, though even their design scheme is commendable as all the artwork is from Casem (see p204). Minibars in the rooms, a TV lounge, and transportation from the bus stop are all part of the deal, but the biggest bonus is right out back: this is the trailhead for Cerro Amigos (p194). And you can be sure that the management works continuously to minimize its environmental impact – even the excess water from the mountainside Jacuzzi and pool is reused in the organic gardens, which of course makes for some great dishes at the on-site restaurant.

TOP END

Many of the pricier hotels are taking it upon themselves to experiment with alternative technologies, from solar-heated showers to elaborate gray-water systems. Owners are usually more than happy to offer impromptu tours with full explanations of how these technologies work, and can offer suggestions to folks who'd like to implement similar systems back home.

Hotel de Montaña Monteverde (☎ 645 5046; www.monteverdemountainhotel.com; standard/superior US$63/ 113; P) Opened in 1978 as the first high-end accommodation in Monteverde, this hotel was undergoing major renovation at the time of writing to create a new reception, restaurant and bar. Standard rooms have wood accents, thick mattresses and cable TV, and they can sleep up to three people. The superior rooms are definitely pricey, though they can accommodate up to four people, and they have a huge bathtub, a private balcony and a minibar. The spacious gardens and forests of the 15-hectare property are pleasant to walk around, and there's also a sauna and Jacuzzi.

Trapp Family Lodge (☎ 645 5858; www.trappfam .com; d/tr US$80/92; s/d ste US$95/107; P ☒) The closest lodge to the reserve entrance (just under 1km away) has 20 spacious rooms with high wooden ceilings, big bathrooms, and fabulous views from the picture windows (which overlook either gardens or cloud forest). Suites come complete with TV and refrigerator, and there's no smoking anywhere (so you can breathe easy at night). There's a homey restaurant (mains US$10 to US$16) for guests only; a bar and sitting room with cable TV is open till 10pm. The emphasis here is on creating a family atmosphere, so bring the kids along and teach them a thing or two about nature.

El Establo Mountain Resort (☎ 645 5110; www .hotelelestablo.com; d US$84-250; **P** **✕** **�writ**) This is a seriously upscale lodge offering a variety of rooms, some of which are among the most luxurious that the Monteverde–Santa Elena area has to offer. Unfortunately, rooms here are located on two different properties, and travelers often complain that some of the standard rooms near the parking lot are overpriced, cinderblock prisons. This is of course a marked contrast with the newer rooms, some of which feature personal, flagstone-trimmed Jacuzzi – be smart and ask to see a room first before you pay. Since this is Monteverde, you'll be happy to know that the new deluxe property comes complete with solar power, gray-water systems, a well-insulated underground electrical network and a good restaurant where buffet-style meals usually include locally grown produce. It's a steep hike to the best rooms, but the resort runs a shuttle on request.

Hotel Heliconia (☎ 645 5109, www.hotelheliconia .com; d standard/junior ste US$85/95, f ste US$115; **P**) Located in Cerro Plano, this attractive, wooden, family-run hotel consists of the main lodge and several bungalows that are spread out across a mountainside. Standard rooms have breezy views while junior suites are ridiculously luxurious with two double beds, full baths and stained-glass windows. The two family suites, which can each accommodate up to six people or be connected for a party of 12, are downright palatial with huge sitting areas and outdoor terraces overlooking the Gulf of Nicoya. Owners arrange all the usual tours, and operate a spa and esthetic center where you can soak your stresses away in the Jacuzzi, or indulge in an endless list of beauty treatments. The reader-recommended Restaurante Mediterráneo (mains US$8 to US$12, open 6:30am to 9pm) offers innovate Italian and seafood specialties as well as a smattering of typical Costa Rican dishes.

Hotel El Sapo Dorado (☎ 645 5010; www.sapodo rado.com; d/ste US$89/99, extra person US$17; **P** **✕**) This hotel is owned by the Arguedas family, which first settled in the Monteverde area 10 years prior to the Quakers. Today the family is extremely active in the community, and they're regular promoters of the virtues of sustainable tourism. The 'Golden Toad' has 30 spacious rooms mostly in duplex cabins. All have two queen-size beds, a table and chairs, and private hot showers. Various deluxe suites have minibars, refrigerators and French doors that open to private terraces with views of the Golfo de Nicoya. The private forest behind the hotel has an extensive system of trails, and the restaurant (mains US$10 to US$20, open 6:30am to 9am, noon to 3pm and 6pm to 9pm) is renowned for its use of locally grown produce and wide range of vegetarian dishes.

Vista Verde Lodge (☎ 380 1517; www.info-monte verde.com; d incl breakfast standard/junior US$92/99; **P**) When you really want to get away from it all, take the signed side road just east of Selvatur and head 2.5 rough kilometers (4WD only) to this marvelous lodge, where you can be assured that nothing will disturb your night's sleep (except maybe the sounds of the surrounding rain forest). Wood-paneled rooms with picture windows take in views of Volcán Arenal, and the recent shift in the direction of the lava flow means that on a clear night, there will be plenty of fireworks. There is also a great common area where you can unwind in front of the TV and warm your feet beside the fire. Some 4km of trails through the primary forest surrounding this gorgeous spot can be explored on horseback; tours further into the forest can be arranged at the desk. The staff may be able to pick you up in Santa Elena, but if not it's a US$15 taxi ride from town.

Monteverde Lodge & Gardens (☎ 257 0766; www .costaricaexpeditions.com; d garden/standard US$112/148, additional person US$22; **P** **✕** **☐** **�writ**) A progressive recycling strategy, a solar-energy system, and a huge solar-powered – but nice and hot – Jacuzzi are among this non-smoking hotel's noteworthy environmentally sound practices. Large rooms with full bathrooms and wraparound picture windows have garden or forest views. The large lobby is graced by a huge fireplace, and there's an impeccable bar that looks down on the huge Jacuzzi. The grounds are attractively landscaped with a variety of native plants, emphasizing ferns, bromeliads and mosses, and a short trail leads to a bluff with an observation platform at the height of the forest canopy, with good views of the forest and a river ravine. Most folks are here on all-inclusive package deals that include three meals, served à la carte and featuring quality international cuisine, as well as guided tours and transportation from San José.

Eating

Pricier hotels often have good restaurants – many are open to the public. Santa Elena has most of the budget eateries.

These restaurants are listed from Santa Elena to the Monteverde preserve.

Restaurante El Nido (mains US$3-7; ⊙ 8:30am-9pm) Located in the heart of downtown Santa Elena, El Nido serves top-quality typical food including casados of every sort, plus burgers and snacks.

Panadería Jiménez (⊙ 5am-6:30pm Mon-Sat, 5-10am Sun) Downstairs from Restaurante El Nido, this has the best baked goods in town, plus coffee for folks booked on the early bus.

Pizzeria Pepe (slice US$1-2; ⊙ 8am-9pm) This unpretentious, no-frills local joint packs in budget travelers looking for a slice of 'za while still saving a buck or two.

Café Rainforest (light meals US$2-3; ⊙ 8am-8pm) Grab the best cup of coffee in town (which is certainly saying something) at this hip, downtown café that's also a great meeting place for travelers. Mellow the buzz a bit with a homemade pastry or a sandwich packed to the brim with local cheeses and organic veggies.

Restaurante Campesino (mains US$2-8; ⊙ 9am-11pm) Relax beneath about 80 stuffed animals won from machines by the dexterous owner, who also serves up amazing casados, beautiful salads and lots of good seafood with a smile.

Morpho's Restaurant (☎ 645 5607; mains US$4-8; ⊙ 7:30am-9:30pm) This romantic, downtown restaurant spices up typical Costa Rican food by adding a gourmet flair. Casados feature a variety of European-influenced sauces (think sea bass in a fruity demiglaze), and are served with a traditional *batido* (fruit shake) or a more sophisticated glass of wine.

Nuestra Tierra (☎ 645 5861; mains US$6-12; ⊙ 11am-10pm) This recommended restaurant is a branch of the celebrated San José eatery that's famous for the incredible quality of its casados. Don't let the prices fool you – typical food here is anything but typical, and you'll be impressed with the freshness of the produce and the richness of the meats and fishes.

Moon Shiva Restaurant (☎ 645 6270; dishes about US$4-8; ⊙ 10am-10pm) We get a lot of reader mail about this Israeli-run bohemian eatery. By day, Moon Shiva is a good spot for Mediterranean- and Middle Eastern–inspired dishes. By night it turns into the hippest spot in town for live music. Keep your eyes open for fliers in town advertising different shows and events, as this is *the* place for everything from rock and jazz to salsa and electronica.

Sabores (⊙ 10am-9pm; cones US$0.30-3) With longer hours than La Lechería, this place serves Monteverde's own brand of ice cream, plus coffee and a variety of homemade desserts. It's the perfect place for a civilized scoop after a morning hike through primitive forest.

Sofia (☎ 645 7017; mains US$10-18; ⊙ 5-10pm) This new addition to the Monteverde restaurant scene is quickly winning everyone over with its *nuevo Latin cuisine*, which is a modern fusion of traditional Latin American cooking styles. The ambience is flawless – soft lighting, hip music, picture windows, romantic candle settings, sloping wooden ceilings, pastel paints and potent cocktails to lighten the mood.

Restaurant de Lucía (☎ 645 5337; ⊙ 11am-8:30pm; mains US$7-15) On the same road as the Butterfly Garden, this Chilean-owned place is Monteverde's most famous restaurant. Chef José Belmar, who speaks more languages then you and your friend put together, regularly chats up guests and asks for feedback on the cuisine, though dishes here (a good mix of Italian and South American specialties) are always flawless (and reasonably priced).

Paradise Cafe (☎ 645 6081; plates US$2-5; ⊙ 8am-7pm) In our humble opinion, there's one simple question you can ask to figure out if a place is developed – does it have a bagel shop? And, if we're talking about Monteverde, the answer is yes. This relaxed café has a number of homemade salads and some tempting sandwiches, but you know why you're here. We like ours with poppy seeds, a slice of tomato and some local cheese, but you're an independent traveler, so don't be afraid to get a little wild.

Flor de Vida (☎ 645 6081; mains US$4-10; ☟ 7am-9:30pm) This branch of the popular vegetarian restaurant makes everything in-house, from spicy, lentil stews to cruelty-free casados. Still hungry? Treat yourself to a slice of carrot cake or heavenly *tiramisu*.

Pizzería Tramonti (☎ 645 6120; mains US$5-11; ☟ 11:30am-3pm & 5:30-10pm, closed Mon in low season) This is a good choice for Italian as the pizzas are baked in a wood-fired oven, and the pastas and seafood are consistently fresh. The atmosphere is also relaxed yet romantic, and the picture windows are perfect for admiring the cloud forest or the khaki-fashions of the passer-bys.

Stella's Bakery (☎ 645 5560; mains US$2-5; ☟ 6am-6pm) Order your choice of sandwich on delicious homemade breads with a convenient order form (one side is in English), and don't skimp on the veggies, many of which are locally grown (and organic). You can also get soups, salads, savory pastries stuffed with meats and cheeses, and lots of tempting sweet pastries.

La Cocina de Leña de Doña Flory (☎ 645 5306; mains US$4-6; ☟ 8am-8pm Sun-Fri) On a tiny turnoff close to La Colina Lodge, this 'Restaurante Rustico' is owned by Marvin Rockwell, one of the area's original Quaker settlers. Not surprisingly, food at this outdoor *soda* is simple yet healthy and filling, and it probably has the best tamales in town as well as its own special stew on Sunday.

Well-stocked **Supermercado Esperanza** (☎ 758 7351; ☟ 7am-8pm) has organic groceries, too. **Coop Santa Elena** (☟ 7:30am-6pm) in Cerro Plano has a smaller selection, but profits are reinvested in the community.

Entertainment

There are a few spots that have regular cultural offerings, which are usually heavily advertised around town with fliers. Look for events at the Galeron Cultural, the amphitheatre at Bromelia's and Moon Shiva.

Monteverde and Santa Elena's nightlife generally involves a guided hike into one of the reserves, but there are a few places for more inebriating amusements.

Unicornio Discotec (Santa Elena) A local hangout next to the soccer field at the northern end; can get a little rough in the evening, though

it's the only place in town that has Imperial on tap (and damn does it taste good).

Moon Shiva (☎ 645 6270; Santa Elena) Has regular offerings of live music.

Two popular tourist bars in the town of Santa Elena are **Amigos Bar**, a great place to drink and shoot pool, and the **Taberna Los Valverde**, which has a dance floor that's perfect for shaking what your mama gave ya.

Shopping

These are just some of the galleries, listed in order from Santa Elena to Monteverde reserve.

Compleja Atmosphera (☎ 645 6555; ☟ 9am-7pm) An upscale Cerro Plano gallery that specializes in wood sculpture, particularly pieces by Fabio, Marco and Tulio Brenas, part of a family of wood sculptors who carve exceptional and usually figurative pieces with a fluidity that's impressive in this material, and animals created by David Villalobos. Pieces run from US$6 to more than US$5000.

Luna Azul (☎ 645 6638; ☟ 9am-6pm) This funky boutique is decked out in celestial murals, and it's a relaxing spot to do a little souvenir shopping for your friends back home (or yourself if you're feeling generous). There's a great variety of clothing, jewelry and local art up for grabs as well as various aromatherapy products. The shop is run by the cheerful Nicolette from Austin, TX.

Community Art Center (☎ 645 6121; ☟ 10am-6pm) A great spot to score an early work by a soon-to-be-renowned Costa Rican artist – local kids make much of the pottery, jewelry and other artwork and they staff the place. Local art instructor Marco Tulio Brenes sells a variety of his creations here including wood reliefs, paintings and ceramics.

Alquimia Artes (☎ 645 5837; ☟ 8:30am-6pm) Has work that is a tad more affordable – check out the jewelry by Tarcicio Castillo from the Ecuadorian Andes – but this doesn't mean this collection of work by artists from throughout Costa Rica isn't astounding. Don't miss Helen Rodas' brightly colored portraits of women on banana paper and Justo Aguilar's surreal scenes.

Casem (Cooperativa de Artesanía Santa Elena Monteverde; ☎ 645 5190; ☟ 8am-5pm Mon-Sat, 10am-4pm Sun high season) Begun in 1982 as a women's cooperative representing eight female artists, today it has expanded to include almost

150 area artisans, eight of which are men. Embroidered and hand-painted clothing, polished wooden tableware, handmade cards and other work, some priced even for budget souvenir shoppers, make for an eclectic selection.

Bromelia's Books (☎ 645 6272; ⏱ 10am-5:30pm) Don cute felt shoes before entering, with its polished-wood Cerro Plano expanse of local arts and crafts, including some intricate batik. There are also books about the region, in particular natural history, in English and Spanish, plus lots of Costa Rican music. There's a small amphitheatre outside the bookstore that has regular theatre and musical performances. Be on the lookout for posters advertising events.

Hummingbird Gallery (☎ 645 5030; ⏱ 8:30am-5pm) Just outside Monteverde reserve, this has beautiful photos, watercolors, art by the indigenous Chorotega people of Guanacaste and, best of all, feeders that constantly attract several species of hummingbird. Great photo ops include potential hot shots of the violet sabrewing (Costa Rica's largest hummer) and the coppery-headed emerald, one of only three mainland birds endemic to Costa Rica. An identification board shows the nine species that are seen here. If you'd like a closer look, slides and photographs of the jungle's most precious feathered gems (and other luminous critters) by the renowned British wildlife photographers Michael and Patricia Fogden are on display; the smaller prints are for sale.

Getting There & Away

The government has been planning to build a series of bridges across the several rivers that feed Laguna de Arenal's southwestern shore for about 20 years. If completed, this would provide a road connection between Monteverde and La Fortuna, which would probably be the end of the ecoparadise formerly known as Monteverde. There are always a few scattered spots where some construction work is going on, but fortunately it doesn't look like they're going to make too much progress (at least in this century).

BUS

All intercity buses stop at the **bus terminal** (☎ 645 5159; ⏱ 6-11am & 1:30-5pm Mon-Fri, closes 3pm Sat & Sun) in downtown Santa Elena, and

most continue on to the cheese factory in Monteverde. On the trip in, keep an eye on your luggage, particularly on the San José–Puntarenas leg of the trip, as well as on the Monteverde–Tilarán run.

Purchase tickets to Reservas Monteverde and Santa Elena at Hotel Camino Verde (p197), which can also make reservations for pricier trips with private companies. Destinations, bus companies, fares, journey times and departure times are as follows:

Las Juntas US$2, 1½ hours, departs from bus station at 4:30am. Buses to Puntarenas and San José can drop you off in Las Juntas.

Managua, Nicaragua (Tica Bus) US$11, eight hours; a small shuttle bus (US$1.50) departs from the bus station at 6am and brings you to the highway where you can pick it up.

Puntarenas US$2.50, three hours, departs from the front of Banco Nacional at 6am.

Reserva Monteverde US$0.50, 30 minutes, departs from front of Banco Nacional at 6:30am, 7:30am, 9:30am, 11:30am, 1pm and 2:30pm, returns 6:40am, 8am, 10:40am, noon, 2:10pm and 3pm.

Reserva Santa Elena US$2, 30 minutes, departs from front of Banco Nacional at 6:30am, 8:30am, 10:30am, 2:30pm and 3:30pm, returns 11am, 1pm and 4pm.

San José (TransMonteverde) US$4.50, 4½ hours, departs from La Lechería at 6:30am and 2:30pm, with pick-up at the bus station in Santa Elena.

Tilarán, with connection to La Fortuna US$2, seven hours, departs from the bus station at 7am. This is a long ride as you will need to hang around for two hours in Tilarán. If you have a few extra dollars, it's recommended that you take the jeep-boat-jeep (see p207) option to La Fortuna.

CAR

While most Costa Rican communities regularly request paved roads in their region, preservationists in Monteverde have done the opposite. All roads here are shockingly rough, and 4WD is necessary all year, especially in the rainy season. Many car-rental agencies will refuse to rent you an ordinary car during rainy season if you admit that you're headed to Monteverde.

There are four roads from the Interamericana: coming from the south, the first turnoff is at Rancho Grande (18km north of the Puntarenas exit); a second turnoff is at the Río Lagarto bridge (just past Km 149, and roughly 15km northwest of Rancho Grande). Both are well signed and join one another about a third of the way to

TO RIDE OR NOT TO RIDE?

Though the top two tourist destinations in the region, La Fortuna and Monteverde–Santa Elena, are only about 25km apart, there are a few roadblocks that have thus far stopped anyone from paving a direct route between them: an erupting volcano, the country's largest lake, seven rivers, and the Cordillera de Tilarán for starters, not to mention mountains of bureaucratic red tape in San José. Currently, it takes several very bumpy hours by bus to make the trip.

In the mid-1990s, local entrepreneurs began offering transportation on horseback between the towns, calling it 'the shortest and most convenient connection.' The idea enchanted tourists and quickly became a booming business; as demand for the scenic trip grew, so did the number of outfitters. The result was severe price-cutting, and someone had to suffer for the savings. It was usually the horses.

Unethical practices such as buying cheap old horses and literally working them to death were reported: Lonely Planet received scores of horrified letters describing thin, diseased mounts that could barely make it through the mud; at least one overworked animal died on the Castillo Trail. Author Rob Rachowiecki wrote about the problem, angering local businesspeople who complained that his 'job was to write a guidebook, not harass them.' But the letters kept coming, so Rachowiecki kept reporting. Many companies went out of business.

Today, standards are high for reputable operators, in part (we like to think) because of informed tourists who asked hard questions and insisted on examining their horses before setting out, two precautions we still ask you to take. Although incidents of abuse are still reported, these are happily the exception rather than the rule. Costs have risen, the advertising revolves around how healthy the horses are, and most operators offer mellower alternatives.

There are now three main routes: The gorgeous and infamous **Castillo Trail** (five-hour hike, three hours on horseback), also called the 'Mountain Trail' or 'Mirador Trail,' crosses the fierce Caño Negro three times. It's still in use, but should only be done during the dry months (if then) from mid-March through May (assuming that it's actually dry) by experienced riders. Some businesses offer the trek year-round, as it saves operators about US$25 per person in transport costs compared to other options – but don't do it in the rainy season, no matter what your operator says.

The **Chiquito Trail** (six-hour hike, four hours on horseback) is still scenic and slippery, but doesn't require crossing the deepest rivers. This trail should also be avoided during wet weather, particularly by inexperienced riders. Finally, the flat and somewhat-less-scenic **Lake Trail** (six-hour hike, 2½ hours on horseback) is fine year-round, great for newbies, and basically skirts Laguna de Arenal between the boat taxi and jeep taxi that provide the actual transportation.

A good operator will never guarantee these or any other horseback trip, particularly along the Castillo Trail, as safety for both you and the horse depends completely on the weather. If they aren't offering some kind of refund in the event of rain, and/or an alternate lake trail or jeep-boat option, something's wrong. Also note that some hotels will imply that they are booking you through an established operator, but actually deliver you to a pal's independent company: ask if anything seems fishy.

And yes, budget travelers, you can find cheaper rides or even bargain reputable operators down by a few dollars in the low season. Hey, it's your choice. But consider this: When you save US$5, it's got to come out of someone's hide. Whose do you think it will be?

If you happen to witness any instance of horse abuse, talk to the equine-loving folks at the Pension Santa Elena (p199) – they know the scene well, and will make sure that the complaint reaches the right people.

Monteverde. Both routes boast about 35km of steep, winding, and scenic dirt roads with plenty of potholes and rocks to ensure that the driver, at least, is kept from admiring the scenery.

A third road goes via Juntas (p186), which starts off paved, but becomes just as rough as the first two a few kilometers past town, though it's about 5km shorter than the previous two. Finally, if coming from the north, drivers could take the paved road from Cañas via Tilarán (p257) and then take the rough road from Tilarán to Santa Elena.

HORSE

There are a number of outfitters that offer transportation on **horseback** (per person US$65-100, 5-6hr) to La Fortuna, usually in combination with jeep rides. The Castillo Trail has long been the source of some hand-wringing on the part of animal lovers and guidebook writers, but today there are three different trails available of varying difficulty. Use your own best judgment (see the boxed text To Ride Or Not To Ride?, opposite).

JEEP-BOAT-JEEP

The fastest route between Monteverde/Santa Elena and La Fortuna is a jeep-boat-jeep combo (around US$30, three hours), which can be arranged through almost any hotel or tour operator in either town. A 4WD jeep taxi takes you to Río Chiquito, meeting a boat that crosses Laguna de Arenal, where a taxi on the other side continues to La Fortuna. This is increasingly becoming the primary transportation between La Fortuna and Monteverde as it's incredibly scenic, reasonably priced and it'll save you half a day of rough travel.

RESERVA BIOLÓGICA BOSQUE NUBOSO MONTEVERDE

When Quaker settlers first arrived, they agreed to preserve about a third of their property in order to protect the watershed above Monteverde. By 1972, however, encroaching squatters began to threaten the region. The community joined forces with organizations such as the Nature Conservancy and the World Wildlife Fund to purchase 328 hectares adjacent to the already preserved area. This was called the Reserva Biológica Bosque Nuboso Monteverde (Monteverde Cloud Forest Biological Reserve), which the Centro Científico Tropical (Tropical Science Center) began administrating in 1975.

In 1986 the Monteverde Conservation League (MCL) was formed to buy land to expand the reserve. Two years later they launched the International Children's Rainforest project, which encouraged children and school groups from all over the world to raise money to buy and save tropical rain forest adjacent to the reserve. Today the reserve totals 10,500 hectares.

The most striking aspect of this project is that it is the result of private citizens working for change rather than waiting around for a national park administered by the government. The reserve relies partly on donations from the public (see Information opposite). Considering that the ridiculously under-funded Minae struggles to protect the national-park system, enterprises like this are more important than ever for maintaining cohesive wildlife corridors.

Visitors should note that some of the walking trails are very muddy, and even during the dry season (late December to early May) the cloud forest is rainy (folks, it's a rain forest – bring rainwear and suitable boots). Many of the trails have been stabilized with concrete blocks or wooden boards and are easy to walk on, though unpaved trails deeper in the preserve turn into quagmires during the rainy season.

Because of the fragile environment, the reserve allows a maximum of 160 people at any time. During the dry season this limit is almost always reached by 10am, which means you could spend the better part of a day waiting around for someone to leave. The best strategy is to get there before the gates open, or better (and wetter) to come during the off season, usually May through June and September through November.

Here are a couple of important points to consider, so read this part very carefully. If you only have time to visit either the Monteverde or Santa Elena reserve, you should know that Monteverde gets nearly 10 times as many visitors, which means that the infrastructure is better and the trails are regularly maintained, though you'll have to deal with much larger crowds. Also, most visitors come to Monteverde (and Santa Elena) expecting to see wildlife, though it's important to realize that both reserves cover large geographic areas, which means that the animals have a lot of space to move around in. Taking a night tour or staying overnight in one of the lodges deep within the reserve will maximize your chances of spotting wildlife, though it's best to enter the parks without any expectations. The trees themselves are primitive and alone worth the price of admission, though a lot has changed since the quetzal-spotting days of 1983. The animals have adapted to the increased tourist volume by avoiding the main trails, though the majority of people who visit either reserve are more than satisfied with the whole experience.

Information

The **information office** (☎ 645 5122; www.cct.or.cr; park entry adult/child under 6/student US$13/6.50/6.50; ⊙ 7am-4pm) is adjacent to the gift shop, where you can get information and buy trail guides, bird and mammal lists, and maps. The shop also sells T-shirts, beautiful color slides by Richard Laval, postcards, books, posters and a variety of other souvenirs, and rents binoculars (US$10); you'll need to leave your passport. The annual rainfall here is about 3000mm, though parts of the reserve reportedly get twice as much. It's usually cool (high temperatures around 18°C/65°F), so wear appropriate clothing.

It's important to remember that the cloud forest is often cloudy (!) and the vegetation is thick – this combination cuts down on sound as well as vision. Also keep in mind that main trails in this reserve are among the most trafficked in Costa Rica. Some readers have been disappointed with the lack of wildlife sightings. The best bet is, as always, to hire a guide.

Donations to the **Friends of Monteverde Cloud Forest** (friends@cct.or.cr; www.cloudforestalive .org) are graciously accepted at the following address: PO Box 1964, Cleveland, OH 44106, USA.

If you're looking for a great volunteer opportunity, the **Cloud Forest School** (☎ 645 5161; www.cloudforestschool.org; info@cloudforestschool .org) is a kindergarten-through-11th-grade bilingual school locally known as the Centro de Educación Creativa. The school was founded in 1991 to increase educational opportunities for a growing population of school-age children in the area. This independent school offers creative, experiential education to 220 students with an emphasis on integrating environmental education into all aspects of the school. For more information about volunteering as well as a few intern positions, you can contact the Volunteer Coordinator at opportunities@ cloudforestschool.org.

Activities

HIKING

There are currently 13km of marked and maintained trails – a free map is provided with your entrance fee. The most popular of the nine trails, suitable for day hikes, make a rough triangle (El Triángulo) to the east of the reserve entrance. The triangle's sides are made up of the popular **Sendero Bosque Nuboso** (1.9km), an interpretive walk (booklet US$0.75 at gate) through the cloud forest that begins at the ranger station, paralleled by the more open, 2km **El Camino**, a favorite of bird-watchers. The **Sendero Pantanoso** (1.6km) forms the far side of El Triángulo, traversing swamps, pine forests and the continental divide. Returning to the entrance, **Sendero Río** (2km) follows the Quebrada Cuecha past a few photogenic waterfalls.

Bisecting the triangle, gorgeous **Chomogo Trail** (1.8km) lifts hikers 150m to 1680m, the highest point in the triangle, and other little trails crisscross the region, including the worthwhile **Sendero Brillante** (300m), with bird's-eye views of a miniature forest. There's also a 100m suspension bridge about 1km from the ranger station. However, keep in mind that despite valiant efforts to contain crowd sizes, these shorter trails are among the most trafficked in the country, and wildlife learned long ago that the region is worth avoiding unless they want a good look at hominids.

There are also more substantial hikes, including trails to the three backcountry shelters (opposite) that begin at the far corners of the triangle. Even longer trails, many of them less developed, stretch out east across the reserve and down the Peñas Blancas river valley to lowlands north of the Cordillera de Tilarán and into the Children's Rainforest. If you're strong enough and have the time to spare, these hikes are highly recommended as you'll maximize your chances of spotting wildlife, and few tourists venture beyond the triangle. If you're serious about visiting the backcountry shelters, you should first talk to the park service as you will be entering some fairly rugged terrain, and a guide is highly recommended and, at times, essential. Camping is normally not allowed.

WILDLIFE-WATCHING

Monteverde is a birding paradise, and though the list of recorded species tops out at over 400, the one most visitors want to see is the resplendent quetzal (see the boxed text Local Lore, p210). The Mayan bird of paradise is most often spotted during the March and April nesting season, though you could get lucky anytime of year.

For mammal-watchers, the cloud forest's limited visibility and abundance of higher primates (namely human beings) can make wildlife-watching quite difficult, though commonly sighted species (especially in the backcountry) include coatis, howlers, capuchins, sloths, agoutis and squirrels (like squirrel-squirrels, not squirrel monkeys).

Tours & Guides

Although you can hike around the reserve on your own, a guide is highly recommended, and not just by us but by dozens of readers who were inspired by their adventures to email us. The park runs a variety of guided tours: make reservations *at least* one day in advance. As size is limited, groups should make reservations several months out for dry season and holiday periods. Guides speak English and are trained naturalists, and proceeds from the tours benefit environmental-education programs in local schools.

The reserve offers guided **natural history tours** (reservations ☎ 645 5112; tours excl entry fee US$15) at 7:30am daily, and on busy days at 8:30am as well. Participants meet at the Hummingbird Gallery (p205), where a short 10-minute orientation is given. A half-hour slide show from renowned wildlife photographers Michael and Patricia Fogden is followed by a 2½- to three-hour walk. Once your tour is over, you can return to the reserve on your own, as your ticket is valid for the entire day.

The reserve also offers recommended two-hour **night tours** (tours incl entry fee with/without transportation US$15/13) at 7:15pm nightly. These are by flashlight (bring your own for the best visibility), and offer the opportunity to observe the 70% of regional wildlife with nocturnal habits.

Guided **birding tours** (5hr tours incl entry fee per person US$40-50) in English begin at Stella's Bakery at 6am, and usually sight more than 40 species. There's a two-person minimum and six-person maximum. Longer tours go on by request at a higher fee, and usually more than 60 species are seen.

Several local businesses can arrange for a local to guide you either within the reserve or in some of the nearby surrounding areas. Staff can also recommend **private guides** (guide@monteverdeinfo.com), or ask at your hotel or any tour operator.

The reserve can also recommend excellent guides, many of which work for them, for a private tour. Costs vary depending on the season, the guide, and where you want to go, but average about US$60 to US$100 for a half-day. Entrance costs may be extra, especially for the cheaper tours. Full-day tours are also available. The size of the group is up to you – go alone or split the cost with a group of friends.

Sleeping & Eating

Near the park entrance are **dormitories** (☎ reservations 645 5122; www.cct.or.cr; dm adult/student US$37/33) with 43 bunks and shared bathrooms. These are often used by researchers and student groups but are often available to tourists – make reservations. Full board can be arranged in advance.

There are also three **backcountry shelters** (dm US$5), with drinking water, showers, propane stoves, and cooking utensils. You need to carry a sleeping bag, candles, food and anything else (like toilet paper) you might need. El Valle (6km, two hours) is the closest, Alemán Hut (8km, four hours) is near a cable car across Río Peñas Blancas, and Eladios Hut (13km, six hours) is the nicest, with separate dorm rooms and a nice porch. Trails are muddy and challenging, scenery mossy and green, and the tourist hordes that inundate the day hikes a far-off memory. This may be the best way to appreciate the reserve. Reservations are highly recommended, and they can be made at the park office prior to setting out on your hike.

There is a small **restaurant** (plates US$2-5; ☼ 7am-4pm) located at the entrance to the reserve, which has a good variety of healthy sandwiches, salads and typical dishes.

Getting There & Away

Public buses (US$2, 45 minutes) depart the Banco Nacional in Santa Elena at 6:30am, 7:30am, 9:30am, 11:30am, 1pm and 2:30pm daily. Buses return from the reserve at 6:40am, 8am, 10:40am, noon, 2:10pm and 3pm. You can flag down the buses from anywhere on the road between Santa Elena and the reserve – enquire at your hotel about what time they will pass by. Taxis are also available for around US$5.

The 6km walk from Santa Elena is uphill, but lovely – look for paths that run parallel to the road. There are views all along the way, and many visitors remark that some of the best birding is on the final 2km of the road.

RESERVA SANTA ELENA

Though Monteverde Reserve gets all the attention, this exquisitely misty entry, at 310 hectares just a fraction of that other forest's size, has plenty to recommend it. While Monteverde Crowd...er...Cloud Forest entertains almost 200,000 visitors annually, many of whom spend peak-season mornings waiting around to meet strict quotas before entering, Santa Elena sees fewer than 20,000 tourists each year, which means its dewy trails through mysteriously veiled forest are usually far quieter. It's also a bit cheaper and much less developed, plus your entry fee is helping support another unique project.

One of the first community-managed conservation projects in the country, this cloud-forest reserve was created in 1989 and opened to the public in March 1992. It is now managed by the Santa Elena High School board and bears the quite unwieldy official name of Reserva del Bosque Nuboso del Colegio Técnico Profesional de Santa Elena. You can visit the **reserve office** (☎ 645 5693; ⏰ 8am-4pm Wed-Fri) at the high school.

The reserve is about 6km northeast of the village of Santa Elena. This cloud forest is slightly higher in elevation than Monteverde, and since some of the forest is secondary growth, there are sunnier spots for spotting birds and other animals

throughout. There's a stable population of monkeys and sloths, many of which can be seen on the road to the reserve. Unless you're a trained ecologist, the old-growth forest in Santa Elena is fairly similar in appearance to Monteverde, though the lack of cement blocks on the trails means that you'll have a much more authentic (note: muddy) trekking experience.

This place is moist, and almost all the water comes as fine mist, and more than 25% of all the biomass in this forest are epiphytes – mosses and lichens – for which this place is a humid haven. Though about 10% of species here won't be found in Monteverde, which is largely on the other side of the continental divide, you can see quetzals here too, as well as Volcán Arenal exploding in the distance – theoretically. Rule No 407 of cloud forests: it's often cloudy.

Information

You can visit the **reserve** (☎ 661 8290; www.monte verdeinfo.com/reserve-santa-elena-monteverde; adult/ student US$10/6; ⏰ 7am-4pm) on your own, but just as at Monteverde, a guide will enhance your experience 10-fold (see opposite).

There's also a simple restaurant, coffee shop and gift store. Note that all proceeds go towards managing the reserve and to environmental-education programs in local schools. Donations are most graciously accepted.

If you have some extra time, there's a good volunteer program here – possible projects include trail maintenance, surveying, administration and biological research.

LOCAL LORE

The Central American lore of the resplendent quetzal originated during the era of the Maya and the Aztecs, who worshipped a deity known as Quetzalcoatl (Plumed Serpent). This mythical figure was often depicted as wearing a crown of male quetzal tail feathers, and was believed to be responsible for bestowing corn upon humans.

A popular legend regarding the scarlet-red breast of the quetzal originated during the colonial period. In 1524 in the highlands of Guatemala, the Spanish conquistador Pedro de Alvarado defeated Tecun Uman, the last ruler of the Quiché people. As Uman lay dying, his spiritual guide, the quetzal, stained its breast with Uman's blood and then died of sadness. From that day on, all male quetzals bore a scarlet breast, and their song hasn't been heard since.

Even today, quetzals are regarded in Central America as a symbol of freedom, and it's commonly believed that they cannot survive if held in captivity. In Guatemala, the quetzal is the national bird, and its image is still depicted on the currency. And in Costa Rica, the quetzal is something of a legend as birders from far and wide continue to brave the elements for the chance to see the most famous bird in Central America.

You're expected to make at least a one-week commitment, and very basic (no electricity, very cold showers) dorm-style accommodations are available free to volunteers, though all but the most rugged will prefer a US$10-per-day homestay, including three meals. Although at times it's possible to simply show up and start volunteering, it's best to contact the reserve in advance.

Activities

More than 12km of trails are currently open for hiking, featuring four circular trails offering walks of varying difficulty and length, from 45 minutes to 3½ hours (1.4km to 4.8km) along a stable (though not 'concrete-blocked') trail system. Rubber boots (US$1) can be rented at the entrance. Unlike Monteverde, Santa Elena is not developed enough to facilitate backcountry hiking, and at the time of writing it was not possible to overnight in the reserve.

Tours & Guides

The reserve offers guided **daylight tours** (3hr tours excl admission per person US$15) at 7:30am and 11:30am daily; try to make the earlier hike. Popular **night tours** (1½-hr tours excl admission per person US$13) leave at 7pm nightly. Tours have a two-person minimum and six-person maximum, so reservations are recommended for both tours during the dry season. The reserve can also arrange three-day private tours through various guides for US$20.

Getting There & Away

A daily shuttle (US$2 each way) between the village of Santa Elena and the reserve departs from the Banco Nacional in town at 6:30am, 8:30am, 10:30am and 2:30pm, and returns at 11am, 1pm and 4pm. A taxi from Santa Elena costs US$8.

ECOLODGE SAN LUIS & RESEARCH STATION

Formerly a tropical-biology research station, this facility now integrates research with ecotourism and education, and is administrated by the University of Georgia. The 70-hectare site is on the Río San Luis and adjoins the southern part of the Monteverde reserve. Its average elevation of 1100m makes it a tad lower and warmer than Monteverde, and birders have recorded some 230 species attracted by the

slightly nicer weather. There are also a number of trails into primary and secondary forest, and there's also a working farm with tropical fruit orchards, and a coffee harvest from November to March.

A variety of comfortable accommodations at the **lodge** (☎ 645 8049; www.ecolodgesanluis .com; dm US$65, s/d cabin US$85/160; **P**) is available for anyone interested in learning about the cloud-forest environment and experiencing a bit of rural Costa Rican life. Rates include all meals and most activities. There are a host of day and night hikes guided by biologists, as well as slide shows, seminars, horse rides and even an introduction to research activities. Discounts can be arranged for students, researchers, large groups and long stays.

The ecolodge also runs a resident naturalist volunteer program, though there is a preference for University of Georgia students and graduates, and a six-month commitment is required. The position entails running a number of teaching workshops and guided walks as well as participating in development projects on the station and in the community. Training, room and board are provided.

From the main road between Santa Elena and Monteverde, it's a steep 3km walk from the signed road where the bus will drop you off. A 4WD taxi from town runs about US$12 each way, and the lodge can also arrange transportation from San José in advance.

PUENTE LA AMISTAD

About 23m south of Cañas on the Interamericana is a turnoff, which continues for another 25km to the Puente La Amistad. The 'Friendship Bridge' was constructed with the help and funding of the Taiwanese government, and greatly reduced transit time to and from the beaches in Nicoya. (Prior to the construction of the bridge, drivers had to take a ferry across).

CAÑAS

If you're cruising north on the Interamericana, this is the first town of any size (population 25,000) in Costa Rica's driest and dustiest province, Guanacaste. *Sabanero* culture is evident on the sweltering and quiet streets, where full-custom pickup trucks share the road with wizened cowboys on horseback, fingering their machetes with a swagger you just don't see outside the province. It's a typically Latin American town, where everyone walks slowly and businesses shut down for lunch, all centered on the Parque Central and Catholic church – which are most definitely not typical.

Although the town is popular with truckers looking for a cheap bed, travelers prefer nearby Liberia since it's more geared towards tourists. However, there are a few interesting sights in otherwise uninteresting Cañas worth checking out. It's also a good base for organizing rafting trips on the nearby Río Corobicí or for exploring Parque Nacional Palo Verde.

Information

You can find public phones, a post office, library and a Banco Nacional, as well as many simple *sodas* and hotels here.

Emergency clinic (☎ 669 0092; cnr Av Central & Hwy 1; ☾ 7am-4pm Mon-Fri) Has 24-hour on-call service.

Internet Ciberc@ñas (Av 3 btwn Calles 1 & 3; per hr US$1.25; ☾ 8am-9pm Mon-Sat, 2-9pm Sun) Has fast computers, air-con and, if you get here at 8am, two hours for the price of one.

Minae/ACT office (☎ 669 0533; Av 9; ☾ 8am-4pm Mon-Fri) Has limited information about nearby national parks and reserves.

Sights & Activities

Though most visitors simply use the town as a base for visits to nearby **Parque Nacional Palo Verde** (p216) or rafting the **Río Corobicí**, it's worth the trip just to see the Catholic church's **psychedelic mosaics** designed by famed local painter Otto Apuy. Sinewy vines and colorful starbursts that have enveloped the modern church's once clean lines are enhanced by jungle-themed stained glass that's completely different from anything on offer at the Vatican. In **Parque Central** opposite, park benches and the pyramid-shaped bandstand are equally elaborate.

RAFTING

Gentle rafting trips down the Río Corobicí can be made with **Safaris Corobicí** (☎ 669 6091, www.nicoya.com; Km 193 Interamericana Hwy; ☾ departures 7am-3pm). Bookings can be made at its office on the Interamericana about 4.5km north of Cañas. The emphasis is wildlife observation rather than exciting white water. The river is Class I–II (in other words, pretty flat) but families and nature-lovers enjoy

these trips. Swimming holes are found along the river. Per person, based on a two-person minimum, a two-hour float costs adult/child under 14 US$37/18.50, a three-hour birding float covering 12km costs US$45/22.50, and a half-day 18km float including lunch costs US$60/30. The company also rents out a little guesthouse nearby.

A branch office of the popular **Rio Tropicales** (☎ 233-6455; www.riostropicales.com/english.htm; ☾ departures 7am-3pm) operates out of the Rincón Corobicí restaurant (p214).

LAS PUMAS

Directly behind the office of Safaris Corobicí is **Las Pumas** (☎ 669 6044; admission by donation; ☾ 8am-5pm), a wild-animal shelter started in the 1960s by Lilly Hagnauer, a Swiss woman, and said to be the largest shelter of its kind in Latin America. Pumas, jaguars, ocelots, and margays – plus peccaries and a few birds that were either orphaned or injured – are taken care of here and it has clearly been a labor of love to save and raise them. Unfortunately, Lilly herself died in 2001, though the shelter is still managed by her family. Las Pumas is not officially funded and contributions help offset the high costs of maintaining the shelter.

REFUGIO DE VIDA SILVESTRE CIPANCI

New in 2001, this small wildlife refuge is at the confluence of the Ríos Tempisque and Bebedero, at the southern end of Parque Nacional Palo Verde. It's a good spot for **birding** and **fishing**, though it's not virtually untouristed. Local fishers offer passenger boats for tours on these two rivers. A three-hour guided tour costs around US$20 per person (US$150 minimum), and can usually be arranged at the docks; show up early.

The Minae/ACT office in Cañas has more information on the park. Boats leave from the Níspero dock, just north of the Tempisque ferry.

Sleeping

Cañas is a cheaper place to stay than Liberia, though the following places cater more to truckers than travelers. Rooms have cold showers unless otherwise stated.

Hotel Central/Hotel Parque (☎ 669 1101; s with/without bathroom US$8/4, d with/without bathroom US$12/8) Right on Parque Central, grungy rooms at this joint-hotel have a high-school-gym

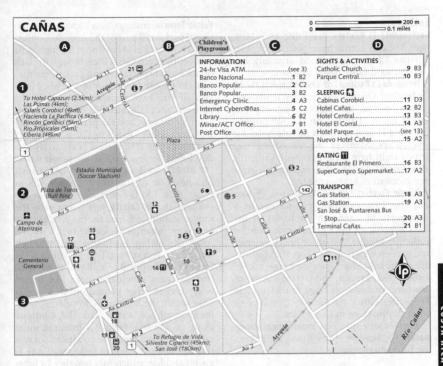

CAÑAS

| 0 | 200 m |
| 0 | 0.1 miles |

INFORMATION
24-hr Visa ATM.....................(see 3)
Banco Nacional..........................**1** B2
Banco Popular............................**2** C2
Banco Popular............................**3** B2
Emergency Clinic.......................**4** A3
Internet Cyberc@ñas.................**5** C2
Library.......................................**6** B2
Minae/ACT Office......................**7** B1
Post Office.................................**8** A3

SIGHTS & ACTIVITIES
Catholic Church.........................**9** B3
Parque Central.........................**10** B3

SLEEPING
Cabinas Corobicí.......................**11** D3
Hotel Cañas...............................**12** B2
Hotel Central.............................**13** B3
Hotel El Corral...........................**14** A3
Hotel Parque.......................(see 13)
Nuevo Hotel Cañas...................**15** A2

EATING
Restaurante El Primero.............**16** B3
SuperCompro Supermarket.......**17** A2

TRANSPORT
Gas Station...............................**18** A3
Gas Station...............................**19** A3
San José & Puntarenas Bus
   Stop.....................................**20** A3
Terminal Cañas.........................**21** B1

To Hotel Capazuri (2.5km);
Las Pumas (4km);
Safaris Corobicí (4km);
Hacienda La Pacifica (4.5km);
Rincón Corobicí (5km);
Rio Tropicales (5km);
Liberia (48km)

Plaza

Estadio Municipal
(Soccer Stadium)

Plaza de Toros
(Bull Ring)

Campo de
Aterrizaje

Cementerio
General

To Refugio de Vida
Silvestre Cipanci (45km);
San José (180km)

Río Cañas

**NORTHWESTERN
COSTA RICA**

ambience, though they're cheap and somewhat clean. It's worth springing for the private bathrooms – truckers are generally not the cleanest of people.

Cabinas Corobicí (☎ 669 0241; cnr Av 2 & Calle 5; r per person US$9; P) At the southeastern end of town, this is a better budget option as the friendly management maintains comfortable, good-sized rooms with warmish private showers, and the area is fairly quiet at night.

Hotel Cañas (☎ 669 0039; hotelcanas@racsa.co.cr; cnr Calle 2 & Av 3; s/d US$10/18, with TV & air-con US$15/25; P) Basic rooms surrounding the parking lot are dark and uninviting, though guests are permitted to use the pool at Nuevo Hotel Cañas. The restaurant (mains US$2 to US$6, open 6am to 9pm Monday to Saturday, 7am to 2pm Sunday) serves up a number of Western dishes including chicken cordon bleu and beef Stroganoff, so dine here if you're pretty sure you can't stomach another casado.

Hotel El Corral (☎ 669 1467; s/d US$15/25) Right on the Interamericana, ask for your absolutely standard room (some with air-con, hot shower and/or TV) in the back, away from the highway noise. The attached restaurant

(mains US$2 to US$5, open 6am to 10pm) overlooks the Interamericana, so you can watch (and smell) the big rigs blast by while enjoying your casado.

Nuevo Hotel Cañas (☎ 669 5118; hotelcanas@racsa .co.cr; Av 3 btwn Calle 4 & Hwy 1; s/d US$30/45; P) This is by far the best option in town, and although it's a bit pricey, the Nuevo Hotel Cañas is consistently packed with vacationing Ticos who adore the swimming pool and Jacuzzi. All rooms have air-con, cable TV and private hot showers, so you're definitely getting bang for your buck here.

Hotel Capazuri (☎ 669 6280; capazuri@racsa.co.cr; camping US$5, d incl breakfast with/without air-con US$36/25; P) Though it's inconveniently located about 2.5km northwest of Cañas on the Interamericana, this is the best option if you have your own transport. A small Tico resort, it has rather frilly rooms, most sleeping three, with TV and private hot-water bathroom. There's also a festive, on-site restaurant and, best of all, a huge pool (admission US$1.25 for nonguests). The friendly management will also let you pitch a tent on the well-maintained grounds.

Eating

Restaurante El Primero (mains US$2-4; ☿ 11am-10pm) Located across from the church, this popular Chinese restaurant arguably has the best food (and views) in town.

Hacienda La Pacífica (☎ 669 6050; mains US$7-12; ☿ 7am-9pm) Once a working hacienda and nature reserve, this elegant restaurant is 4.5km north of Cañas on the Interamericana and is now part of a private hotel for researchers. Many of the ingredients are grown right here on experimental organic plots, including the only large-scale organic rice cultivation in the country.

Rincón Corobicí (☎ 669 6162; US$3-10; ☿ 8am-8pm) This attractive Swiss-run restaurant is 5km north of Cañas on the banks of the Río Corobicí, and is a great lunch stop for authentic fondue. A terrace provides river and garden views, and a short trail follows the riverbank where you can take a cool dip. English, French, and German are spoken here, and you can book tours with Rio Tropicales either on the Río Corobicí or other destinations in Costa Rica.

There's an enormous **SuperCompro supermarket** (☿ 8am-8pm) that's situated right on the Interamericana.

Getting There & Away

All buses arrive and depart from **Terminal Cañas** (☿ 8am-1pm & 2:30-5:30pm) at the northern end of town. There are a few *sodas* and snack bars, and you can store your bags (US$0.50) at the desk. There's a taxi stand in front. Destinations and departure times for buses:

Juntas US$0.50, 1½ hours, departs 9am and 2:15pm.
Liberia US$1.35, 1½ hours, 6:45am, 8:30am, 9am, 10:30am, 1pm, 2pm, 3pm and 5:30pm.
Puntarenas US$2, two hours, 6am, 6:40am, 9:30am, 10:30am, 11:30am, 12:30pm, 1:45pm, 3:30pm and 4:30pm.
San José US$3, 3½ hours, 4am, 4:50am, 6am, 9:30am, 12:30pm, 1:40pm and 5pm.
Tilarán US$0.75, 45 minutes, 6am, 8am, 9am, 10:30am, noon, 1:45pm, 3:30pm and 5:30pm.
Upala US$2, two hours, 4:30am, 6am, 8:30am, 11:15am, 1pm, 3:30pm and 5:15pm.

VOLCÁN TENORIO AREA

A paved road 6km northwest of Cañas branches off the Interamericana and heads north to Upala, passing between Volcán Miravalles (2028m) to the west and Volcán Tenorio (1916m) to the east. **Parque Nacional**

Volcán Tenorio, among Costa Rica's newest national parks and part of the Area de Conservación Arenal (ACA), is one of the highlights of Northwestern Costa Rica, though the lack of public transportation and park infrastructure contribute to the lack of tourists. However, if you have your own transport, the park entrance is located just a few kilometers south of Bijagua, and the park is an easy day trip from either Liberia or Cañas.

Though the trail system is relatively undeveloped, grab a map at the **ranger station** (☎ 200 0135; admission US$6; ☿ 7am-4pm), which outlines one of the finest short hikes in Costa Rica. On the northeast flanks of the volcano, the **Río Celeste**, just 1.5km from the ranger station, is famed for the blue created by many minerals dissolved in its waters. After navigating a winding trail through secondary forest, you'll find yourself in front of an impossibly milky-blue **waterfall** that cascades down the rocks like it was heavy cream being poured out of a jug. If after seeing the falls you're wondering what the thermal headwaters look like, continue along on the trail for a few hundred more meters until you reach the confluence of two rivers – one is brownish yellow and one is a whitish blue, which mix together to form blueberry milk. Another 3km hike through epiphyte-laden cloud forest takes you past a series of hot springs and boiling mud pots – take great care not to scald yourself when you're exploring the area.

Since volcanic activity at Tenorio is limited to fumaroles, hot springs, and mud pots, it's possible to hike to the top of the crater on a two-day trek where you can camp next to a small lake that'll make your evening surreally beautiful. The trail system here is unmarked and passes through rough terrain, so you're going to need the services of a local guide, who can be hired either at the ranger station or at any of the lodges following.

Sleeping & Eating

There are a few simple *sodas* in Bijagua, but other than that, you'll probably be eating at the lodge.

Rio Celeste Lodge (☎ 365 3415; camping US$2, r per person US$5) This simple set of rustic cabinas is the cheapest accommodation in the area, and is a good option if your day trip suddenly turns into an overnight. Rooms have fans and warm showers, and the lodge is conveniently located on the hill near the trailhead.

Posada Cielo Roto (☎ 352 9439, 466 8692; r per person incl 3 meals & horse rides US$40; **P**) On expansive grounds with horse stables and several kilometers of private trails, owner Mario Tamayo, who speaks English, has built several lovely, rambling houses with shared kitchens that are just perfect for groups. Some rooms are doubles, but most are dorm-style, all with private bathrooms and lots with big windows overlooking the stunning scenery. There's no electricity, but kerosene lamps and candles are provided. Mario accepts walk-ins, but it's better to make reservations so he can bring in food, ice and whatnot for your stay.

La Carolina Lodge (☎ 380 1656; www.lacarolina lodge.com; s/d incl 3 meals & horse rides US$65/120; **P** 🐎) This isolated lodge run by a gracious North American named Bill is located on a working cattle ranch on the slopes of the volcano, and is highly recommended for anyone looking for a beautiful escape from the rigors of modern life. The remote location means no electricity – it's candles only (provided). The highlight here is the amazing meals (organic beans, rice, fruits, cheeses, chicken and pork from the farm), which are cooked over an outdoor wood-burning stove. The 'nightlife' is also a treat, which consists of stoking the campfire and soaking in the wood-fired hot tub. Rooms with warm showers are basic, though you'll be spending most of your time in the nearby hot springs, swimming holes or on the riverside (where you can lounge, swim, fish or go birding). The lodge is located about 6km north of Bijagua and 7km east of the highway on the road towards the village of San Miguel.

VOLCÁN MIRAVALLES AREA

Volcán Miravalles (2028m) is the highest volcano in the Cordillera de Guanacaste, and although the main crater is dormant, the geothermal activity beneath the ground has led to the rapid development of the area as a hot-springs destination. With the recent increase in tourist traffic to Liberia, travelers are starting to discover that there exists a nearby refuge from the ubiquitous cold shower.

Volcán Miravalles isn't a national park or refuge, though the volcano itself is afforded a modicum of protection by being within the Zona Protectora Miravalles. You can also take guided tours of the government-run Proyecto Geotérmico Miravalles, north of Fortuna, an ambitious project inaugurated in 1994 that uses geothermal energy to produce electricity, primarily for export to Nicaragua and Panama. A few bright steel tubes from the plant snake along the flanks of the volcano, adding an eerie touch to the remote landscape. But the geothermal energy most people come here to soak up comes in liquid form. Note that all of the listed hot springs are located north of Fortuna.

Thermo Manía (☎ 673 0233; admission US$4; ⏱ 8am-10pm) has seven developed springs of different temperatures, shapes and decor that are connected by all manner of waterslides, heated rivers, waterfalls and whatnot. But there weren't enough for the very friendly owners. Nope, there are little boats for kids, a playground, go-cart racing and a 170-year-old colonial cabin furnished with museum-worthy period pieces, just to give folks a glimpse into Costa Rica's pre-banana culture. There are also some newly constructed cabinas (US$18 per double) that have private hot-water bathrooms, though what's the point really as you'll have free access to the hot springs all day and night. There's also a restaurant-bar (mains US$4 to US$10) where you can cook up the tilapia you catch in the pond.

Nearby **Yökö Hot Springs** (☎ 673 0410; adult/child US$4/2; ⏱ 7am-10pm) has four attractively landscaped hot springs with a small waterslide and waterfall, though the real draw is the elegant cabinas (single/double US$57/91), with huge bathrooms and gleaming wood floors, where you can relax after soaking all day. Extra amenities include a Jacuzzi, sauna and a restaurant (mains US$2 to US$10) serving everything from burgers to filet mignon.

For some local flavor, **Miravalles Thermales** (☎ 305 4072; admission US$2) has a real family feel to it, with Ticos grilling meats and kiddies swimming in the hot springs and cold pools. The owner is usually there on weekends, though the springs are open more regularly during the high season.

Las Hornillas (☎ 673 0045; admission US$10; ⏱ 9am-5pm), on the southern slopes of Miravalles, is the center of volcanic activity in the area. The entrance fee allows you to soak in some of the thermal pools and hike around the bubbling mud pools and steam vents, though there are no guardrails – stay away from the edges which can easily collapse. For the not-exactly bargain price of US$30, you're also granted access to the nearby waterfall and hanging bridges.

Near the base of the volcano is the newly opened **Adventure Center** (☎ 673 0662), which has a number of offerings including a canopy tour (US$30), rappelling (US$10), horse riding (US$25 to US$50), and a guided tour through a nearby macadamia-nut farm (US$40). There are also some brightly painted cabinas (doubles US$20), which have private hot-water bathrooms and are centered on a pool that's fed by mountain springwater.

There's a rumor about a two-day hike to the top of Miravalles that departs from behind the adventure center and passes through a box canyon, though you're going to have to inquire locally about finding a guide to take you.

Volcán Miravalles is 27km northeast of Bagaces and can be approached by a paved road that leads north of Bagaces through the communities of Salitral and Torno, where the road splits. From the left-hand fork, you'll reach **Guayabo**, with a few *sodas* and basic cabinas; to the right, you'll find **Fortuna** (not to be confused with La Fortuna), with easier access to the hot springs. Both towns are small population centers, and are not of much interest to travelers. The roads reconnect north of the two towns and toward Upala, and also make a great scenic loop. Though the region is relatively remote, it's well served by buses from Bagaces.

BAGACES

This small town is about 22km northwest of Cañas on the Interamericana, and is the headquarters of the **Area de Conservación Tempisque** (ACT; ☎ 200 0125; ⏰ 8am-4pm Mon-Fri) which, in conjunction with Minae, administers Parque Nacional Palo Verde, Reserva Biológica Lomas de Barbudal, and several smaller and lesser-known protected areas. The office is on the Interamericana opposite the signed main entry road into Parque Nacional Palo Verde. The office is mainly an administrative one, though sometimes rangers are available. Any buses between Cañas and Liberia can drop you off in Bagaces. If you're heading to Miravalles,

there are hourly local buses to both Fortuna and Guaybo.

If you have your own car, 3km south of Bagaces on the road to Palo Verde is the turnoff for **Llano de Cortés**, a hidden waterfall that's free to enter and perfect for an afternoon swim. Follow the dirt road for about 1.5km until you reach the small parking area.

PARQUE NACIONAL PALO VERDE

The 18,417-hectare Parque Nacional Palo Verde is a wetland sanctuary in Costa Rica's driest province that lies on the northeastern banks of the mouth of Río Tempisque at the head of the Golfo de Nicoya. All of the major rivers in the region drain into this ancient intersection of two basins, which creates a mosaic of habitats including mangrove swamps, marshes, grassy savannahs and evergreen forests. A number of low limestone hills provide lookout points over the park, and the park's shallow, permanent lagoons are focal points for wildlife.

The park derives its name from the *palo verde* (green tree), which is a small shrub that's green all year round and abundant within the park. It's also contiguous in the north with the 7354-hectare **Caballero Wildlife Refuge** and the **Reserva Biólogico Lomas de Barbudal** (opposite) which join with the **Parque Nacional Barra Honda** (p287) to form the **Tempisque Megapark**, a large conservation area containing some of the remaining strands of dry tropical forest. A recent addition to this project was the **Refugio do Vida Silvestre Cipancí**, which protects the corridors linking the various parks from being clearcut by local farmers.

Palo Verde has the greatest concentrations of waterfowl and shorebirds in Central America, and over 300 different bird species have been recorded in the park. Birders come particularly to see the large flocks of herons (including the rare blackcrowned night herons), storks (including the endangered jabiru stork), spoonbills, egrets, ibis, grebes and ducks, though forest birds including scarlet macaws, great curassows, keel-billed toucans and parrots are also common. Frequently sighted mammals include deer, coatis, armadillos, monkeys, and peccaries as well as the largest population of jaguarundi in Costa Rica. There are also numerous reptiles in the wetlands including crocodiles that are reportedly up to 5m in length.

The dry season, from December to March, is the best time to visit as flocks of birds tend to congregate in the remaining lakes and marshes and the trees lose their leaves allowing for clearer viewing. However, the entire basin swelters during the dry season, so bring adequate sun protection. There are also far fewer insects in the dry season, and mammals are occasionally seen around the waterholes. Take binoculars or a spotting scope if possible. During the wet months, large portions of the area are flooded, and access may be limited.

Orientation & Information
The **park entrance** (☎ 200 0125; admission US$6) is located 28km along the turnoff from the Interamericana near the town of Bagaces. However, your best source of information on the park is the Hacienda Palo Verde Research Station (below). There is a fairly extensive system of roads and hiking trails that originate from the park entrance and lead to a series of lookout points and observation towers.

Tours
To fully appreciate the size and topography of the park, it's worth organizing a boat trip. Travelers recommend the guided tours (half-/full day adult US$15/30, child US$10/20) that can be arranged through the Hacienda Palo Verde Research Station. The station also offers horseback tours (per person, per hour US$6) through the park. A number of tour operators in San José and La Fortuna run package tours to Palo Verde, though you'll save yourself a bit of money by arranging everything yourself.

Sleeping & Eating
Overnight visitors should make reservations, and remember you'll need to pay the US$6 entry fee, too.

Hacienda Palo Verde Research Station (☎ 661 4717; www.ots.ac.cr; s/d US$55/100) Run by the Organization of Tropical Studies (OTS), this conducts tropical research and teaches university graduate–level classes. Researchers and those taking OTS courses get preference for dormitories with shared bathrooms. A few two- and four-bed rooms with shared bathrooms are also available. Meals are

about US$10 each. The research station is located on a well-signed road 8km from the park entrance.

Camping (per person US$2) is permitted near the Palo Verde ranger station where toilets and hot-water showers are available. You can also stay at the **ranger station** (☎ 200 0125; dm US$10), which has 36 beds in six rooms with fans, mosquito nets and private cold showers, though they are occasionally occupied by student groups. Meals are available here for a small fee by advance arrangement.

Getting There & Away
The main road to the entrance, usually passable to ordinary cars year-round, begins from a signed turnoff from the Interamericana, opposite Bagaces. The 28km gravel road has tiny brown signs that usually direct you when the road forks, but if in doubt, take the fork that looks more used. Another 8km brings you to the limestone hill, Cerro Guayacán (and the Hacienda Palo Verde Research Station), from which there are great views; a couple of kilometers further are the Palo Verde park headquarters and ranger station. You can drive through a swampy maze of roads to the Reserva Biológica Lomas de Barbudal without returning to the Interamericana.

Buses connecting Cañas and Liberia can drop you at the ACT office, opposite the turnoff to the park. If you call the ACT office in advance, rangers may be able to pick you up in Bagaces. If you're staying at the Hacienda Palo Verde Research Station, the staff can also arrange to pick you up in Bagaces.

RESERVA BIOLÓGICA LOMAS DE BARBUDAL
The 2646-hectare Lomas de Barbudal reserve forms a cohesive unit with Palo Verde, and protects several species of endangered trees such as mahogany and rosewood as well as the common and quite spectacular *corteza amarilla*. This tree is what biologists call a 'big bang reproducer' – all the yellow cortezes in the forest burst into bloom on the same day, and for about four days the forest is an incredible mass of yellow-flowered trees. This usually occurs in March, about four days after an unseasonal rain shower.

Nearly 70% of the trees in the reserve are deciduous, and during the dry season they shed their leaves as if it were autumn in a temperate forest. This particular habitat is known as tropical dry forest, and occurs in climates that are warm year-round, though characterized by a long dry season that lasts several months. Since plants lose moisture though their leaves, the shedding of leaves allows the trees to conserve water during dry periods. The newly bare trees also open up the canopy layer, enabling sunlight to reach ground level and facilitate the growth of thick underbrush. Dry forests were once common in many parts of the Pacific slopes of Central America, though very little remains. Dry forests also exist north and south of the equatorial rain-forest belt, especially in southern Mexico and the Bolivian lowlands.

Aside from the trees, Lomas de Barbudal is also known for its abundant and varied wasps, butterflies, moths and other insects. There are about 250 different species of bee in this fairly small reserve – representing about a quarter of the world's bee species. Bees here include the Africanized 'killer' bees – if you suffer from bee allergies, this is one area where you really don't want to forget your bee-sting kit.

There are more than 200 bird species, including the great curassow, a chickenlike bird that is hunted for food and is endangered, as well as other endangered species including the king vulture, scarlet macaw and jabiru stork. Much like Palo Verde, Lomas de Barbudal is also home to a variety of mammal species as well as some enormous crocodiles – you might want to leave your swim trunks at home.

Orientation & Information

At the reserve entrance, there's a small **information center** (entry to the park US$6; ☺ 7am-4pm) though the actual reserve is on the other side of the Río Cabuyo, behind the museum. The infrastructure of the park is less geared to tourists than Palo Verde, though there is a small network of hiking trails that radiate from the information center. A small map is provided, though it is not possible to overnight in the park and backcountry hiking is not permitted.

Getting There & Away

The turnoff to Lomas de Barbudal from the Interamericana is near the small community of Pijije, 14km southeast of Liberia or 12km northwest of Bagaces. It's 7km to the entrance of the reserve. The road is unpaved, but open all year – some steep sections may require 4WD in rainy season. Buses between Liberia and Cañas can drop you at the turnoff to the reserve.

LIBERIA

Before the boom in Costa Rican tourism, deciphering the bus timetables and fighting your way through the crowds at Coca-Cola terminal in San José was a rite of passage for the uninitiated traveler. As little as three years ago, getting to the beaches on the Península de Nicoya took determination, patience and – depending on the state of the Costa Rica's dreadful roads – a little luck. These days however, an increasing number of travelers are getting their first glimpse of *pura vida* Costa Rica at Liberia's own Daniel Oduber Quirós International Airport, which is roughly the size of a Wal-Mart parking lot.

Previously, the sunny capital of Guanacaste served as a transportation hub connecting the capital with both borders, as well as the standard bearer of Costa Rica's *sabanero* culture (see the boxed text Las Fiestas de Guanacaste, p220). Even today, a large part of the greater Liberia area is involved in ranching operations, and still much enamored of Clint Eastwood movies, cowboy hats and machetes. However, as more and more gringos are stumbling off their international flights and seeking out the nearest *cerveza* in broken Spanish, Guanacastecos are starting to realize how lucrative the tourism industry can be.

These days, the public schools in Liberia have expanded the number of English courses on offer, private clinics catering to moneyed foreigners are popping up all over, and some folks are even looking into renovating the 150-year-old downtown with a full facelift and expanded pedestrian mall. But, like most tourism projects in Costa Rica, development is a double-edged sword, and the nearby Papagayo Project is no exception.

Liberia has long been a base for visiting the nearby volcanoes, national parks and beaches, though the multinational corporations who've already invested heavily in the project have other ideas. Located only

50km away from Liberia, the Golfo de Papagayo is being tagged by hopeful tourist-industry magnates as 'the new Cancún,' though the difference is that here you can actually drink the water. Liberia's airport, which recently unveiled plans to build a second parking lot…er, runway, is slated to become the most important entry point for package tourists in search of tropical sun (without all that fuss of actually having to speak a foreign language). In this rapidly unfurling master plan, the city will redefine itself as a service community, providing much needed jobs in the daiquiri-mixing industry. (For more information, see the boxed text Playa Panamá & the Papagayo Project, p266).

Clearly, this new development raises the stakes – grass-roots groups have been pressuring the government to enforce strict regulations on new resorts, though Liberia has already started ramping up its own infrastructure to make sure local talent stays put to guide the city's transformation. Whistle-blowers are already rallying to the call of 'overdevelopment' and 'sustainability,' though it's difficult to know who's actually listening. Regardless of how the drama unfolds, Liberia is a much safer and surprisingly pleasant alternative to San José, and it's a great base for exploring destinations in both the northwest and the Península de Nicoya. And, though most of the historic buildings in the city center are a little rough around the edges and in desperate need of a paint job, Liberia is a fairly pleasant city (at least by Costa Rican standards), and there is a good range of accommodations and services aimed at travelers of all budgets.

Information

INTERNET ACCESS

Cyberm@nia (Av 1 btwn Calles 2 & Central; per hr US$1; ☽ 8am-10pm) Also good for cheap long-distance calls, charging US$0.25 a minute to most parts of the world.

Planet Internet (Calle Central btwn Avs Central & 2; per hr US$1; ☽ 8am-10pm) Has speedy machines in spacious air-conditioned cubicles, making this one of Costa Rica's finest emailing experiences.

MEDICAL SERVICES

Hospital Dr Enrique Baltodano Briceño (☎ 666 0011, emergencies 666 0318) is behind the stadium on the northeastern outskirts of town.

MONEY

Most hotels will accept US dollars, and may be able to change small amounts. If not, Liberia probably has more banks per square meter than any other town in Costa Rica.

Banco Centro America (Ave 25 de Julio btwn Calles 10 & 12; ☽ 8am-5pm Mon-Fri, to noon Sat) Also gives US dollars.

Banco de Costa Rica (cnr Calle Central & Av 1; ☽ 8:30am-3pm Mon-Fri) Has a 24-hour ATM.

Banco Nacional (Av 25 de Julio btwn Calles 6 & 8; ☽ 8am-5pm Mon-Fri, to noon Sat) Has a 24-hour ATM.

TOURIST INFORMATION

Sabanero Art Market & Tourist Information Center (☎ 362 6926; www.elsabanero.8k.com; Calle 8 btwn Avs Central & 1) Travelers seeking guidance will be best off here. It has bus schedules, information on tours and lodging, and will arrange taxi pick-ups.

Tourist office (☎ 666 4527; cnr Av 6 & Calle 1) Has hours that remain a mystery. One local explained it this way: 'Sometimes it's open. Sometimes it's closed.'

Sights & Activities

There are a number of good hotels, restaurants, and bars, and the main activity is relaxing in one of them as you plan your next trip to a beach or volcano.

The tourist office has a tiny **museum** of local ranching artifacts – cattle-raising is a historically important occupation in Guanacaste. There has also been talk of reopening a museum of *sabanero* culture in **La Gobernación**, the old municipal building at the corner of Av Central and Calle Central.

In the meantime, a **statue** of a steely-eyed *sabanero*, complete with an evocative poem by Rudolfo Salazar Solorzano, stands watch over Av 25 de Julio, the main street into town. The blocks around the intersection of Av Central and Calle Central contain several of the town's oldest houses, many dating back about 150 years.

The pleasant Parque Central frames a modern church, **Iglesia Inmaculada Concepción de María**. The park is also the seasonal hangout of Nicaraguan grackle, a tone-deaf bird that enjoys eating parrot eggs and annoying passers-by with its grating calls.

Walking six blocks northeast of the park along Av Central brings you to the oldest church in town, popularly called **La Agonía** (though maps show it as La Iglesia de la Ermita de la Resurrección). Strolling to La Agonía and around the surrounding blocks makes a fine walk.

Tours

Hotel Liberia and La Posada del Tope (see opposite) are great budget hotels that can organize trips and tours throughout Costa Rica. La Posada del Tope has the best deals on rental cars around.

Sleeping

Liberia is at its busiest during the dry season – reservations are strongly recommended during Christmas, Easter, Día de Guanacaste and on weekends. During the wet season, however, most of the midrange and top end hotels give discounts.

Note that although streets are labeled on the map, very few of them are signed, especially once you get away from Parque Central (see boxed text What's That Address?, p539).

BUDGET

Hospedaje Real Chorotega (☎ 666 0898; cnr Av 6 & Calle 2; s/d US$4/8) For all you shoestringers out there, here it is – the cheapest accommodation in town – though with small, windowless rooms and rough-looking shared bathrooms, spend the extra dollar and treat yourself right. All showers are cold, which (trust us) is definitely a good thing.

Hotel Liberia (☎ 666 0161; Calle Central btwn Avs Central & 2; s with/without bathroom US$10/5, d with/ without bathroom US$20/10; P) Rooms in this rambling, century-old building surround an outdoor lounge complete with TV, hammocks and jetlagged backpackers chatting about their past and present travel plans. Rooms here are slowly being renovated and in the meantime are pretty basic. But the hotel is recommended for its vibrant atmosphere that's in part created by the Peruvian manager Beto, who's an absolute riot.

La Posada del Tope (☎ 666 3876; www.posadadeltope .com; Calle Central btwn Avs Central & 2; r per person US$5-12; P ✗) This budget hotel is housed in an attractive mid-19th-century house that's decorated with old photos, antiques and mosquito nets, and has a bit of an old-plantation feel to it. Rooms here with shared private bathrooms are also fairly basic, though the hotel is recommended as the bilingual Tico owner, Dennis, is a wealth of information. The annex across the street, Hotel Casa Real, has rooms with private bath and TV.

Hotel La Casona (☎ 666 2971; marijozuniga@ hotmail.com; cnr Calle Real Av 6; s with/without bathroom US$12/7, d with/without bathroom US$15/10; P ✗) This pink, wooden house has three simple rooms sharing three bathrooms, while the annex has newer rooms (some with air-con) with private bathrooms. There is also a small living room with TV that's

---

LAS FIESTAS DE GUANACASTE

Guanacastecos love their horses, almost as much as they love their fiestas. And what better way to get the best of both worlds then with a *tope* (horse parade), a mix of a Western rodeo and a country fair complete with a cattle auction, food stalls, music, dancing, drinking and, of course, bull riding. The main event is the *tope* itself, which is where you can see the high-stepping gait of the *sabanero*, which demands endurance and skill from both horse and rider. However, the bull riding usually draws the biggest crowds, though in Costa Rica the bulls are fortunately never killed. There's nothing like watching a young man in the throes of machismo cross himself before he enters the ring, and it's fairly common for the local drunks to jump around in the bullring, which is always an amusing spectacle.

Topes are also a great place to see the region's traditional dance, which is known as the Punto Guanacasteco. Perhaps the most noticeable aspect of the dance is the long, flowing skirt worn by each woman. This skirt is meant to resemble an ox-cart wheel, which is a traditional Costa Rican craft that is most often associated with the town of Sarchí. Punto Guanacasteco traditionally served as a means of courtship, and it's common for the dance to be frequently interrupted by young men who shout rhyming verses in order to try to win over a love interest. The dance and accompanying music are fast paced and full of passion, and they're fairly similar to most other Central American styles.

Topes are a fairly common occurrence in Guanacaste, so ask a local about where you can see one or keep your eyes peeled for posters. Generally, *topes* occur on Costa Rican civic holidays (p536), though you can be assured of a big party during Semana Santa (the week before Easter), the week between Christmas and New Year's and on July 25, the anniversary of Guanacaste's annexation.

LIBERIA

0	300 m
0	0.2 miles

INFORMATION
Banco Centro America..................1 B4
Banco de Costa Rica.....................2 C3
Banco Nacional............................3 B3
Cyberm@nia.................................4 C3
ICE (Telephone)...........................5 B4
Planet Internet.............................6 D4
Post Office..................................7 B3
Sabanero Art Market & Tourist
   Information Centre.....................8 D4
Tourist Office...............................9 D4
Western Union.........................(see 5)

SIGHTS & ACTIVITIES
Iglesia Inmaculada Concepción de
   María.......................................10 C3
La Agonía...................................11 D2
La Gobernación..........................12 D4
Museum..................................(see 9)
Sabanero Monument....................13 B3

SLEEPING 🏠
Best Western Hotel El Sitio.........14 A4
Hospedaje Puente Real................15 C4

Hospedaje Real Chorotega............16 C4
Hostal Ciudad Blanca..................17 D3
Hotel Boyeros.............................18 B4
Hotel Casa Real..........................19 C3
Hotel El Bramadero....................20 B4
Hotel El Punto............................21 B4
Hotel Guanacaste.......................22 B3
Hotel La Casona.........................23 D4
Hotel La Siesta...........................24 D4
Hotel Liberia..............................25 D4
Hotel Primavera.........................26 D4
La Posada del Tope.....................27 C3

EATING 🍴
Café Calle Real...........................28 C3
Café Liberia................................29 B3
Casa Pueblo...............................30 D4
Food Mall de Burger King............31 B4
Guanaburger..............................32 D3

Kleaver......................................33 C3
Las Tinajas.................................34 C3
Los Camales................................35 C2
Pan y Miel..................................36 C3
Paso Real....................................37 D4
Pizza Pronto...............................38 D3
Restaurante Elegante..................39 D4
Soda Rancho Dulce.....................40 D4
SuperCompro..............................41 C3

DRINKING 🍸
Bar Mexico.................................42 D3
Hpnotiq......................................43 C3
Las Tinajas.............................(see 34)

ENTERTAINMENT 🎭
Discoteque Kuru Kuru..................44 A4
Pooles Liberia.............................45 D4

TRANSPORT
Main Intersection (Gas Stations)......46 B4
Terminal Liberia..........................47 A3
Terminal Pullmitan (Buses to San
   José)......................................48 B3

To Hospital Dr Enrique
Baltonado Briceño (600m)

Jardin y
Parque Infantil

Barrio La
Victoria

Río Liberia

To San Jorge (18km);
Parque Nacional Rincón
de la Vieja (25km)

To Nicaragua
(77km)

Market

Plaza

Parqué Hector
Zuniga Bovera

Parque
Central

See Enlargement

Av 25 de Julio

To Airport (12km);
Peninsula de Nicoya

To Centro Plaza Liberia
(1 km); Best Western Hotel
Las Espuelas (2km);
Cañas (48km);
San José (234km)

To San Jorge (18km)

Av Central

**NORTHWESTERN
COSTA RICA**

perfect for lounging or chatting up other travelers.

Hospedaje Puente Real (☎ 666 1112; Calle 2 btwn Av 8 & 10; r per person with/without bathroom US$14/10; **P**) This beautiful colonial mansion with wooden sloping ceilings and original fixtures was recently transformed into a pleasant hotel by a young Colombian couple. Simple rooms with a fan come with both shared and private bathrooms, and there's a barbecue in the enclosed backyard.

Hotel Guanacaste (☎ 666 0085; www.higuana caste.com; cnr Av 3 & Calle 12; r per person with/without bathroom US$17/10; **P**) This HI-affiliated hostel near the bus terminal has all the style and personality you've come to expect from

Hostelling International (read as: sterile and boring), though rooms are clean and the knowledgeable staff organizes tours.

MIDRANGE
Hotel El Punto (☎ 665 2986; www.elpuntohotel.com; Interamericana btwn Ave 25 de Julio & Av 2; s/d/tr/q US$21/41/48/53, all incl breakfast; **P**) This converted elementary school is now one of the chicest hotels in Liberia, though it would definitely feel more at home in NYC than in humble Guanacaste. Rooms here are ultramodern loft apartments with private showers, small kitchens, Japanese minimalist accents and plenty of MOMA-worthy art. This spot is recommended as rooms are severely underpriced.

Hotel Primavera (☎ 666 0464; Av Central btwn Calles Central & 2; s/d/tr US$26/38/48; **P** **✖**) Right on the Parque Central, rooms at this small hotel are a little worn, but they have attractive wood accents and come furnished with microwaves, cable TV and private cold showers. Rooms with air-con cost US$5 more.

Hotel La Siesta (☎ 666 0678; hotellasiesta@hotmail .com; Calle 4 btwn Avs 4 & 6; s/d/tr incl breakfast US$30/ 42/48; **P** **✖** **≋**) Clean, standard rooms with cable TV and private cold showers are arranged around a pretty poolside garden. Slightly larger upstairs rooms have air-con and cost US$5 more. The real reason to stop by, however, is the attached restaurant (US$4 to US$7), which is regarded by locals as having the best *casado* in town.

Hotel El Bramadero (☎ 666 0371; bramadero@racsa .co.cr; cnr Interamericana & Hwy 21; s/d US$30/42; **P** **✖** **≋**) This *sabanero*-themed spot is a comfortable, midrange hotel that has well-appointed rooms with air-con, hot showers and cable TV. Its restaurant (US$10 to US$16) has some of the thickest and juiciest steaks you've ever feasted on.

Hostal Ciudad Blanca (☎ 666 3962; Av 4 btwn Calles 1 & 3; s/d US$30/50; **P** **✖**) One of Liberia's most attractive hotels is located in a historic colonial mansion that has been completely refurbished. Rooms have air-con, fan, cable TV, nice furnishings, and private hot-water bathrooms. There is a charming little restaurant-bar that's perfect spot for a nightcap.

Hotel Boyeros (☎ 666 0995; www.hotelboyeros.com; cnr Interamericana & Av 2; s/d US$48/68; **P** **✖** **✖** **≋**) The largest hotel in Liberia feels like a cross between a dude ranch and the Holiday Inn, though immaculate rooms all have new furnishings, air-con and cable TV, and the upstairs rooms have private balconies. There's also a 24-hour restaurant, pool with water slide and a kiddie pool.

Not one, but two, Best Western Hotels are available for all your generic, overpriced chain-hotel needs. The **Best Western Hotel Las Espuelas** (☎ 666 0144; espuelas@racsa.co.cr; s/d incl breakfast US$60/70; **P** **✖** **✖** **≋**) is located about 2km south of Liberia, and has all the standard amenities and characterless rooms you've come to expect from the chain. In case you want to be closer to town, you can also try the **Best Western Hotel El Sitio** (☎ 666 1211; htlsitio@racsa .co.cr; s/d incl breakfast US$60/70; **P** **✖** **✖** **≋**), which is located on the road to Nicoya.

Eating

Café Liberia (Calle 8 btwn Avs 25 de Julio & 2; snacks US$1-2; ⏰ 10am-6pm Mon-Fri) This hip spot that's popular with travelers is perfect for savoring a strong espresso or indulging in a homemade pastry.

Café Calle Real (cnr Calle Central & Av 2; snacks US$1-4; ⏰ 9am-6pm Mon-Sat) This cutesy café is run by a Swiss-Tica couple, and has dreamy coffees and fresh pastries as well as a small assortment of salads and sandwiches.

Soda Rancho Dulce (Calle Central btwn Avs Central & 2; mains US$2-4; ⏰ 7:30am-10pm) Sometimes a casado is more than a casado, and this outstanding open-air *soda*, with groovy wooden tables and good *batidos*, serves some of the best.

Guanaburger (cnr Calle 3 & Av 1; burger, fries & drink combo US$2.50; ⏰ noon-2:30pm & 5:30-10pm) This famous homegrown institution packs in the locals with its US$2.50 bargain combo.

Los Camales (Calle Central btwn Avs 7 & 5; plates US$2-5) This popular local spot is run by a woman's collective, and serves native Guanacaste dishes as well as typical cuisine. The specialty is chicken and salsa, and it's mighty tasty.

Kleaver (cnr Av 1 & Calle Central; plates US$2-5) This greasy spoon specializes in fried chicken and other less-than-healthy treats, and it's open 24 hours for all your drunken needs.

Pan y Miel (☎ 665 3733; Av 3 btwn Calle Central & 2; mains US$2-5; ⏰ 7am-8pm Mon-Fri, 7am-2pm Sat) The best breakfast in town can be had at this branch of the local bakery, which serves its excellent bread as sandwiches and French toast, or alongside a long list of salads, pastas and other entrees.

DAY TRIPPER

Looking for something to do? Here are a few suggestions:

■ Scan the murky depths for 5m crocs at **Palo Verde** (p216)

■ Soak your cares away in the hot springs near **Volcán Miravalles** (p215)

■ See how blue blue can be at the waterfall near **Volcán Tenorio** (p214)

■ Step carefully near the fuming fumaroles of **Rincón de la Vieja** (p224)

■ Swim, sunbathe and sweat it up on the dance floor at nearby **Playa del Coco** (p259)

Restaurante Elegante (Calle Real btwn Av Central & 2; dishes US$3-4) This cheap Chinese joint is famous in Liberia for its huge portions and low prices. Our favorite dish is the shrimp with curry paste, though you really can't go wrong here.

Las Tinajas (Calle 2 btwn Avs Central & 1; meals US$4-7) This parkside pub is an ideal place to watch the town mutts run around while sipping a cold beer and noshing on some greasy fries.

Pizza Pronto (cnr Av 4 & Calle 1; pizzas from US$5) Situated in a handsome 19th-century house, this pizzeria is in a class of its own. You can choose from a long list of toppings, including fresh, local seafood, pineapple and some of the more 'traditionalist' toppings.

Paso Real (☎ 666 3455; Av Central btwn Calles Central & 2; mains US$6-20; ☘ 11am-10pm) Liberia's most famous restaurant has a breezy balcony overlooking Parque Central, and is locally known for its inventive cuisine, like sea bass served in a cream sauce of puréed spinach.

Casa Pueblo (Calle Central btwn Avs 6 & 8; ☘ 5:30-10pm; dishes US$12-20) This romantic restaurant is housed in an old Spanish colonial building, and blends European and Tico cooking styles to created sophisticated fusion dishes.

Food Mall de Burger King (cnr Interamericana & Hwy 21; ☘ 7am-11pm) Weak-stomached gringos of the world rejoice! Thou hast thy choice of Burger King, Church's Chicken, Papa John's Pizza, Subway, TCBY and Pizza Hut. Amen.

There are lots of inexpensive *sodas* around town, or you could grab groceries at the **SuperCompro** (Av Central btwn Calles 4 & 6; ☘ 8am-8pm Mon-Fri, to 6pm Sat & Sun). For a good selection of gringo groceries including tahini, Entemann's, curry paste and olives, check out the **Superplaza Supermercado** (Centro Plaza Liberia).

Drinking

Despite the recent tourist influx, Liberia surprisingly feels dead in the evening, though there are a number of local spots where you can get hammered for under US$10.

Las Tijanas (Calle 2 btwn Avs Central & 1) Sometimes has live music, and there's always bound to be good people-watching in the Parque Central at night.

Pooles Liberia (Calle Central btwn Avs Central & 2; ☘ 11am-11pm) Lets you enjoy a cold brew and a hot game inside the historic Calle Real building.

Bar Mexico (Calle Central btwn Avs 3 & 5; ☘ 11am-11pm) A mellow local spot for a cold Imperial in the hot town.

Hpnotiq (cnr Av 25 de Julio & Calle 4; ☘ 11am-11pm) The English tagline is 'something different,' though the reality is a bunch of hard-drinking cowboys listening to Mexican ballads.

Entertainment

Cinema (Centro Plaza Liberia) If you're looking for your Hollywood fix, this has a decent offering of mainstream American films.

Discoteque Kuru Kuru (Av 25 de Julio) Across from the Best Western El Sitio, lets the DJs do their thing Thursday through Sunday nights.

Cultural offerings are unfortunately slim to none in Liberia, though your best chance of seeing *Punto Guanacasteco* is to be in town for a *tope*.

Getting There & Away

AIR

Since 1993, Aeropuerto Internacional Daniel Oduber Quirós (LIR), 12km east of Liberia, has served as the country's second international airport, providing easy access to all those beautiful beaches without the hassle of dealing with less-than-pristine San José. It's a tiny airport, jam-packed with increasing traffic, and a serious (and potentially schedule-busting) overhaul is planned for the 'near future.' All international flights are through the USA, though there are talks of starting direct flights to Europe.

NatureAir and Sansa both make multiple daily runs between Liberia and San José, with connections all over the country, for about US$80 one way, US$160 round-trip.

There are no car-rental desks at the airport; make reservations in advance, and your company will meet you at the airport with a car. There are plans to open a tourist-information desk, but at press time, there weren't even racks of flyers available. A taxi to Liberia costs US$10.

It is likely that this list of airlines will have expanded by the time you read this. Although there's a lot of talk about airport expansion, at time of writing the first three are still the only airlines that actually fly into and out of Liberia from the USA.

American Airlines (☎ 800-421 0600; www.aa.com) Fights to/from Miami, Florida.

Continental (☎ 800-231 0856; www.continental.com) To/from Houston, Texas.

Delta (☎ 800-241 4141; www.delta.com) To/from Atlanta, Georgia.

NatureAir (☎ 220 3054; www.natureair.com) To/from San José.

Sansa (☎ 668 1047; www.flysansa.com) To/from San José.

BUS

Buses arrive and depart **Terminal Liberia** (Av 7 btwn Calles 12 & 14) and **Terminal Pullmitan** (Av 5 btwn Calles 10 & 12). Routes, fares, journey times and departures are as follows:

Cañas US$1, 1½ hours, departs Terminal Liberia 5:45am, 1:30pm, 4:30pm and 5:10pm. It's quicker to jump off the San José–bound bus in Cañas.

La Cruz/Peñas Blancas US$1.25, 1½ to two hours, departs Pullmitan 5:30am, 8:30am, 9am, 11am, noon, 2pm, 4:45pm and 8pm.

Managua, Nicaragua US$10, five hours, departs Pullmitan 8:30am, 9:30am and 1pm (buy tickets one day in advance).

Nicoya, via Filadelfia & Santa Cruz (Alfaro Buses) US$1.25, two hours, hourly from 4am to 8pm.

Playa del Coco US$0.75, one hour, departs Pullmitan 5:30am, 8am, 9am, 12:30pm, 2pm, 4pm and 6pm.

Playa Hermosa, Playa Panamá (Tralapa) US$0.75, 1¼ hours, departs Terminal Liberia 7:30am, 11:30am, 3:30pm, 5:30pm and 7pm.

Playa Tamarindo US$1.25, two hours, departs Terminal Liberia 5:15am, 7am, 10:15am, 12:15pm, 2:30pm and 6pm.

Puntarenas US$1.40, 3 hours, seven services from 5am to 3:30pm. It's quicker to jump off the San José–bound bus in Puntarenas.

San José US$5, four hours, departs Pullmitan hourly 6am to 7pm.

CAR

Liberia lies on the Interamericana, 234km north of San José and 77km south of the Nicaraguan border post of Peñas Blancas. Hwy 21, the main artery of the Península de Nicoya, begins in Liberia and heads southwest. A dirt road, passable to all cars in dry season (4WD is preferable), leads 25km from Barrio la Victoria to the Santa María entrance of Parque Nacional Rincón de la Vieja; the gravel road to the Las Pailas entrance begins from the Interamericana 5km north of Liberia (passable to regular cars, but 4WD is recommended).

There are several rental-car agencies in the region (none of which have desks at the airport) that charge about the same amount as those in San José. Most can arrange pick-up in Liberia and drop-off in San José, though they'll try to charge you extra. Rental

agencies are on Hwy 21 between Liberia and the airport, but should be able to drop off your car in town. La Posada de Tope (p220) arranges the cheapest car rental in Liberia. At last count, there were 28 car-rental agencies in Liberia, though here are a few of the more popular ones:

Adobe (☎ 667 0608; www.adobecar.com)

Avis (☎ 666 7585; www.avis.co.cr)

Budget (☎ 668 1024; www.budget.com)

Dollar (☎ 668 1061; www.dollarcostarica.com)

Economy Rent-A-Car (☎ 666 2816; www.econ omyrentacar)

Europcar (☎ 668 1022; www.europcar.co.cr)

Hola (☎ 667 4040; www.hola.net)

Mapache (☎ 665 4444; www.mapache.com)

National (☎ 666 5595; www.natcar.com)

Payless (☎ 257 0026; www.paylesscr.com)

Toyota Rent a Car (☎ 666 8190; www.carrental-toyota -costarica.com)

Tricolor (☎ 665 5412; www.tricolorcarrental.com)

PARQUE NACIONAL RINCÓN DE LA VIEJA

This 14,161-hectare national park is named after the active Volcán Rincón de la Vieja (1895m), the steamy main attraction, but within the same volcanic range are several other peaks, of which Volcán Santa María (1916m) is the highest. The region bubbles with multihued fumaroles, lukewarm hot springs, lively mud pots hurling clumps of ashy gray mud in flatulent (the sulfur smell in these hills is strong) Dr Seuss-style fun, a young and feisty *volcancito* (small volcano), plus a cacophony of popping, hissing holes in the ground. All these can be visited on well-maintained but sometimes-steep trails, and if you've never visited Yellowstone National Park, this is a good substitute.

The park was created in 1973 to protect the 32 rivers and streams that have their sources within the park, an important watershed. Its relatively remote location means that wildlife, rare elsewhere, is out in force here, with the major volcanic crater a rather dramatic backdrop to the scene. Volcanic activity has occurred many times since the late 1960s, with the most recent eruption of steam and ash in 1997. At the moment, however, the volcano is gently active and does not present any danger (ask locally to be sure, as volcanoes do have a habit of occasionally blowing their tops).

Elevations in the park range from less than 600m to 1916m, so visitors pass through a variety of different habitats as they ascend the volcanoes, though the majority of the trees in the park are typical of those found in dry tropical forests throughout Guanacaste. One interesting tree to look out for is the strangler fig, a parasitic tree that covers the host tree with its own trunk and proceeds to strangle it by competing for water, light and nutrients. Although the host tree eventually dies and rots away, the strangler fig continues to survive as a hollow, tubular lattice. The park is also home to the highest density of Costa Rica's national flower, the increasingly rare purple orchid (*Cattleya skinneri*), locally known as *guaria morada*.

Most visitors to the park however flock to the hot springs, where you can soak the day away to the tune of howler monkeys bleating overhead. Many of the springs are reported to have therapeutic properties, which is always a good thing in case you've been hitting the Guaro Cacique a little too hard. In the past, the park was not heavily visited due to its remote location, though things are slowly picking up due to increased tourist traffic in nearby Liberia. There are several lodges just outside the park that provide access and arrange tours, though most tourists these days arrange transportation directly from Liberia.

Orientation & Information

There are two main entrances to the park, each with its own ranger station, where you sign in and get free maps. Most visitors enter through the **Las Pailas ranger station** (☎ 661 8139; admission US$6; ☺ 7am-5pm, no entry past 3pm, closed Mon) on the western flank. Trails to the summit and the most interesting volcanic features begin here. Note that on the way to Las Pailas, you will pass through the private property of Hacienda Lodge Guachipelín, and be forced to pay a fee of US$2 per person. This is absolutely absurd as there is little evidence that the money is used for anything other than padding the pockets of the hotel owners.

The **Santa María ranger station** (☎ 661 8139; admission US$6; ☺ 7am-5pm, no entry past 3pm, closed Mon), to the east, is in the Casona Santa María, a 19th-century ranch house with a small public exhibit that was reputedly once

owned by US President Lyndon Johnson. It's closest to the sulfurous hot springs and also has an observation tower and a nearby waterfall.

Activities
WILDLIFE-WATCHING
The wildlife of the park is extremely varied. Almost 300 species of bird have been recorded here, including curassows, quetzals, bellbirds, parrots, toucans, hummingbirds, owls, woodpeckers, tanagers, motmots, doves, and eagles – to name just a few.

Insects range from beautiful butterflies to annoying ticks. Be especially prepared for ticks in grassy areas – long trousers tucked into boots and long-sleeved shirts offer some protection. A particularly interesting insect is a highland cicada that burrows into the ground and croaks like a frog, to the bewilderment of naturalists.

Mammals are equally varied; deer, armadillos, peccaries, skunks, squirrels, coatis, and three species of monkey are frequently seen. Tapir tracks are often found around the lagoons near the summit. Several of the wild cat species have been recorded here, including the jaguar, puma, ocelot, and margay, but you'll need patience and good fortune to observe one of these.

HIKING
A circular trail east of Las Pailas (about 8km in total) takes you past the boiling mud pools (Las Pailas), sulfurous fumaroles, and a miniature volcano (which may subside at any time). About 700m west of the ranger station along the **Sendero Cangreja** is a swimming hole, which is prescribed for lowering your body temp after too much time in the hot springs. Further away along the same trail are several waterfalls – the largest, **Catarata La Cangreja**, 5km west, is a classic, dropping straight from a cliff into a small lagoon where you can swim. Dissolved copper salts give the falls a deep blue color. This trail winds through forest, then onto open grassland on the volcano's flanks, where you can get views as far as the Golfo de Nicoya. The slightly smaller **Cataratas Escondidas** (Hidden Waterfalls) are 4.3km west on a different trail.

The longest and most adventurous hike in the area is the 16km round-trip trek to the summit of Rincón de la Vieja and to nearby **Laguna de Jilgueros**, which is reportedly where you may see tapirs – or more likely their footprints, if you are observant. The majority of this hike follows a ridge trail, and is known for being extremely windy and cloudy – come prepared for the weather. It's also advised that you hire a guide from the ranger station or a nearby hotel as the trail is dotted with sulfurous hot springs and geysers, and hikers have been severely burned (and occasionally boiled) in the past.

From the Santa María ranger station, a trail leads 2.8km west through the 'enchanted forest' and past a waterfall to sulfurous **hot springs** with supposedly therapeutic properties. Don't soak in them for more than about half an hour (some people suggest much less) without taking a dip in one of the nearby cold springs to cool off. An observation point is 450m east of the station.

Tours

All of the tourist lodges following can arrange a number of tours including horse riding (US$12 to US$20), mountain biking (US$10 to US$30), guided waterfall and hot springs hikes (US$10 to US$15), rappelling (US$10 to US$15), rafting (US$45 to US$60), hanging bridges (US$15 to US$20) and everyone's favorite cash-burner, canopy tours (US$35 to US$50). Rates vary depending on the season, and there are a number of package deals available. If you're staying in Liberia, it's possible to organize these activities in advance either through your hotel, or by contacting the lodges directly.

Sleeping & Eating

INSIDE THE PARK

Both ranger stations have camping (per person US$2). Each campground has water, pit toilets, showers, tables and grills. There is no fuel available, so bring wood, charcoal, or a camping stove. Mosquito nets or insect repellent are needed in the wet season.

Camping is allowed in most places within the park, but you should be self-sufficient and prepared for cold and foggy weather in the highlands – a compass is very useful. The wet season is very wet (October is the rainiest month), and there are plenty of mosquitoes then. Dry-season camping in December, March, and April is recommended. January and February are prone to strong winds.

OUTSIDE THE PARK

Note that all of these places are a long way from a restaurant, so you're stuck with paying for meals at your hotel restaurant.

Rinconcito Lodge (☎ 200 0074; www.rinconcito lodge.com; camping per person US$3, s/d US$18/30; meals US$4-6; P) Just 3km from the Santa María sector of the park, this recommended budget option offers attractive, rustic cabins with private showers, and is surrounded by some of the prettiest pastoral scenery imaginable. Since the lodge primarily caters to budget travelers, it's the best place in the area for booking inexpensive package deals, and staff regularly shuttles travelers to and from Liberia (and points further).

Hacienda Lodge Guachipelín (☎ 666 8075; www .guachipelin.com; s/d US$46/67, incl 3 meals US$76/126; ☑) Located on the road to Las Pailas, this attractive 19th-century working cattle ranch is located on 1200 hectares of primary and secondary forest, and has 30 spacious duplex cabins with private hot-water bathrooms and porches. Unfortunately, since the only access road to Las Pailas passes through its private property, it engages in the fairly despicable practice of charging US$2 per person, and it's doubtful that any of this money is actually put toward park conservation.

Rincón de la Vieja Mountain Lodge (☎ 661 8198; www.rincondelaviejalodge.net; s/d standard US$57/86, bungalow US$86/97; P ☐ ☑) Closest to the Las Pailas entrance to the park, this rustic hacienda is located on 400 hectares of protected land and has 49 spacious standard rooms, some with wildly painted walls or exposed-beam roofs, and even larger cottages with balconies. All the electricity is produced by water falling into a turbine, so you can enjoy your steaming hot shower without any ecoguilt. Meals cost US$6 to US$12.

Hotel Borinquen (☎ 6660363; www.borinquenresort .com; s/d incl breakfast US$188/227; P ☒ ☒ ☐ ☑) If you've got money to burn then burn it here. The most luxurious resort in the area features fully air-conditioned bungalows with private decks, minibars and satellite TV. There's also a private trail system you can negotiate with the help of golf carts, especially if you're too drained from soaking in the on-site hot springs and mud baths or from sweating the day away in the natural saunas.

Getting There & Away

The Las Pailas sector is accessible via a good, 20km gravel road that begins at a signed turnoff from the Interamericana 5km north of Liberia; a private road is needed to reach the park and costs US$2 per person. The Santa María ranger station, to the east, is accessible via a rougher road beginning at Barrio La Victoria in Liberia. Both roads are passable to regular cars throughout the dry season, but a 4WD is required during the rainy season and is highly recommended at all other times (or it will take you twice as long). There's no public transportation, but any of the above lodges can arrange transport from Liberia for around US$15 per person each way with the requirement of a two or three person minimum. Alternately, you can hire a 4WD taxi for about US$25 to Las Pailas, or US$45 to Santa María, each way.

PARQUE NACIONAL SANTA ROSA

Among the oldest (established in 1971) and largest national parks in Costa Rica, Santa Rosa's sprawling 38,674 hectares of the Península Santa Elena protects the largest remaining stand of tropical dry forest in Central America, and some of the most important nesting sites of several species of sea turtle. However, Santa Rosa is also famous among Ticos as a symbol of historical pride – Costa Rica has only been invaded by a foreign army three times, and each time the attackers were defeated in Santa Rosa.

The best-known of these events was the Battle of Santa Rosa, which took place on March 20, 1856 when the soon-to-be-self-declared President of Nicaragua, an American named William Walker, invaded Costa Rica. William Walker was the head of a group of foreign pirates and adventurers known as the 'Filibusters' that had already seized Baja and southwest Nicaragua, and were attempting to gain control over all of Central America. In a brilliant display of military prowess, Costa Rican President Juan Rafael Mora Porras guessed Walker's intentions, and managed to assemble a rag-tag group of fighters that proceeded to surround Walker's army in the main building of the old Hacienda Santa Rosa, known as **La Casona**. The battle was over in just 14 minutes, and Walker was forever driven from Costa Rican soil.

Santa Rosa was again the site of battles between Costa Rican troops and invading forces from Nicaragua in both 1919 and 1955. The first was a somewhat honorable attempt to overthrow the Costa Rican dictator General Federico Tinoco, while the second was a failed coup d'état led by Nicaraguan dictator Anastasio Somoza. Today, you can still see Somoza's abandoned tank, which lies in a ditch beside the road just beyond the entrance to the Park. However, the military history surrounding the park didn't end with Somoza as Santa Rosa was later used as a staging point for the US military during the Sandinistas–Contra War.

Although the park was established mainly due to historical and patriotic reasons, in a surprising coincidence Santa Rosa has also become extremely important to biologists. With its acacia thorn trees and tall *jaragua* grass, first impressions of the park are likely to make you believe you've suddenly landed in the African savannah, though closer inspection reveals more American species of plants including cacti and bromeliads. Santa Rosa is also home to **Playa Nancite**, which is famous for its *arribadas* (mass nesting) of olive ridley sea turtles that sometimes number up to 8000 at a single time. Although the exact reason for mass nesting is unknown, scientists believe that this may be an attempt to overwhelm predators and ensure species survival.

However, a good number of travelers are here for one reason – the chance to surf the near-perfect beach break at **Playa Naranjo**, which is created by the legendary offshore monolith known as **Witch's Rock**. The park is also home to another break of arguably equal fame, namely **Ollie's Point**, which was immortalized in the film *Endless Summer II,* and is named after US Marine Lieutenant Colonel Oliver North. North is most famous for illegally selling weapons to Iran during the Reagan Era, and using the profits to fund the Contras in Nicaragua – Ollie's Point refers to the nearby troop staging area that everyone but the US Congress knew about.

Difficult access means that Santa Rosa is fairly empty, though it can get reasonably busy on weekends in the dry season when Ticos flock to the park in search of their often-hard-to-find history. In the wet months from July through December, particularly

September and October, you can observe the sea turtles nesting and often have the rest of the park virtually to yourself.

Orientation & Information

Parque Nacional Santa Rosa's entrance is on the west side of the Interamericana, 35km north of Liberia and 45km south of the Nicaragua border. The Santa Rosa Sector **park entrance** (☎ 666 5051; admission US$6, camping per person US$2; ☼ 8am-4pm) is close to the Interamericana, and it's another 7km to park headquarters, with the administrative offices, scientists quarters, an information center, an immaculate campground, museum, and nature trail. This office administers the Area de Conservación Guanacaste (ACG).

From this complex, a 4WD trail leads down to the coast to Playa Naranjo, 12km away. During the dry season, this road is passable to 2WD, though the road is usually closed to all cars from May to November (wet season). During the rainy months, the road is open to hikers and horses, though surfers can access the beach by hiring a boat from Playa del Coco or Tamarindo. Be aware that rangers can and will shut down the beach to all visitors during the turtle nesting season. From the campsite at the southern end of the beach, it's a 13km hike along the beach or through a wooded trail to Witch's Rock.

The coastal road branches a few kilometers before Playa Naranjo and heads north where it eventually connects to a hiking trail that leads to Playa Nancite. However, the beach is generally closed to visitors unless you have permission from the park office.

The park's Sector Murciélago (Bat Sector) encompasses the wild northern coastline of the Península Santa Elena, though it's not accessible from the main body of the park. From the Interamericana, continue north past the entrance to the Santa Rosa sector for 10km and then turn left once you pass through the police checkpoint. Continue on this road for a few more kilometers until you reach the village of Cuajiniquíl, and then bear left. Continue on this road for another 15km, which will bring you past such historic sights as the former hacienda of the Somoza family (it's currently a training ground for the Costa Rican 'police') and the old airstrip that was used by Oliver North

to 'secretly' smuggle goods to the Nicaraguan Contras in the 1980s. Just after the airstrip is the **park entrance** (admission US$6; camping US$2 per person; ☼ 8am-4pm), which is located in the village of Murciélago. From here, it's another 16km to the isolated white-sand beach of **Playa Blanca** and the trailhead for the **Poza el General** watering hole, which attracts birds and animals year-round.

Ollie's Point in **Playa Portero Grande** is located in this sector of the park, though it can only be reached by hiring a boat from Playa del Coco or Tamarindo. Or you can do as Patrick and Wingnut did in *Endless Summer II* and crash-land your chartered plane right on the beach (note: this is not actually recommended).

Sights

The historic **La Casona**, the main building of the old Hacienda Santa Rosa, is located near the park headquarters in the Santa Rosa sector. Unfortunately, the original building was burnt to the ground by arsonists in May 2001, though it was rebuilt in 2002 using historic photos and local timber. The battle of 1856 was fought around this building, and the military action, as well as the region's natural history, is described with the help of documents, paintings, maps, and other displays (mostly in Spanish). If you remember your dictionary, this will be an inspiring (and perhaps humbling) history lesson in how not to invade a country (you'd think the US government would have learned by now).

The arson was set by a local father-son team of poachers who were disgruntled at being banned from hunting here by park rangers. They were caught and sentenced to 20 years in prison for torching a building of national cultural and historical value. Unfortunately, poaching continues in the park since it's difficult for rangers to effectively patrol such a large landmass.

Activities
WILDLIFE-WATCHING

The wildlife is certainly both varied and prolific, especially during the dry season when animals congregate around the remaining water sources and the trees lose their leaves. More than 250 bird species have been recorded, including the raucous white-throated magpie jay, unmistakable with its

A WHOPPER OF A PROBLEM

Although there is a long history of deforestation in Costa Rica, massive clear-cutting of the rain forests (particularly in Guanacaste) intensified during the 1970s. Currently, there is much debate regarding the causes of this wide-scale deforestation, though research suggests that a shift in governmental philosophy likely sparked the event. Specifically, national policies were implemented at the time that promoted increased land use relating to agriculture, wood production, pasture land creation and improved transit infrastructure. It is argued that these initiatives were aimed at speeding up the country's economic development, especially in response to the decrease in the international demand for Costa Rican coffee.

Clearly, development is a double-edged sword as it's impossible to argue that the philosophies of the 1970s did not in fact improve the quality of life in Costa Rica. Today, Guanacaste is one of the richest provinces in Costa Rica, and the country as a whole is often regarded as the gem of Central America. Quality of life in Costa Rica is among the highest in Latin America, and Ticos have never had to starve like their neighbors to the north and south. However, cattle ranchers in Costa Rica produce an abundance of meat, much of which is destined for the international fast-food market. Thus the devastation to the rain forest is not solely a product of national improvement, but in fact the result of fast-food companies importing beef that has been raised on recently deforested land.

The body of evidence supporting these claims is astounding, and consists of everything from court testimonials to recorded data on imports and exports. Officially, most fast-food companies maintain that they are in favor of rain-forest preservation, and that they do not use hamburger meat of foreign origin in their products. However, although imported beef is only a small portion of the total meat consumed in the USA, this accounts for a significant percentage of Central American beef production. One documented problem is that when Central American beef arrives at a US point of entry, it is often marked as 'US inspected and approved,' which disguises the origin of the product. Furthermore, since the meat in a single burger can be derived from multiple cows, it's difficult to verify that a product is in fact free of foreign beef.

As a consumer, it's virtually impossible to ensure that you're not eating beef that's been raised on recently deforested areas, aside from boycotting the major fast-food retailers. And, with Cafta looming on the horizon, it's likely that Central American beef exports will increase dramatically. Fortunately, Western diets have recently shifted away from beef and processed meats, and several fast-food companies have started adopting healthier menus (though much of this is attributable to recent declines in profits). And you can take comfort in knowing that researchers in Costa Rica are currently hard at work investigating the natural processes of reforestation (for more information, see Parque Nacional Guanacaste on p231).

NORTHWESTERN COSTA RICA

long crest of maniacally curled feathers. The forests contain parrots and parakeets, trogons and tanagers, and as you head down to the coast, you will be rewarded by sightings of a variety of coastal birds.

Bats are also very common; about 50 or 60 different species have been identified in Santa Rosa. Other mammals you have a reasonable chance of seeing include deer, coatis, peccaries, armadillos, coyotes, raccoons, three kinds of monkey, and a variety of other species – about 115 in all. There are also many thousands of insect species, including about 4000 moths and butterflies – bring bug spray.

Reptile species include lizards, iguanas, snakes, crocodiles, and four species of sea turtle. The olive ridley sea turtle is the most numerous, and during the July to December nesting season, tens of thousands of turtles make their nests on Santa Rosa's beaches. The most popular beach is Playa Nancite, where, during September and October especially, it is possible to see as many as 8000 of these 40kg turtles on the beach at the same time. The turtles are disturbed by light, so flash photography and flashlights are not permitted. Avoid the nights around a full moon – they're too bright and turtles are less likely to show up. Playa Nancite is strictly protected and entry restricted, but permission may be obtained from park headquarters to observe this spectacle.

The variety of wildlife reflects the variety of habitat protected within the boundaries of the park. Apart from the largest remaining stand of tropical dry forest in Central America, habitats include savannah woodland, oak forest, deciduous forest, evergreen forest, riparian forest, mangrove swamp, and coastal woodland.

HIKING

Near La Casona is **El Sendero Indio Desnudo**, a 1km trail with signs interpreting the ecological relationships among the animals, plants and weather patterns of Santa Rosa. The trail is named after the common tree, also called *gumbo limbo,* whose peeling orange-red bark can photosynthesize during the dry season, when the tree's leaves are lost (resembling a sunburned tourist). Also seen along the trail is the national tree of Costa Rica, the *guanacaste (Enterolobium cyclocarpum).* The province is named after this very large tree species, which is found along the Pacific coastal lowlands. You may also see birds, monkeys, snakes, iguanas, and petroglyphs (most likely pre-Columbian) etched into some of the rocks on the trail.

Behind La Casona a short trail leads up to the **Monumento a Los Héroes** and a lookout platform. There are also longer trails through the dry forest, including a gentle 4km hike to the Mirador, with spectacular views of Playa Naranjo, which is accessible to hikers willing to go another 9km along the deeply rutted road to the sea. The main road is lined with short trails to small waterfalls and other photogenic natural wonders as well.

From the southern end of Playa Naranjo, there are two hiking trails – **Sendero Carbonal** is a 20km trail that swings inland and then terminates on the beach at Cerros Carbonal, while **Sendero Aceituno** parallels Playa Naranjo for 13km and terminates near the estuary across from Witch's Rock. There's also a roughly 6km hiking trail that starts where the northern branch of the access road terminates – this leads to the biological research station at Nancite, though you will need prior permission to access the beach.

Although it's not officially recommended by the park service, the opportunities for long-distance beach hiking abound, especially if you're an experienced hiker who's prepared to carry large quantities of food and water. Inquire locally about the feasibility of long-distance trekking (especially in regards to permanent water sources), though we have heard a rumor that it's possible to hike from Santa Rosa to Playa del Coco (if you make it, let us know!).

SURFING

The surfing at Playa Naranjo is truly world-renowned, especially near Witch's Rock, which is famous for its totally tubular 3m curls (these are some serious waves, and not recommended for beginners). Note that this is a beach break, though there are rocks near the river mouth, and you need to be especially careful near the estuary as it's a rich feeding ground for crocodiles during the tide changes. The surfing is equally legendary at Ollie's Point off of Playa Portero Grande, which has the best right in all of Costa Rica. The bottom here is a mix of sand and rocks, and the year-round offshore is perfect for tight turns and slow closes. Shortboarding is preferred by surfers at both spots, though if you're a Wingnut-wannabe you'll be fine with your longboard.

Sleeping & Eating

Research station (dm US$20) Make reservations well in advance to stay here, with eight-bed bunkrooms, cold showers and electricity. Researchers get priority, but there's usually some room for travelers. Good meals (US$3 to US$7) are available, but make arrangements the day before. There's also a snack bar.

There is a shady developed **campground** (per person US$2) close to the park headquarters, with picnic benches, grills, flushing toilets and cold-water showers. Playa Naranjo has pit toilets and showers, but no potable water – bring your own. Other camping areas in the park are undeveloped. There's a 25-person, two-night maximum for camping at Playa Naranjo. There's also a small camp site with pit toilets and showers near the ranger station in the Bat Sector, though you'll have to carry in your own food and water.

Getting There & Away

The well-signed main park entrance can be reached by public transport: take any bus between Liberia and the Nicaragua border and ask the driver to set you down at the park entrance; rangers can help you catch a return bus. You can also arrange private transportation from the hotels in Liberia for about US$15 per person round-trip.

To get to the northern Sector Murciélago of the park, go 10km further north along the Interamericana, then turn left to the village of Cuajiniquíl, with a couple of *sodas* and a *pulpería*, 8km away by paved road. Keep your passport handy, as there may be checkpoints. The paved road continues beyond Cuajiniquíl and dead-ends at a marine port, 4km away – this isn't the way to Sector Murciélago but goes toward Refugio Nacional de Vida Silvestre Bahía Junquillal. It's about 8km beyond Cuajiniquíl to the Murciélago ranger station by poor road – 4WD is advised in the wet season, though the road may be impassable. You can camp at the Murciélago ranger station, or continue 10km to 12km on a dirt road beyond the ranger station to the remote bays and beaches of Bahía Santa Elena and Bahía Playa Blanca.

REFUGIO NACIONAL DE VIDA SILVESTRE BAHÍA JUNQUILLAL

This 505-hectare wildlife refuge is part of the Area de Conservación Guanacaste (ACG), administered from the park headquarters at Santa Rosa. There is a **ranger station** (☎ 679 9692; admission incl Parque Nacional Santa Rosa US$6, camping per person US$2; ☾ 7am-4pm) in telephone and radio contact with Santa Rosa.

The quiet bay and protected beach provide gentle swimming, boating, and snorkeling opportunities, and there is some tropical dry forest and mangrove swamp. Short trails take the visitor to a lookout for marine birding and to the mangroves. Pelicans and frigatebirds are seen, and turtles nest here seasonally. Volcán Orosí can be seen in the distance. Campers should note that during the dry season especially, water is at a premium and is turned on for only one hour a day. There are pit latrines.

From Cuajiniquil, continue for 2km along the paved road and then turn right onto a signed dirt road. Continuing 4km along the dirt road (passable to ordinary cars) brings you to the entrance to Bahía Junquillal. From here, a poorer 700m dirt road leads to the beach, ranger station, and camping area.

PARQUE NACIONAL GUANACASTE

This newest part of the ACG was created on July 25 (Guanacaste Day), 1989. The park is adjacent to Parque Nacional Santa Rosa, separated from it by the Interamericana, and is only about 5km northwest of Parque Nacional Rincón de la Vieja.

The 34,651 hectares of Parque Nacional Guanacaste are much more than a continuation of the lowland habitats found in Santa Rosa. In its lower western reaches, the park is indeed composed of the dry tropical rain forest characteristic of much of Guanacaste, though the terrain soon begins to climb toward two volcanoes – Volcán Orosí (1487m) and Volcán Cacao (1659m). Here the landscape slowly transitions to the humid cloud forest that's found throughout much of the highland Cordillera de Guanacaste. This habitat, which is similar in function to Parque Nacional Carara, provides refuge for altitudinal migrants that move between the coast and the highlands. Thus the national park allows for the ancient migratory and hunting patterns of various animal species to continue as they have for millennia.

However, this ecosystem is more the domain of biologists than tourists (it's among the least visited parks in Costa Rica), and there are three major research stations within the borders of the park. In addition to observing animal migratory patterns, researchers are also monitoring the pace of reforestation as much of the park is composed of ranch land. Interestingly enough, researchers have found that if the pasture is carefully managed (much of this management involves just letting nature take its course), the natural forest will reinstate itself in its old territory. Thus crucial habitats in the national park are not just preserved, but in some cases they are also expanded.

For information on this park, contact the **ACG headquarters** (☎ 666 5051) in Parque Nacional Santa Rosa.

Sights & Activities

The three **research stations** located within the park borders are open to tourists, and they're great spots for wildlife observation. If you have a relevant background in biology or ecology, volunteer positions are available, though it's best to contact ACG well in advance of your arrival.

MARITZA BIOLOGICAL STATION

This is the newest station and has a modern laboratory. From the station, at 600m above sea level, rough trails run to the summits of Volcán Orosí and Volcán Cacao (about five to six hours). There is also a better trail to a site where several hundred petroglyphs have been found that are chipped into volcanic rock. As with most indigenous sites in Costa Rica, little is known about the origins of the petroglyphs, though the area was believed to be inhabited by the Chorotega (p183). There is also another trail that leads to the Cacao Biological Station.

To get there, turn east off the Interamericana opposite the turnoff for Cuajiniquil. The station is about 17km east of the highway along a dirt road that may require a 4WD vehicle, especially in the wet season.

CACAO BIOLOGICAL STATION

High on the slopes of Volcán Cacao (about 1060m), this station offers access to rough trails that lead to the summit of the volcano and to Maritza Biological Station. Cacao Biological Station is reached from the southern side of the park. At Potrerillos, about 9km south of the Santa Rosa park entrance on the Interamericana, head east for 7km on a paved road to the small community of Quebrada Grande (marked 'Garcia Flamenco' on many maps). A daily bus leaves Liberia at 3pm for Quebrada Grande. From the village plaza, a 4WD road that is often impassable during the wet season heads north toward the station, about 10km away.

PITILLA BIOLOGICAL STATION

This station lies on the northeast side of Volcán Orosí, which is located on the eastern side of the continental divide. The surrounding forests here are humid, lush and atypical of anything you'll find in the rest of Guanacaste.

To get to the station, turn east off the Interamericana about 12km north of the Cuajiniquil turnoff, or 3km before reaching the small town of La Cruz. Follow the paved eastbound road for about 28km to the community of Santa Cecilia. From there, a poor dirt road heads 11km south to the station – you'll probably need 4WD. (Don't continue on the unpaved road heading further east – that goes over 50km further to the small town of Upala.)

Activities

Hiking trails in the national park are among the least developed in the entire country, and are principally used by researchers to move between each of the stations. It's advisable to talk to the staff before setting out on any of the hikes, as infrastructure in the park is almost nonexistent. If you're interested in summiting Volcán Cacao, it's strongly recommended that you hire a guide, which can be arranged through any of the biological stations or at Hacienda Los Inocentes (see below).

Sleeping & Eating

INSIDE THE PARK

If there's space, you may be able to reserve dorm-style accommodations at Maritza or **Cacao** (☎ 666 5051; dm US$20). Pitilla is the province of research biologists and students. The stations are all quite rustic, with room for about 30 people, and shared cold-water bathrooms. Meals are also available for US$3 to US$7, and should be arranged in advance.

You can also camp (per person US$2.50) near the stations, though there aren't any facilities.

OUTSIDE THE PARK

Hacienda Los Inocentes (☎ 679 9190; www.losinocenteslodge.com; d with/without 3 meals US$70/45) This former cattle ranch on the northern edge of the park was the former property of the Inocente family, who used to own nearly one-third of Guanacaste. Today, it's part biological research station, part ecolodge, and the principal aim is to convert much of the 1000-hectare ranch from pasture land to rain forest. The ranch has a spectacular location below the Volcán Orosí, and nearly two-thirds of the property has returned to secondary forest (not surprisingly, there are great opportunities here for wildlife-watching). The hacienda building itself is a very attractive, century-old wooden house, and has 11 spacious wooden bedrooms with private (but separate) bathroom, plus several larger separate cabins. The upper floor is surrounded by a beautiful, shaded, wooden veranda with hammocks and also volcano views – a good spot for sunset/moonrise. The staff can arrange guided hikes throughout the park as well as to the top of Volcán Cacao.

Previous page:
Family life (p45)
ERIC L WHEATER

TOM BOYDEN

Granite spheres, Reserve Biólogica Isla del Caño (p413)

Hiking, Parque Nacional Volcán Poás (p157)

ERIC L WH

The hacienda is 15km east of the Interamericana on the paved road to Santa Cecilia. Buses from San José to Santa Cecilia pass the lodge entrance at about 7:30pm, returning at around 4:15am. Taxis from La Cruz charge about US$10.

LA CRUZ

La Cruz is the closest town to the main border crossing with Nicaragua (p237), and it's the principal gateway to Bahía Salinas (right), one of Costa Rica's premier wind- and kite-surfing destinations. Although it's a fairly boring provincial town with the same drab architecture characteristic of most Costa Rican settlements, its hilltop location is awash with scenic views of the coastline, and it's a rather pleasant place to spend the night (at least by border-town standards).

Information

It's reportedly easiest to change money at the border post.

Banco Nacional (☎ 679 9296) At the junction of the short road into the center and the Interamericana.

Banco Popular (☎ 679 9352) In the center.

Clinic (☎ 679 9116) There is a small clinic located just north of the town center on the road towards the border.

Sleeping

Cabinas Santa Rita (☎ 679 9062; s/d US$3/6, s/d with bathroom US$9/13, air-con US$13/21; P ✿) The best budget option in town has clean though dark rooms with shared bathrooms and is popular among migrant workers. Across the street, the newer annex has frillier rooms with private bathroom, cable TV, hot showers, and air-con.

Hotel Bella Vista (☎ 679 8060; hotelbellavista.tripod.com; per person incl breakfast US$15, dinner extra US$5; P ▣ ✿) This German-run hotel, located on the hilltop with scenic views of the gulf, is a terrific value. Well-furnished rooms have private hot-water bathrooms, cable TV and terraces, and you can relax in the spotless pool or have a beer and a casado at the attached restaurant.

Amalia's Inn (☎ 679 9618; s/d US$20/35; P ✿ ✿) Not just the best hotel in town, but one of the finest nonresort accommodations in the region, this spot offers seven enormous rooms furnished with 1980s-style leather modular couches, comfy beds and lots of absolutely incredible paintings by the deceased North American husband of Amalia, the Tica owner. The mural by the pool and fabulous views of the gulf through each room's huge picture windows make this a great reason to spend the night in a border town. Go figure.

Eating

It's not the gastronomic capital of Costa Rica, but you can always get a good *gallo* (tortilla sandwich).

Soda Candy (mains US$1-3; ✷ 6am-8pm) There's no menu at this basic *soda* across from the bus terminal, but in addition to casados and *gallos* 'made with a lot of love,' Candy knows all the bus schedules by heart and can fill you in if the station happens to be closed.

Bar/Snacks Pizotes (bocas US$1, mains US$2-4; ✷ 11am-10pm) With colorful murals of coatis on its walls, this inviting spot welcomes hungry travelers with its cheap selection of *bocas* and light meals.

Pollo Rico Rico (mains US$2-4; ✷ 10am-10pm) Folks who love fried chicken should stop by this spot, right on the park, or try the roasted chicken, which is even tastier (and a whole lot better for your poor arteries).

Getting There & Away

A **Transportes Deldú counter** (✷ 7am-1pm & 3-5:30pm) sells tickets and stores bags. To catch a TransNica bus to Peñas Blancas, you'll need to flag a bus down on the Interamericana.

Bahía Salinas US$1, one hour, departs at 7am, noon and 4pm.

Liberia (Transportes Deldú) US$1, two hours, 6:15am, 7:30am, 9:30am, 11:30am, 3:15pm, 3:30pm, 5:30pm and 6:30pm.

Peñas Blancas US$1, 45 minutes, 5am, 7am, 7:45am, 10:45am, 1:20pm and 4:10pm.

San José (Transportes Deldú) US$5, five hours, 5:45am, 8am, 10am, 11am, 12:20pm, 2pm and 4:15pm.

BAHÍA SALINAS

Bahía Salinas is the second-best place in all of Costa Rica (only after Laguna de Arenal) for windsurfing, and is arguably the best place in the country for kiteboarding because the vegetation around Arenal can be quite dangerous for folks in the air. The bay is also home to **Isla Bolaños**, which protects a large colony of seabirds including the endangered brown pelican (from January to May).

NORTHWESTERN COSTA RICA

Sights & Activities

A dirt road (normally passable to cars) leads down from the lookout point in La Cruz past the small coastal **fishing community** of Puerto Soley and out along the curve of the bay to where there are a couple of newer resorts. Boats can be rented in the town of **Jobo** to visit Isla Bolaños (you can't land, but you can approach and view the nesting seabird colonies). As well, you can try **Frank Schultz** (☎ 827 4109; franks_diving@costaricense .co.cr), who also organizes fishing and diving trips.

WINDSURFING & KITEBOARDING

The strongest and steadiest winds blow from December through March, but it blows pretty well year-round here. The shape of the hills surrounding the bay funnel the winds into a predictable pattern, and the sandy, protected beaches make this a safe place for beginners and experienced windsurfers and kiteboarders alike. In regards to kiteboarding, it's important to remember that there are inherent dangers in the sport (namely the risk of losing a limb – yikes!), so it's best to seek professional instruction unless you're an experienced rider.

Tico Wind (☎ 692 2002; www.ticowind.com; half-/full-day rentals US$38/68) is a recommended windsurfing company at Ecoplaya Beach Resort. Like its flagship operation on Laguna de Arenal (p255), it maintains the same high standards, with new equipment purchased every year and top-notch instruction.

If windsurfing is too tame for you, then enroll at **Kitesurf School 2000** (☎ 826 5221; ⓨ Nov-May; www.suntoursandfun.com/kitesurfing.htm) a sporty combination of wind and waves (which school instructors insist is much easier to learn than regular surfing) where you are attached to a large kite, seriously, then pulled across the bay by the breeze, allowing more advanced students to do flips and other aerial acrobatics above the froth and swells – way cool. If you want to give this a try, make reservations a couple of days in advance for 10 hours of lessons (US$250) or just equipment rental (basic gear US$40 per day). If the school isn't full of grinning students, they'll rent you **basic dorms** (dm US$15) with hot showers and a shared kitchen.

Sleeping & Eating

Proyecto Pura-Vida (☎ 389 6784; velrey@racsa.co.cr; apt & houses per night US$30-100) Though geared toward long-term stays, this agency rents several wicker-furnished apartments and houses, priced according to size and amenities, which may include a pool or, perhaps, a bidet (they're Italian-owned). Smaller apartments can accommodate up to four people while the larger villas can house seven. Each property is reasonably spaced from one another, and they all overlook a pristine stretch of white sand. There are weekly and monthly discounts available.

Restaurant Copal (☎ 676 1006; mains US$4-7; ⓨ 5pm-party is over) Though there's not much competition, that doesn't stop this excellent eatery from turning out top-quality seafood, salads and other beautifully prepared mains. Try the *pizza del mar*, with shrimp and the catch of the day – outstanding. It's located on Playa Copal, and is popular with folks escaping Ecoplaya Beach Resort, about 3km away.

Ecoplaya Beach Resort (☎ 676 1010; www.eco playa.com; villa US$90-203; Ⓟ Ⓧ Ⓧ Ⓠ Ⓡ) About 16km from La Cruz, you're really getting away from it all on this isolated stretch of paradise, where bungalows range from upscale elegance (big bathroom, nice furniture) to full luxury (minibar, sitting room, private porch). Smaller studio villas can accommodate three people, while the larger luxury villas can hold up to eight people. There's not much around here in the way of *sodas*, so you'll probably be eating at the on-site thatch-roofed restaurant (mains US$5 to US$11). The pristine white-sand beach in front of the hotel is about as perfect as they come, though there are plenty of activities and tours available to ward off the boredom including kayaking, mountain biking, fishing, diving, windsurfing, horse riding and a pool with a swim-up bar.

Getting There & Away

Buses along this road depart the La Cruz bus terminal at 7am, noon and 4pm daily and return approximately one hour later. A taxi to either beach area costs about US$11, and you can usually catch a *colectivo* (US$3.50) from La Cruz, close to the taxi stand, though you may have to wait a while for it to fill up.

ARENAL ROUTE

Sure, the Interamericana is the fastest way around the region, but then there's this route, the road less traveled – probably because of all the potholes. The Arenal Route starts in Ciudad Quesada, the largest population center in this mostly agrarian area, and then winds northwesterly toward La Fortuna, the gateway to the region's undisputed highlight, Volcán Arenal. Along the way (if the weather cooperates), the continuously smoking volcano looms ominously in the distance while patches of tropical rain forest and scattered fincas line the road.

Past La Fortuna, the road wraps around the oblong expanse of Laguna de Arenal, passing through the small Tico towns (for the time being at least) of Nuevo Arenal and Tilarán. Although these spots are well served by public transportation, this is a five-star road trip just made for folks lucky enough to have rented their own vehicle. This vista-packed trip is lined with lakeside picnic spots, wacky art galleries, wonderful restaurants and weird hotels galore, all just waiting to be explored by travelers with a little time on their hands.

Although this region has historically been home to farmers and ranchers, the cool climate of the hills around Lake Arenal has, in recent year, resulted in the increased migration of North American and European hominids. Baby boomers, to be exact, are starting to buy up property along the lakeside in record numbers, and it's unfortunately only a matter of time now before the condo crazy kicks into high gear.

CIUDAD QUESADA (SAN CARLOS)

The official name of this small city is Ciudad Quesada (sometimes abbreviated to 'Quesada'), but all the locals know it as San

NICA VS TICO

Ticos have a well-deserved reputation for friendliness, and it's rare for travelers of all sexes, races and creeds to experience any instance of racism in Costa Rica. However, it's unfortunate and at times upsetting that the mere mention of anything related to Nicaragua is enough to turn your average Tico into a hate-spewing bigot. Despite commonalities in language, culture, history and tradition, Nica vs Tico relations are at an all-time low, and rhetoric (on both sides) of *la frontera* isn't likely to improve anytime soon.

So why is there so much hostility between Nicas and Ticos? The answer is as much a product of history as it is of misunderstanding, though economic disparities between both countries are largely to blame.

Though Nicaragua was wealthier than Costa Rica as little as 25 years ago, decades of civil war and a US embargo quickly bankrupted the country, and today Nicaragua is the second-poorest country in the western hemisphere (after Haiti). For example, the 2005 CIA World Fact book lists the GDP per capita purchasing-power parity of Costa Rica as US$10,000, while Nicaragua is listed at only US$2800. The main problem facing Nicaragua is its heavy external debt, though debt relief programs implemented by the IMF and the pending free-trade zone created by Cafta are both promising signs.

In the meantime, however, Nica families are crossing the border In record numbers, drawn to Costa Rica by its growing economy and impressive education and health systems. Unfortunately, immigration laws in Costa Rica make it difficult for Nicas to find work, and the majority end up living in shantytowns. Also, crime is on the rise throughout Costa Rica, and though it's difficult to say what percentage is actually attributable to Nica immigrants, Ticos are quick to point their finger.

It's difficult to predict whether relations will improve between both countries over the next several years, though current signs are fairly negative. Costa Rica, whose civil guard is better funded than most country's militaries, has a bad habit of being caught on the river San Juan with a patrol boat of fatigued combat troops brandishing M16s. Nicaragua, which has the power to simultaneously defuse Tico racism and promote tourism, recently passed a law requiring all visiting Ticos to be in possession of a valid visa. Like all instances of deep-rooted prejudice, the problem is easy to address, though the solution is anything but clear.

Carlos, and local buses often list San Carlos as the destination. It's long been a bustling ranching and agricultural center, known for its *talabaterías* (saddle shops). They make and sell some of the most intricately crafted leather saddles in Costa Rica; a top-quality saddle can cost US$1000. The city is also home to the **Feria del Ganado** (cattle fair and auction), which is held every April and accompanied by carnival rides and a *tope*.

Although San Carlos is surrounded by pastoral countryside, the city of 31,000 has developed into the commercial center of the region – it's also gritty and congested, and driving here can be harrowing for the uninitiated driver. Fortunately, there's no real reason to enter the city, except to either change buses or to visit one of the area's fine hot springs.

Check your email at **Internet Café** (per hr US$1; ☽ 8am-9pm Mon-Sat, 3-7pm Sun), 100m north of the parque. Banco de San José, 200m north of the parque, and the Mutual de Alajuela across the street both have ATMs on the Cirrus and Plus systems.

If you're not staying at one of the two private hot-springs resorts, you can visit the budget-friendly **Aguas Termales de la Marina** (☎ 460 1692; admission US$2). The springs are located on the outskirts of town, and locally referred to as 'El Tucanito' (El Tucano is the name of the most expensive resort in town).

Sleeping

Hotel del Norte (☎ 460 1959; s/d US$6/9, s/d with bathroom US$9/13) Small, clean rooms with TV have ridiculously thin walls (so pray that you like what your neighbor is watching), though the excellent security and professional staff make this the best budget option in town; 200m north of Banco Nacional.

Hotel Don Goyo (☎ 460 1780; s/d US$12/22; P) This is the most established hotel in San Carlos proper, and has small, pleasant, salmon-colored rooms with private hot showers. The attached restaurant (mains US$4 to US$10) is well respected for its high-quality food including traditional Tico favorites and a good variety of Western dishes. It's 100m south of Parque Central.

Termales del Bosque (☎ 460 4740; www.termales delbosque.com; s/d incl breakfast US$49/61; P ☎) Several airy cottages are arranged around the jungly grounds at this recommended resort designed with Tico tourism in mind,

though it's popular with foreigners who don't want to fork out the cash at nearby El Tucano. Luxury here is low-key with therapeutic soaking taking place in a series of seven natural hot- and warm-water springs, which are arranged on the riverbank in a forested valley populated by morpho butterflies. To reach the resort, turn right behind the cathedral, and continue for 7km to the east; you will see a sign on the left.

El Tucano Resort & Thermal Spa (☎ 460 6000; www.1costaricalink.com/eng/hotels/hota/tucano/home .htm; d US$75-140; P ☒ ☎) This posh Mediterranean-style resort, 8km northeast of Ciudad Quesada, is located in primary forest and comes complete with an Italian restaurant, swimming pool, Jacuzzi, spa and sauna, plus various sports facilities ranging from tennis courts to miniature golf. However, the real draw is the nearby thermal springs, which are tapped into three small hot pools that are perfect for soaking away your ills. If you're not staying at the hotel, you can access the pools for US$11.

Eating

San Carlos has gone urban – chain restaurants abound throughout the city, though there are a few decent local spots on or near the park.

Charlie's Burger (Parque Central; burgers US$2; ☽ 11am-10pm) This San Carlos institution is the place to go when you really need a burger – they're big, juicy and oh-so-cheap.

Restaurant Los Geranios (mains US$2-5) On a 2nd-story terrace 100m south of the church, overlooking the bustling street below, this popular meeting spot for the city's 20-somethings has cheap casados and cold beer – a perfect combination.

Restaurant El Parque (mains US$3-6; ☽ 11am-9pm) If you're looking for a break from the standard rice and beans, head to this small *soda* 50m north of the *parque*, which specializes in Italian pastas.

Getting There & Away

The new Terminal Quesada is about 2km from the center of town. Taxis (US$1) and a twice-hourly bus (US$0.20) make regular runs between town and the terminal. (Walking there is fine if you don't mind hauling your luggage uphill.) Popular bus routes (and their bus companies) from Ciudad Quesada:

GETTING TO RIVAS, NICARAGUA

Peñas Blancas is a busy border crossing, and it's good to get there early, if only to avoid the sliding entry fee into Nicaragua, which runs US$7 until noon, US$9 afterward; your car will cost another US$22. You won't be charged to enter Costa Rica, but leaving Nicaragua costs US$2, payable in US dollars only. (There are banks on either side that will change local colones and córdobas for dollars, but not for each other, though independent moneychangers will happily make the exchange at a ridiculous rate.) And those are just the base fees.

The border posts, open 6am to 8pm daily, are 1km apart; if you're feeling saucy you can hire a golf cart (US$2) to make the run. Hordes of totally useless touts will offer to 'guide' you through the simple crossing; if you let them carry your luggage, they will charge you whatever they want. And should you have any hard currency left, there's a fairly fabulous duty-free shop, with fancy makeup and lots of liquor, waiting for you in Sipoá, the Nicaraguan equivalent of Peñas Blancas.

Relax with your purchases on the 37km bus ride (US$0.75, 45 minutes), departing every 30 minutes, to Rivas, a quiet, colonial city that's primarily used by travelers as a transport hub, though its well-preserved 17th-century center is worth exploring (think a more rundown version of Granada without all the crowds).

Alternatively, if you're good at bargaining (and you will have to bargain hard), there are a number of taxis waiting on the Nicaraguan side of the border to whisk travelers to Rivas (US$6), the San Jorge ferry (US$8), San Juan del Sur (US$8) and Granada (US$25).

La Fortuna (Coopatrac) US$0.75, 1½ hours, departs 6am, 10:30am, 1pm, 3:30pm, 5:15pm and 6pm.

Los Chiles (Chilsaca) US$3, two hours, 12 times daily from 5am to 7:15pm.

Puerto Viejo de Sarapiquí (Empresarios Guapileños) US$1.50, 2½ hours, 4:40am, 6am, 9:15am, 10am, 3pm and 5:30pm.

San José (Autotransportes San Carlos) US$2.50, 2½ hours, hourly from 5am to 6pm.

Tilarán (Transportes Tilarán) US$4, 4½ hours, 6:30am and 4pm.

LA FORTUNA & AROUND

Even without an active volcano spewing smoke and fireworks overhead, the quiet, rural town of La Fortuna de San Carlos would be a relaxing place to kick back for a few days. The surrounding area is home to cascading waterfalls and luxurious hot springs, though there are seemingly more tour operators in town than insects. Of course, these distractions are all probably good things if you're going to need lots of patience if you want to see the notoriously shy Volcán Arenal unveil itself from beneath the cloud cover.

Prior to 1968, La Fortuna was a sleepy agricultural town located 6km from the base of Cerro Arenal (Arenal Hill). However, on the morning of July 29, 1968, Arenal erupted violently after nearly 400 years of dormancy, and buried the small villages of Pueblo Nuevo, San Luís and Tabacón (yes, Tabacón Hot Springs (p238) is in fact located in the eruption path). Suddenly, like moths to the flame, tourists from around the world started descending on La Fortuna in search of fiery night skies and the inevitable blurry photo.

Despite the influx of tourists who have swollen the economy in recent years, La Fortuna still retains that *sabanero* vibe and real Tico feel – probably because it's quite consciously holding on to it. Brilliant flowers, not fences, still guard the edges of family-run hotels and restaurants throughout the town, and the nearby jungle still echoes with the cries of howler monkeys and the occasional rumble from the looming volcano.

But things have changed in recent years, and it would be naive to say that overdevelopment hasn't taken its toll on the once-humble town of La Fortuna. These days, arriving visitors descend from their buses into a gauntlet of touts and hawkers, and the small-town charm that makes La Fortuna so pleasant is rapidly disappearing. Tour operators, in search of the almighty dollar, have set up shop in virtually every storefront in town, and tourists have responded with distrust, even when intentions are honorable. Even worse is the recent string of McResorts that popped up on the road heading west from La Fortuna to Arenal. However, in a fitting twist of irony, the lava has recently switched directions, and forced high-paying customers to endure a bumpy bus ride each evening to the southwestern side of the volcano.

La Fortuna serves as the principal gateway for visiting Volcán Arenal, and it's one of the top destinations for travelers in Costa Rica. The town is well connected by public transport to San José, and travelers are increasingly arriving from or heading to Monteverde via the scenic and unusual Jeep-Boat-Jeep transfer. If you have your own transport, however, consider staying at the Arenal Observatory Lodge (p250) or in the small town of El Castillo (p251) as you'll be rewarded with less crowds and better views of the lava flows.

Orientation & Information

Though streets in La Fortuna are named, there are few street signs, and most locals will give better directions using landmarks. The town is centered on a small park, which is adjacent to the bus stop and taxi stand. The clinic, police station, and post office are shown on the La Fortuna map.

INTERNET ACCESS

Expediciones (per hr US$1.55; ☺ 9am-10pm Mon-Sat) Most tour operators in town also provide Internet access, but if you're not interested in hearing a sales pitch, there's no hassles here. Across from Parque Central.

LAUNDRY

Lavandería Alice (☎ 479 9084, per kg US$0.50; ☺ 8am-9pm) Here you get the full fluff-and-fold treatment, 100m north of the park.

MEDICAL SERVICES

Clinic (Calle 3; ☺ 9am-8pm Mon-Fri, 10am-7pm Sat & Sun)

MONEY

Despite being a relatively touristy town, some hotels and restaurants won't accept US dollars, though things will probably change in the near future.

Banco de Costa Rica (Av Central) Has a Visa Plus ATM.

TOURIST INFORMATION

Not surprisingly, there is no unbiased tourist information center in La Fortuna, though any tour operator or hotel front desk will be happy to give you information out of enlightened self-interest.

Lunática (☎ 479 8255; ☺ 9:30am-7:30pm) For cultural offerings in the La Fortuna area, information on events and happenings, though unfortunately they're infrequent to rare. The store, across from the school, also displays the work of area artists, including baskets, masks and jewelry made by Muleka Indians.

Sights
HOT SPRINGS

What's the consolation prize if you can't actually see the volcano? Why, hot springs, of course, and La Fortuna has some doozies.

If Steven Spielberg ever needed a set for the Garden of Eden sequence in Genesis, **Tabacón Hot Springs** (☎ 319 1900; www.tabacon.com; adult/child US$29/17; after 7pm US$19/17; ☺ 10am-10pm), 13km west of La Fortuna, is what it would look like. Enter through the gratuitously opulent ticket counter, flanked by an outrageous buffet (adult/child US$12/9 extra) on one side and glittering gift shop on the other. Then, with a thundering announcement, rare orchids and more florid tropical blooms part to reveal, oh yes, a 40°C waterfall pouring over a cliff, concealing naturalish-looking caves complete with camouflaged cup holders. And lounged across each well-placed stone, in various stages of sweat-induced exhaustion, relax reddening tourists all enjoying what could be called a hot date.

Just know however, that hedonism comes at a price – the spa is actually on the site where a volcanic eruption ripped through in 1975, killing one local (there weren't any tourists here in those days), and several times a year the resort is evacuated whenever Arenal has a bit of indigestion and decides to belch some poisonous gas (and we haven't even told you about the threat of avalanches). Sure, chances are you'll be fine, but imagine how bad the cover of the *Tico Times* is going to look when a bunch of rich Americans and Europeans get toasted (or crushed).

If you're looking for a hot bath without all the glitz, glamour and gargantuan entrance fee, head across the street to **Las Fuentes Termales** (☎ 460 2020; weekday/weekend US$10/8; ☺ 10am-10pm), which is operated by Tabacón and popular with Tico families, who love to break up their soaking sessions with some serious grilling.

Baldi Thermae Hot Springs (☎ 479 9651; with/without buffet US$27/17; ☺ 10am-10pm) Sporting concrete Roman pillars and a Mayan pyramid sprouting waterslides, the whole ambience at these springs 5km west of La Fortuna falls somewhere between Caesar's Palace and Epcot Center. Furthermore, the 10 thermal pools here can only be considered understated in comparison to Tabacón, and the hefty admissions fee is probably better spent elsewhere.

Eco-Termales (☎ 479 8484; admission US$16; 🕙 10am-9pm) Across the street is this unsigned gate that leads to this recommended hot-spring complex, which is by appointment only. The theme here is minimalist elegance, and everything from the natural circulation systems in the pools to the soft, mushroom lighting is understated yet luxurious. Just 100 visitors per four-hour slot are welcomed at 10am, 1pm and 5pm, and you can phone ahead, make a reservation next door at Hotel el Silencio del Campo (p246), or take your chances by just showing up. During the evening session, guests have the option to choose from one of three set menus (US$13/15/20), which feature home-style food served in earthenware pots.

We're certainly not going to let out the secret, but there are several free **hot springs** in the area that any local can take you to.

DAY SPAS

Masajes Serenity (☎ 479 8261; massages US$20-70; 🕙 9am-10pm) treats weary muscles with a variety of massages, and skin with a selection of facials and spa treatments. It's 50m southeast of Parque Central.

Herrera Day Spa (☎ 479 9016; massages US$20-85; 🕙 9am-10pm), 200m northeast of Parque Central, has an intimate, European atmosphere and sells its own line of homemade beauty products.

WATERFALLS

Even if you can't see Arenal, La Fortuna has another natural wonder that pales only in comparison with an erupting volcano: **La Catarata de la Fortuna** (admission US$6; 🕙 8am-5pm), a sparkling 70m ribbon of clear water pouring through a sheer canyon of dark volcanic rock arrayed in bromeliads and ferns. It's photogenic, and you don't have to descend the canyon – a short, well-maintained and almost-vertical hike paralleling the river's precipitous plunge – to get the shot, though you do have to pay the steep entry fee.

It's worth the climb out (think Stairmaster with a view) to see the rare world at the jungle floor. Though it's dangerous to dive beneath the thundering falls, a series of perfect swimming holes with spectacular views tiles the canyon in aquamarine – cool and inviting after the hike or ride here. Keep an eye on your backpack.

Though the signed turnoff from the road to San Ramón claims it's 5km to the falls, this is a cruel hoax. It's 7km (at least), it's all uphill, and folks enjoying the trip through pastureland and papaya trees will appreciate a stop at **Neptune's House of Hammocks** (☎ 479 8269; hammocks US$50-150), which sells soft drinks and hammocks (cat-sized models also available) that you'll want to give a test run.

You can also get to the *catarata* on horseback (US$20 to US$30 per person) or by car or taxi (US$7 one way); several outfits also offer overpriced tours that include a shuttle. A handful of snack and souvenir stands are at the entrance to the falls, but it's worth packing your own lunch and making a day of it.

The falls are also the trailhead for the steep, five-hour **Cerro Chato** climb, a seriously strenuous trek to a lake-filled volcanic crater, where you can see two Arenals fuming for the price of one.

Can't handle the hike? Just past the turnoff to the *catarata*, at the third bridge as you leave La Fortuna for San Ramón, there's a short trail on the left leading to a pretty **swimming hole** just under the road, with a rope swing and little waterfall of its own, thank you very much.

ECOCENTRO DENAUS

This reader-recommended **ecological center** (☎ 460 8005; admission US$5; 🕙 8am-3:30pm), 3km east of town then 500m on a dirt road, has a well-developed trail system that's good for birding, and there are frequent sightings of sloths, coatis and howler monkeys. The price of admission also includes a visit to a butterfly garden, a ranarium featuring poison-dart frogs and a small lake containing caiman and turtles. Various tour operators in town run guided night tours (US$25) to the ecological center.

VALLE COCODRILO

Part crocodile conservation program, part seat-of-its-pants tourist attraction, this

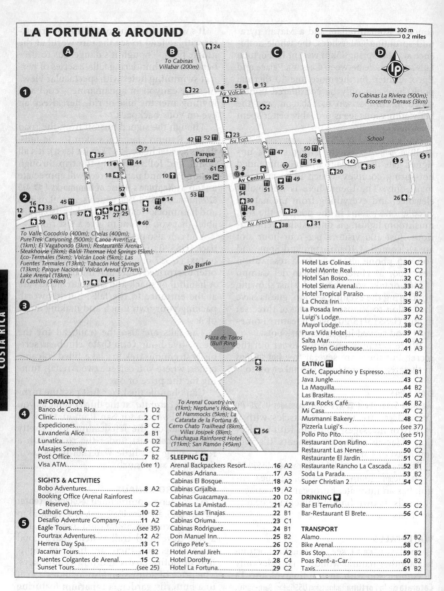

LA FORTUNA & AROUND

0 ——— 300 m
0 ——— 0.2 miles

To Cabinas
Villabar (200m)

To Cabinas La Riviera (500m);
Ecocentro Denaus (3km)

Av Volcán

Av Fort

Parque
Central

School

Av Central

Av Arenal

Río Burío

To Valle Cocodrilo (400m); Chelas (400m);
PureTrek Canyoning (500m); Canoa Aventura
(1km); El Vagabondo (3km); Restaurante Arenas
Steakhouse (3km); Baldí Thermae Hot Springs (5km);
Eco-Termales (5km); Volcán Look (5km); Las
Fuentes Termales (13km); Tabacón Hot Springs
(13km); Parque Nacional Volcán Arenal (17km);
Lake Arenal (18km);
El Castillo (34km)

Plaza de Toros
(Bull Ring)

To Arenal Country Inn
(1km); Neptune's House
of Hammocks (5km); La
Catarata de la Fortuna &
Cerro Chato Trailhead (8km);
Villas Josipek (8km);
Chachagua Rainforest Hotel
(11km); San Ramón (45km)

INFORMATION		
Banco de Costa Rica	1	D2
Clinic	2	C1
Expediciones	3	C2
Lavandería Alice	4	B1
Lunática	5	D2
Masajes Serenity	6	C2
Post Office	7	B2
Visa ATM	(see 1)	
SIGHTS & ACTIVITIES		
Bobo Adventures	8	A2
Booking Office (Arenal Rainforest Reserve)	9	C2
Catholic Church	10	B2
Desafío Adventure Company	11	A2
Eagle Tours	(see 35)	
Fourtrax Adventures	12	A2
Herrera Day Spa	13	C1
Jacamar Tours	14	B2
Puentes Colgantes de Arenal	15	C2
Sunset Tours	(see 25)	

SLEEPING		
Arenal Backpackers Resort	16	A2
Cabinas Adriana	17	A3
Cabinas El Bosque	18	A2
Cabinas Grijalba	19	A2
Cabinas Guacamaya	20	D2
Cabinas La Amistad	21	A2
Cabinas Las Tinajas	22	B1
Cabinas Oriuma	23	C1
Cabinas Rodríguez	24	B1
Don Manuel Inn	25	B2
Gringo Pete's	26	D2
Hotel Arenal Jireh	27	A2
Hotel Dorothy	28	C4
Hotel La Fortuna	29	C2

Hotel Las Colinas	30	C2
Hotel Monte Real	31	C2
Hotel San Bosco	32	C1
Hotel Sierra Arenal	33	A2
Hotel Tropical Paraíso	34	B2
La Choza Inn	35	A2
La Posada Inn	36	D2
Luigi's Lodge	37	C2
Mayol Lodge	38	C2
Pura Vida Hotel	39	A2
Salta Mar	40	A2
Sleep Inn Guesthouse	41	A3
EATING		
Cafe, Cappuchino y Espresso	42	B1
Java Jungle	43	C2
La Maquila	44	B2
Las Brasitas	45	A2
Lava Rocks Café	46	B2
Mi Casa	47	C2
Musmanni Bakery	48	C2
Pizzería Luigi's	(see 37)	
Pollo Pito Pito	(see 51)	
Restaurant Don Rufino	49	C2
Restaurant Las Nenes	50	C2
Restaurante El Jardín	51	C2
Restaurante Rancho La Cascada	52	B1
Soda La Parada	53	B2
Super Christian 2	54	C2
DRINKING		
Bar El Terruño	55	C2
Bar-Restaurant El Brete	56	C4
TRANSPORT		
Alamo	57	B2
Bike Arenal	58	C1
Bus Stop	59	B2
Poas Rent-a-Car	60	B2
Taxis	61	B2

locally operated **crocodile ranch** (☎ 479 9279; admission US$2; ☑ 8am-6:30pm) guides visitors past various fenced-in ponds where you can see crocodiles and caimans at various stages in their lives (sure, a full-on crocodile is frightening, but aren't the little guys just so cute?). It's situated 700m west of the church.

Unfortunately, readers often complain about the treatment of the animals, and have written letters describing abuse at the hands of the operators.

ARENAL RAINFOREST RESERVE

The Arenal Rainforest Reserve (p251) in nearby El Castillo is a spectacular ecopark complete with zip lines, aerial trams, hanging bridges and perfect views of the lava. The booking office is located east of the park.

Activities

There's no shortage of things to do in the La Fortuna area, but it's going to cost you.

ATV RIDING

Ecotourism and ATV riding go together like topless sunbathing and the Middle East, but whatever – to each their own. There are a surprising number of companies, though **Fourtrax Adventures** (☎ 479 8444; www.fourtraxadventure.com; Av Central) is the most established operator in town, located on the western edge of town. A four-hour tour that brings you to the base of the Arenal costs US$75 per ATV, and each of these little gas-guzzlers can carry two.

CANOEING

Canoa Aventura (☎ 479 8200), highly recommended and about 1km west of town on the road to Arenal, this does one thing: canoe trips. Most are geared toward wildlife-watching, in particular birds, certain species of which (green macaws, roseate spoonbills, honeycreepers etc) are the focus of various tours. The most popular paddles include the full-day tri-colored heron trip to Caño Negro (US$90) and the four-hour, early-morning tanager paddle on Río Fortuna (US$45), but overnights (US$250) are also on offer.

CANYONING

PureTrek Canyoning (☎ 479 9940; www.puretrek.com) leads guided rappels down four waterfalls, one of which is 50m in height. The four-hour tour costs US$80 and includes transportation and lunch. Find it 500m west of town.

HORSE RIDING

Desafío Adventure Company (☎ 479 9464; www.desafiocostarica.com) This company, behind the church, treats its horses well and has been recommended for the trek to Monteverde (US$65), with a couple of caveats (see the boxed text To Ride Or Not To Ride?, p206). It also offers a four-hour guided horseback tour to the La Fortuna waterfall (US$35), a two-hour 'forest and farm' ride (US$20) and it's possible to arrange multiday advanced rides.

KITESURFING & WINDSURFING

You're only a short drive from the premier spot in Costa Rica for wind sports – Laguna de Arenal (p252).

RAFTING & KAYAKING

Desafío Adventure Company (☎ 479 9464; www.desafiocostarica.com) is also recommended for its expertise in river running. White-water rafting and kayaking on the Ríos Toro, Peñas Blancas and Sarapiquí are convenient day trips from La Fortuna, and rapids ranging from Class I to Class IV cater to all skill levels. Depending on access and the difficulty of the rapids, trips cost between US$45 and US$100.

Courses

The **Adventure Education Center** (☎ 479 8390; www.adventurespanishschool.com; 1 week with/without homestay US$415/315) is an unusual Spanish school that includes outdoor healthy and safety courses as well as various guided hikes and adventures in the curriculum (most adventures cost a little extra). There's another campus in Turrialba.

Tours

The tour-operator business is exploding in La Fortuna, though its growth is not sustainable, and it's likely that there will be a shakedown in the near future. In the meantime, however, you need to be a smart consumer, so shop around, compare prices, and never buy a tour on the streets. If you rented a car, this is one region where having your own wheels can save you money and hassles.

There's usually a two-person minimum for any trip, and groups can work out discounts in advance with most outfitters. If you don't want to deal with the tour operators, most hotels can arrange trips for you, though you will probably be charged a US$5-per-person commission. It's also becoming standard practice in La Fortuna to sell tourists pricey tours to distant destinations such as Caño Negro. If you're turned off by the idea of public transportation, this is a fine option, though you'll save yourself a ton of money (and have a much better experience) if you actually go to these places on the local bus and then organize a tour upon arrival.

Most tourists are interested in taking the obligatory trip to Volcán Arenal, which is generally an afternoon excursion to either the national park or a private overlook to appreciate the mountain by day, combined with a trip to one of the hot springs and usually dinner. Then it's off to another overlook in the evening, where lucky souls will see some lava. Prices vary widely, but generally run US$25 to US$65 per person. Make sure your tour includes entry fees to the park and hot springs, which could easily add another US$25 to the total. Also remember that there's a better-than-even chance that Arenal will remain demurely wrapped in cloud cover for the duration of your trek, and there are no refunds if you can't see anything.

Most agencies in town can also arrange Jeep-Boat-Jeep transportation to Monteverde (see p207), which is the easiest, most scenic and recommended (if you have the cash) way to visit the cloud forests.

The tour operators listed below are recommended by travelers, though this list is by no means exhaustive.

Bobo Adventures (☎ 479 1952; tours US$40) Specializes in guided tours of the spectacular Venado Caves. It's 200m west of the park.

Eagle Tours (☎ 479 7080; www.eagletours.net; solarenal@racsa.co.cr) Budget travelers rave about this professionally run tour agency, which operates out of the recommended La Choza Inn (opposite).

Jacamar Tours (☎ 479 9767; www.arenaltours.com; jacamar@racsa.co.cr) Recommended for its incredible variety of naturalist hikes.

Puentes Colgantes de Arenal (p242) A recommended day trip as you can explore the rain-forest canopy through a series of suspended bridges and cement-blocked hiking trails. The booking office is located 300m east of the park.

Sunset Tours (☎ 479 9800; www.sunsettourcr.com; sunsettours@racsa.co.cr) Located at the Don Manuel Inn, this is La Fortuna's most established tour company, and is recommended for its high-quality tours with bilingual guides.

Festivals & Events

The big annual bash is **Fiestas de la Fortuna**, which is held in mid-February and features two weeks of Costa Rican–rules bullfights, colorful carnival rides, greasy carnival food, craft stands and unusual gambling devices. It's free, except for the beer (which is cheap) and you'll have a blast trying to decide between the temporary disco with go-go dancers getting down to reggaeton or the rough and wild tents next door with live ranchero and salsa.

Sleeping

La Fortuna is popular among foreign and domestic travelers alike, all eager for a glimpse of the famous erupting volcano. Try to make reservations in advance on weekends and during Costa Rican holidays.

The great thing about La Fortuna is the number of small, family-run places, usually a few simple rooms with electric showers and maybe a private bathroom, offering meals by arrangement and good conversation. Some aren't well signed, and you may hear about them through word of mouth. These places will help arrange local tours and are a good way to help locals cash in on the tourism boom. Hotel touts meet the buses and are a little more aggressive with their wares than in most of Costa Rica; not all are trustworthy (see the boxed text Scams, opposite).

Note that hotels west of town are listed separately.

The rates given are high-season rates, but low-season rates could be as much as 40% lower.

IN TOWN
Budget

Gringo Pete's (☎ 479 8521; gringopetes2003@yahoo .com; camping per person US$2, dm US$3, r per person with/without bathroom US$5/4; P) With a clean and cozy hostel vibe, it's hard to believe that this place, 100m south of the school, is so cheap! Whether you're in the comfy dorms sleeping four or your own private room, you'll flock to the breezy covered common areas, which are great spots to chat with other backpackers. Pete, from Washington State, can point you toward cut-rate tours and store your bags for you while you're on them. There's also a book exchange, and lockers in every room.

Sleep Inn Guesthouse (☎ 394 7033; carlossleepinn@ hotmail.com; r without bathroom per person US$5) If you're looking for a welcoming Tico family to stay with, you've found them – Cándida will invite you into her home, 250m west of MegaSuper, as if it were yours, and Carlos, whose nickname is Mr Lava Lava man, guarantees you'll see lava (or you get to go again for free), and his tours (US$25) are the cheapest in town.

Hotel Dorothy (☎ 479 8068; noelsamuelsdouglas@ hotmail.com; r per person downstairs/upstairs US$6/8; P 🖳) At 300m south of town next to the bullring, although it's a bit far from

SCAMS

If you're taking the bus to La Fortuna, they start before you even get there, boarding a few kilometers out of town, then working the crowd: 'That hotel is overpriced, but I have a friend…' You know this scam, right? But it gets worse.

In addition to steering travelers to poor hotels, which discredits reputable hoteliers who meet the bus because they can't afford flashy brochures and still charge US$5 per room, there's a family in La Fortuna who'll also book you on 'half-price tours.' Usually you'll just show up for your tour and learn that your receipt is invalid, though we've also heard about folks taken to pricey hot springs, then abandoned without transportation or their entry fees paid as promised. In a disturbing recent development, we've even heard of touts selling vouchers for phony tours in such far-flung locales as Monteverde and Caño Negro.

After milking a batch of tourists, family members trade off between La Fortuna, Monteverde and other hot spots for a couple of weeks; it's worked hassle-free for years. Why haven't the police done anything? That's a good question, but basically it comes down to the fact that no one wants to wait around for months to bring these folks to trial. Any police report you file will be for insurance purposes only – period.

It's worth going through a reputable agency or hotel to book your tours around here. You may pay twice as much, but at least you'll get to go. On the bright side, the recent upswing in tourism in the La Fortuna area has brought promises from the ICT that there will be a crackdown on touts, though remember that the government is in the business of making promises it can't keep. Don't believe us – just look at the state of the roads!

town and a little rough around the edges, this spot is highly recommended simply because Noel, the bilingual Limónese owner, is positively beaming with Caribbean warmth. Noel is also something of a local hero – upon noticing that the nearby bullring was on fire, Noel saved the day by alerting the fire department, and saving the scores of undocumented Nicaraguan workers that were being detained inside.

La Choza Inn (☎ 479 9007; solarenal@racsa.co.cr; Av Fort; dm US$7; r per person with/without air-con US$12/10; P ✗ 🖳) This popular budget inn 100m west of Parque Central has a great variety of rooms, a well-stocked communal kitchen, an extremely personable staff and it's consistently packed with discriminating travelers. The on-site location of the recommended Eagle Tours (opposite) is a huge bonus.

Hotel Las Colinas (☎ 479 9305; www.lascolinasarenal.com; Calle 1; r per person incl breakfast with/without bathroom US$15/10) Rooms with shared bathroom are old and underground, though the ones with private bathrooms are sunny and have private balconies (Nos 33 and 27 have volcano views). The owners are superfriendly.

Cabinas Adriana (☎ 479 9474; Av Arenal; r per person US$10) Rooms in this ageing pink wooden house 300m west of the supermarket have private hot-water bathrooms, though the

real draw is the friendly manager, Adriana, who will start your day right with a hot breakfast (US$2).

La Posada Inn (☎ 479 9793; Av Central; r per person US$10; P) The management is very welcoming, though the rooms at this inn across from the school with unpainted concrete walls and warmish showers are pretty dreary.

Don Manuel Inn (☎ 479 9585; donmanuelinn@racsa.co.cr; cnr Calle 2 & Av Central; r per person US$12; P) Southeast of the church, the three wood-paneled rooms here with air-con and hot-water bathrooms are a steal, and you're sleeping upstairs from one of the recommended tour operators in town, namely Sunset Tours (opposite).

Cabinas La Amistad (☎ 479 9364; Av Central; r per person US$15-25; ✗) Ask to see a few cabins as they all have varying combinations of kitchenette, air-con, balcony and/or cable TV.

Hotel La Fortuna (☎ 479 9197; cnr Calle 3 & Av Central; s/d incl breakfast US$16/26; 🖳) This recently renovated budget hotel is run by Lorena and Jose, a delightful Tico couple who work hard to offer professional service and a relaxed, mellow vibe.

Mayol Lodge (☎ 479 9110; Av Arenal; s/d US$16/32; P 🖳) Small but bright rooms here are centered on a cool, refreshing pool with volcano views. It's 200m southeast of Parque Central.

Cabinas El Bosque (☎ 479 9365; Calle 2; s/d US$20/25; P) Standard rooms with private hot-water bathrooms become something more whenever the helpful host Edwin is around. Just 100m west of Parque Central.

Cabinas Oriuma (☎ day 479 9111; cnr Calle 1 & Av Fort; s/d/tr US$20/30/40) You've never seen a bathroom sparkle quite like they do at this family-run place above the hardware store on the northeast corner of Parque Central. Orderly rooms with double bed and private hot shower should be reserved in advance on Sunday, when the hardware store is closed and they need to leave the key next door.

Cabinas Grijalba (☎ 479 9129; cnr Calle 4 & Av Central; d US$30; P ☒) Though the exterior isn't so inviting, rooms are surprisingly plush, and the tiled bathrooms are a nice touch, 150m west of Parque Central.

Midrange

All of the listed accommodations have private bathrooms with hot water.

Cabinas La Riviera (☎ 479 9048; Av Fort; camping per tent US$6, s/d/tr incl breakfast US$20/30/40; P ☒) A pretty 10-minute walk east from town, this recommended spot has nine basic, fan-cooled cabinas scattered around absolutely fantastic gardens, where fruit trees attract all manner of birds.

Cabinas Rodríguez (☎ 479 9843; Calle 1; s/d incl breakfast US$35/45; P) Frilly and fancy, this immaculate option has a lady's touch, obvious from the moment you see the bedspreads. It's 200m north of Banco Nacional.

Cabinas Las Tinajas (☎ 479 9308; Av Volcán; d US$40; P) Located on a quiet residential street 150m north of Banco Nacional, this homey option comes complete with rocking chairs on the front porch for all your 'rocking' needs.

Hotel Sierra Arenal (☎ 479 9751; Av Central; d bottom/top fl US$35/45; P ☒) Everything you're looking for is right here – hot showers, good mattresses, cable TV, private balconies and some of the best volcano views in town from 300m west of the church. The Tico owners are laid back and really helpful.

Hotel Monte Real (☎ 479 9357; Av Arenal; d US$35-60; P ☒ ☒) The paint is still gleaming at this newly constructed hotel 150m southeast of Parque Central, which is run by an attentive Tico couple named Francisco and Nury. Room prices vary depending on proximity to the inviting pool.

Hotel Tropical Paraíso (☎ 479 9222; Av Central; d US$45; P ☒) It's the small touches that make these rooms so special – wooden furniture, picture windows, an electric jug, a microwave and even your own phone. Find it 100m west of Parque Central.

Cabinas Guacamaya (☎ 479 9393; cnr Av Central & Calle 5; s/d/tr/q incl breakfast US$40/50/60/70; P ☒) Good-sized though spartan rooms seem a bit overpriced, though the garden patio with volcano views is mighty nice.

Hotel Arenal Jireh (☎ 479 9004; Av Central; s/d/tr US$45/60/75; P ☒ ☒) Modern comforts, volcano views and a central location come at a price at this place 150m west of Parque Central, though there are cheaper options.

Luigi's Lodge (☎ 479 9909; www.luigislodge.com; cnr Av Central & Calle 4; s/d incl breakfast US$48/60; P ☒ ☒) This is one of the most upscale options in town that caters mainly to moneyed travelers (to help lighten their pockets a bit, the management has constructed an on-site casino). Rooms here are modern and spacious, though the Italian restaurant, Pizzería Luigi's (p247), is more memorable.

Hotel San Bosco (☎ 479 9050; www.arenal-volcano .com; Av Volcán; s/d/tr US$50/55; P ☒ ☒) The most established hotel in town is certainly the priciest, though you're paying for such amenities as a pool, Jacuzzi and guarded parking lot. If you're traveling in a group, there are two furnished houses with kitchens that cost US$80 (maximum eight people) and US$100 (maximum 14 people).

Top End

Villas Josipek (☎ 430 5252; www.villasjosipek.com; s/d US$89/99; P ☒) Located about 8km south of La Fortuna in the village of Chachagua, these beautifully crafted wooden cabins with volcano views are surrounded by private rain forest trails that penetrate the Children's Eternal Rainforest. Groups can arrange meals in advance, served beside the substantial outdoor pool, and anyone can book horse-riding tours throughout the region.

Arenal Country Inn (☎ 479 9670; www.arenalcoun tryinn.com; d US$86; P ☒ ☒) About 1km south of town is this old cattle ranch that has been converted into an private inn. Rooms here are relatively simple affairs, though the beautiful property and the friendly, helpful staff make for a quiet and relaxing stay. Be sure to dine at the restaurant-bar, which is housed in a restored cattle corral.

THE AUTHOR'S CHOICE

Budget

Arenal Backpackers Resort (☎ 479 7000; www.arenalbackpackersresort.com/main.htm; camping US$6, dm US$10, d/tr/q US$50/66/80; P ⊠ 🖳 🛋) This self-proclaimed 'five-star hostel' 300m west of the church is the newest addition to the La Fortuna scene, and is among the top hostels in all of Costa Rica. Dorm rooms with private (steaming) hot-water bathrooms are kept comfortable and cool with state-of-the-art air-conditioners, and you'll sleep easy on the thick, orthopedic mattresses. Private rooms definitely cater to midrange travelers, though with flat-screen TVs and tiled-bathrooms, they're worth the splurge. However, the real draw is the landscaped pool where backpackers spend lazy days lounging with a cold beer, and there are even talks of building an on-site movie theater! Other amenities include unlimited Internet access (US$1) including wi-fi, a professional-quality shared kitchen, pool table, barbecue pit and a gated parking lot.

Midrange

Pura Vida Hotel (☎ 479 9495; s/d/tr US$25/35/50; P ⊠) If you want a hotel to be successful, just stick to the basics – hot showers with good pressure, real mattresses (not foam!), modern air-conditioning units, simple design schemes and an attentive maid service. Although Pura Vida is nothing too out of the ordinary, it's recommended for being reasonably priced, extremely comfortable and all-around pleasant. The Chinese family that owns the hotel also runs a restaurant (US$3 to US$10) downstairs that serves (you guessed it!) Chinese food. It's 300m west of the church.

Top End

Chachagua Rainforest Hotel (☎ 468 1010; www.chachaguarainforesthotel.com; s/d US$72/84, P ⊠ 🛋) This hotel is a naturalist's dream – located just 11km south of La Fortuna, the Chachagua Rainforest Hotel is situated on a private reserve that abuts the Bosque Eterno de Los Niños. Part of the property is a working orchard, cattle ranch and fish farm while the rest is humid rain forest that can be accessed either through a series of hiking trails or on horseback. Request the older, Frank Lloyd Wright–esque wooden cabins, which have indoor jungles and low windows for watching the birds. There is also an exquisitely landscaped pool with waterfall and two restaurants (meals US$8 to US$16) that feature local produce and meats.

From La Fortuna, head 8km south to the village of Chachagua where you'll see a sign pointing to the entrance. From here, it's another 3km on a dirt road that may require 4WD in the rainy season.

WEST OF TOWN

The road to Arenal is one of the most depressing stretches in the country. For kilometers on end, McResorts line both sides of the road, though Mother Nature is not without her sense of humor. Although these resorts once enjoyed the nightly fireworks of Arenal, the recent switch in the direction of the lava flow deprived them of their coveted views.

Although it's tempting to drive through this area as quickly as possible, there are a few recommended places to stay. Note that hotels are listed according to their distance from La Fortuna, and that they do not appear on the map.

Hotel Arenal Rossi (☎ 479 9023; www.hotelarenalrossi.com; d standard/deluxe US$42/47; P ⊠ 🛋)

This dude ranch–themed hotel 2km west of town complete with cowboy paraphernalia is an excellent value as rooms with two double beds, private hot showers, cable TV and refrigerators come with air-con for a few dollars more. Everyone gets to use the palm-shaded pool in the gardens, and there's a little playground for kids. The attached steakhouse (p247) serves up juicy, sizzling cuts of locally raised beef.

Cabinas Las Flores (☎ 479 9307; r per person incl breakfast US$15, camping per person US$5; P) This is a great budget option! Attractive, wood-paneled cabinas 2.5km west of town with hot-water bathrooms are pleasantly located on a quiet farm, which is a world away from La Fortuna. If you have a tent, feel free to pitch it here.

Hotel Vagabondo (☎ 479 9565; with/without air-con US$59/41; **P**) This continually expanding complex 2.5km west of town (it started out as a pizzeria, **right**) now has a disco bar, souvenir shops and a very laid-back hotel with tons of good vibes. Rooms with hot-water bathrooms are decorated with southwestern pastels and arranged around a flower-filled courtyard where you can stop and listen to the birds chirp.

Lomas del Volcán (☎ 479 9000; www.lomasdelvolcan.com; d incl breakfast US$75; **P** ☒) Although Lomas del Volcán is one of the original resorts lining this stretch of road, it's recommended because of its quiet location (you can hear monkeys in the trees) and stunning volcano views (especially when you're soaking in the outdoor hot tub). Comfy, hardwood cabins have private hot-water bathrooms with stained-glass accents, and there are plenty of opportunities for hiking through the surrounding primary forest. Find it 4km west of La Fortuna then 5km down a dirt road; follow the signs.

Hotel el Silencio del Campo (☎ 479 7056; s/d/tr incl breakfast US$108/120/132; **P** ☒) This recently constructed resort 5km west of town was built by the same owners as Eco-Termales and reflects the same understated elegance that makes their hot springs so memorable. Cabins here are luxurious without being showy, and have attractive tiling, plush bedding and soft lighting. Bonus: if you stay here, you get a discount at Eco-Termales.

Posada Colonial (☎ 460 5955; d breakfast US$145; **P**) For the time being, Canadian-owner Grant rents a fully furnished guesthouse 9km west of town complete with garage, sundeck and volcano vistas. However, at the time of writing, the foundation was just being laid for the Emily Grace Hotel, a four-story luxury hotel that Grant insists will be a future landmark on the road to Arenal.

Los Erupciones B&B (☎ 460 8000; 9km west of La Fortuna; d incl breakfast US$55; **P**) This small B&B is a refreshing sight after passing countless all-inclusive resorts on both sides of the road. Cabinas here are colored with vibrant paints and adorned with ornamental tiles and windows. And each one comes with its own private patio with chairs – perfect for relaxing while taking in the sights and sounds of the surrounding cattle farm.

Tabacón Resort (☎ 256 1500; www.tabacon.com; d incl breakfast US$175-290; **P** ☒ ☒ ☐ ☒) Well,

the best part of staying here (aside from obviously being rich) is that you have unlimited access to Tabacón Hot Springs, which is about 400m away (in the path of the eruption). But, you'll probably want to spend most of your time at the hot springs considering that the large, modern rooms here are completely uninspiring (surprisingly no one seems to care really). It's 13km west of La Fortuna.

Eating
BUDGET
Mi Casa (Calle 3; pastries US$1-2; ☺ 8am-5pm) This European-style café (with a splash of Tico charm) has a good variety of strong coffees and homemade pastries. It's 200m east of Parque Central.

Cafe, Cappuchino y Espresso (Av Fort; ice cream US$1-3; ☺ 8am-9pm Mon-Thu, to 11pm Fri-Sun) Your parkside spot for, well, coffee, cappuccino and espresso (and ice cream too!). North side of *parque*.

Java Jungle (Calle 1; mains US$1-4) In addition to supplying a serious java jolt, this place south of Hotel Las Colinas fries up a massive 'Huevos McGringo' breakfast sandwich that could raise the dead.

Soda La Parada (Av Central; mains US$1-5; ☺ 24hr) Across from the bus terminal, 50m south of the church, this place stays open serving great steak casados, decent pizza and a couple of bizarre Tico health drinks, *chan* (slimy) and *linaza* (good for indigestion), to after-hours revelers and folks waiting for their buses.

Lava Rocks Café (Av Central; mains US$2-5; ☺ 7:30am-10pm) Big breakfasts, hearty casados and fresh salads are all big draws at this cutesy café that's a popular hang-out spot for tourists.

El Vagabondo (☎ 479 9565; mains US$3-10) This laid-back pizza joint 3km west of La Fortuna, with mellow vibes and relaxing tunes, has been popular for years with backpackers.

Restaurante El Jardín (☎ 479 9360; cnr Av Central & Calle 3; mains US$2-7; ☺ 5am-1pm) You can either relax over a shrimp pizza in this bustling eatery 100m east of the *parque*, or grab a chair beneath the Pollo Pito Pito sign and snack on a few pieces of greasy (but delicious) fried chicken.

La Maquilla (Av Fort; mains US$3-4) This huge, open-air *soda* behind the church is more like a German beer garden, though the home-style food is as typical as it gets.

Chelas (☎ 479 9594; mains US$3-7) This popular, open-air spot next to Valle Cocodrilo has great *bocas* including *chicharrrones* (stewed pork) and *ceviche de pulpo* (raw octopus marinated in lemon juice). The bar stays open until 1am, so wash your meal down with a cold Imperial (or four).

Super Christian 2 (cnr Av Central & Calle 1; ☻ 7am-9pm) Located on the southeast corner of Parque Central, this place has the best selection of groceries.

MIDRANGE & TOP END

Restaurante Rancho La Cascada (☎ 479 9145; Av Fort; breakfast US$2-4; dinner US$4-15; ☻ 7-11am & 6pm-2am) This thatch-roofed landmark is probably a better bet for an evening beer or cocktail as dishes are pricey and unmemorable, though if you've got the cash, it's got an impressive list of imported wines.

Restaurant Las Nenes (☎ 479 9192; Calle 5; mains US$5-15; ☻ 10am-11pm) This classic La Fortuna establishment 200m east of Parque Central is adored by locals and tourists alike. If you're in the mood for fine dining, the seafood platters here can't be beat, and the *ceviche* (US$3) is as good as it gets.

Restaurante Arenas Steak House (☎ 479 9023; mains US$5-12; ☻ 6:30am-10pm) Go West! (for 3km) – this *sabanero*-themed steakhouse does *churrasco* (steak) just right.

Las Brasitas (☎ 479 9819; Av Central; mains US$5-15; ☻ 11am-11pm) Sometimes you just need some good Mexican food – nothing against Lizano sauce, but there's just no burn. Check out this breezy but elegant open-air spot 200m west of Parque Central with good fajitas (US$6) and something called a *choriqueso*, sort of like a sausage fondue. Hey, if you're going to have a heart attack, go happy.

Pizzería Luigi's (☎ 479 9909; cnr Av Central & Calle 4; breakfast US$5, dinner US$6-15; ☻ 7-9:30am & 11am-11pm) This spacious, Italian restaurant 200m west of Parque Central is formal enough to justify buttoning up your shirt and putting on a little lipstick (or at least washing your hair for once). The buffet breakfast is a popular option if you've got a long day of hiking ahead of you, though the pizzas, calzones and pastas are a better bet. The bar-casino stays open till 3am or so.

Restaurant Don Rufino (Av Central; mains US$7-15; ☻ 11am-10pm) The newest, gourmet-dining option in town is staffed by a former Four Seasons chef – the specialty here is continental cuisine with a splash of Tico flavors. It's 100m east of Parque Central.

Salta Mar (☎ 479 9879; Av Central; mains US$8-15; ☻ 11am-10pm) This romantic, open-air spot 300m west of Parque Central specializes in seafood, right down to the fishing nets strung up on all the walls.

Entertainment

Despite the tourist influx, La Fortuna unfortunately remains a cultural wasteland. Occasionally, offerings are advertised at Lunatíca (p238), though entertainment in the area tends to be more of the liquid kind, and is aimed more at locals looking to get hammered and hopefully score with a gringa.

Restaurante Rancho La Cascada (☎ 479 9145; Av Fort; ☻ 7-11am & 6pm-2am) The only real nightspot in La Fortuna, which serves as the town bar, and occasionally the town disco and town movie theatre.

Bar El Terruño (cnr Av Central & Calle 3) A basic local drunks' bar that serves somewhat-edible *bocas*.

Bar-Restaurant El Brete (☎ 479 9982; mains US$2-6; ☻ 11am-close) Just south of town on the road to San Ramón, this has ladies' nights and other specials on cheap beer.

Volcán Look (☎ 479 9690/1) Reportedly the biggest discotheque in Costa Rica outside of San José is 5km west of town, though it's virtually abandoned except on weekends and holidays.

El Vagabondo El Vagabondo (☎ 479 9565) Has a small disco bar that's popular with travelers and Ticos working in the tourist industry. It's 3km west of La Fortuna.

Getting There & Away

BUS

All buses currently stop at Parque Central, though a real bus terminal is currently in the works.

Keep an eye on your bags, particularly on the weekend San José run.

Ciudad Quesada (Auto-Transportes San José-San Carlos) US$1, one hour, departs 5am, 8am, 12:15pm and 3:30pm.

Monteverde US$2, six to eight hours, 8am (change at Tilarán at 12:30pm for Monteverde).

San José (Auto-Transportes San José-San Carlos) US$3, 4½ hours, 12:45pm & 2:45pm.

Tilarán (Auto-Transportes Tilarán) US$1.40, 3½ hours, 8am and 5:30pm.

THINK GREEN

The following lodges are recommended to anyone looking to put a little 'eco' back into this whole 'ecotourism' thing. All of these lodges are members of a collective known as Cultourica, which actively promotes sustainable tourism initiatives. Aside from being nice places to stay, they are good spots to inquire about volunteer opportunities in the area. At the time of writing, the lodges were involved in reforestation projects, recycling initiatives and reproductive health education. From La Fortuna, head 1.5km west and then make a left onto a dirt road when you see a small, faded Mariposario sign. The lodges are listed in order of their proximity to the highway.

Arenal Oasis Lodge (☎ 479 9526; aoasis@racsa.co.cr; s/d/tr/q US$30/40/50/60, all incl breakfast; **P** **☐**) The Rojas Bonilla family, which operates a sustainable farm, has recently built three adorable cabins, 800m south of the highway, which are equipped with hot water and bathtubs. There are a number of walking trails through the surrounding rain forest, though you'll spend most of your time marveling at the beautiful botanic garden. The family is warm and hospitable, and also great cooks!

Cerro Chato Lodge (☎ 479 9494; www.cerrochato.com; camping US$3, s/d US$23/32; **P**) This lodge is owned by Miguel Zamora, an avid naturalist who delights in leading tourists on nature tours. Rooms here are simple and sweet, with hot-water bathrooms and great views of the volcano. It's 1km south of the highway. Campers will love the solitude and security and everyone will want breakfast (US$2). Other meals can be arranged.

Albergue la Catarata (☎ 479 9522; www.cataratalodge.com; s/d/tr/q US$30/45/55/65; **P** **☐**) This lodge 1.5km south of the highway is managed by a local cooperative for sustainable tourism, and features a small *mariposario* and a medicinal plant garden. There are nine cabinas for rent, each with wooden, sloping ceilings and private hot-water bathrooms. There is also a small restaurant (US$4 to US$8) that serves local meats and vegetables, and the staff can arrange for guided nature walks and night tours.

HORSEBACK

Several companies also make the trip partially by horseback, including Desafío Adventure Company (p241). There are a few other options, one of which is not always recommended. See the boxed text, p206, for a full description of the trip.

JEEP-BOAT-JEEP

The fastest route between Monteverde–Santa Elena and La Fortuna is a jeep-boat-jeep combo (around US$30, three hours), which can be arranged through almost any hotel or tour operator in either town. A taxi from La Fortuna takes you to Laguna de Arenal, meeting a boat that crosses the lake, where a 4WD taxi on the other side continues to Monteverde. This is increasingly becoming the primary transportation between La Fortuna and Monteverde as it's incredibly scenic, reasonably priced and it'll save you half a day of rough travel.

Getting Around
BICYCLE

Some hotels rent bikes to their guests, though **Bike Arenal** (☎ 479 9454; www.bikearenal .com; Av Volcán; half-day US$6-12, full day US$9-18) has the best variety in town. It also offers guided bike tours. Note that cycling after dark is illegal in La Fortuna.

The classic mountain-bike trip to La Catarata is a fairly brutal, if nontechnical, 7km climb, although we've heard stories of hardy pack-a-day smokers who've made it (just barely). Another good trip is cycling the paved Laguna de Arenal loop, though you need to be prepared to change a flat tire or two as the road is in a truly terrible condition.

CAR

La Fortuna is easy to access by public transportation, but nearby attractions such as the hot springs, national park and Laguna de Arenal require a bit more of an effort without internal combustion. Luckily, you can rent cars at **Alamo** (☎ 479 9090; www.alamo costarica.com; cnr Av Central & Calle 2; ☾ 7:30am-6pm) or **Poas Rent-a-Car** (☎ 479 8418; www.carentals.com; Calle 2), 100m west of the church, for similar rates to those you will find in San José or in Liberia. Trust us – it's worth having your own wheels.

PARQUE NACIONAL VOLCÁN ARENAL

Arenal was just another dormant volcano surrounded by fertile farmland from about AD 1500 until July 29, 1968, when something snapped. Huge explosions triggered lava flows that destroyed three villages, killing about 80 people and 45,000 cattle. The surrounding area was evacuated and roads throughout the region were closed. Eventually, the lava subsided to a relatively predictable flow and life got back to normal. Sort of.

Although it occasionally quiets down for a few weeks or even months, Arenal has been producing menacing ash columns, massive explosions, and streamers of glowing molten rock almost daily since 1968. Miraculously, the volcano has retained its picture-perfect conical shape despite constant volcanic activity, though its slopes are now ashen instead of green.

The degree of activity varies from year to year and week to week – even day to day.

Sometimes it can be a spectacular display of flowing red-hot lava and incandescent rocks flying through the air; at other times the volcano subsides to a gentle glow. During the day, the lava isn't easy to see, but you might still see a great cloud of ash thrown up by a massive explosion. Between 1998 and 2000, the volcano was particularly active (which is when many of those spectacular photos you see in tourist brochures were taken), and while the lava of late hasn't been quite that photogenic, it's still an awe-inspiring show.

The best night-time views of the volcano are usually from its northern side, which you can appreciate by taking a night tour or by spending the night at either the Arenal Observatory Lodge or one of several accommodations in El Castillo. However, be aware that clouds can cover the volcano at any time, and on rainy days a tour can be a miserably cold affair – thank goodness for all those hot springs!

FEELIN' HOT, HOT HOT!

Volcanoes are formed over millennia as a result of the normal shifting processes of the earth's crust. For example, when oceanic crust slides against continental crust, the higher-density oceanic crust is pushed into a deep region of the earth known as the asthenosphere. This process, along with friction, melts the rocky crust to form magma, which rises through weak areas in the continental crust due to its comparatively light density. Magma tends to collect in a chamber below the Earth's crust until increasing pressure forces it upward through a vent and onto the surface as lava. Over time, lava deposits can form large, conical volcanoes with a circular crater at the apex from which magma can escape in the form of gas, lava and ejecta.

Although our understanding of volcanoes has greatly progressed in the past few decades, scientists are still unable to predict a volcanic eruption with certainty. However, it is possible to monitor three phenomena – seismicity, gas emissions and ground deformation – in order to predict the likelihood of a volcanic eruption. Seismicity refers to the ongoing seismic activity that tends to accompany active volcanoes. For example, most active volcanoes have continually recurring low-level seismic activity. Although patterns of activity are difficult to interpret, generally an increase in seismic activity (which often appears as a harmonic tremor) is a sign that an eruption is likely to occur.

Scientists also routinely monitor the composition of gas emissions as erupting magma undergoes a pressure decrease that can produce a large quantity of volcanic gases. For example, sulphur dioxide is one of the main components of volcanic gases, and an increasing airborne amount of this compound is another sign of an impending eruption. Finally, scientists routinely measure the tilt of slope and changes in the rate of swelling of active volcanoes. These measurements are indicators of ground deformation, which is caused by an increase in subterranean pressure due to large volumes of collecting magma.

Since Volcán Arenal is considered by scientists to be one of the 10 most active volcanoes in the entire world, comprehensive monitoring of the volcano occurs daily. Although there is constant activity and frequent eruptions, nothing has thus far rivaled the deadly 1968 eruption. In recent years, the lava flow switched directions to the southwest (much to the chagrin of hotel owners in La Fortuna), though scientists are currently predicting that the flow might reverse itself in years to come.

Orientation & Information

The **ranger station** (☎ 461 8499; admission to the park US$6; ☺ 8am-4pm) is on the western side of the volcano. Most people arrive as part of a group tour, but you can reach it independently. Drivers (who have at least a half-tank of gas!) can head west from La Fortuna for 15km, then turn left at the 'Parque Nacional' sign and take a 2km dirt road to the entrance. You can also take an 8am bus toward Tilarán (tell the driver to drop you off at the park) and catch the 2pm bus back to La Fortuna.

From the 'Parque Nacional' sign off the main road, a 2km dirt road leads to the ranger station, information center and parking lot. From here, trails lead 3.4km toward the volcano. Rangers will tell you how far you are allowed to go. At the time of writing, this area was not in a danger zone.

From the ranger station and information center, the road splits – head left unless you want to go back to the main highway or to the park headquarters. After heading right for about 5.5km, you'll come to another split in the road – left will bring you to Arenal Observatory Lodge (about 9km), right will bring you to the village of El Castillo (about 4km). Even in the dry season, this is most definitely 4WD country. A taxi to either the lodge or to El Castillo will run about US$20.

Sights & Activities

ARENAL OBSERVATORY LODGE

The **Arenal Observatory Lodge** (reservations ☎ 290 7011, lodge 692 2070; www.arenalobservatorylodge.com; day-use US$7; ℗) was built in 1987 as a private observatory for the University of Costa Rica. Scientists chose to construct the lodge on a macadamia-nut farm on the south side of Volcán Arenal due to its proximity to the volcano (only 2km away) and its relatively safe location on a ridge. Since its creation, volcanologists from all over the world, including researchers from the Smithsonian Institute in Washington, DC, have come to study the active volcano. Today, the majority of visitors are tourists, though scientists regularly visit the lodge, and a seismograph in the hotel continues to operate around the clock. The lodge is also the only place inside the park where you can legally bed down.

The lodge also offers massages (from US$60), guided hikes and all the usual tours at good prices. You can swim in the pool, wander around the macadamia nut farm

or investigate the pine forest that makes up about half of the 347-hectare site. You can also rent horses for US$8 per hour.

A tiny **museum** (admission free) on the old observation deck has a seismograph and some cool newspaper clippings.

WILDLIFE-WATCHING

Arenal was made a national park in 1995, and it is part of the Area de Conservación Arenal, which protects most of the Cordillera de Tilarán. This area is rugged and varied, and the biodiversity is high; roughly half the species of land-dwelling vertebrates (birds, mammals, reptiles, and amphibians) known in Costa Rica can be found here.

Birdlife is very rich in the park, and includes such specialties as trogons, rufous motmots, fruitcrows and lancebills. Commonly sighted mammals include howlers, white-faced capuchins and surprisingly tame coatis (please folks, don't feed the wild animals, see the boxed text Don't Feed the Monkeys! Dammit We're Serious!, p359).

HIKING

From the ranger station (which has trail maps available), you can hike the 1km circular **Sendero Los Heliconias**, which passes by the site of the 1968 lava flow (vegetation here is slowly sprouting back to life). A 1.5km-long path branches off this trail and leads to an overlook, though the view here is foreshortened (but the explosions sure do sound loud!).

The **Sendero Las Coladas** also branches off the Heliconias trail, and wraps around the volcano for 2km past the 1993 lava flow before connecting with the **Sendero Los Tucanes**. This trail extends for another 3km through the tropical rain forest at the base of the volcano. To return to the car-parking area, you will have to turn back, though you'll get good views of the summit on the way back since you're now at a better angle to view it.

From the park headquarters (not the ranger station), there is also the 1.2km **Sendero Los Miradores**, which leads you down to the shores of the lake, and provides a good angle for viewing the volcano.

Every once in a while, perhaps lulled into a sense of false security by a temporary pause in the activity, someone tries to climb to the crater and peer within it. This is very dangerous – climbers have been killed and maimed by explosions. The problem is not so much that the climber gets killed (that's a risk the foolhardy insist is their own decision) but rather that the lives of Costa Rican rescuers are placed at risk.

If you're not staying at the Arenal Observatory lodge, it's worth visiting as there are 6km of **trails** in total, and it's only US$7 to access. A handful of short hikes includes views of a nearby waterfall, while sturdy souls could check out recent lava flows (2½ hours), old lava flows (three hours), or the climb to Arenal's dormant partner, Volcán Chato, whose crater holds an 1100m-high lake only 3km southeast of Volcán Arenal (four hours). For the best night-time views, a guided hike is suggested. Maps and local English-speaking guides are available for these hikes. The lodge also has a 4.5km bike trail that winds through secondary forest, as well as a 1km sidewalk trail that is completely wheelchair-accessible.

Note that camping is not allowed inside the park, though people do camp (no facilities) off some of the unpaved roads west of the volcano by the shores of the lake.

Sleeping & Eating

Arenal Observatory Lodge (reservations ☎ 290 7011, lodge 692 2070; www.arenalobservatorylodge.com; s/d/tr/q La Casona US$56/72/92/107, standard r US$81/101/112/132, Smithsonian r US$110/137/147/158, White Hawk Villa 8 people US$425; [P] [X] [💻] [🏊]) Although most of the lava flows are on the southwest side of Arenal (the lodge is positioned to the west), the views of the eruptions are excellent, and the constant rumbling is enough to make you sleep a bit uneasy at night. The lodge has a variety of rooms spread throughout the property, five of which are wheelchair-accessible (along with the pool and several trails – this lodge hasn't slouched). Rates include a buffet breakfast and guided hike. La Casona is about 500m away in the original farmhouse. It now houses four rustic double rooms sharing two bathrooms; there are volcano views from the house porch. Standard rooms, adjacent to the main lodge, were originally designed for researchers but have been renovated to acceptably plush standards. Smithsonian rooms, accessible via a suspension bridge over a plunging ravine, are the best and have the best views. The White Hawk Villa, with a kitchen and several rooms, is perfect for groups.

The restaurant (lunch/dinner US$10/25), which has a good variety of international dishes, is decorated with jars of venomous snakes in formaldehyde.

EL CASTILLO

The tiny mountain village of El Castillo is a wonderful alternative to staying in La Fortuna – it's bucolic, untouristed and perfectly situated to watch the southwesterly lava flows. There are also some delightful accommodation options, a number of worthwhile sights and what promises to be the biggest achievement in ecotourism since the invention of safari vests.

The recently constructed **Arenal Rainforest Reserve** (☎ 479 9944; www.arenalreserve.com; all-access admission US$60) was just starting operations at the time of writing. The ecocenter features an aerial tram with dead-on view of the lava flows as well as a canopy tour, hanging bridges, expansive hiking trails and promises of more to come. For more information, visit the booking office in La Fortuna. The reserve is located on the main access road to El Castillo.

On the only road in town, you'll find two noteworthy ecological attractions. The **El Castillo-Arenal Butterfly Conservatory** (☎ 306 7390; www.arenalbutterfly.com; with/without guide US$10/8; 🕗 8am-5pm) is run by an American ex-pat named Glenn, whose conservation project far exceeds your normal butterfly garden. He is seeking to understand life cycles and hatching times for different species, and routinely works with students and volunteers to rigorously catalog every scrap of data. Here you'll find seven different gardens pertaining to each habitat as well as a ranarium, an insect museum, a medicinal herb garden, botanic garden trails and a river walk. Glen is also actively involved in local reforestation programs, and is always looking for a few good volunteers.

Next door is the Tico-run **Jardin Zoologico de Serpientes del Arenal** (☎ 692 2087; admission US$8; 🕗 8am-9pm), where local snake-handler Victor Hugo Quesada will introduce you to six species of frog, four species of turtle, 35 species of snake and a fair number of lizards and iguanas.

Sleeping & Eating

Hotel Linda Vista del Norte (☎ 380 0847; www.linda vistadelnorte.com; s/d/tr standard US$60/70/80, ste US$90/

NORTHWESTERN
COSTA RICA

100/110; (P)) The first accommodation you'll pass on the road into town is a honeymoon-worthy lodge consisting of 11 simple but smashing rooms that are perched high on a mountaintop (though only some of the rooms have volcano views). The real draw however is the restaurant-bar (mains US$10 to US$15), which is lined with picture windows and has spectacular views of the lava flows from Arenal.

Nido del Colibri (☎ 835 8711; www.hummingbird nestbb.com; r per person incl breakfast US$25; (P)) At the entrance to town, you'll see a small path that leads up the hill to one of our favorite B&Bs in all of Costa Rica. It is owned by Ellen, a former Pan Am stewardess and all-round world traveler who has finally found a small slice of paradise to call her own. Her quaint little home has two guest bedrooms with private hot showers and enough frilly pillows to make you miss home – but that's not even the best part! In her immaculately landscaped front garden, you can soak the night away in a huge outdoor Jacuzzi while watching the lava flow down Arenal. You can even arrange to have a massage (US$45) while watching the lava. A well-stocked kitchen is available for self-caterers. Ellen (who's also charming and full of grace) is active in the local schools, and is a good person to talk to about volunteering in the area.

Cabanitas El Castillo Dorado (☎ 383 7196; r per person US$17; (P)) If there isn't space at Ellen's try next door, which has simple cabins with private warm-water bathrooms and volcano views. The on-site restaurant (mains US$2 to US$6) is recommended for its fresh tilapia and, needless to say, volcano views.

Villa Volcan Suites (☎ 302 5568; villavolcan suites@yahoo.com; ste US$75; (P)) Glenn, who also owns the butterfly conservatory, rents out two suites in his luxurious guesthouse opposite the conservatory. Each suite has orthopedic pillows and mattresses, plush bedding, steamy showers, designer furniture and (yup, you guessed it!) volcano views.

Rancho Margot (☎ 302 7318) One of the most exciting ecotourism initiatives in Costa Rica right now is the construction of Rancho Margot, which is described by Juan, the Chilean owner, as 'a cross between a dude ranch and a kibbutz.' The aim of the 152-hectare ranch, which is located past El Castillo in Pueblo Nuevo, is to be entirely self-sufficient, and you only need to speak with Juan for a moment to grasp the beauty of his vision. Electricity will be produced by turbines, dairy cows will be raised for cheese and milk, orchards and organic gardens will be sown for produce, pigs and chickens will be raised for food, biodigestors will convert animal waste into energy to heat the thermal pools etc (the list goes on and on). And, as if this wasn't impressive enough, Juan also flexes his muscle in the local community, and has already paid off school debts, purchased shuttle buses and built an animal rescue center, veterinary hospital and a ranger station. Juan plans on catering to students, researchers, farmers, horticulturists, backpackers and high-end tourists alike, so make sure you stop by, and be sure to let us know what's going on.

LAGUNA DE ARENAL AREA

18km west of La Fortuna, you'll arrive at a 750m-long causeway across the dam that created Laguna de Arenal, an 88 sq km lake that is the largest in the country. Although a number of small towns were submerged during the lake's creation, the lake currently supplies valuable water to Guanacaste, and produces hydroelectricity for the region. High winds also produce power with the aid of huge, steel windmills, though wind- and kitesurfers frequently steal a breeze or two.

If you have your own car (or bicycle), this is one of the premier road trips in Costa Rica. The road is lined with odd and elegant businesses, many run by foreigners who have fallen in love with the place, and the scenic views of lakeside forests and Volcán Arenal are about as romantic as they come. Strong winds and high elevations give the lake a temperate feel, and you'll be forgiven if you suddenly imagine yourself in the English Lakes District or the Swiss countryside.

But (you already know what's coming), things are changing – quickly. Baby boomers, who are lured to the area by the cool climate and premier fishing, are buying up every spot of land with a 'For Sale' sign on it. The problem is that Costa Rican law does not require would-be-realtors to possess a valid real-estate license, and these days it seems like every idiot is looking to speculate in the hopes of turning a quick buck.

Costa Ricans are not happy about the impending loss of their lakeside paradise, and it doesn't seem likely that the construction boom is going to slow.

While most of the road is supposedly paved, repairs have been infrequent, and there are some huge potholes – don't expect to drive this stretch quickly. Buses run about every two hours, and hotel owners can tell you when to catch your ride. Also, if you're heading to Monteverde via the jeep-boat-jeep transfer, you're in for a beautiful ride.

Dam to Nuevo Arenal

This beautiful stretch of road is lined on both sides with cloud forest, and there are a number of fantastic accommodations strung along the way. They are described here in the order you will pass them, and distance are given from the dam.

AROUND THE DAM

The **Puentes Colgantes de Arenal** (Hanging Bridges of Arenal; ☎ 479 9686; www.hangingbridges.com; adult/senior/student US$20/15/10, child under 12 free, guided tour US$30; ☘ 8am-8pm), 50m west of the dam, are probably what you imagined the first time you heard the term 'canopy tour,' before realizing that those were mere carnival rides. Here, some 4km of trails and bridges span across canyons while silently lifting you up into the canopy. There are also 6am birding trips and guided 6pm night walks with volcano views.

This bridges are easily accessible by car and well signed, though most tourists arrive on a package tour from La Fortuna. The Tilarán bus can drop you off at the entrance, though it's a 3km climb from the bus stop.

Arenal Lodge (☎ 228 3189; www.arenallodge.com; s/d standard US$64/71, junior ste US$114/119, chalet US$117/125, extra person US$23) is 400m west of the dam, located at the top of a steep 2.5km, though the entire lodge is awash with views of Arenal and the surrounding cloud forest. Standard rooms are pretty standard, but junior suites are spacious, tiled and have wicker furniture, a big hot-water bathroom and a picture window or balcony with volcano views. Ten chalets sleep four and have kitchenettes and good views. The lodge also has a Jacuzzi, a billiards room, a sophisticated restaurant (mains US$6 to US$15), complimentary mountain bikes and private stables.

UNIÓN AREA

You can't miss **Hotel Los Heroes** (☎ 692 8012/3; www.hotellosheroes.com; d with/without balcony US$65/55, tr US$85, apt US$115, all incl breakfast; ☐ ☒), a slightly incongruous alpine chalet 14km west of the dam, complete with carved wooden balconies and Old World window shutters – and that's just on the outside. Large, immaculate rooms with wood paneling and private hot bathrooms are decorated in thickly hewn wood furniture that may get Swiss-Germans a little homesick, particularly when viewing paintings of tow-headed children in *Lederhosen* smooching innocently. There are also three apartments (each sleeps up to six) with full kitchen, huge bathroom and balcony overlooking the lake. Facilities include a Jacuzzi, swimming pool, a church complete with Swiss chimes and a restaurant (mains US$5 to US$12, open 7am to 3pm and 6pm to 8pm) that gets Swiss folks on the road too long to indulge in authentic *Zuercher Geschnetzelts* and fondues. Bonus: the owners have built a **miniature train** (US$10) that brings you up a hill to an underground station beneath the Rondorama Panoramic Restaurant (mains US$8 to US$15), a revolving restaurant (seriously!) that's reportedly one-of-a-kind in Mexico and Central America. There's also a **hiking trail** that leads to the restaurant and is great for wildlife-watching.

Toad Hall (☎ 692 8020; www.toadhall-gallery.com; mains US$3-8; ☘ 8am-5pm) is quite simply a great place to stop for coffee (espresso drinks or regular) and one of its heavenly macadamia chocolate brownies, Costa Rica's best! The restaurant, 16km west of the dam, overlooks the forest and serves a short, delicious and beautifully presented menu that tends toward California cuisine, with homemade focaccia, spectacular sandwiches and hot dishes, all made with organic veggies grown outside; don't skip the yummy fruit drinks. While there, you can browse the art gallery, which has a small but very high-quality collection of local and indigenous art and jewelry, as well as a bookstore (travel and wildlife guides in English) and the *pulpería*, where local farmers stop for sundries.

Just beyond Toad Hall, a dirt road to the right goes to the **Venado Caves**, which can be explored with guides.

Rates for the simply gorgeous two-person cottages – works of art, really – at **La Mansion**

Inn Arenal (☎ 692 8018; www.lamansionarenal.com; cottages incl breakfast US$175-550; P ⊠ ⚊) also include a champagne breakfast, fruit basket, welcome cocktail, canoe access and horse rides, all conspiring with the magnificent views to make this the most romantic inn in the region. The cottages feature huge split-level rooms with private terraces, lake views, high ceilings, Italianate painted walls, and arched, bathroom doors. There's also an ornamental garden featuring Chorotega pottery, an infinity swimming pool that appears to flow into the lake, a pool table, a formal restaurant (four-course dinner excluding wine US$35) and a cozy bar shaped like the bow of a ship. It's 17km west of the dam.

La Ceiba Tree Lodge (☎ 814 4004; www.ceibatree -lodge.com; d US$49; P) is a wacky, German-run retreat, 21km west of the dam, centered on a most impressive ceiba tree, and has five spacious, cross-ventilated rooms that are entered through Mayan-inspired carved doors and decorated with original paintings. The views of Lake Arenal along with the lush, tropical gardens make this mountaintop spot a tranquil retreat from whatever ails you. A small apartment (price negotiable) is available for rent.

ARENAL BOTANIC GARDENS & AROUND

About 25km west of the dam is a well-signed turnoff for the **Jardín Botánico Arenal** (☎ 694 4305; adult/child US$8/4; ⏰ 9am-5pm), a private reserve and living library of over 2000 tropical and subtropical plants. Self-guided tours (booklets are available in English, German and Spanish) lead visitors along an immaculate trail through primary rain forest that is frequented by countless species of birds and butterflies. There is also a small, on-site butterfly garden and *serpentario*. This is a great spot for families to take a breather and stretch their legs for a while.

Villa Decary B&B (☎ 694 4330, 383 3012; www.villa decary.com; s/d US$90/100, casita with kitchen US$145, additional person US$15, all incl breakfast) is an all-round winner with bright, spacious, well-furnished rooms, delicious full breakfasts and fantastic hosts. Five rooms have private hot showers, a queen and a double bed, bright Latin American bedspreads and artwork, and balconies with excellent views of the woodland immediately below and the lake just beyond. There are also three separate casitas with a kitchenette. Paths into the woods behind the house give good opportunities for birding and watching wildlife, and there's a good chance that howlers will wake you in the morning. Guests can borrow binoculars and a bird guide to identify what they see. Jeff, one of the US owners, has gotten the bird bug and can help out with identification. His partner, Bill, is a botanist specializing in palms (Decary was a French botanist who discovered a new species of palm). Credit cards accepted.

A few kilometers past Villa Decary on the left-hand side of the highway is **Nuevo Arenal** (camping per tent US$5), a small lakeside park with camp sites, cold showers and bathrooms.

Nuevo Arenal

The only good-sized town between La Fortuna and Tilarán is the small Tico settlement of Nuevo Arenal, which is located 29km west of the dam. In case you were wondering what happened to the old Arenal (no, it wasn't wiped out by the volcano, but good guess), it's about 27m below the surface of Lake Arenal. You see, in order to create a large enough reservoir for the dam, the Costa Rican government had to make certain, er, sacrifices, which ultimately resulted in the forced relocation of 3500 people. Today, the humble residents of Nuevo Arenal don't seem to be fazed by history, especially since they now own premium lakeside property.

Nuevo Arenal is something of a rest stop for travelers heading to Tilarán and points beyond, though it's certainly a pleasant (and cheap) place to spend the night. The town also has a gas station (finally!), a Banco Nacional, and a bus stop near the park.

SLEEPING & EATING

Cabinas Rodríguez (☎ 694 4237; r per person with bathroom US$6) Located near the soccer field, this is pretty much the cheapest place you're going to find in the whole Lake Arenal region. Rooms are clean though a bit dark, and guests can share the kitchenette.

Cabinas Catalina (☎ 819 6793; d US$20; P) Also near the soccer field is this budget option, which consists of sterile cabinas with concrete walls and warmish showers that aren't exactly welcoming, but they'll do in a pinch.

WORLD-CLASS WINDSURFING (AND KITESURFING TOO!)

Some of the world's most consistent winds blow across northwestern Costa Rica, and this consistency attracts windsurfers from all over the world. Laguna de Arenal is rated one of the three best windsurfing spots in the world, mainly because of the predictability of the winds. From December to April, the winds reliably provide great rides for board sailors who gather on the southwest corner of the lake for long days of fun on the water. Windsurfing is possible in other months, too, but avoid September and October, which are considered the worst.

Although there are plenty of fly-by-night operators, there are really only two places you should consider for all your surfing needs. The best company for windsurfing is **Tico Wind** (☎ 695 5387; www.ticowind.com; rentals incl lunch half/full day US$38/68), which sets up a camp on the western shores of the lake each year from December 1 to April 15. It has state-of-the-art boards and sails that are replaced every year. There are 50 sails to allow for differing wind conditions, experience, and people's weights, but it rents only 12 at a time so that surfers can pick and choose during the day as conditions change – a class act. Staff will arrange nearby hotel accommodations. Serious surfers book boards weeks ahead of time; newbies and those wishing to improve their skills can take lessons. Tico Wind also offers rentals and lessons through Ecoplaya Beach Resort (p234) on the Bahía Salinas, Costa Rica's second windsurfing destination.

Hotel Tilawa (p256) has emerged as a popular destination for windsurfers (and increasingly kitesurfers too), and has an excellent selection of sailboards for rent at comparable rates. Although some folks think that the high winds, waves, and world-class conditions are too much for a beginner to handle, the folks at Tilawa disagree. They run a reader-recommended windsurfing and kitesurfing **school** (half-/full day US$100/150), and if you don't enjoy your first day of lessons, which takes place on land using stationary boards, they'll refund your money. After the first day, lessons become more expensive (US$60 per hour) and cater to all skill levels – once you've learned the basics, self-motivated practice with short instructional periods is the best way to learn. If you're staying at the hotel, you can also take advantage of discount rates on rental equipment (half-/full day US$45/55).

It gets a little chilly on Laguna de Arenal, and rentals usually include wet suits, as well as harnesses and helmets (serious boarders bring their own for the best fit, just renting the board and sail). For a warm change, head down to Bahía Salinas on Costa Rica's far northwestern coast. Resorts here offer windsurfing year-round, and though the wind may not be quite as world-class as at Lake Arenal, it comes pretty close. The seasons are the same as for the lake.

Hotel Aurora Inn (☎ 694 4245; aurorainn@hotmail.com; s/d incl breakfast US$41/54; P ⚡) Located on the shoreline and next to the soccer field, this midrange option is a good choice as American ex-pat Tom has several well-furnished cabinas with private hot showers, cable TV and gorgeous views of the lake. The attached restaurant, Maverick's Restaurant and Saloon (mains US$4 to US$10), has a good reputation in town for steaks, ribs, chicken and seafood.

Bar y Restaurant Bambú (☎ 694 4048; mains US$2-4; ⏲ 6am-10pm) In addition to doing good casados and *gallos* (not to mention another round of beer on Friday night when there's live music), owner Randall has tourist information and can arrange tours including fishing trips, guided hikes and horse rides.

Tom's Pan (☎ 694 4547; mains US$1-6, d incl breakfast US$55; ⏲ 7am-4pm Mon-Sat; P) This small, German bakery is a famous rest stop for road-trippers heading to Tilarán. Its breads, strudels and cakes are all homemade and delicious, though heartier eaters will rave over the big German breakfasts, goulash with homemade noodles, and a deli stocking *Leiberkäs* and *Weisswurst*. Behind the restaurant, there is a cozy room for rent with huge windows and an outdoor Jacuzzi.

Nuevo Arenal to Tilarán

Continue west and around the lake from Nuevo Arenal, where the scenery gets even more spectacular just as the road gets progressively worse. Tilarán is the next 'big' city, with a reasonable selection of hotels and restaurants, plus roads and buses that can take you to Liberia, Monteverde or beyond.

NORTHWESTERN COSTA RICA

SLEEPING & EATING

Lake Arenal Hostel (☎ 694 4218; dm incl breakfast US$10; P ⊠) The newest accommodation on the lake is an old mansion situated in a jungle canyon next to the Río Coté, 1km west of Nuevo Arenal. The owner, Professor Will, spent a number of years teaching philosophy around the world, so he can not only answer questions, but also ask them too. Rooms share hot showers, and Will's a bit of a gourmand, so you can expect a delicious breakfast. Private rooms are available.

Chalet Nicholas (☎ 694 4041; www.chaletnicholas .com; s/d incl breakfast US$48/68; P ⊠) This attractive mountain chalet 2km west of Nuevo Arenal is owned by Catherine and John Nicholas, though their co-owners, five very playful Great Danes (don't be alarmed when they come bounding out to greet you), really know how to steal the show. Two downstairs rooms have private bathrooms while the upstairs loft has two linked bedrooms (for families or groups) and shares a downstairs bathroom. On clear days, all rooms have views of the volcano at the end of the lake. The owners enjoy natural history and have a living collection of dozens of orchids, which attract numerous species of birds. This place has many repeat guests.

Caballo Negro Restaurant (☎ 694 4515; mains US$3-10; ☺ 8am-8pm high season, to 5pm low season) The Caballo Negro (Black Horse) serves recommended vegetarian and European fare handcrafted by owner Monica, who speaks English and German (hence the excellent schnitzel). The cozy restaurant has forest and lake views, and you can look for iguanas, turtles and birds while you are dining. Also here is the fabulously quirky Lucky Bug Gallery, which features high-quality work from local and national artisans, not least of whom are Monica's teenage triplets Kathryn, Alexandra, and Sabrina. The artistry really is outstanding, and should you fall in love with a painting of a bug or something bigger, they can ship it for you. It's 3km west of Nuevo Arenal.

Lago Coter Ecolodge (☎ 440 6768; www.ecolodge costarica.com; d standard/cabin US$54/60; meals US$10; P ⊠) This environmentally friendly lodge caters mostly to visitors that come on a complete package including meals, rental equipment and guided naturalist hikes. Standard rooms with private hot showers are located in a handsome wood-and-stone lodge that has a large fireplace and a relaxation area with billiards, TV and a small library. There are also 14 larger cabins that have picture windows overlooking the lake. Go 5km west of Nuevo Arenal then turn 3km down an unpaved road.

Rock River Lodge (☎ 695 5644; www.rockriverlodge .com; d incl breakfast room/bungalow US$76/94; P) This outdoorsy lodge 9km west of Nuevo Arenal deals exclusively with Tico Wind (p255), and is a popular option for well-to-do windsurfers looking for a comfortable place to call home. Six rooms in a rustic wooden building have private hot showers and volcano views, while separate bungalows have excellent (if small) tiled tubs and private terraces. There is also a small spa, a restaurant (breakfast US$6, dinner US$12, no lunch) and a cozy bar with brilliant views and a warm fireplace. The staff can arrange a number of activities included reader-recommended mountain-bike tours (US$45).

Equus Bar-Restaurant (13km west of Nuevo Arenal; mains US$4-8; ☺ 11am-close) This lakeside spot is perennially popular among windsurfers looking to brag about their exploits over a cold Imperial. There's a good mix of Costa Rican and Western dishes, and on some nights there's live music here.

Mystica Resort (☎ 692 1001; mystica@racsa.co.cr; s/d incl breakfast US$60/70; P) This hillside retreat 1km after the Tierras Morenas turnoff also deals exclusively with Tico Wind (p255), and is another good midrange option. The resort has six comfortable, uniquely decorated rooms with hot showers and volcano views. Even if you're not staying here, it's worth stopping by to eat at the pizzeria (open 7:30am to 9:30pm, mains US$5 to US$10), which has a real wood-burning oven on the premises. The Essence, a yoga and meditation center, is located on the grounds for all your holistic-healing needs.

Hotel Tilawa (☎ 695 5050; www.hotel-tilawa.com; d US$68-98; P ⊠ ⊠ 🖵 ⊠) This hotel is something of a legend among windsurfers and kitesurfers, and whether you're semiprofessional or just starting out, you'll find a great community of surfers here. As for the rooms, well, they're definitely spacious and they cater to different budgets, though the theme (Grecian?!) takes a bit of getting used to – hey, at least it's consistent, straight down to the classical frescos. Tilawa also has the best collection of amenities on the lake including a skateboard park, pool, tennis courts and free bike rental.

TILARÁN

Located near the southwestern end of Laguna de Arenal, the small town of Tilarán has a prosperous air to it – probably because it has served as a regional ranching center long before there was a lake to speak of. Every year, this tradition is honored on the last weekend in April with a rodeo that's popular with Tico visitors, and on June 13 with a bullfight-filled fiesta that's dedicated to patron San Antonio.

Aside from getting a closer look at all those windmills (and soaking up the friendly Western feel), travelers stop here primarily to break up the trip between La Fortuna and Monteverde.

It's easy to check email while waiting for your bus at **Cybercafé Tilarán** (☎ 695 9010; per hr US$1.25; ☯ 9am-10pm Mon-Sat), which has computers with speedy connections, 25m west of the bus terminal.

Sleeping & Eating

All of the hotels listed following have private warm(ish) showers.

Hotel Tilarán (☎ 695 5043; s/d US$6/12) On the west side of Parque Central, this is an excellent budget choice as rooms with cable TV are clean and quiet (if you can get one facing the rear).

Hotel y Restaurant Mary (☎ 695 5479; s/d/tr US$10/15/20) Another good option as clean rooms feature linens your grandma would love. Plan on street noise in the parkside rooms, or just enjoy it from the balcony. The attached restaurant (mains US$3 to US$6; open 6am to midnight) has a mix of Tico and Chino favorites.

Hotel & Restaurante y Cafetería Guadalupe (☎ 695 5943; d US$20) Quiet upstairs rooms are arranged around a few nice common areas for rocking and reading. The downstairs cafeteria (mains US$2 to US$6, open 6am to 9pm Monday to Friday, 7am to 5pm Saturday) is consistently packed with hungry locals.

Hotel El Sueño (☎ 695 5347; s/d standard US$15/30, s/d with balcony US$20/35) Near the bus terminal, this beautiful hotel (in an ageing, baroque sort of way) has antique decorated rooms, but it's worth splurging for the balcony where you can bask in the faded glory. Downstairs is Restaurante El Parque (☎ 695 5425; mains US$3 to US$5; open 7am to 11pm) with a selection of *bocas* that discriminating barflies also appreciate.

La Carreta (☎ 695 6693; s/d US$30/55; ℗) The most established hotel in town is well accustomed to catering to tourists, so feel free to stop by if you're in the market for souvenirs or you need directions. Rooms are kept spotlessly clean, though the ones near the garden are more pleasant. Even if you're not staying here, grab lunch or dinner at the pizzeria (pizzas US$5 to US$8), which has a real wood-fired oven.

Cheap meals can be found in the *mercado*, beside the bus terminal, or pop into the **SuperCompro** (☯ 8am-8pm), just across from the park, for groceries.

Getting There & Away

Tilarán is usually reached by a 24km paved road from the Interamericana at Cañas. The route on to Santa Elena and Monteverde is unpaved and rough, though ordinary cars can get through with care in the dry season.

Buses arrive and depart from the terminal, half a block west of Parque Central. Be aware that Sunday-afternoon buses to San José may be sold out by Saturday. The route between Tilarán and San José goes via Cañas and the Interamericana, not the Arenal–La Fortuna–Ciudad Quesada route. Buses offer regular service to the following locations:

Cañas US$0.50, 45 minutes, departs 5am, 6:40am, 7:30am, 8am, 10am, 11:30am and 3:30pm.

Ciudad Quesada, via La Fortuna US$2.50, four hours, 7am and 12:30pm.

Nuevo Arenal US$0.75, 1¼ hours, 5am, 6am, 8am, 9am, 10am, 11am, 1pm, 2:30pm and 3:30pm.

Puntarenas US$2.50, two hours, 6am and 1pm.

San José (Auto-Transportes Tilarán) US$3.50, three hours, 4:45am, 7am, 9:30am, 2pm and 5pm.

Santa Elena US$1.75, three to four hours, 12:30pm.

NORTHWESTERN COSTA RICA

Península de Nicoya

The Nicoya Peninsula, a hook-shaped, beach-fringed and sun-drenched strip of land, has always figured prominently in the history of Costa Rica. Following the independence of Central America from Spain, the peninsula (along with Northwestern Costa Rica) comprised the bulk of Guanacaste, a province of the newly formed country of Nicaragua. However, on July 25, 1824, Guanacastecos voted to secede and join Costa Rica, creating yet another grievance between Nicas and Ticos (p235).

Today, the region still holds on to its dream of independence, and it's not uncommon to see the Guanacaste flag flying high (sometimes higher than the national one). However, like most Ticos, Guanacastecos are fierce adherents to the philosophy of *pura vida*, and their separatist plans usually play second fiddle to something much more important, namely enjoying a coastal sunset.

Much of the Nicoya Peninsula is the domain of the *sabanero*, Guanacaste's equivalent of the American cowboy. However, in true Tico fashion, *sabaneros* are peaceful and honorable, and most carry themselves with an air that will remind you as much of a samurai or knight as of a cowboy.

In the past, poor roads and slow ferries kept development in check, though the recently constructed Friendship Bridge and new international airport in Liberia have made the region easier to access than ever. Today, record numbers of foreigners are flocking to Nicoya, and the government's 'ambitious' Papagayo Project (p266) will ensure that they keep coming.

PENÍNSULA DE NICOYA

HIGHLIGHTS

- Following the well-trodden gringo trail from **Playa Tamarindo** (p274) to **Montezuma** (p307)

- Surfing killer waves at **Playas Avellana** and **Negra** (p281) and **Playa Grande** (p271)

- Sunbathing on the cool white sands of Costa Rica's most elegant beach, **Playa Sámara** (p295)

- Driving the coastal 'road' from **Playa Carillo** (p298) to **Mal País** (p313)

- Visiting Costa Rica's first wildlife park, **Reserva Natural Absoluta Cabo Blanco** (p315)

★ Playa Grande
★ Playa Tamarindo
★ Playa Avellana
★ Playa Negra

★ Playa Sámara
★ Playa Carillo

Montezuma
★
Mal País ★   Reserva Natural
★ Absoluta Cabo
Blanco

NORTHERN PENINSULA

Like most of Nicoya, the dry forests of the northern peninsula have been cut down over the generations and transformed into farms and pastureland. Lifestyles here have always revolved around the harvest and the herd, though today Ticos are adapting to a different cycle – the tourist season. Each year from December to April, when the snows falls on Europe and North America (which is coincidently when Guanacaste experiences its dry season), tourists descend en masse to soak up a little sun, catch a little surf and buy a little property.

Today, the northern peninsula is one of the most rapidly changing areas in Costa Rica. The Gulf of Papagayo is slowly earning its place on glossy leaflets in travel agencies throughout the world, while the coastline, which was once the domain of the leatherback turtle, is increasingly occupied by the leather handbag.

Highway 21 runs from Liberia southwards, with coastal access roads branching out from the small towns of Comunidad, Belén and Santa Cruz.

PLAYA DEL COCO

Thirty-seven kilometers west of Liberia and connected by good roads to San José, Playa del Coco is the most easily accessible of the peninsula's beaches. Its name is derived from the cocoa-colored sand that lies between its two rocky headlands, though it can appear a bit dirty at times, especially with the detritus of all the beachside bars. With nearby Tamarindo rapidly becoming the enclave of moneyed foreigners, Playa del Coco has emerged as a party destination for young Ticos on weekends, when the town has a beach-party atmosphere, though it's fairly quiet during the week.

Although most travelers either pass through quickly or skip El Coco in favor of beaches further south, the town is a growing scuba-diving center, and it's a convenient jumping off point for surfers heading to the celebrated Witch's Rock and Ollie's Point (see p227).

Information

The police station and post office are both on the southeast side of the plaza by the beach. The Banco Nacional, south of the center on the main road into town, exchanges US dollars and traveler's checks. The few people arriving at Playa del Coco by boat will find the *migración* office near the Banco Nacional.

Hospedaje Catarino (☎ 670 0156) Email access and English-language newspapers are available.

Internet Juice Bar (per hr US$2; ☺ 8am-9pm) Surf the Internet, get your laundry done (US$0.50 per kg), drink fresh juice (US$2) or rent a mountain bike (per day US$8).

Activities

DIVING & SNORKELING

All of the following agencies are thoroughly recommended.

Bill Beard's Diving Safaris (☎ 453 5004; www.bill beardcostarica.com) At the Villas Sol Hotel (p265) in Playa Hermosa, these folks have been scuba diving and snorkeling here since 1970.

Deep Blue Diving Adventures (☎ 670 1004; www .deepblue-diving.com) Inside the Hotel Coco Verde (p263), this is one of the cheaper outfitters in town.

El Ocotal Resort (☎ 670 0321; www.ocotalresort.com) In Playa Ocotal, this resort has a dive shop that can handle groups of up to 40 divers.

Rich Coast Diving (☎ 670 0176, in the USA and Canada 800-434 8464; www.richcoastdiving.com) On the main street, this American-owned dive shop has a trimaran for overnight diving trips.

SWIMMING

Travelers are generally dissatisfied with the quality of the beach at Playa del Coco, though it's just a 4km drive or walk along the paved road to Playa Ocotal (p267), which is clean, quiet and perfect for swimming and snorkeling.

SURFING

There is no surfing in Playa del Coco, but the town is a base for Costa Rica's most legendary surf destinations: Witch's Rock and Ollie's Point, which are inside Parque Nacional Santa Rosa. The best way to reach them is by boat, and boat operators *must* be licensed by Minae (Ministry of Environment and Energy) to enter the park.

Roca Bruja Surf Operation (☎ 381 9166; www.roca bruja.50g.com) is a local licensed operator. An eight-hour tour to both breaks is US$250 for five people. A number of surf shops in Tamarindo (p276) also offer trips to Santa Rosa.

PENÍNSULA DE NICOYA

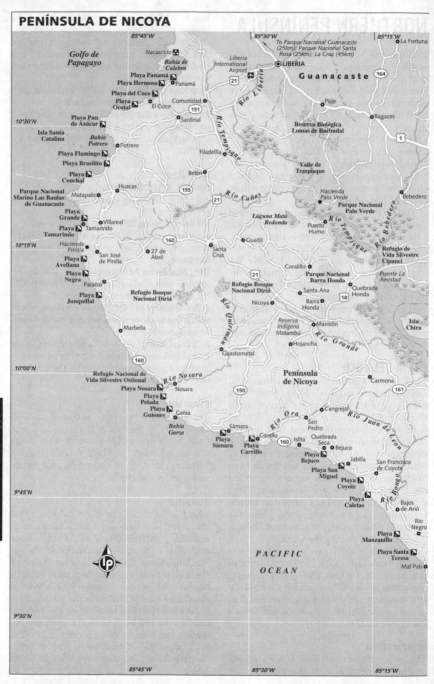

PENÍNSULA DE NICOYA

OTHER ACTIVITIES

Sportfishing, sailing and sea kayaking are other popular activities. Many places will rent sea kayaks, which are perfect for exploring the rocky headlands to the north and south of the beach as well as the nearby beaches.

Papagayo Marine Supply (☎ 670 0354; papagayo@ infoweb.co.cr) has bounteous information and supplies for anglers. Nearby, **R & R Tours** (☎ 670 0573) offers fishing charters and runs day trips to Parque Nacional Palo Verde (p216) for US$65.

Just outside Playa del Coco, **El Ocotal Resort** (☎ 670 0321; www.ocotalresort.com) offers fishing charters (it has six boats) and kayak rentals. Complete fishing packages are also available. In Playa Hermosa, **Hotel El Velero** (see p265) has a yacht and runs daily sunset cruises (minimum four people). Also in Hermosa, **Aqua Sport** (☎ 672 0050) has boats for fishing, water tours and snorkeling.

Festivals

In late January the town hosts a **Fiesta Cívica**, with bullfights, rodeos, dancing and plenty of drinking. But the biggest festival in El Coco is the **Fiesta de la Virgen del Mar**, celebrated in mid-July with a vivid religious-themed boat procession in the harbor and a horse pageant.

Sleeping
BUDGET

All lodgings listed below have cold-water showers and fans unless otherwise noted, and primarily cater to Tico weekenders. It's popular for Ticos to camp near the beach, though you need to be careful as things can get dodgy when the clubs let out.

Camping Chopin (☎ 391 5998; per person US$4; P) Camping isn't allowed on the beach, though this is the next best thing; bathroom facilities and water are available.

Cabinas Luna Tica (☎ 670 0127; r per person US$10; P) This budget hotel is right on the beach, though the rooms and shared bathrooms have seen better days, and you're definitely going to want to keep track of your stuff.

Cabinas Jivao (☎ 670 0431; r per person US$10; P) This is a solid choice as these homey cabinas are super-clean and in a quiet part of town. Each cabina has a private bathroom and also has a small outdoor deck with a table and hammocks.

PENÍNSULA DE NICOYA

DIVERS DO IT DEEPER

The northern area of the peninsula is one of the best and most easily accessible sites in the country for diving. There's no good beach diving in this area, so dives are made either around volcanic rock pinnacles near the coast, or from a boat further off at **Isla Santa Catalina** (about 20km to the southwest) or **Isla Murciélago** (40km to the northwest, near the tip of Península Santa Elena).

Diving here is not like diving the Caribbean – do not expect to see colorful hard coral on the scale of Belize. Conditions can be mediocre from a visibility standpoint (9m to 15m visibility, and sometimes up to 20m) but the sites make up for it in other ways: namely, their abundant marine life. The richness, variety and sheer number of marine animals is astonishing. This is the place to see large groupings of pelagics like manta rays, spotted eagle rays, sharks, whales, dolphins and turtles, as well as moray eels, starfish, crustaceans and huge schools of native tropical fish. Most of the dive sites are less than 25m deep, allowing three dives a day. Keep in mind however that since February 2006, it is now illegal to swim in close proximity with dolphins and whales.

The Papagayo winds blow from early December to late March and make the water choppy and cooler, cutting down on visibility, especially for the four days around the full moon. June and July are usually the best months for visibility.

Isla Santa Catalina and Isla Murciélago both boast a rich variety of marine life living and cruising around these rocky outcrops. Manta rays have been reported from December to late April and at other times you can expect to spot eagle rays, eels, Cortez angelfish, hogfish, parrot fish, starfish, clown shrimp and other bottom dwellers. The far point of Murciélago is known for its regular sightings of groups of bull sharks, which can be a terrifying sight if you're not an accustomed diver. Divers also head to **Narizones**, which is a good deep dive (about 27m), while **Punta Gorda** is an easy descent for inexperienced divers.

The good thing about scuba diving is that the sheer cost of starting and maintaining a dive center discourages fly-by-night operators from setting up shop. As a general rule, though, it's good to feel out a dive shop before paying for a trip – talk to the divemaster, inspect the equipment and make sure you're comfortable with everything before heading out (you should never feel pressured into diving!).

If you haven't been scuba diving before, consider taking a 'Discovery Course,' which costs about US$80 and will teach you all the basics. If you're interested in getting your Open Water Diver certification, which allows you to dive anywhere in the world, a three- to four-day course is about US$350. Compared to what these courses can cost in either North America or Europe, consider this price a bargain.

Hospedaje Catarino (☎ 670 0156; r per person US$10; P 🖳) Conveniently (or inconveniently) located near the discotheque, rooms here have a mix of shared and private bathrooms, though they're all pretty uninspiring.

Mar y Mar (☎ 670 1212; r per person US$12; P 🖳) Across the road from Luna Tica is this slightly more expensive hotel, though the US$2 doesn't get you a whole lot more in terms of quality.

MIDRANGE
Coco Palms Hotel (☎ 670 0367; hotelcocopalm@racsa .co.cr; d US$45-135; P 🐾) This low-key resort hotel has a variety of rooms and apartments for travelers of all budgets. The hallways are light and airy and have high ceilings but some of the cheaper interior rooms are

a little dark. There's an outdoor deck and pool for relaxing, and the small sushi bar (sushi US$5 to US$10) keeps guests happy and well fed.

Pato Loco Inn (☎ 670 0145; d US$45-80; P 🐾 🐾) If you're going to spend the night in Playa del Coco, do it here. This small inn is run by an American artist who spends his free time painting murals on the few remaining white walls. Each room has a design motif and range of amenities depending on your budget. The backyard surrounds an inviting pool, and the hanging lights on the trees are absolutely adorable. The small restaurant (dishes US$4 to US$8) specializes in fresh pastas.

Villa del Sol B&B (☎ 670 0085, in the USA 866-815 8902, in Canada 866-793 9523; www.villadelsol;

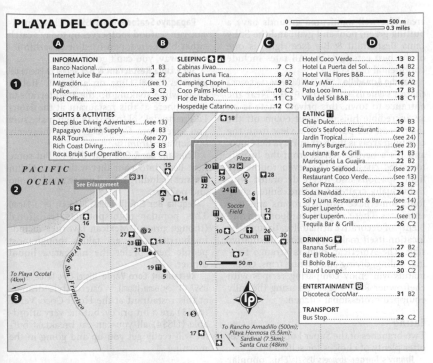

PLAYA DEL COCO

INFORMATION
Banco Nacional..................................1 B3
Internet Juice Bar.............................2 B2
Migración....................................(see 1)
Police..3 C2
Post Office..................................(see 3)

SIGHTS & ACTIVITIES
Deep Blue Diving Adventures.....(see 13)
Papagayo Marine Supply..................4 B3
R&R Tours.................................(see 27)
Rich Coast Diving..............................5 B3
Roca Bruja Surf Operation............6 C2

SLEEPING
Cabinas Jivao....................................7 C3
Cabinas Luna Tica............................8 A2
Camping Chopin................................9 B2
Coco Palms Hotel...........................10 C2
Flor de Itabo...................................11 C3
Hospedaje Catarino........................12 C2

Hotel Coco Verde.............................13 B2
Hotel La Puerta del Sol...................14 B2
Hotel Villa Flores B&B.....................15 B2
Mar y Mar...16 A2
Pato Loco Inn...................................17 B3
Villa del Sol B&B..............................18 C1

EATING
Chile Dulce......................................19 B3
Coco's Seafood Restaurant............20 B2
Jardín Tropical.............................(see 24)
Jimmy's Burger.............................(see 23)
Louisiana Bar & Grill.......................21 B3
Marisquería La Guajira....................22 B2
Papagayo Seafood......................(see 27)
Restaurant Coco Verde...............(see 13)
Señor Pizza......................................23 B2
Soda Navidad...................................24 C2
Sol y Luna Restaurant & Bar........(see 14)
Super Luperón.................................25 C2
Super Luperón..............................(see 1)
Tequila Bar & Grill..........................26 C2

DRINKING
Banana Surf.....................................27 B2
Bar El Roble.....................................28 C2
El Bohío Bar.....................................29 C2
Lizard Lounge..................................30 C2

ENTERTAINMENT
Discoteca CocoMar.........................31 B2

TRANSPORT
Bus Stop...32 C2

PACIFIC OCEAN

See Enlargement

Plaza

Soccer Field

Church

To Playa Ocotal (4km)

To Rancho Armadillo (500m);
Playa Hermosa (5.5km);
Sardinal (7.5km);
Santa Cruz (48km)

0 ————— 500 m
0 ————— 0.3 miles

0 ——— 50 m

---

d/ste US$60/75; **P** **X** **R**) This quiet French-Canadian–run place is 1km north of the main road and offers a good mix of well-furnished rooms and studio apartments. There are also six pricey villas that sleep up to 16, though these cater primarily to long-term renters. The hotel is about 100m from the beach, which is little visited at this end.

Hotel Villa Flores B&B (☎ 670 0787; www.hotel-villa-flores.com; d standard/deluxe incl breakfast US$75/85; **P** **X** **R**) An American-owned B&B, the Villa Flores has nine, brightly painted rooms with sparkling tiled floors and private bathrooms with modern fixtures. Upstairs quarters have nice terraces overlooking the palm-fringed pool, and larger deluxe units have cable TV. Credit cards accepted.

TOP END

In addition to the hotels listed here, see also the listings under Playa Ocotal (p267), 4km to the south, and Playa Hermosa (p265), 7km to the north.

Hotel Coco Verde (☎ 670 0494/544; www.bestwestern.com; s/d/tr incl breakfast US$75/95/105; **P** **X** **R**) This overpriced hotel primarily caters to

high-end tourists, most of whom are here on pricey package holidays. The name of the game is fishing and diving trips, though guests seem happy enough spending their free time in the casino. People, Costa Rica is right there if you just venture out a bit and open your eyes.

Flor de Itabo (☎ 670 0438; www.flordeitabo.com; d bungalows US$45; r standard/deluxe US$70/90, apt US$120-140; **P** **X** **R**) If you're into sportfishing this is your spot, as the owners have a reputation for catching big game and can organize expeditions throughout Nicoya and the Pacific coast. Standard units sleep two and have air-con, cable TV, phone, minifridge and coffee maker, while deluxe units also have whirlpool tubs and accommodate four. Apartments sleep four or six and have full kitchens. There's a restaurant serving Italian-international food, a casino and a bar.

Hotel La Puerta del Sol (☎ 670 0195; s/d/tr/ste US$60/80/100/110; **P** **X** **R**) A five-minute walk from town, this stunning, Mediterranean-inspired hotel has eight pastel-colored rooms, each with its own spacious sitting

PENINSULA DE NICOYA

area. The well-manicured grounds have a putting green, pool and gym, and the Sol y Luna Restaurant & Bar (see right) is one of the best eats in town. All rates include continental breakfast.

Rancho Armadillo (☎ 670 0108; www.ranchoarmadillo.com; s/d/ste US$111/122/171; ℗ ☒) Near the entrance to town, this private estate is on an incredible hillside about 600m off the main road (all paved). The view from the common areas is the best in Playa del Coco, and it's a perfect retreat from the heavily touristed coastline. The seven rooms are light, spacious and nicely decorated with individually crafted furniture. Suites sleep four; some have two bathrooms and two entrances. There's a pool, outdoor gym and plenty of decorative armadillos, though the location itself makes a relaxing, meditative stay. The American owners arrange fishing, sailing, diving and surfing trips. Gourmands will enjoy comparing recipes with chef/owner Rick Vogel and using the fully equipped professional kitchen.

Eating

Two branches of the Super Luperón market offer plenty of choices for self-caterers.

Jimmy's Burger (burgers US$2) This popular institution has gut-filling cheeseburgers – perfect when you've been hitting the Guaro Cacique a little too hard.

Soda Navidad (meals US$2-4) On the west end of the soccer field, this popular local spot is your best bet for cheap, filling casados.

Jardín Tropical (meals US$3-6) Also on the soccer field, this slightly more sophisticated *soda* (basic eatery) has a wider selection of menu items including filling pizzas and freshly caught fish.

Coco's Seafood Restaurant (meals US$3-6) This is a good choice for fish casados and *ceviche* – everything here is cheap, filling and oh-so-fresh.

Chile Dulce (sandwiches US$4-5, mains US$8; ☒ 12:30-10:30pm) Whips up well-reviewed and highly inventive sandwiches, natural energy shakes, veggie specials and seafood courses. (Try the dorado in citrus-spiced coconut milk.)

Señor Pizza (pizzas US$4-6) Here you'll find small pies and nachos, and it's open until 11:30pm for all your late-night, drunken munchies.

Marisquería La Guajira (dishes US$5-8) The beach setting is almost as good as the shellfish chowder and pan-seared mahi-mahi.

Papagayo Seafood (plates US$5-9) This American-run seafood spot serves up today's catch either blackened, pan-fried or as sashimi – either way, you can't go wrong.

Sol y Luna Restaurant & Bar (Hotel La Puerto del Sol; dishes US$6-8) Dine on authentic Italian pasta while soaking up the Mediterranean atmosphere at this restaurant at the Hotel La Puerto del Sol (p263), though make sure you save room for a slice of the heavenly homemade *tiramisu*.

Louisiana Bar & Grill (plates US$6-10) Put some heat back into your diet with spicy Cajun classics including jambalaya, seafood gumbo and po'boys.

Tequila Bar & Grill (dishes US$6-11; ☒ 5-11pm) This popular nightspot has traditional (though pricey) Mexican favorites including burritos, tacos and fajitas, though most people here prefer the margarita liquid dinner.

Restaurant Coco Verde (Hotel Coco Verde; steaks US$7-14; ☒ 6am-10pm) Western-style dinners at this restaurant at the Hotel Coco Verde (p263) are a bit pricey, but the very affordable (US$4) all-you-can-eat breakfast buffet will really get you up and going in the morning.

Drinking

Playa del Coco has a strong following of Ticos looking to get toasted, so follow the crowds to see what's hip and hot at any moment. If you're looking for entertainment that doesn't involve drinking, you've obviously gone to the wrong town.

The restaurants surrounding the plaza double as bars, with El Bohío Bar earning the reputation as long-standing favorite. The open-air Bar El Roble is preferred by heavy drinks, while the Lizard Lounge attracts a livelier crowd of dancers. One of the top places for liver damage is Banana Surf, serving perennial favorites such as Jaegermeister and Red Bull. Tequila Bar & Grill (see above) is the spot for slamming a few pitchers of margaritas.

Boogie 'til the break of dawn at Discoteca CocoMar on the beach, which is the biggest (and sweatiest) dance-fest around.

Getting There & Away

All buses arrive and depart from the main stop on the plaza, across from the police station.

Filadelfia, for connection to Santa Cruz US$0.75, 45 minutes, depart at 11:30am and 4:30pm.
Liberia US$0.75, one hour, depart at 5:30am, 7am, 9am, 11am, 1pm, 3pm, 5pm and 6pm.
San José (Pullmitan) US$5.25, five hours, depart at 4am, 8am and 2pm.

A taxi from Liberia to Playa del Coco costs US$15. Taxis between Playa del Coco and Playa Hermosa or Ocotal cost between US$5 and US$7.

Note that there's no gas station in town; the nearest one is in Sardinal, about 9km inland from Playa del Coco.

PLAYA HERMOSA

If you're looking for the legendary surf beach, see p339. For those of you still with us, Playa Hermosa is a gently curving and tranquil grey-sand beach that stretches for about 2km. Although it's only 7km (by road) north of Playa del Coco, Hermosa is much less developed than Coco, though you should enjoy the peace and tranquility right now as this area is about to boom. With the Papagayo Project (p266) slowly transforming the coastline to the north, the development craze is spreading like wildfire and the hills above Hermosa are already full of signs advertising condo complexes with such ridiculous names as 'El Oasis,' 'Crystal Court' and (are you ready for it?) 'Graceland.'

From the main road, there is a southern and northern access road leading to the beach.

Sleeping

If you want to do things the Tico way, there is free camping under a few shady spots near the main beach, though don't expect any facilities.

Hotel Playa Hermosa (☎ 672 0046; s/d US$40/60, s/d with air-con US$55/75; P ✗) Right on the southern end of the beach (via the first entrance road), this hotel was being completely renovated from the ground up at the time of writing. The location is perfect as there is less development on the southern access road.

On the second (or northern) entrance to the beach, you'll find several other lodging options.

Iguana Inn (☎ 672 0065; d US$24; ☟) Set 100m back from the beach, this rambling bi-level

terracotta inn has 10 simple, slightly beat-up rooms with private bathroom, though the price is definitely right. The Tico owners are also super laid-back, which makes for a relaxing, worry-free stay.

Cabinas La Casona (☎ 672 0025; d US$36; P) Another good budget option, the seven cutesy cabinas with whitewashed rooms, small kitchenettes, minifridges and private hot-water bathrooms are ideal for self-caterers, and they're just steps from the beach.

Hotel El Velero (☎ 672 0036/16, 672 1017; www.costa ricahotel.net; d US$64; P ✗ ☟) Also just steps from the beach, this resort hotel has 22 spacious and fully equipped rooms decorated with woodwork and colorful spreads. The complex features a pool, patio lounge and American-style restaurant and bar, though the real draw is the owner's incredible yacht. Guests are invited on a number of cruises through the crystal-blue waters of the Bahía Culebra, including daily sunset cruises (minimum four people).

Villas Sol Hotel (☎ 257 0607; www.villassoltc.com; d US$150, villas US$280-360; P ✗ ☟) If you've got the cash, you really can't do much better than this spectacular hill-side resort (though wait a few years and there'll be plenty to choose from). Standard rooms are equipped with everything you'd want, and the views of the gulf are breathtaking. The villas are definitely a lot pricier, but they have three bedrooms, a kitchen and there's the option of a private pool, so gather a few of your rich friends and live it up. There are also tennis courts, a restaurant and a bar. The owners can arrange all types of activities. Bill Beard's Diving Safaris (p259) is based here. Credit cards accepted.

Eating & Drinking

Whether you're just passing through Playa Hermosa or spending the night, there are some great spots to eat here. Food and other basic supplies are available at Mini Super Cenizaro, on the paved road into town.

Restaurant Pescado Loco (☎ 672 0017; dishes US$5-14) The 'Crazy Fish' serves up some of the freshest seafood around, including Costa Rican standards like red snapper and *ceviche*, though we got excited about the *pulpo de gallego* (Galecian octopus). The restaurant is between the first and second entrances to Playa Hermosa.

Ginger (☎ 672 0041; dishes US$15-20) If you're driving north, look to the hills on the right and you'll see this stunner of an open-air restaurant (it was designed by the famous Costa Rican architect Victor Cañas). Chic ambience (that would probably be more at home in NYC) is complimented by a gourmet list of Asian and Mediterranean-inspired tapas.

Monkey Bar (☺ 5pm-midnight Mon-Sat, noon-midnight Sun) For all your liquid needs visit this huge tree house between the first and second entrances to Playa Hermosa, where you can sip a sundowner to the tune of howlers bleating overhead.

Getting There & Away

There is a daily bus from San José, but you can always take a bus to Liberia and switch there for more frequent buses to Playa Hermosa. A taxi from Liberia costs about US$15, and a taxi from Coco costs about US$5. If you're driving from Liberia, take the signed turnoff to Playa del Coco. The entire road is paved.

Buses to Liberia and San José depart from the main road on the northern end of the beach and make a stop in Sardinal.

Liberia US$0.75, 1¼ hours, depart at 5am, 6am, 10am, 4pm and 5pm.

San José (Empresa Esquivel) US$5, five hours, departs at 5am.

PLAYA PANAMÁ & THE PAPAGAYO PROJECT

If anyone reading this right now thinks that Costa Rica is a virtual eco-paradise where environmental conservation always takes precedence over capitalist gains, put your reading glasses on and educate yourself about Costa Rica's darker side.

In the mid-1970s the Costa Rican Tourism Board, known as the ICT (whose slogan, in case you're curious, is 'No Artificial Ingredients'), hatched a long-term development plan for Gulf of Papagayo, particularly focusing on the Nacascolo Peninsula, a tiny strip of land that juts out into the Bahía de Culebra. The 'harmless' idea was to use Costa Rica's image as a happy, sloth-hugging tropical wonderland to lure package tourists away from traditional resort destinations like Cancún. With a high record of safety and a targeted PR campaign of well-tanned European models frolicking

on white sands, government bigwigs patted themselves on the back and waited for the dollars to roll in.

The project took off during the administration of President Rafael Calderón, who adamantly backed the development proposal. Soon after, the Grupo Papagayo conglomerate was formed, headed by Mexico's Grupo Situr (which was reportedly investing US$2.5 billion in the project). Although no environmental impact studies were done, the group unveiled plans to raze most of the peninsula's *dry* tropical forest to make way for 20,000 hotel rooms, two golf courses, a marina, racetrack, athletic center and (of course) condos. Developers, in their infinite wisdom, never stopped to consider the availability of fresh drinking water, let alone the pre-Columbian archaeological sites that dotted the peninsula.

However, when an independent commission appointed by Calderón expressed concerns that the Papagayo Project was, to put it bluntly, an environmental disaster, *it* really hit the fan. The tourism minister was indicted on charges of corruption, and all of the ICT was embroiled in scandal (it didn't help much that bulldozers were occasionally digging up pre-Columbian sites). In a quick scramble, Calderón seized control of the entire peninsula, while Grupo Papagayo put on a fresh coat of PR paint by changing its name to Ecodesarrollo Papagayo (Papagayo Eco-development). Very cute. For a quick lesson in what it *actually* means to be 'eco,' see the boxed text How to Know if a Business is Really Eco Friendly, p350.

Fortunately, the company went bankrupt, and development stalled until a group of North American investors seized the straggled remains of the project in 1999. In 2004 the Four Seasons Resort opened up for business, and has the dubious distinction of being the most expensive hotel in the country. Currently, there are a number of high-end resorts popping up along the bay, and it looks like interest is starting to peak again. The resort mania has already spread south to Playa Panamá, and it's just a matter of time before it reaches Hermosa and points beyond.

It's worth noting that some locals appreciate the extra jobs, though adding umbrellas to fancy blended drinks isn't exactly the most coveted of professions. However, the most upsetting development to Ticos is being told that they're not permitted to camp on the dark sand beaches that line the front of the Four Seasons and other resorts to come. Since there are no camping facilities on these beaches, it is unclear whether the letter of the law allows it. The ICT claims that camping isn't allowed, while local and environmental groups argue otherwise. In the end, however, the courts will determine who has the law (or more money) on their side.

To access the Nacascolo Peninsula, turn north at Comunidad and follow the highway until the end (though don't expect to just turn up and say hi – security here makes US Customs seem lax). To reach Playa Panamá, just follow the road for 1km past Playa Hermosa.

Sleeping & Eating
NACASCOLO PENINSULA
There are currently a few all-inclusives on the Nacascolo Peninsula (ranging from US$250 to US$1300 per night), though simply ringing the doorbell and asking to see a room is not recommended. For more information, visit a travel agent as we're certainly not going to list them all here.

PLAYA PANAMÁ
The all-inclusives have spread south to Playa Panamá, though there are plenty of cheaper accommodations 1km south in Playa Hermosa (p265).

Most Ticos prefer to camp for free on the beach (while they can), though if you'd prefer to have a shower and a toilet then pitch a tent (US$4) at **Bar y Restaurante Guanacaste** (☎ 672 0295), which also serves burgers, fries and other fast-food favorites for around US$1 to US$3.

PLAYA OCOTAL
This small but attractive grey-sand beach with tidal pools on both ends is 4km southwest of Playa del Coco by paved road. Aside from a few privately owned villas (which are mostly rented as vacation houses), there isn't an actual town here, though it's close enough to Coco that you can either drive or take a leisurely stroll here along the road. Although it's a fairly quiet beach, Ocotal can get mobbed on weekends by Ticos looking to escape the Coco scene.

Sleeping & Eating
Villa Casa Blanca (☎ 670 0518/448; www.costa-rica-hotels-travel.com; d standard/honeymoon/condo incl breakfast US$95/125/145, additional person US$10; **P** 🕱 🕿) Between Playa del Coco and Ocotal, this attractive villa is perched on a pleasant hilltop just a few minutes' walk from the beach. The 10 rooms here are beautifully decorated with either Victorian motifs or more modern accents. Three honeymoon suites are larger and feature a step-up bathtub and ocean views. Two fully equipped condos with kitchens are available. The pool is crossed by a garden bridge and has a swim-up bar.

Ocotal Inn B&B (☎ 670 0835; www.ocotalinn.com; d incl breakfast US$55; **P** 🕱 🕿) This is a great option, especially if you want to enjoy the Playa del Coco scene without actually having to stay in the town. Comfortable rooms with air-con and hot water are arranged around a well-landscaped pool, and there's even a hammock loft where you can swing, sun and love life.

Father Rooster Restaurant (dishes US$5-10; 🕙 11am-11pm) Apart from eating at Playa del Coco, try the beachside Father Rooster, which is inexpensive and has a good variety of grilled dishes, including fish, snacks and burgers. The staff makes a good margarita and a killer frozen cocktail which they call the 'kamikaze.'

BEACHES SOUTH OF PLAYA OCOTAL
Although they're next to one another, Playas **Azucar**, **Potrero**, **Flamingo**, **Brasilito** and **Conchal** have relatively nothing in common except for their proximity. The beaches range in color from grey to white to crushed seashells, while development ranges from years away to way past its expiration date.

Although it's tempting to take the 'road' from Sardinal to Potrero, there's a reason why locals call this route the 'monkey trail.' Although the first 9km of dirt road leading to the small town of Arola isn't so bad, the second half is pretty brutal, and should only be tackled if you have a 4WD (and after you've talked to a few locals).

If you want to avoid the rough roads, return to the main peninsular highway then head south through Filadelfia and on to Belén (a distance of 18km), from where a paved road heads 25km west to Huacas (where there is a gas station). Then take the

PENINSULA DE NICOYA

road leading north until you hit the ocean at the village of Brasilito. Turn right and head north and you'll pass Playa Flamingo and Bahía Potrero before reaching Playa Pan de Azucár. If you make a left instead and head south, you will end up at Playa Conchal.

Buses from San José, Liberia or Santa Cruz can also get you to most of the beaches. If you're into sea kayaking, the proximity of the beaches to one another makes for some great day trips.

In the small village of Arola you can take the **Congo Trail Canopy Tour** (☎ 666 4422; US$35), which is a fitting consolation prize if you're looking for adventure *sans* broken axles.

Playa Brasilito

Somehow, Brasilito managed to avoid the overdevelopment that's plagued much of northern Nicoya. One possible reason is that the grey-sand beach here is not nearly as pretty as nearby strips of white sand, and the lack of resorts and big hotels give the town a laid-back atmosphere. Playa Brasil-ito is popular with weekending Ticos and travelers 'in the know,' who are drawn here for the relaxed beach scene, pleasant swim-ming, cheap accommodations and spectac-ular Pacific sunsets.

Brasilito Excursiones (☎ 654 4237; www.brasilito .com), which operates out of Hotel Brasilito (right), can book two-hour guided horse-back rides (US$25), sunset sails (US$60) and two-tank dives ($75).

Internet is available (US$2 per hour) at Rancho Nany (right).

SLEEPING

The town of Brasilito consists of a few small stores and *sodas* as well as some great budget and midrange accommodations.

Cabinas Ojos Azules (☎ 654 4346; r downstairs per person US$5, d upstairs US$35; P ☘) The best budget option in town is a somewhat ram-shackle collection of rooms featuring big, comfy beds complete with saucy mirrored headboards. Fancy doubles are upstairs and simpler downstairs quarters fit up to eight people. All units have private bathrooms with hot water. It's 200m south of the plaza.

Brasilito Lodge (☎ 654 4452; www.brasilito-conchal .com; camping adult/child under 6 US$3/free, r per person US$9; P) This German-run lodge is also a great budget option. Rooms here are sim-ple but comfortable with private hot-water

showers and kitchenettes, and they're just steps from the beach. If you're camping, the sites are well maintained and very shady.

Hotel Brasilito (☎ 654 4237; www.brasilito.com; d/ tr/q US$30/35/40, d/q with view US$40/50; P) On the beach side of the plaza, this recommended hotel is the perfect place to slow down and chill out for a few days. The rooms are sim-ple and clean, though you'll scream with joy when you take a steamy shower with some serious pressure. If it's available, splurge for the sea-view room in the front that has a private hammock-strung patio that's ideal for soaking up the sunset. The hotel bar is open late. The owners speak German, English, Spanish and French, and will help arrange tours. Credit cards accepted.

Cabinas Gloria (☎ 654 4353; camping adult/child under 6 US$3/free, tr US$50; P ☘) Run by an ami-able Tico named Santos, these spruced-up rooms with air-con and cable TV are a great deal if you're a traveling trio. This place is definitely a bit more upmarket even though the modest, painted-black sign on the road looks pretty budget. It's 200m south of the plaza.

Rancho Nany (☎ 654 4343; d/q US$50/90; P ☘ 🖥 🍴) Between Playas Brasilito and Con-chal, Rancho Nany is an impressive Tico-run complex complete with its own Internet café, steakhouse, supermarket, swimming pool and cabinas. Large rooms here are painted in cheerful tropical colors, and come with cable TV, air-con and warm showers. The hotel is managed by the López family, who have been in the area for four decades.

Conchal Hotel (☎ 654 9125; www.conchalhotel.com; d incl breakfast US$75; P ☘ 🖥 🍴) Rooms at this recommended hotel are simply stun-ning – white-washed walls are offset by exposed wooden beams, ceramic tiling and elegant bathrooms. The owner, a French-man named Michel, invites guests every night to dine on French and international cuisine at the *table d'hôtes*, a 12-person ob-long table that sits beneath a thatched roof. English, Spanish and French spoken.

EATING

Indira Bar y Restaurant (☎ 654 4028; dishes US$3-10) This large beachfront spot has a great vibe, especially in the evening when its outdoor ta-bles are packed with tourists and locals alike. The *ceviche* here is killer, especially when it's washed down with an Imperial (or four).

Restaurant Happy Snapper (☎ 654 4413; meals US$6-10) Situated on the beach side of the plaza, this cheerful restaurant with solid ocean views serves steaks and seafood, and has occasional live music during the evening.

Il Forno Restaurant (☎ 654 4125; meals US$5-12) This recommended Italian restaurant is in a romantic garden, and has such delightful menu items as thin-crust pizza, homemade pastas and risottos, and enough fresh eggplant dishes to keep vegetarians happy and healthy.

Geckos at the Beach (☎ 654 4596; breakfast US$2-4, lunch US$5-8, dinner US$10-15; ☽ 11am-10pm) This restaurant is attached to the Hotel Brasilito (opposite), and has a good reputation for its sophisticated and international menu featuring seasonal soups, exotic sauces and fresh meats and produce.

GETTING THERE & AWAY
Buses to and from Playa Flamingo travel through Brasilito; see p270 for details.

Playa Flamingo
The crescent-strip of white sand known as Playa Flamingo is postcard-worthy, which is probably why it was billed decades ago as Costa Rica's most sophisticated beach destination. These days the beach has gone completely upscale, though the scene is far from pretty. The hills above the bay are lined with private villas and expensive condos, and the area has an awful reputation for rampant cocaine use, high-end prostitution and more dirty old men than you can shake a cigar at. Package tourists and sportfisherman still frequent the old resorts that line the bay, though there are definitely better places to spend your time and money.

Interestingly enough, the original name of the beach was Playa Blanca; it changed its name in the 1950s to coincide with the construction of the area's first major hotel, the Flamingo Beach Resort. Oh, and in case you're wondering, the flamingo season runs from never to never.

Across from the Flamingo Marina Resort, **Banco de Costa Rica** (☎ 654 4984; ☽ 8:30am-3:30pm) can exchange US dollars and traveler's checks. The Super Massai, on the main north–south road, is good for all kinds of food supplies and toiletries.

ACTIVITIES
At the entrance to Flamingo beach, the **Edge Adventure Company** (☎ 6544946,3503670;www.costaricaexotic.com) has a range of rentals and tours. A two-tank dive is US$75, and snorkeling gear, bikes and body boards are available for rent. Fishing charters are also available.

Samonique III (☎ 388 7870) is a 15.5m ketch available for sunset cruises for US$60 per person (minimum four). Overnight tours are available by arrangement. You can find the office at the Mariner Inn.

Spanish classes are operated by **Centro-Panamericano de Idiomas** (☎ 265 6306; www.cpi-edu.com; classes without/with homestay US$255/380), which also has locations in Heredia (p159) and Monteverde (p197), with the opportunity to transfer from campus to campus.

SLEEPING & EATING
Budget options are nonexistent in Playa Flamingo. If you want to visit the beach but save a few bucks, consider staying in nearby Brasilito (opposite).

Guanacaste Lodge (☎ 654 4494; d/tr US$45/50; ⓟ ⓧ ⓡ) The only really affordable option in town is a good choice as the well-furnished rooms with air-con, cable TV and private hot showers are surrounded by shady, tropical grounds. There's a nice pool for cooling off, and the attached restaurant (dishes US$3 to US$6) has good casados and grilled meats.

Flamingo Beach Resort (☎ 654 4444; www.resortflamingobeach.com; r US$120-300; ⓟ ⓧ ⓡ) If you're going to get down and dirty in Flamingo, do it at the granddaddy of the area's resorts. This 91-room complex on the beach has a 1950s air about it, complete with fat, balding men and their fine young Latina escorts (She's your girlfriend, you say? Sure, why not?). Rooms are heavy on the amenities, and there's a pool and two bars where you can meet new 'friends.'

Marie's (meals US$3-6; ☽ 6:30am-9:30pm) One of the longest-established eateries in town offers a variety of affordable snacks and meals. The pancakes, burgers and rotisserie chicken are locally famous.

GETTING THERE & AWAY
Air
You can fly to Tamarindo (p280), which has regular scheduled flights and is about 8km away by paved road.

PENÍNSULA DE NICOYA

Bus

Buses depart from the Flamingo Marina on the point and travel through Brasilito on the way out. Schedules change often so ask locally about departure times as well as the best place on the road to wait for the bus.

Liberia US$1.50, two hours, depart at 5:30am and 2:30pm.

San José (Tralapa) US$6.50, five hours, depart at 2:45am, 9am and 2pm Monday to Saturday, 10:30am on Sunday.

Santa Cruz US$1.50, one hour, eight buses depart from 5:45am to 10pm.

Bahía Potrero

This stretch of bay is separated from Playa Flamingo by a rocky headland. Although the overdeveloped nightmare that is Playa Flamingo can be seen across the bay, monkeys can still be heard in the trees here, and you don't have to worry about coked-up retirees spoiling your groove. Unfortunately, by the time you read this things will probably be different, as the hillsides were being zoned for villas and condos at the time of writing.

Several undeveloped beaches are strung along the bay. The black-sand beach is **Playa Prieta**, the white-sand beach is **Playa Penca**, and **Playa Potrero**, the biggest, is somewhere in between – these names, it should be noted, are used loosely. Hotels on the beaches rent water-sports equipment. The rocky islet 10km due west of Playa Pan de Azúcar is **Isla Santa Catalina**, a popular diving spot (see the boxed text Divers Do It Deeper, p262).

There's a small community at **Potrero**, just beyond the northern end of the beach. This is where the bus line ends, though the beaches here don't get the weekend rush found at Brasilito.

SLEEPING & EATING

If you're looking for budget accommodation, consider staying 7km south in Brasilito (p268).

Mayra's (☎ 654 4213, 654 4472; camping per person US$3, d/tr/q US$25/30/43; **P**) Right on the southern beach, this friendly, tranquil place has shady camping with beach showers and five rustic rooms with refreshing cold showers, fridge and kitchenette. A small *soda* prepares meals. Mayra is helpful and friendly, and her husband, Álvaro, a retired journalist, is well stocked with stories.

Cabinas Isolina (☎ 654 4333; www.isolinabeach .com; d/tr/q US$40/50/60, d/tr/q villas US$90/110/130;

P ☒ ☲) These Italian-run cabinas are set back from the northern end of the beach and completely surrounded by huge bushes of fragrant hibiscus. Rooms have tiled hot showers, cable TV and air-con, while larger villas have two bedrooms and a fully equipped kitchen. Rates include continental breakfast, and the attached restaurant serves up Tico-Mediterranean specialties.

Bahia Esmeralda (☎ 654 4480; www.hotelbahia esmeralda.com; d/tr/q/apt/villas US$55/65/85/120/170; **P** ☒ ☲) About 50m east of the village center, this Italian-owned resort offers luxurious surroundings at a bargain price. Standard rooms are a little on the small side, though the palm-fringed pool and sophisticated ambience more than make up for it. The apartments sleeping up to four have fold-out futons and a kitchen, while larger villas can sleep six. The on-site restaurant (open for breakfast and dinner, meals from US$3 to US$12) specializes in pizzas, pastas and other Italian treats. Credit cards accepted.

Las Brisas Bar & Grill (☎ 654 4047; casados US$3.75) There are a number of *sodas* in Potrero if you're looking for cheap eats, and this local favorite is at the far end of the bay past the village. Villagers pack the joint nightly for *bocas*, beers and brilliant sunsets. The pool table here is probably the most exciting entertainment offering in town.

GETTING THERE & AWAY

Many buses begin their route in Potrero on the southeast corner of the soccer field. See Playa Flamingo (left) for schedules. Ask locally before setting out as not every bus goes all the way into Potrero.

Playa Pan de Azúcar

Although the buses stop at Potrero, those with their own ride (it'd better be a 4WD in the rainy season) can head 3km north on a rough dirt road to 'Sugar Bread Beach,' which derives its name from the crystalline strip of white sand that's protected at both ends by rocky headlands. Difficult access and the lack of cheap accommodations create an atmosphere of total seclusion, and the ocean here is calm, clear and perfect for snorkeling.

Although the beach is fronted by the Hotel Sugar Beach, don't be afraid to walk down to the shore as beaches are public property in Costa Rica.

Luxury at the **Hotel Sugar Beach** (☎ 654 4242; www.sugar-beach.com; d standard/deluxe US$110/155, ste/apt US$195/222, beach house US$475-600; P 🏊 💻 🐚) is simple and understated, which is the right approach considering how difficult it is to compete with the natural beauty of the beach. The 22 lovely rooms are brightly painted and entered via elaborately hand-carved wooden doors. Deluxe rooms are slightly larger and have stunning ocean views. There are also four two-bedroom apartments, two beach houses (with two or three bedrooms sleeping 10 to 12) and a small restaurant. But the real reason you're here is to slow down and linger on one of the most isolated beaches in all of Costa Rica.

Playa Conchal

Just 2km south of Brasilito is Playa Conchal, which is widely regarded as *the* most beautiful beach in all of Costa Rica. The name comes from the billions of *conchas* (shells) that wash up on the beach, which are gradually crushed by tourists' flip-flops into a fine powder. The ocean water is an intense turquoise blue, which is indeed a rarity on the Pacific coast. If you have snorkeling gear, this is the place to break it out.

The beach is bounded on the north by an expansive resort that can make beach access frustratingly difficult. However, it's easy enough to stay in nearby Brasilito (p268) and then simply walk south along the road for 2km.

Why is it that the most expensive resorts always seem to have the most ridiculous names? With 285 hectares of property, including an over-the-top free-form pool and a championship golf course, it's not like **Paradisus Playa Conchal Beach & Resort** (☎ 654 4123; www.paradisusplayaconchal.com; d US$350-630; P 🏊 🐚) really needs a fancy name to compensate for any inadequacies. Guests have got it all here, and everything from the marble columns to the gold-trimmed toothbrush holder is a class act. Needless to say, the whole shebang is about as *un*-Costa Rican as you can get.

GETTING THERE & AWAY

If you're staying in Conchal, it's probably best to catch buses in Brasilito; see opposite for details.

PLAYA GRANDE

From Huacas, the southwesterly road leads to Playa Grande, an undeveloped wilderness beach that's equally famous among conservationists and surfers alike. By day, the offshore winds create steep and powerful waves, especially at high tide and in front of the Hotel Las Tortugas. By night, an ancient cycle continues to unfurl as leatherback sea turtles bearing clutches of eggs follow the ocean currents back to their birthplace.

Since 1991 Playa Grande has been part of the **Parque Nacional Marino Las Baulas de Guanacaste** (p272), which prevents beachfront development and ensures that one of the most important leatherback nesting areas in the world is preserved for future generations. Although there are a few accommodations near the beach, they are set back from the shoreline and carefully managed to ensure that ambient light is kept to a minimum.

Some travelers prefer to stay in nearby Tamarindo (p276), as there is a better range of accommodations, and national parks aren't exactly known for their wild nightlife. However, there are a number of beautiful hotels on Grande, and if you're not looking to get tanked with a bunch of package holidaymakers, you might enjoy the peaceful solitude that comes with sleeping in a national park. And, of course, there's nothing like waking up in the morning and being the first one in the water.

Sleeping & Eating

Hotels are listed from north to south, and high-season rates are given.

Hotel Las Tortugas (☎ 653 0423; www.cool.co.cr /usr/turtles; s/d/ste US$50/80/120, apt US$25-100; P 🐚 💻) The owner of this hotel, Louis Wilson, is a local hero as he was instrumental in helping to designate Playa Grande as a national park. Although his hotel is near the beach, it was carefully designed to keep ambient light away from the beach area, and to block light from development to the north. Eleven spacious rooms with air-con have private bathrooms with hot water, plus thick walls and small windows to enable daytime sleep after a night of turtle-watching. The hotel also has two apartments with kitchens for rent up the hill. Surfboards, body boards, sea kayaks, snorkels and horses are rented. There's a pool, Jacuzzi and a popular restaurant, and all tours can be arranged.

Rip Jack Inn (☎ 653 0480; d US$75; P ⊠ ▣) Just south of Las Tortugas on the inland road, this recently renovated inn has a handful of clean, modern rooms with private bathrooms and air-con. There is also a beautiful open-air bar-restaurant with stunning ocean views, and there are regular yoga classes here.

Playa Grande Inn (☎ 653 0719; www.playagrande inn.com; r/apt/ste US$60/85/90; P ⊠ ▣) Around the corner from the Rip Jack Inn, air-conditioned rooms here are beautifully appointed with polished stained-wood floors, ceilings and walls, and there are a variety of different sizes depending on your budget.

Casa Verde (☎ 653 0481; casaverdecr@yahoo.com; cabinas US$55-75, casa US$100-110; P ⊠ ▣) This small property, just off the center of the beach on the inland road, is owned by Brian and Bonnie, two American ex-pats who were some of the first foreigners to settle in the area. Brian is an incredible surfer who delights in riding the waves with his guests, and Bonnie is an absolute doll who's always ready to chat about whatever ails you. The two cabins and one casa all have air-con and hot water, and vary in size (the largest option, the casa, can accommodate up to four people and has a full kitchen).

Hotel Bula Bula (☎ 653 0975; www.hotelbulabula .com; s/d US$80; P ⊠ ▣) A few hundred meters inland near the Tamarindo estuary is this recommended hotel, owned by two Americans (one of whom is a professional chef). The rooms are simply exquisite, with full amenities and original artwork on all the walls, and the landscaped grounds and free-form pool are perfect for relaxing after a hard day of surfing. But one of the biggest draws is the Great Waltini's (dishes US$9 to US$16), the on-site restaurant that serves up only the freshest local fish and shrimp, as well as some truly excellent grilled meats.

El Manglar (☎ 653 0952; www.hotel-manglar.com; d standard/deluxe US$41/64; P ⊠ ▣) Near the southern end of the beach is this funky, laid-back spot with brightly painted stuccoed rooms and lush, tropical grounds. Standard rooms have private cold showers while deluxe rooms have hot water and slightly more space.

Playa Grande Surf Camp (☎ 653 1074; www.playa grandesurfcamp.com; r per person without/with air-con US$15/25; P ⊠ ▣) Next to El Manglar is this great budget option which is run by two surfing brothers, Gerry and Patrick. The three two-person cabinas with *palapa*-thatched roofs and two four-person elevated cabinas with private hammock-strung porches all have private bathrooms, and are just steps from the beach.

Villa Baula (☎ 653 0644/493; www.hotelvillabaula .com; d/tr US$60/70, bungalows US$100-125; P ⊠ ▣) Across from the estuary near the southern end of the beach, this rustic beachfront hotel emits virtually no ambient light at night. All rooms have private hot-water bathrooms, while more expensive bungalows have air-con and optional kitchens. There's an attractive pool, and this end of the beach is much quieter as it's further from the best surfing.

Los Maunche's (meals US$5-9; ⏱ 7:30am-3pm & 6-8pm) Aside from eating at the hotels try Los Maunche's, where you can dine on fresh seafood underneath a giant thatched hut.

There's a small **grocery** (⏱ 7:30am-8pm) if you're self-catering.

Getting There & Away

There are no buses to Playa Grande. You can drive to Huacas and then take the paved road to Matapalo, followed by a 6km dirt road to Playa Grande. If you don't have your own car and are staying in Playa Grande, call ahead and the hotel owners can arrange for a pickup from the Matapalo turnoff (where the bus from San José can drop you off). You can also get a local boat captain to take you across the estuary from Tamarindo to the southern end of Playa Grande (around US$1.25 per person).

PARQUE NACIONAL MARINO LAS BAULAS DE GUANACASTE

Playa Grande is considered one of the most important nesting sites in the entire world for the *baula*, or leatherback turtle. In 1991 the entire beach and adjacent land (379 hectares), along with 22,000 hectares of ocean, was designated as Marino Las Baulas National Park. This government act followed a 15-year battle between conservationists and various self-motivated parties including poachers, developers and tour operators.

However, lest you think that the Costa Rican government was particularly concerned about the welfare of the turtles, the actual impetus for the creation of the national park came from the owner of the Hotel Las Tortugas (see p271). In fact, the sole stipulation for designating Playa Grande as a protected area was that the beach needed to generate revenue based on tourism. Fortunately, tourists perennially pay the park fees to watch the turtles nest, and local guides ensure that the beach (and their economic livelihood) stays intact.

The ecology of the park is primarily composed of mangrove swamp, and it's possible to find here all of the six mangrove species native to Costa Rica. This habitat is ideal for caimans and crocodiles, as well as numerous bird species, including the beautiful roseate spoonbill. Other creatures to look for when visiting are howler monkeys, raccoons, coatis, otters and a variety of crabs. But, as is to be expected, the main attraction is the nesting of the world's largest turtles, which can weigh in excess of 400kg. Nesting season is from October to March, and it's fairly common for three or four leatherbacks to lay their eggs here on any given night.

The leatherback is critically endangered from over-hunting, a lack of protected nesting sights, and coastal overdevelopment (beachside lights disorient the turtles when they come up to nest). Despite increased conservation efforts, fewer and fewer leatherbacks are nesting on Playa Grande each year. In 2004 an all-time low of 46 leatherbacks visited the beach, which was a vast departure from the estimated 1000 turtles that nested here in the 1990s. While it's easy to point fingers at developers in Tamarindo, park rangers attribute the decline in nesting turtles to longline commercial fishing (see the boxed text Sportfishing, p300), though the construction of high-rise apartments and beachside Pizza Huts certainly isn't helping.

In an effort to protect the dwindling leatherback population, park rangers collect the eggs daily and incubate them to increase their chances of survival. Even so, sea turtles must hatch on the beach and enter the water by themselves, otherwise memory imprinting does not occur, and the hatchlings will never return to their birthplace to nest. It's estimated that only 10% of hatchlings will survive to adulthood, though leatherbacks can live over 50 years, and females can lay multiple clutches of eggs during a single nesting season.

During the day, the beach is free and open to all, which is a good thing as the breaks off Grande are fast, steep and consistent. During the nighttime, however, it is only possible to visit the beach on a guided tour, which is also a good thing as it ensures that the nesting cycles of the leatherback will continue unhindered.

Turtle-Watching

The **park office** (☎ 653 0470; admission US$16) is by the northern entrance to Playa Grande. Reservations for turtle-watching can be made up to seven days in advance, and they're highly recommended as there are a limited number of places each evening. If you phone ahead, you will be promised a spot within a week, though there is usually a vacancy within a day or two. You can also show up in the evening as there are frequent no-shows, though this is less likely on weekends and during the busy winter holiday season.

Many hotels and tourist agencies in Tamarindo can book tours that include transport to and from Playa Grande, admission to the park and the guided tour. The whole package costs about US$35. If you don't have your own transport, this is the best way to go. When making a reservation, passport numbers and full names are required as this prevents big hotels in Tamarindo from reserving blocks for their guests.

The show kicks off anytime from 9pm to as late as 2am, though there is no guarantee that you will see a turtle – this is nature, not the San Diego Zoo. This also means that you may only have to wait for 10 minutes before a turtle shows up, or you could be there for five hours. A small stand at the exhibit sells snacks and *sodas,* but bring a (thick) book or a deck of cards for entertainment. It could be a very long night – but well worth it. While you're waiting, a good way to begin your tour is with a visit to **El Mundo de la Tortuga** (☎ 653 0471; admission US$5; ☯ 4pm-dawn), a small and informative self-guided exhibit about leatherback turtles near the northern end of the park.

To minimize the impact of viewing the turtles, guidelines for the tours are very strict (though not always enforced; see the boxed

---

CAMERA SHY

Sure, a picture is worth a thousand words, but sometimes it's better to say nothing at all. You see there's a reason why turtles no longer nest on Playa Tamarindo – they're extremely sensitive to ambient light, and a beachside fast-food restaurant isn't exactly conducive to pale nights. So, you can imagine how upset we get when we hear that tourists are taking photos of the leatherbacks, and thus reducing the chances that the turtles will return to Grande to nest. Let's be clear about this: photography (and filming) is not allowed while you're watching the turtles, and just because the Tico rangers are too polite to tell you to put your Nikon away doesn't mean that we are. And, while we have your attention, if you do see someone sneaking a photo or two, say something, because all it takes is one idiot and their bright flash to ruin a fragile cycle that has progressed continually for millions of years. Thank you.

---

text Camera Shy, above). Tourists are not allowed on the beach until the turtles have made it to dry sand. Guards with two-way radios are posted on the beach and they will alert your guide when a turtle is ready for its close-up. As a group, you will be accompanied by a guide to a designated viewing area, though photography, filming or lights of any kind are *not* allowed. Over the span of one to two hours, you can watch as the turtle digs its nest, lays about 150 silver shiny eggs and then buries them in the sand (while grunting and groaning the whole time).

If you're looking for a worthwhile volunteer project, the park office usually accepts volunteers to help monitor and catalog each nesting.

PLAYA TAMARINDO

If there are any aging hippies in your family who traveled through Costa Rica back in the day, make a point of asking them about Tamarindo when you return home – you'll no doubt be regaled with dreamy tales of watching sea turtles nest on an abandoned beach. And, of course, when they in turn ask you what it's like now, consider the sanctity of their nostalgia and lie through your teeth.

Tamarindo has long been on the radar of jet-setting surfers. In the immortal classic *Endless Summer II*, Patrick and Wingnut stopped here to visit their buddy Robert August (who still leaves here), though in recent years Tamarindo is playing host to a different breed of traveler.

Today, the beach is full of blubbery North American and European holidaymakers who spend most of their time frying in the sun like beached whales. After their complexion darkens from a pasty white to a rosy shade of skin cancer, they spend a little time perusing the town's eclectic mix of tourist shops, tourist restaurants, tourist bars and tourist cafés. And then it hits them – 'This place is booming! Let's buy some property here!'

In the span of only a few years, Tamarindo changed from a small beach town into a well-to-do (and oh so fashionable!) suburb of North American and European ex-pats. You can go boutique shopping in air-conditioned strip malls while sipping a cold mocha latte. Or why not slip in a quick Botox session before taking your dog to the groomer?

To be fair, plenty of people do enjoy themselves in Tamarindo, and it's a great place to meet tourists from every corner of, well, America. It's easy to criticize Tamarindo, but it is what it is. If you came to Costa Rica to party all night long, sleep with strangers and surf some great (but crowded) waves, welcome to paradise. But if an overdeveloped beachfront full of gringo tourists and Dolce & Gabbana-clad 'locals' isn't your thing, remember that Costa Rica is just a few kilometers away.

Information

Tourist information is available from any of the tour operators in town, but for less self-serving information try the helpful website www.tamarindobeach.org. For a refreshingly honest look at the sad, sad state of modern Tamarindo, pick up a copy of the local 'zine *Flyswatter*.

@Internet (per hr US$4; 🕑 9am-9pm) There are almost as many Internet cafés in town as there are realtors (OK, that was an exaggeration), but this place is as good as any.

Backwash (🕑 Mon-Sat) As in the wave (not the spittle), charges US$1.25 per kg for wash and dry.

Jaime Peligro Bookstore (☎ 820 9004; ⏰ 10am-8pm Mon-Sat, noon-5pm Sun) A local spot for new and used books (including Lonely Planet!), CDs and DVDs.
San Jose Bank (☎ 653 1617; ⏰ 8:30am-3:30pm) Has an ATM, and exchanges US dollars and traveler's checks.

Dangers & Annoyances

The tourist invasion has left Tamarindo with a growing drug (and prostitution) problem. Vendors openly ply their wares (and their women) on the main road by the rotunda, and some bars can get rough at closing time.

Theft is a problem. Leave your hotel room locked, use room safes and don't leave valuables on the beach. If you're driving, never leave anything in your car.

Activities

BIKING

The local expert on mountain biking, distance cycling and repairs is **Blue Trax** (☎ 653 1705; www.bluetraxcr.com).

DIVING

Agua Rica Diving Center (☎ 653 0094; www.aguarica .net), the area's scuba-diving expert, offers snorkeling and an assortment of dives, including diving certification classes.

GOLF

Just outside Tamarindo, near the village of San José de Pinilla, lies a new residential development project that boasts one of the finest golf courses in Central America.

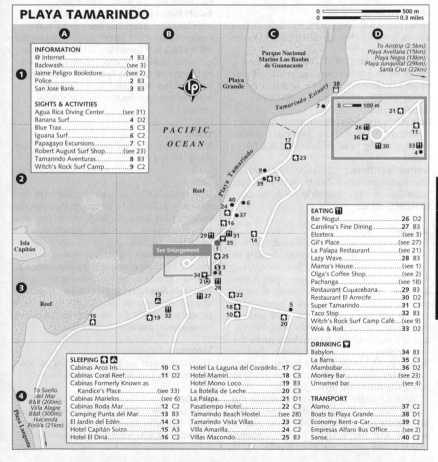

PLAYA TAMARINDO

Parque Nacional Marino Las Baulas de Guanacaste

To Airstrip (2.5km); Playa Avellana (15km); Playa Negra (18km); Playa Junquillal (29km); Santa Cruz (22km)

Playa Grande

Tamarindo Estuary

Playa Tamarindo

PACIFIC OCEAN

Reef

Isla Capitán

Reef

See Enlargement

To Sueño del Mar B&B (200m); Villa Alegre B&B (300m); Hacienda Pinilla (21km)

Playa Langosta

PENÍNSULA DE NICOYA

Hacienda Pinilla (☎ 680 7000; www.haciendapinilla .com) has a 7500-yard par 72 course that was designed by noted architect Mike Young. Greens fees are US$125/150 per person during the low/high season.

SAILING

For sunset and day-long sailing excursions book in advance via phone or online with one of the following outfits:

Blue Dolphin Sailing (☎ 653 0867, 842 3204; www .sailbluedolphin.com) Reader-recommended trips on Captain Jeff's catamaran include a sunset sail (US$60) and snorkel sail (US$75).

Mandingo Sailing (☎ 653 0623, 831 8875; www.tama rindosailing.com) A gaff-rigged schooner is available for snorkeling and sunset sails for US$50 per person.

SPORTFISHING

None of the following outfitters have offices so you'll have to book excursions by phone or online.

Capullo Sportfishing (☎ 653 0048, 837 3130; www .capullo.com) Has a 10.8m custom Topaz and a 6.6m Boston Whaler; both inshore and offshore trips are available for half-day (US$350 to US$600) and full-day (US$450 to US$1100) charters.

Lone Star Sportfishing (☎ 653 0101; www.lonestar sportfishing.com) Captain Gaylord Townley has a 9m Palm Beach boat available for half-day/full-day (US$450/750) charters.

Tantrum Sportfishing (☎ 653 0357; www.tamarindo fishingcharters.com) Captain Philip Leman has a 7.8m Boca Grande custom sportfisher available for half-day/full-day (US$450/725) charters.

SURFING

The most popular wave in Tamarindo is a medium-sized right that breaks directly in front of the Diriá Hotel. Unfortunately, the waters here are full of virgin surfers learning to pop up, most of whom seem to enjoy playing aquatic bumper cars. There is also a good left that's fed by the river mouth, though be advised that crocodiles are occasionally sighted here, particularly when the tide is rising (which is coincidently the best time to surf). Locals know a few other spots in the area, but we're certainly not going to ruin their fun – ask around.

More advanced surfers will appreciate the bigger, faster and less crowded waves at **Playas Langosta** (on the other side of the point), **Avellana** and **Negra** (p281) and **Junquillal** (p283) to the south, and **Playa Grande** (p271)

to the north. Note that the best months for surfing coincide with the rainy season.

A number of surf schools and surf tour operators line the main stretch of road in Tamarindo. Surf lessons hover at around US$30 for 1½ to two hours and most operators will let you keep the board for a few hours beyond that to practice. All outfits can organize day-long and multiday excursions to popular breaks, rent equipment and give surf lessons. Try:

Banana Surf (☎ 653 1270; www.bananasurfclub.com) This Argentinean-run outfit has the fairest prices in town on new and used boards, and is reminiscent of the way surf shops used to be (ie before they rented space in shopping malls).

Iguana Surf (☎ 653 0148; www.iguanasurf.net) Operates a surf taxi service to neighboring beaches (US$10 per person to Playa Grande, US$25 per person to Playa Negra).

Robert August Surf Shop (☎ 653 0114; rasurfshop@ yahoo.com) Based at Tamarindo Vista Villas (p278), this famous name-brand shop is something of an obligatory stop.

Witch's Rock Surf Camp (☎ 653 0239; www.witchs rocksurfcamp.com) Board rentals, surf camps, lessons and regular excursions to Witch's Rock and Ollie's Point are available, though they're pricey. There are beachside accommodations for surfers who sign up for multiday packages.

YOGA

Daily yoga classes are offered at the Cabinas Arco Iris (p278).

Tours

Boat tours, ATV tours, snorkeling trips and scooter rentals can be arranged through the various tour agencies in town. Many also rent equipment. The most reputable ones include the following:

Papagayo Excursions (☎ 653 0254; www.papagayoexcur sions.com) The longest-running outfitter in town organizes a variety of tours including visits to turtle-nesting sites.

Tamarindo Aventuras (☎ 653 0108; www.tamarindo adventures.net; scooters per 4hr US$25, ATVs per 4hr US$60, dirt bikes per 4hr US$34) Also rents water-sports equipment including kayaks, snorkeling gear and surfboards.

Sleeping

The rates given are high-season rates; low-season rates can be about 25% lower.

BUDGET

Note that we constantly receive complaints about hotels in Tamarindo, so choose your accommodations wisely. All the hotels below have cold water (and you won't mind a bit).

THE AUTHOR'S CHOICE

Budget

Tamarindo Beach Hostel (☎ 653 0944; dm US$12; P ✕ 💻) This hostel, formerly known as 'La Botella de Leche,' is recommended for its fantastic building and bustling backpacker vibe. Common areas, including the kitchen, big-screen TV lounge with DVD player and cold-water bathrooms, are centrally air-conditioned during the day. During the night, the air-con is switched to the six-person dorms, ensuring a comfortable night's sleep. The hostel is perfectly suited to meet the needs of surfers, right down to the surf racks and ample supply of beer.

Midrange

Villas Macondo (☎ 653 0812; www.villasmacondo.com; s/d/tr US$30/35/45, s/d/tr with air-con US$50/55/65; 2-/4-person apt US$90/125, additional person US$5; P ✕ 💻) Although it's only 200m from the beach, this German-run establishment is an oasis of serenity in an otherwise frenzied town – it's also one of the best deals around. Beautiful modern villas with private hot showers and hammock-strung patios surround a solar-heated pool and tropical garden, while larger apartments are equipped with cable TV, a full kitchen and air-con. Credit cards accepted.

Top end

Hotel Capitán Suizo (☎ 653 0075/353; www.hotelcapitansuizo.com; d with fan/air-con US$150/175, bungalows/apt US$210/250, additional person US$20; P ✕ 💻 🐾) On the southern end of the beach is this Swiss-run hotel, which belongs to the group of 'Small Distinctive Hotels of Costa Rica.' The 22 rooms and 18 larger, thatched-roof bungalows are decorated with natural stone floors, polished hardwoods and soft, pastel hues. The entire complex is centered on a free-form pool that's shaded by expansive gardens, and all units are just steps from a quiet strip of sand. Credit cards are accepted.

Camping Punta del Mar (per person US$2) This basic campground has toilets, showers, water and electricity, and it's open all year.

Cabinas Coral Reef (☎ 653 0291; r per person US$8; P) The cheapest place in town has disheveled and cramped wooden cabins with reasonably clean shared bathrooms, though the communal areas are good places to chat up other shoestringers.

Cabinas Roda Mar (☎ 653 0109; r per person without/with bathroom US$7/11; P) Dark and airless concrete rooms with private bathrooms are spacious and clean by prison standards. Avoid the rooms with shared bathrooms – the toilets are a biohazard, even by prison standards.

La Botella de Leche (☎ 653 0189; www.botelladeleche.com; dm/s/d US$12/14/28; P ✕) First, let's clear up some confusion: the new La Botella de Leche, or 'Milk Bottle', is not the Author's Choice. But this Argentinean-run spot is highly recommended for its over-the-top cow theme, warm and attentive management, fully air-conditioned rooms and dormitories, and quiet location at the eastern edge of town. Facilities include a shared kitchen, surfboard racks, big-screen

TV lounge and free bike rentals. The lovely owner will even lend you a spare umbrella if you're here in the rainy season!

Cabinas Marielos (☎ 653 0141; d without/with air-con US$30/35; ✕) This is a good budget option. The comfortable cabins are decidedly lacking in personality, though they do have firm beds and private bathroom (some cabins have decks facing a garden).

Hotel Mono Loco (☎ 653 0238; elmonoloco@racsa.co.cr; d with fan/air-con US$36/45; ✕ 🐾) This reader-recommended hotel is on the back road into town, so you can definitely sleep quietly at night. The hotel itself is a yellow-stuccoed and thatched building that surrounds a beautifully landscaped pool. Bright and airy rooms have cable TV and optional air-con. The on-site restaurant serves reasonably priced Costa Rican fare all day long.

MIDRANGE

All the hotels below have private hot-water bathrooms unless otherwise stated.

Villa Amarilla (☎ 653 0038; carpen@racsa.co.cr; d US$30, d with bathroom US$45, additional person US$10; ✕) This quaint, French-owned inn is one of the safest beachfront hotels in Tamarindo.

PENÍNSULA DE NICOYA

There are four rooms with private bathroom, air-con and cable TV as well as three cheaper units with shared hot-water showers. All have a fridge and safe, and share an outdoor kitchen. Credit cards accepted.

Cabinas Formerly Known as Kandice's Place (s/d US$30/40; 🕮 🖳) These funky, hidden-away boutique cabinas are great value for anyone in need of some creature comforts. Three air-conditioned rooms (one with private hot shower) have thick mattresses, cable TV and plenty of breathing space. The real draw, however, is the professional open-air kitchen (there's even a juicer and rice-cooker), the wi-fi Internet and the intimate feel. The Korean-Spanish owners rely on a speakeasy-like word of mouth, so walk-ins only.

Hotel Mamiri (☎ 653 0079; www.hotelmamiri.com; d/tr US$46/51; 🅿) This delightful open-air hotel is decorated with memorabilia from the Italian owners' travels through Asia and Central America. Each room is unique, and some feature attractive volcanic stone tiling on the floors and walls. The relaxed and breezy grounds are strung up with hammocks, and there's a well-equipped communal kitchen for all your self-catering needs. The attached restaurant, Pachanga (p280), is the top spot to dine in town.

Cabinas Arco Iris (☎ 653 0330; www.hotelarcoiris .com; s/d US$40/50; 🅿) A cluster of four distinctively decorated hillside cabinas make up this wonderfully reclusive Italian-owned place. Every unit is whimsically painted with artsy motifs, and the talented owners truly have a good idea for detail. The hotel offers weekday yoga (and occasional martial arts) classes in the shaded 'Dojo-gym.' Guests can also use the communal open-air kitchen.

Hotel La Laguna del Cocodrilo (☎ 653 0255; www .lalagunadelcocodrilo.com; r US$65-80; 🅿 🕮) This simple but charming French-owned hotel has modest, well-kept rooms of varying sizes and shapes (some can accommodate up to four people), either overlooking the shady grounds or the ocean and estuary. The property is adjacent to a crocodile-filled lagoon (hence the name), and has a private trail leading to the beach. There is also a restaurant that specializes in sushi and Asian-fusion cuisine. Credit cards accepted.

Pasatiempo Hotel (☎ 653 0096; www.hotelpasatiem po.com; d standard/grande/ste incl breakfast US$79/89/99, additional person US$15; 🅿 🕮 🖳) This well-established Tamarindo landmark is widely known for its popular live-music nights, though it's also a great place to stay. Sixteen standard and larger 'grande' rooms are awash in tropical-themed murals, and feature comfortable beds, modern bathrooms, air-con and a private hammock-strung patio. Suites have a living room with fold-out couch, which is perfect if you're traveling with the offspring. There's a pool and a popular bar-restaurant. Credit cards accepted.

TOP END

All hotels can arrange tours in the area.

Tamarindo Vista Villas (☎ 653 0114; www.tama rindovistavillas.com; d/tr US$89/99, ste US$139-229; 🅿 🕮 🖳) Perched on a hill overlooking the entrance to Tamarindo, this hotel is best known for being featured on the TV show 'Wild on E!,' which dubbed Tamarindo one of the three 'top destinations in the world.' We can assure you that a) you shouldn't believe the hype; and b) most of the show was staged anyway. Regardless, the Best Western Tamarindo Vista Villas is one of the most popular places in town for well-to-do travelers, and the 33 rooms and suites have all the amenities (and institutionalized blandness) you associate with the Best Western chain. The hotel also has an ocean-view pool, the popular Monkey Bar (p280), a dive shop, the Robert August Surf Shop and a tour desk. Rates include continental breakfast, and credit cards are accepted.

La Palapa (☎ 653 0362; www.lapalapa.info; s/d/tr US$90/110/130; 🅿 🕮) Despite the attached bar-restaurant (opposite), which is one of the most popular spots in town, this beachfront hotel is surprisingly quiet and secluded. La Palapa is definitely luxurious – all seven loft-style rooms have king-size beds, ocean views and big-screen TVs with DVD players. However, the hotel is overpriced, especially considering the quality of other top-end hotels in town. Still, you are on the beach, and that's enough for most people. A small travel agency, Destination Adventures (☎ 814 6900), operates out of the hotel.

El Jardín del Edén (☎ 653 0137/11; www.jardindel eden.com; d US$110-150, apt US$145; 🅿 🕮 🖳) On a hill overlooking Tamarindo, this luxurious French-run hotel has 18 exquisite rooms, each with a sitting area and private patio or balcony (and some of Tamarindo's best views). Rooms are fully equipped and come in a variety of sizes and shapes depending on the price. There are also two apartments (sleeping five) with kitchenette, plus a Jacuzzi, pool with swim-up bar and Mediterranean-inspired bar-restaurant. Credit cards accepted.

Hotel El Diriá (☎ 653 0031/2, in San José 291 2821, in the USA 510-315 1294; d garden/ocean/premium US$140/160/180; P ⊠ ⊠) In the center of town and right on the beach is Tamarindo's first luxury hotel. Bland rooms are offset by three pools, a Jacuzzi, bar-restaurant and a private beachfront, which is, of course, technically illegal in Costa Rica.

Villa Alegre B&B (☎ 653 0270; www.villaalegrecos tarica.com; r US$170-185, villas US$230; P ⊠ ⊠ ⊛) This beachside B&B in nearby Playa Langosta has five rooms of various sizes, each decorated with memorabilia from the owners' world travels (you can choose from the Caribbean, USA, California, Guatemala or Mexican rooms). Or stay in the Japan or Russia villas, which are equipped with full kitchens. There's an honor bar, a comfortable guest living room and plenty of games for children. Bounteous breakfasts (included in the rates) are served on the deck. Two units are wheelchair-accessible. Credit cards are accepted.

Sueño del Mar B&B (☎ 653 0284; www.sueno-del -mar.com; d standard/honeymoon US$185/295, casita US$210-230; P ⊠ ⊠) This delightful Spanish *posada* in nearby Playa Langosta is affectionately run by innkeepers Paul and Nancy, and decorated with handcrafted rocking chairs, heavenly hammocks and a cozy living room that's perfect for relaxing with the other guests. The six rooms have four-post beds, artfully placed crafts and open-air garden showers, while the romantic honeymoon suite has a wraparound window with sea views. A delicious breakfast is included in the price, and there's private beach access through a tropical garden. All tours can be arranged. No children aged under 12 allowed. Credit cards accepted.

Eating

You can't have sophisticated modern living without boutique gourmet eateries, so it's not surprising that Tamarindo has some of the best restaurants in Costa Rica. But be prepared to pay – a cheap meal in this town is about as common as a nesting turtle.

If you're self-catering, the Super Tamarindo is well stocked with (pricey) international groceries.

Olga's Coffee Shop (snacks US$1-3) This adorable Russian-owned café serves up organic coffees and homemade pastries – even lactose intolerants will feel at home while sipping an ice-cold soy-milk latte.

Taco Stop (meals US$3-5) Mexican foodies will appreciate the quality of offerings at this popular eatery while shoestringers will revel in the generous portions and low prices.

Gil's Place (meals US$4-6) Gil's pretty famous in these parts, and it's not hard to see why – his Mexican cuisine caters to both veggies and carnivores alike, and emphasizes fresh produce and potent sauces.

Restaurant El Arrecife (meals US$4-6) This is one of the few places in town where you can get a cheap casado, though it's definitely a tourist-only affair.

Mama's House (meals US$4-7) Italian-inspired salads, sandwiches and pastas at this open-air restaurant are reasonably priced and very filling – our favorite is Mama's meatloaf sub.

Witch's Rock Surf Camp Café (meals US$4-7) The best snack in town is at this American-run surf camp, where you can order 'nachos as big as your ass' while sucking down cold ones on the outdoor deck until 2am. Sweet!

Wok & Roll (meals US$4-7) Korean-American owner Kandice routinely inspires fear in local fishermen throughout the Nicoya. She is famous for scrutinizing daily tuna and mahi-mahi catches, and will only buy the freshest of fish. The result: some of the best sushi we've ever eaten. Her woks and Vietnamese spring rolls are also popular.

Restaurant Copacabana (meals US$4-9) The 'poor-man's La Palapa' (see below) has the same damn view without all the pretence. Sunset is predictably a good time to visit, though it's worth getting up in the morning for the killer crepes.

Bar Nogui (meals US$6-11) This beachside restaurant offers upscale casados featuring grilled fish, mixed meats and unbelievable shrimp and lobster. It's consistently popular with locals and tourists alike, so come early for dinner or you'll have to wait.

La Palapa Restaurant (meals US$7-15) The restaurant at La Palapa is an intriguing mix of Thai beach-bar ambience, big-city prices and school-cafeteria quality. Still, it's one of the most popular places in town, though

PENÍNSULA DE NICOYA

discerning tourists tend to avoid pricey beach bars to begin with.

Pachanga (☎ 653 0021; mains US$7-15; ☯ 6-10pm Mon-Sat) Don't leave town without eating here – it may be the best meal you have in Costa Rica. The Israeli chef, Shlomy, serves innovative dishes with Mediterranean accents that change daily depending on the availability of local ingredients. The restaurant is understated yet elegant, which focuses your attention on the perfection of Shlomy's cuisine.

Carolina's Fine Dining (meals US$10-25) Sure, it's a splurge, but the continental cuisine at this sophisticated eatery highlights skillfully prepared sauces, tender cuts of meat, delectable fish and an impressive selection of imported wines.

Lazy Wave (meals US$10-25) This hip (and pricey) nightspot is built around a huge tree, and attracts sophisticated (and wealthy) travelers. The Lazy Wave has an assorted mix of cocktails, *bocas* (the Costa Rican equivalent of tapas), and Asian and European-inspired dishes.

Etcetera (meals US$15-35) Welcome to the next generation of Tamarindo eateries. Toronto chef Derek Furlani is famous in town for his culinary excellence, though his new LA-inspired spot (it is next to a strip mall, after all) is arguably a little heavy on the flash. The food is decent but definitely overpriced, and the VIP tables and velvet ropes somehow seem a little un-Costa Rican.

Drinking

About the only culture you're going to find in Tamarindo is the roaming band of mariachis. Sure, Mexican ballads seem a little out of place in Central America, but remember that a surprising number of visitors to Tamarindo think that Costa Rica is an island. However, if you're looking to get wasted, you picked the right town.

The wild spot in town is Mambobar, which attracts a steady crowd of sexual predators – things can get rough here, and local Ticos love roughing up the occasional drunk, belligerent gringo.

The Monkey Bar, inside the Tamarindo Vista Villas (p278), has a mellower ladies' night on Friday. Also recommended is the Tuesday-night live-music jam at the Pasatiempo Hotel (p278), Wednesday-night Latin dancing at La Barra and Thursday reggae night at Babylon. Any night of the week you can expect the music to be pumping *loudly* at the unnamed bar, even if no one is there.

Getting There & Away

AIR

The airstrip is 3km north of town; a hotel bus is usually on hand to pick up arriving passengers or you can take a taxi. Sansa has 14 daily flights to and from San José (one way/return US$78/114), while NatureAir has five (US$80/160).

Sansa (☎ 653 0012) has an office on the main road, and the travel desk at Hotel El Diriá (p279) can book trips on NatureAir. The airstrip belongs to the hotel and all passengers must pay a US$3 departure tax to use it.

BUS

Buses from San José (US$5, six hours) depart from the Empresas Alfaro office next to the police station at 3:30am, 5:45am and 1pm.

Catch the following buses at any point on the main road:

Liberia US$1, two hours, depart at 5:30am, 9am, 11:30am, 3pm and 5pm.

Santa Cruz US$0.75, 1¼ hours, depart at 6am, 9am, 11am, 3:30pm and 4pm.

CAR & TAXI

If driving to Tamarindo, the better road is from Belén to Huacas and then south. It's also possible to drive from Santa Cruz to 27 de Abril on a paved road and then northwest on a dirt road for 19km to Tamarindo – this route is rougher, though passable to ordinary cars. A taxi from Santa Cruz costs about US$20 and it's twice that from Liberia.

Getting Around

Boats on the northern end of the beach can be hired to cross the estuary for daytime visits to the beach at Playa Grande. The ride is roughly US$1.25 per person, depending on the number of people.

Many visitors arrive in rental cars. If you get here by air or bus, you can rent bicycles and dirt bikes in town (see p275). There's no gas station, but you can buy expensive gas from drums at the hardware store near the entrance to town. (It's cheaper to fill up in Santa Cruz or at the station in Huacas.) Cars can be rented from:

Alamo (☎ 653 0727)

Economy Rent-a-Car (☎ 653 0752)

PENÍNSULA DE NICOYA

PLAYAS AVELLANA & NEGRA

These popular **surfing beaches** have some of the best, most consistent waves in the area, made famous in the surf classic *Endless Summer II* (one of the breaks off Avellana is known as 'Pequeño Hawaii'). The beaches begin 15km south of Tamarindo and are reached by a dismal dirt road requiring 4WD most times of the year (in the wet season there are three rivers to cross). The difficult access keeps the area refreshingly uncrowded, though the recent boom in Tamarindo is likely to spread here in the years to come (there are plans to build a pedestrian promenade along the waterfront, and much of the area is already residentially zoned).

Avellana is a long stretch of white sand, and Negra, a few kilometers further south, is a darker beach broken up by rocky outcrops. At Avellana, **Little Hawaii** is a powerful and open-faced right at medium tide, while **Beach Break** barrels at low tide (though the surfing is good anytime of the day). Negra has a world-class right that barrels, especially with a moderate offshore wind.

If you're not coming from Tamarindo, head west on the paved highway from Santa Cruz, through 27 de Abril to Paraíso, then follow signs or ask locals (this is a confusing area to drive through as there's just a scattering of accommodations here instead of an actual town).

While you are on the beach, be absolutely certain that nothing is left visible in your car as professional thieves operate in this area, and they will remove your window even for a broken flip-flop or moldy sarong.

Café Playa Negra (p283) has a laundry service (per load US$6), Internet access (per hour US$2) and a small book exchange.

Sleeping & Eating

PLAYA AVELLANA

The following places to stay and eat are very spread out and are listed approximately from north to south.

Cabinas Las Olas (☎ 658 8315; www.cabinaslasolas .co.cr; s/d/tr US$60/70/80; **P**) On the road from San José de Pinilla into Avellana, this pleasant hotel is set on spacious grounds only 200m from the beach. Ten airy, individual bungalows have shiny woodwork, stone detailing, hot-water showers and private decks. There's a restaurant and a specially built

---

WHAT TO DO IF YOU'RE CAUGHT IN A RIPTIDE

Riptides account for the majority of ocean drownings, though a simple understanding of how these currents behave can save your life. Rip currents are formed when excess water brought to shore by waves returns to the sea in a rapidly moving depression in the ocean floor. They are comprised of three parts: the feeder current, the neck, and the head.

The feeder current consists of rapidly moving water that parallels the shore, though it's not always visible from the beach. When this water reaches a channel, it switches direction and flows out to sea, forming the neck of the rip. This is the fastest-moving part of the riptide, and can carry swimmers out to sea at a speed of up to 10km/h. The head of the riptide occurs past the breakers where the current quickly dissipates.

If you find yourself caught in a riptide, immediately call for help as you only have a few seconds before being swept out to sea. However, it's important to conserve your energy and not to fight the current – this is the principal cause of drownings. It's almost impossible to swim directly back to shore. Instead, try one of two methods for escaping a rip. The first is to tread water and let yourself be swept out past the breakers. Once you're in the head of the rip, you can swim out of the channel and ride the waves back to shore. Or you can swim parallel or diagonally to the shore until you're out of the channel.

Rip currents usually occur on beaches that have strong surf, though temporary rips can occur anywhere, especially when there is an offshore storm or during low tide. Fortunately, there are indicators such as the brownish color on the surface of the water that is caused by swept-up sand and debris. Also look for surface flattening, which occurs when the water enters a depression in the ocean floor and rushes back out to sea. If you're ever in doubt about the safety of a beach, it's best to inquire locally about swimming conditions.

Remember, rips are fairly survivable as long as you relax, don't panic and conserve your energy.

boardwalk leads through the mangroves down to the beach (good for wildlife spotting). Kayaks and surfing gear are for hire.

Cabinas Gregorios (☎ 658 8319; camping US$3, r per person US$4) You can't get much cheaper than this small but popular shoestringer's spot on the access road to Avellana. 'Rooms' are minuscule open-air stalls with shared bathroom (bring repellent), though you'll survive to surf another day. There is a small *soda* that's about as cheap as it gets.

Rancho Iguana Verde (☎ 658 8310; r per person US$10) About 50m past Gregorios, this is a better choice (that is, if you can afford the extra US$6 splurge). The six rooms are definitely dark but reasonably clean, and share cold-water showers. There is a small *soda* that's also very cheap.

Lola's on the Beach (meals US$5-10) This recommended spot is on a palm-fringed stretch of Avellana sand, and is a great place to spend the day if the water is looking a bit glassy.

ORGANIC COSTA RICA *Elizabeth Hart*

Among their many other accomplishments, the Maya of Central America were known for their efficient methods of sustainable agriculture – that is, farming to meet the nutritional demands of their people without robbing future generations' ability to meet their own needs. The dawn of agriculture shone on the Maya, and their croplands had some of the longest stretches of continual production in the history of mankind – all without the use of synthetic pesticides or fertilizers. Yet, today, if you ask Central American farmers what is essential to crop production, first on their list will most likely be the use of deadly chemicals. In Costa Rica, however, the dangerous cycles of agricultural chemical use are beginning to change.

Much of Costa Rica's economy depends on agriculture, and annual chemical use is heavy – about 173,000 metric tons of synthetic fertilizer in a country about the size of West Virginia. But with Costa Rica having one of the highest occurrences of stomach cancer in the world, and the obvious effects of pollution in many rivers and coastal waters, people are becoming more conscious of the lasting consequences of using synthetic chemicals in agriculture. With help from numerous nonprofit organizations, schools like Earth University (a nonprofit university offering education in agricultural sciences) and an ever-expanding number of green-conscious people visiting and moving to Costa Rica, organic produce is becoming easier to find and research in sustainable farming techniques is compounding.

Going organic does not just mean cutting out the chemicals – all it takes is a glance at the jungle to see how well plants thrive in the tropics. But also thriving are the diseases, insects and animals that can decimate a crop overnight. An integrated approach of soil enrichment, the introduction of beneficial organisms and keeping a close watch over the garden help keep the negative influences at bay. While they are usually more time-consuming than chemical use, the majority of organic methods cost less to the farmer and bring in much greater returns – financially and physically – for workers and their families than dangerous 'traditional' methods of growing food.

As a popular tourist destination, Costa Rica has an important opportunity to educate visitors from all over the world about the necessity of keeping such ecologically diverse places thriving. When they learn that chemical fertilizers and pesticides are becoming less and less effective, and become aware of the lasting consequences of such chemicals poisoning the environment and their bodies, visitors want to become more active in promoting organic farming. And tourists visiting Costa Rica play an important role in the fate of the organic movement by choosing to support eco-friendly tours, hotels and products.

How can you help? There are restaurants and markets all over Costa Rica that offer organic meats and produce. Most grocers carry organic fruits, veggies and products like those made by BioLand. There are work/trade programs at organic farms, and also hotels that offer free or discounted room and board in exchange for a hand in the garden. A visit to Earth University (p448) or countless other nonprofit organizations can educate and guide you toward making organic choices while visiting Costa Rica and upon returning to your home country. For more information on the organic movement and eco-friendly destinations in Costa Rica visit www.earth.ac.cr or www.sustainabletravel.com.

Food here is top quality, and you can linger in the comfortable hammocks or grab an African-style wooden chair and watch the sun go down. Oh, and in case you're curious, Lola is the owner's pet pig who's seemingly infected with gigantism. And no, the pig doesn't surf (they get this question all the time!).

More or less between Playas Avellana and Negra, you'll find **Mono Congo Surf Lodge** (☎ 658 8261; www.monocongolodge.com; d incl breakfast US$35; P) This large, open-air, Polynesian-style tree-house lodge is surrounded by howler-filled trees (which are reliable wake-up calls if you want to catch the morning surf). Polished wood rooms are exquisite and private bathrooms have hot water and Spanish tiles. A patio has hammocks and a star-watching deck on the roof provides 360-degree views of the area. A variety of French/international meals are available from the gourmet kitchen (dinner US$7 to US$18).

PLAYA NEGRA

In Playa Negra to the south there are a variety of surfer-oriented places.

Cabinas Pablo Picasso (☎ 658 8158; dm US$9, r per person US$15, deluxe d US$45; P ☒) This long-standing surfer outpost is run by an American ex-pat named Hank, and has a variety of accommodations for travelers of all budgets. Dorms and standard rooms share cold-water bathrooms, while deluxe rooms have private hot-water showers, air-con and kitchenettes. If you're in the area, be sure to stop by and take on the restaurant's half-kilo 'burger as big as your head.'

Aloha Amigos (☎ 658 8023; r per person US$10, d with bathroom US$30, 6-person cabin US$50; P) This Hawaiian-run surfer's retreat has simple rooms with shared cold-water bathrooms and more expensive doubles with private hot-water bathrooms and kitchenettes. The grounds are grassy and hibiscus-lined, and the atmosphere is about as chilled as it gets.

Kontiki (☎ 658 8038; dm US$10) Next door to Aloha Amigos, this Peruvian-run place has a ramshackle collection of tree-house dorms on stilts that are frequented by both surfers and howlers. There's a small restaurant serving up traditional Peruvian dishes.

Hotel Playa Negra (☎ 658 8034; www.playanegra .com; s/d/tr/q US$60/72/81/92; P ☒) This charming hotel is a collection of 10 spacious, circular bungalows with thatched roofs, bright tropical colors and traditional indigenous-style tapestries and linens. Each cabin has a queen-sized bed, two single beds and a private bathroom with hot water.

Pasta Mike's (☎ 658 8270; r per person without/with air-con US$15/35; ☒) Further south, this mellow surfers' retreat is run by a friendly Floridian. Rooms here are simple and standard, though the communal area is a nice place to unwind.

Playa Negra Surf Camp (☎ 658 8140; playanegrasc@ hotmail.com; s/d US$25/30) Before leaving the area you'll pass this great French-owned option for self-caterers, where guests are permitted to use the fully equipped kitchen. Alan, the friendly owner, is eager to teach you anything you want to know about surfing, and gives both private and group lessons for reasonable prices.

Café Playa Negra (☎ 658 8348; dishes US$3-6; ☒ 7am-9pm; ☐) For anything else you might need, head straight to this local eatery serving Tico/Peruvian food. There's also a bakery, a laundry service and Internet access here.

La Vida Buena Pizzeria (☎ 658 8082; pizzas US$4-8; ☒ 4pm-late) A good spot for an excellent slice of thin-crust pizza or a cold beer and some hot tunes, La Vida Buena is run by a laid-back Californian who knows how to make a good pizza.

Getting There & Away

There is no public transportation to Avellana or Negra, though surf outfitters in Tamarindo (p276) organize trips, and just about every local in town is willing to give you (and your surfboard) a ride – bargain hard.

PLAYA JUNQUILLAL

Junquillal is a 2km-wide grey-sand wilderness beach that's absolutely stunning and always deserted – probably because the surf is high and the rips are fierce (see the boxed text What to Do if You're Caught in a Riptide, p284). It's best to leave your swimming trunks at home, though there are clean lefts and rights when the waves drop a bit in size. Ridley turtles nest here from July to November, with a peak from August to October, though in smaller numbers than at the refuges. The nearest village is 4km inland at **Paraíso**, which has a few local *sodas* and bars. Accommodations are spread out along the beach.

Sleeping & Eating

The following places are listed in order as you drive in from Paraíso and most are well signed.

Hotel Iguanazul (☎ 658 8124; www.iguanazul.com; s/d/tr US$60/70/80, s/d/tr with ocean view US$80/90/100, s/d/tr with air-con US$90/100/110; P 🞨 🖳) This funky, well-established resort hotel is by far the nicest place to stay in the area. There are 24 brightly painted and cool tiled rooms with garden or ocean views, and some have air-con. Amenities include a pool (check out the palm island), games room, volleyball and a restaurant-bar with killer views. All rates include breakfast.

Camping Los Malinches (☎ 658 8429; per person US$5) Just south of the Iguanazul, this pretty campground has toilets, showers, electricity until 9pm and ocean views.

Hotel El Castillo Divertido (☎ 658 8428; www.costa rica-adventureholidays.com; d without/with ocean view US$30/35; P) On a hilltop about 500m down the road, you'll find the entrance to this quirky inn owned by an affable German/Tica couple and son. The hotel's rooftop bar has panoramic views – a breezy place to laze in a hammock. Paulo, one of the owners, plays his guitar for guests during sunsets. Tiled rooms are clean and have private hot showers, and it's worth splurging for the ones with ocean views. The restaurant (dishes US$3 to US$10) has good breakfasts and dinners with plenty of German favorites.

Guacamaya Lodge (☎ 658 8431; www.guacamaya lodge.com; s/d US$50/55, apt s/d/tr/q US$70/75/80/85, villas US$120; P 🖳 🖳) Next door to El Castillo, this quiet Swiss-run place has six quaint bungalows, a two-bedroom villa with a kitchen and an apartment with balcony views. There's also a pool and a restaurant-bar with ocean views and a smattering of Swiss delicacies. The warm and wonderful brother and sister owners speak a remarkable seven languages. Credit cards accepted.

El Lugarcito (☎ 658 8436; ellugarcito@racsa.co.cr; d incl breakfast US$50; P) This hospitable Dutch-run, two-room B&B is intimate, quaint and full of personality. The rooms are fairly simple, though the house itself is decorated with indigenous pottery and has beautiful stone floors and vaulted ceilings.

Hotel Tatanka (☎ 658 8426; www.crica.com/tatanka; s/d/tr US$25/36; P 🖳) Ten rancho-style rooms with private hot-water bathrooms are pretty in pink, and have rustic wooden furnishings.

There's an inviting pool as well as an open-air pizzeria (pizzas US$4 to US$7) that serves wood-fired pizza pies in the evenings. Credit cards accepted.

Hotel Hibiscus (☎ 658 8437; d incl breakfast US$40) This charming Tica/German-run hotel has five spotless rooms with private bathrooms and hammock-strung patios overlooking the palm-fringed garden. There's a small restaurant that has a good variety of international cuisine.

Aside from the hotel restaurants, your best option for cheap eats is to head to nearby Paraíso, though there a few small spots on the beach, including the locally popular **Bar y Restaurant Junquillal** (dishes US$3-6).

Getting There & Away

Buses arrive and depart from Hotel Playa Junquillal on the beach. Daily buses to Santa Cruz depart at 5:45am, noon and 4pm.

If you're driving, it's about 16km by paved road from Santa Cruz to 27 de Abril, and another 17km by unpaved road via Paraíso to Junquillal. From Junquillal, you can head south by taking a turnoff about 3km east of Paraíso on a road marked 'Reserva Ostional.' This is for 4WD only and may be impassable in the rainy season. There are no gas stations on the coastal road and there is little traffic, so ask before setting out. It's easier to reach beaches south of Junquillal from Nicoya.

A taxi from Santa Cruz to Junquillal costs about US$25.

SANTA CRUZ

A stop in Santa Cruz, a *sabanero* town typical of inland Nicoya, provides some of the local flavor missing from foreign-dominated beach towns. Unfortunately, since there are no real sights in town to hold your attention, most travelers' experience in Santa Cruz consists of changing buses and buying a mango or two. It doesn't help much either that Santa Cruz (with Liberia a close second) holds the dubious title of being the hottest city in Costa Rica (we're talking temperature, not sex appeal). However, the town is an important administrative center in the region, and serves as a good base for visiting Guaitil (see the boxed text Guaitil, p286).

About three city blocks in the center of Santa Cruz burned to the ground in a devastating fire in 1993. An important landmark in town is a vacant lot known as the

Plaza de Los Mangos, which was once a large grassy square with three mango trees. However, soon after the fire the attractive and shady **Parque Bernabela Ramos** was opened up 400m south of Plaza de Los Mangos.

Information

Kion, on the southwest plaza corner, is a Wal-Mart–style department store selling English-language newspapers and more.

Banco de Costa Rica (☎ 680 3253) Change money at this bank, three blocks north of Plaza de Los Mangos.

Ciberm@nia (per hr US$2) Check your email here, 100m north of Parque Ramos.

Festivals & Events

There is a rodeo and fiesta during the second week in January and on July 25 for **Día de Guanacaste** (p220). At these events, you can check out the *sabaneros*, admire prize bulls and drink plenty of beer while listening to ear-popping music.

Santa Cruz is considered the folklore center of the region and is home to a long-time marimba group, Los de la Bajura. The group plays traditional *bombas*, a combination of music with funny (and off-color) verses. Keep an eye out for wall postings announcing performances or ask hotel staff.

Sleeping & Eating

Any directions that mention the 'plaza' are making reference to Plaza de Los Mangos. All showers are cold, though you'll wish they were even colder.

Pensión Isabel (☎ 680 0173; r per person US$6) The cheapest beds in town are housed in bare whitewashed rooms, though they're reasonably firm, the shared bathrooms are acceptable and the owner's quite friendly. It's southeast of the plaza.

Hotel La Estancia (☎ 680 0476; s/d US$20/32; P ✖) Though it's definitely a step up in price from Isabel, Estancia has 16 very comfortable rooms with air-con, cable TV and private bathroom set around a motor court. You'll find it 100m west of the plaza.

Hotel La Pampa (☎ 680 4586; d without/with air-con US$30/37; P ✖) Another good midrange option, 50m west of the plaza, this terracotta-colored building houses 33 simple and clean modern rooms, all with private bathroom and cable TV.

Hotel Diriá (☎ 680 0080/402; hoteldiria@hotmail .com; s/d US$30/45; P ✖ ✖) On the northern outskirts of town, 500m north of the plaza, you'll find this long-standing hotel on the intersection with the peninsular highway. This is the best hotel in town and has a land-scaped garden, adult and children's pools, a restaurant and 50 rooms with air-con, private bathrooms and cable TVs. Credit cards accepted.

La Fábrica de Tortillas (casados US$2.50; ☺ 6am-6:30pm) Feast on tasty, inexpensive casados at this place 700m south of the plaza. Also referred to by its official name, Coopetortillas, it's a huge corrugated-metal barn that looks like a factory. Inside are plain communal wooden tables, and you eat whatever's available – all of it cooked right in front of you in the wood-stove kitchen.

El Milenio (dishes US$3-6) Chinese food is mighty popular in Santa Cruz, though

---

GUAITIL

An interesting excursion from Santa Cruz is the 12km drive by paved road to the small pottery-making community of Guaitil. Attractive ceramics are made from local clays, using earthy reds, creams and blacks in pre-Columbian Chorotega style. Ceramics are for sale outside the potters' houses in Guaitil and also in San Vicente, 2km beyond Guaitil by unpaved road. If you ask, you can watch part of the potting process, and local residents would be happy to give you a few lessons for a small price.

If you have your car, take the main highway toward Nicoya and then follow the signed Guaitil road to the left, about 1.5km out of Santa Cruz. This road is lined by yellow corteza amarilla trees and is very attractive in April when all of them are in bloom. There are local buses from Santa Cruz, though they're infrequent and unreliable. However, a round-trip cab should only cost about US$10 to US$15, depending on how long you stay.

If you don't have time to get to Guaitil, visit the small *depósito* (outlet) selling ceramics on the peninsular highway, about 10km north of Nicoya on the eastern side of the road. You can also buy them on every street corner in Tamarindo, though you can expect to pay quintuple the price.

El Milenio tops them all with its colossal portions of fried rice, decent stir-fries, big-screen TV and blessed air-con. It's 100m west of the plaza.

Getting There & Away

Santa Cruz is 57km from Liberia and 25km south of Filadelfia. It's on the main peninsular highway and is often an overnight stop for people visiting the peninsula. A paved road leads 16km west to 27 de Abril, from where dirt roads continue to Playa Tamarindo, Playa Junquillal and other beaches.

Some buses depart from the terminal on the north side of Plaza de Los Mangos.

Liberia (La Pampa) US$1, 1½ hours, depart every 30 minutes from 5:30am to 7:30pm.

Nicoya (La Pampa) US$0.50, one hour, depart every 30 minutes from 6am to 9:30pm.

San José US$5.50, 4¼ hours, Tralapa has nine buses from 3am to 5pm, Empresas Alfaro buses depart at 5:30am, 7:30am, 10am, 10:30am, 11:30am, 12:30pm, 3pm and 5pm. (For Alfaro, buy tickets at the Alfaro office, 200m south of the plaza, but catch the bus on the main road north of town.)

Other local buses leave from the terminal 400m east of the plaza. These schedules fluctuate constantly, so ask around.

Bahía Potrero US$1.50, 1¼ hours, depart every two to three hours.

Playa Brasilito US$1.50, one hour, depart in the morning and afternoon.

Playa Flamingo US$1.50, one hour, departs in the afternoon.

Playa Junquillal US$2, 1½ hours, departs in the afternoon.

Playa Tamarindo US$2, 1½ hours, depart every two to three hours.

CENTRAL PENINSULA

The central peninsula has always served as the political and cultural heart of Guanacaste. In 1824 the residents of the city of Nicoya were instrumental in driving the secession of Guanacaste from Nicaragua. Today, however, most Ticos in the region are more concerned with the price of cattle than they are with politics, though the central peninsula is still awash with Guanacasteco pride.

Coastal development in the region is considerably less than the north of the peninsula, though the areas around Sámara and Nosara are growing slowly. Foreigners are particularly drawn to this region because of its lush rain forests and rugged coastal landscape, and for the most part they're actively committed to its conservation.

From Nicoya, Highway 151 runs south to Playa Sámara while Highway 21 continues along the interior of the peninsula.

NICOYA

Situated 23km south of Santa Cruz, Nicoya was named after an indigenous Chorotega chief, who welcomed Spanish conquistador Gil González Dávila in 1523 (a gesture he no doubt regretted; see the boxed text Garabito, p38). In the following centuries, the Chorotegas were wiped out by the colonists, though the sharp facial features of the local residents is a testament to their heritage.

Although Nicoya is in fact a colonial city, very little still remains of the original architecture, and what is left is usually in a state of disrepair. However, Nicoya is one of the most pleasant cities in the region, and the bright buildings and bustling streets contribute to the welcoming atmosphere.

For travelers Nicoya primarily serves as a transportation hub for the region, though the city serves as a good base for exploring Parque Nacional Barra Honda (opposite). It's also a good base for visiting **Puerto Humo**, a small town about 27km northeast on the road to Corallilo that has good opportunities for birding.

Information

Área de Conservación Tempisque (ACT; ☎ 685 5667; ☻ 8am-4pm Mon-Fri) The office of the ACT can help with accommodations and cave exploration at Parque Nacional Barra Honda.

ATH ATM (A Toda Hora ATM) This 24-hour ATM accepts cards on the Cirrus system.

Banco de Costa Rica (☻ 8:30am-3pm Mon-Fri) Exchanges US dollars.

Banco Popular (☻ 9am-4:30pm Mon-Fri, 8:15-11:30am Sat) Also exchanges US dollars.

Ciber Club (per hr US$1; ☻ 9am-9pm Mon-Sat, 1-8pm Sun) Has air-con and roughly a dozen terminals with very good connections.

Clínica Médica Nicoyana (☎ 685 5138) For lesser illnesses, visit this clinic.

Hospital La Anexión (☎ 685 5066) The main hospital on the peninsula is north of town at Hospital La Anexión.

Sights

In Parque Central, a major town landmark is the attractive white colonial **Iglesia de San Blas**, which dates back to the mid-17th century.

The appealingly peaceful, wooden-beamed church is under continuous restoration, and its mosaic tiles are crumbling, but it can be visited. It has a small collection of colonial religious artifacts. The park outside is an inviting spot to stroll and people-watch.

On the opposite side of the park is **La Casa de la Cultura**. This small exhibit area has cultural exhibits a few times a year and features work by local artists. The exhibit schedule and hours of operation are erratic, but it's worth a peek if the doors are open.

Festivals & Events
The town goes crazy for **Día de Guanacaste**, on July 25, so expect plenty of food, music and beer in the plaza to celebrate the province's annexation from Nicaragua. The **Festival de La Virgin de Guadalupe** (see the boxed text A Brief History of the Chorotega, p288) is one of the most unique festivals in Costa Rica.

Sleeping & Eating
All showers are cold unless otherwise stated.

Hotel Chorotega (☎ 685 5245; r per person US$4, s/d with bathroom US$7/9) A pleasant family keeps bare-bones rooms that could use a face-lift, but are reasonably clean and neat, and you're not going to find a cheaper bed elsewhere.

Hotel Las Tinajas (☎ 685 5081; s/d US$10/15; **P**) Decent and mercifully far from the noise of the plaza, the 28 clean (though rough around the edges) rooms have private bathrooms

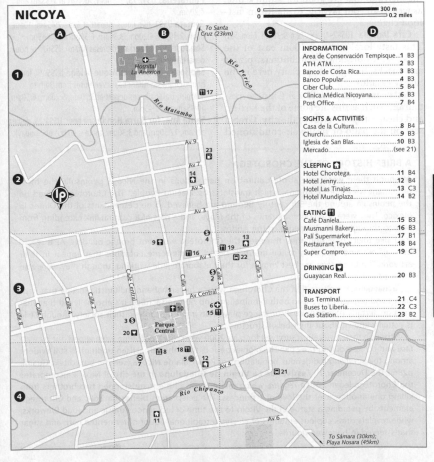

NICOYA

0 ——— 300 m
0 ——— 0.2 miles

INFORMATION
Area de Conservación Tempisque...1 B3
ATH ATM.................................2 B3
Banco de Costa Rica....................3 B3
Banco Popular...........................4 B3
Ciber Club..............................5 B4
Clínica Médica Nicoyana.................6 B3
Post Office.............................7 B4

SIGHTS & ACTIVITIES
Casa de la Cultura......................8 B4
Church.................................9 B3
Iglesia de San Blas....................10 B3
Mercado..............................(see 21)

SLEEPING 🛏
Hotel Chorotega........................11 B4
Hotel Jenny...........................12 B4
Hotel Las Tinajas......................13 C3
Hotel Mundiplaza......................14 B2

EATING 🍴
Café Daniela..........................15 B3
Musmanni Bakery.......................16 B3
Palí Supermarket......................17 B1
Restaurant Teyet......................18 B4
Super Compro.........................19 C3

DRINKING 🍷
Guayacan Real.........................20 B3

TRANSPORT
Bus Terminal..........................21 C4
Buses to Liberia......................22 C3
Gas Station...........................23 B2

PENÍNSULA DE NICOYA

To Santa Cruz (23km)

Río Perico

Hospital La Anexión

Río Matambo

To Sámara (30km); Playa Nosara (45km)

Río Chipanzo

Parque Central

and are a good choice if you want a quiet night's rest.

Hotel Jenny (☎ 685 5050; s/d US$16/25; 🗙) This is a great choice – all 24 spic-and-span rooms have air-con, cable TV and private bathrooms. This is among the best value in town, so it's no wonder it's always packed.

Hotel Mundiplaza (☎ 685 3535; s/d US$25/35; 🗙) If you've got a bit of extra cash in your pocket, you can't do better than the newest hotel in town, which has 25 sparkling, modern rooms offering private hot shower, cable TV and air-con. Go on – treat yourself. Credit cards accepted.

Super Compro and Palí supermarkets provide food and supplies for self-caterers. There are also a number of cheap *sodas* in the *mercado* that are good for a quick bite, as well as all your favorite Costa Rican fast-food chains.

Café Daniela (US$2-4; 🕑 7am-9:30pm Mon-Sat) This tasty local favorite, 100m east of the park, serves breakfast, hamburgers, pizzas and snacks, though the specialty here is the hearty casados.

Restaurant Teyet (meals US$2-5) Chinese restaurants such as this are some of the tastiest and cheapest spots to eat in the city. Grab a seat on the patio or in the air-conditioned interior and feast on huge portions of chow mein and other noodle dishes.

Guayacan Real (meals US$2-4) The best place for a drink and delicious *bocas* is the consistently packed Guayacan Real. The *ceviche* and *patacones* (fried plantain with bean dip) are exceptional and there is cable TV.

Getting There & Away

Most buses arrive at and depart from the bus terminal southeast of Parque Central.

Liberia US$1.25, 2½ hours, depart every 30 minutes from 3am to 8pm.

Playa Naranjo, connects with ferry US$1.75, three hours, depart at 5am, 9am, 1pm and 5pm.

Playa Nosara US$1.50, four hours, depart at 5am, 10am, noon and 3pm.

Puntarenas US$2.75, 2½ hours, depart at 7:35am and 4:20pm.

Sámara US$1, two hours, depart at 6am, 7:45am, 10am, noon, 2:30pm, 4:20pm, 3:30pm, 6:30pm and 9:45pm.

San José, via Liberia (Empresas Alfaro) US$6, five hours, depart five times daily.

San José, via Río Tempisque bridge US$5.25, four hours, Empresas Alfaro has seven buses from 3am to 5:20pm, Tralapa buses depart at 3:20am, 5:20am, 6:50am, 10:45am and 1:45pm.

Santa Ana, for Barra Honda one hour, US$1.25, depart at 8am, 12:30pm and 3:30pm (there is no bus on Sunday).

A BRIEF HISTORY OF THE CHOROTEGA

Although there were several pre-Columbian populations in the Nicoya peninsula, the most prominent were the Chorotega, which translates as 'Fleeing People.' The Chorotega arrived on the peninsula around the 8th century BC, and are believed to be descendants of the Olmec in Mexico. They were also contemporaries of the Maya, and a part of a cultural link extending from Mexico through Central America to the Andes.

Unlike their contemporaries, however, the Chorotega were not prolific builders. As a result, most of our understanding of the group is based on the representations that appear in their artwork. The Chorotega are best known for their elaborate jade working, though they were also talented potters and sculptors.

Archaeologists believe that the Chorotega were a hierarchal and militaristic society that kept slaves and regularly practiced both cannibalism and human sacrifice. It's also believed that shamanism, fertility rites and ritualistic dance played an important role in their society, though little is actually known about their belief structure.

Although their civilization survived for over 2000 years, the Chorotega were wiped out by warfare and disease during the Spanish colonial period, though their artisan tradition is still evident among the surviving indigenous populations of Península de Nicoya (see the boxed text Guaitil, p286). The December 12 **Festival de La Virgin de Guadalupe** in the city of Nicoya incorporates the Chorotega legend of *La Yequita,* which relates how a little mare stopped two brothers from killing one another over the love of a princess. The celebration blends Catholic and Chorotega elements by parading a statue of the Virgin to the tune of indigenous music and loud fireworks, while revelers drink copious amounts of *chicha,* a traditional liquor of fermented corn and sugar that's served in hollowed gourds.

PENÍNSULA DE NICOYA

Other buses depart from the terminal northeast of the park. Buses for Santa Cruz, Filadelfia and Liberia depart every 30 minutes from 3:50am to 8:30pm.

if you need a taxi, try calling **Cootagua** (☎ 686 6490, 686 6590) or **Taxis Unidos de Nicoya** (☎ 686 6857).

PARQUE NACIONAL BARRA HONDA

Situated about halfway between Nicoya and the mouth of the Río Tempisque, this 2295-hectare national park protects a massive underground system of more than 40 caves, and is one of the most unusual (and also highly memorable) national parks in all of the country. The caverns, which are composed of soft limestone, were carved by rainfall and erosion during a period of about 70 million years. Speleologists have discovered just more than 40 caverns, with some of them reaching as far as 200m deep, though to date only 19 have been fully explored. There have been discoveries here of pre-Columbian remains dating back to 300 BC.

The caves come with the requisite cave accoutrements: stalagmites, stalactites and a host of beautiful formations with intriguing names such as fried eggs, organ, soda straws, popcorn, curtains, columns, pearls, flowers and shark's teeth. However, unlike caverns in your own country perhaps, Barra Honda is not developed for widescale tourism, which means that the caves here feel less like a carnival attraction and more like a scene from *Indiana Jones*. So, don your yellow miner's hat, put on some sturdy boots and be prepared to get down and dirty.

Information

The dry season is the only time that tourists are allowed to enter the caves, though hiking is good anytime of year. In the dry season, carry several liters of water and let the rangers know where you are going. Two German hikers died at Barra Honda in 1993 after getting lost on a short hike – they had no water, and succumbed to dehydration. Sneakers or preferably boots are necessary if you will be caving.

The **ranger station** (☎ 659 1551; ⊙ 8am-4pm) in the southwest corner of the park takes the US$6 admission fee and provides information.

Sights

You can only explore the **caves** with a guide from the Asociación de Guías Ecologistas de Barra Honda, which can be arranged in the national park offices in Nicoya (☎ 686 6760), Santa Cruz (☎ 680 1920) and Bagaces (☎ 671 1455). A guide charges about US$20 for a group of up to four cavers, US$25 for five to eight people, and US$30 for groups larger than nine. Equipment rental is an additional US$15 per person. The descent involves using ladders and ropes, so you should be reasonably fit.

A guide service is available for hiking the trails within the park and also for descending into the most popular caves. Guides speak Spanish, though a few of the rangers speak some English.

The only cave with regular access to the public is the 62m-deep **La Terciopelo**, which has the most speleothems – calcite figures that rise and fall in the cave's interior. The best known of these is **El Órgano**, which produces several notes when lightly struck. Scientists and other visitors are required to have permits from the park service to enter other caves. These include **Santa Ana**, the deepest (249m); **Trampa** (Trap), 110m deep with a vertical 52m drop; **Nicoya**, where early human remains were found; and, our favorite, **Pozo Hediondo**, or Fetid Pit, which is famous for its huge piles of bat droppings. Note that caves cannot be entered after 1pm.

Activities

Wildlife-watching underground, you'll have the chance to see such fun-loving creatures as bats, albino salamanders, blind fish and a variety of squiggly little invertebrates. On the surface, howler and white-faced monkeys, armadillos, coatis and white-tailed deer are regularly spotted, as are striped hog-nosed skunks and anteaters.

For **hiking**, the Barra Honda hills have a few trails through deciduous, dry tropical rain forest that lead to waterfalls (in the rainy season) adorned with calcium formations. It's also possible to hike to the top of Cerro Barra Honda, which boasts a lookout with a view that takes in the Río Tempisque and Golfo de Nicoya. Since this national park is comparatively undertouristed and undeveloped, it is advised that you either inquire about the state of the trails before setting out, or hire the services of a guide.

Sleeping & Eating

At the entrance to the park, there is a **camping area** (per person US$2) with bathrooms and showers. There is also a small park-administered area that has three basic dorm-style **cabins** (per person US$12), each with a shower and six beds. Meals can be pre-arranged (breakfast US$1.75, lunch and dinner US$3). Reserve accommodations and meals through the **ACT office** (☎ 685 5667) in Nicoya or by calling the ranger station. Spanish is necessary.

Getting There & Away

The easiest way to get to the park is from Nicoya. No bus goes directly to the park; however, buses to Santa Ana (1km away) will get you close. These leave Nicoya at 8am, 12:30pm and 3:30pm. Return buses leave Santa Ana at 1pm and 6pm. There are no buses on Sunday. The better option is to take a taxi from Nicoya, which will cost about US$10. You can arrange for your driver to pick you up later at a specified time.

If you have your own vehicle, take the peninsular highway south out of Nicoya toward Mansión and make a left at Tony Zecca's restaurant on the access road leading to Puente La Amistad. From here, continue another 1.5km and make a left on the signed road to Barra Honda. The dirt road will take you to the village of Barra Honda and will then wind to the left for another 6km before ending up at the entrance to the national park. The community of Santa Ana is passed en route. The road is clearly marked and there are several signs along the way indicating the direction of the park. After the village of Barra Honda, the road is unpaved, but in good condition. However, there is no telling what the next rainy season will do to it, so ask locally before setting out.

If you are coming from Puente La Amistad you will see the access road to Barra Honda signed about 16km after leaving the bridge. From this point, follow the above directions.

PUENTE LA AMISTAD

Once made exclusively by ferry (car and passenger), the trip over the Río Tempisque has been completely transformed by the recent construction of a brand-new 780m bridge, now the largest in Costa Rica (but tiny by US standards). The Puente La Amistad (Bridge of Friendship) was built with Taiwanese financial support and opened in July 2003. There is a small parking area and observation platform on the western side of the river so that you can admire it and take photos (as the locals proudly do).

NOSARA AREA

The attractive beaches near the small Tico village of Nosara are backed by a pocket of luxuriant vegetation that attracts birds and wildlife. The area has seen little logging, partly because of the nearby wildlife refuge, and partly because of real-estate development – an unlikely sounding combination.

There are a few hundred foreigners living permanently in the Nosara area (mainly North Americans), the majority of them keen on protecting the rain forests. One resident describes the area as 'sophisticated jungle living,' and indeed blending retirement with conservation is an interesting experiment. However, Ticos remain hostile to the development of the area, mainly because land prices have been driven through the roof in just under a decade.

The Nosara area is a magical destination as you can sometimes see parrots, toucans, armadillos and monkeys just a few meters away from the beaches. There are three distinct beaches here. North of the river is **Playa Nosara**, which is difficult to access and primarily used by fishermen. Further south is **Playa Pelada**, a small crescent-shaped beach with an impressive blowhole that sends water shooting through the air at high tide. The southernmost beach is **Playa Guiones**, a 7km stretch of sand that's one of the best surf spots on the central peninsula.

Orientation

The accommodations options are spread out along the coast and a little inland (making a car a bit of a necessity). Nosara village (where you'll find supplies and gas) and the airport are 5km inland from the beach. There are many unidentified little roads, which makes it hard to get around if you don't know the place – look for hotel and restaurant signs, and ask for help. Log on to Nosara Travel's website (www.nosaratravel .com/map.html) for a handy map, or pick one up at Tuanis (opposite).

PENÍNSULA DE NICOYA

Information

There is a public phone by Sodita Vanessa.

Mini Super Delicias del Mundo (per hr US$6; 8:45am-1pm & 2:30-6:15pm) Expensive Internet access is available here, on the second access road to Playa Guiones.

Nosara Office Center (682 0181; www.nosaratravel .com; Internet per hr US$3) Near the airstrip, the office also books NatureAir tickets and arranges car rentals and hotel reservations. Tickets for Sansa airlines can be booked at Rancho Tico (right).

Police (682 0317) Next to the Red Cross and post office on the southeast corner of the soccer field in the village center.

Post office (7:30am-noon & 1-6pm)

Super Nosara (8am-7pm Mon-Sat, 8am-3pm Sun) There is no bank or ATM here but Super Nosara, southwest of the soccer field, will change US dollars and traveler's checks. This is also a good place to stock up on supplies – and it's cheaper than anything by the beaches.

Tuanis (682 0249) By the soccer field, the Dutch-American Tuanis serves as an unofficial tourist information center. It has bike rentals (per day US$8), a notice-board, local crafts, a book exchange, Internet access and rooms for rent in the Backpacker's Bunkhouse (right).

Activities
HIKING

The **Reserva Biológica Nosara** behind the La-garta Lodge has private trails leading through a mangrove wetland down to the river (five minutes) and beach (10 minutes). This is a great spot for birding, and there's a good chance you'll see some reptiles as well (look up in the trees as there are occasionally boa constrictors here). Nonguests can visit the reserve for US$6.

SURFING

Playa Guiones has the best beach break in the central peninsula, especially when there is an offshore wind. Although the beach is usually full of surfers, there are fortunately plenty of take-off points.

On the main road into Guiones, past Café de Paris, **Nosara Surf 'n' Sport** (682 0186; www.nosarasurfshop.com; 7am-6pm) rents ATVs (US$35 to US$50), repairs surfboards and arranges surf lessons and tours.

TURTLE-WATCHING

Most hotels in the area can arrange guided tours to Refugio Nacional de Fauna Silvestre Ostional (p294), where you can watch the mass arrivals of olive ridley turtles.

YOGA

In the hills near Playa Guiones is the famous **Nosara Yoga Institute** (682 0071; www.nosarayoga .com), which has regular classes, weeklong workshops, instructor training and offers massage.

Sleeping & Eating
NOSARA

Backpacker's Bunkhouse (682 0249; nosarabunk house@yahoo.com; camping US$6; r per person US$10;) Swiss Family Robinson meets Alice in Wonderland at this laid-back, dilapidated tree house that's a recommended base for exploring the area – that is, when you're not chilling out with Queenie, the hippie manager. There are trails leading from the bunkhouse down to the nearby river and then up the mountain, and at the time of writing the Dutch owner was in the process of building a small wading pool of continu-ously rushing water. Open-air rooms share warm-water bathrooms, and there's a small communal kitchen.

Rancho Tico (dishes US$4-6) The best casados are served here, at the western end of town, or try the catch of the day, which is usually farm-raised tilapia or red snapper.

There are a few grocery stores in town as well as a number of small *sodas*.

NEAR THE BEACHES

The following places are listed roughly in order as you drive into town from south to north.

Café de Paris (682 0087; www.cafédeparis.net; d without/with kitchen US$60/70, 4-person bungalows US$100, 6-person villas US$120, additional person US$10;) This pleasant hotel is run by a French couple and located at the corner of the main road and the first access road that leads to Playa Guiones. Shiny, clean rooms feature plenty of polished wood-work, a private bathroom and air-con, while larger bungalows and villas are great deals if you're traveling in a group. The bakery-café (ummm, French bread) is perfect for breakfast. Credit cards accepted.

Marlin Bill's (682 0548; meals US$6-14; 11am-2:30pm & 6pm-late Mon-Sat) Across the main road is this popular bar-restaurant with fantas-tic ocean views. It's worth grabbing lunch here when the menu is cheaper, though it's worth the price anytime for a hearty filet of blackened tuna and a slab of key lime pie.

Harbor Reef Lodge (☎ 682 0059; www.harborreef .com; d US$69-85, Pelada/Guiones ste US$102/123, casas per wk US$850-1050; P ⊠ ⊕) These cool tiled rooms with private bathroom, air-con, hot water and fridges have wood detailing and attractive Latin American textiles. Suites are located on Playas Pelada and Guinoes, and are much more expansive and have full kitchens. There are also two- and three-bedroom casas available for rent. They are pristine, secluded and guests can use the hotel's facilities. Credit cards accepted. To get here, continue beyond Nosara Surf 'n' Sport to where the road bends to the left as it hits the shore.

Giardino Tropicale (☎ 682 0258; www.giardinotropi cale.com; tr standard US$58-76, tr deluxe US$64-82; P ⊕) On the main road, north of Marlin Bill's, this collection of white-walled cabins have various sizes and views. The pleasant quarters with solar-heated showers all look out onto a lawn shaded by a huge tree, and there's a pool for taking a cool dip. There's also a rambling, rustic restaurant (dishes US$5 to US$9) that's popular among area residents for its thin-crust pizzas.

Blew Dog's Surf Camp (☎ 682 0080; www.blew dogs.com; dm US$10, d cabin US$45, houses US$40-80) The heart of this reader-recommended, sprawling surfer's retreat is the dorm-style accommodations in the 'flop house,' though the shared bathrooms are spotless and the pool with waterfall shower is perfect for cooling off. There are also a few cabins with private hot-water bathrooms and a few houses for rent in the back of the property. A restaurant serves American-style food and the Reggae Bar plays a continuous stream of surf videos. It's down the road toward the

beach on the right-hand side, past the Mini Super Delicias del Mundo.

Gilded Iguana Bar & Restaurant (☎ 682 0259; www.gildediguana.com; d US$45-65; P ⊠ ⊕) This popular hotel for anglers and surfers has well-furnished, tiled rooms of varying sizes with private hot-water bathrooms and refrigerators. Fishing charters can be arranged and kayaking, snorkeling and nature tours are offered by congenial, English-speaking Joe (☎ 682 0450). The tasty restaurant will grill your catch for you, and the attached bar is a popular gringo hang-out. Credit cards accepted.

Casa Romántica (☎ 682 0019; www.hotelcasaroman tica.com; d casas US$70-76; P ⊠ ⊕) Right next to Playa Guiones is this recommended Spanish colonial mansion with six rooms with private bathrooms in the downstairs arcade. They've all been recently renovated, and have views of the manicured gardens surrounding the thatch-covered pool. There is also private beach access, a small restaurant featuring international cuisine, and well-being services (yoga and massage) and tours can be arranged. Rates include breakfast and credit cards are accepted.

Almost Paradise (☎ 682 0173; www.nosaravacation .de; d US$40; P) Housed in a vintage wooden building high on a hill overlooking Playa Pelada, the six pleasant rooms here have plenty of character and are decorated with Tico crafts, while the wraparound balcony provides fine ocean views. By day, the attached restaurant is the Sunrise Cafe (dishes US$2 to US$4), which is a great place for a Brooklyn style 'caw-fee with shu-gah.' By night, it's Allison's Sunset Bar, which has designer sushi for US$4 to US$6 per roll.

LOCAL LORE

There is a legend of a Tarascos warrior named Curime, who journeyed from Mexico to the Nicoya where he was welcomed by Nambí, the chief of the Chorotega. After his arrival, Curime met a beautiful Chorotega princess named Nochari, whose name in Nahuatl, the language of the Aztecs, meant Land of the Prickly Pear, though Curimeo soon gave her the Tarascos name of Nosara.

One evening, Nambí's village was ambushed by Chiras warriors. Nosara quickly awakened and cried out to Curime. Realizing that the Chiras were heading for the temple, Curime fought back the warriors while Nosara retrieved the temple's treasure and headed to the mountains. After safely burying the treasure Nosara returned to Curime, but moments later he was killed by an arrow to the breast. Although the Chorotega soon swept down from the mountains and drove the Chira away, Nosara was overcome with grief and took her own life with a dagger.

Today, it is believed that when the moon is full you can still hear the voice of Curime calling out to Nosara in the distance.

PENÍNSULA DE NICOYA

To get here, follow the main road from Casa Romántica for a winding 1km, then take the left-hand turnoff for Playa Pelada. Turn right at the fork in the road and you will come to another winding road that leads to several other sleeping and eating options. Almost Paradise is the first of these choices.

Hotel Playas Nosara (☎ 682 0121; d US$70; ℗ ☎) Follow the road all the way down and left and you'll reach this famous Nosara landmark, perhaps the most unusual hotel in Costa Rica. With its whitewashed minaret-style tower and unique architecture, it's somewhere between *1001 Nights* and a Salvador Dalí painting. Balconied rooms offer beautiful beach views and there's a restaurant and pool, but the place feels like it's been abandoned for years.

La Luna (dishes US$9-12; ☺ 11am-11pm) On the beach and to the right of the Hotel Playas Nosara, you'll find this impressive stone building that houses a trendy restaurant-bar. The eclectic menu has Asian and Mediterranean flourishes, and the views (and the cocktails) are intoxicating.

Olga's Bar & Restaurant (casados US$3) A few hundred meters to the north, on a separate side road, lies this perennially popular beachside institution. The Tico-owned joint whips up cheap, yummy casados and very reasonable fish dinners (US$6).

La Mariposa Panaderia Café-Bar (☎ 682 0545; snacks US$1-5) From Olga's, continue north on the road until your reach this much-adored Swiss-run bakery that has everything from fresh breads and homemade brownies to heartier quiches and sandwiches.

Rancho Suizo Lodge (☎ 682 0057; www.nosara.ch; s/d/tr incl breakfast US$38/55/87; ℗ ☎) Make a left in front of La Mariposa and follow the road to the left for another 200m to the end and you'll come to Rancho Suizo. It's only a few minutes' walk from Playa Pelada and is run by René and Ruth, a charming Swiss couple. Rustic, tiled-bungalows all have private hot-water bathrooms, and there's an inviting pool and whirlpool. The Piratabar is a popular spot for drinking and beachside barbecues, while El Pelicano (meals US$6 to US$12) has innovative Swiss-Tico dishes using fresh local ingredients.

Nosara B&B (☎ 682 0209; s/d/tr incl breakfast US$39/49/65) Further north, on a private access road, this cute, clean and quiet option is set back in the trees near a quiet strand of beach. All rooms have private hot-water bathrooms and simple decorative motifs.

Lagarta Lodge (☎ 682 0035; www.lagarta.com; s/d/tr US$70/76/82; ℗ ☐ ☎) Further north, a road dead-ends at this seven-room hotel, a recommended choice high on a steep hill above the private 50-hectare Reserva Biológica Nosara. Birding and wildlife spotting is good here – and you can watch from the comfort of the hotel balcony or see many more species if you go on a hike. Large rooms have high ceilings, hot showers and small private patios or balconies. The balcony restaurant (breakfast and lunch US$4 to US$7, dinner US$9 to US$15) is worth a visit just for the spectacular sunsets, though the rotating menu of international and Tico specialties is equally appealing.

Pancho's Resort (☎ 682 0591; panchsnosara@rasca .co.cr; d without/with air-con US$50/60; ℗ ☒ ☐ ☎) On the main road leading back to Nosara village, this huge complex comes complete with supermarket, bar, restaurant and cabinas. Bungalows with private hot-water bathrooms have attractive tiled floors and high ceilings, and you're just steps from one of the most beautiful pools in Nosara.

Red Lion (meals US$3-8; ☺ 7am-late) Every neighborhood needs a proper British pub, and now Nosara has one, just up the road from Pancho's. The owners serve up traditional English staples like fish and chips, roast beef and meat pies, though it's worth saving some stomach space for the wide selection of imported beers, including Leffe, Guinness and Hoegaarden. There's a satellite TV with all the sports channels and a pool table for all your drunken gaming needs.

Drinking & Entertainment

Aside from the bars and restaurants previously listed, there are a few spots in the village of Nosara.

Near the soccer field are two Tico-riffic spots, Tropicana and Bar Bambú, though travelers enjoy the gringa-run La Vida Buena. Or you can have a beer served by a hard-working prostitute at Beatle Bar, a branch of the nefarious Jacó institution (p339).

Getting There & Away

AIR

Both Sansa and NatureAir have three daily flights to and from San José for about US$80 each way.

BUS

Local buses depart from the *pulpería* by the soccer field. Traroc buses depart for Nicoya (US$2.25, two hours) at 5am, 7am, 12:25pm and 3pm. Empresas Alfaro buses going to San José (US$5, five to six hours) depart from the pharmacy by the soccer field at 12:30pm.

For US$0.25, any of these buses will drop you off at the beach. To get to Sámara, take any bus out of Nosara and ask the driver to drop you off at *la bomba de Sámara* (Sámara gas station). From there, catch one of the buses traveling from Nicoya to Sámara. It's also easy to hitch at this point (see p552 for tips).

CAR

From Nicoya, a paved road leads toward Playa Sámara. About 5km before Sámara (signed), a windy, bumpy (and, in the dry season, dusty) dirt road leads to the village (4WD recommended). It's also possible to continue north (in the dry season), to Ostional, Paraíso and Junquillal, though you'll have to ford rivers. Ask around before trying this road in the rainy season, when the Río Nosara becomes all but impassable.

The nearest gas station is on the paved road leading to Sámara. Otherwise, vendors in Nosara sell gas from drums around town.

REFUGIO NACIONAL DE FAUNA SILVESTRE OSTIONAL

This 248-hectare coastal refuge extends from Punta India in the north to Playa Guiones in the south, and includes the beaches of Playa Nosara and Playa Ostional. It was created in 1992 to protect the *arribadas,* or mass nesting of the olive ridley sea turtles, which occurs from July to November with a peak from August to October. Along with Playa Nancite in Parque Nacional Santa Rosa, Ostional is one of two main nesting grounds for this turtle in Costa Rica.

The olive ridley is one of the smallest species of sea turtle, typically weighing around 45kg. Although endangered, there are a few beaches in the world where ridleys nest in large groupings that can number in the thousands. Scientists believe that this behavior is an attempt to overwhelm predators, which contributes to increased species survival.

Prior to the creation of the park, coastal residents used to harvest eggs indiscriminately (drinking raw turtle eggs is thought to increase sexual vigor). However, an imaginative conservation plan has allowed the inhabitants of Ostional to continue to harvest eggs from the first laying, which are often trampled by subsequent waves of nesting turtles. By allowing locals to harvest the first batches, the economic livelihood of the community is maintained, and the villagers in turn act as park rangers to prevent other poachers from infringing on their enterprise.

Rocky **Punta India** at the northwestern end of the refuge has tide pools that abound with marine life, such as sea anemones, urchins and starfish. Along the beach, thousands of almost transparent ghost crabs go about their business, as do the bright-red Sally Lightfoot crabs. The vegetation behind the beach is sparse and consists mainly of deciduous trees, and is home to iguanas, crabs, howler monkeys, coatis and many birds. Near the southeastern edge of the refuge is a small mangrove swamp where there is good birding.

Activities

Mass arrivals of **nesting turtles** occur during the rainy season every three or four weeks and last about a week (usually on dark nights preceding a new moon), though it's possible to see turtles in lesser numbers almost any night during nesting season. In the dry season, a fitting consolation prize is the small numbers of leatherback and green turtles that also nest here. Many of the upmarket hotels and tour operators in the region offer tours to Ostional during nesting season, though you can also visit independently.

Aside from turtle-watching, **surfers** can catch some good lefts and rights here just after low tide, though the beach is notorious for its strong currents and huge, crashing surf – it's definitely not suitable for swimming unless you're green and have flippers.

Sleeping & Eating

Camping (per person US$3) is permitted behind the centrally located Soda La Plaza, which has a portable toilet available. The *soda* is open for breakfast, lunch and dinner.

Hospedaje Guacamaya (☎ 682 0430; r per person US$5) In the village of Ostional, this place has several small and dark rooms with shared cold showers, though you'll be thrilled to spend the night here as demand is high during nesting season. The same folks run the attached *pulpería*, which can sell you basic supplies.

Cabinas Ostional (☎ 682 0428; r per person US$10) The rooms are slightly better here, with private cold-water shower and a cozy garden. It too fills up quickly.

Rancho Brovilla (☎ 839 2327; r per person US$36; 🅡) In the hills, 2km north of town, Rancho Brovilla is an upscale lodge that's a world away from the more modest accommodations in Ostional. Rooms are adorned with stained-wood accents and come equipped with private hot-water bathrooms. There's also a restaurant-bar (dishes US$6 to US$10) featuring Thai, Mexican, Italian and Tico favorites, as well as an Aikido studio and a telescope for viewing the Pacific sunsets.

Getting There & Away

Ostional village is about 8km northwest of Nosara village. During the dry months there are two daily buses from Santa Cruz (times change, so ask around), but at any time of the year the road can get washed out by rain. Hitching from Nosara is reportedly easy.

If you're driving, plan on taking a 4WD as a couple of rivers need to be crossed. From the main road joining Nosara beach and village, turn north just before Supermercado La Paloma. Continue north for about 400m and you will see a pedestrian bridge over the Río Nosara. The river becomes deep in the rainy season, so approach it with respect; see the boxed text Driving Through Rivers, p551 before attempting to drive across a river. After the bridge, there's a T-junction; take the right fork and continue 1.2km to another T-junction, where you take the left fork. From here, continue on the main road north to Ostional, about 6km away.

Beyond Ostional, the dirt road continues onto Marbella before arriving in Paraíso, northeast of Junquillal. Ask carefully before attempting this drive and use 4WD.

PLAYA SÁMARA

The crescent-shaped strip of pale-grey sand at Sámara is one of the most beloved beaches in Costa Rica – it's safe, tranquil, reasonably developed and easily accessible by public transportation. Not surprisingly, it's popular with vacationing Tico families, backpackers, wealthy tourists, snorkelers

and surfers alike (even President Oscar Arias has a vacation house near here).

In recent years the village has undergone a bit of a transformation. Sámara is becoming increasingly more sophisticated, and Tico and ex-pat residents are giving face-lifts to tired-looking shops, restaurants and storefronts. Although the village is trying to hang on to the authenticity of its relaxed vibe, Sámara is without a doubt the most upscale destination on the central peninsula.

Information

A good source of inform n is www.samara beach.com.

Banco Nacional (☎ 656 0086; ⏰ 9am-5pm Mon-Fri) Change money at this bank behind the church.

Lava Ya (☎ 656 0059; ⏰ 8am-5pm) Drop your dirty shirts off here; it's 75m east of the main road and 100m north of the beach. The amiable American owner can provide you with information on everything there is to do in town.

Tropical Latitude (☎ 656 0120; per hr US$2) Check your email here, 100m east of the main road.

Activities

BIKING

Ciclo Sámara (☎ 656 0438) rents bicycles for US$2.50 an hour or US$12 per day. It's 100m west of Cabinas Arenas.

CANOPY TOUR

The local zip-line operator is **Wingnuts** (☎ 656 0153; US$40), on the eastern outskirts of town off the main paved road.

FLIGHTS

Several kilometers west, in Playa Buenavista, the **Flying Crocodile** (☎ 656 8048; www.flying-croco dile.com) offers ultralight flights for US$60.

SWIMMING

Though the surf can pick up just before high tide, Sámara is safe for swimming.

SNORKELING & DIVING

When the water's calm and visibility high, snorkelers should check out the coral reef in the center of the bay. Divers can go to **Pura Vida Dive** (☎ 398 8655), 100m west of the church, which arranges trips to nearby sites.

SURFING

Experienced surfers will probably be bored with Sámara's inconsistent waves, though beginner surfers can have a blast here.

If you need a little schooling, the experienced and personable Jesse at **Jesse's Samara Beach Gym & Surf School** (☎ 656 0055; whiteagle@racsa.co.cr) has been teaching wannabe surfers for years, and his expert instruction is highly recommended by readers. If you need a workout, his gym has machines and free weights (per day US$3). If you need a massage, his daughter Sunrise has professional certifications.

Another great choice is the **C&C Surf School & Adventure Center** (☎ 656 0628; samarasurfcamp .com), at the northern end of town, which donates US$3 from every surf lesson to a local children's school and a turtle conservation project. It also arranges a variety of tours and trips throughout Costa Rica.

Courses

Centro de Idiomas Intercultura (☎ 656 0127; www .interculturacostarica.com) has a campus right on the beach. Language courses begin at US$260 a week without homestay.

Tours

Tío Tigre (☎ 656 0098; www.samarabeach.com/ps35 .html) and **Carrillo Tours** (☎ 656 0543; www.carrillo tours.com), on opposite sides of the street near the Super Sámara, offer all kinds of excursions: snorkeling, dolphin-watching, turtle-watching, kayaking and horseback riding.

Sleeping

BUDGET

Showers are all cold unless otherwise noted. High-season prices are listed.

Camping Los Coco (☎ 656 0496; camping per person US$3) On the eastern edge of the beach, this attractive site has well-maintained facilities.

Cabinas Playa Sámara (☎ 656 0190; r per person US$7; **P**) Off the soccer field, this is the number one choice for Tico travelers (who must be completely immune to the sound of the pounding nightclub next door). Clean lime-green rooms with private bathrooms are yours for a cheap price, but don't expect to get much sleep here.

Cabinas Kunterbunt (☎ 656 0235; www.cabinas -villa-kunterbunt.com; r per person US$10; **P** ✗ ☎) Though it's about 3km outside of town on the road to Playa Carillo, this is a great choice if you have your own wheels. Tommy, the German owner, has built a handful of 'multi-colored' (in case you were wondering what Kunterbunt meant) cabinas right beside a

quiet section of beach that has a good reef break. There are larger private rooms with hot water available for US$35, and guests can use the communal kitchen.

Bar Restaurant Las Olas (☎ 656 0187; camping per person US$3; d cabin/thatched hut US$25/30, additional person US$5) This beachside place is about 200m west of Soda Sheriff Rustic, and offers the most unusual accommodations in town: one- and two-story thatched huts with private bathroom. There are no screens, so plan on bugs. It also offers camping and there are several regular cabinas as well. As the name implies, there is also a bar-restaurant.

Posada Matilori (☎ 656 0314; d/tr US$25/35; **P**) Without a doubt, this is the best budget option in town. The Italian-Tica owners are simply delightful, and their rustic and tranquil farmhouse just outside of the town center (yet only 50m from the beach) is the perfect place to call home for a few days (or weeks). Need more reasons to stay? How about hot showers, free laundry, free coffee and tea, free use of the boogie boards, a fully equipped outdoor kitchen and lots of comfy hammocks.

Casa Paraiso (☎ 656 0471; s/d/q incl breakfast US$20/36/60; **P**) This comfortable B&B run by a pleasant Tico family is on the road to Playa Carillo. Rooms with private bathrooms are basic, though the owners fill the place with warmth, and the freshly cooked breakfasts are a great way to start your day.

Cabinas Arenas (☎ 656 0320; s/d US$25/32; **P**) On the main drag you'll find this unremarkable budget option, though it's clean and one of the cheaper places in town. Rooms have private bathrooms and are fairly quiet at night.

MIDRANGE & TOP END

All showers are hot unless otherwise stated.

Casa Valeria B&B (☎ 656 0511; casavaleria_af@ hotmail.com; d/bungalows US$30/50) This intimate little B&B is right on the beach about 100m east of the main road. The rooms and bungalows vary in size and are fairly simple, though it's the hammock-strung palm trees and tranquil garden setting that make this place a winner. A communal kitchen is available, and in the mornings you can sit back and enjoy Valeria's home-cooked meals.

Entre Dos Aguas B&B (☎ 656 0641; www.samara .net.ms; s/d/tr/q incl breakfast US$30/40/57/62; **P** ☐ ☎) This fantastic hilltop inn, on the way into town, is what one reader accurately describes as 'Mercedes Benz accommodations on a Toyota budget.' Seven freshly painted rooms have private stone showers. There is a well-manicured garden surrounding the pool, free Internet access and bike rental. English, Spanish, Italian and German are spoken.

Hotel Belvedere (☎ 656 0213; www.samara-costarica .com; d/tr/q US$35/40/60, d bungalows US$65; P ⊠ ⊠ ⊠) Set in a breezy garden with nice views at the northern end of town, the Hotel Belvedere has 10 whitewashed rooms with exposed-wooden beams, a solar-heated private shower, cable TV and a small private terrace. Two larger bungalows include a kitchenette – perfect for self-caterers looking for a quiet spot in town. The German owners also speak English. All rates include breakfast, and credit cards are accepted.

Hotel Casa del Mar (☎ 656 0264; www.casadelmar samara.com; d without/with bathroom incl breakfast US$29/65, additional person US$10; P ⊠) Just east of the Super Sámara and close to the beach is this agreeable American-run hotel, which has a good mix of rooms for travelers of all budgets. If you don't need your own bathroom, rooms here are a steal (and you can still use the Jacuzzi), though those with private bathrooms are bright, airy and well worth the money.

Tico Adventure Lodge (☎ 656 0628; www.ticoad venturelodge.com; d US$45, tree-top apt US$90, poolside house US$120; P ⊠ ⊠) The American owners are proud of the fact that they built this lodge without cutting down a single tree, and they have every reason to be – it's stunning. Nine double rooms with private bathrooms and wood accents are surrounded by lush vegetation and old-growth trees while the tree-top apartment for four lets you swing on the patio hammock from three stories high. Or you can stay in the poolside house for five with a fully equipped kitchen and dining room and dream about a life in the tropics. Cheaper weekly and monthly rates are available.

Hotel Giada (☎ 656 0132; www.hotelgiada.net; s/d/ tr/q incl breakfast US$50/75/85/100; P ⊠ ⊠) On the main road down to the beach is this charming boutique hotel. Well-placed tropical plants and bamboo give it a tropical feel, while Mediterranean-washed rooms with sparkling tiles and private bathrooms make for a comfortable night's sleep.

Hotel Mirador de Sámara (☎ 656 0044; www.mira dordesamara.com; sky-room/apt US$95/105, additional person US$15; P ⊠) Perched on a hill on the northern edge of town is this architecturally unusual hotel, complete with looming towers that offer dizzying views of the area. The sky-rooms can accommodate up to three while the large apartments with kitchens can sleep up to six. There's also a small private restaurant with panoramic views of the entire area. Credit cards accepted.

Villas Kalimba (☎ 656 0929; www.villaskalimba.com; d/tr/q US$110/130/150; P ⊠ ⊠) This reader-recommended collection of Spanish-colonial villas is perhaps the best-appointed accommodations in the Sámara area. Each self-contained and climate-controlled unit is awash in bright Mediterranean colors, and features lush bedding, rich ceramic tiles, regal bathrooms and kitchens fit for a chef (complete with long wooden tables for family-style dining). The villas surround a garden pool, and are just steps from the beach.

Eating

Out with the old and in with the new is the name of the game in Sámara. There are still some simple *sodas* left in town, though with each passing year the restaurant scene is reinventing itself to cater to a more sophisticated palate. Self-caterers can stock up on supplies at the Super Sámara Market, east of the main road.

Soda Sheriff Rustic (dishes US$2-5) One of a few classic *sodas* in town, the beachside location sells itself, though the filling breakfasts, killer casados and low, low prices aren't too bad either.

Soda Ananas (☎ 656 0491; dishes US$2-5) Near the entrance to town, this health-conscious *soda* run by Tica owner Beatriz has delicious veggie burgers, fresh salads, fruit smoothies and (our favorite) scooped-out pineapple sundaes with homemade ice cream.

Pizza & Pasta a Go-Go (dishes US$4-9) This place on the main road has a huge list (we're talking over 50 choices!) of thin-crust pizzas and fresh pastas with all the fixings.

Shake Joe's (☎ 656 0252; dishes US$5-10) This hip beachside spot is awash with chilled-out electronica and cool, calm travelers lounging on the huge wooden outdoor couches. The French toast will start your day right, though the ambience is tops when the sun goes down and the drinks start to flow.

Restaurant El Dorado (☎ 656 0145; dishes US$5-10; 🕑 5-10pm, closed Thu) It's not hard to have the best Italian food in Sámara when all your pasta is homemade, your meats and cheeses are imported directly from Italy, and you have the Pacific Ocean in your backyard.

Restaurant Las Brasas (☎ 656 0546; dishes US$7-12) This upscale Spanish restaurant on the main street has all the signature dishes including tortillas, paellas and roast suckling pig. It also has a well-stocked wine cellar, and the upstairs balcony is perfect for people-watching.

Drinking & Entertainment

The coolest nightspot in town is La Vela Latina, on the beach, which serves sophisticated *bocas* and perfectly blended cocktails and sangria to guests sitting on wooden seats or rocking in comfy leather chairs. On the main road, La Gondola is also a fun late-night spot for drinks, pool and darts – check out the full-on mural of Venice. Shake Joe's (see p297) really gets going in the evenings with soft lighting and trendy tunes. Tutti Frutti Discotheque (on the beach) keeps the music pumping hard most weekends of the year, and is perennially popular with Ticos.

Shopping

Numerous vendors sell crafts and hand-made jewelry at stands along the main road.

Koss Art Gallery (☎ 656 0284) Visit Jaime at his outdoor studio on the beach, where he frequently displays his richly hued works in the high season. Call ahead for a viewing.

Also worth a stop is Mama Africa, which sells beautiful beaded leather sandals from Kenya. The Italian owners work directly with a Maasai collective that crafts the sandals, and purchases support this work.

Getting There & Away

The beach lies about 35km southwest of Nicoya on a well-paved road.

AIR

The airport is between Playa Sámara and Playa Carrillo (actually closer to the latter), and serves both communities. Sometimes the airport is referred to as Carrillo. Sansa flies daily to and from San José (one way/round trip US$78/156). It has an office in Hotel Giada (see p297).

BUS

Empresas Alfaro has a bus to San José (US$5, five hours) that departs from the main road at 4:30am and 8:30am. There is an added departure at 3pm on Sunday.

Traroc buses to Nicoya (US$1, two hours) depart from the *pulpería* by the soccer field at 5:30am, 7am, 8:45am, 11:30am, 1:30pm and 4:30pm.

PLAYA CARRILLO

This beach begins about 4km southeast of Sámara and is a smaller, quieter, less-developed version. With its clean sand, rocky headlands and curving boulevard of palm trees, Carrillo is a postcard-perfect tropical beach. During weekends and holidays, the beach can get crowded with Tico families who descend from San José and Nicoya for a little fun in the sun.

The town is on a hillside above the beach and attracts a trickle of surfers working their way down the coast, as well as schools of American sportfishers chasing billfish (see the boxed text Sportfishing, p300).

Activities

SPORTFISHING

Kingfisher Sportfishing (☎ 656 0091; www.costari cabillfishing.com) is a well-known local outfit, offering full-day offshore excursions for US$850. **Kitty Cat Sportfishing** (☎ 656 0170; www .sportfishcarrillo.com) is another reputable operation, with full-day charters at US$750.

SURF CASTING

You don't have to drop big bucks to catch some nice-sized fish – do as the Ticos do and try your hand at surf casting. Most hotels and tour outfitters can set you up for a few dollars.

SURFING

Surfing here is better than at nearby Playa Sámara, though it's nothing great. Mid to high tide is when you can catch some decent waves.

Tours

Popos (☎ 656 0086; www.poposcostarica.com) offers exciting, well-orchestrated and reasonably priced kayak tours, including a few designed for families. Prices start at US$55.

Carrillo Tours (☎ 656 0543; www.carrillotours.com; 🕑 8am-7pm), on the road up the hill, organizes snorkeling, dolphin-watching, kayaking, horseback riding and trips to Palo Verde (p216). It also offers Internet access for US$3 per hour.

Sleeping & Eating

Camping Mora (☎ 656 0118; per person US$3; P) At the western end of the beach, this camp site has showers, bathrooms, electricity and potable water.

All of the following hotels are at the eastern end of the beach on a hill. The beach is a five- to 10-minute walk down from most of these places.

Casa Pericos (☎ 656 0061; camping per person US$5, dm/d US$9/25; P) This laid-back place to the left up the hill is a great budget option for campers, hostellers and couples alike. Four dorm beds and three double rooms have ocean view and private bathroom, and there's also a deck with amazing views, a living room and communal kitchen. The welcoming owners speak German and English, and offer surfing, diving and horseback trips.

Carrillo Club (☎ 656 0316; www.carrilloclub.com; s/d incl breakfast US$45/55, apt US$75; P 🏊) This pretty yellow inn near the top of the hill has a clutch of cabinas with great views as well as a nice pool and spa. All rooms have private hot-water bathrooms, and the larger four-person apartments also have kitchens.

Cabinas El Colibrí (☎ 656 0656; www.hotelcabinas elcolibri.com; s/d/tr incl breakfast US$50/58/66; P) These Argentinean-run cabinas are high on the hilltop, and come fully equipped with private hot-water bathrooms and kitchenettes. It's a relaxed and comfortable spot, and you'll be well fed at the attached restaurant (open from 5pm to midnight, dishes US$4 to US$10), which serves traditional Argentinean *parrilladas* (grilled meats) and *empanadas*.

Hotel Esperanza B&B (☎ 656 0564; www.hotel esperanza.com; d incl breakfast US$58, additional person US$10; P) A multilingual French-Canadian couple are your wonderful hosts at this recommended B&B. Cheerful rooms set back from a columned promenade have private hot showers, and the attached restaurant, El Ginger (open from 5:30pm to 9pm, dishes US$5 to US$9), is famous for its fresh fish and heavenly banana flambé desserts.

Pizzería Restaurant y Bar El Tucán (dishes US$3-7; 🕔 5:30-10:30pm Thu-Tue) On the turnoff to the beach, this restaurant is recommended for its great pizzas and hearty Italian favorites.

There are a number of small *sodas* near the beach.

Getting There & Away

Regularly scheduled Sansa flights to and from San José (one way/round trip US$78/156) use the airstrip just northwest of the beach. Some Traroc buses from Nicoya to Sámara continue on the well-paved road to Playa Carrillo – check with the driver first.

ISLITA AREA

The coast southeast of Playa Carrillo remains one of the most isolated and wonderful stretches of coastline in the Nicoya, mainly because it's largely inaccessible and lacking in accommodation. Regardless, if you're willing to tackle some rugged roads or venture down the coastline in a sea kayak (or possibly on foot), you'll be rewarded with abandoned beaches backed by pristine wilderness and rugged hills.

There is some very good surfing north of Punta Islita on **Playa Camaronal**, as well as some smaller breaks in front of the Hotel Punta Islita. **Playa Corzalito** and **Playa Bejuco** to the south of the Punta Islita are both backed by mangrove swamps, and offer good opportunities for birding and wildlife-watching.

Also worth a visit is the small town of **Islita**, which is home to the Museo de Arte Contemporáneo al Aire Libre, an open-air exhibition of contemporary art featuring mosaics, murals, carvings and paintings that adorn everything from houses to tree trunks. This project was organized by the Hotel Punta Islita, which sells local art in its gift shops and invests proceeds in the community. If you're interested in helping with the project, inquire at the hotel about volunteer possibilities in the community.

Sleeping & Eating

You can camp on the beaches (without facilities) if you have a vehicle and are self-sufficient.

Hotel Punta Islita (☎ 661 3324/32, in San José 231 6122; www.hotelpuntaislita.com; d/ste US$200/350, villas US$450-800; P 🅿 🖥 🏊) This luxury resort should serve as an example of how to ethically

SPORTFISHING

Sportfishing is a form of recreational fishing that emphasizes the thrill of finding and catching a fish instead of focusing on its culinary value (though plenty of sports fish like tuna and swordfish are delicious). Primarily, anglers are interested in large, deep-sea fish like marlin and tarpon that put up a good fight when they're hooked. Sportfishing is almost always done with a hook, rod and reel instead of nets or other aids.

With two coastlines of tropical water, Costa Rica is regarded as one of the top sportfishing destinations in the world. However, the sportfishers themselves are among the most vilified groups in the country, and it's common for Tico fishermen to go on strike protesting their presence. It's difficult to say who is in the right, though there is merit to the arguments on both sides.

Ticos resent sportfishers mainly because they tend to be extremely wealthy. With high fuel prices and expensive boat and equipment rentals, a typical sportfishing outing can cost upwards of US$1000 per day. It also doesn't help that most anglers tend to be rich Americans with a penchant for young women. Indeed, anyone who travels throughout Costa Rica for a long period of time soon realizes that hotels that cater to 'anglers' are, more often than not, nothing more than high-end brothels.

However, although sportfishing does interfere slightly with commercial fishing operations, its environmental impact is comparably much less. For example, although anglers in the past killed their catches so that they could be weighed and preserved as trophies, today it's standard to practice 'catch and release.' This is a drastic difference from commercial fishing operations, which typically use longlines containing hundreds or thousands of baited hooks. Longlines tend to hook a variety of other animals, including dolphins and whales, and conservationists believe that the method is responsible for declining sea turtle populations.

With Baby Boomers continuing to colonize the Pacific coastline, it's not likely that sportfishing is going to (or even should) stop anytime soon. But it's evident that high-end prostitution is on the rise, and although the link is not causal, there is certainly a correlation.

---

operate a hotel in Costa Rica. In addition to organizing community arts projects, the hotel has sponsored the construction of various public buildings, including a new church, and is consistently working to integrate the rural community of Islita into its development. The hotel is on a hilltop, and has 40 fully equipped rooms with staggering ocean views (some of the pricier units even have private Jacuzzis). The pool and surrounding grounds are simply stunning, and the impeccable staff can arrange any tour you desire.

1492 Restaurant (dishes US$10-25) The movie *1492* was shot on location in Punta Islita and many of the set pieces can be seen in this restaurant, which is inside the Hotel Punta Islita and open to the public. Dishes here are top quality, and there is a continuously rotating array of specialty *ceviches* and seafood.

Restaurant Mirador Barranquilla (dishes US$3-5; 11am-10pm Wed-Mon) On the crest of a hill about 2km southeast of the hotel, the Mirador Barranquilla has breathtaking 180-degree views of Punta Islita and Playas Bejuco and San Miguel, and is the top place in the area for a sunset beer.

Getting There & Away

AIR

NatureAir flies once daily between San José and Punta Islita (one way/round trip US$80/160).

BUS

The closest you can get to Islita by bus is Empresa Arza's two daily buses from San José that go through San Francisco de Coyote and on to Playas San Miguel and Bejuco. Keep in mind, though, that from Bejuco there is still a long uphill hike to Islita – and hitching is almost impossible due to the lack of traffic.

CAR

Although Punta Islita is less than 10km by road southeast of Playa Carrillo, the road is wicked and requires some river crossings that are impossible in the wet season (see the boxed text Along the West Coast by 4WD, p302). The 'easiest' route is for you to head inland from Playa Carrillo through the communities of San Pedro and Cangrejal, which is also known as Soledad, and then down to Bejuco on the coast. From there, you can head to Islita (to the northwest).

PLAYAS SAN MIGUEL & COYOTE

Just south of Playa Bejuco are arguably two of the most beautiful (and least visited) beaches in Costa Rica. Playa San Miguel, to the north, and Playa Coyote, to the south, are wilderness beaches of fine, silver-grey sand that are separated by the mouth of the Río Jabillo. Despite opportunities for great surfing, kayaking and just about anything else you want to do on a sandy strip of paradise, the beaches are nearly always abandoned (though the lack of reliable public transportation is probably to blame). As if there weren't enough reasons to visit, San Miguel and Coyote also serve as nesting grounds for olive ridley turtles (see the boxed text Have More Time?, p304).

There are no coastal villages to speak of, though a number of in-the-know foreigners have settled in the area and have built some beautiful accommodations near the shoreline. The nearest village is **San Francisco de Coyote**, which is 4km inland and has a few small *sodas* and cabinas.

Activities

Surfers will revel in the crowd-free beach breaks off of San Miguel, particularly when the tide is rising. At Coyote there is an offshore reef that can be surfed at high tide.

Swimmers are advised to take precautions as the surf can pick up, and there are not many people in the area to help you in an emergency.

If you have your own sea kayak, these beaches (as well as nearby Islita) are perfect for coastal exploration.

Sleeping & Eating

If you're self-sufficient, you can camp on both beaches (just don't expect services).

Chez Bruno B&B (☎ 655 8157; r per person US$25) This perfect retreat for couples is 1km before the turnoff for San Miguel, and has sweeping views of the coastline from its hilltop location. Pleasant bungalows have private hot showers and attractive tiling, though the real appeal of staying here is being able to use the private trail which winds down the hillside to a pristine section of Playa San Miguel that's only visited by fishermen.

Blue Pelican (☎ 390 7203, 655 8046; www.theblue pelicaninn.com; d US$30, 4-person surfer room US$40; **P**) Near the center of Playa San Miguel is this recommended, quirky purple wooden house owned by a friendly Floridian named Ronnie. Whether you're traveling with your significant other or your best mates, Ronnie's got a room for you, and they're all just steps from the beach. The bar-restaurant (dishes US$4 to US$12) has a mixed menu of international dishes emphasizing fresh seafood, and the beer is always cold (this is a hard thing to find in these parts).

Azul Plata B&B (☎ 655 8080; azul-plata@gmx.net; d incl breakfast US$30, studio US$45; **P**) This homey, German-run inn has five modern and comfortable rooms with private hot showers. There is also a larger studio apartment for rent that has a living room and a deck overlooking the ocean.

Hotel Arca de Noé (☎ 655 0065; www.hotelarcade noe.com; d incl breakfast US$60, d surfer US$20, additional person US$5; **P**) Inland from the beach, this pleasantly landscaped complex has 10 attractive doubles with private hot showers and air-con. Five cheap 'surfer' rooms have bunk beds and cold-water showers. There is also an Italian restaurant and a bar.

Soda Familiar y Cabinas Rey (☎ 655 1055; s/ d/tr US$6/15/20; **P**) For those taking the more direct (and treacherous) route to Mal País, this Tico-run *soda* in the village of San Francisco de Coyote is a good place to stock up on provisions and get some local advice. If it's getting late, you might want to stay here as there are simple cabinas with private cold showers for rent. And, believe it or not, it is also a wireless hot spot – seriously. We didn't believe it either until we tested it!

Bar.Co Nico (boras US$3-6; ☉ 5pm-late) A few kilometers past the village on the turnoff for Costa de Oro, this German-run beachfront restaurant (which looks like a giant ship) has reinstated the old Tico tradition of giving away a free *boca* with every beer. The beer is cold and the *bocas* are delicious – what are you waiting for?

ALONG THE WEST COAST BY 4WD

If you are truly adventurous, have a lot of time on your hands and have some experience driving in places where there is nary a road in sight, then you might be ready to take on the southern Pacific coast of Península de Nicoya. Make sure that you have a 4WD with high clearance though, as well as a comprehensive insurance policy. Do *not* attempt this drive during the rainy season.

Mal País, Montezuma and Cabo Blanco are most frequently reached by the road that follows the eastern part of the peninsular coast and connects with the ferry from Puntarenas in Playa Naranjo. However, if you're looking for some adventure in your life, it's possible to take a 4WD from Playa Carrillo along the southeast coast to Islita, Playa Coyote, south to Mal País and points beyond. Again, don't even *think* of trying to do any of this in a regular car.

As the crow flies, it's about 70km of 'road' from Playa Carrillo to Mal País, though you should allow at least five hours for the trip (provided you encounter no delays). Several rivers have to be forded, including the Río Ora about 5km east of Carrillo, which is impassable at high tide during the dry season – even to 4WDs; check tide schedules.

From Playa Coyote, drivers will cross a few more rivers, including the Río Bongo and Río Arío, and pass by Playas Caletas, Arío and Manzanillo (you can camp on any of these beaches if you're self-sufficient). There are some pretty hairy river crossings throughout this stretch, so it certainly pays to talk to locals before setting out. In some cases the road doesn't cross directly through the river, and you'll have to drive up the river a bit to find the egress. In these cases, it is best to walk the river first, double-check the egress and then drive in so that you don't plunge your rental car into thigh-deep mud or onto a pile of rocks. Many a rental vehicle has been lost to this stretch of road, so it definitely pays to be cautious (see the boxed text Driving Through Rivers, p551).

From Playa Manzanillo you can either head inland to Cóbano (p307), which is well connected to Montezuma, Mal País and Cabo Blanco by reasonable dirt roads, or finish up the drive in rock-star fashion by driving along the beach from Manzanillo to Mal País (again, be sure to check the tides!).

For the majority of the trip, there are no facilities, a couple of villages and few people that can help you if you get stuck. Also, the roads are unsigned, so getting lost will be part of the deal, though you can always navigate with a compass and the sun. Take a jerry can of gas, your favorite snack foods and plenty of water – if you break down, plan on spending some quality time on your own or with your traveling companion.

For very good reason, Costa Rica's tourist office recommends *against* undertaking this journey.

Getting There & Away

BUS

Empresa Arza has two daily buses from San José that cross the Golfo de Nicoya on the Puntarenas ferry and continue through Jicaral to San Francisco de Coyote, and on to Playa San Miguel and Bejuco. Buses depart San José at 6am and 3pm, pass through San Francisco de Coyote at about 11:30am and 10pm, and arrive at Playa San Miguel at noon and 10:30pm. Return buses leave Bejuco at 2:30am and 12:30pm, pass through Playa San Miguel at around 3am and 1:30pm, and San Francisco de Coyote at 3:30am and 2:30pm. This service is sketchy in the rainy season and the trip may take longer if road conditions are bad.

There aren't any other bus services frequenting this area from Nicoya or from any other of the peninsula towns for that matter.

In addition, there is no bus service (because there is barely an actual road) traveling south along the coast between Playa Coyote and Mal País.

CAR

Turn to p300 for valuable information about heading north along the coast from here.

Also consult the boxed text Along the West Coast by 4WD, above, for details on how you could *possibly* travel further south along the coast.

SOUTHEASTERN PENINSULA

Locally known as Nandayure, the southeastern peninsula is the least developed region in the Nicoya, and traditionally the most difficult one to access. In the past, arriving at the southern tip of the peninsula to catch the afternoon swell at Mal País or a sunset spliff at Montezuma involved a combination of dusty bus rides and sluggish ferries – but not anymore. These days, even 'one-weekers' are including a day or two in Nandayure on their whirlwind tours, aided in part by the speedboats that now race across the Gulf of Nicoya from Jacó to Montezuma.

As in the rest of the peninsula, Ticos in this region primarily live rural lives centered on agriculture and ranching, though the recent influx of travelers has created a number of jobs in the tourism market. Although the coastline here is still comparatively underdeveloped, the government is pegging Nandayure as the next hot destination, and you can bet that people are listening.

PLAYA NARANJO

This tiny village next to the ferry terminal is nothing more than a few *sodas* and small hotels that cater to travelers either waiting for the ferry or arriving from Puntarenas. There really isn't any reason to hang around, and thankfully you probably won't have to as the ferries tend to run reasonably on time.

If you get stuck at the port for a night, the **Hotel El Ancla** (☎ 661 3887; d without/with air-con US$45/55; P 🅿 🕮) is just 200m from the pier. Rooms with cold-water bathrooms seem a bit pricey, but there's a pool, bar and restaurant to help kill the time.

There's a small *soda* next to the ferry port, as well as a few vendors selling shaved ice and other goodies.

Getting There & Away

All transportation is geared to the arrival and departure of the Puntarenas ferry, so don't worry – if either is running late, the other will wait.

BOAT

The **Coonatramar ferry** (☎ 661 1069; passenger US$2, car US$9) to Puntarenas operates daily at 7:30am, 12:30pm, 5pm and 9pm, and can accommodate both cars and passengers. The trip takes 1½ hours. If traveling by car, get out and buy a ticket at the window, reboard your car and then drive onto the ferry. You cannot buy a ticket onboard. Show up at least an hour early on holidays and busy weekends as you'll be competing with a whole lot of other drivers to make it on.

BUS

Buses meet the ferry and take passengers to Nicoya (US$1.75, three hours). Departures are at approximately 7:20am, 12:20pm, 4:50pm and 8:50pm.

Regular buses ride from Paquera to Montezuma, though there are none that go southeast from here.

CAR & TAXI

It's possible to get to Paquera via a scenic, bumpy and steep dirt road with some great vistas of Bahía Gigante. For this a 4WD is recommended, especially in the rainy season when there are rivers to cross. The only public transportation is to take a 4WD taxi at about US$25, depending on the number of passengers and road conditions.

ISLANDS NEAR BAHÍA GIGANTE

The waters in and around the isolated Bahía Gigante, 9km southeast of Playa Naranjo, are studded with rocky islets and deserted islands, 10 large enough to be mapped on a 1:200,000 map. Since there is no public transportation here, and a 4WD is a necessity almost year-round, the area feels quiet and unhurried (read as completely abandoned).

However, travelers are drawn to this off-the-beaten-path destination for its range of activities, namely sportfishing, snorkeling, diving and kayaking, which can all be arranged through hotels and travel agencies in the area. There are also plenty of opportunities for some serious adventure here: kayak between the islands, camp on a deserted island or explore the crumbling ruins of an island prison – the choice is yours.

Isla San Lucas

The largest island in Bahía Gigante (just more than 600 hectares) is about 5km off the coast from Playa Naranjo, and from a distance seems like a beautiful desert island. On the contrary, the 'Island of Unspeakable

Horrors' has a 400-year history as one of the most notorious jails in Latin America. The island was first used by Spanish conquistadors as a detention center for local tribes in the 16th century. In 1862 the job of warden was inherited by the Costa Rican government, which used the island to detain political prisoners up until 1992. The prison was also the inspiration for Costa Rica's most internationally famous memoir: *La isla de los hombres solos* (available in English as *God was Looking the Other Way*) by José León Sánchez, who was imprisoned on the island for stealing *La Negrita* from the cathedral in Cartago (see the boxed text Local Lore, p168).

Visitors to the island can expect to see the 100-year old overgrown remains of the prison. Although there are still guards living on the island, their primary purpose is to discourage poachers, which means that travelers are usually permitted to wander freely through the prison grounds and even camp on the island.

Isla Gigante

In the middle of Bahía Gigante is the 10-hectare Isla Gigante, which is shown on most maps as Isla Muertos (Island of the Dead) because it is home to a number of Chara burial sites (and believed by locals to be haunted).

The almost 10-hectare island once served as a rustic resort for yachters, but is now completely abandoned and covered with cacti. Isla Gigante is an interesting place to explore, especially since most Ticos are afraid to set foot on the island (good luck trying to convince anyone to spend the night).

Isla Guyabo, Islas Negritos & Los Pajaros

This cluster of islands was recently established as a biological reserve to protect nesting seabird populations, including the largest breeding colony of brown pelicans in Costa Rica as well as frigate birds, boobies, egret, peregrines and petrels. Although they're not geographically close to one another, the islands are managed as a single unit. For the protection of the birds, no land visitors are allowed except researchers with permission from the park service. However, the reserves can be approached by boat, and the bird populations are large enough to be visible from the ocean.

Isla Tortuga

Isla Tortuga, which consists of two uninhabited islands just offshore from Curú, is widely regarded as the most beautiful island in Costa Rica. The white-sand beaches feel like baby powder, there are gargantuan coconut palms overhead, and the coral reef is perfect for snorkeling. Unfortunately, Tortuga receives heavy boat traffic from tour operators in Montezuma and Jacó, though if you can visit during the week in low season it can be a magical place.

Tours

Most travelers arrange tours either through the hotels listed below or with an operator in Montezuma (p308) or Jacó (p332). However, this is one region where independence (and language skills) can make for a good adventure – inquire locally to find out if someone with a boat is willing

HAVE MORE TIME?

Looking to give back before heading back home? Since 1998 Programa Restauracíon de Tortugas Marinas (Pretoma; Marine Turtle Restoration Program) has collaborated with locals to monitor turtle nesting activity and the operation of hatcheries in order to guarantee the efficient protection of nesting sea turtles and the production of hatchlings. Members of the community are hired as field assistants, and environmental education activities are held with the children in town. The project also involves tagging, measuring and protecting nesting turtles, which has resulted in a drastic reduction in poaching levels.

At the time of writing, Pretoma was operating projects in Playa San Miguel, Playa Caletas (7km south of San Miguel) and Punta Banco, near the border with Panama. For more information on volunteering, visit the website at www.tortugamarina.org or contact Pretoma at tortugas@tortugamarina.org.

to take you where you want to go for a fair price.

The most luxurious excursion is with **Calypso Tours** (☎ 256 8585; www.calypsotours.com). The company transports passengers to Isla Tortuga in a luxurious 21m motorized catamaran called the *Manta Raya*. It's all flash with this boat, which has air-con, a couple of outdoor Jacuzzis and an underwater viewing window. The cost is US$100 – not a bad deal considering the price includes transportation from San José, food and drinks.

Sleeping

Hotels come and go quickly in these parts, though there are two recommended places that have stood the test of time. Both are located on the road between Naranjo and Paquera.

Hotel Paradiso (☎ 641 8193; d US$50; P ❌ ☎) This Italian and American-run hotel has recently renovated rooms with private hot showers set around an attractive pool. There's a small pizzeria (pizzas US$4 to US$8) and bar on the grounds, as well as a pool table, darts and table tennis (why not – you're on holiday!). The owners are very helpful in organizing tours around the area.

Hotel Bahía Luminosa Resort (☎ 641 0386; d with fan/air-con US$60/70, q US$90; P ❌ ☎) Set back in the hills and overlooking the bay is this 15-room resort complex with well-appointed rooms, attractive hammock-strung gardens and an inviting pool. This is also a good spot for organizing tours around the bay.

Getting There & Away

There is no public transportation in the area. The dirt road from Playa Naranjo to Paquera requires 4WD for most of the year.

PAQUERA

The tiny village of Paquera is about 25km by road from Playa Naranjo and 4km from the ferry terminal. Paquera is more of a population center than Playa Naranjo, though there's little reason to stay here longer than you have to.

Banco Popular (✆ 8:15am-4pm), on the side street, can change US dollars and traveler's checks. On the main road, across from the gas station, you'll find the new **Turismo Curú** (☎ 641 0004; luisschutt@hotmail.com; ✆ 7am-9pm),

operated by the knowledgeable Luis Schutt of the Curú refuge (below). Luis offers a two-in-one tour that combines a visit to Curú and a snorkeling trip to Isla Tortuga for US$25 per person (this is a great deal!).

There are a number of cabinas in the village, though the best option is **Cabinas & Restaurant Ginana** (☎ 641 0119; s/d US$11/19, s/d with air-con US$16/23; P ❌), which has 28 simple and clean rooms with private bathroom and optional air-con. There's also a good restaurant (dishes US$3 to US$5) in case you need a bite to eat before getting on the ferry.

Getting There & Away

All transportation is geared to the arrival and departure of the Puntarenas ferry. If either is running late, the other will wait.

BOAT

Ferry Peninsular (☎ 641 0118/515, 661 8282; passenger US$2, car US$9) operates daily at 4:30am, 6:30am, 8:30am, 10:30am, 12:30pm, 2:30pm, 4:30pm and 10pm. The trip takes an hour. Buy a ticket at the window, reboard your car and then drive onto the ferry; you can't buy a ticket onboard. Show up at least an hour early on holidays and busy weekends.

BUS

Buses meet passengers at the ferry terminal and take them to Paquera, Tambor and Montezuma. The bus can be crowded so try to get off the ferry early to get a seat.

Most travelers take the bus from the terminal directly to Montezuma (US$2.25, two hours). Many taxi drivers will tell you the bus won't come, but this isn't true. There are no northbound buses.

TAXI

Getting several travelers together to share a cab is a good option since the ride will take half as long as the bus. The ride to Montezuma is about US$7 per person and to Mal País it's about US$10 – provided you can get enough people together.

A 4WD taxi to Playa Naranjo costs about US$25.

REFUGIO NACIONAL DE VIDA SILVESTRE CURÚ

This small 84-hectare **refuge** (day fee US$8; ✆ 7am-3pm), which is now part of a larger protected area of almost 1500 hectares, is a wilderness gem in the largely deforested peninsula. Situated at the eastern end of the peninsula and only 6km south of Paquera, the tiny Curú holds a great variety of landscapes including dry tropical forest, semideciduous forest and five types of mangrove swamp. The rugged coastline is also home to a series of secluded coves and white-sand beaches that are perfect for snorkeling and swimming.

The refuge is privately owned by the Schutts, a Tico family whose roots in the area go back more than 70 years. They have long been active in environmental efforts, and were instrumental in having the area designated a wildlife refuge. Currently, they are working to reintroduce species to the area including the scarlet macaw and the rare *mono titi* or spider monkey.

The entrance to the refuge is clearly signed on the paved road between Paquera and Tambor (it's on the right-hand side). Day visitors can show up anytime during operating hours and pay the day fee to hike the trails and visit the reserve. In addition, a variety of tours are available – from horseback riding and kayaking through the estuary to snorkeling and guided hikes. The Schutts can arrange transport to the reserve from Paquera and travel agencies in Montezuma (p308) can arrange guided day tours.

Seventeen well-marked, easy to moderate trails take visitors through the variety of different ecosystems; maps are available at the entrance. Readers recommend hiring a guide as it greatly increases your chances of spotting wildlife. The forested areas are the haunts of deer, monkeys, agoutis and pacas, and three species of cat have been recorded. Iguanas, crabs, lobsters, chitons, shellfish, sea turtles and other marine creatures can be seen on the beaches and in the tide pools. Birders have recorded more than 232 species of bird throughout the reserve, though there are probably more.

Camping is not allowed in the reserve, though there are six rustic **cabinas** (r per person with 3 meals US$35) with private cold showers. Stays must be arranged in advance either through the office in Paquera, your tour operator or at the entrance. There is no electricity, so take a flashlight and batteries.

PLAYAS POCHOTE & TAMBOR

These two mangrove-backed grey-sand beaches are protected by Bahía Ballena, the largest bay on the southeastern peninsula, and are surrounded by a few small fishing communities. In the past 15 years, however, the area has slowly been developed as a resort destination, though the outcome has been less than green (see the boxed text Clamor in Tambor, p309). Fortunately, there are a few good choices for accommodations in the area and for the most part Pochote and Tambor are undertouristed, providing plenty of opportunities for hiking, swimming, kayaking and even whale-watching.

The beaches begin 14km south of Paquera, at the community of Pochote, and stretch for about 8km southwest to Tambor – they're divided by the narrow and wadable estuary of the Río Pánica.

Activities

Both beaches are safe for **swimming**, and there are occasional **whale sightings** in the bay. The gentle waters are also conducive to **kayaking**. Although the mangroves are not set up for hiking, Curú (p305) is just down the road.

Sleeping

There are a number of very expensive, all-inclusive, environmentally questionable resorts around here – if you want more information, talk to your travel agent.

Cabinas Tambor Beach (☎ 683 0057; q US$25) This is a good, cheap option. Rooms are neatly tiled and painted in bright blues, and there are private warm-water bathrooms. There is also a patio with hammocks and a restaurant that provides inexpensive meals.

Cabinas Cristina (☎ 683 0028; s/d with shared bathroom US$10/15, d with private bathroom without/with air-con US$20/30; ✷) These recommended cabinas are run by the always-welcoming Eduardo and Cristina, a Tico couple who are eager to show you the *real* beauty of the area. Rooms are simple and spotless, and accommodate travelers of all budgets. There's also a small restaurant, and the owners can give you good advice about booking tours in the area.

Hotel Dos Lagartos (☎ 683 0236; aulwes@costarica .net; d without/with bathroom US$20/30; ℗) At the southern end of the bay, in the village of Tambor, this clean, simple American-run

CLAMOR IN TAMBOR

Few sites are better examples of how *not* to be environmentally sustainable than Playa Tambor. In 1991 Spanish hotel chain Grupo Barceló began the construction of a massive beachside resort on this tranquil bay that was to include 2400 hotel rooms, a golf course and a marina. The following year, Barceló and the regional government overseeing the project were challenged by grassroots groups alleging environmental violations – from the draining of mangrove swamp to the removal of sand and gravel from a nearby riverbed (causing erosion). The hotel chain was ultimately fined the paltry sum of US$14,000 for its actions. The project proceeded – though the plans were significantly scaled down – and Hotel Barceló Playa Tambor opened its doors to the public in 1992. Ironically, the hotel's website now touts the resort as ideal for 'nature lovers.'

The small fine outraged Noemi Canet, a Costa Rican biologist who was active in Ascona (Costa Rican Association for the Protection of Wildlife), an organization that helped lead the charge against Barceló. But for her, the main issue shouldn't be one hotel chain's alleged actions but the compliant attitude of her own government, which in turn opens the door for other developers to do the same thing.

Canet says that a number of things need to improve. For one, all tourism projects should require an environmental impact study conducted by a biologist knowledgeable about the area. In addition, she reports that the permit process is so Byzantine that sometimes it's difficult to know who is in charge of what, much less enforce environmental laws. Unfortunately, groups such as Ascona are fighting a continuing battle – one that pits the influence of money against the interests of local communities. 'This belongs to the people of Costa Rica,' says Canet of the country's natural wonders. 'It's a national treasure – we should start treating it as such.'

As the massive developments at the equally controversial Papagayo Project (p266) continue on the northern Península de Nicoya, it's easy to be skeptical about whether this will happen soon enough.

For more information on the Costa Rican Tourism Institute's sustainable tourism program, visit www.turismo-sostenible.co.cr/en/home.shtml.

hotel has beach views, a nice restaurant and a pleasant garden. Seventeen tidy rooms share clean bathrooms, while five pricier units have private bathrooms.

Hotel Costa Coral (☎ 683 0105; www.costacoral .com; d incl breakfast without/with air-con US$50/60, additional person US$16; P ⊠ ⬛) Slightly more upscale (though you don't have to wear those ridiculous bracelets), the Costa Coral's 10 colorful Spanish-colonial villas accommodate up to four people and have hot-water bathrooms, cable TV, kitchenettes and optional air-con. There's a pool and Jacuzzi, and there's also a small bar-restaurant. Credit cards are accepted.

Getting There & Away

The airport is just north of the entrance to Hotel Barceló Playa Tambor. Hotels will arrange pickup at the airport for an extra fee. Sansa (one way/round trip US$63/126) and NatureAir (US$66/132) have two daily flights each to San José.

Paquera–Montezuma buses pass through here.

CÓBANO

Cóbano has a post office, gas station, clinic and bank, which makes it the only real 'city' (it's hardly even a town) in the southeastern peninsula. Although there are a few hotels and restaurants here, there's no reason to stay since Montezuma is only 5km away.

Paquera–Montezuma buses pass through here, and a 4WD taxi to Montezuma costs about US$6.

MONTEZUMA

Up until the late 1990s a traffic jam in Montezuma was getting off your bike to shoo some cows off the road, a tourist was someone who left after only a month, a night out was rolling a spliff on the beach instead of in your hammock, a good time was – OK, you get the idea. Montezuma was one of the original 'destinations' in Costa Rica, and its remote location and proximity to Costa Rica's first nature reserve, Cabo Blanco (p315), attracted hippies, artists and dreamers alike. You had to work to get here, and no one had plans to leave quickly.

HAVE MORE TIME (PART II)?

Since 1992 Programa para la Conservación de Felinos (Profelis; Feline Conservation Program) has taken care of confiscated felines that were given to the center by Minae. The project concentrates on smaller felines including the margay, ocelot and jaguarundi, and aims to rehabilitate and, when possible, reintroduce animals into the wild. In addition, a large component of the program involves the environmental education of the public.

Profelis is headquartered in Hacienda Matambú, a private wildlife reserve in San Rafael de Paquera, about 5km west of Paquera. Volunteers are sought after, especially if you have experience in either keeping animals or veterinary science. For more information on volunteering, visit the website at www.seibermarco.de/profelis or contact Profelis at profelis@racsa.co.cr.

Montezuma is still a charming village, and foreign travelers continue to be drawn here by the laid-back atmosphere, cheap hotels, sprawling beaches and, yes, the kind bud. But just keep in mind that a good number of the 'hippie travelers' in town are returning to NYC in a week to work in an investment bank, and the expensive hotels and raging bars are a vast departure from the beach-side camping and 'free-love' atmosphere that once made this place unique.

Information

The nearest bank is in Cóbano (left). For money exchange, tour operators in town will take US dollars, euros or traveler's checks, though you can expect to pay a heavy commission. Laundry service is available at most hotels for about US$1.50 per kg. A couple of good web resources are www.nicoyapeninsula.com and www.playamontezuma.net.

Aventuras en Montezuma (☎ 642 0050; per hr US$2) Internet access.

El Sano Banano (☎ 642 0638; per hr US$2) Internet access.

Librería Topsy (🕓 8am-4pm in the high season) Has American newspapers and magazines, and a large lending library in several languages. It also serves as the unofficial post service, selling stamps and making regular mail drops at Cóbano's post office.

Activities

BEACHES

Picture-perfect white-sand beaches are strung out along the coast, separated by small rocky headlands and offering great beachcombing and tide-pool studying. Unfortunately, there are strong rips along the entire coastline, so inquire locally before going for a swim and take care (see the boxed text What to Do if You're Caught in a Riptide, p284).

The beaches in front of the town are nice enough, but the further northeast you walk, the more isolated and pristine they become. During low tide, the best **snorkeling** is in the tide pools, while decent **surf** can be had further up the coastline during rising high tide.

Because of the town's carefree 'hippie' feel, topless and (sometimes) nude sunbathing have become *de rigueur* on some beaches. No one is likely to say anything to you if you choose to sunbathe topless, but keep in mind that Ticos are fairly conservative and many residents find the whole scene disrespectful of their town (see the Boxed text Going Topless?, p340).

HIKING & HORSEBACK RIDING

Inland from Montezuma is the **Nicolás Wessburg Absolute Reserve**, a private conservation area that was the original site of Olof Wessburg and Karen Mogensen's homestead (for more information, see p315). Although the reserve is closed to visitors, you can either hike or go horseback riding along its perimeter – tours can be arranged through operators in town or at the Nature Lodge Finca Los Caballos (p311).

YOGA

Daily **yoga classes** (www.montezumayoga.com; per person US$10) are offered at the open-air studio at Hotel Los Mangos (p310).

Tours

Tour operators around town rent everything from snorkeling gear and body boards to bikes and ATVs. Prices vary depending on the season, and it pays to shop around. They can also arrange speed-boat transfers to Jacó as well as private shuttle transfers (also known as 'Gringo Buses').

The most popular tour is a boat trip to Isla Tortuga, which costs around US$40 a person and should include lunch, fruit, drinks and snorkeling gear. Although the island is certainly beautiful, travelers complain that the whole outing feels like a tourist circus, especially during high season when the entire island is full of boat tours.

Another popular excursion is to take a guided hike (US$25) or a half-day horseback ride (US$25) to nearby Cabo Blanco.

The following three tour operators are recommended:

Aventuras en Montezuma (☎ 642 0050; www.zuma tours.com)

Cocozuma Traveller (☎ 642 0911; www.cocozuma.com)

Montezuma Expeditions (☎ 440 8078; www.monte zumaexpeditions.com)

Festivals & Events

Keep your eyes open for posters advertising special events as there always seems to be something going on in town. There is also an annual music festival in July, though the dates change each year.

Sleeping

The high season gets crowded, though with so many hotels dotting such a small town you're bound to find something. High-season prices are listed throughout.

BUDGET

All the hotels listed below have shared cold showers unless otherwise stated. Also, be careful with your stuff – travelers frequently complain of thefts from hotel rooms in Montezuma.

Camping is illegal on the beaches, though some travelers seem to have not had a problem outside the town limits. If you want to play it safe, there is a small, shaded **campground** (per person US$3) with bathrooms and cold showers only a 10-minute walk north of town.

Pensión Arenas (☎ 642 0306; r per person US$5) The cheapest place in town is certainly cheap, though the management is unwelcoming, and the rooms are run-down and poorly maintained. There are definitely better options.

Pensión Lucy (☎ 642 0273; r per person US$6) This beachside pension is popular with shoestring travelers, and was the first budget place to open up in town. Ask for a room upstairs –

the ocean views and verandas make all the difference.

Cabinas Tucán (☎ 642 0284; d US$6) Just north of the soccer field, the Tucán is attentively managed by the crotchety Doña Marta. Rooms are spotless, as are the communal showers.

Pensión Jenny (r per person US$6) This lovely white and blue country house north of the soccer field is a bit removed from the action, which makes it a good option if you want a quiet night's sleep.

Hotel Lys (☎ 642 0642; www.hotellysmontezuma .net; camping US$6, d US$15) This recommended beachside budget hotel is run by a group of funky Italians who are bursting with creativity. In addition to creating a laid-back vibe that's perfect for slowing down and reflecting on your travels, the owners have also launched a project known as Libre Universidad de Montezuma or LUDM. This rapidly evolving concept is based on communication through artistic expression, and the aim is for travelers to bring an idea to the resident artisans and explore a part of their personality that may not have been previously expressed. Past 'graduates' have studied music, sculpture, painting, cooking, photography and fashion, though the founders believe that the possibilities are endless as long as you arrive with an open mind.

Mochila Inn (☎ 642 0030; d US$15, d/tr cabin without kitchen US$20/25, d/tr cabin with kitchen US$25/30) On a quiet hillside north of town, this secluded inn is brimming with wildlife and silent (except for the sounds of the rain forest) at night. There are a variety of rooms available that cater to different budgets, though everyone can use the outdoor toilets, which offer only a thin curtain between you and nature. (Bring binoculars and watch nature from the throne.)

Hotel Moctezuma (☎ 642 0058; s/d US$11/25) This hotel right in the center of town has 21 worn-out rooms containing private warm-water bathrooms (certainly a plus), though the loud (and we mean very, very L-O-U-D) bar next door won't allow for any beauty rest.

Luna Llena (☎ 642 0390; s/d US$15/20; **P**) On the northern edge of town at the base of the hills is this delightful German-run budget option that's terrific value. Rooms at the edge of the forest share kitchens and

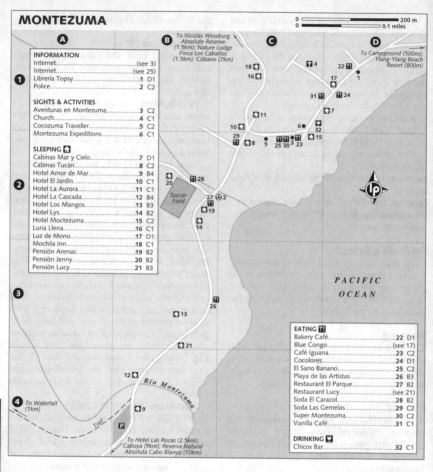

MONTEZUMA

0 — 200 m
0 — 0.1 miles

To Nicolás Wessburg
Absolute Reserve
(1.5km); Nature Lodge
Finca Los Caballos
(1.5km); Cóbano (7km)

To Campground (500m);
Ylang-Ylang Beach
Resort (800m)

INFORMATION
Internet.............................(see 3)
Internet............................(see 25)
Librería Topsy.......................1 D1
Police................................2 C2

SIGHTS & ACTIVITIES
Aventuras en Montezuma.............3 C2
Church..............................4 C2
Cocozuma Traveller..................5 C2
Montezuma Expeditions...............6 C1

SLEEPING
Cabinas Mar y Cielo.................7 D1
Cabinas Tucán.......................8 C2
Hotel Amor de Mar...................9 B4
Hotel El Jardín....................10 C1
Hotel La Aurora....................11 C1
Hotel La Cascada...................12 B4
Hotel Los Mangos...................13 B3
Hotel Lys..........................14 B2
Hotel Moctezuma....................15 C2
Luna Llena.........................16 C1
Luz de Mono........................17 D1
Mochila Inn........................18 C1
Pensión Arenas.....................19 B2
Pensión Jenny......................20 B2
Pensión Lucy.......................21 B3

Soccer
Field

*PACIFIC
OCEAN*

To Waterfall
(1km)

Trail

Río Montezuma

P

To Hotel Las Rocas (2.5km);
Cabuya (9km); Reserva Natural
Absoluta Cabo Blanco (10km)

EATING
Bakery Café........................22 D1
Blue Congo........................(see 17)
Café Iguana........................23 C2
Cocolores..........................24 D1
El Sano Banano.....................25 C2
Playa de las Artistas..............26 B3
Restaurant El Parque...............27 B2
Restaurant Lucy...................(see 21)
Soda El Caracol....................28 B2
Soda Las Gemelas...................29 C2
Super Montezuma....................30 C2
Vanilla Café.......................31 C1

DRINKING
Chicos Bar.........................32 C1

hot-water bathrooms, and for an extra US$5 you can upgrade to the honeymoon suite, an incredible pavilion that overlooks the bay.

Cabinas Mar y Cielo (☎ 642 0261; s/d US$25/35) Although slightly overpriced, this is a decent option as rooms with beach views and clean ocean breezes are right in town, though a bit removed from the bar scene.

Hotel Los Mangos (☎ 642 0076; www.hotellosman gos.com; d without bathroom US$33, tr bungalows US$82; P ⓡ) This is a charming hotel offering double rooms with shared bathroom in the main building and bungalows with private bathrooms scattered around the mango-dotted gardens. There is also a small wooden pavilion near the base of the hills where daily yoga classes (US$10) take place.

Hotel La Cascada (☎ 642 0056/7; d US$40, additional person US$15) By the river en route to the waterfalls, this classic Montezuma hotel has 19 simple wooden rooms with ocean views and a 2nd-floor deck that's fully strung with cozy hammocks – perfect for swinging or snoozing.

MIDRANGE
Montezuma
All hotels have private hot showers.

Hotel La Aurora (☎ 642 0051; www.playamontezuma .net/aurora.htm; d US$25-50, additional person US$5, house per week US$250; P ⓡ) La Aurora has been around for more than 20 years and the pretty, vine-covered yellow building houses an assortment of 15 delightful rooms. All of the units come with fan and mosquito net, and others come with varying degrees of cold or hot water and air-con. There's a communal kitchen and plenty of hammocks for chilling out. The hotel rents a six-person wooden house on the road leading up to the waterfalls (the price above is for two, and each additional person is US$25). Credit cards accepted.

Hotel Amor de Mar (☎ 642 0262; www.amordemar .com; d US$50-95) At the southern end of town, this quiet place has a well-manicured garden (think golf course quality) that's strung up with luxurious hammocks and a beautiful shorefront with a tide pool big enough to swim in. There are 11 rooms of varying shapes and sizes that have varying amenities depending on your budget.

Luz de Mono (☎ 642 0090; www.luzdemono.com; d/ ste US$65/86, casita without/with Jacuzzi US$120/160; P ⛒ ⛵) Between the beach and the forested hills, this hotel has a variety of rooms and casitas, though they're all well appointed with solar-heated showers, ceramic tiles and wooden accents (it's worth the splurge to have a private outdoor Jacuzzi). The bar-restaurant Blue Congo (dishes US$5 to US$12) serves a good mix of international and Tico dishes, though the real reason you're here is to try the restaurant's own brand of wine (yes, you can grow grapes in the tropics!), which comes

in red and white and is known as 'monkey shine.' Credit cards accepted, and rates include breakfast.

Hotel El Jardín (☎ 642 0548; www.hoteleljardin .com; d US$85-95, 4-person villas US$135; P ⛒ ⛵) This hotel has 15 luxurious stained-wood cabinas of various sizes and amenities (some have stone bathrooms and ocean views). The grounds are landscaped with tropical flowers and lush palms, and there's also a pool and Jacuzzi for soaking your cares away.

Around Montezuma

Hotel Las Rocas (☎ 642 0393; d/apt US$30/50, additional person US$10; P ⛵) About 2.5km south of Montezuma on the road to Cabuya (the perfect getaway), this simple, quiet spot near rocky tide pools has a few basic doubles with shared bathroom, mosquito nets and nice ocean breezes. Rustic one-bedroom apartments have private bathrooms, kitchens, a terrace with hammocks and a little garden. There are free bikes, body boards and snorkeling gear for guests to use. Visa is accepted.

Nature Lodge Finca Los Caballos (☎ 642 0124; www.naturelodge.net; d US$80-130, additional person US$18; P ⛵) North of Montezuma on the road to Cabano, this 16-hectare ranch is adjacent to the Nicolás Wessburg Absolute Reserve. The lodge has a variety of rooms

---

THE MONTEZUMA WATERFALL

A 20-minute stroll south of town takes you to a set of three scenic waterfalls. The main attraction here is to climb the second set of falls and jump in. Though countless people do this every day, be aware that even though there is a warning sign, about half a dozen people have died attempting this.

The first waterfall has a good swimming hole but it's shallow and rocky and not suitable for diving. From here, if you continue on the well-marked trail that leads around and up, you will come to a second set of falls. These are the ones that offer a good clean leap into the deep water below – and at 10m high, they are also the tallest. To reach the jumping point, continue to take the trail up the side of the hill until you reach the diving area. Do *not* attempt to scale the falls. The rocks are slippery and this is how most jumpers have met their deaths. From this point, the trail continues up the hill to the third and last set of falls. Once again, these are not suitable for jumping. However, there is a rope swing that will drop you right over the deeper part of the swimming hole.

A lot of travelers enjoy this activity, but as with anything of this nature, you undertake it at your own risk. To get there, follow the main Montezuma road south out of town and then take the trail to the right after Hotel La Cascada, past the bridge. You'll see a clearly marked parking area for visitors (US$2.50 per car) and the beginning of the trail that leads up.

It probably doesn't *need* to be said, but let's just be clear about one thing – weed and waterfall jumping do *not* go hand in hand. Thanks.

scattered around the property with either jungle or ocean views. The Canadian owner prides herself on having some of the best looked-after horses in the area, and there are great opportunities here for riding on the trails around the reserve. You can also rent bikes, go hiking, have a meal in the restaurant or splash around the infinity pool.

Ylang-Ylang Beach Resort (☎ 642 0636; www .ylangylangresort.com; d standard/ste US$105/130, bungalows US$150-180; ⚫) About a 15-minute walk north of town along the beach is this resort catering to holistic holiday seekers. Here you'll find a collection of beautifully appointed rooms, suites and polygonal bungalows with private hot showers (some open-air) as well as a palm-fringed swimming pool, yoga center, gourmet restaurant and spa. Oh, and you can't actually drive here, though they'll pick you up in their custom beach cruisers. Rates include breakfast and dinner, and credit cards are accepted.

Eating

Self-caterers should head on over to the Super Montezuma for fresh food.

Bakery Café (dishes US$1-3) Grab a chair on the outdoor patio and feast on homemade banana bread and French toast, or get some tasty whole-grain bread to go and have a picnic on the beach (or on the ferry).

Soda Las Gemelas (dishes US$2-4) This famous local eatery is the cheapest place in town for a heaping and delicious fish casado accompanied by a frothy *batido* (fruit shake).

Restaurant El Parque (dishes US$3-6) For beachside ambience and cheap seafood, this small *soda* is a good choice.

Soda El Caracol (dishes US$4-6) Although the building looks like it's seen better days, don't let appearances fool you – the casados here are tops.

Café Iguana (dishes US$4-6) In the center of town is this vegetarian-friendly spot where you can get hummus sandwiches, veggie lasagne and a variety of healthy salads.

Vanilla Café (dishes US$4-7) This little café is full of warmth, and serves delicious gourmet pastries and sandwiches. Sit outside where you can watch the freak show that is Montezuma over a frothy cappuccino.

Restaurant Lucy (dishes US$5-8) Though it's aimed at tourists, the beachside dining here is relaxed and even romantic, and the dishes are a welcome change from the standard rice and beans offering – try the fish in coconut curry sauce (it's as good as it sounds).

El Sano Banano (☎ 642 0638; dishes US$4-12) This restaurant has a multipage menu that offers everything from spicy curries to mixed meat stir-fries. Come during the evening when the restaurant shows nightly films for US$6 minimum consumption.

Cocolores (☎ 642 0348; dishes US$5-12; ⏱ 2-9:30pm) This pleasant patio restaurant offers candle-lit dinners and heaping portions of French-influenced cuisine as well as a few Tico standards.

Playa de las Artistas (mains US$8-12; ⏱ 10:30am-10:30pm) This artfully decorated beachside spot is the most adored restaurant in town. The international menu with heavy Mediterranean influences changes daily depending on locally available ingredients, though you can always count on fresh seafood and impeccable culinary sophistication.

Drinking & Entertainment

True to its roots, most entertainment in Montezuma is of the herbal kind, though there are two recommended spots in town for getting blotto.

Chico's Bar is a sprawling complex of bars, tables, beach chairs, dance space and a sushi restaurant – because nothing goes better than binge drinking and raw fish.

Luz de Mono (see p311) has an open-air discotheque that plays house music on Thursday and reggae on Saturday (smoke 'em if you got 'em).

Getting There & Away

BOAT

Travelers are increasingly taking advantage of the jet-boat transfer service that connects Jacó to Montezuma. Several boats per day cross the Gulf of Nicoya, and the journey only takes about an hour. At US$35 it's definitely not cheap, but it'll save you about a day's worth of travel. It's a beach landing, so wear the right shoes.

BUS

Buses depart Montezuma from in front of Café Iguana. Buy tickets directly from the bus driver.

Cabo Blanco US$1, 30 minutes, depart at 8:15am, 10:15am, 2:15pm and 6:15pm.

Paquera US$2, 1½ hours, depart at 5:30am, 8am, 10am, noon, 2pm, 4pm and 6pm.

San José US$10, nine to 12 hours, departs at 4:45am.
Santa Teresa US$1.25, 45 minutes, depart at 10:30am and 2:30am.

CAR & TAXI
During the rainy season, the stretch of road between Cóbano and Montezuma is likely to require 4WD. In the village itself, parking can be a problem, though it's easy enough to walk everywhere.

A 4WD taxi can carry five people, and can take you from Montezuma to Cóbano (US$6), Cabo Blanco (US$12), Tambor (US$25), Mal País (US$30) or Paquera (US$30).

MAL PAÍS & SANTA TERESA
OK, first let's make a little sense of the nomenclature. Mal País (Bad Country) refers to the southwestern corner of Nicoya that's famous among surfers for its consistent waves. Santa Teresa refers to the largest village in the area, though this is not to be confused with the smaller villages of Mal País and Carmen. ¿Comprende? Don't worry if you're lost – this area is booming, and it's only a matter of time before it all becomes one big city anyway.

The legendary waves at Mal País have been attracting surfers since the 1970s, so it's not surprising that many of them grew up and decided to stay. In the last several years, this once isolated corner of the peninsula has become a 'destination,' and widespread development is rapidly carving up the beachfront. Although it's still too early to tell what the future holds for Mal País, it's difficult to be optimistic, especially considering the fates of beach towns like Jacó and Tamarindo.

It's worth saying that Mal País is not for everyone. If you're an experienced surfer looking for a 'scene,' throw away your itinerary because you're going to get stuck here. But if you're looking for an authentic Costa Rican beach town, and 'surf culture' isn't exactly your thing, don't waste your time coming here.

Orientation & Information
The road from Cóbano meets the beach road next to Frank's Place (see right), on the western side of the peninsula. To the left (south) lies Mal País and to the right (north) there's Santa Teresa.

A useful website is www.malpais.net. Super Santa Teresa (300m north of Frank's place), on the road to Santa Teresa, will change US dollars and traveler's checks.
Surf Shop Malpaís (☎ 640 0173) Rents and fixes boards.
Tuanis (☎ 640 0370) Has Internet access, various gifts and sundries, and can help book taxi services around the area. It's 2km north of Frank's.

Activities
Although surfing is on everyone's mind, the beaches stretch both north and south for kilometers on end, so whether you're a hiker or a kayaker the possibilities for adventure and exploration are endless.

SURFING
One surfer we spoke with described Mal País as follows:

> There's a consistent beach break at high and low tide, and it can get real big in the winter. The waves are playful and not super steep, so they're a bit more forgiving then you'd expect. There are plenty of peaky rights and lefts, though they're not super hollow.

The following beaches are listed from north to south.
Playa Manzanillo is a combination of sand and rock that's best surfed when the tide is rising and there's an offshore wind.

The most famous break in the Mal País area is at **Playa Santa Teresa**, and is characterized as being fast and powerful. This beach can be surfed virtually anytime of day, though be cautious as there are scattered rocks.
Playa El Carmen is a good beach break that can also be surfed anytime.

The town is saturated with surf shops, and competition has kept prices low – this is a good place to pick up a cheap surfboard, and there's a good chance you can make most of your money back if you sell it elsewhere.

Sleeping & Eating
Frank's Place (☎ 640 0096; www.frankplace.com; r per person US$16; P 🖳 🖴 🕿) Coming into town from Cóbano, the first place you'll see is this local landmark and historic surfer outpost. Roomy, tiled cabinas are comfortable,

and the shared bathrooms and communal kitchen are well kept. This place is always full of travelers, and the freeform pool, whirlpool and restaurant are great places to hang out and get the latest surf report.

Playa Carmen restaurant (pizzas US$3-8) On the road that leads down to the beach from Frank's, this is another Mal País institution that's recommended for its good variety of pizza and pasta.

You'll find all of the following places heading south into Mal País.

Ritmo Tropical (☎ 640 0174; www.ritmo.malpais .net; d/tr US$47/57; P) Tropical-themed cabins with airy rooms, hot showers and shady verandas are scattered around simple but peaceful grounds. There is an on-site bar-restaurant (dishes US$3 to US$7) that does pancakes and *gallo pinto* in the morning, and Italian-inspired dishes for lunch and dinner.

The Place (☎ 640 0001; www.theplacemalpais.com; d US$45-90, additional person US$10; P ✗) Cheaper rooms in this Swiss-run guesthouse are air-conditioned and have private hot-water bathrooms, though it's absolutely worth it to splurge on the more expensive cabinas – each one is wildly decorated according to a different theme (our favorite is 'Spicy Colors of Mexico,' though 'Out of Africa' is a close second). The Swiss owners are multilingual and can arrange surfing lessons and tours and the small restaurant serves Mediterranean-style seafood by candlelight in the evenings.

Malpaís Surf Camp & Resort (☎ 640 0061; www .malpaissurfcamp.com; camping per person US$7, dm/d/q US$12.50/20/45, d/tr/q villas US$85/97.50/110; P ☺) Whether you're looking for a breezy bunkhouse or poolside villa, this 'surfer's lodge' caters to travelers of all budget levels. However, regardless of how much you're paying each night, all guests can wander the landscaped tropical grounds, swim in the lavish pool or grab a cold beer in the open-air bar-restaurant.

Blue Jay Lodge (☎ 640 0089; www.bluejaylodge costarica.com; d incl breakfast US$85, additional person US$20; P) This traveler-recommended Tico-owned lodge has seven stunning private bamboo bungalows that are surrounded by lush forest and feature huge, screened half-walls (protected with an awning), hot showers and shady verandas. Credit cards accepted. It's 1km south of Frank's Place.

Star Mountain Eco Resort (☎ 640 0101 www .starmountaineco.com; s/d/tr incl breakfast US$65/95/110, casita per person US$32; P ☺) This intimate and secluded lodge was built without cutting down a single tree, and today the grounds of the resort abound with wildlife. There are trails leading through the property that have good birding, and a viewpoint overlooks both sides of the peninsula. There are four hillside rooms, each painted in cool tropical pastels. The Argentinean-American owners will prepare home-cooked meals on request. The resort is off the rough road (4WD only) between Mal País and Cabuya, alongside the Cabo Blanco reserve (follow the signs), 5.5km south of Frank's Place.

You'll find all of the following places heading north into Santa Teresa – all distances are in relation to Frank's Place.

Las Piedras (meals US$3-7) This Argentinean-run chicken shack proclaims that, 'Our chicken is the sh%t.' One bite and you'll agree – its chicken really is the sh%t.

Tranquilo Backpackers (☎ 640 0589; www.tran quilobackpackers.com; dm US$10, d/tr with shared bathroom US$30/45, d with private bathroom US$35, 4-/5-person loft apt US$60/75; P ☐) This brand-new hostel is the best budget option in the area. Everything has been designed from the ground up to be smart, hip and functional – you can even flush the toilet paper here! The owners know exactly how to create a chilled-out atmosphere, and it helps when your guests get to eat their fill of free pancakes every morning. Amenities and services include shared kitchen, shared hot-water bathrooms, free Internet, free bike rental and free surfboards.

Casa Zen (☎ 640 0523; www.casazencr.com; dm US$12, d with shared bathroom US$22-30, apt US$50; P) This recommended Asian-inspired guesthouse is decked out in Zen art, celestial murals and enough happy Buddha sculptures to satisfy all your belly-rubbing needs. The owner, Kelly, is committed to helping guests 'chill and recreate on their own time.' She also runs an eclectic restaurant (dishes US$3 to US$7) that has everything from veggie sandwiches and burgers to fresh sushi and Thai curries.

Tropico Latino Lodge (☎ 640 0036; www.tropico .malpais.net; d US$77-103; P ✗ ☺) The beautifully decorated and roomy wooden bungalows here are scattered around a tropical garden and along the beach, and feature air-con, king-size beds, hammock-strung patios and private hot-water bathrooms (one bungalow also has a full kitchen). There's a dreamy pool right next to the beach and a surfside restaurant (dishes US$4 to US$8) that specializes in Italian food.

Funky Monkey (☎ 640 0317; www.funky-monkey -lodge.com; d/q bungalows US$65/85, 8-person bungalows US$120; P ☲) Up the hill from Tuanis, this 'funky' lodge is situated at the top of a natural rock hill, and consists of rustic-style bungalows built out of bamboo. Each bungalow has a 'garden-shower,' and the larger ones have a fully equipped kitchen. A popular sushi restaurant (sushi rolls US$4 to US$8) packs in the crowds with good raw fish and excellent sunsets.

On the beach, **Roca Mar** (per person US$3; P) and **Paraíso Azul** (per person US$2.50; P) both offer camping and shared bathrooms with cold showers.

Milarepa (☎ 640 0023; www.milarepahotel.com; cabinas US$125-150; P ☲) This self-proclaimed 'small hotel of luxurious simplicity' has beachfront bungalows constructed of bamboo and Indonesian teak. Each bungalow is adorned with four-post beds that are drenched in voluminous mosquito nets, and comes complete with a private bathroom and garden shower. The French owners run a good restaurant (mains US$6 to US$9) serving southern French cuisine.

Hotel Flor Blanca (☎ 640 0232; www.florblanca .com; 1-/2-bedroom villas incl breakfast US$375-655; P ☒ ☐ ☲) The most elegant and sophisticated hotel in Santa Teresa is truly in a class of its own – not surprisingly, it belongs to the group of 'Small Distinctive Hotels of Costa Rica.' Ten romantic villas are scattered around 3 hectares of land next to a pristine white-sand beach. Each one is awash in gentle cream-colored hues, and is highlighted by garden showers and outdoor sunken bathtubs. Yoga and Pilates classes are offered as well as guided tours around the area. Its Asian-fusion restaurant, Nectar (dishes US$7 to US$20), is open to the public and is highly recommended for its innovative dishes and unbelievably fresh sushi. Credit cards accepted. It's 4km north of Frank's Place.

Getting There & Away
From Mal País, there's a bus to Cóbano at 7am. From Santa Teresa there are buses

at 6:45am and 11am. A taxi to these areas from Cóbano costs about US$18, depending on road conditions.

CABUYA
This tiny village is scattered along a dirt road about 9km south of Montezuma. Although it's rather uninteresting, it's worth visiting the town **cemetery**, which is on Isla Cabuya to the southeast and can only be reached at low tide. Here you'll find a few modest graves marked by crosses, though make sure you keep an eye on the tides!

Aside from the cemetery, most travelers either pass through Cabuya on their way to Cabo Blanco or use the town as a base for exploring Cabo Blanco.

Coming from Montezuma, the first hotel you'll come to is the Belgian-owned **Hotel Celaje** (☎ 642 0374; www.celaje.com; d/tr/q with full board US$70/82/93; P ☒ ☐ ☲), which has a collection of four-person thatched bungalows scattered around a nice pool and Jacuzzi. Prices include full board, which consists of European-style cuisine and *real* Belgian beer.

Further up is the American-run **Hotel Cabo Blanco** (☎ 642 0332; www.playamontezuma.net /caboblanco.htm; d with fan/air-con US$50/60; P ☒ ☲), which is certainly an attractive hotel, but it's lacking in character compared to the other two hotels in town.

Ancla de Oro (☎ 642 0369; www.caboblancopark .com/ancla; d US$22, d/tr bungalows US$35/41, tr bungalows with kitchen US$46; P) is the last hotel before the park. The Dutch-owned Ancla de Oro, which was one of the original places to stay in the area has rooms that are simple and cater to travelers on a budget, though it's worth springing for the 'jungalows,' which are raised bungalows that will fulfil all your childhood tree-house fantasies. The on-site restaurant specializes in seafood.

For everything else, make a pit stop at **Café Coyote** (dishes US$5-6; ☐). The owners serve up pizza, seafood and veggie meals, and offer Internet access.

RESERVA NATURAL ABSOLUTA CABO BLANCO
Just 11km south of Montezuma is Costa Rica's oldest protected wilderness area. Cabo Blanco is comprised of 1272 hectares of land and 1700 hectares of surrounding ocean, and includes the entire southern tip

of the Península de Nicoya. The moist microclimate present on the tip of the peninsula fosters the growth of evergreen forests, which are unique when compared with the dry tropical forests typical of the Nicoya. The park also encompasses a number of pristine white-sand beaches and offshore islands that are favored nesting areas for various species of bird.

The park was originally established by a Danish-Swedish couple, the late Karen Mogensen and Olof Wessberg, who settled in Montezuma in the 1950s and were among the first conservationists in Costa Rica. In 1960 the couple was distraught when they discovered that sections of Cabo Blanco had been clear-cut. At the time, the Costa Rican government was primarily focused on the agricultural development of the country (see the boxed text A Whopper of a Problem, p229), and had not yet formulated its modern-day conservation policy. However, Karen and Olof were instrumental in convincing the government to establish a national park system, which eventually led to the creation of the Cabo Blanco reserve in 1963. The couple continued to fight for increased conservation of ecologically rich areas, but tragically Olof was murdered in 1975 during a campaign in the Osa Peninsula. Karen continued her husband's work until her death 1994, and today they are buried in the Nicolás Wessburg Absolute Reserve, which was the site of their original homestead.

Cabo Blanco is called an 'absolute' nature reserve because prior to the late 1980s visitors were not permitted. Even though the name has remained, a limited number of trails have been opened to visitors, though the reserve remains closed on Monday and Tuesday to minimize environmental impact.

Information

The **ranger station** (☎ 642 0093; admission US$8; ☽ 8am-4pm Wed-Sun) is 2km south of Cabuya at the entrance to the park, and trail maps are available. It is not possible to overnight

in the park, though there are plenty of options in nearby Cabuya (p315) or Montezuma (p308). Bring drinks and snacks as there is no food or water available.

The average annual temperature is about 27°C and annual rainfall is some 2300mm at the tip of the park. Not surprisingly, the trails can get muddy, so it's best to visit from December to April – the dry season.

Activities

WILDLIFE-WATCHING

Monkeys, squirrels, sloths, deer, agoutis and raccoons are usually present, and armadillos, coatis, peccaries and anteaters are occasionally sighted.

The coastal area is known as an important nesting site for brown boobies, which are mostly found 1.6km south of the mainland on **Isla Cabo Blanco** (White Cape Island). The name 'Cabo Blanco' was coined by Spanish *conquistadores* when they noticed that the entire island consisted of guano-encrusted rocks. Other seabirds in the area include brown pelicans and magnificent frigatebirds.

HIKING

From the ranger station, the **Swedish Trail** and **Danish Trail** lead 4.5km down to a wilderness beach at the tip of the peninsula. Note that both trails intersect at various points, and it's possible to follow one down and return on the other. Be advised that the trails can get very muddy (especially in the rainy season), and are fairly steep in certain parts – plan for about two hours in each direction. From the beach at the end of the trails it's possible to follow another trail to a second beach, though check first with park rangers as this trail is impassable at high tide.

Getting There & Away

Buses depart from the park entrance for Montezuma at 7am, 9am, 1pm and 4pm.

A 4WD taxi (for six passengers) from Montezuma to the park costs about US$12. You can prearrange for a pickup if you so desire.

Central Pacific Coast

With its varied landscape of both wet and dry tropical rain forests and a sun-drenched coastline teeming with big fish and even bigger surf, the central Pacific coast is one of the most popular destinations in Costa Rica for hikers, anglers, surfers and sun-worshippers alike. National parks hug the coastline providing refuge for rare species of animals such as the squirrel monkey and scarlet macaw, while more commonly sighted creatures like iguanas and white-faced capuchins ensure that every outing is memorable. The region also boasts well-paved roads leading from San José and the Central Valley out to the coastline, so it's no surprise that Ticos flock to the Pacific looking for the perfect weekend escape.

Not surprisingly, this stretch of the Pacific has always been popular with the North American package holiday crowd as it's easy to squeeze in a one week retreat and be back to work on Monday. In recent years however, North American Baby Boomers nearing retirement began snatching up property, lured to Costa Rica by a combination of good weather, safety and a low cost of living. Beach towns like Jacó that were once the exclusive enclaves of vacationing Tico families are now quickly being colonized by American-style strip malls, gated communities and 4x4 car dealerships. Foreign investment blessed this region with continuous development and solid infrastructure, though Ticos are starting to wonder if they will soon feel like tourists in their own backyard.

Things are indeed changing quickly, and it's difficult to say which interests will win out in the end. A new marina at Quepos will bring in a larger volume of tourists visiting Costa Rica on cruise ships, though it's difficult to imagine that the authenticity of the coastal fishing villages and palm-oil plantations could ever be lost.

HIGHLIGHTS

- Watching squirrel monkey troops scamper along the beaches at **Parque Nacional Manuel Antonio** (p356)

- Surfing the breaks at **Matapalo** (p360), **Playa Hermosa** (p265) and **Dominical** (p362)

- Watching crocodiles sunbathe and scarlet macaws fly overhead at **Parque Nacional Carara** (p325)

- Clambering up the canopy platforms to admire wildlife and the views at **Hacienda Barú National Wildlife Refuge** (p361)

- Whale-watching at **Parque Nacional Marino Ballena** (p368) near Uvita

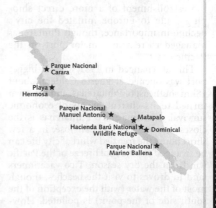

★ Parque Nacional Carara

Playa ★ Hermosa

Parque Nacional Manuel Antonio ★   ★ Matapalo

Hacienda Barú National ★ ★ Dominical Wildlife Refuge

Parque Nacional ★ Marino Ballena

PUNTARENAS TO QUEPOS

The northern stretch of the central Pacific coastline was initially developed in the colonial era as a gateway for commodity exports. For much of the 19th and 20th centuries, goods such as coffee were hauled by ox cart from the highlands down the Pacific slope and then shipped off around Cape Horn to Europe. Although the maritime business is still bustling, the proximity of the region to San José and the Central Valley means something much more important to your average Tico – convenient beach access.

Heading from north to south, Puntarenas is of interest to travelers heading to the Península de Nicoya by ferry, while the beaches stretching south to Jacó and beyond offer some of the most consistent surf breaks in the country. This stretch of the pacific is also home to Parque Nacional Carara, which is a great place for spotting crocodile and scarlet macaw.

PUNTARENAS

Prior to the mid-20th century, Puntarenas was the largest and most significant openwater port in Costa Rica. Some of the finest coffees to grace European tables were carried to the continent on Puntarenas-registered freighters, and the steady flow of capital back into the city transformed it into the 'Pearl of the Pacific.' However, after the construction of the railway leading from the Central Valley to Puerto Limón, the establishment of a more direct shipping route to Europe initiated the city's decline in importance, though Puntarenas managed to remain a major port on the Pacific coast.

This all changed in 1981 when a bigger port was opened at Puerto Caldera, about 18km southeast of Puntarenas, and the town turned to its current means of economic survival: tourism. Since Puntarenas is the closest coastal town to San José, in a few short hours the frenzied whirl of city life can be swapped for the cool breeze of the Pacific winds. In the dry season, Tico vacationers land in droves to visit the beaches, though most of the water (with the exception of the south side of the point) is polluted. However, the beaches are regularly cleaned, the

views across the Golfo de Nicoya are scenic, and future plans to continue overhauling the beachfront are ambitious.

Despite its popularity with land-locked Ticos, Puntarenas has an unjustified reputation among travelers as a filthy port city that should be avoided at all costs. And, in the age of gringo buses and jet-boat transfers to the Península de Nicoya, this is becoming easier to achieve. The reality is that although Puntarenas will never be a destination for foreigners, its ferry terminal does provide the cheapest option for reaching the beaches of Southern Nicoya. And as far as port cities are concerned, it's relaxed and brimming with local flavor, and you'll probably be the only gringo sunning yourself on a well-kept beach full of Tico families.

Orientation

Situated at the end of a sandy peninsula (8km long but only 100m to 600m wide), Puntarenas is Costa Rica's most significant Pacific coastal town and is just 110km west of San José by paved highway. The city has 60 calles running north to south but only five avenidas running west to east at its widest point. As in all of Costa Rica, street names are largely irrelevant and landmarks are used for orientation (see p539).

Information

INTERNET ACCESS
Coonatramar (☎ 661 9011, 661 1069; www.coonatramar.com; cnr Calle 31 & Av 3; per hr US$1.50; ☼ 8am-5pm) Has three computer terminals with speedy connections. This is a good place to check email while waiting for the car ferry.

MEDICAL SERVICES
Hospital Monseñor Sanabria (☎ 663 0033; 8km east of town)

MONEY
The major banks along Avenida 3, to the west of the market, exchange money and are equipped with 24-hour ATMs.
Banco de San José (cnr Av 3 & Calle 3) Connected to the Cirrus network.

TOURIST INFORMATION
Puntarenas tourism office (Catup; ☼ 8am-5pm Mon-Fri) Opposite the pier on the 2nd floor above the Báncredito. It closes for lunch.

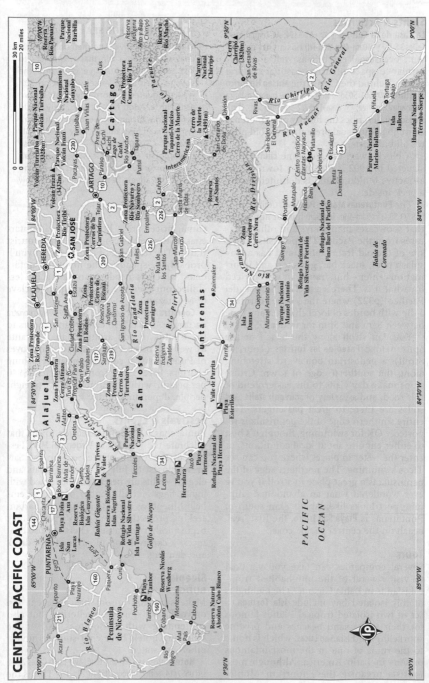

CENTRAL PACIFIC COAST

Sights & Activities

La Casa de la Cultura (☎ 661 1394; Av Central btwn Calles 3 & 5; ☷ 10am-4pm Mon-Fri) has an art gallery with occasional exhibits as well as a performance space offering seasonal cultural events. Behind the Casa is the **Museo Histórico Marino** (☎ 661 5036, 256 4139; www.museocostarica .com; admission free; ☷ 8am-1pm & 2-5pm Tue-Sun). The museum describes the history of Puntaranas through audiovisual presentations, old photos and artifacts.

A block away, the old stone **church** constructed in 1902 is one of the town's most attractive buildings and is definitely worth a peek inside.

The **Puntarenas Marine Park** (adult/child under 12 US$7/1.50; ☷ 9am-5pm Tue-Sun) has an aquarium that showcases manta rays and other creatures from the Pacific. The park sits on the site of the old train station and has a tiny splash pool, snack bar, gift shop and information center – but, frankly, it's overpriced for what it is. There's a **pool** at El Oasis del Pacífico (p322) where the kiddies can take a dip with hordes of local children any time between 8am and 5pm for under US$2.

You can stroll along the beach or the aptly named **Paseo de los Turistas** (Tourist's Stroll), a pedestrian boulevard stretching along the southern edge of town. Cruise ships make day visits to the eastern end of this road, and a variety of **souvenir stalls** and sodas are there to greet passengers. This entire southern edge of the peninsula is reportedly OK for swimming, though it's best to either enquire about local conditions, or enter the water in places where you can see Ticos swimming. The northern edge of the peninsula is a great place to stroll if you've ever wondered what an abandoned shipping port looks like. About 8km south of Puntarenas is **Playa San Isidro**, the first 'real' beach on the central pacific coast.

Tours

Several companies can take you via boat to visit several of the uninhabited tropical islands in Bahía Gigante. The highlights of this isolated bay include **Isla Tortuga**, a set of two isolated tropical islands famous for their white sand beaches and pristine snorkeling, and **Isla San Lucas**, which is home to the ruins of one of the most infamous prisons in Latin America. Although most tourists organize these tours in Monte-

FIVE AGAINST THE SEA

In January 1988 five fishermen from Puntarenas set out on a trip that was meant to last seven days. Just five days into the voyage, their small vessel was facing 30ft waves triggered by northerly winds known as El Norte. Adrift for 142 days, they would face sharks, inclement weather, acute hunger and parching thirsts. They were finally rescued – 7200km away – by a Japanese fishing boat. *Five Against the Sea* by American reporter Ron Arias, recounts in gripping detail the adversities they faced and how they survived.

zuma, prices are a little lower in Puntarenas as it receives considerably less tourist traffic. The trade-off of course is that you'll probably be spending the night in Puntarenas, which is needless to say, a lot less chilled out then the former hippie enclave of Montezuma.

Coonatramar (☎ 661 9011, 661 1069; www.coonatramar.com; cnr Av 3 & Calle 31) can organize tours to the islands in and around Bahía Gigante as well as to the estuaries and mangroves of Puntarenas. It can also organize fishing charters. Fares range from US$10 to US$40 per person, with a minimum of five to eight people, depending on the tour.

Festivals & Events

Puntarenas is one of the seaside towns that celebrate the **Fiesta de La Virgen del Mar** (Festival of the Virgin of the Sea) on the Saturday closest to July 16. Fishing boats and elegant yachts are beautifully bedecked with lights, flags and all manner of fanciful embellishments as they sail around the harbor, seeking protection from the Virgen as they begin another year at sea. There are also boat races, a carnival and plenty of food, drink and dancing.

Sleeping
BUDGET

Make sure your room has a decent fan or you'll not only be sweltering, but also contending with mosquitoes. All of the following hotels have cold showers unless otherwise stated.

Hotel Cabezas (☎ 661 1045; Av 1 btwn Calles 2 & 4; s/d US$7/14, with bathroom US$10/20; ℗) This is the

PUNTARENAS

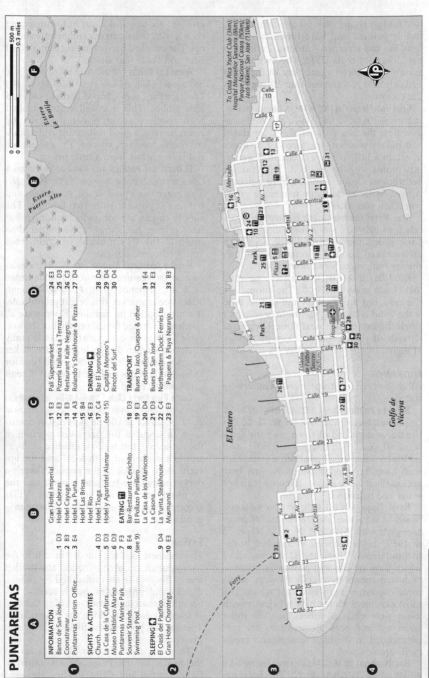

INFORMATION	
Banco de San José................	1 D3
Coonatramar........................	2 B3
Puntarenas Tourism Office....	3 E4

SIGHTS & ACTIVITIES	
Church..................................	4 D3
La Casa de la Cultura............	5 D3
Museo Histórico Marino.........	6 D3
Puntarenas Marine Park.........	7 F3
Souvenir Stands....................	8 E4
Swimming Pool.....................	(see 9)

SLEEPING	
El Oasis del Pacífico.............	9 D4
Gran Hotel Chorotega...........	10 E3

Gran Hotel Imperial..............	11 E3
Hotel Cabezas......................	12 E3
Hotel Cayuga.......................	13 E3
Hotel La Punta.....................	14 A3
Hotel Las Brisas...................	15 B4
Hotel Río.............................	16 E3
Hotel Tioga.........................	17 C4
Hotel y Apartotel Alamar.....	(see 15)

EATING	
Bar-Restaurant Cevichito.......	18 D3
El Pollazo Parrillero..............	19 E3
La Casa de los Mariscos........	20 D4
La Casona............................	21 D3
La Yunta Steakhouse............	22 C4
Musmanni...........................	23 E3

Palí Supermarket.................	24 E3
Pizzería Italiana La Terraza...	25 D3
Restaurant Kaite Negro........	26 C3
Rolando's Steakhouse & Pizzas...	27 D4

DRINKING	
Bar El Joroncito...................	28 D4
Capitán Moreno's.................	29 D4
Rincón del Surf....................	30 D4

TRANSPORT	
Buses to Jacó, Quepos & other	
destinations......................	31 E4
Buses to San José................	32 E3
Northwestern Dock: Ferries to	
Paquera & Playa Naranjo.....	33 B3

Estero La Bodija

Estero Puerto Alto

El Estero

Golfo de Nicoya

Mercado

Ferry

To Costa Rica Yacht Club (3km);
Hospital Monseñor Sanabria (8km);
Parque Nacional Carara (50km);
Jacó (66km); San José (110km)

500 m
0.3 miles

best budget choice. Rooms are calm, clean, freshly painted and have functional overhead fan and screened windows. Parking in the locked lot costs US$3. The owners operate a small travel agency out of the hotel and can help you arrange tours throughout the country.

Gran Hotel Imperial (☎ 661 0579; Paseo de los Turistas btwn Calles Central & 2; s/d US$14/24; **P**) Well situated near the bus stations, this dilapidated and rickety wooden structure still manages to retain a little old-world charm. Cavernous rooms with several beds have private bathrooms. Upstairs rooms have balcony. A beer cooler of the same namesake greets you when you enter.

Gran Hotel Chorotega (☎ 661 0998; cnr Av 3 & Calle 1; s/d US$9/15, d with bathroom US$25) Fairly basic rooms are clean and well kept with an overhead fan and a small TV, though they're nothing to write home about.

Hotel Río (☎ 661 0331; 100m west of the market; s/d US$5/11, with air-con US$8/16; ❄) The rooms are like cells, but they're clean and secure. And if the wind is blowing just right, you won't smell the fish market next door. Keep your wits about you as this area can get dodgy at night.

MIDRANGE
All showers are cold-water unless otherwise stated.

Hotel La Punta (☎ 661 1900, 661 0696; cnr Av 1 & Calle 35; d with fan/air-con US$30/40; **P** ☎ ❄ ❄) At the far-western end of town near the ferry terminal, you'll find this pleasant little hotel with a cozy bar, small pool and a restaurant with hanging wooden lamps. Rooms here are excellent value as they all come with hot water and balconies.

Hotel Tioga (☎ 661 0271; www.hoteltioga.com; Paseo de los Turistas btwn Calles 17 & 19; d standard/deluxe/balcony incl breakfast US$64/82/99; **P** ❄ ❄) Opened in 1959, this is the most established hostel in Puntarenas. There are 52 rooms, all of which have air-con and private bathrooms. Standard rooms have cold showers, while more expensive units have hot water. The most expensive rooms have a balcony with a sea view while all others face the inner courtyard and pool. Reservations are recommended in the high season, and credit cards are accepted.

Hotel Cayuga (☎ 661 0344; Calle 4 btwn Avs Central & 1; d US$19, s/d with TV US$25/33; **P** ❄) This hotel has

efficient air-con and clean but uninspiring rooms with faded carpets and private showers. The attached bar-restaurant does decent beer and *bocas* (bar snacks).

Hotel Las Brisas (☎ 661 4040; hbrisas@racsa.co.cr; cnr Paseo de los Turistas & Calle 31; s/d US$61/88; ❄ ❄) Look for the candy-striped barber poles and blue globes. This is a well managed hotel with spotless accommodations, friendly management, a good restaurant and a pool. All rooms have fan, air-con, TV and private hot showers but seem a little pricey.

El Oasis del Pacífico (cnr Paseo de los Turistas & Calle 5; s/d US$22/35, d with air-con US$40; **P** ❄ ❄) This place has a pool, disco, restaurant and bar and is popular with Tico families. The simple rooms are somewhat rundown but have private hot showers. Be prepared to listen to the DJ's musical selection from your bedroom all night.

Hotel y Apartotel Alamar (☎ 661 4343; www.alamarcr.com; cnr Paseo de los Turistas & Calle 31; d/tr/q standard US$70/94/105, d/q apt US$105/141; **P** ❄ ❄) Though a bit more upmarket, this bright yellow hotel is a great option for families. Rooms are all spotless, with tiled floors, private hot shower, cable TV and air-con. Apartments have fully equipped kitchen that includes coffee maker and rice cooker. There are two pools (one for kids) and all rates include breakfast. Credit cards are accepted.

Costa Rica Yacht Club (☎ 661 0784; cryacht@racsa.co.cr; s/d US$26/38, with air-con US$32/45, villa with air-con US$90; **P** ❄ ❄ ❄) Some 3km east of downtown in Cocal at the narrowest portion of the peninsula, this well-established club caters to members of both local and foreign yacht clubs as well as the public. There's a decent restaurant-bar and a pool, and the 25 rooms are spartan but spotless. Villas accommodate a gaggle of five fishermen – good value. Credit cards are accepted.

Eating
The cheapest food for the destitute is in the *sodas* (lunch counters) around the market area. This area is also inhabited by sailors, drunks and prostitutes, but it seems raffish rather than dangerous – during the day, at least. Restaurants along the Paseo de los Turistas are, predictably, filled with *turistas* (tourists).

There's a row of fairly cheap *sodas* on the beach by the Paseo de los Turistas, Calle Central and Calle 3. They are good for people-watching and serve snacks and nonalcoholic drinks. You'll also find a collection of Chinese restaurants on Avenida 1 east of the church.

La Casona (cnr Av 1 & Calle 9; casados US$2) This bright yellow house is marked with a small, modest sign, but it's an incredibly popular lunch spot, attracting countless locals who jam onto the large deck and into the interior courtyard. Portions are heaping, and soups are served in bathtub-sized bowls. Bring your appetite.

Bar-Restaurant Cevichito (cnr Calle 3 & Av 2; meals US$2-5) Though small and unassuming, this is the best place in town for (you guessed it) *ceviche* (marinated fish cocktails).

Restaurant Kaite Negro (☎ 661 2093; cnr Av 1 & Calle 17; dishes US$2-9) On the north side of town, this is a rambling restaurant popular with locals. It serves good seafood and generous *bocas*. The open-air courtyard comes to life on weekends with live-music and all-night dancing.

Pizzería Italiana La Terraza (Av 1, west of Calle 3; pizzas from US$3; ◷ noon-9pm Mon-Sat, 5-9pm Sun) This pleasant corner restaurant on a small plaza is a good place for a personal-sized pie, pasta or cheap lunch special (US$2). It displays artwork, all for sale.

El Pollazo Parrillero (cnr Av Central & Calle 2; half chicken US$3.50; ◷ 11am-10pm) Grills up tasty chicken 'butterflied' over coals, which is a healthy 'change from all the fried chicken you've been eating.

La Casa de los Mariscos (Paseo de los Turistas btwn Calles 7 & 9; meals US$5-10) Puntarenas is a big fishing port, so you know the fresh catches on offer here are going to be good.

Rolando's Steakhouse & Pizzas (cnr Paseo de los Turistas & Calle 3; dishes US$4-12) Your unassuming corner pizzeria/steakhouse/*cevichiera*/cotton candy stand (OK, not the last one). There's a popular bar serving a long list of *bocas*.

La Yunta Steakhouse (☎ 661 3216; Paseo de los Turistas btwn Calles 19 & 21; meals US$6-10) Your culinary mecca for every imaginable cut of meat has professional service, great ocean views and enough hunks of dead animal to arouse your doctor's anger.

For baked goods, there's always the omnipresent **Musmanni** (Av 1 btwn Calle Central & 1) and self-caterers can head to the **Palí supermarket** (Calle 1 btwn Av 1 & 3) to stock up on just about anything.

Entertainment

Like most port towns, entertainment tends to revolve around boozing and flirting, though the occasional cultural offering does happen at La Casa de la Cultura. If you're looking for the more traditional liquid entertainment, do as the Ticos do and head for the countless bars that line Paseo de los Turistas. The current hot spot for shaking some booty is **Capitán Moreno's** (Paseo de los Turistas at Calle 13), which has a huge dance floor right on the beach. On this same bend in the street, you'll find Bar El Joroncito and Rincón del Surf, two popular waterfront bars offering cheap beer and loud music. Another older, but still popular, spot is **El Oasis del Pacífico** (cnr Paseo de los Turistas & Calle 5), which has a lengthy bar and a warehouse-sized dance floor. Discos may close or have shorter hours in the low season.

Getting There & Away
BOAT

Car and passenger ferries bound for Paquera and Playa Naranjo depart several times a day from the **northwestern dock** (Av 3 btwn Calles 31 & 33). (Other docks are used for private boats.) If you are driving and will be taking the car ferry, arrive at the dock early to get in line. The vehicle section tends to fill up quickly and you may not make it on. In addition, make sure that you have purchased your ticket from the walk-up ticket window *before* driving onto the ferry. You will not be admitted onto the boat if you don't already have a ticket.

Schedules change seasonally and can be affected by inclement weather. Check with the ferry office by the dock for any changes. Many of the hotels in town also have up-to-date schedules posted. The free publication *Península de Nicoya* includes the schedule, or you can check online at www.peninsula denicoya.com.

To Playa Naranjo (for transfer to Nicoya and points west) **Coonatramar** (☎ 661 1069; northwestern dock) departs at 6am, 10am, 2:20pm and 7pm (passenger/car US$2/9, two hours).

To Paquera (for transfer to Montezuma and Mal País) **Ferry Peninsular** (☎ 641 0118, 641 0515; northwestern dock) departs at 4:30am, 6:30am, 8:30am, 10:30am, 12:30pm, 2:30pm, 4:30pm, 6:30pm and 8:30pm (passenger/car US$2/9, 1½ hours).

CENTRAL PACIFIC COAST

BUS

Buses for San José depart from the large navy blue building on the north corner of Calle 2 and Paseo de los Turistas. Book your ticket ahead of time on holidays and weekends.

Buses for other destinations leave from across the street, on the beach side of the paseo.

Cañas & Tilarán US$2.50, 1½ hours, departs 11:45am and 4:30pm.

Costa de Pájaros US$0.50, 1½-two hours, 5:50am, 10:45am, 1:15pm and 5pm.

Jacó/Quepos US$1.50/3, 1½/3½ hours, 5am, 11am, 2:30pm and 4:30pm.

Liberia US$1.50, 2½ hours, 4:40am, 5:30am, 7am, 8:30am, 9:30am, 11am, 2:30pm and 3pm.

Nicoya, Santa Cruz & Filadelfia US$2.75, three to five hours, 6am and 3:45pm.

San José US$2.50, 2½ hours; every hour from 4am to 9pm.

Santa Elena, Monteverde US$2, three hours, 1:15pm and 2:15pm.

Getting Around

Buses marked 'Ferry' run up Av Central and go to the ferry terminal, 1.5km from downtown. The taxi fare from the San José bus terminal in Puntarenas to the northwestern ferry terminal is about US$2.

Buses for the port of Caldera (also going past Playa Doña Ana and Mata de Limón) leave from the market about every hour and head out of town along Av Central.

PUNTARENAS TO TURU BA RI TROPICAL PARK

Boca Barranca, Playa Doña Ana & El Segundo

The road heading south from Puntarenas skirts along the coastline, and a few kilometers out of town you'll start to see the forested peaks of the Cordillera de Tilaran in the distance. The first place of interest is about 12km south of Puntarenas at the river mouth of the **Boca Barranca**, which boasts the 3rd longest left-hand surf break in the world. Conditions here are best at low-tide, and it is possible to surf here all year round.

Just beyond the river mouth is a pair of beaches known as **Playa Doña Ana** and **El Segundo**, which are relatively undeveloped and have an isolated and unhurried feel to them. Surfers can find some decent breaks here, though they are more popular for Tico beachcombers on day trips from Puntarenas, especially during weekends in high season.

Buses heading for Caldera Port depart hourly from the mercado central in Puntarenas, and can easily drop you off at any of these spots. If you're driving, the break at Boca Barranca is located near the bridge on the Costanera Sur (South Coastal Highway), while the entrance to Playa Doña Ana and El Segundo is a little further south (look for a sign that says 'Paradero Turístico Doña Ana.') At the beach entrance there is a parking lot (US$0.60). Day-use fees for the beach are US$1.50/0.75 per adult/child and the beach is open 8am to 5pm. There are snack bars, picnic shelters and changing areas, and the swimming is good.

Mata de Limón & Beyond

This sleepy little place has long been popular with local day trippers from Puntarenas as it's a picturesque little hamlet situation on a mangrove lagoon. Mata de Limón is located near the port of Caldera, and the buses from Puntarenas to Caldera can take you there. If you're driving, the turnoff is 5.5km south of Playa Doña Ana.

The mangrove lagoon is a great spot for **birding** (especially at low tide when the swarms of feathered creatures flock here to scrounge for tasty morsels), though unfortunately it's not very good for swimming. Mata de Limón is divided by a river, with the lagoon and most facilities on the south side.

The major port on the Pacific coast is **Puerto Caldera**, which you pass soon after leaving Mata de Limón. There aren't any sights here (unless you've ever wondered what a container yard looks like), and the beach is unremarkable unless you're a surfer. There are a few good breaks to be had here, though be careful as the beach is rocky in places. Further south, **Playa Tivives** and **Playa Valor** are also of interest to surfers, offering beach breaks at the river mouth, though occasional sightings of crocodiles and sharks are a bit of a deterrent. Any Puntarenas–Jacó bus can drop you at the turnoffs – but you may have to walk 500m or more to find your waves.

Turu Ba Ri Tropical Park

If you've ever thought that the 'eco-adventure' tag just isn't profitable, consider a day trip to the newest project aimed at emptying tourists' wallets under the guise of conservation. For years, tour operators in Puntarenas wondered what to do with all the cruise ship tourists who quickly tired of shopping for plastic baubles on the Paseo de los Turistas. Now, for the simple price of air-conditioned private transportation, park admission, an adrenaline tour or two and possibly a buffet lunch (Costa Rican style of course!), visitors can be assured that as long as their cash keeps flowing, they'll have an 'eco-adventure.'

The **Turu Ba Ri Tropical Park** (☎ 250 0705; www .turubari.com; adult/student US$45/40; ☯ 9am-5pm) is a collection of botanical gardens reflecting each of the topographic zones native to Costa Rica. As you walk along impeccably manicured trails, you'll pass through palm forests, pasture lands, herbariums, cactus fields, bamboo groves, bromeliad gardens, orchid beds and a loma canopy. The gardens are accessed by an aerial tram, which is included in the price of admission. There's no denying the ecological impressiveness of the grounds, but the hefty price tag accompanied by the sounds of package tourists marching in file kinda gets rid of the whole 'adventure' element. If you're an adrenaline junky, there is also a canopy tour (adult/ student US$60/55) in the park, though it's one of the most expensive in the country.

The park is accessed by buses from Orotina (US$0.50, 30 minutes), which depart at 5:30am, noon and 4:30pm. However, most tourists organize private transportation to the park either from Puntarenas or San José. If you're driving, look for a road to the east, just south of Orotina signed 'Coopebaro, Puriscal.' This road goes over an Indiana Jones–worthy wooden suspension bridge to the park. The park is about 9km beyond the bridge, and half the road is paved.

PARQUE NACIONAL CARARA
Situated at the mouth of the Río Tárcoles, the 5242-hectare park is only 50km southeast of Puntarenas by road or about 90km west of San José via the Orotina highway. Its significance cannot be understated. This reserve is at a crucial meeting point between the dry tropical forests to the north and the wet rain forests to the south, which means that it's possible to see strangler figs and deciduous kapok trees alongside acacias and cacti. Since the park is surrounded by pasture and agricultural land, it forms a

necessary oasis for all the wildlife inhabiting the transitional zone.

With the help of a hired guide, it's also possible to visit the archaeological remains of various indigenous burial sites located within the park, though they're tiny and unexciting compared to anything you might see in Mexico or Guatemala. At the time of the Europeans' arrival in Costa Rica, these sights were located in an area inhabited by an indigenous group known as the Huetar (Carara actually means 'crocodile' in the Huetar language). Unfortunately, not much is known about this group as little cultural evidence was left behind. Today, the few remaining Huetar are confined to several small villages in the Central Valley. (For more on the area's indigenous history, see the boxed text Garabito, p38).

Over 400 different species of birds inhabit the reserve, though your chances of spotting rarer species will be greatly enhanced with the help of an experienced guide. The most exciting bird for many visitors to see, especially in June or July, is the brilliantly patterned scarlet macaw, a rare bird that is common to Parque Nacional Carara. Other birds to watch for include antbirds, parrots, trogons, manakins, herons and shorebirds. Monkeys, squirrels, sloths, agoutis and white-tailed deer are among the more common mammals present.

The dry season from December to April is the easiest time to go, though the animals are still there in the wet months. March and April are the driest months. Rainfall is almost 3000mm annually, which is less than in the rain forests further south. It's fairly hot, with average temperatures of 25°C to 28°C – but it's cooler within the rain forest. An umbrella is important in the wet season and occasionally needed in the dry months. Make sure you have insect repellent. According to the park rangers, the best chance of spotting wildlife is at 7am when the park opens.

If you're driving from Puntarenas or San José, pull over to the left immediately after crossing the Río Tárcoles bridge, also known as **Crocodile Bridge**. If you scan the sandbanks below the bridge, you'll have a fairly good chance of seeing as many as 30 basking crocodiles. Although they're visible year-round, they best time for viewing is low-tide during the dry season. Binoculars help a great deal.

Crocodiles this large are generally rare in Costa Rica as they've been hunted vigorously for their leather. However, the crocs are tolerated here as they feature prominently in a number of wildlife tours that depart from Tárcoles. And of course, the crocs don't mind as they're hand-fed virtually every day. Please people, we're asking you nicely – don't feed the animals.

Some 600m further south on the left-hand side is a locked gate leading to the **Sendero Laguna Meándrica** trail. This trail penetrates deep into the reserve and passes through open, secondary forest and patches of dense, mature forest and wetlands. About 4km from the entrance is Laguna Meándrica, which has a large population of herons, smoothbills and kingfishers. If you continue past the lagoon, you'll have a good chance of spotting mammals and the occasional crocodile, though you will have to turn back to exit. Another 2km south of the trailhead is the **Carara ranger station** (admission US$8; 7am-4pm), where you can get information and enter the park. There are bathrooms, picnic tables and a short nature trail. Guides can be hired for US$15 per person (two minimum) for a two-hour hike. About 1km further south are two loop trails. The first, **Sendero Las Araceas**, is 1.2km long and can be combined with the second, **Sendero Quebrada Bonita** (another 1.5km). Both trails pass through primary forest, which is characteristic of most of the park.

Increased tourist traffic along the Pacific coast has unfortunately resulted in an increase in petty theft. Vehicles parked at the trailheads are routinely broken into, and although there may be guards on duty, it is advised that drivers leave their cars in the lot at the Carara ranger station and walk along the Costanera Sur for 2km north or 1km south. Also, be sure to travel in a group and don't carry unnecessary valuables as muggings are reported here occasionally. Alternatively, park beside the Restaurante Ecológico Los Cocodrilos (below).

Sleeping & Eating
Camping is not allowed, and there's nowhere to stay in the park, so most people come on day trips.

Restaurante Ecológico Los Cocodrilos (428 9009; d with bathroom US$20) Located on the north side of the Río Tárcoles bridge, this is the

nearest place to stay and eat. Rooms are boring and unexciting, though it's cheap and convenient base for getting to the park before the tour buses arrive. Its restaurant (casados US$3, open 6am to 8pm) is extremely popular with travelers stopping to check out the crocodiles.

Getting There & Away
There are no buses to Carara, but any bus between Puntarenas and Jacó can leave you at the entrance. You can also catch buses headed north or south in front of the Restaurante Ecológico Los Cocodrilos. This may be a bit problematic on weekends, when buses are full, so go midweek if you are relying on a bus ride. If you're driving, the entrance to Carara is right on the Costanera and is clearly marked.

TÁRCOLES AREA
The Tárcoles area is centered on the small, unassuming town of Tárcoles, which is a small population center of modest houses, strung along a series of dirt roads that parallel the ocean. The main reason for visiting the area, however, are the area's two noteworthy attractions, mainly low-tide birding on the mudflats of the Río Tárcoles and hiking trails near one of the country's tallest waterfalls.

About 2km south of the Carara ranger station is the Tárcoles turnoff to the right (west) and the Hotel Villa Lapas turnoff to the left. To get to Tárcoles, turn right and drive for 1km, then go right at the T-junction to the village. To reach the mudflats of the Río Tárcoles, continue past the village for 2km or 3km.

Sights & Activities
A 5km dirt road past Hotel Villa Lapas leads to the primary entrance to the **Catarata Manatial de Agua Viva** (8312980; admission US$10; 8am-3pm), which is about 200m high and claims to be the highest in the country. From here, it's a steep 3km climb down into the valley, though there are plenty of benches and viewpoints where you can rest. Be sure to keep an eye out for the beautiful, but deadly, poison-dart frogs as well as the occasional scarlet macaw. The falls are more dramatic in the rainy season when they're fuller, though the serene rain-forest setting is beautiful anytime of year. At the

bottom of the valley, the river continues through a series of natural swimming holes where you can take a dip and cool off. A camping area and outhouse are located at the bottom. Local buses between Orotina and Bijagual can drop you off at the entrance to the park.

Although the man at the top of the waterfall will tell you that he operates the only entrance to Manatial de Agua Viva, you can also access the trails by heading 2km further up the road to the 70-hectare **Jardín Pura Vida** (☎ 637 0346; admission US$15; ☽ 8am-5pm) in the town of Bijagual. Although it costs a few more dollars here to enter the waterfall, the admission price also includes access to a private botanical garden that is impeccably manicured, and offers great vistas of Manatial de Agua Viva cascading down the side of a cliff. There is a small restaurant on the grounds, and you can also arrange horse riding and tours through the area.

Before leaving Jardín Pura Vida, be sure to stop by the small kiosk near the parking lot to say hi to Lauri and Howard, a charming American–South African couple who roast small batches of Tarrazu coffee under the brand name **Costa Rica Coffee Roasting Company**. Lauri and Howard will delight in explaining the intricacies of the coffee roasting process, and they certainly know how to make a powerful brew. Lauri and Howard live in Jacó, and are the owners of a delightful guesthouse called Sonidos del Mar (p337).

If you want to get the adrenaline pumping, check out a crocodile tour on the mudflats of the Río Tárcoles. Bilingual guides in boats will take you out in the river for croc spotting and some hair-raising croc tricks. And you know it's going to be good when the guide gets *out* of the boat and *into* the water with these massive beasts – it's *Crocodile Hunter* without the Australian accent. Both **Crocodile Man** (☎ 637 0426; crocodileman@hotmail.com) and **Jungle Crocodile Safari** (☎ 637 0338; www.costarica naturetour.com) have offices in the town. Unfortunately, although the tours are definitely a spectacle to behold, it's frustrating to watch the crocodiles being hand-fed by the tour guides. Furthermore, several travelers report that these tours may not be worth it if you've already been to Tortuguero. Tours usually cost US$25 per person for two hours.

If you're still looking to kill a few hours, Hotel Villa Lapas operates the **SkyWay Tour** featuring 2.5km of suspended bridges (US$25) and yet another canopy tour ($35).

Sleeping & Eating

The Tárcoles area can be almost deserted midweek in the wet season, which can make finding a hot meal problematic.

Hotel Carara (☎ 637 0178; d US$20; P ☒) Situated in the village and right on the beach, this pink building was undergoing a complete overhaul at the time of writing. Rooms on the 2nd floor have an ocean view, though Tárcoles village is not exactly the most exciting place to stay.

Hotel Villa Lapas (☎ 221 5191; www.villalapas.com; s US$160-190, d US$210-280; P ☒ ☒) Although this hotel claims to be an eco-destination, it's really nothing more then an expensive all-inclusive resort. There's no denying the beauty of the place as all the buildings are Spanish colonial in design, and its proximity to primary rain forest makes it the perfect retreat, if you can afford the price tag. There are 55 well-maintained and spacious tiled rooms that have private hot shower, air-con, coffee maker and a nice terrace,

---

BATTLING THE BLOOD SUCKERS

Whether you call them skeeters, mozzies or midges, everyone can agree that fending off mosquitoes is one of the most annoying parts of traveling in the tropics. Although the scientific evidence surrounding effective mosquito bite prevention is circumstantial at best, the following is a list of road-tested, combat strategies for battling the blood suckers:

- Wear socks, trousers and a long sleeve shirt, especially at dusk when mosquitoes feed.

- Eat lots of garlic (not recommended if you're traveling with your significant other).

- Fill your room with the smoke of the ever-present burnable Costa Rican mosquito coils.

- Invest in a good quality mosquito-net, preferably one that has been chemically treated.

- Never underestimate the power of spraying yourself with DEET.

and there's a pool and immaculate gardens. There is good birding along trails that wind up the Río Tárcoles in a private reserve, and there is a SkyWalk and canopy tour on the hotel grounds. The restaurant (open 7am to 9pm) is open to the public and the bar area has a pool table. Credit cards are accepted.

PUNTA LEONA AREA

This tiny headland is about halfway between Tárcoles and Jacó on the Costanera, and is renowned for its crystal blue waters and exquisite natural surroundings. Unfortunately, accommodation here is top end, so most tourists blow through Punta Leona on their way to Jacó and points further south. However, if you have your own wheels, it's worth stopping for a quick drink at the Hotel Villa Caletas (below), arguably one of the most spectacular hotels in all of Costa Rica.

US-based **JD's Watersports** (☎ 256 6391; www .jdwatersports.com) operates a complete watersports center inside Hotel Punta Leona and offers sportfishing packages, scuba diving trips, half-day jungle river cruises, sunset cruises and ocean-kayak rental. Other gear and boat charters to various destinations are also available.

Sleeping & Eating

Hotel Punta Leona (☎ 231 3131; www.hotelpuntaleona .com; s/d/tr US$80/90/100, apt US$170-240; P ⊠ ⌨ ⌘) About 6km south of Tárcoles, a guarded gate lets guests onto the 4km dirt road that leads to this complex. The bland-looking rooms and apartments all come with the usual top-end amenities. However, the beaches lining the property are exquisite, though unfortunately the hotel has tried, on several occasions, to shut down public access to them. This is illegal in Costa Rica, where beaches are public property. Credit cards are accepted.

Hotel Villa Caletas (☎ 637 0505; www.hotelvilla caletas.com; reservations@hotelvillacaletas.com; r US$170-420; P ⊠ ⌘) This property is one of only six hotels in all of Costa Rica belonging to the 'Small Distinctive Hotels of Costa Rica Group,' and from the moment you enter the property you'll understand why. Since it's perched high on a dramatic hillside, you'll first have to navigate a 1km-long serpentine driveway adorned with cacti and Victorian lanterns. The drive will be worth it as upon entering the property, you'll be rewarded with panoramic views of the Pacific coastline. But, what makes the hotel truly unique is its fusion of architectural styles, incorporating elements as varied as tropical Victorian, Hellenistic and French colonial. Unlike most luxury hotels, Villa Caletas is solely comprised of 35 units, each sheltered in a tropical gardens and dense foliage that gives the appearance of total isolation. The interiors of the rooms are individually decorated with art and antiques, but nothing is nearly as magnificent as the views you'll have from your room. There is also a French-influenced restaurant, an inviting infinity pool and a private 1km trail leading to the beach. Credit cards are accepted.

Even if you're not staying at the hotel, it's worth stopping by to have a drink (US$2 to US$4) at the amphitheatre, which is built according to Grecian specifications and is carved into the hillside facing the ocean. For a few dollars, you will be rewarded with what may be the best Pacific sunset you've ever seen.

PLAYA HERRADURA

Until the mid-1990s, Playa Herradura was a rural, palm-sheltered beach of grayish-black sand that was popular mainly with campers. However, in the late 1990s the beach was thrown into the spotlight when it was used as the stage for the movie *1492*. As with all things 'discovered,' rapid development ensued, and soon Playa Herradura had a marina, several condominium complexes and one of the most expensive hotels in the country, the Los Sueños Marriott Beach & Golf Resort (opposite). The beach was also an easy sell since the off-shore waters were teeming with dolphin and sportfish like marlin, which brought in wealthy American anglers by the thousands.

Today, the road out to the beach is starting to look like one giant construction site. And, with Jacó only a few kilometers down the road, it's not likely that the pace of development is going to slow anytime soon. However, regardless of all the foreign investment taking place, Playa Herradura still attracts a slew of locals who come to take a dip in the tranquil waters, and the beach scene is still very much 'Tico' in character.

Although most activities in Herradura revolve around beachcombing, the reader-recommended **Herradura Divers** (☎ 637 7123, 846 4649; www.herraduradivers.com) can organize a variety of dive tours as well certification classes and snorkeling trips.

A few hundred meters before the beach on the main road is a large grass campground, **Campamento Herradura** (per person US$3.50), which has showers and basic facilities.

About 500m from the beach on the main road is **Cabañas el Río** (☎ 643 8891; s/d/tr US$10/18/24; P), a German-owned place with six cabins of varying comfort and size spread out near a tiny creek. Rooms are well-kept, and some come with a small kitchenette. If you're not camping, this is the only budget accommodation in the area as most people prefer to stay in Jacó and then take trips to Playa Herradura.

Los Sueños Marriott Beach & Golf Resort (☎ 630 9000; www.lossuenosresort.com; d US$300-400; P ▣ ▣ ▣) is a US$40 million hotel-and-condo project at the northern end of the bay. It features a 250-ship marina, golf course, tennis courts, pool, shopping center, casino, sportfishing and enough other stuff that'll hopefully make the US$300-plus room rate seem worth it. And, if you ask anyone with the slightest bit of knowledge regarding sustainable tourism, they'll also tell you it's one of the most universally hated hotels in the country. Needless to say, American package holiday travelers, who don't engage with any locals other then their waiter and bartender, absolutely love it. The **golf course** (green fee guest/nonguest US$95/140) is one of the principal attractions, which is a good way to pass the time when you're afraid to leave your compound. And, as if the whole package wasn't ridiculous enough, the hills above the bay have been bulldozed to make way for million-dollar homes (that only a rich foreigner could afford). To be fair, the Spanish colonial–style complex is attractive, though it does reek of pre-fabricated sameness.

On the beach are many locally popular seafood restaurants including Marisquería Juanita, El Rey Marino and El Pelícano, which are jam-packed with locals in the know.

The Herradura turnoff is on the Costanera Sur, 3.5km north of the turnoff to Jacó. From here, a paved road leads 3km west to Playa Herradura. There are frequent local buses connecting Playa Herradura to Jacó.

JACÓ

Jacó (pronounced ha-*ko*, not *ja*-ko and never *ya*-ko) has a special place in the hearts of Ticos as it is the quickest oceanside escape for landlocked denizens of the Central Valley. Many joséfinos recall fondly the days when weekend shuttle buses would pick up beach-seekers in the city center and whisk them away to the undeveloped Pacific paradise of Jacó. With warm water, year-round consistent surf, world-class fishing and a relaxed, beachside setting, it was hard to believe that a place this magical was only a short bus ride away from San José.

The secret got out in the early 1990s when Canadians on package tours started flooding Jacó, though for the most part tourism remained pretty low key. Things picked up a bit in the late 1990s when surfers and anglers from North America and Europe started visiting Costa Rica en masse, though Jacó remained the dominion of Central Valley Ticos looking for a little fun and sun. And then, something happened that was completely beyond anyone's control – Baby Boomers started getting old.

In only a few years time, Jacó became the most rapidly developing town (some would argue city) in all of Costa Rica due to the constant stream of Western retirees looking for their own little slice of beachside paradise. Plots of land were subdivided, beachfronts were cleared, hillsides were leveled and almost overnight Jacó became the exclusive enclave of moneyed expats. Ticos were happy that development brought coveted Western institutions like paved roads and fast-food restaurants, but suddenly the majority of residents in Jacó were pronouncing the beach's name without the soft 'j'.

And then, the problems started. Costa Rica's carefree attitude towards drugs meant that Dick and Jane could buy a little reefer on the street and relive their misspent youth. Jack's wife left him three years ago, but since prostitution is decriminalized in Costa Rica, his pension checks made him the most popular guy at the bar. It all started out as fun and games, but when the drugs got harder and the women younger, people started to worry.

Not surprisingly, most people in Costa Rica will tell you that you shouldn't go to Jacó, though this is certainly unwarranted

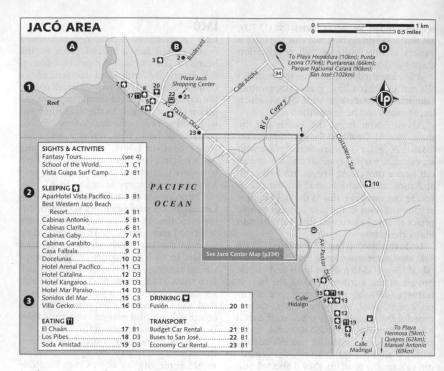

JACÓ AREA

SIGHTS & ACTIVITIES	
Fantasy Tours	(see 4)
School of the World	**1** C1
Vista Guapa Surf Camp	**2** B1

SLEEPING	
AparHotel Vista Pacifico	**3** B1
Best Western Jacó Beach	
Resort	**4** B1
Cabinas Antonio	**5** B1
Cabinas Clarita	**6** B1
Cabinas Gaby	**7** A1
Cabinas Garabito	**8** B1
Casa Falbala	**9** C3
Docelunas	**10** D2
Hotel Arenal Pacifico	**11** C3
Hotel Catalina	**12** D3
Hotel Kangaroo	**13** D3
Hotel Mar Paraíso	**14** D3
Sonidos del Mar	**15** C3
Villa Gecko	**16** D3

EATING	
El Chaán	**17** B1
Los Pibes	**18** D3
Soda Amistad	**19** D3

DRINKING	
Fusión	**20** B1

TRANSPORT	
Budget Car Rental	**21** B1
Buses to San José	**22** B1
Economy Car Rental	**23** B1

To Playa Herradura (10km); Punta Leona (17km); Puntarenas (66km); Parque Nacional Carara (90km); San José (102km)

Reef

PACIFIC OCEAN

Río Copey

Costanera Sur

See Jacó Center Map (p334)

Calle Hidalgo

Calle Madrigal

To Playa Hermosa (5km); Quepos (62km); Manuel Antonio (69km)

Plaza Jacó Shopping Center

Calle Ancha

0 ——— 1 km
0 ——— 0.5 miles

as the majority of people who stay there enjoy themselves thoroughly. The beach is also *the* party destination on the central Pacific coast and attracts a slew of sportfishing enthusiasts, surfers, spring-breakers, cruise-shippers (who disembark in Puntarenas) and package-holiday makers who all come to paint the town red at night and pass out on the beach during the day. The surf is also a killer, and on most days of the year you're guaranteed consistent swells that are dreamy if you're a beginner or intermediate surfer. But, if you're looking for an authentic Costa Rican beach scene, it's probably better to head to the beaches further south or west to Nicoya.

Jacó is expensive and during the high season it's jam-packed with tourists, so reservations are recommended, especially around the winter holidays.

Orientation

Playa Jacó is about 2km off the Costanera, 3.5km past the turnoff for Herradura. The beach itself is about 3km long, and hotels and restaurants line the road running

behind it. The areas on the northern and southern fringes are the most tranquil and attractive and are the cleanest.

In an effort to make foreign visitors feel more at home, the town has placed signs with street names on most streets. These names are shown on the map, but the locals continue to use the traditional landmark system (see the boxed text What's That Address?, p539).

Information

There's no unbiased tourist information office, though several tour offices will give information. Look for the free monthly *Jaco's Guide* which includes tide charts and up-to-date maps, or go to www.jacoguide.com. The free monthly magazine *Central Pacific Way* has information on tourist attractions up and down the coastline.

There are pay phones on the main street. If you're on the beach and your bladder needs relief, there are public toilets (US$0.30) just north of Hotel Balcón del Mar (p336). For a fee (US$1.50) the staff will also let you check in belongings.

Aquamatic Coin Laundry (Map p334; Av Pastor Díaz; ☼ 7:30am-12:30pm & 1-5pm) The best place to get the skivvies clean; do-it-yourself and drop-off service.

Banco de San José (Map p334; Av Pastor Díaz, north of Calle Cocal; ☼ 8am-5pm Mon-Fri, 8am-noon Sat) Has a Cirrus ATM open during bank hours on the 2nd floor of the Il Galeone shopping center.

Banco Popular (Map p334; Av Pastor Díaz at Calle La Central) Exchanges US dollars and traveler's checks.

Books & Stuff (Map p334; Av Pastor Díaz btwn Calles Las Olas & Bohío) Has books in several languages as well as US newspapers.

Mexican Joe's (Map p334; Av Pastor Díaz btwn Calles Las Olas & Bohío; per hr US$0.75; ☼ 9am-9pm Mon-Sat, 10am-8pm Sun) The best place to check email; has multiple computers with high-speed connections and air-con.

Red Cross (Map p334; ☎ 643 3090; Av Pastor Díaz btwn Calles El Hicaco & Las Brisas) Medical clinic.

Activities

SWIMMING

Jacó is generally safe for swimming, though you should avoid the areas near the estuaries, which are polluted. Be advised that the waves can get crowded with beginner surfers who don't always know how to control their boards, so be smart and stay out of their way. Riptides do occasionally occur (see the boxed text What To Do If You're Caught in a Riptide, p284), especially when the surf gets big, so enquire about local conditions and keep an eye out for red-flags marking the paths of rips.

SURFING

Although the rainy season is considered best for Pacific coast surfing, Jacó is blessed with consistent year-round breaks. Although more advanced surfers head further south to Playa Hermosa, the waves at Jacó are strong, steady and a lot of fun. Jacó is also a great place to start a surf trip as it's easy to buy and sell boards here. If you're looking to rent a board for the day, shop around as the better places will rent you a board for US$15 to US$20 for 24 hours, while others will try to charge you a few dollars per hour.

There are too many surf shops to list, and it seems like every store in town does ding repair and rents long boards. One shop that stands out is **Chuck's W.O.W. Surf** (Map p334; ☎ 643 3844; www.wowsurf.net.com; Av Pastor Díaz at Calle Anita), which is owned and managed by Chuck Herwig, one of Jacó's original surf gurus. He's an all-around knowledgeable

---

CHUCK'S SIMPLE RULES

Chuck Herwig, who runs W.O.W. Surf (left) and Chuck's Cabinas (p333) offers the following simple rules for staying safe and enjoying your time in Costa Rica:

- Be wary of instant friendships.
- Don't bring strangers back to your room.
- Don't leave anything unattended; hygiene or personal goods.
- Treat locals as you would want to be treated as a local.

---

dude (see the boxed text Chuck's Simple Rules, above), and a great source of information on anything from surf conditions to the future of Jacó. He also runs Chuck's Cabinas (p333) around the corner. Oh, and in case your curious W.O.W. can stand for 'walking on water' or a 'world of waves.'

Six-time national surf champion Alvaro Solano runs the highly respected **Vista Guapa Surf Camp** (Map p330; ☎ 643 2830, in the USA 409-599 1828; www.vistaguapa.com), which comes recommended by readers. Weekly rates including full board are US$775 to US$1300.

SURFCASTING

Several shops in town rent fishing gear and sell bait for a few dollars each, and there are plenty of spots along the beach where you can crack a beer and try your luck. Surfcasting is extremely popular with locals, so dust off your Spanish vocab and strike up a conversation or two.

HIKING

A popular local pastime is following the trail up Miros Mountain, which winds through primary and secondary rain forest, and offers spectacular views of Jacó and Playa Hermosa. The trail actually leads as far as the Central Valley, though you only need to hike for a few kilometers to reach the viewpoint. Note that the trailhead is located near the entrance to the canopy tour though it's unmarked, so it's a good idea to ask a local to point it out to you.

HORSE RIDING

Readers have reported incidents of horse abuse in Jacó, specifically operators uses malnourished and mistreated animals.

However, one recommended company is **Discovery Horseback Tours** (☎ 838 7550; www.discoveryhorsetours.com; from $70) which is run by an English couple.

HANG GLIDING

Hang Glide Costa Rica (☎ 778 8710; www.hangglidecostarica.com; from $70) will pick you up in Jacó and shuttle you to an airstrip south of Playa Hermosa where you can ride tandem in a hang glider or fly in a three-seat ultralight plane.

KAYAKING

If you're interested in organizing kayaking and sea canoeing trips that include snorkeling excursions to tropical islands, contact **Kayak Jacó Costa Rica Outriggers** (☎ 643 1233; www.kayakjaco.com) which offers a wide variety of customized day trips.

SPAS

A branch of the exceedingly professional **Serenity Spa** (Map p334; ☎ 643 1624; serenity@racsa.co.cr; Av Pastor Díaz, east of Calle Bohio) offers the full range of spa services.

Courses

City-Playa Language Institute (Map p334; ☎ 643 2123; www.costarica-spanishschool.com; Av Pastor Díaz btwn Calle Las Palmeras & Calle Las Olas) offers inexpensive courses in Spanish for as little as US$80 per week. Ask about group rates.

School of the World (Map p330; ☎ 643 1064; www.schooloftheworld.org; 1-4 week packages US$540-1900; P 🞸) is a popular school and cultural-studies center offering classes in Spanish, surfing, art and photography. The sweet new building also houses a café and art gallery. Rates include kayaking and hiking field trips and on-site lodging. Spanish and surfing are the most popular programs.

Tours

Tours around the area include visits to Parque Nacional Carara (US$40) as well as longer-distance trips around the country. Another popular destination is Isla Damas – you can organize tours here or in Quepos, further south. Isla Damas is not 100% an island, but the tip of a pointed mangrove forest that juts out into a small bay just south of Parrita. During high tide, as the surrounding areas fill with water, this point becomes an island – offering an incredible opportunity for birders and other wildlife

watchers. Boating tours can be arranged from Jacó for US$60 per person, but more avid adventurers can opt for a sea-kayaking expedition with Amigo Tico Complete Adventure Tours in Quepos. There are also two nearby canopy tours, **Canopy Adventure Jacó** (☎ 643 3271; www.adventurecanopy.com; tours US$55) and **Waterfalls Canopy Tour** (☎ 632 3322; www.waterfallscanopy.com; tours US$55).

You can also appreciate the beauty and grandeur of Mother Nature by burning liters upon liters of her precious natural resources. **Paraiso Adventure** (☎ 643 2920; www.paraisocostarica.com; from $55) runs guided jungle and safari tours.

Virtually every store in town books tours as Jacó operates on a lucrative commission-based system, so save yourself a few dollars and go directly to one of the following agencies:

Fantasy Tours (Map p330; ☎ 220 2126; www.fantasy.co.cr; Best Western, Av Pastor Díaz)

King Tours (Map p334; ☎ 643 2441, 388 7810; www.kingtours.com; Av Pastor Díaz, north of Calle Cocal)

Sleeping

The center of town, with its many bars and discos, can mean that noise will be a factor in where you choose to stay. The far northern and southern ends of town have more relaxed and quiet accommodations. Reservations are highly recommended during dry-season weekends and become critical during Easter and the week between Christmas and New Year's. If you plan on a lengthy stay (more than five days), ask about long-term rates.

The rates given are high-season rates, but low-season rates could be as much as 30% to 40% lower. Hotels below are listed from north to south.

BUDGET

Cabinas Antonio (Map p330; ☎ 643 3043; cnr Av Pastor Díaz & Boulevard; d US$15; P 🞸) At the northern end of town, basic cabins here are clean and come with private cold shower and cable TV. Rooms are uninteresting, though you won't care as it's cheap and close to a quiet part of the beach.

Cabinas Garabito (Map p330; ☎ 643 3321; Av Pastor Díaz; d US$20; P) Cabins here are slightly more expensive than Cabinas Antonio and nearly identical, though the Tico owners are friendly and you're still in a quiet part of town.

GOT DRUGS, WILL TRAVEL

Drugs are plentiful in Costa Rica, and a good number of tourists would never give a second thought to lighting up a joint on the beach (or, more recently, blowing a line of coke in a discotheque). However, drugs are 100% illegal in Costa Rica, and if you are charged with possession you can be fined and imprisoned depending on the severity of the offense. There are currently foreigners serving out terms, and occasionally a big drug bust will make the headlines. The bad news is that there is little that your embassy can do on your behalf. The good news is that as far as Latin American penal systems are concerned, there are places a hell of a lot worse than a Costa Rican prison.

The reality is that most police officers would rather collect a bribe or confiscate a joint and smoke it themselves than send a bunch of backpackers to jail. Unlike other destinations on the hippie trail like Morocco, Thailand and India, Costa Rica has a squeaky-clean, ecofriendly image that it needs to uphold, and the last thing the tourist board wants is the mugs of a bunch of American teenagers plastered on the front page of *USA Today*. However, things are changing rapidly, and as more gringos start packing their bags and heading to Costa Rica, you can expect that the supply will meet the demand.

The main problem with the market in Costa Rica right now is that a greater number of hard drugs are becoming readily available for purchase. On beaches with a growing international scene like Jacó and Tamarindo, it's possible to buy just about any drug on any street corner in any language. The drug of choice in the bars is quickly becoming cocaine, and although there's no guarantee you're actually getting ecstasy, backpackers are popping pills in the clubs like they are Tic-Tacs.

Ticos will tell you that the Colombians, Jamaicans, Panamanians and just about every other nationality are to blame for importing drugs into their country, but the truth is that they share an equal amount of blame. An 8-ball of cocaine yields a much larger profit than a wood-carving of a tree-frog, and most backpackers are happy to pay in US dollars for a dime-bag of dubious quality.

The moral of the story is that at some point during your travels in Costa Rica, there is a good chance that you will be offered drugs. And there's a good chance that if you're reading this right now, you might say yes. So, remember to use your judgment, consider the consequences and don't say that we didn't warn you.

Cabinas Clarita (Map p330; ☎ 643 2615; western end of Boulevard; r per person US$9; P) This fading, pink complex on the beach wows guests with the beauty and grandeur of concrete walls. Rooms have a private bathroom, and there is a bar and restaurant.

Chuck's Cabinas (Map p334; ☎ 643 3328; chucks@ racsa.co.cr; Calle Anita; r per person US$7.50, d/tr/q with bathroom US$25/30/35; P) This cool, budget hangout is usually packed to the gills with surfers from around the world. Concrete-block rooms are small and clean and come with high-powered fan. A couple of larger rooms come with private bathroom. Owner Chuck, who runs W.O.W. Surf (p331), will obligingly answer any questions you might have as he is a solid, dependable dude.

Cabinas Emily (Map p334; ☎ 643 3513; Av Pastor Díaz btwn Calles Anita & Bri Brí; d US$13; P) Situated right behind Wahoo's, rooms with shared bathroom are cheap and within crawling distance of the pubs, but don't expect a quiet night of sleep in this part of town.

Hotel de Haan (Map p334; ☎ 643 1795; www.hotel dehaan.com; Calle Bohío; r per person US$10, child under 10 free; P) This Dutch/Tico outpost is one of the top budget bets in town and is perennially popular with backpackers. Freshly tiled rooms with hot-water showers are clean and secure, and there's a shared kitchen with fridge, a pool and free Internet. The upstairs balcony is a great place for swapping stories with fellow backpackers, or checking out the parade of paying customers at the brothel next door. Ask about long-term rates.

Cabinas Roblemar (Map p334; ☎ 643 3173; Calle Bohío; d US$20; P) Comfy doubles here come with private bathroom, and there's a room for five with a kitchenette that's great value (US$38). There are also a number of smaller, dank rooms with tired-looking shared bathroom (rates vary), though they're not recommended.

Cabinas La Cometa (Map p334; ☎ 643 3615; Av Pastor Díaz, south of Calle Bohío; d with/without bathroom US$32/22) Rooms are fairly basic at this

French-Canadian–run inn, though they're fresh, clean, secure and good value. Four units share a clean bathroom with cold shower, while another three have private restroom with hot water. There is a spotless shared kitchen.

Cabinas Marilyn (Map p334; ☎ 643 3215; Calle Cocal; s/d US$16/25; r for 4/5/6 persons with kitchen

US$36/50/72) Bare rooms here are seriously musty and not at all well kept, but they're cheap and they'll definitely do in a pinch. All come with private bathroom, and a couple of units have a fridge.

Nathon's Place (Map p334; ☎ 355 4359; Calle Hicaco; dm/d US$10/25; 🅿 🖳 🗷) White-washed, bunker-like rooms are devoid of any personality,

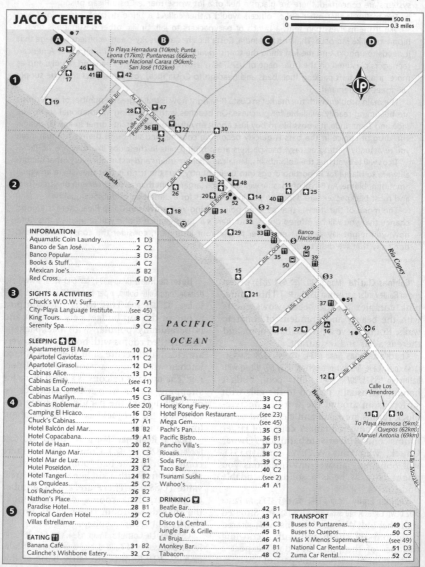

JACÓ CENTER

0 ___ 500 m
0 ___ 0.3 miles

PACIFIC OCEAN

To Playa Herradura (10km); Punta Leona (17km); Puntarenas (66km); Parque Nacional Carara (90km); San José (102km)

Banco Nacional

Río Copey

Calle Los Almendros

To Playa Hermosa (5km); Quepos (62km); Manuel Antonia (69km)

INFORMATION	
Aquamatic Coin Laundry	1 D3
Banco de San José	2 C2
Banco Popular	3 C2
Books & Stuff	4 C2
Mexican Joe's	5 B2
Red Cross	6 D3

SIGHTS & ACTIVITIES	
Chuck's W.O.W. Surf	7 A1
City-Playa Language Institute	(see 45)
King Tours	8 C2
Serenity Spa	9 C2

SLEEPING 🏠 ⌂	
Apartamentos El Mar	10 D4
Apartotel Gaviotas	11 C2
Apartotel Girasol	12 D4
Cabinas Alice	13 D4
Cabinas Emily	(see 41)
Cabinas La Cometa	14 C2
Cabinas Marilyn	15 C3
Cabinas Roblemar	(see 20)
Camping El Hicaco	16 D3
Chuck's Cabinas	17 A1
Hotel Balcón del Mar	18 B2
Hotel Copacabana	19 A1
Hotel de Haan	20 B2
Hotel Mango Mar	21 C3
Hotel Mar de Luz	22 B1
Hotel Poseidon	23 C2
Hotel Tangerí	24 B2
Las Orquídeas	25 C2
Los Ranchos	26 B2
Nathon's Place	27 C4
Paradise Hotel	28 B1
Tropical Garden Hotel	29 C2
Villas Estrellamar	30 C1

EATING 🍴	
Banana Café	31 B2
Calinche's Wishbone Eatery	32 C2

Gilligan's	33 C2
Hong Kong Fuey	34 C2
Hotel Poseidon Restaurant	(see 23)
Mega Gem	(see 45)
Pachi's Pan	35 C3
Pacific Bistro	36 B1
Pancho Villa's	37 D3
Rioasis	38 C2
Soda Flor	39 C3
Taco Bar	40 C2
Tsunami Sushi	(see 2)
Wahoo's	41 A1

DRINKING 🍷	
Beatle Bar	42 B1
Club Olé	43 A1
Disco La Central	44 C3
Jungle Bar & Grille	45 B1
La Bruja	46 A1
Monkey Bar	47 B1
Tabacon	48 C2

TRANSPORT	
Buses to Puntarenas	49 C3
Buses to Quepos	50 C3
Más X Menos Supermarket	(see 49)
National Car Rental	51 D3
Zuma Car Rental	52 C2

but the Texan owners know how to run a good show. Rooms are fully air-conditioned, there are shared hot-water bathrooms, a TV lounge and free bike rentals all-day.

Camping El Hicaco (Map p334; ☎ 643 3004; Calle Hicaco; campsites per person US$3; P) The best campground in town: there are picnic tables, bathrooms and a lockup for gear. (Don't leave valuables in your tent.)

MIDRANGE

Villas Estrellamar (Map p334; ☎ 643 3102; www.estrellamar.com; eastern end of Calle Las Olas; d US$59, bungalow US$69; P 🐾 🔊) Twenty-eight spacious, pristine rooms have massive bathrooms with hot-water shower, cable TV, fridge, lock box, air-con, phone and private balcony. Villas accommodate from two to seven people and have equipped kitchen with coffee maker. There's a pool, Jacuzzi, restaurant and bar, and the new American owners have big plans for the place. Be sure to take a relaxing swing in the hammock pavilion, and keep an eye out for the huge

iguanas that live on the grounds and feed off the mango tree. Credit cards are accepted.

Cabinas Gaby (Map p330; ☎ 643 3080; Av Pastor Díaz; tr with air-con US$56; P 🐾 🔊) At the far northern end of town, this bright yellow place is popular with Tico families and has pleasant rooms with kitchenette, hot water and a choice of fan or air-con. It's by far the nicest cabina on this stretch of road. There's a small pool and a shady garden.

Paradise Hotel (Map p334; ☎ 643 2563; www.paradisehoteljaco.com; Av Pastor Díaz; d US$35; P 🔊 🐾) This recently renovated hotel has simple, well-maintained rooms that are equipped with air-con, hot water and cable TV, though the whole place is lacking in personality. There's also a pool, a lounge with comfortable couches and a pool table.

Hotel Mar de Luz (Map p334; ☎ 643 3259; www.mardeluz.com; Av Pastor Díaz btwn Calles Las Palmeras & Los Olas; d/tr/q incl breakfast US$75/80/95; P 🐾 🔊) This adorable hotel with Dutch-inspired murals of windmills and tulips on the walls has tidy and attractive air-con rooms with

---

THE AUTHOR'S CHOICE

Budget

Hotel Kangaroo (Map p330; ☎ 643 3351; www.hotel-kangaroo.com; 300m from Hotel Jacó Fiesta; dm US$12, d US$35; P 🖳 🐾 🔊) The newest accommodation in town is located 100m from one of the quietest and most beautiful strips of sand. This chilled-out nine-room hotel is run by a pair of French surfers, Stef and Nico, and completely draped in Nepali prayer flags and adorned with huge dream catchers. All the rooms have air-con, there's a free breakfast, 24-hour free Internet, a shared kitchen and a refreshing pool (check out the awesome mural!). Shared bathrooms are equipped with hot water. If you're arriving by bus, the owners will pay for a cab from the center of town.

Midrange

AparHotel Vista Pacifico (Map p330; ☎ 643 3261; www.vistapacifico.com; top of the hill off Boulevard; d incl breakfast from US$55, additional person US$10; P 🗶 🔊) Located on the crest of a hill just outside Jacó, this Canadian-run hotel is an absolute gem. The views of the coastline are phenomenal, particularly at sunset when you'll have panoramic views of a fiery sky, and the mountain-top location means that it's a few degrees cooler (and a whole lot quieter) than Jacó. Homey and comfortable rooms have hot water, cable TV and tremendous views. There is a pool-side BBQ that guests can use.

Top End

Docelunas (Map p330; ☎ 643 2277; Costanera Sur; d/jnr ste incl breakfast US$130/150; P 🖳 🐾 🗶 🔊) Situated in the foot hills across the highway, 'Twelve Moons' is a heavenly mountain retreat consisting of only 20 rooms sheltered in a pristine landscape of tropical rain forest. Each teak-accented room is intimately decorated with original artwork that's available for purchase, and the luxurious bathrooms feature double sinks and bathtubs. Yoga classes are given daily, there's a full spa that uses the hotel's own line of beauty products and you can dip in a free-form pool that's fed by a waterfall. The open air restaurant serves everything from marlin ceviche to vegan delicacies. To reach the hotel, make a left off the Costanera between the two entrances for Playa Jacó.

patio, hot-water shower, microwave, fridge and coffee maker. Several larger stone rooms in the back are also a good option. There are two pools and barbecue grills for guests to use. The friendly Dutch owners also speak Spanish, English, German and Italian and are knowledgeable about the area. This is a perfect family option. The owners are also committed to fighting drugs and prostitution in Jacó. Credit cards are accepted.

Los Ranchos (Map p334; ☎ 643 3070; Calle Las Olas; d with/without kitchen US$58/50, bungalow US$100; P ⛱) This popular place is near the beach and attracts many repeat clients from Europe. It has a sparkling pool, pleasant garden, small paperback library and friendly staff offering information on local tours and surfing. Rooms are clean, well kept and quiet and all have fan and private bathroom with hot water. Larger bungalows sleep up to seven. Credit cards are accepted.

Hotel Balcón del Mar (Map p334; ☎ 643 3251; btwn Calles Las Olas & El Bohío; d/tr US$92/104; P ⛱ ⛱) This beachfront place has a prime location and rooms all have hot-water shower, private balcony, ocean view, minifridge, air-con and cable TV, though the hotel was undergoing a major renovation at the time of writing. There's a pool and a good restaurant. Credit cards are accepted.

Tropical Garden Hotel (Map p334; ☎ 643 3003; d/tr/q US$70/80/90; P ⛱ ⛱) This Israeli-run hotel comprises cabinas centered on a large pool and, not surprisingly, a tropical garden. Each cabina has a full kitchen, private porch, air-con, hot water cable TV and wireless Internet. The owner also runs the Las Orquideas hotel.

Apartotel Gaviotas (Map p334; ☎ 643 3092; d with/ without air-con US$52/42; P ⛱ ⛱) Here you'll find 12 spacious and modern apartments that are well-furnished with a kitchenette, fridge, sitting area, cable TV and hot water. There's a fine pool and a TV room. Significantly lower rainy-season rates are available.

Las Orquideas (Map p334; ☎ 643 4056; d with/ without air-con US$48/42; P ⛱ ⛱) Las Orquideas is essentially a kitchenless version of the Tropical Garden Hotel, though it's much further from the beach. Rooms have been recently renovated with attractive furnishing, and have hot water, cable TV, refrigerator and coffeemaker.

Hotel Mango Mar (Map p334; ☎ 643 3670; Calle Cocal; d US$60, apt US$100-120; P ⛱ ⛱) This

whitewashed hotel with a prime beachfront location has a dozen air-con rooms with kitchenette, hot water, and balcony overlooking the pool and Jacuzzi. It also has two fully equipped apartments that can accommodate up to six. Credit cards are accepted.

Cabinas Alice (Map p334; ☎ 643 3061; Calle Los Allmendros; d with fan/air-con US$37/47, q with kitchen US$68; P ⛱ ⛱) Alice is a long-time Tica resident, who's friendly, outspoken and oozes personality. Here you'll find decent, clean rooms with private bathroom, hot water and fan or air-con. The beach is steps away. Credit cards are accepted.

Apartamentos El Mar (Map p334; ☎ 643 3165; Calle Los Almendros; d/tr/q US$35/45/55; P ⛱) Spacious rooms here surround a cactus-landscaped courtyard with a pool. Apartments are clean and have hot water, kitchenette and fan. They can sleep up to five and are a good deal. Credit cards are accepted.

Hotel Catalina (Map p330; ☎ 643 1237; www.hotel catalinacr.com; Calle Hidalgo; d with/without air-con US$70/55; P ⛱ ⛱) This beachfront hotel has large and spotless tiled rooms with private hot shower, fan, kitchenette and a small balcony or patio that overlooks a garden courtyard. Several units have air-con and there is a barbecue grill available for guest use. Monthly rates are available.

Casa Falbala (Map p330; ☎ 643 1687; www.falbala -costarica.com; Calle Hidalgo; d US$65; P ⛱ ⛱) This small and personal French-owned pension has prime beach front on a relaxed stretch of sand at the southern end of town. The rooms are spacious and comfortable, and are all equipped with air-con, cable TV and hot water. The real sell here is the well-landscaped grounds that surround the pool and outdoor Jacuzzi.

Villa Gecko (Map p330; ☎ 643 1314; www.villagecko .net; Calle Hidalgo; 2-3 person studio US$80, 3-5 person ste US$150; P ⛱ ⛱) By far the most charming accommodation on the beach, Villa Gecko is managed by a French artist whose artistic touch can be seen throughout the property. From stenciled drawings on the walls to mosaic murals in the bathrooms, every corner of the property projects European sensibility and imaginative design. Rooms have air-con and hot water, and there's a shared kitchen and a pool.

Hotel Mar Paraíso (Map p330; ☎ 643 1947, 643 3277; southern end of Av Pastor Díaz; d/tr/q US$68/78/88; P ⛱ ⛱) Twenty clean rooms come with private hot shower, cable TV and air-con at this refurbished bright yellow hotel. The grounds are well landscaped and the hotel is situated at the end of the road (where you just might see wildlife). There are adult and kiddie pools and a pleasant restaurant-bar overlooking the ocean. Some units sleep six. Credit cards are accepted.

TOP END

All of the hotels here accept credit cards. Listings are from north to south.

Best Western Jacó Beach Resort (Map p330; ☎ 643 1000; www.bestwestern.com; Av Pastor Díaz btwn Boulevard & Calle Ancha; s/d US$112/125; P ✗ ⚲) This hotel offers all the amenities of a full-service beach resort: more than 100 rooms have air-con, cable TV, private bathroom, hot water and, of course, the laundry list of resort activities – from biking, surfing and horse riding to lounging by one of the hotel's pools. There's a restaurant and bar. Nice, but totally uninteresting, and chock full of Americans incapable of pronouncing the town's name correctly.

Hotel Tangerí (Map p334; ☎ 643 3001; www.hotel tangeri.com; Av Pastor Díaz btwn Calles Las Palmeras & Las Olas; d/tr/q US$94/107/124, villa US$144, grand villa US$256; P ✗ ⚲) This pleasant resort complex is in the middle of it all, but surprisingly manages to remain tranquil. The grounds are well manicured and there are three pools. Rooms have air-con, cable TV, private hot shower and fridge; villas sleep up to five people and come with fully equipped kitchen, chalets accommodate eight. All rates include breakfast, and there is a restaurant, BBQ Tangerí, attached. Low-season rates available.

Hotel Copacabana (Map p334; ☎ 643 1005; www .copacabanahotel.com; Calle Anita; d/ste US$99/159; P ✗ ⚲) This three-story resort hotel is fairly bland inside and out, though it's in a great location and the swim-up bar is a terrific place to spend your day. Standard tile-floor rooms have fan, hot shower and air-con. Suites sleep up to four people and have kitchenette and private balcony. There's also a restaurant serving international cuisine and a sports bar with satellite TV and pool table.

Hotel Poseidon (Map p334; ☎ 643 1642; www.hotel -poseidon.com; Calle Bohío; d economy/standard/premium US$88/98/108; P ✗ ⚲) It's hard to miss the huge Grecian wood carvings that adorn the exterior of this small, modern hotel. Hotel Poseidon has 14 sparkling, attractive rooms with bathroom and hot water. Some units have cable TV, and hair dryers are available. The elegant open-air restaurant specializes in fresh fish, and its one of the best spots in town. There's a pool, bar, Jacuzzi and private parking. French, Spanish, English and German are spoken.

Apartotel Girasol (Map p334; ☎ 643 1591; www .girasol.com; Calle Las Brisas; d/tr/q US$105/132/144; P ✗ ⚲) With luxury apartment units surrounding a landscaped garden, this complex looks like it would be more at home in Santa Monica. All units have a private bathroom, hot water and a fully equipped kitchen with fridge. Weekly and monthly rates are available. The complex has private beach access.

Hotel Arenal Pacífico (Map p330; ☎ 643 3419; www .arenalpacifico.com; Av Pastor Díaz, north of Calle Hidalgo; r standard/superior incl breakfast US$105/125; P ✗ ⚲) The entrance doesn't look like much, but you'll be pleasantly surprised once you step into this pretty, wooded hotel which has 26 rooms with private hot shower, air-con and cable TV. Standard rooms surround a lagoon and slightly more expensive superior rooms line the beach. All units are priced for two adults and two children. There is an ocean-front pool.

Sonidos del Mar (Map p330; ☎ 643 3924, 643 3912; www.sonidosdelmar.com; Calle Hidalgo; house US$200-250; P ✗ ⚲) Howard and Lauri, a South African–American couple, will welcome you to their guesthouse as if you were family. And, when you see their house, you'll wish you were! Set within a mature garden at the bend of a river, 'Sounds of the Ocean' may be one of the most beautiful guesthouses in Costa Rica. Lauri is a skilled artist and a collector who has lovingly filled each room with original paintings, sculptures and indigenous crafts. The house itself is impeccable, incorporating stylistic elements such as vaulted Nicaraguan hardwood ceilings and black, volcanic rock showers. The house is equipped with a full kitchen, which comes stocked with Howard and Lauri's own brand of fresh-roasted coffee (see p327). Guests have free use of kayaks and surfboards, and the beach is only 50m away. Full spa services are also available. The house can accommodate up to six people, and cheaper weekly and monthly rates are available.

Eating

Plenty of restaurants busily cater to the crowds and new ones open (and close) every year. Hours can fluctuate wildly, especially in the rainy season, so it's best to eat early.

BUDGET

Soda Flor (Map p334; Av Pastor Díaz, north of Calle La Central; casados US$3) This Jacó institution is a perennial favorite of locals and budget travelers. Food is fresh, tasty, cheap and served in huge portions.

Soda Amistad (Map p330; southern end of Av Pastor Díaz; dishes US$2-4) For a more local atmosphere, head to this small *soda* on the southern edge of town. Portions are generous, and the staff is friendly.

Pachi's Pan (Map p334; Av Pastor Díaz, south of Calle Cocal; pastries US$1-2) Pick up steaming fresh bread, cinnamon rolls, donuts, croissants and empanadas here and make your own picnic on the beach.

Los Pibes (Map p330; southern end of Av Pastor Díaz) This small, Argentinean-run joint has authentic empanadas (US$1) and great lunch deals – two slices of pizza and a soda is just US$2.

Mega Gem (Map p334; Av Pastor Díaz, across from the Hotel Tangerí; falafels US$2-4) The only place in town where you can get real, homemade falafel, prepared daily by a group of Israelis. Mega Gem also sells fresh bread and pizza.

Hong Kong Fuey (Map p334; Calle Bohío; dishes US$2-5) It's cheap, quick and filling, which makes it the perfect lunch spot for hungry surfers.

Rioasis (Map p334; cnr Calle Cocal & Av Pastor Díaz; medium pizza US$5) This place is good for beer and pizza from a wood-burning oven, all on the outdoor deck. Check out the US$3 'beer and a slice special.'

MIDRANGE & TOP END

Wahoo's (Map p334; Av Pastor Díaz btwn Calles Anita & Bri Brí; mains US$4-8) From *ceviche* to sea bass, this is one of the best spots in town for all things fishy.

Taco Bar (Map p334; mains US$5-10) Your place for 'Fish, Shakes + Salads.' Note the comma. Smoothies come in 1L sizes, and the salad bar has over 20 different kinds of exotic salads.

Pancho Villa's (Map p334; cnr Av Pastor Díaz & Calle Hicaro; dishes US$6-8) The greasy food here is hardly worth the price, but you'll probably end up here since the kitchen is open until the wee hours. It's also located downstairs

from a rowdy strip club, so you know you're bound to see some interesting characters.

Calinche's Wishbone Eatery (Map p334; Av Pastor Díaz, south of Calle Bohío; meals US$6-12) Overseen by the charming Calinche, this is the most famous restaurant in town. The eclectic menu includes pizza, pitas, stuffed potatoes, pan-seared seabass and tuna-sashimi salads. Everything is fresh, delicious, and good value.

Pacific Bistro (Map p334; Av Pastor Díaz, south of Calle Las Palmeras; mains US$7-12) This popular place offers Southeast Asian fusion-style dishes. Noodle dishes are good, but one local claims he can't live without the shrimp in spicy Thai sauce.

Gilligan's (Map p334; Av Pastor Díaz, north of Calle Cocal; breakfast US$3-5, mains US$8-12) The best place in town if you're feeling homesick for your mom's meatloaf. Come for breakfast and get a short-stack of pancakes or French toast.

Tsunami Sushi (Map p334; Av Pastor Díaz, north of Calle Cocal; sushi & rolls US$3-11) If you've got a hankering for raw fish, don't miss Tsunami. This modern, lively, beautifully decorated restaurant serves up an exquisite assortment of sushi, sashimi and rolls.

El Chaán (Map p330; ☎ 643 1642; Calle Jardin; dishes US$9-15) This beachfront, open-air restaurant has an eclectic menu featuring traditional Peruvian delicacies as well as a number of Tico classics including a killer *ceviche* and pan-fried red snapper.

Hotel Poseidon Restaurant (Map p334; ☎ 643 1642; Calle Bohío; dishes US$10-20) One of the most sophisticated restaurants in town, the specialty here is fresh seafood served up with an Asian flare. Sauces are inventive, the staff professional and the atmosphere upscale yet relaxing. A good bet for top-quality food.

Drinking & Entertainment

Jacó is a wasteland as a cultural offering, but it's a great place to get hammered and do something you'll regret in the morning. There are several dance clubs and in this fast-changing town it's worth asking around to find the latest hot spots. Foam parties are popular in the high season; ask about locations if you're feeling sudsy. Be advised that a good portion of Jacó nightlife revolves around prostitution, so be wary of suddenly being the most attractive guy in the bar.

All of these places (unless otherwise stated) are located on Av Pastor Díaz and only cross street information is provided.

Tabacon (Map p334; at Calle Bohío) Definitely one of the more respectable night spots, and there's a good chance there will be live music here.

Monkey Bar (Map p334; at Calle Las Palmeras) Don't let the cutesy jungle themes distract you – this place is a meat market.

Jungle Bar & Grille (Map p334; south of Calle Las Palmeras) The 2nd-story terrace gives you a good vantage point for sizing up your prey.

La Bruja (Map p334; south of Calle Anita) Also in the center of town, La Bruja is an old standby that offers a mellow atmosphere for downing a few beers. Try the Maudite – it's the best beer you'll ever taste.

Beatle Bar (Map p334; btwn Calles Bri Brí & Anita) If Beatle Bar were a piece of candy, it'd have a crunchy outer shell of Latina prostitutes and a creamy white-filling of old, dirty men.

Disco La Central (Map p334; Calle La Central) This disco sets the volume at 11, whether or not there's anyone on the dance floor.

Club Olé (Map p334; north of Calle Anita) Completely unmemorable, which isn't a problem as you'll be tanked before you walk in the door.

Fusión (Map p330; cnr Boulevard & Av Pastor Díaz) This dance spot (with air-con) is at the northern end of town, so it's popular with locals.

Getting There & Away
BOAT
Travelers are increasingly taking advantage of the jet boat transfer service that connects Jacó to Montezuma. Several boats per day cross the Golfo de Nicoya, and the journey only takes about an hour. At US$35 it's definitely not cheap, but it'll save you about a day's worth of travel. Reservations can be made at most tour operators in town. It's a beach landing, so wear the right shoes.

BUS
Buses for San José (US$2.50, three hours) stop at the Plaza Jacó mall (Map p330), north of the center. Buses depart at 5am, 7:30am, 11am, 3pm and 5pm.

The bus stop for other destinations is opposite the Más X Menos supermarket (Map p334). (Stand in front of the supermarket if you're headed north; stand across the street if you're headed south.) Buses to Puntarenas (US$1.50, 1½ hours) depart at 6am, 9am, noon and 4:30pm. Buses to Quepos (US$2, 1½ hours) depart at 6am, noon, 4:30pm

and 6pm. These are approximate departure times since buses originate in Puntarenas or Quepos. Get to the stop early!

Getting Around
BICYCLE & SCOOTER
Several places around town rent bicycles, mopeds and scooters. Bikes usually cost about US$2 an hour or US$6.50 a day, though prices can change depending on the season. Mopeds and small scooters cost from US$35 to US$50 a day (many places ask for a cash or credit card deposit of about US$200).

CAR
There are several rental agencies in town, so shop around for the best rates.

Budget (Map p330; ☎ 643 2665; Plaza Jacó mall; ⏱ 8am-6pm Mon-Sat, 8am-4pm Sun)

Economy (Map p330; ☎ 643 1719; Av Pastor Díaz, south of Calle Ancha; ⏱ 8am-6pm)

National (Map p334; ☎ 643 1752; Av Pastor Díaz at Calle Hicaco; ⏱ 7:30am-6pm)

Zuma (Map p334; ☎ 643 3207; Av Pastor Díaz, south of Calle Bohío; ⏱ 7am-noon & 1-5:30pm Mon-Sat)

TAXI
Taxis to Playa Hermosa from Jacó cost about US$3 to US$5. To arrange for a pickup, call **Taxi 30-30** (☎ 643 3030), or negotiate with the any of the taxis along Av Pastor Díaz.

PLAYA HERMOSA
The monster waves that pound the 10km-long Playa Hermosa are among the most consistent in the world, which means that just about any day, any time, there'll be a wave here waiting for you to thrash. Located only 5km south of Jacó, Playa Hermosa is fronted by a number of hotels and cabinas, though development here is relatively low key. As a result, most travelers choose to stay in Jacó since there is a better variety of accommodations, and taxis (with surf racks) are abundant. Note that this beach can only be recommended to advanced surfers as the huge waves and strong rip tides are unforgiving. Needless to say, this is not one of the better places on a Pacific coast for a refreshing swim. An annual contest is held here in August.

Sleeping & Eating
All of the following hotels (listed north to south) offer easy access to the waves.

CENTRAL PACIFIC COAST

Terraza del Pacífico (☎ 643 3222; www.terraza-del -pacifico.com; d US$102; P ⊗ ☒ ☒) The most famous hotel on Playa Hermosa has prime beachfront property that overlooks some killer breaks. The hotel has Spanish colonial accents, spacious tile-floor rooms with ocean views, air-con, cable TV and private bathroom with hot water. There are two pools and a restaurant-bar, and all the usual tours are available. This is a popular choice with upmarket surfers. Credit cards accepted.

Hotel Fuego del Sol (☎ 643 3737; www.fuegodelsol hotel.com; s/d US$57/67; P ⊗ ☒ ☒) Head south on the Costanera and make a right at the Jungle Surf Café to find this cheaper and slightly more personal hotel. The whitewashed rooms have a small balcony, air-con and hot water. There's also a pool, restaurant and beachside bar. Credit cards accepted.

Villa Hermosa Hotel (☎ 643 3373; taycole@racsa .co.cr; r from $40; P ⊗ ☒ ☒) This is another small, intimate hotel that has 13 beachside rooms with private bath, air-con and kitchenette. There are a few units accommodating up to six for US$80 that are good value. There's a garden-shaded pool and a happening poolside bar. Credit cards accepted.

Cabinas Rancho Grande (☎ 643 3529; r per person US$10; P) Further down the Costanera, this surfer joint is run by a friendly couple from Florida. There are eight rustic cane-paneled rooms with private hot shower and cable TV. An A-frame room on the top floor has killer views and some units sleep up to seven. There's an outdoor communal kitchen.

Brisa del Mar (☎ 643 2076; d US$35-50, r per person US$10; P ⊗) Another Floridian-run hotel, Brisa del Mar has a few rooms of varying size with air-con, private hot shower and cable TV. They also have some cheaper 'surfer rooms' which are only US$10 per person and next to a communal kitchen.

Costanera B&B (☎ 643 1942; d incl breakfast US$30- 50; P) This Italian-run B&B is situated in a beautiful, mustard-colored building and has a sophisticated ambience that is popular with European travelers. There are five rooms of various sizes, some with garden and others with ocean view. A small Italian restaurant is open for dinner.

Cabinas Las Olas (☎ 643 3687; www.lasolashotel .com; r per person US$20; P ☒) This hotel consists of a three-story A-frame building and several beachside bungalows that have kitchens, fan and hot water. Some larger rooms sleep up

to six. Check out the awesome skybox room with sweeping views of the nearby surf. It has a pool and a good restaurant.

Cabinas Vista Hermosa (☎ 643 3422; d/tr with shared bathroom US$35/45, r for 6/8 people with bathroom US$100/140, r for 2/4/6 people with air-con & bathroom US$50/80/120; P ⊗ ☒) These plain oversized concrete-block quarters are designed to maximize occupancy and minimize comfort, but they're popular with surfers looking for a cheap place to crash. There's a beachfront restaurant, two pools, cable TV and foosball. All rates include breakfast.

Jungle Surf Café (dishes US$3-5; ⊗ 7am-3pm & 6-10pm Thu-Tue) Don't miss this locally recommended spot. Specialties include meaty burritos, kebabs and serious fish tacos.

Goola (sandwiches US$2-4; ⊗ 7am-3pm & 6-10pm Thu-Tue) Next door to the Jungle Surf Café is where you'll find deli sandwiches and thick smoothies that are a good for a quick boost between sets.

PLAYA HERMOSA TO QUEPOS

The paved Costanera continues southeast from Playa Hermosa to Quepos, a 60km stretch that most tourists pass through quickly on their way to Manuel Antonio. The Costanera parallels the Pacific coastline, though unfortunately views are mostly of pastureland as the road is mostly inland. However, the scenery gets interesting once you get closer to Quepos as you'll start to see endless rows of African palms. These palms are cultivated on large plantations for their fruits, which are pressed in large vats to produce palm oil. The route has a

---

GOING TOPLESS?

Though it's the cultural norm for European women and American college girls on spring break, going topless is heavily frowned upon in Costa Rica. This of course shouldn't be surprising as more than 75% of Ticos are practicing Catholics. Sure, if you bear it all the guys on the beach will hoot and holler, but remember Costa Rican beaches are often frequented by families. If the temptation to get a little extra sun is too much to bear, please be considerate and move to an isolated stretch of sand. And remember, if you're spending your spring break in Costa Rica, be generous with the sunscreen.

few good beaches (some with surf) that are off the beaten track but easily visited by car, though you could disembark from buses going to Quepos or Manuel Antonio and walk down to them.

Esterillos Area

About 22km south of Jacó is **Playa Esterillos**, a deserted beach with a few good surf spots that's relatively undiscovered and little visited. Unfortunately, the building craze has reached here too, and the 'Condos For Sale' billboards on the sides of the road is a frustrating sign of things to come. In the meantime, Esterillos is very much an off-the-beaten path destination, and it's a great place to have a few waves all to yourself.

This area can be a little confusing to navigate as there are three towns with access to the beach – Esterillos Oeste, Esterillos Centro and Esterillos Este. These towns are all off the Costaneara about 22km, 25km and 30km southeast of Jacó, respectively. Most surfers camp underneath the trees at the northern edge of the beach, though there are two comfortable places to stay in Esterillos Este.

One is the **Hotel El Pélicano** (☎ 778 8105; www .pelicanbeachfronthotel.com; d US$60; P ⊠ ⊠), which is a homey, beachfront hotel that's only steps away from the surf. All rooms have a rustic ambience and are equipped with air-con and a private bathroom with hot water. There's a pool, a restaurant serving Tico and international specialties all day, and plenty of hammocks for lounging. Surfboards, body boards and bikes are available for guests; boat tours can be arranged.

Just south of El Pélicano, you'll find the lovely French Canadian-run **Flor de Esterillos** (☎ 778 8045, 778 8087; d US$65; P ⊠). Ten comfortable cabins of various sizes have tiled floors, colorful detailing, kitchenettes and pristine bathrooms with hot shower.

Rarely visited beaches to the south of Esterillos include **Playa Bejuco** (there's great surfing here) and **Playa Palma**, which are two beautiful stretches of grey sand that are reached by short side roads from the Costanera. If you're swimming here, be careful of riptides, especially at Playa Bejuco.

In Bejuco, you'll find **Hotel El Delfín** (☎ 778 8054; esuperglide@yahoo.com; s/d US$53/76, deluxe r with air-con US$94), a whitewashed building at the end of the beach road. The hotel is owned by an American family that has completely renovated the entire building. The simple rooms and deluxe units feature teak accents. There is a small restaurant.

Parrita

Parrita is a bustling town on a river of the same name and is home to a tremendous palm oil processing plant (see the boxed text Ever Wonder Where Palm Oil Comes From?, p342). From the Costanera, it is possible to see huge trucks hauling full cargos of the ripened fruits. Parrita is about 40km south of Jacó, and has a couple of basic hotels and *sodas*. The primary reason for coming here is to visit **Playa Palo Seco**, a quiet, unhurried grey-sand beach located near mangrove swamps that provide good opportunities for **birding**. A 6km dirt road connects the eastern edge of town to the beach. Another popular excursion is to visit **Isla Damas**, which is actually the tip of a mangrove peninsula that becomes an island at high tide. Most people arrive here on package tours from Jacó and Quepos, though you can hire a boat to bring you to and from the island for US$4.

If you're looking to stay on Playa Palo Seco, **Beso del Viento B&B** (☎ 779 9674; d/q US$70/ 150; P ⊠) has four apartments for rent which have private tiled bathrooms, kitchens and fans. Kayaks, bikes and horses can be rented, and there is also a pool. French and English are spoken.

After Parrita, the coastal road dips inland through more African oil-palm plantations on the way to Quepos. The road is a mix of a badly potholed pavement and stretches of dirt, with several rickety one-way bridges.

Rainmaker Aerial Walkway

Rainmaker was the first aerial walkway through the forest canopy in Central America and its tree-to-tree platforms offer spectacular views. From the parking lot and orientation area, visitors walk up a beautiful rain forest canyon with a pristine stream tumbling down the rocks. A wooden boardwalk and series of bridges across the canyon floor lead to the base of the walkway. From here, visitors climb several hundred steps to a tree platform, from which the first of six suspension bridges spans the treetops to another platform. The longest span is about 90m, and the total walkway is about 250m long. At the highest point, you are some 20 stories above the forest floor.

In addition, there are short interpretive trails that enable the visitor to identify some of the local plants, and some long and strenuous trails into the heart of the 2000-hectare preserve. Keep your eye out for countless birds, poison-dart frogs and various insects. Tours with naturalist guides leave hotels in Manuel Antonio and Quepos daily except Sunday; reservations can be made at most hotels or by calling

the **Rainmaker office** (in Quepos ☎ 777 3565; www .rainmakercostarica.com). Tours cost US$65 and include a light breakfast and lunch. Binoculars are invaluable for watching wildlife. Bring sun protection and water.

A large colorful sign marks the turnoff for Rainmaker on the Costanera at the northern end of Pocares (10km east of Parrita or 15km west of Quepos). From the turnoff, it is 7km to the parking area.

EVER WONDER WHERE PALM OIL COMES FROM?

African palms (Elaesis guineensis) are native to West Africa and primarily cultivated for their large, reddish fruits, which are pressed to produce a variety of oils that have several domestic uses. Each fruit is about the size of a baseball, though they grow in huge pods that can weigh as much as 40kg each. Within each fruit is a single seed or palm kernel (also known as an oil date) that is surrounded by a soft, greasy pulp. Oil that is extracted from the pulp of the fruit is used for edible palm oil, while palm kernel oil is used mainly for the manufacturing of soap and cosmetics. For every 100kg of fruit, it is possible to extract about 22kg of palm oil and 1.6kg of palm kernel oil.

Palm oil is dark-yellow to reddish in color and used primarily in cooking oil, margarine and processed foods. It is extremely high in Vitamin E, though it is one of the few vegetable oils that is high in saturated fat. If refined properly, it can provide the necessary quantity of vegetable oils needed to synthesize biodiesel. Today, the world's largest producers and exports of palm oil are Malaysia and Indonesia (with a combined volume of 83% of the market share), though African palms are cultivated throughout the tropics.

African palms were first introduced to the Quepos area by the United Fruit Company (also know as Chiquita Banana) during the 1940s in response to a banana blight that afflicted plantations across most of Central America. At the time, Quepos was one of the largest banana ports in operation on the Pacific coast, which meant that the local economy was dependant on finding an alternate source of income.

Although the banana blight finally ended in the 1960s, the palm plantations were already firmly entrenched and starting to turn a profit. Since palm oil is easily transported in tanker trucks, Quepos was able to close its shipping port in the 1970s, which freed up resources and allowed the city to invest more heavily in the oil palm industry. In 1995, the plantations were sold to Palma Tica, which continues to operate the plantations today. With the exception of commercial fishing and tourism, the oil palm plantations serve as the primary source of employment in the Quepos area.

Unlike banana harvesting, plantation fieldwork is specialized, and requires a smaller but more skilled workforce. One problem with African palms is that they can live to be over 200 years old, and grow too tall to be properly maintained. As a result, plantation owners have started replacing their palms with hybrid dwarfs, though digging up and replanting is extremely labor intensive. Another major problem is keeping the palms clear of insects, which is accomplished by clearing growth on the forest floor and applying poison to the trunks. Finally, fronds must be regularly clipped in order to encourage fruit growth, and to provide easy access to the pod. In terms of harvesting, mature pods are cut from the ground and transported to processing plants where the fruits are separated and pressed. The main processing plant is located in Parrita (see p341), though there are several smaller plants further south on the Costanera.

The main complaint from workers is that the industry does not provide as many job opportunities as banana harvesting, though workers are generally paid higher wages as their work is specialized. However, the work is laborious as the pods are heavy and extremely unwieldy, and it can get brutally hot underneath the tropical sun. Also, job dissatisfaction is on the rise, especially as lucrative jobs in the tourism market start to open up.

So, the next time you bite into a Snickers bar and wonder how such a little treat can have so much saturated fat, remember everything you've learned about the wondrous oil date.

QUEPOS & MANUEL ANTONIO

The sleepy, provincial town of Quepos never had ambitions of being anything more than a community of fisherman, merchants and plantation workers. But, when tourists clad from head to toe in designer khaki started inquiring about squirrel monkey colonies in nearby Parque Nacional Manuel Antonio, people caught on. As the closest town to the national park, Quepos suddenly found itself with an opportunity to cash in on something even more lucrative then fish and palm oil: tourism.

Located only 7km from Manuel Antonio, Quepos serves as a convenient base for exploring the park as it has all the goods and services common to a small town. Manuel Antonio is famous for its pristine beaches that are fronted by tropical rain forest, though nearby overdevelopment is starting to pose a considerable threat. Some people prefer to stay outside of Quepos as it's closer to the beaches and the national park, though accommodation is generally more expensive.

QUEPOS

This town's name was derived from the indigenous Quepoa, a subgroup of the Borucas, who inhabited the area at the time of the conquest. As with many indigenous populations, the Quepoa declined because of European diseases and slavery. By the end of the 19th century, no pure-blooded Quepoa were left, and the area began to be colonized by farmers from the highlands.

Quepos first came to prominence as a banana-exporting port in the early 20th century, though crops declined precipitously in subsequent decades due to disease and labor issues (underpaid workers had the gall to demand raises). African oil palms, which currently stretch towards the horizon in dizzying rows around Quepos, soon replaced bananas as the major local crop, though unfortunately they generated a lot less employment for the locals.

But, the future is looking bright for locals as tourists are coming to Manuel Antonio by the boat load, and the construction of the new marina in the next few years means

that cruise liners will no longer have to dock at Puntarenas. More visitors means more jobs in the area's rapidly expanding tourist market, though no one's talking about how hard it's getting to spot wildlife. The Pez Vela Marina is scheduled to open sometime in the next few years, but it is too early to tell what effect this will have on this provincial town.

Information

BOOKSHOP
Books2Go (☎ 777 1754, 371 3476; tours2go@racsa.co.cr; ◷ 10am-6pm) Susan runs a quaint little bookshop that also serves as a traveler's meeting place. You can post messages, store your bags, burn photos onto CDs, check the Internet or just hang out and read a good book. Susan also books tours in the area, and guarantees that she has the lowest prices around (per hour US$2).

INTERNET ACCESS
Internet Quepos.com (per hr US$2; ◷ 8am-8pm Mon-Sat) You can check email here on several computers with decent connections.

LAUNDRY
Aquamatic Laundry (per load US$4.50; ◷ 8am-noon & 1-5pm Mon-Sat) Self-service machines, or they'll do it for you for an additional US$1.

MEDICAL SERVICES
Dr Max Teran Vals (☎ 777 0200) A hospital that provides emergency medical care for the Quepos and Manuel Antonio area. It's on the Costanera Sur en route to the airport. However, this hospital doesn't have a trauma center and seriously injured patients are evacuated to San José.

MONEY
Banco de San José and Coopealianza both have 24-hour ATMs on the Cirrus and Plus systems. Other banks will all change US dollars and traveler's checks.

TOURIST INFORMATION
Quepolandia (www.quepolandia.com) The latest happenings are listed in this free English-language monthly magazine, found in many of the town's businesses.

Dangers & Annoyances

The town's large number of easily spotted tourists has attracted thieves. In response, the Costa Rican authorities have greatly increased police presence in the area, but travelers should always lock hotel rooms and never leave cars unattended on the street – use guarded lots instead. The area is far from dangerous, but the laid-back atmosphere should not lull you into a false sense of security.

In addition, women should keep in mind that the town's bars attract rowdy crowds of plantation workers on weekends. So walking around town in your swimsuit will most certainly garner the wrong kind of attention.

Note that the beaches in Quepos are polluted and not recommended for swimming. Go over the hill to Manuel Antonio instead.

Activities
SPORTFISHING

Sportfishing is big in the Quepos area. Offshore fishing is best from December to April, when sailfish are being hooked. Some of the main charter outfits are listed following. Not all charters have offices in Quepos, so it's usually best to call ahead. If you don't have a reservation, any hotel in the area can help put you in contact with a charter outfit.

Bluefin Sportfishing (☎ 777 1676, 777 2222; www .bluefinsportfishing.com) Across from the soccer field.

Costa Mar Dream Catcher (☎ 777 0725; www.costa marsportfishing.com) Next to Cafe Milagró.

Luna Tours (☎ 777 0725; www.lunatours.net) In Best Western Hotel Kamuk.

DIVING

The dive sites are still being developed in the Quepos and Manuel Antonio area, though the following operators have both been recommended by readers.

Manuel Antonio Divers (☎ 777 3483; www.manuel antoniodivers.com)

Oceans Unlimited (☎ 777 3171, 390 0626)

Tours

There are numerous reputable tour operators in the Quepos area.

Amigo Tico Complete Adventure Tours (☎ 777 2812; www.puertoquepos.com) Offers a range of tours, including rafting, walks in national parks, mountain biking and fishing. A full day of rafting on the Savegre is US$95 and this outfit also offers boat and kayaking tours of Isla Damas (see p341). Amigo Tico doesn't have an office in Quepos; book by phone or through your hotel.

Brisas del Nara (☎ 779 1235; www.horsebacktour.com) Locally recommended for horse-riding tours; half-day tours are US$55 and include pickup at your hotel and breakfast. Brisas doesn't have an office in Quepos; book by phone or through your hotel.

Canopy Safari (☎ 777 0100) The obligatory canopy tour costs US$65 and includes all transfers to and from the site, which is 45 minutes inland.

Four Trax Adventure (☎ 777 1825; www.fourtraxad venture.com) Four-hour ATV tours are US$95 per person.

Iguana Tours (☎ 777 1262; www.iguanatours.com) An adventure travel shop offering river rafting, sea kayaking, horse rides, mangrove tours and dolphin-watching excursions.

Lynch Travel (☎ 777 1170; www.lynchtravel.com) From airline reservations to fishing packages to rain forest tours, this travel shop has it all.

Ríos Tropicales (☎ 777 4092; www.riostropicales.com) The venerable Costa Rican rafting company now has an office in Quepos.

Sleeping

Staying in Quepos offers a cheaper alternative to the sky-high prices at many lodges on the road to Manuel Antonio. It can also be more convenient as all the banks, supermarkets and bus stops are in Quepos. Reservations are recommended during high-season

---

LOCAL LORE

Locals have long believed that a treasure worth billions of dollars lies somewhere in the Quepos and Manuel Antonio area waiting to be discovered. The lore was popularized by the English pirate John Clipperton, who befriended the coastal Quepoa during his years of sailing to and from the South Pacific. Clipperton's belief stemmed from a rumor that in 1670, a number of Spanish ships laden with treasure escaped from Panama City moments before it was burned to the ground by Captain Henry Morgan. Since the ships were probably off-loaded quickly to avoid being raided at sea, a likely destination was the San Bernadino de Quepo Mission, which had a strong loyalty to the Spanish crown.

John Clipperton died in 1722 without ever discovering the legendary treasure, and the Mission closed permanently in 1746 as most of the Quepoa had succumbed to European diseases. Although the ruins of the mission where discovered in 1974, they were virtually destroyed and were long since looted. However, if the treasure was indeed as large as it's described in lore, then it is possible that a few gold doubloons could still be lying somewhere, waiting to be unearthed.

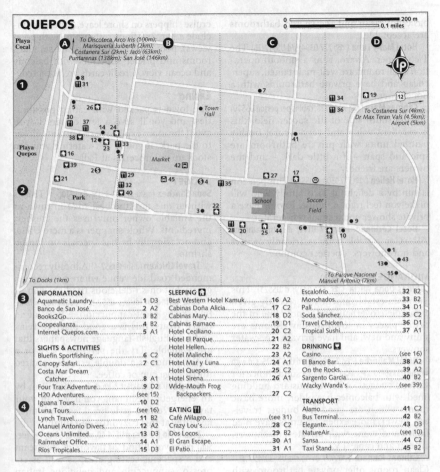

QUEPOS

weekends and are necessary during Easter and the week between Christmas and New Year's. High-season rates are listed, but many places have less expensive green-season rates.

BUDGET
All these hotels have cold-water showers unless otherwise stated.

Wide-Mouth Frog Backpackers (☎ 777 2798; dm US$7, d with/without bathroom US$30/20; Ⓟ ▢ ▨ ▨) This backpacker outpost is run by a welcoming British–New Zealand couple who are determined to make their little spot one of the best accommodations in Costa Rica. And so far, they've done everything right. Brightly tiled rooms are centered on an inviting pool with plenty of lounge chairs where backpackers can congregate and swap stories. There's also a communal kitchen with a huge dining area, a TV lounge with a free DVD rental library and free Internet. Shared bathrooms have hot water. Breakfast is served in the high season. Credit cards are accepted. Air-con is available for US$10.

Hotel Quepos (☎ 777 0274; d US$14) Small cramped rooms will make you feel a bit claustrophobic, but it's fairly clean and cheap. Ask for lodging in the back or you'll be enjoying the loud TV near reception.

Hotel El Parque (☎ 777 0063; s/d US$10/15) It's certainly cheap, though the linoleum floors and lime-green walls will make you feel like you're staying in a hospital. The rooms are basic but clean and the shared bathrooms are acceptable.

Hotel Mar y Luna (☎ 777 0394; s/d US$12/16) The Tico-owner, Alvaro, runs a smooth operation as all rooms are well-maintained, super-cheap and have private bathrooms with a hot shower.

Cabinas Mary (☎ 777 0128; cabins per person US$10) On the south side of the soccer field, this is excellent value and very secure; freshly painted units with private bathroom are spic and span – if a little dark – and the owners are friendly.

Hotel Hellen (☎ 777 0504; d US$20) This pension is run by a delightful Tico family who will make you feel right at home. Rooms have a private shower and a small refrigerator.

Hotel Ceciliano (☎ 777 0192; d with bathroom US$24) Comfortable doubles, friendly owners and hot showers: a perfect combo.

MIDRANGE & TOP END

Cabinas Doña Alicia (☎ 777 0419; d US$25) This Tico-run establishment was recently given a complete overhaul and is now one of the better places in town to stay. Rooms are shiny and new, and have private, hot-water showers.

Hotel Malinche (☎ 777 0093; s/d US$15/25, s/d with air-con US$36/50; P ✖) This is a solid choice for various budgets. A pretty mustard building lined with balconies has older, more basic rooms which are good for budget travelers. Newer, more expensive units have tiled floors and come with private hot shower, air-con and cable TV.

Cabinas Ramace (☎ 777 0590; s/d US$30/45; P) Clean rooms offer private bathroom with hot water and a fridge, though it's a bit overpriced considering the range of alternatives in town.

Hotel Sirena (☎ 777 0572; info@lasirenahotel.com; s/d US$59/69/79; P ✖) This intimate boutique hotel is the best midrange option in town. Whitewashed walls are subtly lit by blue tiffany lamps, which give the hotel a soothing, Mediterranean ambience. Recently renovated rooms are awash in soft pastels and fresh coats of white paint, and feature hot showers with good pressure.

Best Western Hotel Kamuk (☎ 777 0379; www.kamuk.co.cr; d standard/superior incl breakfast US$85/110; P ✖) The most upscale hotel in town has air-con rooms with hot water and phone. It's also completely characterless, and full of

cruise shippers on shore leave. Amenities include a bar, 3rd-floor restaurant (with good views), pool and casino. There are standard rooms and pricier superiors with balcony and ocean view. Credit cards are accepted.

Eating

The town is packed with eating possibilities, and you'll save a few dollars if you avoid the more expensive restaurants closer to the park. If you're self-catering you can stock up on groceries at Palí.

BUDGET

Soda Sánchez (dishes US$2-3 6am-10pm) This is without question the best *soda* in town as the amiable owner only uses the freshest ingredients. Whole snapper is a mere US$3, and occasionally he has specials on jumbo shrimp.

Travel Chicken (dishes US$2-4) A locally recommended roadside venue where you can get greasy but oh-so-delicious fried chicken.

Café Milagro (dishes US$2-5; 6am-10pm Mon-Fri) Serving great cappuccino, espresso and baked treats, this is a good place to relax and read English-language newspapers that are available. Try the *perezoso* (lazy or a sloth), which is a double espresso poured into a large cup of coffee.

Crazy Lou's (breakfast & lunch from US$3) Run by an energetic Irishman, you'll get all your favorite Western-style breakfast and lunch favorites at this cozy little restaurant.

Escalofrío (ice-cream US$1.50, meals US$3-6; Tue-Sun) Here you'll find 20 flavors of ice-cream and a spacious seating area, as well as espresso, cappuccino and delicious Italian food.

MIDRANGE & TOP END

Marisquería Juiberth (☎ 777 1292; dishes US$3-8) Though it's located a little south of town on the road towards Dominical, it's always packed as locals report it has the best seafood around.

Dos Locos (☎ 777 1526; dishes US$4-14; 7am-11pm Mon-Sat, 11am-10pm Sun) This popular Mexican restaurant also serves some of the best steaks in town, and is a popular drinking spot for the local ex pat community. Expect live bands on Wednesday and Friday nights in the high season.

Tropical Sushi (platters US$5-7; 5-10pm) For Japanese, try this colorfully decorated restaurant, which has a handful of tables and serves sushi rolls and sashimi. It has an all-you-can-eat special for US$12.

Monchados (dishes US$5-12; ☼ 5pm-midnight) This bustling Mex-Carib spot is a great place to try traditional Limónese dishes as well as your Mexican favorites. The walls are adorned with bright murals, and occasionally there's live music.

El Gran Escape (☎ 777 0395; dishes US$8-12; ☼ 6am-11pm) This restaurant caters primarily to gringo anglers and their palates, and is a popular night spot for telling tales about the one that got away. Check out the old fishing caps that hang from the ceiling.

El Patio (breakfast US$3-4, dinner mains US$8-15; ☼ 6am-10pm) This innovative Nuevo Latino spot is recommended for its innovative menu that changes daily. It's definitely a favorite of tourists staying in Quepos, though with good reason – meats and seafood are consistently fresh, and the homemade salsas are spot-on.

Drinking & Entertainment
Nightlife in Quepos is good blend of locals and travelers, and it's cheaper than anything you'll find on the road to Manuel Antonio. If you are looking for something a bit more sophisticated (note: read as expensive), it's easy enough to jump in a cab.

The mellow On the Rocks is good for a beer and chit-chat, while Wacky Wanda's will chill you out with cheap cocktails and air-con. For the best hangout in town, head to Sargento García, which has lounge nights on Tuesdays and Thursdays.

The bar at El Gran Escape (above) restaurant is the place for swapping fish tales, and **El Banco Bar** (☼ noon-midnight) around the corner is good for sports on satellite TV. And, if you feel like giving away your cash, there's the **casino** (opposite; ☼ 7pm-3am) at the Best Western Hotel Kamuk. The industrial-sized Discoteca Arco Iris brings out the locals with thumping dance beats.

Shopping
Café Milagro (opposite) and nearby El Patio (above) both sell roasted coffee, as well as other assorted souvenirs.

Getting There & Away
AIR
The airport is 5km out of town and taxis make the trip for US$3 to US$5 (depending

on traffic). Sansa has six daily flights between San José and Quepos (one way/round-trip US$44/88), and NatureAir (US$50/95) has four. In Quepos, the office for **Sansa** (☎ 777 0683) is on the southwest corner of the soccer field, while **NatureAir** (☎ 777 2548) is on the 2nd floor above Iguana Tours.

Lynch Travel (☎ 777 1170; www.lynchtravel.com) can book charter flights to and from the Quepos area.

Flights are packed in the high season, so book (and pay) for your ticket well ahead of time and reconfirm often.

BUS
All buses arrive and depart from the main terminal in the center of town. Buy tickets for San José well in advance at the **Transportes Morales ticket office** (☎ 777 0263; ☼ 7-11am & 1-5pm Mon-Sat, 7am-1pm Sun) at the bus station. Buses from Quepos depart for the following destinations:

Jacó US$1.50, 1½ hours, 4:30am, 7:30am, 10:30am and 3pm.
Puntarenas US$3, 3½ hours, departs 8am, 10:30am and 3:30pm.
San Isidro, via Dominical US$2, four hours, 5am and 1:30pm.
San José (Transportes Morales) US$4, four hours, 5am, 8am, 10am, noon, 2pm, 4pm and 7:30pm.
Uvita, via Dominical US$2.50, 4½ hours, 10am and 7pm.

Getting Around
BUS
Buses between Quepos and Manuel Antonio (US$0.20) depart roughly every 30 minutes from the main terminal between 6am and 7:30pm, and less frequently after 7:30pm. The last bus departs Manuel Antonio at 10:25pm. There are more frequent buses in the dry season.

CAR
The following car-rental companies operate in Quepos; reserve ahead and reconfirm to guarantee availability:
Alamo (☎ 777 3344; ☼ 7:30am-noon & 1:30-5:30pm)
Elegante (☎ 777 0115; ☼ 7:30am-5pm Mon-Fri)

TAXI
Colectivo taxis between Quepos and Manuel Antonio will usually pick up extra passengers for about US$0.50. A private taxi will cost about US$5. Call **Quepos Taxi** (☎ 777 0425/734) or catch one at the taxi stand south of the market.

QUEPOS TO MANUEL ANTONIO

From the port of Quepos, the road swings inland for 7km before reaching the beaches of Manuel Antonio village and the entrance to the national park. The serpentine road passes over a number of hills awash with picturesque views of forested slopes leading down to the palm-fringed coastline. Unfortunately, virtually every hilltop vista has been commandeered by a hotel that lists 'ocean views' as a major attraction, and the wave of construction seems to be building momentum. The problem with the proliferation of hotels is that the sewage system in the area is primitive at best, which has led to serious threats of marine pollution. The park is also being overwhelmed by visitors, which is disruptive to the wildlife as some tourists are insistent on feeding wild animals (see the boxed text Don't Feed the Monkeys! Dammit, We're Serious!, p359).

This area is regarded as the most popular gay destination in Costa Rica with gay-friendly establishments lining the road. Although homosexuality has been decriminalized in Costa Rica since the 1970s, the recent relocation of gay ex-pats to the Manuel Antonio area has resulted in a blossoming gay scene that is unique in conservative Latin America. During the day there are a few popular hangout spots on the local gay beach, La Playita (p354), though the scene moves into the upscale bars and clubs at night.

Note that the road is steep, winding and very narrow. Worse, local bus drivers love to careen through at high velocities. There are almost no places to pull over in the event of an emergency. Drive and walk with care.

Information

INTERNET ACCESS

Cantina Internet Café (per hr US$2; opposite Hotel Costa Verde)

El Chante Internet (per hr US$2; adjacent to Hostal Vista Serena)

MONEY

Banco Promerica (opposite Tulemar Bungalows; ⏰ 8am-5pm Mon-Fri, 9am-1pm Sat) Has a 24-hour ATM on the Cirrus network and can exchange US dollars.

TOURIST INFORMATION

La Buena Nota (☎ 777 1002; buennota@racsa.co.cr; Manuel Antonio) A good source of tourist information for this area.

Rafiki Safari Lodge (☎ 777 2250; www.rafikisafari .com) The booking and information office for this lodge is across the street from the Kekoldi Beach Hotel.

Sights & Activities

Equus Stables (☎ 777 0001) offers horse rental and a variety of excursions.

You can relax after a day's activities at the **Serenity Spa** (☎ 777 0777, ext 220; inside Si Como No hotel), a good place for couple's massages, sunburn-relief treatments, coconut body scrubs and tasty coffee.

Belonging to the Si Como No hotel, and situated just across the street is **Fincas Naturales** (www.butterflygardens.co.cr; admission US$15), a private rain-forest preserve and butterfly garden. About three dozen species of butterfly are bred here. The garden has a sound-and-light show at night (US$40 per person) and is surrounded by nature trails.

Amigos del Rio (☎ 777 1084; www.adventuremanuel antonio.com; trips from $69) runs white-water rafting trips for all skill levels on the Savegre and Naranjo rivers.

Courses

Escuela de Idiomas D'Amore (☎ 777 1143, in the USA 310-435 9897, 262-367 8589; www.escueladamore.com) has Spanish immersion classes at all levels; local homestays can be arranged. Two-week classes start at US$845 without homestay.

Centro de Idiomas del Pacífico (☎ 777 0805) provides personalized Spanish tutorials and offers a variety of housing options. One-week classes (four hours of class time) start at US$290 without homestay.

Sleeping

This stretch of winding, forested road has mostly top-end hotels, but there are a few midrange and budget options as well. Some places require that you pre-pay your stay – so choose carefully (see the boxed text Reserving By Credit Card, p527). High-season rates are provided throughout, and reservations are a must for weekends. Low-season rates can be as much as 40% lower in some hotels.

Hotels listed here are in the order they're passed traveling from Quepos to Manuel Antonio. They all accept credit cards unless otherwise stated.

MIDRANGE

Cabinas Pedro Miguel (☎ 777 0035; www.cabinaspedro miguel.com; d/tr/q US$50/60/80; P ⏰) Just up the hill and out of Quepos is this 100% Costa Rican managed and owned property. The 18 spic-and-span rooms are lovingly decorated with a mother's touch. Larger units sleep four and five people and have a kitchenette. There's a pool and breakfast is available upon request. Long-term rates are available.

Kekoldi Beach Hotel (☎ 777 0368; www.kekoldi beachhotel.com; d standard/studio US$60/70, villa US$85; ✗ ⛱) Back on the Quepos–Manuel Antonio road, this quaint little hotel only has four simple rooms awash in pastel hues that feature picture windows, air-con and private hot-water shower. Four villas have fully equipped kitchen. There's a pool and the helpful staff can arrange local tours. The hotel is gay-friendly, and has a recommended sister hotel in San José.

Mimo's Hotel (☎ 777 2217; www.mimoshotel.com; d US$65, junior ste US$85, additional person US$18, child under 12 free; P ✗ ⛱) Run by a delightful Italian couple, this whitewashed hotel has spacious, clean, terracotta-tiled rooms that are awash with bright, colorful murals. All units have an ample bathroom, hot water, air-con, kitchenette and cable TV. There's a pool, a 'fiber-optic' Jacuzzi and restaurant-bar (mains US$10, open to the public) serving Italian-influenced dishes. The Italian owners speak half a dozen languages and can share with you a wealth of knowledge about Costa Rica.

Hotel Mono Azul (☎ 777 2572; www.monoazul .com; s/d/tr from US$55/60/65, child under 12 free; P ✗ ⛶ ⛱) This is a great family option as the entire hotel is decorated with animal murals, rain-forest paraphernalia and you'll sleep well at night knowing that your money is going to a good cause. There are 27 pleasant rooms, all of which have private hot shower and ceiling fan. Deluxe units also have air-con and patio, and villas have two bedrooms and a kitchen. There are three pools, sunning decks, a games room with cable TV, a small gym, Internet access and a good restaurant (p353).

The Mono Azul is home to 'Kids Saving the Rain forest' (KSTR), started by two local schoolchildren who were concerned about the endangered *mono tití* (Central American squirrel monkey). Many monkeys were run over on the narrow road to the national park, or electrocuted on overhanging electrical cables, so KSTR purchased and erected seven monkey 'bridges' across the road (you can see them, often in use, as you head to the park). Ten percent of hotel receipts are donated to the organization. (To learn how you can work with other worthwhile local organizations to support protection and conservation of the *mono tití*, see the boxed text Saving the Squirrel Monkey, p356.)

Hotel Las Tres Banderas (☎ 777 1284/521; d standard/superior US$75/81, ste US$116, apt US$174; P ✗ ⛱) Located about 2.5km south of Quepos, this place is owned by a Polish-born US citizen who lives in Costa Rica – hence *tres banderas* (three flags). Fourteen attractive, spotless doubles and three suites have air-con, large bathroom, hot water, cable TV and private balcony. Suites have bathtub, microwave and fridge. A two-bedroom apartment accommodates eight and has air-con, cable TV and kitchen. There's a pool, a huge Jacuzzi and a bar-restaurant.

La Colina (☎ 777 0231; www.lacolina.com; d incl breakfast from US$80; P ✗ ⛱) Down the road, this pleasant B&B is tucked away in a peaceful, forest setting that's almost as magnificent as the ocean views you'll have from your room. There are five small, clean, colorfully decorated air-conditioned rooms with hot water and fan, and six air-conditioned suites with cable TV, small private terraces and ocean views. Two units have kitchenettes. There is a split-level pool with swim-up bar, as well as a small restaurant.

BaBaLoo Inn (☎ 777 3461; www.babalooinn.com; d standard/king US$85/145; P ✗ ⛱) This American run establishment is reader recommended, and offers standard rooms overlooking a lush, tropical garden with a private balcony or porch. Though they're a bit more expensive, the larger king rooms feature dramatic, ocean views, a comfortable sitting area, oversized beds and showers and a small kitchenette. All rooms have been recently renovated and come with air-con, hot water, cable TV, a fully stocked mini-bar and DVD players. There's also a small pool.

Banana Tree Hotel (☎ 777 1585; www.bananatree hotel.com; d standard/deluxe incl breakfast US$65/85; P ✗ ⛱) It's hard to miss this brightly painted hotel that blinds anyone who passes by with its florescent yellow, green and pink color scheme. The rooms are equally vibrant, and the bamboo accents make for a subtle, rustic touch. All rooms have air-con, hot water and cable TV, and there is a small pool. The hotel is gay friendly.

HOW TO KNOW IF A BUSINESS IS REALLY ECOFRIENDLY

Ecotourism means big business in Costa Rica, and sometimes it can seem like every hotel, restaurant, souvenir stall, bus company, surf shop and ATV tour operator is claiming to be a friend and protector of Mother Earth. It's certainly easy to dupe your average package tourist with business cards printed on recycled paper and a bunch of tree-frog stickers plastered on an office wall, but sometimes in Costa Rica it's difficult even for the discerning traveler to know whether a business is truly 'eco.' Sure, you didn't cut down a single tree when you built your canopy tour, but can you explain why your grey water trickles down the hillside into the stream below?

The guiding principle behind ecotourism is striking a balance between the positive and negative impacts of tourism, specifically traveling in a manner that is sensitive to the conditions of your destination while simultaneously minimizing negative impacts on the environment. Unfortunately, the problem is that it is becoming increasingly popular for destinations to label themselves as 'ecodestinations', yet there are no universal guidelines dictating exactly what it means to be 'eco'. However, there are various environmental, economic and socio-cultural aspects of running an ecofriendly business that every traveler should be aware of.

Since most ecotourism destinations are located in areas where the natural environment is relatively untouched, it is important for a business to adhere to strict conservation guidelines. At the bare minimum, an ecofriendly business should participate in recycling programs, effectively manage their wastewater and pollutants, implement alternative energy systems, use natural illumination whenever possible and maintain pesticide-free grounds using only native plants. When it is possible, a business should also participate in environmental conservation programs as well as be an active member of regional or local organizations that work on solving environmental problems.

The economics of an ecotourist destination is a major issue concerning tourists, local communities and developers as the misdistribution of economic benefits generated by a business can have harmful consequences on the sustainability of an area. This is especially important as tourists are increasingly interested in visiting the most undeveloped areas possible, which is a problem as the individuals living in these locales are relatively removed from the greater economy. An ecofriendly business can address these realities by hiring a majority of its employees from the local population, associate with locally owned businesses, provide places where native handicrafts can be displayed for sale, serve foods that support local markets and use local materials and products in order to maintain the health of the local economy.

The socio-cultural aspect of ecotourism refers to the ability of a community to continue functioning without social disharmony as a result of its adaptation to an increased volume of tourists. Although tourism contributes to the loss of cultural integrity, it can also alleviate poverty and help maintain natural resources that might otherwise be exploited. An ecofriendly business can achieve these goals by fostering indigenous customs, protecting sites of historical, archaeological and/or spiritual importance, educating visitors about local customs and practices, regulating the tourist flow to indigenous areas and when possible, donating a portion of profits to the local community.

Tourism will never be a completely harmless venture, but there are ways of minimizing its damage and distributing its benefits to local communities. Travel responsibly, think green, and be critical the next time you see the word 'eco.'

Hotel Karahé (☎ 777 0170/52; www.karahe.com; d US$80-120; P ✖ ⧉) This is a great option as its conveniently located on the final hill before the park entrance, so it's only a 10-minute walk to the beach and 20-minutes to the park. There's a pool, spa, restaurant and three levels of rooms. The oldest cabins have superb views and are reached by climbing a flight of steep stairs. All have hot water and air-con; rates depend on the location of your room and include breakfast.

A few minutes' walk further, the beach level is reached; there are more accommodations along here and in Manuel Antonio village (p355).

TOP END

Hotel California (☎ 777 1234; www.hotel-california .com; d standard/deluxe US$110/130; P ✖ ⧉) Look for a driveway to the left to find this quiet hotel, which is well set back from the road and has 10km of hiking trails into rain forest surrounding the property. The 22 rooms are cool, spacious and comfortable, and feature hardwood floors, light-colored walls with attractive hangings, air-con, cable TV, minibar and a large bathroom with hot shower. The deluxe rooms are slightly larger and have a private terrace with ocean views. There's a pool with a waterfall, and the adjacent restaurant has views.

The Hotel California is home to the 'Roberta Felix Foundation,' a nonprofit organization whose mission is to improve the quality of life for handicapped children in the rural Pacific coast.

Tulemar Bungalows (☎ 777 1325; www.tulemar .com; bungalows incl breakfast US$270; P ☒ ☎) This luxurious private complex has 20 modern bungalows that sleep six. Each has air-con, huge picture windows with great views, two queen-sized beds, sitting room with two more foldout queen-sized beds, well-equipped kitchenette, phone, TV, VCR and hair dryer. There's an infinity pool and you can hike 15 minutes to the beach, where complimentary kayaks and snorkeling gear are available for guests' use.

El Parador (☎ 777 1411, in the USA 800-648 1136; www.hotelparador.com; r from US$210-800, additional person US$30; P ☒ ☎) This hotel, which was created for admirers of lavish excess, a la *Lifestyles of the Rich and Famous*, is situated on a formerly forested hilltop that was dynamited away. The resulting El Parador is a 68-room, 10-suite complex, complete

---

THE AUTHOR'S CHOICE

Budget

Hostal Vista Serena (☎ 777 5162; www.vistaserena.com; dm/d US$12/50; P ☐) In an area that is hopelessly overpriced, it's a relief to find such a great budget hostel. Perched on a hillside, this hostel allows guests to enjoy spectacular, ocean sunsets from a hammock-filled terrace, and most travelers find themselves getting stuck here for longer than they planned. The white-tiled dorms are spic-and-span, shared bathrooms have hot water and there's a communal kitchen. There are a couple of neighboring doubles with shared bathroom and kitchen. A lounge has cable TV and there is laundry service (US$4 per load). Sonia and her son Conrad, the super-helpful Tico owners, are fully bilingual. A small trail leads down through a farm to a remote beach.

Midrange

Hotel Plinio (☎ 777 0055; www.hotelplinio.com; d without/with air-con US$65/75, 2-/3-story ste US$85/110, jungle house US$100; P ☒ ☎) This cozy hotel is nestled on the verdant edge of the rain forest, and is the perfect retreat from all of your stresses. Rooms have super-high ceilings which create a tranquil, relaxed atmosphere. Larger suites are two and three stories tall and have great polished-wood decks for lounging. (Suites don't have air-con, but the high ceilings keep rooms fresh.) Attractive units have private hot shower and there are plenty of hammocks. A jungle house accommodates five. The grounds boast 10km of trails into the forest, where you'll find a 17m-high lookout tower (open to the public). There is a highly recommended restaurant (p353) and the staff is friendly. Rates include breakfast during the high season. Credit cards are not accepted.

Top End

Makanda by the Sea (☎ 777 0442; www.makanda.com; studio/villa incl breakfast US$265/400, additional person US$35; P ☒ ☎) Even in the hopelessly overdeveloped area of Manuel Antonio, Makanda stands alone in a class of its own. The entire hotel is solely comprised of six villas and five studios, which give Makanda an air of intimacy and complete privacy. Villa 1 (the largest) will take your breath away – the entire wall is open to the rain forest and the ocean. Several of the units can be interconnected and have every conceivable amenity. Every room (except Villa 1) has air-con, and a breakfast fit for a king is delivered straight to your room. There is a beautiful infinity pool, a Jacuzzi with a superb view and flawless, Japanese gardens that you can stroll through and reflect on the beauty of your surroundings. And, if you're still not impressed, you can access a remote beach by taking the 552 steps down the side of the mountain. Children under 16 years are not admitted. There is an exclusive poolside restaurant, the Sun Spot (p353).

CENTRAL PACIFIC COAST

with a private helicopter landing pad, two Jacuzzis, an infinity pool with swim-up bar, a sauna, a tennis court and mini-golf. Splendiferous rooms of various types and sizes have all the usual goodies: private terrace, cable TV, air-con, hot water and minibars. Rates include breakfast.

Hotel La Mariposa (☎ 777 0355/456; www.lamariposa.com; r from US$195-430; P ⊠ ⓢ) This internationally acclaimed hotel was the area's first luxury accommodation, so not surprisingly it snatched up the best view of the coastline. Fifty-seven pristine rooms of various sizes are elegantly decorated with hand-carved furniture and cool, tiled floors. All quarters come with one king-sized or two double beds, private bathroom, hot water, air-con, phone and private terrace or balcony. The penthouse suite has a terrace Jacuzzi. The grounds and pools are meticulously kept and there are hammocks for lounging. This hotel was recently listed in the book *1000 Places to See Before you Die*. The hotel's restaurant, Le Papillon (opposite), is recommended.

Mango Moon (☎ 777 5323; www.mangomoon.net; r incl breakfast US$225/240; ⊠ ⓢ) This intimate boutique hotel is run by an American couple, though it has a woman's touch as there are fresh flowers in every corner of the property, luxurious linens on all the beds and heavenly bathrooms with steaming hot water. The rooms also face out onto a crystal blue bay, which you can hike down to on the hotel's private trail. The owners organize tours on their private boat. Rooms can accommodate two to four people.

Si Como No (☎ 777 0777, in the USA ☎ 800-237 8201; www.sicomono.com; d standard/superior/deluxe US$1170/195/210, ste US$240-270, additional person US$29, child under 6 free; P ⊠ 🖥 ⓢ) This flawlessly designed hotel is an example of how to build a resort while maintaining your environmental sensibility. Rooms are insulated for comfort and use energy-efficient air-con units; water is recycled into the landscape, and solar-heating panels are used to heat the water. The rooms feature picture windows and balconies, so you'll never feel closed in from the surrounding rain forest. Standard rooms are spacious; superior suites have wet bar or kitchen, and there are larger deluxe suites, some with stained-glass windows. The hotel has two pools (one with a slide for kids; one for adults only; both with

swim-up bars), two solar-heated Jacuzzis and two good restaurants. All rates include breakfast.

La Plantación (☎ 777 1332, 777 1115, in the USA & Canada 800-477 7829; www.bigrubys.com; d standard/deluxe/apt/house US$165/180/615/1050; P ⊠ ⓢ) If you're a gay man, welcome to paradise. The 24 impeccable rooms at the Plantation are cool, light and spacious with regal bathroom, air-con, cable TV and huge mosquito nets romantically draped over king-sized beds. There are eight standard rooms as well as a handful of larger deluxe rooms with patio overlooking the gardens and free-form pool. Two deluxe rooms have sea views and share a private pool with a luxurious two-bedroom apartment. A larger three-bedroom house has every amenity imaginable. There's a pool and clothing-optional sundeck and an adjacent bar. Rates include breakfast and a cocktail hour.

Hotel Casitas Eclipse (☎ 777 0408, 777 1738; www.casitaseclipse.com; d standard/junior ste US$112/155; P ⊠ ⓢ) The soothing curves of this architecturally arresting, pure white complex hint at the beauty within. The hotel consists of nine attractive, split-level houses spread around three swimming pools. The bottom floor of each house is a spacious junior suite with air-con, queen-sized and single beds, bathroom with hot water, living room, kitchen and patio. The upper floor is a standard room with queen-sized bed, bathroom and terrace. These have a separate entrance but a staircase (with lockable door) combines the two and, *voilà*, you have a house sleeping five. There are also 11 unconnected rooms and suites. There's an excellent Italian restaurant, Gato Negro (opposite), on the premises.

Hotel Costa Verde (☎ 777 0700, 777 0584, 777 0187; www.costaverde.com; efficiency/studio US$104/135; P ⊠ 🖥 ⓢ) This is the sister hotel of the Costa Verde Inn (p133) in Escazú and has been recommended by several readers for its lush, tropical setting and frequent monkey sightings. The attractive, tile-floor rooms have kitchenettes, fridges, private hot water bathrooms and air-con. Efficiency units have two queen-sized beds, while studios have partial ocean views and more expensive 'studio-plus' rooms have full ocean views. There are also two swim-up pool bars with ocean views.

Eating

Many hotels mentioned earlier have good restaurants open to the public, and there are also several good independent places; the following are particularly recommended. Reservations are a good idea in the high season. Restaurants are also listed from north to south.

Café Milagro (breakfast US$3-4, sandwiches US$4-6) The sister café to the one in Quepos is an obligatory stop on the way to the park as its coffee is pure, black gold. Breakfast and sandwiches are reasonably priced and filling.

Hotel Mono Azul (☎ 777 2572; pizza US$4-8, dishes US$5-12; ☺ 6am-10pm) Dig into a hot, gooey slice of cheese pizza in the original 'rain forest café.' You can also choose from a variety of Tico and American dishes, and they'll always cater to vegetarians.

Ronny's Place (☎ 777 5120; mains US$5-12; ☺ 7:30am-10pm) Head 800m west from the main drag, on the good, well-signed dirt road opposite Manuel Antonio Experts – it's worth the trip as the view here won't disappoint. Ronny, the bilingual Tico owner, has worked hard to make his rest-stop a favorite of locals and travelers alike. Feast on a big burger or some fresh seafood, and then wash down your meal with some of the best *sangría* in the country while enjoying views of two pristine bays and 360° of primitive jungle.

Hotel Plinio (☎ 777 0055; dishes US$7-12) The restaurant at this popular hotel has an incredible Southeast Asian menu that also includes a smattering of Italian and German specialties. The food is, without a doubt, inventive and delicious, and there is enough variety to make anyone happy. The Asian *bocas* menu allows you to put together a multitude of tapas-sized dishes to make a main course of your choosing.

Restaurant Barba Roja (☎ 777 0331; dishes US$8-15; ☺ 4-10pm Mon, 10am-10pm Tue-Sun) The energetic, new American owner is freshening up this classic spot, so expect big things to come. In the meantime, it's still got great views, a good mix of American standards with a bit of Mexican flair, and the margaritas are as potent as ever.

Bar Restaurante Karola's (☎ 777 1557; dishes US$5-15; ☺ 11am-10pm) Behind Barba Roja is this small outpost serving Mexican dishes, steaks, ribs and seafood in a relaxed, garden

setting. Try the coconut margaritas and the macadamia nut pie to inject a little bit of local flavor into your life.

Sun Spot (☎ 777 0442; Makanda by the Sea; dishes US$7-10) OK, so your budget won't allow you to stay at Makanda by the Sea, though trust us – it's worth checking out its exclusive little poolside restaurant for its breathtaking rain forest and ocean views. The kitchen whips up delicious seafood, sandwiches and salads, though the real reason you're here is to soak up the atmosphere. Reservations are required at all times if you are not a guest at the hotel. No children under 16 allowed.

La Hacienda (☎ 777 3473; Centro Comercial Plaza Yara; dishes US$9-20) One of the newest restaurants on the Manuel Antonio scene, this Canadian-run venture blends Latin American, Asian and Mediterranean elements with local ingredients to create gourmet dishes that would satisfy even the strictest of critics. Original creations include tamarind-rum-soy soaked chicken skewers and onion-mango-brie quesadillas.

Restaurant Gato Negro (☎ 777 0408, 777 1738; Hotel Casitas Eclipse; dishes US$12-35) The glitziest restaurant in Manuel Antonio comes with a huge price tag, though you're here for one reason – it's one of the hippest spots in the area to be scene. The European-influenced food is consistently flawless, and every detail from the presentation of the meat to the thickness of the sauce is simply perfect.

Le Papillon (☎ 777 0355/456; Hotel La Mariposa; lunch US$6-10, dinner US$12-40) You're paying for the view at this class institution, though when the sun dips below the horizon and lights up the Pacific sky, you'll stop caring about the price. The food is largely continental cuisine, and if you're pinching your pennies the lunch menu is a good deal.

Also see Manuel Antonio (p356) and Quepos (p346) for nearby eating suggestions.

Drinking & Entertainment

Most people choose to spend the evenings drinking over-priced cocktails in their hotels, though the area's reputation as a gay magnet means that there is a constantly evolving scene. Things change quickly as popularity waxes and wanes, though there are a few consistently popular spots. If you're looking to strut your stuff on the dance floor, head to Mar y Sombra (p356) in Manuel Antonio.

CENTRAL PACIFIC COAST

BOMBS AWAY!

On the Quepos to Manuel Antonio road, you'll find **El Avión** (☎ 777 3378; sandwiches US$6, dishes from US$7), an airplane bar constructed from the body of a 1954 Fairchild C-123. The plane was originally purchased by the US government in the '80s for the Nicaraguan Contras, but it never made it out of its hangar in San José because of the ensuing Iran-Contra scandal that embroiled Oliver North and his cohorts in the US government. (The plane is lovingly referred to as 'Ollie's Folly.') In 2000 the enterprising owners of El Avión purchased it for US$3000 and then proceeded to cart it piece by piece to Manuel Antonio. It now sits on the side of the main road, where it looks as if it had crash-landed into the side of the hill. It's now a great spot for a beer, guacamole and a Pacific sunset, and on evenings in the dry season there is live music.

Bambú Jam (in Hotel Mirador del Pacífico) is a popular music and drinking spot on Friday nights when there are live bands. The upstairs bar at **Restaurant Gato Negro** (p353) is consistently packed with stylish gay men, so dress your best. The trendiest spot is the **Lounge**, which is run by two women from Los Angeles who know how to throw a good party. The club is bouncing on Tuesdays and Thursdays while Monday reggae nights bring in a mellower crowd.

Getting Around

Many visitors who stay in this area arrive by private or rented car (see p347) for rental agencies in Quepos). Drive carefully on this narrow, steep and winding road – and keep an eye out for pedestrians. There's no shoulder, so everyone walks in the street.

Buses between Manuel Antonio and Quepos (US$0.20) operate up and down the main road and run every 30 minutes between 6am and 7:30pm, and less frequently after 7:30pm. The last bus departs Manuel Antonio at 10:25pm. Taxis going to Quepos will usually pick up extra passengers for about US$0.50.

MANUEL ANTONIO

Here's an analogy for you – Mainstreet USA is to Walt Disney World as Manuel Antonio village is to the national park (minus the mouse ears of course). Run the tourist gauntlet of roadside vendors selling squirrel monkey stuffed animals (made in China) and commemorate your trip to the rain forest with a tree-frog sarong (hecho en Guatemala). If you've still got some cash left to burn, there are some lovely little beach chairs to rent on **Playa Espadilla** as you wouldn't want to get any sand on your bathing suit, now would you? Yes, things

have indeed changed in Manuel Antonio, so if you're coming here expecting deserted beaches frequented by hundreds of monkeys, you're in for a surprise.

The village of Manuel Antonio is the closest base for exploring the national park, though reservations are a must for the high season, especially on weekends, and lengthy advance planning is needed for Easter week. The town is generally safe, but don't leave belongings unattended on the beach and make sure your hotel room is securely locked when you are out, even briefly.

Information

La Buena Nota (☎ 777 1002; buennota@racsa.co.cr), at the northern end of Manuel Antonio village, serves as an informal information center. It sells maps, guidebooks, books in various languages, English-language newspapers, beach supplies and souvenirs; it also rents body boards. You can inquire here about guesthouses available for long-term stays. Look for a free copy of the English-language *Quepolandia*, which details everything to see and do in the area.

Internet access is available at **Top Tours** (per hr US$1.50; ⦿ 9am-8:30pm Mon-Fri, 9am-6pm Sat & Sun).

Sights & Activities

There's a good beach, **Playa Espadilla**, but swimmers should beware of rip currents (p284). There are some lifeguards working at this beach (but not at the others in the area). At the far western end of Playa Espadilla, beyond a rocky headland (wear sandals) is **La Playita**, a gay beach frequented primarily by young men and offering nude sunbathing (trust us on the sunscreen). This point is inaccessible one hour before and after the high tide, so time your walk well or you'll get cut off. Don't be fooled –

you do not need to pay to use the beaches as they're outside the park.

Steve Wofford at **Planet Dolphin** (☎ 777 2137; www.planetdolphin.com; inside Cabinas Piscis) runs dolphin- and whale-watching tours; starlight sailing cruises are also offered. Outings start at US$65 for four hours, including lunch and snorkeling. The Tico-run **Marlboro Horse Stables** (☎ 777 1108), opposite Cabinas Piscis, rents horses. The owners can organize trips through the rain forest. Snorkeling gear, body boards and kayaks can be rented all along the beach at Playa Espadilla. If you're looking to surf, the gentle ankle-slappers here are perfect for getting your sea-legs, and **Manuel Antonio Surf School** (☎ 777 4842) and **Monkey Surf** (☎ 777 5240) both have kiosks near the beach. White-water rafting and sea kayaking are both popular in this area – see p344 for details of companies that offer these and other options.

Sleeping
BUDGET
Cabinas ANEP (☎ 777 0565; cabinas US$28; P) These cabinas were originally built as a resort for public employees, so they're perfectly located near the park exit and a few minutes from the beach. Each bare, dorm-style cabin accommodates up to five people.

Cabinas Ramirez (☎ 777 5044; r per person US$10, camping per person US$3; P) This popular budget spot is located just steps from the beach, though the ambience is reminiscent of a trailer park. Double rooms are respectable and clean, and there's a communal kitchen. Camp sites are adequate. The nearby disco may discourage sleep.

Cabinas Irarosa (☎ 777 5085; d without/with bathroom US$10/25; P) Another great budget option near the park offer reasonably clean rooms with shared bathrooms and newer, much nicer units with private bathroom, TV and the occasional burst of hot water.

Cabinas Piscis (☎ 777 0046; d without/with bathroom US$20/40, apt US$65, additional person US$5; P) An amiable family runs this shaded inn with quick, private access to the beach. Large, well-maintained rooms have fan and private hot shower. A few cheaper units share bathrooms. An apartment accommodates three and has a kitchenette, air-con and cable TV. A restaurant serves local specialties.

Cabinas Los Almendros (☎ 777 0225, 777 5137; tr with air-con/fan US$50/40; ▯ ⌨) A good option if you're a traveling trio, rooms here come with hot water and the friendly Doña Emilia runs a tight ship. There's also a pool, restaurant and slow Internet access (per hour US$2).

MIDRANGE & TOP-END
Hotel Vela Bar (☎ 777 0413; www.velabar.com; s/d/tr US$40/50/63; ⌨) This hotel is relatively unremarkable, though its has 19 pleasant rooms with air-con and hot shower for a very fair price. The owners also run a consistently popular restaurant (p356).

Hotel Ola del Pacífico (☎ 777 1944/74; s/d/tr/q US$60/70/85/95; P ⌨) This popular midrange option has eight rooms awash in pastel pinks with private hot shower, air-con, cable TV and ocean views. The attached restaurant, Al Mono Loco (p356), is one of the busiest in the area. Credit cards are accepted.

Hotel del Mar (☎ 777 0543; www.hoteldelmar-costarica .com; d without/with air-con US$70/80, d with king-size bed US$90 P ⌨) This gay-friendly hotel has 12 smartly decorated rooms, some with oversized king beds and private balconies. All rooms have hot water and it's a short walk to the beach.

La Posada (☎ 777 1446; www.laposadajungle.com; bungalows US$115; P ⌨) Your private jungle bungalow can accommodate you and three of your friends, though you might have some furry visitors as you're adjacent to the exit of the national park. All bungalows have air-con, hot water, a refrigerator, microwave, private porch with hammock and occasionally a few monkeys clambering on the rooftop.

Hotel Playa Espadilla (☎ 777 0416; www.espadilla .com; s/d US$105/125, s/d with kitchenette US$126/142; P ⌨ ⌨) This comfortable, modern hotel complete with tennis courts is located near the park entrance, and is one of the most expensive hotels in the village. However, its 16 brightly painted rooms with air-con, cable TV and private hot shower are utterly bland and not worth the hefty price tag. Four pricier units have kitchenette, though if you're self catering you're probably staying elsewhere.

Cabinas Playa Espadilla (standard d/tr/q US$80/85/ 100, deluxe d/tr/q US$85/90/105; P ⌨) A much better option, slightly cheaper and granting access to the hotel's tennis courts and pools are these cabinas. They are equipped with hot water and there's the option of air-con and a kitchenette. There is also a small pool.

SAVING THE SQUIRREL MONKEY

With its expressive eyes and luxuriant coat, the *mono tití* (Central American squirrel monkey) is one of the most beautiful of Costa Rica's four monkey species. Unfortunately, it is also in danger of extinction. Roughly 1500 of these charming animals are left in the Manuel Antonio area, one of their last remaining habitats. Unfortunately, the area is in constant environmental jeopardy due to overdevelopment. To remedy this problem, the folks at **Ascomoti** (Asociación para la Conservación del Mono Tití, Association for the Conservation of the Titi Monkey; ☎ 224 5703; www.ascomoti.org) have begun to take measures to prevent further decline.

The organization is creating a biological corridor between the hilly Cerro-Nara biological protection zone in the northeast and the Parque Nacional Manuel Antonio on the coast. To achieve this, they are reforesting the Río Naranjo, a key waterway linking the two. Already more than 10,000 trees have been planted along 8km of the Naranjo. This not only has the effect of extending the monkeys' habitat, but also provides a protected area for other wildlife. Scientists at the Universidad Nacional de Costa Rica have mapped and selected sites for reforestation and the whole project is supported financially by business owners in the area. (Ascomoti's website has a list of all the local businesses supporting this valuable effort.)

If you want to volunteer, Ascomoti is looking for individuals interested in planting trees or tracking monkey troops. Volunteers must be able to devote at least one month. The cost is US$350 per person per month to cover room and board. Inquire months ahead of your desired travel date as opportunities are not always immediately available.

Eating & Drinking

There are a number of stands on the beach that cater to hungry tourists, though everything is expectedly overpriced. Plus, it leads to the temptation to feed the monkeys (see the boxed text Don't Feed the Monkeys! Dammit We're Serious!, p359), though we know you're smarter than that.

Al Mono Loco (casados US$6) Just north of the rotunda, Al Mono Loco sits under a thatched *rancho* (small house or house-like building) and serves Tico and international specialties, including pasta (US$7) and burgers (US$4). It has a long list of tapas for US$2 a plate.

Marlin Restaurant (breakfast US$2-5, fish dishes US$6-8; ☺ 7am-10pm) This restaurant is packed to the gills with hungry gringos in search of fresh fish and filling breakfasts.

Hotel Vela Bar (dishes US$7-15) specializes in seafood and has the best and priciest restaurant in Manuel Antonio, though its nothing compared to the restaurants on the road towards Quepos.

Restaurant Mar y Sombra (casados US$3, fish dinners US$6) The food is hit or miss, but the beachside setting can't be beat. On weekends, the restaurant turns into a discotheque that's recommended by locals and travelers alike.

Getting There & Away

All flights for Manuel Antonio land at the airport in Quepos (p347).

Buses depart Manuel Antonio for San José (US$4, four hours) at 6am, 9:30am, noon and 5pm. These will pick you up in front of your hotel if you are on the road to flag them down or from the Quepos bus terminal, after which there are no stops. Buy tickets well in advance at the Quepos bus terminal. This bus is frequently packed and you will not be able to buy tickets from the driver. Buses for destinations other than San José also leave from the main terminal in Quepos (see p347 for more details).

PARQUE NACIONAL MANUEL ANTONIO

Parque Nacional Manuel Antonio was declared a national park in 1972, preserving it (with minutes to spare) from being bulldozed and razed to make room for a crucial development project – namely an all-inclusive resort and beachside condominiums. Although Manuel Antonio was enlarged to its present-day size of 1625 hectares in 2000, it remains the country's second-smallest national park. Unfortunately, the volume of visitors that descend on Manuel Antonio can sometimes make it feel like you're tromping through a safari park at Six Flags.

To be fair, Manuel Antonio is absolutely stunning, and on a good day at the right time it's easy to convince yourself that you've died and gone to a coconut-filled paradise. The

MANUEL ANTONIO AREA

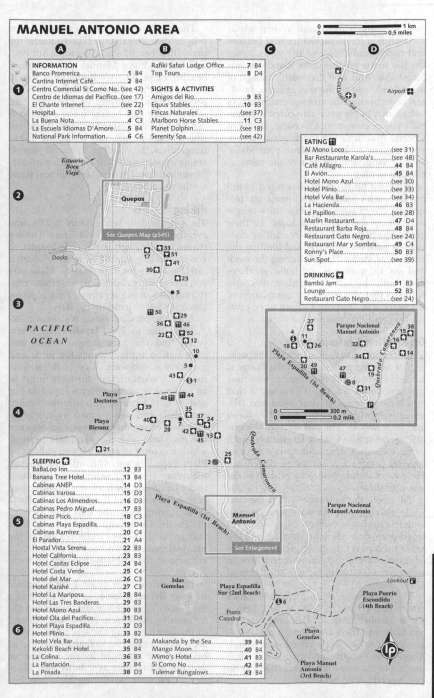

| 0 | 1 km |
| 0 | 0.5 miles |

INFORMATION
Banco Promerica	**1** B4
Cantina Internet Café	**2** B4
Centro Comercial Si Como No	(see 42)
Centro de Idiomas del Pacifico	(see 17)
El Chante Internet	(see 22)
Hospital	**3** D1
La Buena Nota	**4** C3
La Escuela Idiomas D'Amore	**5** B4
National Park Information	**6** C6
Rafiki Safari Lodge Office	**7** B4
Top Tours	**8** D4

SIGHTS & ACTIVITIES
Amigos del Rio	**9** B3
Equus Stables	**10** B3
Fincas Naturales	(see 37)
Marlboro Horse Stables	**11** C3
Planet Dolphin	(see 18)
Serenity Spa	(see 42)

EATING
Al Mono Loco	(see 31)
Bar Restaurante Karola's	(see 48)
Café Milagro	**44** B4
El Avión	**45** B4
Hotel Mono Azul	(see 30)
Hotel Plinio	(see 33)
Hotel Vela Bar	(see 34)
La Hacienda	**46** B3
Le Papillon	(see 28)
Marlin Restaurant	**47** D4
Restaurant Barba Roja	**48** B4
Restaurant Gato Negro	(see 24)
Restaurant Mar y Sombra	**49** C4
Ronny's Place	**50** B3
Sun Spot	(see 39)

DRINKING
Bambú Jam	**51** B3
Lounge	**52** B3
Restaurant Gato Negro	(see 24)

Estuario Boca Vieja

Quepos

See Quepos Map (p345)

Docks

PACIFIC OCEAN

Parque Nacional Manuel Antonio

Playa Espadilla (1st Beach)

| 0 | 300 m |
| 0 | 0.2 mile |

Playa Doctores

Playa Biesanz

SLEEPING
BaBaLoo Inn	**12** B3
Banana Tree Hotel	**13** B4
Cabinas ANEP	**14** D3
Cabinas Irarosa	**15** D3
Cabinas Los Almendros	**16** D3
Cabinas Pedro Miguel	**17** B3
Cabinas Piscis	**18** C3
Cabinas Playa Espadilla	**19** D4
Cabinas Ramírez	**20** C4
El Parador	**21** A4
Hostal Vista Serena	**22** B3
Hotel California	**23** B3
Hotel Casitas Eclipse	**24** B4
Hotel Costa Verde	**25** C4
Hotel del Mar	**26** C3
Hotel Karahé	**27** C3
Hotel La Mariposa	**28** B4
Hotel Las Tres Banderas	**29** B3
Hotel Mono Azul	**30** B3
Hotel Ola del Pacífico	**31** D4
Hotel Playa Espadilla	**32** D3
Hotel Plinio	**33** B2
Hotel Vela Bar	**34** D3
Kekoldi Beach Hotel	**35** B4
La Colina	**36** B3
La Plantación	**37** B4
La Posada	**38** D3
Makanda by the Sea	**39** B4
Mango Moon	**40** B4
Mimo's Hotel	**41** B3
Si Como No	**42** B4
Tulemar Bungalows	**43** B4

Airport

Parque Nacional Manuel Antonio

Quebrada Camaronera

Manuel Antonio

See Enlargement

Islas Gemelas

Playa Espadilla Sur (2nd Beach)

Punta Catedral

Playa Gemelas

Playa Manuel Antonio (3rd Beach)

Lookout

Playa Puerto Escondido (4th Beach)

park's clearly marked trail system winds through rain forest-backed tropical beaches and rocky headlands, and the views across the bay to the pristine outer islands are unforgettable. And, as if that wasn't enough of a hard sell, add to the mix iguanas, howlers, capuchins, sloths and squirrel monkeys (which may be the gosh-darn cutest little furballs you've ever seen). Of course, as one of Central America's top tourist destinations, you're going to have to share your idyllic spot of sand with the rest of the camera-clicking hordes.

Increased tourist traffic has taken its toll on the park's wildlife as animals are frequently driven away or – worse still – taught to scavenge for tourist handouts. To their credit, the park service has reacted by closing the park on Mondays and limiting the number of visitors to 600 during the week and 800 on weekends and holidays. However, with the inevitable influx of cruise shippers that will follow the completion of the marina in Quepos, it's hard to be optimistic about the future of the park.

Orientation & Information

Visitors must leave their vehicles in the parking lot near the park entrance; the charge is US$3. However, the road here is very narrow and congested and it's suggested that you leave your car at your hotel and take an early-morning bus to Manuel Antonio and then walk in. The **park entrance** (admission US$7; ⏱ 7am-4pm Tue-Sun) is a few meters south of the rotunda. Count your change as many tourists complain about being ripped off. Here you can hire naturalist guides to take you into the park.

To reach the entrance, you'll have to wade through the Camaronera estuary, which can be anywhere from ankle to thigh deep, depending on the tides and the season. However, in an impressive display of opportunism, there are boaters here to transport you 100m for the small fee of US$1.

The park ranger station and **information center** (Map p357; ☎ 777 0644) is just before Playa Manuel Antonio. Drinking water is available, and there are toilets, beach showers, picnic tables and a refreshment stand. There is no camping and guards will come around in the evening to make sure that no one has remained behind.

The beaches are often numbered – most people call Playa Espadilla (outside the park) 'first beach,' Playa Espadilla Sur 'second beach,' Playa Manuel Antonio 'third beach,' Playa Puerto Escondido 'fourth beach,' and Playa Playita 'fifth beach.' Some people begin counting at Espadilla Sur, which is the first beach in the park, so it can be a bit confusing trying to figure out which beach people may be talking about. Irregardless, they're all pristine, and provide ample opportunities for snorkeling or restful sunbathing. There is a refreshment stand on the third beach.

Hiking

The average daily temperature is 27°C and average annual rainfall is 3875mm. The dry season is not entirely dry, merely less wet, so you should be prepared for rain (although it can also be dry for days on end). Make sure you carry plenty of drinking water, sun protection and insect repellent. Pack a picnic lunch if you're spending the day.

After the park entrance, it's about a 30-minute hike to **Playa Espadilla Sur**, where you'll find the park ranger station and information center; watch for birds and monkeys as you walk. West of the station, follow an obvious trail through forest to an isthmus separating Playas Espadilla Sur and Manuel Antonio. This isthmus is called a *tombolo* and was formed by the accumulation of sedimentary material between the mainland and the peninsula beyond, which was once an island. If you walk along Playa Espadilla Sur, you will find a small mangrove area. The isthmus widens into a rocky peninsula, with a forest in the center. A trail leads around the peninsula to **Punta Catedral**, from where there are good views of the Pacific Ocean and various rocky islets that are bird reserves and form part of the national park. Brown boobies and pelicans are among the seabirds that nest on these islands.

You can continue around the peninsula to **Playa Manuel Antonio**, or you can avoid the peninsula altogether and hike across the isthmus to this beach. At the western end of the beach, during the low tide, you can see a semicircle of rocks that archaeologists believe were arranged by pre-Columbian Indians to function as a **turtle trap**. (Turtles would swim in during high tide, but

DON'T FEED THE MONKEYS! DAMMIT WE'RE SERIOUS!

We at Lonely Planet respect the environment, so you can imagine how irate we become when we hear that tourists are feeding the monkeys their left-over Cheetos. Sure, they're cute, and you may think that you're doing them a favor, but you're not. Really. Here are few reasons why:

- Monkeys are susceptible to bacteria transmitted from human hands.
- Irregular feeding leads to aggressive behavior and creates a dangerous dependency.
- Bananas are NOT their preferred food, and can cause serious digestive problems.
- Increased exposure with humans facilitates illegal poaching.

This list could go on and on. Please people, we're on our hands and knees. Don't feed the monkeys, and if you see someone else doing so, be responsible and say something. The problem has become so bad in Manuel Antonio that an initiative has been started in which the names (and sometimes photos) of violators are published in the local press. To report an irresponsible soul, call ☎ 777 2592.

when they tried to swim out after the tide started receding, they'd be trapped by the wall.) The beach itself is an attractive one of white sand and is popular for swimming. It's protected and safer than the Espadilla beaches.

Beyond Playa Manuel Antonio, the trail divides. The lower trail is steep and slippery during the wet months and leads to the quiet Playa Puerto Escondido. This beach can be more or less completely covered by high tides, so be careful not to get cut off. The upper trail climbs to a **lookout** on a bluff overlooking Puerto Escondido and Punta Serrucho beyond – a stunning vista. Rangers reportedly limit the number of hikers on this trail to 45.

The trails in Manuel Antonio are well-marked and heavily traversed, though there are some quiet corners near the ends of the trail. Off-trail hiking is not permitted without prior consent from the park service.

Tours & Guides

Hiring a guide costs US$20 per person for a two-hour tour. The only guides allowed in the park are members of Aguila (a local association governed by the park service) who have official ID badges, and recognized guides from tour agencies or hotels. This is to prevent visitors from getting ripped off and to ensure a good-quality guide – Aguila guides are well trained and multi-lingual. (French-, German-, or English-speaking guides can be requested.) Visitors report that hiring a guide virtually guarantees wildlife sighting.

Wildlife-Watching

Monkeys abound in the park, and indeed it's difficult to spend a day walking around without seeing at least some. White-faced monkeys are the most common, but rarer squirrel monkeys are present and howler monkeys can usually be seen (and heard). Apart from monkeys, sloths, agoutis, peccaries, armadillos, coatis, and raccoons can also be spotted on a regular basis. More than 350 species of bird have been reported in the park and the surrounding area, and a variety of lizards, snakes, iguanas and other animals may also be observed.

All the trails within the park are good for wildlife-watching, but it's always wise to ask the rangers about recent sightings. Some trails may limit the number of hikers to minimize disturbance of the animals. There's a small coral reef off Playa Manuel Antonio, but the water is rather cloudy and the visibility limited. Despite this, snorkelers can see a variety of fish, as well as marine creatures such as crabs, corals, sponges and sea snails.

Immediately inland from the beaches is an evergreen littoral forest. This contains many different species of tree, bush and other plants. Watch out for the *manzanillo* tree *(Hippomane mancinella)*. It has poisonous fruits that look like little crab apples, and the sap exuded by the bark and leaves is toxic, causing the skin to itch and burn. Warning signs are prominently displayed beside examples of this tree near the park entrance.

QUEPOS TO UVITA

About 4km south of Quepos, the paving on the Costanera Sur suddenly stops. Most travelers never give this much thought, though they later scratch their heads when they reach Dominical and realize that the paving starts up again. Curious? So were we.

The reason (are you ready for this one?) is that this stretch of road is owned by the Quepos regional government, and the last thing they want is tourists dividing their time between Manuel Antonio and points further south. Sure, backpackers could care less about a couple of potholes, but most tour buses wouldn't dare proceed. Isn't feudalism great?

Of course, the real losers in this sad state of affairs are the local Ticos who perennially beg the government to pave the road, though the bright side is that overdevelopment of the coastline virtually ceases south of Quepos. For the intrepid traveler, this means you can have your pick of deserted beaches and great surf spots, and it's a great place to look back at the Costa Rica of 10 years ago.

QUEPOS TO DOMINICAL

It's 44km from Quepos before you reach the next village of any size, Dominical. The road is bone-shaking gravel, easily passable in the dry season but requiring care to negotiate in the wet. At the time of writing, the bridge was out, so it's best to inquire about the state of the road as you will have to ford a river, which may necessitate a 4WD. The drive is through kilometer after kilometer of African oil-palm plantations, with minor centers for palm oil processing along the way (see the boxed text Ever Wonder Where Palm Oil Comes From?, p342).

Rafiki Safari Lodge

About 15km south of Quepos you'll come to the town of Savegre. From here a 4WD dirt road parallels the Río Savegre and leads 7km inland, past the towns of Silencio and Santo Domingo, to the **Rafiki Safari Lodge** (☎ 777 2250, 777 5327; www.rafikisafari.com; s/d with 3 meals US$152/260, child under 5 free; P ⛶). Nestled into the rain forest, with a prime spot right next to the river, the lodge combines all the

comforts of a hotel with the splendor of a jungle safari – all with a little bit of African flavor. The owners, who are from South Africa, have constructed nine luxury tents on stilts equipped with private bathrooms, hot water, private porches and electricity. All units are screened in, which allow you to see and hear and the rain forest without actually having creepy-crawlies in your bed. There's a spring-fed pool with a waterslide and ample opportunity for horse riding, bird-watching (more than 350 species have been identified), hiking and white-water rafting. There's a well-equipped bar and a rancho-style restaurant serving Tico and South African specialties.

The lodge has an office on the Quepos to Manuel Antonio road, and transportation to and from can be arranged. Credit cards are accepted.

Matapalo

Matapalo is off of most travelers' radar, though without good reason as this palm-fringed, grey-sand beach has some truly awesome surf. With two river mouth breaks, a spattering of reasonably priced accommodation and some wicked, wicked waves, the fact that Matapalo hasn't blown up is a bit of a mystery (though we're blaming the Quepos regional government). Not surprisingly, Matapalo is not the best beach for swimming as the transient rips here are about as notorious as they get (see the boxed text What To Do if You're Caught in a Riptide, p284).

Just south of Matapalo are the **Terciopelo Waterfalls**, which are famous for their swimming pools. The falls are located a few kilometers south of Rió Hatillo Viejo, though it's best to ask someone to point out the trailhead for you as it's tough to find.

The turnoff to this tiny village from the main road is at the **Chasa Matapalo** (dishes US$3-6), which does a decent *casado*, though it's more memorable as a reference point.

The first hotel you'll see after turning off the Costanera is the German-run **El Coquito del Pacífico** (☎ 787 5028, 384 7220; www .elcoquito.com; s/d/tr/q US$45/55/65/75; P ⛶ ⛶) which consists of six spacious, whitewashed bungalows equipped with air-con and hot water. There's a shady garden with almond and mango trees as well as a pool, restaurant and bar.

The next place you'll come to is **Cabina Matapalo** (☎ 787 5246; d US$30; **P**), which is also German-run and great value as all the rooms have a bathtub.

Across the street is **Terraza del Sol** (☎ 787 5081; cabinas US$30; **P**), which is run by a Canadian-Tica couple and has large A-frame cabins for rent that can accommodate up to four people. All cabins have a private bathroom with hot water.

Tico Gringo (☎ 787 5023; dishes US$3-10) is owned by an American ex pat and his Tica wife who've lived in Matapalo for decades. Seafood, burgers and wings are the standard here, though the real draw is the display of old black and white photos of Costa Rica.

Just down the road on the beach side is **Dos Palmas B&B** (☎ 787 5037; d US$47, additional person US$5; **P**) a tiny, bright-yellow inn with some of the best views of the crashing surf in town. The owners are a charming Canadian couple who are very welcoming to their international guests. The two rooms for rent here each have a private hot shower, mini-fridge and a king-sized bed.

The American-owned **Jungle House** (☎ 787 5005, 777 2748; www.junglehouse.com; d incl breakfast US$65; **P** 😋) provides the epitome of relaxation, with five polished-wood quarters that are all nicely decorated and come with private bathroom, cable TV, air-con, kitchenette and hammock. The bamboo 'honeymoon' cabin in the back is a large open-air unit with incredible views of the hills. Charlie, the friendly owner, is active locally and supports local education initiatives and trash pickup efforts on the beach. A pool table provides a great gathering spot.

At the end of the road you'll find the new **Bahari Beach Bungalows** (☎ 787 5057/14; andrealudwig10@hotmail.com; d cabin US$55, d tent US$90; **P** 🐾) with four safari-style beachfront tents and two cabins. All of the tents are fully furnished and have electricity, tiled private bathroom with hot shower, hand-painted sink and ocean views. The cabins, across the road, are also beautifully decorated and come ornamented with fresh flowers. There's a pool overlooking the ocean, a spa and an excellent restaurant featuring continental cuisine. Credit cards are accepted.

The most expensive lodging on the beach is **Dreamy Contentment** (☎ 787 5223; www.dreamy contentment.com; bungalow/house US$125/200; **P** 😋), a beautiful, Spanish colonial property with impressive woodworking throughout. The bungalows are fully equipped with air-con, hot water and kitchenettes, though the real star attraction is the main house, which has the kitchen of your dreams, a beachfront veranda and princely bathroom complete with tub.

There's a campsite on the beach by the main access road, but it gets quite crowded on high-season weekends.

Buses between Quepos and Dominical can drop you off at the turnoff to the village; from there it's a couple of kilometers to the beach.

Hacienda Barú National Wildlife Refuge

Located on the Pacific coast 3km northeast of Dominical on the road to Quepos, **Hacienda Barú National Wildlife Refuge** (☎ 787 0003; www.haciendabaru.com; admission US$6, each subsequent day US$2) forms a key link in a major biological corridor called 'The Path of the Tapir.' It is comprised of more than 330 hectares of private and state owned land that has been protected from hunting since 1976. The range of tropical habitats that may be observed there include pristine beaches, river banks, mangrove estuaries, wetlands, selectively logged forests, secondary forests, primary forests, tree plantations and pastures. This diversity of habitat plus its key position in the Path of the Tapir Biological Corridor accounts for the multitude of species that have been identified on Hacienda Barú. As of January 2006, these included 351 birds, 69 mammals, 94 reptiles and amphibians, 87 butterflies and 158 species of trees, some of them over 8.5m (27.5ft) in circumference. Ecological tourism provides this wildlife refuge with its only source of funds with which to maintain its protected status, so guests are assured that money spent there will be used to further the conservation of tropical rain forest.

TOURS

There are an impressive number of guided tours (US$20 to US$60) on offer. You can experience the rain-forest canopy in three different ways – a platform 36m above the forest floor, tree climbing and a zip line called 'The Flight of the Toucan.' In addition to the canopy activities, Hacienda Barú offers bird watching tours, hiking tours and two overnight camping tours in both tropical rain forest and lowland beach habitats.

Hacienda Barú's naturalist guides come from local communities and have lived near the rain forest all of their lives.

For people who prefer to explore the refuge by themselves, there are 7km of well kept and marked, self-guided trails, a birdwatching tower, 3km of pristine beach, an orchid garden and a butterfly garden.

SLEEPING & EATING
Hacienda Barú Lodge (d US$60, additional person US$10) consists of six clean, two-bedroom cabins located 350 meters from Barú Beach. Children ten years or under are free. The red-tile-roofed, open air restaurant (meals US$6 to US$10) serves a variety of tasty Costa Rican dishes.

GETTING THERE & AWAY
The Quepos–Dominical–San Isidro bus stops outside the hacienda entrance. The San Isidro–Dominical–Uvita bus will drop you at the Río Barú bridge, 2km from the hacienda office. A taxi from Dominical costs about US$5.

If you're driving, the El Ceibo gas station, 50m north of the Hacienda Barú Lodge, is the only one for a good way in any direction. Groceries, fishing gear, tide tables, and other useful sundries are available, and there are clean toilets.

Centro Turístico Cataratas Nauyaca
Just north of the turn-off for Dominical is the junction for San Isidro. If you turn left towards San Isidro and travel for about 10km, you'll see an entrance to the right that leads to **Centro Turístico Cataratas Nauyaca** (☎ 787 0198, 771 3187; www.ecotourism.co.cr/nauyacawaterfalls/index .html). There's no vehicle access to this tourist center, but you can hire horses for a guided ride to two waterfalls that plunge into a deep swimming hole. With a day's notice, a tour can be arranged, including the guided ride, swimming, and country meals with the local family. Tours leave at 8am, take six to seven hours and cost US$40 per person. A campground with dressing rooms and toilets is available. Tour companies in Dominical can also arrange tours to the falls.

DOMINICAL
With monster waves, a laid-back vibe and enough reefer to inspire a Snoop Dog song, Dominical is one of the most popular destinations on the Pacific coast for surfers, backpackers and do-nothings. Most travelers get stuck here for longer than they intended, though no one seems to care so long as the surf's up and the spliff's not out.

Difficult access has spared Dominical from the fate suffered by other beaches on the central Pacific coast. Development remains low-key, the few roads around the village are still dusty and pot-holed and the majority of the beach is fronted by forests not fast food. The town is definitely gringofied and growing slowly, though for the time-being it's a great place to get stoked (or stoned).

Orientation & Information
The main Costanera highway bypasses Dominical; the entrance to the village is immediately past the Río Barú bridge. There's a main road through the village, where many of the services mentioned are found, and a parallel road along the beach.

There are no banking facilities, but San Clemente Bar & Grill (see p364) will exchange both US dollars and traveler's checks. It has a postal service upstairs.
Dominical Internet (per hr US$4.50; ⊙ 9:30am-7pm Mon-Sat) Check email here, above the San Clemente Bar & Grill.
Lavandería Las Olas (⊙ 7am-9pm) Have your laundry done here, inside the minisuper of the same name.
Police (☎ 787 0011)

Dangers & Annoyances
Waves, currents and riptides in Dominical are very strong and many people have drowned here (don't smoke and swim!). Watch for red flags (which mark riptides), follow the instructions of posted signs and swim at beaches that are patrolled by lifeguards.

In addition, because of the heavy-duty party crowd Dominical is attracting, there is a burgeoning drug problem and some of the bars can get a little rough at night.

Sights & Activities
The **Green Iguana Surf Camp** (☎ 815 3733; www .greeniguanasurfcamp.com), on a side road leading to the beach, is run by experienced surfers Jason and Karla Butler. It offers a variety of surf lessons and tours as well as seven- to 10-day surfing camps.

Dominical is emerging as a base for day trips to Parque Nacional Corcovado and

Parque Nacional Marino Ballena. Get details at **Southern Expeditions** (☎ 787 0100; www .dominical.biz/expeditions/; tours from US$55) at the entrance to the village. The staff can also organize trips to the Guaymi indigenous reserve near Boruca.

The San Clemente Bar & Grill (p364) rents bicycles and surfboards.

Courses

Adventure Spanish School (☎ 787 0023, in the USA & Canada 800-237 730; www.adventurespanishschool.com) runs one-week Spanish-language programs starting at US$315, without homestay. Private lessons are available.

Sleeping

The hotels listed here are in the main village. If you're camping, watch your stuff as theft is a regular occurrence here. The rates given are for high-season, but low-season rates could be as much as 30% to 40% lower.

Antorchas Camping (☎ 787 0307; camping per person US$5, s/d US$10/15; P) Just a few meters from the beach, this campground provides lockers and showers. It rent out tents for US$1 per night and there are six prison-like rooms with zero amenities that share cold showers. For an extra fee of US$3 per stay, basic kitchen privileges are available.

Dominical Backpackers Hostel (dm US$10; P) This is the most popular option in town, though it's not recommendable as there are no locks on the individual rooms, and the front door is not always closed. The booking office is next door at the San Clemente Inn.

San Clemente Inn (☎ 787 0026; d US$30-60; ✗ P) A much safer option than the hostel. Shiny wooden units of various sizes are spacious and clean; pricier ones have air-con, hot water and ocean views.

Cabinas Coco (☎ 787 0235; camping per person US$4, r with/without bathroom US$34/12; P) It'll do in a pinch, though you could definitely do better. The cabinas are run-down and the adjacent disco won't allow you to get any beauty sleep.

Cabinas Thrusters (☎ 787 0127; d without/with air-con US$25/30; P ✗) A steady stream of surfers and skaters flock to these simple and clean wood cabins with private, cold showers. The attached bar is one of the most popular in town, so stay here if you want a short crawl back to bed, or elsewhere if you want to be able to hear yourself think.

Tortilla Flats (☎ 787 0033; s/d US$20/30, s/d with air-con US$30/40; ✗) This popular budget option has 19 rooms with private hot-water bathrooms and a patio hammock, though the attached restaurant can get very noisy. More expensive units have air-con and face the beach.

Cabinas Arena y Sol (☎ 787 0140; small/large cabins US$35/50; P 🖭) This recently renovated property has small cabins for one to three people and large cabins for four to six. All come equipped with private, hot water showers and kitchenettes. Great value if you're traveling in a group. There's also a pool, restaurant and a mini-super.

Posada del Sol (☎ 787 0085; d US$36; P) Rooms here are well decorated and have spotless, private bathrooms with hot water and a patio hammock that'll satisfy all your swinging needs.

Sundancer Cabinas (☎ 787 0189; d US$40; P 🖭) A good option if you're looking for a quiet night's sleep. Rooms with private, hot shower are in a pleasant family home and share a communal kitchen.

Domilocos (☎ 787 0244; s/d US$30/50; P ✗ 🖳 🖭) This recent addition to the Dominical hotel scene is surprisingly luxurious. The mattresses are thick and comfortable, the water is hot and steamy and the air-con will make you forget you're in the tropics. There's also a pool, restaurant and lounge bar.

Hotel DiuWak (☎ 787 0087; www.diuwak.com; standard/deluxe/bungalow incl breakfast US$60/80/80; P ✗ 🖳 🖭) This resort complex is the most upscale accommodation in the town center, though the rooms here are bland and overpriced. However, the grounds surrounding the waterfall-fed pool are palm-fringed, which makes for relaxing days of idle laziness.

The following places are a few minutes out of town by car:

Hotel Villas Río Mar (☎ 787 0052; www.villasriomar .com; bungalow/junior ste/superior ste US$70/115/125; P ✗ 🖳 🖭) Just beyond the edge of town, a sign points under the bridge to this hotel about 800m from the village. This is the most expensive and sophisticated hotel in the area which consists of 40, polished-wood bungalows each with a private hammock-strung terraces, hot-water showers and mini-fridges. There are also luxury suites available with Internet, air-con and a bathtub. Room service is available and for an extra US$15 a day per person, you can have breakfast and dinner. There's a pool, Jacuzzi, tennis court, restaurant and bar. The hotel can arrange all local tours and has surfboards for rent. Credit cards are accepted.

Hotel y Restaurante Roca Verde (☎ 787 0036; www.rocaverde.net; r US$85; P ⚒ ⚔) Overlooking the beach about 1km south of the village, this stylish, American-owned hotel is decorated with hardwoods, tile mosaics, festive murals and rock inlays. The 12 tropical-theme rooms with air-con and hot showers can accommodate up to four people. On certain nights, the hotel turns into a theater when local theater groups and dancers perform in the hotel lobby.

Eating & Drinking

Soda Nanyoa (☉ 7am-10pm) The cheapest eatery in town, so it's consistently packed with hungry surfers snatching up casados for around US$2.

Thrusters Bar (at Cabinas Thrusters) The local party people congregate here for beer and skateboarding around the pool tables. Patrons have evidently spent quality time at the tattoo parlor upstairs, conveniently situated if you feel the need to drink and redecorate yourself. Next door is Fifi's Sushi Bar 787 (rolls US$3 to US$5), because there's no better combination than sharp needles and raw tuna.

San Clemente Bar & Grill (dishes US$3-8) This classic, Dominical watering hole complete with broken surfboards on the walls serves up big breakfasts and Tex-Mex dishes, though it's more popular as a place to get tanked during the weekly club night on Fridays. There is a pool table and foosball.

Maracutú (dishes US$4-10 ☉ 6-11pm) The self-proclaimed world music beach bar and Italian kitchen. Each night features a different genre of music from Brazilian beats to reggae and hip-hop, and live music is common. Vegetarian and vegan food is available.

Tortilla Flats (dishes US$4-7) Here you'll find a great beach-side atmosphere, highly drinkable margaritas and a good variety of salads, sandwiches and gringo patrons.

Jungle Bistro (dishes US$5-10; ☉ 5-11pm) We are not entirely sure if *tropical fusion* is actually a type of cuisine, but we do know that the food here is damn good. Dig into

an eclectic mix of dishes featuring fresh, tropical ingredients.

Restaurant Wachaca (dishes US$6-12; ☉ 11am-11pm Tue-Sun) is your spot for Limónese-inspired Caribbean dishes, served in an open-air courtyard underneath a giant, old ceiba tree.

If you're looking for a cinematic fix, check out the boxed text Movies in the Jungle, p366.

Getting There & Away
BUS
All buses arrive and depart at the end of the road next to Cabinas Coco. These schedules change regularly, so ask about times before setting out. (Most hotel owners have current schedules.)

Ciudad Cortés US$2.50, two hours, departs 4:15am and 10am.

Palmar US$2, 1¾ hours, 4:30am and 10:30am.

Quepos US$2, four hours, 7:30am, 8am, 10:30am, 1:45pm, 4pm and 5pm.

San Isidro US$1, one hour, 6:45am, 7:15am, 2:30pm and 3:30pm.

Uvita US$0.75, one hour, 4:30am, 10:30am, noon and 6:15pm.

TAXI
Taxis to Uvita cost US$10, while the ride to San Isidro costs US$20 and the ride to Quepos is US$50. Cars can accommodate up to five people. Minivans for up to 28 passengers can also be arranged. For service call **Del Tabaco Real & Taxi Dominical** (☎ 814 444), which can arrange pick ups and drop offs anywhere in the region.

ESCALERAS AREA
The Escaleras area refers to a small community of houses and hotels scattered around a steep and narrow dirt loop-road that branches off the Costanera. A 4WD vehicle is an absolute necessity as the locals weren't kidding when they named it Escaleras (staircase). Aside from the scenic views, travelers primarily brave the road to either have a relaxing, mountain retreat or to check out the boxed text Movies in the Jungle, p366).

The first entrance is 4km south of the San Isidro turn off before Dominical, and the second is 4.5km past the first. Both are on the left-hand side of the road and poorly signed.

Sleeping & Eating

Finca Brian y Emilia (☎ 396 6206; r per person without/ with bathroom US$36/50; P) If you take the first entrance to Escaleras, you'll pass this sustainable fruit farm run by an American farmer Brian and his daughter Emilia. Brian has spent over 25 years experimenting with various methods of subsistence agricultural, and runs a volunteer program (two-week minimum) that focuses on fruit harvesting and farm maintenance. Screened cabins here sleep up to six, and there's a heated rock pool to soak in. Rates include three meals and a guided hiking tour.

Bellavista Lodge & Ranch (☎ 388 0155, in the USA 800-909 4469; www.bellavistalodge.com; d room/cabin US$55/75; P) Further up the road is this remote lodge owned by long-time resident Woody Dyer. The lodge itself is in a revamped farmhouse surrounded by a balcony providing superb ocean views. Accommodations are in four shiny wood rooms with private, solar-heated shower. A two-floored private cabin comes with a kitchen and living room and accommodates six. Rates include breakfast or an evening snack of beer and chips. Tasty home-cooked meals (and pies!) are available (breakfast and lunch US$5, dinner US$10). The ranch has electricity 24 hours a day. There are guided horse-riding excursions to waterfalls (US$35 to US$55). If you don't have a 4WD, Woody will pick you up in Dominical for US$10.

Villa Escaleras (☎ 823 0509, in the USA 773-279 0516; www.villa-escaleras.com; villas for 4/6/8 people US$240/280/320; P) About another 1km up the Escaleras road, this spacious villa has gorgeous views and a pool and is a great getaway spot for a large family or a group of friends. There are four bedrooms, five bathrooms, an equipped kitchen, cathedral ceilings, Spanish tiled floors and a TV with DVD player. Twice-weekly maid service, coffee supplies and a wraparound balcony make the setting complete. Local tours can be arranged and there are special weekly rates available.

Pacific Edge (☎ 531 8000; www.pacificedge.com; cabin d/tr/q US$60/68/77, bungalow d/tr/q US$75/92/108, additional person US$10; P) This hotel is located on a different road that's 1.2km south of the first entrance. The owners are a worldly North American–British couple who delight in showing guests their slice of paradise. Four cabins are perched on a knife-edge ridge about 200m above sea level and have solar-heated hot shower, balcony, coffee maker and fridge. Family bungalows accommodate up to six and have kitchen. You can add breakfast and dinner to the rate for US$25 per person.

Sun Storms Mountain (☎ 305 2414; d US$30; P) This is the only real budget option on the mountain, and is easiest to reach via the second entrance to Escaleras. Basic wood cabins are clean and rooms have private bathroom with hot water – a great value. The hotel is most popular for its bar, the Jolly Roger (open to 1am), run by American pirate, er, proprietor, Roger.

DOMINICAL TO UVITA

Just southeast of Dominical, the paved road continues through lush vegetation another 17km towards Uvita. This is a quiet stretch of coastline that is bypassed by most tourists on their way south to Uvita and Osa, though there are a number of pleasant places to stay and two wild reserves worth visiting. If you're driving, note that the smooth tarmac has speed bumps at inopportune and unmarked places, and the rainy season regularly produces ditch-sized potholes.

The attractive, tranquil and comfortable **Costa Paraíso Lodge** (☎ 787 0025; www.costaparaiso dominical.com; d US$90-105, additional person US$12; P) is about 2km south of Dominical on the northern end of **Playa Dominicalito** (which has small waves if you're tired of being thrashed at Dominical). Here you'll find five rooms of various sizes housing up to four people. All units have private bathroom, living room and porch overlooking the ocean. Several rooms have air-con and a few with kitchenette. Credit cards are accepted.

Cabinas Punta Dominical (☎ 787 0016/34, 787 0241; puntadominical@racsa.co.cr; q incl breakfast US$60, additional person US$6; P), about 4km south of Dominical and then to the right on a dirt road to the beach, are situated high on the rocky **Punta Dominical**. The four attractive cabins are isolated yet comfortable and have fan, private bathroom, electric shower and a porch. Each cabin will sleep up to four people and reservations are recommended. Boat trips can be arranged. Credit cards are accepted. **Restaurant La Parcela** (meals US$6-16; ☯ 7am-9:30pm), is widely regarded as the best spot in the area for thick, juicy steaks.

About 2km further on, **Las Casitas de Puer-tocito** (☎ 393 4327, 200 0139; www.lascasitashotel .com; d/tr incl breakfast US$54/72, additional person US$18; P ❄) has eight beautifully appointed cabins with private hot shower, fan and patio. One unit has a kitchenette and fridge. There's a pool, bar, Italian restaurant and beach access nearby. Lara, the manager, speaks Italian, English, Spanish and French. Guests can rent horses and arrange hiking, snorkeling, diving and boat trips.

A few kilometers before Uvita, you'll see a signed turnoff to the left on a rough dirt road (4WD only) that leads 3.5km up the hill (look over your shoulder for great views of Parque Nacional Marino Ballena) to **Reserva Biológica Oro Verde** (☎ 743 8072, 843 8833; P). This private reserve is on the farm of the Duarte family, who have homesteaded the area for more than three decades. Two-thirds of the 150-hectare property is rain forest and there are guided hikes (US$15 per person), horse-riding tours (US$25) and birding walks (US$30). The birding walks take three hours and depart at 5am and 2pm.

Opposite the turnoff to Oro Verde is **La Merced National Wildlife Refuge**, a 506-hectare national wildlife refuge (and former cattle ranch) with primary and secondary forests and mangroves lining the Río Morete. Here, you can take guided nature hikes (US$25), horseback tours to Punta Uvita (US$35) and half-day birding walks (US$35). The latter can be turned into full-day tours with lunch for an extra US$20. You can stay at La Merced in a 1940s **farmhouse** (r per person with 3 meals US$60), which can accommodate 10 people in double rooms of various sizes. There is a separate cabin that has space for up to seven people. Rooms are very well maintained and all of them share hot-water bathrooms, a living room and porch. Electricity is available by generator from 6pm to 9pm. Rates include a guided tour.

UVITA

This small hamlet just 17km south of Dominical will give you an idea of what Costa Rican beach towns looked like before the tourist boom. The village itself is nothing more than a loose straggle of farms, houses and *sodas*, though several of the nearby beaches are part of the **Parque Nacional Marino Ballena**, a pristine marine reserve famous for its migrating pods of humpback whales.

MOVIES IN THE JUNGLE

Every Friday night, an Escaleras resident named Toby invites locals and travelers to screen his favorite flicks. Cinema Escaleras is built on a hilltop with panoramic views of jungle-fronted coastline and features state of the art projection equipment and surround sound. Seriously, this guy loves his movies. Films are shown every Friday at 6pm, and a small donation to pay for the projector bulbs is requested. To get to the cinema, follow the first entrance to Esclaeras a few hundred meters up the mountain and look for a white house on the left hand side.

Unfortunately, the secret is out about the Brunca coast, and the recent paving of the Costanera Sur has seen in an influx of developers and speculators. Real-estate offices are popping up over town, and rich gringos like Jack and Susan think that Spanish tiles and sea-green stucco would look great against the rain forest backdrop. Visit quickly, because the building orgy is about to begin.

The area off the main highway is referred to locally as Uvita, while the area next to the beach is called Playa Uvita and Playa Bahía Uvita (the southern end of the beach).

Orientation & Information

The beach area is reached through two parallel dirt roads that are roughly 500m apart. The first entrance is just south of the bridge over the Río Uvita and the second entrance is in the center of town. At low tide you can walk out along Punta Uvita, but ask locally before heading out so that you don't get cut off by rising water.

Banco Coopealianza (☎ 743 8231) will change small amounts of US dollars. Steve at Hotel Toucan will exchange traveler's checks for a 3% service charge.

Sights & Activities

Uvita serves as the perfect base for exploring nearby Parque Nacional Marina Ballena. Beaches here are perfect for swimming, though there are occasionally some swells at **Playa Hermosa** to the north and **Playa Colonia** to the south.

The **Jardín de Mariposas** (admission US$4; ☼ 8am-4pm) is in Playa Uvita (just follow the signs).

This Tico-run outfit raises butterflies for export and education and this is a good opportunity to get up-close-and-personal with breeds such as the morpho. Go early in the morning when butterflies are at their most active. Admission includes a guided tour.

Sleeping & Eating

The main entrance to Uvita leads inland, east of the highway, where you'll find the following places. All showers are cold unless otherwise stated.

Hotel Toucan (☎ 743 8140; www.tucanhotel.com; dm US$10, d without/with bathroom US$18/25, tr with bathroom US$40, camping per person US$4; **P** **✕** **▯**) Located 100m inland of the main highway in Uvita, this is the most popular hostel in Uvita – and with good reason. Excitable American owner Steve is just bursting at the seams with news on the area and his clean rooms are a bargain. Even though the beach is right down the road, most guests never escape the evil clutches of the hammock movie theatre. The hotel offers free Internet, laundry service, free luggage storage, communal kitchen, movie nights and the reader-recommended Sunday spaghetti dinners.

Cabinas Los Laureles (☎ 743 8235; s/d US$16/18; **P**) About 200m up the road you'll find this pleasant, locally run spot which has eight clean, polished wood cabins with private bathroom set in a beautiful grove of laurels. The family can arrange horse-riding tours and any other activities you might be interested in.

Cascada Verde (www.cascadaverde.org; dm US$7, shared loft per person US$9, s/d house US$10/16, s/d lodge US$20/36) About 2km inland and uphill from Uvita is this alternative-living organic permaculture farm that also functions as a holistic retreat. Rooms are simple and bathrooms are all shared, though there is ample outdoor communal space for yoga and quiet meditation. A restaurant serves vegetarian, raw-food specialties, and all the produce is grown on the property. A taxi here will cost about US$3 from the highway area.

Balcón de Uvita (☎ 743 8034; www.balcondeuvita.com; tr US$55, additional person US$10; **P** **▯**) About 1km inland on a 4WD access road across from the gas station and run by a Dutch-Indonesian couple, this place consists of a lovely collection of rustic, stone-walled bungalows featuring huge, walk-in solar-powered showers. It also has a highly rec-

ommended restaurant (dishes US$8, open 11am to 9pm Tuesday to Sunday) that specializes in Thai and Indonesian delicacies.

There are also a number of cabinas that line the shores of Playa Uvita.

Cabinas Punta Uvita (☎ 771 2311, 743 8015; d/tr/q US$12/15/20, cabin for 5 people US$25; d with bathroom US$15, camping per person US$3; **P**) Close to the beach on the southern access road to Playa Uvita this offers the traveler a variety of rooms.

South of Uvita on the road towards Osa, you'll find a few more accommodations.

Villas Bejuco (☎ 743 8093; meals US$3-5; d/tr US$50/60; **P** **▯**) Just 2km south of the bridge, a clearly signed turnoff leads to this comfortable, hillside lodge that's only 500m from the beach. There are 10 modern cabins with private showers and screens. There's a bar and an inexpensive restaurant.

La Colonia (☎ 743 8021; tr/q US$15/30; **P**) A few hundred meters further down the Costanera, you'll see a dirt road leading to the beach. Here you'll find this family-run establishment, which has no-frills cabins with private cold-water bathrooms.

Whales & Dolphins Ecolodge (☎ 770 3557; www.whalesanddolphins.net; d standard/ste US$100/120; **P** **✕** **▯** **▯**) A little further down the road on a hilltop overlooking Playa Hermosa this place (at the time of writing) is the only resort in the area (wait a few years). Rooms are equipped with all amenities, though it's main appeal is the stunning location, which provides constant whale-watching opportunities. There is a pool, gym, bar and restaurant.

There are a number of small sodas on the Costanera in Uvita. One popular option is **Soda Salem** (casados US$2), which is located across the street from Hotel Tucan. There's no menu; just sit at the counter and ask what's cooking.

Getting There & Away

Most buses depart from the two sheltered bus stops on the Costanera in the main village.

Ciudad Cortés/Palmar US$1/1.50, one/1½ hours, buses originate in Dominical and pick up passengers in Uvita at about 4:45am and 10:30am (times depend on whether the driver stops for breakfast).

San Isidro de El General, via Dominical US$1.50, 1½ hours, departs 6am and 2pm.

San José, via Dominical & Quepos US$5, seven hours, 5am 6am, and 2pm.

PARQUE NACIONAL MARINO BALLENA

This pristine marine park protects coral and rock reefs in more than 5300 hectares of ocean and 110 hectares of land around Isla Ballena, south of Uvita. Although the park gets few human visitors, the beaches are frequently visited by a number of different animal species, including nesting seabirds, bottle-nosed dolphins and a variety of lizards. And, from May to November with a peak in September and October, both olive ridley and hawksbill turtles bury their eggs in the sand nightly.

However, the star attractions are the pods of humpback whales that pass through the national park from August to October and December to April. Scientists are unsure as to why humpback whales migrate here, though it's possible that Costa Rican waters may be one of only a few places in the world where humpback whales mate. There are actually two different groups of humpbacks that pass through the park – whales seen in the fall migrate from California waters, while those seen in the spring originate from Antarctica.

From Punta Uvita, heading southeast, the park includes 13km of sandy and rocky beaches, mangrove swamps, estuaries and rocky headlands. All six kinds of Costa Rican mangrove occur within the park. There are coral reefs near the shore, though they were heavily damaged by sediment run-off from the construction of the coastal highway.

The **ranger station** (☎ 743 8236; admission US$3) is in Playa Bahía, the seaside extension of Uvita. While there's a set admission, the guards at the gate will often charge less because of the limited number of visitors. The station is run by Asoparque (Association for the Development of the Ballena Marine National Park), a joint protection effort launched by local businesses in conjunction with Minae. It has worked hard at installing services, so be considerate and don't litter, cook with driftwood and use biodegradable soap when bathing.

Sights & Activities

The beaches at Marino Ballena are a stunning combination of golden sand and polished rock, and all of them are virtually deserted and perfect for peaceful swimming and sunning. And, the lack of visitors means you'll have a number of quiet opportunities for good **birding**.

From the station, you can walk out onto Punta Uvita and snorkel (best at low tide). Boats from Playa Bahía to Isla Ballena can be hired for US$30 per person for a two-hour snorkeling trip, though you are not allowed to stay overnight on the island.

If you're looking to get under the water, **Mystic Dive Center** (☎ 788 8636; www.mysticdivecenter .com; Playa Ventanas) is a PADI operation that offers scuba trips in the national park. There is also some decent surfing near the river mouth at southern end of **Playa Colonia**.

Sleeping

There are a few recommended lodges on the road alongside the national park, though most visitors choose to stay in Uvita.

The park has a free campground just 300m from the entrance, with toilets and showers. There is no electricity.

La Cusinga (☎ 770 2549, www.lacusingalodge .com; Finca Tres Hermanas; d US$116; P) About 5km south of Uvita, you'll see a sign on the beachside for this attractive place. The grounds have a small stream that provides hydroelectricity, a farm growing organic crops, five cabins with two to four beds, and two dorms sleeping eight. Each unit has a private hot shower. Food served is 'rural Tico' and includes fish, vegetarian options, and chicken, but no beef. Boat trips to the national park, hiking on several kilometers of trails, birding, snorkeling, surfing and other activities are offered.

Finca Bavaria (www.finca-bavaria.de; d US$64; additional person US$12; P ☼) On the inland side of the road, you'll see a signed dirt road leading to this quaint rain-forest inn decorated with wood accents and bamboo furniture. There are five spacious, clean, tiled rooms with private bathroom and mosquito nets draped over the beds. There's a hilltop pool with views of the ocean, and meals (cooked on request) are served in an open-air *rancho*. And of course, there's plenty of great German beer served by the stein. The owners speak German and English and can book local tours.

SOUTHEAST OF UVITA

Beyond Uvita, the road (all paved) follows the coast as far as Palmar, almost 40km away. There are several remote beaches along here that are becoming discovered as hotels begin opening their doors to visitors who travel the Costanera all the way through. This route provides a coastal (and less congested) alternative to the Interamericana, and provides convenient access to points in Osa. Daily buses between Dominical/Uvita and Cortés/Palmar can drop you near any of the places described here, though this area is best navigated by car. Telephone links here are poor; be patient when sending messages, faxes and emails.

About 14km south of Uvita is **Playa Tortuga**, though there is a bit of confusion regarding its name as it's called Turtle Beach by ex-pats, listed as Tortuga Abajo on maps and referred to by locals as Ojochal, which is the name of the nearest town. Whatever you call it, just be aware that it has fierce riptides and not recommended for swimming.

Diving trips of all types are offered at **Crocodive** (☎ 382 0199; www.crocodive.com; ☼ 8:30am-5pm Mon-Sat). It is situated across from the police station and behind the Ventana del Pacífico real estate office. The French owners also speak Spanish, English and German.

A signed turnoff on the eastern side of the road leads to the beautiful hilltop **Lookout at Turtle Beach** (☎ 350 9013, 378 7473; www .hotelcostarica.com; d US$70-80; P ⊠). The hotel has 12 brightly painted rooms featuring hot showers, ocean views and private balconies. A large deck in a tower above the pool is excellent for early-morning birding or slothful lounging. The hotel caters mostly to large groups but the pleasant California and South African owners will take drop-in guests from December to May. All local tours can be arranged. Rates vary, depending on the number of people in the group and the length of stay.

Along the beach side of the road is the beautifully kept **Hotel Villas Gaia** (☎ 256 9996, 282 5333, 382 8240; www.villasgaia.com; d US$70, large bungalow US$129; P ⊠). Set in tranquil forested grounds, 12 shiny wooden cabins are decorated with light, tropical colors and feature private terraces and steamy, hot water showers. There is also a restaurant, bar and a hilltop pool where you can swim a few laps while enjoying the panoramic view. The beach is a 20-minute hike down the hill. Credit cards are accepted.

A few hundred meters south of the Gaia, **Villas El Bosque** (☎ 398 2112; www.villaselbosque .com; d US$50, cabin with kitchen per wk US$300; P ⊠) is a friendly little place perched on a hilltop about 15 minutes from the beach. Guests can stay in one of three villas, each with hot showers, patios and ocean views. There are two private cabins with kitchen and hot shower. All rates include breakfast, and credit cards are accepted.

Just south and inland is the charming hilltop **El Perezoso** (in the USA ☎ /fax 435-518 8923; www.elperezoso.net; d incl breakfast US$55-70; P ⊠) with great views, a pool, and seven rooms in a small vine-covered villa. The British owner, Roger, is helpful and will pick guests up at the Palmar airport with prior arrangement. All units have private, hot-water bathroom, though some of the more expensive rooms have balconies overlooking the ocean and are slightly larger. It's definitely worth splurging for the room in the 'tower,' where you can pretend you're royalty and stare down at the fiefdom below. There is also a small on-site bar and restaurant.

Southern Costa Rica

In the oft-overlooked southern zone, the mist-shrouded peaks of the Cordillera de Talamanca descend dramatically into agricultural lowlands and raging river valleys, offering a completely different landscape to the rain forests and beaches on the coasts.

The well-trodden tourist trail does not traverse the southern sector – at least not yet. You'll be hard-pressed to find the resort hotels and fast-food chains that cater to *norteamericanos* in other parts of the country. Instead, you'll find limitless opportunities for bird-sighting, fly-fishing and mountain trekking. Not to mention the country's friendliest, most welcoming Ticos (though you may have to speak Spanish to appreciate them).

These hard-working, simple life–loving locals are employed primarily in agriculture. The countryside in the northern part of the region is carpeted with coffee plantations and family-run fincas (farms); while further south, African palms and banana plants dominate the landscape.

Southern Costa Rica is home to the country's single largest swath of protected land – the virtually unexplored Parque Internacional La Amistad, which extends across the border into Panama. The regional capital – the bustling town of San Isidro de El General – also serves as a gateway to nearby Parque Nacional Chirripó, home to the nation's highest mountains.

And while Monteverde is the country's most famous cloud forest, southern Costa Rica offers many other equally enticing opportunities to explore this mystical habitat. If you hope to spy the quetzal, you can start looking at the Parque Nacional Los Quetzales, the country's newest national park that was named in his honor. Note that this chapter refers to the numbered posts along the Interamericana, which count the kilometers from San José.

HIGHLIGHTS

- Catching a glimpse of the vibrant greens, reds and blues of the resplendent quetzal in the **Parque Nacional Los Quetzales** (p375)

- Following in the footstep's of one of Costa Rica's greatest ornithologists at **Los Cusingos Bird Sanctuary** (p379)

- Wandering around with your head in the clouds at **Cloudbridge Nature Preserve** (p382)

- Reaching Costa Rica's highest summit at **Cerro Chirripó** (p383)

- Witnessing the Festival de los Diablitos at the **Reserva Indígena Boruca** (p388)

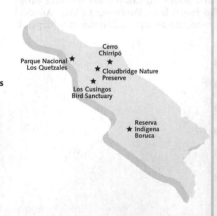

ZONA DE LOS SANTOS

Also called Zona Santa, or 'Saint's Zone,' this region of redolent coffee plantations and cool cloud forests isn't exactly a destination, but rather a collection of highland villages at the heart of relaxed, rural Costa Rica. They famously bear sainted names: San Pablo de León Cortés, Santa María de Dota, San Marcos de Tarrazú, San Cristóbal Sur, San Gerardo de Dota.

Birders flock to this area, no pun intended. The area around San Gerardo de Dota and the Cerro de la Muerte, especially, are famed for attracting high-altitude species. The elusive quetzal is such a celebrity in these parts that they named a national park after him – Costa Rica's newest – Parque Nacional Los Quetzales (see p375). Besides the rich, dark coffee that is grown and processed here, the local specialty is rainbow trout, which abound in the river steams and stocked ponds (see p374).

SAN MARCOS DE TARRAZÚ

San Marcos de Tarrazú bustles a bit more than the other Santos. For travelers passing through, it has a decent range of hotels and restaurants, but not much else. To learn what San Marcos is all about, find a spot on a bench in the central park, a prime locale for people-watching and coffee-drinking. There is a Banco Populaire with an ATM (Plus system only) next to Hotel Zacatecas.

Sleeping & Eating

Hotel Arbolado (☎ 546 5073; s/d/tr US$8/10/14; P ⚑) The most comfortable option for spending the night in San Marcos is this new motor lodge on the west side of the park. The salmon-colored rooms are a little cramped, but they have tasteful decorations and shiny new bathrooms with faux marble sinks and hot showers. A simple restaurant overlooks the covered parking lot.

Hotel Tocayos (☎ 546 6898, 546 6236; s/d US$8/12; ⚑) This strip of rooms is located downstairs from the Restaurante Chico. They are clean, comfortable and secure; however, the whole place is pretty dark since it is actually in the basement. There is a shared lounge area with windows if you need your Vitamin D.

Pizzeria las Tejas (☎ 546 6620; meals US$2-5) This popular lunch spot offers several varieties of pizza pies, as well as more traditional Tico fare. Around the corner from the church.

Los Santos Café (☎ 546 7881; coffee drinks US$1-3) A highlight of Los Santos. This little café showcases the region's finest, with straight-up coffee, elaborate espresso drinks and sweet coffee cocktails. Most of the people who come in here seem to know each other; or maybe they are that friendly to everybody.

SANTA MARÍA & VALLE DE DOTA

Centered on a green, grassy soccer field, Santa María de Dota is surrounded by lavish plantations. It's a great place to stretch your legs, though it's so quiet you can practically hear the coffee drying.

Coffee production is the economic lifeblood of this little village, from the surrounding farms to the Coopedota processing facility in town (which you'll find on the east side of the soccer field). Coopedota can give you the complete picture of where your caffeine fix comes from: the **Coffee Experience** (☎ 541 2828; coffee-experience@coopedota.com; tour US$12) is a half-day tour that takes guests to an organic coffee farm, visits the production facility and – most importantly – offers tastings of several different kinds of coffee.

A tree-hugger paradise, **Actividades Arboreales** (☎ 874 0817, in Canada 456 2477; www.treewalking .com; Providencia de Dota; 6hr tour for 2 people US$60) offers all sorts of adventures in the treetops. The farm, La Cabana, is rigged with treetop platforms, linked by suspension bridges and slack lines, creating a 'canopy maze.' For the purist, this place is also great for good old-fashioned tree climbing (or not so old-fashioned, like climbing up the *inside* of a 30m strangler fig). The price includes transportation from Copey de Dota or Ojo del Agua. Otherwise, if you have your own vehicle, drive east from Santa María and continue 12km past El Toucanet Lodge. Coming from the south, turn off the Interamericana at Ojo de Agua; drive about 21km south and west.

Tours

Cloudy Mountain Tour (☎ 283 1792; www.ecotourcr .com; adult/child US$73/60) is an all-day tour from San José that includes a hike around the cloud forest in the morning and a coffee-tasting tour in the afternoon.

SOUTHERN COSTA RICA

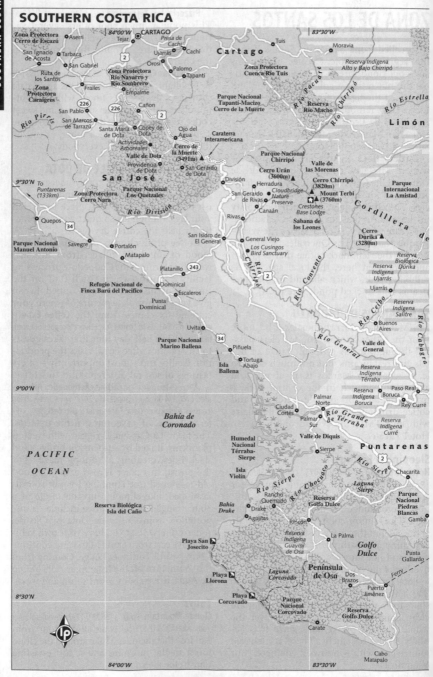

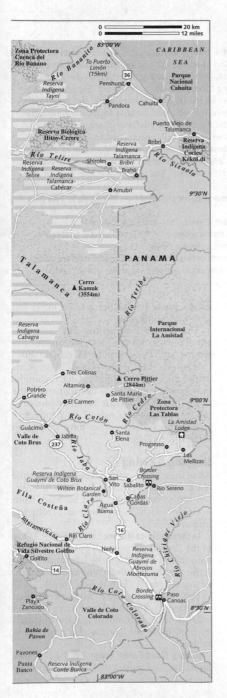

Sleeping & Eating

There is little reason to spend the night in Santa María proper, although there are some excellent lodges nearby.

Hotel Dota (☎ 541 1025; r per person US$10) This place is in the dead center of Santa María, diagonally opposite the soccer field. Ten rooms are equipped with TV and hot-water bathrooms. The place was closed for renovations at the time of research, so you can expect a price increase when it reopens.

El Toucanet Lodge (☎ 541 3131; www.eltoucanet .com; Copey de Dota; s/d incl breakfast US$45/65; P) At 1850m, this lovely country lodge offers seven rustic hardwood cabins with wonderful views of the Dota Valley. The valley and the surrounding cloud forest are excellent for birding, and co-owner Gary leads daily tours. Fruit birds are commonly sighted, as well as the resplendent quetzal and the namesake toucanet. The Flintstones-style hot tub is an excellent place to recover from the day's activities. Breakfast often features delicious fresh-baked whole wheat bread. Reach this place by driving east from Santa María, or turn off the Interamericana at Km 58.

La Casona de Sara (☎ 541 2258; mains US$2-4; ☷ 6am-7pm Mon-Sat) This traditional *soda*, 50m south of soccer field, is the most inviting place to eat in town, with daily specials and inexpensive *casados*.

Artesanías Café Amanecer (☎ 541 1616; ☷ sporadic) This sunny spot opposite the soccer field has homemade ice cream and specialty coffee drinks, as well as some handicrafts made by the local women's association. It's a treat, if you happen to be here when it's open.

Los Santos Café (☎ 571 1118; Interamericana Km 52; ☷ 10:30am-5:30pm) If you are traveling south on the Interamericana, this Coopadota café is a convenient place to stop and sample the fruits of the region, including fancy espresso drinks. Incidentally, the gas station at this intersection is the last place to fill your tank before San Isidro de El General.

Getting There & Away

Most drivers take the Interamericana south to Empalme almost 30km from Cartago. Just south of the station a signed turnoff leads west on a paved road and turns to Santa María de Dota (10km away), San Marcos de Tarrazú (7km beyond) and San Pablo (4km further). Six daily buses (US$2, 2½ hours) connect these towns to San José.

A RIVER RUNS THROUGH IT

While most sportfishers flock to the coast for the thrill of the big catch, the mountain rivers of the Cordillera de Talamanca offer a different kind of fishing experience. The crystal-clear waters and the cool air of the cloud forest are a delightfully tranquil setting, and the fish – here, rainbow trout – are no less tasty. The trout that populate these rivers are not endemic. Supposedly they were first introduced to Central American rivers by the US military in Panama, and the healthy fish made their way north into Costa Rican waters. The most popular spot for trout fishing is the Río Savegre, although the nearby Río Blanca and Río Dota also attract local anglers.

In order to maintain healthy populations, fishers are strongly encouraged to limit stream fishing to catch and release. If you want to take home your trout for dinner, fish in one of the local spring-fed ponds, which are well stocked with 30cm to 50cm trout. Success is guaranteed, and you just pay for what you take home (about US$4 per kilo). This is a great option for kids and other folks with less fishing karma.

Finca Madre Selva (☎ 224 6388; Copey de Dota) Grounds include a trout pond and hiking trails for a full day of fun.

Pesca Deportiva Río Blanca (☎ 541 1818, 541 1816; Copey de Dota) Near Santa María de Dota.

Ranchos La Isla (☎ 740 1038; San Gerardo de Dota) Borrow equipment to fish in the river or in nearby ponds. Bring your catch back to the restaurant, where staff will fry it up for your dinner.

Savegre Hotel de Montaña (☎ 740 1028; San Gerardo de Dota) This lodge provides equipment and guides for fly-fishing in the Río Savegre (US$30); or you can fish in the picturesque pond and pay for what you catch.

SAN GERARDO DE DOTA

The banks of the Río Savegre were long protected by the steep flanks of the Talamanca mountains, prohibiting settlement in this area. It was not until 1952 that Efrain Chacón and his brothers – driven by drought – made their way south from Copey de Dota and established a farm on the western slopes of Cerro de la Muerte – which would become the village of San Gerardo.

In the early days, they planted cubano beans, a typical subsistence crop in this region. That's as far as the Chacón family followed the typical trend, however. Eschewing coffee (which would not thrive at these high altitudes) and beef cattle (which would destroy the surrounding cloud forest), the Chacón family instead raised dairy cattle.

Later, they supplemented dairy-farm activity by stocking their streams with trout and planting apple orchards and other fruit trees. The former had the effect of attracting anglers from San José, while the latter (along with the wild avocado trees that were abundant) attracted the resplendent quetzal, in turn attracting birders. As tourism in Costa Rica flourished, so did San Gerardo.

Today this little farming village has become famous for highland birding. Quetzals are spotted frequently every April and May (during breeding season), but are seen all year. Indeed, San Gerardo is the easiest access point to the Parque Nacional Los Quetzales (opposite).

The trout fishing in the Río Savegre is good: the seasons are May and June for fly-fishing and December to March for lure-fishing (see the boxed text A River Runs Through It, above). And the Chacón family, now several generations deep, operates the well-established Savegre Hotel de Montaña (above) on the grounds of its productive farm, while other facilities have sprung up around the village.

Sleeping & Eating

All of these places offer access to the Parque Nacional Los Quetzales. Water is hot, unless otherwise noted. Listed in order from north to south, along the road from the Interamericana:

La Comida Tipica Miriam (cabins US$30; P) One of the first places you will pass in San Gerardo (about 6km from the Interamericana) is the cozy house advertising comida tipica, or 'typical meals'. Eating here (meals US$3 to US$6) is almost like receiving a personal invitation to dine in a Tico home: the food is delicious and abundant and the hospitality even more so. Miriam also rents a few cabins.

Dantica Cloud Forest Lodge (☎ 352 2761; www .dantica.com; d incl breakfast US$122; P) Definitely the slickest place in San Gerardo, if not the whole southern sector. Three beautiful, upscale cabins have two bedrooms, each with private bathroom, a full kitchen and a Jacuzzi. The walls are graced with artwork from the owner's native Colombia, some of which you can buy in the on-site gallery, while modern furniture and stone and hardwood floors provide a contemporary contrast. The kicker, though, is the wall of windows, with an extraordinary vista over the cloud forest. A romantic breakfast is served on your private terrace.

Trogon Lodge (☎ in Costa Rica 293 8181, in San José 223 2421; www.grupomawamba.com; standard s/d US$51/73, junior ste US$116/140; P) The Trogon Lodge is part of the Grupo Mawamba, which caters mostly to package tourists escaping the coastal heat in the cloud forest. Wooden cabins are clustered around a manmade pond, on grounds overflowing with flowers. Horseback riding (US$25), mountain-biking (US$10) and canopy-riding (US$35) are all on the agenda.

Ranchos La Isla & Restaurant Los Lagos (☎ 740 1038; camping per person US$4; P) The Chinchilla family goes all out to make sure its guests are entertained, from guiding hikes to nearby waterfalls to seeking the illusive quetzal. Shady campsites are down along the river. Meals cost US$3 to US$5. Make sure you have a sleeping bag as it gets cold at night!

Cabinas El Quetzal (☎ 740 1036; r per person incl 3 meals US$35; P) About 1km after the Trogon Lodge turnoff, four quaint cabins enjoy a pleasant riverside setting. Each cabin is a little different: birders will appreciate the one with a balcony overlooking the river, while cold-blooded creatures will prefer the fireplace.

Savegre Hotel de Montaña (☎ 740 1028; www .savegre.co.cr; d standard/ste incl 3 meals US$156/210; P) Set on a 160-hectare orchard and reserve, this famous place has been owned and operated by the Chacón family since 1957. It's now something of a Costa Rica institution, especially among birders. A feeder hangs near every window, attracting an amazing variety of hummingbirds; while the edge of the grounds is lined with avocado trees, the favorite perch of the quetzal. The Savegre suites are gorgeous: wrought-iron chandeliers hang from the high wood ceilings; rich wood furniture is arranged around a stone fireplace. The standard rooms are less inspiring and perhaps overpriced, although

they are still comfortable. Buffet-style meals receive mixed reviews.

Suria Mountain Lodge (☎ 740 1004; www.geo cities.com/suriacabins; r per person incl 3 meals US$60; P) Just past the Savegre, this is a friendly, family-run lodge. The cabins are immaculate and new, with high wood ceilings and shiny tiled bathrooms. Each has a private porch, overlooking relatively barren grounds. Meals are served in the inviting restaurant.

Getting There & Away
The turnoff to San Gerardo de Dota is near Km 80 on the Interamericana. From here, the dirt road descends 8km to the village. The road is very steep: be careful if you're in an ordinary car. Buses between San José and San Isidro de El General (US$4, three hours) can drop you off at the turnoff. Both the Trogon Lodge and Savegre Hotel de Montaña will pick you up if you call ahead.

PARQUE NACIONAL LOS QUETZALES
Costa Rica's newest national park, formerly the Reserva Los Santos, was made official in 2005. Spread along both banks of the Río Sevegre, the park covers 5000 hectares of rain and cloud forest. At altitudes of 2000 to 3000m, this is the heart of the Cordillera de Talamanca, which means picturesque mountain streams and glacial lakes at a range of altitudes.

The Sevegre, which starts high up on the Cerro de la Muerte, pours out into the Pacific near the coastal town of Savegre. This area is extremely important to biodiversity in Costa Rica: although it covers a relatively small area, the Savegre watershed contains approximately 20% of all the registered species of Costa Rica.

As the park's new name implies, this area is rich in birdlife. The emerald green and ruby red quetzal is only one of the many species that call this park home. Trogons, hummingbirds, great tinamous and sooty robins are some bird favorites. Many lodges cater to hopeful birders in this area, and some even 'guarantee' sightings during certain seasons. Besides the quetzal, the park is home to several other endangered species, including the jaguar, Baird's tapir, black guan and squirrel monkey.

The flora at these higher altitudes is very different from what you will see in the lowland forests. It is mostly classified as montane and premontane forests, the latter being the second-most endangered life zone in Costa Rica. Massive oak trees and other alpine plants are characteristic.

The park does not have any facilities for tourists, although all of the lodges around San Gerardo de Dota offer hiking and birding tours. If you wish to explore on your own, follow the road to San Gerardo to its end, from where a trail will lead you through lush lower-montane forest to a spectacular waterfall. It's worth inquiring about more specific directions before you set out.

EMPALME TO SAN ISIDRO

Along the stretch between Empalme and San Isidro de El General, the highway passes the highest point along the Interamericana, the famed **Cerro de la Muerte** (3491m). This is the northernmost extent of the *páramo*, a highland shrub and tussock grass habitat more common in the Andes than in Costa Rica. When the fog clears, this area offers exquisite panoramic views of the Cordillera Talamanca on all sides – but only for a moment, as the fog undoubtedly rolls back in almost immediately. Welcome to the cloud forest.

The so-called 'Mountain of Death' received this moniker before the road was built; but the steep, fog-shrouded highway, which climbs into the clouds, is still considered one of the most dangerous in Costa Rica. The road itself is paved and smooth, but it twists and turns around the mountain, making overtaking treacherous. During the rainy season landslides may partially or completely block the road. As in most places in rural Costa Rica, it's best to avoid driving at night.

This area is actually part of the Parque Nacional Tapantí-Macizo Cerro de la Muerte (p172), which is accessible from the north.

Sleeping & Eating

All the lodges in this area offer access to hiking trails and opportunities for birding. Listed from north to south:

Albergue de Montaña Tapantí (☎ 232 0386, 301 5022; Interamericana Km 62; d/q US$30/36; P) You can't miss the brightly painted, pink-and-green edifice of this family-run mountain lodge, just north of the signed turnoff at Km 62. This welcoming building is the restaurant, which is highly recommended for its traditional Tico food (meals US$4 to US$8). Big two-room cabins have stucco walls, parquet floors and slightly worn furniture. A network of trails leads down the mountain for birders and other adventurers to explore.

Mirador de Quetzales (☎ 771 8456; www.exploring costarica.com/mirador/quetzales.html; Interamericana Km 70; r/cabin per person incl 2 meals US$32/45; P) About 1km west of the Interamericana, Eddie Serrano's farm – as this place is known – is an excellent-value midrange lodging option. Painted wood walls and colorful curtains brighten up the eight cozy cabins that line the farm's ridge (and electric heaters warm them up). They have cramped, clean bathrooms with lukewarm water. In the main lodge, four simple rooms share bathrooms. Prices include an early-morning 'quetzal walk'. Those bright beauties reside in these forested hills year-round, but sightings are guaranteed between November and April.

Iyök Ami (☎ 387 2238, 772 0222; www.iyokami.com; Interamericana Km 71; reserve admission US$5, r per person US$30-40; P) Meaning 'Mother Earth' in Bribrí, Iyök Ami is a wonderful cloud-forest reserve, rustic lodge and quaint coffee shop, all in one. Guests have access to 6km of trails and a picturesque lake, as well as delicious Tico meals (US$10 per day). This place is run by one Tica woman, so be sure to call in advance so she will be there to greet you.

Cabinas Georgina (☎ 771 1299, 770 8043; Interamericana Km 95; d US$13; P) About 5km beyond the highest point on the Interamericana, this roadside joint is a popular stop for drivers heading south, including public buses, which sometimes make a pit stop. Everyone appreciates the hot coffee and filling fare, served up cafeteria-style, not to mention the sparkling clean bathrooms. Simple rooms provide hot showers and extra blankets, all of which are needed at this high altitude (3100m).

Bosque del Tolomuco (☎ 847 7207; www.bosque deltolomuco.com; Interamericana Km 118; d incl breakfast US$55-70; P ☻) Named for the sly tayra (tree otter) spotted on the grounds, this new lodge is run by a lovely, loquacious Canadian couple. There are four spacious, light-filled cabins, the most charming of which is the secluded 'Hummingbird Cabin'. The grounds offer 5km of hiking trails, ample opportunities to indulge in bird-watching and some magnificent views of Los Cruces.

A made-to-order gourmet dinner is also available with advance notice.

Mirador Vista del Valle (☎ 384 4685, 836 6193; www.vistadelvallecr.com; Interamericana Km 119; d US$55, extra person US$15; **P**) Aptly named, this restaurant (meals US$3 to US$8) boasts one of the best views of the valley. Windows on three sides allow you to take it all in, while feasting on local specialties like fried trout fillet, and fresh-brewed coffee. Below the restaurant, rustic wood cabins (built only from cultivated wood) are brightened by colorful tapestries. Set on 40 hectares, 11km of trails allow for excellent bird-watching and a very interesting tour about coffee production.

VALLE DE EL GENERAL

Although the Valle de El General is home to southern Costa Rica's largest town, the area is decidedly rural. Small, family-run fincas dot this fertile valley, growing subsistence crops like beans, corn, coffee and sugar cane.

The highest mountains of the Cordillera Talamanca grow from these foothills, with massive peaks like the Cerro Chirripó (3820m) and the Cerro Ventisqueros (3812m) towering above. The high altitudes are the main draw to these parts: peakbaggers can't resist Costa Rica's highest summit; while birdwatchers visit the many nature preserves and wildlife sanctuaries to tick off their highland and southern endemic species.

SAN ISIDRO DE EL GENERAL

San Isidro de El General (population 45,000), 136km south of San José, is the 'big city' as far as southern Costa Rica is concerned. Built right on the Interamericana, it is always bustling, as travelers and truck drivers whiz through on their way to or from the capital. The town has sprouted up along this route, with motels, gas stations, supermarkets and even a McDonald's vying for drivers' attention.

The heart of San Isidro, however, is south of here, in the narrow streets that are clustered around Parque Central. Normally a meeting place for townsfolk, the park was blocked off at the time of research; rumor has it that San Isidro will be enjoying a brand new landscaped park by the end of 2006. An uncharacteristic but impressive cathedral lords over the eastern end of this square. Travelers are well cared for, with plenty of banks, Internet access and good lodging facilities.

Most travelers who stop in San Isidro are making their way east to Parque Nacional Chirripó or south to Dominical. But the immediate outskirts also offers breathtaking mountain scenery, prime birding opportunities and plenty of day-trip excursions.

Locals sometimes refer to San Isidro as Pérez (the county is Pérez Zeledón). Though labeled on the map, streets are poorly signed and everyone uses landmarks to orient themselves (see the boxed text What's That Address?, p539).

Information

Banco Coopealianza (Av 4 btwn Calles 2 & 4) Have 24-hour ATMs on the Cirrus network. There's a second branch at Avenida 2 between Calles Central & 1.

Brunc@Net Café (☎ 771 3235; Av Central btwn Calles Central & 1; per hr US$1.20; 8am-8pm Mon-Sat, 9am-5pm Sun)

BTC Internet (☎ 771 3993; Av 2 btwn Calles Central & 1; per hr US$1; 8:30am-9pm Mon-Fri, 8:30am-8pm Sat, 10am-4pm Sun)

Ciprotur (☎ 770 9393; www.ecotourism.co.cr; Calle 4 btwn Avs 1 & 3; 7:30am-5pm Mon-Fri, 8am-noon Sat) Tourist office with information about the southern Pacific region.

Clínica El Labrador (☎ 771 7115, 771 5354; Calle 1 btwn Avs 8 & 10) This medical service has 10 private doctors in a variety of specialties.

Hotel San Isidro (☎ 770 6389; Interamericana; per hr US$0.80; 9am-8:30pm Mon-Sat) Internet access. Conveniently located on the highway, 2km south of the center.

Minae park service office (Sinac; ☎ 771 3155; aclap@sinac.go.cr; Calle 2 btwn Avs 2 & 4; 8am-noon & 1-4pm Mon-Fri) Dispenses a minimal amount of information about Parque Nacional Chirripó. On the first working day of the month, you can try to make reservations for the mountaintop hostel at Chirripó for following months – see p385 for details.

Selva Mar (☎ 771 4582, 771 4579; www.exploringcostarica.com; Calle 1 btwn Avs 2 & 4; 8am-noon & 1:30-6pm) Useful for booking area hotels and buying plane tickets. Also houses offices for Costa Rica Trekking Adventures.

Tours

Aratinga Tours (☎ 770 6324; www.aratinga-tours .com) Pieter Westra specializes in bird tours in his native

Dutch, but he is fluent in English, Spanish and many dialects of bird. His website provides an excellent introduction to birding in Costa Rica. Based at Talari Mountain Lodge (p380).

Sunny Travel (☎ 771 9686; www.sunnycostarica.com) Organizes a wide variety of tours, including a two-day rafting trip on the Ríos Savegre and División (US$250 per person) and a variety of birding programs.

Courses

SEPA (☎ 770 1457; www.sabalolodge.com/sepaschool .html; western end of Av 1) runs Spanish-language programs; they start at with/without home-stay US$333/195. Additional options include a longer-term course with environmental classes or volunteering at a local school or park.

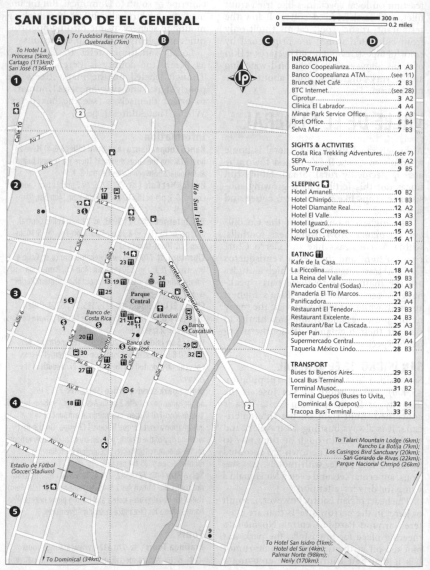

SAN ISIDRO DE EL GENERAL

0 ————— 300 m
0 ————— 0.2 miles

INFORMATION
Banco Coopealianza.............................**1** A3
Banco Coopealianza ATM.............(see 11)
Brunc@ Net Café................................**2** B3
BTC Internet..................................(see 28)
Ciprotur...**3** A2
Clínica El Labrador............................**4** A4
Minae Park Service Office...................**5** A3
Post Office..**6** B4
Selva Mar...**7** B3

SIGHTS & ACTIVITIES
Costa Rica Trekking Adventures.......(see 7)
SEPA...**8** A2
Sunny Travel.....................................**9** B5

SLEEPING
Hotel Amaneli...................................**10** B2
Hotel Chirripó...................................**11** B3
Hotel Diamante Real..........................**12** A2
Hotel El Valle...................................**13** A3
Hotel Iguazú....................................**14** B3
Hotel Los Crestones...........................**15** A5
New Iguazú......................................**16** A1

EATING
Kafe de la Casa.................................**17** A2
La Piccolina......................................**18** A4
La Reina del Valle..............................**19** B3
Mercado Central (Sodas).....................**20** A3
Panadería El Tío Marcos.....................**21** B3
Panificadora.....................................**22** A4
Restaurant El Tenedor........................**23** B3
Restaurant Excelente..........................**24** B3
Restaurant/Bar La Cascada..................**25** A3
Super Pan..**26** B4
Supermercado Central........................**27** A4
Taquería México Lindo.......................**28** B3

TRANSPORT
Buses to Buenos Aires........................**29** B3
Local Bus Terminal............................**30** A4
Terminal Musoc.................................**31** B2
Terminal Quepos (Buses to Uvita,
    Dominical & Quepos)......................**32** B4
Tracopa Bus Terminal.........................**33** B3

To Fudebiol Reserve (7km);
Quebradas (7km)

To Hotel La
Princesa (5km);
Cartago (113km);
San José (136km)

Av 7
Av 5
Av 3
Av 1

Calle 10
Calle 8
Calle 6
Calle 4
Calle 2
Calle Central

Río San Isidro

Carretera Interamericana

Av Central

Parque
Central

Cathedral

Banco de
Costa Rica

Banco de
San José

Banco
Cuscatlán

Av 4
Av 6
Av 8
Av 10
Av 12
Av 14

Estadio de Fútbol
(Soccer Stadium)

To Talari Mountain Lodge (6km);
Rancho La Botija (7km);
Los Cusingos Bird Sanctuary (20km);
San Gerardo de Rivas (22km);
Parque Nacional Chrripó (26km)

To Hotel San Isidro (1km);
Hotel del Sur (4km);
Palmar Norte (98km);
Neily (170km)

To Dominical (34km)

DAY TRIPPER

Not to disparage El General, but there's no point in hanging around town if you don't have to. Here's what you can do with your free day instead:

Fudebiol Reserve (Las Quebradas Biological Center; ☎ 771 4131; admission US$2; ☽ 8am-4pm Tue-Sun) Heading in the opposite direction, Fudebiol is a community reserve along the Río Quebradas. Its 750-hectare grounds include extensive hiking trails, some with rewarding lookout spots, a cooling pond and a butterfly farm (always a treat for kids). Fudebiol offers volunteer opportunities for travelers who want to live with a local family and work at the reserve; this educational facility also has lodging for visiting groups. For information, contact Ciprotur (p377).

Los Cusingos Bird Sanctuary (☎ 200 5472; www.cct.or.cr; Quizarrá; adult/child US$10/5; ☽ 7am-4pm Tue-Sun) This sanctuary and a museum are on the grounds of the farm that was once home to the great ornithologist Dr Alexander Skutch. Author of the birder's bible, *A Guide to the Birds of Costa Rica,* Dr Skutch enjoyed a long and fruitful career studying the birds of the tropics. Much of his work took place at this 78-hectare reserve, which is now open to the public. The grounds are wonderful for watching wildlife, wandering the trails and meditating on the mysteries of nature, as Dr Skutch often did. The great scientist's home is due to open as a museum dedicated to his life and work. To get to Los Cusingos, drive 8km north on the road to San Gerardo de Rivas. Turn right at Rivas and continue 5km through General Viejo, then turn east to Quizarrá. Aratinga Tours and Sunny Travel both lead birding walks here (p377).

Rancho La Botija (☎ 770 2146, 770 2147; www.rancholabotija.com; Rivas; admission US$5; ☽ 8:30am-5pm Tue-Sun, guided tours 9am) A great option for families with kids, this is a working coffee and sugar farm. Trails traverse the grounds, and a daily guided hike leads to the famous 'Indian Rock,' an ancient stone carved with pre-Columbian petroglyphs. There is entertainment for all ages, whether you paddle a kayak around the lake or a raft around the swimming pool. A restaurant and a few cabins (wheelchair accessible; double including breakfast US$61) are on-site. The rancho is 7km from the Interamericana along the road to San Gerardo de Rivas.

Sleeping

In addition to the places to sleep listed here, all three private reserves (see the boxed text Day Tripper, above) offer lodging options.

Hotel El Valle (☎ 771 0246; fax 771 0220; Calle 2 btwn Avs Central & 2; s/d US$10/15; P) If you don't lose yourself in the cavernous lobby, you will find the rooms here are spacious and clean with large windows letting in plenty of light. Cheaper rooms share slightly grotty bathrooms. This place is blessedly quiet – an anomaly for its central location and low price.

Hotel Chirripó (☎ 771 0529; Av 2 btwn Calles Central & 1; s/d/tr/q with bathroom US$10/17/20/27, s/d without bathroom US$6/10; P) Popular with budget travelers, here you'll find bare, whitewashed rooms that are barren but dirt-free. A few flowering plants and a festive mural in the lobby brighten otherwise stark surroundings. The *soda* out front is a good spot to see who else is in town.

Hotel Amaneli (☎ 771 0352; cnr Calle 2 & the Interamericana; r per person US$9-10) This sprawling place does not have the best location, but its 30 rooms offer good value. Dark, polished wood detailing and matching curtains and bedspreads make the place rather attractive, and all rooms have cable TV and electric water heaters. Ask for a room away from the highway so the roar of the trucks won't disturb you.

Hotel Iguazú (☎ 771 2571; cnr Av 1 & Calle Central; s/d/tr US$12/20/28; P) Just one block south of the Interamericana, this centrally located hotel offers plain, spacious rooms with white-paneled walls and linoleum floors, plus fans and TV. The place looks slightly foreboding from the outside but the staff is friendly and accommodating.

New Iguazú (☎ 771 0076; Calle 10; s/d/tr US$16/ 22/ 38; P ⚇) A new facility, this is an upgrade of Hotel Iguazú.

Hotel San Isidro (☎ 770 3444; www.hotelsanisidro .com; Interamericana; s/d US$12/24; P ⚇ 🖳 🖳) This roadside motel does not have much character, but it is clean, comfortable and convenient for those travelers who have no business in San Isidro. Everything you need – from bank to Internet to pizza place – is right here in this complex, 2km south of the center.

Hotel Los Crestones (☎ 770 1200, 770 1500; www .hotelloscrestones.com; Calle Central at Av 14; s/d US$30/40, with air-con US$40/45, extra person US$10; P ⚇) This sharp motor court is decked with blooming flowerboxes and climbing vines outside, while inside, rooms feature attractive furniture, TV and ceiling fans. The attentive staff keeps this place running efficiently. An attached café is an excellent choice for fresh coffee and fluffy omelettes.

Hotel Diamante Real (☎ 770 6230; www.hotel diamantereal.com; cnr Av 3 & Calle 4; d/tr/q/ste US$34/53/58/68; P ✆ ⌨ ⌘) 'Executive Elegance' is the boast of this upscale business hotel. Indeed all the expected amenities are there, including telephones with voice mail and wi-fi access. The classy quarters are painted bright yellow and fitted with shiny black lacquer furniture.

AROUND SAN ISIDRO

Hotel La Princesa (☎ 772 0324; www.laprincesahotel .com; San Rafael; d/q US$25/30; P) If sitting in the hot tub and watching the sun drop behind the Talamanca mountains sounds appealing, La Princesa is for you. Eight brand-new rooms are decorated tastefully, with wood furniture and fabulous views. Lovely gardens are filled with blooms and birds. Turn off the Interamericana 5km north of San Isidro in the barrio of San Rafael.

Talari Mountain Lodge (☎ 771 0341; www.talari .co.cr; Rivas; s/d incl breakfast US$36/56, extra child/adult US$10/20; P ✆) This secluded mountain lodge exudes charm, as does the Dutch-Tica couple who runs the place. They are ever-accommodating, also offering arrangements for treks to Chirripó (US$165 per person) and customized bird tours (Pieter Westra of Aratinga Tours is their son). Accommodations are simple: clean cabins, all equipped with refrigerators and fans. Breakfast is hearty. Birdlife is prolific on these grounds, and 2km of trails wind through the forest and along the Río El General. Drive 7km south of San Isidro on the road to San Gerardo de Rivas.

Hotel del Sur (☎ 771 3033; http://hoteldelsur.net; standard/superior US$53/75; P ✆ ⌨ ⌘) This is an option for guests who don't want to leave the hotel; it's 5km south of the center, convenient to the highway but not much else. The hotel offers every facility you might desire, plus a few you probably don't (read: casino). The business complex has 48 guestrooms (huge by local standards), several conference rooms and an upscale restaurant and bar. Rooms are very comfortable, with modern though nondescript decor. Don't stay too long: you will forget you are in Costa Rica.

Eating & Drinking

Kafe de la Casa (☎ 770 4816; Av 3 btwn Calles 2 & 4; meals US$4-6; ⏱ 7am-8pm) Set in an old Tico house, this bohemian café features an open kitchen and shady garden seating. Inside, each room is painted in bright colors and decorated with eclectic artwork. With a menu featuring excellent breakfasts, light lunches and plenty of coffee drinks, this funky place receives a stream of regulars.

La Piccolina (☎ 71 0031; Calle Central btwn Avs 8 & 10; dishes US$5; ⏱ 11am-10pm Wed-Mon) The terrace filled with greenery and the Latin ballads in the air create an inviting atmosphere for pizzas, pasta and Tico food.

Taquería México Lindo (☎ 771 8222; Av 2 btwn Calles Central & 1; dishes S$3-5; ⏱ 10am-8:30pm) For a welcome change of pace, stop by this *taquería* for tasty tacos, of course, as well as burritos, nachos, fajitas and more. All the Mexican favorites are available with beef, chicken, pork or vegetables, not to mention homemade guacamole and several kinds of salsa. Photos of Mexico and festive piñatas will send you south – er, north – of the border.

La Reina del Valle (☎ 771 4860; cnr Calle Central & Av Central; dishes US$3-5) A beautiful, tile and teak restaurant is on the 1st floor, while mosaic-tiled steps lead up to the 2nd-floor open-air bar. Both offer views over Parque Central – a nice place to witness the sights and sounds of San Isidro.

Restaurant/Bar La Cascada (☎ 771 6479; cnr Calle 2 & Av 2; dishes US$3.50-9) Pleasant restaurant by day, trendy bar by night. The well-stocked bar, massive TV screens showing music videos, and an extensive menu of pub grub attract plenty of local youth, who spend quality time, getting to know the beer, the burgers and each other.

Restaurant El Tenedor (☎ 771 0881; Calle Central btwn Avs Central & 1; dishes US$1-7; ⏱ 10am-11pm) Though pizza is the specialty, this informal joint also serves pasta, burgers, gyros and more. This family-friendly place has the atmosphere of a fast-food restaurant, with a few tables on the balcony overlooking the busy street below. There is another outlet on the Interamericana near the Hotel San Isidro.

Restaurant Excelente (☎ 771 8157; Av Central btwn Calles Central & 1; dishes US$4-6; ⏱ 11:30am-10:30pm Thu-Tue) Excellent, indeed. With white table linens and soft lighting, this Chinese restaurant is upscale, by San Isidro standards.

It's a fine place to take a break from casados and chow down on some chow mein.

Travelers watching their colones should head for the inexpensive *sodas* in the **Mercado Central** (Av 4 btwn Calles Central & 2), while self-caterers can shop at the **Supermercado Central** (Ave 6 btwn Calles Central & 2; ☼ 7am-9pm Mon-Sat, 8am-2pm Sun), one block south.

There is no shortage of freshly baked goods:

Panadería El Tío Marcos (Av 2 btwn Calles Central & 1) Small seating area, but no coffee.

Panificadora (☎ 771 5878) Open early for breakfast, but no seating area.

Super Pan (☎ 771 1353; Calle 1 btwn Avs 4 & 6)

Getting There & Away

BUS
In San Isidro the local bus terminal on Avenida 6 serves nearby villages. Long-distance buses leave from various points near the Interamericana and are frequently packed, so buy tickets early.

From Tracopa Terminal
The following buses originate in other destinations and pick up passengers on a space-available basis. The **Tracopa terminal** (☎ 771 0468) is on the Interamericana, just southwest of Avenida Central. Times are approximate, so get there early.

Agua Buena Depart 9:30am, 11:30am, 2:30pm and 5:45pm.

Ciudad Cortés Depart 11:30am and 5:30pm.

Coto 47 Depart 1:30pm.

David, Panama Depart 10:30am.

Golfito Depart 10am and 6pm.

Palmar Norte/Ciudad Neily $2.75/5, three/six hours, depart 4:45am, 7:30am 12:30pm and 3pm.

Paso Canoas Five hours, depart 8:30am, 10:30am, 2:30pm, 4pm, 7:30pm and 9pm.

San José US$3, three hours, depart 7:30am, 8am, 9:30am, 10:30am, 11am, 1:30pm, 4pm, 5:45pm and 7:30pm.

San Vito 3½ hours, depart 5:30am and 2pm.

From Terminal Quepos
Terminal Quepos (☎ 771 2550) is on the side street south of the Tracopa terminal. Buses originate in San Isidro.

Dominical US$1, 2½ hours, depart 7am, 8am, 1:30pm and 4pm.

Palmar Norte/Puerto Jiménez US$2.75/5, three/six hours, depart 6:30am and 3pm.

Quepos US$3, three hours, depart 7am and 1:30pm.

Uvita US$1.25, 1½ hours, depart 8:30am and 4pm.

From Other Bus Stops
These buses all originate in San Isidro:

Buenos Aires (Gafeso) US$1.50, one hour, depart hourly 5am to 5pm from north of Terminal Quepos.

San Gerardo de Rivas, for Parque Nacional Chirripó US$1, 2½ hours, depart from Parque Central at 5am and from the main terminal on Av 6 at 2pm.

San José US$3, three hours, depart from Terminal Musoc on Interamericana btwn Calles 2 and 4 every hour from 5:30am to 5:30pm.

TAXI
A 4WD taxi to San Gerardo de Rivas will cost at least US$17. A taxi all the way up to Albergue Urán will cost US$20. (As always, these rates vary depending on road conditions.)

SAN GERARDO DE RIVAS
The road to San Gerardo de Rivas winds its way 22km up the valley of the Río Chirripó. The road is paved for the first 10km or so; after the town of Rivas, however, it is a gravel road that is bumpy, narrow and steep. The 'center' of San Gerardo – as it is – consists of the ubiquitous soccer field and the *pulpería* opposite. Otherwise, there's not much to this village – just the family-run farms and cabinas that are strung along this road.

The backdrop to this village scene is the rushing Río Chirripó and the rocky peak of the same name. The river is fierce in these parts, crashing over cliffs and boulders as it tumbles down the mountain. It's breathtaking, alpine scenery, though at this altitude (1350m) it's often cloudy. Temperatures are noticeably cool and birdlife is bounteous.

While most travelers to San Gerardo are on their way up Cerro Chirripó, you don't have to climb the mountain to be able to walk around with your head in the clouds. Cloudbridge Nature Preserve is a perfect alternative for those who don't have the time (or energy) to go all the way to the summit. And even a simple stroll around the village provides a cool reprieve from the coastal heat.

Information
Chirripó ranger station (Sinac; ☎ 200 5348; ☼ 6:30am-noon & 1-4:30pm) Located about 1km below the soccer field on the road from San Isidro. Stop by here (the earlier the better) to check for space availability at Los Crestones mountaintop hostel, and to confirm and pay your fee before setting out.

Sights & Activities

About 2km past the trailhead to Cerro Chirripó you will find the entrance to the mystical, magical **Cloudbridge Nature Preserve** (in the USA ☎ 212-362 9391; www.cloudbridge.org; admission by donation; ☼ sunrise-sunset). Covering 182 hectares on the side of Cerro Chirripó, this private reserve is an ongoing reforestation and preservation project, spearheaded by New Yorkers Ian and Genevieve Giddy. A network of trails traverses part of the property, which is easy to explore independently; maps are available. Hike to two waterfalls, including the magnificent **Catarata Pacífica**, which is close to the entrance. You are bound to see some amazing birdlife, including the vibrant emerald toucanet, the endangered black guan and many other cloud-forest species. Check out the website if you are interested in volunteering on the reforestation program at Cloudbridge. You can drive up here if you have a 4WD; otherwise it's a steep but rewarding hike.

If you can't stand the thought of going for another hike, you will undoubtedly appreciate a soak in the **thermal hot springs** (☎ 391 8107; Herradura; admission US$3; ☼ 7am-6pm) that are about 2km north of San Gerardo. Just above the ranger station the road forks; take the left fork and walk for about 1km on a paved road. Turn right and take the rickety suspension bridge over the river. A switchback trail will lead you another 1km to a house with a *soda*, which is the entrance to the springs.

Sleeping & Eating

Hotels are all situated along the narrow road that runs parallel to the river. All these options offer hot-water showers (a necessity in these parts). They are listed in order from south to north (uphill):

Río Chirripó Retreat (☎ 364 9527, in the USA 707-937 3775; www.riochirripo.com; Canaán; s/d/tr incl breakfast US$49/69/79; Ⓟ Ⓡ) About 1.5km below the ranger station, in Canaán, this upscale lodge is sometimes used for group retreats. The space is ideal, with a beautiful new yoga studio overlooking the river and a vast open-air, Santa Fe–style communal area. You can hear the rush of the river from eight secluded cabins, where woven blankets and stenciled walls evoke the southwest USA. Grounds include hiking trails and a heated pool and hot tub with views.

Hotel El Pelicano (☎ 382 3000; www.hotelelpelicano.net; d/tr with bathroom US$30/60, r per person without bathroom US$10; Ⓟ Ⓡ) About 300m below the ranger station, this rustic, wood lodge has 10 spotless, simple rooms that share a bathroom and a balcony overlooking the river valley. Spacious cabins have private facilities and a few other perks. The highlight is the gallery of the owner, a late-blooming artist who sculpts whimsical wood pieces. A restaurant and recreation room are onsite; all rates include transport to the park entrance.

Cabinas La Marín (☎ 393 7894; r per person with/without bathroom US$14/7) Next door to the ranger station, this very basic place has eight stuffy rooms with wood walls and not much else. With the exception of the hot showers, sleeping here is almost like camping. Reception is friendly, and the restaurant opens early to serve breakfast before you hike. The small store on site is useful for stocking up on snacks before you hit the trails.

Cabinas y Restaurante El Bosque (☎ 771 4129; d with bathroom US$12, r without bathroom per person US$8) Set in the midst of overflowing gardens, this family affair offers sunless rooms with shared bathrooms, as well as newer, more spacious units with private facilities. Some kitsch art by a local painter adorns the restaurant-bar, where you can enjoy fantastic views of the forest and river from the outdoor deck. Service is lackluster and slow, but at least you have something to look at while you wait. Just north of the ranger station.

Cabinas y Restaurante El Descanso (☎ 369 0067; marlaequ@costarricense.cr; camping per person US$4, r per person with/without bathroom US$10/8; Ⓟ) This quaint and quiet homestead, run by the ever-accommodating Elizondo family, is an excellent budget option. Skip the cheaper, cell-like rooms and spring for a brighter, more spacious unit on the 2nd floor, with private bathroom and balcony. Transport to the park entrance for trekkers is included in the rate.

Hotel y Restaurant Roca Dura Café (☎ 262 7218; luisrocadura@hotmail.com; camping per person US$5, d with bathroom US$20-30, r without bathroom per person US$5; Ⓟ) Opposite the soccer field, this hip hostelry is built right into the side of a giant boulder, lending a Flintstones ambience to the quarters. Wall murals brighten the smallest, stone rooms. Pricier rooms have tree-trunk furniture and fixtures and wonderful views of the forest-covered hillside leading down to the river. The restaurant (open 6am to 7:30pm) upstairs is a popular local pit stop.

Vista al Cerro Lodge (☎ 373 3365) This lodge is just 300m above the soccer field and offers simple and clean rooms as well as a rough camping ground overlooking the river. Closed at the time of research, but it's worth inquiring if you are stuck for some place to stay.

Talamanca Reserve (☎ 772 1715; d US$77-92, q US$175; Ⓟ 🖵) This huge, 1600-hectare private reserve contains San Gerardo's first full-service lodge, catering to guests who want their creature comforts, even at 2500m. Ominous Talamanca Indian sculptures pose among the spacious stone cabins, but that's the only thing that is primitive about this place. The cabins are furnished with lacquered wood, brand-new bathrooms and big, light-filled windows. In the modern, glass-walled restaurant (open for nonguests), the menu is the length of a Russian novel, featuring any item of American cooking you might be craving. The lodge boasts a very impressive network of trails, all of which are accessible not only on foot, but also by ATV (US$30 per hour). The entrance is about 1km south of the trailhead.

Albergue Urán (☎ 388 2333, 771 1669; www.hotel uran.com; dm/d US$7/22; Ⓟ) Just 50m below the trailhead, this recommended hostel has 12 simple, spotless rooms with clean sheets, fresh paint and shared showers. Spiffy, newer doubles have private bathrooms and majestic views. The affable and accommodating owner loves sending hikers off on their way to Chirripó. A small store, restaurant and laundry facilities all cater to the backpacker set.

Casa Mariposa (☎ 816 7573; jrm_olas@hotmail .com; r per person US$12, cabin US$30) This warm and welcoming casa contains four tiny rooms that share a bathroom, plus two more spacious cabinas with private bathrooms and kitchens. Guests are also very welcome to lounge about the comfy couches in the library. The stone walls, carved out of the inside of the mountain, are adorned with colorful tapestries. The cuarters are close but cozy.

Getting There & Away

Buses to San Isidro depart from the soccer field at 7am and 4pm (US$1, two hours). Any of the hotels can call a taxi for you.

Driving from San Isidro, head south on the Interamericana and cross the Río San Isidro at the southern end of town. About 500m further cross the unsigned Río Jilguero and take the first, steep turn up to the left, about 300m beyond the Jilguero. Note that this turnoff is not marked.

The ranger station is about 18km up this road from the Interamericana. The road is paved as far as Rivas but beyond that it is steep and graveled. It is passable to ordinary cars in the dry season, but a 4WD is recommended. If you are driving past the village of San Gerardo de Rivas, to Albergue Urán or to Cloudbridge Nature Preserve, you will need a 4WD.

PARQUE NACIONAL CHIRRIPÓ

Costa Rica's principal mountain park is named for its highest peak, the majestic **Cerro Chirripó**. Towering 3820m above sea level, the Chirripó massif is part of the Cordillera de Talamanca, which stretch divides the country northwest to southeast.

While Chirripó is the highest and most famous summit in Costa Rica, it is not unique: two other peaks inside the park top 3800m, and most of its 502 sq km lie above 2000m.

At these highest elevations (especially above 3400m), the landscape is *páramo*, which is mostly scrubby trees and grasslands. Between January and May, the *páramo* on the Pacific side is susceptible to forest fires (no smoking on the trails!). Rocky outposts – such as the unmistakable facade of Los Crestones – punctuate the otherwise barren hills. A series of glacial lakes (many of which are visible from the summit) earned the park the name Chirripó, which means 'eternal waters' or *aguas eternas*.

The bare *páramo* contrasts vividly with the lushness of the cloud forest, which dominates the hillsides between 2500m and 3400m. Oak trees (some more than 50m high) tower over the canopy, which also consists of evergreens, laurels and lots of undergrowth. Epiphytes – the scraggy plants that grow up the trunks of larger trees – thrive in this climate. The low-altitude cloud forest is being encroached by agricultural fields and coffee plantations in the areas near San Gerardo de Rivas.

The varying altitude means an amazing diversity of flora and fauna in Parque Nacional Chirripó. The forests are home to several endangered species, including the harpy eagle and the resplendent quetzal (especially visible between March and May). Even besides these highlights, the birding is phenomenal. If you are not too tired to look up while you are climbing, you might see highland birds like three-wattled bellbird, black guan and tinamou. The Andean-like *páramo* guarantees volcano junco, sooty robin, slaty finch, large-footed finch and the endemic volcano hummingbird, which is found only in Costa Rica's highlands. Unusual high-altitude reptiles like green spiny lizard and highland alligator lizard are common. Mammals include spider monkey, capuchin and – at higher elevations – Dice's rabbit and their predator coyote.

The dry season (from late December to April) is the most popular time to visit Chirripó. February and March are the driest months, though it may still rain. On weekends, and especially during holidays, the park is crowded with Tico hiking groups and the mountaintop hostel is often full. The park is closed in May, but the early months of the rainy season are still good for climbing, as it usually doesn't rain in the morning.

In any season, temperatures can drop below freezing at night, so warm clothes (including hat and gloves), rainwear and a three-season sleeping bag are necessary. In exposed areas, high winds make it seem even colder. The ranger station in San Gerardo de Rivas is a good place to check weather conditions.

Information

It is essential that you stop at **Chirripó ranger station** (Sinac; ☎ 200 5348; ⊙ 6:30am-noon & 1-4:30pm) at least one day before you intend to climb Chirripó so you can check availability at the mountaintop hostel and pay your entry fee (US$15 for two days, plus US$10 for each additional day). Space at the hostel is limited, so it's best to arrive early – first thing in the morning – to inquire about space on the following day. Even if you have a reservation, you must stop here the day before to confirm (bring your reservation and payment confirmation). You can also

make arrangements here to hire a porter (US$22 for 14kg) or to store your luggage while you hike.

MAPS

The maps available at the ranger station are fine for the main trails. Good topographical maps are available from the Instituto Geográfico Nacional in San José (p538). Chirripó lies frustratingly at the corner of four separate 1:50,000-scale maps, so you need maps 3444 II *San Isidro* and 3544 III *Dúrika* to cover the area from the ranger station to the summit of Chirripó, and maps 3544 IV *Fila Norte* and 3444 I *Cuerici* to cover other peaks in the massif. Topographical maps are useful but not essential.

Climbing Chirripó

The park entrance is at San Gerardo de Rivas, which lies 1350m above sea level; from here the summit is 2.5km straight up! An easy-to-follow 16km trail leads all the way to the top, and no technical climbing is required.

Allow seven to 14 hours to cover the 10km from the trailhead to the hostel, depending on how fit you are: the recommended departure time is 5am or 6am. The trailhead lies 50m beyond Albergue Urán in San Gerardo de Rivas (about 4km from the ranger station). The main gate is open from 4am to 10am to allow climbers to enter; no one is allowed to begin the ascent after 10am. Inside the park the trail is clearly signed at every kilometer.

The open-sided hut at **Llano Bonito**, halfway up, is a good place for a lunch break. There is shelter and water, but it is intended for emergency use, not overnight stays.

About 6km from the trailhead, the **Monte Sin Fe** (which translates as 'Mountain without Faith'; this climb is not for the faint of heart) is a preliminary crest that reaches 3200m. You then enjoy 2km with gravity in your favor, before making the 2km ascent to the Crestones Base Lodge at 3400m.

Reaching the hostel is the hardest part. From there the hike to the summit is about 6km on relatively flatter terrain (although the last 100m is very steep): allow at least two hours if you are fit, but carry a warm jacket, rain gear, water, snacks and a flashlight just in case. From the summit on a clear day, the vista stretches to both the Atlantic and the Pacific Oceans. The deepblue lakes and the plush-green hills carpet the Valle de las Morenas in the foreground. One reader recommends leaving the base camp at 3am to arrive in time to watch the sunrise from the summit.

A minimum of two days is needed to climb from the ranger station in San Gerardo to the summit and back, leaving no time for recuperation or exploration. It is definitely worthwhile to spend at least one extra day exploring the trails around the summit and/or the base lodge.

Other Trails

Most trekkers follow the main trail to Chirripó and return the same way, but there are several other attractive destinations that are accessible by trails from the base camp. An alternative, longer route between the base lodge and the summit goes via **Cerro Terbi** (3760m), as well as **Los Crestones**, the moon-like rock formations that adorn many postcards. If you are hanging around for a few days, the glorious, grassy **Sabana de los Leones** is a popular destination that offers a stark contrast to the otherwise alpine scenery. Peak-baggers will want to visit **Cerro Ventisqueros** (3812m), which is also within a day's walk of Crestones. These trails are fairly well-maintained, but it's worth inquiring about conditions before setting out.

For hard-core adventurers an alternative route is to take a guided three- or four-day loop trek that begins in Herradura and spends a day or two traversing cloud forest and *páramo* on the slopes of Fila Urán. Hikers ascend **Cerro Urán** (3600m) before the final ascent of Chirripó, and then descend through San Gerardo. This trip requires camping and you must be accompanied by a local guide at all times. Costa Rica Trekking Adventures can make arrangements for this tour. Alternatively, contact the **guides' association** (☎ 771 1199) in Herradura. The number is for the local *pulpería*. Ask for Dennis Elizondo, who is a recommended guide.

Tours

Prices vary depending on the size of the party.
Costa Rica Trekking Adventures (☎ 771 4582; www.chirripo.com; Calle 1 btwn Avs 2 & 4; ☯ 8am-noon & 1:30-6pm) Several different guided excursions around Chirripó, ranging from a one-day trek to Llano Bonito

(US$90 per person) to a four-day trek around the Urán loop (US$300 to US$435 per person).
Sunny Travel (☎ 771 9686; www.sunnycostarica.com) Offers the traditional three-day trek (US$270 to US$355 per person) to the summit.

Sleeping & Eating

The only accommodation in Parque Nacional Chirripó is at **Crestones Base Lodge** (dm US$10), housing up to 60 people in dorm-style bunks. The basic stone building has a solar panel that provides electric light from 6pm to 8pm and sporadic heat for showers. The lodge rents a variety of gear including sleeping bags (US$1.60), blankets (US$0.80), cooking equipment (US$0.80) and gas canisters (US$2); all rates are per day.

Reservations are absolutely necessary at Crestones Base Lodge. Your tour company will likely make reservations for you; but for those traveling independently it is virtually impossible to make reservations before your arrival in Costa Rica. To do so, it is necessary to contact the **Minae office** (☎ 771 3155; fax 771 3297; aclap@sinac.go.cr) in San Isidro on the first working day of the month, at least one or two months prior to your trip. If space is available, you will be required to send your payment by wire transfer to confirm the reservation. You must present your reservation and payment confirmation at the ranger station in San Gerardo de Rivas on the day before you set out.

Fortunately, the lodge reserves 10 spaces per night for travelers who show up in San Gerardo and are ready to hike on the following day. This is the more practical option for most travelers, although there is no guarantee that there will be space available on the days you wish to hike. Space is at a premium during holiday periods and on weekends during the dry season. The ranger station opens at 6:30am – the earlier you arrive, the more likely you will be able to hike the following day.

Crestones Base Lodge provides drinking water, but no food. Hikers must bring all of their own provisions. Camping is allowed only at a special designated area near Cerro Urán – not at Crestones or anywhere else in the park.

Getting There & Around

See details under San Gerardo de Rivas (p383) for directions on how to get here.

CHIRRIPÓ CHECKLIST

Costa Rica might be in the tropics, but Chirripó lies at some chilly altitudes. Don't get caught without the necessities when hiking Costa Rica's highest mountain.

■ Water bottle (there is one water stop between the trailhead and the base camp)

■ Food (including snacks for the hike)

■ Warm jacket, gloves and hat (temperatures can dip below freezing)

■ Good sleeping bag (also available to rent at the lodge)

■ Rain gear (even when it's not raining, the summit is misty)

■ Plastic bags (to protect your clothing and personal items from the rain)

■ Sunblock (it may be chilly but the sun is powerful and much of the route is not shaded)

■ Flashlight (there's no electricity for much of the evening at the mountaintop hostel)

■ Compass and map (especially if you are planning to hike one of the lesser-used trails)

■ Camera (photographic evidence that you reached the top!)

From opposite the ranger station, in front of Cabinas El Bosque, there is free transportation to the trailhead at 5am. Also, several hotels offer early-morning trailhead transportation for their guests.

BUENOS AIRES

A small town about 64km southeast of San Isidro, Buenos Aires is in the center of an important pineapple-producing region. If you don't notice the farms, you will surely spot the Del Monte plant that is just north of town along the Interamericana.

It is also something of an administrative center for the indigenous groups in the surrounding regions. The Ujarrás, Salitre and Cabagra groups all have reserves north of here, while the Reserva Indígena Boruca is to the south. The **Asociacíon Regional Aborigen del Dikes** (Aradikes; ☎ 730 0289; www.aradikes.org) is a local organization that works to increase the capacity of indigenous communities in the Buenos Aires region. Efforts range from reforestation to cultural tourism to activism against the Boruca hydroelectric project (p388). This is a good source of information about visiting Boruca.

Buenos Aires is a hot, tranquil town centered around a tree-filled plaza. This shady Parque Central is – at times – the town's only relief from the searing heat. There is a handful of places to stay, but few facilities catering to travelers. That's probably because very few travelers pass through this town, which does not offer much in the way of sights or activities. Nonetheless, it is a useful

entry point for the indigenous reserves in the region, as well as the **Reserva Biológica Dúrika** (☎ 730 0657; www.durika.org), which has an office here. Take the right-hand turn off the main road into town and follow the signs. (See opposite for a description of the reserve.)

Information & Orientation

Turn off the Interamericana just south of the Del Monte plant. A paved road leads 3km north to Buenos Aires. This main road into town forks about 1km south of town: the left fork passes the Dúrika office and heads into the center of town, near the Parque Central; the right fork bypasses the center, but passes the hospital and most of the places to stay.

There is a Banco Nacional on the northeast corner of Parque Central. **Terr@net** (☎ 730 5050; per hr US$1; ☟ 10am-10pm Mon-Sat, 2-8pm Sun) offers Internet access, one block south of Parque Central, diagonally opposite the Nuevo Maracaibo.

Sleeping & Eating

A cluster of cabinas are south of the center, along the main road into town. Heading south to north:

Cabinas Mary (☎ 730 0187; r per person US$10; **P**) These boxy cabinas form a horseshoe around a flower-filled courtyard (which loses some of its charm when it fills up with cars). Rooms are looking a little worse for wear, with cracked plaster and tattered curtains, but they do have fans, cable TV and lukewarm water. It's 100m south of the clinic.

Aradikes (☎ 730 0289; d US$12; P ⊠) Although this facility is sometimes used for meetings and such, it's a great option for travelers when rooms are available. The sparkling new cabins have whitewashed walls and sturdy wood furniture. They are arranged around a thatch-roof rancho which houses a small exhibit of handicrafts. A small restaurant is also on-site. It's 100m south of the clinic.

Nuevo Maracaibo (☎ 730 2759; bocas US$600-800, meals US$1500-2500) There's only one proper restaurant in town, but it's a good one. The 2nd-story outdoor terrace is removed from the street noise, but ideally located to catch the breeze – often the only relief in this sunburned town. Decent food, friendly service and the big-screen TV attract a regular stream of contented customers. It's at the southeast corner of the park.

A number of *sodas* operate out of Mercado Central, west of Parque Central.

Getting There & Away

Besides the buses listed here, many buses travel between Palmar Norte, San Vito, San Isidro and San José without stopping in Buenos Aires. You can flag them down as they pass on the Interamericana. There is no marked bus shelter, so be sure that you are visible so the bus driver knows to stop for you.

The following buses (except San Isidro) leave from the *mercado*, west of Parque Central:

Boruca US$1.75, 1½ hours, depart at noon and 3:30pm, returns the following morning.

San Isidro US$1.50, one hour, depart from the Gafeso terminal, diagonally opposite the *mercado* at 5:30am, 6am, 6:30am, 7:30am, 8am, 10am, 11am, 12:15pm, 2pm, 2:45pm and 5pm.

San José (Tracopa) US$5, four hours, buses from Neily stop here around 6:15am, 9:15am and 4:30pm.

RESERVA BIOLÓGICA DÚRIKA

Within the Parque Internacional La Amistad, on the flanks of Cerro Dúrika, this is a 7500-hectare **biological reserve** and a **working farm**, where a group of committed individuals live in an independent, sustainable community. About 30 community members – both Tico and foreign – are committed to local conservation, natural medicine and preservation of indigenous culture.

Since 1992, Dúrika welcomes travelers to stay and work on the finca, which is about 17km north of Buenos Aires. It is a unique opportunity to explore the remote wilderness and communities around the reserve and to participate in this inspiring social experiment. Interesting all-day tours of the finca demonstrate the principles and processes of organic agriculture that Dúrika employs (eg fertilizer made from chili peppers). Guests can also take shorter hikes in the reserve or multiday treks to the Continental Divide.

Staff here can arrange daylong forays to the Cabécar indigenous village of **Ujarrás**, providing a glimpse of contemporary indigenous life in Costa Rica. Travelers with a strong interest in indigenous cultures or medicinal plants should inquire about the **Shaman Tour**, a weeklong journey that visits several of these communities.

Visitors are also welcome to stay closer to home, participating in the life of the farm, checking out local waterfalls (which fuel the community's hydroelectric power) and otherwise exploring the grounds. On-site facilities include 10 cabins of various sizes sleeping two to eight people (US$35 per person). All the cabins have a bathroom and porch with mountain views. Guests are invited to relax in the sauna and Jacuzzi. Rates include reader-recommended organic vegetarian meals made from locally grown foods. There are special nightly rates for large groups, students (US$25) and also volunteers (US$15). Reservations and information are available from the **Fundación Dúrika office** (☎ 730 0657; www.durika.org) in Buenos Aires. Make reservations at least 10 days in advance.

The office can arrange transport to the reserve (US$30 for up to five passengers). If driving to the finca on your own (not recommended), a 4WD is necessary.

INTERAMERICANA SUR

From San Isidro the Interamericana winds its way southeast through hillside agricultural towns. Along this stretch, a series of narrow, steep, dirt roads lead to some of the country's most remote areas – some nearly inaccessible due to the prohibitive presence of the Cordillera de Talamanca. This dry, hot area is home to the Brunka peoples – one

SOUTHERN COSTA RICA

of the few indigenous reserves that is accessible and welcoming to visitors.

Further south, the Interamericana then dips to sea level at Palmar, where the scenery is dominated by banana and palm plantations. From this point the Panamanian border lies a little more than 100km away.

More than anything, this unremarkable stretch of highway serves the transportation needs of travelers heading west to the Península de Osa and the Golfo Dulce or north to the Valle del Coto Brus.

RESERVA INDÍGENA BORUCA

The picturesque valley of the Río Grande de Térraba is the setting for this reserve for the Brunka indigenous peoples (also called Boruca). Historians believe that the present-day Brunka have evolved out of several different indigenous groups, including the Coto, Quepos, Turrucaca, Burucac and Abubaes, whose territories stretched all the way to the Península de Osa in pre-Columbian times. These days, the Brunka population is centered in the small villages of **Rey Curré**, which is bisected by the Carratera Interamericana, and **Boruca**, 8km north.

The Brunka are celebrated craftspeople, and their traditional art plays a leading role in the survival of indigenous culture (see the boxed text Endangered Cultures, p49). The tribe is most famous for its ornate masks, carved from balsa or cedar, and sometimes colored with natural dyes and acrylics. These elaborate creations are used in the annual Fiesta de los Diablitos (right). Brunka women also use pre-Columbian back-strap looms to weave colorful, natural cotton bags, placemats and other textiles. While most people make their living from agriculture, some indigenous people have begun producing these fine handicrafts for sale to tourists.

Rey Curré (usually just 'Curré' on maps) is about 30km south of Buenos Aires, right on the Interamericana. Drivers can stop to visit a small **cooperative** (☺ 9am-5pm Mon-Fri, 2-5pm Sat) that sells handicrafts. In Boruca, local artisans post signs outside their homes advertising their handmade balsa masks and woven bags. Exhibits are sometimes on display in the **museo**, a thatch-roof rancho 100m west of the *pulpería*.

Other than a few artisans selling their handiwork, these towns hardly cater to tourists. In fact, at first glance, they're hard to differentiate from any typical Tico village. For a more in-depth understanding of the Brunka culture and lifestyle, make arrangements for a longer-term homestay (see below). In any case, always be particularly sensitive when visiting indigenous communities. Dress modestly and avoid photographing people without asking permission.

Festivals & Events

The **Fiesta de los Diablitos** is a three-day Brunka event that symbolizes the struggle between the Spanish and the indigenous population. Sometimes called the Danza de los Diablitos, or 'dance of the little devils,' the culmination of the festival is a choreographed battle between the opposing sides. Villagers wearing wooden devil masks and burlap costumes play the role of the natives in their fight against the Spanish conquerors. The Spaniards, represented by a man in a bull costume, lose the battle. This festival is held in Boruca from December 31 to January 2 and in Curré from February 5 to 8.

Many outsiders descend on Boruca and Curré during these events. While the Brunka welcome visitors, they request that guests respect their traditions. Tourists are generally required to pay a fee for the right to take photographs or video. No flash photography or artificial lighting is allowed, and tourists are not allowed to interfere with the program.

The lesser-known **Fiesta de los Negritos**, held during the second week of December, celebrates the Virgin of the Immaculate Conception. Traditional indigenous music – mainly drumming and bamboo flutes – accompanies dancing and costumes.

Tours

Asociación Regional Aborigen del Dikes (Aradikes; ☎ 730 0289; www.aradikes.org; Buenos Aires) Inquire about homestays and local tour guides.

Galería Namu (☎ 256 3412; www.galerianamu.com; Ave 7, San José; per person per day US$45) This San José gallery – which specializes in indigenous art – can arrange tours to Boruca, which include homestay, hiking to waterfalls, handicraft demonstrations and storytelling. Transportation to Boruca not included.

Sleeping & Eating

The only regular place to stay is the *soda* in Boruca, **Bar Restaurante Boruca** (☎ 730 2454; d US$10). Five basic rooms have two single beds and private cold-water bathrooms. It's run by Memo Gomez, who can also help you find a private home to stay in.

Getting There & Away

Buses (US$1.75, 1½ hours) leave the central market in Buenos Aires at noon and 3:30pm daily, traveling to Boruca via a very poor dirt road. The bus returns the following morning, which makes Boruca difficult for a day trip relying on public transportation. A taxi from Buenos Aires to Boruca is about US$20.

Drivers will find a better road that leaves the Interamericana about 3km south of Curré – look for the sign. It's about 8km to Boruca; a 4WD is recommended.

PALMAR

This unremarkable, flat village lies right in the center of the banana-growing region of the Valle de Diquis. The Río Grande de Térraba bisects the town, creating Palmar Sur and Palmar Norte.

Most of the facilities – hotels, banks and buses – are in Palmar Norte, clustered around the intersection of the Carratera Interamericana and the Costanera Sur (Pacific Coast Hwy). About 1km to the south, linked by a sturdy metal bridge, Palmar Sur is the locale of the airstrip. On any given day, you'll find a large percentage of the population lounging in the shade outside the local *pulpería* watching the traffic on the Interamericana. This is a hot, dusty, uneventful place.

At the intersection of the country's two major highways, Palmar is a transportation hub. It serves as a gateway to the Península de Osa, as travelers arrive by airplane and bus and pass en route to Sierpe. This route goes straight through the **banana plantations**, so keep your eyes peeled. Situated strategically between San Isidro (125km to the north) and the Panamanian border (95km to the southeast), Palmar is also a key transportation link in any north–south migrations.

Lack of charm aside, Palmar is one of the best sites in the country to see the **granite spheres** *(esferas de piedra)*, a legacy of pre-Columbian cultures – some of which exceed 2m in diameter. They are scattered all over town, including at the airstrip; some of the largest and most impressive are in front of the peach-colored school *(el colegio)* on the Interamericana.

To get from Palmar Norte to Palmar Sur, take the Interamericana southbound over the Río Grande de Térraba bridge, then take the first right beyond the bridge.

Information

If you are heading to the Osa, Palmar represents your best chance to get some cash before less-serviced areas.

Banco Coopealianza (Interamericana; ☾ 8am-5pm Mon-Fri, 8am-noon Sat) Has an ATM on the Cirrus network.

Banco Popular (☎ 786 7033; Interamericana) Changes traveler's checks and cash.

Brunka Lodge (☎ 786 7944; brunkalodge@costaricense .cr; per hr US$0.20) This may be the only place in town offering public Internet access .

Osa Tours (☎ 786 6534, 786 7825; catuosa@racsa.co.cr; ☾ 8am-noon & 2-6pm) Home of the local tourist board.

Sleeping & Eating

You'll not want to linger in Palmar, but if you miss a connection you may find yourself spending the night.

THE BORUCA DAM

Rey Curré has been proposed as the site of a huge hydroelectric project (reportedly the largest in Central America), a 220m dam across the Río Grande de Térraba. The proposal for the so-called Boruca dam has caused much controversy, as it would flood 25,000 hectares of land in this area and displace thousands of residents.

Brunka ties to their land are strong, not only due to their subsistence from agriculture and dependence on plants for medicinal use, but also due to the presence of ancestral burial grounds. Furthermore, the Brunka recognize that relocation would inevitably result in physical division of their community (something they have already experienced – to a smaller degree – with the construction of the Interamericana). In theory, the hydroelectric project cannot go forward without the consent of the residents, but many of the Brunka feel helpless and hopeless in the face of the well-funded electricity company ICE.

SOUTHERN COSTA RICA

Cabinas & Restaurante Wah Lok (☎ 786 6262; s/d US$6/8; P) This roadside motel along the highway has a strip of plain, clean rooms, each with a bathroom and a fan, but not much else. The attached restaurant serves Chinese food.

Hotel Vista al Cerro (☎ 786 7744; s/d US$13/16, with air-con US$19; P ⊠ 💻) On the western edge of town, the Vista al Cerro is a larger hotel, where 20 clean guestrooms have the required amenities like fans and cold-water showers. Breakfast is included in all rates and is served in the attached restaurant.

Brunka Lodge (☎ 786 7944; brunkalodge@costa rricense.cr; s/d/tr with air-con US$25/35/40, without air-con US$15/20/25; ⊠ 💻) The Brunka Lodge is undoubtedly the most inviting option in Palmar. Sun-filled, clean swept bungalows are clustered around a swimming pool and a popular, pleasant open-air restaurant. All rooms have hot-water bathrooms and cable TV.

Self-caterers will want to visit the **Supermercado Térraba** (Transportes Térraba bus stop) before heading to the Osa, as shopping opportunities are limited in Bahía Drake. The

Panadería Palenquito (Tracopa bus stop) is a useful breakfast spot if you are catching an early-morning bus.

If you are looking for a convenient lunch break:

Bar/Restaurante El Puente (dishes US$2.50-4) Serves a tasty *arroz con pollo*.

Lapa Rojo (dishes US$3-4) A popular choice, serving good seafood and plenty of rice dishes.

Getting There & Away

AIR

Sansa has two daily flights to and from San José (one way/round trip US$72/144), while NatureAir has one (US$80/160). Taxis meet incoming flights and charge about US$3 to Palmar Norte and US$15 to Sierpe. Otherwise, the infrequent Palmar Norte–Sierpe bus goes through Palmar Sur – you can board it if there's space available.

BUS

Buses to San José and San Isidro stop on the east side of the Interamericana. Other buses leave from in front of Panadería Palenquito or Supermercado Térraba a block apart on

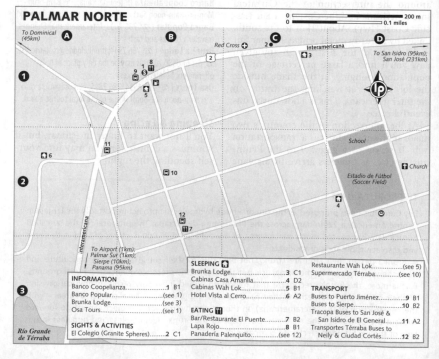

PALMAR NORTE

0 _____ 200 m
0 _____ 0.1 miles

To Dominical (45km) — Ⓐ

Ⓑ

Red Cross ✚ 2● Ⓒ

Interamericana

🏛3 Ⓓ

To San Isidro (95km); San José (231km)

School

Church

Estadio de Fútbol (Soccer Field)

To Airport (1km); Palmar Sur (1km); Sierpe (10km); Panama (95km)

Río Grande de Térraba

INFORMATION	
Banco Coopelianza	1 B1
Banco Popular	(see 1)
Brunka Lodge	(see 3)
Osa Tours	(see 1)

SIGHTS & ACTIVITIES	
El Colegio (Granite Spheres)	2 C1

SLEEPING 🛏	
Brunka Lodge	3 C1
Cabinas Casa Amarilla	4 D2
Cabinas Wah Lok	5 B1
Hotel Vista al Cerro	6 A2

EATING 🍴	
Bar/Restaurante El Puente	7 B2
Lapa Rojo	8 B1
Panadería Palenquito	(see 12)
Restaurante Wah Lok	(see 5)
Supermercado Térraba	(see 10)

TRANSPORT	
Buses to Puerto Jiménez	9 B1
Buses to Sierpe	10 B2
Tracopa Buses to San José & San Isidro de El General	11 A2
Transportes Térraba Buses to Neily & Ciudad Cortés	12 B2

the town's main street. The bus ticket office is inside the Palenquito.

Ciudad Cortés (Transportes Térraba) Six buses depart from 6:30am to 6:30pm.

Dominical Depart 8am.

Neily (Transportes Térraba) Depart 5am, 6am, 7am, 9:30am, noon, 1pm, 2:20pm & 4:50pm.

Puerto Jiménez Depart from in front of Banco Coopealianza at 8am, 11am & 5pm (these buses originate in San Isidro, so pick-up times are approximate).

San Isidro (Tracopa) US$3.50, three hours, depart 8:30am, 11:30am, 2:30pm and 4:30pm.

San José (Tracopa) US$6.50, five hours, 5:25am, 6:15am, 7:45am, 10am, 1pm, 3pm and 4:45pm.

Sierpe US$0.60, one hour, depart 4:30am, 7am, 9:30am, 11:30am, 2:30pm and 5:30pm.

Uvita US$1.25, 1½ hours, depart 12:30pm.

RÍO CLARO

This little town is at the junction of the Carratera Interamericana and Route 14, which is the road that heads south to Golfito on the Golfo Dulce. It is more of a major intersection (complete with traffic light) than a destination. If you are looking for somewhere to stop, however, there are a few hotels and restaurants as well as a gas station. And there is one delightful attraction that is worth extending your visit, or even making a day trip from Golfito.

At the **Paradise Tropical Garden** (☎ 789 8746; http://paradis-garden.tripod.com; admission by donation; ⏱ 6am-5pm), Robert and Ella Beatham have created a wonderfully sensual introduction to tropical fruits and rain-forest remedies that they call the 'Tropical Fruit See, Smell, Taste & Touch Experience'. Besides this interactive display, visitors also learn about the production of African palm oil and how it came to be the dominant crop of this region (with the destruction of the banana trees). Robert and Ella are wonderful hosts, but you should call a day in advance if you want their full attention. To get here from Río Claro, go west on the Interamericana for 1km and cross the Río Largarto. Turn right at the end of the bridge; the garden is 200m on.

There are more lodging options in Golfito. Otherwise, the **Hotel y Restaurant Papili** (☎ 789 9038; s/d US$10/15; ✖) and the **Cabinas y Restaurant Impala** (☎ 789 9921; s/d US$9/17; P) offer tidy rooms with TV and private bathrooms (cold water only at the Impala).

Any bus between Neily and Golfito can drop you off in Río Claro. If you're traveling

to Golfito and don't want to wait for the bus, semiregular collective taxis usually cruise through town soliciting passengers for the ride, which costs US$1.50 per person if you have a full car.

NEILY

Just 50m above sea level, this steamy city is a transportation hub and an agricultural center. From here the Interamericana continues 17km to Panama, while Rte 16 makes a beeline north to the attractive mountain village of San Vito.

Neily sits on the west bank of the Río Corredor, on the north side of the Interamericana. An asymmetrical web of streets is woven between the river and the smaller Quebrada Neily.

Although Ciudad Neily – as it is often called – is Southern Costa Rica's second-largest 'city,' it retains the friendly atmosphere of a rural town. To the south, the lowlands are carpeted in the banana and palm plantations of the Valle de Coto Colorado, and in the north, the Fila Costeña is the source of spectacular mountain scenery.

Information

Banco Coopealianza, southwest of the Mercado, has a 24-hour ATM on the Cirrus network.

Banco de Costa Rica (⏱ 8am-3pm Mon-Fri) Changes traveler's checks.

Technoplanet Internet (☎ 783 4744; per hr US$1; ⏱ 9am-5pm) Opposite the lyceum.

TPC Doctor (☎ 783 9020; per hr US$3; ⏱ 8am-10pm) More convenient and more expensive Internet access.

Sights & Activities

About 15km north of Neily on the road to San Vito, the **Cavernas de Corredores** are a network of little-explored caverns on a private banana plantation. Besides the huge, impressive stalactites, several species of bats are also in the caves. It's not geared toward tourists, but it is usually possible to visit. William Hidalgo is a **local guide** (☎ 770 8225) who leads travelers through the cavern. Otherwise, La Purruja Lodge (p433) in Golfito has tours to the site (US$35 per person). If you have a 4WD, turn off about 15km north of Neily, just before the school. The small *pulpería* (look for the 'telefono publico' sign) has more information. Otherwise, you can hire a 4WD taxi from Neily for about US$6.

SOUTHERN COSTA RICA

Sleeping

All hotels have cold showers unless otherwise indicated.

Hotel Musuco (☎ 783 3048; r per person with/without bathroom US$6/5) Close to the highway, these rooms are clean and secure, if not particularly inspiring. The friendly management does not always hang around if there are no guests, so you may have to hunt somebody down to let you in.

Cabinas Heileen (☎ 783 3080; s/d US$5/9; **P**) The welcoming, flower-filled porch (that also serves as the reception) is Heileen's private home. Unfortunately, the cabinas for rent are not quite as charming, but they are adequate. Ceiling fans, linoleum floors and peach-painted walls are the extent of the decor.

Hotel El Rancho (☎ 783 3060, 783-4210; s/d/tr US$7/8/12, with TV US$9/13/15, with TV & air-con US$15/18/20; **P** **X**) Right off the Interamericana, this big, charmless hotel resembles a storage facility, with 52 turquoise blocks set around a gravel parking lot. The spartan rooms are not superclean, but the wood-panel walls and curtains in the windows add a touch of hominess.

Cabinas Helga (☎ 783 3146; d US$20; **P**) Helga runs a tight ship, ensuring immaculate rooms and good security at this friendly, family-run motel. Cool, clean cabinas have linoleum floors, cable TV and tiled bathrooms straight out the 1950s.

Hotel Andrea (☎ 783 3784; s/d/tr US$19/20/24, s/d/tr/q with air-con US$23/24/26/28; **P** **X**) Diagonally opposite the *mercado*, this is the top place in town. The 40 white-tiled units (all with hot shower and cable TV) sparkle; upstairs guests enjoy a terrace with views. The attached open-air restaurant is also among Neily's nicest places to eat. Beers, bocas and big screen TVs attract small crowds in the evenings; in the morning, pick up a tasty *gallo pinto* for a little more than a dollar.

Centro Turistico Neily (☎ 783 3031; r per person with/without air-con US$19/13, cabins US$30-32; **P** **X** **R**) This rambling resort is on the northern edge of town in a quiet residential neighborhood 300m northwest of the school, about a 20-minute walk from the center. The handsome colonial-style building contains sparkling new guestrooms, all with decorative details like lace curtains and carved wood furniture and with spacious, hot-water bathrooms. A tranquil open-air restaurant overlooks the grounds.

Eating & Drinking

Neily's most inviting places to eat and drink are the restaurants attached to the Hotel Andrea and the Centro Turistico Neily.

Restaurant La Moderna (☎ 783 3097; dishes US$2-6; ⏱ 7am-10:30pm) One block east of the park, this is an inviting indoor restaurant with a full menu of Tico meals, plus pasta, pizza and tacos. The woody interior and designated play area for kids make it a popular family spot.

Restaurant Nuevo Mundo (☎ 783 3111; dishes US$3-5; ⏱ 11am-midnight) Neily's top spot for

---

LOCAL LORE

Indigenous groups use tropical flowers, herbs and plants to treat all kinds of illness, from diabetes to a slipped disk. Here are a few of our favorites, courtesy of Paradise Tropical Garden (p391).

■ Most doctors treat stomach ulcers with antibiotics, but natural-medicine connoisseurs recommend the seeds from the spiny red annatto pod. Remove the seeds from the pod and wash away the red paste. You can eat the seeds straight from the pod, or dry them and grind them into your food.

■ The leaves of the avocado tree are said to cure high blood pressure. Just boil them for three minutes and let them steep for another three. Strain the murky drink and store it in the fridge. Apparently you should drink three cups a day, but beware: this brew is a diuretic.

■ If you suffer from a slipped disk, you might try this natural remedy, made from the bracts of the beautiful red plume ginger (alpinia purpurata), which is bountiful in the rain forest. The bracts are the small leaves at the base of the bloom. Pull them off the stem of the ginger and stuff as many as you can fit into a small bottle, then fill the bottle with rubbing alcohol. Let it sit for three days, before rubbing this tincture onto your sore back. This remedy should ease your pain within a few days.

Playa Manuel Antonio (p358), Parque Nacional Manuel Antonio

Forest canopy walk, Reserva Biológica Bosque Nuboso Monteverde (p207)

Scarlet macaws, Parque Nacional Corcovado (p413)

Reserva Biológica Bosque Nuboso Monteverde (p207)

Butterfly (p58)

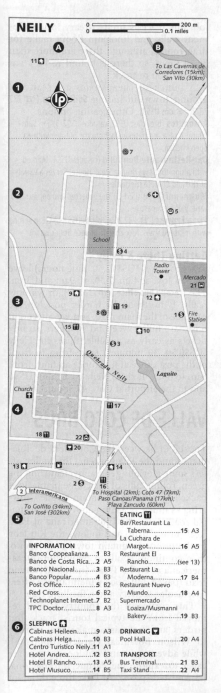

NEILY

0 _____ 200 m
0 _____ 0.1 miles

To Las Cavernas de
Corredores (15km);
San Vito (30km)

School

Radio
Tower

Mercado
21

Fire
Station

Quebrada Neily

Laguito

Church

Interamericana

To Golfito (34km);
San José (302km)

To Hospital (2km); Coto 47 (7km);
Paso Canoas/Panama (17km);
Playa Zancudo (60km)

INFORMATION
Banco Coopealianza....**1** B3
Banco de Costa Rica....**2** A5
Banco Nacional...........**3** B3
Banco Popular.............**4** B3
Post Office..................**5** B2
Red Cross....................**6** B2
Technoplanet Internet.**7** B2
TPC Doctor.................**8** A3

SLEEPING
Cabinas Heileen...........**9** A3
Cabinas Helga............**10** B3
Centro Turistico Neily.**11** A1
Hotel Andrea.............**12** B3
Hotel El Rancho.........**13** A5
Hotel Musuco............**14** B5

EATING
Bar/Restaurant La
Taberna....................**15** A3
La Cuchara de
Margot.....................**16** A5
Restaurant El
Rancho..................(see **13**)
Restaurant La
Moderna..................**17** B4
Restaurant Nuevo
Mundo......................**18** A4
Supermercado
Loaiza/Musmanni
Bakery......................**19** B3

DRINKING
Pool Hall...................**20** A4

TRANSPORT
Bus Terminal.............**21** B3
Taxi Stand.................**22** A4

Chinese. A spacious, light-filled dining room is furnished with shiny varnished wood tables and constantly running ceiling fans to keep things cool. The menu has a huge selection of chop suey (US$3) and creative combos like 'tacos chinos' (US$3) and 'wanton fritos' (US$4).

La Cuchara de Margot This friendly *soda*, north of the Interamericana, serves hamburgers and snacks and has a couple of outside tables. It's convenient for drivers looking for a light lunch.

Supermercado Loaiza (one block west of Hotel Andrea) useful for self-caterers. Also an excellent breakfast option, as there is a small Musmanni bakery and café inside.

Attached to the hotel of the same name, **Restaurant El Rancho** (☎ 783 3060; dishes US$3; 🕐 11-2am Mon-Sat) is a boisterous local eatery, popular for karaoke evenings. The **pool hall** shown on the map is friendly but is surrounded by rough bars, uninviting to women. **Bar/Restaurant La Taberna**, one block north of the park, is a better option, where you'll find a mixed crowd admiring the monster TV.

Getting There & Away
AIR
Sansa has a daily flight (one way/round trip US$78/156) between San José and Coto 47, the airport located 7km southwest of Neily. The bus to Finca 40 makes a stop by the airport.

BUS
These buses leave from the main terminal on the east side of town:
Ciudad Cortés Depart 4:45am, 9:15am, 11am, 12:30pm, 2:30pm, 4:30pm and 5:45pm.
Dominical Depart 6am and 2:30pm.
Finca 40 (airport) US$0.50, 30 minutes, depart 7:30am, 9:15am, 11:30am, 1:15pm, 3:15pm, 5:30pm and 6pm.
Golfito US$0.50, 1½ hours, depart 13 times daily from 6am to 7:30pm.
Palmar Depart 4:45am, 9:15am, noon, 12:30pm, 2:30pm, 4:30pm and 5:45pm.
Paso Canoas Thirty minutes, depart 19 times daily from 6am to 6pm.
Puerto Jiménez Depart 7am and 2pm.
San José (Tracopa) US$8.50, seven hours, depart 4:30am, 5am, 8:30am, 11:30am and 3:30pm.
San Isidro (Tracopa) US$5, five hours, depart 7am, 10am, 1pm and 3pm.
San Vito, via Agua Buena (Capul) US$1, two hours, depart 6am, 7:30am, 9am, noon, 1pm, 4pm and 5:30pm.

San Vito, via Cañas Gordas (Capul) US$1, two hours, depart 11am and 3pm.
Zancudo US$1.50, three hours, depart 9:30am and 2:15pm.

TAXI

Taxis with 4WD wait at the taxi stand southeast of the park. The fare from Neily to Paso Canoas is about US$6; to Coto 47 it's about US$3. Taxis between Coto 47 and Paso Canoas cost about US$8.

PASO CANOAS

This small town is the main port of entry between Costa Rica and Panama and, like most border outposts, is largely devoid of charm. (Neily, only 17km away, is far more pleasant.) Hotels are often full of Tico bargain hunters looking for duty-free specials, especially on weekends and holidays.

Báncredito (� 8am-4:30pm) near Costa Rican *migraciónes* changes traveler's checks and there is an ATM on the Visa Plus system near the border. Rates for converting excess colones into dollars are not good, but they will do in a pinch. Colones are accepted at the border, but are difficult to get rid of further into Panama.

The **Instituto Panameño de Turismo** (☎ 727 6524; ☺ 6am-11pm), in the Panamanian border post, has information on travel to Panama. If you are arriving in Costa Rica, you'll find sparse tourist information at a small office in the Costa Rican *migraciónes* office. Hours are irregular.

Sleeping & Eating

The hotels in Paso Canoas aren't particularly inviting, but you'll have no problem finding a decent, secure place to crash. All showers are cold.

Cabinas Romy (☎ 732 2873; s/d US$8/12; P) Set around a pleasant courtyard, shiny and spotless new rooms are decked with pastel-colored walls, wooden doors and floral bedspreads. This bright yellow building is the best-value place in Paso Canoas, but a few other decent options are along this strip.

Hotel Real Victoria (☎ 732 2586; r per person US$6; P ✕ ⊛) This is a proper-looking hotel, with facilities like guarded parking, swimming pool and restaurant. The lack of windows means dark rooms, but they are clean and cool. Good value.

Hotel Azteca (☎ 732 2217; d with/without air-con & TV US$25/10; ✕) Despite the colorful paint

job, this place is pretty dreary inside. Cement walls and linoleum floors make for drab rooms, although there are more than 50 of them, so there is bound to be a vacancy if you're stuck.

A bunch of cheap *sodas* are scattered around town, including **Soda Hilda** (☎ 732 2873; casados US$3). Other eating options:
Antonjitos (breakfast US$2, casados US$2-3; ☺ 5am-10pm) A pleasant patio away from the hubbub with an open kitchen.
Bar-Restaurante Don Julio (casados US$4) Marked with a sign that says Brunca Steak House. Serves a variety of Tico and Chinese specialties.
Musmanni (items US$1-3) The expected and appreciated variety of fresh pastries.
Pizza Express (☎ 732 2656; pizzas US$2-6) Clean setting with mirrored walls. Nice change of pace from casados.

Getting There & Away

Tracopa buses (US$12.50, nine hours) leave for San José at 4am, 7:30am, 9am and 3pm. The **Tracopa bus office** (☎ 732 2201), or window really, is north of the border post, on the east side of the main road. Sunday-afternoon buses are full of weekend shoppers, so buy tickets as early as possible. Buses for Neily (US$0.50, 30 minutes) leave from in front of the post office at least once an hour from 6am to 6pm. Taxis to Neily cost about US$6 and to the airport at Coto 47 about US$8.

VALLE DE COTO BRUS

Tucked in between the Cordillera de Talamanca and the Fila Costeña, this valley offers some glorious geography, featuring the green, rolling hills of the coffee plantations backed by striking mountain facades, towering as much as 3350m above. The principal road leaves the Interamericana at Paso Real (near Curré) and follows the Río Jaba to the pretty mountain town of San Vito, then continues south to rejoin the Interamericana at Neily. This winding mountain road (paved, but poorly maintained) offers spectacular scenery and a thrilling ride.

This corner of the country is well removed from the typical tourist track. But birders and botanists make the journey to Wilson Botanical Garden (opposite), while adventurers and outdoorsy types are eager to explore the Parque Internacional La Amistad (p398). At least three different

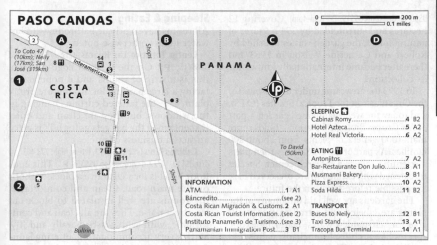

PASO CANOAS

0   200 m
0   0.1 miles

To Coto 47
(10km); Neily
(17km); San
José (319km)

COSTA
RICA

Shops

PANAMA

Shops

Bullring

SLEEPING
Cabinas Romy............................**4** B2
Hotel Azteca.............................**5** A2
Hotel Real Victoria....................**6** A2

EATING
Antonjitos................................**7** A2
Bar-Restaurante Don Julio..........**8** A1
Musmanni Bakery......................**9** B1
Pizza Express...........................**10** A2
Soda Hilda..............................**11** B2

INFORMATION
ATM..**1** A1
Báncredito............................(see 2)
Costa Rican Migración & Customs.**2** A1
Costa Rican Tourist Information..(see 2)
Instituto Panameño de Turismo...(see 3)
Panamanian Immigration Post.....**3** B1

TRANSPORT
Buses to Neily..........................**12** B1
Taxi Stand...............................**13** A1
Tracopa Bus Terminal................**14** A1

indigenous groups inhabit parts of the international park, while the Guaymí also have a reserve near San Vito.

SAN VITO

At 980m, the cool, green hills around San Vito (population 15,000) offer a delicious respite from the heat of the nearby lowlands. Overlooking the Valle de Coto Brus, this pleasant town is a convenient base for excursions to the Wilson Botanical Garden and to the infrequently visited Parque Internacional La Amistad.

As provincial Costa Rica goes, San Vito is downright culturally diverse.

It was founded by Italian immigrants in the 1950s. Italian is still spoken in these parts and – more importantly – still eaten. Plus the proximity of the Reserva Indígena Guaymí de Coto Brus means that indigenous peoples pass through this region (Guaymí enclaves move back and forth undisturbed across the border with Panama). You might spot women in traditional clothing – long, solid-colored *pollera* dresses trimmed in contrasting hues – riding the bus or strolling the streets. The Guaymí is one of the few indigenous groups that preserve such traditional customs (see the boxed text Endangered Cultures, p49).

The drive north from Neily is a scenic one, with superb views of the lowlands dropping away as the road winds up the hillside. The paved road is steep, narrow and full of hairpin turns. You can also get

to San Vito from San Isidro via the Valle de Coto Brus – an incredibly scenic and less-used route offering fantastic views of the Cordillera de Talamanca to the north and the lower Fila Costeña to the south.

Information

Banco Coopoleanza (8:30am-3:30pm Mon-Fri) An ATM on the Cirrus network. South of the church.

Banco de Costa Rica (8:30am-3:30pm Mon-Fri) South of the church.

Centro Cultural Dante Alighieri (773 4934; 1-7pm Mon-Fri) Opposite the park. Historical information on Italian immigration (or Italian lessons).

El Kiosko (per hr US$1; 6:30am-7pm) Offers Internet access.

Minae parks office (773 3955; 9am-4pm) In theory, this office provides information about Parque Internacional La Amistad, but it's not particularly helpful.

Sights & Activities

About 3km south of town, **Finca Cántaros** (773 3760; admission US$1; 9:30am-5pm Tue-Sun) is a recreation center and reforestation project. The 10 hectares of grounds – which used to be coffee plantations and pasture land – are now a lovely park with garden trails, picnic areas and a dramatic lookout over the city. The reception is housed in a pretty, well-maintained cabin that contains a small but carefully chosen selection of local and national crafts.

About 6km south of San Vito is the world-class **Wilson Botanical Garden** (Las Cruces Biological Station; 773 4004; www.esintro.co.cr; admission

US$6, guided tours US$15; ☺ 8am-4pm). Covering 12 hectares and surrounded by 254 hectares of natural forest, the garden was established by Robert and Catherine Wilson in 1963 and thereafter became internationally known for its collection.

In 1973 the area came under the auspices of the Organization for Tropical Studies (OTS), and today the well-maintained garden – part of Las Cruces Biological Station – holds more than 1000 genera of plants from about 200 families. As part of the OTS, the garden plays a scientific role as a research center. Species threatened with extinction are preserved here for possible reforestation in the future.

The gardens are well laid out, many of the plants are labeled and a trail map is available for self-guided walks, featuring exotic species like orchids, bromeliads, palms and medicinal plants. The many ornamental varieties are beautiful, but the tours explain that they are useful too (such as the delicate cycad, used by Cabécar and Bribrí indigenous people as a treatment for snakebite). The gardens are especially popular among bird-watchers, who may see scarlet-thighed dacni, silver-throated tanager, violaceous trogon, blue-headed parrot, violet sabrewing hummingbird and turquoise cotinga.

Buses between San Vito and Neily pass the entrance to the gardens. Make sure you take the bus that goes through Agua Buena; buses that go through Cañas Gordas do not stop here. A taxi from San Vito to the gardens costs US$3.

Sleeping & Eating

All rooms have a private bathroom with hot water unless otherwise noted.

Centro Turístico Las Huacas (☎ 773 3115; s/d US$9/15; P) On the western edge of town, this is a strip of rooms and a popular bar facing a large parking lot. Rooms are pretty plain, save the tattered curtains hanging in the windows, but they are clean and quiet (except when the bar gets going). This place attracts a business clientele.

Cabinas Rino (☎ 773 3071, late at night 773 4030; s/d/tr US$12/14/22, d with air-con US$35; P) This 2nd-floor hotel is located above a block of shops on the main road. Clean and comfortable, the rooms are well insulated to block out the street noise. They are all clean and comfortable, with whitewashed walls and TV. Staff is very accommodating, offering laundry service and other useful perks.

La Riviera (☎ 773 3295; r per person US$15) Next to the Dante Alighieri center, the Riviera has six spacious rooms with curtained windows and tiled bathrooms. Ask for one at the back, for a sensational view over the valley. More interesting, perhaps, is the restaurant (dishes US$3 to US$8, open 6am to 10pm) next door. In front, it's a popular fast-food joint serving burgers and burritos; in the back, the place goes upscale, with dim lights and a full bar.

Hotel El Ceibo (☎ 773 3025; apapilic@racsa.co.cr; s/d/tr US$25/35/45; P) With 40-odd immaculate rooms, this larger hotel is the only midrange option in town. It is conveniently

---

GETTING TO DAVID, PANAMA

On the Carratera Interamericana, Paso Canoas is the major border crossing with Panama. It is crowded and confusing, especially during holiday periods, when hordes of Ticos arrive for shopping sprees. Note that it's very easy to walk across the border without realizing it. No harm done, but don't go too far without getting the proper stamps in your passport.

Costa Rican *migraciónes* is on the eastern side of the highway, north of the Tracopa bus terminal. After securing an exit visa, walk 400m east to the Panamanian immigration post, in the huge new yellow cement block. Here you can purchase the necessary tourist card (US$5 for US citizens) to enter Panama. You might be asked for an onward ticket and evidence of financial solvency (presenting a credit card does the trick). From here dozens of minivans go to David, 1½ hours away (US$2 per person).

If you are in a private vehicle, you must have your car fumigated (US$4). Keep a copy of the fumigation ticket as roadside checkpoints often request it. Note that you cannot cross the border in a rental vehicle.

The border is open 24 hours. The Panamanian currency is the US dollar, which they call *balboa*, as well as Panamanian coins that are the same size and value as US coins. For more information about border crossings, see the boxed text Border Crossings, p546).

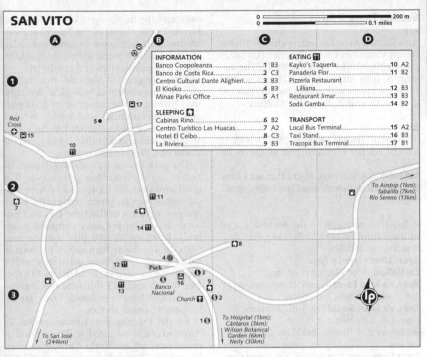

SAN VITO

INFORMATION
Banco Coopoleanza.........................1 B3
Banco de Costa Rica.......................2 C3
Centro Cultural Dante Alighieri.......3 B3
El Kiosko.......................................4 B3
Minae Parks Office.........................5 A1

SLEEPING
Cabinas Rino..................................6 B2
Centro Turístico Las Huacas............7 A2
Hotel El Ceibo................................8 C3
La Riviera......................................9 B3

EATING
Kayko's Taquería...........................10 A2
Panadería Flor...............................11 B2
Pizzería Restaurant
    Lilliana....................................12 B3
Restaurant Jimar...........................13 B3
Soda Gamba.................................14 B2

TRANSPORT
Local Bus Terminal........................15 A2
Taxi Stand....................................16 B3
Tracopa Bus Terminal....................17 B1

located about 100m west of the main intersection, on its own private road allowing for safety and tranquility (or peace and quiet, as they say). Some rooms have pretty forest views; others face the parking lot, which is less scenic. An upscale bar-restaurant (dishes US$4 to US$5) has good Italian and Tico dishes, including pasta varieties that you won't see in other parts of the country.

Wilson Botanical Garden (☎ 773 4004; www.esintro.co.cr; s/d incl meals US$85/156) If you want to stay overnight at the botanical gardens, make your reservations well in advance: facilities are often filled up with researchers and students. Accommodation is in comfortable cabins in the midst of the gorgeous grounds. The rooms are simple, but they each have a balcony with an amazing view of the surrounding flora. Rates include entry to the gardens.

Pizzería Restaurant Lilliana (pizzas US$3-5; ☼ 10:30am-10pm) The tables are often all occupied on Lilliana's terrace, which is filled with greenery and flowering plants, attracting tanagers and fruit birds. Locals come for

15 different kinds of pizza, plus tasty pasta and salads, everything made from scratch. The lovely mountain views and the friendly, familiar service make this a pleasant place to while away an afternoon.

Restaurant Jimar (dishes US$2-3) Jimar has a pleasant terrace too; but this restaurant is right on the highway to San José, and traffic can be disruptive. Otherwise, this is a fun, family place. Clean plastic booths create a fast-food feel, appropriate for the burgers and sandwiches that are on the menu.

Kayko's Taquería (dishes US$3-5) This is a colorful, friendly place with only one table, which allows Kayko to devote his attention to guests while he works in the open kitchen. Daily specials are posted above the counter.

Soda Gamba (☎ 773 3072; casados US$2) On San Vito's main road, one of many *sodas* serving cheap Tico fare.

Do not miss **Panadería Flor** (pastries US$0.50-$3.00; ☼ 6am-4pm), also on the main road, which has fresh flaky pastries and opens early for breakfast.

Getting There & Away

AIR

Alfo Romeo Aero Taxi offers charter flights to San Vito from Puerto Jiménez (US$472) and Golfito (US$432), respectively. The airstrip is 1km east of town. Otherwise, the nearest airports with scheduled services are at Coto 47 near Neily and in Golfito.

BUS

The main **Tracopa terminal** (☎ 773 3410) is located on the northern end of the main street.

San Isidro US$4, three hours, depart 6:45am and 1:30pm.

San José US$7.60, six hours, depart 5am, 7:30am, 10am and 3pm.

A local bus terminal on the northwest end of town runs buses to Neily and other destinations as follows:

Agua Caliente Depart at 3pm.

Las Mellizas Depart 9:30am, 2pm and 5pm.

Neily, via Agua Buena (Capul) US$1, two hours, depart 7am, 7:30am, 9am, noon, 2pm and 5pm.

Neily, via Cañas Gordas (Capul) US$1, two hours, depart 5:30am and 11am.

Río Sereno US$1, 1½ hours, depart 7am, 10am, 1pm and 4pm.

Santa Elena Depart 10am, 11:30am, 2pm, 4pm and 6pm.

PARQUE INTERNACIONAL LA AMISTAD

This huge 1950-sq-km park is by far the largest single protected area in Costa Rica. It is known as an international park because it continues across the border into Panama, where it is managed separately. The Panamanian side of the park is another 2070 sq km.

The backbone of this park is the Cordillera de Talamanca, which not only includes the peaks of the Chirripó massif but has many mountains higher than 3000m. The thickly forested northern Caribbean slopes and southern Pacific slopes of the Talamancas are also protected in the park, but it is only on the Pacific side that ranger stations are found.

Combined with two adjoining national parks and a host of indigenous and biological reserves, La Amistad is part of a huge biological corridor protecting a great variety of tropical habitats. Above 3200m, the landscape is characterized by the shrubby, stunted vegetation of the *páramo,* while slightly lower altitudes yield impressive oaks and the thick vegetation of the cloud forest. The lowlands of the Talamanca valley are fertile rain forest – a canopy of cedar, cypress and oak trees, with a thick undergrowth of palms, ferns and epiphytes.

This diversity of altitude and habitat creates unprecedented biological diversity, thus attracting the attention of ecologists and conservationists worldwide. In 1982 Unesco declared La Amistad to be a Biosphere Reserve, and in 1983 it was given the status of a World Heritage Site.

The park has the nation's largest population of Baird's tapirs (see p415), as well as giant anteaters, all six species of neotropical cats – jaguar, puma (mountain lion), margay, ocelot, oncilla (tiger cat) and jaguarundi – and many more-common mammals. In excess of 500 bird species have been sighted (more than half of the total in Costa Rica); 49 of these exist only within the biosphere reserve. In addition, 115 species of fish and 215 different reptiles and amphibians have been listed. There are innumerable insect species.

Besides the countless animal species, La Amistad is also home to five different indigenous reservations for the Cabécar and Bribrí groups. These tribes originally inhabited lands on the Caribbean coast (and many still do). But over the past century, they have migrated west into the mountains and as far as the Pacific coast. It is possible to visit the Cabécar via the Reserva Biológica Dúrika, and the Bribrí via ATEC in Puerto Viejo de Talamanca.

Within the park, tourist infrastructure is almost nonexistent, which means trekkers are limited to specific areas and/or the services of guides.

Orientation & Information

Limited information is available at local **Minae offices** Buenos Aires (☎ 730 0846); San Isidro (☎ 771 3155, 771 4836, 771 5116; Calle 2 btwn Avs 4 & 6); San Vito (☎ 773 4090). They are all minimally helpful.

To make reservations to camp or to stay in a refuge, it's better to call directly to park headquarters at **Altamira** (☎ 200 5355; park fee per person per day US$5). This is the best-developed area of the park, with a camping area, showers and drinking water, electric light and a lookout tower. A group of parataxonomists studying insects in this area has created a small display of butterflies and moths.

GETTING TO RÍO SERENO, PANAMA

East of San Vito a little-transited road leads to the border post at Río Sereno, from where you can continue on to the village of Volcán near Parque Nacional Volcán Barú in Panama. Río Sereno is a tranquil, pleasant place – atypical of border towns. The crossing here is hassle-free.

Migración (8am-6pm) is beside the police station. Panamanian immigration officials may require an onward ticket, plus US$500 to show solvency. The latter isn't usually demanded if you have a passport from a first-world country and look reasonably affluent.

US passport holders will need to purchase a tourist card (US$5), which is sold at the bank, about 100m past the *migración* office. Officials can direct you there. Note that the bank is closed on Sundays and Saturday afternoons.

There are no facilities on the Costa Rican side, but Río Serena, Panama has a decent hotel, a good pizza place and Internet access. The banking facilities at the border do not handle foreign exchange; the Panamanian currency is US dollars, or *balboa*. Buses depart hourly to David via Volcán.

Besides the headquarters at Altamira, there are additional, little-used ranger stations at **Potrero Grande** (742 8090), north of Paso Real and **Santa María de Pittier**, 15km south of Altamira on the slopes of Cerro Pittier. While there is apparently a hostel with toilets and fresh water at Santa María, these stations are not really set up to accommodate tourists.

Hiking

Behind Altamira station, **Los Gigantes del Bosque** is a short 3km circuit that is named for the 40m trees along the way. Signposts in Spanish provide simple explanations of some of the flora, although this is clearly designed for kids. Nonetheless, the trail is an easy means of seeing some ancient rain forest. It passes two lookout points, one on the edge of the primary forest, and the other overlooking the rural landscape outside the park. Note that this trail is marked, but it is not well maintained. Be prepared to climb over fallen branches and wade through high grass. More importantly, make sure you bring plenty of water and snacks and pay close attention to the markers. Normally the loop takes two hours, but it can be much longer if you lose the trail.

The longest trail (20km) – known as the **Valle del Silencio** – departs from the Estación Altamira and winds its way through pristine and hilly primary forest, before ending up at a camping area and refuge at the base of Cerro Kamuk. The walk takes anywhere from eight to 12 hours, provided you are in very good physical condition. It is reportedly spectacular and traverses one of the most isolated areas in all of Costa Rica.

A local guide is required to make the journey. Contact the association of guides **Asoprola** (743 1184) in Altamira to inquire about these arrangements. Asoprola can also provide food and lodging in the village of Altamira, just below the park headquarters.

Hardy adventurers can also hike to the summit of Cerro Kamuk (3549m) from the village of Potrero Grande or Tres Colinas. This journey requires three days to ascend and two days to descend and – again – the services of a guide. Lodging is in tents, and hikers must transport all of their own supplies and provisions. Contact the **Tres Colinas guides' association** (814 0889) for more information.

Sleeping & Eating

Besides the options listed here, see also the Reserva Biológica Dúrika, which is contained within the borders of the park.

All of the ranger stations have **camping facilities** (per person US$5), including freshwater and toilets. There are **basic hostels** (per person US$6) at Santa María de Pittier and at the base of Cerro Kamuk. These facilities offer drinking water and toilets, and – in the case of Altamira – electricity. All food and supplies must be packed in and out.

Asoprola (743 1184) can make arrangements for lodging in local homes in the village of Altamira.

South of Altamira, in the village of El Carmen, **Soda La Amistad** (El Carmen; r per person US$6) has simple cabins with cold-water showers – useful if you are heading in or out of the park.

Situated about 3km by poor dirt road from the village of Las Mellizas (not near

Altamira), **La Amistad Lodge** (☎ 200 5037, in San José 289 7667; www.laamistad.com; s/d/tr US$96/170/240; Ⓟ) sits on 100 sq km of wilderness and organic farm that constitutes Costa Rica's third-largest reserve. Since 1940, the congenial Montero family has operated this organic coffee farm, and has long worked to balance the needs of development with protecting the environment. The main lodge has tropical hardwood cabins with hot water and electricity provided by a low-impact hydroelectric plant.

Four additional jungle camps have been built at different altitudes and habitats, allowing visitors to do a multiday trek around the area without leaving the comforts of a solid bed and good cooking. The staff will transport your belongings from one site to another and provide meals at each camp, which has full-sized walk-in tents, toilets and running water. The extensive network of trails (40km) is excellent for birding and horseback riding. Guests are also invited to participate in the harvesting and processing (and drinking) of the homegrown coffee.

Rates include three meals a day (and lots of fresh-brewed coffee), as well as the entry fee into the park. Buses to Las Mellizas can get you close to the lodge, but the owners will come get you if you call ahead.

Getting There & Away

To reach Altamira, you can take any bus that runs between San Isidro and San Vito and get off in the town of Guácimo (often called Las Tablas). From Guácimo buses depart at noon and 5pm daily and travel the 16km to the town of El Carmen; and if the road conditions permit, they continue 4km to the village of Altamira. To return to Guácimo, buses depart from Altamira at 5am and 2:30pm daily. From the village of Altamira, follow the Minae sign (near the church) leading to the steep 2km hike to the ranger station.

Vehicles with 4WD go all the way to Altamira station. In theory, it is possible to hire a 4WD taxi to bring you here, either from San Vito or Buenos Aires. Keep in mind, however, that the roads are grueling, and bad conditions can make it pretty tough for anyone. If you are driving here, inquire about road conditions prior to your departure.

Península de Osa & Golfo Dulce

It's not uncommon to use superlatives when describing the Península de Osa and the Golfo Dulce. *National Geographic* famously described it as 'the most biologically intense place on earth.' That's right, on earth. Residents claim it is the most picturesque, the most pristine, the most perfect spot in Costa Rica.

Certainly, indisputably, it is the most remote (which goes a long way toward explaining why the other adjectives also apply).

Containing a huge swathe of Pacific rain forest, the Osa is crammed with life. What's more, you can actually see it. From the army ants toiling away, to the scarlet macaws squawking in the almond trees, from Baird's tapirs hanging around Sirena ranger station, to the four species of monkeys swinging in the trees, this is undoubtedly Costa Rica's top spot to witness life at its wildest. And not only in Parque Nacional Corcovado – although that's the obvious place – but also in the surrounding reserves that create a biological corridor around the gulf.

The peninsula protects the Golfo Dulce from the powerful Pacific, attracting groups of whales and dolphins to its tranquil waters. Fringing the bay, miles of shoreline are populated with swaying palms and prodigious birdlife, but hardly a human soul.

While the Guaymí Indians were the earliest inhabitants of the Osa and still live here, much of this area was never populated or developed by Ticos. It means that roads are poor and most of the peninsula is still off the grid. In recent years, all those superlatives have attracted the attention of gringos who want to trade in their workaday world for a piece of paradise.

HIGHLIGHTS

- Watching the sunrise over the Golfo Dulce and the sunset over the Pacific Ocean from the deserted beaches on **Cabo Matapalo** (p427)
- Encountering Baird's tapir on the trails around **Sirena station** (p415)
- Exploring the mangroves around **Puerto Jiménez** (p422) by kayak
- Feasting on the catch of the day, which you reeled in yourself from the **Golfo Dulce** (p424 or p431)
- Spotting the stunning, squawking scarlet macaw in the palm trees lining **Playa San Josecito** (p410)

★ Playa San Josecito

★ Golfo Dulce

Puerto Jiménez ★

Sirena station ★

Cabo Matapalo ★

TO CORCOVADO VIA BAHÍA DRAKE

At the northern base of the Península de Osa, the Valle de Diquis is named for the indigenous group that originally inhabited this area (probably the same folks responsible for the strange stone spheres that still decorate the region). The valley stretches from the basin of the Río Grande de Térraba west to the mouth of the river and south to Sierpe, from where the Río Sierpe flows out to Bahía Drake. Inland, this flat terrain is covered with palm plantations, but closer to the coast line, the Humedal Nacional Térraba-Sierpe protects an amazing array of jungly swampland and overgrown mangroves.

SIERPE

Almost 30km from the Pacific Ocean, this sleepy village on the Río Sierpe sees bursts of activity when travelers pass through to Bahía Drake. Boats can be hired here – though most lodges in Bahía Drake will arrange boat pickup in Sierpe for guests with reservations.

The **Centro Turistico Las Vegas** (next to the boat dock; ☯ 6am-10pm) has become a sort of catchall place for tourist information, distributing a wide selection of maps and brochures. It also offers Internet access.

Sleeping & Eating

Hotel Margarita (☎ 786 7574; west side of soccer field; d US$10-12; **P**) Margarita's cheapest rooms are very basic, sharing cold showers and clean toilets. Five more comfortable rooms have tile floors, much needed fans and private bathrooms, some with hot water. A pleasant terrace overlooks the soccer field. This is a good choice if you need somewhere cheap to crash before catching the water taxi to Bahía Drake in the morning.

Hotel Oleaje Sereno (☎ 786 7580; oleajesereno@ racsa.co.cr; r US$35-50; **P** 🎇) This surprisingly stylish little motel offers a prime dockside location overlooking the Río Sierpe. Ten renovated rooms have wood floors, sturdy furniture, crisp but mismatched linens, and aqua blue walls that match the color of the sky on a clear day. The open-air restaurant is one of the Sierpe's most welcoming, with

linen tablecloths and lovely river views. This is a safe and convenient place to leave your car when you continue on to Drake. Credit cards are accepted.

Eco Manglares Sierpe Lodge (☎ 786 7414; eco siepa@racsa.co.cr; 2km north of Sierpe; s/d US$41/53; **P**) Across the river from the Estero Azul Lodge, this secluded lodge is accessible by a narrow, metal suspension bridge: it looks dodgy but it will support your car! Ten spacious, thatched-roof cabins are nicely furnished, featuring artistic cane and mangrove pieces. Owned and managed by a long-time resident Italian family, which explains the excellent pizzas and homemade pastas served in the on-site restaurant (meals US$7 to US$14, open 7am to 10pm). Drive north on the road to Palmar.

Veragua River House (☎ 786 7460; 2km north of Sierpe; d US$50; **P** 🎇) This property's amiable Italian owner, Ven, is well loved for his fresh-baked bread, his extensive classical music collection, and especially, his hospitable nature. About 1km past the Eco Manglares Sierpe Lodge (yes, you have to cross the bridge), this B&B has four elegant bungalows hidden behind blooming hibiscus and shady fruit trees. A wraparound porch, a comfy lounge well stocked with games and a discrete plunge pool all comprise the inviting common areas.

Estero Azul Lodge (☎ 786 7422; esteroazul@hotmail .com; 2km north of Sierpe; r per person $80; **P** 🎇) Named for the peaceful flowing river, the Estero Azul Lodge is set on several acres of primary forest along the road to Palmar. Safari-style rooms feature ceiling fans, hardwood floors, screened porches and tile bathrooms. Rates include all three meals – a perk, considering co-owner Patricia Kirk is an award-winning chef. She uses homegrown herbs to highlight fresh river fish and seafood, with delectable results. The lodge offers fishing tours in the mangroves (US$150 per day) and offshore (US$500 per day).

Las Vegas Bar/Restaurant (next to the boat dock; casados US$5; ☯ 6am-10pm) Impressive for its wide ranging menu, offering everything from pancakes to pork chops.

Getting There & Away

AIR

Scheduled flights and charters fly into Palmar Sur (see p390), 14km north of Sierpe.

PENÍNSULA DE OSA & GOLFO DULCE

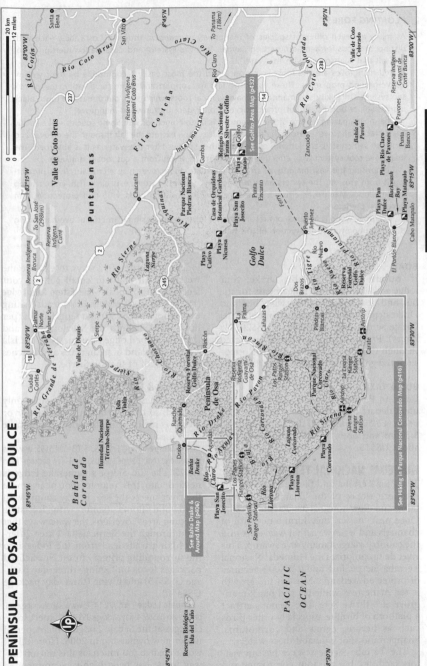

FLOATING FOREST

As many as seven different species of mangrove, or *manglar*, thrive in Costa Rica, each with distinct methods for aeration (getting oxygen into the system) and desalination (getting rid of the salt that is absorbed with the water).

Red mangroves are the most common – and the most easily recognizable by their web of above-ground prop roots. These roots are less for support and more for aerating the plant's sap system. Other kinds of mangroves have vertical roots which stick out above the mud (black mangrove), or buttresses that provide access to oxygen (buttonwood mangrove).

The most amazing feature of the mangrove is its tolerance for salt. Some species – like Pacific coast black mangrove – absorb the salinated water, then excrete the salt through their leaves and roots, so salt crystals are sometimes visible. Other species filter the water as it is absorbed. The mangrove root system is so effective a filter that the water from a cut root is drinkable.

Comprising the vast majority of tropical coastline, mangroves play a crucial role in protecting it from erosion. The waters are a refuge for countless critters, especially fish, crab, shrimp and mollusks. Mangroves also act as a sanctuary for roosting birds, who find protection from terrestrial predators.

Mangrove wood is a source of fuel and tannin (used in processing leather). But overharvesting is contributing to the destruction of this habitat.

BOAT

If you are heading to Bahía Drake, your lodge will likely make arrangements for the bus and boat transfer. Otherwise, boats to Drake depart from the dock in front of Hotel Oleaje Sereno daily at 10:30am (US$20, 1½ hours). Private boats can also be chartered through Corcovado Expeditions (see opposite); the going rate is about US$100.

BUS & TAXI

Buses to Palmar Norte (US$0.50, 30 minutes) depart from in front of the Pulpería Fenix at 5:30am, 8:30am, 10:30am, 12:30pm, 3:30pm and 6pm. A taxi to Palmar costs about US$15.

HUMEDAL NACIONAL TÉRRABA-SIERPE

The Ríos Térraba and Sierpe begin on the southern slopes of the Talamanca mountains and flow toward the Pacific Ocean. Once near the sea, they form a network of channels and waterways that weave around the country's largest mangrove swamp. This river delta comprises the Humedal Nacional Térraba-Sierpe, just under 33,000 hectares of protected wetlands. Most of the growth is red mangrove, while tea and black mangrove also thrive here. The swamps attract a plethora of birdlife, especially water birds such as herons, egrets and cormorants. Snapper and snook inhabit these waters.

The Térraba-Sierpe reserve has no visitors facilities, but the tour companies and

lodges in Sierpe offer ways to explore the wetlands. All of them entail getting your feet wet, so to speak. The **Estero Azul Lodge** (☎ 786 7422; esteroazul@hotmail.com) leads fishing expeditions (US$150) and rents kayaks (per hour US$15). Both the Sábalo Lodge and the Río Sierpe Lodge take guests to the Isla Violin, an island of mangroves and beaches at the mouth of the Río Sierpe.

Sleeping & Eating

Both of these options are accessible only by boat, so transportation from Palmar or Sierpe is included in the price, as are three daily meals.

Río Sierpe Lodge (☎ 253 5203, 384 5595; www.rio sierpelodge.com; per person US$65, 3-day package from US$175) The Río Sierpe's namesake lodge is nestled into this remote spot near where the river meets the sea. Breezy rooms with hardwood floors (some with loft-style sleeping areas) overlook the waterways that wind through the Sierpe delta. Three different hiking trails lead from the lodge into the surrounding primary forest. Specialized packages focus on fishing (three-day package US$375) and diving (three-day package US$450).

Sábalo Lodge (☎ 770 1457; www.sabalolodge.com; per person US$65, 4-day package US$395) Expect some changes at the Sábalo Lodge, which opened under new ownership in 2006. Hopefully it won't change too much, as this out-of-the-way lodge has been highly recommended for hiking, horse riding and wildlife-watching. (Most of the treks incorporate a cooling visit to a nearby waterfall and/or swimming hole.)

BAHÍA DRAKE

Nestled into the western side of the Península de Osa, between the thick jungle of Parque Nacional Corcovado and the crystalline waters of Bahía Drake, this little settlement is actually composed of two tiny towns: Agujitas, spread out along the southern shore of the bay; and Drake, a few kilometers to the north.

The bay is named for Sir Francis Drake himself, who visited this area in March 1579, during his circumnavigation in the Golden Hind. History has it that he stopped on the nearby Isla del Caño, but locals speculate that he probably landed here as well. A monument at Punta Agujitas (on the grounds of the Drake Bay Wilderness Resort, p409) states as much.

Agujitas is a friendly community of about 300 residents, whose ramshackle houses are clustered around a school and a clinic at the mouth of the Río Agujitas. Typically, the centre of village life is the *pulpería* (corner grocery store), where you'll find a public phone and the town's main boat dock. Drake is the site of the airstrip, and a few places to stay.

It's not easy to visit Bahía Drake on the cheap: only few budget options exist in Agujitas. Supplies, food and just about everything else are shipped in, a logistical fact that is reflected in local prices. Furthermore, the only way to get around is by boat or by foot; so if you are counting your colones, get ready to hoof it. Fortunately, walking is not only transportation, but also recreation, as sightings of macaws, monkeys and other wildlife are practically guaranteed.

Orientation

Agujitas is a one-road town (and not a very good road, at that). It comes south from Rincón and past the airstrip in Drake. At the T, the right branch dead-ends at the water, where the *pulpería*, clinic and school constitute the heart of Agujitas; while the left branch heads out of town southeast to Los Planes. From the eastern end of Agujitas, a path follows the shoreline out of town. A swinging, swaying pedestrian bridge crosses the Río Agujitas to Punta Agujitas. From here, the trail picks up and continues south along the coast, all the way to Parque Nacional Corcovado.

Information

B&B Bambú Sol (☎ 214 2711; per hr US$1) This little hotel has Internet access for the public.

Corcovado Expeditions (☎ 818 9962; info@corcovadoexpeditions.net; per hr US$1; ☼ 8am-6pm) A wealth of information on the area, including maps (a rarity!) and Internet access.

Activities

No matter what activity you undertake, rest assured that it will also involve hiking.

HIKING

All of the lodges offer tours to Parque Nacional Corcovado, usually a full-day trip to San Pedrillo station (US$50 to US$75 per person), including boat transportation, lunch and guided hikes. Indeed, if you came all the way to the Península de Osa, it's hard to pass up a visit to the national park that made it famous.

Some travelers, however, come away from these tours disappointed. The trails around San Pedrillo station attract many people, usually hiking in groups, which inhibits animal sightings; furthermore, most tours arrive at the park well after sunrise, when activity in the rain forest has already quieted down. Considering their hefty price tag, these tours are not necessarily the most rewarding way to see wildlife. The lodges strongly encourage their guests to take these tours (because they are money makers), but you have other options.

The easiest and most obvious one is the long, coastal trail that heads south out of Agujitas and continues about 10km to the border of Parque Nacional Corcovado. Indeed, a determined hiker could make it all the way to San Pedrillo station on foot in three to four hours (make sure you reserve a spot at the ranger station if you intend to spend the night – see p417). But there is little need to go all the way, as the same species that inhabit the park are frequently spotted in the surrounding buffer zone. Macaws, monkeys and other exotic species travel this trail as often as humans!

Playa San Josecito (see p411) is a popular destination for a day-hike, but it's easy to

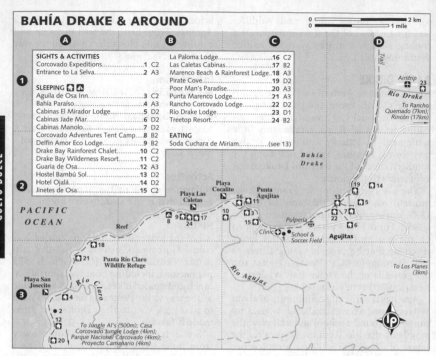

BAHÍA DRAKE & AROUND

SIGHTS & ACTIVITIES
Corcovado Expeditions.....................1 C2
Entrance to La Selva........................2 A3

SLEEPING
Aguila de Osa Inn...........................3 C2
Bahía Paraíso..................................4 A3
Cabinas El Mirador Lodge.................5 D2
Cabinas Jade Mar............................6 D2
Cabinas Manolo...............................7 D2
Corcovado Adventures Tent Camp....8 B2
Delfín Amor Eco Lodge.....................9 B2
Drake Bay Rainforest Chalet...........10 C2
Drake Bay Wilderness Resort...........11 C2
Guaria de Osa................................12 A3
Hostel Bambú Sol...........................13 D2
Hotel Ojalá...................................14 D2
Jinetes de Osa...............................15 C2

La Paloma Lodge.............................16 C2
Las Caletas Cabinas.........................17 B2
Marenco Beach & Rainforest Lodge..18 A3
Pirate Cove...................................19 D2
Poor Man's Paradise.......................20 A3
Punta Marenco Lodge.....................21 A3
Rancho Corcovado Lodge................22 D2
Río Drake Lodge.............................23 D1
Treetop Resort..............................24 B2

EATING
Soda Cuchara de Miriam.............(see 13)

PENÍNSULA DE OSA & GOLFO DULCE

---

tailor a hike to any distance and destination that you like.

If you want to head inland, you can explore the **Punta Río Claro Wildlife Refuge** (also called the Marenco Rain Forest Reserve). Both Marenco Beach & Rain Forest Lodge (p412) and Punta Marenco Lodge (p412) offer access to this private reserve. Otherwise, you can access it from the Río Claro Trail (see p411) or from Playa San Josecito (see p411).

When hiking without a guide, make sure that somebody knows when and where you are going. Should you get lost, try to find a river or stream, which you can follow to the ocean.

SWIMMING & SNORKELING

Isla del Caño is commonly considered the best place for snorkeling in this area. Lodges and tour companies all offer day-trips to the island (US$60 to US$80 per person), which usually includes the park fee, snorkeling equipment and lunch, as well as a guided island hike in the afternoon. As anywhere, the clarity of the water and the variety of

the fish fluctuate according to water and weather conditions: it's worth inquiring before dishing out the cash for a tour.

Other opportunities for snorkeling exist on the coast between Agujitas and Corcovado. **Playa San Josecito** (see p411) attracts scores of colorful species, who hide out amongst the coral reef and rocks. Another recommended spot is **Playa Las Caletas**, just in front of the Corcovado Adventures Tent Camp. Most lodges rent equipment to guests.

Closer to Agujitas, **Playa Cocalito** is a small, pretty beach that is pleasant for swimming and sunbathing, although it disappears at high tide.

SCUBA DIVING

About 20km west of Agujitas, **Isla del Caño** is one of Costa Rica's top spots for diving, with attractions including intricate rock and coral formations and an amazing array of underwater life, teeming with colorful reef fish and incredible coral formations. Divers report that the schools of fish swimming overhead are often so dense that they block the sunlight from filtering down.

While the bay is rich with dive sites, a local highlight is undoubtedly the **Bajo del Diablo** (Devil's Rock), an astonishing formation of submerged mountains that attracts an incredible variety of fish species, including jack, snapper, barracuda, puffer, parrotfish, moray eel and shark.

A two-tank dive runs US$90 to US$110, or you can do an open-water course for US$325 to US$400. Area lodges that offer diving packages include Pirate Cove (p409), Jinetes de Osa (p409), Aguila de Osa Inn (p409), Drake Bay Wilderness Resort (p409) and La Paloma Lodge (p410).

KAYAKING & CANOEING

A fantastic way to explore the region's biodiversity is to paddle through it. The idyllic **Río Agujitas** attracts a huge variety of birdlife and lots of scaly reptiles. Paddling at high tide is recommended because it allows kayakers to explore more territory. The river conveniently empties out into the bay, which is surrounded by hidden coves and sandy beaches ideal for exploring in a sea kayak. Several lodges have kayaks available for their guests, including La Paloma Lodge (p410), Aguila de Osa (p409), and Drake Bay Wilderness Resort (p409). Corcovado Expeditions (p408) also rents kayaks (per hour/day US$5/25) and leads a wide variety of kayaking tours (half/full day US$35/50).

HORSE RIDING

The **coastal trail** between Agujitas and Corcovado is perfect for horse riding, especially if you relish the idea of galloping wildly across deserted beaches while the waves crash below you. **Los Planes** is another popular destination for horse riders, with ample opportunities for wildlife-watching along the way. Many lodges offer guided tours for about US$60 per day, including Cabinas El Mirador Lodge (p408). Poor Man's Paradise (p412) rents horses for US$10 per hour, while Jungle Al's (p412) includes beach riding in the price of all packages.

SPORTFISHING

Bahía Drake claims more than 40 fishing records, including sailfish; black, blue and striped marlin; yellow fin tuna; wahoo; cubera snapper; Spanish and sierra mackerel; and roosterfish. Fishing is excellent year-round, although the catch may vary

according to the season. The peak season for tuna and marlin is from August to December. Sailfish are caught year-round, but experience a slow-down in May and June. Dorado and wahoo peak between May and August. Other species are abundant year-round, so you are virtually assured to reel in something.

Many lodges will arrange fishing excursions, but the best lodge dedicated to offshore anglers is Aguila de Osa (p409), which arranges half-/full-day excursions for US$550/800. More off the beaten track, Jungle Al's (p412) offers a variety of multiday fishing packages. If you are on a budget, you will appreciate the opportunities at Hotel Ojalá (p408) and the aptly named Poor Man's Paradise (p412).

DOLPHIN- & WHALE-WATCHING

As of 2006, swimming with dolphins and whales is illegal in Costa Rica. These measures are a result of an increase in tourist activity, often led by inexperienced guides who did not respect the best interests of these amazing creatures. Dolphin- and whale-watching tours still provide opportunities to get up-close and personal with these sea creatures – but only from the comfort and safety of the boat.

Bahía Drake is rife with marine life, including more than 25 species of dolphins and whales which pass through on their migrations throughout the year. This area is uniquely suited for whale-watching: humpback whales come from both the north and the south hemispheres to calve, resulting in the longest humpback whale season in the world. Humpbacks can be spotted in Bahía Drake year-round (except May), but the best months to see whales are late July through early November.

Several of the lodges are involved with programs to protect and preserve marine life in Bahía Drake, as well as to offer tourists a chance for a close encounter. Tours generally cost about US$100 per person.

The program at Drake Bay Wilderness Resort (p409) is highly recommended. Marine biologist Shawn Larkin has an infectious enthusiasm about marine mammals. He spends his time researching and filming dolphins and whales for his educational organization, the **Costa Cetacea Research Institute** (www.costacetacea.com).

Delfín Amor Eco Lodge (p411) also specializes in educational marine tours, with an excellent website detailing the species of dolphins and whales and their migratory patterns. Under the auspices of the nonprofit **Fundación Vida Marina** (www.vidamarina.org), staff are involved in collecting data to work towards the goal of establishing a protected marine sanctuary in this area. They use an amazing 'Flying Inflatable Boat' to track and monitor dolphins, whales and commercial fishing in the area.

Tours

Corcovado Expeditions (☎ 818 9962, 833 2384; www.corcovadoexpeditions.net) Competitively priced tours to Corcovado and Caño Island, as well as specialty hikes to look for birds (per person US$25) and poison-dart frogs (per person US$25). Corcovado Expeditions also rents mountain bikes (per hour/day US$10/35) and leads biking tours (half-/full day US$35/50).

Night Tour (www.thenighttour.com; admission US$35; ⊙ 7:45-10pm) Tracie the 'Bug Lady' and her spotting partner Victor have created quite a name for themselves, with this fascinating nighttime walk in the jungle. Tracie is a walking encyclopedia on bug facts. Participants use night-vision scopes as an added bonus. Make reservations well in advance.

Original Canopy Tour (☎ 371 1598; admission US$55; ⊙ 8am-4pm) Bahía Drake's only such facility is located at Jinetes de Osa (p409). Nine platforms, six cables and one 20m observation deck provide a new perspective on the rain forest. Reservations recommended.

Sleeping & Eating

This area is off the grid, so many places do not have electricity (pack a flashlight) or hot water. Reservations are recommended in the dry season (mid-November to the end of April). High-season rates are quoted; prices are per person, including three meals, unless otherwise stated.

For other accommodations, check out the area from Bahía Drake to Corcovado, beginning on p411.

BUDGET

Cabinas Manolo (r US$10) Any place you choose to stay is going to be rustic; Manolo drops all pretenses and prices his rooms accordingly. They are very simple with shared cold-water bathrooms. But the place is friendly and clean and it provides easy access to all that Bahía Drake has to offer. Meals are not included in this rock bottom price, but there are a few places to eat nearby.

Río Drake Lodge (☎ 817 2035; edu_pop@hotmail.com; r US$20) This budget option near the Drake airstrip offers quaint, thatch-roof cabins with no electricity. Amenities are limited, but opportunities for fun are not: spend your days lounging in a hammock on a 200m stretch of beach, hiking on several kilometers of jungle trails or swimming in the Río Drake. Meals (not included) are available at the attached restaurant, which specializes in barbecue.

MIDRANGE

Cabinas El Mirador Lodge (☎ 836 9415, 387 9138; www.miradordrakebay.com; r US$42) High up on a hill at the northern end of Agujitas, El Mirador – which means Lookout Point – lives up to its name, offering spectacular views of the bay from its eight cozy cabins. Catch the sunset from your balcony, or climb up to the lookout that perches above. The hospitable

---

JUNGLE NIGHTS

As night falls in the jungle, an amazing transformation takes places. That is, all the birds that were squawking all day long are suddenly quiet. And a whole new host of noises fills the air. The sounds of crickets, cicadas and other tropical bugs, awakening at dusk, are utterly overwhelming: the buzz emanates from all sides, vibrating throughout the forest. This is also when the aptly named vesper bats come out, seemingly flying circles around your head.

As the darkness engulfs you, your other senses are heightened. That is the only way to explain the amazing otherworldly quality of the exotic night sounds, like the mournful coo of the puaraque calling his mate, or the scream of fighting coatis in the distance.

Most of the night tours in Bahía Drake focus on finding nocturnal critters like river shrimps, frogs, spiders and insects (see Night Tour, above). But many mammals are nocturnal: night tours around Sirena station (p415) are the best way to spot Baird's tapir, kinkajou and skunk, as well as American crocodile. It doesn't happen often, but if you're going to see a feline it will likely be at night.

Vargas family ensures that all guests receive a warm welcome. They also run the very simple Hostel Bambú Sol (rooms US$15), which is just down the road, and the Soda Cuchara de Miriam, next door.

Rancho Corcovado Lodge (☎ 786 7903; camping/unit US$10/45) This family-run lodge is amazingly secluded, considering its location in the middle of the village. Fruit trees and coconut palms shade the grounds, which face a wide stretch of sandy beach. One set of cabinas is beachside, while others are set back on the ridge, offering more privacy and sweeping views. The grounds are also open to campers, who can access the cold showers and other facilities, but electricity is available only in the evenings.

Cabinas Jade Mar (☎ 845 0394; r US$45; P) Doña Marta and Don Rafa rent out seven clean and comfy cabinas in the center of town. In the main building, concrete rooms share a breezy porch, which provides lovely ocean vistas and plenty of hammocks. But the prime real estate is the private beachside house, which goes for US$50 to US$80, not including meals. Electricity in the evenings only.

Corcovado Jungle Eco Lodge (☎ 7708209; www.corcovadojungleecolodge; Los Planes; camp/cabin/ranch US$15/30/50, meal plan US$35) Surrounded by miles and miles of primary rain forest, this new jungle lodge is inland from Bahía Drake on the northern edge of the Parque Nacional Corcovado. Standard accommodations are clean and comfortable cabinas (and one fun tree house), constructed out of hardwood. A common terrace enjoys a view over the botanical garden, lush with fruit trees that attract incredible birdlife. Ranchos are more secluded – accessible only by a series of wooden walkways and elevated observation platforms. A network of trails crosses the 100-hectare private reserve, providing ample opportunities for wildlife-watching and hiking, including a trek to a nearby waterfall and swimming hole.

Hotel Ojalá (Fred's Place; ☎ 380 4763, 815 1080, in the USA 877-769 8747; www.hotelojala.com; r US$58; P 😣) The Hotel Ojalá, known locally as Fred's Place, is ideal for the traveler who wants to enjoy fishing and relaxing, 'without unnecessary frills.' A quaint two-storey house has three small, comfortable rooms; a shared balcony overlooks two hundred meters of mangroves and the wide blue ocean

beyond. Fred's focus is fishing, but lots of activities can be arranged.

Jinetes de Osa (☎ 371 1598, 236 5637, in the USA 800-317 0333; www.costaricadiving.com; r standard/superior from US$60/76) Jinetes de Osa boasts a choice bayside location that is – literally – a few steps from the ocean. The small black-sand beach disappears at high tide, but the views are wonderful around the clock (especially at sunrise, when your fresh-brewed coffee is delivered to your room). The convivial open-air cantina is Bahía Drake's top spot for sipping fruity cocktails. Jinetes is home to Drake's only canopy tour and is also a PADI dive facility.

Pirate Cove (☎ 234 6154; www.piratecovecostarica.com; r US$75, 4-day package US$570) Breezy, tent-like bungalows and spacious hard-wood cabins both offer an element of luxury at Pirate Cove. All of the options have private terraces with swinging hammocks and wonderful views. They are set amidst the lush rain forest, fronting 2km of deserted beach. If you can tear yourself away, the typical tours are offered, including PADI dive instruction.

TOP END
Listed in order from north to south:

Aguila de Osa Inn (☎ 296 2190; www.aguiladeosa.com; r adult/child US$180/110, 4-day package US$769/506) On the east side of the Río Agujitas, this swanky lodge caters to a fishing and diving clientele. The roomy quarters have shining wood floors and high ceilings, tiled bathrooms and private decks. With this oceanfront site, the sunrise views are worth waking up for. The downstairs restaurant is one of the lodge's main attractions: comfortable yet elegant, the open-air *rancho* (small house-like building) has the liveliest bar and best *bocas* (snacks) in Bahía Drake. The kitchen will prepare your catch – grilled or sashimi – as you like.

Drake Bay Wilderness Resort (☎ 770 8012; www.drakebay.com; 4-day package US$660; 😣) Sitting pretty on Punta Agujitas, this resort occupies the optimal piece of real estate in all of Bahía Drake. Naturalists will be won over by the lovely landscaping, from flowering trees to the ocean-fed pool; while history buffs will appreciate the memorial to Drake's landing. Most of the accommodations are in comfortable cabins, which have mural-painted walls and private patios with ocean views. Several cheaper cabanas with shared bathroom are also available (four-day package US$560). Family-style meals feature ingredients from your congenial host's organic farm. This place is popular with families, probably because kids under 16 get a hefty discount.

La Paloma Lodge (☎ 239 7502; www.lapalomalodge .com; 4-day package standard/deluxe/sunset deluxe US$1050/1190/1250; 🖭) Perched on a lush hillside, this exquisite lodge provides guests with an incredible panorama of ocean and forest, all from the comfort of the sumptuous, stylish quarters. Rooms have shiny hardwood floors and queen-size orthopedic beds, draped in mosquito netting. Shoulder-high walls in all the bathrooms offer rainforest views while you bathe. Each room has a large balcony (with hammock, of course) that catches the breeze off the ocean. Five additional deluxe *ranchos* are secluded, spacious and ideal for families. For scuba enthusiasts the lodge has an 11m pontoon boat that makes fast time to Isla del Caño. Rates include air transfer from San José.

Drake Bay Rainforest Chalet (☎ 382 1619; www .drakebayholiday.com; 4-/7-day package US$760/1150, additional night US$100) Set on 45 acres of pristine rain forest, this luxurious jungle get-away is a remote, romantic adventure. Huge, French windows provide a panoramic view of the surrounding jungle, enjoyed from almost every room in the house. Sleeping quarters feature a king-sized bed with giant mosquito net, flanked by a luxurious tiled bathroom with a sunken shower and a decadent two-person hot tub. The modern Moroccan-style kitchen is fully stocked for self catering, or chef service is available (three/six nights US$120/270).

Getting There & Away
AIR
Departing from San José both NatureAir (one way/round trip US$87/174) and Sansa (US$80/160) have four flights daily into the Drake airstrip, which is 2km north of Agujitas. Most lodges provide transportation, which involves a jeep or a boat or both.

BOAT
All of the hotels offer boat transfers between Sierpe and Bahía Drake. The trip to Drake is scenic and – at times – exhilarating. Boats travel along the river through the rain forest and the mangrove estuary. Captains then pilot boats through tidal currents and surf the river mouth into the ocean. Most hotels in Drake have beach landings, so wear reef-walkers.

If you have not made advanced arrangements with your lodge for a pick-up, you can catch the collective water taxi, which departs at 10am from the dock in front of the Hotel Oleaje Sereno in Sierpe (US$15, 1½ hours).

BUS & CAR
A rough dirt road links Agujitas to Rincón, from where you can head south to Puerto Jiménez or north to the Interamericana. A 4WD is recommended for this route, especially from June to November. There are several river crossings, the one at Río Drake being the most significant. (Locals fish many a water-logged tourist vehicle out of the river, see p551). Once in Agujitas, you will likely abandon your car, as most places are accessible only by boat or by foot.

If you are hiking through Parque Nacional Corcovado but you want to avoid the arduous San Pedrillo trail, you can hire a 4WD vehicle to La Palma (US$50) and start the hike there. In theory, a bus also goes to La Palma (US$5), departing Drake at 4am during the dry season only.

HIKING
From Bahía Drake, it's a four- to six-hour hike along the beachside trail to San Pedrillo ranger station at the north end of Corcovado. If you are heading into the park, make sure you have reservations to camp at the ranger stations (see p417).

BAHÍA DRAKE TO CORCOVADO
The craggy shore stretches 10km from Bahía Drake to Corcovado, a series of sandy inlets that disappear at high tide, leaving only the rocky outposts and luxuriant rain forest. Besides the lodges that dot the coastline, this beautiful stretch is uninhabited and undeveloped. The setting is magnificent and wild, but be aware that travelers are more or less dependent on their lodges. There are no other facilities outside of Agujitas.

A public trail follows the coastline for the entire spectacular stretch. It is easy to follow and wonderful for wildlife. Among the multitude of bird species, you are likely to spot (and hear) squawking scarlet macaws, often traveling in pairs, and the hooting chestnut-mandible toucan. White-faced capuchins and howler monkeys inhabit the treetops, while eagle-eyed hikers might also spot a sloth or a kinkajou.

This entire route is punctuated by pretty little inlets, each with a wild, windswept beach. Just west of Punta Agujitas, a short detour off the main trail leads to the picturesque **Playa Cocalito**, a secluded cove perfect for sunning, swimming and body surfing. With no lodges in the immediate vicinity, it is often deserted. **Playa Las Caletas**, in front of the Corcovado Adventures Tent Camp, is supposed to be excellent for snorkeling.

Further south, the Río Claro empties out into the ocean. Water can be waist deep or higher, and the current swift, so take care when wading across. This is also the start of the Río Claro trail, which leads inland into the 1000-acre **Punta Río Claro Wildlife Refuge** (formerly known as the Marenco Rain Forest Reserve) and passes a picturesque waterfall along the way. Be aware that there are two rivers known as the Río Claro: one is located near Bahía Drake, while the other is inside Corcovado near Sirena station.

South of Río Claro, the **Playa San Josecito** is the longest stretch of white sand beach on this side of the Península de Osa. It is popular with swimmers, snorkelers and sunbathers, though you'll rarely find it crowded.

From here you can access another private reserve, labeled **La Selva**. A short, steep climb leads from the beach to a lookout point, offering a spectacular view over the treetops and out to the ocean. A network of trails continues inland, and eventually connects La Selva to the Río Claro reserve. Be advised that La Selva does not have any facilities: the trails are not labeled; there is no water or maps; you will likely meet no one along the way. If you choose to continue past the lookout point, make sure you have food, water and a compass.

The border of Parque Nacional Corcovado is about 5km south of here (it takes three to four hours to hike the entire distance from Agujitas to Corcovado). The trail is more overgrown as it gets closer to the park, but it is a well-traveled route.

Sleeping & Eating

The lodges offer varying degrees of comfort, but they are the only development in this area. Most have generators or solar power, providing electricity for at least part of the day. Nonetheless, 'early to bed, early to rise' is the norm in these parts. Reservations are recommended for the high season (December through April). Rates are per person, including three meals, unless otherwise stated. In order from Bahía Drake to Corcovado:

Las Caletas Cabinas (☎ 381 4052, 826 1460; www .caletas.co.cr; r US$50-70; 🖳) This sweet little hotel is set on the picturesque beach of the same name. Five cabins vary in terms of size and views, but they are all cozy wooden structures with tile bathrooms (with hot water), private terraces and rustic decor. The Swiss-Tico owners are warm hosts who are passionate about environmental sustainability. Solar and hydroelectric power provides electricity around the clock.

Treetop Resort (in the USA ☎ 310-748 6844; www .drakebayresort.com; r US$65) Another intimate resort with four rustic cabins, all constructed from scavenged hardwood and bamboo. Wide porches and huge screened windows allow for cooling breezes and magnificent vistas – guaranteed by the beachside setting. This place was closed at the time of research for the construction of all-new deluxe cabins with kitchens, but was scheduled to re-open in 2006.

Delfín Amor Eco Lodge (☎ 847 3131, in the USA 831-345-8484; www.divinedolphin.com; r US$95, 4-day package US$658; 🖳) Six light-filled cabanas – all with ocean views – are set on 10 acres of tropical gardens (featuring an impressive collection of exotic heliconia). An underwater motif pervades this place, from the mural-painted walls to the colorful comforters (appropriate, as this place specializes in marine tours and conservation, see p407).

Corcovado Adventures Tent Camp (☎ 384 1679; www.corcovado.com; r US$65, 4-day package US$355) Less than an hour's walk from Drake brings you to this fun, family-run spot. It's like camping, but comfy: spacious, walk-in tents are set up on covered platforms and fully equipped with sturdy wood furniture. Fifty acres of rain forest offer plenty of opportunity for exploration, while the beachfront setting is excellent for water sports (all equipment included), not to mention magnificent sunsets from your deck. Solar power provides electricity in the common *rancho* only.

PENÍNSULA DE OSA & GOLFO DULCE

Marenco Beach & Rainforest Lodge (☎ 770 8002, in San José 258 1919, in the USA 800-278 6223; www .marencolodge.com; d US$50-65, d bungalow US$75; 🖳) One of Bahía Drake's more institutional options, this lodge is set on 1500 acres of tropical forest reserve, also known as the Punta Río Claro Wildlife Refuge. Accommodation is basic – cold water showers, minimal decor – but the grounds are nicely landscaped and the flowering trees attract hummingbirds, toucans and capuchins. This place has electricity in the evenings only, provided by a noisy generator. Buffet-style meals are not included in the price.

Punta Marenco Lodge (☎ 234 1308, 234 1227; www.corcovadozone.com; r US$65) Not to be confused with its next door neighbor, this more intimate, family-run lodge shares access to the Punta Río Claro Wildlife Refuge, providing excellent opportunities for independent hiking and wildlife-watching. Accommodation is in thatch-roof cabanas in the style of the Boruca indigenous peoples, with private terraces, ocean views and 360 degrees of screened windows, creating a wonderful cross-breeze. A generator provides electricity in the evening.

Bahía Paraíso (☎ 293 2121; www.bahiaparaiso.com; tent US$55, cabin US$70-85, 4-day package US$405-495) The Bahía Paraíso is less atmospheric than some of the other options, but its beachside setting – steps from Playa San Josecito – makes up for it. The priciest cabins have private verandahs with panoramic views of the ocean, while the cheaper option is furnished walk-in tents with shared bathrooms. In all cases, kayaks, snorkeling gear and beachside hammocks are included in the price.

Guaria de Osa (☎ 235 4313, in the USA 510-235 4313; www.guariadeosa.com; tent/r US$55/90, 4-day package US$459) Cultivating a new-age ambiance, this Asian-style retreat center offers yoga, tai chi and all kinds of massage, along with the more typical rain-forest activities. The lovely grounds include an 'ethnobotanical garden' (guided tour US$15), which features exotic local species used for medicinal and other purposes. The architecture of this place is unique: the centerpiece is the Lapa Lapa Lounge, a spacious multi-storey pagoda, built entirely from reclaimed hardwood.

Poor Man's Paradise (☎ 771 4582; www.mypoor mansparadise.com; tent/ranch/cabin US$45/50/60, 4-day package US$316-367) While sportfishing can be an expensive prospect, local fisherman Pincho Amaya aims to make it more accessible to everyone. He offers some of Bahía Drake's most reasonably priced fishing excursions and accommodation. The place is pretty straight-forward: furnished walk-in tents built on sturdy wood platforms with shared clean bathrooms; and breezy light-filled cabins with private cold-water facilities. Traditional Tico fare might include your catch of the day, which the kitchen will prepare to order.

Jungle Al's (www.jungleals.com; camping US$20, cabin/ villa 4-day package US$638/860) Bargain-hunters take note: this is the cheapest place to stay north of Agujitas, as long as you don't mind sleeping in a tent (available to rent for an additional fee). Other accommodation is in hardwood cabins and villas, with screened windows and wide porches. Jungle Al caters to anglers, so all guests can look forward to meals of fresh fish, in addition to organic fruits and an open beer bar!

Proyecto Campanario (☎ 258 5778; www.cam panario.org; 4-day package US$407) Run by a former Peace Corp volunteer, this biological reserve is more of an education center than a tourist facility, as evidenced by the dormitory, library and field station. Behind the main facility, five spacious platform tents with 'garden' bathrooms offer a bit more privacy and comfort. Ecology courses and conservation camps are scheduled throughout the year, but individuals are also invited to take advantage of the facilities. The whole place is set on 150 hectares of tropical rain forest, which provides countless opportunities for exploration and wildlife observation.

Casa Corcovado Jungle Lodge (☎ 256 3181, in the USA 888-896 6097; www.casacorcovado.com; r US$135, 4-day package US$1015; 🖳) A spine-tingling boat ride takes you to this luxurious lodge on 175 hectares of rain forest, bordering the national park. Each bungalow is tucked away in its own private tropical garden, each with a hammock. Artistic details – such as Mexican tiles and stained glass – make the Casa Corcovado one of this area's classiest accommodation options. On site, the Margarita Sunset Bar lives up to its name, serving up 25 different 'ritas and great sunset views over the Pacific.

Getting There & Away

This section of coast is accessible by boat from Sierpe or Bahía Drake – most lodges provide transportation with prior arrangements (be prepared to get your feet wet during your beach landing). Otherwise, you can reach them from Agujitas by hiking along the coastal trail.

RESERVA BIOLÓGICA ISLA DEL CAÑO

This 326-hectare island – surrounded by 2700 marine hectares of ocean – is among Bahía Drake's most popular destinations, not only for fish and marine mammals, but also for snorkelers, divers and biologists.

The island is the tip of numerous underwater rock formations, which is evident from the rocky cliffs along the coastline, some towering 70m over the ocean. This is not your stereotypical tropical island: the few white sand beaches are small to start with and they disappear to nothing when the tide comes in.

The submarine rock formations are among the island's main attractions, drawing divers to explore the underwater architecture. Snorkelers can investigate the coral and rock formations along the beach right in front of the ranger station. The water is much clearer here than along the mainland coast, though rough seas can cloud visibility. Fifteen different species of coral have been recorded, as well as threatened animal species that include the Panulirus lobster and the giant conch. The sheer numbers of fish attract dolphins and whales, frequently spotted swimming in outer waters. Hammerhead sharks, manta rays and sea turtles also inhabit these waters.

A steep but well-maintained trail leads inland from the ranger station. Once the trail plateaus, it is relatively flat, winding through evergreen forest to a lookout point at about 110m above sea level. These trees are primarily milk trees (also called 'cow trees' after the drinkable white latex they exude), believed to be the remains of an orchard planted by pre-Columbian indigenous inhabitants.

Near the top of the ridge there are several pre-Columbian **granite spheres**. Archaeologists speculate that the island may have been a ceremonial or burial site for the same indigenous tribes.

Vegetation on the island includes the West Indian locust tree and the wild cocoa. Birders may spot both coastal and oceanic species: look for cattle egret and brown booby, as well as raptors like osprey and black hawk. Other rain-forest inhabitants are here, but wildlife is not as varied or prolific as on the mainland.

Camping is prohibited, and there are no facilities except a ranger station by the landing beach. Most visitors arrive on tours arranged by the nearby lodges. Corcovado Expeditions (p408) offers a day trip for US$70 per person. Admission is US$8 per person, although this fee is usually included in your tour price.

PARQUE NACIONAL CORCOVADO

Famously labeled by *National Geographic* as 'the most biologically intense place on earth', this national park is the last great original tract of tropical rain forest in Pacific Central America. The bastion of biological diversity is home to Costa Rica's largest population of scarlet macaws, as well as countless other endangered species, including Baird's tapir, the giant anteater and the world's largest bird of prey, the rare harpy eagle. Its amazing biodiversity has long attracted the attention of tropical ecologists, as well as a devoted stream of visitors who descend from Bahía Drake and Puerto Jiménez to explore the remote location and spy on a wide array of wildlife.

The 42,469-hectare park is nestled in the southwestern corner of the Península de Osa and protects at least eight distinct habitats, ranging from mangrove swamps to primary and secondary rain forest to low altitude cloud forest. The most accessible and visible habitat is the 46km of sandy coastline.

Because of its remoteness, the park remained undisturbed until loggers invaded in the 1960s. The destruction was halted in 1975 when the area was established as government-administered parklands. The early years were a challenge as park authorities, with limited personnel and resources, sought to deal with illegal clear-cutting, poaching and gold-mining, the latter of which was causing severe erosion in the park's rivers and streams.

Unfortunately, poaching remains a severe problem in Corcovado. The highest-profile victims are the highly-endangered Central American jaguar and its main food source, the white-lipped peccary. Heavily-armed hunters gun down peccaries en masse and sell their meat, resulting in a drastic 85% decline in their populations in the last five years. Jaguars, suffering from a diminishing food supply, prey on domestic animals in the area, making them a target of local residents (not to mention the fact that jaguar pelts and bones fetch hefty sums as well). Minae has stepped up its police patrols but has been unable to curb the poaching.

Meanwhile, the Fundacíon Corcovado spearheaded a local effort to propose Parque Nacional Corcovado as a Unesco World Heritage Site, in recognition of its stunning aesthetic appeal and scientific importance. Sadly, ongoing reports of uncontrolled hunting highlighted the government's inability to protect and preserve this valuable site, and the nomination was temporarily withdrawn.

Information

Information and maps are available at the **Oficina de Área de Conservación Osa** (☎ 735 5036, 735 5580; park fee per person per day US$10; ☿ 8am-4pm) in Puerto Jiménez. Contact this office to make reservations for lodging and meals at all of the ranger stations and to pay your park fee. Be sure to make these arrangements well in advance – 15 to 30 days during the dry season – as facilities are limited.

Park headquarters are at Sirena ranger station, located on the coast in the middle of the park. Other ranger stations are located on the park boundaries: San Pedrillo station in the northwest corner on the coast; the new Los Planes station on the northern boundary (near the village of the same name); La Leona station in the southeast corner on the coast (near the village of Carate); and Los Patos station in the northeast

corner (near the village of La Palma). Always check with rangers before setting out about trail conditions and possible closures (especially during the wettest months from June to November).

Wildlife-Watching

The best wildlife-watching in Corcovado is at Sirena, but the coastal trails have two advantages: they are more open and the constant crashing of waves covers the sound of noisy walkers. White-faced capuchin, red-tailed squirrel, collared peccary, white-nosed coati and northern tamandua are regularly seen on both trails.

On the less traveled San Pedrillo trail, Playa Llorona is a popular nesting spot for marine turtles, including leatherback, olive ridley and green turtles. Nesting turtles attract ocelot, jaguar and other predators, though they are difficult to spot.

Both coastal trails produce an endless pageant of birds. Scarlet macaw are guaranteed; the tropical almond trees lining the coast are a favorite food. The sections along the beach produce mangrove blackhawk by the dozens and numerous waterbird species. The little rock island opposite Salsipuedes serves as a roost for hundreds of magnificent frigate bird and brown booby.

The Los Patos trail attracts lowland rain forest birds such as great curassow, chestnut-mandibled toucan, fiery-billed aracari, turquoise cotinga and rufous piha; trogon, hummingbird and wood creeper are plentiful. Encounters with mixed flocks are common. Mammals are similar to those sighted on the coastal trails, but Los Patos is better for primates and white-lipped peccaries.

GREEN GRASSROOTS

The impressive **Fundación Corcovado** (☎ 297 3013; www.corcovadofoundation.org) is a network of local business people – mostly hoteliers – who have teamed up to raise money and raise awareness to support their most valuable resource: the biodiversity of the national park. Through their own fundraising efforts, they have hired additional rangers to crack down on poaching, implemented various community education programs and worked toward establishing a code for sustainable tourism for local businesses to follow.

The Fundación Corcovado invites volunteers to work in the community and in the park. Tasks might include teaching about waste management and conservation at local schools, maintaining trails and bridges in the park, patrolling beaches and collecting data during turtle season, and providing assistance and expertise to visiting tourists. The daily fee of US$24 includes transportation from San José as well as room and board with a local family; two weeks minimum.

PENINSULA DE OSA &
GOLFO DULCE

BAIRD'S TAPIR PROJECT

The Baird's Tapir Project has been studying the populations of Baird's tapir around Sirena station since 1994 in the hope of enhancing conservation efforts. Scientists use radio telemetry (that's radio collars to you and me) to collect data about where the tapirs live, how far they wander, whom they associate with and how often they reproduce. So far, 28 tapirs around Sirena are wearing collars, which allows scientists to collect the data without disrupting the animals.

Sirena station is an ideal place to do such research, because there is no pressure from deforestation or hunting, which gives researchers the chance to observe a healthy, thriving population. The animals' longevity and slow rate of reproduction mean that many years of observation are required before drawing conclusions.

So, what have we learned about these river rhinos so far? The nocturnal animals spend their nights foraging – oddly, they prefer to forage in 'disturbed habitats' (like along the airstrip), not in the dense rain forest. They spend their days in the cool waters of the swamp, out of the hot sun. Tapirs are not very social, but a male-female pair often shares the same 'home range,' living together for years at a time. Scientists speculate that tapirs may in fact be monogamous – who knew these ungainly creatures would be so romantic!

For wildlifers frustrated at the difficulty of seeing rain forest mammals, a stay at Sirena ranger station is a must. Topping the list, Baird's tapir are practically assured. Check out the airstrip after dusk. Sirena is excellent for other herbivores, particularly red brocket (especially on Sirena trail) and both species of peccary. Agouti and tayra are also common.

The profusion of meat on the hoof means there are predators aplenty, but they are not nearly as confiding. Jaguar are occasionally sighted near the airstrip in the very early morning (midnight to 4am). While spotlighting at night you are more likely to see kinkajou and crab-eating skunk (especially at the mouth of the Río Sirena). Ocelot represents your best chance for observing a cat, but again, it's difficult.

Corcovado is the only national park in Costa Rica with all four of the country's primate species. Spider monkey, mantled howler and white-faced capuchin can be encountered anywhere; Sirena trail is best for the fourth and most endangered species, the Central American squirrel monkey. Sirena also has fair chances for the extremely hard-to-find silky anteater, a nocturnal animal which frequents the beachside forests between the Río Claro and the station.

The Río Sirena is a popular spot for all kinds of heron, as well as waders like ruddy turnstone and western sandpiper. You may be more excited to spot the other riverside regulars, which include American crocodile, three-toed sloth and bull shark.

Hiking

Paths are primitive and the hiking is hot, humid and insect-ridden; but the challenge of the trek and the interaction with wildlife at Corcovado are thrilling. Hiring a local guide is highly recommended. Obviously, your guide will know the trails well, thus avoiding the unmitigated disaster of getting lost; furthermore, he or she will have a keen eye for spotting and identifying wildlife.

Otherwise, travel in a small group. Bring a compass, as it is impossible to navigate using the sun or stars underneath the rain forest canopy. Carry plenty of food, water and insect repellent. And always verify your route with the rangers before you depart.

The most popular route traverses the park from Los Patos to Sirena, then exits the park at La Leona (or vice versa). This allows hikers to begin and end their journey in or near Puerto Jiménez, offering easy access to La Leona and Los Patos. The trek between Sirena and San Pedrillo is more difficult, both physically and logistically. The travel times listed are conservative: fit hikers with light packs can move faster, unless you spend a lot of time birding or taking photos.

Hiking is best in the dry season (from December to April), when there is still regular rain but all of the trails are open. It's still muddy, but you won't sink quite as deep.

SIRENA TO SAN PEDRILLO

The route between Sirena and San Pedrillo is the longest trail in Corcovado, covering 23km in 10 to 15 hours. The first 18km of

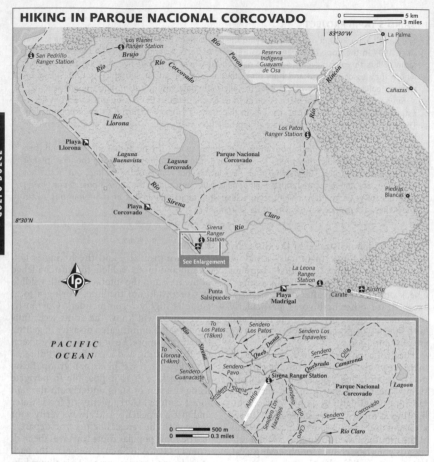

this hike are along the beach, which means loose sand and little shade – grueling, especially with a heavy pack. One local guide recommends doing this portion of the hike at night to avoid the hot sun.

Another tricky factor is the three river crossings, which become very difficult or impossible at high tide. As a result, the time of departure from Sirena station depends on the tides; the recommended departure time is about two hours before low tide.

The first river crossing – Río Sirena – is about 1km north of Sirena. The largest river on the hike, it is the neighborhood hangout for sharks and crocodiles, so cross with caution. The final river, the cascading Río Llorona, also marks the end of the beach

trail. Here, you will be rewarded with a fantastic photo op – a breathtaking waterfall plunging onto the wild beach of Playa Llorona. The final 7km of the trail traverse coastal forest.

This trail is only open from December through April, since heavy rains can make the Río Sirena impassable. Due to the complexity of this route, taking a guide is strongly recommended.

SIRENA TO LA LEONA

The 16km hike from Sirena to La Leona is another sizzler, following the shoreline through coastal forest and along deserted beaches. It involves one major river crossing at Río Claro, just south of Sirena station.

The journey between Sirena and La Leona takes six or seven hours. You can camp at La Leona; otherwise, it takes another hour to hike the additional 3.5km to Carate, where you can stay in a local lodge or catch the collective taxi to Puerto Jiménez.

SIRENA TO LOS PATOS

The route to Los Patos goes 18km through the heart of Corcovado, affording the hiker an opportunity to pass through plenty of primary and secondary forest. The trail is relatively flat for the first 12km. You will hike through secondary forest and wade the Río Pavo and the Río Sirena before reaching the Laguna Corcovado. From this point, the route undulates steeply (mostly uphill!) for the remaining 6km. One guide recommends doing this hike in the opposite direction – from Los Patos to Sirena – to avoid this exhausting, uphill ending. Near Los Patos, a lovely waterfall provides a much-needed shower at the end of a long trek.

The largest herds of peccaries are reportedly on this trail. Local guides advise that peccaries sense fear, but they will back off if you act aggressively. (Alternatively, if you climb about 2m off the ground you'll avoid being bitten in the unlikely event of running into a surly bunch.)

You can camp at Los Patos, or continue an additional 14km to the village of La Palma. This four-hour journey is a shady and muddy descent down the valley of the Río Rincón. If you are traveling from La Palma to Los Patos, be prepared for a steep climb.

If you don't plan on traversing the park, a 6km day hike from Los Patos to the Laguna Corcovado is feasible. (This requires spending two nights at Los Patos.)

Tours

The main routes across Parque Nacional Corcovado are well marked and well traveled, making this journey easy enough to complete independently. However, hiring a guide can greatly enhance this experience, not only because you will not have to worry about taking a wrong turn. Besides their intimate knowledge of the trail, local guides are amazingly knowledgeable about flora and fauna, including the best places to spot various species. Many guides carry telescopes, allowing for up-close inspection of the various creatures. One excellent, independent guide is **Alexis Rojas Gonzalez** (alexis 20cr@yahoo.es; per day US$80-100), based in Bahía Drake.

Tour companies charge a per person rate, inclusive of park fees, meals and transportation to the park:

Corcovado Expeditions (☎ 833 2384, 818 9962; www.corcovadoexpeditions.net; Agujitas, Bahía Drake) Corcovado Expeditions employs only local, bilingual guides, who are extremely knowledgeable about the wildlife and carry telescopes for your viewing pleasure.

Osa Aventura (☎ 735 5670, 830 9832; www.osaaven tura.com; Puerto Jiménez) 'Crocodile Mike' Boston and his colleagues specialize in multiday adventure tours up and down the Osa. Mike doesn't have an office, so ring ahead.

Eating & Sleeping

Camping costs US$5 per person per day at any station; facilities include potable water and latrines. Sirena station has a covered platform, but other stations have no such luxuries. Remember to bring a flashlight or a kerosene lamp, because the campsites are pitch black at night. Camping is not permitted in areas other than the ranger stations.

Simple dormitory lodging (US$10) and meals (breakfast US$8, lunch or dinner US$11) are available at Sirena station only. Food and cooking fuel have to be packed in, so reserve at least 15 to 30 days in advance through the **Oficina de Área de Conservación Osa** (☎ 735 5036) in Puerto Jiménez. Scientists and researches working at the Sirena biological station get preference over travelers for accommodations and meals.

Otherwise, campers must bring all of their own food. Note that ranger stations face a challenge with trash disposal, so all visitors are required to pack out all of their trash.

Getting There & Away
FROM BAHÍA DRAKE

From Bahía Drake, you can walk the coastal trail that leads to San Pedrillo station (about four hours from Agujitas), or any lodge can drop you here as a part of their regular tours to Corcovado. Alternatively, you can charter a boat to San Pedrillo (US$80) or Sirena (US$120).

FROM LA PALMA

From the north, the closest point of access is the town of La Palma, from where you can catch a bus or taxi south to Puerto Jiménez or north to San José.

IT'S A JUNGLE OUT THERE

The birds are brilliant, the animals are enchanting and the forest is fantastic. But Parque Nacional Corcovado is the real deal, 100% wilderness, and the dangers should not be underestimated. Every season, travelers to Corcovado become injured, sick or even dead; take some precautions to make sure this is not you:

- The number one danger for hikers is suffering from heat exhaustion and dehydration. This is the rain forest: it is hot and humid and you are going to sweat more than you realize. Make sure you carry enough water: a 1L or 1.5L bottle (which you can refill at each ranger station) is the bare minimum per person.
- Do not drink water from any stream; this is a surefire way to get a nasty case of giardia.
- Wear sunblock and insect repellent. The number two danger for hikers is mosquito bites, followed closely by sunburn (especially on coastal trails). Both of these are easily avoided.
- Travel light! The pleasure of the hike is inversely proportionate to the weight of your pack.
- Always check with the rangers about trail conditions and tide charts before setting out. This is extremely valuable, not only so that you are up-to-date on this information, but also so that the rangers know the route you are planning to follow and your time of departure. Pay attention to their recommendations about river crossings: the Río Sirena can be very dangerous.
- Bring a compass and know how to use it. Bring plenty of food and water. Always travel with a flashlight.
- Do not hike alone. If you have limited wilderness experience, hire a guide. You will get your money back many times over in peace of mind.

Heading to Los Patos, you might be able to find a taxi to take you partway; however, the road is only passable to 4WD vehicles (and not always), so be prepared to hike the 14km to the ranger station. The road crosses the river about 20 times in the last 6km. It's easy to miss the right turn shortly before the ranger station, so keep your eyes peeled.

FROM CARATE

In the southeast, the closest point of access is Carate, from where La Leona station is a one-hour, 3.5km hike west along the beach.

Carate is accessible from Puerto Jiménez via a poorly maintained, 45km dirt road. This journey is an adventure in itself, and often allows for some good wildlife spotting along the way. A collective 4WD jeep taxi travels this route twice daily.

BY AIR

Alfa Romeo Aero Taxi (☎ 735 5353; Puerto Jiménez) offers charter flights from Carate to Drake, Sirena and Palmar Sur for about US$350. You can also fly to the Carate/Sirena airstrip from Puerto Jiménez (US$153/371), Golfito (US$275/357) or Quepos (US$633/633).

TO CORCOVADO VIA PUERTO JIMÉNEZ

The western side of Parque Nacional Corcovado has a little more going on than the east side – meaning a road that goes all the way to the park and a few villages sprinkled along the coast of the Golfo Dulce. The landscape is cattle pastures and rice fields, while much of the inland area is protected by the Reserva Forestal Golfo Dulce.

This is not a heavily populated area – far from it – but the gold rush of the 1960s and 1970s fueled the growth of towns like Dos Brazos del Río Tigre and Puerto Jiménez. These days, most locals are engaged in agriculture, and the only impetus in the economy is the slow and steady growth of tourism. With the exception of Puerto Jiménez, these sleepy villages still have few facilities.

THE INTERAMERICANA TO PUERTO JIMÉNEZ

A 78km road links the Interamericana (at Chacarita) with Puerto Jiménez. It is paved as far as Rincón, where a poor and potholed dirt road heads west towards the Pacific, passing Rancho Quemado (unmarked on most maps) and continuing to Bahía Drake. The coastal road continues all the way to Puerto Jiménez.

Rincón & Around

The northern shore of the Golfo Dulce is part of the **Reserva Forestal Golfo Dulce**, a protected zone that links the Parque Nacional Corcovado to the Parque Nacional Piedras Blancas. This connecting corridor plays an important role in preserving the biodiversity of the peninsula and allowing the wildlife to migrate to the mainland. Unfortunately, the forest area around Rincón is threatened by illegal logging practices.

Several lodges are doing their part to preserve this natural resource by protecting their own little pieces of this wildlife wonderland. While there is not much going on in Rincón itself, these are some lovely places to stay. In any case, you may want to stop and admire the amazing panorama of the Golfo Dulce. From the highway just east of Rincón you can gaze over the gulf and see as far as Panama on a clear day.

SLEEPING & EATING

Suital Lodge (☎ 826 0342; www.suital.com; 15km east of Rincón; s/d/tr US$37/56/70; P) On the northern shore of the Golfo Dulce, the Suital Lodge is set on 70 acres of hilly, forested property. Lots of love has gone into the construction of three rustic cabins, but not a single tree was felled. Each cabin has a private porch with a hammock and beautiful view. A network of trails winds through the property

and down to the beach. This tranquil place is 27km from the Interamericana along the road to Rincón.

Cabinas & Restaurante Ventana al Golfo (☎ 837 2169; r US$25, meals US$3-5; P) 'Window to the Gulf', indeed! The wide verandah of this quaint, family-run restaurant is a perfect place to recover from a grueling road trip. Typical Tico fare is prepared by a chef trained in the USA. If you want to spend the night, hardwood cabins are built on stilts up behind the restaurant, allowing for plenty of privacy. It's 2km north of Rincón.

Villa Corcovado (☎ 817 6969; www.villacorcovado.com; 500m Este Parada, Rincón; s/d US$289/376; P) Rincón seems an unlikely setting for a brand new top-of-the-line resort, but you'll understand when you glimpse the 70 acres of exquisite, unspoiled rain forest and the magnificent unobstructed vista of the Golfo Dulce. Eight light-filled, luxurious villas have private porches, wood-beamed ceilings and hardwood floors, not to mention classy, contemporary decor. Gourmet meals (included) feature organic produce straight from the garden; you can request yours packed in a picnic to enjoy on a nearby deserted beach.

La Palma & Around

About 9km southeast of Rincón, the town of La Palma is the origin of the rough road that turns into the trail to the Los Patos ranger station. The *soda* (eating establishment) at the village's only intersection serves as bus depot, information center and breakfast nook. If you are hiking across Corcovado,

---

LOCAL LORE

In 1526, the Isla del Coco – far off Costa Rica's southwestern coast – was 'discovered' by Spanish explorer Joan Cabezas. It was noted on a map drawn by French cartographer Nicolas Desliens in 1541. Heavy rainfall attracted the attention of sailors, pirates and whalers, who frequently stopped for fresh water and coconuts.

Between the late 17th and early 19th century, Isla del Coco became something of a way-station for a band of pirates, who supposedly hid countless treasures here. The most famous was the storied Treasure of Lima, which consisted of gold and silver ingots, gold laminae scavenged from church domes and a solid-gold, life-size sculpture of the Virgin Mary. Isla del Coco is so renowned for its hidden treasures that authors have speculated it was the inspiration for Robert Stevenson's *Treasure Island*. Nonetheless, more than 500 treasure-hunting expeditions have found only failure.

In 1869, the government of Costa Rica organized its own official treasure hunt. No gold or jewels were discovered, but this expedition did result in Costa Rica unfurling its flag and taking possession of the island, a treasure in itself.

PARQUE NACIONAL ISLA DEL COCO

In the opening minutes of the film *Jurassic Park,* a small helicopter swoops over and around a lushly forested island with dramatic tropical peaks descending straight into clear blue waters. That island is Isla del Coco and that scene turned Costa Rica's most remote national park into more than a figment of our collective imaginations.

Isla del Coco is more than 500km southwest of the mainland in the eastern Pacific and is often referred to as the Costa Rican Galapagos. The island has two large bays with safe anchorages and sandy beaches: **Chatham** is located on the northeast side and **Wafer Bay** is on the northwest. Just off Coco are a series of smaller basaltic rocks and islets, which constitute some of the best dive sites. **Isla Manuelita** is a prime spot, home to a wide array of fish, rays and eels. Sharks also inhabit these waters, including huge schools of white tip shark, which are best spotted at night. **Dirty Rock** is another main attraction – a spectacular rock formation that harbors all kinds of sea creatures. Isla del Coco boasts more than a dozen dive sites. More than anything else, Coco is famous for its huge schools of hundreds of scalloped hammerhead sharks.

The island is rugged and heavily forested, with the highest point at **Cerro Iglesias** (634m); a network of trails leads to a spectacular viewpoint. Because of its remote nature a unique ecosystem has evolved, earning the island the protective status of national park. More than 70 animal species (mainly insects) and 70 plant species are endemic, and more remain to be discovered. Birders come to see the colonies of seabirds, some of which are endemic and many of which nest on Coco. There are also two endemic lizard species. The marine life is varied, with sea turtles, more than 18 species of coral, 57 types of crustaceans, three types of dolphin and tropical fish in abundance. Needless to say, the diving is excellent and is the main attraction of the island.

Settlers who lived on the island in the late 19th and early 20th centuries left behind domestic animals that have since converted into feral populations of pigs, goats, cats and rats. Today it's the pigs that are the greatest threat to the unique species native to the island: they uproot vegetation, cause soil erosion and contribute to sedimentation around the island's coasts, which damages coral reefs. Unregulated fishing poses further, more ominous, threats, especially to populations of shark, tuna and billfish that get caught in logline sets. The Servicio de Parques Nacionales (Sinac) is aware of the problem, but a lack of funding has made regulation of these illegal activities difficult, if not impossible.

Information

Apply for a permit at the **Área de Conservación de la Isla del Coco** (☎ 258 7350) in San José. (Dive operators usually make these arrangements for their clients.) Park fees are US$35 per person per day. On the island, there is also a **ranger station** (☎ 0087-468712 0010), with staff surveillance stations at Wafer Bay and Chatham Bay. Drinking water is available, but there is no camping; visitors must spend the night on their boats.

Tours

Trips depart from San José. Park fees are not included in the price.

Okeanos Aggressor (in the USA ☎ 985-385 2628, in the USA & Canada 800-348 2628; www.aggressor.com; 8-day charter per person from US$2495) Includes five days of diving

Undersea Hunter (☎ 228 6613, in the USA 800-203 2120; www.underseahunter.com; 10-day dive trip per person from US$3440) Includes seven days of diving.

---

this will likely be the starting point or ending point of your trek. Note that travelers have reported getting mugged on the road from La Palma to Los Patos, so keep your wits about you and travel in a group.

There's not much to this town, save a few *pulperías* and the requisite *soda*. If you are headed into Corcovado, you can stock up on provisions for your hike here. The surrounding landscape is flat farmland – a stark contrast to the lush greenery in the park. A beautiful sand and coral beach, known as **Playa Blanca**, is at the east end of town. The **Reserva Indígena Guaymí** is southwest of here, on the border of Parque Nacional Corcovado (for information about the Guaymí, see p442).

SLEEPING & EATING

Danta Corcovado Lodge (☎ 378 9188, 819 1860; www.dantacorcovado.net; s/d/tr US$20/30/36, camping per person US$6) Conveniently located midway between Los Patos and La Palma, Danta is a new lodge set on the finca of the congenial Sanchez family. Rustic cabins – constructed of wood and painted in warm hues – are furnished with hand-crafted furniture and share clean bathrooms. A covered platform is also available for campers. Delicious, home-cooked meals are prepared on a wood stove (breakfast US$6, lunch or dinner US$8.50). Guided tours include hiking, horse riding and kayaking, as well as a visit to the Guaymí reserve.

Tamandu Lodge (☎ 821 4525; www.tamandu-lodge.com; r per person US$45) The Carreras – a Guaymí family – have started welcoming tourists to their home and farm on the grounds of the indigenous reserve. This unique lodge provides a rare chance to interact directly with an indigenous family and experience firsthand the Guaymí lifestyle. This is hands-on stuff: gather crabs and fish with palm rods; hunt for palmito or harvest yucca; learn how to prepare these specialties over an open fire. Accommodations are in rustic, wooden houses, built on stilts with thatch roofs. Home-cooked meals are included in the price. A member of the Carrera family will meet you in La Palma, from where it is a two-hour journey on horseback to the lodge. Getting there is half the fun!

GETTING THERE & AWAY

Catch a taxi to Puerto Jiménez for US$20. Otherwise, buses depart La Palma for:
Drake 1½ hours, noon (dry season only).
Neily 2½ hours, 2:30pm.
Puerto Jiménez 30 minutes, 8:30am, 10am, 11:30am, 1:30pm, 7pm and 8:30pm.
San Isidro 3½ hours, 1:30pm.
San José eight hours, 5:30am & 11am.

La Palma to Puerto Jiménez

Heading south from La Palma, the gravel road passes through a series of small towns ('small', meaning you might not realize it's a town). The surrounding plains are speckled with family farms and tall palms and not much else.

About 8km south of La Palma, the Ticorun **Köbö Farm** (☎ 351 8576; www.kobofarm.com; 3-hr tour in Spanish/English US$20/30) is a chocolate-lover's dream come true. In fact, *köbö* means 'dream' in Guaymí. The 50-hectare finca is dedicated to organic cultivation of fruits and vegetables and – the product of choice – cacao. Tours give a comprehensive overview of the life cycle of cacao plants and the production of chocolate (with dégustation!). To really experience life on the farm, you can stay in simple, comfortable teak **cabins** (r per person US$11-15, meals US$6-8).

About 21km south of La Palma (4km north of Puerto Jiménez), a right turn leads 8km to **Dos Brazos**, formerly a gold-mining town. This place has a colorful history: apparently in its heyday, its population grew exponentially, as gold diggers came seeking their fortune. Some locals still pan for gold with a sluice; the Bosqué del Río Tigre (p422) offers tours to show you how its done (and yes, you might be lucky enough to take home a nugget or two).

Dos Brazos is in the midst of the **Reserva Forestal Golfo Dulce**, a protected area that provides an important buffer zone around Parque Nacional Corcovado. (Incidentally, it's also possible to access Corcovado through the forest reserve.) As in the national park, the birding is excellent in this area. Keel-billed toucan and scarlet macaw are guaranteed; birders have reported lesser-known but equally exotic species such as blue-hooded parrot, brown-billed scythebill, cedar waxwing and wattled jacana. The Bosqué del Río Tigre (p422) offers highly recommended half-/full-day birding tours in the river valley for US$25/40 per person.

Just before entering Puerto Jiménez, a turn-off in the road leads 16km to the hamlet of **Río Nuevo**, also in the forest reserve. A good trail network leads to spectacular mountain viewpoints, some with views of the gulf. Again, birding is excellent in this area: visitors can expect to see the many species they would find in Corcovado. Cacique Tours (p424) offers a day-long excursion in this area.

SLEEPING & EATING

Los Mineros (eckico@yahoo.com; Dos Brazos; r per person US$15; meals US$6-10; **P**) This place evokes the atmosphere of the old gold-rush town; indeed, back in the day it was the local bar and brothel. Four cozy cabins have private bathrooms and swinging hammocks. The spacious, open air restaurant serves international cuisine.

Bosque del Río Tigre (in Puerto Jiménez ☎ 735 5062, 824 1372, in the USA 888-875 9453; www.osaadventures.com; Dos Brazos; s/d US$128/216, 4-day package from US$349; **P**) On the edge of the Reserva Forestal Golfo Dulce, in the midst of a 31-acre private reserve, this off-the-beaten-track ecolodge is a birder's paradise. Four well-appointed guest rooms and one private, open-air cabana have huge windows for viewing the feathered friends that come to visit; and the downstairs lodge contains a library well-stocked with wildlife reference books. Rates include three meals, afternoon snacks and plenty of fresh-brewed coffee.

Río Nuevo Lodge (☎ 735 5411, 365 8982; www.rionuevolodge.com; s/d US$65/100) Who knew that former gold-miners would be so friendly? The Aguirre family now owns and operates this popular tent lodge set on a forested mountainside 2km west of Río Nuevo. This is camping made easy: guests sleep in comfortable, furnished tents on covered platforms, with access to shared cold-water facilities. Tasty meals (included) are served family style in a traditional thatch-roof *rancho*. Communal areas have solar-powered electricity, but tents do not. Rates include transportation from Puerto Jiménez (don't try to drive here yourself).

GETTING THERE & AWAY

Buses for Dos Brazos leave Puerto Jiménez from the Super 96 at 5:15am, 11am and 4pm. Buses return to Puerto Jiménez from Dos Brazos at 6am, noon and 5pm. Schedules may vary so be sure to double check.

PUERTO JIMÉNEZ

The main attraction of this dusty town is undoubtedly its proximity to Parque Nacional Corcovado, which has an information office here. But Puerto Jiménez is something of a natural wonder in itself, sliced in half by the swampy, overgrown Quebrada Cacao, and flanked on one side by the emerald waters of the Golfo Dulce. This untamed environment often brings wildlife to your doorstep, so it's not unusual to spot scarlet macaws roosting on the soccer field or white-faced capuchins swinging in the treetops around your hotel.

Although it appears on maps dating to 1914, Puerto Jiménez was little more than a cluster of houses built on a mangrove swamp. With the advent of logging in the 1960s and the subsequent discovery of gold in the local streams, Jiménez became a small boomtown. The logging industry still operates in parts of the peninsula, but the gold rush has quieted down in favor of the tourist rush.

Even so, Port Jim (as the gringos call it) retains a frontier feel. Now, instead of gold miners descending on the town's bars on weekends, it's the naturalist guides, who come to have a shot of *guaro* and brag about the snakes, sharks and alligators they've allegedly tousled with.

Parts of Puerto Jiménez are currently being threatened by seemingly indiscriminate enforcement of maritime zone laws. As in coastal areas around the country, townsfolk are rallying against the municipality's threats to demolish some 200 odd homes that are built within the zone.

Information

Banco Nacional de Costa Rica (◷ 8:30am-3:45pm Mon-Fri) ATM on the Plus system only.

Cafenet El Sol (☎ 735 5719; www.soldeosa.com; per hr US$3; ◷ 7am-10pm) Internet access is painfully slow (and often nonexistent), however, it is one of the few places on the Osa with wi-fi access. Also makes hotel reservations, arranges tours and maintains a useful website.

Colectivo Transportation (☎ 735 5539; Soda Deya, 200m south of the bus station) Will exchange US dollars and euros when the bank is closed.

Oficina de Área de Conservación Osa (☎ 735 5036, 735 5580; ◷ 8am-noon & 1-4pm Mon-Fri) Information about Corcovado, Isla del Caño, Parque Nacional Marino Ballena and Golfito parks and reserves. Make reservations here (at least 15 days in advance) to camp in Corcovado.

Osa Tropical (☎ 735 5062, 735 5722; www.osaviva.com) Doña Isabel is the NatureAir agent and the best and most reputable source of local travel information. She handles hotel and transportation arrangements of all kinds and has a radio that reaches all the lodges on the peninsula and in the Golfo Dulce areas.

Red Cross (☎ 735 5109) For medical emergencies.

Sights & Activities

About 5km east of town, the secluded – and often deserted – **Playa Platanares** is excellent for swimming, sunning and recovering from too much adventure. The nearby mangroves of Río Platanares are a paradise for kayaking and bird-watching. Rent kayaks at the Pearl

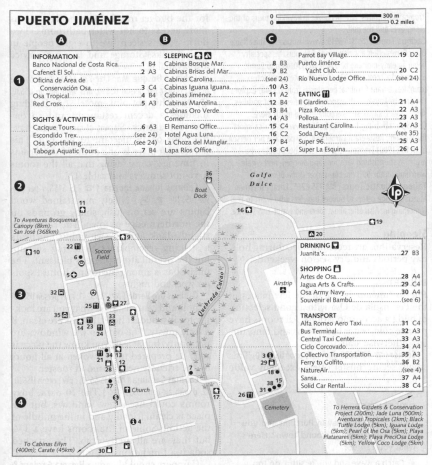

PUERTO JIMÉNEZ

0 _____ 300 m
0 _____ 0.2 miles

INFORMATION
Banco Nacional de Costa Rica.........1 B4
Cafenet El Sol..............................2 A3
Oficina de Área de
    Conservación Osa.....................3 C4
Osa Tropical................................4 B4
Red Cross...................................5 A3

SIGHTS & ACTIVITIES
Cacique Tours..............................6 A3
Escondido Trex.........................(see 24)
Osa Sportfishing.......................(see 24)
Taboga Aquatic Tours....................7 B4

SLEEPING
Cabinas Bosque Mar.......................8 B3
Cabinas Brisas del Mar....................9 B2
Cabinas Carolina.......................(see 24)
Cabinas Iguana Iguana...................10 A3
Cabinas Jiménez..........................11 A2
Cabinas Marcelina........................12 B4
Cabinas Oro Verde........................13 B4
Corner....................................14 A3
El Remanso Office........................15 C4
Hotel Agua Luna..........................16 C2
La Choza del Manglar.....................17 B4
Lapa Ríos Office.........................18 C4

Parrot Bay Village.......................19 D2
Puerto Jiménez
    Yacht Club............................20 C2
Río Nuevo Lodge Office................(see 24)

EATING
Il Giardino...............................21 A4
Pizza Rock...............................22 A3
Pollosa...................................23 A3
Restaurant Carolina......................24 A3
Soda Deya.............................(see 35)
Super 96.................................25 A3
Super La Esquina.........................26 C4

DRINKING
Juanita's.................................27 B3

SHOPPING
Artes de Osa.............................28 A4
Jagua Arts & Crafts......................29 C4
Osa Army Navy............................30 A4
Souvenir el Bambú.....................(see 6)

TRANSPORT
Alfa Romeo Aero Taxi.....................31 C4
Bus Terminal.............................32 A3
Central Taxi Center......................33 A3
Ciclo Corcovado..........................34 A4
Collectivo Transportation................35 A3
Ferry to Golfito.........................36 B2
NatureAir.............................(see 4)
Sansa....................................37 A4
Solid Car Rental.........................38 C4

Golfo Dulce

Boat Dock

To Aventuras Bosquemar Canopy (8km); San José (368km)

Soccer Field

Airstrip

Quebrada Cacao

Church

Cemetery

To Cabinas Eilyn (400km); Carate (45km)

To Herrera Gardens & Conservation Project (200m); Jade Luna (500m); Aventuras Tropicales (2km); Black Turtle Lodge (5km); Iguana Lodge (5km); Pearl of the Osa (5km); Playa Platanares (5km); Playa PreciOsa Lodge (5km); Yellow Coco Lodge (5km)

PENÍNSULA DE OSA & GOLFO DULCE

of the Osa or take a tour with Aventuras Tropicales or Escondido Trex.

On the east side of the airstrip, **Herrera Gardens & Conservation Project** (☎ 735 5267; admission US$4, guided tour US$15-30; ☻ 6am-5pm) is a 250-acre reserve with beautiful botanical gardens. This innovative, long-term reforestation project offers an ecologically and economically sustainable alternative to cattle-grazing. Visitors can explore the 5km of garden trails or 15km of well-marked forest trails. Guided tours focus on birding, botany or even tree climbing! Stop by Jagua Arts & Crafts (p426) to buy a map or arrange your tour.

If you prefer to tour the rain forest at high speed, the brand new **Aventuras Bosquemar Canopy** (☎ 735 5102; admission US$75; Miramar) is the

first zip-line canopy tour on this side of the peninsula. Five lines stretch between five platforms, winding 600m through primary forest. It's about 8km from Jiménez near the village of Miramar; prices include transportation from Puerto Jiménez.

Boat tours around the Golfo Dulce are becoming increasingly popular. The all-day outing often includes a mangrove tour, snorkeling excursion and dolphin watch. Remember that it is illegal to swim with the dolphins, despite your tour guide's best intentions.

Tours

Aventuras Tropicales (☎ 735 5195; www.aventuras tropicales.com) A Tico-run operation that offers all sorts of 'tropical adventures' but specializes in kayaking tours of the mangroves and the gulf.

Cacique Tours (☎ 815 8919; www.lasosas.org) The affable Oscar Cortés offers a variety of wildlife tours, his specialty being an early-morning bird walk (US$30, 6am to 9am).

Escondido Trex (☎ 735 5210; www.escondidotrex .com; Restaurant Carolina; per person from US$40) Explore the area by kayak, with mangrove paddles, night paddles, sunset tours, kayak-snorkel combos and much more.

Osa Sportfishing (☎ 735 5675; www.costa-rica-sport fishing.com; Restaurant Carolina; 4-day package per person from US$1900) Transplanted Florida fisher people who organize sportfishing vacations and dolphin- and whale-watching on the 50ft double-decker *Delfin Blanco*.

Taboga Aquatic Tours (☎ 735 5265) Local fisherman Marco Loaiciga caters to budget travelers who want to reel something in. Also offers boat tours and water-taxi service.

Sleeping

Reservations are recommended during holiday periods and dry-season weekends.

BUDGET

Puerto Jiménez is one of the few places in the Península de Osa with a good selection of budget accommodations. All rooms have private cold-water bathrooms and fans, unless otherwise stated.

Corner (☎ 735 5328; dm/r per person US$6/10) This small, secure hostel offers excellent value

---

DAY TRIPPER

You've got a free day in Port Jim and you don't want to hang around town? Here's what you can do:

■ Catch a wave and you're sittin' on top of the world. Check out the point break at Playa Pan Dulce in Cabo Matapalo (p427).

■ Indulge your sweet tooth. See (and taste) where chocolate comes from at Köbö Farm (p421).

■ Go panning for gold and see if you get lucky. Tours are offered by Bosqué del Río Tigre (p422).

■ Get a bird's eye view from the top of a 200ft ficus tree. Tree-climbing tours offered by Everyday Adventures (p427).

■ Experience tropical paradise among the orchids, bromeliads and heliconia at the Casa de Orquídeas (p436).

---

for the budget traveler. Immaculate rooms share access to hot-water bathrooms. Two dorm rooms sleep five to eight people in basic bunks. Storage and laundry service also available.

Cabinas Bosque Mar (☎ 735 5681; www.bosque marosa.com; r per person US$10, d/tr with air-con US$30; P 🕸) This hot-pink motel-style building includes a decent restaurant and an on-site tour agency. Super clean rooms have the odor of disinfectant to prove it. This family-run place is one of the best bargains in Jiménez, considering that all the rooms have hot showers and cable TV.

Cabinas Iguana Iguana (☎ 735 5158; r per person US$10; P 🕸) Nicely maintained wood cabins are set on lush, shady grounds on the northern edge of town. The rooms are slightly dank, and the swimming pool bears a striking resemblance to a frog swamp, but the overall atmosphere is pleasant. The onsite bar is among the town's hottest spots on weekend nights.

Cabinas Oro Verde (☎ 735 5241; r per person US$10) Simple and central: this is what you are looking for in a budget hotel. Rooms are clean, if a little musty. The bars on the windows are not pretty, but at least you know the place is safe. Be prepared to be awoken at all hours by the friendly neighborhood rooster.

Cabinas Carolina (☎ 735 5696; r per person US$10-12, d with air-con US$35; 🕸) The 10 dark, boxy rooms could use a few windows, but the place is clean, friendly and in the middle of the action. Some of the rooms have a TV, but they are all pretty drab. The attached soda is a Jiménez institution.

Campers should head to **Herrera Gardens & Conservation Project** (☎ 735 5267; camping per person US$6-8) or the ironically-named **Puerto Jiménez Yacht Club** (☎ 735 5051; camping per person US$3).

MIDRANGE

All listings feature private bathrooms with hot water.

Cabinas Marcelina (☎ 755 5286; cabmarce@hotmail .com; d without/with air-con US$30/40; P 🕸) Marcelina's place is a long-standing favorite: the concrete building is painted salmon pink and decked with blooming trees, lending it a homey atmosphere. Rooms have new furniture, fluffy towels and tile bathrooms.

Cabinas Eilyn (☎ 735 5465; cabinaseilyn@hotmail .com; r US$40; P 🕸) Hospitality is a family affair at these quiet quarters on the edge of

LUKE HUNTER

Savannah, Parque Nacional
Chirripó (p383)

Previous page:
Rain forest, Parque Nacional Tortuguero (p459)
STEPHEN SAKS

CHARLOTTE HINDLE

Bus traveling on the Interamericana

Young local drinking the popular *pipa* (p83)

AARON

town. High ceilings, tile floors and a loungey porch enhance the decor of the four cozy cabinas which are attached to the Tico owners' home. Prices include a home-cooked breakfast.

Cabinas Brisas del Mar (☎ 735 5012, 735 5028; r US$35-55; P ☒ ☐) Closed for renovation at the time of research, the Brisas del Mar is going upscale. The waterside location has always been prime; after renovations are complete, guests will also enjoy upgraded rooms and wi-fi access.

Cabinas Jiménez (☎ 735 5090; www.cabinasjimenez.com; standard s/d US$25/40, deluxe s/d US$35/50, cabina s/d/tr/q US$46/60/75/90; P ☒) The efforts of the new American ownership are evident: all of the rooms have been recently renovated, now featuring jungle scenes painted on the walls and underwater murals in the bathrooms. Refrigerators and safes are practical, while details like carved wooden furniture, woven textiles and batik curtains add an artistic flare. The pricier rooms have fantastic views of the lagoon.

La Choza del Manglar (☎ 735 5002; www.manglares.com; standard s/d US$46/64, deluxe s/d/tr US$57/79/89; P ☒ ☐) Set on the edge of the mangrove swamp, this tropical inn is – as it claims – 'a *very* natural place.' Wildlife sightings are de rigueur on these beautifully landscaped grounds – from crocodiles to kinkajous, monkeys to macaws. Recently revamped rooms have hand-carved furniture and mural-painted walls.

Playa Preci-Osa Lodge (☎ 818 2959; www.playa-preciosa-lodge.de; Playa Platanares; tents s/d US$30/40, bungalows s/d/tr/q US$48/62/75/80; P) All of the options at this romantic beach lodge offer excellent value: four spacious thatch-roof bungalows have a sleeping loft and plenty of living space (great for families); eight screened platform tents are set in the secluded garden. The grounds are filled with fruit trees and flowering plants that attract loads of birdlife, monkeys and iguanas. A hearty breakfast is included; other meals are available (lunch US$3 to US$5, dinner US$8 to US$10).

Hotel Agua Luna (☎ 735 5393; www.hotelagualuna.com; s/d US$45/65; ☒) This place bears a striking resemblance to a Motel 6: it's clean enough and comfortable enough, but it's utterly bland. Spacious, tiled rooms are all equipped with cable TV, telephones and refrigerators, so all your practical needs are met.

TOP END

Black Turtle Lodge (☎ 735 5005; www.blackturtlelodge.com; Playa Platanares; cabinetta s/d US$99/163, cabina s/d US$128/198; P) A peaceful retreat along Playa Platanares. Choose between the two-storey cabinas, which have magnificent views over the treetops to the Golfo Dulce, and the less spacious cabinettas, which are nestled into the tropical garden below. All feature bamboo furniture and hardwood floors, but the cabinettas share hot-water bathrooms. Gourmet meals (included) receive rave reviews from readers.

Pearl of the Osa (www.thepearloftheosa.com; Playa Platanares; d US$116-130; P) A bright, beachfront bungalow with eight breezy rooms. They all share a wide hardwood balcony with Adirondack chairs to lounge about. A delightful tropical breakfast is included, but other meals are available next door at the Iguana Lodge.

Yellow Coco Lodge (☎ 827 2741, in the USA 941-376 0910; www.yellowcocolodge.com; Playa Platanares; s/d US$110/135; P) Two cheerful bungalows are just a few steps from the beach. They feature wide balconies with jungle views, fully-equipped kitchens and stylish bedrooms with hardwood floors and citrus-colored walls.

Parrot Bay Village (☎ 735 5180, 735 5748; www.parrotbayvillage.com; d US$146; P ☒) With the beach on one side and the mangrove swamp on the other, Parrot Bay Village enjoys a prime locale and a laidback beach-bum atmosphere. Eight spacious, screened cabins are clustered loosely around an open-air restaurant. Each is exquisitely decorated with ceramic tile floors, uniquely carved doors and polished hardwood detailing. Prices include breakfast.

Iguana Lodge (☎ 735 5205; www.iguanalodge.com; Playa Platanares; s/d US$220/256; P) This luxurious lodge fronting Playa Platanares has the most architecturally alluring cabins in the area: four two-story bungalows have huge breezy decks, bamboo furniture, orthopedic beds draped in mosquito netting and lovely stone bathrooms with garden showers. Rates include three delectable meals a day: the creative cuisine is a highlight.

Eating

Restaurant Carolina (☎ 735 5185; dishes US$3-8) This is *the* hub in Puerto Jiménez. Expats, nature guides, tourists and locals all gather here for food, drinks and plenty of carousing.

The food is decent and the service indifferent, but the fresh fruit drinks and cold beers go down pretty easily on a hot day.

Soda Deya (meals US$3-6) One of many *sodas* around town. This friendly place is excellent for very early breakfasts for passengers departing on the jeep-taxi to Carate, which stops right in front.

Pizza Rock (☎ 735 5295; pizzas US$3-6; ☺ 6-10pm) Sizzling pizzas come straight out of the wood-burning oven and on to your plate at this informal, open-air diner.

Pollosa (☎ 735 5667; meals US$4-8; ☺ noon-9pm Sun-Fri) Renowned for juicy, delectable rotisserie chicken (US$6), but also offers a good selection of salads, sandwiches and spaghetti. Carry-out is available, so this is an excellent option for packing a picnic.

Il Giardino (☎ 735 5129; meals US$10-12; ☺ 10am-2pm & 5-10pm) Specialties of the house are homemade pasta and fresh seafood (including, oddly, sushi). Pick out a nice Italian red to accompany your feast, which you can enjoy in this lovely, shaded garden setting.

Jade Luna (☎ 735 5735; meals US$25-40; ☺ 6-9pm Mon-Sat) A delectable dining experience, starting with the linen napkins and candle-lit tables, and ending with tropical-flavored homemade ice cream. Not to gloss over what comes in between: the menu varies, but always features fresh Cajun-style fish and garlicky jumbo shrimp straight from the gulf, plus a host of appetizers and salads prepared with the freshest organic produce. Open for ice cream throughout the day; reservations recommended for dinner.

Stock up on food items, bug repellent and other necessities at the Super La Esquina or the smaller **Super 96 Store** (☎ 735 5168).

Drinking

You can get greasy Mexican food at **Juanita's** (☎ 735 5056; ☺ 5-2am, happy hr 4-6pm) but it's better to stick to the beer. **Iguana Iguana** (☺ 4pm-midnight), at the cabins of the same name, is a popular watering hole, especially on weekends.

Shopping

Artes de Osa (☎ 735 5429) Handcrafted furniture and hand-painted pottery (mostly featuring monkeys, toucans and the creatures of the Osa).

Jagua Arts & Crafts (☎ 735 5267; ☺ 6:30am-5pm) A great collection of art and jewelry by local and ex-pat craftspeople, including some amazing painted masks.

Osa Army Navy (☺ 8am-7pm Mon-Sat, 9am-4pm Sun) has sportswear, boogie boards, fishing gear, bug nets, knives, backpacks and a selection of Costa Rican arts and crafts. Expect to pay American prices.

Souvenir el Bambú (☎ 816 3815) Anglers can buy a high-quality hardwood reproduction of 'the one that got away'.

Getting There & Around

AIR

To and from San José **Sansa** (☎ 735 5017) has three flights daily for US$78/156 one way/ round trip and **NatureAir** (☎ 735 5062, 735 5722; at Osa Tropical) has four flights daily for US$87/174. Both offices are closed on Sunday.

Alfa Romeo Aero Taxi (☎ 735 5353) has charter flights. Five-seat aircraft fly to Sirena inside Corcovado (US$371), Carate (US$153), Golfito (US$153), Drake (US$350), Palmar Sur (US$350), San Vito (US$472), Quepos (US$633), San Isidro (US$552), Punta Banco (US$230), San José (US$935) and Limón (US$1450); book two days in advance.

BICYCLE

Rent a bike at **Ciclo Corcovado** (☎ 735 5429; per hr US$1; ☺ 8am-5pm).

BOAT

The **passenger ferry** (admission US$2) leaves at 6am for the 1½-hour run to Golfito, returning at 11:30am. At the time of research, a second ferry was also running, departing Puerto Jiménez at 6:15am and returning at 1:30pm. **Taboga Aquatic Tours** (☎ 735 5265) runs water taxis to Zancudo for US$35. Other journeys can be arranged.

BUS

Most buses arrive at the new peach-colored terminal on the west side of town. All of these pass La Palma (23km away) for the eastern entry into Corcovado. Buy tickets to San José in advance.

Neily US$3, three hours, departs 5:30am and 2pm.

San Isidro US$4.25, four hours, 1pm.

San José, via San Isidro (Autotransportes Blanco Lobo) US$6.50, nine hours, 5am and 11am.

CAR & TAXI

Colectivo Transportation (☎ 837 3120, 832 8680; Soda Deya) runs a collective jeep-taxi service to Matapalo (US$3) and Carate (US$6) on the southern tip of the national park. Departures are from the Soda Deya at 6am and 1:30pm, returning at 8:30am and 4pm.

Otherwise, you can hire a 4WD taxi from **Taxi 348** (☎ 849 5228; taxicorcovado@racsa.co.cr) or from the **central taxi center** (☎ 735 5481). Taxis usually charge US$60 for the ride to Carate, US$25 for the ride to Matapalo and US$100 for the overland trek to Drake.

It is also possible to rent a vehicle from **Solid Rental Car** (☎ 735 5777; per day US$75).

CABO MATAPALO & AROUND

About 17km south of Puerto Jiménez, the forested Cabo Matapalo juts out into the Pacific Ocean marking the entrance to the Golfo Dulce. It's prime real estate, containing miles of pristine beaches (some of which offer the Osa's best surfing). A network of trails traverses theses foothills, which are largely uninhabited except for the creatures that come down from the Reserva Forestal Golfo Dulce. The wildlife sighting opportunities in this area are excellent: scarlet macaw, brown pelican and all breeds of heron are frequently sighted on these beaches; while four species of monkey, sloth, coati, agouti and anteater also roam these parts. This little cape is also home to its own little community of luxurious lodges and beachside rental properties. Otherwise, facilities are extremely limited.

Sights & Activities

Cabo Matapalo is an attractive destination for adventurers who wish to go it alone. All of the lodges have easy access to miles of trails which you can explore without a guide. Indeed, you are likely to spot a good selection of wildlife just walking along the Cabo's tree-line dirt road. A fantastic and easy hiking destination is **King Louis**, a magnificent, 90ft waterfall which can be accessed by trail from Playa Matapalo. For ocean adventures, most of the lodges also offer kayaks; and the wild, beautiful beach – surrounding on three sides – is never more than a short walk away.

These pristine beaches around Cabo Matapalo offer three breaks that are putting this little peninsula on the surfing map. **Playa Pan Dulce** is a double point break. The inside break is a small wave that is ideal for beginners; experts can find the point on the outside break and ride it all the way into

shore. **Backwash Bay** offers a nice beach break at low-tide. The steep beach makes it excellent for long-boarding. **Playa Matapalo** also has an A-plus right break, with the biggest and best waves in the area. Conditions are usually good with a west swell; surfing season coincides with the rainy season, which is April to October.

Naturalist Andy Pruter runs **Everyday Adventures** (☎ 353 8619; www.everydaycostarica.com), which offers all kind of adventures in Cabo Matapalo. His signature tour is tree climbing (US$55 per person): scaling a 200ft ficus tree, aptly named 'Cathedral'. Also popular – and definitely adrenaline inducing – is waterfall-rappelling (US$75) down cascades ranging from 50ft to 100ft.

Sleeping

Cabo Matapalo is off the grid, so many places do not have electricity around the clock. Prices include three meals, unless otherwise stated. Listed in order from east to west:

Ojo del Mar (☎ 735 5531; www.ojodelmar.com; r per person US$45; **P**) Tucked in amidst the windswept beach and the lush jungle, this is a little plot of paradise. The four beautifully handcrafted bamboo bungalows are entirely open-air, allowing for all the natural sounds and scents to seep in (thatch roofs and mosquito nets provide protection from the elements). Solar power provides electricity in the *casa grande*. Hammocks swing from the palms, while howler monkeys swing above. Rates include breakfast, but Niko – co-owner and cook – also serves an excellent, all-organic dinner (US$15). Look for this gem on the road to Carate, just before the Buena Esperanza Bar.

Casa Bambú (www.casabambu.addr.com; Cabo Matapalo; d US$155, additional adult/child US$25/10; **P**) Three secluded *casas* comprise this property on the pristine Playa Pan Dulce. All three houses feature solar power, bamboo and hardwood construction, and screen-free half-walls, allowing nothing to come between you and the ocean breezes (except maybe a mosquito net). Fully-equipped kitchens and twice-weekly maid service make this an excellent option for longer-term guests who want to get back to nature (weekly rates available). Meals are not included; kayaks, boogie boards and other beach toys are.

Osa Vida (☎ 735 5062; osatropi@racsa.co.cr; Cabo Matapalo; r per person US$20) This hidden retreat is as budget as it gets on Cabo Matapalo. Follow the leafy, overgrown footpath to the Tico-owned hostel, where clean, plain rooms are furnished with bunk beds; they share cold-water bathrooms. Meals are not included, but the restaurant on site serves *casados* and other filling fare. Reserve through **Osa Tropical** (☎ 735 5062, 735 5722; www .osaviva.com).

Encanta La Vida (☎ 735 5678, in the USA 805-969 4270; www.encantalavida.com; Cabo Matapalo; r per person US$76-87; ℗) Three varied houses dot the lush grounds of Encanta La Vida, ranging from the cozy, Spanish-style 'Honeymoon Cabin' to the two-storey, family-friendly 'La Casona'. A trail winds through cacao and mango trees to the Playa Pan Dulce; surfboards and kayaks are provided.

Ranchos Almendros (Kapu's Place; ☎ 735 5531; http://home.earthlink.net/~kapu/; Cabo Matapalo; r per person US$75; ℗) This is the end of the line on the Cabo Matapalo, where the road stops pretending and turns into a sandy beach path. The property includes three cozy cabanas that are completely equipped with solar power, large screened windows, full kitchens and garden showers. As per the name, 'Almond Tree Ranch' is part of an ongoing project dedicated to the refor-estation of Indian almond trees to create habitat for the endangered scarlet macaw.

Lapa Ríos (☎ 735 5130; www.laparios.com; road to Carate, 17km; s/d US$359/484; ℗ ℞) A few hundred meters beyond El Portón Blanco along the road to Carate, this top-of-the-line wilderness resort combines the right amount of luxury with a rustic, tropical ambience. Scattered over the site are 16 spacious, thatch bungalows, all decked out with queen-sized beds, bamboo furniture, garden showers and private decks boasting panoramic views. An extensive trail sys-tem allows exploration of the 400-hectare reserve, while swimming, snorkeling and surfing are at your doorstep. If you can't afford to stay here, it's worth stopping by for a sunset drink at Brisa Azul, the inviting open-air restaurant.

Bosque del Cabo (☎ 381 4847, in Puerto Jiménez 735 5206; www.bosquedelcabo.com; road to Carate, 18km; standard s/d US$195/300, deluxe US$205/330; ℗ ℞) Nine quaint cabins are perched on a bluff overlooking the ocean. Modern bathrooms,

garden showers and personal hammocks in lush surrounding are the norm; deluxe cabins have added perks like king-size beds, dressing rooms and wrap-around porches. Explore the surrounding 200 hectares of rain forest at canopy level (by zip-line or by suspension bridge) or at ground level (on miles of marked trails).

El Remanso Rain Forest Beach Lodge (☎ 735 5569; www.elremanso.com; road to Carate, 18km; per person US$90-154; ℗ ℞) Set on 140 acres of rain forest, El Remanso is another tropical para-dise. Constructed entirely from fallen tropi-cal hardwoods, the secluded, spacious and sumptuous cabins have shiny wood floors and beautifully finished fixtures. Several units have folding French-style doors that open to provide unimpeded vistas of the foliage and the ocean in the distance. Stop by the office in Puerto Jiménez for more information.

Eating & Drinking

About 1km before El Portón Blanco, you'll find the trendy, tropical **Buena Esperanza Bar** (☎ 735 5531; road to Carate, Carbonera; meals US$5-10; ☉ 9am-midnight), a festive, open-air tropical bar on the east side of the road. The limited menu includes lots of sandwiches and veg-etarian items, plus a full bar. It's Cabo Mata-palo's only place to eat or drink, so often attracts a decent crowd of locals, resident ex-pats and tourists. Ask here about renting surfboards or renting the cabinas out back.

Getting There & Away

From the Puerto Jiménez–Carate road, the turnoff for the Cabo Matapalo is on the left-hand side, through a white cement gate (called 'El Portón Blanco'). If you are driv-ing, a 4WD is highly recommended, even in the dry season. Otherwise, the transport colectivo will drop you here; it passes by at about 6:30am and 2pm heading to Car-ate, and 10am and 5:30pm heading back to Jiménez. A taxi will come here for about US$30.

CARATE

It's 45km by dirt road from Puerto Jiménez around the Cabo Matapalo to the end of the road at Carate, near La Leona ranger station in Parque Nacional Corcovado. This ride is an adventure in itself, as the nar-row, bumpy dirt road winds its way around dense rain forest, through gushing rivers and across windswept beaches. Birdlife and other wildlife are prolific along this stretch: keep your eyes peeled and hang on tight. The 'village' of Carate consists of the airstrip, the *pulpería*, and that's it.

Sleeping & Eating

Communication is often through Puerto Jiménez, so messages may not be retrieved every day; book well in advance. Prices are per person, including three meals a day, unless otherwise noted. Listed in order from east to west:

Laguna Vista (☎ 735 5062; www.lagunavistavillas .com; s/d US$100/170; P ☎) As the name suggests, this brand new lodge is perched up on a hillside, overlooking the picturesque Laguna Pejeperrito, 2.5km east of the Carate airstrip. Three unusual villas are built in a Mediterranean style, with stucco walls and tile roofs. Thanks to carefully planned construction, all units feature both sunrise and sunset views (some from the comfort of their king-sized beds!).

Terrapin Lodge (☎ 735 5603; www.terrapinlodge .com; r US$75; P ☎ ☐) Under new ownership, this family-friendly lodge is getting revamped, starting with the new hydroelectric system (don't miss the chance to hike up the river to see how this environmentally sound system works). The five simple, screened cabins are very private, with ocean views from the balconies and cold water in the bathrooms. The custom cuisine is reader recommended.

Lookout Inn (☎ 735 5431; www.lookout-inn.com; r US$99-125; P ☎ ☐) 'Look out' for the signs advertising this place, starting in Puerto Jiménez. Despite this billboard pollution, it's a sweet retreat once you arrive. Comfortable quarters feature mural-painted walls, hardwood floors, beautifully carved doors and – you guessed it – unbeatable views. The 'tiki huts' (US$99) are the best value: open-air, A-frame huts that are accessible only by a wooden walkway winding through the giant Joba trees (prime birding territory). Behind the inn, 360 steps – known as the 'stairway to heaven' – lead straight up the side of the mountain to four observation platforms and a waterfall trail.

Carate Jungle Camp (☎ 735 5062; camping per person US$6-10, r with shared/private bathroom US$15/20; P) Carate's only nod to the budget traveler.

Very basic cabins with torn screens and worn linen are scattered across pleasant, shady grounds. Or you can also pitch your tent under a thatch-roof gazebo. Meals are not included but kitchen facilities are available. You can also camp for US$15 per person at the *pulpería*, which offers hot meals and cold showers.

Luna Lodge (☎ 380 5036, in the USA 888-409 8448; www.lunalodge.com; bungalows s/d US$240/330, hacienda s/d US$150/250, tents s/d US$125/170; P) A steep road goes through the Río Carate and up the valley to this enchanting retreat center, located about 2km north of the *pulpería*. The hillside location offers fantastic forest views, reaching to the ocean. Taking full advantage of the vista, the high-roofed, open-air restaurant is a marvelous place to indulge in the delights of the gardens and orchards that are on the grounds. Seven spacious, thatch-roof bungalows each have a huge garden shower and private patio. The open-air meditation studio is nothing less than inspirational.

Corcovado Lodge Tent Camp (in San José ☎ 227 0766, 222 0333; www.corcovadolodge.com; tent without/ with meals US$20/70) On the beach south of Parque Nacional Corcovado 1.7km west of the *pulpería*, this long-established lodge is owned and operated by Costa Rica Expeditions. Twenty platform tents have two single beds, clean linens and access to shared bathrooms (but no electricity). The grounds are sort of stark, but a steep trail leads into a 160-hectare private reserve, which is ripe for exploration. A highlight of the reserve is the canopy platform – high up in a 45m guapinol tree – where you can spend the day/night (US$69/125).

La Leona Eco-Lodge & Tent Camp (☎ 735 5704; www.laleonalodge.com; s/d shared bath US$75/120, s/d private bath US$99/150; ☎) On the edge of Parque Nacional Corcovado 2km west of the *pulpería*, this friendly, family-run lodge offers all of the thrills of camping, without the hassles. Sixteen comfy forest-green tents are nestled between the palm trees, with decks facing the beach. All are fully screened and comfortably furnished; solar power provides electricity in the restaurant. Behind the accommodations, 30 hectares of virgin rain-forest property offer opportunities for waterfall hiking, horse riding and wildlife-watching. Lodging-only rates are available.

Getting There & Away

Transportation Colectivo (US$6, 2½ hours) departs Puerto Jiménez for Carate at 6am and 1:30pm, returning at 8:30am and 4pm. Note that the colectivo often fills up on its return trip to Puerto Jiménez, especially during the dry season. Arrive at least 30 minutes ahead of time or you might find yourself stranded.

Alternatively, catch a taxi from Puerto Jiménez (US$60). If you are driving, you'll need a 4WD – even in the dry season as there are a couple of river crossings. You can leave your car at the *pulpería* (per night US$5) and hike to a tent camp (one hour) or to La Leona station (1½ hours).

NORTHERN GOLFO DULCE

While the eastern shore of the Golfo Dulce is less celebrated than the Península de Osa, it offers a surprisingly similar landscape. Indeed, the rich rain forest within the Parque Nacional Piedras Blancas used to be part of Corcovado and still protects the same amazing biodiversity. The breathtakingly beautiful beaches on the northern Golfo Dulce are accessible only by boat – making them even more isolated and perhaps more intriguing than their Osa counterparts. And while Golfito lacks the charm of Puerto Jiménez, it evokes the rise and fall of the banana industry, which took place right around here.

GOLFITO

Formerly a bustling banana port, Golfito retains the same rough-around-the-edges and slightly sketchy atmosphere that beleaguers many port cities. It serves primarily as a departure point for tourists passing through to the beach resorts to the north or south. Attracted by the fish-filled waters of the Golfo Dulce, sportfishers also dock their vessels here, while they catch up on their beer drinking and tale telling.

This fading town is slowly being reclaimed by the jungle behind it. Covering the steep slopes surrounding Golfito, the little visited Refugio Nacional de Fauna Silvestre Golfito provides a picturesque backdrop and inviting retreat, harboring many species of flora and fauna. Tellingly, Warner Brothers chose Golfito as the site to film

Chico Mendes, the true story of a Brazilian rubber tapper's efforts to preserve the rain forest. One of the few remnants of the movie set is an old steam locomotive that graces the park.

From 1938 to 1985, Golfito was the headquarters of United Fruit's operations in the southern part of Costa Rica, but in the 1980s, declining markets, rising taxes, worker unrest and banana diseases forced its departure. Some of the plantations now produce African palm oil, but it has not alleviated the economic hardship caused by United Fruit's departure.

In an attempt to boost the region's economy, the federal government built a duty-free facility *(déposito libre)* in the northern part of Golfito. This surreal shopping center attracts Ticos from around the country, who descend on the otherwise dying town for 24-hour shopping sprees. The duty-free shopping is for Costa Rica residents only, so you can put away your credit card. Indeed, the primary impact on foreign tourists is that tax-free shoppers are required to spend the night in Golfito, so hotel rooms can be in short supply on weekends and during holiday periods.

Orientation

Golfito is named after a tiny gulf that forms an inlet into the eastern shore of the much larger Golfo Dulce. The town is strung out along a dusty, coastal road with a backdrop of steep, thickly forested hills. The southern part of town is where you find most of the bars and businesses, including a seedy red-light district. Nearby, is the so-called Muellecito (Small Dock), where the ferry to Puerto Jiménez departs on a daily basis.

The northern part of town was the old United Fruit Company headquarters, and it retains a languid, tropical air with its large, verandah-decked homes. Now, the so-called *Zona Americana* is home to the airport and the duty-free zone.

Information

Banco Coopealianza (☽ 8am-5pm Mon-Fri, 8am-noon Sat) Has a 24-hour ATM on the Cirrus network and a Western Union office.

Golfito On-line (☎ 775 2424; Hotel Golfito; per hr US$1.20; ☽ 8am-9pm Mon-Sat, noon-6pm Sun; ☷) Speedy Internet connections and delicious air-con.

Hospital de Golfito (☎ 775 0011) Emergency medical attention.

Land Sea Tours (☎ 775 1614; www.realestate-costarica
.info; Km 2) Books airline tickets, makes hotel reservations
and provides info on local real estate. Katie Duncan is an
enthusiastic advocate for Golfito: if she can't connect you
with what you're looking for, she'll know who can.

Migración (☎ 775 0423; ☺ 8am-4pm) Situated away
from the dock, in a 2nd-story office above the Soda Pavas.

Port captain (☎ 775 0487; opposite the large Muelle
de Golfito; ☺ 7:30-11am & 12:30-4pm Mon-Fri)

Activities
SPORTFISHING & BOATING
The Golfo Dulce offers 'the best fishing in
the world', according to one enthusiast.
And he may not be exaggerating when it
comes to dorado, marlin, sailfish and tuna.
You can fish year-round, but the best season for the sought-after Pacific sailfish is
from November to May.

Golfito is also home to several full-service
marinas that attract coastal-cruising yachters. If you didn't bring your own boat, you
can hire local sailors for tours of the gulf at
any of the docks.

Banana Bay Marina (☎ 775 0838; www.bananabay
marina.com; d US$85; ✕ ▣) This floating dock marina
accommodates up to 155 yachts with a full range of services,
including on-shore lodgings and a restaurant boasting the
best burgers in town. Charters can be arranged; a full day of
all-inclusive fishing on a 6m or 17m boat starts at US$750
per day.

C-Tales (in the USA ☎ 772-335 9425; www.c-tales.com;
3-day package per person from US$1065) Operates out of
Las Gaviotas Hotel.

King & Bartlett (☎ 775 1624; www.kingandbartlett
sportfishing.com; 3-day package per person from US$1700;
✕ ▣) This slick new operation offers all-inclusive
fishing packages, including meals and lodging in luxurious
quarters overlooking the gulf.

Sleeping
Note that the area around the soccer field in
town is Golfito's red-light district.

BUDGET
Cabinas Mazuren (☎ 775 0058; r per person US$4) The
locked entry and barred windows don't create
the most inviting atmosphere, but they speak
well for security at this tiny hostel. The place
is musty, but the seven dark, woody rooms
are reasonably clean and adequately equipped
with fan and private cold-water bath.

Cabinas Marisquera (☎ 775 0442; s/d US$8/10)
This little inn, popular with shopping Ticos,
operates out of a big old house near the

Muelle de Golfito. Quaintly painted white
with red trim, the homey place is surrounded
by welcoming, shady gardens. Simple, comfortable rooms have private hot-water bathrooms and televisions.

Cabinas El Tucán (☎ 775 0553; r per person without/
with air-con US$6/12; ▣ ✕ ▣) This friendly, family-
run hotel is a wonderfully welcoming place
to stay, with kids playing in the courtyard
and mothers cooking in the kitchen nearby.
Clean spacious rooms are clustered around
the shady, tiled courtyard. Rooms vary to
suit the size of your party; pricier rooms
have televisions and refrigerators.

Hotel Golfito (☎ 775 0047; r per person US$10;
▣ ✕ ▣) This bright yellow building overlooking the gulf is convenient to the Muellecito. Despite the location, the plain, modern
rooms do not enjoy water views, but you
can sit out back on the shared balcony and
watch the sunset. Considering the friendly
accommodating service, this place offers
excellent value.

Cabinas Mar y Luna (☎ 775 0192; maryluna@racsa
.co.cr; s/d/tr US$15/17/24, with air-con US$21/23/30;
▣ ✕) This motel-style lodging set right on
the main drag does not offer guests much
privacy. But the rooms are well-maintained
and comfortable, with TVs and private hot-
water bathrooms. The attached restaurant
serves fresh seafood and cold beer on its
open-air waterside terrace.

MIDRANGE
Some of the marinas also provide upscale
lodging.

Hotel El Gran Ceibo (☎ 775 0403; hotelelgranceibo@
yahoo.com; s/d US$18/20, d with air-con US$30; ▣ ✕ ☎)
At the southern end of Golfito, this is a nondescript but perfectly acceptable motel-style
lodging with friendly management. What it
lacks in atmosphere, it makes up for in value.
The pricier rooms are worth the extra investment, not for the hot showers or air-con, but
for the poolside location.

Hotel Golfo Azul (☎ 775 0871; golfazul@racsa.co.cr;
d US$28; ▣ ✕) This family-run hotel is in a
quiet location, set away from the street, in
the northern end of town. Immaculate,
white-tiled rooms have heavy wood doors,
crisp clean linens and attractive wood furniture. The restaurant serves a bounteous
breakfast on request.

Cabinas Buena Vista (☎ 775 2065; petergolfito@
hotmail.com; 2km south of Golfito; d US$25-30; ▣ ☎)

GOLFITO AREA

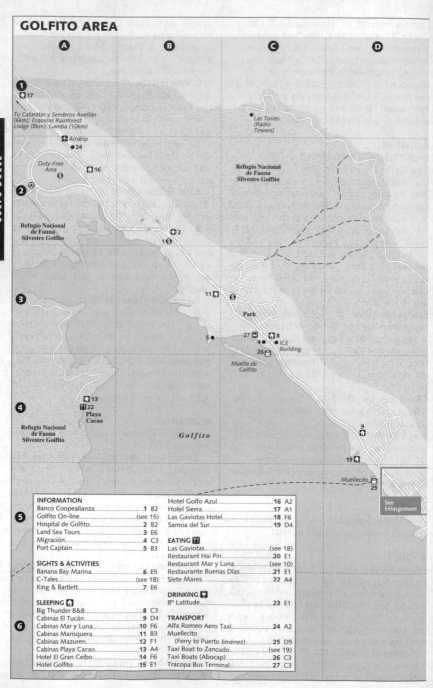

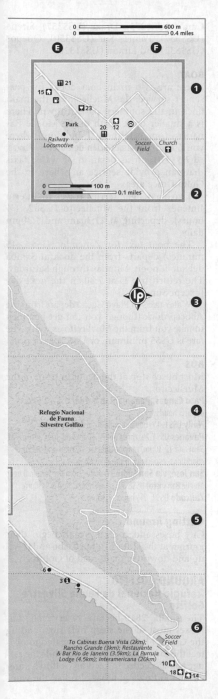

PENINSULA DE OSA & GOLFO DULCE

On the outskirts of Golfito, set on 50 acres of rain forest, these four pleasant cabinas offer a wonderful getaway. The highlight is the stream which runs down the side of the mountain and cascades into the swimming pool.

La Purruja Lodge (☎ 775 1054; www.purruja.com; 4.5km south of Golfito; s/d/tr US$20/30/35; P ☒) A delightful Swiss-Tica couple run this secluded place. Five simple but sparkling cabins have the necessary comforts, including ceiling fans and private showers. The tranquil and tree-filled grounds are renowned for bird sightings. Besides running the lodge, Walter organizes several unique tours, including a boat trip to the Río Coto mangroves (US$35) and trips to the Cavernas de San Rafael (US$35). Breakfast (included) is served in a pleasant outdoor *rancho* that attracts plenty of local birdlife.

Las Gaviotas Hotel (☎ 775 0062; www.resortlas gaviotas.com; s/d/tr/q US$42/48/54/84; P ☒ ☒) The classiest place to stay in Golfito is this full-service hotel at the southern end of town. The cozy cabins have stucco walls and tile floors, colorful woven bedspreads and private porches. They are set amidst a lovely tropical gardens, the centerpiece of which is a pre-Columbian granite sphere.

Hotel Sierra (☎ 775 0666, 775 0336; www.hotel sierra.com; s/d US$50/55; P ☒ ☒) Appropriate to its location in the *Zona Americana*, this place feels like an American-style motor lodge. It is efficient but anonymous, a peaceful retreat from Golfito's grime, but sanitized of its flavor. A large restaurant and casino are on site.

Samoa del Sur (☎ 775 0233, 775 0264; www.samoa delsur.com; r US$58, RV US$10; P ☒ ☐ ☒) This French-run facility includes a restaurant and boat dock, in addition to the handsome lodgings. Fourteen spacious rooms (sleeping up to four people) have stucco walls, tile floors and stylish wood furniture. The bar is a popular spot in the evenings, when guests congregate to play pool or darts. Many services are available, including laundry and bike rental. Kids will appreciate the swimming pool and play area and (on rainy days) the on-site shell museum.

Big Thunder B&B (☎ 775 9191; www.bigthunderbed andbreakfast.com; opposite Muelle de Golfito; d US$75; P ☒ ☒) Colorful depictions of marlin and sailfish adorn the walls of this upscale B&B. Backed by the forested hills of the reserve, the property was formerly the home of a banana manager. Six very spacious rooms are equipped with two double beds, a fridge and coffeemaker and a huge hot-water bathroom. It's a pleasant alternative to the more anonymous resorts in town.

Eating & Drinking

Most of the midrange hotels have restaurants and bars on-site.

Restaurante Buenos Días (☎ 775 1124; opposite the Muellecito; meals US$4-6; ☼ 6am-10pm) Rare is the visitor who passes through Golfito without stopping at this cheerful spot opposite the Muellecito. Brightly colored booths, bilingual menus and super convenient location ensure a constant stream of guests – whether for an early breakfast, a typical Tico casado or a good old-fashioned burger.

Rancho Grande (☎ 775 1951; dishes US$5-12) About 3km south of Golfito, this rustic, thatched-roof place serves country-style Tico food cooked over a wood stove. Margarita, the Tica owner, is famous for her *patacones*. Her hours are erratic, so stop in during the day to let her know you're coming for dinner.

Las Gaviotas (☎ 775 0062; meals US$8; ☼ 6am-10pm) In a spacious *rancho* overlooking the gulf, this hotel restaurant offers excellent international cuisine, an impressive wine list and a fully stocked bar. The place is stylishly decorated with teak and rosewood picnic tables and lots of potted plants.

Restaurant Hai Pin (☎ 775 0032; dishes US$3-7) When you tire of *gallo pinto* (rice and beans), you can change it up with some Chinese food. This popular open-air restaurant enjoys views of the activity on the main drag.

8° Latitude (☎ 775 0235; ☼ noon-midnight) Northwest of the soccer field, this popular ex-pat bar is frequented by Americans into sportfishing (including some women). Its laidback and friendly atmosphere make it the perfect place to tipple a few and listen to fish tales.

Getting There & Away

AIR

The airport is 4km north of the town center near the Duty-Free Zone. Sansa flies five times a day to/from San José (one way/round trip US$78/156).

Alfa Romeo Aero Taxi (☎ 775 1515) has light aircraft (three and five passengers) for charter flights to Puerto Jiménez (US$153),

Carate (US$275), Drake (US$357), Sirena (US$357), Palmar Sur (US$350), Quepos (US$632) and Limón (US$1320).

BOAT

There are two main boat docks for passenger service: the Muellecito is the main dock in the southern part of town. There is a smaller dock north of the Muelle Bananero (opposite the ICE building) where you'll find the **Associación de Boteros** (Abocap; ☎ 775 0357), an association of water taxis that can provide service anywhere in the Golfo Dulce area.

Two passenger ferries travel to Puerto Jiménez from the Muellecito (US$2, 1½ hours), departing at 11:30am and 1:30pm daily.

The boat taxi for Zancudo (US$4, 45 minutes) departs from the dock at Samoa del Sur at noon, Monday through Saturday. The return trip is at 7:30am the next day (except Sunday).

Water taxis to Playa Cacao depart from the Abocap dock (though you can get boatmen to take you from the Muellecito as well). The fare is US$5 minimum or US$2 per person.

BUS

Most buses stop at the depot in front of the Muellecito.

Paso Canoas, Panamanian border US$1, 2½ hours, departs hourly.

Neily US$1, 1½ hours, hourly from 6am to 7pm.

Pavones US$1.20, three hours, 10am and 3pm, returns at 5am and 12:30pm, may be affected by road and weather conditions, especially in the rainy season.

San José, via San Isidro (Tracopa; from the terminal near Muelle Bananero) US$8.50, seven hours, 5am & 1:30pm.

Zancudo US$1, 1½ hours, 1:30pm.

Getting Around

City buses and collective taxis begin their journey at the Hotel El Gran Ceibo and travel up and down the main road of Golfito.

AROUND GOLFITO
Refugio Nacional de Fauna Silvestre Golfito

The small, 2810-hectare reserve encompasses most of the steep hills surrounding the Golfito. It was originally created to protect the town's watershed. And while the refuge has succeeded in keeping Golfito's water clean and flowing, it has also had the wonderful side effect of conserving a number of rare and interesting plant species, for example, the Zamia, which are cycads. Cycads are called 'living fossils' and are among the most primitive of plants. They were abundant before the time of the dinosaurs, but relatively few species are now extant. Other species of interest include many heliconias, orchids, tree ferns, and tropical trees including copal, the kapok tree, the butternut tree and the cow tree.

The vegetation attracts a variety of birds such as parrot, toucan, tanager, trogon and hummingbird. Although the scarlet macaw has been recorded here, poaching in this area has made it rare. Peccary, paca, raccoon, coati, and the four types of monkey are among the mammals that have been sighted here.

There are no facilities for visitors, save a gravel access road and a few poorly maintained trails. About 2km south of the center of Golfito, a gravel road heads inland, past a soccer field, and winds 7km up to some radio towers (Las Torres) 486m above sea level. This access road is an excellent option for hiking, as it has very little traffic. In any case, you'll probably see more from the cleared road than from the overgrown trails.

A very steep hiking trail leaves from Golfito, almost opposite the Samoa del Sur hotel. A somewhat strenuous hike (allow about two hours) will bring you out on the road to the radio towers. The trail is easier to find in Golfito than at the top.

Another option is to walk along the poor dirt road heading toward **Gamba**. This road begins a couple of kilometers northwest of the duty-free area and crosses through part of the refuge. The local bus stops at the beginning of this dirt road, from where it is about 10km to Gamba.

Finally, there are several trails off the road to Playa Cacao. Hikers on these routes will be rewarded by waterfalls and views of the gulf. They are often obscured, however, so it's worth asking locally about maps and trail conditions before setting off.

As always, be sure that somebody knows when and where you are going before you set off on an independent hike.

Cataratas y Senderos Avellán

This Tico family-run **reserve and adventure camp** (☎ 378 7895; www.waterfallsavellan.com; admission US$2.50) is an excellent option for adventur-

ers who like a little guidance. Guided hikes (US$18) and horse riding tours (US$8 per hour) explore the extensive, rain forest–covered grounds, including three impressive waterfalls. Camping (US$5) and meals (US$2 to US$4) are also available.

Playa Cacao

Just a hop, skip and a jump across the bay, this small beach offers a prime view of Golfito stretched out along the coast, with the rain forest as a backdrop. It is, perhaps, the most appealing spot from which to enjoy the old port. The small beach is cleaner than the polluted waters just off Golfito, but the water isn't exactly pristine.

Cabinas Playa Cacao (in San José ☎ 221 1169; www.kapsplace.com; d US$50) is a beach retreat with six spacious cabins with screened windows, high thatched roofs and tiled floors. Units are equipped with kitchenettes, or you can make use of the well-stocked communal kitchen that overlooks the gulf. With hammocks on the beach and hiking trails in the wildlife refuge, you'll not want for entertainment. And the amiable owner, Doña Isabel Arias, provides excellent company.

Siete Mares (☎ 824 5058; dishes US$4-8; ☷ 8am-8pm) is a waterside shack and a popular gathering spot for Golfito residents, who come in for the good beachside atmosphere, plenty of beer, garlic fish and good *ceviche* (US$2.50). Ask here about boat tours or transport around the gulf.

Catch a water taxi from Golfito for about US$5. You can also get to Playa Cacao by walking or driving about 6km along a dirt road west and then south from the airport. A 4WD is recommended.

PARQUE NACIONAL PIEDRAS BLANCAS

This park, formerly called Parque Nacional Esquinas, was established in 1992 as an extension of Corcovado. Piedras Blancas covers 30,000 acres of undisturbed tropical primary rain forest, as well as 5000 acres of secondary forests, pasture land and coastal cliffs and beaches.

One of the last remaining stretches of lowland rain forest, the park is home to a vast array of flora and fauna. According to a study conducted at the biological station at Gamba, the biodiversity of trees in Piedras Blancas is the densest in all of Costa Rica, even surpassing Corcovado. Tree enthusiasts will have a field day identifying species such as ceiba, nazareno, manú, fruta dorada, cristóbal, cedro macho and many, many more.

Parque Nacional Piedras Blancas borders the Refugio Nacional Fauna Silvestre Golfito in the east. In the west, the Reserva Forestal de Golfo Dulce connects Piedras Blancas with Corcovado, forming an important biological corridor for resident wildlife, especially large mammals and predators that cover vast areas. Unfortunately, the forests around Rincón are threatened by illegal logging, jeopardizing this route.

Because Piedras Blancas is so remote and so little visited, it is the site for several ongoing animal projects, including the reintroduction of scarlet macaws with the hopes of establishing a self-sustaining population, and the re-integration of wild cats, like ocelot and margay that were confiscated from private homes. Look for all of the wildlife that you might see in Corcovado: all five big cats and all four monkeys, collared and white-lipped peccary and lots of smaller mammals; caiman, American crocodile and various species of poison dart frog (including the endemic Golfo Dulce dart frog); not to mention more than 330 species of bird.

Parque Nacional Piedras Blancas does not yet have facilities for visitors. However, it is possible to access the park from the Esquinas Rainforest Lodge in Gamba and all of the coastal lodges north of Golfito.

The **Esquinas Rainforest Lodge** (☎ 775 0140, 775 0901; www.esquinaslodge.com; Gamba; s/d/tr US$130/200/240; P ☒) was founded by the nonprofit Rainforest for the Austrians, which was also vital in the establishment of Piedras Blancas as a national park. Now, surrounded by the primary and secondary rain forest of the park, Esquinas is integrally connected with the community of Gamba, employing local workers and reinvesting profits in community projects. Accommodations at Esquinas Lodge are in spacious, high-ceilinged cabins with ceiling fans and private porches; meals are included. The lodge's extensive grounds comprise a network of well-marked trails and a welcoming stream-fed pool. Gamba is 8km north of Golfito and 6km south of the Interamericana.

Playas San Josecito, Nicuesa & Cativo

The northeastern shore of the Golfo Dulce is defined by idyllic deserted beaches,

backed by the pristine rain forest of Parque Nacional Piedras Blancas. The appeal of this area is only enhanced by its inaccessibility: part of the charm is that very few people make it to this untouched corner of Costa Rica. All of the lodges offer boat transportation from Puerto Jiménez and/or Golfito, or you can catch a water taxi.

The beaches along this stretch are excellent for swimming, snorkeling and sunning. Lodges also provide kayaks for maritime exploration. Hiking and wildlife-watching opportunities are virtually unlimited, as the lodges provide direct access to the wilds of Piedras Blancas. Miles of trails lead to secluded beaches, cascading waterfalls and other undiscovered attractions.

CASA DE ORQUÍDEAS

This private **botanical garden** (Playa San Josecito; admission & tour US$5; ☼ tours at 8:30am Sat-Thu), surrounded on three sides by primary rain forest, is a veritable Eden. The garden's plants have been lovingly collected and tended by Ron and Trudy MacAllister, who have lived in this remote region since the 1970s. Self-taught botanists, they've amassed a wonderful collection of tropical fruit trees, bromeliads, cycads, palms, heliconias, ornamental plants and more than 100 varieties of orchid, after which their garden is named.

The two-hour guided tours titillate all of the senses: chew on a 'magic' seed that makes lemons taste sweet; smell vanilla beans; see insects trapped in bromeliad pools; or touch ginger in its flower. Casa de Orquídeas is at the west end of Playa San Josecito and can be reached from the lodges on that beach by foot. Otherwise, it's accessible only by boat; **Land-Sea Tours** (☎ 775 1614; www.realestate-costarica .info) can make these arrangements (US$50).

SLEEPING

The following lodges may be difficult to contact directly, but you can leave a message with an agent in Golfito. They are all accessible only by boat (with beach landings). Prices include three meals per day. Listed in order from south to north:

Golfo Dulce Lodge (☎ 821 5398; www.golfodulce lodge.com; Playa San Josecito; standard/deluxe 4-day package from US$285/315; ☒) Set back from the rocky beach, this Swiss-owned place is on the edge of a 275-hectare property, much of which is rain forest. The owners are clued in about local flora and fauna, dedicating their efforts to a nearby wildcat rehabilitation project. Deluxe units consist of five individual wooden cabins, each with a large veranda containing a rocking chair and hammock; three standard adjoining rooms with smaller verandahs surround the spring-fed pool.

Dolphin Quest (☎ 775 8630, 775 0373; www.dolphin questcostarica.com; Playa San Josecito; s/d camping US$30/ 55, cabins US$60/100, house US$70/120) This jungle lodge offers as much privacy as a mile of beach and 280 hectares of mountainous rain forest can offer. Three round, thatched-roof cabins and one large house are spread out around two hectares of landscaped grounds. Meals – featuring many organic ingredients from the garden – are served communally in an open-air pavilion near the shore. Access to many miles of trails is free after an introductory tour outlining the beauties and dangers of the forest (US$10), but many other tours and activities are also available.

Playa Nicuesa Rain Forest Lodge (☎ 735 5237, in the USA 866-348 7610; www.nicuesalodge.com; Playa Nicuesa; guesthouse/cabins per person US$150/170) Nestled into a 65-hectare private rain-forest reserve north of Casa de Orquídeas, this lodge is barely visible from the water (though its dock gives it away). The open-air accommodations are beautifully decorated with canopied beds and indigenous textile spreads; private hot-water bathrooms have garden showers. Meals are served in a thatched *rancho*, featuring a sparkling, polished wood bar. Electricity is provided by solar power, but the lodge usually uses candlelight to conserve energy and enhance the romantic atmosphere.

Rainbow Adventures Lodge (in the USA ☎ 503-297 2682; www.rainbowcostarica.com; Playa Cativo; s/d US$235/355, penthouse US$250/375, beachfront cabins US$275/395, additional adult/child US$95/80; ☒) The rustic appearance of the wide wood balconies adorning this lodge belies the elegance within: handmade furniture, silk rugs, early 20th-century antiques and fresh flowers make this a special place. In the 1st-floor library, guests are welcome to relax and peruse one of thousands of natural history publications. Upstairs, the rooms are partially exposed to the elements (but protected by mosquito nets) to allow unimpeded views of the rain forest, beach and gulf.

Caña Blanca Beach & Rain Forest Lodge (☎ 813 3803; www.canablanca.com; r per person US$150) About 2km (by boat) north of Playa Cativo and Rainbow Adventures, three breezy, comfortable hardwood cabins front a small beach that is ideal for snorkeling, swimming and star-gazing. The place is designed for the optimum privacy: each cabin has a spacious verandah and a hot-water garden shower (both with unobstructed forest views).

SOUTHERN GOLFO DULCE

Departing the Interamericana at Río Claro, a gravel road travels south to the forested Valle de Coto Colorado on the south shore of the Golfo Dulce. It's worth noting that the road does not actually cross the Río Coto Colorado: that is done on a slow-moving barge, carrying three cars and a handful of humans, which gives you a pretty good idea of how things work in these parts. Nonetheless, many travelers make this arduous journey in search of the country's longest left-hand break at Pavones or the more tranquil waters at Zancudo. Other than the transplants who came to surf and sun and decided to stay, this far corner is also home to a significant indigenous population, who inhabit the Reserva Indígena Guaymí de Conte Burica near Pavones.

ZANCUDO

The tiny town of Zancudo sits on a slender finger of land that juts into the Golfo Dulce, 15km south of Golfito. On the west side, gentle, warm, Pacific waters lap up onto its black sands, inviting swimmers, sunbathers and surfers to frolic on these shores. On the east side, a tangle of mangrove swamps attracts birds, crocodiles and plenty of fish, which in turn attract fisher people hoping to reel them in.

In the midst of these natural habitats, the town of Zancudo is constituted by one dirt road, which leads from the boat dock in the north, past the lodges that are strung along the shore and out of town south toward Pavones.

Zancudo is a popular destination for Ticos, especially around New Year and during the annual **Fishing & Blues Festival** held in early February. Nonetheless, seeing another person on the beach means it's 'crowded.'

The surf is gentle, and at night the water sometimes sparkles with bioluminescence, tiny phosphorescent marine plants and plankton that light up if you sweep a hand through the water – the effect is like underwater fireflies.

The largest store in town is the **Super Bellavista** (opposite Cabinas Tío Froylan), where there is also a public phone. **Oceano** (☎ 776 0921; www.oceanacabinas.com) offers Internet access. There is no bank in town and very few places accept credit cards, so bring your cash from Golfito.

Activities

The main activities at Zancudo are undoubtedly swinging on hammocks, strolling on the beach and swimming in the aqua blue waters of the Golfo Dulce. The southern end of the beach (in front of Latitude 8) attracts surfers, although this is not one of Costa Rica's hottest surfing spots, due to inconsistent conditions. Locals report that the beach break makes it an ideal place to learn. Stop by **Coloso del Mar** (☎ 776 0050; www.coloso-del-mar.com) to inquire about the surf and rent surfboards.

Oasis on the Beach (☎ 776 0087; www.oasisonthebeach.com) offers an early-morning **horse riding** tour, which starts at its horse farm in La Virgen, about 7km from Zancudo. The guided tour (per person US$50) traverses the mountains and the beach and concludes with a bountiful breakfast.

The **mangrove swamps** offer plenty of opportunities for exploration: birdlife is prolific, while other animals such as crocodile, caiman, monkey and sloth are also frequently spotted. The boat ride from Golfito gives a glimpse of these waters, but you also paddle them yourself: rent kayaks from **Cabinas Los Cocos** (☎ 776 0012; www.loscocos.com).

Zancudo is a base for inshore and offshore fishing, river fishing (mangrove snapper, snook and corbina) and fly fishing. The best **sportfishing** is from December to May for sailfish and May to September for snook, though many species bite year-round. The outfits listed following offer all-inclusive, multiday fishing packages:

Arena Alta Sportfishing (☎ 282 3370, in the USA 631-731 1737; www.costaricasailfish.com; 5-day package per person US$1800-2500) Based in Golfito, but lodging is also offered in Zancudo.

Golfito Sportfishing (☎ 776 0007; www.costaricafishing.com; 5-day fishing package per person US$2700-3600)

Roy's Zancudo Lodge (☎ 776 0008; www.royszancudolodge.com; 5-day fishing package per person US$2900-4300) Claims over 50 world records.

Sleeping & Eating

Most of these places fill up during the high season, so reservations are recommended (especially on weekends). Listed in order from north to south:

Roy's Zancudo Lodge (☎ 776 0008; www.royszancudolodge.com; r per person US$120; P ☒ ☖) North of the dock you'll find one of the oldest places in Zancudo – catering to a faithful clientele of anglers. Clean but bland rooms have all the amenities you would expect from a western hotel. Family-style meals (included in the price) usually feature the daily catch. If you don't like to fish, you will still appreciate the huge pool overlooking the ocean and the luxurious hot tub nearby. The lodge closes in October.

Soda Katherine (☎ 776 0124; dishes US$2-4; ☼ 6am-8pm) Backed by the mangrove swamp, this atmospheric, open-air *soda* is full of locals and savvy visitors enjoying fresh fruit juices, *gallo pinto* and casados. Katherine also has one cabina which she rents for US$20. Just south of the dock.

Cabinas Tío Froylan (☎ 776 0128; r per person US$7) Plain and cheap whitewashed rooms with private cold shower and fan attract a loyal Tico following. This place is good for groups, as some of the rooms have four or five beds. There's a shady patio, beach access and an attached restaurant and disco with a pool table. Expect to hear the disco from your room on weekend nights.

Oceano (☎ 776 0921; www.oceanacabinas.com; d US$80; ☐) With its back to the beach, this friendly little inn has just two rooms, both spacious and airy with wood-beamed ceilings and tile bathrooms. The decor features quaint details like throw pillows and folk art – a rarity in these parts. The open-air restaurant is also inviting for dinner or drinks: it advertises the best ceviche on the beach, a claim worth investigating.

Macondo (☎ 776 0157; d/tr US$35/45; P ☒ ☖) Set back from the road, this excellent midrange choice has lovely landscaped grounds surrounding an inviting tiled swimming pool. Six spacious rooms share a balcony overlooking the garden. Your host Daniele is also the chef at the Italian restaurant (dishes US$5 to US$10), serving homemade pastas, fresh pastries and aromatic espressos and cappuccinos.

Bar/Cabinas Sussy (☎ 776 0107; s/d US$5/10) Possibly the cheapest place in town, Sussy offers clean, dark concrete rooms with no windows. It's a friendly place, attracting plenty of late-night revelers to drink at the bar and play pool.

Iguana Verde (☎ 776 0910; cabins US$60; 😮) About 500m south of the dock, the Iguana Verde consists of three simple tiled cabins, set on palm-lined beachfront grounds. Sleeping up to four people, the cabins have sturdy wood furniture and private bathrooms decorated with whimsical fish and rubber ducks. The staff is accommodating, but ownership of this place was in flux at the time of research so it's subject to change.

Cabinas BM (☎ 776 0045; camping US$7, cottages US$40) New owners are upgrading this unfortunately-named property, starting with landscaping the grounds and building a children's play area. Four cottages (sleeping up to four) are equipped with kitchens, bathrooms and televisions. Good option for families.

La Puerta Negra (☎ 776 0181; meals US$10-15; 😮 6-9pm Tue-Sun). More than just a dinner, eating here is a culinary and cultural experience. Alberto – chef, waiter, maitre d' and musical entertainer – cooks delicious seafood and fresh pasta dinners and will consume bottles of good wine right along with you. Stop in during the day to make a reservation.

Cabinas Los Cocos (☎ 776 0012; www.loscocos .com; cabins US$70; Ⓟ) Two North American artist transplants run this wonderful beachfront lodge that is about 1km south of the dock. The well-groomed gardens are dotted with Andrew's sculptures, while Susan's magnificent mosaic work adorns the showers. Two quaint cabins, which used to be banana company homes in Palmar, were transported to Zancudo, reassembled and completely refurbished. The other two more spacious cabins are also charming, with loft sleeping areas under palm frond roofs. All the cabins have kitchenettes and private porches overlooking the garden.

Cabinas Sol y Mar (☎ 776 0014; www.zancudo .com; d economy s/d US$18/23, standard s/d US$38/43, deluxe US$42/48; Ⓟ) Just south of Los Cocos on the beach, this popular place offers lodging options for all budgets: smallish economy dwellings that are farther from the water;

larger standard units with a shared terrace overlooking the beach; and private, deluxe units with fancy tile showers and unobstructed ocean views. The open-air restaurant (dishes US$5 to US$8) is a Zancudo favorite, especially among carnivores: Rick's barbecue night is legendary, as is the specialty 'Cheeseburger in Paradise'.

Latitude 8 (☎ 776 0168; www.latitude8lodge.com; d US$70, additional person US$10; Ⓟ) Known locally as 'Ty's Place,' these two shiny hardwood cabins have a huge hot-water shower, pretty floral sink, and refrigerator stocked with drinking water. There is also an outdoor kitchen and barbecue grill that's wonderful for whipping up a beachside meal.

Coloso del Mar (☎ 776 0050; www.coloso-del-mar .com; d garden/beachfront US$40/45; 🖳) Four simple cabins are nestled into the tropical gardens that front the black sand beach at Coloso del Mar. Fun sea-themed murals decorate the showers, as a reminder of what's outside your door. The cabins are otherwise pretty plain, but they are equipped with refrigerators, coffee makers and semi-private porch. A beachside observation platform offers Zancudo's best sunset views (bring your own drinks).

Cabinas y Restaurant Tranquilo (☎ 776 0131; dm US$5, s/d with bathroom US$7.50/12.50) This simple lodge at the southern end of Zacundo has small, clean rooms and a pleasant terrace restaurant, all overseen by the motherly María, whose delicious cooking has earned her loyal fans.

Oasis on the Beach (☎ 776 0087; www.oasisonthe beach.com; d without/with air-con US$50/60, ste US$65; Ⓟ) Beachy grounds are dotted with spacious, airy cabins, each with mosquitonetted beds, tile floors and huge bathrooms. The cabins are looking a little worn, but new owners have intentions of sprucing the place up. The moniker 'Oasis on the Beach' definitely describes the spacious restaurant (lunch US$6, dinner US$10 to US$15), which is now enclosed, air-conditioned and painted with a jungle mural.

Getting There & Away
BOAT
The boat dock is near the north end of the beach on the inland, estuary side (3km from Oasis on the Beach, at the opposite end of town). A water taxi to Golfito departs from this dock at 7am, returning at noon,

Monday through Saturday. **Zancudo Boat Tours** (☎ 776 0012; www.loscocos.com) at Cabinas Los Cocos can provide private taxi-boat service to and from Puerto Jiménez (per person US$15, four person minimum) and Golfito (US$12.50, two person minimum).

BUS
A bus to Neily leaves from the *pulpería* near the dock at 5:30am (US$1.50, three hours). The bus for Golfito leaves at 5am for the three-hour trip, with a ferry transfer at the Río Coto Colorado. Service is erratic in the wet season, so inquire before setting out.

CAR
It's possible to drive to Golfito by taking the road south of Río Claro for about 10km. Turn left at the Rodeo Bar and go another 10km to the Río Coto Colorado ferry, which carries three vehicles (per car US$1.20) and runs all day except during the lowest tides. From there, 30km of dirt road gets you to Golfito. To get to Pavones, take a right at the first major intersection, instead of a left. A 4WD is necessary in the rainy season.

PAVONES
About 15km south of Zancudo, the Bahía de Pavón is legendary among surfers for its long left-hand break. The name Pavones is used to refer to both Playa Río Claro de Pavones and Punta Banco, which is 6km south. Here, near Costa Rica's most southern point, the wide sandy beaches lined with palms and the coastal hills covered with rain forest provide a breathtaking backdrop to the waves crashing in across the gulf.

This village used to be off-the-beaten-track. (And it's still not so easy to get to.) But surfers have their ways. Both foreigner and Ticos are transforming this town from an off-beat backwater into a hip, happening hotspot. A small but significant ex-pat community has relocated to Pavones on a semi-permanent basis; old, dilapidated houses are being demolished in favor of modern construction with rental units. Fortunately, the tranquil air remains (especially outside of surf season). The palm-lined streets are still not paved and the pace of life is slow.

Of course, Pavones has much more to offer than a good wave. This is Costa Rica, after all, and the flora and fauna of the rain forest are never far away.

Note that the best season for surfing coincides with the rainy months, so getting here offers an adventure of its own. A 4WD vehicle is highly recommended in the rainy season.

Orientation & Information
The road into Pavones comes south and deadends at the Río Claro, which is where you'll find the Esquina del Mar Cantina and the soccer field. About 200m to the east, a parallel road crosses the Río Claro and continues the 6km to Punta Banco. The dirt path by the soccer field leads to the Pavones–Banco road. Otherwise, you can reach it by taking the turnoff by the fishing boats, about 500m north of Esquinas del Mar.

Many places in Pavones do not have a telephone; the only public telephone is at **Doña Dora's** (☎ 770 8221), by the soccer field. Local lodging information is available at the **real estate office** (www.pavoneslocal.com). Pavones has no bank or gas station, so make sure you have plenty of money and petrol.

Sights
Set on a verdant hillside between Pavones and Punta Banco, the **Tiskita Jungle Lodge** (in San José ☎ 296 8125; www.tiskita-lodge.co.cr; guided hike US$15) consists of 100 hectares of virgin forest and a huge orchard, which produces more than 100 varieties of tropical fruit from all over the world. A network of 14 trails wind through surrounding rain forest, which contains waterfalls and fresh-water pools suitable for swimming.

The combination of rain forest, fruit farm and coastline attracts a long list of birds. About 300 species have been recorded here. The fruit farm is particularly attractive to fruit-eating birds such as parrots and toucans. The forest is home to more reticent species such as yellow-billed cotinga, fiery-billed aracari, green honeycreeper and lattice-tailed trogon. Hikes are usually guided by the owners – personable conservationist and conversationalist Peter Aspinall and his wife Elizabeth – or their son; reservations recommended.

About 8km east of Pavones, the **Reserva Indígena Guaymí de Conte Burica** is an interesting destination for a hiking or horseback riding. The reserve is home to as many as 3000 inhabitants, the largest concentration of indigenous people in the area. Ask at

Doña Dora's: her son Marvin will provide horses and lead the way for US$40 per person. The trip takes about five hours, and you will have the chance to share a meal with an indigenous family, buy some handicrafts and stop for a swim at a local watering hole. Lily at Cabinas Mira Olas (p442) also organizes this trek.

Activities
SURFING

Pavones is one of Costa Rica's most famous surf breaks: when the surf's up, this tiny beach town attracts hordes of international wave riders and Tico surfer dudes. Conditions are best with a southern swell, usually between April and October. However, because Pavones is inside Golfo Dulce, it is protected from many swells so surfers can go for weeks without seeing any waves.

Pavones has become legendary among surfers for its wicked long left. Some claim it is among the world's longest, offering a two- or three-minute ride on a good day. Legend has it that the wave passes so close to the Esquina del Mar Cantina that you can toss beers to surfers as they zip by. Be warned: when the wave is big, it can deposit surfers on the sharp rocks at the far end of the bay.

Locals know that when Pavones has nothing (or when it's too crowded), they can head south to **Punta Banco**, a reef break with decent rights and lefts. The best conditions are at mid- or high-tide, especially with swells from the south or west.

For more surf info:

Sea Kings (☎ 393 6982; www.surfpavones.com; at Arte Nativo) Rents surf boards and body boards, and sells new and refurbished boards and plenty of other gear. Inquire here about lessons (per hour US$50).

Venus Surf Adventures (☎ 840 2365, in the USA 800-793 0512; www.venussurfadventures.com; 6-night package per person US$1450) Offers surf-centered package tours for women, which include surf lessons, yoga classes, jungle spa sessions and other adventures.

OTHER ACTIVITIES

Chen Taiji International (in the USA ☎ 305-931 0918; www.chentaijiinternational.com) Another way to find inner peace in a tropical paradise is through the ancient art of Tai Chi.

Shooting Star Studio (☎ 393 6982; www.yogapavones .com; per class US$10) Ashtanga yoga, traditional shotokan karate and other classes designed especially for surfers occur on a daily basis. Located 400m south of the point.

Sleeping
Pavones is exploding as a tourist destination, and locals are definitely trying to get in on it – building, renovating and opening cabinas faster than we can review them. If you show up and ask around, you are sure to find someone to put you up.

PAVONES
There is a cluster of places to stay around the soccer field and along the dirt path that cuts up to the main road to Punta Banco. A few places are further north. Listed in order (roughly) from west to east:

Esquina del Mar Cantina (☎ 844 9454; r per person US$6; **P**) The heart of Pavones, right here. Three basic but breezy upstairs rooms have incredible views (but no mosquito nets). All units have shared, cold-water shower. The bar is open until 1am on weekends, so if you're staying here, plan on staying up too.

Hotel Maureen (r per person US$8; **P**) The bright exterior – painted with a wild, jungle mural – belies the dark, drab rooms within. Upstairs from the small grocery, the seven basic cabins have hardwood floors and walls, heavy wood furniture, powerful fans and dim light bulbs. Shared cold-water facilities.

Cabinas Willy Willy (☎ 770 8221; r per person US$20; **P** 🔁) On the soccer field, three brand-new, concrete cabins are behind the pulpería of the same name. Boxy but bright, they are painted in pastel colors and fully furnished with comfortable beds and televisions.

Cabinas Carol (☎ 827 3394; r per person US$10; **P**) Carol's cabinas (50m east of the soccer field) are Pavones' best budget option. The cabinas are nothing to write home about, but the friendly Kiwi management and the shady garden setting guarantee a good time. White stucco walls keep things cool inside, and each room has a pretty, private garden with an outdoor shower. Guests have access to open-air kitchen facilities and plenty of hammocks strung up around the grounds.

Cabinas Casa Olas (☎ 826 3693; r per person US$10; **P** 🔁) About 100m east of the soccer field, five cabins of varying sizes have wide-plank wood floors, brightly painted walls and an attractive unfinished feel that might appeal to the laidback surfer set. All the rooms share access to outdoor kitchen facilities and a covered hammock lounge – an excellent chill-out zone. A good choice if friendliness takes precedence over cleanliness.

Riviera (☎ 823 5874; www.pavonesriviera.com; d US$60, additional person US$15; P ☒) The slickest option in Pavones proper is this resort on the road to Banco. The three villas are brand spanking new, each with a fully-equipped kitchen, cool tile floors and attractive hardwood ceilings. Big shady porches overlook the landscaped gardens.

Vista Dulce (☎ 383 2739, 488 0700; www.vistadulce -pavones.com; d US$25-30, additional person US$10-15) This little lodge is high up in the hills overlooking Pavones: take the turn-off at the fishing boats, and continue straight instead of turning south to Banco. Follow signs to this two-room perch with tile floors, wooden beds and private bathrooms. (Prices vary according to size of the room and temperature of the showers.)

Cabinas Mira Olas (☎ 393 7742; www.miraolas .com; d/tr rustic US$25/30, modern US$35/40, deluxe US$45/53; P) This 4.5-hectare farm is full of wildlife and fruit trees and cabins to suit all tastes. The 'rustic' cabin, incidentally, boasted the first flush toilet in Pavones, so it's not *that* rustic. However, it contrasts with the 'jungle deluxe', a beautiful, open-air lodging with a huge balcony and elegant cathedral ceiling. Both include

fully equipped kitchens, offering excellent value. At the front of the property, the aptly labeled 'modern' cabinas are yellow concrete blocks that are relatively characterless. To find Mira Olas, turn off at the fishing boats and follow the signs up the steep hill: it's worth the climb!

Casa Siempre Domingo (☎ 820 4709; d/tr US$80/ 120; www.casa-domingo.com; P) The most unbelievable views of the gulf are from this luxurious bed and breakfast, high in the hills above Pavones. Lodging is elegant and simple, with cathedral ceilings and a wonderful sense of openness. You'll need a car to get here: take the left fork at the Río Claro crossing.

PUNTA BANCO

Note that the morning bus from Golfito stops at the Esquinas del Mar Cantina in Pavones and does not pass these places in Punta Banco. If you want door-to-door service, take the afternoon bus at 3pm. Listed in order from north to south:

Cabinas La Ponderosa (☎ 824 4145, in the USA 954-771 9166; www.cabinaslaponderosa.com; r per person without/with air-con US$50/55; P ☒) Set on 14 acres, these cozy cabins feature clean white

GUAYMÍ

The earliest inhabitants of Costa Rica's far southern corner were the Guaymí, or Ngöbe, who migrated – over generations – from Panama. The Guaymí inhabit indigenous reserves in the Valle de Coto Brus, on the Osa peninsula and in southern Golfo Dulce, though they retain some semi-nomadic ways, and are allowed to pass freely over the border into Panama. This occurs frequently during the coffee harvesting season, when many Guaymí travel to work on plantations.

The Guaymí have been able to preserve – to some degree – their customs and culture, and it is not unusual to see women wearing traditional dress. These vibrant, solid-colored pollera dresses hang to the ankles, often trimmed in contrasting colors and patterns. Unlike other indigenous groups, the Guaymí still speak their native language and teach it in local schools.

The Guaymí traditionally live in wooden huts with palm roofs and dirt floors, although most families have now upgraded to wooden houses on stilts. All food is prepared over a wood-burning stove. They live off the land, cultivating corn, rice and tubers, while fruit and palmitos grow in the wild.

The Guaymí reserves are largely inaccessible, which may be one reason the culture persists. It is now at a precipitous point, however. As tourism filters into the farthest corners of the country, there is a growing interest in indigenous traditions and handicrafts, and this demand may actually encourage their preservation. Without proper management and community participation, however, an influx of tourists (and tourist dollars) can also lead to cultural dilution and bastardization.

Visit the reserves. Take time to learn about the lifestyles, traditions and folklore. Whenever possible, travel with local guides. And most importantly, be respectful of these endangered cultures. For more information on visiting the reserves, see the Tamandu Lodge on p421 or the Reserva Indígena Guaymí de Conte Burica on above.

walls, powerful ceiling fans and lots of varnished hardwood detailing. Balconies overlook the lovely landscaped gardens (diminished only by the poor captive coati that paces in his cage out front). The common lounge offers all kinds of entertainment, including a ping-pong table and a massive video library.

Tiskita Jungle Lodge (in San José ☎ 296 8125; www .tiskita-lodge.co.cr; s/d/tr US$145/240/315, child under 12 US$60; P ☎ ⅏) Set amidst extensive gardens and orchards, the lodge's accommodations are in one of 16 beautiful, shiny wood rooms. Private bathrooms have hot water, stone garden shower and one unit even has a garden toilet with pretty forest views. (You won't need magazines; just binoculars.) Daily rates include fresh, home-cooked meals and guided walks. The lodge is closed from mid-September to mid-October.

Sotavento (☎ 391 3468; Casa Poinsetta US$60, Casa Vista Grande US$80; P) These two tropical hardwood, furnished houses are set on a picturesque pepper and cacao plantation, perched above Punta Banco. Casa Poinsetta and the larger Casa Vista Grande both feature rustic, open-air architecture that takes advantage of the breeze and the views. The houses sleep six to eight people, so they are a great deal if you can get a pack of friends together to split costs. The place is managed by the personable American surfer Harry, who makes his own boards. Follow signs from the soccer field.

Rancho Burica (www.ranchoburica.com; r per person US$7-14; P) This is a friendly and youthful Dutch-run outpost is literally the end of the road in Banco. All rooms have bathrooms and fans, while the pricier ones boast mosquito-netted beds and attractive wood furniture. Hammocks interspersed around the property offer ample opportunity for chilling out. Reservations are not accepted: 'just show up… like everyone else does.'

Yoga Farm (www.yogafarmcostarica.org; dm US$20) This yoga retreat center, conservation project and working farm is a unique and welcome addition to Pavones. Simple clean rooms have wood bunk beds, while tent space is also available. All bathrooms are shared. The price includes three vegetarian meals, prepared primarily with ingredients from the organic garden. The daily yoga classes are not required, but they are definitely recommended, especially considering

the fabulous open-air studio overlooking the ocean. This place is a 15-minute walk from Rancho Burica: take the road going up the hill to the left, go through the first gate on the left and keep walking up the hill.

Eating & Drinking
Listed from north to south:

Perch (☎ 848 9145; ☽ 5:30-9:30pm Tue-Thu) This new American-owned restaurant and bar is popular for its grilled burgers, fresh salads and homemade ice cream. The signature mango salsa is making 'Taco Tuesdays' a Pavones institution. The Perch has the only properly stocked bar in town, although it's only open midweek, so it's really not a proper bar at all. It's 3km north of Pavones.

La Manta (☽ 6-10pm Tue-Sun) The best dining in Pavones is at this airy *rancho*, which catches the breezes off the bay. The menu features an impressive variety of Mediterranean food. Surfing videos on the big screen set the vibe. This place fronts the beach, 200m north of Esquina del Mar.

Esquina del Mar Cantina (dishes US$3-6; ☽ 6:30am-9pm) More for drinking than eating, but the pub grub is not bad either.

Café de la Suerte (breakfast US$4; ☽ 8am-dusk) The health-conscious and animal-lovers will appreciate this open-air vegetarian joint. The specialty is tropical fruit smoothies, but daily specials offer all sorts of wholesome and delicious veggie fare. There is a comfortable cabina out back that is available for rent.

Also recommended:
La Puesta del Sol (meals US$3-6) This beachside bungalow gets an A-plus for its *ceviche* (local dish of uncooked but well-marinated seafood).
Aleri Pizzeria (meals US$8-10; ☽ 6-9pm) Tasty pizzas and pasta.

Getting There & Away
Two daily buses go to Golfito (US$1.20, three hours): the first leaves at 5:30am and departs from the end of the road at Rancho Burica (but you can pick it up at the bus stop opposite the Riviera); the second leaves at 12:30pm from the Esquina del Mar Cantina. Buses from Golfito depart at 10am (to Pavones) and 3pm (to Punta Banco via Pavones) from the stop at the Muellecito.

A 4WD taxi will charge about US$50 from Golfito. If you are driving, follow the directions to Zancudo and look for the signs to Pavones.

Caribbean Coast

The cloud-covered mountains of the Cordillera de Talamanca and the volcanic peaks of the Cordillera Central effectively split Costa Rica down its spine, creating a very real division between the 'Caribbean side' and the rest of Costa Rica.

Over here, the jungle meets the sea in a smooth arc of sandy beaches that stretch – nearly uninterrupted – from the Nicaraguan border to the Panamanian border. More than a quarter of this coast is protected, including the country's last living coral reefs. And the lack of a dry season results in river-crossed wetlands in the north and lush rain forest in the south.

The difference between the Caribbean and the Pacific is not only geographic. Even more noteworthy is the cultural distinction: this is 'Carib,' and not only in name. Descended from Jamaican and Barbadian immigrants who came to work in the banana industry, more than one-third of the population has Afro-Caribbean roots. Spicy seafood, calypso music and colorful carnivals are reminiscent of Jamaica, mon, as is the local patois.

The Afro-Caribbean clan joined the original inhabitants of the Talamanca region – the KéköLdi, Bribrí and Cabécar indigenous peoples – intermingling and intermixing. Successive waves of immigrants came from Panama, China, Nicaragua and, most recently, Europe and North America, resulting in Costa Rica's most ethnically diverse region.

One resident compares it to the local specialty stew, *rondón*, which is made by mixing together whatever the cook can 'run down.' As the individual ingredients are stirred together, they contribute their own flavors and absorb each others', with a richly layered and tantalizingly spicy outcome.

HIGHLIGHTS

- Spotting the tree-bound sloths along the canals of **Parque Nacional Tortuguero** (p459)
- Surfing the gnarly 'Salsa Brava' off **Puerto Viejo de Talamanca** (p481)
- Riding a bike from Puerto Viejo to Manzanillo, through the **Refugio Nacional de Vida Silvestre Gandoca-Manzanillo** (p496)
- Savoring the flavors of coconut, the sounds of calypso and the allure of the Caribbean in **Cahuita** (p470)
- Patrolling the beaches to see and save the turtles of **Parismina** (p458)

THE ATLANTIC SLOPE

The idea was simple: build a port on the Caribbean coast and connect it to the Central Valley by railroad, thus opening up important shipping routes for soaring coffee production. In 1867 present-day Puerto Limón was chosen as the site, perhaps not accounting for the 150 unexplored kilometers of dense jungles, malaria-ridden swamps and steep, muddy mountainsides along the Atlantic slope.

Though things did not go exactly according to plan, the Costa Ricans eventually got their port and their railroad. They also got a booming banana business, which dominated this region for 100 years.

The railroad, once the lifeline of the region, is no longer. Today, a cloudy highway links the Central Valley to the Caribbean coast, starting in the foothills of the Cordillera Central, traversing a landscape dominated by banana and pineapple plantations, and ending in the swampy lowlands around Limón.

GUÁPILES & AROUND

This pretty, prosperous town in the northern foothills of the Cordillera Central is the transport center for the Río Frío banana-growing region. Some 60km northeast of San José, Guápiles is a bustling place, its main streets lined with shopping centers and other services. A lively agricultural market takes place on Saturdays.

Guápiles is about 1km north of Hwy 32. The two major streets are one way, running parallel to each other. Most of the services are located on the loop these streets make through the busy downtown. The convenient **Café Internet Caribe** (☎ 771 0631; per hr US$1; ☯ 8am-10:30pm) is opposite the bus terminal.

Jardín Botánico Las Cusingas

Exhibits at this family-run **botanical garden** (☎ 710 2652; guided tour US$5; ☯ by appointment) emphasize medicinal plants, rural life, conservation and the ethical use of plants. Eighty medicinal-plant species, 80 orchid species, 30 bromeliad species and more than 100 bird species have been recorded on the flower-filled property. There are several easy trails, as well as courses, research projects and a library.

In the middle of the gardens, a rustic two-room wood **cabin** (r per person US$5; P) houses up to four people. Its cozy living area is equipped with a wood-burning stove; meals are also available. Turn south at the Servicentro Santa Clara (the opposite direction from Cariari), then go 4km by rough paved road to the signed entrance.

Ecofinca Andar

Combining organic agriculture, environmental conservation and community activism, this **ecological farm** (☎ 272 1024; www.andarcr.org; Santa Rosa; 1-day admission US$14, homestays US$17; P) is an impressive educational facility. Demonstrations focus on plants cultivated for medicinal use, sources of renewable energy and the biodiversity of the surrounding rain forest. If you stick around for more than a day you can really get your hands dirty, planting or harvesting in the gardens, fishing and maintaining trails. The farm is 3km northeast of the village of Santa Rosa.

La Danta Salvaje

Make advance arrangements to visit **La Danta Salvaje** (☎ 750 0012; www.greencoast.com/ladanta /ladantasalvaje.htm; 3-night package per person US$210). On the Caribbean slope at 800m above sea level, this private 410-hectare rain-forest reserve is part of the critical buffer zone that protects Parque Nacional Braulio Carrillo (p163). The rustic lodge hosts small groups for three days of hiking in the jungle, swimming under waterfalls and spotting wildlife like spider monkeys and tapirs. Prices include three meals a day, as well as transportation (45 minutes by 4WD, followed by a three-hour hike to the lodge).

Sleeping

Hotel y Cabinas Wilson (☎ 710 2217; d/tr US$14/16; P ☷) This clean, comfortable spot is on the left-hand side as you drive into Guápiles north from the highway. A vibrant wall mural brightens up the otherwise nondescript decor on the open-air lobby, which overlooks the busy street.

Hotel Cabinas Lomas del Toro (☎ 710 2934; d US$10-15; P ☷ ☲) If you'd rather not brave Guápiles proper, this ramp motel off Hwy 32 (about 3km before Guápiles) is efficient and easy to find. Besides the spotless guestrooms, you'll find a good restaurant and a recreation room with table-tennis and pool tables.

CARIBBEAN COAST

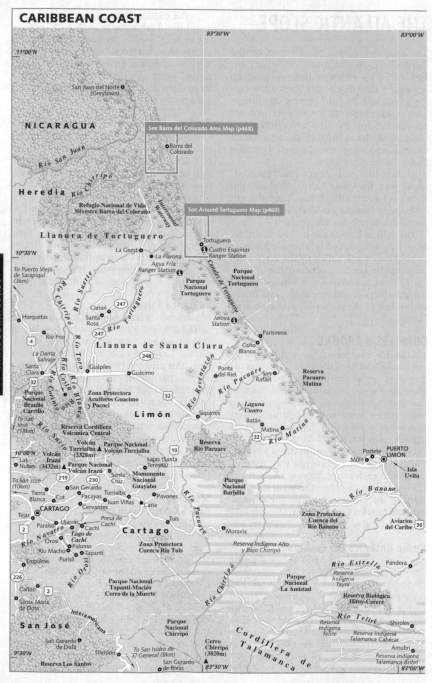

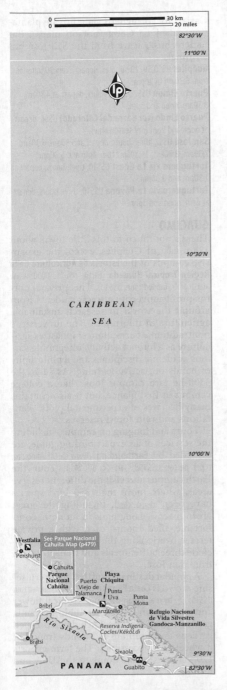

Cabinas Quinta (☎ 710 7016; d with fan/air-con US$40/46; P 🏍) Much nicer than the average cabinas, these large, spotless rooms have cable TV, hot showers and cold refrigerators. The 19-hectare grounds have private trails, two rivers, horses and a motocross track. It's on the road to Cariari just as you leave Guápiles.

Casa Río Blanco (☎ 710 4124; www.casarioblanco .com; s/d/tr US$45/65/80) Four rustic little cabins are perched high above the Río Blanco, offering great canopy views from private porches. Each is individually and creatively decorated, with bright bedspreads and woody interiors. Rates include breakfast and guided hikes on private trails, which provide excellent birding and wildlife-watching opportunities. Turn off the highway 300m east of Restaurant La Ponderosa and drive about 1.5km south.

Country Club Suerre (☎ 710 7551; www.suerre.com; s/d/ste US$70/87/140; P 🍽 🏍 🐾) Join banana executives and other VIPs at this swish spot, 1km north of the Servicentro Santa Clara. Spacious but sanitized rooms have all the required amenities. The Olympic-sized pool, tennis courts and children's play area make this a great spot for families, while everyone will appreciate the luxurious sauna and spa.

Eating

There is an assortment of *sodas*, bakeries and fast-food joints in town.

Restaurant La Ponderosa (☎ 710 2075; mains US$3-10; 🕙 11am-midnight) This roadside joint is about 5km west of Guápiles. A popular stop for a steak, or just *bocas* (snacks) and a beer.

Happy's Pizza (☎ 710 2434; mains US$1-5; 🕙 9am-10pm) More than just pizza, this place anchors a food court with all sorts of independent fast food. Happy's is 100m from the Catholic church.

Restaurant El Unico (☎ 710 6250; meals US$3-5; 🕙 10am-11pm) Around the corner from the bus station, this popular restaurant specializes in chop suey, General Chau's chicken and other Chinese fare.

There's also a huge **Más X Menos supermarket** (🕙 9am-9pm), 200m from the bus terminal.

Getting There & Away

The Guápileños bus terminal is just south of the center.

Cariari US$0.50, 20 minutes, depart every 20 minutes from 6am to 10pm.

Puerto Limón via Guácimo & Siquirres US$2, two hours, depart hourly from 6am to 7pm.

Puerto Viejo de Sarapiquí US$1, 45 minutes, depart at 5:30am, 8am, 10:30am, noon, 2:30pm and 5pm.

San José US$1.75, 1¼ hours, depart every 30 minutes from 6:30am to 7pm.

CARIARI

Due north of Guápiles, Cariari is a blue-collar, rough-around-the-edges banana town. There's a gas station, a bank and an Internet café, **Compuser** (☎ 767 8286; Tracopa bus terminal; per hr US$1; ☷ 7am-10pm Mon-Fri, 11am-8pm Sun).

The reason why tourists cruise through Cariari is to catch a boat to Tortuguero (p461), which can usually be accomplished in an hour or two. If you get stuck, you can spend the night at the **Hotel Central** (☎ 767 6890; r per person US$10; ℗), which is conveniently located close to the bus terminals. The proprietor Patricia – known as 'la mama en Cariari' – takes care of her guests, providing breakfast, luggage storage, long-term parking and other services. Plus she used to work in a hospital, so her brightly painted rooms (with shared bathrooms) are spotless.

Getting There & Away

The turnoff for the paved road to Cariari is about 1km east of Guápiles, at the Servicentro Santa Clara. If you are heading to Tortuguero, you can leave your car at the Hotel Central (per day US$2) or at the guarded parking in La Pavona. (Do not drive to La Geest, as parking is not available.)

Cariari has two bus terminals: the one serving San José is at the southern end of town, while the one serving Guápiles and Caribbean destinations is about five blocks closer to the center, behind the police station.

Despite what you might hear from overzealous tour operators, the most common route to Tortuguero is through La Pavona, a private farm on the Río Suerte (this is not a town, and does not show up on most maps). Buses for La Pavona depart from the central bus terminal behind the police station; buy tickets from the Coopetraca window. Boats from La Pavona to Tortuguero are timed to meet the buses, so you won't have to wait long for your connection.

The private **Bananero** (☎ 709 8005) boat company also provides transportation from

Cariari to Tortuguero via a private plantation called La Geest (not on maps). Bananero buses leave from the San José bus terminal.

Guápiles US$0.50, 20 minutes, depart every 20 minutes from 6:30am to 10pm.

Puerto Limón US$2.25, 2½ hours, depart at 4:30am, 8:30am, noon and 3pm.

Puerto Lindo (for Barra del Colorado) US$6, depart at noon and 2pm (dry season only).

San José US$2, three hours, depart at 5:30am, 6:30am, 7:30am, 8:30am, 11:30am, 1pm, 3pm and 5:30pm.

Tortuguero via La Geest US$10, three hours, depart at 1:30pm and 3:30pm.

Tortuguero via La Pavona US$10, three hours, depart at 6am, noon and 3pm.

GUÁCIMO

There's not much to this little town, about 12km east of Guápiles, except the expansive campus of the **Escuela de Agricultura de la Región Tropical Húmeda** (Earth; ☎ 713 0000; www .earth.ac.cr; guided tours US$10). This private, not-for-profit university attracts students from around the world to research sustainable agriculture in the tropics. The university's nontraditional curriculum emphasizes agriculture as a human activity, integrating various academic disciplines and a philosophy of hands-on, active learning. As such, the 3300-hectare campus looks like a college campus at first glance, but it also contains many hectares of experimental plots, plantations and rain-forest reserves.

Tours and lodging on campus, including the services of an expert birding guide, are provided by **Earthbirding** (www.earthbirding.org; r per person US$198; ℗ ✗ ☐ ✦). Tour the Earth campus and visit the different reserve areas, where more than 350 bird species have been recorded, including the great green macaw. Lodging is in modern, comfortable, tiled rooms, each with a private terrace overlooking the campus. Prices include three buffet meals and transportation from San José.

A popular destination of the Limón cruise-ship crowd is **Costa Flores** (☎ 717 6457; guided tour US$15; ☷ by reservation), a huge tropical flower and palm farm, with incredible heliconia gardens. Its 48 hectares include landscaped gardens and fountain-fed ponds (much of it wheelchair accessible). The farm exports 120 varieties of blossoms to the USA and Europe.

TALLYING THE TRUE COST OF BANANAS   *Beth Penland*

Banana cultivation, the second-largest industry (trailing tourism) in Costa Rica, began in 1878 when Minor Keith, the American entrepreneur contracted to build the Atlantic Railway (see p39), planted those first Panamanian cuttings to provide cheap food for his workforce. The sweet crop was a surprise hit in the USA and, after the completion of the Atlantic Railway in 1890, the banana boom began in earnest.

Mostly foreign investors bought and cleared the land that would become the 'banana coast.' In 1909 Keith consolidated his holdings as United Fruit, a banana empire that would influence Central American affairs for the next half century.

The banana industry has created an enormously lucrative monoculture that has been susceptible to a variety of parasites and other diseases, including a series of blights that swept through the region in the early 20th century, decimating banana crops throughout the northern lowlands and Caribbean coast. To combat these diseases and other parasitic organisms that might compromise the bottom line, growers use an arsenal of ecologically destructive methods to guarantee a profitable harvest.

For example, while still on the trees, bananas are wrapped in blue plastic bags impregnated with petrochemicals that shield them from pests, while also inducing the fruit to ripen more quickly. These baggies often end up in streams and canals around the fincas. The bags can kill wildlife directly by suffocation, or indirectly by contaminating the environment with chemicals. Moreover, runoff from the fincas, which are kept free of weeds and other undergrowth that could naturally stop serious erosion, is enriched with fertilizers that often promote radically increased growth in some plants, potentially denying space and light to organisms less capable of using the fertilizers for themselves.

These synthetic products can also affect humans. At least 280 pesticides are authorized for use in the cultivation of the fruit, including five that the World Health Organization (WHO) ranks as 'extremely hazardous.' Plantation owners and chemical companies have faced lawsuits from more than 24,000 Latin American workers over the effects of Dibromochloropropane (DBCP), which has been linked to birth defects, tissue damage and sterility in male workers. Although it was banned in 1977 by the USA, where it is manufactured, it was used here until 1990.

In Costa Rica the right to acceptable working conditions is protected under the Declaration of Human Rights, but this does not include protection from hazardous toxins. Workers had to petition US courts to seek recourse against the producers and distributors of DBCP. Though Nicaraguan courts ordered US corporations in 2002 to pay out US$490 million to 583 workers affected by DBCP, most of the 9000 Costa Rican workers who claim to have been rendered sterile are still waiting for a settlement. A Dow Chemical representative called the ruling 'unenforceable.'

Conditions for many Costa Rican banana workers are still poor. Wages are low, particularly among the under-regulated indigenous workforce along the Caribbean coast. Efforts to organize the labor force have reportedly resulted in the blacklisting of union representatives. Paraquat, a chemical that is banned in several European countries because of links to problems including blurred vision, tissue damage and death, is still used to the tune of 65kg per worker annually.

In the late 1990s a loose coalition of organizations began certifying bananas as 'Fair Trade;' these labeled, premium-priced fruits are usually grown on smaller farms, and companies must prove that they pay living wages and offer workers minimal protection from agrochemicals. This increased focus on social responsibility is finally moving US corporations such as Chiquita Brands to work with auditors including the Rainforest Alliance, European Good Agriculture Practices and Social Accountability International to meet labor, human-rights and food-safety standards.

Despite efforts toward change, the long-term ecological damage done by the banana trade will be evident throughout Costa Rica for years to come. Fortunately, socioeconomic and sustainable growth in the industry are seemingly on the right track.

CARIBBEAN COAST

Hotel Restaurant Río Palmas (☎ 760 0330; d with/without air-con US$45/39; P ⊠ ⬚ ⬚) Some 600m east of Earth, this hotel stands out with its lush gardens and hiking trails. Very comfortable rooms have cable TV, hot showers and other amenities, and the restaurant is recommended. It's an excellent deal, in the middle of nowhere.

SIQUIRRES

Siquirres has long served as an important transportation hub as it sits at the intersection of Hwy 32 (the main road that crosses the Atlantic slope to Puerto Limón) with Hwy 10, the old road that connects San José with Puerto Limón via Turrialba.

Even before the roads came, Siquirres administered the most important junction in the San José–Limón railway. And for the first part of the 20th century, the town delineated Costa Rica's segregated interior: without special permission, blacks were barred from traveling west of this internal border (see p41). Until the constitution of 1949 outlawed racial discrimination, black conductors and engineers would change places with their Spanish counterparts here, then head back to Limón.

Today, Siquirres still seems to mark the place where Costa Rica proper takes a dip into the Caribbean – and it's not just the geography. The lack of infrastructure to the east of Siquirres is subtle, but you'll notice it when you're charged twice as much for painfully slow Internet access, then spend half a day locating an ATM to pay for it.

There is little reason to stop in Siquirres, unless you are heading north to Parismina (in which case you should definitely make use of the bank in town). If you need somewhere to crash for the night, head 800m north of the plaza to **Chito's Lodge** (☎ 768 9293; per person US$20; 🏊), which also has a lively bar and restaurant, as well as lovely grounds inhabited by many animals. Chito is something of a local celebrity, as he has appeared on TV, wrestling with crocodiles. **Castellana** (central plaza; meals US$1-3) is a friendly *soda* and bakery serving tasty, typical Tico fare.

Getting There & Away

If you are heading to Parismina, take the **Caño-Aguilar bus** (☎ 768 8172) to Caño Blanco (US$1.50, two hours) at 4:15am or 12:30pm Monday through Friday, 7:15am or 3:15pm Saturday and Sunday. Boats to Parismina (US$2, 10 minutes) wait for the buses in Caño Blanco, departing at 6am and 3pm Monday through Friday, and 9am and 5pm Saturday and Sunday.

Siquirres is a regular stop on the San José–Limón route, so you can catch a bus to either destination every hour between 6am and 7pm.

PUERTO LIMÓN

This is the great city of Costa Rica's Caribbean coast, birthplace of United Fruit (see the boxed text Tallying the True Cost of Bananas, p449) and capital of Limón Province. In many ways, it's still removed from San José's sphere of influence. Around here, business is measured by truckloads of bananas, not busloads of tourists, so don't expect much pampering. Cruise ships do deposit passengers between October and May; we can only hope that they weren't expecting to spot a quetzal.

Most travelers simply pass through on their way to more user-friendly destinations, as this hard-working port city doesn't float everyone's boat. Breezes blow in off the Caribbean, but the seaside stretch is underutilized, at best. Only the guests at the Park Hotel and the workers at the cruise-ship pier can appreciate that this is a coastal city. Further inland, the orderly grid of streets is lined with run-down buildings and overgrown parks, and the sidewalks are crowded with shoppers and street vendors.

If you're the rare traveler inclined to a little urban exploration, Limón is an interesting place. It is the heart of Costa Rica's Afro-Caribbean culture, reflected in the laid-back hospitality, a growing music scene and the country's best African cultural festival (see p452). The city's dilapidated charm is giving way to more modern growth, as federal funds are slowly invested in this side of the country.

Some urban-renewal programs have already been implemented, such as the pedestrian mall from the market to the sea wall, and the new bus station. But Limón – both port and province – has a long and difficult history of complications with the capital, and locals don't expect their city to get a full federally funded face-lift anytime soon. (This might not seem such a bad thing for visitors who need a break from the zip-line economy anyway.)

History

Christopher Columbus first dropped anchor in Costa Rica in 1502 at Isla Uvita, just off the coast of Puerto Limón. The Atlantic coast, however, was left largely unexplored by Spanish settlers until the 19th century. In 1867, construction began on an ambitious railroad connecting the highlands to the sea.

THE GREAT MALARIA DEBATE

According to the Center for Disease Control (CDC), travelers to Costa Rica face a risk of contracting malaria in Alajuela, Limón, Guanacaste and Heredia Provinces. The greatest risk is outside urban areas, especially where greater rainfall occurs. Limón Province, which covers the entire Caribbean coast, has the highest risk of malaria in the country.

The most important precaution to take against malaria is to protect yourself from mosquitoes.

■ Wear long-sleeved shirts and long pants, especially between dusk and dawn.

■ Use an insect repellent containing DEET. Don't bother with repellents that have a concentration higher than 50%, as they do not provide any additional protection.

■ Consider taking a flying-insect spray to clear your room of critters.

■ Sleep in a screened area or under a mosquito net. Nets can be treated with permethrin to repel and kill mosquitoes and ticks.

Even the most vigilant bug sprayer can still get bitten. The CDC recommends that travelers to the above areas take an antimalarial for further protection. Malaria pills are infamous for their side effects, which can include insomnia, nightmares and hallucinations. High doses (usually used to treat malaria, not prevent it) can even lead to depression and psychosis. These dire side effects, however, refer to mefloquine (also called Lariam), which used to be the most common preventative.

These days, more user-friendly antimalarials are available. And while side effects do occur, they are usually not serious enough to prevent a traveler from using the drug. In Costa Rica, the CDC recommends taking chloroquine (also known by the brand name Aralen), which should be taken for the duration of your trip and continued for four weeks after you get home. There can be side effects, but most people do not suffer much.

In any case – but especially if you decide against taking an antimalarial – be aware of the symptoms of malaria, which occur seven to nine days after being bitten by an infected mosquito. See a doctor immediately if you develop fever and flu-like illness, including chills, headache, muscle aches and fatigue.

Limón was chosen as the site of a major port, which would facilitate exports of the coffee from the Central Valley.

The railroad project changed Costa Rica in dramatic ways. The freed Jamaican slaves that provided cheap labor for the railroad construction settled on the coast, introducing the English language and Caribbean culture to the previously homogeneous population. The bananas that were planted alongside the tracks as a cheap food source for the workers became the country's number-one export. And the American-owned United Fruit, which controlled the booming business, made Costa Rica a part of its banana empire (see p39).

In 1913 a banana blight shut down many Caribbean fincas, and much of the banana production moved to the Pacific coast. Afro-Caribbean workers, however, were restricted by visa regulations to Limón Province, so they were forbidden from following the employment opportunities.

Stranded in the least-developed part of the country, many turned to subsistence farming, fishing or working on cocoa plantations. Others organized and staged bloody strikes against United Fruit (see p41).

In 1948 Limón provided key support to José Figueres during the 40-day civil war (see p41). In 1949 the new president enacted a constitution that finally granted blacks the right to work and travel freely throughout Costa Rica.

Orientation

Limón's streets are poorly marked and most do not have signs. Most locals can give better directions using city landmarks such as the market, the old Radio Casino and Parque Vargas. Avenida 2 begins as the pedestrian mall, stretching from the sea wall past Parque Vargas to the market, where it becomes a main street. Several banks, bars, restaurants and hotels are within a few blocks, as is the main bus terminal.

CARIBBEAN COAST

Information

Note that banks are a rarity in other parts of the Caribbean coast, so whether you're headed north or south, stock up here with as many colones as you think you're going to need.

Banco de Costa Rica (☎ 758 3166; cnr Av 2 & Calle 1) Exchanges US dollars cash and has an ATM.

Centro Médico Monterrey (☎ 798 1723, emergency 297 1010) Opposite the cathedral.

Hospital Tony Facio (☎ 758 2222) On the coast at the northern end of town; serves the entire province.

Internet Café (☎ 798 0128; per hr US$1; ☼ 8am-7pm Mon-Fri, noon-7pm Sat) Ten fairly fast computers, conveniently located upstairs at Terminal Caribeño.

La Casona de Parque (per hr US$1; ☼ 7am-6pm) Another option for Internet access, servicing the cruise-ship crowd.

Post office (Calle 4 btwn Avs 1 & 2; ☼ 9am-4pm)

Scotiabank (☎ 798 0009; cnr Av 3 & Calle 2; ☼ 8:30am-4:30pm Mon-Fri, 8:30am-3:30pm Sat) Exchanges cash and traveler's checks. Also has a 24-hour ATM on the Plus and Cirrus systems that dispenses US dollars.

Dangers & Annoyances

Limón is what you'd call gritty: take precautions against pickpockets during the day, particularly in the market. People do get mugged here, so stick to well-lit main streets at night, avoiding the sea wall and Parque Vargas. Park in a guarded lot and remove everything from the car, as vehicle break-ins are common.

Sights & Activities

The city's main attraction is the waterfront **Parque Vargas**, an incongruous expanse of bench-lined sidewalks beneath a lost little jungle of tall palms and tropical flowers, centered on an appealingly decrepit bandstand.

From here, you can head inland along Avenida 2, the **pedestrian mall** that caters to the cruise-ship traffic. Keep an eye out for vendors selling home-burned CDs by local bands – Limón is getting a reputation for its growing hip hop and Latin-reggae fusion scenes. You'll end up at the colorful **mercado central**. Two blocks away, the **Museo Etnohistórico de Limón** (Calle 4 btwn Avs 1 & 2; admission free), on the 2nd floor of the post office, was closed for renovations at press time (and has been for years). Past exhibits of Afro-Caribbean artifacts sound intriguing, so it's worth checking out if it ever opens again.

From the park, it's a pleasant walk north along the **sea wall**, where views of the rocky headland are set to a steady baseline of waves crashing against the concrete. After dark, it's a popular mugging and make-out spot.

Although there are no beaches for swimming or surfing in Limón, **Playa Bonita** (p456), 4km northwest of town, has a sandy beach, while **Isla Uvita** (p456), 1km offshore, has one of the country's most powerful lefts.

Festivals & Events

El Día de la Raza (Columbus Day; October 12) Columbus' historic landing on Isla Uvita inspires Limón to go all out, with a four- or five-day carnival of colorful street parades and dancing, music, singing and drinking. Book your hotel in advance.

Festival Flores de la Diáspora Africana (late August) A celebration of Afro-Caribbean culture. While it is centered in Puerto Limón, the festival sponsors events showcasing African heritage throughout the province and San José.

Sleeping

Hotels all along the Caribbean coast are in demand on weekends and vacations, when prices rise. Reserve ahead if possible during those periods.

BUDGET

The hotels listed here are at the more wholesome end of the budget spectrum, but they are still pretty gloomy; ask to see a room and check security.

Nuevo Hotel Internacional (☎ 798 0545, 798 7532; Av 5 btwn Calles 2 & 3; s/d with fan US$7/11, with air-con US$9/14; P ﹩) Linoleum floors and paper-thin walls (some without windows) constitute the rooms at this drab place near the sea. All rooms have a private hot shower, accessed through a sliding accordion door. The same family runs Hotel Continental (across the street) with the same prices for slightly less comfortable accommodations. Some of these rooms have excellent balcony windows so it's worth inquiring.

Hotel King (☎ 758 1033; Av 2 btwn Calles 4 & 5; s/d/tr with private bathroom US$9/11/13, r with shared bathroom per person US$5) This safe, friendly option is conveniently located about 250m from the bus station. The small rooms are dark but clean; those with shared bathrooms are particularly cramped.

Hotel Costa del Sol (☎ 798 0909; cnr Calle 5 & Av 5; s/d with shared bathroom US$7.50/10, with private bathroom US$14/16, with air-con US$16/18; P ﹩) Limón's

PUERTO LIMÓN

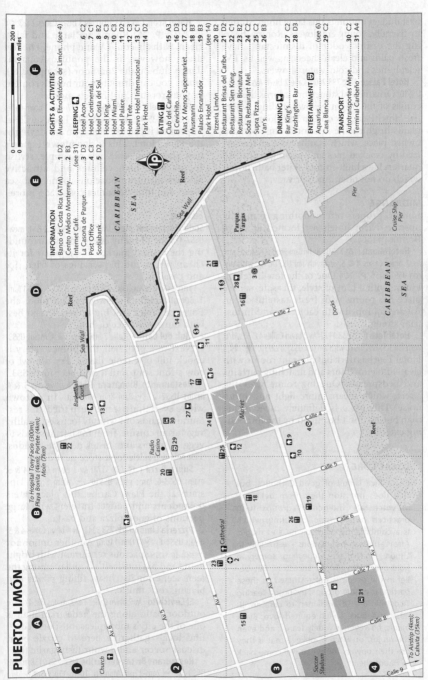

0   200 m
0   0.1 miles

INFORMATION
Banco de Costa Rica (ATM)........1 D2
Centro Médico Monterrey...........2 B3
Internet Café............................(see 31)
La Casona de Parque.................3 D3
Post Office..............................4 C3
Scotiabank..............................5 D2

SIGHTS & ACTIVITIES
Museo Etnohistórico de Limón...(see 4)

SLEEPING
Hotel Acon..............................6 C2
Hotel Continental......................7 C1
Hotel Costa del Sol...................8 B2
Hotel King...............................9 C3
Hotel Miami............................10 C3
Hotel Palace...........................11 D2
Hotel Tete..............................12 C3
Nuevo Hotel Internacional........13 C1
Park Hotel..............................14 D2

EATING
Club del Caribe........................15 A3
El Cevichito.............................16 D3
Mas X Menos Supermarket.......17 C2
Musmanni..............................18 B3
Palacio Encantador...................19 B3
Park Hotel...........................(see 14)
Pizzeria Limón........................20 B2
Restaurant Brisas del Caribe.....21 D2
Restaurant Sien Kong..............22 C1
Restaurante Bionatura.............23 B2
Soda Restaurant Meli...............24 C2
Supra Pizza............................25 C2
Yan's.....................................26 B3

DRINKING
Bar King's...............................27 C2
Washington Bar.......................28 D3

ENTERTAINMENT
Aquarius...............................(see 6)
Casa Blanca............................29 C2

TRANSPORT
Autotransportes Mepe..............30 C2
Terminal Caribeño...................31 A4

best budget option is this large hotel, staffed by friendly, young employees. Rooms, bearing the distinct odor of disinfectant, have fresh paint and clean sheets, as well as TV, telephones and cold-water showers.

Hotel Palace (☎ 798 2604; Calle 2 btwn Avs 2 & 3; d US$10) Ornamental stonework adorns the balconies of the bright yellow building, where the Hotel Palace is on the 2nd floor. Potted plants brighten the interior at this woman-owned place, which is otherwise characterized by cracked tiles and peeling paint. All quarters have built-in cold-water bathrooms, which do not offer much privacy.

MIDRANGE

Limón proper offers nothing remotely upscale. Nicer hotels are located at Playa Bonita (p456).

Hotel Miami (☎ 758 0490; hmiamilimon@yahoo.com; Av 2 btwn Calles 4 & 5; s/d with fan US$14/18, with air-con US$18/25; P 🞶) One of the few hotels in Limón with a hint of style, this safe, secure place has rooms with fresh, tasteful decor. All are equipped with cable TV and industrial-strength fans.

Hotel Tete (☎ 758 1122; Av 3 btwn Calles 4 & 5; s/d/tr with fan US$12/21/28, with air-con US$15/22/30; P 🞶) Hotel Tete has dark but pleasant rooms with clean linoleum floors and matching curtains and bedspreads. One big room faces the street, which means more light and more noise. This place is definitely nicer inside than out, so don't be put off by the foreboding exterior.

LOCAL LORE

Costa Rica is full of good Catholics, but that does not stop them from believing in witchcraft. Indigenous groups long practiced *curanderismo,* or curing, which is a combination of medicine and magic. Afro-Caribbean populations – especially in Limón – may practice *obeah,* or sorcery, a hold-over from African ancestors. But belief in the occult is not restricted to these particular ethnic groups; even god-fearing Ticos might visit a shaman to cure an illness or seduce an unrequited love. Black magic, however, is widely feared; and even the *brujos,* or witches, believe that if they use their powers for evil, it will come back to haunt them.

Hotel Acon (☎ 758 1010; Av 3 btwn Calles 2 & 3; s/d US$25/32; P 🞶) Rooms are large and fairly clean, with air-con, TV and phone. The real draw, however, is the popular Aquarius dance club on the 2nd floor (see opposite), where you can drink to your heart's content as your room is just meters away.

Park Hotel (☎ 798 0555, 758 3476; Av 3 btwn Calles 1 & 2; s/d US$35/48; P 🞶 🞶 🖳) Locals will act impressed if you tell them you are staying at the Park Hotel. This is downtown Limón's best stab at upscale, where simple, stylish rooms have high ceilings and attractive wooden furniture. Spacious rooms with sea views and little balconies cost US$5 more.

Eating

Soda Restaurant Meli (Av 3 btwn Calles 3 & 4; meals US$2-4) One of many cheap *sodas* surrounding the central market. It's popular for its cheap prices and big servings of fried rice and casados.

Yan's (Av 2 btwn Calles 5 & 6; mains US$1-5; 🕙 11am-11:30pm) Limón's answer to fast food, the Formica tables and big-screen TV go best with burgers or rice dishes.

Club del Caribe (Calle 7 btwn Avs 3 & 4; mains US$3-6) Next to a pool hall, this homey eatery is chock-full of Creole flavor. Try a bowl of cow's-foot soup and a cold beer for US$3.

Restaurante Bionatura (Calle 6 btwn Avs 3 & 4; mains US$2-5; 🕙 8am-8pm Mon-Sat) In a town where everything seems deep fried, this restaurant stands out with its focus on healthy vegetarian cuisine, from fresh fruit salads to veggie burgers and 'bistek de soya' casados. There's a health-food store next door.

Supra Pizza (☎ 758 3371; Av 3 btwn Calles 4 & 5; mains US$3-6, large pizza US$10; 🕙 10am-11pm) Upstairs at the Plaza Caribe, this place caters to students and budget travelers with large portions of good pizza and pasta.

Pizzeria Limón (☎ 758 3341; Av 4 btwn Calles 4 & 5; meals US$4-6; 🕙 11am-11pm) Another option for pizza is this spacious restaurant with bright lights and big music. It's popular among the teen scene for its cheap, filling pizzas and blaring rock music.

El Cevichito (Av 2 btwn Calles 1 & 2; mains US$4) The outdoor patio along the pedestrian mall is one of the city's more pleasant spots. You'll find locals gathering here to guzzle beer, discuss soccer and devour tasty garlic fish.

Restaurant Brisas del Caribe (☎ 758 0138; mains US$3-5; 🕙 7am-11pm Mon-Fri, 10am-11pm Sat & Sun)

The best view in town isn't over the waves: right by the Parque Vargas, outdoor tables and a breezy balcony make for excellent people-watching and delicious Caribbean fare.

Park Hotel (☎ 798 0555; Av 3 btwn Calles 1 & 2; meals US$6-10; 🕐 6am-10pm) Go upscale at the semiswanky restaurant attached to Limón's top hotel. With white linen tablecloths and big windows catching Caribbean breezes, it exudes a tropical, colonial ambience. The menu features seafood and many mysterious (but delicious) specialties of the house.

A budget traveler's best bet is the **mercado central** (🕐 6am-8pm Mon-Sat), with several *sodas* and plenty of groceries. The big supermarket **Más X Menos** (🕐 8am-9pm) across the avenue is useful for self-caterers. If you are looking for breakfast, you can't go wrong at **Musmanni** (🕐 6am-6pm), located near the bus terminal.

Puerto Limón boasts the country's largest Chinese population, so pass up on the chop suey:

Palacio Encantado (Av 2 btwn Calles 5 & 6; mains US$3-9; 🕐 11am-11pm) This recommended spot for quality Chinese cuisine is two blocks from the market.

Restaurant Sien Kong (cnr Av 6 & Calle 3; dishes US$5-10; 🕐 11am-10pm) Further from the center, this place is worth the walk for some of the best Chinese food in town.

Drinking & Entertainment

No one in Limón need ever go thirsty, considering the wide selection of bars. Those by Parque Vargas and a few blocks west are popular hang-outs for a variety of coastal characters: sailors, ladies of the night, entrepreneurs, boozers, losers and the casually curious. The standard warnings for solo women travelers go double here. This is a lousy town for getting drunk – keep your wits about you.

Washington Bar (cnr Calle 1 & Av 2; 🕐 9-3am) With a few outdoor tables and big wicker chairs, this is a pleasant place to observe the activity along the pedestrian mall and around Parque Vargas.

Casa Blanca (cnr Calle 4 & Av 4) On weekends this is the best place to check out the local music scene. On any day of the week it is packed from about 5pm onward with a primarily male clientele. It's easy to find; just follow the reggae beat emanating from the jukebox.

Aquarius (☎ 758 1010; Av 3 btwn Calles 2 & 3; 🕐 8pm-2am) Inside the Hotel Acon, this is the hottest disco in town, with salsa, reggae and pop spinning on different nights.

Bar King's (Calle 3 btwn Avs 3 & 4) More Latin and less Carib. Women travelers may feel more comfortable here, as some local señoritas usually make an appearance.

Getting There & Away

Puerto Limón is the transportation hub of the Caribbean coast.

AIR

The airstrip is about 4km south of town. There are no regularly scheduled flights, but you can charter a flight to Puerto Jiménez (US$1450) or Golfito (US$1320) through Alfa Romeo Aero Taxi (see p434).

BOAT

Cruise ships occasionally dock in Limón, but most boats providing transportation use the major port at Moín, about 7km west of Limón. For information on boats to Tortuguero, see p456.

BUS

Buses to and from San José, Moín, Guápiles and Siquirres arrive at **Terminal Caribeño** (Av 2 btwn Calles 7 & 8) on the west side, walking distance from all the hotels. Buses to points south all depart from **Autotransportes Mepe** (Mepe; Av 4 btwn Calles 2 & 4).

Bribrí & Sixaola (Mepe) US$3, three hours, depart at 5am, 7am, 8am, 10am, noon, 1pm, 4pm and 6pm.

Cahuita (Mepe) US$1, 1½ hours, depart at 5am, 6am, 8am, 10am, 1pm, 2:30pm, 4pm and 6pm.

Guápiles via Siquirres & Guácimo (Empresarios Guápileños; Terminal Caribeño) US$2, two hours, depart hourly 6am to 6pm.

Manzanillo (Mepe) US$2, 2½ hours, depart at 6am, 10:30am, 3pm and 6pm.

Moín, for boats to Tortuguero (Tracasa; Terminal Caribeño) US$0.25, 20 minutes, depart hourly 5:30am to 6:30pm.

Puerto Viejo de Talamanca (Mepe) US$1.75, 2½ hours, depart at 5am, 8am, 10am, 1pm, 4pm and 6pm.

San José (Autotransportes Caribeños; Terminal Caribeño) US$3.50, three hours, depart hourly 5am to 8pm.

CAR

There is only one gas station on the coast south of Limón, at the crossroads just north of Cahuita.

CARIBBEAN COAST

AROUND PUERTO LIMÓN
Isla Uvita

This island just 1km off the coast of Limón is most famous as the site of Columbus' landing on his last trans-Atlantic voyage. It is also a popular destination for surfers, for its thrilling – and often punishing – left that breaks on a reef. Those in the know claim that this is the most powerful left in Costa Rica, with 3m waves on good days. Isla Uvita is a 20-minute boat ride from Limón – ask around the pier to try to hire a boat. Pack a picnic, as there are no facilities on the island.

Playa Bonita

While not the finest beach in the Caribbean, **Playa Bonita** offers sandy stretches of seashore and good swimming convenient to Limón. Surfers make their way to Bonita for its point/reef break, which makes for a powerful (and sometimes dangerous) left. Just north, **Portete** is a small bay with a wicked right working off the southerly point. Any Limón–Moín bus will drop you at these places.

SLEEPING & EATING

The road between Limón and Moín is home to some decent accommodations. Listed in order from Limón (east to west):

Oasys del Caribe (☎ 795 0024; oasysdelcaribe@racsa .co.cr; s/d/tr US$30/35/40; P ⊠) About 3km northwest of Puerto Limón, these cozy pink bungalows are decorated with lace curtains and bamboo furniture, worn sheets and clean towels. They are clustered around a small swimming pool, which is critical, as this place does not have beach access.

Hotel Maribú Caribe (☎ 795 2543/2553; maribu@ racsa.co.cr; s/d/tr US$55/65/75; P ⊠ ⊠) Just west of Oasys del Caribe, several spacious white stucco bungalows are arranged atop a small hill amid tropical gardens. They all catch ocean breezes and enjoy good views, as does the Afro-Caribbean restaurant.

Cabinas Cocori (☎ 795 1670; s/d/tr US$35/50/60; P ⊠ ⊡ ⊠) Enjoy your free continental breakfast as you watch the waves crash on the rocks below. This citrus-colored motel is the best deal on the beach, with cute, clean rooms and a breezy restaurant. About 4km out of Limón (2.5km from the Moín dock).

Hotel Happy Land (☎ 795 2828; hotel_happyland@ yahoo.com; s/d/q US$35/41/52; P ⊠ ⊠) You can't miss the shocking-pink entrance to this happy land. Despite what the sign says, there is no casino here, but there are a couple of big swimming pools with fun slides, tennis courts and a recreation area, making this an excellent stop with kids in tow. It's about 6km from downtown Limón, very close to the Moín dock.

Two side-by-side beach restaurants provide excellent seaside dining, about 5km from Limón. At **Reina's** (☎ 798 0879; mains US$6-8; ⊠ 8am-last guest) loud music and good vibes make for a popular nighttime spot. Next door, **Quimbamba** (☎ 795 4805; mains US$5-7; ⊠ 8am-close) is similar, offering a shady spot to watch the soccer game on the beach. *Mariscos* (seafood) and *cervezas* (beer) are on the menus.

Moín

The reason you're here, no doubt, is to catch a boat through the canals to Parismina (opposite), Tortuguero (p459) or perhaps Barra del Colorado (p467). There has always been a series of natural waterways between Limón and Barra del Colorado, but they could only be used by small dugouts during the rainy season. In 1974 canals linking the system were completed, eliminating the need for boats to go out to sea when traveling north from Moín.

GETTING THERE & AWAY

The journey by boat to Tortuguero can take anywhere from 1½ hours to five hours, depending on how often the boat stops to observe the copious wildlife along the way (many tours also stop for lunch). Indeed, it is worth taking your time. As you wind your way through these jungle canals, you are likely to spot howler monkeys, morelot's crocodiles, both two- and three-toed sloths and an amazing array of waterbirds.

While this route is often used by tourist boats, it is not necessarily a regular transportation route to Tortuguero or Parismina (boats rarely go to Barra del Colorado). When canals north of Moín are blocked by water hyacinths or logjams, the route might be closed altogether. Schedules exist in theory only and they change frequently, depending on the boatload. If you are feeling lucky, you can just show up in Moín in the morning and try to get on one of the outgoing tour boats. But you are better off making a reservation in advance.

Asociación de Boteros de los Canales de Tortuguero (Abacat; ☎ 360 7325; US$30; ⊗ 10am) In theory, Abacat operates a daily collective to Tortuguero, although it may not run if there are not enough passengers.

Caribbean Tropical Tours (William Guerrero) (☎ 371 2323; wguerrerotuca@hotmail.com) A highly recommended tour guide, with excellent sloth-spotting skills.

Moín–Parismina–Tortuguero water taxi (☎ 709 8005; ⊗ depart Moín 11am, depart Tortuguero 1:30pm) Reservations are essential, especially if you are requesting a stop in Parismina.

Viajes al Tortuguero (Benjamin Gomez) (☎ 795 0937; localbenjamin@hotmail.com; one way/round trip US$30/50; ⊗ 9:30-10am) A member of the association of Boteros Independentes de Moín. Again, the schedule is subject to change if there are not enough passengers.

Tracasa buses to Moín from Puerto Limón (US$0.25, 20 minutes) depart from Terminal Caribeño hourly from 5:30am to 6:30pm. Get off the bus before it goes over the bridge. If you are driving, it's worth leaving your car in a guarded lot in Limón.

NORTHERN CARIBBEAN

A vast network of rivers and canals wind their way through this remote region – Costa Rica's wettest. Lush forests, filled with waterbirds and sleepy sloths, line the edges of these waterways. The long stretches of otherwise empty beaches are nesting grounds for three kinds of sea turtles, and more green turtles are born here than anywhere else on earth. It's not easy to get here – in fact it's accessible only by boat – but the Amazonian atmosphere is well worth the journey.

PARISMINA

At the southern end of Parque Nacional Tortuguero, and at the mouth of Río Parismina, this friendly village attracts two kinds of travelers: turtle lovers and tarpon lovers. Though not as famed as the beaches of Tortuguero, Parismina is the preferred breeding ground of hundreds of discriminating leatherback, green and hawksbill turtles; and the coastal waters are rife with record-breaking Atlantic tarpon.

Surrounded on all sides by jungle rivers and the Caribbean Sea, Barra de Parismina is accessible only by boat, which has allowed it to preserve a remote 'island' atmosphere. Legend has it that the village was founded by a pregnant woman named Mina, who was traveling down the Caribbean coast. When the time came for her to have her baby, her traveling companion told her, 'Here you give birth, Mina,' or *'Aqui pares, Mina.'* Thus the village was named.

Sportfishing is the traditional tourist draw to Parismina. Top tarpon season is from January to mid-May, while big snook are caught in Río Parismina from September to November.

More recently, with the growth of ecotourism, many travelers come to see (and

CARIBBEAN COAST

PUENTE

Many spots along the Caribbean coast are used as *puentes,* or bridges, for drug trafficking. Locals are quick to blame the Colombians, as Colombia is the source of the product and they often oversee the trade. But it wouldn't work without local participation as well.

Huge boats cruise up and down the coastline, carrying shipments of cocaine north to the primary market, the USA. At strategic places along the coast, the traffickers drop nets – full of cocaine – into the water and anchor them at the bottom of the ocean. Then with a quick GPS reading and a phone call, they make arrangements for a pickup at a later time, thus avoiding prickly situations with the Coast Guard. It's an efficient system, which usually only involves those that want to be involved.

There is the occasional mishap, where the net breaks and the valuable cocaine floats out to sea. It usually washes ashore within a few days, and it's easy to stroll the beach and salvage the stray packages. In villages like Tortuguero and Parismina local kids have a field day collecting these packages, because they know the local point-person will buy them back for a few colones (a fraction of their value, of course, but a windfall for the *niños*).

Drug use is a growing problem in Puerto Limón and Puerto Viejo, and a cause of increased crime. No doubt, those nets are strategically placed so the packages of cocaine do not wash up around here, or they would surely disappear forever.

protect) the endangered sea turtles. Leath-erbacks nest on Parisimina's beach between late February and early October, with the peak season in April and May. Green turtles begin nesting in June and the peak season is August and September. Hawksbills are not as common, but they are sometimes seen between February and September.

Information

There are no banks or post office in Paris-mina. Credit cards and traveler's checks are not accepted, so be sure to bring as much cash as you need.

Asociación Salvemos Las Tortugas de Parisimina Information Center (Astop, Save the Turtles of Parisimina; ☎ 710 7703; www.costaricaturtles.org; ☾ 9am-8pm daily Mar-Oct, 2-6pm Mon-Sat Nov-Feb) Organizes homestays (US$15), offers Internet access (per hour US$1.50) and posts information about local tour guides (US$20), activities and events.

Sights & Activities

The locally grown conservation group **ASTOP** (above) has built a guarded turtle hatchery to deter increasing numbers of poachers and egg thieves. Travelers can volunteer as a turtle guard to patrol the beaches along-side local 'turtle guides.' The daily fee of US$20 to US$25 includes three meals a day, lodging with a local family and turtle train-ing (three-night minimum).

This local association is a wonderful way for travelers to get involved with the com-munity; locals also offer Spanish lessons, Latin dance lessons, fishing trips and boat tours into Parque Nacional Tortuguero.

While villagers have traditionally de-pended on farming and fishing, the turtle project has become a crucial part of the local economy, as families depend on the income they receive from homestays and other activities. As explained in the ASTOP orientation materials, 'If you...support our turtle project, you support not only the tur-tles, but the whole town.'

The beach near Parisimina is very rough, strewn with rubble and dangerous for swim-ming. However, a nearby lagoon – known as the **Barrita** – is a popular spot for a cool-ing dip or a picnic. Walk south along the beach or follow the road from the airstrip.

Across the river in Caño Blanco, Don Victor and his wife Isaura run the **Jardin Tropical** (☎ 200 5567; admission free; ☾ 8am-5pm),

an amazing heliconia farm. ASTOP organ-izes day trips to Caño Blanco, which in-clude visiting a traditional Tico farm and riding horses to the Jardin Tropical (US$20 including transportation from Parisimina).

Sleeping & Eating

Besides the options listed here, the **Soda Paris-mina**, at the boat dock, serves simple meals.

Don Alex (☎ 710 1892; camping per person with/ without kitchen use US$3/2, cabinas per person US$5) Alex at the hardware store offers sheltered tent sites with access to showers, bathrooms and a kitchen for a small charge, as well as simple cabinas.

Carefree Ranch (☎ 710 3149; r per person US$6) Opposite the Catholic church, this simple clapboard house – bright yellow with green trim – gives you a lot of charm for your colón. Perks include newish bathrooms with hot water and family-style meals (available for an additional charge).

Mono Cariblanco Lodge (☎ 710 1161; r per person US$8; ☒) In a nice beachfront location, this lodge offers 10 dark but clean rooms, each with brightly colored curtains and private cold-water bathrooms. The rooms do not face the ocean, but you can catch the breezes from the inviting open-air restaurant and bar, the on-site White-Faced Monkey (meals US$6 to US$8). Locals complain that the owner of the Mono Cariblanco does not support the goals of the turtle project.

Iguana Verde (☎ 710 1528; d with/without air-con US$25/10; ☒) Crazy Rick (or 'Loco Rico' as he is known) and his wife Yenri run this friendly spot, offering three clean rooms

---

TORTUGUERO BY KAYAK

Unbeknown to many, you can explore Parque Nacional Tortuguero from Parisimina, but the only access is by water. The wildlife is just as abundant as at the northern end of the park, and you are unlikely to run into any tour boats in this neck of the woods. Local guides take passengers in dugouts (inquire at ASTOP, left) for about US$20. The truly adventurous (and experienced) can hire a kayak from Iguana Verde lodgings (above) and go it alone, but make sure you have a detailed map and a compass. And don't forget to stop at Jalova Station (see p460) to pay your park admission fee.

with private hot-water bathrooms. Rick is also a popular guide, offering highly entertaining guided hikes and boat tours. They are both active in the turtle-conservation project, but who is looking out for the poor blue macaw that is caged out front?

Asociación Salvemos Las Tortugas de Parismina (☎ 710 7703; www.costaricaturtles.com; r per person US$15) Although volunteers get first choice of accommodations, this organization can arrange homestays, including three meals, with a local family. All lodging is in private rooms with locking doors and shared bathroom facilities.

Río Parismina Lodge (☎ 229 7597, in the USA 800- 338 5688, 210-824 4442; www.riop.com; s/d 3 days US$2050/3700, 7 days US$3350/6200; ☒ ☑) Employing many Parismina residents, this deluxe fishing lodge caters to top-end tourists on all-inclusive vacations. Package prices include fishing, lodging in cushy cabins and transfers from San José, as well as three meals a day, which feature plenty of freshly brewed coffee and fabulous seafood. Private trails lead through 20 hectares of jungle, and other tours are available. Located on the opposite side of the river from Parismina village; accessible only by boat.

Getting There & Away

Parismina is only accessible by boat, and the only regular service is to Siquirres, via Caño Blanco.

From Siquirres, take the **Caño-Aguilar bus** (☎ 768 8172) to Caño Blanco (US$1.50, two hours) at 4:15am or 12:30pm Monday through Friday, 7:15am or 3:15pm Saturday and Sunday. Taxis make this run for about US$40. Boats to Parismina (US$2, 10 minutes) wait for the buses in Caño Blanco, departing at 6am and 3pm Monday through Friday, and 9am and 5pm Saturday and Sunday.

Boats leave from the Parismina dock to Caño Blanco at 5:30am and 2:30pm Monday through Friday, and at 8:30am and 4:30pm on Saturday and Sunday. Again, the buses wait for these water taxis, departing to Siquirres at 6am and 3pm Monday through Friday, and at 10am and 5pm on Saturday and Sunday.

A **water taxi** (☎ 709 8005; each way US$20) is supposed to travel the route between Moín and Tortuguero every day, and he can stop and pick up passengers in Parismina if they make advance arrangements. In theory, the taxi departs Moín at 11am, stopping in Parismina at noon, en route to Tortuguero. The return trip is at 1:30pm, stopping in Parismina at 2:30pm and continuing south to Moín. The boat driver will not stop in Parismina unless he knows passengers are waiting.

Otherwise, if you are trying to get to Tortuguero or Moín, your best bet is to hang around the dock in Caño Blanco and try to snag a spot on one of the tour boats passing through.

PARQUE NACIONAL TORTUGUERO

Parque Nacional Tortuguero is accessible from the village of Tortuguero in the north or from Parismina in the south.

'Humid' is the driest word that could truthfully be used to describe Tortuguero. With annual rainfall of up to 6000mm in the northern part of the park, it is one of the wettest areas in the country. There is no dry season, although it does rain less in February, March and October.

The famed **Canales de Tortuguero** are quite the introduction to this important park. Created to connect a series of naturally lazy lagoons and meandering rivers in 1969, this engineering marvel finally allowed inland navigation between Limón and the coastal villages in something sturdier than a dugout canoe (though you'll still see plenty of those). There are regular flights, sure, but a leisurely ride through the banana plantations and wild jungle is equal parts recreation and transportation.

This 31,187-hectare coastal park (plus about 52,000 hectares of marine area) is the Caribbean's most important breeding ground for the green sea turtle *(Chelonia mydas)*. Of the world's eight species of sea turtles, six nest in Costa Rica and four lay their eggs right here in Tortuguero.

These black-sand hatching grounds gave birth to the sea turtle–conservation movement. The Caribbean Conservation Corporation (p462), the first program of its kind in the world, has continuously monitored turtle populations here since 1955. Today, green sea turtles are increasing in numbers along this coast, but both the leatherback and hawksbill turtles are in decline (see the boxed text Dream of the Bountiful Turtles, p55).

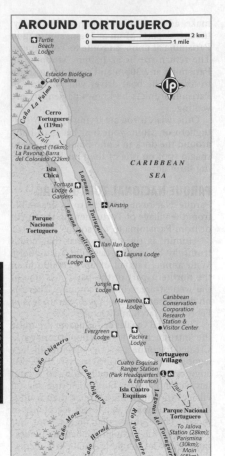

AROUND TORTUGUERO

0 ——— 2 km
0 ——— 1 mile

Turtle Beach Lodge

Estación Biológica Caño Palma

Caño La Palma

Cerro Tortuguero (119m)

Tortuguero Trail

To La Geest (16km); La Pavona; Barra del Colorado (22km)

Isla Chica

Tortuga Lodge & Gardens

Laguna del Tortuguero

Laguna Penitencia

Parque Nacional Tortuguero

Airstrip

CARIBBEAN SEA

Ilan Ilan Lodge

Laguna Lodge

Samoa Lodge

Jungle Lodge

Mawamba Lodge

Caribbean Conservation Corporation Research Station & Visitor Center

Evergreen Lodge

Pachira Lodge

Caño Chiquero

Tortuguero Village

Cuatro Esquinas Ranger Station (Park Headquarters & Entrance)

Isla Cuatro Esquinas

Caño Chiquero

Caño Mora

Caño Harold

Río Tortuguero

Laguna del Tortuguero

Trail

Parque Nacional Tortuguero

To Jalova Station (28km); Parismina (30km); Moín (65km)

CARIBBEAN COAST

But Tortuguero is more than just turtles: from sloths and howler monkeys in the treetops, to the tiny frogs and green iguanas that crawl among the roots, to the mighty tarpon and endangered manatee that swim the waters, this place is thick with life.

Orientation & Information

Park headquarters is at **Cuatro Esquinas** (☎ 709 8086; 1-/3-day admission US$7/10; ◷ 5:30am-6pm with breaks for breakfast & lunch), just north of Tortuguero village. It is an unusually helpful ranger station, with maps, information and access to a 2km-loop nature trail. Wear your boots: it's muddy, even in the dry season.

Jalova Station (◷ 6am-6pm), accessible from Parismina by boat, is on the canal at the south entrance to the national park. Tour boats from Moín often stop here for a picnic; you will find a short nature trail, bathroom, drinking water and camping facilities.

Activities

HIKING

Behind Cuatro Esquinas station, **El Gavilan Land Trail** is the only public trail through the park that is on solid ground. Visitors can hike the muddy, 2km loop that traverses the tropical humid forest and follows a stretch of beach. Green parrots and several species of monkeys are commonly sighted here. The short trail is well marked and does not require a guide.

BOATING

Four aquatic trails wind their way through Parque Nacional Tortuguero, inviting canoe paddlers, kayakers and other boaters to explore the ins and outs of this wild place. **Río Tortuguero** acts as the entrance way to the network of trails. This wide, beautiful river is often covered with water lilies and frequented by aquatic birds like herons (especially the great blue heron and the night heron), kingfishers and anhingas. The **Caño Chiquero** is thick with vegetation, especially red guacimo trees and epiphytes. Black turtles and green iguanas like to hang out here. Caño Chiquero leads to two more waterways. **Caño Mora** is about 3km long but only 10m wide, so it feels like it's straight from *Jungle Book*. **Caño Harold** is actually an artificially constructed canal, but that doesn't stop the creatures – like Jesus Christ lizards and caimans – from inhabiting its tranquil waters. Canoe rental and boat tours are available in Tortuguero village (p463).

TURTLE-WATCHING

Sea turtles usually nest every two or three years. Depending on the species, a female may nest up to 10 times during one season. She comes ashore about two weeks after mating to lay her eggs on the beach.

Most female turtles share a nesting instinct that drives them to return to the beach of their birth, or natal beach, in order to lay their eggs. Often, a turtle's ability to successfully reproduce depends on the ecological health of this original habitat. Only the leatherback returns to a more general region, instead of a specific natal beach.

The female turtle digs a cavity in the sand using her flippers, and then lays 80 to 120 eggs in the cavity. She diligently covers the nest with sand to protect the eggs, and she may even create a false nest in another location in an attempt to confuse predators. Then she makes her way back to the sea and the eggs are on their own.

Incubation ranges from 45 to 70 days. Hatchlings break out of their shells with a caruncle, or temporary tooth. Sometimes it takes several days for a group of hatchlings to dig their way up out of the nest cavity. The tiny hatchlings are small enough to fit in the palm of your hand. They crawl to the ocean in small groups, moving as quickly as possible to avoid dehydration and predators. Once they reach the surf, they must swim for at least 24 hours to get to deeper water, away from predators.

Visitors are allowed to check out the turtle rookeries at night from March to October (late July through August is prime time) and observe eggs being laid or hatching. Obviously, turtle sightings are not guaranteed. A licensed guide must accompany all visitors. Local lodges operate these tours for between US$10 and US$30 per person. Local guides charge about US$10. Flashlights and any type of camera or video camera are not allowed on the beach (see the boxed text Camera Shy, p274). Dark clothing is strongly recommended.

If you're unable to visit during the peak green turtle–breeding season, the next best time is April, when leatherback turtles nest in small numbers. Hawksbill turtles nest sporadically from March to October, and loggerhead turtles are also sometimes seen. For information about volunteering with turtle patrols, see the boxed text Doing Time for the Turtles, p463).

OTHER WILDLIFE-WATCHING

Parque Nacional Tortuguero is, without a doubt, one of Costa Rica's top wildlife destinations. To get the best from Tortuguero, be on the water early or go out following rain. As soon as the downpour clears, mammals, birds and reptiles come out into the open to sunbathe and dry out. They're most conspicuous on the rain forest edges lining the wide main canals.

More than 300 bird species, both resident and migratory, have been recorded in Tortuguero. Due to the wet habitat, the park is especially rich in herons (14 different kinds), kingfishers and waders. In September and October, look for huge flocks of migratory species like eastern kingbirds, barn swallows and purple martins. The Caribbean Conservation Corporation (p462) conducts a biannual monitoring program, in which volunteers can participate. Great green macaws are a highlight. They are most common from December to April, when the almendro trees are fruiting.

Certain species of mammals are particularly evident and relaxed in Tortuguero, especially mantled howlers, Central American spider monkeys and white-faced capuchins, as well as both two- and three-toed sloths. Normally shy Neotropical river otters are reasonably habituated to boats.

Turtles and turtle eggs are one of the favorite foods of jaguars, and turtle-watchers occasionally encounter these big cats, who swim the Laguna del Tortuguero to patrol the beach for nesting turtles.

Tortuguero is also possibly Costa Rica's best chance to spot West Indian manatees (see the boxed text Elephants of the Sea, p462).

Sleeping

Cuatro Esquinas ranger station has been closed to camping for the foreseeable future, but you can camp at **Jalova Station** (per person US$2) at the southern end of the park. Choose your spot (and season) carefully, as parts of the camping area can be submerged after heavy rainfall.

TORTUGUERO VILLAGE

Wholly surrounded by protected forest and sea, accessible only by air or water, this magical spot is best known for the hordes of hatchling turtles that lurch across its dark sands. Indeed, the name Tortuguero means 'turtle place.' For the 'turtle season,' which peaks from late July through August, make all reservations well in advance.

Once the turtles are safely at sea, however, both park and village sort of fall off the radar screen. Perhaps it is because these luxuriant jungles rank among the rainiest of all rain forests, and thus are threaded by canals and rivers that are your only way into this place. It's not easy to get to, but it's worth it.

Tortuguero is a quieter destination than others on the Caribbean coast, and the

ELEPHANTS OF THE SEA

Belonging to a unique group of sea mammals comprising only four species worldwide, manatees are thought to be distantly related to elephants. However, with at least 55 million years separating the two, their kinship is only apparent in a few fairly obscure anatomical similarities and a broadly similar diet.

Like elephants, manatees are herbivore and require huge amounts of vegetation each day. Grazing on a wide variety of aquatic plants, a large adult can process as much as 50kg every 24 hours, producing a prodigious amount of waste in the process; fresh floating droppings (similar to a horse's) and almost continuous bubbling streams of flatulence are useful ways to find them. Not too appetizing, but it does make them easier to spot. The best chances for observing manatees are around 'blowing holes' or *sopladeros* (deep hollows in the riverbed where manatees congregate to wait for high tide).

Manatees are reputed to have excellent hearing, but they're most sensitive to fairly high frequency sounds such as their squeaking vocalizations. It means that quiet approaches are often rewarded with good viewing, although sadly it also makes them vulnerable to collisions with motorboats.

vine-draped trails that weave through the lush, slender peninsula are frequented by a host of wild creatures. This is where the line between sea and dry land is blurred, which may be the reason why so many sea turtles, caught by a trick of evolution between these two worlds, begin their lives here.

It's certainly why so many fishermen originally settled this spot, and the recipes they stirred from the jungle and ocean are still served up faithfully by folks around town.

Information

Small hotels, tour operators and transportation providers compete fiercely for business in Tortuguero. Unfortunately, that means you won't always get a straight answer when you ask for information. Places offering 'Free Tourist Information' are often hawking tours; and friendly 'advice' about lodging and transportation is sometimes outright lies.

Note that there are no banks or ATMs in town. Only a few businesses accept credit cards, so bring all the cash that you will need.

La Casona (☎ 709 8092; per hr US$2; ☽ 8:30am-9pm) There is a small Internet café with two computers behind the La Casona restaurant.

Paraíso Tropical Store (☎ 710 0323) Sells souvenirs and NatureAir airline tickets and cashes traveler's checks.

Tortuguero Info Center (☎ 709 8055; tortuguero _info@racsa.co.cr; per hr US$3; ☽ 8am-7pm) An independent information center that sells Sansa airline tickets and provides Internet access. It's across from the Catholic church.

Sights

About 200m north of Tortuguero village, the **Caribbean Conservation Corporation** (CCC; ☎ 709 8091, in the USA 800-678 7853; www.cccturtle.org; admission US$1; ☽ 10am-noon & 2-5pm Mon-Sat, noon-5pm Sun) operates a research station which has a small visitor center and museum. Exhibits focus on all things turtle-related, including a video about the history of local turtle conservation. For volunteer opportunities, see the boxed text Doing Time for the Turtles, opposite.

The **Canadian Organization for Tropical Education and Rainforest Conservation** (Coterc; ☎ 709 8052, in Canada 905-831 8809; www.coterc.org; admission free) is the nonprofit organization that operates the Estación Biológica Caño Palma, 7km north of Tortuguero village. The on-site *rancho* (thatched-roof or open-air building) houses a museum which contains the station's collection of biological specimens – mainly an impressive though eerie collection of skulls from the area. You can also get up close with some serious insects, and there is a growing display of labeled seeds and fruit. If you'd rather look at live animals, a network of trails leads into the rain forest. This place is surrounded on three sides by water, so you'll have to hire a boat to get here. Coterc also has a volunteer program (see the boxed text Doing Time for the Turtles, opposite).

Activities
CANOEING

Signs all over Tortuguero advertise boat tours and boats for hire. This is obviously the best way to explore the waterways of the national park and the surrounding environs (see p460).

For boat tours, see below. You can paddle yourself in a dugout canoe for about US$2 per person per hour, but make sure you have a good map. Rent canoes at accommodations such as Hotel Miss Junie and La Casona or other places around town. This is an excellent way to see nature without disturbing wildlife and with full access to all the nooks and crannies of the park.

HIKING

Apart from hiking in the park (p460), hikers can climb the 119m **Cerro Tortuguero**, an extinct volcano about 6km north of the village within the Refugio Nacional de Silvestre Barra del Colorado. You need to hire a boat and guide to get there, and the 45-minute hike to the top is muddy, steep and strenuous. The trek offers an excellent chance of spotting colorful poison-dart frogs. And it is the highest point right on the coast anywhere north of Puerto Limón, so the views of the forest, canals and village are unparalleled. Unfortunately, this trail was closed for maintenance at the time of research; inquire further when you arrive in Tortuguero.

Tours

Guides have posted signs all over town advertising their services for canal tours and turtle walks. Ask at the **Tortuguero Info Center** (☎ 709

8055; tortuguero_info@racsa.co.cr) or at **Soda El Muelecito** (☷ 6:30am-8pm), across from Super Morpho Pulpería, to get in touch with a guide. Going rates are about US$10 per person for a two-hour turtle tour, and US$15 for a three- or four-hour hiking or boat excursion.

Recommended local guides:

Barbara Hartung (☎ 709 8004; www.tinamontours .com) Offers hiking, canoe and turtle tours in German, English, French or Spanish. Also offers a unique tour about Tortuguero history, culture and medicinal plants.

Castor Hunter Thomas (☎ 709 8050; ask at Soda Doña María)

Chico (☎ 709 8033; ask at Cabinas Miss Miriam) Chico's hiking and canoe tours receive rave reviews from readers.

Daryl Loth (☎ 833 0827, 709 8011; safari@racsa.co.cr) This knowledgeable Canadian naturalist (formerly of Coterc) offers excellent boat trips in an environmentally friendly, supersilent electric motorboat, as well as turtle tours (in season) and guided hikes to Cerro Tortuguero.

Sleeping

Competition for business is fierce. Unfortunately, it often results in unethical 'touts' trying to lure tourists to an establishment where they will get a commission. Don't make any decisions about where to stay without exploring your options and looking at the rooms being offered.

TORTUGUERO VILLAGE

There is a wide range of budget and midrange options here. The following places are

---

DOING TIME FOR THE TURTLES

There are many opportunities to volunteer your time for the greater good of the turtles (and other creatures).

Asociación Nacional de Asuntos Indígenas (ANAI; ☎ 759 9100, in San José 277 7549; www.anaicr.org; Gandoca; registration US$30, camping US$7-15, homestays US$15, cabins US$30) At the other end of the Caribbean coast in the Refugio Nacional de Vida Silvestre Gandoca Manzanillo (see p498).

Canadian Organization for Tropical Education and Rainforest Conservation (Coterc; ☎ 709 8052, in Canada 905-831 8809; www.coterc.org; per day US$65) Volunteers help with the upkeep of the station and assist ongoing research projects, including sea turtle conservation, bird banding, and animal- and plant-diversity inventories. The daily fee covers room and board. Lodging is in a brand-new dormitory building, with full access to the facilities and grounds at the research station. Make advance arrangements for transportation from Tortuguero village.

Caribbean Conservation Corporation (CCC; ☎ 709 8091, in the USA 800-678 7853; www.cccturtle.org) From March through October volunteers can assist scientists with turtle tagging and research on green and leatherback turtles. During bird-migration seasons (March through May and August through October) volunteers can receive training and assist with mist-netting, walking transects and point-counts. Programs range from one week (US$1400 to US$1600) to three weeks (US$2100 to US$2500); prices include dorm lodging, meals and transport from San José.

Save the Turtles of Parismina (ASTOP; ☎ 710 5183, in the USA 538 8084; www.costaricaturtles.org; registration US$25 fee, per day US$30) Good deeds for the financially challenged. Volunteers assist with turtle patrols and otherwise participate in the community of Parismina. See p458.

listed in order from south (near the park entrance) to north.

Tropical Lodge (☎ 826 6246; r per person US$10) This colorful and classically Caribbean setup behind the food store Tienda Bambú has cute yellow cabinas right on the river. While the exterior is bright, the interior is dank concrete.

Cabinas Tortuguero (☎ 709 8114; s/d with shared bathroom US$10/16, d/tr with private bathroom US$25/30) This festive spot, just a few steps south of the main dock, is set among pretty gardens, well hung with hammocks. The pricier rooms are spacious, with elegant wood floors and private hot-water bathrooms. A few smaller, simpler rooms share a bathroom in the building above the restaurant (breakfast US$3, mains US$4 to US$7).

Cabinas Meriscar (☎ 709 8132; r with shared/private bathroom per person US$5/7; 🖳) An enthusiastic new owner is giving this place a complete overhaul, starting with planting trees, hanging hammocks and inviting campers onto the extensive grounds. The cheapest accommodations are in cramped, clapboard quarters with shared cold-water showers. Brand-new concrete cabinas have whitewashed walls and hot-water bathrooms (per person US$10). Walk 100m east from Cabinas Tortuguero.

Cabinas Aracari (☎ 709 8006; s/d US$10/14) With their backs to the sea, these cabinas enjoy a quiet, out-of-the-way location (east of Cabinas Meriscar). The superclean, Spanish-tiled rooms contrast with the pleasantly overgrown gardens.

Cabinas Princesa (☎ 709 8107; s/d US$15/20) One of Miss Miriam's hospitable clan runs this new seaside place, south of the soccer field. The grand colonial-style building has three comfortable, clean rooms with private bathrooms and fans. They all share a balcony that provides a panorama of the waves crashing over the beach.

La Casona (☎ 709 8092; lacasonadetortuguero@yahoo.com; s/d US$15/20; 🖳) Long a favorite for eating, this friendly, family-run spot opposite the main dock is now an excellent sleeping option too. Handsome new rooms have tiled floors and sparkling hot-water bathrooms. Jenny and her sons offer canoe rental, as well as an interesting tour to an ecological finca in Guápiles. This is one of the few places that accepts credit cards.

Cabinas Miss Miriam (☎ 709 8002, 821 2037; s/d US$15/20) A top choice, at the soccer field.

Miss Miriam's rooms (actually run by her daughter) have tiled floors and firm beds, while the ones upstairs share a balcony with dramatic sea views. Miss Miriam's restaurant is one of Tortuguero's top spots for Caribbean fare.

Casa Marbella (☎ 833 0827; http://casamarbella.tripod.com; s/d US$35/40) Filling the void between budget hotels and luxury lodges, this five-room B&B opposite the Catholic church features light-filled rooms with fans suspended from the high ceilings and private hot-water showers. Room rates include a hearty breakfast, perhaps served on the shady riverside patio. Owner Daryl Loth also organizes excellent area tours.

Hotel Miss Junie (☎ 709 8029, in San José 709 7102; s/d US$22/32) At the northern end of the village, Miss Junie's place is set on wide, grassy grounds, shaded by palm trees and strewn with hammocks. One side faces the river, while the other looks out to sea, so you can't go wrong. The clean, comfortable rooms smell of disinfectant, so you'll appreciate the big screened windows which let in the breeze. Prices include a full breakfast by Tortuguero's most celebrated cook (see p466).

NORTH OF THE VILLAGE

Lodges north of town cater primarily to groups who have arranged a package deal, usually including transportation from San José, all meals and a guided tour through the park. Note that lodges on the west side of the lagoon don't have beach – or turtle – access. All these lodges will accept walk-ins if they aren't full, but only Mawamba and Laguna Lodges can actually be walked to; others will pick you up. The following are listed from south to north, and all rates are per person, based on double occupancy, including meals.

Pachira Lodge (☎ 256 7080, in the USA 800-644 7438; www.pachiralodge.com; 2-night package per adult/child US$269/100; 🖳) Rocky, Flintstones-style pathways lead through the landscaped jungle grounds, from the beautiful buffet-style restaurant to your pastel room in the rain forest. This place is right on the Laguna Tortuguero, opposite the CCC visitor center at the north end of the village. Across Laguna Penitencia, the lodge also operates the Evergreen Lodge, which has more privacy but smaller rooms. This is also where you will find the region's only canopy tour (US$25).

Mawamba Lodge (☎ in San José 293 8181; www .grupomawamba.com; 2-night package per adult/child US$262/131; ☑) Rustic rooms are airy and spacious, with fan and hot shower, all fronted by a veranda with hammocks and rocking chairs. A network of trails leads into the rain forest and to the beach, while the fully equipped recreation room will entertain kids of all ages. But the real draw is that you can walk to town, unlike guests at most of the other lodges.

Jungle Lodge (☎ 223 1200; www.grupopapagayo .com; 2-night package per adult/child US$278/121; ☑) This is one of the largest lodges, with 44 spacious, hardwood rooms with ceiling fans and big windows. On hot days guests appreciate the excellent outdoor bar, serving up tropical cocktails, and the waterfall-fed swimming pool, offering impressive jungle views.

Samoa Lodge (☎ 258 6244; www.samoalodge.com; 2-night package US$240; ☑) On the far side of Laguna Penitencia, colorful A-frame bungalows are nestled into tropical gardens. The rooms are simple, but brightly painted in citrus tones and furnished with bamboo and hardwood. The restaurant is recommended for the fusion creations from the kitchen.

Laguna Lodge (☎ 709 8082, in San José 225 3740; www.lagunatortuguero.com; 2-night package US$249; ☐ ☑) Sparkling rooms are hewn from beautiful hardwood, with bathroom tiles that match the wild mosaics spicing up the grounds. It also offers pedestrian access to town (2km).

Ilan Ilan Lodge (☎ 296 7378, 296 7502; www.mi tour.com; r US$40, 2-night package US$215; ☑) Named for the pretty-scented yellow-flowered tree that adorns the grounds. Smallish, fan-cooled rooms are arranged around a rather overgrown courtyard that the birds adore. This hotel is set on 8 hectares between the Lagunas Tortuguero and Penitencía, with a network of trails connecting them. It's a good place to spot poison-dart frogs and other critters.

Tortuga Lodge & Gardens (☎ 257 0766, 222 0333; www.costaricaexpeditions.com; s/d US$116/140, 2-night package per person US$379; ☑) This cushy lodge is operated by Costa Rica Expeditions. Superior rooms are spacious and screened, and rocking chairs and hammocks await invitingly in covered walkways outside. Beyond the restaurant, an enticing free-form swimming pool flows serenely by, mirroring the

languid movement of the canals. The lodge is on 20 hectares of landscaped gardens, with private trails and a quiet pond.

Turtle Beach Lodge (☎ 248 0707, after hours 837 6969; www.turtlebeachlodge.com; 2-night package per adult/child US$255/100; ☑) Flanked on either side by the beach and the river, this newest lodge is surrounded by 70 hectares of tropical gardens and rain forest. Spacious, elegant rooms have hardwood furniture and huge screened windows to let in the breezes. You can explore the grounds on the network of jungle trails, or lounge around the turtle-shaped pool or in the thatch-roofed hammock hut.

Eating

One of Tortuguero's unsung pleasures is the cuisine: the homey restaurants lure you in from the rain with steaming platters of Caribbean-style seafood. The following restaurants are listed from south to north.

Soda Doña María (☎ 709 8050; ☯ 7am-8pm) Recover from a hike in the park at this riverside *soda*, serving fresh *jugos* (juices) and other cold drinks. Located just north of the park entrance.

Miss Miriam's (☎ 709 8002; mains US$3-5, lobster US$7) It's worth blowing off your lodge's meal plan and getting a boat into town just for this fine food, from delicious rice and beans to whole lobsters served up by Miss Miriam's friendly and fabulous daughter. It's at the soccer field.

La Casona (☎ 709 8092; mains US$4-7; ☯ 11am-10pm) Conveniently located opposite the boat dock, this rancho restaurant is an excellent choice for a romantic dinner. The specialty of the house is the *palmito* (hearts of palm) lasagna, but the menu offers a host of delicious Italian and Tico options.

Buddha Cafe (☎ 709 8084; meals US$4-6; ☯ 9am-9pm) If the New Age music doesn't lure you inside, the aromas of fresh-from-the-oven pizza certainly will. Peruse the menu before deciding, however, as it features many tempting options: savory crepes, filled with grilled shrimp or chicken and cheese; and the namesake Buddasalata, with avocado, sweet corn and *palmito*. It's just a short walk north of the boat dock.

Mundo Natural (☯ 9am-10pm Nov-Feb, 7am-10pm Mar-Oct) This cute little clapboard house, 50m north of the Catholic church, is an excellent place for an afternoon refresher; order your fresh juice or homemade ice cream and take a seat at a shady table outside. This place also sells delicious organic coffee and other culinary souvenirs.

Dorling Bakery (☎ 845 6389; pastries US$1-3; ☽ 6am-8pm) Outstanding homemade breads and pastries baked fresh every day get you even more wired when combined with good coffee and espresso beverages. It's cozy.

Miss Junie's (☎ 709 8029; dinner US$8-10; ☽ 6-9pm) The great thing about high-quality Caribbean-style meals – and this place is Tortuguero's best-known restaurant – is that the longer seafood and veggies simmer in coconut sauce, the better they taste. This is why you should order dinner early in the day. It's worth it.

Grab groceries at the **Super Morpho Pulpería** (☎ 709 8110; ☽ 6:30am-9pm Mon-Sat, 8am-8pm Sun).

Drinking

La Taberna (☎ 710 6716; ☽ 11:30am-close) Adjacent to Tropical Lodge, and overlooking Laguna Tortuguero, this tavern is Tortuguero's most popular and pleasant spot for a drink. It's particularly enjoyable in the afternoon, when you'll appreciate the cool breezes off the canal, the ice-cold *cerveza* and the sun dropping behind the trees.

La Culebra (☽ 8pm-close) Next to the boat dock, this is the only nightclub in town. The barren concrete space and thumping music make for a good dance floor, or you can retire to the waterside bar area for a beer and a *boca*. This place rocks during turtle season.

Getting There & Away

First of all, it is not *that* hard to get here on your own. However, if you do not care to go it alone, the options for package tours are everywhere, from the moment your airplane lands in San José. Most include meals, lodging, transportation and at least one canal tour. Costs vary widely depending on accommodations and transportation.

Jungle Tom Safaris (☎ 280 0243; www.jungletom safaris; 2-night package US$119-240) Also offers a one-day trip from San José (US$79) or just round-trip transportation (US$59) – useful for independent travelers who want to be free upon arrival, but don't want the hassle of getting here alone.

Learning Trips (☎ 258 2293, 396 1979; www.costa-rica .us; 1-/2-night package US$155/195) Packages include lodging, meals, boat tours and transportation from San José.

Riverboat Francesca Nature Tours (☎ 226 0986; www.tortuguerocanals.com; 2-day package US$175-190) Highly recommended tours on the riverboat *Francesca*. Prices include food and lodging, canal tours and a nighttime turtle walk (in season).

AIR

The small airstrip is 4km north of Tortuguero village. **NatureAir** (☎ 220 3054; one way/round trip US$68/136) and **Sansa** (☎ 709 8055; one way/round trip US$63/126) both have daily flights to and from San José. Many of the upscale lodges offer transportation by charter flight as a part of their package tours.

BOAT

Tortuguero is accessible by boat from Cariari or Moín. If you are traveling to Parismina, you should be able to get one of the boats to Moín to drop you off on the way.

To/From Cariari

The most common and least expensive route to/from Tortuguero is through Cariari, from where you can catch buses to San José or Puerto Limón (via Guápiles). Three companies provide transportation along this route for US$10 per person:

Clic Clic (☎ 844 0463) Via La Pavona, 6am and 11:30am.
Coopetraca (☎ 767 7137) Via La Pavona, 6am, 11:30am and 3pm.
Viajes Bananeros (☎ 709 8005) Via La Geest, 7am and 11am.

Buy tickets on the boat or at any of the information centers around Tortuguero. Once you arrive in La Pavona or La Geest, a bus will pick you up and take you to Cariari (buses are timed to the boats, so you will not wait long). If you are traveling to San José, you are better off taking a 6am boat because bus connections are better earlier in the day.

If you are coming to Tortuguero through Cariari, you may be greeted by touts luring you onto their buses and boats. Despite what they insist, the common route to Tortuguero is through La Pavona. Coopatreca buses for La Pavona depart from the central bus terminal in Siquirres, behind the police station, at 6am, noon and 3pm. The private Bananero boat company also provides transportation from Cariari to Tortuguero via Geest. Bananero buses leave from the San José bus terminal at 1:30pm and 3:30pm.

For more information, see p448. Transportation schedules and fares to Tortuguero change frequently. For the latest details, see www.geocities.com/tortugueroinfo /main.html.

To/From Moín

Moín–Tortuguero is primarily a tourist route. While tour boats ply these canals frequently, there is not a reliable, regularly scheduled service.

In theory, **Viajes Bananeros** (☎ 709 8005; www .tortuguero-costarica.com; US$30) offers a daily transfer to Moín at 10am in the high season.

Otherwise, you can check with the **Tortuguero Info Center** (☎ 709 8015; tortuguero_info@racsa .co.cr) to try to find out about tour boats going to Moín that might have space for independent travelers. In any case, call to confirm: schedules change, or they may not run if there are not enough passengers.

BARRA DEL COLORADO

At 90,400 hectares, including the frontier zone with Nicaragua, **Refugio Nacional de Vida Silvestre Barra del Colorado**, or 'Barra' for short, is the biggest national wildlife refuge in Costa Rica.

It forms a regional conservation unit with the adjacent Parque Nacional Tortuguero, and their landscapes are similar. The refuge has 50km of coastline, and countless square kilometers of canals, lagoons, rivers and marshes. Some hilly areas, none higher than 230m, are ancient volcanic cones (like Cerro Tortuguero). Rain – lots of it – falls year-round.

The Ríos San Juan, Colorado and Chirripó all wind through the refuge and eventually make their way to the Caribbean Sea. The alluvial plain is often flooded, which means the whole place is very marshy, with various islets occasionally appearing and disappearing. The only feasible way to get around is by boat.

Barra is much more remote, more expensive and more difficult to visit than Tortuguero, but adventurous travelers will be rewarded with a wildlife bonanza. The area is home to the endangered West Indian manatee, caymans, crocodiles and tarpon. Mammals that live here include four kinds of big cats and two species of monkeys, as well as Baird's tapirs and three-toed sloths. The bird population includes the colorful keel-billed toucan and the great green macaw; raptors such as osprey and white hawks; as well as many waterbirds.

The northern border of the refuge is the Río San Juan, the border with Nicaragua (many local residents are Nicaraguan nationals). This area was politically sensitive during the 1980s, which contributed to the isolation of the reserve. Since the relaxing of Sandinista–Contra hostilities in 1990, it has become straightforward to journey north along the Río Sarapiquí and east along the San Juan, technically entering Nicaragua (see the boxed text Getting to San Juan del Nicaragua, p469). However, while Costa Ricans have right of use, the Río San Juan is Nicaraguan territory. Other territorial disputes in this area mean that tensions between the countries still exist; carry your passport when you are out fishing.

Orientation & Information

The village of Barra del Colorado lies near the mouth of the Río Colorado and is divided by the river into Barra del Norte and Barra del Sur. There are no roads. The airstrip is on the south side of the river, but more people live on the north side. The area outside the village is swampy and travel is almost exclusively by boat, though some walking is possible around some of the lodges.

The Servicio de Parques Nacionales (SPN) maintains a small **ranger station** (refuge admission US$6) near the village, on the south side of the Río Colorado. However, there are no facilities here. Stop by **Diana's Souvenirs** (☎ 710 6592), close to the airport, for weather reports, tourist information, Internet access or a public telephone.

Activities

FISHING

Despite the incredible wildlife-watching opportunities, fishing is still the bread and butter of most of the area's lodges. Anglers go for tarpon from January to June and snook from September to December. Fishing is good year-round, however, and other tasty catches include barracuda, mackerel and jack crevalle, all inshore; or bluegill, rainbow bass (*guapote*) and machaca in the rivers. There is also deep-sea fishing for marlin, sailfish and tuna, though this sort of fishing is probably better on the Pacific.

Dozens of fish can be hooked on a good day, so 'catch and release' is an important conservation policy of all the lodges.

CANOEING AND KAYAKING

Just like in Parque Nacional Tortuguero, the best way to explore the rivers and lagoons of the refuge is by boat. If you are not fishing, you can paddle these waterways in a canoe or kayak, available from some of the local lodges. Silver King Lodge rents 5m aluminum canoes, which are used both for fishing and for exploring the backwater lagoons.

Sleeping & Eating

From the airport, only Tarponland Cabinas and Río Colorado Lodge are accessible on foot. All other lodges require a boat ride (a boat operator will be waiting for you at the airport if you have a reservation). Packages include air transfers from San José, all fishing, accommodations, meals and an open bar. Trips of varying lengths can be arranged.

Tarponland Cabinas (☎ 710 2141; r per person US$20, d with sportfishing US$275; ☒) This is it as far as budget lodgings go in Barra. Walking distance from the airport, these basic hardwood rooms are pretty run-down, but there is a good on-site restaurant.

Casa Mar Lodge (☎ in the USA 800-543 0282; www .casamarlodge.com; 5-night package per person US$2250-2795) When CEOs hang a 'gone fishing' sign on the office door, you can bet this is the type of place they've gone to. Luxurious cabins with nicely tiled hot showers are set in a pleasant 2.8-hectare garden that attracts lots of birds, and meals are home-cooked. But the real drawcards are the big-engine boats and the impressive 75kg tarpon that make the covers of all those sportfishing magazines. Incidentally, you may have seen the owner, Bill Barnes, in one of those magazines, as he currently holds the world record for catching a 12kg snook on a fly rod.

Río Colorado Lodge (☎ 232 4063, in the USA 800-243 9777; www.riocoloradolodge.com; r per person with/without fishing US$400/120; ☒ ⅋) Built in 1971, this is the longest-established lodge on the Caribbean coast. The rambling tropical-style buildings near the mouth of the Río Colorado are constructed on stilts, with covered walkways that make a lot of sense in the rain forest. Rooms are breezy and pleasant. For relaxation after a day of fishing the lodge features a happy hour with free rum drinks, a pool table, a breezy outdoor deck and satellite TV. This is the only upscale lodge from which you can walk to the airport; the local crowd it attracts has earned it a reputation as a 'party lodge.' Rates include meals.

Silver King Lodge (☎ 711 0708, in the USA 800-847 3474; www.silverkinglodge.net; r per person US$135, 3-day package per person US$1875, extra day US$325; ☒ ▯ ☒) This excellent sportfishing lodge caters to couples and families, besides just fishers. Huge hardwood guestrooms have beautiful 3.5m cane ceilings, colorful woven tapestries and plenty of amenities. Outside, covered walkways lead to the waterfall-filled pool, an international buffet-style restaurant and an open-air bar serving tropical drinks (like the specialty 'Funky Monkey'). This lodge closes in July and December.

Getting There & Away

The easiest way to Barra by far is by air, and both Sansa (one way/round trip US$63/126) and NatureAir (US$68/136) will drop you off here on their daily Tortuguero run.

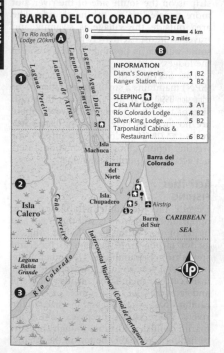

BARRA DEL COLORADO AREA

0 ——— 4 km
0 ——— 2 miles

INFORMATION	
Diana's Souvenirs	1 B2
Ranger Station	2 B2

SLEEPING ⌂	
Casa Mar Lodge	3 A1
Río Colorado Lodge	4 B2
Silver King Lodge	5 B2
Tarponland Cabinas & Restaurant	6 B2

To Río Indio Lodge (20km)

Laguna Pereira
Laguna de Emmedio
Laguna de Agua Dulce
Laguna de Arras

Isla Machuca
Barra del Norte
Barra del Colorado
Isla Chupadero
Airstrip
Barra del Sur

Isla Calero
Caño Pereira

Laguna Bahía Grande
Río Colorado

CARIBBEAN SEA

Intercoastal Waterway (Canal de Tortuguero)

GETTING TO SAN JUAN DEL NICARAGUA

Day trips along the Río San Juan and some offshore fishing trips technically enter Nicaraguan territory. Carry your passport and US$10, in the unlikely event that you are stopped and checked.

If you are planning to head further into Nicaragua, you can make arrangements with your lodge (or hire a boat independently for about US$300) to take you to the border town of San Juan del Norte – now called San Juan del Nicaragua, in light of the recent border disputes. Though you can get your passport stamped here, you should probably check with immigration officials in San José before doing this independently. (If you are coming from Nicaragua into Costa Rica here, you will need to get your passport stamped in Limón.)

San Juan del Nicaragua, at the mouth of the Río San Juan, is a tranquil village with very few services but an interesting history. Founded in 1549, it became something of a boomtown when English settlers took over in 1847, naming it 'Greytown.' During the gold rush, the Río San Juan became an important transportation route connecting the Atlantic and the Pacific. Huge amounts of cargo, travelers and money passed through this town. Today, the former Greytown is more of a ghost town: only ruins remain from this heyday.

The 'living' (though very wet) village of San Juan del Nicaragua is across the bay. **Río Indio Lodge** (☎ 381 1549, 296 0095, in the USA 866-593 3176; www.rioindiolodge.com; San Juan del Nicaragua; s/d US$225/400; 🖳 💺) has 34 spacious rooms, a gourmet restaurant and a well-stocked bar. Sportfishing is the lodge's forté, but you can also hike on the old railroad track that remains from the Greytown days or kayak on Laguna Silico.

San Juan del Norte is linked with the rest of Nicaragua by irregular passenger boats sailing up the San Juan to San Carlos, on Lago de Nicaragua.

There is no regular boat service to Barra, although you may be able to arrange a boat ride from Tortuguero (US$50 per boat), Puerto Viejo de Sarapiquí (p522; US$60 per boat) or Moín (p456), for a price. During the dry season, buses run from Cariari (p448) to Puerto Lindo, from where you can try to hop on a lodge boat or a water taxi continuing on to Barra.

SOUTHERN CARIBBEAN

This is the heart and soul of Costa Rica's Afro-Caribbean community, where Jamaicans brought here by United Fruit to build the backbone of the original banana republic learned to call this country home. For more than half a century, the communities of the southern Caribbean existed almost independent of the rest of the country, turning to subsistence farming and fishing when the banana plantations, and later cacao fincas, fell to devastating blights.

These Afro-Caribbean communities found good neighbors among the ancient indigenous groups, now encompassed by the nearby Cocles/KéköLdi, Talamanca Cabécar and Bribrí reserves. The two peoples,

isolated from the goings-on of mainstream Costa Rica, exchanged the ancient wisdom of medicinal plants, agriculture and jungle survival. And thrived.

Though the racial borders fell in 1949, electricity, roads and phones all came late to this perfect stretch of beachfront property. The result of all this isolation is a culture still largely independent of everyday Costa Rica.

Inevitably, however, improved infrastructure and an expanding tourism industry are inexorably wearing away the cultural quirks that many folks come to experience. Puerto Viejo in particular has experienced an influx of North American and European transplants, starting with surfers but now including all kinds of folks looking for a change of pace. (And with this picture-perfect setting and low-key vibe, who can blame them?)

Not to worry, not yet anyway: the music of the islands is everywhere, reggae and calypso pouring from homes and businesses into the streets. The cuisine is extraordinary, where even the simplest rice-and-beans dish conjures flavors of Jamaica. And while most residents speak Spanish, a patois of English remains common, if a little bit difficult to decipher for those unused to it.

Dangers & Annoyances

The southern Caribbean gets a bad rap for being dangerous, with Pacific-coasters warning about hurricane-like weather, prohibitively bad roads and rampant theft and drug use. Most of these warnings are exaggerated. But as in the rest of Costa Rica, it is wise to take the usual precautions: lock your hotel room; don't leave anything in your car; never leave gear unattended on beaches; don't walk the beaches alone at night. While drug use is not uncommon in some places, most residents do not condone or appreciate this activity. Remember that buying drugs is illegal as well as dangerous.

RESERVA BIOLÓGICA HITOY-CERERE

One of the most rugged and rarely visited reserves in the country, **Hitoy-Cerere** (☎ 795 1446; admission US$6; ☒ 8am-4pm) is only about 60km south of Limón (half that distance as the crow flies). The 9950-hectare reserve sits on the edge of the Cordillera de Talamanca, characterized by varying altitudes, evergreen forests and rushing rivers. This may be one of the wettest reserves in the parks system; its evergreen forests are inundated with 4000mm to 6000mm of rain annually.

The reserve is named for two rivers: the Hitoy (which means 'woolly,' referring to its moss-covered rocks) and the Cerere (meaning 'clear waters'). Indeed, these rivers define much of the landscape in the reserve. Aided and abetted by heavy rainfall, they rush down the side of the mountains and spill off into glorious cascades that make for marvelously picturesque scenery. The surrounding rain forest is dominated by Spanish cedar, wild tamarind, possum-wood and silk cotton tree. But the most evident flora is the thick, soft carpeting of moss that covers the ground and trees alike.

Wildlife is abundant in this moist, humid forest. The most commonly sighted mammals include the woolly opossum, grey four-eyed opossum, tayra, howler monkey and white-faced capuchin. You can hardly miss the Montezuma oropendola, whose nests are suspended from trees like unexpected pendulums. Other ornithological highlights include the keel-billed toucan, spectacled owl and green kingfisher.

The biological reserve is surrounded by some of the country's most remote indigenous reserves, which you can visit with a local guide (see Tours, opposite). See also the boxed text Bribrí & Cabécar, p498.

Although there is a ranger station at the reserve entrance, there are no other facilities. A 9km trail leads south from the ranger station, but it is steep, slippery and poorly maintained.

Getting There & Away

By car (4WD recommended), head west on the signed road to Valle de la Estrella and Penshurst (just south of the Río Estrella bridge). Another small sign at the bus stop sends you down a good dirt road about 15km to the reserve.

By public transport, catch a bus from Limón to Valle de la Estrella. From the end of the bus line (Fortuna/Finca 6) you can hire a taxi to take you the rest of the way and pick you up at a prearranged time (US$25).

You can also arrange taxis and guided hikes, including transportation, from Cahuita. **Cahuita Tours** (☎ 755 0000/0232) offers an all-day guided hike, departing at 6am for optimal wildlife-sighting, for US$100 per person.

CAHUITA

While neighboring Puerto Viejo is rapidly developing into a can't-miss destination on the groovier travel circuit, Cahuita has managed to maintain a more relaxed relationship with folks discovering the Caribbean coast. Most of the businesses are still locally owned and the vibe is still very laid-back.

What's more, the place is breathtakingly beautiful. The black sand gives the very swimmable Playa Negra an unusual and ethereal presence.

While the Bribrí and Cabécar Indians were the original inhabitants of this area (see the boxed text Bribrí & Cabécar, p498), Cahuita claims the first Afro-Caribbean settler, one turtle fisherman named William Smith, who moved his family to Punta Cahuita in 1828. Mr Smith's descendents – and the descendents of many other immigrants – are now cooking with coconuts in the kitchen and playing reggae music on the radio, giving this town a decidedly Afro-Caribbean flavor.

Along with excellent meals and quality beach time, an itinerary in this relaxed paradise certainly includes a wander into neighboring Parque Nacional Cahuita, only a five-minute walk from 'downtown.' Here are even more perfect beaches, trails through protected jungle and one of Costa Rica's two living coral reefs.

With the Playa Negra stretching out to the north of town, and the Parque Nacional Cahuita immediately to the south, Cahuita's little center is nestled into a small point that sticks out into the Caribbean Sea. It consists of only two gravel roads, neither of which sees too much traffic. But that doesn't stop the townsfolk from spending the afternoon sitting in the shade and watching it pass by.

Information

There are no banks in Cahuita – the closest are in Puerto Limón and Puerto Viejo – so bring the cash you need.

Centro Turístico Brigitte (☎ 755 0053; www.brigit tecahuita.com; Playa Negra; per hr US$2; ◑ 7am-6pm) Internet access.

Internet Palmer (per hr US$2; ◑ 9am-8pm)

Mercado Safari (◑ 6am-4pm) Changes US and Canadian dollars, euros, Swiss francs, British pounds and traveler's checks but has a steep commission.

Spencer Seaside Lodging (☎ 755 0210/027; per hr US$2; ◑ 8am-8pm) Internet access.

Willie's Tours (☎ 843 4700; per hr US$2; ◑ 8am-8pm Mon-Sat, 4-8pm Sun) Internet access.

Dangers & Annoyances

Women should know that Cahuita enjoys a free-love reputation and evidently some female travelers do come here for a quick fling. Be prepared to pay your gent's way around town and bring (and use!) your own condoms.

Activities

SWIMMING & SURFING

At the northwest end of Cahuita, **Playa Negra** is a long, black-sand beach flying the *bandera azul ecológica* (see p533). This is undoubtedly Cahuita's top spot for swimming. Most importantly, it is far enough from town to never be crowded.

Unknown to many surfers, Playa Negra has an excellent beach break. It is not one of the regular stops on the Costa Rica surfer circuit, which means more waves for you. Conditions are best in the early morning, especially with a swell from the south or east. Sign up for a lesson (US$25 for two hours) or just rent a board at the Beach House (p477). Closer to the beach, the Centro Turístico Brigitte (below) may also give lessons.

The relatively remote Playa Negra contrasts with the **Playa Blanca** at the entrance to the national park (see p479).

Incidents of theft in broad daylight at these two beaches have been reported, so why not store your stuff at Mister Big J Tourist Service (p472)?

Tours

Snorkeling, sportfishing and horseback riding are standard offerings:

Cahuita Tours (☎ 755 0000/0232) One of the oldest established agencies in town, this place offers guided hikes to the Hitoy-Cerere (opposite) and all-day trips to the Bribrí Indigenous Reserve (US$55).

Centro Turístico Brigitte (☎ 755 0053; www.brigit tecahuita.com) Brigitte specializes in horseback-riding tours (three/five hours per person US$35/45) along the beach or to jungle waterfalls. Also an excellent place to rent a bike (per day US$8). She also rents a few cabinas (s/d/q US$25/30/40).

SELVA BANANITO LODGE

At the foot of Cerro Muchito, on the edge of La Amistad biosphere reserve, this family-run **farm and ecolodge** (☎ 253 8118; www.selvabananito.com; 3-day package US$330-350; Ⓟ) has about 1200 hectares of pasture, plantation and reforested areas. Conscious of the environmental impact of all their activities, the Stein family employs solar energy, recycled hardwood for construction and biodegradable products. And they are deeply committed to preserving the Limón watershed. While this lodge does not offer beach access, there is plenty to keep the adventurous traveler occupied: tree climbing, tree planting, waterfall hiking and horseback riding. Rates, based on double occupancy, include three meals daily and transportation from San José, as well as the above-mentioned activities.

If you are driving yourself, the turnoff is just south of the Río Vizcaya crossing (about 19km south of Limón). The lodge is about 8km inland. Detailed driving directions are posted on the website.

Mister Big J Tourist Service (☎ 755 0328; ⏱ 8am-7pm) Big 'J' is Mr Joseph Spencer. Besides the standards, he leads guided hikes to visit an indigenous family in the Bribrí reserve.

Roberto's Tours (☎ 755 0117) Arranges snorkeling trips and dolphin tours in the national park, but Roberto's real claim to fame is inshore/offshore sportfishing (per person US$60/300). Bonus: after all your hard work, Roberto can have your haul cooked for dinner in his recommended restaurant.

Willie's Tours (☎ 843 4700; www.willies-costarica -tours.com) Willie's signature tour takes visitors to visit a Bribrí family and a KéköLdi iguana farm (US$35).

Sleeping

There are two possible areas for lodgings in Cahuita – the town center or north of town along the Playa Negra.

CENTER

Within the town, hotels are mostly cheaper and noisier (though there are a few upscale options). The advantage is being close to many restaurants and to the national park.

Budget

Budget accommodations dominate in Cahuita. Most are clean and basic, geared for folks content with a cold shower and decor revolving around mosquito nets.

Backpacker's Dream (☎ 755 0174; r per person US$6) 'Backpacker's Reality' is probably a better name for this place. Basic, cramped clapboard rooms are furnished with a bed and a fan; shared bathrooms have clean, cold-water showers. There's not much to it, but it's the cheapest place in town and it works.

Cabinas Rhode Island (☎ 755 0264; r per person US$8; P) Good-sized, reasonably clean rooms with comfy chairs and cold showers surround a grassy parking lot. The office is in the yellow house across the street.

Villa Delmar (☎ 755 0392/75; d with/without air-con US$30/14, additional person US$6; P ✕) In a quiet, out-of-the-way spot close to the national park, the Villa Delmar has colorful cabins, ranging in size from small singles to more spacious family-sized quarters. Set around a grassy yard, the rooms are dark and musty, brightened only moderately by the pleasant pastel paint job.

Cabinas Riverside (☎ 553 0153; s/d US$15/20; P) German management ensures efficient service and superclean rooms at this spot near

Kelly Creek. With painted wood furniture and colorful woven hammocks strung up around the grounds, this charming place is definitely the best of the budget bunch. Simple rooms have mosquito nets and stone showers with hot water.

Cabinas Surfside (☎ 755 0246; evadarling1930@ yahoo.com; s/d/tr US$15/20/25, d annex US$30; P) These concrete-block rooms do not look like much, but they are spotless, from the tiled floor to the wood ceiling. The less expensive cabinas surround a pleasant courtyard, while slightly pricier rooms are in the adjacent annex, facing the waterfront.

Cabinas Smith (☎ 755 0068; s/d/tr US$15/20/25; P ✕) These basic concrete cabinas are much nicer on the inside than they appear from the outside. The rooms are fresh, each furnished with a firm bed, a refrigerator and plenty of storage space. There is an annex with similar quarters around the corner.

Cabinas Safari (☎ 755 0405; s/d/tr/q US$15/18/22/25; P) These basic but well-maintained rooms all have tiled floors and a few frilly details. The helpful owners also provide money-changing services. Big breakfasts are worth the extra US$2 charged.

Cabinas Bobo Ashanti (☎ 755 0128, 829 6890; tr US$25; P) Come here if you are in a reggae mood. This place is characterized by Rasta colors, plenty of hammocks and *very* laid-back service. The rooms are a good deal if you can fill the beds, but single travelers may want to look elsewhere. The outdoor kitchen facilities are useful for self-caterers.

Cabinas Palmer (☎ 755 0046; kainepalmer@racsa .co.cr; s/d US$15/20) The faded rooms could use a paint job at this otherwise pleasant place. If your room is a bit dreary, you can always retire to the hammock hut in the garden.

You can camp in Parque Nacional Cahuita (p479) or just north of town at Reggae Restaurant (p477).

Midrange

The midrange options have private bathrooms with hot water, unless otherwise noted.

Spencer Seaside Lodging (☎ 755 0210; spencer@ racsa.co.cr; s/d downstairs US$16/22, upstairs US$22/28; P ▦) A seaside setting makes this the perfect place to take advantage of hammocks strung beneath the coconut palms. The cottages are nothing fancy, but the lizards, turtles and other creatures stenciled on

CAHUITA

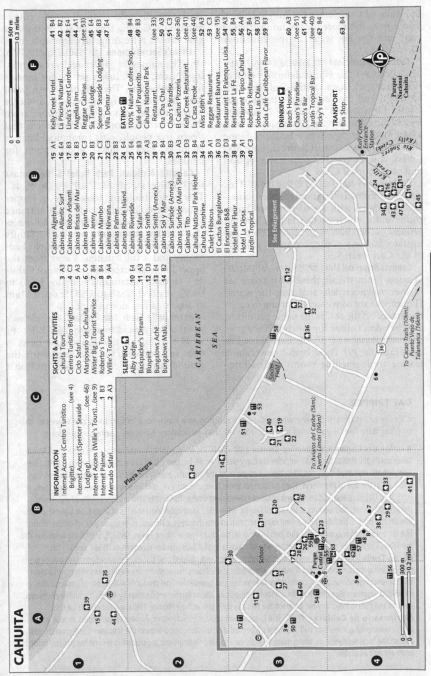

0   500 m
0   0.3 miles

CARIBBEAN COAST

INFORMATION

Internet Access (Centro Turístico	
Brigitte)..	(see 4)
Internet Access (Spencer Seaside	
Lodging).......................................	(see 46)
Internet Access (Willie's Tours)......	(see 9)
Internet Palmer.................................	1 B3
Mercado Safari.................................	2 A3

SIGHTS & ACTIVITIES

Cahuita Tours.......................................	3 A3
Centro Turístico Brigitte......................	4 C3
Ciclo Safari...	5 A3
Mariposario de Cahuita........................	6 C4
Mister Big J Tourist Service..................	7 B4
Roberto's Tours....................................	8 B4
Willie's Tours.......................................	9 A4

SLEEPING

Alby Lodge..	10 E4
Backpacker's Dream............................	11 A3
Blusipirit...	12 D3
Bungalows Aché.................................	13 E4
Bungalows Malú..................................	14 B2
Cabinas Algebra..................................	15 A1
Cabinas Atlantic Surf...........................	16 E4
Cabinas Bobo Ashanti..........................	17 B3
Cabinas Brisas del Mar.........................	18 B3
Cabinas Iguana...................................	19 C3
Cabinas Jenny.....................................	20 B3
Cabinas Mambo..................................	21 C3
Cabinas Nirwana.................................	22 C3
Cabinas Palmer...................................	23 B3
Cabinas Rhode Island...........................	24 E4
Cabinas Riverside................................	25 E4
Cabinas Safari.....................................	26 B3
Cabinas Smith.....................................	27 A3
Cabinas Smith (Annex).........................	28 B3
Cabinas Sol y Mar................................	29 B4
Cabinas Surfside (Annex)......................	30 A3
Cabinas Surfside (Main Site)..................	31 A3
Cabinas Tito..	32 D3
Cahuita National Park Hotel.................	33 B4
Cahuita Sunshine................................	34 E4
Chalet Hibiscus...................................	35 A1
El Cactus Bungalows............................	36 D3
El Encanto B&B...................................	37 D3
Hotel Belle Fleur.................................	38 B4
Hotel La Diosa....................................	39 A1
Jardín Tropical....................................	40 C3

EATING

Kelly Creek Hotel................................	41 B4
La Piscina Natural................................	42 B2
Linda's Secret Garden..........................	43 E4
Magellan Inn......................................	44 A1
Reggae Cabinas..................................	(see 53)
Sía Tami Lodge...................................	45 E4
Spencer Seaside Lodging......................	46 B3
Villa Delmar.......................................	47 E4

EATING

100% Natural Coffee Shop....................	48 B4
Café del Parquecito..............................	49 B3
Cahuita National Park	
Restaurant...	(see 33)
Cha Cha Chá.......................................	50 A3
Chao's Paradise..................................	51 C3
El Cactus Pizzería...............................	(see 36)
Kelly Creek Restaurant.........................	(see 41)
La Casa Creole....................................	(see 44)
Miss Edith's.......................................	52 A3
Reggae Restaurant..............................	53 C3
Restaurant Bananas.............................	(see 15)
Restaurant El Palenque Luisa................	54 A3
Restaurant La Fé.................................	55 B4
Restaurant Típico Cahuita....................	56 A4
Roberto's Restaurant...........................	57 B4
Sobre Las Olas....................................	58 D3
Soda Café Caribbean Flavor.................	59 B3

DRINKING

Beach House......................................	60 A3
Chao's Paradise..................................	(see 51)
Coco's Bar...	61 A4
Jardín Tropical Bar..............................	(see 40)
Ricky's Bar...	62 B4

TRANSPORT

| Bus Stop.. | 63 B4 |

the walls add an element of jungle charm. You'll pay a bit more for the unobstructed view and the hot water in the 2nd-floor rooms.

Cabinas Atlantic Surf (☎ 755 0116, 846 4622; s/d/tr US$20/25/30; P) The vibe is definitely cool at this sweet spot, thanks to the cool manager, Kenneth, and the cool reggae tunes emanating from within. Attractive hardwood rooms have semiprivate porches, each with a hammock for optimum relaxation. Stone showers – straight out of Bedrock – are hot, unless you choose the cold-water option and save yourself US$5.

Cabinas Sol y Mar (☎ 755 0237; d US$20) This good-value motel offers immaculate rooms – each equipped with a well-scrubbed bathroom and a much-needed fan – clustered around rather barren gardens. From the upstairs balcony you can catch a glimpse of the Caribbean Sea.

Cabinas Brisas del Mar (☎ 755 0011; s/d US$21/25) Spotless if not stylish, these cabinas are set in overgrown gardens that face the water. Hammocks are conveniently strung to catch the breeze off the sea, as the name promises, but they don't allow for much privacy.

Cahuita Sunshine (☎ 371 0049; www.hotelsunshine .net; d US$23-30; P) These brand-new cabins feature fresh-smelling rooms with white-washed walls and stained wood ceilings and doors. Ceiling fans and starched sheets guarantee a refreshing, airy atmosphere.

Linda's Secret Garden (☎ 755 0327; dm/d US$7/25; P) The namesake garden really is an enticing retreat, and a lovely setting for Linda's four airy cabins. They all have fresh paint jobs and bamboo furniture, with a wicker screen that separates the bathroom from the rest of the room. The new dorm that sleeps five people, plus communal kitchen facilities, makes this a good option for families.

Cahuita National Park Hotel & Restaurant (☎ 755 0244; s/d/tr/f US$25/30/35/65; P ✗ ✷) This large building looks like a proper hotel, overlooking the beach at the entrance to the park. Wood paneling and balconies characterize the rooms, while the family room comes complete with multiple bedrooms and a full kitchen. Views from the upper floors are excellent, and one of Cahuita's favorite restaurants (casados US$3 to US$5, seafood US$8 to US$15; open 11am to 10pm) is just downstairs.

Hotel Belle Fleur (☎ 755 0283; hotelbellefleur@ hotmail.com; d standard/deluxe/king US$25/35/55; P ▢ ▣) Although this brand-new hotel is right smack dab in the middle of town, the grounds are completely enclosed, making it

---

DAY TRIPPER

It's easy to let time slip away while you are lounging in a hammock or catching the waves in this tropical paradise. If you need a break from all that relaxation, here are some suggestions:

Avarios del Caribe & Buttercup Center (☎ 750 0725; www.ogphoto.com/aviaros; ☽ 6am-5pm) About 10km north of Cahuita, this small wildlife sanctuary sits on an 88-hectare island in the delta of the Río Estrella. The now-famous orphaned sloth named Buttercup reigns over the grounds, ever since she was adopted by owners Luis and Judy at the age of five weeks. Their passion for these funny creatures is contagious; informative guided tours (US$20 to US$30) allow visitors to meet some of the resident sloths. The center also offers a variety of excursions through the canals and lagoons of the Estrella delta, where 312 (and counting!) species of birds have been recorded. Besides the prolific birdlife, this lowland rain forest is home to monkeys, caimans, river otters and, of course, sloths. The recommended way to explore this lush tropical setting is by canoe (three hours, US$30), but hiking tours are also available. The reserve and research center also contains a restful B&B (double rooms from US$87 to US$110).

Cacao Trails (☎ 812 7460; www.cacaotrails.com; Hone Creek; guided tour US$25; ☽ 8am-5pm) Visit this exquisite new botanical garden and outdoor museum, where educational tours demonstrate the various uses of medicinal plants and the workings of a cacao plantation (plus you can see and sample the final product), with plenty of opportunities for wildlife sightings along the way. An additional expedition allows further exploration by kayak. It's midway between Cahuita and Puerto Viejo; any bus between the two can drop you at the entrance. This is a great outing for kids.

Mariposario de Cahuita (☎ 755 0361; admission US$7; ☽ 9am-4pm) Almost all local tours include a visit to this wonderful garden that's all aflutter with beautiful butterflies. Stroll around the fountain-filled grounds and admire the local residents, including many friendly caterpillars. Descriptions are posted in several languages; guided tours are also available.

a private, peaceful site. The exception is the standard rooms, which are above the Vaz supermarket on the main drag. The pricier rooms are clustered around lovely gardens in the back. A cool hammock hang-out and a refreshing swimming pool make it a welcome retreat in a superconvenient locale.

Cabinas Jenny (☎ 755 0256; d US$30-35; additional person US$5; P) A stone's throw from the advancing waves, this straightforward place has great views from the shared porches. Linoleum floors, fresh paint and mosquito nets constitute the decor, but the rooms are functional and offer plenty of storage space. Upstairs, the more private rooms are a few dollars more. Give a call in advance to make sure that somebody is here when you arrive.

Top End

Bungalows Aché (☎ 755 0119; www.bungalowsache .com; s/d/tr US$40/45/50; P &) In Nigeria, *Aché* means 'Amen,' and you'll likely say the same thing when you arrive at this little piece of paradise. With its back to the national park, it is surrounded by wildlife, but these spacious octagonal bungalows have almost every amenity. High ceilings and spacious woody interiors are brightened by colorful print curtains and linens.

Alby Lodge (☎ 755 0031; www.albylodge.com; d/tr/ q US$40/45/50; P) On the edge of the park, this fine German-run lodge has spacious landscaped grounds, littered with trees that attract loads of howler monkeys. Four thatch-room bungalows are spread out across the grounds, allowing for plenty of privacy. High ceilings, mosquito nets and driftwood details make for a pleasant jungle decor. A common rancho has excellent communal kitchen facilities.

Sia Tami Lodge (☎ 755 0374; www.siatamilodge .com; d/q US$55/61, extra person US$14; P) A gravel road leads from town, past the other lodges, to this tranquil spot on the edge of the park. This place is ideal for families, as the 10 casas are fully equipped with two bedrooms, living space and kitchen. From each, a terrace overlooks a large private garden. With rain forest all around, this the next best thing to staying in the park itself.

Kelly Creek Hotel & Restaurant (☎ 755 0007; www.hotelkellycreek.com; d US$58; additional person US$10; P X R) This snazzy hotel is on a busy stretch of beach, right next to the park entrance. The location allows for welcome sea breezes, which blow right into the rooms; it's also not a bad spot for wildlife-watching, as animals sometimes sneak out from the park. Four hardwood rooms each have high ceilings, two double beds with mosquito nets, and two big windows letting in plenty of light. The on-site Spanish restaurant (dishes US$8 to US$10, open 6:30pm Thursday to Tuesday) serves up a mouthwatering paella.

PLAYA NEGRA

Northwest of town, along Playa Negra, you'll find more expensive hotels and a few pleasant cabinas, which offer more privacy and quiet but a limited choice of restaurants and services. All of the options have private bathrooms with hot water.

Budget

Cabinas Nirwana (☎ 755 0110; nirwana99@racsa.co.cr; d US$20-35; R) This good budget choice offers a range of lodging options, from small doubles to larger quarters (sleeping up to four) with kitchenettes. Built by a friendly Italian, the wooden cabins are cool and comfortable, with plenty of windows for cross-ventilation. A wide porch overlooks the grounds, which are perhaps too well maintained.

Cabinas Algebra (☎ 755 0057; d US$18, d/tr with kitchen US$25/39; P) This friendly, family-run option is a 2km trek from town. But the owners will pick you up (for free!) if you call in advance. The rooms are cheerful and inviting, as is the on-site Restaurant Bananas (meals US$7 to US$12), serving top-notch Creole food.

Midrange

Cabinas Tito (☎ 755 0286; s/d incl breakfast US$20/25; P) Surrounded by extensive tropical gardens and banana plants, this atmospheric spot offers excellent value. The bright rooms are furnished in wicker, with mosquito nets and jungly accents. If you absolutely love it, there is a furnished house available for long-term rental.

Cabinas Iguana (☎ 755 0005; www.cabinas-iguana .com; d with shared bathroom US$20, cabins US$35-40; P R) Set back from the beach, these cabinas are in the middle of the jungle: agoutis and sloths have been sighted on the grounds. Three comfortable, small rooms share warm showers and a small terrace. More spacious cabins have handsome woody interiors, big beds with mosquito nets and hammock-hung porches. One large furnished house with a kitchen sleeps up to six (US$65).

La Piscina Natural (☎ 755 0146; d US$27; **P**) This gem is about 2km out of town and 100% worth the walk or cab ride. The comfortable rooms are recently renovated, but what makes this place are the gorgeous grounds fronting a scenic stretch of beach and the neat natural pool for which the complex is named. With drinks available from the breezy bar, you may never feel the need to trek back into town.

Bluspirit (☎ 755 0122; bluspirit_@hotmail.com; d US$30) Three delightful blue A-frame cabins are lined up on this pleasant stretch of waterfront property. They each have a thatch-roofed porch – hung with a hammock, of course – for maximum breeze-catching. The on-site seaside restaurant (pasta US$5 to US$7, seafood US$9 to US$15) is Cahuita's most romantic dining spot.

Jardín Tropical (☎ 811 2754; jardintropical@racsa .co.cr; cabins US$35-40, house US$50-60) Deep in the middle of overgrown tropical gardens, two cozy cabins have high ceilings and porch hammocks. It doesn't get more tranquil than this, unless of course there's a rowdy crowd at the popular bar on-site. The same fine folks also run Cabinas Mambo (double/triple room US$30/40) opposite. Inquire at Jardín Tropical about these spacious rooms that share a shady porch.

El Cactus Bungalows y Pizzería (☎ 755 0276; www.elcactuscahuita.com; d US$40-50; **P** ⊠) With four cute, comfortable bungalows, El Cactus ensures that you never have to be far from a delicious pizza (US$8 to US$10). The stucco bungalows have high wood ceilings and sparkling green marble bathrooms, as well as a shaded porch facing the parking lot. If you are not staying here, you can eat an extra slice and work it off on the 1km walk back into town.

Top End

Chalet Hibiscus (☎ 755 0021; www.hotels.co.cr/hibiscus .html; d/q US$45/55, chalets US$100-120; **P** ⊠) The rooms in the 'principal chalet' are very comfortable, with all the necessary amenities, plus wide balconies and a few artsy touches. The two-story private chalets, however, are fabulous. The balconies, strung with ham-

mocks, overlook private gardens; other practical perks include full kitchens and separate bedrooms. The chalets sleep six to 10 people.

Bungalows Malú (☎ 755 0114; www.bungalows malu.com; s/d/tr/q US$46/58/64/70; **P** ⊠ ⊠) At this new lodge along Playa Negra, five stone bungalows are scattered across the palm-shaded grounds, surrounding an open-air rancho and a sunken swimming pool. They feature cool Stone Age bathrooms and tropical hardwood interiors, individually decorated with poignant paintings by local artist Alessandra Bucci.

El Encanto B&B (☎ 755 0113; www.elencantobed andbreakfast.com; s/d 49/59; **P**) This B&B, run by French-Canadian artists Pierre and Patricia, is set in lovingly landscaped grounds, with statuettes and nooks reflecting the creative nature of the owners. An Asian-style pavilion has hammocks and lounge chairs – yoga, massage and meditation also take place here. Attractive wooden bungalows have ceiling fans and private patios.

Hotel La Diosa (☎ 755 0055; www.hotelladiosa .net; s/d US$58/63, with air-con US$76/87, with air-con & Jacuzzi US$88/99; **P** ⊠ ⊠) Cabins with names like Aphrodite and Isis evoke the feminine energy of La Diosa, or 'the goddess.' This place is designed to please the senses, from the spacious, cool, tiled cabins with king-size beds, to the swimming pool set amid tropical gardens, to the new hardwood yoga and meditation space. Prices include breakfast – with plenty of fresh-brewed coffee – served in the open-air *rancho*.

Magellan Inn (☎ 755 0035; www.magellaninn.com; d with fan/air-con US$92/115, additional person US$17; **P** ⊠ ⊠) At the northern end of Playa Negra, this elegant, upscale inn isn't really within a casual stroll of town, but it is worth the extra effort. Comfortable, classy rooms with king-size beds have beautiful wood furniture, and their private terraces look out into the tropical garden, which is filled with orchids and bromeliads. Prices include breakfast.

Eating

CENTER

A few excellent restaurants situated in the town center are conveniently attached to hotels, including the Kelly Creek Hotel & Restaurant and Cahuita National Park Hotel & Restaurant.

100% Natural Coffee Shop (☎ 755 0317; ☯ 6am-8pm) There is no better place in Cahuita to greet the morning with a cup o' joe or unwind in the afternoon with a refreshing *jugo*. A few tapas are also on the menu. Rare is the individual who can walk by this place on the main drag without being lured over to the beckoning bar.

Café del Parquecito (☎ 775 0279; breakfast US$3-5; ☯ 6:30am-noon) Early risers come for the coffee, but breakfast lovers at any hour of the morning will delight in this menu. The specialty is the huge crepes, wrapped around fresh fruit or other fillings.

Miss Edith's (☎ 755 0248; mains US$7-12; ☯ 11am-10pm) As local people earn respect in the community, they are called Miss or Mister, followed by their first name – hence, Miss Edith. Miss Edith's is undoubtedly Cahuita's most famous restaurant, and deservedly so, for mouthwatering, cooked-to-order Caribbean cuisine. Reserve in advance so your dinner has time to simmer.

Restaurant La Fé (meals US$5-10; ☯ 7am-11pm) You can't miss this inviting spot on the main drag, draped in swinging oropendola nests. It's particularly atmospheric in the evening, when the open-air terrace is lit by candles. The specialty is anything in coconut sauce, from octopus to marlin to delectable shrimp, served up with a side of plantains.

Cha Cha Cha! (☎ 394 4153; mains US$6-9; ☯ noon-10pm Tue-Sun) In a corner veranda of an old blue-painted clapboard house, this attractive eatery offers recommended *cuisine del mundo*. Well-prepared dishes range from Jamaican jerk chicken to Tex-Mex cuisine. There are plenty of vegetarian options, including the 'zen salad' (mandarin oranges with basil, sprinkled with cashews and macadamia nuts). It's all savored against a background of world music and jazz.

Restaurant El Palenque Luisa (☎ 755 0400; dishes US$5-8) Tree-trunk beams, bamboo roof and plant-filled interior create quite the jungle decor in this inviting open-air restaurant. It's an ideal spot to feast on tasty vegetarian fare, as well as fish and meat dishes cooked Caribbean Creole style.

Roberto's Restaurant (☎ 755 0117; seafood dishes US$3-8; ☯ 7am-10pm) Owned by one of the top fishing guides in the region, you know the seafood is fresh. The restaurant uses organic ingredients and fresh produce whenever possible.

You can't really go wrong in Cahuita if you stop for lunch at one of the local *sodas*:

Soda Café Caribbean Flavor (mains US$2-5; ☯ 6am-9pm) Caribbean-style Tico standards, particularly fresh juices, and rice and beans.

Restaurant Típico Cahuita (mains US$4-8; seafood US$5-15; ☯ 8am-close) A spacious spot beneath a *palapa* (a palm-thatched umbrella) with a wide-ranging menu.

PLAYA NEGRA

Near Playa Negra, you can also head to El Cactus Bungalows y Pizzeria, the restaurant at Bluspirit and Restaurant Bananas at Cabinas Algebra.

Sobre Las Olas (☎ 755 0109; meals US$8-10; ☯ noon-10pm Wed-Mon) Cahuita's top option for waterfront dining. The Italian owners guarantee excellent homemade pasta and an impressively stocked wine cellar, while the location ensures the freshest of ingredients straight from the sea. Vegetarians will also find plenty to sate their appetites.

Chao's Paradise (☎ 755 0421; seafood mains US$6-10; ☯ 11am-close) It's worth the short beachside jaunt out of town to enjoy the catch of the day simmered in spicy Chao sauce. The open-air restaurant-bar also has a pool table and live reggae and calypso music some nights.

Reggae Restaurant (☎ 755 0515; mains US$4-9; ☯ 7-11am & noon-9pm) Exuding a friendly, laid-back vibe, this *soda* serves Caribbean-style standards, from inexpensive casados to the house specialty, shrimp in coconut milk. This place also has facilities for camping (per person US$3), plus some comfortable cabins (US$20 to US$30).

La Casa Creole (☎ 755 0035; mains US$7-20; ☯ 6-9pm Mon-Sat) Set in the tropical gardens of the Magellan Inn (see p476), this candlelit restaurant is perhaps Cahuita's finest dining. The French-fusion cuisine emphasizes seafood and Caribbean flavors. The house specialty is the shrimp Martinique (that's ginger and garlic sauce to make your mouth water). Reservations are required.

Drinking & Entertainment

Though low-key, Cahuita certainly has some fine spots for a few drinks or live music.

Beach House (☎ 369 4254; cariberen@yahoo.com) 'Eat, Drink and Go Surfing.' So implores Rennie Leone, owner of this ex-pat hangout. By day, the place rents surfboards; by night, it serves sandwiches (US$5), quesa-dillas (US$6) and cold beers – at the cozy bar or on the breezy terrace. Live calypso music plays Thursday through Saturday.

Coco's Bar (⊙4pm-midnight) You can't miss Coco's at the main intersection, painted in Rasta red, yellow and green. It embodies Cahuita's Caribbean atmosphere, so it comes as no surprise that it's famous for fruity rum concoctions and Friday 'reggae night.'

Ricky's Bar (☎755 0228; ⊙4pm-midnight or so) Opposite Coco's, Ricky's has a jungly vibe, outdoor seating and a nice dance floor. This place really gets hopping on Wednesday and Saturday nights, when live bands sometimes take the stage.

Along Playa Negra, stop by Chao's Paradise restaurant-bar or the bar at Jardín Tropical cabins.

Getting There & Away

Grayline (☎ 262 3681; www.graylinecostarica.com) runs a daily bus, departing at 11am to San José (US$27) and on to Arenal (US$38). All public buses arrive and depart from the terminal half a block southwest of Parque Central.

Puerto Limón/San José (Autotransportes Mepe) US$1/7, 1½/four hours, depart at 7:30am, 8:30am, 9:30am, 11:30am and 4:30pm, additional bus at 2pm on weekends.

Puerto Viejo de Talamanca/Bribrí/Sixaola US$1/2/3, 30 minutes/one hour/1½ hours, depart hourly from 7am to 9pm.

Getting Around

The best way to get around Cahuita – especially if you are staying out along Playa Negra – is by bicycle. In town, rent bikes at **Ciclo Safari** (☎ 755 0020; per hr/day US$1.50/8; ⊙7am-6pm). Near the Playa Negra, bikes are available at Centro Turistico Brigitte (see p471) for similar prices. Many lodges also provide bikes for their guests.

PARQUE NACIONAL CAHUITA

This small park – just 1067 hectares – is one of the more frequently visited national parks in Costa Rica. The reasons are simple: the nearby town of Cahuita provides attractive accommodations and easy access; more importantly, the white-sand beaches, coral reef and coastal rain forest are bursting with wildlife.

Declared a national park in 1978, Cahuita is typical of the entire coast in that it is very

humid, resulting in dense tropical foliage – mostly coconut palms and sea grapes. The area includes the swampy **Punta Cahuita**, which juts out into the sea between two stretches of sandy beach. Often flooded, the point is populated with cativo and mango trees, as well as green ibises, yellow-crowned night herons, boat-billed herons and the rare green-and-rufous kingfisher.

The dark Río Perezoso, or 'Sloth River,' bisects the Punta Cahuita (and sometimes prevents hiking between the ranger stations). This is the discharge for the swamp that covers the point.

Red land and fiddler crabs live along the beaches, attracting mammals like crab-eating raccoons and white-nosed coatis. White-faced capuchins, southern opossums and three-toed sloths also live in these parts. The mammal you are most likely to see (and hear) is the mantled howler monkey, which makes its presence known.

The coral reef represents another rich ecosystem that abounds with life. See the boxed text Under the Sea, p481.

Information

The **Kelly Creek ranger station** (☎ 755 0461; admission by donation; ⊙6am-5pm) is convenient to the town of Cahuita, while 1km down Hwy 32 takes you to the well-signed **Puerto Vargas ranger station** (☎ 755 0302; admission US$6; ⊙8am-4pm).

Technically, you do not have to pay the US$6 admission fee if you enter at Kelly Creek. This is the result of a local stir-up in the 1990s, when locals feared high park fees would deter the tourists. Keep in mind, however, that these fees provide important income for the park service. These tourist dollars support education about and maintenance and conservation of the national park, so it is important to pay the fee, or donate it, as the case may be.

Activities

HIKING

An easily navigable 7km **coastal trail** leads through the jungle from Kelly Creek to Puerto Vargas. At times the trail follows the beach; at other times hikers are 100m or so away from the sand. At the end of the first beach, Playa Blanca, hikers must ford the Río Perezoso. Inquire about river conditions before you set out: under

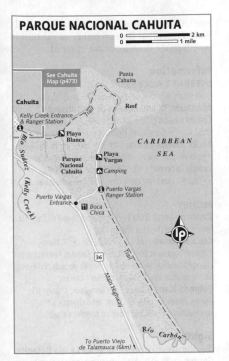

PARQUE NACIONAL CAHUITA

normal conditions, this river can be thigh-deep at high tide. During the rainy season, it is often too dangerous to cross.

The trail continues around Punta Cahuita to the long stretch of Playa Vargas. The trail ends at the southern tip of the reef, where it meets up with a road leading to the Puerto Vargas ranger station. From the ranger station, it is another 2km along a gravel road to the park entrance. From here, you can hike back to Cahuita along the coastal highway, or you can catch a ride going in either direction.

SWIMMING

Almost immediately upon entering the park, you'll see the 2km-long **Playa Blanca** stretching along a gently curving bay to the east. The first 500m of beach may be unsafe for swimming, but beyond that, waves are gentle. These conditions may change, so inquire at the ranger station before diving in. The rocky Punta Cahuita headland separates this beach from the next one, **Playa Vargas**. It is unwise to leave clothing or other belongings unattended when

you swim. Near the entrance, Mister Big J (p472) stores valuables in individual security boxes.

SNORKELING

Parque Nacional Cahuita contains one of the last living coral reefs in Costa Rica (see the boxed text Under the Sea, p481). The reef is accessible from the beach, but the best way to see the creatures under the sea is to hire a guide with a boat in Cahuita. If you prefer to walk, hike along the beach trail. After about 6km, you will come to a sandy stretch that is cut off from the coastline by a rocky headland of Punta Cahuita. The offshore coral reef represents Cahuita's best snorkeling.

In an attempt to protect the reef from further damage, snorkeling is permitted only with a licensed guide. Local guides include Mister Big J, Roberto and Willie (see p471). The going rate is US$15 to US$25 per person, but prices vary according to the size of your group and the mood of the guide. Cahuita Tours (p471) offers an all-day trip on a glass-bottom boat, which includes snorkeling and hiking (US$35 per person).

Snorkeling conditions vary greatly, depending on the weather and other factors. In general, the drier months in the highlands (from February to April) are best for snorkeling on the coast, as less runoff occurs in the rivers and there is less silting in the sea. Conditions are often cloudy at other times. Indeed, conditions are often cloudy, period.

Sleeping & Eating

Within the park, **camping** (per person US$3; **P**) is permitted at Playa Vargas, less than 1km from the Puerto Vargas ranger station. The limited facilities include cold outdoor showers, drinking water and pit latrines.

After the long, hot hike through the jungle, you may think you are hallucinating when you see the Italian restaurant beckoning at the end of the road. But **Boca Chica** (☎ 755 0415; meals US$6-8) is not a mirage, just a well-placed eatery, offering cold *jugos,* homemade pasta and fresh *mariscos* to hungry and tired trekkers coming out of the park. If you stop for lunch, they'll spot you the bus fare for your return all the way to Cahuita.

PUERTO VIEJO DE TALAMANCA

Puerto Viejo de Talamanca (not to be confused with Puerto Viejo de Sarapiquí in the northern lowlands) is a decidedly Caribbean concoction of perfect beaches, spectacular surfing and laid-back attitude, spiced up with the most happening music, nightlife and restaurant scene on the coast. It's touristy – and more and more expats are moving here every year. But if you can let go of getting in touch with 'the real Costa Rica' for a moment, you'll have a blast.

As throughout the southern Caribbean coast, the Afro-Caribbean presence is strong here: locals sometimes refer to the town by its patois name 'Walaba,' and coconut-scented odors and reggae music emanate from the doorways. With the influx of foreigners, however, you might hear German or French on the streets sooner than patois. Puerto Viejo's kitchens are now turning out fantastic fusion cuisine, incorporating influences from Mexico, Italy and China. Music lovers are mixing up their play lists with salsa, hip-hop and rock and roll. Some might claim the 'authentic' Caribbean flavor is diluted; but others argue it is enhanced.

'Downtown' Puerto Viejo is little more than one long paved road that follows the coastline. And that one long road is crowded with ice-cream parlors and surf shops and open-air bars, all exuding good music and good vibes. What makes Puerto Viejo what it is, however, are the miles and miles of beach stretching along the coast in both directions from the center. Playa Negra to the northwest and Salsa Brava, Playa Cocles and Punta Uvita to the southeast: this is what draws the surfers and sun-worshippers.

Puerto Viejo is most certainly a party town, but the road to Manzanillo is strewn with mellow bungalows and empty beaches. And if you would rather watch wildlife than engage in it, the Refugio Nacional de Vida Silvestre Gandoca-Manzanillo (p496) is a beautiful bike ride away.

Dangers & Annoyances

Do keep in mind that as tourism grows, a cottage industry of sketchy drug dealers and irritating touts is growing with it. Stay alert late at night, choose your own accommodations (and use the hotel safe!) and always remember that an ounce of caution is worth more than a pound of weed.

Information

INTERNET ACCESS

Internet access is expensive and slow.
Asociación Talamanqueña de Ecoturismo y Conservación (ATEC; ☎ 750 0191, 750 0398; per hr US$2.40; ☼ 8am-9pm) Painfully slow Internet access.
books librería y bazar (☎ 750 2005; per hr US$2.40; ☼ 9am-9pm) Ten machines with decent Internet speeds.
Jungle Internet (☎ 750 2003; per hr US$3.40; ☼ 8am-11pm) Fast computers plus free wireless access.

MONEY

Banco de Costa Rica (☼ 9am-4pm Mon-Fri) The ATM here works on the Plus system only.
Cabinas Almendras (☎ 750 0235; ☼ 7:30am-7:30pm) Stop in at the front desk at Cabinas Almendras to change Canadian and US dollars, British pounds and euros at 1% commission, 2.5% on traveler's checks.
Pulpería Manuel León (☼ 8am-8pm) Change US dollars and euros with 'El Chino,' who charges 1.5% commission on cash and more on traveler's checks.

Sights

To the west of town is **Finca La Isla Botanical Garden** (☎ 750 0046; www.greencoast.com/garden .htm; self-guided/guided tour US$2/5; ☼ 10am-4pm Fri-Mon), a working tropical farm where the owners have been growing local spices, tropical fruits and ornamental plants for more than a decade. Part of the farm is set aside as a botanical garden, which is also good for birding and wildlife observation (look for sloths and poison-dart frogs). The informative guided tour (in English) includes admission, fruit tasting and a glass of homemade juice to finish, or you can buy a booklet and take yourself on a self-guided tour.

West of Puerto Viejo, the **Jungles of Talamanca** is actually a small tropical nursery and cacao finca. This Bribrí family welcomes visitors to its home, where you can see cacao toasted over an open fire then hand ground into delicious chocolate or rich cocoa butter. For flavor, nutmeg, black pepper or cinnamon, all grown on-site, may be added. The resulting product is truly decadent – it's amazing that something so luscious comes from such humble origins. It's on the road to Bribrí; look for the sign just past the clinic.

CARIBBEAN COAST

UNDER THE SEA

The monkeys and other forest creatures are not the only wildlife attractions of Parque Nacional Cahuita. About 200m to 500m off Punta Cahuita is the largest living coral reef in Costa Rica (though it's very small compared to the huge barrier reef off Belize, for example). Corals are tiny, colonial, filter-feeding animals (cnidarians, or, more commonly, coelenterates) that deposit a calcium-carbonate skeleton as a substrate for the living colony. These skeletons build up over millennia to form the corals we see. The outside layers of the corals are alive, but, because they are filter feeders, they rely on the circulation of clean water and nutrients over their surface to remain so.

Since the opening up of the Caribbean coastal regions in the last couple of decades, increased logging (and the consequent lack of trees on mountainous slopes) has led to increased erosion. The loosened soil is washed into gullies, then streams and rivers, and eventually the sea. By the time they reach the ocean, the eroded soils are no more than minute mud particles – just the right size to clog up the filter-feeding cnidarians. The clogged animals die and the living reef dies along with them.

After deforestation, the land is often given over to plantations of bananas or other fruit. These are sprayed with pesticides which, in turn, are washed out to sea. These chemicals also cause damage to creatures that pass large quantities of water through their filtering apparatus to extract the nutrients they need.

The 1991 earthquake, which was centered near the Caribbean coast, also had a damaging effect on the reef. The shoreline was raised by more than a meter, exposing and killing parts of the coral. Nevertheless, some of the reef has survived and remains the most significant in Costa Rica.

It is important never to step on or touch corals. A reef is not just a bunch of colorful rocks – it is a living habitat. Coral reefs provide a solid surface for animals such as sponges and anemones to grow on, and a shelter for a vast community of fish and other organisms – octopi, crabs, algae, bryozoans and a host of others. Some 35 species of coral have been identified in this reef, along with 140 species of mollusk (snails, chitons, shellfish and octopi), 44 species of crustacean (lobsters, crabs, shrimps and barnacles), 128 species of seaweed and 123 species of fish. Many of these seemingly insignificant species represent important links in various food chains. Thus logging has the potential to cause much greater and unforeseen damage than simply destroying the rain forest.

Activities
SURFING

Outside the reef in front of Stanford's Restaurant Caribe, the famed **Salsa Brava** is known as the country's best wave (see the boxed text, p484). The reef here is shallow, so if you lose it, you're liable to smash yourself and your board on the reef; this is not for beginners. Salsa Brava offers both rights and lefts, although the right is usually faster. Conditions are best with an easterly swell.

Almost as impressive are the less-damaging waves at **Playa Cocles**, about 2km east of town (an area known as 'Beach Break,' which is an accurate description). Lefts and rights both break close to the steep beach. Conditions are usually best early in the day, before the wind picks up.

The waves are generally at their peak here from December to March, and there is a miniseason for surfing in June and July. From late March to May, and in September and October, the sea is at its calmest.

There are several surf schools around town, more or less independent operations charging US$30 to US$35 for two hours of lessons. Note that Puerto Viejo isn't the best spot for true beginners to pick up the sport; the Pacific coast has smaller, more user-friendly waves. Folks with some experience will benefit from local advice before tackling the big breaks. It's not a bad deal as boards rent for about US$10 to US$15 per day at several places around town.

Surf schools around town:

Aventuras Bravas (☎ 750 2000, 849 7600) Rents boards and gives lessons.

Cut Bak (☎ 366 9222, 885 9688) Also a popular place for surfers to pitch a tent (per person US$3, rent-a-tent US$4) and sleep on the beach.

Salsa Brava Surf School (☎ 750 0689; salsabravasurfshop@hotmail.com) Adjacent to the Hotel Puerto Viejo.

CARIBBEAN COAST

PUERTO VIEJO DE TALAMANCA

INFORMATION
Asociación Talamanqueña de
  Ecoturismo y Conservación
  (ATEC).................................1 B2
Banco de Costa Rica..................2 A3
books librería y bazaar................3 A3
Jungle Internet..........................4 B3
Laundry Los Ticos...............(see 40)
Lavandería Fash & Book Trade....5 E4
Pulpería Manuel León.................6 A2

SIGHTS & ACTIVITIES
Aventuras Bravas........................7 E3
Cut Bak..............................(see 28)
Exploradores Outdoors................8 B3
Finca La Isla Botanical Garden......9 B4
Juppy & Tino Adventures...........10 A2
Puerto Viejo Tours....................11 A3
Reef Runner Divers....................12 A2
Salsa Brava Surf School.............13 B2
Terra Venturas.........................14 A3

SLEEPING
Agapi....................................15 F3
Bungalows Calalú.....................16 F3
Cabinas Almendras...................17 A2
Cabinas David.........................18 B3
Cabinas Guaraná......................19 B3
Cabinas Jacaranda....................20 B3
Cabinas Tropical......................21 C3
Camping Mis Helena..................22 E4
Casa Verde.............................23 B2
Cashew Hill Jungle Lodge...........24 E4
Chimuri Jungle Lodge................25 A4
Coco Loco Lodge......................26 D4
Coconut Grove.........................27 F3
Cut Bak................................28 C4
El Pizote Lodge........................29 F3
Escape Caribeño......................30 F3
Hotel Los Sueños......................31 D4
Hotel Maritza..........................32 A2
Hotel Puerto Viejo....................33 B3
Hotel Pura Vida.......................34 B4
Jordan's Jacuzzi Suites..............35 C3
Kaya's Place............................36 D4
Las Olas Beach........................37 B3
Lizard King Resort.....................38 F3

Monte Sol..............................39 F3
Rocking J's.............................40 F3

EATING
Amimodo...............................41 F3
Bread & Chocolate....................42 B3
Café El Rico............................43 B2
Café Pizzería Coral...................44 B3
Café Viejo..............................45 B3
Chile Rojo..............................46 B2
Clapboard House
  (homemade ice cream)............47 B2
El Loco Natural.........................48 A3
EZ-Times...............................49 B2
Heidi's Café....................(see 27)
Lechería Las Lapas....................50 A3
Lotus Garden..................(see 35)
Miss Lidia's Place......................51 C3
Organic Market.........................52 A3
Pan Pay.................................53 A2
Patagonia Steak House..............54 A3
Restaurant Salsa Brava...............55 C3
Soda Mis Helena................(see 22)
Soda Miss Sam........................56 C3

Soda Tamara...........................57 B2
Stanford's Restaurant Caribe.......58 E3
Super el Buen Precio.................59 A3
Trattoria da Cesare...................60 D4
Veronica's Place.......................61 E3

DRINKING
Baba Yaga.............................62 B2
El Dorado..............................63 B3
Mi Bar..................................64 B3

ENTERTAINMENT
Café Hot Rocks........................65 B2
Johnny's Place.........................66 A2
Sunset Bar.............................67 A3

TRANSPORT
Bus Stop...............................68 A3
Dragon Scooter.......................69 A3
Los Ticos......................(see 40)
Peter's Bikes on the Beach..........70 B2
Tienda Marcos.........................71 A3

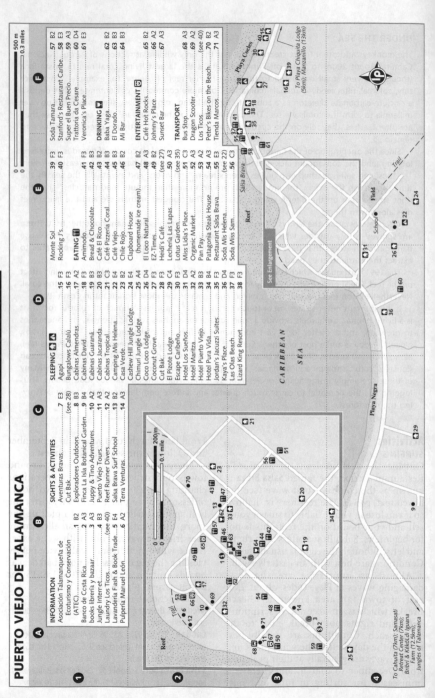

To Cahuita (7km); Samasati
Retreat Center (7km);
Bribri & KéköLdi Iguana
Farm (12.5km);
Jungles of Talamanca

To Playa Chiquita Lodge
(5km); Manzanillo (13km)

SWIMMING

The entire southern Caribbean coast – from Cahuita all the way south to Punta Mona – is lined with unbelievably beautiful beaches. Just northwest of town, **Playa Negra** offers the area's safest swimming, as well as excellent body boarding.

But southeast of town is where you will find the region's gems. This is where the jungle meets the sea; stretches of smooth sand (quite slender at high tide) are caressed by waves perfect for swimming and body surfing, all fringed with the requisite swaying coconut palms. Toucans, monkeys and sloths frolic in these treetops, making it all the more exotic. So take your pick: **Playa Cocles** (2km east of town), **Playa Chiquita** (4km east), **Punta Uva** (6km east) and **Manzanillo** (see p497) all offer picture-perfect beach paradise.

Of course, conditions vary and they can be dangerous. Riptides and undertows can be deadly. It is always wise to inquire at your hotel or with local tour operators about current conditions.

SNORKELING

The waters from Cahuita to Manzanillo are protected by Costa Rica's only two living reef systems, which form a naturally protected sanctuary, home to some 35 species of coral and more than 400 species of fish, not to mention dolphins, sharks and, occasionally, whales; see the boxed text Under the Sea, p481. Generally, underwater visibility is best when the sea is calm, ie when surfing is bad, snorkeling is good.

Just south of **Punta Uva**, in front of the Arrecife restaurant, is a decent spot for snorkeling, when conditions are calm. The reef is very close to the shore and features some stunning examples of reindeer coral, sheet coral and lettuce coral. The reef at **Manzanillo** (p497) is also easily accessible for snorkeling. Rent equipment at Juppy & Tino Adventures (p484) in Puerto Viejo or Aquamor Talamanca Adventures (p496) in Manzanillo. Most of the tour companies offer snorkeling trips for about US$45 per person.

DIVING

Divers in the southern Caribbean will discover upwards of 20 dive sites, from the coral gardens in shallow waters to deeper sites with amazing underwater vertical walls. Literally hundreds of species of fish

BUS STOP MADNESS

Expect to be greeted at the bus terminal in Puerto Viejo by a crew of local solicitors offering sweet deals on hotel rooms. Some are honest people representing their businesses, while others will say just about anything to get you to the hotel that pays them the highest commission. You might be told that, shockingly, your chosen hotel for the night is teeming with rats and scabies, or, coincidentally, your new friend is a representative from that very place and, sadly, it's overbooked. Don't believe everything you hear. And if you have any doubts about your hotel, simply ask to see a room before agreeing to stay.

swim around here, including angelfish, parrotfish, triggerfish, sharks and different species of jack and snapper.

The only dive operation in Puerto Viejo is **Reef Runner Divers** (☎ 750 0480; www.reefrunnerdivers.net; 1-/2-tank dive US$55/80; ☒ 7am-8pm). If you are not certified, you can use a temporary license for US$55, or spring for the full PADI certification for US$325. Aquamor Talamanca Adventures (p496), in Manzanillo, also coordinates diving trips.

HIKING

The immediate vicinity of Puerto Viejo is not prime hiking territory: the proximity of the Parque Nacional Cahuita (p478) and the Refugio Nacional de Vida Silvestre Gandoca-Manzanillo (p497) means that most trekkers will head to these protected areas to look for toucans and sloths. Getting to the indigenous reserves often requires a pretty serious trek, usually with a guide (see Tours, below).

Still, the edge of town is the edge of the jungle. So, if you are up for some independent exploring, you can discover your own destination. Pack a picnic and follow the town's most southerly road, which goes past the soccer field and the Cashew Hill Jungle Lodge. Once out of the village, the road dwindles to a path and leads into the hills.

Tours

Tour operators generally require a minimum of two people on any excursion. Rates are per person, but they may be discounted for larger groups.

SALSA BRAVA

The biggest break in Costa Rica, for expert surfers only and dangerous even then, Salsa Brava is named for the heaping helping of 'sauce' it serves up on the sharp, shallow reef, continually collecting its debt of fun in broken skin, boards and bones. There are a couple of take-off points: newbies waiting around to catch the popular North Peak should keep in mind that there are plenty of people in this town who gave up perks like mom's cooking and Wal-Mart just to surf this wave regularly. Don't get in their way.

In a sense, it was the Salsa Brava that swept Puerto Viejo into the relaxed limelight it enjoys today. Although discrimination against the primarily black residents of the southern Caribbean was officially outlawed in 1949, luxuries like paved roads, electricity and telephone lines came more slowly here than elsewhere in Costa Rica. Most tourists – nationals and foreigners – still spend most of their beach time on the more accessible and developed Pacific coast.

But surfers are a special breed. Even 30 years ago, they would not be dissuaded by the bumpy bus rides and rickety canoes that hauled them and their boards from San José on the week-long trip (assuming that the bus didn't get stuck in the mud for a night or two) to this once-remote outpost. Bemused locals first opened their homes, then basic cabinas and *sodas,* to accommodate those rugged souls on their quest.

In the wake of the wave riders came other intrepid explorers, eager to see those storied sunrises over perfect coastlines and monster curls; residents, who were by this time surfing with the best of them, happily developed a grassroots tourist infrastructure to keep everyone happy – *pura vida,* baby.

And though today's visitors enjoy Internet access, fine dining and a paved route that's shortened travel time by several orders of magnitude, the magnificence of Salsa Brava and its attendant waves still flood Puerto Viejo with tanned troopers on a mission.

So if you find yourself wondering what stirred up this marvelous mix of Caribbean culture and tourist trappings amid all this natural beauty, grab a beer at the Stanford and watch the waves roll in.

Asociación Talamanqueña de Ecoturismo y Conservación (ATEC; ☎ 750 0191, 750 0398; www .greencoast.com/atec.htm; half-day US$20-25, day trip US$35-55, overnight US$55-70; ☽ 8am-9pm) This nonprofit organization promotes environmentally sensitive local tourism by working with local guides and supporting local communities. Hiking, horseback riding and canoeing trips involve birding, visiting indigenous reserves and visiting local farms.

Exploradores Outdoors (☎ 750 0641; www.explora doresoutdoors.com) Besides the signature one-day trip down the Río Pacuare (US$95), this outfit offers a canopy tour, a glass-bottom boat trip to Parque Nacional Cahuita and a guided hike to Punta Mona.

Juppy & Tino Adventures (☎ 750 0621; juppytino adventures@yahoo.com) Specializes in kayak tours in the Gandoca-Manzanillo refuge or Talamanca Indigenous Reserve (US$60). Or you can rent a kayak and paddle yourself around the reef.

Puerto Viejo Tours (☎ 829 8216; www.ptoviejotours .com; opposite bus stop; ☽ 7am-7pm Tue-Sun) A good source of information about local real estate. Tours include fishing in a dugout canoe (six hours, US$100), as well as the typical hiking, horseback riding and snorkeling.

Terra Venturas (☎ 750 0750/489; www.terraventuras .com; ☽ 8am-7pm) Offers overnights in Tortuguero (US$120), hiking (US$38) and snorkeling (US$55) in Cahuita, white-water rafting (US$95), plus its very own 18-platform, 2.1km-long canopy tour (US$50), with a Tarzan swing.

Festivals & Events

The **South Caribbean Music & Arts Festival** (☎ 750 0062; www.playachiquitalodge.com) fills weekends in March and April with eclectic offerings, all home-grown on the Caribbean coast. Calypso to jazz, reggae to Celtic and classical artists perform; dancing troupes take the stage with Jamaican and African flair; and Costa Rican–produced films are shown. This is a family event, with many programs for kids. Dates for the festival vary but are usually weekends in March and April (for about five weeks before Easter). Most performances are held at the Playa Chiquita Lodge.

Sleeping

BUDGET

Cold water is the norm in budget places, but you won't miss the hot water. Rockin'

J's (see the boxed text Author's Choice, p486) is the author's selection for budget accommodation.

Hotel Puerto Viejo (☎ 750 0620; r per person with/without bathroom US$10/7, d with air-con US$25; P ❌ ▣) 'No shoes, no shirt, no problem,' dude, and that goes for the clean, functional rooms with hot showers and the shared kitchen. Boards can be hung in the reception area, where talk revolves around surfing big waves, a topic about which owner Kurt Van Dyke is a respected local expert.

Chimuri Jungle Lodge (☎ 750 0119; www.green coast.com/chimurilodge.htm; dm/d/q US$10/30/46; P) On the edge of the KéköLdi reserve, this is about as private and peaceful as it gets in Puerto Viejo. Four bungalows mimic the indigenous architecture, with thatched roofs, mosquito nets and private balconies, while one dormitory sleeps eight. All units share a communal kitchen. Follow the 2km walking trail to explore the jungly grounds, which attract an amazing array of birds and wildlife.

Hotel Maritza (☎ 750 0003; per person with shared bathroom US$15, s/d with private bathroom US$25/35; P ❌) This motel-style place has 14 modern rooms with porches and balconies that face the parking lot. What they lack in style, they make up for in comfort, with private hot-water bathrooms and air-conditioning. The building facing the street has older wood-paneled rooms that are dark but cozy. It's not the most efficient service you will ever encounter, but it's friendly.

Cabinas Jacaranda (☎ 750 0069; www.cabinasjaca randa.com; s/d/tr/q US$15/25/30/40; P) In a beautiful blooming garden woven with mosaic walkways, this colorful spot proves that personal touches and attention to detail are what constitutes luxury. Magic inhabits each uniquely decorated room, with fanciful stenciled designs on the walls, tropical hardwood furniture and mosaic-tiled, hot-water bathrooms. The rooms all have access to a security box – use it!

Hotel Pura Vida (☎ 750 0002; www.hotel-puravida .com in German; s/d/tr with shared bathroom US$15/20/25, with private bathroom US$20/25/30) This place is getting an overhaul, thanks to new German owners. They started with the beautiful, breezy terrace, which has been spruced up with polished-wood floors and furniture, and surrounded with gardens. Comfortable, airy rooms feature high ceilings and big

windows; four have brand-new bathrooms with stone floors, elaborate tile work and solar-heated showers.

Hotel Los Sueños (☎ 750 0369; www.costaricaguide .info/lossuenos.htm; d US$18-20; P) This homey, hospitable Swiss-run spot is in a quiet location east of the main drag. The clean, comfortable rooms are simple, with wood floors, fans and mosquito nets. Catch a glimpse of the sea from the upstairs porch, or just enjoy the overgrown gardens. Bathrooms are shared; showers are hot. New kitchen facilities are also available.

Monte Sol (☎ 750 0098; www.montesol.net in German; d US$20-30; P ▣) Away from the noise of the main road, this German-run place has a lovely, laid-back atmosphere. Simple, stylish cabins have stucco walls and tile bathrooms, with a welcoming hammock-hung terrace. An awesome jungle house, sleeping up to eight, is available for weekly or monthly rental.

Coconut Grove (☎ 750 0093; s/d with shared bathroom US$20/25, with private bathroom US$25/35; P) Attentive and efficient, Heidi oversees this two-story complex just east of town. Wood-beamed rooms – painted in tropical colors – have mosquito nets, fans and hammocks overlooking the street. Your first stop in the morning should be downstairs at Heidi's Cafe (open 7am to noon), serving pancakes, eggs and terrific smoothies.

Las Olas Beach (☎ 750 0424; masterservicios@yahoo .com; tents per person US$6, d/q US$25/40; P) Watch the big waves roll in from the porch of your rustic room or from a sandy, covered tent site. This place is perhaps overpriced, considering how basic the facilities are, but you can't beat the location. A friendly open-air *soda* is attached.

Camping Mis Helena (☎ 750 0580; camping US$10, rent-a-tent US$4) Campers who are not interested in the surfer party scene should seek out this family-oriented site off the main drag. It offers covered campsites in the likely event of rain. The on-site Soda Mis Helena (mains US$2 to US$4, open 7am to 6pm Tuesday to Sunday) serves inexpensive Caribbean-Tico standards and daily soup specials made over a wood-burning stove. Cool off with a glass of spicy home-made ginger ale.

Several hotels offer camping, including Rocking J's and Las Olas Beach. There's also camping in Manzanillo (see p494).

AUTHOR'S CHOICE

Budget

Rocking J's (☎ 750 0657; www.rockingjs.com; pitch-a-tent/rent-a-tent US$4/6, hang-a-hammock/rent-a-hammock US$4/5, dm/d/tr/q US$7/20/30/50, treehouse US$60; **P**) Walk into this backpackers' mecca and you are presented with a free slushy – how's that for an icy welcome? This place has everything a budget traveler needs, including lockers, kitchen facilities, beachside bonfires and all-you-can-eat bananas. Accommodations fit all budgets, from the clean but crowded 'hammock hotel' to the fully equipped, canopy-level treehouse, dumbwaiter included. The most unusual perk at Rocking J's is the art supplies that are available to guests with artistic urges: the resulting paintings and mosaics are incredible. J's also rents surfboards (per day US$15), bikes (per day US$5) and other fun stuff. A word of warning: nonsmokers may feel out of place.

Midrange

La Costa de Papito (☎ 750 0704; www.lacostadepapito.com; Playa Cocles; d US$42-60, additional person US$10; **P**) Relax in Rasta luxury in sculpture-studded jungle grounds. Hardwood bungalows vary in size, but they all feature artistically tiled showers, hand-carved furniture and private porches. For an extra US$6 you can have breakfast delivered to your table (or hammock) on the porch – nice. Set amid these gorgeous grounds is the thoroughly decadent **Pure Jungle Spa** (☎ 750 0536; www.purejunglspa.com), which offers a one-hour facial/massage for US$50/60. Indulge in the signature chocolate facial or a 'Rain forest Immersion' massage, using locally grown, hand-mixed natural products.

Top End

Tree House (☎ 750 0706; www.costaricatreehouse.com; Punta Uva; tree or beach house/beach ste US$144/245, additional person US$35; **P**) The 'tree house' is only one of three ecologically sound and architecturally amazing options on this property, but it *is* our favorite. This bilevel beauty is constructed around a living sangrillo tree, whose roots and branches accentuate the gorgeous hardwood decor. The open-air, canopy-level accommodations are only for the adventurous! If you prefer to remain closer to the ground – or closer to the ocean – the beautiful 'beach house' is for you. With equally enticing (but nonphotosynthesizing) hardwood construction, the beach house has a wide veranda with a spectacular Caribbean view. The newest option is the fantasy-filled 'beach suite,' which features (among other perks) a roof terrace and an amazing Jacuzzi á la Gaudí. All three houses offer total seclusion, courtesy of the jungle setting, as well as easy access to a pristine stretch of beach. Prices are based on double occupancy; weekly rates are available.

MIDRANGE

Midrange hotels offer private bathrooms with hot water, unless otherwise indicated. La Costa de Papito, in Playa Cocles, is the our pick for midrange lodging (see the boxed text Author's Choice, above).

Kaya's Place (☎ 750 0690; www.kayasplace.com; s/d/tr/q with shared bathroom US$22/31/41/50, with private bathroom from US$29/40/52/64, s/d/tr garden rooms US$46/58/70) This rustic lodge on Playa Negra has been completely renovated and now features inviting lounge areas on two floors, furnished with hammocks and couches and ocean views. The guestrooms facing the ocean are a bit dark and dreary; airy, light-filled rooms facing the garden are more pleasant and more private (thus the price difference). Lackadaisical service reflects the supersweet and easygoing manner of new owners JT and Sarah.

Cashew Hill Jungle Lodge (☎ 750 0256; www.cashewhilllodge.co.cr; s/d/tr with shared bathroom US$23/35/46, with private bathroom US$29/40/52, with private patio US$46/58/70; **P**) Set on a hectare of land in the far southeast corner of town, this lodge is surrounded by jungly gardens. The brightly painted bungalows feature lots of hardwood and whimsical decor, with simple, sturdy beds draped in mosquito nets. Two rooms share kitchen facilities – useful for families – while the pricier rooms boast ocean views in the distance. Daily yoga classes are offered at the studio on-site.

Cabinas Guaraná (☎ 750 0244; www.hotelguarana .com; s/d/tr US$25/35; P ♿) A lot of attention has gone into the details in these delightful cabinas, set amid tropical gardens. Painted wood furniture, colorful *molas* (indigenous tapestries made with layers of colorful cloth cut into patterns depicting local flora and fauna) and other local handicrafts decorate each room, while a private terrace with a woven hammock are just outside. On the practical side, all rooms have access to a communal kitchen. Grab a drink and climb up to a perch in the treehouse for a spectacular view of the sun setting over the Caribbean Sea.

Coco Loco Lodge (☎ 750 0281; www.cocolocolodge .de; s/d/tr/q US$30/35/40/45, with kitchen US$40/45/50/55; P ❷) Eight spacious bungalows dot these well-manicured lawns. Choose between quaint thatch-roofed cabañas or newer (more expensive and more spacious) stone bungalows. They all feature fans suspended from hardwood ceilings, handsome wood furniture, modern tiled bathrooms and private porches with the requisite hammocks.

Bungalows Calalú (☎ 750 0042; www.bungalow scalalu.com; s/d/tr/q US$26/34/42/50, with kitchen US$40/40/50/60; P ❷) You hear a lot of talk about 'tropical paradise' in Puerto Viejo, but Calalú has actually created it. This hidden gem is set in gardens blooming with exotic flora like heliconia and bromeliads. A rock-formation swimming pool is fed by a gushing waterfall. Breakfast is served at the 'butterfly balcony' with hundreds of the beauties fluttering around. The bungalows themselves are attractive but simple, with tiled floors and wood-beam ceilings, as well as private porches overlooking the gardens.

Casa Verde (☎ /50 0015; www.cabinascasaverde.com; s/d standard US$32/36, s/d/tr/q deluxe US$60/76/96/110; P ❷) Tiled walkways wind through gardens showcasing local flora to 14 sparkling rooms, each with spacious interiors decorated with local artwork and dark stained wood furniture, and private terraces with hammocks. The new swimming pool and hot tub are straight out of *Fantasy Island*. Bikes are available (US$6 a day) and breakfast is served daily except Monday.

Agapi (☎ 750 0446; www.agpisite.com; r/ste from US$35/65; P) In a prime seaside location east of town, this sweet spot is run by a Greek-Tico couple. All the accommoda-

tions are individually decorated, ranging from simple, colorful single rooms to more-spacious multiroom suites with kitchenettes. The pricier rooms have private balconies with ocean views, but all guests have access to lovely beachfront grounds that are sprinkled with gazebos and towering palm trees.

Cabinas Tropical (☎ 750 0283; www.cabinastropi cal.com; s/d US$30/35, tr with kitchen US$45; P ❌ ❷) Ten spacious rooms – decorated with varnished wood and shiny tiles – surround a primly landscaped garden on the edge of town. The comfortable quarters are just part of the appeal: the biologist owner leads jungle hikes for birders from dawn until about 11am (per person US$40, three minimum, breakfast provided).

Cabinas David (☎ 750 0542; cabinas_david@yahoo .com; d US$32; P) East of town, this row of concrete cabins is not – on first impression – the most welcoming place. The nondescript architecture and bars on the windows may deter travelers in search of aesthetic appeal, but their simple sturdy construction and comfortable interiors offer decent value for the money. Breakfast, included in the price, is served on the shady terrace.

Escape Caribeño (☎ 750 0103; www.escapecari beno.com; s/d/tr US$55/65/75, air-con extra US$10; P ❷) Take your pick from bungalows facing the beach or others surrounded by lush tropical gardens, about 500m east of town. They range in size, but all 14 are equipped with refrigerators and fans and – most importantly – hammocks hanging on the porches.

Cabinas Almendras (☎ 750 0235/46; flchwg@racsa .co.cr; d US$60; P ❷) These comfortable cabinas lack the charm of their competition – and that goes for the plain, pastel-painted rooms with views of the parking lot, as well as the disinterested staff at the front desk. Nonetheless, amenities like satellite TV and kitchenettes have their appeal. And the location in the center of town is prime.

El Pizote Lodge (☎ 750 0227; d/q standard US$66/82, bungalows US$82/115; P ❌ ❷) On a quiet back road 1km west of town, this comfortably rustic lodge is a 10-minute walk from town, but just a few steps from the waves lapping at Playa Negra. Spacious but simple standard rooms have shared bathrooms, while the nicer wooden bungalows offer more privacy.

TOP END

The Tree House, at Punta Uva, is our selection for top-end accommodations (see the boxed text Author's Choice, p486).

Jordan's Jacuzzi Suites (☎ 750 0232; jordansjacuzzi suites@hotmail.com; d US$60-90; P ⊠ ⊒) Luxury suites feature king-size, four-poster beds, rich varnished wood floors and the namesake in-room whirlpools. Set in tropical gardens, the place has a distinctive Asian elegance. To complete the mood, the on-site Lotus Garden restaurant (open 7am to 11pm) offers an impressive menu of pan-Asian cuisine, including an all-you-can-eat sushi special for US$14.

Lizard King Resort (☎ 750 0614; lizardkingresort@ net.com; d US$80; ⊒) This slick new resort features 15 spacious hardwood cabins overlooking a sweet swimming pool. Rates include a hearty breakfast. If you can't afford these cushy quarters, stop by the laid-back lounge, upstairs, for Mexican food, movie night or – bonus – happy hour.

Samasati Retreat Center (☎ 750 0315, in the USA 800-563 9643; www.samasati.com; s/d with shared bathroom US$94/150, s/d/tr with private bathroom US$162/230/282) Set on a lush hillside 8km north of Puerto Viejo, this well-built, attractive complex affords sweeping views of the coast and the village far below. Nine private bungalows have cool, wraparound screened walls, while the guesthouse has simple rooms with wood interiors and single beds. Tasty vegetarian meals (included) are served buffet-style on a wooden terrace with ocean views. Daily yoga classes (US$12) are open to all guests.

Eating

Cooking up the most impressive restaurant scene on the coast, Puerto Viejo has the cure for casado overkill. Besides the listings here, see also the Lotus Garden at Jordon's Jacuzzi Suites and Heidi's Cafe at Coconut Grove accommodations.

CAFÉS

Pan Pay (☎ 750 0081; light meals US$2-4; ⏱ 7am-7pm) This beachside spot is excellent for strong coffee and freshly baked goods, not to mention delicious sandwiches that are a perfect picnic for a long hike or a beach day. This is a popular spot for tourists and Ticos to meet, post announcements and exchange books.

Bread & Chocolate (☎ 830 3223; breakfast US$2-4, lunch US$4-8; ⏱ 6:30am-2:30pm Wed-Sun) This classy café invites early-risers to sit on the spacious, covered porch, sip fresh-brewed coffee and peruse the Tico Times. Breakfast favorites include oatmeal like your mom used to make; big, fluffy omelets; and the classic crunchy granola and yogurt.

Café El Rico (⏱ 8am-4pm) Dark, rich coffee – iced, even – is served alongside light breakfasts and lunches. Bonus: you earn yourself a free cappuccino by doing your laundry (US$5 for 4kg) on-site. Bikes are rented here, too.

Café Pizzería Coral (☎ 750 0051; breakfast US$2-3, pizza US$4-6; ⏱ 7am-noon & 5:30-9:30pm Tue-Sun) Beloved for healthy breakfasts and homemade wholemeal bread, this old stand-by now serves excellent pizza, including lots of vegetarian options.

You've got two options for dessert: homemade ice cream or homemade ice cream. Opposite the Hotel Puerto Viejo, a darling old woman sells creamy concoctions out of her clapboard house (US$0.30). Described by one reader as 'frozen bliss,' this is kind of like a milkshake in a bag, and it hits the spot. For a more traditional helado, the **Lechería Las Lapas** (⏱ 11am-11pm) is in a little kiosk fronting the beach, near the bus stop. The creamy, cool stuff comes in a wide variety of tropical flavors (the macadamia nut is highly recommended), and there is also arroz con leche (rice pudding).

BUDGET

Veronica's Place (☎ 750 0132; meals US$3-5; ⏱ 7am-9pm Sun-Thu, 7am-4:30pm Fri) This vegetarian café behind Supermercado El Pueblo is a delightful find, and not only for nonmeat-eaters. Veronica offers a fresh, healthy interpretation of Caribbean food, focusing on fresh fruits and vegetables. This is the only place in town where you'll find veggie favorites like soy burgers and soy milk.

Soda Tamara (☎ 750 0148; breakfast US$2-4, seafood dinners US$6-10; ⏱ 7am-10pm) With its signature red, green and yellow paint job, this is a popular spot to grab breakfast overlooking the street and watch the village wake up. During the day seafood is the specialty, but don't skip the coconut bread.

EZ-Times (☎ 750 0663; mains US$5-9; ⏱ 10-2:30am) The reggae music and groovy vibe lure in hungry beach bums for pizza, pasta and salads. The outdoor terrace is strewn with colorful cushions, making it a comfy place to sit back and enjoy the fine food, not to mention the live music on Friday nights.

If you can't get enough of the Caribbean flavors, **Soda Miss Sam** (☎ 750 0108; mains US$2-6) and **Miss Lidia's Place** (☎ 750 0598; mains US$2-6) are the local favorites for rice and beans and spicy coconut sauce. Both of the ladies have been around for years, pleasing the palates and satisfying the stomachs of locals and tourists alike.

The best spot for groceries is **Super el Buen Precio** (🕑 6:30am-8:30pm). Don't miss the weekly **Organic Market** (🕑 6am-6pm Sat), when area vendors and growers sell snacks typical of the region.

MIDRANGE & TOP END

El Loco Natural (☎ 750 0263; meals US$8-12; 🕑 6-11pm) This upstairs open-air music café features creative fusion cuisine, combining elements of Italian, Asian and Caribbean cooking. Tropical gazpacho soup and Caribbean fish tacos are some of the delicacies you can enjoy while watching the street scene below. There is live music on Thursday and Saturday, and local artwork on display every night of the week.

Chile Rojo (☎ 750 0025; mains US$8-12; 🕑 noon-10pm) If you are yearning for something spicy, head to this popular spot for excellent Thai and Middle Eastern fare. It's a tiny place (formerly a garage, apparently). But one whiff of the curry – or whatever daily special is on the menu – and you'll know it's worth whatever wait it takes.

Patagonia Steak House (☎ 390 5677; meals US$10-15; 🕑 5-11pm) This friendly, family-run restaurant is a real-deal Argentinean-owned steak house. There is not much going on in the basic interior – just plain wood tables and chairs – and there's an open kitchen, where you can see (and smell) the steaks sizzling on the grill. Washed down with a delicious red from Mendoza, it's a meal you won't forget.

Stanford's Restaurant Caribe (☎ 750 0016; mains US$5-14; 🕑 11am-11pm) Folks who have been around for decades marvel at how little this community landmark has changed – the beer is still cold, the seafood is still spectacular and the views remain absolutely perfect.

Restaurant Salsa Brava (☎ 750 0241; meals US$10-15; 🕑 11am-11pm) This well-recommended hot spot specializes in seafood and open-grill cooking in an intimate atmosphere. The ever-popular on-site 'juice joint' is an oasis for thirsty surfers and beachcombers.

Café Viejo (☎ 750 0817; mains US$6-15; 🕑 11am-close) Elegant and a little bit pricey, this fine Italian restaurant gets high marks for the excellently dressed fresh pastas and fancy cocktails. The upscale, romantic ambience makes it a definite date destination if you've got someone to impress. But it's also an excellent people-watching spot if you are on your own.

Amimodo (☎ 750 0257; meals US$10-15; 🕑 11am-10pm) The beachside tropical garden setting here is among Puerto Viejo's most romantic spots. The menu is a fusion of Mediterranean, Caribbean and 'exotica,' which basically means 'delicious.' Pasta, pizza and fresh seafood.

Trattoria da Cesare (☎ 750 0161; meals US$10-15; 🕑 5:30-10pm Thu-Tue) West of town, this lovely trattoria features wonderful homemade pastas with fresh cheeses and sauces made from locally grown produce.

Drinking

Restaurants often metamorphose into rollicking bar scenes after the tables are cleared. Try Soda Tamara for some people-watching over a beer, or Café Viejo for being seen over a fancy cocktail. If you want a cool ocean breeze with your frosty mug, stop by the bar at Stanford's during happy hour.

Baba Yaga (☎ 388 4359) Puerto Viejo's trendiest place for cold drinks and hot music. Come on Tuesday for ladies' night, Sunday for reggae night or any day for happy hour.

El Dorado (☎ 750 0604; 🕑 11am-close) This thatch-roofed restaurant has one of the quieter and more relaxed bars in town, though it picks up at happy hour. Grab a burger and beer and catch a breeze on the outdoor terrace; or sidle up to the town's only pool table.

Mi Bar, near Jungle Internet, is basically a row of brightly painted seats topped with equally colorful characters, all fronting a narrow bar. It's a fine spot to sip a cold brew and watch the town's goings-on.

Entertainment

As you might expect from such a hip town, there is plenty to do after the sun goes down. So put away that surfboard and fluff those dreadlocks – Puerto Viejo is an entirely different sort of paradise after dark.

CINEMA

Café Hot Rocks (☎ 750 0525; meals US$3-8; ⊗ 11-2:30am) In a big red tent in the center of town, this place shows fine flicks for free most evenings and also hosts live (and often new) calypso, reggae and rock bands. Recommended for fun, not for food.

Cine Playa Cocles (☎ 750 0128, 750 0507; Playa Cocles; admission free, minimum purchase US$4.50; ⊗ screenings 7pm Mon-Fri, 5:30pm Sat & Sun) At Cabinas El Tesoro (see opposite), this popular big screen shows a cool selection of camp, cult and classic movies plus plenty of Hollywood blockbusters. Weekend showings are specially for kids.

LIVE MUSIC & DANCING

Sunset Bar (☎ 750 0025; ⊗ noon-close) Closed at the time of research, but locals insist that this local favorite will be open to host the weekly open-mike night – a long-standing Wednesday-night tradition in Puerto Viejo (we lost track of how many weeks it has been, but somebody is counting).

El Loco Natural (☎ 750 0263; ⊗ 6-11pm) This music café (see p489) hosts mellow live music on Thursday and Saturday at 8:30pm. The bar is otherwise a low-key inviting place to catch a breeze and enjoy a tropical cocktail.

Johnny's Place A Puerto Viejo institution. DJs spin reggae, hip-hop and salsa, and patrons light beach bonfires outside.

Getting There & Away

Grayline (☎ 262 3681; www.graylinecostarica.com) runs a daily bus departing at 11am to San José (US$27) and on to Arenal (US$38). Call for a reservation so the bus will pick you up at your hotel. All public buses arrive and depart from the terminal half a block southwest of Parque Central.

Bribrí/Sixaola US$1/2, 30 minutes/1½ hours, depart at 6:30am, 8:30am, 9:30am, 10:30am; 12:30pm, 1:30pm, 2:30pm, 3:30pm, 5:30pm, 6:30pm and 7:30pm.

Cahuita/Puerto Limón US$1/2, 30 minutes/1½ hours, depart every hour on the half-hour from 5:30am to 7:30pm.

Manzanillo US$1.50, 30 minutes, depart at 7:30am, 11:45am, 4:30pm and 7:30pm.

San José US$7.50, five hours, depart at 7am, 9am, 11am and 4pm.

Getting Around

Bicycle is a fine way to get around town, and pedaling out to Manzanillo or to the other beaches east of Puerto Viejo is one of the highlights of this corner of Costa Rica. You'll find bicycle rentals all over town (including at many lodges):

Dragon Scooter (☎ 750 0728; per 4hr from US$15; ⊗ 8am-late) If you prefer your wheels motorized.

Los Ticos (☎ 750 0611; ⊗ 7am-6pm) Next to Rocking J's.

Peter's Bikes on the Beach (per day US$5) Opposite Stanford's Restaurant.

Tienda Marcos (☎ 750 0303; per day US$3; ⊗ 7am-6pm)

PUERTO VIEJO TO MANZANILLO

The 13km road heading east from Puerto Viejo was paved for the first time in 2003, dramatically shortening the time it takes to drive or bike past the sandy, driftwood-strewn beaches and rocky points, through the small communities of Punta Uva and Manzanillo, through sections of Reserva Indígena Cocles/KéköLdi and Refugio Nacional de Vida Silvestre Gandoca-Manzanillo.

The road is still considered the property of folks without internal combustion, and drivers should be particularly careful at night as cyclists and pedestrians make their way between the different bars, restaurants and lodges. Hitching is quite common on this stretch, which does not mean it is risk-free.

This route more or less follows the shoreline, but you usually can't see the beach from the road, once past Playa Cocles. The vegetation is thick – coconut palms and sea grapes protect the coast, while tropical rain forest covers the lowland hills further inland.

A wide variety of places to stay and eat is spread out along this road, with a few clusters in the community of Cocles and at Punta Uva. The paving has inspired increased interest in this real estate, with new resorts and restaurants opening every year. Luckily for local monkeys, wild boars and other wildlife, the southern stretch of road is within the Gandoca-Manzanillo refuge, which has strict rules for development.

It's probably just as easy to head into Puerto Viejo to take care of business, but **Playa Chiquita Services** (☎ 750 0575; Playa Chiquita; ⊗ 9am-8pm), across from Miraflores Lodge, has a public phone, Internet access (US$2 for 30 minutes) and a small café. Buses heading from Puerto Viejo to Manzanillo will drop you at any of these places along the way.

Sights

MARIPOSARIO PUNTA UVA

This **butterfly farm** (☎ 750 0086; Punta Uva; adult/child US$5/free; ☑ 8am-4pm) is less of a tourist attraction and more of a breeding center. Some 70 species of butterfly are bred annually, including four species they claim exist in captivity nowhere else in the world: Prepona, Filaetinias, Mintorio and Inmanius. What you'll see depends on the time of year. Lydia, the biologist in charge of the project, can lead interesting guided tours in Spanish by request.

CRAZY MONKEY CANOPY TOUR

Affiliated with Punta Uva's Almonds & Corals Lodge (see p494), this is the only **canopy tour** (☎ 759 9057/56, in San José 272 2024; www.almondsandcorals.com; US$40; ☑ 8am-2pm) in the south Caribbean. Set in the heart of Refugio Nacional de Vida Silvestre Gandoca-Manzanillo, this tour starts in the rain forest and ends on the beach, offering plenty of opportunities for wildlife-spotting and adrenaline-rushing.

Activities

The region's biggest draws involve surf, sand, wildlife-watching and attempts to get a decent tan between downpours. Playa Cocles is known for it's great **surfing** and organized lifeguard system, which helps offset the dangers of the frequent riptides, while Punta Uva features the best and safest beaches for **swimming**. At the north end of the Punta Uva beach, a footpath leads out to the point, with some interesting rock formations and a wonderful lookout along the way.

While the best **hiking** opportunities are in the wildlife refuge south of Manzanillo (p497), the stretch of road between Puerto Viejo and Manzanillo is largely undeveloped and so offers plenty of forest and beach trails to explore, too. While cars and buses ply this main road, any turnoff between Playa Chiquita and Manzanillo is bound to be free of traffic and full of birdlife and other creatures. The road to El Toucan

Lodge, for example, is little more than a wide dirt path winding through dense rain forest and rife with wildlife.

Sleeping & Eating

PLAYA COCLES

Known for big waves, this stretch begins about 1.5km south of Puerto Viejo. The following places are listed from west to east and the accommodations have hot water, unless otherwise noted.

Echo Books (desserts US$1-3; ☑ 11am-6pm Fri-Tue; ☒) Admittedly, it seems a strange place for a bookstore, but resident ex-pats and tourists alike are overjoyed at the opening of this new coffee and bookshop – call it a Caribbean-style Borders. Serving coffee and desserts in a deliciously cool, air-conditioned spot, this place also has thousands (really, thousands) of new and used books.

Cabinas El Tesoro (☎ 750 0128; www.puertoviejo.net; dm/s/d/tr US$9/21/28/41; P ☒ ☐) Accommodations to suit every budget, from the basic Beach Break hostel with shared bathroom and bunk beds, to the fully loaded 'executive suites' (US$68) with air-con and TV. El Tesoro offers a list of perks a mile long, from free coffee and free Internet access to community kitchens. Evening entertainment is also included: movies every night and a fun mobile disco on Saturdays.

La Isla Inn (☎ 750 0109; islainn@racsa.co.cr; d with/without air-con US$93/64; P ☒) You can't miss the magical mosaic welcoming guests into La Isla, one of Playa Cocles' upscale options. The elegant lodging features sparkling new bathrooms and unobstructed ocean views. The rooms are furnished with exotic handmade wood pieces, created from the slightly curved outer boards that are discarded during lumber processing. These rates include breakfast, but they are still on the high side.

Totem (☎ 750 0758; www.totemsite.com; d US$82, extra person US$15, air-con extra US$10; P ☒) This Cocles newcomer offers unique modern suites decorated in jewel tones, with terracotta floors and bamboo furniture. This is the Caribbean with a contemporary edge. By day there's the on-site Totem Beach Bar; by night, the Italian restaurant Osteria (mains US$7 to US$10) serves up fresh-baked bread, homemade pasta and fresh seafood prepared by a talented European chef.

Cariblue (☎ 750 0518; www.cariblue.com; d US$99, bungalows US$116, extra person US$16; P ⚡) Set in lovely gardens (plants and trees are labeled for the botanically curious), this complex has nine standard cabins with fans and high ceilings that keep them airy, quiet and cool. Four spacious hardwood bungalows – each decorated with mosaics – have thatched roofs and hammock-hung porches. Prices include breakfast.

Cabinas Garibaldi (☎ 750 0101; r US$20; P) Many surfers stay at this place, which is among the cheapest along this stretch. The concrete row of reasonably clean cabinas share kitchen facilities and a porch with sea views. The waves are right across the street.

Azania Bungalows (☎ 750 0540; www.azania-costa rica.com; s/d with breakfast US$76/87; P ⚡) Spacious but dark thatch-roofed bungalows are hidden away in these landscaped jungle grounds. The details here are delectable, including woven bedspreads, elegant bathrooms and wide-plank hardwood floors. A loft allows sleeping space for four people; rates include breakfast. The new free-form swimming pool, fringed with greenery and topped with a hot tub, adds to the exotic ambience.

El Tucán Jungle Lodge (☎ 750 0026; www.eltucan junglelodge.com; s/d/tr US$25/30/35) You may wonder if you missed your turn, as you follow the signs into the depths of the jungle in search of this little lodge on the banks of the Caño Negro. It's only 1km off the road, but it feels miles from anywhere. Four brand-new wood cabins have balconies that are perfect for bird-watching in the treetops. You are guaranteed to see at least one howler monkey: the orphan, Rubio, who is being raised by the lodge's loving owners.

Hotel Yaré (☎ 750 0106; www.hotelyare.com; s/d/ tw US$30/41/58, bungalows US$70; P) Somewhere between Playa Cocles, Playa Chiquita and Wonderland is Hotel Yaré. Vine-strewn covered walkways weave through a marshy setting, connecting fanciful citrus-colored cabañas. Inside, the dark rooms are not as stylish as some of your other options, but they are fully equipped (some with kitchens). At night, the air is filled with the music of frogs, which drifts across the complex to the pleasant on-site restaurant.

El Living (snacks US$2-4, pizza US$4-6; ⊙ 11:30am-3pm & 5:30-9:30pm Thu-Sun) This quaint yellow house is the perfect place to take a break from the beach and get some lunch. You'll find fresh-brewed coffee, crispy-crust pizza and other home-baked goodies, plus fresh juice and smoothies.

La Finca Chica (☎ 750 0643; www.fincachica.com; d/q US$50/100) Three hand-built Caribbean-style casas (with kitchens) are scattered across these jungle grounds. The smallest – sleeping two – is a sweet little bungalow with one bedroom; two houses – sleeping four to six people – have multiple bedrooms and living space. Ask about long-term rates.

La Pecora Nera (☎ 750 0490; mains US$10-15; ⊙ 11am-close, closed Mon in low season) Arguably the region's finest dining, this recommended spot is marvelously free of pretensions, as you savor delicacies like starfruit-and-shrimp carpaccio, fresh pasta dishes, steak and seafood – all perfectly prepared by the amicable Italian chef Ilario. No menu makes an appearance; the chef or a server will consult about what you'd like and suggest an Italian red to accompany it.

PLAYA CHIQUITA

It isn't exactly clear where Playa Cocles ends and Playa Chiquita begins, but conventional wisdom applies the name to a series of beaches 4km to 6km east of Puerto Viejo. The following are listed in order from west to east.

Villas del Caribe (☎ 750 0202, in San José 233 2200; www.villascaribe.net; standard with/without air-con US$92/80, ste with/without air-con US$104/92, villa US$115; P ✂ ⚡) Stressing function over form, these 20 motel-style beachside villas offer a comfortable, convenient lodging option. The pricier rooms include kitchens and private terraces with sea views, but even the standard lodgings have king-size beds.

Aguas Claras (☎ 750 0131; www.aguasclaras-cr .com; 1-/2-/3-room cottages US$70/130/220; P 🖥) Five cozy cottages are distinguished by their color of the rainbow, each one brighter than the next. They offer fully equipped kitchens and easy access to the beach. The delightful gazebo out front – this one sea blue with yellow trim – is Miss Holly's Kitchen (open 8am to 4pm), which serves delicious breakfast, lunch and snacks on the breezy porch.

Cabinas Slothclub (☎ 750 0358; d with kitchen US$30, bungalows US$58; P) Five clean wood cabins have great views, beach access and a snorkeling reef out front. This is the best and only budget option along Playa Chiquita. These little places often attract long-term renters so call in advance.

Cabinas Yemanya (☎ 750 0110; www.yemanya.tk; q US$60-80) The most rustic option along this stretch of the coast is this funky Dutch-run outpost, on a strip of land between the road and the beach. Little trails run through the wild unkempt jungle right up to the door of three basic wood cabins on stilts. The larger ones have an outdoor kitchen and hot showers, while the smaller one is a cold-water affair.

Jungle Love Garden Café (☎ 750 0356; mains US$6-8; 🕒 1-9:30pm Tue-Sat & 3-9:30pm Sun) It's hard to resist this bohemian, Caribbean, cosmopolitan café. The eclectic menu features fusion masterpieces like mango chicken with cilantro (US$7) and Tokyo tuna with tamarind and ginger sauce (US$8). The garden setting is always inviting, but it's particularly romantic after sunset.

Kashá (☎ 750 0205, in the USA 800-521 5200; www.costarica-hotelkasha.com; s/d/q US$97/105/163; P 🐾) These stucco bungalows are pretty basic, for what you are paying, though semiprivate porches and custom-designed furniture are nice perks. Most guests come here on all-inclusive packages. Breakfast is included in the rates quoted; you'll surely want to return for dinner at Magic Ginger (mains US$5 to US$10, open 6pm to 10pm Tuesday to Sunday), the only French restaurant (featuring a chef straight from *la belle France!*) on the Caribbean coast.

Miraflores Lodge (☎ 750 0038; www.miraflores lodge.com; d from US$40) Ten rooms with refrigerator, hot water, hammocks and nice decor are tucked away on beautiful grounds. Each one is different and prices vary accordingly. Owner Pamela Carpenter is an expert on local botany and medicinal plants. Breakfast (included) consists of seasonal fruits grown on the grounds.

Bar y Restaurante Elena Brown (☎ 750 0265; mains US$4-7; 🕒 8am-11pm) The culinary-gifted Brown family scores high marks once again with Elena's famed whole red snapper, shrimp dishes and big breakfasts. The rice and beans get raves. The bar is festive and features a big TV and occasionally live music.

Playa Chiquita Lodge (☎ 750 0408; www.playa chiquitalodge.com; s/d US$52/70; P) After spending an afternoon at the namesake Playa Chiquita, wind your way through the jungly grounds and stop along the way to rinse off in the funky shower in the roots of a huge sangrillo tree, before retiring to your cozy bungalow. Rooms are simple but elegant, with white stone walls, ceiling fans, big bathrooms and private hammock-hung terraces. Rates include breakfast.

Shawandha Lodge (☎ 750 0018; www.shawandha lodge.com; d incl breakfast US$116; P 🐾) This upscale lodge has 10 large, airy bungalows, all with fabulous bathroom mosaics – a feature that seems to represent a minor cultural movement along this stretch of coast. The elegant French-Caribbean restaurant (mains US$5 to US$14, open 7am to 9:30pm) adds *flambé panache* and Provençale flavorings to Caribbean classics.

PUNTA UVA

Punta Uva is known for the region's most swimmable beaches, each lovelier than the next. Don't miss the turnoff to the point, about 7km east of Puerto Viejo. The following places are listed in order from west to east.

Itaitá Villas (☎ 750 0414; labvaco@racsa.co.cr; d US$47; P) Huge, no-nonsense rooms offer festive furnishings and kitchenettes, not to mention the private porches, excellent for catching a coastal breeze. Jungle and beach setting, all in one.

Selvin's Bar (mains US$4-12; 🕒 8am-8pm Wed-Sun) Selvin is a member of the extensive Brown family, noted for their charm and unusual eyes, which have attracted both romantic and scientific attention. His place is considered one of the region's best, specializing in shrimp, lobster and chicken *caribeño*.

Albergue Walaba (☎ 750 0147; per person from US$12) This very basic spot has colorful rooms – some dorms and some with private bathroom, but all heavenly hippy havens. The place is tucked away in its own personal jungle. Kitchen facilities, friendly, funky management and groovy vibe make it a popular spot for budget travelers.

Casa Viva (☎ 750 0089; www.puntauva.net; d per night/week US$175/500; P 🐾) Enormous, elegantly constructed and fully furnished hardwood houses, each with tiled shower, kitchen, two bedrooms and wrap-around veranda, are set on property that fronts the beach. Hang out on your hammock and spy on the sloths, howler monkeys, hummingbirds and toucans that frequent these tropical gardens.

Chawax (☎ 750 0219) This friendly spot has good music, original food and a cool vibe. Open for breakfast, lunch and – most importantly – happy hour.

Ranchito Beach Restaurant (☎ 759 9048; mains US$3-8; ☻ 10am-6pm) Fronting a fine, palm-lined swimming beach, this mellow out-post features a thatch-roofed outdoor bar and a few romantic little tables scattered about beneath their own personal *palapas*. Fruity cocktails, pizzas and seafood are happily served to folks in swimsuits and sandy feet.

Cabinas & Marisquería Arrecife (☎ 759 9200; q US$50; ☻ 7am-9pm) This breezy beachside bar and seafood restaurant now operates eight comfortable cabins. This is an excellent deal if you can fill the beds. Fans suspended from high ceilings lend the place an open airy atmosphere. Balconies provide round-the-clock amazing ocean views. You can also rent kayaks here and spend the day paddling around the point. Turn off the main road to Manzanillo about 7km east of Puerto Viejo.

Cabinas Angela (☎ 759 9092; r per person US$10) If you are counting your colones but you still want to be right next to the beach, Angela's got the place for you. It could use some maintenance, to say the least, but Angela keeps the cabinas adequately clean and some of them have kitchen facilities. Did we mention it's right next to the beach? Take the turnoff to Punta Uva.

Almonds & Corals Lodge (☎ 759 9057/56, in San José 272 2024; www.almondsandcorals.com; s/d/tr US$100/150/200; ℗ ᗺ) These 'campsites' are actually huge, fully furnished canvas tents with hardwood floors, big beds draped in mosquito nets and hot-water bathrooms nearby. Set in the middle of the wild-life refuge, it offers all the adventure of camping – including the nighttime serenade of insects and frogs, and the wake-up call from resident howler monkeys – without any of the discomfort. Rates include break-fast and dinner, served family-style in the main lodge.

MANZANILLO

The idyllic little village of Manzanillo has long been a destination off the beaten track. Until 2003 the 13km road from Puerto

Viejo de Talamanca was a rutted, bumpy affair that could take 45 minutes by car or bus. Today, a paved road has cut drive time down to 15 minutes; even better, cycling the gorgeous stretch of perfect, palm-lined beaches is now a relatively smooth option.

Though some worry that the easier access will funnel too many tourists in from Puerto Viejo, this region remains among the most pristine on the coast, thanks to ecologically minded locals and the 1985 establishment of the Refugio Nacional de Vida Silvestre Gandoca-Manzanillo, which actually encompasses the village and imposes strict regulations on further development of the region.

The pristine stretch of sandy white beach – protected by a rocky headland – is the focal point of the village. Most of Manzanillo's activity takes place right here, including sunning, snorkeling and surfing (see p497). A few simple cabinas and *sodas* are sprinkled along the dusty streets that run parallel to the beach. Beyond that, it's just trees and monkeys.

Wildlife, not nightlife, is the main attraction on this end of the road, where folks wake up early to take advantage of the fog-shrouded beauty of the morning, while those in Puerto Viejo are still rocking out. (Though Manzanillo does have its moments, courtesy of Maxi's.) Beaches are pristine and postcard perfect, but note that the stretch from the Almonds & Coral Lodge all the way to Punta Mona has potentially dangerous riptides. Swimmers are cautioned to inquire locally about conditions before diving in.

The **Casa de Guías** (☎ 759 9064) provides Internet access (per hour US$3), camping facilities (per person US$8) and local tours.

Sleeping & Eating

Most of the facilities for sleeping and eating are concentrated in the village of Manzanillo, with a few additional options scattered along the road to Punta Uva. The following hotels have hot water, unless otherwise noted, and are listed from east to west.

Maxi's Cabinas (☎ 759 9042; deluxe/basic q US$35/15; ℗) This family-owned landmark close to the entrance of the park has two sets of cabinas: the older portion with rustic, cold-water, rather ramshackle (but clean and cozy) rooms; the newer, much nicer rooms with TV, hot water and refrigerator, set back a bit further.

Cabinas Something Different (☎ 759 9014/97; d/tr/q US$30/35/45; **P**) In a quiet setting one block off the beach, these quaint cabinas are named for local fauna. So, in theory, you could spot a sloth from your porch perch in the 'Sloth.' In reality, the private terraces face the parking lot, so this scenario is unlikely, but it's still a pleasant spot.

Pangea B&B (☎ 759 9204; r per person incl breakfast US$35; **P**) Tucked into a corner of the wildlife refuge, this sweet spot has only two rustic rooms that are completely secluded. The wood cabins are equipped with mosquito nets and ceiling fans, and surrounded by extravagant gardens. The included breakfast features organic produce (grown on-site).

Cabinas Las Veraneras (☎ 759 9050; s/d with fan US$16/26; **P**) About 100m off the main drag, these 13 simple cabinas smell of fresh paint and disinfectant. They are all equipped with televisions and hot water. The pleasant *soda* (breakfast US$2, other meals US$4 to US$8, open 7am to 9pm), serves Caribbean and Tico standards.

Cabinas Manzanillo (☎ 759 9033, 839 8386; d US$20) The ever-helpful Sandra Castrillo and Pablo Bustamante have eight brand-new cabinas at the west end of town. All the rooms have fresh coats of pastel-colored paint, hardworking ceiling fans and spacious bathrooms. Other facilities include bicycle rental, laundry and a recommended restaurant (seafood mains US$4 to US$8, open 11am).

Congo Bongo (☎ 759 9016; mvleevwenzegueld@wxs .nl; d/q US$75/120, per week US$450/720; **P**) On the road between Manzanillo and Punta Uva, four beautiful houses are totally secluded, surrounded by a reclaimed chocolate plantation (now dense forest). They offer fully equipped kitchens and plenty of living space, including open-air terraces and strategically placed hammocks that are perfect for spying on the wildlife. The hardwood construction blends seamlessly with the surroundings, especially the thatch-roofed Bribrí 'Indian rancho.' A network of trails leads through the six hectares of grounds to the beautiful beach.

El Colibrí Lodge (☎ 759 9036; www.elcolibrilodge .com; d/tr US$75/85; **P**) Designed with romance in mind, six bright and comfortable rooms open onto a terrace surrounded by gardens alive with interesting insects and colorful birds. Breakfast is included, served on the terrace or in the privacy of your room. A 300m trail winds through the rain forest to the beach.

CHICKEN OF THE TREE

As the Caribbean coast heats up each February and March, plump pregnant green iguanas make ready to lay their eggs, anticipating a new generation of young lizards to rule the jungle canopy. At the same time, local kids eager for a real treat set out with slingshots, hoping to bring a tasty 'chicken of the tree' to the family table. Although hunting iguanas is now federally forbidden (except for indigenous folks), some residents believe that they are still legally entitled to harvest one iguana each year. The results of these traditional hunts have been devastating.

According to Edsart Besier, a Dutch conservationist who founded **Iguanaverde** (☎ 750 0706; www.iguanaverde.com; guided tour US$8/5; ☽ by appointment) in 2005, there are only between 500 and 2000 green iguanas left in the Gandoca-Manzanillo reserve – less than a quarter of a stable population. The species is found from Northern Mexico down into South America, but is becoming increasingly rare throughout the range. Climate change and loss of habitat, along with barbecues, have probably contributed to the crisis.

Iguanaverde, which began collecting eggs and endangered lizards in cooperation with the federal ministry (Minae), now boasts an 800-sq-meter enclosure stocked with the trees and plants iguanas enjoy in the wild. Besier has been raising and releasing the camouflaged critters into the protected refuge, often with the help of local schoolchildren who are in turn educated about the iguanas' plight. Bessier, who has largely funded the project out of his own pocket, offers supporters the chance to 'adopt an iguana' for US$15 (entitling you to a certificate and email updates on the project).

To visit the refuge, take the first entrance on the right after the Punta Uva turnoff. Be sure to call in advance to arrange your visit.

Maxi's Restaurant (mains US$2-3, seafood US$4-10; ☻ 6am-close) Maxi's Cabinas' on-site restaurant features inexpensive red snapper casados and extravagant fresh lobster served by weight. It's all topped off with good mixed drinks, local color and occasional live music, plus it's a fine spot to ask around about trail conditions and local guides.

Soda Miskito (casados US$3; ☻ 7am-9pm) Wood furniture, Indian lamps and lots of greenery and bamboo adorn the terrace of this friendly *soda*. Place your order for a home-cooked casado and sit back and relax, because this place operates on Caribbean time.

Getting There & Away

The most rewarding way to get to and from Manzanillo is to bike along the 13km road. It is paved (but it's not the smoothest ride you will ever take) and not heavily trafficked. In Manzanillo, you can rent bikes at Cabinas Manzanillo (per day US$6).

Buses to Manzanillo depart from Puerto Viejo (US$1.50, 30 minutes) at 7:30am, 11:45am, 4:30pm and 7:30pm. They return from Manzanillo to Puerto Viejo at 5am, 8:15am, 12:45pm and 5:15pm, departing from the Sodita La Playa.

REFUGIO NACIONAL DE VIDA SILVESTRE GANDOCA-MANZANILLO

This refuge (called Regama for short) protects nearly 70% of the southern Caribbean coast, extending from Manzanillo southeast to the Panama border. It encompasses 5013 hectares of land plus 4436 hectares of sea, making this the ultimate in surf-and-turf exploration.

The park was created with special provisions for folks already living here, and the dry (well, drier) land portion encompasses various habitats including farmland. This was once a productive cocoa-growing region, but after a devastating blight swept through, the monoculture was replaced by a patchwork of fincas, ranches and encroaching jungle.

The peaceful, pristine stretch of sandy white beach is one of the area's main attractions. It's the center of village life in Manzanillo, and stretches for miles in either direction – from Punta Uva in the west to Punta Mona in the east. Just off the coast, the colorful coral reef comprises almost 5 sq km, providing a nutrient-rich habitat for lobster, sea fans and long-spined urchins.

Besides the farmland and the marine areas, the wildlife refuge is mostly rain forest. Cativo trees form the canopy, while there are many heliconia in the undergrowth. A huge 400-hectare swamp – known as **Pantano Punta Mona** – provides a haven for waterfowl, as well as the country's most extensive collection of holillo palms and sajo trees. Beyond Punta Mona, protecting a natural oyster bank, is the only red mangrove swamp in Caribbean Costa Rica. In the nearby Río Gandoca estuary there is a spawning ground for Atlantic tarpon, and caimans and manatees have been sighted.

The variety of vegetation and the remote location of the refuge attract many tropical birds; sightings of the rare harpy eagle have been recorded here. Other birds to look out for include the red-lored parrot, the red-capped manikin and the chestnut-mandibled toucan, among hundreds of others. The area is also known for incredible raptor migrations, with more than a million birds flying overhead in the fall.

This southeastern corner of Costa Rica is widely considered one of the most scenic spots in the country. Hopefully, this will not change as a result of an ongoing dispute about the status of the wildlife refuge. The federal ministry (Minae) and the local municipality are struggling over who has the right and responsibility to administer the refuge – an issue that is currently hung up in a drawn-out court case. In the meantime, nobody seems to be taking the right or the responsibility very seriously, resulting in a lack of signage, no official park entrance and no entrance fee.

Information

Aquamor Talamanca Adventures (☎ 759 0612; www.greencoast.com/aquamor.htm) An excellent source of general information about the refuge (particularly if you don't speak much Spanish), with an informative display of articles and tips about enjoying the park and reef, as well as the many conservation programs on the coast.

Casa de Guías (☎ 759 9064) Prominently placed opposite the Minae office, this operation offers Internet access (per hour US$3), as well as camping facilities (per person US$8) and local tours.

Minae (☎ 759 9100; ☻ 8am-noon & 1-4pm) In the green wooden house as you enter town. Offers maps of the refuge and trails. An excellent book of photos featuring local flora and fauna, including the folks who live here, with commentary in Spanish and English, is *Refugío Nacional de Vida Silvestre Gandoca-Manzanillo* by Juan José Pucci, available locally and online.

Activities

HIKING

The trails within the wildlife refuge are not marked, but they are well traveled and easy enough to follow, should you wish to explore independently. However, readers have reported armed robberies in the depths of the reserve, so it is advisable to hire a guide, or at least avoid hiking alone.

There is a coastal trail leading 5.5km from Manzanillo to **Punta Mona**. From the east end of Manzanillo, follow the dirt road until it turns into a path and continue along the coastline all the way. This hike is spectacularly beautiful and rewards hikers with amazing scenery, as well as excellent (and safe) swimming and snorkeling at the end.

Another more difficult 9km trail leaves from just west of Manzanillo and skirts the southern edges of the Pantano Punta Mona, continuing to the small community of **Gandoca**. Again, this trail is fairly easy to follow, but a guide is recommended for enhancing your experience and your knowledge of local flora and fauna. In any case, be sure to pick up the Instituto Geografico Nacional map of the wildlife refuge (available at the Minae office) before you set out.

SNORKELING & DIVING

The undersea portion of the park cradles one of two living coral reefs in the country. Comprising five different types of coral, the reefs begin in about 1m of water and extend 5km offshore to a barrier reef that local fishers have long relied on and researchers have only recently discovered. This colorful undersea world is home to some 400 species of fish and crustaceans. **Punta Mona** is a popular destination for snorkeling, though it's a bit of a trek so you may wish to hire a boat (see p498). Otherwise, you can snorkel right offshore at **Manzanillo** at the eastern end of the beach (the riptide can be dangerous here; be sure to inquire about conditions).

As at Punta Uva and in Cahuita, conditions vary widely, and clarity can be adversely affected by weather changes. Visit the excellent **coral reef information center** at Aquamore Talamanca Adventures (see opposite), where you can also rent snorkeling equipment (per day US$8) or organize dive excursions.

KAYAKING

If you prefer to stay dry, you can explore the wildlife refuge in a kayak, also available from Aquamore Talamanca Adventures (per hour US$8). Paddle out to the reef, or head up the **Quebrada Home Wark**, in the west of the village, or the tiny **Simeon Creek**, at the east end of the village.

SPORTFISHING

Manzanillo does not have the same high-falutin facilities that many fishers expect, but it does have the same fish-filled waters that attract them to places like Barra del Colorado, Parismina and Cahuita. So if you don't mind more rustic accommodations, the waters off the coast of Manzanillo are filled with tarpon, sailfish, tuna, snook, wahoo, grouper, jacks, barracuda and even blue marlin – all waiting for your hook, line and sinker. **Los Cielos Charters** (☎ 827 4834; www.loscieloscharters.com; half/full-day charters from US$300/500) organizes fishing trips, as does the manager at Pangea B&B in Manzanillo.

DOLPHIN OBSERVATION

In 1997 a group of local guides in Manzanillo identified tucuxi dolphins, a little-known species previously not found in Costa Rica, and began to observe their interactions with the bottlenose dolphins. Meanwhile, a third species – the Atlantic spotted dolphin – is also common in this area. This unprecedented activity has attracted the attention of marine biologists and conservationists, who are following these animals with great interest.

The **Talamanca Dolphin Foundation** (☎ 759 0715/612; www.dolphinlink.org), housed at Aquamore Talamanca Adventures, is dedicated to the study and preservation of local dolphins through outreach programs. It offers daily dolphin-observation outings, as well as a four-day, all-inclusive tour (US$380 per person).

TURTLE-WATCHING

Marine turtles, especially leatherbacks but also green, hawksbill and loggerheads, all endangered, nest on the beaches between

Punta Mona and Río Sixaola. Leatherbacks nest from March to July, with a peak in April and May. Local conservation efforts are under way to protect these nesting grounds – the growth in the human population of the area has led to increased theft of turtle eggs and contributed to the declining local population.

During turtle season, no flashlights, beach fires or camping are allowed on the beach. All tourists must be accompanied by a local guide (see below) to minimize the disturbance to the nesting turtles.

The **Asociación Nacional de Asuntos Indígenas** (ANAI; ☎ 759 9100, in San José 277 7549; www .anaicr.org; Gandoca; registration US$30, camping US$7-15, homestays US$15, cabins US$30), or National Association of Indigenous Affairs, is a grassroots organization that works with locals to protect the sea turtles. Volunteers assist efforts to collect nesting and size data, patrol beaches and move eggs that are in danger of being destroyed by high tides or predation. Rates include training, accommodations and meals; minimum commitment seven days.

Tours

Sure, you can explore the refuge on your own (if you've made it to Manzanillo, you already are). But without a guide you'll probably be missing out on the refuge's incredible diversity of medicinal plants, exotic birds and earthbound animals. Most guides charge US$20 to US$30 per person for a four- to five-hour trek, depending on the size of the group. Ask around at Maxi's (p496) or at the Casa de Guías (below).

Recommended local guides include **Florentino Grenald** (☎ 759 9043, 841 2732), who used to serve as the reserve's administrator; **Ricky Alric** (☎ 759 9020), a specialist in birding and medicinal plants; and **Abel Bustamonte** (☎ 759 9043). A local boat captain, Willie Burton, will take you boating and snorkeling from Manzanillo.

Aquamor Talamanca Adventures (☎ 759 9012; www.greencoast.com/aquamor.htm; 1-/2-tank dives US$45/60, PADI certification US$300) This unique outfit is devoted as much to conservation as recreation. Besides diving packages, also leads kayak and snorkeling tours (per person US$40) and rents equipment for independent use.

Asociación Talamanqueña de Ecoturismo y Conservación (ATEC; ☎ 750 0191, 750 0398; www .greencoast.com/atec.htm) This community organization, based in Puerto Viejo de Talamanca offers a variety of tours into the refuge, including day and overnight trips on foot, horseback or by boat.

Casa de Guías (☎ 759 9064) A much-needed though poorly organized initiative to hook up travelers with local guides. Offers guided hikes (four hours US$25), snorkeling (US$25), turtle-watching (US$100) and sportfishing (US$150).

Sleeping & Eating

Many options for sleeping and eating are in the village of Manzanillo, which is contained within the Refugio Nacional de Vida Silvestre Gandoca-Manzanillo and is the easiest access point.

Punta Mona (www.puntamona.org; dm US$30, transportation US$10; 🖳) Five kilometers south of

---

BRIBRÍ & CABÉCAR

At least two indigenous groups occupied the territory on the Caribbean side of the country from pre-Columbian times. The Bribrí tended to inhabit lowland areas, while the Cabécar made their home high in the Cordillera de Talamanca. Incidentally, this choice of homeland is no coincidence, as even today the Bribrí tend to be more acculturated, while the Cabécar remain more isolated.

Over the last century many of these folks migrated across the mountain range to the Pacific side. But many stayed on the coast, intermingling with Jamaican immigrants, and even seeking employment in the banana industry. The most significant populations of Bribrí and Cabécar are still in the Talamanca region, where several indigenous reserves are found today.

The Bribrí and Cabécar have distinct languages, which are preserved to some degree. They share similar architecture, weapons and canoe style.

Tellingly, these indigenous groups share an enlightened spiritual belief that the planet – and the flora and fauna contained therein – are precious gifts from Sibö, or God, and should be conserved and respected. *Taking Care of Sibö's Gifts*, by Juanita Sanchez, Gloria Mayorga and Paula Palmer, is a remarkable record of Bribrí oral history that provides some rare insights into this culture.

VISITING INDIGENOUS COMMUNITIES

There are several reserves on the Caribbean slopes of the Cordillera de Talamanca, including the Talamanca Cabécar reserve (which is the most remote and difficult to visit) and the Bribrí reserve, where locals are a bit more acculturated and tolerant of visitors.

The most interesting destination is **Yorkín**, in the Upper Talamanca Indigenous Reserve (it's a long trip, so it's best to spend the night). While you are there, you can meet with a local women's artisan group, **Mujeres Artesanas Stibrawpa** (☎ 375 3372). These women offer demonstrations of basket-weaving (with plenty of fine examples you can purchase), roof thatching and cooking, not to mention lots of storytelling. Yorkín is a rewarding trip, but it is not easy to get there: it requires traveling in a traditional dugout canoe from the village of Bambú (midway between Puerto Viejo and Cahuita). To make arrangements contact Stibrawpa or **ATEC** (☎ 750 0191, 750 0398; www.greencoast.com/atec.htm; ✆ 8am-9pm).

Alternatively, you can visit the larger village of **Shiroles**, about 20km west of Bribrí. This is one of the most populous indigenous communities in the country and one of the easiest to access. It's a relatively modern place, and so it's very interesting to see how the indigenous people are adapting to outside influences and preserving their traditional customs.

ATEC is a comprehensive source of information about finding local guides to visit the reserves. Note that it is not really recommended to visit the reserves independently, for two reasons: these places are remote and very difficult to reach; and the villages do not have facilities for tourists. A guide will make arrangements for you to visit a local family, participate in daily life and learn about their customs and traditions.

Manzanillo, this organic farm and retreat center is a unique experiment in permaculture design and sustainable living that covers some 40 hectares. More than 200 varieties of edible fruits and veggies are grown here, which make up about 85% of the huge vegetarian meals that are included in the daily rate. You can visit Punta Mona on a guided day trip (US$35 including transportation). Or, volunteers (per day/week/month US$15/125/300) work on trail maintenance, community cooking and tending gardens (one week minimum); advanced arrangements required.

Finca Lomas (☎ 759 9100, in San José 277 7549; www .anaicr.org; per month US$90) Besides the turtle conservation project, ANAI has an agroforestry and crop experimentation project at nearby Finca Lomas, where volunteers work on trail maintenance, data recording and caring for species of tropical lowland flora, including fruit, nut and spice trees. The work can be physically demanding and conditions are very basic (no electricity or running water). Six-week minimum; a one-time US$160 registration fee covers training.

BRIBRÍ

This small, pleasant town is en route from Cahuita to Sixaola and the Panama border, at the end of the paved (and badly potholed)

coastal road. From Bribrí, a 34km gravel road takes the traveler to the border. Bribrí is a lively little town, with little to offer the casual tourist except for a handful of restaurants and a few accommodations options.

Bribrí is the center for the local indigenous communities in the Talamanca mountains, but there's not too much to see here. These indigenous communities are only now starting to welcome tourists and take advantage of this growing interest in their culture. See the boxed text Visiting Indigenous Communities, above.

Sleeping & Eating

There are a couple of basic lodging options, a good-sized supermarket and some restaurants, including the requisite Musmanni Bakery, in Bribrí. Accommodations tend to fill up on market days (Monday and Tuesday).

Cabinas El Piculino (☎ 751 0130; d US$12-25; Ⓟ ⊠) Fifteen clean, pleasant rooms have private hot showers; some have TV and aircon. A recommended *soda* (mains US$2 to US$3, open 7am to 10pm Monday to Saturday) run by the same family serves a fine *sopa consomé de pollo* and good rice dishes.

Complejo Turístico Mango (☎ 751 0115; s/d/tr/q US$7/10/12/14; Ⓟ) Various configurations of basic rooms, some with hot water, are adjacent to a large restaurant on the outskirts of town.

Delicias de Mi Tierra (mains US$2-5; 6am-9pm Mon-Sat) You can't miss this wide-open and popular spot close to the bus terminal, with a steam table and quality local meals.

Restaurant Bribrí (mains US$2-5; 5am-5pm Mon-Sat) A bit more plush, this restaurant not only serves good casados, *gallos* (tortilla sandwiches) and recommended fried plantains, but is also an excellent place to ask about tours to indigenous villages.

Getting There & Away

Buses to and from Sixaola usually stop in front of Restaurante Bribrí. Buses going north then continue to Puerto Viejo de Talamanca (30 minutes) and Cahuita (one hour), departing at 6:30am, 8:30pm, 10:30am and 3:30pm.

SIXAOLA

This is the end of the road as far as the Costa Rican Caribbean is concerned. Sixaola marks the country's secondary border crossing with Panama, though most foreign tourists travel overland via Paso Canoas on the Carratera Interamericana. Sixaola is a border town, which – by definition – is not a nice place. But the crossing here is more relaxed than Paso Canoas; it's popular among expats without residency visas who take their required 72-hour vacation on the lovely islands of Bocas del Toro, Panama.

Sixaola is centered on the optimistically named Mercado Internacional de Sixaola, a gravelly square where you can find taxis, a handful of *sodas* and several small stores selling a wide selection of rubber boots. The *mercado* is about two blocks from the border crossing.

If you need to change money or use the toilet, ask at Restaurante La Prada, just north of the bridge on the main drag. For details on crossing the border at this point, see the boxed text Getting to Guabito & Bocas del Toro, Panama, below.

Sleeping & Eating

While it's not exactly a layover in Tokyo, there are worse places to be stuck if you miss immigration hours. Accommodations and restaurants are basic, but certainly acceptable for any seasoned budget traveler.

Cabinas Sanchez (☎ 754 2196; d US$10) This squat orange building has six clean rooms, offering cracked tiles in the bathroom and mismatched sheets. But it's a clean place to spend the night, about one block west of the main drag.

Hotel Imperio (☎ 754 2289; d with/without bathroom US$9/7) Cleaner and quieter, this basic motel's biggest selling point is its enviable location,

GETTING TO GUABITO & BOCAS DEL TORO, PANAMA

With a reputation as one of Costa Rica's most relaxed border crossings, Sixaola is popular among folks embarking on their three-day 'visa vacation' to the islands of Bocas del Toro. The picturesque archipelago of jungle islands has more than a dozen beaches, home to everything from endangered red frogs and leatherback turtles to a dilapidated *Survivor* set, plus a range of accommodations, all accessible by convenient water taxis. Paradise.

Get to Sixaola as early as possible. The border is open 7am to 5pm (8am to 6pm in Guabito, Panama, which is an hour ahead of Costa Rica); one or both sides may close for lunch at around 1pm. Begin crossing the high metal bridge over the Río Sixaola, stopping at Costa Rica **migración** (☎ 754 2044) to process your paperwork. Cars can cross here, but be prepared for a long wait.

Once over the bridge, stop in the small office on the left-hand side which is home to Panama *migración*. US citizens will be required to pay an entry fee of US$5. There is no bank, but in a pinch you can change your colones at the *mercado* across the street. Guabito has no hotels or banks, but it has plenty of taxis ready to take you further into Panama.

There are two ways to get to Bocas del Toro. The easiest, cheapest route is to take a taxi to Finca 63 near Changuinola (US$5), from where a water taxi goes regularly to Bocas (US$5, 45 minutes). Note that the last water taxi departs at 5:30pm Panama time (so if you are crossing the border at 5pm Costa Rica time you already missed it). Alternatively, you can take a taxi to Almirante (US$20, one hour), where there is another water taxi (US$3, 45 minutes) that runs every hour between 6:30am and 6:30pm.

1km from the border but directly across the street from the police checkpoint.

Soda Navi (mains US$2-4; ☑ 6am-9pm) Facing the Mercado Internacional, it's a nice spot with crocheted decor specializing in *gallo pinto* (rice and beans) and fried fish casados.

Restaurante Las Cabinas (mains US$2-5; ☑ 7am-9:30pm) This is as upscale as it gets in Sixaola, with pretty checkered tablecloths, fried chicken and to-go food.

Getting There & Away

The bus station is one block north of the border crossing, on the east side of the main drag. Buses to either San José or Puerto Limón all stop at Bribrí and Cahuita, but only some go through Puerto Viejo.

Puerto Limón US$3, three hours, depart at 5am, 7am, 8am, 10am, noon, 1pm, 4pm and 6pm.

San José US$9.50, five hours, depart at 6am, 8am, 10am and 3pm.

Northern Lowlands

Life in the northern lowlands has always revolved around the seasonal rains. When river banks swelled and flooded across the plains, the landscape was transformed into a vast swamp that enabled people to subsist on fish, fowl and small game. However, as populations flourished and resources were strained, the earth was altered with the swing of a hoe, and the lowlands were slowly reshaped by farming interests.

Today, the name of the game is agribusiness, and from the Atlantic slopes of the Cordillera Central to the rich, tropical plains stretching to the Nicaraguan border, farmers coax from the red earth staples such as corn, rice, beans and the big money-earner – sugar cane. These days, sugar is destined for the domestic market where it's used to sweeten an orange Fanta or fermented to create *Guaro Cacique*. But, with a decision regarding Cafta looming, farmers are already eyeing the lucrative market of sweet-toothed North Americans.

From the traveler's perspective, this is the least-visited region in Costa Rica, and folks here are more likely to know how to saddle a horse than what the latest dollar-to-colón exchange rate is. However, the rapid changes sweeping across Costa Rica can be felt here as well, and in recent years tour operators have started promoting the region's natural attractions. It's unlikely that the region will experience the overdevelopment characteristic of the coasts, though tour operators as far-flung as La Fortuna and Quepos will gladly take you to Caño Negro for a price.

Tourism is also picking up in the region as more travelers each year are lacing up their boots, tying their bandanas and heading upriver to Nicaragua. And, they're discovering that it's simply wonderful.

HIGHLIGHTS

- Watching raptors and spoonbills frolic at **Refugio Nacional de Vida Silvestre Caño Negro** (p511)
- Taking a boat ride along the **Río San Juan**, the remote boundary between Costa Rica and Nicaragua (p523)
- Dangling on the 267m-long suspension bridge between **Centro Neotrópico Sarapiquís** and **Tirimbina Rainforest Center** (p518)
- Sniffing the fragrant blooms of rare flowers at **Heliconia Island** (p523)
- Running a different section of river each day near **La Virgen** (p516)

HIGHWAY 126 TO SAN MIGUEL

Hwy 126 is well known to most josefinos as the principal commuter freeway between San José and Heredia, though north of Heredia the road takes on a whole different character.

As the urban bustle of the Central Valley fades into the distance, the highway climbs over a dramatic pass in the Cordillera Central, and then descends into a rural landscape of fincas (farms) and pastureland. This is campesino (farmer) country, and it's as authentic as a plate of gallo pinto (stir-fry of rice and beans served with eggs), a Guanacaste sunset or a guaro (local firewater) hangover.

The highway passes through a number of small towns before reaching San Miguel, which is the main transport hub in the southeast corner of the region. From San Miguel, you can head northwest towards Los Chiles or northeast towards Puerto Viejo de Sarapiquí. Buses from San José to Puerto Viejo de Sarapiquí follow this route.

VARA BLANCA & AROUND

Hwy 126 climbs to just more than 2000m before reaching the tiny village of Vara Blanca, and, if you are lucky, on a clear day you can see Volcán Poás to the west and Volcán Barva to the east. At the gas station in town, continue straight if you're heading to Poás or make a right turn for San Miguel. A few kilometers past the turnoff, the road starts to descend at a dizzying speed. If you're on a tour or driving your own car, there are numerous viewpoints to stop for a photograph as well as ample opportunities for high- and middle-elevation bird-watching.

About 8km north of Vara Blanca, Río La Paz is crossed by a bridge on a hairpin bend; to your left you will find an excellent view of the absolutely spectacular Catarata La Paz.

Several other waterfalls may also be seen, particularly on the right-hand side (if you are heading north) in the La Paz Valley, which soon joins up with the Sarapiquí Valley.

SAN MIGUEL TO LOS CHILES

The papaya-plantation and jungle-trimmed route from San Miguel to Muelle winds through the mountains in a series of hairpin turns. But just as the patchwork of fincas and wildflowers gives way entirely to sugar cane, the road opens to a long, straight and usually steaming-hot stretch across the lowlands to the border crossing at Los Chiles.

This is the agricultural heartland of Costa Rica, and the majority of the towns in this area revolve around the harvest. Although the younger generation is increasingly moving to the Central Valley in search of employment, most Ticos greatly respect and admire the campesino culture. Life here is peaceful and uncomplicated

This is the principal route if you're heading to either Caño Negro or to the border crossing with Nicaragua, though there are a number of pleasant towns and minor sights along the way.

VENECIA & AROUND

The westbound road hugs the northern limits of the Cordillera Central as flowering vines scramble down the mountains and threaten to overtake the road. In the distance, the northern lowlands appear as a patchwork quilt of cane fields and rice paddies. The road momentarily straightens out as it enters the rural town of Venecia, 14km west of San Miguel, though it passes by in a heartbeat as the road continues its dizzying wind towards Muelle.

If you're looking to break up the driving, what better place to spend the night than Venecia's famous 'Medieval castle' of **Torre Fuerte Cabinas** (☎ 472 2424; s/d US$12/25; [P] [X]), about 2.5km west of town. Though it looks like it would feel more at home on the Las Vegas Strip, rooms are clean and have a private bathroom with hot water. Plus, now you can tell all your friends and family that you spent the night in a Costa Rican castle.

A great place to relax and rejuvenate your body after a long drive is **Recreo Verde** (☎ 472 1020; www.recreoverde.com; camping US$15; s/d incl dinner US$35/55), which has a number of rustic

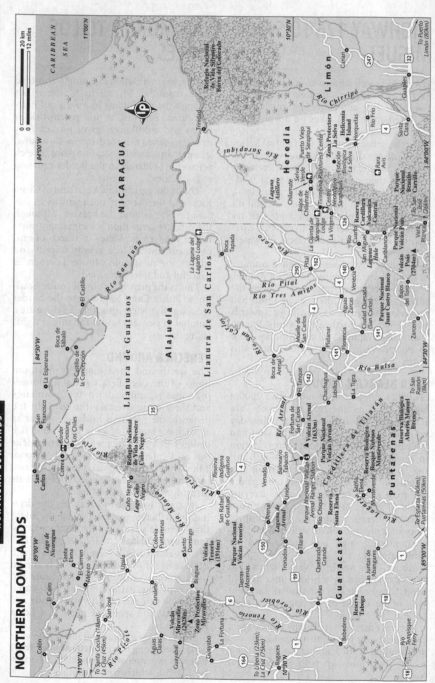

NORTHERN LOWLANDS

SUGAR IN THE RAW

The origins of the sugar industry lie in the European colonization of the Americas, particularly on the islands of the Caribbean. Although it was possible for Europeans to import sugar from the colonies in Asia, the advent of slavery in the New World meant that sugar cane could be grown for a fraction of the cost. This in turn led to lower prices for the European consumer, which took precedent over the lives of the slaves forced to work in the fields.

During the 18th century, European diets started to change dramatically as sugar increased in popularity. Coffee, tea and cocoa were consumed in greater frequency, and processed foods such as candies and jams became commonplace items. The demand for increased production fueled the slave trade, though the actual process of refining sugar became increasingly mechanized.

In industrial countries, sugar is one of the most heavily subsidized agricultural products. Sugar prices in the USA, the EU and Japan are on average three times the international market cost as governments maintain elevated price floors by subsidizing domestic production and imposing high tariffs on imports. As a result, sugar-exporting countries are excluded from these markets, and thus receive lower prices than they would under a system of free trade. Brazil, which exports more than a quarter of the world's supply of refined sugar and heads a coalition of sugar-exporting nations, has repeatedly lobbied the World Trade Organization to reform the market.

For countries like Costa Rica, sugar production is mainly a domestic industry as it's not profitable to export sugar to countries that levy a high tariff on imports. However, if Cafta is ratified, then the USA would be forced to open its markets to Costa Rican sugar. Although sugar farmers in Costa Rica are unsure about the future of Cafta, they continue to eagerly eye the US market, which consumes more sugar than any other industrialized country in the world.

Harvesting sugar cane manually is exhausting work as the stalks can grow to a height of 4m, and their thick stalks are fibrous and difficult to cut down. However, it's becoming increasingly common in Costa Rica for sugar cane to be harvested using self-propelled harvesting machines, which has made it difficult for rural Ticos to find employment.

The next time you're driving through cane country, look for signs advertising *jugo de caña* as there's nothing quite like a glass of fresh sugar-cane juice.

cabinas with private bathrooms near a river bend. Guests have access to four mineral baths featuring a variety of different colored mud as well as three cold-water pools fed by mountain-spring water. There's also a football pitch for a quick pick-up game, and a number of rain-forest trails that you can hike and explore. You can also go spelunking in the Cueva de la Muerte (Cave of Death), though the only real danger is the risk of catching a cold.

Halfway between San Miguel and Venecia is the hamlet of Río Cuarto, from where an unpaved road heads southeast past the beautiful **waterfall** near Bajos del Toro, through Parque Nacional Juan Castro Blanco, and on to Zarcero.

LA LAGUNA DEL LAGARTO LODGE

One of the most isolated places in the country, this environmentally sensitive **ecolodge** (☎ 289 8163; www.lagarto-lodge-costa-rica.com; s/d US$44/58) is surrounded by 1300 hectares of virgin rain forest and is something of a

legend among birders. Simple but pleasant screened rooms, some with a private bathroom, have fan and large veranda. Package tours include transportation from San José, all meals and guided tours. Otherwise, breakfast is US$6, lunch US$7.50 and dinner US$14.

Most of the 500-hectare 'grounds' of the lodge is rain forest. Some is swamp, some is lagoon, and canoes are available to explore it all. There are also about 10km of foot trails, and horseback trips and boat tours down along the Nicaraguan border can be arranged. This is one of the few places where the increasingly rare great green macaw, subject of an on-site study, can be seen frequently.

To get here by car, take the paved road to Pital (north of Aguas Zarcas) and continue on a decent gravel road 29km to the tiny community of Boca Tapada, from where it's 7km further to the lodge (there are signs). Buses from San José (US$4.30, five hours) depart from the Atlántico Norte terminal twice daily, with a connection to Boca

FINE, FEATHERED FRIENDS

The northern lowlands have suffered from heavy deforestation in recent years due to the demand for increased agricultural and pasture land. As a result, species such as the green macaw or *Ara ambigua* are on the brink of extinction. Although it's difficult to estimate their population size, some studies suggest there may be as few as 30 breeding pairs left in Costa Rica.

The green macaw also faces another risk beyond deforestation – pet owners. Illegal sales of green macaws can fetch as much as US$5000 for a single bird, and the international trade has decimated the population. The irony of the situation is that green macaws are actually less talkative then other parrots, and generally do not fare well in captivity. Fortunately, green macaws are protected by the Convention on International Trade in Endangered Species (Cites), though it's difficult to enforce these laws on the ground.

In response to their perilous state, the National Green Macaw Commission was created to help establish the San Juan–La Selva Biological Corridor, which would protect existing green macaw populations as well as other species in the area. The proposed corridor would bridge the gap between the Central Volcanic Mountain Range, the Barra del Colorado Wildlife Reserve, Tortuguero National Park and the Indio Maíz, Punta Gorda and Cerro Silva Reserve in Nicaragua. The core conservation unit of the corridor would be the proposed 'Maquenque National Park,' which would protect an estimated 6000 species of vascular plants, 139 mammals, 515 birds, 135 reptiles and 80amphibians. The creation of the new national park would also generate employment opportunities for an economically depressed area that depends on limited forestry and agriculture for subsistence.

Perhaps the most interesting aspect of this proposal is that it was intended to serve as a binational park for Nicaragua and Costa Rica. The idea was proposed by both governments in 1974, though it first took shape in 1985 when Nicaraguan President Daniel Ortega endorsed the plan as a way of demilitarizing the border and halting the activities of the anti-Sandinista rebels. Not surprisingly, Costa Rican President Oscar Arías also supported the initiative in the hopes that it would remove the US-backed Contras from Costa Rican soil while simultaneously improving relations between the two countries. Unfortunately, the project failed to materialize due to the political instability in Nicaragua and a general lack of funding.

Since the end of the civil war in Nicaragua, both governments have funneled money towards the initiative. However, the major obstacle remains the relocation and compensation of the farmers currently living within the proposed boundaries. Current estimates hover just above US$56 million, though with each passing year the project moves closer towards realization. For more information, go to www.lapaverde.or.cr.

Tapada, where you will be picked up by prior request. The lodge can also arrange round-trip transportation from San José for US$90 per person (two-person minimum).

MUELLE DE SAN CARLOS

This small crossroads village is locally called Muelle, which means 'dock,' seemingly because 'Cañas' was already taken – this is sugar cane country. Breaks in the sweet scenery include huge sugar cane-processing facilities, always interesting to ponder over a soda, and very slow sugar cane-hauling trucks, so drive carefully. This was, actually, an important dock (hence the shipping infrastructure still here) as it's the most inland spot from which the Río San Carlos is navigable.

The main tourist activity in Muelle is pulling over to have a look at the map. A 24-hour gas station lies at the intersection of Hwy 4 (which connects Ciudad Quesada and Upala) and Hwy 35 (running from San José to Los Chiles). From Hwy 4 you can easily catch Hwy 32, the main artery serving the Caribbean coast. Can't decide? A range of accommodations will let you sleep on it, and they're convenient to just about everything.

Sleeping & Eating

Cabinas Beitzy (☎ 469 9100; camping US$4, d US$10; P ⱬ) The cheapest accommodation in town is on the road to Los Chiles. It's perfectly acceptable if you need a place to crash, and the pool is surprisingly well-maintained.

Rooms are (not surprisingly) bare and share cold showers. If you're counting every dollar, you can also pitch a tent here and save yourself a few bucks.

La Quinta Lodge (☎ 475 5260, 475 5921, 817 9679; s/d US$30/35, cabinas per person US$10; P ☒) About 5km south of Muelle in the tiny community of Platanar, this rustic inn has a B&B feel thanks to the eclectic antiques splashed around, plus a pool with a small waterslide and sauna. It's run by the Ugaldes, a friendly Tico couple who taught in the USA for years and who both speak excellent English. Birds have adopted the grounds, and there's a small river behind the inn where fish and caimans can be seen. This is a popular option with Tico families as the atmosphere is warm and inviting.

Hotel La Garza (☎ 475 5222; d/tr US$85/100; P ☒ ☒) Also near Platanar, this attractive, upscale lodge sits on a 600-hectare working dairy ranch and citrus plantation with views of the Río Platanar and far-off Volcán Arenal. Visitors enter the landscaped compound via a graceful suspension footbridge, and 12 polished wooden bungalows with big porch, ceiling fan, telephone and good-size private bathroom have a touch of class. Tennis, basketball and volleyball courts are available, as are 4km of private trails, a swimming pool and Jacuzzi. Meals are served in the adjoining farmhouse (US$9 for breakfast, US$15 for lunch and dinner). A number of tours are available, including horseback rides through the extensive grounds (US$25/40 for two/four hours).

Tilajari Resort Hotel (☎ 469 9091; www.tilajari .com; s/d incl breakfast US$81/91, additional person US$15; P ☒ ☒ ☒ ☒) This former country club turned luxury resort has well-landscaped grounds and an impressive number of tours and activities, though it feels a bit neglected and past its expiration date. Rooms in a modern building are comfortable, and have private hot shower, cable TV, refrigerator and a terrace, though they're nothing memorable. A few of the rooms and private trails are wheelchair accessible. Other amenities include pools, racquetball and tennis courts, a restaurant, sauna, spa and butterfly garden (admission US$3), plus access to the neighboring 400-hectare private rain-forest reserve with several trails. The resort is 800m west of the intersection at Muelle, on the road to Ciudad Quesada.

There are a number of *sodas* (eating establishments) and a small supermarket on the road toward Los Chiles that will do just fine if you're looking for your casado-fix. However, one recommended spot is **Restaurant/Bar La Subasta** (☎ 467 8087; mains US$3-7; ☼ 11am-11pm) which overlooks a bullpen and is bustling with hungry *campesinos*. It has an expansive menu of local dishes, and it's a great spot for a cold beer. If you speak Spanish, strike up a conversation here as you're bound to meet some interesting characters.

SAN RAFAEL DE GUATUSO AREA

The small town of Guatuso (shown on some maps as San Rafael) is 19km northeast of Nuevo Arenal and 40km east of La Fortuna, and is the main population center of this predominantly agricultural area. Although the town itself is rather unremarkable, it's a good base for exploring the recommended Venado Caves. The area is also home to the few remaining Maleku, one of Costa Rica's indigenous populations.

Venado Caves

Four kilometers south of Venado (Spanish for 'deer') along a good dirt road, the **Venado Caves** (☎ 478 8071; admission US$10; ☼ 7am-4pm) are a popular rainy-day attraction that can be organized as a day trip from La Fortuna, San José and many other cities for US$45 to US$65 per person (including transportation and lunch). It's cheaper to visit by yourself, though bus service is inconvenient.

The caves were discovered by chance in 1945 when a farmer fell through a hole in the ground and found himself in an underground chamber surrounded by stalactites and stalagmites (we also don't know which one's which). The exploration that followed uncovered an eight-chamber limestone labyrinth that extends for almost 3km. The entire area, which is composed of soft, malleable limestone, was carved over the millennia by a series of underground rivers.

The caverns get rave reviews from folks fond of giant spiders, swarms of bats, eyeless fish and getting wet and muddy (obviously a big hit with certain families). A guide takes you through the caves, including a few tight squeezes, pointing out various rock formations and philosophizing about what they sort of look like.

Drop-ins are welcome, but it's best to make reservations so you don't need to wait around for a group. You're provided with a guide (some speak English), lights, helmets and showers afterward. It's strongly recommended that you bring an extra set of clothes. There's a small *soda* on site, and a few nicer spots for a snack in Venado, but no lodging.

A 1pm bus from Ciudad Quesada drops you off at a steep 4km slog from the cavern entrance at about 2pm, with pickup at 4pm – hurry! A taxi from Guatuso will cost from US$15 to US$20. If you're driving, the caves are well-signed.

Sleeping & Eating

There are several clean, basic cabinas in San Rafael de Guatuso, sometimes used on a long-term basis by farm workers, as well as a good selection of *sodas* and stores.

Cabinas Milagro (☎ 464 0037; s/d US$6/10; P) This quiet, family-run place on the edge of town is a tranquil budget option. From the center, go past the church toward the Río Frío bridge and turn right just past the soccer field. Rooms have cold showers and fan.

Cabinas Tío Henry (☎ 464 0344; r per person US$9; P 🕸) Big, clean, air-conditioned rooms here are relatively plush, with cable TV and

---

A BRIEF HISTORY OF THE MALEKU

The Maleku (colloquially referred to as the Guatuso) are one of the few remaining indigenous groups in Costa Rica. Unlike other pre-Columbian populations, the Maleku are closer in stature to Europeans, and their skin tone is comparatively lighter than other groups in Central America. Historically, the Maleku were organized into 12 communities that were scattered around the Tilaran–Guanacaste Range and the San Carlos Plains.

Although their numbers dwindled following the arrival of Spanish colonists, the population survived relatively intact until the early 20th century. With the invention of the automobile, the US rubber industry started searching for new reserves to meet the increasing demand for tires. With the aid of Nicaraguan mercenaries, industry representatives scoured Central America for stable reserves, which were found on Maleku-inhabited land. The resulting rubber war virtually wiped out the population, and confined the survivors to a handful of communities. Today, the Maleku number around 400, and live in the three settlements of Sol, Margarita and Torjibe.

As is the situation with most indigenous groups in Costa Rica, the Maleku are one of the poorest communities in the country, and survive by adhering to a subsistence lifestyle. Their diet revolves around corn and the *tipuisqui* root, a traditional food source that grows wild in the region. Fortunately, since the Maleku have a rich, artisan tradition, they are able to earn a small income by selling traditional crafts to tourists. Although their modern crafts primarily consist of pottery, jewelry, musical instruments and other small trinkets that are desirable to tourists, historically they were renowned for their impressive jade work and arrow craftsmanship.

The Maleku are also famous for their unique style of clothing known as *tana*. Although it's rare to see modern Maleku wearing anything other then Western-style clothing, *tana* articles are often offered to tourists for purchase. *Tana* is actually tree bark that has been stripped of its outer layer, soaked in water and then pounded thin on wooden blocks. After it has been dried and bleached in the sun, it can be stitched together like leather, and has a soft texture similar to suede.

Despite being small in number, the Maleku have held on to their cultural heritage, perhaps more than any other indigenous group in Costa Rica. This is especially evident in their language, which is one of the oldest in the Americas and linguistically unique from the Amazonian and Mayan dialects. Today, the Maleku still speak their language to one another, and a local radio station, Radio Sistema Cultural Maleku, airs daily programs in the Maleku language. The Maleku have also maintained their ceremonial traditions, such as the trimonthly custom of crying out to Mother Nature for forgiveness through ritualistic song and dance.

As with all indigenous reservations in Costa Rica, the Maleku welcome tourists as craft sales are vital to their survival. You can access the reservation via Rte 143, though it's best to inquire locally for directions as the roads are poorly maintained and unsigned. While you're at the reservation, please be sensitive to their situation and buy a few small crafts. If you can, it's also recommend that you give a few some small, useful gifts such as pencils, pens and paper. And of course, avoid giving hand-outs such as money and candy as this will only create a culture of begging.

private hot shower. The cabinas are centrally located in town, though the reception is at the vet and feed store next door.

Cabinas El Bosque (☎ 464 0335; s/d with fan US$7/11, with air-con US$10/15; **P** ☒) Just a bit north of town on the road toward Upala, this 10-room hotel is a bit impersonal, though it has clean, simple rooms with private, cold-water showers and optional air-con.

Soda La Macha (☎ 464 0393; mains US$3; ☺ 6am-9pm) You don't exactly get a menu at this fine *soda*, on the main road across from the bus stop. Everything here is cooked using a wood-fired oven. Just request your casado or *gallo* (tortilla sandwich) preferences and they'll be made on the spot.

Getting There & Away

Guatuso lies on Hwy 4, about 40km from both Upala, to the northwest, and Muelle, to the southeast. Buses leave about every two hours for either Tilarán or Ciudad Quesada, some of which continue to San José. Ciudad Quesada is the most frequent destination.

UPALA

Just 9km south of the Nicaraguan border in the northwestern corner of the northern lowlands, Upala is a small but thriving town that serves a widespread community of some 15,000 people. A center for the area's cattle and rice industries, Upala is linked to the Interamericana by an excellent paved road and regular bus service, and it enjoys some apparent affluence. Most visitors are Costa Rican businesspeople, who arrive in town to negotiate for a few dozen calves or a truckload of grain.

In the past, the only real reason to come to Upala was, for instance, to enjoy Nicaraguan radio. However, more travelers are passing through these days as the town serves as a comfortable base for visiting Caño Negro, and it's a good jumping off point for the border crossing at Los Chiles.

Sleeping

Rooms fill up quicker then you'd expect, though there are plenty of options in town. Showers are cold, and you probably won't mind a bit.

Cabinas Ebenezer (☎ 837 7830; d US$10; **P**) On a dirt path on the left-hand side of the road,

this is the first place you'll see when you enter town. Cabinas with private showers have a certain cement-block ambience to them.

Hotel Rosita (☎ 470 0198; s/d US$8/12; **P**) Across from the bridge, this small hotel has a few fairly basic rooms with private cold showers, though its perfectly acceptable and the price is right.

Hotel Upala (☎ 470 0169; s/d with fan US$9/12, with air-con US$12/15; **P** ☒) The most established hotel in town is always a good choice as all the rooms are spotless and bright, and you can watch the soccer games from your private porch. Rooms have a private cold shower and cable TV.

Cabinas Maleku (☎ 470 0142; s/d with fan US$12/16, with air-con US$14/20; **P** ☒) Though it's a few dollars more, this is the best option in town. Big, high-ceilinged rooms with colorful cartoon murals have folksy furniture, including really cute Sarchí-style rocking chairs in front of the rooms. All rooms have a private bathroom and a large cable TV.

Eating

The busy market, just behind the bus terminal, opens early with several nice *sodas* dishing up good *gallos*, *empanadas* (meat or chicken turnovers) and just about everything else. There are also a few Chinese restaurants and produce vendors.

Soda Norma (☎ 819 7048; mains US$2-4; ☺ 6:30am-9pm) With outdoor tables overlooking the park, this is a seriously top-notch *soda*, serving some of the most beautiful casados, with all the trimmings, you've ever seen.

Rancho Don Horacio (☎ 470 0905; mains US$5-8; ☺ 11am-10pm) Right off the plaza and far more atmospheric is this romantic restaurant with red tablecloths, mood lighting and a nice bar. The specialty is steak, and chances are it was born, raised and slaughtered right here in Upala.

Heladería Baloons (☎ 470 0041; ice cream US$1; ☺ 8am-9pm) Do as the locals do and relax in the central park with some cool ice cream on your tongue.

Restaurant Buena Vista (☎ 470 0063; mains US$3-6; ☺ 11am-9pm) This breezy spot serves a good mix of typical Chinese food. It's also aptly named (Good View) as the river views are wonderful.

Just down the street, **Waka's Discoteque** (☺ 9pm-late) does dancing, rave-style parties and sometimes live music (all with a campesino spin of course), while Bar Baja Mundo is more of a get drunk with your mates kinda place.

Getting There & Away

Upala is connected to the Interamericana north of Cañas by Hwy 6, an excellent paved road, and also to La Fortuna and Laguna de Arenal by the somewhat more potholed Hwy 4. A rough, unpaved road, usually passable to all cars, skirts the Refugio Nacional de Vida Silvestre Caño Negro on the way to Los Chiles, the official border crossing with Nicaragua.

Other dirt roads cross the Nicaraguan border, 9km away, but these are not official entry points into either Costa Rica or Nicaragua. Sometimes there's a passport check by the bridge at the south end of Upala (coming from San Rafael de Guatuso) and another near Canalete (coming from the Carratera Interamericana on the paved road from Cañas). Make sure you have your passport accessible, though most times foreigners are simply waved through since the police are here primarily to stop illegal immigrants from Nicaragua.

The bus terminal is right off the park; a **ticket booth** (⌚ 4:30-5:15am, 7:30am-1pm & 6:45-8pm Mon-Sat) has information and can store bags for US$1. Taxis congregate just outside the Upala bus terminal, by the park.

Caño Negro US$1, one hour, depart 11am and 4pm.
Los Chiles US$2.50, two hours, 5am and 4pm.
San José, via Cañas US$6, four hours, 5am, 2pm and 4:30pm.
San José, via Ciudad Quesada/San Carlos US$6, four hours, 9am and 3:30pm.

REFUGIO NACIONAL DE VIDA SILVESTRE CAÑO NEGRO

Because of the region's relative remoteness (although this has changed in recent years with the improvement of roads), this 102-sq-km refuge has long been frequented primarily by two sorts of specialists. Anglers come in search of that elusive 18kg snook, though they abandon ship April through July, when the park is closed to fishing (a good time to get a bargain price on accommodations). Birders flock here each year from January through March to spot an unequalled assortment of waterfowl. During the dry season water levels drop, with the

effect of concentrating the birds (and fish) in photogenically (or tasty) close quarters. From January to March, when migratory birds land in large numbers, avian density is most definitely world class.

The Río Frío defines the landscape – a table-flat, swampy expanse of marsh that is similar in appearance to other famous wetlands such as the Florida Everglades or the Mekong Delta. During the wet season, the river breaks its banks to form an 800-hectare lake, and then contracts during the dry months from January through April, when water levels drop to the point where the river is barely navigable. By April it has almost completely disappeared – until the May rains begin. This cycle has proceeded without fail for millennia, and the small fishing communities that live around the edges of the reserve have adapted to each seasonal nuance of their environment.

Unfortunately, the stability of the reserve is in grave danger. Bird counts are at an all-time low, caimans are being hunted for their leather in record numbers, and satellite images clearly show that the lagoon is shrinking with each passing year. Illegal poaching and logging operations are largely to blame, though the unwieldy size of the park and the lack of available funds and manpower are difficult obstacles to overcome.

Thanks to improved roads, dozens of tour operators are now able to offer relatively inexpensive trips to Caño Negro from all over the country. However, it's advisable to book your trip through a reputable tour company as it's fairly common practice for operators to save on park fees by taking tourists on a boat ride through swampy private property that is by all accounts lovely, though not Caño Negro. If you're more independently minded, you'll save yourself a little money (and have a much better experience) by heading directly to the park without a tour operator, and hiring a local guide in town. This practice is recommended as it puts money directly in the hands of locals, and encourages communities in the area to protect the wildlife.

Orientation & Information

The refuge is part of the Area de Conservación Arenal–Huetar Norte and is accessible primarily by boat. Close to the park

THE WEEPING FOREST

Extensive deforestation of the Caño Negro area began in the 1970s in response to an increase in population density and the subsequent need for more farmland. Although logging was allowed to proceed in the area for almost 20 years, the government took action in 1991 with the creation of the Refugio Nacional de Vida Silvestre Caño Negro. Since its creation, Caño Negro has served as a safe habitat for the region's aquatic and terrestrial birds, and has acted as a refuge for numerous migratory birds.

However, illegal logging has continued around the perimeter of the park, and the wildlife has accordingly suffered. In the last two decades, one-time residents of the park including ocelot, manatee, shark and macaw have vanished. Tarpon and caiman populations are decreasing, and fewer migratory birds are returning to the park each year. Additionally, anglers are reporting record lows in both the size and number of their catches.

It gets worse. Aerial photography shows that the lake is shrinking each year, and that water levels in the Río Frío are dropping rapidly. It's difficult to say with certainty what is causing these changes, though the farms surrounding Caño Negro require extensive irrigation, and sugar cane is nearly 10 times as water intensive as wheat.

Locals are extremely worried about the stability of the park as entire communities are dependent on fishing and tourism for their survival. In response to the growing need to regulate development in the region, area residents have formed a number of organizations aimed at controlling development in the northern lowlands. While you're visiting Caño Negro, talk to your guide about conservation initiatives in the area and make a small donation if it's within your means. For these reasons, it is recommended that you avoid booking your tour in another town as your money is better spent within the Caño Negro community.

entrance (that'd be the dock) is the tiny community of Caño Negro, which has no grocery stores, banks or gas stations, though there is a **Minae office** (☎ 471 1309; 🕒 8am-4pm), where you pay your entrance fees (US$6).

You can get all other information and arrange guided tours at the **ranger station** (☎ 471 1309; 🕒 8am-4pm), located at the dock. In addition to administering the refuge, rangers are contact points for local guides and a few community projects, including a butterfly garden put together by a local women's association (Asomucan). You can camp (US$2 per person) by the river, or stay in the rangers' house for US$6 with advance reservations. There are cold showers, and meals can be arranged.

Local guides for fishing and ecological tours can also be arranged at most hotels and restaurants in town. You can usually find a guide (US$10 to US$20 per hour) on short notice, but they can get booked up during peak fishing and birding seasons.

Wildlife-Watching

Caño Negro is regarded among birders as one of the premier destinations in Central America. During the dry season, the sheer density of birds in the park is astounding,

and you'll be impressed with the number and variety of different species that inhabit the park. In the winter months, migratory duck congregations can be enormous, and very-well represented groups include kingfisher, heron, egret, ibis, rail, anhinga, roseate spoonbill and stork. The refuge is also the only reliable site in Costa Rica for olivaceous cormorant, Nicaraguan grackle and lesser yellow-headed vulture.

Reptiles are easily seen in the park, especially spectacled caimans, green iguana and striped basilisk. Commonly sighted mammals in Caño Negro include howler monkeys, white-faced capuchin and two-toed sloth. Despite increasing incursions from poachers, puma, jaguar and tapir have also been recorded here in surprising numbers.

Caño Negro also possesses an abundant number of river turtle, which historically were an important part of the Maleku diet (see the boxed text A Brief History of the Maleku, p508). Prior to a hunt, the Maleku would appease the turtle god Javara by fasting and abstaining from sex. If the hunt was successful, the Maleku would later celebrate by feasting on smoked turtle meat and consuming large quantities of *chicha*, an alcohol derived from maize.

Mosquitoes in Caño Negro are huge, abundant and most definitely classifiable as wildlife. Bring bug spray, or you'll regret it.

Tours

If you don't have your own car or you're not a fan of public transportation, then it's recommended that you organize a day trip to Caño Negro from La Fortuna, San José or any hotel within a 150km radius. Tours are geared toward wildlife-watching, though travelers report that a boatload of noisy tourists tends to scare away most animals. If you're looking to do a little sportfishing, it's recommended that you organize your trips through one of the lodges in the park. Fishing licenses can be arranged through the lodges for US$30 for two months, though you will need a photocopy of your passport and a small photo.

However, Caño Negro is not as difficult to access as it once was, and you'll have a much better experience if you avoid the tour operators and head directly to the park. Hiring a local guide is quick, easy and full of advantages – you'll be supporting the local economy, you'll have more privacy when you're out on the water and, of course, there's the satisfaction of doing things independently.

Either way, the key to Caño Negro is to get there as early in the morning as possible when wildlife is still active, and it's worth paying extra for an overnight adventure that puts you in the water early. Folks staying in town basically have the refuge to themselves at daybreak, with boat-trippers from Puerto Viejo de Sarapiquí and Los Chiles arriving by 9am.

Sleeping & Eating

There are a few budget lodging options in town, plus a handful of nicer accommodations down the road, most of which are geared toward fishing – they're still pretty rustic by ecolodge standards. Businesses are listed according to their distance from the park – none is more than 1.5km from the dock.

Soda La Palmera (☎ 816 3382; mains US$3-10; ☽ 6am-9pm) Right at the entrance to the refuge, this pleasant *soda* serves Tico standards and fresh fish, including your personal catch of the day. The staff can also arrange

local guides for fishing and naturalist trips (US$40, two hours, up to three people). Advance reservations are recommended in the high season.

Cabinas Martín Pescador (☎ 471 1369; r per person US$10, with air-con US$14, with air-con & hot water US$25; **P**) These rustic cabins are about 100m from the town center, and feature a variety of rooms to accommodate travelers of all budgets. They're owned and operated by the Sequera brothers, who are recommended refuge guides and boat captains. Two-hour fishing or naturalist trips for up to five people cost US$40, and you can also arrange horseback riding here.

Caño Negro Natural Lodge (☎ 471 1426; www .canonegrolodge.com; s/d incl breakfast US$80/90; **P** **⊠** **⊜**) Perched on land that becomes a virtual island in the Río Frío during the high-water season, this Italian-run lodge is surprisingly upscale considering its remote location. Well-appointed rooms have hot showers, air-con and satellite TV. The friendly staff can arrange all your trips while you relax in the pleasant pool, Jacuzzi or game room. The restaurant is here is open to the public and is popular among anglers.

Albergue Caño Negro (r per person US$8; **P**) The cheapest accommodation in the area is a family-run venture of small cabinas that overlook the lagoon. Rooms are simple and have cold water showers, but the family is relaxed and friendly, and they're happy to organize trips to the reserve on their small boat.

Hotel de Campo y Caño Negro Fishing Club (☎ 471 1021; www.welcometocostarica.com; d incl breakfast US$65; **P** **⊠** **⊜**) Set in a lakeside orchard of mango and citrus trees, this hotel is a fisherman's paradise. You can rent any combination of boats, guides and fishing equipment here at the well-stocked tackle shop. And after a hard day of fighting monster fish, relax in clean, light rooms with air-con and private hot showers. There's also a restaurant (mains US$7 to US$12, open 7am to 9am, noon to 2:30pm and 6pm to 8:30pm) specializing in, you guessed it, fish. The owner of the lodge is committed to preserving Caño Negro for future generations, and is involved in a number of conservation initiatives in the area.

Restaurante Las Vegas Sunset Bar (☎ 399 4164; US$4-10; ☽ 10am-10pm Tue-Sun) At the bridge over the Río Frío just outside the village is this recommended riverside oasis run by a charming Dutch-Belgian couple. Sit among the bamboo groves and feast on fresh sea bass or tilapia while you watch the caimans drift idly by. English, French, Dutch, German, Spanish and Flemish spoken. The owners can also organize tours.

Getting There & Away

The village of Caño Negro and the entrance to the park lie on the rough road connecting Upala and Los Chiles, which is passable to all cars during the dry season. However, this road is frequently washed out during the rainy season, and a 4WD is usually required. Two buses daily run past the park entrance from both Upala and Los Chiles.

During the rainy season and much of the dry season, you can also catch a boat here from either Los Chiles or Puerto Viejo de Sarapiquí. This is becoming increasingly popular, especially as more and more travelers are exploring the Río San Juan (see the boxed text Boating to Nicaragua, p523) and crossing into Nicaragua (see the boxed text Getting to San Carlos, Nicaragua, p516).

LOS CHILES

Seventy sweltering kilometers north of Muelle on a smooth, paved road through the sugar cane, and just three dusty, red and heavily rutted kilometers south of the Nicaraguan border, lies the sleepy farming and fishing town of Los Chiles. The humid lowland village, arranged with dilapidated grace around a grassy soccer field and along the unmanicured banks of the leisurely Río Frío, is pleasant enough – almost charming by border-town standards. It was originally settled by merchants and fisherman who worked on the nearby Río San Juan, much of which forms the Nicaragua–Costa Rica border. In recent history, Los Chiles served as an important supply route for the Contras in Nicaragua, and was home to a strong US military presence throughout the 1980s.

Gringo traffic is on the rise in Los Chiles as it's a great base for enjoying the scenic water route to Caño Negro, and an early-morning excursion by small motorized boat is an adventure in itself. The second big draw is the scenic boat route to Nicaragua, a one- to two-hour boat ride across the border that is becoming increasingly popular among foreign tourists. Assuming your

papers are in order, the border crossing is fairly relaxed and often hassle-free.

Although the road continues past Los Chiles to Nicaragua, this border is closed to Ticos, Nicas and tourists alike. The police patrolling this line in the sand are heavily armed and extremely bored, so save your sweet-talking for another day, and don't give them any excuses to work on their marksmanship.

Information & Orientation

The last stretch of paved road along Hwy 35 is home to a few restaurants, the post office and a gas station. If you continue north past Los Chiles on the rutted dirt road, you'll find yourself in the dusty no-man's-land en route to a border crossing you probably won't be allowed to use.

Drivers must head west through town to reach the town center and the docks of the Río Frío, close to the bus station. It's a small town. Banco Nacional, close to the central park and soccer field, changes money. Folks heading to Nicaragua must stop at **migración** (☎ 471 1223; ☼ 8am-5pm), about 100m east of the park, on the way to the dock.

Tours

Los Chiles is a convenient base to organize your tours to Caño Negro. You'll be able to get on the river early, which means you'll probably see more wildlife than folks being shuttled in from La Fortuna and San José. The port is also a good jumping-off point if you want to explore Lake Nicaragua or Tortuguero.

Cabinas Jabirú (☎ 471 1055) Well-established and run by friendly Manfred Vargas Rojas. In addition to offering trips to Caño Negro, the hotel runs tours to the nearby private reserve of Medio Queso where you can go horseback riding, observe indigenous farming techniques, and have a traditional farm lunch. Tours start at US$15 per person. Other tours and guided camping trips go to the islands in Lake Nicaragua.

Rancho Tulipán (☎ 471 1414; cocas34@hotmail.com) As the most established hotel in town, it's not surprising that it offers a variety of different tours to Caño Negro (a three-hour tour for two people is around US$60). The staff can also arrange transportation to Nicaragua, plus accommodations when you get there.

At the boat dock you can also hire individual boat captains to take you up the Río Frío during the dry season and all the way

US MEDDLING & THE SANDINISTAS

The Sandinista era roughly started in 1978 with the assassination of Pedro Joaquín Chamorro, a newspaper journalist who was critical of the Nicaraguan dictatorship. The event sparked a countrywide revolt that resulted in the FSLN (Frente Sandinista de Liberacíon Nacional) overthrowing the Somoza regime on July 19, 1979. Although the Sandinistas inherited a poverty-stricken country, they managed to establish farming cooperatives, raise literacy rates and introduce an immunization program that eliminated polio and reduced infant mortality. They also angered the good friends of the Somozas, namely the US government, who feared that a successful popular revolution would 'set a bad example' to the other countries in the region.

After taking office in 1981, President Ronald Reagan suspended aid to Nicaragua and allocated more than US$10 million to counter-revolutionary groups that became known as the Contras. In response to the brewing civil war, the Sandinistas responded by using much of the nation's resources to defend themselves against the US-funded insurgency. Although the leader of the Sandinistas, Daniel Ortega, won 63% of the popular vote in 1984, the US government continued its attacks on Nicaragua. Dissatisfied with the pace of the war, the US government imposed a trade embargo in 1985 that lasted for five years and bankrupted the Nicaraguan economy. As it became publicly known that the CIA was covertly funding the Contras, the US Congress passed a number of bills aimed at ending US involvement. However, US support for the Contras continued secretly until the famous Iran-Contra Affair, which revealed that the CIA was using profits from illegal weapons sales to Iran (who were fighting a war with Uncle Sam's old friend Iraq) to fund the Contras.

US meddling ended in 1990 when Nicaraguans elected Violeta Chamorro, leader of the opposition party and widow of the martyred Chamorro. Although she was unable to revive the economy, the civil war was over, though the USA did threaten to withhold aid on several occasions since Chamorro continued to rely on Sandinista support. However, economic reform has proceeded relatively smoothly since the early 1990s, though per-capita income in Nicaragua is nearly 10 times less than it is in Costa Rica.

into Lago Caño Negro during the rainy season, as well as to San Carlos, Nicaragua (see the boxed text Getting to San Carlos, Nicaragua, p516). Three- to four-hour trips cost about US$45 to US$80 for a small group, depending on the size and type of boat.

Viajes y Excurciones Cabo Rey (☎ 471 1251, 839 7458) provides a boat service to the refuge (from US$45) as well as to El Castillo and the Solentiname islands in Nicaragua. Cabo himself can usually be found by the dock.

Festivals & Events
This sleepy little town bursts to life during the October 4 **Feast of San Francisco**. Occasionally, festivities are held in Los Chiles during the irregularly scheduled **Bi-national Green Macaw Festival**, so keep your eyes peeled for information.

Sleeping & Eating
Accommodations in town are surprisingly limited, though most people aren't too keen on sticking around.

Rancho Tulípan (☎ 471 1414; cocas34@hotmail .com; s/d incl breakfast US$25/30; P ✗ ➠) Rancho Tulípan is the most respectable accommodation in town, though it's also the most expensive. All the rooms have air-con, private hot-water bathrooms and cable TV, and it's conveniently located right next to the docks. The on-site restaurant (mains US$3 to US$7, open 7am to 10pm) will start your day off right with a good breakfast, and the pan-fried sea bass is not to be missed.

Cabinas Jabirú (☎ 471 1055; d with shared/private bathroom US$10/20; P ➠) Well positioned near the bus terminal, this popular budget option has bare rooms and cold water, though it'll save you a few bucks, and it's much nicer than anything you'll find immediately across the border.

Hotel Río Frío (☎ 471 1127; r per person US$3) Old plank rooms arranged in a row, with shared cold showers at the end, are kept sparkling clean at this very basic budget option. A great place to meet migrant workers, if that's your thing.

Soda Pamela (casados US$2-5) This small kiosk near the bus station will cook up your casados to order, and it's a good spot for getting reliable bus info.

Restaurant El Parque (☎ 471 1373, 471 1090; mains US$3-5; ⏰ 6am-9pm) This popular spot has some of the best eats in town, and it's open early if you're looking to get your coffee fix before setting out on the river.

There's no real grocery store in town, though a couple of well-stocked markets should do the trick.

Getting There & Away

You can charter a plane to a nearby landing strip (the US government did it routinely in the 1980s), though there is currently no regular passenger service.

Drivers usually get here via Hwy 35 from Muelle, about 70 smooth, straight kilometers where huge trucks completely disregard the posted 40km/h signs, except when confronted with those awkward sugar cane–hauling contraptions lurching along at 20km/h. Skid marks do break up the monotony of endless sugar cane plantations. More scenic, if a little harder on your chassis, is the decent dirt road running for 50km to Upala, through Caño Negro, passable for normal cars throughout the dry season.

Note that you can't drive across the border at the Los Chiles checkpoint without special permission, which is rarely granted in San José.

All buses arrive and leave from the stop on the main street across from the park. Time tables are flexible, so play it safe and inquire locally.

Ciudad Quesada US$3; two hours; depart 12 times daily from 5am to 7:15pm.

San José US$5; five hours; depart 5:30am & 3:30pm.

Upala via Caño Negro US$2.50; 2½ hours; depart 5am & 2pm.

Regular boat transport is only limited to quick shuttles across the Nicaraguan border (US$7) and various day trips throughout the region.

For most of the year, boats can be arranged to travel to Caño Negro, Puerto Viejo de Sarapiquí, Barra del Colorado and Tortuguero (US$250 to US$300) and just about everywhere else in northeastern Costa Rica that has a dock.

SAN MIGUEL TO PUERTO VIEJO DE SARAPIQUÍ

This flat, steaming stretch of finca-dotted lowlands was once part of the United Fruit Company's cash-cow of banana holdings. Harvests were carried from the plantations to Puerto Viejo de Sarapiquí where they were packaged and shipped down the river on boats destined for the lucrative North American market. However, with the advent of the railway in 1880 that connected most of the country to the new shipping port in Puerto Limón, Puerto Viejo de Sarapiquí became a sleepy backwater.

Banana harvesting continued in the area through most of the 20th century, though in recent years farmers have switched to a more lucrative cash crop – sugar cane. Although Puerto Viejo de Sarapiquí has never managed to recover its faded glory, the area around the town is still one of the premier destinations in Costa Rica for kayakers and rafters. There are also a number of stellar ecolodges in the region that are open to nonguests, and feature everything from rainforest hiking and suspension bridges to pre-Columbian ruins and chocolate tours.

The road north from San Miguel drops for 12km to the village of La Virgen and then flattens out as it bisects agricultural country for an additional 13km to Bajos de Chilamate. The old port town of Puerto Viejo de Sarapiquí lies 6km further along this road. Buses linking either San José or Ciudad Quesada with Puerto Viejo de Sarapiquí are the primary means of public transportation along this route.

LA VIRGEN

Tucked into the densely jungled shores of the wild and scenic Río Sarapiquí, La Virgen was one of a number of small towns that grew and prospered during the hey-day of the banana trade. Although United Fruit has long since packed up and shipped out, the town is still dependent on the river, though most people today earn a living by either mongering fish or guiding gringos through the rapids.

Welcome to one of the premier kayaking and rafting destinations in Costa Rica. Surprisingly, most travelers have never even heard about La Virgen, and those who have would be hard-pressed to find it on a map. But, to the dedicated groups of hard-core rafters and kayakers that spend days running the Río Sarapiquí, La Virgen is an off-the-beaten-path paradise. As an added bonus, the three luxurious lodges east of town feature a number of interesting attractions including museums, private trails and a Maleku archaeological site – so there's plenty to do in the area even on a rest day.

Information

Most of La Virgen's businesses are strung out along the highway, including a gas station, a Banco Nacional with 24-hour ATM, a couple of small supermarkets and many bars. **Internet Cafe** (☎ 761 1107; per hr US$1.25; ☻ 8am-9pm Mon-Sat, 2-9pm Sun) has fairly fast computers.

Sights & Activities
RAFTING

The Río Sarapiquí isn't as wild as the white water on the Río Pacuare near Turrialba, though it will still get your heart racing, and the dense jungle that hugs the riverbank is lush and primitive. You can run the Sarapiquí year-round, but July through December are considered peak months. Although it's possible to get a rafting trip on short notice, it's far better to make reservations at least two days in advance. Several tour operators in La Fortuna organize trips (p241).

GETTING TO SAN CARLOS, NICARAGUA

Although there's a 14km dirt road between Los Chiles and San Carlos, Nicaragua, using this crossing requires special permission generally reserved for federal employees. Most folks go across by boat, which is easily arranged in Los Chiles proper. You must first have your paperwork processed at **migración** (☎ 471 1223; ☻ 8am-5pm), 100m west of the dock, which is also your first stop when entering from Nicaragua.

Regular boats (US$7, 1½ hours) leave Los Chiles at 1pm and 4pm daily, with extra boats at 11am and 2:30pm if demand is high. Boats leave San Carlos for Los Chiles at 10:30am and 1:30pm, with extra boats scheduled as needed. Of course, the Nicaragua–Costa Rica border is not known for its reliability, so make sure you confirm these times before setting out. Nicaragua charges a US$9 entry fee, though Costa Rica is more gracious (so long as you're not Nicaraguan) as entry is free. Fees should be paid in US dollars.

Border officials are generally patient with travelers making day trips to Lago de Nicaragua or El Castillo, and those folks probably won't be charged the fee for entering Nicaragua – probably. Bring your passport and a few US dollars, just in case.

While you're cruising down the Río San Juan, consider keeping your fingers and toes in the boat as there in fact river sharks (seriously, we're not kidding). Sharks are one of several euryhaline species that are able to survive in both fresh- and salt-water conditions. Every year, sharks that have been tagged by scientists in the Caribbean Sea are later found swimming in Lake Nicaragua. Although the rapids of the Río San Juan are a deterrent to most species of marine fish, sharks are apparently able to negotiate the river without problems, and presumably head for fresh water in search of food.

From San Carlos, which has a similar range of services as Los Chiles, you can arrange bus, boat and plane transportation to Managua, Granada and other destinations in Nicaragua. If you're looking to experience the Nica side of life, here's a quick list of the country's highlights:

- Admire the Spanish-colonial architecture in **Granada**, one of Central America's most beautiful cities.
- Catch a wave on the beaches near **San Juan del Sur**, years before it becomes the Nicaraguan Tamarindo.
- Explore the twin volcanoes of **Isla Ometepe**, a strong contender for the world's most beautiful island.
- Stroll through the mango tree–lined streets of colonial **Rivas**, a mellower alternative to Granada.
- Get lost in the produce markets of **Managua**, Nicaragua's sprawling, lakeside capital.

You can also call directly to the companies listed in this section.

There are three basic runs offered by several companies, and all have a minimum age of nine or 10; prices and times vary a bit, but the following are average. The Class I-II Chilamate put-in (per person US$45, three hours) is a gentle float more suited to younger kids and wildlife-watching. The Class III-IV Lower Sarapiquí (US$45 to US$65, three hours) puts in close to La Virgen and is a scenic and challenging trip that's a good choice for healthy people without white-water experience. The Class IV-V Upper Sarapiquí (US$80, five hours) is seven screaming miles of serious white water, perfect for thrill-seekers.

Sarapiquí Outdoor Center (☎ 761 1123; sarapaquioutdoor@hotmail.com) is an established, family-run operation that offers top-quality rafting trips, as well as camping and good budget accommodations.

Aguas Bravas (☎ 292 2072; www.aguas-bravas.co.cr), in addition to offering rafting trips from La Virgen, San José and La Fortuna, can also arrange horseback rides and bike tours.

Aventuras del Sarapiquí (☎ 766 6768; www.sarapiqui.com) and **Hacienda Pozo Azul Adventures** (☎ 438 2616, 761 1360) also organize rafting trips.

HIKING

For the truly rugged do-it-yourself adventures, it's possible to hike from La Virgen to the southernmost rangers stations in Parque Nacional Braulio Carrillo. For more information, see p164.

KAYAKING

If you're a kayaker, several accommodations in town are directly on the river, which means that you can roll out of bed, brush your teeth and have a quick paddle before breakfast. In particular, Rancho Leona has evolved into a famous meeting spot for kayakers, which isn't surprising as its stunning riverside allows for easy launches and free kayak storage. Staff can also provide information regarding launches in the area, and it's recommended that you stop by and visit before setting out on the river.

SERPENTARIO

A great, locally run attraction is La Virgen's famous **snake garden** (☎ 761 1059; adult/student US$5/3; ⏰ 9am-6:30pm), where you can get face-to-face with more than 60 different species of reptiles and amphibians, including poison-dart frogs, anaconda and the star-attraction, an 80kg Burmese python. The owner of the serpenario, Lydia, gives impromptu tours and takes certain snakes out of their cages for big hugs and memorable photo ops. The mural outside is most definitely tattoo-worthy.

Sleeping & Eating

Rancho Leona (☎ 761 1019; www.rancholeona.com; dm US$12) This shady, riverside spot is a gem – kayakers congregate here to swap tales of white-water adventure, backpackers detox in the Native American–style sweat lodge and artistically minded travelers admire the incredible on-site collection of stained glass. A variety of rooms (some private) share hot-water showers and a communal kitchen, there's a small bathing pool for taking a cool dip and spa services are available. The friendly staff prepares family-style dinners each evening for guests, and they've got the best water in Costa Rica (we're not going to spoil the surprise – ask for a test). Kayaking trips (per person including lunch US$75, six hours) and guided hikes can also be arranged on an ad hoc basis.

Hotel Claribel (☎ 761 1190; s/d US$10/16; P) At the eastern edge of town, rooms here are a bit neglected and run-down, though the price is right; they have cable TV and hot showers.

Sarapiquí Outdoor Center (☎ 761 1123; sarapaqui@hotmail.com; camping US$5, d US$25; P) Excellent campsites here are laid out on impeccable grounds that overlook the river, and have access to showers and bathrooms. Private rooms are simple and have river views, though they're nothing special and a bit overpriced. There's also a communal kitchen and a covered terrace in case of rain. In addition to rafting and kayaking trips, the owners can also arrange horseback rides and guided hikes to a nearby waterfall.

Hacienda Pozo Azul Adventure (☎ 438 2616; s/d/tr luxury tent US$55/86/117; P 💻 🐾) Beside the bridge over the Río Sarapiquí is, if you've been paying attention, one of the most heavily advertised lodges in the entire region. Accommodation here is in a number of luxury tents scattered on the edge of the tree-line, and there's also a secondary campsite (single/double/triple luxury tents US$60/96/132) deep in the jungle if you really want to get away from it all. Tents have polished, wooden floorboards, air mattresses, mosquito nets and enclosed showers with hot water. It's certainly expensive, though the young, package travelers that flock here for the range of activities on offer don't seem to mind. You can rent horses (US$30, two hours), take a canopy tour (US$45), go mountain-biking (US$60, one day), milk a cow in the dairy (US$20) or take a guided hike (US$15).

Restaurante y Cabinas Tía Rosita (☎ 761 1032, 761 1125; meals US$2-5; ☉ 8am-9pm; P) Not only is Tía Rosita the most highly recommended *soda* in town, with excellent spaghetti, *chiles rellenos* (stuffed fried peppers) and fish dishes, it also rents four clean, cute cabinas (single/double/triple rooms US$8/12/17) with private hot shower, TV, fan and plenty of breathing space. Both rooms and meals are very popular with truckers.

Restaurant La Costa (☎ 761 1117; mains US$3-7; ☉ 11am-9pm) On the eastern edge of town, the specialty here is Chinese-style seafood dishes, and the portions are huge, so you know it's going to be packed with hungry kayakers and rafters.

Restaurant Mar y Tierra (☎ 761 1603; mains US$4-9) La Virgen's favorite finer-dining (but still very relaxed) option is this comfortable seafood and steak restaurant that's popular with both locals and travelers. The specialty here is shrimp, and it's damn good.

Getting There & Away

La Virgen lies on Hwy 126, about 30km from both San Miguel, to the south, and Puerto Viejo de Sarapiquí, to the northeast. Buses originating in either San José, San Miguel or Puerto Viejo de Sarapiquí make regular stops in La Virgen. If you're driving, the road is paved between San José and Puerto Viejo de Sarapiquí, though irregular maintenance can make for a bumpy ride.

LA VIRGEN TO PUERTO VIEJO DE SARAPIQUÍ

This scenic stretch of Hwy 4 is home to a few lovely ecolodges that are extremely popular among well-heeled tourists. However, if you're the kind of traveler that scraps together a few hundred colones every morning to buy a loaf of bread from Palí, then fear not as these place do allow nonguests to see their unusual attractions and private trails for a small fee. Any bus between La Virgen and Puerto Viejo de Sarapiquí can drop you at the entrances, while a taxi from La Virgen (or Puerto Viejo for Selva Verde) will cost from US$4 to US$6.

Centro Neotrópico Sarapiquís & Tirimbina Rainforest Center

About 2km east of the village of La Virgen is **Centro Neotrópico Sarapiquís** (☎ 761 1004; www .sarapiquis.org; d standard/deluxe US$82/90; P ⊠ ✕), a unique ecolodge that aims to foster sustainable tourism by educating its guests about environmental conservation and pre-Columbian history and culture. The entire complex consists of Palenque-style, thatch-roofed buildings modeled after a 15th-century pre-Columbian village, and contains a clutch of luxuriously appointed hardwood rooms with huge, solar-heated bathrooms and private terraces. However, the main reason guests rave about this ecolodge is the variety of exhibits and attractions located on the grounds.

Even if you're not staying at the lodge, it's worth stopping by just to visit the lodge's real claims to fame, namely the **Alma Ata Archaeological Park**, **Rainforest Museum of Indigenous Cultures** and **Sarapiquís Gardens** (adult/child under 8/child over 8 US$12/free/10; ☉ 9am-5pm). Admission includes entry to all three places. The archaeological site is estimated to be around 600 years old, and is attributed to the Maleku (see the boxed text A Brief History of the Maleku, p508). Currently, about 70 small stone sculptures marking a burial field are being excavated by Costa Rican archaeologists, and have thus far revealed a number of petroglyphs and pottery. Although the site is modest, and is definitely not comparable in size or scope to other Central American archaeological sites, it's one of the few places in Costa Rica where you can get a sense of pre-Columbian history.

The museum chronicles the history of the rain forest (and of human interactions with it) through a mixture of displays and videos, and also displays hundreds of Costa Rican indigenous artifacts including some superbly-crafted musical instruments. Finally, the gardens boast the largest scientific collection of medicinal plants in Costa Rica.

An on-site **restaurant** (mains US$7-20; ⓨ 7am-2pm & 5-9pm) serves meals incorporating fruits, vegetables, spices and edible flowers used in indigenous cuisine, many of which are grown on the premises.

As if this wasn't spectacular enough, following the museum tour visitors are invited to enter the **Tirimbina Rainforest Center** (☎ 761 1579; www.tirimbina.org), a 300-hectare private reserve that is reached by crossing two suspension bridges, 267m and 111m long, that span the Río Sarapiquí. Halfway across, a spiral staircase drops down to a large island in the river. The reserve has more than 6km of trails, some of which are paved or woodblocked. There are also a number of different guided tours on offer (US$14 to US$20) including birding, 'bat-ing' and a recommended guided chocolate tour, which lets you explore a working cacao plantation and learn about the harvesting, fermenting and drying processes. Student discounts are available.

La Quinta de Sarapiquí Lodge

About 5km north of La Virgen, this pleasant family-run **lodge** (☎ 761 1300, 761 1052; www.laquintasarapiqui.com; d/tr US$65/80; P 🏊 ♿) is on the banks of the Río Sardinal. The lodge has covered paths through the landscaped jungle connecting thatch-roofed, hammock-strung pagodas to beautiful and secluded bungalows. All the rooms have a terrace, ceiling fan and private hot shower.

Owner Beatriz Gámez is active in local environmental issues and helps administer the Cámara de Turismo de Sarapiquí (Cantusa), which works to balance conservation and tourism in the area. Activities at the lodge include swimming in the pretty pool or river (there's a good swimming hole near the lodge), horseback riding, fishing, boat trips, mountain-biking and birding, and you can spend time in the large **butterfly garden** or hike the 'frog land' trail where poison-dart frogs are commonly seen. Fishing and horseback riding are free for lodge guests. You can also get meals in the lovely restaurant (mains US$8 to US$13).

La Galleria (admission US$8.50, free for lodge guests), on the hotel grounds, features an eclectic collection of regional ephemera, including an extensive collection of insect specimens such as *la machaca*.

Even more interesting are the unusual exhibits on Costa Rican history. Indigenous artifacts, including some worthwhile copies of the area's more important archaeological finds, are a treat. The collection of Spanish-colonial relics is even more impressive, featuring not only antiques collected by the owners, but interesting family heirlooms as well – Gámez's great-grandmother was pen pals with famed Nicaraguan poet Rubén Darío. The fee also includes access to the lodge's private trails and gardens.

Selva Verde

In Chilamate, about 7km west of Puerto Viejo, this former finca is now an elegant **lodge** (☎ 766-6800, in the USA 800-451 7111; www.selvaverde.com; s/d/tr/q incl meals US$98/162/201/220, child 12-15 yrs US$32) that protects over 200 hectares of rain forest. Guests can choose to stay in the river lodge, which is elevated above the rain-forest floor on wooden platforms, or in a private bungalow, quietly tucked away in the nearby rainforest. Rustic rooms have a private hot shower, great views and of course, your very own hammock.

The lodge works closely with Elderhostel (a tour company for over-55s; see p554) and offers educational opportunities, guided tours and other interesting diversions, many of which nonguests can enjoy for a fee.

There are several kilometers of walking trails through the grounds and into the

LOCAL LORE

Young men throughout Costa Rica delight in telling the story of *la machaca*, an insect famously possessed of venom with an odd antidote: women bitten by the bug must make love within 24 hours...or die. The sad reality for amorous men on the prowl is that the insect does not actually bite young women, and is in fact completely harmless.

The machaca is about 7.5cm long, and most likely one of the strangest looking critters you've ever seen. It has a huge protuberance on its head that is reminiscent of a lizard, and is believed to be luminescent. It also has a number of fake eyes on its wings as a defense mechanism against predators.

pre-montane tropical wet forest; you can either get a trail map or can hire a bilingual guide from the lodge (per person US$15, three hours). There's also a garden of medicinal plants, as well as a **butterfly garden** (admission US$5, free for lodge guests). Various boat tours on the Río Sarapiquí are also available, from rafting trips to guided canoe tours; locally guided horseback rides (US$20 for two to three hours) can also be arranged.

The Holbrook family, which owns the lodge, also funds the nonprofit Sarapiquí Conservation Learning Center nearby, where guests can visit (US$20), buy their arts and crafts, chat with locals and perhaps make a donation.

PUERTO VIEJO DE SARAPIQUÍ & AROUND

At the scenic confluence of Río Puerto Viejo and Río Sarapiquí, Puerto Viejo de Sarapiquí was once the most important port in Costa Rica. Boats laden with bananas, coffee and other commercial exports plied the Sarapiquí as far as the Nicaraguan border, then turned east on the Río San Juan to the sea. Today, Puerto Viejo (the full name distinguishes it from Puerto Viejo de Talamanca on the Caribbean coast) is simply a jungle border town – slightly seedy in a film-noir sort of way. There are, however, numerous opportunities in the surrounding area for birding, rafting, boating and jungle exploration.

Migraciónes is near the small wooden dock, sometimes avoided by visiting Nicaraguans who share the river with local fishers and visiting birders. Adventure seekers can still travel down the Sarapiquí in motorized dugout canoes.

There is no dry season, but late January to early May is the 'less wet' season. On the upside, when it rains there are fewer mosquitoes.

Banco Popular has an ATM and changes money. **Internet Sarapiquí** (☎ 766 6223; per hr US$2; ☺ 8am-10pm) is at the west end of town. **Souvenir Río Sarapiquí** (☎ 766 6727), on the main street, has tour information on birding, kayaking, white-water rafting and zip lining.

Activities

Grassroots environmental activity is strong in this area. Local guide Alex Martínez, owner of the Posada Andrea Cristina B&B, maintains an **ecotourism center** (☎ 766 6265; ☺ 8am-3pm), which focuses on conservation activities and wilderness tours – **birding** trips in particular. You can also arrange transportation and make other reservations here, as well as learn about worthwhile volunteer opportunities in the region.

If you're looking to organize a rafting or kayaking trip, a branch of **Aguas Bravas** (☎ 292 2072; www.aguas-bravas.co.cr) is across the road from the bank. You can also try **Costa Rica Fun Adventures** (☎ 290 6015; www.crfunadventures.com), which is 2km north of town and offers a good variety of guided hiking and horse riding trips.

Sleeping

The region boasts a huge range of accommodations, from budget bunks, designed for local long-term plantation workers, situated in town, to several extraordinary lodges on the outskirts, the most exclusive of which are on the road to La Virgen. Lodges in the area north of Puerto Viejo are also listed, including one in the river town of Trinidad, on the Nicaraguan border.

BUDGET

Cabinas Restaurant Monteverde (☎ 766 6236; s/ d US$4/8 P) Fairly dark and dingy rooms here are the cheapest in town, but if you're not counting every dollar then it's worth heading elsewhere. The attached restaurant, with similarly low prices, serves great typical Tico food.

DAY TRIPPER

Looking for something to do? Here are a few suggestions:

- Getting your adrenaline fix in a **kayak** or **raft** on the Río Sarapiquí (see above).
- Seeing biologists in action at the **Estación Biológica La Selva** (p522).
- Learning how to distinguish different species of heliconia at **Heliconia Island** (p523).
- Journeying to Nicaragua (and back) in a motorized canoe on the **Río San Juan** (p523).
- Spotting rare species while **birding** with local hero Alex Martínez (left).

Mi Lindo Sarapiquí (☎ 766 6281; s/d US$12/20; **P**) On the south side of the soccer field, this is the best budget option in the town center. Rooms here are simple but spacious and clean, and have a private hot shower and fan. The on-site restaurant (mains US$4 to US$9, open 8am to 10pm) is slightly pricey, though it offers some of the freshest seafood in town.

Trinidad Lodge (☎ 213 0661, 381 0621; s/d US$15/20) Situated on the Río San Juan in the community of Trinidad, this budget lodge is right across from the Nicaraguan border crossing, and gets rave reviews from travelers. It is accessible only by boat (US$5), which departs at 11am from the main dock of Puerto Viejo de Sarapiquí (35km away) and returns at 2pm. It's a working ranch, and several rustic cabins comfortably sleeping three have a private bathroom. Home-cooked meals (US$4 to US$8) are available, and you can arrange horse rentals and also boat tours at the desk.

MIDRANGE
Posada Andrea Cristina B&B (☎ 766 6265; www .andreacristina.com; s/d/tr US$25/45/65) About 1km west of the center, this recommended B&B has six quiet little cabins in its garden, each with fan and a private hot-water bathroom. It's also situated on the edge of the rain forest, so there are plenty of opportunities for birding while you sit outside and eat breakfast (US$20 extra). The owner, Alex Martínez, is an excellent, charming guide as well as a passionate frontline conservationist. He arrived here 30 years ago as a tough young hunter exploring what was virgin forest, and saw the jungle's rapid destruction in the hands of humankind. He changed his philosophy and is now a volunteer game warden – who will abandon a Saturday-night soccer match to chase down poachers on the river. He helped found Asociación para el Bienestar Ambiental de Sarapiquí (ABAS), a local environmental-protection and education agency. Alex, who speaks excellent English, runs an on-site ecotourism center (see opposite), and can tell you as much as you want to know about environmental issues in the area. Alex's latest project involves planting mass tracts of wild almond trees, which are the preferred trees for nesting green macaw (see the boxed text Fine, Feathered Friends, p506).

Los Cuajipales (☎ 283 9797, 766 6608; camping per person US$10, r per person US$17-25; **P** **🐕**) About 3km north of town on a good gravel road, this rustic complex is geared toward Tico tourists. Comfortable thatch-roofed cabinas sleeping up to five were designed according to Huetar Indian techniques that keep them naturally cool (cable TV and private cold showers are, however, less authentic). All rates include meals at the casually elegant restaurant and access to the rather extravagant pool, table-tennis and billiard tables, 4km of private trails and tilapia pond.

Hotel Ara Ambigua (☎ 766 6743; www.gavilan lodge.com; s/d/tr US$28/40/60; **P** **🐕**) One kilometer west of Puerto Viejo near La Guaíra, this countryside retreat has 19 rustic cabinas that are well equipped with private hot-water showers and cable TV. The real draw is the varied opportunities for wild-life-watching – you can see poison-dart frogs in the *ranario* (frog pond), caiman in the small lake and occasionally rare green macaw in the treetops.

Hotel El Bambú (☎ 766 6359; www.elbambu.com; s/d incl breakfast US$55/70; **P** **🐕** **🐕**) You really can't miss the sign for downtown Puerto Viejo's finest lodging, which caters mostly to package tourists looking for a clean and comfortable base when they're not out on 'adventure tours.' Rooms are all equipped with air-con and hot water, and there's a big pool and a popular restaurant, though the whole package just doesn't seem to justify the price.

El Gavilán (☎ 766 6743; www.gavilanlodge.com; s/d incl breakfast US$50/75; **P**) Sitting on a 100-hectare reserve about 4km northeast of Puerto Viejo, this former cattle hacienda is cozy, quaint and a birding paradise. Birders can watch the colorful action in the attractive gardens from the porches of spacious cabins that have big hot-water shower and fan; some have river views. The grounds feature 5km of private trails and a good restaurant, plus a nice outdoor Jacuzzi to relax in after a long hike. Boat trips are also a big attraction here, and range from short jaunts down the Río Sarapiquí to overnights in Tortuguero. Multi-day package deals are available that include meals, tours and transportation from San José.

A taxi or boat from Puerto Viejo costs US$4. There's a signed turnoff from Hwy 4 about 2km from town.

Eating

Most of the lodging in and around Puerto Viejo have on-site restaurants or provide meals.

There are several *sodas* in Puerto Viejo de Sarapiquí, including the excellent **Soda Judith** (mains US$2-4; ☺ 6am-7pm), one block off the main road, where early risers grab brewed coffee and big breakfasts or an *empanada* (meat or chicken turnover) to start their day. **Restaurant La Casona** (meals US$4-10) at the Hotel Ara Ambigua is particularly reader-recommended for its homemade, typical cuisine served in an old barn complete with old farming equipment adorning the walls.

There's also a **Palí Supermarket** (☺ 8am-9pm) at the west end of town.

Getting There & Away

Puerto Viejo de Sarapiquí has been a transport center longer than Costa Rica's been a country, and is easily accessed by paved major roads from San José, the Caribbean coast and other population centers. There is a taxi stop across from the bus terminal, and taxis will take you to the nearby lodges and Estación Biológica La Selva for US$3 to US$6.

BUS

Right across from the park, the **bus terminal** (☎ 233 4242; ☺ 5am-7pm) sells tickets and stores backpacks (US$1.50).

Ciudad Quesada/San Carlos via La Virgen (Empresarios Guapileños) US$1.50, three hours, depart 5:30am, 9am, 2pm, 3:30pm and 7:30pm.

Guápiles (Empresarios Guapileños) US$1.50, one hour, eight times daily from 5:30am to 6:40pm.

San José (Autotransportes Sarapiquí) US$2.50, two hours, 5am, 5:30am, 7am, 7:30am, 8am, 11am, 11:30am, 1:30pm, 3pm, 4:30pm and 5:30pm.

BOAT

The small port has a regular service to the Trinidad Lodge in Trinidad, and you are able to arrange transportation anywhere along the river (seasonal conditions permitting) through independent boat captains. Short trips cost about US$10 per hour per person for a group of four, or US$20 per hour for a single person. Serious voyages to Tortuguero or Barra del Colorado and back cost about US$350 for a boat holding five.

SOUTH OF PUERTO VIEJO DE SARAPIQUÍ

South of Puerto Viejo de Sarapiquí, the legacy of United Fruit is still evident in the endless banana plantations that stretch as far as the Caribbean coast. To the west, the rugged hills of the Cordillera Central mark the northeastern boundary of Parque Nacional Braulio Carrillo. Travelers on this scenic stretch of highway are either heading to points on the Caribbean Coast or in the Central Valley. However, it's worth slowing down a bit as this area is home to a working biological research station, a world-class botanical garden and perhaps the most isolated lodge in the entire country.

About 4km and 10km southeast of Puerto Viejo are, respectively, the entrances to Estación Biológica La Selva and Heliconia Island. About 15km further is the village of Horquetas, from where it's another 15km on a dirt road to the rain-forest preservation project and lodge at Rara Avis. From Horquetas the paved road continues for about 17km through banana plantations to Hwy 32, which connects San José to the Caribbean coast. The route to San José takes you through the middle of Parque Nacional Braulio Carrillo.

ESTACIÓN BIOLÓGICA LA SELVA

Not to be confused with Selva Verde in Chilamate, **Estación Biológica La Selva** (☎ 524 0629; www.ots.ac.cr; s/d with bathroom US$62/78, without bathroom US$56/70; P) is a working biological research station that is well equipped with laboratories, experimental plots, a herbarium and an extensive library. On any given day, the station is usually teeming with scientists and students, who use the station as a headquarters for researching the nearby private reserve. Although most guests are affiliated with an institution of higher learning, La Selva does welcome drop-ins, though it's best to phone ahead and reserve your accommodation. Rooms are basic, with fan and bunk beds (a few have doubles), but rates include all meals and guided hikes.

La Selva is operated by the **Organization for Tropical Studies** (OTS; ☎ 240 6696; www.ots.ac.cr), a consortium founded in 1963 to provide leadership in the education, research and wise use of tropical natural resources. In fact, many well-known tropical ecologists have trained at La Selva. Twice a year OTS offers a grueling eight-week course open mainly to graduate students of ecology, along with various other courses and field trips that you can apply for.

The area protected by La Selva is 1513 hectares of pre-montane wet-tropical rain forest, much of it undisturbed. It's bordered to the south by the 476 sq km of Parque Nacional Braulio Carrillo, creating a protected area large enough to support a great diversity of life. More than 430 bird species have been recorded at La Selva, as well as 120 mammal species, 1900 species of vascular plants (especially from the orchid, philodendron, coffee and legume families) and thousands of insect species.

Hiking

Reservations are required for guided hikes (US$26/40 per person for four/eight hours, children half price; 8am and 1:30pm daily) across the hanging bridge and into 50km of well-developed jungle trails, some of which are wheelchair accessible. Unguided hiking is forbidden, although you'll be allowed to wander a bit after your guided tour. You should make reservations for the popular

guided birding hikes, led at 6am and 7pm, depending on demand. Profits from these walks help to fund the research station.

No matter when you visit La Selva, it will probably be raining. Bring rain gear and footwear that's suitable for muddy trails. Insect repellent and a water bottle are also essential.

For the truly rugged do-it-yourself adventures, it's possible to hike from La Selva to the southernmost ranger stations in Parque Nacional Braulio Carrillo. For more information, see p164.

Getting There & Away

Public buses between Puerto Viejo and Río Frío/Horquetas can drop you off 2km from the entrance to La Selva. It's about 3km from Puerto Viejo, where you can catch a taxi for around US$3 to US$5.

OTS runs buses (US$10) from San José on Monday. Make reservations when you arrange your visit, and note that researchers and students have priority.

HELICONIA ISLAND

This self-proclaimed 'oasis of serenity' is arguably the most beautiful garden in all of Costa Rica. **Heliconia Island** (☎ 764 5220; www .heliconiaisland.com; tour with/without lunch US$25/15) is

---

BOATING TO NICARAGUA   Rob Rachowiecki

Sailing down the Río Sarapiquí to the Río San Juan is a memorable trip. If the water is low, dozens of crocodiles can be seen sunning themselves on the banks. If the water is high, river turtles climb out of the river to sun themselves on logs. Birds are everywhere. North of Puerto Viejo much of the land is cattle pasture with few trees, but as you approach the Nicaraguan border more stands of forest are seen. In trees on the banks you may see monkeys, iguanas or maybe a snake draped over a branch.

On my trip the boat captain suddenly cut the engine, so I turned around to see what the matter was. He grinned and yelled and it was not until the dugout had gently nosed into the bank beneath the tree that I saw a sloth raise a languid head to see what was going on. How he managed to make out that the greenish-brown blob on a branch (the color is caused by the algae that grows in the fur of this lethargic animal) was a sloth is one of the mysteries of traveling with a sharp-eyed *campesino*.

We continued on down to the confluence of the Sarapiquí with the San Juan, where we stopped to visit an old Miskito Indian fisher named Leandro. He claimed to be 80 years old, but his wizened frame had the vitality of a man half his age. From the bulging woven-grass bag in the bottom of his fragile dugout, Leandro sold us fresh river lobster to accompany that evening's supper.

The official border between Nicaragua and Costa Rica is the south bank of the San Juan, not the middle of the river, so you are technically traveling into Nicaragua when on the San Juan. This river system is a historically important gateway from the Caribbean into the heart of Central America. Today it remains off the beaten tourist track and allows the traveler to see a combination of rain forest and ranches, wildlife and old war zones, deforested areas and protected areas.

NORTHERN LOWLANDS

a masterpiece of landscape architecture that was started in 1992 by New York City native Tim Ryan, a former professor of art and design. Today, this 2-hectare island is home to more than 80 varieties of heliconia, tropical flowers, plants and trees, and is a refuge for 228 species of birds (hummingbirds are the sole pollinators of heliconias). There are also four resident howler monkeys, three species of river otters and a couple of friendly (and large) dogs that will greet you upon arrival.

Tim will guide you through the property with grace and expertise, and you'll see a number of memorable plants including the Madagascar traveling palm, rare hybrids of heliconia found only on the island and the *Phenakospermum guyannense* (or Phenomenal sperm), a unique flowering plant native to Guyana. The tour lasts for about 1½ hours, and it's most definitely worth sticking around for lunch as Tim's riverside house is almost as beautiful as the gardens themselves.

Heliconia Island is about 5km north of Horquetas, and there are signs along the highway pointing to the entrance. When you arrive at the entrance, park your car, walk across the metal bridge and turn left on the island to reach Tim's house.

RARA AVIS

When they say remote, they mean remote: this **private reserve** (☎ 764 3131; www.rara-avis .com; **P**), which is comprised of 1335 hectares of high-altitude tropical rain forest, is accessible only to overnight guests willing to make the three-hour tractor ride (seriously!) up a steep, muddy hill to get there.

Rara Avis was founded by Amos Bien, an American who came to Costa Rica as a biology student in 1977. Amos is dedicated to environmental conservation, and has been involved in a number of ongoing sustainability projects since his arrival. The private reserve borders the eastern edge of Parque Nacional Braulio Carrillo and has no real dry season. **Birding** here is excellent, with more than 350 species sighted so far, while mammals including monkeys, coatis, anteaters and pacas are often seen. Visitors can use the trail system alone or on guided hikes included in the cost of lodging. A popular jaunt is the short trail leading from the lodge to **La Catarata**, a 55m-high waterfall that cuts an impressive swath through the forest.

The accommodations, although lovely, are rustic – most don't have electricity, though the kerosene lamps and starry skies are unforgettable. Room prices, which include all meals, transportation and a guided hike, seem high, but it's because of the remote location – you, the groceries and the guides all have to be hauled up that mountain from Horquetas.

Very basic **cabins** (r per person US$45) in the woods sleep four and have shared cold-water bathrooms, while nicer rooms in the **Waterfall Lodge** (s/d/tr US$80/140/180) have private hot-water shower and balcony overlooking the rain forest. Even when it's pouring outside you can watch birds from your private balcony. The **River-Edge Cabin** (s/d/tr US$90/160/210) is the nicest spot, with solar-powered electricity, hot water and separate rooms. It's a dark (or romantic, depending on the company) 10-minute hike from the rest of the lodge.

Because access is time consuming and difficult, a two-night stay is recommended. The bus to Puerto Viejo de Sarapiquí leaves San José (US$4.50, four hours) from the Guápiles-Limón terminal at 6:30am, though you'll need to get off at Horquetas. Here, you'll embark on the famed tractor ride. You can also arrange to be taken by jeep or on horseback, both of which require hiking the last 3km yourself.

Directory

CONTENTS

ACCOMMODATIONS

The hotel situation in Costa Rica ranges from luxurious and sparkling all-inclusive resorts to dingy, I-can't-believe-I'm-paying-for-this barnyard-style quarters. The sheer number of hotels means that it's rare to arrive in a town and find nowhere to sleep.

In touristy towns, you'll find plenty of cabinas, a loose term for cheap to midrange lodging. Apartotels are like a hotel room but with equipped kitchens. This type of accommodation can usually be rented for a cheaper rate for week- and month-long stays.

High-season (December to April) prices are provided throughout this book, though many lodges lower their prices during the rainy season. Some beach towns will also charge high-season prices in June and July, when travelers from the northern hemisphere arrive in their droves. During Semana Santa (Easter Week) and the week between Christmas and New Year, hotels raise their rates beyond what's listed throughout this book. During this time, you should make reservations well in advance. During school-vacation weekends in January and February it's advisable to book your accommodation before arriving at your destination.

PRACTICALITIES

- **Electricity** Electrical current is 110V AC at 60Hz and plugs are two flat prongs (same as USA).

- **Newspapers** The most widely distributed newspaper is *La Nación* (www.nacion.co.cr), followed by *Al Día* (a tabloid), *La República* and *La Prensa Libre* (www.prensalibre.co.cr). The *Tico Times* (www.ticotimes.net), the English-language weekly newspaper, hits the streets every Friday afternoon.

- **Magazines** The Spanish-language *Esta Semana* is the best local weekly news magazine.

- **TV** Cable and satellite TV are widely available for a fix of CNN, French videos or Japanese news, and local TV stations have a mix of news, variety shows and *telenovelas* (Spanish-language soap operas).

- **Radio** 107.5FM is the English-language radio station, playing current hits and providing a regular BBC news feed.

- **Video Systems** Videos on sale use the NTSC image registration system (same as USA).

- **Weights & Measures** Costa Ricans use the metric system for weights, distances and measures.

If you're traveling in from another part of Central America, note that prices in Costa Rica will generally be much higher than in the rest of the region. The boxed text Bargaining (p540) has more advice about costs.

Sleeping options are listed in order of budget, unless otherwise specified.

B&Bs

Almost unknown in the country in the 1980s, the B&B phenomenon has swept Costa Rica. They vary from midrange up to top-end options. While some B&Bs are reviewed in this guide, you can also find this type of accommodation on several websites (although they are far from exhaustive):

Bed and Breakfast dot-com (www.bedandbreakfast.com/costa-rica.html)

Costa Rica Innkeepers Association (☎ 441 1157; www.costaricainnkeepers.com)

Pamela Lanier's Bed and Breakfasts (www.lanierbb.com/costa_rica)

Camping

Camping is the way many Ticos (Costa Ricans) enjoy the more expensive seaside towns. Most destinations have at least one campsite, and if not, many budget hotels outside San José accommodate campers on their grounds. The sites usually include toilets and cold showers and can be crowded, noisy affairs. Campsites are available at many national parks as well; take all food and supplies in and out with you.

Camping can be a challenge anywhere because of the bounteous mosquitoes. Pack repellent or you'll be a human buffet. In addition, camping fuel can be difficult to find in remote areas, so stock up in San José. The Cemaco (see p140) in Escazú stocks it. Camping prices in this book are listed per

person, per night. In some places it is possible to camp on public beaches for free.

Hostels

There are some Hostelling International (HI) hostels, but offerings in Costa Rica tend to be fairly expensive. Most places will charge US$11 to US$40 per person for a bed. Hostal Toruma (p129) in San José is a member and can make reservations in HI-affiliated hostels around the country.

There are numerous independently run hostels in Costa Rica, which are considerably cheaper than the HI ones. San José has several places, as does Manuel Antonio, Puerto Viejo de Talamanca and Tamarindo. The least-expensive private rooms in budget hotels are often as cheap as hostels.

Hotels

It is always advisable to ask to see a room – and a bathroom – before committing to a stay, especially in budget lodgings.

BUDGET

For the most part, this guide's budget category covers lodging in which a typical double costs up to US$20. Cheaper places generally have shared bathrooms, but it's still possible to get a double with a private bathroom for US$10 in some towns off the tourist trail. (Note that 'private' in some low-end establishments consists of a stall in the corner of your hotel room.) On the top end of the budget scale, rooms will frequently include a fan and private bathroom that may or may not have hot water. At the cheapest hotels, rooms will frequently be a stall, with walls that don't go to the ceiling.

Hot water in showers is often supplied by electric showerheads (affectionately termed the 'Costa Rican suicide shower'). Contrary to traveler folklore, they are perfectly safe – provided you don't fiddle with the showerhead while it's on. It will actually dispense hot water if you keep the pressure low.

MIDRANGE & TOP END

Midrange generally covers hotels that charge between US$30 and US$80. These rooms will be more comfortable than budget options and include a private bathroom with hot water, a choice between fans and air-con, and maybe even cable TV. The better places will offer tour services and

---

HOTEL SECURITY

Although hotels give you room keys, it is recommended that you carry a padlock for your backpack or suitcase. Don't leave valuables, cash or important documents lying around your room or in an unlocked bag. Upmarket hotels will have safes where you can keep your money and passport. If you're staying in a basic place, take your valuables with you.

RESERVING BY CREDIT CARD

Some of the pricier hotels will require that you confirm your reservation with a credit card. Before doing so, note that some top-end hotels require a 50% to 100% payment up front when you reserve. Unfortunately, many of them aren't very clear about this rule.

Sometimes visitors end up 'reserving' a room only to find out that they have actually paid for it in advance. Technically, reservations can be cancelled and refunded with enough advance notice. (Again, ask the hotel about its cancellation policy.) However, in Costa Rica it's a lot easier to make the reservation than to unmake it. In addition, many hotels charge a 7% service fee for credit card use.

Have the hotel fax or email you a confirmation. Hotels often get overbooked, and if you don't have confirmation, you could be out of a room.

---

many will have an on-site restaurant or bar and a swimming pool or Jacuzzi. In this price range, many hotels offer kitchenettes and even full kitchens. (This is a popular choice for families.)

Anything more than US$80 is considered top end and includes all-inclusive resorts, business and chain hotels, in addition to a strong network of more intimate boutique hotels, jungle lodges and upmarket B&Bs. Many such lodging options will include amenities such as hot-water bath tubs, private decks, cable TV, air-con, as well as concierge, tour and spa services.

Most midrange and top-end places charge 16.39% in taxes. This book has attempted to include taxes in the prices listed throughout. Note that many hotels charge per person, rather than per room; read rates carefully. See also the boxed text Reserving by Credit Card, above.

ACTIVITIES
Bungee Jumping
No vacation appears to be complete without a head-first, screaming plunge off a bridge. **Tropical Bungee** (☎ 248 2212, 383 9724; www.bungee.co.cr; 1st/2nd jump US$60/30) in San José has been organizing jumps off the Río Colorado bridge since 1992.

Canopy Tours
Life in the rain forest takes place at canopy level. But with trees extending 30m to 60m in height, the average human has a hard time getting a look at what's going on up there. Enter the so-called 'canopy tour.'

Some companies have built elevated walkways through the trees that allow hikers to stroll through. SkyWalk (p195) near Monteverde and Rainmaker (p341) near

Quepos are known for this. A new operation is Actividades Arboreales (p371) near Santa María de Dota. You can also take a ski-lift-style ride through the tree tops, such as the Rainforest Aerial Tram (p165) near Braulio Carrillo or the smaller Aerial Adventures (p196) in Monteverde.

Other outfitters have built viewing platforms into huge trees. Visitors are winched up 20m or more into the canopy where they lie in wait for the wildlife to swing by (which they often do). Good sites are at Hacienda Barú Coast (p361) and Corcovado Lodge Tent Camp (p429). Pack your binoculars.

And, of course, there's nothing quite like sailing through the rain forest at high speeds à la *George of the Jungle*. On zipline tours, adventurers are strapped into harnesses and hooked onto a cable-and-pulley system that allows them to traverse from tower to tower. Operators sell this as a great way to see nature, but plan on viewing broccoli-sized trees as you go whizzing past at full throttle.

One of the top zip-line experiences is at SkyTrek (p195) in Monteverde. The Original Canopy Tour (see the boxed text Canopy Fighting, p196) operates rides at several locations. Nearly every town has an independent operator to indulge wannabe Tarzans.

Zip-line adventures are not without risk. Travelers have been injured, and in a couple of cases killed. Go with well-recommended tour operators and make sure that you're provided with: a secure harness with two straps that attach to the cable (one is a safety strap); a hard hat; and gloves.

Diving & Snorkeling
For sheer numbers and variety of sea life, Costa Rica's underwater world is excellent

for diving and snorkeling. As a general rule, water visibility is not good during the rainy months, when rivers swell and their outflow clouds the ocean. At this time, boats to locations offshore offer better viewing opportunities.

The water is warm – around 24°C to 29°C at the surface, with a thermocline at around 20m below the surface, where it drops to 23°C. If you're keeping it shallow, you can skin dive (ie no wet suit). See p75 for the best dive sites in Costa Rica.

If you want to spend time diving, it's advisable to get diving accreditation ahead of time. Get information from the **Professional Association of Diving Instructors** (PADI; in the USA ☎ 949-858 7234, 800-729 7234, in Canada 604-552 5969, 800-565 8130, in Switzerland 52-304 1414; www.padi.com). **Divers Alert Network** (in the USA ☎ 800-446 2671, 919-684 2948; www.diversalertnetwork.org) is a nonprofit organization that provides diving insurance and emergency medical evacuation.

If you are interested in diving but are not accredited, you can usually do a one-day introductory course that will allow you to do accompanied dives. If you love it, consider accreditation, which takes three to four days and costs around US$350.

Dive companies offering tours to Costa Rica:

JD's Watersports (in the USA ☎ 970-356 1028, 800-477 8971; www.jdwatersports.com)

Okeanos Aggressor (in the USA ☎ 985-385 2628, in the USA & Canada 800-348 2628; www.aggressor.com)

Undersea Hunter (☎ 228 6613, in the USA 800-203 2120; www.underseahunter.com)

For snorkelers, many coastal areas have popular reefs. Leading destinations include Cahuita (p478), Manzanillo (p497), Isla del Caño (p413) and Isla Tortuga (p304).

Fishing

Sportfishing is tremendously popular, and 'catch-and-release' is strongly encouraged (though some fish are kept to eat).

Inland, fishing in rivers and lakes is popular. Particularly recommended are the Río Savegre near San Gerardo de Dota for trout fishing (p374) and Caño Negro for snook (p510). Check with the local operators about closed seasons.

The ocean is always open for fishing. As a general rule, the Pacific coast is slowest from September to November, though

you'll get better fishing on the south coast during that period, while the Caribbean is slowest during June and July. For more information, see p80.

A good resource is **Costa Rica Outdoors** (☎ 282 6743, in the USA 800-308 3394; www.costaricaoutdoors.com), a magazine carrying information on adventure travel, with a focus on fishing. Other companies offering fishing tours:

Discover Costa Rica (☎ 257 5780, in the USA 888-484 8227; www.discover-costa-rica.com) Offers six-day fishing packages based in Quepos.

JD's Watersports (in the USA ☎ 970-356 1028, 800-477 8971; www.jdwatersports.com)

Rod & Reel Adventures (in the USA ☎ 800-356 6982; www.rodreeladventures.com)

Hiking & Trekking

For long-distance hiking and trekking, it's best to travel in the dry season. In Parque Nacional Corcovado rivers become impassable and trails are shut down in the wet. The trek up Cerro Chirripó becomes more taxing in the rain and the bare landscape offers little protection. For more details on trekking options see p73. Maps are not widely available; see p537.

Be sure to pack a hat, sunscreen, insect repellent and plenty of water – and always carry trash out with you. The parks have a limited ability to collect trash, so do them and the environment a favor and dispose of your own garbage after leaving the park.

Assaults and robberies have been reported in some parks, namely Carara and Braulio Carrillo, as well as Gandoca-Manzanillo and on the road between La Palma and Los Patos near Corcovado. For maximum safety, go in a group or with a guide. For other precautions, see p532.

Some companies offering trekking tours include:

Costa Rica Trekking Adventures (☎ 771 4582; www.chirripo.com; San Isidro de General) Offers multiday treks in Chirripó, Corcovado and Tapantí.

Ocarina Expeditions (☎ 229 4278; www.ocarinaexpeditions.com) Naturalist-led treks in Corcovado and Chirripó, as well as volcano and cloud forest hiking.

Osa Aventura (☎ 735 5670; www.osaaventura.com) Specializes in treks through Corcovado.

Horse Riding

Wherever you go in Costa Rica, you will certainly find someone giving riding trips. Rates vary from US$25 for an hour or two to US$100 for a full day. Overnight trips with pack horses can also be arranged. Riders weighing more than 100kg (221lb) cannot expect small local horses to carry them very far.

With the increased demand for riding, some unscrupulous owners have worked their horses past breaking point. In the past, the trail between La Fortuna and Monteverde was a center of such abuse, where overworked horses were forced through muddy trails and chest-deep rivers. Recently, the situation appears to have improved (see p206). Ask to see the condition of the horses before setting out.

Riding along the beach is popular and possible at any number of beach towns, but don't ride through crowded beach areas, especially at high speeds. Isolated beach areas aren't hard to find. Make sure your guide is respectful of this.

Travelers should continue to recommend good outfitters (and give the heads up on bad ones) by writing to Lonely Planet.

Sarapiquí Aguas Bravas (☎ 292 2072; www.aguas -bravas.co.cr) Offers rafting, biking and horse riding day trips around Sarapiquí and La Virgen.

Serendipity Adventures (☎ 558 1000, in the USA 734-995 0111, 800-635 2325; www.serendipityadventures .com) Creates high-quality horse riding itineraries, including journeys to a Cabécar indigenous reserve.

Mountain Biking & Motorcycling

Outfitters in Costa Rica and the USA can organize multiday mountain-biking trips around Costa Rica that cover stretches of highland and beach. Gear is provided on trips organized by local companies, but US outfitters require that you bring your own.

Most international airlines will fly your bike as a piece of checked baggage if you box it. (Pad it well, because the box is liable to be roughly handled.) Other airlines might charge you an extra handling fee.

You can rent mountain bikes in almost any tourist town, but the condition of the equipment varies; you may also be able to buy a decent bike and sell it back at a reduced rate at the end of your trip. It is advisable to bring your own helmet and water bottle. For a monthly fee of US$10, **Trail Source** (www.trailsource.com) can provide you with information on trails all over Costa Rica and the world.

For organized tours:

Backroads (in the USA ☎ 510-527 1555, 800-462 2848; www.backroads.com) Offers a six-day cycling trip around Arenal and the Pacific Coast for US$2400.

Coast to Coast Adventures (☎ 280 8054; www.ctoc adventures.com) Everything from short biking excursions to 14-day coast-to-coast multisport trips.

Costa Rica Expeditions (☎ 257 0766, 222 0333; www.costaricaexpeditions.com) Multisport itineraries including biking, hiking, rafting and other adventures.

Harley Davidson Rentals (☎ 289 5552; www.maria alexandra.com) See p133.

Lava Tours (☎ 281 2458; www.lava-tours.com) Reader-recommended tours include a bike ride (mostly downhill!) from the Cerro de la Muerte to Manuel Antonio. Offers day-trips, multiday packages and riding clinics.

MotoDiscovery (in the USA ☎ 800-233 6564, 830-438 7744; www.motodiscovery.com) Organizes motorcycle tours through Central America – including an annual trip that takes riders from the Río Grande in Mexico to the Panama Canal on their own motorcycles.

Serendipity Adventures (☎ 558 1000, in the USA 734-995 0111, 800-635 2325; www.serendipityadventures .com) Creates custom biking itineraries to fit your schedule and your group.

Western Spirit Cycling (in the USA ☎ 800-845 2453; www.westernspirit.com) Offers a few different eight-day biking itineraries for US$1750 to US$1825.

Wild Rider (☎ 258 4604; www.wild-rider.com) See San José, p127.

River Running & Kayaking

Between June and October are considered the wildest months for rafting, but some rivers offer good running all year. Rafters should bring sunblock, a spare change of clothes, a waterproof bag for your camera and river sandals to protect your feet. The regulation of outfitters is poor, so make sure that your guide is well versed in safety and has had emergency medical training.

River kayaking can be organized in conjunction with rafting trips if you are experienced; sea kayaking is popular year-round.

The Adventure Travel chapter has more detailed information on destinations (p75).

Many companies specialize in kayaking and rafting trips (but will arrange other tours):

Aventuras Naturales (☎ 225 3939, 224 0505, in the USA 800-514 0411; www.toenjoynature.com)

BattenKill Canoe Ltd (in the USA ☎ 802-362 2800, 800-421 5268; www.battenkill.com) Trips include a six-day canoe journey around Monteverde (US$1250) and an 11-day paddle through Talamanca (US$1800).

Coast to Coast Adventures (☎ 280 8054; www.ctoc adventures.com) Trips incorporate rafting, biking and trekking.

Costa Rica Expeditions (☎ 257 0766, 222 0333; www.costaricaexpeditions.com) Multisport itineraries including rafting and other adventures.

Costa Rica Sun Tours (☎ 296 7757; www.crsuntours.com)

Exploradores Outdoors (☎ 222 6262; www.explora doresoutdoors.com) With offices in San José and Puerto Viejo de Talamanca, offers one- and two-day rafting trips.

Gulf Islands Kayaking (in Canada ☎ 250-539 2442; www.seakayak.ca) Tours on offer include five days of sea kayaking in Corcovado (US$1300).

H2O Adventures (☎ 777 4092; www.aventurash2o .com) Two- and five-day adventures on the Río Savegre. Also offers day-long river-rafting and sea-kayaking excursions.

Mountain Travel Sobek (in the USA ☎ 510-594 6000, 888-687 6235; www.mtsobek.com) Offers a 10-day adventure that incorporates sea kayaking and river rafting (US$2400).

Ocarina Expeditions (☎ 229 4278; www.ocarinaex peditions.com)

Ríos Tropicales (☎ 233 6455; www.riostropicales.com) Offers many day-long river-rafting trips, as well as some two- and three-day adventures on the Río Pacuare and two days of kayaking in Tortuguero.

Safaris Corobicí (☎ 669 6191; www.nicoya.com) These slow-moving rafting trips are less for adventurers and more for birders.

Sarapiquí Aguas Bravas (☎ 292 2072; www.aguas -bravas.co.cr) Offers rafting, biking and horse riding day trips around Sarapiquí and La Virgen.

Surfing

Most international airlines accept surfboards (properly packed in a padded board bag) as one of the two pieces of checked luggage. However, domestic airlines offer more of a challenge. They will accept surfboards (for an extra charge), but the board must be under 2.1m (7ft) in length. If the plane is full, there's a chance your board won't make it on because of weight restrictions. It's also possible to buy a board (new or used) in Costa Rica, and then sell it before you leave. Outfitters in many of the popular surf towns rent short and long boards, fix dings, give classes and organize excursions. Jacó (p331), Tamarindo (p276), Pavones (p441) and Puerto Viejo de Talamanca (p481) are good for these types of activities.

For detailed information, including a surf map, turn to p77.

Costa Rica Rainforest Outward Bound (☎ 278 6058, in the USA 800-676 2018; www.crrobs.org) Courses cover the surf in Nicaragua, Panama and Costa Rica eight/15/30 days US$1195/1995/2995).

Discover Costa Rica (☎ 257 5780, in the USA 888-484 8227; www.discover-costa-rica.com) Budget surf packages start at US$304 for six days in Tamarindo or US$513 for 10 days in Jacó and on the Caribbean coast.

Pura Vida Adventures (☎ in the USA 415-465 2162; www.puravidaadventures.com; Malpaís) Six-day packages for women and couples (US$1540).

Tico Travel (☎ in the USA 800-493 8426; www.tico travel.com) Offers a great variety of surfing packages and camps.

Venus Surf Adventures (☎ 840 2365, in the USA 800-793 0512; www.venussurfadventures.com; Pavones) Offers a six-day surf camp for women only, including lessons, yoga and other activities (US$1450).

Wildlife- & Bird-Watching

The national parks are good places for observing wildlife, as are the many private reserves. Perhaps the single best area for spotting wildlife is the Península de Osa, including the Parque Nacional Corcovado (p414). Parque Nacional Santa Rosa (p228), Tortuguero (p461) and Caño Negro (p511) all provide good birding and wildlife-watching opportunities. The areas near the Cerro de la Muerte (p376) and the reserves around Monteverde and Santa Elena (p187) are good for quetzal-watching. A map of the protected areas of Costa Rica appears on p68.

Early morning and late afternoon are the best times to see animals, since most are at rest during the heat of the midday sun. A pair of binoculars – even cheap ones – will improve your powers of observation tremendously. Hiring a guide will also vastly improve your chances; a qualified guide is more than worth the expense.

The Costa Rican-based companies following come highly recommended by our readers. These companies can book everything, from gentle hikes to remote wilderness.

Aratinga Tours (☎ 770 6324; www.aratinga-tours .com) Pieter Westra specializes in bird tours in his native Dutch, but he is fluent in English, Spanish and many dialects of bird. His website provides an excellent introduction to birding in Costa Rica.

Birding Costa Rica (☎ 294 0463; www.birdscostarica .com) Highly recommended agency that creates special birding itineraries or custom adventure and hiking tours.

Condor Journeys & Adventures (in the USA ☎ 318-775 0190, in the UK 01700-841 318, in France 06-14 38 63 94)
Costa Rica Expeditions (☎ 257 0766, 222 0333; www.costaricaexpeditions.com) Offers custom itineraries and a network of eco-lodges. Mixed reviews from readers.
Expediciones Tropicales (☎ 257 4171; www.costa ricainfo.com) Offers a variety of one- and two-week itineraries.
Horizontes (☎ 222 2022; www.horizontes.com) An 11-day itinerary visits Tortuguero, Arenal, Monteverde and Manuel Antonio (US$1706).

Windsurfing

Laguna de Arenal is the nation's undisputed windsurfing (and kitesurfing) center. From December to March, winds are strong and steady, averaging 20 knots in the dry season, with maximum winds often 30 knots, and windless days are a rarity. The lake has a year-round water temperature of 18°C to 21°C with 1m-high swells and winds. Get further information from the boxed text World-Class Windsurfing (& Kitesurfing Too!), p255. For warmer water (but more inconsistent winds), try Puerto Soley in the Bahía Salinas (p234).

BUSINESS HOURS

Restaurants are usually open from 7am and serve dinner until 9pm, though up-scale places may open only for dinner. In remote areas, even the small *sodas* might open only at specific meal times. See other business hours on the inside cover of this book. Unless otherwise stated, count on sights, activities and restaurants to be open daily.

CHILDREN

Children under the age of 12 receive a discount of 25% on domestic airline flights, while infants under two fly free (provided they sit on a parent's lap). Children pay full fare on buses (except for those under the age of three). Infant car seats are not always available at car-rental agencies, so bring your own.

Most midrange and top-end hotels have reduced rates for children under 12, provided the child shares a room with parents. Top-end hotels will provide cribs and usually have activities for children.

If you're traveling with an infant, bring disposable diapers (nappies) and creams, baby aspirin and a thermometer from home,

or stock up in San José. In rural areas, supplies may be difficult to find (though cloth diapers are more widespread and friendlier to the environment).

Top destinations for families with small children include the many beachside communities, particularly Jacó (p331) and Manuel Antonio (p354) on the central Pacific coast, and also Playa Sámara (p295) on the Península de Nicoya. Other popular activities include gentle float trips at La Virgen (p516) or near Cañas (p212). See also p103 for some activities in the capital.

For a near-infinite number of travel suggestions, check out Lonely Planet's *Travel with Children*.

CLIMATE

For a small country, Costa Rica's got an awful lot of weather going on. The highlands are cold, the cloud forest is misty and cool, San José and the Central Valley get an 'eternal spring' and both the Pacific and Caribbean coasts are pretty much sweltering year-round. (Get ready for some bad-hair days.) See p532 for more information.

COURSES
Language

A number of Spanish-language schools operate all over Costa Rica and charge by the hour of instruction. Lessons are usually intensive, with class sizes varying from two to five pupils and classes meeting for several hours every weekday.

Courses are offered mainly in central San José and the suburb of San Pedro, which has a lively university and student scene. See the boxed text Talk like a Tico, p104. In the Central Valley there are a number of institutions offering courses – see the boxed text Spanish Schools in the Central Valley, p147. Other language schools can be found in Santa Elena, near Monteverde (p197), Playa Sámara (p296), Jacó (p332), Manuel Antonio (p348), La Fortuna (p241), San Isidro de El General (p378) and Dominical (p363).

It is best to arrange classes in advance. A good clearing house is the **Institute for Spanish Language Studies** (ISLS; ☎ 258 5111, in the USA 800-765 0025, 626-441 3507, 858-456 9268; www.isls .com) which represents half a dozen schools in Costa Rica.

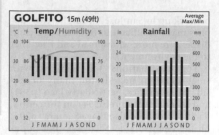

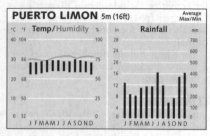

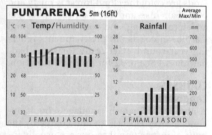

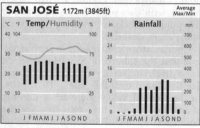

environmental conservation and community development. Prices include meals, homestay and 20 hours of classes. See the boxed text A Natural Education, p165.

SEPA (☎ 770 1457; www.sabalolodge.com/sepaschool .html; San Isidro de General) Spanish-language programs without/with homestay start at US$195/333. Additional options include a longer-term course with environmental classes or volunteering at a local school or park.

CUSTOMS

All travelers over the age of 18 are allowed to enter the country with 5L of wine or spirits and 500g of processed tobacco (400 cigarettes or 50 cigars). Camera gear, binoculars, and camping, snorkeling and other sporting equipment are readily allowed into the country. Officially, you are limited to six rolls of film, but this is rarely enforced.

DANGERS & ANNOYANCES

For the latest official reports on travel to Costa Rica see the websites of the **US State Department** (www.travel.state.gov/travel) or the **UK Foreign & Commonwealth Office** (www.fco.gov.uk).

Earthquakes & Volcanic Eruptions

Costa Rica lies on the edge of active tectonic plates, so it is decidedly earthquake prone. Recent major quakes occurred in 1990 (7.1 on the Richter scale) and 1991 (7.4). Smaller quakes and tremors happen quite often, particularly on the Península de Nicoya, cracking roads and knocking down telephone lines. If you're caught in a quake, the best place to take shelter is under a door frame. If you are in the open, don't stand near walls or telephone poles.

The volcanoes in Costa Rica are not really dangerous as long as you stay on designated trails and don't try to peer into the crater of an active volcano. Always check with park rangers before setting out in the vicinity of active volcanoes.

Hiking Hazards

Hikers setting out into the wilderness should be adequately prepared for their trips. Most importantly, don't bite off more than you can chew. If your daily exercise routine consists of walking from the fridge to the TV, don't start your trip with a 20km trek. There are plenty of 3km and 5km trails that are ideally suited to the less active.

In addition, carry plenty of water, even on very short trips. The hiking is hot and

Environmental Courses

Cerro Dantas Wildlife Refuge (www.cerrodantas .co.cr; Monte de la Cruz, Parque Nacional Braulio Carrillo) This research center runs a variety of educational programs focusing on endangered species preservation, environmental protection, rain-forest ecology and global warming. See the boxed text A Natural Education, p165.

Finca la Flor de Paraíso (www.la-flor-de-paraiso.org; Paraíso; per week US$300) This nonprofit organic farm operates an 'Alternative Spanish Institute,' which combines formal Spanish language education with themes of dehydration sets in quickly. In Corcovado, at least one hiker every year dies of heat exhaustion on the scorching trail between San Pedrillo and Sirena. Hikers have also been known to get lost in rain forests, so carry maps, extra food and a compass. Let someone know where you are going, so they can narrow the search area in the event of an emergency.

There is also wildlife to contend with. Central America's most poisonous snakes, the fer-de-lance (the 'Costa Rican landmine') and the bushmaster, are quite assertive and crocodiles are a reality at many estuaries. Bull sharks love to lounge at the mouth of Río Sirena in Corcovado.

This is no reason to be paranoid. Most animals don't want to mess with you anymore than you want to mess with them, but they will attack if they feel threatened. Hiring a guide can be helpful as they will better know how to spot animals and avoid angst to begin with. To minimize the risk of snake bite, wear sturdy boots.

Some readers have also reported getting mugged along certain trails. Again, it is safer to hike in groups or with a guide.

Ocean Hazards

Approximately 200 drownings a year occur in Costa Rican waters, 90% of which are caused by riptides – a strong current that pulls the swimmer out to sea. Many deaths in riptides are caused by panicked swimmers struggling to the point of exhaustion. If you are caught in a riptide, float. Do not struggle. Let the tide carry you out beyond the breakers, after which it will dissipate. Then swim parallel to the beach and allow the surf to carry you back in. For more information, see the boxed text What To Do if You are Caught in a Riptide, p284.

Some beaches are polluted by litter or, worse, sewage and other contamination. Beaches are now checked by the local authorities, and the cleanest are marked with a blue flag (the *Bandera Azul Ecológica*).

River Running

River-rafting expeditions may be particularly risky during periods of heavy rain – flash floods have been known to capsize rafts. Reputable tour operators will ensure conditions are safe before setting out; some are listed on p529.

Thefts & Muggings

The biggest danger that most travelers face is theft, primarily from pickpockets. There is a lot of petty crime in Costa Rica so keep your wits about you at all times and don't let your guard down. Some tips:

- In public areas keep your daypack on your back, don't wear a lot of jewelry, and never put your wallet in a back pocket.
- Keep your passport and money in the hotel safe. If you are on the road, keep them on your person, preferably in an inside pocket or money belt. (The latter isn't the coolest accessory, but it works).
- Don't put your daypack containing important documents on the overhead bus rack or leave it unattended on a beach.
- Don't leave your belongings inside a parked vehicle, even for a few minutes. Readers have reported car break-ins for something so simple as a T-shirt or a pair of sandals.
- Bring traveler's checks or credit cards. The former can be refunded if lost or stolen; the latter can be canceled and then reissued.
- Keep an emergency packet somewhere separate from your documents that includes photocopies of important papers such as your passport, visa, airline tickets and the serial numbers of traveler's checks.

Of greater concern are the growing number of armed robberies in San José as well as tourist-heavy areas. See p92 so that you'll know what neighborhoods to avoid. In the countryside, don't walk around isolated areas at night by yourself. It is always safest to travel in groups. Solo women travelers would do best to stay away from red-light districts and male-only *cantinas*.

If you are robbed or otherwise attacked, police reports (for insurance claims) should be filed with the **Organismo de Investigación Judicial** (OIJ; ☎ 222 1365; Av 6 btwn Calles 17 & 19, San José) in the Corte Suprema de Justicia (Supreme Court). Bigger towns have police stations that can assist you with this process. If you don't speak Spanish, bring a translator; most policemen do not speak English. It's highly unlikely that the police will be able to recover your property. By law, the tourist board is obliged to represent foreign tourists who are victims of tourist-related crimes in court. Check in with the Instituto Costarricense de Turismo (ICT) in San José (p92) before leaving the country.

For emergency numbers, see the inside cover of this book.

DISABLED TRAVELERS

Independent travel is difficult for anyone with mobility problems. Although Costa Rica has an equal-opportunity law for disabled people, the law applies only to new or newly remodeled businesses and is loosely enforced. Therefore, very few hotels and restaurants have features specifically suited to wheelchair use. Many don't have ramps, while room or bathroom doors are rarely wide enough to accommodate a wheelchair.

Outside the buildings, streets and sidewalks are potholed and poorly paved, making wheelchair use frustrating at best. Public buses don't have provisions to carry wheelchairs and most national parks and outdoor tourist attractions don't have trails suited to wheelchair use. Notable exceptions include Volcán Poás (p156), INBio (p162) and the Rainforest Aerial Tram (p165). Lodges with wheelchair accessibility are indicated in the reviews.

Organizations offering specially designed trips for disabled travelers:

Accessible Journeys (in the USA ☎ 800-846 4537; www.disabilitytravel.com) Organizes independent travel to Costa Rica for people with disabilities.

Vaya con Silla de Ruedas (☎ 454 2810; www.gowith wheelchairs.com) Offers specialty trips for the wheelchair-bound traveler. The company has specially designed vans and its equipment meets international accessibility standards.

DISCOUNT CARDS

Students with an ISIC card or a valid ID from a university offering four-year courses are generally entitled to discounts on museum or guided tour fees. Cards supplied by language schools are not honored.

EMBASSIES & CONSULATES
Costa Rican Embassies & Consulates

For a full list of embassies in Spanish, log on to the Foreign Ministry's website (www .rree.go.cr) and then click on 'Viajando al Exterior.'

The following are the principal Costa Rican embassies and consulates abroad:

Australia (☎ 02-9261 1177; 11th fl, 30 Clarence St, Sydney, NSW 2000)

Canada (☎ 613-562 2855; 325 Dailhouise St, Ottawa, Ontario K1N 7G2)

Denmark (☎ 03-311 0885; Kvasthusgade 3, DK-125 Copenhagen)

France (☎ 01 45 78 96 96; 78 ave Emile Zola, Paris 75015)

Germany (☎ 030-2639 8990; Dessauerstrasse 28-29 D-10963, Berlin)

Israel (☎ 02-2566 6197; Rehov Diskin 13, No 1, Jerusalem 92473)

Italy (☎ 06-84 242 853; Viali Liegi 2, Int 8 Rome)

Japan (☎ 03-3486 1812; Kowa Bldg No 38, fl 12-24, Nishi-Azabu 4, Chome Minato-Ku, Tokyo, 106-0031)

Netherlands (☎ 070-354 0780; Laan Copes Van Cattenburg 46, The Hague 2585 GB)

Nicaragua (☎ 270 3779; 3rd fl, CAR Bldg) It's 4.5km on the road to Masaya, Managua.

Panama (☎ 264 2980, 264 2937; Calle Samuel Lewis, Edificio Plaza Omega, 3rd fl, Panama City) Next to the Santuario Nacional.

Spain (☎ 91 345 9622; Paseo de la Castellana 164, No 17A, Madrid 28046)

Switzerland (☎ 31 37 27 887; Schwarztorstrasse 11, Bern 3007)

UK (☎ 020-7706 8844; Flat 1, 14 Lancaster Gate, London W2 3LH)

USA (☎ 202-234 2945; www.costarica-embassy.org; 2112 S St NW, Washington, DC 20008)

Embassies & Consulates in Costa Rica

Mornings are the best time to go. Australia and New Zealand do not have consular representation in Costa Rica; the closest embassies are in Mexico City. All of the following are in San José. For visa information see p541.

Canada (☎ 242 4400; Oficentro Ejecutivo, 3rd fl, Sabana Sur) Behind La Contraloría.

El Salvador (☎ 257 7855) It's 500m north and 25m west of the Toyota dealership on Paseo Colón.

France (☎ 253 5010) On the road to Curridabat, 200m south and 50m west of the Indoor Club.

Germany (☎ 232 5533) It's 200m north and 75m east of ex-president Oscar Arias' residence, Rohrmoser.

Guatemala (☎ 283 2557; Carr a Curridabat) It's 500m south and 30m east of Pops.

Honduras (☎ 291 5143) It's 250m east, 200m north then another 100m east from Universidad Las Veritas.

Israel (☎ 221 6011; Edificio Centro Colón, 11th fl, Paseo Colón)

Italy (☎ 234 2326; Calle 33, btwn Avs 8 & 10 Los Yoses) It's 50m west of Restaurant Río.

Mexico (☎ 280 5690) It's 250m south of the Subaru dealership, Los Yoses.
Netherlands (☎ 296 1490; Oficentro Ejecutivo La Sabana, Edificio 3, 3rd fl, Sabana Sur) Behind La Contraloría.
Nicaragua (☎ 283 8222; Av Central 2540 btwn Calles 25 & 27, Barrio La California)
Panama (☎ 281 2442) It's 200m south and 25m east from the antiguo higuerón, San Pedro.
Spain (☎ 222 1933; Calle 32 btwn Paseo Colón & Av 2)
Switzerland (☎ 221 4829; Edificio Centro Colón, 10th fl, Paseo Colón btwn Calles 38 & 40)
UK (☎ 258 2025; Edificio Centro Colón, 11th fl, Paseo Colón btwn Calles 38 & 40)
USA (☎ 220 3939; Carretera a Pavas) Opposite Centro Commercial del Oeste.

EMERGENCIES

Emergency numbers are listed on the inside cover of this book, but they may not apply in some remote parts of the country. The ICT (p92) in San José distributes a helpful brochure with up-to-date emergency numbers for every region.

FESTIVALS & SPECIAL EVENTS

The following events are of national significance in Costa Rica:

JANUARY/FEBRUARY

Fiesta de Santa Cruz (mid-January) Held in Santa Cruz de Nicoya, there is a religious procession, rodeo, bullfight, music, dances and a beauty pageant.
Las Fiestas de Palmares (mid-January) Ten days of beer drinking, horse shows and other carnival events in the tiny town of Palmares.
Fiesta de los Diablitos (December 31–January 2 in Boruca; February 5–8 in Curré) Men wear carved wooden devil masks and burlap masks to re-enact the fight between the Indians and the Spanish. In this one, the Spanish lose.

MARCH

Día del Boyero (second Sunday of the month) A parade is held in Escazú in honor of oxcart drivers.
Día de San José (St Joseph's Day; March 19) This day honors the patron saint of the capital.

JUNE

Día de San Pedro & San Pablo (St Peter & St Paul Day; June 29) Celebrations with religious processions held in villages of the same name.

JULY

Fiesta de La Virgen del Mar (Festival of the Virgin of the Sea; mid-July) Held in Puntarenas and Playa del Coco, it involves colorful regattas and boat parades.

Día de Guanacaste (July 25) Celebrates the annexation of Guanacaste from Nicaragua. There's a rodeo in Santa Cruz on this day.

AUGUST

Virgen de Los Angeles (August 2) The patron saint is celebrated with a particularly important religious procession from San José to Cartago.

OCTOBER

El Día de la Raza (Columbus Day; October 12) Puerto Limón celebrates with gusto the explorer's landing at nearby Isla Uvita. The four-day carnival is full of colorful street parades and dancing, music, singing and drinking.

NOVEMBER

Día de los Muertos (All Souls' Day; November 2) Families visit graveyards and have religious parades in honor of the deceased.

DECEMBER

La Inmaculada Concepción (Immaculate Conception; December 8) An important religious holiday.
Las Fiestas de Zapote (December 25–January 1) A week-long celebration of all things Costa Rican (namely rodeos, cowboys, carnival rides, fried food and a whole lot of drinking) in Zapote, southeast of San José.

FOOD

For this book, you can expect that most main dishes at a basic budget eatery will cost under US$5 and between US$5 and US$12 at midrange places. Entrees (main courses) at top-end restaurants will climb to well over US$12. Many midrange and top-end places charge an extra 23% in sales and service taxes.

GAY & LESBIAN TRAVELERS

The situation facing gay and lesbian travelers is better than in most Central American countries. Homosexual acts between two consenting adults (aged 18 and over) are legal, but most Costa Ricans are tolerant only at a 'don't ask; don't tell' level. This is undoubtedly a side affect of the strong role of Catholicism and the persistence of traditionalism in society.

In the recent past, there were outward acts of prejudice. In 1998 a gay-and-lesbian festival planned in San José was cancelled following heavy opposition from Catholic clergy. The church also forced the cancellation of a gay-and-lesbian tour to Manuel Antonio and encouraged the blockade of a coastal hotel hosting a gay group. Things took an embarrassing turn in 1999 when the tourism minister said that Costa Rica should not be a destination for sex tourism or gays. The gay community made it clear that it was against sex tourism, and that linking gay tourism with sex tourism was untrue and defamatory. The official position in Costa Rica was then modified, stating that gay tourism was neither encouraged nor prohibited.

Homosexual acts between consenting adults are legal in Costa Rica; but in actuality, gays and lesbians continue to suffer from discrimination in society. Discrimination usually takes the role of subtle non-acceptance, as opposed to violence or outright persecution. Homophobia has declined in recent years, especially in heavily touristy areas – one positive result of the influx of foreigners.

Thankfully, Costa Rica's gays and lesbians have made some strides. In the 1990s the Supreme Court ruled against police harassment in gay nightspots and guaranteed medical treatment to people living with HIV/AIDS. And in June 2003 the first ever gay-pride festival in San José drew more than 2000 attendants. Gays and lesbians traveling in Costa Rica are unlikely to be confronted with poor treatment; nonetheless, outside of gay spots, public displays of affection are not recommended.

Meeting Places

In San José, hotels that are gay or gay-friendly include Hotel Kekoldi (p108), Joluva Guesthouse (p107) and Colours (p110). **Agua Buena Human Rights Association** (☎ 234 2411; www .aguabuena.org) also offers long-term accommodations.

The Pacific resort town of Manuel Antonio is a popular gay vacation center. Hotels include La Plantación (p352) and Hotel La Mariposa (p352).

In San José there is a good selection of nightclubs, ranging from cruising joints to pounding dance clubs to more intimate places (see p120).

Organizations & Resources

The monthly newspaper *Gayness* and the magazine *Gente 10* (in Spanish) are both available at gay bars in San José (see p120). Other resources:

Agua Buena Human Rights Association (☎ 280 3548; www.aguabuena.org in Spanish) This noteworthy nonprofit organization has campaigned steadily for fairness in medical treatment for people living with HIV/AIDS in Costa Rica.

Cipac (☎ 280 7821; www.cipacdh.org in Spanish) The leading activist organization in Costa Rica.

Gay Costa Rica (www.gaycostarica.com in Spanish) Provides up-to-the-minute information on nightlife, travel and many links.

International Gay & Lesbian Travel Association (IGLTA; in the USA ☎ 800-448 8550, 954-776 2626; www .iglta.org) Maintains a list of hundreds of travel agents and tour operators all over the world.

Tiquicia Travel (☎ 256 9682; www.tiquiciatravel.com) Makes arrangements at gay-friendly hotels.

Toto Tours (in the USA ☎ 800-565 1241, 773-274 8686; www.tototours.com) Gay travel specialists who organize regular trips to Costa Rica, among other destinations.

HOLIDAYS

National holidays (*días feriados*) are taken seriously in Costa Rica. Banks, public offices and many stores close. During this time, public transport is tight and hotels are heavily booked. Many festivals involve public holidays as well (see p535).

New Year's Day January 1

Semana Santa (Holy Week) March or April. The Thursday and Friday before Easter Sunday is the official holiday, though most businesses shut down the whole week. From Thursday to Sunday bars are closed and alcohol sales are prohibited; on Thursday and Friday buses stop running.

Día de Juan Santamaría April 11. Honors the national hero who died fighting William Walker in 1856; major events are held in Alajuela, his home town.

Labor Day May 1

Día de la Madre (Mother's Day) August 15. Coincides with the annual Catholic feast of the Assumption.

Independence Day September 15

Día de la Raza (Columbus Day) October 12

Christmas Day December 25. Christmas Eve is an unofficial holiday.

Last week in December The week between Christmas and New Year is an unofficial holiday; businesses close and beach hotels are crowded.

INSURANCE

In general, signing up for a travel-insurance policy is a good idea. For Costa Rica, a basic theft/loss and medical policy is recommended. Read the fine print carefully as some companies exclude dangerous activities from coverage, which can include scuba diving, motorcycling and even trekking.

You may prefer a policy that pays doctors or hospitals directly rather than you having to pay on the spot and make a claim later.

Make copies of all insurance information in the event that the original is lost. For information on health insurance, turn to p555; for car insurance, see p550.

INTERNET ACCESS

Cybercafés abound in Costa Rica, and, for the most part, finding cheap and speedy Internet access is easy for checking your Web-based email. The normal access rate in San José is US$1 to US$2 per hour, slightly more in other large towns, and up to US$5 per hour in the hard-to-reach places. If you do not have Web-based email, Lonely Planet's **ekit** (www.lonelyplanet.ekit.com/ekit/home) provides a free service.

Wi-fi access is not widespread in Costa Rica, but it is coming. If you keep your eyes open (and computer on), you'll find wireless hotspots in San José, Alajuela, Jacó, Monteverde and Santa Elena, La Fortuna, Tamarindo, Puerto Jiménez and Puerto Viejo de Talamanca.

LEGAL MATTERS

If you get into legal trouble and are jailed, your embassy can offer only limited assistance. This may include an occasional visit from an embassy staff member to make sure your human rights have not been violated, letting your family know where you are and putting you in contact with a Costa Rican lawyer, whom you must pay yourself. Embassy officials will not bail you out and you are subject to Costa Rican laws, not the laws of your own country.

LEGAL AGE

- Driving: 18
- Voting: 18
- Age at which you can marry: 15
- Drinking age: 18
- Minimum age for consensual heterosexual sex: 18. Sex with anyone under 18 is illegal and penalties are severe.
- Minimum age for consensual homosexual sex: no legal age, but sex with anyone under 18 is not advisable.

In many beachside towns, police tend to turn a blind eye to casual marijuana use. However, be forewarned that penalties in Costa Rica for possession of even small amounts of illegal drugs are much stricter than in the USA or Europe. Defendants often spend many months in jail before they are brought to trial and, if convicted, can expect sentences lasting several years.

Prostitution is legal for women over 18. Although prostitutes carry cards showing how recently they have had a medical checkup, these are quite unreliable.

If you are the victim of a crime, report it to the authorities (see p533).

Drivers & Driving Accidents

Drivers should carry their passport and driver's license. For accidents, call the police immediately to make a report (required for insurance purposes) or attend to any injured parties. Leave the vehicles in place until the report has been made and do not make any statements except to members of law-enforcement agencies. The injured should only be moved by medical professionals.

Keep your eye on your vehicle until the police arrive and then call the car-rental company to find out where you should take the vehicle for repairs (do not have it fixed yourself). If the accident results in injury or death, you could be jailed or prevented from leaving the country until legalities are handled.

Emergency numbers are listed on the inside cover of this book.

MAPS

Detailed maps are hard to come by. An excellent option is the 1:330,000 *Costa Rica* sheet produced by **International Travel Map** (ITMB; www.itmb.com; 530 W Broadway, Vancouver, BC, V5Z 1E, Canada), which is waterproof and includes a San José inset.

The **Fundación Neotropica** (www.neotropica.org) has published a 1:500,000 map showing national parks and other protected areas. These are available in San José bookstores.

The Instituto Costarricense de Turismo (ICT; see p92) publishes a 1:700,000 Costa Rica map with a 1:12,500 Central San José map on the reverse. These are free at both ICT offices.

Online, **Maptak** (www.maptak.com) has maps of Costa Rica's seven provinces and their capitals.

DIRECTORY

TOPOGRAPHICAL MAPS

Don't count on any of the national park offices or ranger stations having maps for hikers. Topographical maps are available for purchase from **Instituto Geográfico Nacional** (IGN; ☎ 257 7798; Calle 9 btwn Avs 20 & 22, San José; 🕙 7:30am-noon & 1-3pm Mon-Fri). In the USA, contact **Omni Resources** (☎ 336-227 8300; www .omnimap.com).

The *Mapa-Guía de la Naturaleza Costa Rica* is an atlas published by Incafo, which includes 1:200,000 topographical sheets, as well as English and Spanish descriptions of Costa Rica's natural areas. It is available at Lehmann's (p91) in San José.

MONEY
ATMs

It's increasingly easy to find ATMs (*cajeros automáticos* in Spanish). The Visa Plus network is the standard, but machines on the Cirrus network, which accept most foreign ATM cards, can be found in San José and in larger towns. Some ATMs will dispense US dollars. Note that some machines (eg at Banco Nacional) will only accept cards held by their own customers.

Cash & Currency

The Costa Rican currency is the colón (plural colones), named after Cristóbal Colón (Christopher Columbus). The symbol for colones is written as ¢ and bills come in 500, 1000, 5000 and 10,000 notes; coins come in denominations of 5, 10, 20, 25, 50 and 100 colones. Older coins are silver, newer ones are gold-colored. You can pay for tours, park fees, hotel rooms and large-ticket items with US dollars. Meals, bus fares and small items should all be paid with colones. Paying for things in US dollars should be free of hassle.

Credit Cards

Holders of credit and debit cards can buy colones and sometimes US dollars in some banks. Cards are widely accepted at some midrange and most top-end hotels, as well as top-end restaurants and some travel agencies. All car-rental agencies accept credit cards.

Visa is the most widely accepted, MasterCard less so and American Express (Amex) rarely. Some hotels might charge a 7% fee for using credit cards, in addition to government and service taxes. Check their policies and prices carefully (for more information, see p526).

Exchanging Money

All banks will exchange US dollars, and some will exchange euros; other currencies are more difficult. Most banks have excruciatingly long lines, especially at the state-run institutions (Banco Nacional, Banco de Costa Rica, Banco Popular). However, they don't charge commissions on cash exchanges. Private banks (Banex, Banco Interfin, Scotiabank) tend to be faster. Make sure the dollar bills you want to exchange are in good condition or they may be refused.

Changing money at hotels and travel agencies is even faster and more convenient, though many charge hefty commissions. Changing money on the streets is not recommended, except possibly at land borders. Street changers don't give better rates, and scammers abound.

Non-US travelers should buy US dollars before they arrive in Costa Rica. Carry your passport when exchanging currency and try not to leave the country with many excess colones; it's difficult to buy back more than US$50 at the border or airport.

Taxes

Travelers will notice a 13.39% percent sales tax at midrange and upscale hotels and restaurants, while hotels also charge an additional 3% tourist surcharge. Everybody must pay a US$26 airport tax upon leaving the country. It is payable in US dollars or in colones and credit cards are accepted.

Tipping

It is customary to tip the bellhop/porter (US$0.50 to US$1 per service) and the housekeeper (US$1 per day in top-end hotels, less in budget places). On guided tours, tip the guide US$1 to US$5 per person per day. Tip the tour driver about half of what you tip the guide. Naturally, tips depend upon quality of service. Taxi drivers are not normally tipped, unless some special service is provided.

Upscale restaurants may add a 10% service charge onto the bill. If not, you might leave a small tip to show your appreciation, but it is not required.

Traveler's Checks

Most banks and exchange bureaus will cash traveler's checks at a commission of 1% to 3%. Many hotels will accept them as payment, but check policies carefully as many hotels do not. US dollar traveler's checks are preferred. It may be difficult or impossible to change checks of other currencies.

Amex checks are the easiest to replace quickly in Costa Rica. If your checks are lost or stolen, call **Amex** (☎ 800-012 0039) to have them replaced.

PHOTOGRAPHY

Camera gear is expensive in Costa Rica and film choice is limited, though basic types of Kodak film are available in San José and in popular tourist towns. Slide film tends to only be available in San José. Check expiration dates carefully before purchase.

Guard your film from the particularly intense x-ray machines at the international airport in San José.

If you wish to take pictures of people (particularly in indigenous communities), always ask for permission first. If you are refused, do not be offended.

POST

Airmail letters abroad cost about US$0.35 for the first 20g. Parcels can be shipped at the rate of US$7 per kilogram. You can receive mail at the main post office of major towns. Mail to San José's central post office should be addressed:

Joanne VISITOR, c/o Lista de Correos, Correo Central, San José, Costa Rica.

Letters usually arrive within a week from North America, longer from more distant places. The post office will hold mail for 30 days from the date it's received. Photo identification is required to retrieve mail and you will only be given correspondence with your name on it. In addresses, *apartado* means 'PO Box'; it is not a street or apartment address.

Avoid having parcels sent to you. They are held in customs and cannot be retrieved until you have paid the exorbitant customs fees and dealt with a whole lot of bureaucracy.

SHOPPING

Avoid purchasing animal products, including turtle shells, animal skulls and anything made with feathers, coral and shells. Wood products are also highly suspicious: make sure you know where the wood came from.

Coffee & Alcohol

Coffee is the most popular souvenir, and deservedly so. It is available at gift shops, the Mercado Central (p96) in San José and at any supermarket.

The most popular alcohol purchases are Ron Centenario, the coffee liqueur Café Rica and also *guaro,* the local firewater. All are available at duty-free shops inside the airport, or in supermarkets and liquor stores around the country.

Handicrafts & Ceramics

Tropical hardwood items include salad bowls, plates, carving boards, jewelry boxes and a variety of carvings and ornaments. The most exquisite woodwork is available at Biesanz Woodworks (p139) in Escazú. All of the wood is grown on farms expressly for this purpose, so you needn't

---

WHAT'S THAT ADDRESS?

Though some larger cities have streets that have been dutifully named, signage is rare and finding a Tico who knows what street they are standing on is even rarer. Everybody uses landmarks when providing directions; an address may be given as 200m south and 150m east of a church. (A city block is *cien metros* – literally 100m – so '250 metros al sur' means 2½ blocks south, regardless of the distance.) Churches, parks, office buildings, fast-food joints and car dealerships are the most common landmarks used – but these are often meaningless to the foreign traveler who will have no idea where the Subaru dealership is to begin with. Better yet, Ticos frequently refer to landmarks that no longer exist. In San Pedro, outside of San José, locals still use the sight of an old fig tree (*el antiguo higuerón*) to provide directions.

Confused? Get used to it…

BARGAINING

A high standard of living along with a steady stream of international tourist traffic means that the Latin American tradition of haggling is fast dying out in Costa Rica. The beach communities, especially, have fixed prices on hotels that cannot be negotiated. (Expect some business owners to be offended if you try to negotiate.) Some smaller hotels in the interior still accept the practice.

Negotiating prices at outdoor markets is acceptable though, and some bargaining is accepted when hiring long-distance taxis. Overall, Ticos respond well to courteous manners and gentle inquiries. Don't demand a service for your price or chances are you won't get it.

---

worry about forests being chopped down for your salad bowl.

Uniquely Costa Rican souvenirs are the colorfully painted replicas of traditional oxcarts *(carretas)* produced in Sarchí.

Ceramics are also popular souvenirs and can be found in Guaitil.

SOLO TRAVELERS

Costa Rica is a fine country for solo travelers. Inexpensive hostels with communal kitchens encourage social exchange, while a large number of language schools, tours and volunteer organizations will provide every traveler with an opportunity to meet others. However, it isn't recommended to undertake long treks in the wilderness by yourself.

SUSTAINABLE TRAVEL

For better or for worse, tourism has had an undeniable impact in Costa Rica. The country is constantly trying to balance the economic benefits of investment and development with increasing pressures on its environment and society. For more information, see the boxed text The Price of Ecotourism, p66.

In attempt to encourage more sustainable tourism, the ICT instituted a Certificate for Sustainable Tourism, or el Certificado para la Sostenibilidad de Turismo. This accreditation system rates hotels, on a scale of one to five, on how well they manage their surrounding natural and cultural resources. Search the database of participating hotels at www.turismo-sostenible.co.cr.

TELEPHONE

Public phones are found all over Costa Rica and Chip or Colibrí phonecards are available in 1000, 2000 and 3000 colón denominations. Chip cards are inserted into the phone and scanned. Colibrí cards (the most common) require dialing a toll-free number (☎ 199) and entering an access code. Instructions are provided in English or Spanish. These are the preferred card of travelers since they can be used from any phone. Cards can be found just about everywhere, including supermarkets, pharmacies, newsstands, *pulperías* (corner grocery stores) and gift shops.

The cheapest international calls are direct-dialed using a phonecard. Costs of calls from Costa Rica per minute are approximately US$0.55 to North America and US$0.80 to Europe and Australia. To make international calls, dial '00' followed by the country code and number. Pay phones cannot receive international calls.

Make sure that no one is peeking over your shoulder when you dial your code. Some travelers have had their access numbers pilfered by thieves.

To call Costa Rica from abroad, use the international code (☎ 506) before the seven-digit number. Find other important phone numbers on the inside cover of this book.

TIME

Costa Rica is six hours behind Greenwich Mean Time (GMT), which means that Costa Rican time is equivalent to Central Time in North America. There is no daylight saving time.

TOILETS

Public restrooms are rare, but most restaurants and cafés will let you use their facilities at a small charge – usually between US$0.25 to US$0.50. Bus terminals and other major public buildings usually have lavatories, also at a charge.

If you're particularly fond of toilet paper, carry it with you at all times as it is not always available. Just don't flush it down! Costa Rican plumbing is often poor and has very low pressure in all but the best hotels and buildings. Dispose of toilet paper in the rubbish bin inside every bathroom.

TOURIST INFORMATION

The government-run tourism board, the Instituto Costarricense de Turismo (ICT), has two offices in the capital (see p92). Don't expect to be wowed with any particularly insightful travel advice. It's the staff's job to tell you that it's all good. They speak English.

However, the ICT can provide you with free maps, a master bus schedule and information on road conditions in the hinterlands. Consult the ICT's flashy English-language website (www.visitcostarica.com) for information, or in the US call the ICT's toll-free number (☎ 800-343 6332) for brochures and information.

VISAS

Passport-carrying nationals of the following countries are allowed 90 days' stay with no visa: most western European countries, Argentina, Canada, Israel, Japan, Panama and the USA.

Citizens of Australia, Iceland, Ireland, Mexico, New Zealand, Russia, South Africa and Venezuela are allowed to stay for 30 days with no visa. Others require a visa from a Costa Rican embassy or consulate. Lists of embassies are on p534. These lists are subject to continual change. For the latest info, check the websites of the **ICT** (www .visitcostarica.com) or the **Costa Rican embassy** (www .costarica-embassy.org) in Washington, DC.

Visa Extensions

Extending your stay beyond the authorized 30 or 90 days is a time-consuming hassle. It is far easier to leave the country for 72 hours and then re-enter. Otherwise go to the office of **migración** (Immigration; ☎ 220 0355; ☾ 8am-4pm) in San José, opposite Channel 6, about 4km north of Parque La Sabana. Requirements for extensions change, so allow several working days.

WOMEN TRAVELERS

Most women travelers in Costa Rica rarely experience little more than a *mi amor* or an appreciative hiss from the local men. But in general, Costa Rican men consider foreign women to have looser morals and to be easier

conquests than Ticas. They will often make flirtatious comments to single women, particularly blondes. Women traveling together are not exempt from this. The best way to deal with this is to do what the Ticas do – ignore it completely. Women who firmly resist unwanted verbal advances from men are normally treated with respect.

In small highland towns, dress is generally fairly conservative. Women rarely wear shorts – though belly-baring tops are all the rage. On the beach, skimpy bathing suits are acceptable, though topless bathing and nudity are not.

As in any part of the world, the possibilities of rape and assault do exist. Use your normal caution: avoid walking alone in isolated places or through city streets late at night and skip the hitchhiking. Do not take unlicensed 'pirate' cabs (licensed cabs are red and have medallions) as reports of assaults by unlicensed drivers against women have been reported.

And more mundane, yet still an important point: birth-control pills are available at most pharmacies (without prescription) and tampons can be difficult to find in rural areas – bring some from home or stock up in San José.

The **Centro Feminista de Información y Acción** (Cefemina; ☎ 224 3986; www.cefemina.org; San Pedro) is the main Costa Rican feminist organization. It publishes a newsletter and can provide information and assistance to women travelers.

COMMUNICATING WITH COSTA RICA

Readers have commented that phone messages, faxes and emails sent to Costa Rica can remain unanswered for a week or more. The reason is simply that the remote location of many of the hotels and lodges means that someone must go to the nearest town to recover messages (which might happen once a week or less).

Most commonly, telecommunications systems break down due to bad weather, so you may have to try more than once before you actually get through and someone is able to respond. Some phones don't accept international calls (this is rarely the case for hotels, though).

Just be patient and keep trying.

WORK

Getting a bona fide job necessitates obtaining a work permit, a time-consuming and difficult process. The most likely source of paid employment is as an English teacher at one of the language institutes, or waiting tables or tending bar in a resort town. Naturalists or river guides may be able to find work with private lodges or adventure-travel operators. Don't expect to make more than survival wages from these jobs.

Volunteering

There are numerous volunteer opportunities with placements available around the country:

Amistad Institute (☎ 269 0000; www.amistadinstitute .net) Joint volunteer programs and Spanish instruction allow you to practice your language skills in local community organizations, schools and parks.

Asociación de Voluntarios para el Servicio en las Areas Protegidas de Costa Rica (ASVO; ☎ 233 4989, www.asvocr.com) Has 30-day work programs in the national parks; volunteers pay US$14 per day to defray meal costs and a 15-day commitment is required.

Cross Cultural Solutions (in the USA ☎ 800-380 4777, in the UK 0845-458 2781; www.crossculturalsolutions.org; 2-week program US$2389) A nonprofit group that partners with grassroots organizations for volunteer placement. Volunteers assist with childcare, elderly care, education, women's empowerment issues and other programs in Cartago or San Pedro. Prices include meals and homestay.

Earthwatch (in the USA ☎ 978-461 0081, 800-776 0188; www.earthwatch.org; 2-week program US$2195) All-inclusive 14-day projects allow volunteers to assist with turtle-tagging, tree planting, conducting research about sustainable coffee production or studying the adaptation of monkey populations.

Habitat for Humanity (☎ 447 2330; www.habitat costarica.org) Highly regarded international group that has community-building projects around the country. Construction volunteers pay a US$100 registration fee, plus

US$15 per day for accommodations, and must commit for one week.

International Student Volunteers (in the USA ☎ 714-779 7392; www.isvonline.com) This excellent organization offers four-week programs which include two weeks of volunteer work in local conservation or community development programs, and two weeks of fun and travel.

Volunteer Latin America (☎ 020-7193 9163; www.volunteerlatinamerica.com) Offers a huge array of volunteer opportunities, from working in an orphanage to gardening and trail maintenance to doing research on certain animal species. Some programs require special skills and/or minimum time commitments.

World Teach (☎ in the USA 800-483 2240; www.world teach.org) Volunteers receive a stipend of US$75 per month for their work teaching English in public elementary schools. One-year commitment; lodging and transportation are also included.

Volunteers can also work directly with the local organizations reviewed in the destination chapters, including some environmentally minded lodges around La Fortuna and many organizations around Monteverde. The Fundación Corcovado (see the boxed text Green Grassroots, p414) places volunteers at community organizations or within the national park on the Península de Osa.

During turtle-nesting season (February to October), many different organizations allow volunteers to assist with beach patrols and turtle-tagging, including Programa Restauracíon de Tortugas Marinas (see the boxed text Have More Time?, p304) on the Península de Nicoya, as well as several organizations on the Caribbean coast (see the boxed text Doing Time for the Turtles, p463). If you prefer to work with mammals, you can save the squirrel monkeys with Ascomoti (see the boxed text Saving the Squirrel Monkey, p356).

Transportation

CONTENTS

GETTING THERE & AWAY

ENTERING THE COUNTRY

A few people arrive in Costa Rica by sea, either on fishing or scuba charters or as part of a brief stop on a cruise. Others travel in by bus from neighboring countries. But the vast majority of travelers land at the airport in San José, with a growing number arriving in Liberia.

Entering Costa Rica is usually hassle-free (with the exception of some long queues). There are no fees or taxes payable on entering the country, though some foreign nationals will require a visa. Be aware that those who need visas cannot get them at the border. For information on visas, see p541.

Passport

Citizens of all nations are now required to have a passport that is valid for at least six months beyond the dates of your trip. When you arrive, your passport will be stamped. The law requires that you carry your passport at all times during your stay in Costa Rica.

Onward Ticket

Travelers officially need a ticket out of Costa Rica before they are allowed to enter, but the rules are enforced erratically. Those arriving by land can generally meet this requirement by purchasing an outward ticket from the TICA bus company, which has offices in Managua (Nicaragua) and Panama City.

AIR

Airports & Airlines

International flights arrive at Aeropuerto Internacional Juan Santamaría, 17km northwest of San José, in the town of Alajuela. In recent years Daniel Oduber airport (p223) in Liberia has started receiving international flights from the USA. Although there is a lot of talk about airport expansion, at the time of research only American Airlines, Continental and Delta fly into Liberia. It is expected that many international airlines will start to offer flights in and out of this airport, including some flights direct from Europe (eliminating the layover in Miami or Dallas). Daniel Oduber airport is convenient for travelers visiting the Península de Nicoya.

Costa Rica is well connected by air to other Central and Latin American countries, as well as the USA. The national airline, Lacsa (part of the Central American Airline consortium Grupo TACA), flies to numerous points in the USA and Latin America, including Cuba. The Federal Aviation Administration in the USA has assessed Costa Rica's aviation authorities to be in compliance with international safety standards.

THINGS CHANGE...

The information in this chapter is particularly vulnerable to change. Check directly with the airline or a travel agent to make sure you understand how a fare (and ticket you may buy) works and be aware of current security requirements for international travel. Shop carefully. The details given in this chapter should be regarded as pointers and are not a substitute for your own careful, up-to-date research.

Airlines flying to and from Costa Rica include the following companies; see p123 for details of those with offices in San José.

Air Canada (in Canada ☎ 514-393 3333; www
.aircanada.ca; airline code AC) no office in Costa Rica
America West (in the USA ☎ 480-693 6718; www
.americawest.com; airline code HP) no office in Costa Rica
American Airlines (☎ 257 1266; www.aa.com; airline code AA)
Continental (☎ 296 4911; www.continental.com; airline code CO)
COPA (☎ 222 6640; www.copaair.com; airline code CM)
Cubana de Aviación (☎ 221 7625, 221 5881; www
.cubana.cu; airline code CU)
Delta (☎ 256 7909, press 5 for reservations; www.delta
.com; airline code DL)
Grupo TACA (☎ 296 0909; www.taca.com; airline code TA)
Iberia (☎ 257 8266; www.iberia.com; airline code IB)
KLM (☎ 220 4111; www.klm.com; airline code KL)
Lacsa see Grupo TACA.
Mexicana (☎ 295 6969; www.mexicana.com; airline code MX)
SAM/Avianca (☎ 233 3066; www.avianca.com; airline code AV)
United Airlines (☎ 220 4844; www.united.com; airline code UA)
US Airways (toll-free reservations in Costa Rica ☎ 800-011 0793, 800-011 4114; www.usairways.com; airline code US) no office in Costa Rica

Tickets

Airline fares are usually more expensive during the Costa Rican high season (from December through April), with December and January the most expensive months to travel.

Other Central & Latin American Countries

American Airlines, Continental, Delta and United all have connections to Costa Rica from several other Central and Latin American countries. Grupo TACA gener-

---

DEPARTURE TAX

There is a US$26 departure tax on all international outbound flights, payable in cash (US dollars or colones, or a mix of the two). At the Juan Santamaría airport you can pay with credit cards, and Banco de Costa Rica has an ATM (on the Plus system) by the departure-tax station.

---

ally offers the greatest number of flights on these routes.

Recently, the domestic Costa Rican airlines have begun offering a few international flights. **Nature Air** (www.natureaire.com) now flies to Granada from both Liberia (one way/round-trip US$65/130) and San José (US$120/240) four times a week, and to Bocas del Toro (US$99/199) two times a week.

Grupo TACA offers direct flights to Caracas (US$500, three hours, daily), Guatemala City (US$250, 1½ hours, twice daily) and San Salvador (US$236, 1½ hours, three daily). TACA and Mexicana have daily flights to Mexico City (US$500, three hours), while both TACA and Copa have several flights a day to Panama City (US$300, 1½ hours, three daily). Round-trip prices are quoted unless otherwise indicated.

Australia & New Zealand

Travel routes from these two countries usually go through the USA or Mexico. Fares tend to go up in June and July (the beginning of the rainy season in Costa Rica).

The following are well-known agencies for cheap fares, with branches throughout Australia and New Zealand:

Flight Centre Australia (☎ 133 133; www.flightcentre
.com.au); New Zealand (☎ 0800-243 544; www.flight
centre.co.nz)
STA Travel Australia (☎ 1300-733 035; www.statravel
.com.au); New Zealand (☎ 0508-782 872; www.statravel
.co.nz)
Trailfinders Australia (☎ 1300-780 212; www.trailfind
ers.com.au)

Canada

Most travelers to Costa Rica connect through US gateway cities, though Air Canada has direct flights from Toronto. A good choice for student, youth and budget airfares is **Travel CUTS** (☎ 866-246 9762; www.travelcuts.com). Also see the USA, opposite, since many of the companies listed in that section can arrange travel from Canada.

Europe

Most flights from Europe connect either in the USA or in Mexico City, although this may change once the new airport in Liberia starts attracting more flights. High-season fares may apply during the northern summer, which is the beginning of the Costa Rican rainy season. Some recommended agencies that operate across Europe are **Ebookers.com** (www.ebookers.com) and **STA Travel** (www.sta.com).

THE UK & IRELAND
Discount air travel is big business in London, which means that it's possible to find some bargains there. Advertisements for many travel agencies appear in the weekend broadsheet newspapers, in *Time Out,* the *Evening Standard* and in the free magazine *TNT*. Some recommended agencies include:

Flight Centre (☎ 0870-499 0040; http://flightcentre.co.uk)

Journey Latin America (JLA; in London ☎ 020-8747 3108; www.journeylatinamerica.co.uk)

North-South Travel (☎ 01245-608 291; www.northsouthtravel.co.uk) North-South Travel donates part of its profit to projects in the developing world.

Quest Travel (☎ 0870-442 3542; www.questtravel.com)

Trailfinders (www.trailfinder.co.uk) Dublin (☎ 01-677 7888); Glasgow (☎ 0141-353 2224); London (☎ 020-7628 7628)

Travel Bag (☎ 0800-082 5000; www.travelbag.co.uk)

CONTINENTAL EUROPE
European travelers will most likely find it cheaper to travel to Costa Rica via London or the USA. Some recommended agencies include:

Airfair (☎ 0900-7717 717; www.airfair.nl in Dutch)

Anyway (☎ 0892-302 301; www.anyway.fr in French)

CTS Viaggi (☎ 06-441 111; www.cts.it in Italian) Italian agency that specializes in student and youth travel.

Just Travel (☎ 089-747 3330; www.justtravel.de) German agency.

Lastminute France (☎ 0899-785 000; www.lastminute.fr); Germany (☎ 01805-284 366; www.lastminute.de)

Nouvelles Frontières (☎ 0825-000 747; www.nouvelles-frontieres.fr in French)

OTU Voyages (☎ 0155-82 32 32; www.otu.fr) French agency that specializes in student and youth travel.

Voyageurs du Monde (☎ 0892-23 68 68; www.vdm.com in French)

The USA
More than one-third of all travelers to Costa Rica come from the USA, so finding a nonstop flight from Houston, Miami or New York is quite simple. Schedules and prices are competitive – a little bit of shopping around can get you a good fare.

The following agencies and websites are recommended for bookings:

American Express Travel Services (☎ 800-297 2977; www.itn.net)

Cheap Tickets (www.cheaptickets.com)

Exito Latin America Travel Specialists (☎ 800-655 4053; www.exitotravel.com)

Expedia (www.expedia.com)

Hotwire (www.hotwire.com)

Lowestfare.com (www.lowestfare.com)

STA Travel (☎ 800-781 4040; www.statravel.com)

Tico Travel (☎ 800-493 8426; www.ticotravel.com)

LAND & RIVER
Bus
Costa Rica shares land borders with Nicaragua and Panama and a lot of travelers, particularly shoestringers, enter the country by bus. An extensive bus system links the Central American capitals and it's vastly cheaper than flying.

If crossing the border by bus, note that international buses may cost slightly more than taking a local bus to the border, then another onwards from the border, but they're worth it. These companies are familiar with border procedures and will tell you what's needed to cross efficiently.

There are no problems crossing, provided your papers are in order. If you are on an international bus, you'll have to exit the bus and proceed through both border stations. Bus drivers will wait for everyone to be processed before heading on.

If you choose to take local buses, it's advisable to get to border stations early in the day to allow time for waiting in line and processing. Note that onward buses tend to wind down by the afternoon. See the boxed text Border Crossings, p546.

International buses go from San José to Changuinola (Bocas del Toro), David and Panama City, Panama; Guatemala City; Managua, Nicaragua; San Salvador, El Salvador; and Tegucigalpa, Honduras. For schedules and fares, see p124.

Car & Motorcycle
The cost of insurance, fuel and border permits makes a car journey significantly more expensive than buying an airline ticket. Also, the mountain of paperwork required to drive into Costa Rica from other countries deters many travelers, who prefer to arrive here and then buy or rent a vehicle.

BORDER CROSSINGS

There is no fee for travelers to enter Costa Rica. However, the fee for each vehicle entering the country is US$22. For more information on visa requirements for entering Costa Rica, see p541.

Nicaragua – Sapoá to Peñas Blancas

Situated on the Interamericana, this is the most heavily trafficked border station between Nicaragua and Costa Rica. Virtually all international overland travelers from Nicaragua enter Costa Rica through here. The border station is open from 6am to 8pm daily on both the Costa Rican and Nicaraguan sides – though local bus traffic stops in the afternoon. This is the only official border between Nicaragua and Costa Rica that you can drive across.

The **Tica Bus** (in Managua ☎ 222 6094), **Nica Bus** (in Managua ☎ 228 1374) and **TransNica** (in Managua ☎ 278 2090) all have daily buses to Costa Rica. The fare is US$10 to US$12 and the trip takes nine hours. From Rivas (37km north of the border) twice-hourly buses depart for Sapoá from 5am to 4:30pm. Regular buses depart Peñas Blancas, on the Costa Rican side, for the nearby towns of La Cruz, Liberia and San José.

The Costa Rican and Nicaraguan immigration offices are almost 1km apart; most people travel through by bus or private car. Travelers without a through bus will find golf carts (US$2) running between the borders, but walking is not a problem. While Costa Rica does not charge visitors to cross the border, Nicaragua does: people leaving Nicaragua pay US$2, while folks entering Nicaragua will be charged US$7 until noon, after which the fee becomes US$9. All fees must be paid in US dollars.

Note that Peñas Blancas is only a border post, not a town, so there is nowhere to stay. For detailed information on crossing the border, see the boxed text Getting to Rivas, Nicaragua, p237.

Nicaragua – San Carlos to Los Chiles

International travelers rarely use this route, though it's reportedly hassle-free. There is no land crossing and you cannot drive between the two points. Instead, the crossing must be done by boat. Regular boats (US$7, 1½ hours) depart San Carlos in Nicaragua and head south along the Río Frío for Los Chiles at 10:30am and 1:30pm, returning at 1pm and 4pm. At other times, boatmen can usually be found by the ENAP dock in San Carlos, but remember that the border closes at 5pm. Although there is a road that travels from the southern banks of the Río San Juan in Nicaragua to Los Chiles, it is reserved for federal employees. You will not be able to enter Costa Rica this way (and you certainly will not be able to drive in).

If you are entering Costa Rica, don't forget to get the US$2 exit stamp at the San Carlos *migración* office, 50m west of the dock. Once you enter Costa Rica, you'll have to stop at Costa Rica *migración* for your entry stamp.

Traveling from Costa Rica to Nicaragua, you will need to pay a US$9 fee when you enter. For more information, see the boxed text Getting to San Carlos, Nicaragua, p516.

To enter Costa Rica by car, you'll need the following:

- valid registration and proof of ownership.
- valid driver's license or International Driving Permit (see p550).
- valid license plates.
- recent inspection certificate (not required, but a good idea).
- your passport.
- multiple photocopies of all these documents in case the originals get lost.

One traveler who has made this journey by vehicle recommends arriving at border stations late in the morning or by noon. Border posts tend to be clogged with commercial trucks in the early hours and you'll end up waiting anyhow.

Sometimes border guards can be overzealous when examining a vehicle, so make sure that it doesn't violate any potential existing (or imaginary) safety regulations or you may have to pay a hefty 'fee' (read: bribe) to get it processed. Before departing, check that:

- the head and tail lights, and blinkers are all working properly.
- the spare tire is in good condition.
- there is a jerry can for extra gas (petrol).

Panama – Paso Canoas

This border crossing on the Carretera Interamericana (Pan-American Hwy) is by far the most frequently used entry and exit point with Panama and is open 24 hours a day. The border crossing in either direction is generally straightforward. Be sure to get your exit stamp from Panama at the *migración* office before entering Costa Rica. There is no charge for entering Costa Rica. Travelers without a private vehicle should arrive during the day because buses stop running by 6pm. Travelers in a private vehicle would do better to arrive late in the morning when most of the trucks have already been processed.

Tica Bus (in Panama City ☎ 262 2084) travels from Panama City to San José (US$25, 15 hours) daily and crosses this border post. In David, Tracopa has one bus daily from the main terminal to San José (US$14, nine hours). Here, you'll also find frequent buses to the border at Paso Canoas (US$2, 1½ hours) that take off every 10 minutes from 4am to 8pm.

If traveling to Panama, you will have to pay US$5 for a tourist card. For further details, see the boxed text Getting to David, Panama, p396.

Panama – Guabito to Sixaola

Situated on the Caribbean coast, this is a fairly tranquil and hassle-free border crossing. Immigration guards regularly take off for lunch and you may have to wait a while to be processed. The border town on the Panamanian side is Guabito.

The border is open from 8am to 6pm in Panama and 7am to 5pm in Costa Rica. (Panama is one hour ahead.) Both sides close for an hour-long lunch at around 1pm, which means that there are potentially two hours each day when you'll be unable to make it across the border quickly. Get to Sixaola as early as possible; while there are a couple of places to spend the night, it won't be the highlight of your trip. Before crossing the bridge, stop at Costa Rica **migración** (☎ 754 2044) to process your paperwork. Walking across the bridge is kind of fun, in a vertigo-inducing sort of way.

If you are coming from Bocas del Toro, it's faster and cheaper to take the ferry to Changuinola (US$5, 45 minutes), from where you can take a quick taxi to the border or to the bus station (US$5). One daily bus travels between Changuinola and San José at 10am (US$15, eight hours). Otherwise, you can walk over the border and catch one of the hourly buses that go up the coast from Sixaola. For details, see the boxed text Getting to Guabito & Bocas del Toro, Panama, p500.

Panama – Río Sereno to San Vito

This is a rarely used crossing in the Cordillera de Talamanca. The border is open from 8am to 6pm in Panama and 7am to 5pm in Costa Rica. The small village of Río Sereno on the Panamanian side has a hotel and a place to eat; there are no facilities on the Costa Rican side.

Regular buses depart Concepción and David in Panama for Río Sereno. Local buses (four daily) and taxis go from the border to San Vito. For additional details, see the boxed text Getting to Río Sereno, Panama, p399.

- there is a well-stocked toolbox that includes parts, such as belts, that are harder to find in Central America.
- the car is equipped with emergency flares, roadside triangles and a fire extinguisher.

Another option is to ship a car from Miami to Costa Rica. For specifics, contact **Latii Express International** (in the USA ☎ 800-590 3789, 305-593 8929; www.latiiexpress.com).

Insurance from foreign countries is not recognized in Costa Rica, so you'll have to buy a policy locally. This can be done at the border and costs about US$15 a month. In addition, you'll probably have to pay a US$10 road tax to drive in. You are not allowed to sell the car in Costa Rica. If you need to leave the country without the car, you must leave it in a customs warehouse in San José.

SEA

Cruise ships stop in Costa Rican ports and enable passengers to make a quick (and insignificant) foray into the country. Typically, ships dock at either the Pacific port of Caldera (near Puntarenas, p318) or the Caribbean port of Puerto Limón (p450). It is also possible to arrive by private yacht.

GETTING AROUND

AIR
Scheduled Flights

Costa Rica's domestic airlines are **NatureAir** (☎ 220 3054; www.natureair.com) and **Sansa** (☎ 221 9414; www.flysansa.com); the latter is linked with Grupo TACA.

Both airlines fly small passenger planes, and you're allocated a baggage allowance of no more than 12kg. If the flight is full, your surfboard or golf clubs might not make it on; even if they do, you'll likely be paying extra for excess weight. NatureAir flies from Tobías Bolaños airport, 8km west of the center of San José in the suburb of Pavas. Sansa operates out of the blue building to the right of the international terminal at Juan Santamaría airport. Both airlines fly 14- and 19-passenger aircraft and offer a bumpy ride. These services aren't for people who have phobias about flying. Space is limited and demand is high in the dry season, so reserve and pay for tickets in advance.

Schedules change constantly and delays are frequent because of inclement weather. Be patient: Costa Rica has small planes and big storms; you don't want to be in them at the same time. You should not arrange a domestic flight that makes a tight connection with an international flight back home.

All domestic flights originate and terminate at San José. High-season fares are listed throughout this book. Destinations reached from San José include Bahía Drake, Barra del Colorado, Golfito, Liberia, Coto 47/Neily, Palmar Sur, Playa Nosara, Playa Sámara/Carrillo, Playa Tamarindo, Puerto Jiménez, Quepos, Tambor and Tortuguero.

Charters

Tobías Bolaños airport in Pavas caters to small aircraft that can be chartered to fly just about anywhere in the country. Fares start at about US$300 per hour for three- or four-seat planes, and it takes 40 to 90 minutes to fly to most destinations. You also have to pay for the return flight. You

DOMESTIC AIR ROUTES

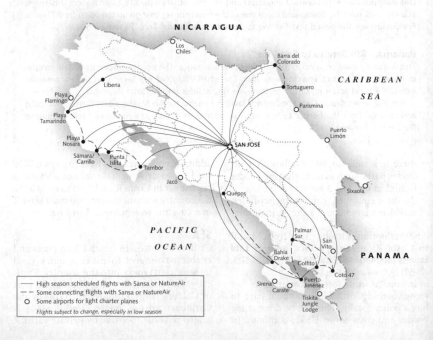

— High season scheduled flights with Sansa or NatureAir
-- Some connecting flights with Sansa or NatureAir
○ Some airports for light charter planes
Flights subject to change, especially in low season

should be aware that luggage space is extremely limited.

Many tour agencies can book charters, but you can book directly as well. For a list of companies, see San José (p124), Golfito (p434) and Puerto Jiménez (p426).

BICYCLE

Mountain bikes and beach cruisers can be rented in towns with a significant tourist presence at US$8 to US$15 per day. A few companies organize bike tours around Costa Rica (see p529).

BOAT

Ferries cross the Golfo de Nicoya connecting the central Pacific coast with the southern tip of Península de Nicoya. The **Countermark ferry** (☎ 661 1069; passenger/car US$2/9) links the port of Puntarenas with Playa Naranjo four times daily. The **Ferry Peninsular** (☎ 641 0515; passenger/car US$2/9) travels between Puntarenas and Vaquero every two hours, for a bus connection to Montezuma (see p323).

On the Golfo Dulce, a daily passenger ferry links Golfito with Puerto Jiménez on the Península de Osa and a weekday water taxi travels to and from Playa Zancudo (see p434). On the other side of the Península de Osa, water taxis connect Bahía Drake with Sierpe (see p402).

On the Caribbean coast, there is a bus and boat service which runs several times a day, linking Cariari and Tortuguero (p466), while another links Parismina and Siquirres (p459). Boats also ply the canals that run along the coast from Moín to Tortuguero, although no regular service exists. A daily water taxi connects Puerto Viejo de Sarapiquí with Trinidad on the Río San Juan. (The San Juan is Nicaraguan territory, so take your passport.) You can try to arrange boat transport in any of these towns for Barra del Colorado.

BUS

For some Latin American Spanish words and phrases useful for catching buses, see p566.

Local Buses

Local buses are the best (if rather slow) way of getting around Costa Rica. You can take one just about everywhere, and they're frequent and cheap, with the longest domestic journey out of San José costing less than US$10.

San José is the transportation center for the country (see p124), but there is no central terminal. Bus offices are scattered around the city: some large bus companies have big terminals that sell tickets in advance, while others have little more than a stop – sometimes unmarked. (One local bus 'station' in San José consists of a guy with a clipboard sitting on a lawn chair.)

Normally there's room for everyone on a bus, and if there isn't, someone will squeeze you on anyhow. The exceptions are days before and after a major holiday, especially Easter, when buses are ridiculously full. (Note that there are no buses on the Thursday to Saturday before Easter Sunday.) There are two types of bus: directo and colectivo. The directo buses presumably go from one destination to the next with few stops. If only this were so! It is against the instinctual nature of Costa Rican bus drivers not to pick up every single roadside passenger. (Directo buses charge more for this largely nonexistent nonstop service.) As for the colectivo, you know you're on one when the kids outside are outrunning your bus.

Trips longer than four hours usually include a rest stop (buses do not have bathrooms). Space is limited on board, so if you have to check luggage watch that it gets loaded and that it isn't 'accidentally' given to someone else at intermediate stops. Keep your day pack with important documents on you at all times. Thefts from overhead racks are rampant.

Bus schedules may fluctuate, so always confirm the time when you buy your ticket. If you are catching a bus that picks up somewhere along a road, get to the roadside early. Departure times are estimated and if the bus comes early, it will leave early.

For information on departures from San José, pay a visit to the ICT office (p92) to pick up the sort of up-to-date copy of the master schedule, which is also on-line at www.visitcostarica.com. Another more thorough but less reliable source of bus schedules and fares is *Costa Rica by Bus,* a self-published e-book that is available at www.costaricabybus.com.

TRANSPORTATION

ROAD DISTANCES (KM)

	Golfito	Liberia	Monteverde	Puerto Limón	Quepos	San Isidro del General	San José
Liberia	447						
Monteverde	499	112					
Puerto Limón	449	379	318				
Quepos	194	255	118	334			
San Isidro del General	205	329	294	294	77		
San José	339	220	160	168	174	134	
Turrialba	364	287	227	136	241	159	67

Shuttle Bus

An alternative to the standard intercity buses is the tourist-van shuttle services provided by **Grayling's Fantasy Bus** (☎ 220 2126; www.gray linecostarica.com) and **Interfuse** (☎ 283 5573; www .interbusonline.com). Both companies run overland transport from San José to the most popular destinations as well as directly between other destinations (see their websites for the comprehensive list). Interfuse fares start at US$19 for trips between San José and Puntarenas, and climb to US$29 for the bumpy ride to Monteverde. Grayline is slightly more expensive. These services will pick you up at your hotel and reservations can be made either online or through local travel agencies and hotel owners.

CAR & MOTORCYCLE

If you plan to drive in Costa Rica, your driver's license from home is normally accepted for up to 90 days. Many places will also accept an International Driving Permit (IDP), issued by the automobile association in your country of origin. After 90 days, you will need to get a Costa Rican driver's license. Most travelers fly into Costa Rica and then rent a car or motorcycle. See p545 if you plan to drive to Costa Rica in your own vehicle.

Gasoline (petrol) and diesel are widely available and 24-hour service stations dot the entire stretch of the Interamericana. The price of gas is about US$0.65 per liter, although it can fluctuate up to US$1 per liter. In more remote areas, fuel will likely be more expensive and might be sold from a drum at the neighborhood *pulpería* (corner grocery store); look for signs that say *'Se vende gasolina.'* Spare parts may be hard to find, especially for vehicles with sophisticated electronics and emissions-control systems.

See p566 for some useful Latin American Spanish words and phrases.

Hire

Most car-rental agencies can be found in San José and in popular tourist destinations on the Pacific coast (Tamarindo, Jacó, Quepos and Puerto Jiménez). Car rental is not cheap, and if you are going to be doing even a small amount of driving, invest in a 4WD. Many agencies will insist on 4WD for extended travel, especially in the rainy season, when driving through rivers is a matter of course. Ordinary cars are pointless as soon as you leave the Interamericana. Most rental vehicles are manual shift.

To rent a car you need a valid driver's license, a major credit card and a passport. The minimum age for car rental is 21. When reserving a car, ask for written confirmation. Carefully inspect rented cars for minor damage, and make sure that any damage is noted on the rental agreement. If your car breaks down, call the rental company. Don't attempt to get the car fixed yourself; most companies won't reimburse expenses without prior authorization.

Prices start at US$450 per week for a 4WD, including *kilometraje libre* (unlimited mileage). Basic insurance will cost an additional US$12 to US$20 per day and rental companies won't rent you a car without it. The roads in Costa Rica are rough and rugged, meaning that minor accidents or damage to the car is not uncommon. You can pay an extra fee (about US$10 per day) for a Collision Damage Waiver, or CDW, which covers the driver and a third party with a US$750 deductible. Above and beyond this, you can purchase full insurance, which is expensive, but it's worth it. Note that if you pay with a gold or platinum credit card, the company will usually take responsibility for damages to the car, in which case you can forego the cost of the full insurance. Make sure you verify this with your credit card company ahead of time. Finally, note that most insurance policies do not cover damages caused by flooding or driving through a river (even though this is sometimes necessary in Costa Rica!), so be aware of the extent of your policy.

Rental rates fluctuate wildly, so make sure you shop around before you commit to anything. Some agencies offer discounts if you reserve online or if you rent for long periods of time. Note that rental offices at the airport charge a 12% fee in addition to regular rates.

Thieves can easily recognize rental cars, and many thefts have occurred from them. *Never* leave anything in sight in a parked car – nothing! – and remove all luggage from the trunk overnight. Park the car in a guarded parking lot rather than on the street.

Motorcycles (including Harleys) can be rented in San José (p127) and Escazú (p133).

All of the major international rental agencies have outlets in Costa Rica, but you can usually get a better deal from a local company:

Adobe (☎ 259 4242, in the USA 800-769 8422; www.adobecar.com) Reader recommended, with offices in Liberia, Tamarindo and Quepos. Each rental vehicle comes with a cell phone with unlimited domestic use.

TRANSPORTATION

DRIVING THROUGH RIVERS

You know all those great ads where monster trucks or 4WD/SUVs splash through rivers full speed ahead? Forget you ever saw them.

Driving in Costa Rica will likely necessitate a river crossing at some point. Unfortunately, too many travelers have picked up their off-road skills from watching TV, and every season Ticos get a good chuckle out of the number of dead vehicles they help wayward travelers fish out of waterways.

If you're driving through water, follow these rules.

- Only do this in a 4WD. Don't drive through a river in a car. (It may seem ridiculous to have to say this, but it's done all the time.) Getting out of a steep, gravel riverbed requires a 4WD. Besides, car engines flood very easily – *adios* rental car.

- Check the depth of the water *before* driving through. To accommodate an average rental SUV (usually a Kia Sportage or similar), the water should be no deeper than above the knee. In a sturdier vehicle (Toyota 4-Runner or equivalent), water can be waist deep. If you're not sure, ask a local.

- The water should be calm. If the river is gushing so that there are white crests on the water, do not try to cross. Not only will the force of the water flood the engine, it could sweep your car away.

- Drive slooooooowly. Taxi drivers all over Costa Rica make lots of money towing out tourists who think that slamming through a river at full speed is the best way to get across. This is a huge mistake. The pressure of driving through a river too quickly will send the water right into the engine and you'll be cooking that electrical system in no time. Keep steady pressure on the accelerator so that the tail pipe doesn't fill with water, but take it slow.

- Err on the side of caution. Car-rental agencies in Costa Rica do not insure for water damage, so if you drown your vehicle, you're paying – in more ways than one.

TRANSPORTATION

THE CASE OF THE FLAT TIRE AND THE DISAPPEARING LUGGAGE

A serious scam is under way on the streets around Aeropuerte Internacional Juan Santamaría. Many readers have reported similar incidents, so take precautions to ensure this doesn't happen to you. Here's how it goes.

After picking up a rental car and driving out of the city, you notice that it has a flat tire. You pull over to try to fix it. Some friendly locals, noticing that a visitor to their fair land is in distress, pull over to help out. There is inevitably some confusion with the changing of the tire, and everybody is involved in figuring it out, but eventually the car repair is successfully accomplished and the friendly Ticos give you a wave and drive off. That's when you get back in your car and discover that your wallet – or your luggage, or everything – is gone.

This incident has happened enough times to suggest that somebody may be tampering with rental cars to 'facilitate' these flat tires. It certainly suggests that travelers should be very wary – and aware – if somebody pulls over to help. Keep your wallet and your passport on your person whenever you get out of the car. If possible, let one person in your party stay inside the car to keep a watchful eye. In any case, lock your doors – even if you think you are going to be right outside. There's nothing like losing all your luggage to put a damper on a vacation.

Dollar (☎ 443 2950, in the USA 866-767 8651; www.dollarcostarica.com) Also has an office at the Liberia airport.

Poas (☎ 442 6178, in the USA 888-607 POAS; www.carentals.com) Service centers in Liberia, Tamarindo, La Fortuna and Guápiles. Includes cell phone, cooler and baby seat, if you reserve on-line.

Solid (☎ 442 6000; www.solidcarrental.com) The only agency with offices in Puerto Jiménez and Golfito.

Toyota (☎ 258 5797, in the USA 894 6709; www.toyotarent.com)

Road Conditions & Hazards

Overall, driving in Costa Rica is for people with nerves of steel. The roads vary from quite good (the Interamericana) to barely passable (just about everywhere else). Even the good ones can suffer from landslides, sudden flooding and fog. Most roads are single lane and winding, lacking hard shoulders; others are dirt-and-mud affairs that climb mountains and traverse rivers.

Drive defensively. Always expect to come across cyclists, a broken-down vehicle, a herd of cattle, slow-moving trucks or an ox cart around the next bend. Unsigned speed bumps are placed on some stretches of road without warning. (The locals lovingly refer to them as *muertos*, 'dead people.')

Most roads (except around the major tourist towns) are inadequately signed and will require at least one stop to ask for directions. Always ask about road conditions before setting out, especially in the rainy season; a number of roads become impassable in the rainy season.

Road Rules

There are speed limits of 100km/h or less on all primary roads and 60km/h or less on secondary roads. Traffic police use radar, and speed limits are enforced with speeding tickets. You can get a traffic ticket for not wearing a seat belt. It's illegal to stop in an intersection or make a right turn on a red. At unmarked intersections, yield to the car on your right. Driving in Costa Rica is on the right, and passing is allowed only on the left.

If you are issued with a ticket, you have to pay the fine at a bank; instructions are given on the ticket. If you are driving a rental car, the rental company may be able to arrange your payment for you – the amount of the fine should be on the ticket. A 30% tax is added to the fine and the proceeds go to a children's charity.

Police have no right to ask for money and shouldn't confiscate a car unless: the driver cannot produce a license and ownership papers; the car lacks license plates; the driver is drunk; or the driver has been involved in an accident causing serious injury. (For more on what to do in an accident, see p537).

If you are driving and see oncoming cars with headlights flashing, it often means that there is a road problem or a radar speed trap ahead. Slow down immediately.

HITCHING

Hitchhiking is never entirely safe in any country, and Lonely Planet doesn't recommend it. Travelers who hitchhike should understand that they are taking a small but potentially serious risk. People who do hitchhike will be safer if they travel in pairs and let someone know where they are planning to go. Single women should use even greater discretion.

Hitching in Costa Rica is not common on main roads that have frequent buses. On minor rural roads, hitching is easier. To get picked up, most locals wave to cars in a friendly manner. If you get a ride, offer to pay when you arrive: *¿Cuanto le debo?* (How much do I owe you?) Your offer may be waved aside, or you may be asked to help with money for gas.

TAXI

Taxis are considered a form of public transport in remote areas that lack good public-transportation networks. They can be hired by the hour, the half-day or full day, or you can arrange a flat fee for a trip.

Meters are not used on long trips, so arrange the fare ahead of time. Fares can fluctuate due to worse-than-expected road conditions and bad weather in tough-to-reach places. The condition of cabs varies wildly, from basic sedans held together by rust to fully equipped 4WDs with air-con. In some cases, taxis are pickup trucks with seats built into the back. Most towns will have at least one licensed taxi, but in some remote villages you may have to get rides from whoever is offering. (Ask at *pulperías*.)

Hiring a car with a driver can cost the same or less than renting a car for the day, and it allows someone else (who knows the roads) to do the driving while you enjoy the scenery.

LOCAL TRANSPORTATION
Bus

Local buses operate chiefly in San José, Puntarenas, San Isidro, Golfito and Puerto Limón, connecting urban and suburban areas. Most local buses pick up passengers on the street and on main roads. The vehicles in service are usually converted school buses imported from the USA, and they are often packed.

Taxi

In San José taxis have meters, called *marías*, but many drivers try to get out of using them, particularly if you don't speak Spanish. (It is illegal not to use the meter.) Outside of San José most taxis don't have meters, and fares tend to be agreed upon in advance; some bargaining is quite acceptable.

In some towns, there are colectivo taxis that several passengers are able to share. Manuel Antonio and Golfito have a collective system in which drivers charge passengers a flat fee of about US$0.50 to take them from one end of town to the other. This service is getting more difficult to find in Manuel Antonio, where foreign travelers seem reticent to share transportation. (Come on folks, loosen up a bit!)

In rural areas, 4WD jeeps are often used as taxis. A 10-minute ride in one will usually cost about US$2. Taxi drivers are not normally tipped unless they assist with your luggage or have provided an above-average service.

TOURS

More than 200 tour operators are recognized by the Costa Rican tourist board (ICT), with the majority based in San José. Scores of tour operators in North America and Europe also run tours to Costa Rica. Many outfits will arrange customized itineraries.

See p527 for trips organized around a specific activity, such as mountain biking or bird-watching. There are also tour companies that cater for gays and lesbians (see p535) and disabled people (see p534). Most of the companies listed following also offer natural-history tours or multiactivity tours.

COSTA RICA-BASED COMPANIES

Ecole Travel (☎ 223 2240; www.ecoletravel.com)
Green Tortoise Adventure Travel (☎ 838 7677, in the USA 800-807 8647; www.greentortoise.com) Budget camping tours.
Green Tropical Tours (☎ 229 4192, 380 1536; www.greentropical.com)
Swiss Travel Service (☎ 282 4898; www.swisstravelcr.com) See p105.

CANADA-BASED COMPANIES

GAP Adventures (in Canada ☎ 1-800-465 5600; www.gapadventures.com)
Trek Holidays (in Canada ☎ 800-661 7265; www.trekholidays.com)

TRANSPORTATION

UK-BASED COMPANIES
Condor Journeys & Adventures (in the UK ☎ 01700-841 318; www.condorjourneys-adventures.com)
Journey Latin America (JLA; in the UK ☎ 020-8747 8315; www.journeylatinamerica.co.uk)
Last Frontiers (in the UK ☎ 01296-653 000; www.lastfrontiers.co.uk)

US-BASED COMPANIES
Costa Rica Connection (in the USA ☎ 805-543 8823, 800-345 7422; www.crconnect.com)
Costa Rica Experts (in the USA ☎ 773-935 1009, 800-827 9046; www.costaricaexperts.com)

Ecotour Expeditions (in the USA ☎ 401-423 3377, 800-688 1822; www.naturetours.com)
Elderhostel (in the USA ☎ 978-323 4141, 877-426 8056; www.elderhostel.org) Tours for travelers aged over 55 (younger companions permitted).
Holbrook Travel (in the USA ☎ 352-377 7111, 800-451 7111; www.holbrooktravel.com) See also Selva Verde Lodge, p519.
International Adventures, Ltd (☎ 800-990 9738; www.intladventures.com)
Nature Expeditions (☎ 800-869 0639; www.natureexp.com)
Preferred Adventures (in the USA ☎ 651-222 8131, 800-840 8687; www.preferredadventures.com)
Pure Trek (☎ 866 569 5723; www.puretrekcostarica.com)

Health Dr David Goldberg

Travelers to Central America need to be vigilant about food-borne as well as mosquito-borne infections. Most of these illnesses are not life threatening, but they can certainly ruin your trip. Besides getting the proper vaccinations, it's important that you bring along a good insect repellent and exercise great care in what you eat and drink.

BEFORE YOU GO

Since most vaccines don't produce immunity until at least two weeks after they're given, visit a physician four to eight weeks before departure. Ask your doctor for an International Certificate of Vaccination (otherwise known as the yellow booklet), which will list all the vaccinations you've received. This is mandatory for countries that require proof of yellow fever vaccination upon entry, but it's a good idea to carry it wherever you travel.

Bring medications in their original containers, clearly labeled. A signed, dated letter from your physician describing all medical conditions and medications, including generic names, is also a good idea. If carrying syringes or needles be sure to have a physician's letter documenting their medical necessity.

INSURANCE

Most doctors and hospitals expect payment in cash, regardless of whether you have travel health insurance or not. If you develop a life-threatening medical problem, you'll probably want to be evacuated to a country with state-of-the-art medical care. As this may cost tens of thousands of dollars, be sure you have insurance to cover this before you leave home. A list of medical evacuation and travel insurance companies is on the website of the **US State Department** (www.travel.state.gov/medical.html).

If your health insurance does not cover you for medical expenses while you are abroad, you should consider supplemental insurance. (Check the Travel Services section of the Lonely Planet website at www.lonelyplanet.com/travel_links for more information.) It might pay to find out in advance if your insurance plan will make payments directly to providers or if they reimburse you later for any overseas health expenditures.

MEDICAL CHECKLIST

- Acetaminophen (Tylenol) or aspirin
- Adhesive or paper tape
- Antibacterial ointment (eg Bactroban) for cuts and abrasions
- Antibiotics
- Antidiarrheal drugs (eg loperamide)
- Antihistamines (for hay fever and allergic reactions)
- Anti-inflammatory drugs (eg ibuprofen)
- Bandages, gauze, gauze rolls
- DEET-containing insect repellent for the skin
- Iodine tablets (for water purification)
- Oral rehydration salts
- Permethrin-containing insect spray for clothing, tents and bed nets
- Pocket knife
- Scissors, safety pins, tweezers
- Steroid cream or cortisone (for poison ivy and other allergic rashes)
- Sun block
- Syringes and sterile needles
- Thermometer

INTERNET RESOURCES

There is a wealth of travel health advice on the Internet. For further information, the website of **Lonely Planet** (www.lonelyplanet.com) is a good place to start. A superb book called *International Travel and Health,* which is revised annually and is available online at no cost, is published by the **World Health Organization** (www.who.int/ith). Another website of general interest is **MD Travel Health** (www.mdtravelhealth.com), which provides complete travel health recommendations for every country, updated daily, also at no cost.

It's usually a good idea to consult your government's travel health website before departure, if one is available:

Australia (www.dfat.gov.au/travel)
Canada (www.phac-aspc.gc.ca/tmp-pmv/pub_e.html)
UK (www.dh.gov.uk/PolicyAndGuidance/HealthAdvice ForTravellers/fs/en)
USA (www.cdc.gov/travel)

FURTHER READING

For further information, see *Healthy Travel Central & South America,* also from Lonely Planet. If you're traveling with children, Lonely Planet's *Travel with Children* will be useful. The *ABC of Healthy Travel,* by E Walker et al, is another valuable resource.

IN TRANSIT

DEEP VEIN THROMBOSIS (DVT)

Blood clots (deep vein thrombosis) may form in the legs during plane flights, chiefly because of prolonged immobility. The longer the flight, the greater the risk. Though most blood clots are reabsorbed uneventfully, some may break off and travel through the blood vessels to the lungs, where they could cause life-threatening complications.

The chief symptom of DVT is swelling or pain of the foot, ankle or calf, usually but not always on just the one side. When a blood clot travels all the way to the lungs, it may cause chest pain and difficulty in breathing. Travelers with any of these symptoms should immediately seek out medical attention.

To prevent the development of DVT on long flights you should walk about the cabin, perform isometric compressions of the leg muscles (ie contract the leg muscles

while sitting), drink plenty of fluids and avoid alcohol and tobacco.

JET LAG & MOTION SICKNESS

Jet lag is common when crossing more than five time zones, resulting in insomnia, fatigue, malaise or nausea. To avoid jet lag try drinking plenty of fluids (nonalcoholic) and eating light meals. Upon arrival, get exposure to natural sunlight and readjust your schedule (for meals, sleep etc) as soon as possible.

Antihistamines such as dimenhydrinate (Dramamine) and meclizine (Antivert, Bonine) are usually the first choice for treating motion sickness. Their main side effect is drowsiness. The herbal alternative ginger works like a charm for some people.

IN COSTA RICA

AVAILABILITY & COST OF HEALTH CARE

Good medical care is available in most major cities, but may be limited in rural areas. For a medical emergency, you should call one of the following numbers:

CIMA San José (☎ 208 1000; Próspero Fernández Fwy, San José) It's 500m west of the tollbooths on the highway to Santa Ana.
Clínica Bíblica (☎ 257 0466, 257 5252; cnr Calle 1 & Av 14, San José)
Hospital Nacional de Niños (☎ 222 0122; Calle 14, Av Central, San José) Only for children under 12.
Poison Center (☎ 223 1028)
Red Cross Ambulance (☎ 911, in San José 221 5818)
San Juan de Dios Hospital (☎ 257 6282; cnr Calle 14 & Av Central, San José)

For an extensive list of physicians, dentists and hospitals go to the US embassy website (usembassy.or.cr). If you're pregnant, be sure to check this site before departure to find the name of one or two obstetricians, just in case.

Most pharmacies are well supplied and the pharmacists are licensed to prescribe medication. If you're taking any medication on a regular basis, be sure you know its generic (scientific) name, since many pharmaceuticals go under different names in Costa Rica. Pharmacies that are open 24 hours include the following:

Farmacia Clínica Bíblica (☎ 257 5252; cnr Calle 1 &
Av 14, San José)
Farmacia Clínica Católica (☎ 283 6616; Guadalupe,
San José)
Farmacia el Hospital (☎ 222 0985)

INFECTIOUS DISEASES
Chagas' Disease
Chagas' disease is a parasitic infection that
is transmitted by triatomine insects (redu-
viid bugs), which inhabit crevices in the
walls and roofs of substandard housing
in South and Central America. In Costa
Rica most cases occur in Alajuela, Liberia
and Puntarenas. The triatomine insect lays
its feces on human skin as it bites, usually at night. A person becomes infected
when he or she unknowingly rubs the feces
into the bite wound or any other open sore.
Symptoms of the disease include fever and
swelling of the spleen, liver and lymph
nodes. Chagas' disease is extremely rare in
travelers. However, if you sleep in a poorly
constructed house, especially one made of
mud, adobe or thatch, you should be sure
to protect yourself with a bed net and a
good insecticide.

Dengue Fever (Breakbone Fever)
Dengue fever is a viral infection found
throughout Central America. In Costa Rica
outbreaks involving thousands of people
occur every year. Dengue is transmitted
by *Aedes* mosquitoes, which bite preferen-
tially during the daytime and are usually
found close to human habitations, often
indoors. They breed primarily in artificial
water containers such as jars, barrels, cans,
cisterns, metal drums, plastic containers
and discarded tires. As a result, dengue is
especially common in densely populated,
urban environments.

Dengue usually causes flu-like symptoms
including fever, muscle aches, joint pains,
headaches, nausea and vomiting, often followed by a rash. The body aches may be quite
uncomfortable, but most cases resolve uneventfully in a few days. Severe cases usually
occur in children under the age of 15 who are
experiencing their second dengue infection.

There is no real treatment for dengue fever
except for you to take analgesics such as
acetaminophen/paracetamol (Tylenol) and
drink plenty of fluids. Severe cases may require hospitalization for intravenous fluids

and supportive care. There is no vaccine.
The cornerstone of prevention is insect
protection measures (see p559).

Hepatitis A
Hepatitis A is the second most common
travel-related infection (after traveler's diarrhea). It's a viral infection of the liver that
is usually acquired by ingestion of contaminated water, food or ice, though it may also
be acquired by direct contact with infected
persons. The illness occurs throughout the
world, but the incidence is higher in developing nations. Symptoms may include
fever, malaise, jaundice, nausea, vomiting
and abdominal pain. Most cases resolve
without complications, though hepatitis
A occasionally causes severe liver damage.
There is no treatment.

The vaccine for hepatitis A is extremely
safe and highly effective. If you get a booster
six to 12 months later, it lasts for at least 10
years. You really should get it before you
go to Costa Rica or any other developing
nation. Because the safety of hepatitis A
vaccine has not been established for pregnant women or children under the age of
two, they should instead be given a gam-
maglobulin injection.

Hepatitis B
Like hepatitis A, hepatitis B is a liver infection that occurs worldwide but is more
common in developing nations. Unlike
hepatitis A, the disease is usually acquired
by sexual contact or by exposure to infected
blood, generally through blood transfusions
or contaminated needles. The vaccine is recommended only for long-term travelers (on
the road more than six months) who expect
to live in rural areas or have close physical
contact with the local population. Additionally, the vaccine is recommended for
anyone who anticipates sexual contact with
the local inhabitants or a possible need for
medical, dental or other treatments while
abroad, especially if a need for transfusions
or injections is expected.

Hepatitis B vaccine is safe and highly effective. However, a total of three injections
are necessary to establish full immunity.
Several countries added hepatitis B vaccine
to the list of routine childhood immunizations in the 1980s, so many young adults
are already protected.

HEALTH

HIV/AIDS

This has been reported from all Central American countries. Be sure to use condoms for all sexual encounters.

Leishmaniasis

Leishmaniasis occurs in the mountains and jungles of all Central American countries. The infection is transmitted by sand flies, which are about one-third the size of mosquitoes. Most cases occur in newly cleared forest or areas of secondary growth. The highest incidence is in Talamanca. In Costa Rica the disease is generally limited to the skin, causing slow-growing ulcers over exposed parts of the body, but more severe infections may occur in those with HIV. There is no vaccine for leishmaniasis. To protect yourself from sand flies, follow the same precautions as for mosquitoes (opposite), except that netting must be finer mesh (at least 18 holes to the linear inch).

Leptospirosis

Leptospirosis is acquired by exposure to water contaminated by the urine of infected animals. Whitewater rafters are at particularly high risk. In Costa Rica most cases occur in Limón, Turrialba, San Carlos and Golfito. Cases have been reported among residents of Puerto Limón who have bathed in local streams. Outbreaks can occur at times of flooding, when sewage overflow may contaminate water sources. The initial symptoms, which resemble a mild flu, usually subside uneventfully in a few days, with or without treatment, but a minority of cases are complicated by jaundice or meningitis. There is no vaccine. You can minimize your risk by staying out of bodies of fresh water that may be contaminated by animal urine. If you're engaging in high-risk activities, such as river running, in an area where an outbreak is in progress, you can take 200mg of doxycycline once weekly as a preventative measure. If you actually develop leptospirosis, the treatment is 100mg of doxycycline twice daily.

Malaria

Malaria occurs in every country in Central America. It's transmitted by mosquito bites, usually between dusk and dawn. The main symptom is high spiking fevers, which may be accompanied by chills, sweats, headache, body aches, weakness, vomiting or diarrhea. Severe cases may involve the central nervous system and lead to seizures, confusion, coma and death.

Taking malaria pills is recommended for the provinces of Alajuela, Limón (except for Puerto Limón), Guanacaste and Heredia. The risk is greatest in the cantons of Los Chiles (Alajuela Province), and Matina and Talamanca (Limón Province).

For Costa Rica the first-choice malaria pill is chloroquine, taken once weekly in a dosage of 500mg, starting one to two weeks before arrival and continuing through the trip and for four weeks after departure. Chloroquine is safe, inexpensive and highly effective. Side effects are typically mild and may include nausea, abdominal discomfort, headache, dizziness, blurred vision or itching. Severe reactions are uncommon.

Protecting yourself against mosquito bites is just as important as taking malaria pills (see opposite), since no pills are 100% effective.

If you may not have access to medical care while traveling, you should bring along additional pills for emergency self-treatment, which you should take if you can't reach a doctor and you develop symptoms that suggest malaria, such as high spiking fevers. One option is to take four tablets of Malarone once daily for three days. If you start self-medication, you should try to see a doctor at the earliest possible opportunity.

If you develop a fever after returning home, see a physician as malaria symptoms may not occur for months.

Rabies

Rabies is a viral infection of the brain and spinal cord that is almost always fatal. The rabies virus is carried in the saliva of infected animals and is typically transmitted through an animal bite, though contamination of any break in the skin with infected saliva may result in rabies.

Rabies occurs in all Central American countries. However, in Costa Rica only two cases have been reported over the last 30 years. Rabies vaccine is therefore recommended only for those at particularly high risk, such as spelunkers (cave explorers) and animal handlers.

All animal bites and scratches must be promptly and thoroughly cleansed with large amounts of soap and water, and local health authorities contacted to determine whether or not further treatment is necessary (see Animal Bites, right).

Typhoid

Typhoid fever is caused by ingestion of food or water contaminated by a species of *Salmonella* known as *Salmonella typhi*. Fever occurs in virtually all cases. Other symptoms may include headache, malaise, muscle aches, dizziness, loss of appetite, nausea and abdominal pain. Either diarrhea or constipation may occur. Possible complications include intestinal perforation, intestinal bleeding, confusion, delirium or (rarely) coma.

Unless you expect to take all your meals in major hotels and restaurants, a typhoid vaccine is a good idea. It's usually given orally, but is also available as an injection. Neither vaccine is approved for use in children under the age of two.

The drug of choice for typhoid fever is usually a quinolone antibiotic such as ciprofloxacin (Cipro) or levofloxacin (Levaquin), which many travelers carry for treatment of traveler's diarrhea. However, if you self-treat for typhoid fever, you may also need to self-treat for malaria, since the symptoms of the two diseases may be indistinguishable.

TRAVELER'S DIARRHEA

To prevent diarrhea, you should avoid tap water unless it has been boiled, filtered or chemically disinfected (iodine tablets); only eat fresh fruits or vegetables if cooked or peeled; be wary of dairy products that might contain unpasteurized milk; and be highly selective when eating food from street vendors.

If you develop diarrhea, be sure to drink plenty of fluids, preferably an oral rehydration solution containing lots of salt and sugar. A few loose stools don't require treatment, but if you start having more than four or five stools a day you should begin taking an antibiotic (usually a quinolone drug) and an antidiarrheal agent (such as loperamide). If diarrhea is bloody or persists for more than 72 hours, or is accompanied by fever, shaking chills or severe abdominal pain, you should seek medical attention.

ENVIRONMENTAL HAZARDS
Animal Bites

Do not attempt to pet, handle or feed any animal, with the exception of domestic animals known to be free of any infectious disease. Most animal injuries are directly related to a person's attempt to touch or feed the animal.

Any bite or scratch by a mammal, including bats, should be promptly and thoroughly cleansed with large amounts of soap and water, followed by application of an antiseptic such as iodine or alcohol. The local health authorities should be contacted immediately for possible postexposure rabies treatment, whether or not you've been immunized against rabies. It may also be advisable to start an antibiotic, since wounds caused by animal bites and scratches frequently become infected. One of the newer quinolones, such as levofloxacin (Levaquin), which many travelers carry in case of diarrhea, would be an appropriate choice.

Insect Bites

No matter how much you safeguard, getting bitten by mosquitoes is part of every traveler's experience in the country. While there are occasional outbreaks of dengue (see p557) in Costa Rica, for the most part the greatest worry you will have with bites is the general discomfort that comes with them, namely itching.

The best prevention is to stay covered up – wearing long pants, long sleeves and a hat, and shoes (rather than sandals). Unfortunately, Costa Rica's sweltering temperatures might make this a bit difficult. Therefore, the best measure you can take is to invest in a good insect repellent, preferably one containing DEET. (These repellents can also be found in Costa Rica.) This should be applied to exposed skin and clothing (but not to eyes, mouth, cuts, wounds or irritated skin).

In general, adults and children over 12 can use preparations containing 25% to 35% DEET, which usually lasts about six hours. Children between two and 12 years of age should use preparations containing no more than 10% DEET, applied sparingly, which will usually last about three hours. Neurologic toxicity has been reported from DEET, especially in children, but appears

HEALTH

to be extremely uncommon and generally related to overuse. DEET-containing compounds should not be used on children under age two.

Insect repellents containing certain botanical products, including oil of eucalyptus and soybean oil, are effective but last only 1½ to two hours.

A particularly good item for every traveler to take is a bug net to hang over beds (along with a few thumbtacks or nails with which to hang it). Many hotels in Costa Rica don't have windows (or screens) and a cheap little net will save you plenty of nighttime aggravation. The mesh size should be less than 1.5mm.

Dusk is the worst time for mosquitoes, so take extra precautions once the sun starts to set.

Snake Bites

Costa Rica is home to all manner of venomous snakes and any foray into forested areas will put you at (a very slight) risk for snake bite.

The best prevention is to wear closed, heavy shoes or boots and to keep a watchful eye on the trail. Snakes like to come out to cleared paths for a nap, so watch where you step. (For more on Costa Rica's fer-de-lance and bushmaster, see p58).

In the event of a bite from a venomous snake, place the victim at rest, keep the bitten area immobilized and move the victim immediately to the nearest medical facility. Avoid tourniquets, which are no longer recommended.

Sun

To protect yourself from excessive sun exposure you should stay out of the midday sun, wear sunglasses and a wide-brimmed sun hat, and apply sunscreen with SPF 15 or higher, with both UVA and UVB protection. Sunscreen should be generously applied to

all exposed parts of the body approximately 30 minutes before sun exposure and should be reapplied after swimming or vigorous activity. Travelers should also drink plenty of fluids and avoid strenuous exercise when the temperature is high.

Water

It is generally safe to drink the tap water everywhere in Costa Rica, other than in the most rural and undeveloped parts of the country. However, if you prefer to be cautious, buying bottled water is your best bet. If you have the means, vigorous boiling for one minute is the most effective means of water purification. At altitudes greater than 2000m (6500ft), boil for three minutes. Another option is to disinfect water with iodine pills: add 2% tincture of iodine to one quart or liter of water (five drops to clear water, 10 drops to cloudy water) and let stand for 30 minutes. If the water is cold, longer times may be required.

TRAVELING WITH CHILDREN

In general, it's safe for children and pregnant women to go to Costa Rica. However, because some of the vaccines listed previously are not approved for use by children or during pregnancy, these travelers should be particularly careful not to drink tap water or consume any questionable food or beverage. Also, when traveling with children, make sure they're up-to-date on all routine immunizations. It's sometimes appropriate to give children some of their vaccines a little early before visiting a developing nation. You should discuss this with your pediatrician.

Lastly, if pregnant, you should bear in mind that should a complication such as premature labor develop while abroad, the quality of medical care may not be comparable to that in your home country.

See p531 for some general information on traveling with children.

Language

CONTENTS

Spanish is the official language of Costa Rica and the main language the traveler will need. Every visitor to the country should attempt to learn some Spanish, the basic elements of which are easily acquired.

A month-long language course taken before departure can go a long way toward facilitating communication and comfort on the road. Alternatively, language courses are also available in all parts of Costa Rica (see Courses on p531 of the Directory chapter). Even if classes are impractical, you should make the effort to learn a few basic phrases and pleasantries. Don't hesitate to practice your new skills – in general, Latin Americans meet attempts to communicate in the vernacular, however halting, with enthusiasm and appreciation.

PHRASEBOOKS & DICTIONARIES

Lonely Planet's *Costa Rica Spanish Phrasebook* will be extremely helpful during your trip. If you're traveling outside of Costa Rica, LP's *Latin American Spanish Phrasebook* is another worthwhile addition to your backpack. Another exceptionally useful resource is the University of Chicago *Spanish-English, English-Spanish Dictionary*.

SPANISH IN COSTA RICA

The following colloquialisms and slang *(tiquismos)* are frequently heard, and are for the most part used only in Costa Rica.

¡Adiós! – Hi! (used when passing a friend in the street, or anyone in remote rural areas; also means 'farewell,' but only when leaving for a long time)
bomba – gas station
Buena nota. – OK/Excellent. (literally 'good note')
chapulines – a gang, usually of young thieves
chunche – thing (can refer to almost anything)
cien metros – one city block
¿Hay campo? – Is there space? (on a bus)
machita – blonde woman (slang)
mae – buddy (pronounced 'ma' as in 'mat' followed with a quick 'eh'; it's mainly used by boys and young men)
mi amor – my love (used as a familiar form of address by both men and women)
pulpería – corner grocery store
¡Pura vida! – Super! (literally 'pure life,' also an expression of approval or even a greeting)
sabanero – cowboy, especially one who hails from Guanacaste Province
Salado. – Too bad/Tough luck.
soda – café or lunch counter
¡Tuanis! – Cool!
¡Upe! – Is anybody home? (used mainly in rural areas at people's houses, instead of knocking)
vos – you (informal, same as *tú*)

It's small, light and has thorough entries, making it ideal for travel. It also makes a great gift for any newfound friends upon your departure.

LATIN AMERICAN SPANISH

The Spanish of the Americas comes in a bewildering array of varieties. Depending on the areas in which you travel, consonants may be glossed over, vowels squashed into each other, and syllables and even words dropped entirely. Slang and regional vocabulary, much of it derived from indigenous languages, can further add to your bewilderment.

Throughout Latin America, the Spanish language is referred to as *castellano* more often than *español*. Unlike in Spain, the plural of the familiar *tú* form is *ustedes* rather than *vosotros;* the latter term will sound quaint and archaic in the Americas. Another notable difference is that the letters **c** and **z** are never lisped in Latin America; attempts to do so could well provoke amusement.

OTHER LANGUAGES

Travelers will find English is often spoken in the upmarket hotels, airline offices and tourist agencies, and some other European languages are encountered in hotels run by Europeans. On the Caribbean coast, many of the locals speak some English, albeit with a local Creole dialect.

Indigenous languages are spoken in isolated areas, but unless travelers are getting off the beaten track they'll rarely encounter them. The indigenous languages Bribri and Cabécar are understood by an estimated 18,000 people living on both sides of the Cordillera de Talamanca.

PRONUNCIATION

Spanish spelling is phonetically consistent, meaning that there's a clear and consistent relationship between what you see in writing and how it's pronounced. Also, most Spanish sounds have English equivalents, so English speakers shouldn't have too much trouble being understood.

Vowels

a	as in 'father'
e	as in 'met'
i	as in 'marine'
o	as in 'or' (without the 'r' sound)
u	as in 'rule'; the 'u' is not pronounced after **q** and in the letter combinations **gue** and **gui**, unless it's marked with a diaeresis (eg *argüir*), in which case it's pronounced as English 'w'
y	at the end of a word or when it stands alone, it's pronounced as the Spanish **i** (eg *ley*); between vowels within a word it's as the 'y' in 'yonder'

Consonants

As a rule, Spanish consonants resemble their English counterparts. The exceptions are listed below.

While the consonants **ch**, **ll** and **ñ** are generally considered distinct letters, **ch** and **ll**

are now often listed alphabetically under **c** and **l** respectively. The letter **ñ** is still treated as a separate letter and comes after **n** in dictionaries.

b	similar to English 'b,' but softer; referred to as 'b larga'
c	as in 'celery' before **e** and **i**; otherwise as English 'k'
ch	as in 'church'
d	as in 'dog,' but between vowels and after **l** or **n**, the sound is closer to the 'th' in 'this'
g	as the 'ch' in the Scottish *loch* before **e** and **i** ('kh' in our guides to pronunciation); elsewhere, as in 'go'
h	invariably silent. If your name begins with this letter, listen carefully if you're waiting for public officials to call you.
j	as the 'ch' in the Scottish *loch* (depicted as 'kh' in our guides to pronunciation)
ll	as the 'y' in 'yellow'
ñ	as the 'ni' in 'onion'
r	a short **r** except at the beginning of a word, and after **l**, **n** or **s**, when it's often rolled
rr	very strongly rolled
v	similar to English 'b,' but softer; referred to as 'b corta'
x	usually pronounced as **j** above; in some indigenous place names **x** is pronounced as the 's' in 'sit'; in other instances, it's as in 'taxi'
z	as the 's' in 'sun'

Word Stress

In general, words ending in vowels or the letters **n** or **s** have stress on the next-to-last syllable, while those with other endings have stress on the last syllable. Thus *vaca* (cow) and *caballos* (horses) both carry stress on the next-to-last syllable, while *ciudad* (city) and *infeliz* (unhappy) are both stressed on the last syllable.

Written accents will almost always appear in words that don't follow the rules above, eg *sótano* (basement), *América* and *porción* (portion).

GENDER & PLURALS

In Spanish, nouns are either masculine or feminine, and there are rules to help determine gender (there are of course some exceptions). Feminine nouns generally end with -**a** or with the groups -**ción**, -**sión** or -**dad**. Other endings typically signify a masculine noun. Endings for adjectives also change to agree with the gender of the noun they modify (masculine/feminine -**o**/-**a**). Where both masculine and feminine forms are included in this language guide, they are separated by a slash, with the masculine form first, eg *perdido/a*.

If a noun or adjective ends in a vowel, the plural is formed by adding **s** to the end. If it ends in a consonant, the plural is formed by adding **es** to the end.

ACCOMMODATIONS

I'm looking for ...	*Estoy buscando ...*	e·stoy boos·kan·do ...
Where is ...?	*¿Dónde hay ...?*	don·de ai ...
a cabin	*una cabina*	oo·na ca·*bee*·na
a camping	*un camping/*	oon *kam*·ping/
ground	*campamento*	kam·pa·*men*·to
a guesthouse	*una casa de*	oo·na ka·*sa* de
	huespedes	*wes*·pe·des
a hostel	*un hospedaje/*	oon os·pe·*da*·khe/
	una residencia	oon·a re·see·
		den·sya
a hotel	*un hotel*	oon o·*tel*
a youth hostel	*un albergue*	oon al·*ber*·ge
	juvenil	khoo·ve·*neel*

Are there any rooms available?

| *¿Hay habitaciones* | ay a·bee·ta·syon·es |
| *libres?* | lee·bres |

I'd like a ...	*Quisiera una*	kee·*sye*·ra oo·na
room.	*habitación ...*	a·bee·ta·syon ...
double	*doble*	*do*·ble
single	*individual*	een·dee·vee·*dwal*
twin	*con dos camas*	kon dos *ka*·mas

How much is it	*¿Cuánto cuesta*	*kwan*·to *kwes*·ta
per ...?	*por ...?*	por ...
night	*noche*	*no*·che
person	*persona*	per·*so*·na
week	*semana*	se·*ma*·na

full board	*pensión*	pen·*syon*
	completa	kom·*ple*·ta
private/shared	*baño privado/*	*ba*·nyo pree·*va*·do/
bathroom	*compartido*	kom·par·*tee*·do
too expensive	*demasiado caro*	de·ma·*sya*·do *ka*·ro
cheaper	*más económico*	mas e·ko·*no*·mee·ko
discount	*descuento*	des·*kwen*·to

Does it include breakfast?

| *¿Incluye el desayuno?* | een·*kloo*·ye el de·sa·*yoo*·no |

May I see the room?

| *¿Puedo ver la* | pwe·do ver la |
| *habitación?* | a·bee·ta·*syon* |

I don't like it.

| *No me gusta.* | no me *goos*·ta |

It's fine. I'll take it.

| *Está bien. La tomo.* | es·*ta* byen la *to*·mo |

I'm leaving now.

| *Me voy ahora.* | me voy a·*o*·ra |

CONVERSATION & ESSENTIALS

In their public behavior, Latin Americans are very conscious of civilities. You should never approach a stranger for information without extending a greeting, such as *buenos días* or *buenas tardes*, and you should use only the polite form of address, especially with the police and public officials.

Central America is generally more formal than many of the South American countries. The polite form *usted* (you) is used in all cases in this guide; where options are given, the form is indicated by the abbreviations 'pol' and 'inf.'

Hi.	*Hola.*	o·la (inf)
Good morning.	*Buenos días.*	*bwe*·nos *dee*·as
Good afternoon.	*Buenas tardes.*	*bwe*·nas *tar*·des
Good evening/	*Buenas noches.*	*bwe*·nas *no*·ches
night.		

The three most common greetings are often abbreviated to simply *buenos* (for *buenos días*) and *buenas* (for *buenas tardes* and *buenas noches*).

LANGUAGE

Bye/See you soon.	*Hasta luego.*	*as*·ta *lwe*·go
Goodbye.	*Adiós.*	a·*dyos* (see

also the boxed text Spanish in Costa Rica on p561)

Yes.	*Sí.*	see
No.	*No.*	no
Please.	*Por favor.*	por fa·*vor*
Thank you.	*Gracias.*	*gra*·syas
Many thanks.	*Muchas gracias.*	*moo*·chas *gra*·syas
You're welcome.	*De nada.*	de *na*·da
Apologies.	*Perdón.*	per·*don*
May I?	*Permiso.*	per·*mee*·so
(when asking permission)		
Excuse me.	*Disculpe.*	dees·*kool*·pe

(used before a request or when apologizing)

How are things?
  ¿Qué tal? ke tal
What's your name?
  ¿Cómo se llama usted? *ko*·mo se *ya*·ma oo·*sted* (pol)
  ¿Cómo te llamas? *ko*·mo te *ya*·mas (inf)
My name is ...
  Me llamo ... me *ya*·mo ...
It's a pleasure to meet you.
  Mucho gusto. *moo*·cho *goos*·to
The pleasure is mine.
  El gusto es mío. el *goos*·to es *mee*·o
Where are you from?
  ¿De dónde es/eres? de *don*·de es/*er*·es (pol/inf)
I'm from ...
  Soy de ... soy de ...
Where are you staying?
  ¿Dónde está alojado? *don*·de es·*ta* a·lo·*kha*·do (pol)
  ¿Dónde estás alojado? *don*·de es·*tas* a·lo·*kha*·do (inf)
May I take a photo?
  ¿Puedo sacar una foto? *pwe*·do sa·*kar* oo·na *fo*·to

DIRECTIONS

How do I get to ...?
  ¿Cómo llego a ...? *ko*·mo *ye*·go a ...
Is it far?
  ¿Está lejos? es·*ta le*·khos
Go straight ahead.
  Siga/Vaya derecho. *see*·ga/*va*·ya de·*re*·cho
Turn left.
  Voltée a la izquierda. vol·*te*·e a la ees·*kyer*·da
Turn right.
  Voltée a la derecha. vol·*te*·e a la de·*re*·cha
Can you show me (on the map)?
  ¿Me lo podría señalar me lo po·*dree*·a se·nya·*lar*
  (en el mapa)? (en el *ma*·pa)

north	*norte*	*nor*·te
south	*sur*	soor
east	*este*	*es*·te
west	*oeste*	o·*es*·te

here	*aquí*	a·*kee*
there	*ahí*	a·*ee*
avenue	*avenida*	a·ve·*nee*·da
block	*cuadra*	*kwa*·dra
street	*calle/paseo*	*ka*·lye/pa·*se*·o

SIGNS	
Entrada	Entrance
Salida	Exit
Información	Information
Abierto	Open
Cerrado	Closed
Prohibido	Prohibited
Comisaria	Police Station
Servicios/Baños	Toilets
Hombres/Varones	Men
Mujeres/Damas	Women

HEALTH

I'm sick.
  Estoy enfermo/a. es·*toy* en·*fer*·mo/a
I need a doctor.
  Necesito un médico. ne·se·*see*·to oon *me*·dee·ko
Where's the hospital?
  ¿Dónde está el hospital? *don*·de es·*ta* el os·pee·*tal*
I'm pregnant.
  Estoy embarazada. es·*toy* em·ba·ra·*sa*·da
I've been vaccinated.
  Estoy vacunado/a. es·*toy* va·koo·*na*·do/a

I'm allergic	*Soy alérgico/a*	soy a·*ler*·khee·ko/a
to ...	*a ...*	a ...
antibiotics	*los antibióticos*	los an·tee·*byo*·tee·kos
nuts	*las fruta secas*	las *froo*·tas *se*·kas
penicillin	*la penicilina*	la pe·nee·see·*lee*·na

I'm ...	*Soy ...*	soy ...
asthmatic	*asmático/a*	as·*ma*·tee·ko/a
diabetic	*diabético/a*	dya·be·*tee*·ko/a
epileptic	*epiléptico/a*	e·pee·*lep*·tee·ko/a

I have ...	*Tengo ...*	*ten*·go ...
a cough	*tos*	tos
diarrhea	*diarrea*	dya·*re*·a
a headache	*un dolor de*	oon do·*lor* de
	cabeza	ka·*be*·sa
nausea	*náusea*	*now*·se·a

LANGUAGE DIFFICULTIES

Do you speak English?
  ¿Habla/Hablas inglés? a·bla/a·blas een·*gles* (pol/inf)

Does anyone here speak English?

¿Hay alguien que hable   ai al·*gyen* ke *a*·ble
inglés?   een·*gles*

I (don't) understand.

(No) Entiendo.   (no) en·*tyen*·do

How do you say ...?

¿Cómo se dice ...?   ko·mo se *dee*·se ...

What does ...mean?

¿Qué significa ...?   ke seeg·*nee*·fee·ka ...

Could you	*¿Puede ..., por*	pwe·de ... por
please ...?	*favor?*	fa·vor
repeat that	*repetirlo*	re·pe·*teer*·lo
speak more	*hablar más*	a·*blar* mas
slowly	*despacio*	des·*pa*·syo
write it down	*escribirlo*	es·kree·*beer*·lo

EMERGENCIES

Help!	*¡Socorro!*	so·*ko*·ro
Fire!	*¡Fuego!*	fwe·go
I've been robbed.	*Me han robado.*	me an ro·*ba*·do
Go away!	*¡Déjeme!*	de·khe·me
Get lost!	*¡Váyase!*	va·ya·se
Call ...!	*¡Llame a ...!*	ya·me a
the police	*la policía*	la po·lee·*see*·a
a doctor	*un médico*	oon *me*·dee·ko
an ambulance	*una ambulancia*	oo·na am·boo·*lan*·sya

It's an emergency.

Es una emergencia.   es oo·na e·mer·*khen*·sya

Could you help me, please?

¿Me puede ayudar,   me pwe·de a·yoo·*dar*
por favor?   por fa·*vor*

I'm lost.

Estoy perdido/a.   es·*toy* per·*dee*·do/a

Where are the toilets?

¿Dónde están los baños?   don·de es·*tan* los ba·nyos

NUMBERS

1	*uno*	oo·no
2	*dos*	dos
3	*tres*	tres
4	*cuatro*	kwa·tro
5	*cinco*	seen·ko
6	*seis*	says
7	*siete*	sye·te
8	*ocho*	o·cho
9	*nueve*	nwe·ve
10	*diez*	dyes
11	*once*	on·se
12	*doce*	do·se

13	*trece*	tre·se
14	*catorce*	ka·tor·se
15	*quince*	keen·se
16	*dieciséis*	dye·see·says
17	*diecisiete*	dye·see·sye·te
18	*dieciocho*	dye·see·o·cho
19	*diecinueve*	dye·see·nwe·ve
20	*veinte*	vayn·te
21	*veintiuno*	vayn·tee·oo·no
30	*treinta*	trayn·ta
31	*treinta y uno*	trayn·ta ee oo·no
40	*cuarenta*	kwa·ren·ta
50	*cincuenta*	seen·kwen·ta
60	*sesenta*	se·sen·ta
70	*setenta*	se·ten·ta
80	*ochenta*	o·chen·ta
90	*noventa*	no·ven·ta
100	*cien*	syen
101	*ciento uno*	syen·to oo·no
200	*doscientos*	do·syen·tos
1000	*mil*	meel
5000	*cinco mil*	seen·ko meel

PAPERWORK

birth certificate	*certificado de nacimiento*
border (frontier)	*la frontera*
car-owner's title	*título de propiedad*
car registration	*registración*
customs	*aduana*
driver's license	*licencia de manejar*
identification	*identificación*
immigration	*migración*
insurance	*seguro*
passport	*pasaporte*
temporary vehicle import permit	*permiso de importación temporal de vehículo*
tourist card	*tarjeta de turista*
visa	*visado*

SHOPPING & SERVICES

I'd like to buy ...

Quisiera comprar ...   kee·*sye*·ra kom·*prar* ...

I'm just looking.

Sólo estoy mirando.   so·lo es·*toy* mee·*ran*·do

May I look at it?

¿Puedo verlo/a?   pwe·do ver·lo/a

How much is it?

¿Cuánto cuesta?   kwan·to kwes·ta

That's too expensive for me.

Es demasiado caro   es de·ma·*sya*·do ka·ro
para mí.   pa·ra mee

Could you lower the price?

¿Podría bajar un poco   po·dree·a ba·khar oon po·ko
el precio?   el pre·syo

I don't like it.
No me gusta. no me *goos·*ta
I'll take it.
Lo llevo. lo *ye·*vo

Do you *¿Aceptan ...?* a·sep·*tan ...*
accept ...?
  American *dólares* do·la·res
  dollars *americanos* a·me·ree·*ka·*nos
  credit cards *tarjetas de* tar·*khe·*tas de
    crédito *kre·*dee·to
  traveler's *cheques de* che·kes de
  checks *viajero* vya·*khe·*ro

less *menos* *me·*nos
more *más* mas
large *grande* gran·de
small *pequeño/a* pe·ke·nyo/a

I'm looking *Estoy* es·*toy*
for the ... *buscando ...* boos·kan·do...
  ATM *el cajero* el ka·*khe·*ro
    automático ow·to·*ma·*tee·ko
  bank *el banco* el ban·ko
  bookstore *la librería* la lee·bre·*ree·*a
  exchange house *la casa de* la *ka·*sa de
    cambio *kam·*byo
  general store *la tienda* la *tyen·*da
  laundry *la lavandería* la la·van·de·*ree·*a
  market *el mercado* el mer·*ka·*do
  pharmacy/ *la farmacia* la far·*ma·*sya
  chemist
  post office *la officina* la o·fee·*see·*na
    de correos de ko·*re·*os
  supermarket *el supermercado* el soo·per·
    mer·*ka·*do
  tourist office *la oficina de* la o·fee·*see·*na de
    turismo too·*rees·*mo

What time does it open/close?
¿A qué hora abre/cierra?
a ke *o·*ra *a·*bre/*sye·*ra
I want to change some money/traveler's checks.
Quisiera cambiar dinero/cheques de viajero.
kee·*sye·*ra kam·*byar* dee·*ne·*ro/che·kes de vya·*khe·*ro
What is the exchange rate?
¿Cuál es el tipo de cambio?
kwal es el *tee·*po de *kam·*byo
I want to call ...
Quisiera llamar a ...
kee·*sye·*ra lya·*mar* a ...

airmail *correo aéreo* ko·*re·*o a·e·re·o
letter *carta* *kar·*ta
registered (mail) *certificado* ser·tee·fee·*ka·*do
stamps *timbres* *teem·*bres

TIME & DATES

What time is it? *¿Qué hora es?* ke *o·*ra es
It's one o'clock. *Es la una.* es la *oo·*na
It's seven o'clock. *Son las siete.* son las *sye·*te
Half past two. *Dos y media.* dos ee *me·*dya

midnight *medianoche* me·dya·*no·*che
noon *mediodía* me·dyo·*dee·*a
now *ahora* a·*o·*ra
today *hoy* oy
tonight *esta noche* es·ta *no·*che
tomorrow *mañana* ma·*nya·*na
yesterday *ayer* a·*yer*

Monday *lunes* *loo·*nes
Tuesday *martes* *mar·*tes
Wednesday *miércoles* *myer·*ko·les
Thursday *jueves* *khwe·*ves
Friday *viernes* *vyer·*nes
Saturday *sábado* *sa·*ba·do
Sunday *domingo* do·*meen·*go

January *enero* e·*ne·*ro
February *febrero* fe·*bre·*ro
March *marzo* *mar·*so
April *abril* a·*breel*
May *mayo* *ma·*yo
June *junio* *khoo·*nyo
July *julio* *khoo·*lyo
August *agosto* a·*gos·*to
September *septiembre* sep·*tyem·*bre
October *octubre* ok·*too·*bre
November *noviembre* no·*vyem·*bre
December *diciembre* dee·*syem·*bre

TRANSPORT
Public Transport

What time does *¿A qué hora ...* a ke *o·*ra ...
... leave/arrive? *sale/llega?* *sa·*le/*ye·*ga
  the bus *el bus/autobús* el bus/ow·to·*boos*
  the ferry *el barco* el *bar·*ko
  the minibus *el colectivo/* el ko·lek·*tee·*vo/
    la buseta/ la bo·*se·*ta/
    el microbus el *mee·*kro·boos
  the plane *el avión* el a·*vyon*
  the train *el tren* el tren

the airport *el aeropuerto* el a·e·ro·*pwer·*to
the bus station *la estación de* la es·ta·*syon* de
  autobuses ow·to·*boo·*ses
the bus stop *la parada de* la pa·*ra·*da de
  autobuses ow·to·*boo·*ses
the train station *la estación de* la es·ta·*syon* de
  ferrocarril fe·ro·ka·*reel*

| the luggage
locker | la consigna para
el equipaje | la kon·*see*·nya para
el e·kee·*pa*·khe |
| the ticket office | la boletería/
ticketería | la bo·le·te·*ree*·ya/
tee·ke·te·*ree*·ya |

A ticket to ..., please.
Un boleto a ..., por favor.
oon bo·*le*·to a ... por fa·*vor*
What's the fare to ...?
¿Cuánto cuesta hasta ...?
kwan·to *kwes*·ta *a*·sta ...

student's	de estudiante	de es·too·*dyan*·te
1st class	primera clase	pree·me·ra *kla*·se
2nd class	segunda clase	se·*goon*·da *kla*·se
single/one-way	de ida	de ee·da
return/round trip	de ida y vuelta	de ee·da e *vwel*·ta
taxi	taxi	*tak*·see

Private Transport

I'd like to hire a ...	Quisiera alquilar ...	kee·*sye*·ra al·kee·*lar* ...
4WD	un todo terreno	oon *to*·do te·*re*·no
car	un auto/carro	oon ow·to/*ka*·ro
motorcycle	una motocicleta	oo·na mo·to·see· *kle*·ta
bicycle	una bicicleta	oo·na bee·see· *kle*·ta

pickup (truck)	camioneta	ka·myo·*ne*·ta
truck	camión ka·myon	
hitchhike	hacer dedo	a·ser *de*·do

Where's a petrol station?
¿Dónde hay una gasolinera/bomba?
don·de ai oo·na ga·so·lee·*ne*·ra/*bom*·ba
How much is a liter of gasoline?
¿Cuánto cuesta el litro de gasolina?
kwan·to *kwes*·ta el *lee*·tro de ga·so·*lee*·na
Please fill it up.
Lleno, por favor.
ye·no por fa·*vor*
I'd like (2000 colones) worth.
Quiero (dos mil colones) en gasolina.
kye·ro (dos meel ko·*lo*·nes) en ga·so·*lee*·na

diesel	diesel *dee*·sel	
leaded (regular)	gasolina con plomo	ga·so·*lee*·na kon *plo*·mo
petrol (gas)	gasolina	ga·so·*lee*·na
unleaded	gasolina sin plomo	ga·so·*lee*·na seen *plo*·mo
oil	aceite	a·*say*·te
tire	llanta *yan*·ta	
puncture	agujero	a·goo·*khe*·ro

ROAD SIGNS

Though Costa Rica mostly uses the familiar international road signs, you should be prepared to encounter these other signs as well:

Acceso	Entrance
Acceso Prohibido	No Entry
Acceso Permanente	24-Hour Access
Construcción de Carreteras	Roadworks
Ceda el Paso	Give Way
Curva Peligrosa	Dangerous Curve
Derrumbes	Landslides
Despacio	Slow
Desvío/Desviación	Detour
Mantenga Su Derecha	Keep to the Right
No Adelantar	No Passing
No Hay Paso	Road Closed
No Pase	No Overtaking
Pare/Stop	Stop
Peligro	Danger
Prohibido Estacionar	No Parking
Prohibido el Paso	No Entry
Puente Angosto	Narrow Bridge
Salida (de Autopista)	Exit (Freeway)
Una Via	One Way

Is this the road to ...?
¿Por acquí se va a ...?
por a·*kee* se va a ...
(How long) Can I park here?
¿(Por cuánto tiempo) Puedo estacionar aquí?
(por kwan·to tyem·po) pwe·do ess·ta·syo·*nar* a·*kee*
Where do I pay?
¿Dónde se paga?
don·de se *pa*·ga
I need a mechanic/tow truck.
Necesito un mecánico/remolque.
ne·se·*see*·to oon me·*ka*·nee·ko/re·*mol*·ke
Is there a garage near here?
¿Hay un garaje cerca de aquí?
ai oon ga·*ra*·khe ser·ka de a·*kee*
The car has broken down in ...
El carro se ha averiado en ...
el *ka*·ro se a a·ve·*rya*·do en ...
The motorbike won't start.
La moto no arranca.
la *mo*·to no a·*ran*·ka
I have a flat tire.
Tengo una llanta desinflada.
ten·go oo·na *yan*·ta des·een·*fla*·da
I've run out of petrol.
Me quedé sin gasolina.
me ke·*de* seen ga·so·*lee*·na
I've had an accident.
Tuve un accidente.
too·ve oon ak·see·*den*·te

LANGUAGE

TRAVEL WITH CHILDREN

I need ...
Necesito ...
ne·se·*see*·to ...

Do you have ...?
¿Hay ...?
ai ...

a car baby seat
un asiento de seguridad para bebés
oon a·*syen*·to de se·goo·ree·*da* pa·ra be·*bes*

a child-minding service
oon club para niños
oon kloob pa·*ra* nee·nyos

a children's menu
un menú infantil
oon me·*noo* een·fan·*teel*

a creche
una guardería
oo·na gwar·de·*ree*·a

(disposable) diapers/nappies
pañales (de usar y tirar)
pa·*nya*·les (de oo·*sar* ee tee·*rar*)

an (English-speaking) babysitter
una niñera (que habla inglesa)
oo·na nee·*nye*·ra (ke *a*·bla een·*gle*·sa)

formula (milk)
leche en polvo
le·che en *pol*·vo

a highchair
una silla para bebé
oo·na *see*·ya *pa*·ra be·*be*

a potty
una bacinica
oo·na ba·see·*nee*·ka

a stroller
una carreola
oona ka·re·o·la

Do you mind if I breast-feed here?
¿Le molesta que dé el pecho aquí?
le mo·*les*·ta ke de el *pe*·cho a·*kee*

Are children allowed?
¿Se admiten niños?
se ad·*mee*·ten *nee*·nyos

Also available from Lonely Planet:
Costa Rican Spanish Phrasebook

Glossary

See p85 for useful words and phrases dealing with food and dining. See the Language chapter for other useful words and phrases.

abrazo – hug
adiós – means goodbye universally, but used in rural Costa Rica as a greeting
aguas negras – sewage
aguila – eagle
aldea – small hamlet
alquiler de automóviles – car rental
apartado – post-office box
árbol – tree
ardilla – squirrel
aspirina – aspirin
ATH – A Toda Hora (open all hours); used to denote ATM machines
auto/automóvil – car
aves – birds; see also *pájaro*
avión – airplane

baño – bathroom, see also *servicio*
barro – mud
barrio – district, neighborhood
beso – kiss
bicicleta – bicycle
billete – banknote, bill
bocas – small savory dishes served in bars
boleto – ticket (bus, train, museum etc)
bomba – gas station; short funny verse; bomb
borracho/a – drunk male/female
bosque – forest
bosque nuboso – cloud forest
bote – boat
buena nota – excellent, right on; literally 'good grade'

caballo – horse
caballeros – gentlemen; the usual sign on toilet doors
cabinas – cabins, cheap hotel
cafetera – coffee-making machine
cafetalero – coffee baron
cajero automático – ATM
cama/cama matrimonial – bed/double bed
caminata – hike
caminata pajarera – birding walk
camión – truck
camioneta – pickup truck
camiseta – T-shirt
campesino – peasant; person who works in agriculture

carretas – colorfully painted wooden ox carts, now a form of folk art
carretera – road
casado – married, also a set meal
cascada – waterfall
catedral – cathedral
caverna – cave
cerro – mountain
ceviche – local dish of uncooked but well-marinated seafood
Chepe – affectionate nickname for José; also used in referring to San José
chicle – gum
chinga – a small boat, see also *panga* and *lancha*; (in other parts of Latin America, this is a description of the sexual act along the lines of 'to screw')
chorizo – used colloquially, *chorizear* or *dejar un chorizo* (leave a *chorizo*) means to make a mess of things or do something illegitimate; also a spicy sausage
chunche – literally 'a thing'
cigarrillo – cigarette
cocina – kitchen, cooking
cochino – pig, the animal; also means filthy
colectivo – buses, minivans, or cars operating as shared taxis; see also *normal*
colibrí – hummingbird
colina – hill
colón – Costa Rican unit of currency; plural colones
condón – condom
cordillera – mountain range
correo – mail service
correo electrónico – email
costarricense – Costa Rican (see also Tico)
cruce – crossing
cruda – often used to describe a hangover; *tengo una cruda*, literally 'raw'
cuadraciclo – ATV
cuchara – spoon
cuchillo – knife
cueva – cave
culebra – snake, see also *serpiente*

damas – ladies; the usual sign on toilet doors
derecha – right
directo – direct; refers to long-distance bus with few stops
dios – god
doble – double as in double room; *una doble*
doble tracción – 4WD
emergencia – emergency

encomienda – sending packages, usually via bus
estación – station, as in ranger station or bus station; can also mean season
estero – estuary
estudiante – student

fauna silvestre – wildlife
farmacia – pharmacy
fiesta – party or festival
finca – farm or plantation
flor – flower
frontera – border
fuego – flame
fútbol – football (soccer)

galón – US gallon; not commonly used
gallo pinto – rice and beans
garza – cattle egret
gasolina – gas, petrol
gracias – thanks
gringo/a – male/female North American or European visitors; can be affectionate or insulting, depending on the tone used
guapote – large fish caught for sport, equivalent to rainbow bass
guaro – local firewater

hacienda – a rural estate
hay – pronounced 'eye,' meaning 'there is' or 'there are'; *no hay* means 'there is none'
hielo – ice
Holdridge Life Zones – classification system developed in the 1960s by US botanist LR Holdridge, whereby climate, latitude, and altitude are used to define 116 distinct natural environmental zones, each with a particular type of vegetation
hombre – man

ICE – Instituto Costarricense de Electricidad; Costa Rican utilities (phone and electricity) company
ICT – Instituto Costarricense de Turismo; Costa Rican tourism institute, which provides tourist information
iglesia – church
IGN – Instituto Geográfico Nacional; National Geographic Institute, which is a publisher of topographic maps of Costa Rica
incendio – fire
indígena – indigenous
invierno – winter; the rainy season in Costa Rica
Interamericana – Pan-American Hwy
isla – island
izquierda – left

jardín – garden
josefino – resident of San José

kilometraje – distance in kilometers; mileage

lancha – boat, usually small; see also *chinga* and *panga*
lapa – parrot
lavabó – hand sink
lavandería – laundry facility, usually offering dry-cleaning services
lentes – eyeglasses
liciado – hurt
llanuras – tropical plains

machismo – an exaggerated sense of masculine pride
macho – a virile figure; typically a man
maje – slang that means 'dude'; used among men
malecón – pier, sea wall, or waterfront promenade
manglar – mangrove
marías – local name for taxi meters
marimba – wood xylophone
menso – dumb
mercado – market
mesa – table
meseta central – central plateau; Central Valley
mestizo – person of mixed descent, usually Spanish and Indian
migración (Oficina de Migración) – immigration (Immigration Office)
Minae – Ministerio de Ambiente y Energía; Ministry of Environment and Energy, in charge of the national park system
minisuper – small convenience store
mirador – lookout point
mochilero – backpacker; though the English word is being used more and more
mono – monkey
mono colorado – spider monkey
mono congo – howler monkey
mono cara blanca – capuchin monkey
mono tití – squirrel monkey
moto/motocicleta – motorcycle
muelle – dock
mujer – woman
murciélago – bat
museo – museum

niñera – nanny or babysitter
niño – child
normal – in bus stations, refers to long-distance bus with many stops

ojalá – hopefully; literally 'if God wills it'
OTS – Organization for Tropical Studies

página web – website
pájaro – bird; birding walks are referred to as *caminatas pajareras*; see also *aves*

palacio municipal – city hall
palma africana – African palm
paloma – pigeon, dove
panga – light boat; see *chinga*
pañales – diapers, nappies
paños – towel or rag
pántano – swamp or wetland
papel higiénico – toilet paper
parada – bus stop
páramo – habitat characterized by highland shrub and tussock grass; common to the Andes of Colombia, Ecuador and Peru, as well as parts of Costa Rica
parche curita – Band-Aid
parque – park
parque central – central town square or plaza
parque nacional – national park
peón – peon; someone who does heavy unskilled labor
perezoso – sloth
perico – mealy parrot
periódico – newspaper
piso – floor, ie as in 2nd floor
pista de aterrizaje – landing strip, tarmac
pista de baile – dance floor
plato – plate
playa – beach
PLN – Partido de Liberación Nacional; National Liberation Party
posada – guesthouse
propina – tip for service
prostituta – prostitute; also shortened for the more vulgar *puta*
puerto – port
pulpería – corner grocery store
puro – cigar; as in *un puro*
PUSC – Partido Unidad Social Cristiana; Social Christian Unity Party

rana – frog or toad
rancho – small house or house-like building
refresco – soda or bottled refreshment
repelente – bug repellent
refugio nacional de vida silvestre – national wildlife refuge
río – river
roja – used to refer to the 1000 colón note, which is red – *dos rojas* is 2000 colones

sabanero – cowboy from Guanacaste
sacerdote – priest
saco de dormir – sleeping bag
salado – literally 'salty'; frequently meant as 'tough luck'
sencilla – single room
sencillo – can mean simple or refer to monetary change (small bills or coinage)
sendero – trail, path
serpiente – snake, see also *culebra*
servicio – toilet; see also *baño*
servicio a domicilio – home delivery
servilleta – napkin
soda – lunch counter; inexpensive eatery
sucio – dirty
supermercado – supermarket

taller mecánico – mechanic's shop
taza – cup
tenedor – fork
tepezcuinte – jungle rodent that is a relative of the guinea pig; locals often eat them
tienda – store
tienda de campaña – a camping tent
Tico/a – Costa Ricans
típica/o – typical; often used to describe food, *comida típica*
trago – cocktail
toallas higienicas – feminine napkins/pads
tortuga – turtle
tuanis – cool, excellent
tucán – toucan

upe – expression used in the countryside when arriving at a home that lets everyone know you're there
Unesco – United Nations Educational, Scientific and Cultural Organization
USGS – US Geological Survey

vaso – glass
vecino – neighbor
venenoso – poisonous
verano – summer; the dry season in Costa Rica
viajero – traveler
vino – wine
vivero – plant nursery

zancudo – mosquito

Behind the Scenes

THIS BOOK

This seventh edition of Costa Rica was written by Mara Vorhees, who also coordinated the book, and Matthew Firestone. David Lukas penned the Wildlife Guide and Environment chapters, Elizabeth Hart wrote the Organic Costa Rica boxed text, and Dr David Goldberg wrote the Health chapter. The first five editions of Costa Rica were written by Rob Rachowiecki, and the 6th edition was written by Paige R Penland and Carolina Miranda. This guidebook was commissioned in Lonely Planet's Oakland office, and produced by the following people:

Commissioning Editor Greg Benchwick
Coordinating Editor Justin Flynn
Coordinating Cartographer Corey Hutchison
Coordinating Layout Designer Margie Jung
Managing Editor Melanie Dankel
Managing Cartographers Alison Lyall, Emma McNicol, Andrew Smith
Assisting Editors Jackey Coyle, Janet Austin, Yvonne Byron, David Andrew
Assisting Cartographers Erin McManus, Jody Whiteoak
Cover Designer James Hardy
Color Designer Pablo Gastar
Indexer Brett Lockwood
Language Content Coordinator Quentin Frayne
Project Manager Chris Love

Thanks to David Burnett, Sally Darmody, Mark Germanchis, Kate McDonald, Celia Wood

THANKS
MARA VORHEES

Many thanks to my team at LP – to Greg, for sending me to work in the tropics and reminding me why I signed up to be a travel writer; and to Matt, for making my job as coordinator all the easier. Here's a shot of *guaro* for you. Cheers to Rob Rachowiecki, Carolina Miranda and Paige Penland for giving us some great material to work with. I am also grateful to Marc Landy and Carlos Muñoz for getting me off in the right direction (and Carlos Gonzalez for making sure I kept going). To my heroes Henry and Olger – the park rangers at Altamira station who rescued me from the jungles of La Amistad – thanks for showing me that park rangers really *do* do something. Many, many other people helped me in Costa Rica – most of whom I don't even know their names. So I'll just say *muchas gracias* and drink another shot to you. And to Jerry – for lugging the heavy pack across Corcovado, for sharing my excitement about every place I go, and for making me 'coffee rica' when I need it most – thanks, B, I couldn't do it without you.

MATTHEW FIRESTONE

First, I'd like to thank my family for their tireless patience and complete support. To my father, thank you for always putting things into perspective, regardless of how many rental cars I crash. To my mother, thank you for always writing me, even though I know you're scared to use computers. To my sister, thank you for being so successful, especially since I continue not to have health in-

---

THE LONELY PLANET STORY

The story begins with a classic travel adventure: Tony and Maureen Wheeler's 1972 journey across Europe and Asia to Australia. There was no useful information about the overland trail then, so Tony and Maureen published the first Lonely Planet guidebook to meet a growing need.

From a kitchen table, Lonely Planet has grown to become the largest independent travel publisher in the world, with offices in Melbourne (Australia), Oakland (USA) and London (UK). Today Lonely Planet guidebooks cover the globe. There is an ever-growing list of books and information in a variety of media. Some things haven't changed. The main aim is still to make it possible for adventurous travelers to get out there – to explore and better understand the world.

At Lonely Planet we believe travelers can make a positive contribution to the countries they visit – if they respect their host communities and spend their money wisely. Every year 5% of company profit is donated to charities around the world.

surance. Second, I'd like to give a big '¡Muchisimo gracias!' to the entire Lonely Planet team. To Greg, thank you for trusting me with such a huge and important project. To Mara, thank you for all the guidance that you've shown me. Finally, I'd like to give a shout out to my friends, both old and new. To Jeff, thank you for co-piloting, and may you never forget the wonders of Costa Rican mechanics. To Drew and Julie, thank you for always taking me down a notch, and reminding me how much fun life can be. To Derek, thank you for always making me laugh, and for sticking it out to the end. To Kandice, Juan Jo and Angela, thank you for keeping me well-rested, well-fed and well-surfed.

OUR READERS
Many thanks to the travelers who used the last edition and wrote to us with helpful hints, useful advice and interesting anecdotes:

A Ruth Abegg, Richard Adams, Colin Alexander, Claudia Allemann, Sandra Amadeo, Allan Ament, Priscilla Anderson, Terrah Anderson, Niels Peter Andreasen, Scott Andrews, Massimo Angelino, Begoña Antonio, Matthew Appelbaum, James Asa **B** Jason B, Dominic Babu, Jonathan Bahnuik, Greg Baker, Ben Banks, Colin Barr, Dave Barry, Jenny Barsby, Gillian Batt, Claudio Battista, Shannon Bauder, Sarah Bauerle, William Beaty, Timo Becker, Hans Beckers, Gilles Belanger, Libby Bell, Dan Bellan, Beke Bello, Kendra Benson, Megan Berkle, Pierre Bernier, Desiree Bilon, Angela Bison, Richard Bles, Laurie Blizzard, Larry Blumenfeld, Elaine Bobbitt, Philippe Boisson, Morena Borghi, Ben Bowell, Randall Bratu, Ute Braun, Lucia Brawley, A & G Bray, Ann Brinson, Mark Brown, Lauren Brownstein, Zack Burnett, Stephen Burnie, Llewella Butland **C** Adam Cairns, Granville Callan, H Caminata, Ingrid Cappel, Annette Carter, Tom Carter, Anne Casement, Marcus Cavelti, Mark Cerniglia, Keith Charabaruk, Shihong Chen, Victoria Chen, Catherine Cheng, Michael Christ, Hsiao-Yun Chu, Michelle Clark, Blaine Clarke, Chip Clarke, Catherine Coates, Nick Coenen, Keith Convery, Anna Cooper, Bettina Costa, John Cotton, Jennifer Cragan, Allison Crawford, Jerome Cretegny, Leon Cukierman, Robert Cummins, Brian Cuttlers **D** Ricardo Daddio, Christine Dahlin, Michelle Dalmau, Addison Dalton, Sara Davidson, Jackie Davison, Caroline Dawes, Pete & Ute Dawn, Maria De Angelo, Miguel De Arriba, Keith Nelson De La Vega, Mathieu de Patoul, Carina De Witt, Kirsten De Witte, Didier Debailleux, Cindy Desir, Heather Diamond, Nicole Diamond, Danielle Diiullo, Margot Diskin, Kelly Dixon, Kevin Dixon, Austin Drill, Rob Duffer, Wil Duits, Lisa Dunn, Linda Duran **E** Lynn Edwards, Adam Eifer, Alexander Erdelt, Charlie EwerSmith **F** Jasper Fase, Jim Fatka, Barry Felberg, Markus Felder, Derek Fenster, Odamis Fernandez-Sheinbaum, Ian Edward Ferns, Andreu Ferrer, Elizabeth Fifer, Robert Fischer, Arnold Flather, Francisco Flores, Stan Ford, Charless & Marjorie Fowlkes, Laura Frey, Giulia Fulci **G** Wyard Gankema, Danika Garby, Michèle Garceau, Skip Garibaldi, Rebecca Garland, Stephan Gaschen, Melissa Geerlings, Nicolas Gendron, Paul Gerhart, Sheryl Gerrard, Diana Gibbs,

Susanne Giegerich, Sierra Goodman, Vicky Goossens, Leigh Gower, Gary Graham, Frederick Grant, Ian Griffiths, Jasper Groos, Denia & Jason Gross, Henning Groß, Megan Gross, Wade Guenther, Joe Gumino, Jochen Gundlach, Hilda Gutierrez **H** Rainer Hagner, Ulf Halbgebauer, Katherine Hamilton, Becca Harber, Paul Harstad, Nicole Henley, Karen Herrgott, Ruth Herscovitch, Miya Hideshima, S Hirsch, Trevor Hodge, Ron Hoglund, Ursula Horst, Nicole Houston, Felipe Howard, Elisabeth Huesmann, Scott Hunter, Lee Hyson **J** Caroline Jacobs, Melanie Jäger, Drew Jeffries, Steven Jehly, Karen Melchior Jensen, Bryan & Chelle Johnson, Milena Johnson, Robert Johnson, Susan Johnson, Sandy Jones, Catherine Jones Roman, Kevin Joseph, Sharon Joseph, Judith Judith **K** Robert Kaplan, Karen Kassy, Caren Katz, Peter Kehoe, Dorothy Kennedy, Heather Kew, Sarah Kilvington, Laura Kimball, Michael King, Andrew Kirk, Doris Klein, Mike Klotz, Margot Kokke, Jason Kolbe, Danielle Koning, Barbara Kortbeek, Richard H Kramer, Ralf Kremer, Julia Kubica, Jeroen Kuiper, Caroline Kuta **L** Jeanne Laduke, Kevin Langel, Raymond Lardinois, Malin Larsson, Mark Lavigne, Hanne & Bruce Lawrence, Natalie Le Cornu, Jeansebastien Leduc, Elsie Lee, Joseph Lee, Joachim Lengacher, Suzanne Lew, Lindsay Lewe, Steve Lidgey, Jim Lillis, Bennett Link, Ina Lockau-Vogel, Miguel Roberto Loew, Rebecca Lukas, Eimear Lynch **M** Barbara Mahan, Patrick Mannens, Raleigh March, Karen Marino, Michelle Marino, Javier Martinez, Pablo Martinez, Daniel Matte, Moira Matthys, Stefanie Mautz, Ginny McIntyre, Jeff Mcbride, Meg Mcclure, Don & Joanne Mccuaig, Taylor McDonald, Daniel Mcginley, Alan McLaughlan, Cathy Meier, Sandra Meissner, Dan Menendez, Nicola Messina, Karen Michalek, Maria Midböe, Nicole Miel-Uken, Danielle Miller,

Julia Milne, Jacques Modiano, Gregory Mogilevsky, Greg Moher, Andrea Morton, Andrea Moxey, Brad Murphy, Arthur Mystek **N** Sartaj Narang, Agnes Nemes, Naomi Neustaedter, Eugenie Nguyen, Ken Nickell, Christine Niho, Jeffrey Nikolas, Johan & Stina Nilsson, Inge Nord, Dj Nordland, Robert Nrouwer **O** Coley O'Brien, Sadie O'Dell, Linda Olenzek, Nancy Ostheimer **P** Bob Packard, Karen Palacios, Patricia Palley, Brad Parker, Angharad Parry, Eri Peles, Giorgio Perversi, Sara Peterson, Jennifer & Tim Pettus, Susan Phillips, John Phippen, Therese Picado, Alaina Pinney, Irit Porat, Chris Powell, R M Puebla, Mary Pug, Minna Puukka **Q** Aaron Quiros Montiel **R** Adam Raffkind, Genevieve Rainville, Pete Reames, Philipp Rest, John Rhodes, Andy Rice, Scott Rick, Chris Riley, Trevor Rix, Anthony Robinson, Deirdre Robinson, Paul Robinson, Cathy Rockoff, Grace Rodriguez, Thomas Roemer, Dirk Roos, Tina Roos, Gerald Rosen, Becca Rosenbaum, Kristie Ross, Mary & Mike Rossignoli, Cerise Roth-Vinson, Shannon Rousey, Jean-Pierre Roy, Brian Rueb, Jodie Ruhl, Ken Rumes **S** Sylvia Saakes, Laurie Saindon, Sherri Sandberg, Allen Sanderson, Raquel Santos, Ben Saperia, John Sargent, Oliver Saria, Caroline Saudek, Katrin Sauer, Nicola Saunders, Desiree Saylor, Lisavette Saylor, Daniel Schatz, Friedemann Scheck, Karen Scheuerer, Tammy Schilbe, Melanie Schlieker, Anne Blume Schmidt, Manuel Scola, Helena & Matilda Shayn, Tim Shedd, Jessica Shull, Tod Sinding, Scott Sinta, Thomas Sippl, Lena Skarby, Mike Skov, Angelina Skowronski, Nika Skvir-Maliakal, Colleen Slack, Rosemary Small, Elisa Smith, Elise Smits, Lida Sparer, William F Steel, Jo Steininger, Alex Stockman, Shirley & Bob Stone, Dave Summerton, Heidi Summerton, Sharifa Suniga, Bjørn Olaf Syvertsen **T** Shari Takenaga, Paule Tetu, Barbara Thomson, Markus Toepler, Derek Tokashiki, Goro Toshima, Erin Tracy, Muriel & Stani Trauwaert, Tracy Turner **U** Chris Uniacke **V** Karen V, Bart Vaes, Nico Van Belleghem, Pieter Van Den Berg, Leo Van der Iaan, Diana Van Der Star, Esther Van Der Wel, Jacqueline Van Driel, Paul Van Rijn, Jeroen Van Wetten, Yves Vandijck, Braulio Vasquez, Joelle Venema, Bob & Mona Vennard, Jeroen Verberk, Laura Verhaeghe, Clem Vetters, Gordon & Sue Vint, Yvonne & Michael Vintiner, Vanessa Voelkel, Willeke Voogd **W** Richard C Walker, Dominic Wall, Michael Walsh, Melanie Wartho, Barbara Watkins, Jane Watson, Peter Watt, Barbara Webb, Nanna Wedendahl Frank, Susan Weeks, David Weinstein, Lara Weiss, Nate Williams, Jeffrey Woldrich, Charlie Woodall, Tim Woolfson, Monty Worth, Daniel Wright, Jen Wyville **Y** Philippa Yool **Z** Alexandra Zachmann, Jeff Zahn, Keren Zaks, Isabel Zaragoza, Brion Ziminski, Manuele Zunelli

ACKNOWLEDGMENTS

Many thanks to the following for the use of their content:

Globe on back cover ©Mountain High Maps 1993 Digital Wisdom, Inc.

Foodcards for the recipe on p82.

Index

000 Map pages
000 Photograph pages

INDEX

000 Map pages
000 Photograph pages

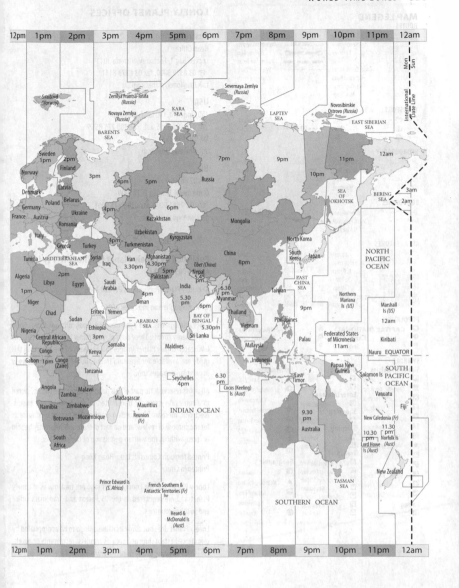

Svalbard (Norway)

Zemlya Frantsa-Iosifa (Russia)

Severnaya Zemlya (Russia)

Novaya Zemlya (Russia)

KARA SEA

LAPTEV SEA

Novosibirskie Ostrovo (Russia)

EAST SIBERIAN SEA

International Date Line

Mon Sun

BARENTS SEA

Sweden 1pm
Norway
2pm Finland
Denmark
Germany Latvia
Poland Belarus
France Austria Ukraine
Italy Romania
Greece Turkey

3pm

4pm

5pm

7pm

9pm

11pm

12am

10pm

SEA OF OKHOTSK

BERING SEA

3am
2am

Russia

Kazakhstan

Mongolia

NORTH PACIFIC OCEAN

Tunisia MEDITERRANEAN SEA
Algeria
Libya 2pm
Niger
1pm Egypt
Chad
Nigeria Sudan
Central African Republic
Congo
Gabon 1pm Congo (Zaire)

Syria
Iraq
Iran 3.30pm
Saudi Arabia
Yemen
Oman 4pm
ARABIAN SEA

Uzbekistan
Turkmenistan 4pm
Afghanistan 4.30pm
Pakistan 5pm
India 5.30 pm

Kyrgyzstan

China 8pm

North Korea
South Korea Japan

EAST CHINA SEA

Taiwan

Northern Mariana Is (US) 9pm

Marshall Is (US) 12am

Tibet (China)
Nepal 5.45 pm

6.30 pm
Myanmar

Eritrea
Ethiopia 3pm
Somalia
Kenya
Tanzania

Maldives

Sri Lanka

BAY OF BENGAL 5.30pm

6pm Thailand
Vietnam

Malaysia

Philippines

Palau

Federated States of Micronesia 11am

Kiribati

Nauru EQUATOR

SOUTH PACIFIC OCEAN

Angola
Namibia Zambia Zimbabwe
Botswana Mozambique
South Africa

Madagascar

Mauritius
Reunion (Fr)

Seychelles 4pm

6.30 pm
Cocos (Keeling) Is (Aust)

Indonesia

East Timor

Papua New Guinea

Solomon Is

Vanuatu

Fiji

INDIAN OCEAN

9.30 pm
Australia

New Caledonia (Fr)

11.30 pm
10.30 pm Norfolk Is (Aust)
Lord Howe Is (Aust)

New Zealand

Prince Edward Is (S. Africa)

French Southern & Antarctic Territories (Fr)

TASMAN SEA

SOUTHERN OCEAN

Heard & McDonald Is (Aust)

AP LEGEND

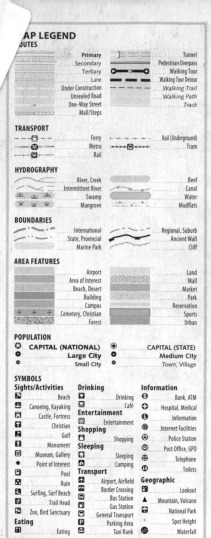

LONELY PLANET OFFICES

Australia
Head Office
Locked Bag 1, Footscray, Victoria 3011
☎ 03 8379 8000, fax 03 8379 8111
talk2us@lonelyplanet.com.au

USA
150 Linden St, Oakland, CA 94607
☎ 510 893 8555, toll free 800 275 8555
fax 510 893 8572
info@lonelyplanet.com

UK
72–82 Rosebery Ave,
Clerkenwell, London EC1R 4RW
☎ 020 7841 9000, fax 020 7841 9001
go@lonelyplanet.co.uk

Published by Lonely Planet Publications Pty Ltd
ABN 36 005 607 983

© Lonely Planet Publications Pty Ltd 2006

© photographers as indicated 2006

Cover photographs: Red eyed tree frog *(agalychris callidryas)*, Brent Ward/Alamy (front); Three boys playing *fútbol* in Puerto Limón, Eric L Wheater/Lonely Planet Images (back). Many of the images in this guide are available for licensing from Lonely Planet Images: www .lonelyplanetimages.com.

Printed through Colorcraft Ltd., Hong Kong
Printed in China